1981	1982	1983	1984	1985	1986	1987	1988	1989	1990	1991	1992	1993	1994
230	232	234	236	238	241	243	245	247	250	253	255	258	261
74.1	74.5	74.6	74.7	74.7	74.7	74.9	74.9	75.1	75.4	75.5	75.7		
3,031	3,150	3,405	3,777	4,039	4,269	4,540	4,900	5,251	5,546	5,725	6,020	6,343	6,738
4,846	4,742	4,926	5,231	5,397	5,554	5,725	5,950	6,101	6,175	6,138	6,279	6,475	6,738
21,078	20,427	21,030	22,138	22,636	23,085	23,584	24,289	24,671	24,717	24,303	24,593	25,091	25,858
3,202	3,238	3,388	3,550	3,705	3,839	3,946	4,088	4,168	4,231	4,214	4,331	4,471	4,628
715	588	643	813	786	763	786	826	845	805	739	783	885	1,034
908	922	947	976	1,036	1,089	1,122	1,129	1,152	1,188	1,202	1,193	1,184	1,175
20	−7	−50	−109	−130	−138	−128	−93	−66	−49	−17	−29	−66	−99
2,954	2,031	2,968	3,109	3,202	3,294	3,403	3,541	3,598	3,664	3,649	3,729	3,856	4,005
1,013	1,133	1,251	1,270	1,264	1,315	1,392	1,413	1,400	1,384	1,352	1,436	1,378	1,453
7.6	9.7	9.6	7.5	7.2	7.0	6.2	5.5	5.3	5.5	6.7	7.4	6.8	6.1
102.0	101.2	102.5	106.7	108.9	111.3	114.2	116.7	119.0	119.6	118.4	119.2	120.8	123.1
162	172	189	204	219	239	261	279	291	310	338	368	407	444
425	453	503	539	587	666	744	775	783	811	859	966	1,079	1,145
1,716	1,877	2,112	2,286	2,491	2,697	2,876	3,027	3,146	3,314	3,421	3,493	3,540	3,605
61.3	65.1	67.1	70.1	72.6	74.0	76.7	79.8	83.6	88.2	91.9	94.7	97.5	100.0
9.9	6.0	3.1	4.3	3.5	1.9	3.6	4.0	4.7	5.3	4.1	3.0	2.9	2.6
14.02	10.61	8.61	9.52	7.48	5.98	5.78	6.67	8.11	7.49	5.37	3.43	3.00	4.25
1,695	1,736	1,799	1,838	1,928	2,010	2,044	2,067	2,112	2,204	2,250	2,377	2,421	2,455
35.0	36.6	36.5	35.1	35.7	36.2	35.7	34.7	34.6	35.7	36.7	37.9	37.4	36.4
18.5	19.3	19.2	18.6	19.1	19.5	19.4	18.7	18.6	18.9	19.2	18.7	18.1	17.4
1,646	1,572	1,597	1,687	1,761	1,819	1,903	1,048	2,022	2,050	2,051	2,108	2,202	2,322
34.0	33.2	32.4	32.2	32.6	32.8	33.2	32.7	33.2	33.2	33.4	33.6	34.0	34.5
−48	−164	−202	−151	−167	−191	−141	−119	−90	−154	−199	−269	−220	−133
−1.0	−3.4	−4.1	−2.9	−3.1	−3.4	−2.5	−2.0	−1.5	−2.5	−3.2	−4.3	−3.4	−2.0
1,256	1,351	1,585	1,774	1,977	2,214	2,374	2,472	2,540	2,697	2,876	3,062	3,271	3,471
25.9	28.5	32.2	33.9	36.6	39.9	41.5	41.5	41.6	43.7	46.8	48.8	50.5	51.5

INTRODUCTION TO
ECONOMICS

ALAN C. STOCKMAN
University of Rochester

The Dryden Press
Harcourt Brace College Publishers

Fort Worth   Philadelphia   San Diego   New York   Austin   Orlando   San Antonio
Toronto   Montreal   London   Sydney   Tokyo

Executive Editor	Emily Barrosse
Acquisitions Editor	Daryl Fox
Project Editor	Amy Schmidt
Art Director	Jeanette Barber
Production Manager	Ann Coburn
Arts & Literary Rights Editor	Annette Coolidge
Product Manager	Craig Johnson
Editorial Assistant	Virginia Warren
Copy Editor	David Talley
Proofreader	Teresa Chartos
Indexer	Linda Webster
Compositor	Monotype Composition Company, Inc.
Text Type	10/12 ITC Garamond

Address for Orders
The Dryden Press
6277 Sea Harbor Drive
Orlando, FL 32887-6777
1-800-782-4479 or 1-800-433-0001 (in Florida)

Address for Editorial Correspondence
The Dryden Press
301 Commerce Street, Suite 3700
Forth Worth, TX 76102

ISBN: 0-03-031129-2 (main version)
        0-03-031132-2 (micro version)
        0-03-031133-0 (macro version)

Library of Congress Catalog Card Number: 94-74006

Credits, which constitute a continuation of the copyright page, appear at the back of the book, following the glossary.

Printed in the United States of America

5 6 7 8 9 0 1 2 3 4   048   9 8 7 6 5 4 3 2 1

The Dryden Press
Harcourt Brace College Publishers

*To Cindy, Gwendolyn,
Madeleine, and Rebecca*

P R E F A C E

WHY I WROTE THIS BOOK

I expected to become a physicist or political scientist when I entered college in the fall of 1969. My interest in political science sprang from my fascination with political philosophy and broad social issues, but most political science courses appeared to focus more on the institutions of government than on fundamental questions. Meanwhile, outside reading led me to the works of Milton Friedman, Friedrich Hayek, and Ludwig von Mises, and inspired me to learn more economics. However, I found my introductory economics course dry and intellectually unsatisfying. The textbook required for the course seemed to imply, contrary to what Freidman and others persuasively argued, that our economy frequently requires government policies to "get things right." Rather than raising and discussing fundamental questions and showing me how to apply economic analysis to such questions, the book implied that most economic issues had already been resolved and that experts could apply economics to correct the failures of markets and fine-tune the economy.

Despite that experience, my outside reading (and some good professors) sustained my interest in economics. When I decided to pursue economics in graduate school, I promised myself that someday I would write a better introductory economics textbook through which I could share with other people the fun and intellectual excitement I found in economics. After getting my Ph.D. at the University of Chicago and spending two years at UCLA, I found myself teaching a principles course at the University of Rochester in the fall of 1979. I have taught principles every year since then but have never been satisfied with the textbooks available. The book you hold in your hands is my attempt to fulfill my promise to myself.

THE IDEAL TEXTBOOK

Surely most professors who teach introductory economics share similar great moments: when a student first exhibits that contagious enthusiasm sparked by a discovery of economic reasoning; when a student spontaneously demonstrates an ability to apply economic principles to new problems; and when a student chooses to major in economics because of that particular professor's course. A textbook should help produce the conditions that create these moments.

Most students enroll in an introductory economics course without knowing what economics is about (aside from general notions of business, finance, and government policy) or why they should care about it. Many expect an economics course to be boring and enroll in it only to satisfy a requirement. The idea that economics could be incredibly interesting and relevant both to their own lives and to broader issues that they care about seldom enters their minds. The first job of a professor is to interest students in economics. Without such an interest, students will neither learn nor retain much of the basic material from their courses, let alone develop the ability to apply it to new situations.

An ideal textbook can help students learn partly by stimulating their interest in economics, by motivating them to think like economists, and by showing them how. Although the factors that shape people's interests are complex, some general themes emerge. We tend to like subjects that satisfy our innate sense of curiosity, that help us make sense of things that we don't understand, and that provide that "Aha!" feeling of new discovery. Of course, this satisfaction requires that we know what it is that we don't understand—that is, what questions to ask. While students who are already curious about economic issues are easy to motivate, most other students have little idea of what questions to ask. It has never occurred to them that our economy, without any central plan or direction, somehow coordinates the activities of millions of people to produce efficiently the goods and services they want. Most students have never been exposed to the kinds of questions that economics answers. Although the results profoundly affect their lives, they take those results for granted.

A good textbook must go well beyond motivating student interest in a subject. It must explain how to *use* basic principles in new situations. Clear explanations of main points, with examples that can serve as memory aids and applications that can deepen understanding, are essential. I believe students learn best if they practice applying concepts to both familiar and new situations, to both everyday life and broader issues. The best way to learn how to think analytically and to apply economics is to practice, and then to practice again. This book tries to provide an opportunity for that practice and to make it easier.

APPROACH

THE APPLIED-PRICE-THEORY APPROACH OF THE MICRO CHAPTERS

The microeconomics chapters of this book take an applied-price-theory approach. Numerous examples help to clarify main points, illustrate the relevance of economics to important real-life issues, show the breadth of economic applications, and help students learn to apply their knowledge outside of class as they read news articles and participate in discussions about current events and public policies. Several chapters (particularly Chapters 6–8, but also more advanced chapters such as those on the economics of information and economic analysis of law) are devoted to applying the logical reasoning of supply and demand to a variety of applied problems, including time prices, safety, bribery, lifestyles, speculation, international trade, and crime. Despite its strong applications approach, the textbook contains separate chapters to explain and apply more advanced theoretical topics, including game theory, the economics of information, and the economic analysis of law and public choice.

THE MODERN, NEOCLASSICAL APPROACH OF THE MACRO CHAPTERS

The macroeconomic chapters take a modern, neoclassical approach. Students learn equilibrium macroeconomics before studying short-run issues involving nominal sluggishness; they study long-run economic growth before business cycles; they learn the distinction between real and nominal variables before studying connections between them. The book's distinctive chapters on monetary and fiscal policies emphasize laissez-faire versus activist views of government policy and examine debates about rules versus discretion. The book also contains a balanced presentation of modern Keynesian theory and evidence and a separate chapter on real business cycle theory. The macroeconomics chapters, like the micro chapters, contain numerous examples designed to clarify main points, illustrate the relevance of economics to important real-life issues, and help students apply economics to current events and public policies.

I have taken this alternative approach to macroeconomics for several reasons. Standard presentations often leave students feeling as if the reasoning of macroeconomics is divorced from the reasoning of microeconomics. Despite the common attempt to make macroeconomics look like microeconomics through the use of aggregate supply and aggregate demand graphs, students seldom learn that the market process, Adam Smith's metaphorical invisible hand, operates for the economy as a whole just as it operates in micro applications. Students who never appreciate the successes of the market process applied to macroeconomic issues will have no basis for understanding where market failures might develop and why some economists advocate active roles for government macroeconomic policies. *This textbook is unique in explaining how the market process applies to macroeconomic issues.*

FUNDAMENTAL ISSUES AND EVERYDAY APPLICATIONS

Throughout the micro and macro chapters, the book emphasizes major social and political issues, enticing students to broaden the set of questions that they ask about the world, to understand both sides of controversial issues, and to combine economic analysis with their own value judgments as they think about current events and fundamental social issues. The book also strives for a real-life flavor through data, examples, applications of economics to personal and business decisions, and the extensive use of real news clippings.

PEDAGOGICAL FEATURES

This book maintains a reader-friendly organization that helps students by separating main points from explanations and examples. This organization increases student understanding by making it easier for readers to identify main points, examples, and explanations. It also helps students to review the chapters with less study time. Some sections of the book deviate from this organization, but always for a reason.

NEWS CLIPPINGS

The book makes extensive use of real news clippings to help students practice applying economic principles as they read about or listen to reports of current or historical events. The news clippings also increase student familiarity with news stories on economic topics, alleviating fears that such stories are beyond their comprehension and elevating their self-confidence not only to read but also to evaluate such stories.

QUESTIONS AND PROBLEMS

Questions and problems appear at the ends of sections, not just the ends of chapters. Some questions are mainly for review, while others require student analysis. This placement of the questions allows students to query themselves about the material in each section before continuing to the next. Questions and problems cover each level of learning, helping students learn to restate main points, to create new examples of those points, to work through applications from the text with small changes, to apply main points to genuinely new applications, and to apply economics to everyday life, current events, and broad social issues. Many problems help students learn to work with graphs (and some with numerical examples) and to state verbally the conclusions of the graphical analysis.

INQUIRIES FOR FURTHER THOUGHT

Inquiries for Further Thought are one of the most important features of the book. These distinctive inquiries supplement other end-of-chapter questions and problems. They challenge students to use economic analysis to formulate positions on issues of fundamental importance. The inquiries raise positive and normative questions on important social issues related to economics, teaching students (a) how to raise new questions and think about issues in new ways, (b) to distinguish between the positive and normative components of such questions, (c) that these positive and normative components are related to each other, (d) that economic analysis helps provide a logical way to approach many questions, and (e) that big-issue questions make economics interesting and important. The inquiries help students practice combining economic analysis with their own values and opinions about fundamental issues. Because most of the inquiries involve value judgments, they have no "correct" answers.

DECISION-MAKING AND SOCIAL AND ECONOMIC ISSUES BOXES

Many chapters also contain boxes presenting the main arguments on both sides of important social and economic issues. The book's strong emphasis on how economics relates to major social issues and political debates stimulates student interest and ties economics to students' lives. Some chapters also have boxes applying economic analysis to business decision making or personal decision making, showing students how they can use economics to help achieve their own goals.

CONCLUSIONS

The concluding sections of each chapter are organized by section, making it easier for students to identify sections that they need to reread. On a second reading, many students will find that they can skip explanation and example sections if they already understand the issues.

SUPPLEMENTARY MATERIALS

FOR THE INSTRUCTOR

▶ *Micro Test Bank.* Prepared by Nancy Ohanian of Macalester College and Dean Croushore of the Federal Reserve Bank of Philadelphia, the micro test bank contains more than 3,500 multiple-choice and critical-thinking questions. Each question is graded by level of difficulty. Also, each critical-thinking question has a suggested correct answer in the printed test bank. All questions were checked for accuracy by Evelyn Smith at West Texas A&M University.

▶ *Macro Test Bank.* Prepared by Alden Shiers of California Polytechnic State University, the macro test bank contains more than 3,500 multiple-choice and critical-thinking questions. Each question is graded by level of difficulty. Also, each critical-thinking question has a suggested correct answer in the printed test bank. All questions were checked for accuracy by David Bishop at the University of Rochester.

▶ *Computerized Test Banks.* Both micro and macro test banks are available on computer disk for IBM and Macintosh users. The ExaMaster system accompanying the computerized test banks makes it easy to create tests, print scrambled versions of the same test, modify questions, and reproduce any of the graphing questions.

▶ *Teaching Transparencies for Microeconomics.* Color acetates of the major exhibits have been prepared for overhead projection. A number of acetates are layered to show what happens graphically when curves shift.

▶ *Teaching Transparencies for Macroeconomics.* Color acetates of the major exhibits have been prepared for overhead projection. A number of acetates are layered to show what happens graphically when curves shift.

▶ *Instructor's Manual.* This supplement contains valuable outlines, teaching tips, and answers to all the questions in the book. This information is also available in WordPerfect 5.1, which allows instructors to customize their lecture notes.

▶ *CD-ROM.* This highly interactive product utilizes animated graphs, audio, video, and text from the book to create a multimedia learning environment. The CD-ROM focuses on core economic concepts that go beyond the linear presentation in the book. The instructor's disk includes LectureActive Presentation Software, which contains all of the graphics and text files from *Introduction to Economics.*

▶ *PowerPoint Presentation Software.* Key concepts and figures from the text are reproduced in an overhead-presentation format designed for lectures. Instructors may pick and choose the information they want to cover by selecting customization options. PowerPoint is a basic program that is very easy to use.

▶ *Video Packages.* The *Economics in Focus* video series facilitates multilevel learning and critical thinking through its up-to-date coverage of current events, while focusing on the economic issues important to students and their understanding of the economy. Recent segments from The MacNeil/Lehrer News Hour are updated quarterly. These videos look at three major topics:

1. "The International Economics Scene" covers free trade, foreign policy, and other issues.
2. "Economic Challenges and Problems" explores topics such as changing incomes, the government budget deficit, and inflation.
3. "The Political Economy" looks at the role of the government, free enterprise, and economic stabilization.

Each segment of *Economics in Focus* closes with a special feature story or one-on-one interview with a noted economist.

Milton Friedman's *Free to Choose* video series is available in 10, half-hour videotapes. These videos update the earlier series, *Milton Friedman Speaks,* and contain introductions by Arnold Schwarzenegger, George Schultz, Steve Allen, David Friedman, and Ronald Reagan.

▶ *Laser Discs.* These discs focus on the core principles of micro- and macroeconomics and present the information interactively. A brief 5- to 7-minute video from CBS begins each learning section. Related animated graphics follow. Once students understand the concepts presented, they are then challenged with critical-thinking questions. A printed *Media Instructor's Manual* explains how the laser disc coordinates with the textbook.

FOR THE STUDENT

▶ *Microeconomics Study Guide.* Written by Dorothy Siden at Salem State College, the micro study guide utilizes numerous strategies for active learning. Elements of this supplement include: learning goals, key-term quizzes, true-false questions, multiple-choice questions, fill-in-the-blank problems, priority lists of concepts, short-answer questions, and basic and advanced problems.

▶ *Macroeconomics Study Guide.* Written by John Dodge at University of Sioux Falls, the macro study guide utilizes numerous strategies for active learning. Elements of this supplement include: learning goals, key-term quizzes, true-false questions, multiple-choice questions, fill-in-the-blank problems, priority lists of concepts, short-answer questions, and basic and advanced problems.

▶ *CD-ROM.* This highly interactive product utilizes animated graphs, audio, video, and the text of the book to create a multimedia learning environment. The CD-ROM focuses on core economic concepts that go beyond the linear presentation of the text. Students can purchase the CD-ROM with or without the printed text.

▶ *Tutorial, Analytical, and Graphical (TAG) Software.* This award-winning software by Tod Porter and Teresa Riley of Youngstown State University has been significantly enhanced to contain an extensive chapter-by-chapter tutorial, a hands-on graphic section in which students are actually required to draw curves (with key strokes or a mouse), and a practice exam for each section. Students receive feedback on their answers. It is available in both DOS and Windows formats.

The Dryden Press will provide complimentary supplements or supplement packages to those adopters qualified under our adoption policy. Please contact your sales representative to learn how you may qualify. If as an adopter or potential user you receive supplements you do not need, please return them to your sales representative or send them to: Attn: Returns Department, Troy Warehouse, 465 South Lincoln Drive, Troy, MO 63379.

ACKNOWLEDGMENTS

How can I begin to thank all the people who have directly or indirectly helped me create this book? I owe a great debt to my former teachers at the University of Chicago, particularly Milton Friedman, George Stigler, Gary Becker, Robert Barro, Jacob Frenkel, Robert E. Lucas, Jr., Tom Sargent, and my fellow students, particularly Tom MaCurdy and Dan Sumner. I also owe special debts of thanks to current and former colleagues, most notably Jeff Banks, Mark Bils, John Boyd, Karl Brunner, Mike Dotsey, Stan Engerman, Lauren Feinstone, Peter Garber, Marvin Goodfriend, Jeremy Greenwood, Eric Hanushek, Ron Jones, Jim Kahn, Robert King, Tony Kuprianov, Steve Landsburg, Ken McLaughlin, Masao Ogaki, Walter

Oi, Charles Phelps, and Sergio Rebelo. I also owe special thanks to Peter Rupert, Lee Ohanian, and Craig Hakkio for their comments on parts of the book.

I also thank all the focus group participants who helped refine the manuscript throughout its development. They include:

Michael Anderson
Washington and Lee University

David Bivin
Indiana University — Purdue University, Indianapolis

David Black
The University of Toledo

Tom Carr
Middlebury College

Mike Dowd
The University of Toledo

Swarna Dutt
Tulane University

Catherine Eckel
Virginia Polytechnic Institute and State University

Sharon Erenburg
Eastern Michigan University

David Gay
University of Arkansas

Y. Horiba
Tulane University

Nasir Khilji
Assumption College

John Lunn
Hope College

John Reid
Memphis State University

Christine Rider
St. John's University

Information received from the following class testers improved the accuracy and made the textbook more student friendly. Class testers include:

David Altig
Cleveland State University

Gerhard Glomm
Michigan State University

Craig Hakkio
Rockhurst College

Jim Irwin
Central Michigan University

Carston Kowalczyk
Tufts University

Catherine McDevitt
Central Michigan University

Lee Ohanian
University of Pennsylvania

Kakkar Vikas
Ohio State University

No successful principles of economics textbook could be written without the help of competent referees. I am indebted to the following people for their insightful recommendations:

Richard Ballman
Augustana College

David Bivin
Indiana University — Purdue University, Indianapolis

Robert T. Bray
California State Polytechnic University, Pomona

James A. Bryan
North Harris Community College

John Chilton
University of South Carolina

Daniel S. Christiansen
Albion College

Richard Claycombe
Western Maryland College

Kenneth A. Couch
Syracuse University

Swarna D. Dutt
Tulane University

Sharon Erenburg
Eastern Michigan University

Paul Farnham
Georgia State University

David Gay
University of Arkansas

Lynn Gillette
Northeast Missouri State University

Stephen F. Gohmann
University of Louisville

Philip J. Grossman
Wayne State University

David L. Hammes
University of Hawaii at Hilo

William Hunter
Marquette University

Stephen L. Jackstadt
University of Alaska at Anchorage

Nasir Khilji
Assumption College

Janet Koscianski
Shippensburg University

Stephen Lisle
Western Kentucky University

Elaine S. McBeth
College of William & Mary

Michael Meurer
Duke University

Joanna Moss
San Francisco State University

Norman Obst
Michigan State University

James A. Overdahl
George Mason University

Deborah J. Paige
McHenry County College

Jim Payne
Kellogg Community College

James Price
Syracuse University

Sunder Ramaswamy
Middlebury College

Kevin Rask
Colgate University

Jose-Victor Rios-Rull
University of Pennsylvania

Peter Rupert
SUNY Buffalo

Robert Rycroft
Mary Washington College

Michael D. Seelye
San Joaquin Delta College

Dorothy R. Siden
Salem State College

Larry Singell
University of Oregon

David L. Sollars
Auburn University at Montgomery

John C. Soper
John Carroll University

Todd P. Steen
Hope College

Michael Taussig
Rutgers University

Abdul M. Turay
Radford University

Ivan Weinel
University of Missouri

James N. Wetzel
Virginia Commonwealth University

Mark Wilkening
Blinn College

Edgar W. Wood
University of Mississippi

Joseph A. Ziegler
University of Arkansas

My deep gratitude goes out to the thousands of my students in introductory economics at the University of Rochester who have helped me with this project either directly (with comments on the manuscript) or indirectly, who have been experimental subjects in pedagogy, and who have helped me learn how to teach economics. Many have made specific comments on the manuscript. I am particularly grateful to Viral Patel, Efrom Sulejmani, and George Yannopoulos. I owe a great debt to all my former teaching assistants, who have taught me new ways to teach and showed me how to improve explanations and examples. I am also grateful to my former Ph.D. students at the University of Rochester, from whom I have learned more than they realize.

I am extremely grateful to Janet Wood, Administrative Assistant in the Department of Economics, for literally hundreds of tasks associated with my introductory classes and the production of this book, which she always did professionally and cheerfully. I also owe a debt to Dave Bishop for proofing the final pages and updating graphs and tables.

I have been extraordinarily fortunate to work with a number of outstanding people at The Dryden Press, including Becky Ryan Kohn and Jan Richardson, who served as editors during the early stages of the book. I am particularly indebted to my project editor, Amy Schmidt, for her excellent professional work and hundreds of supportive phone conversations during the production of this book. I am especially grateful to Daryl Fox, my acquisitions editor at Dryden, for his superb advice and expertise on numerous issues, his outstanding work on all aspects of this book, and his good-natured help and encouragement.

My greatest debt is to my wife, Cindy, and my children, Gwendolyn, Madeleine, and Rebecca, who sacrificed a lot of time with me and endured many burdens while I worked on this book.

Alan C. Stockman

ABOUT THE AUTHOR

Alan C. Stockman is the Marie Curran Wilson and Joseph Chamberlain Wilson Professor of Economics at the University of Rochester, and Chairman of the Department of Economics. He also serves as Research Associate at the National Bureau of Economic Research and as Consulting Economist at the Federal Reserve Bank of Richmond. He has taught introductory economics for 16 years and has been honored for his outstanding teaching of that course.

Professor Stockman received his Ph.D. at the University of Chicago in 1978, and has published widely in the leading professional journals, such as the *Journal of Political Economy, American Economic Review, Journal of Monetary Economics, Journal of International Economics,* and *Journal of Economic Theory.*

He specializes in macroeconomics and international economics, although his research also extends to other areas such as the economics of philosophy. He serves on editorial boards of several professional journals and presents frequent talks at universities and professional conferences around the world. In his spare time, he enjoys music, skiing, and spending time with his wife and three daughters.

BRIEF CONTENTS

C O N T E N T S

Chapter 10   Business Decisions and Supply   267

Chapter 11   Economic Efficiency and the Gains from Trade   303

PART 5   COMPETITION AND STRATEGIC INTERACTIONS   327

Chapter 12   Perfect Competition   329

Chapter 13   Monopoly   355

PART 6   INPUTS AND THEIR EARNINGS   439

PART 7 ADVANCED TOPICS IN MICROECONOMICS 533

PART 8 MACROECONOMIC EQUILIBRIUM 665

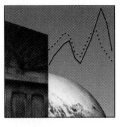

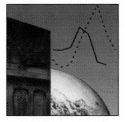

PART 10   BUSINESS CYCLES   855

PART 11   MACROECONOMIC POLICIES   951

PART 12   TOPICS IN MACROECONOMICS   1021

Chapter 34   Financial Markets   1023

Chapter 35   International Trade   1065

Chapter 36   International Money and Finance   1107

ISSUES AND METHODS

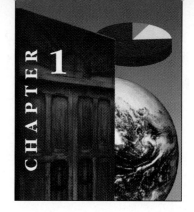

CHAPTER 1

MYSTERIES AND MOTIVES: WHAT ECONOMICS IS ABOUT

WHAT THIS CHAPTER IS ABOUT

▶ The topics of economics

▶ *not plentiful* Scarcity, opportunity costs, and incentives

▶ Property rights, competition, and the market process

ECONOMIC GROWTH

More than 5.8 billion people now live on earth. Each year they produce goods and services worth about $30 trillion ($30,000,000,000,000), or about $5,200 per person. This has not always been true. Back in 1900, production per person was only about one-fifth of today's level. The average person in the world is now about 5 times richer than the average in 1900 (even after adjusting for changes in prices since 1900), and 12 times richer than in 1800.

About 265 million people live in the United States, which produces goods and services worth over $7.5 trillion per year, or about $28,000 per person. The average American is about $1\frac{1}{2}$ times richer than the average 25 years ago, and twice as rich as 40 years ago. If the U.S. economy grows at the same rate over the next 40 years as it did over the last 40 (1.8 percent per year), annual output of goods and services per person in the United States will more than double, rising from $28,000 to $56,000. Whether or not this happens will have a big effect on your life.

Fifty years ago, Japan produced only one-sixth as many goods and services per person as the United States; today, output per person is nearly equal in the two countries. Hong Kong, South Korea, Singapore, and Taiwan have similar economic success stories. Meanwhile, hundreds of millions of people live in countries such as Bangladesh and Ethiopia, which every year produce goods and services worth only a few hundred dollars per person. The average Bangladeshi is only slightly richer now than 100 years ago. People in some countries, such as Madagascar, Mozambique, and Zambia, are poorer today than they were several decades ago.

One of the most important questions in economics concerns how countries grow rich, why some countries are much poorer than others, and why some grow more quickly than others. Why do countries like the United States, Japan, and Germany produce so many more goods and services per person than countries like Bangladesh and Ethiopia? Will output per person in the United States double over the next 40 years as it did over the last 40? How can we best ensure economic growth during your lifetime and after?[1]

refer to ch. 26

RICH AND POOR

The richest 20 percent of people in the world produce and use about 60 percent of everything produced in the world. The poorest 60 percent produce and use only about 20 percent of world output. The relationships within the United States are similar; the 20 percent of households with the highest incomes earn almost half of all income in the country, while the 20 percent with the lowest incomes earn just under 5 percent.

A typical U.S. family with two married adults both working for pay earns about $56,000 per year.[2] A typical family headed by a married couple, only one of whom works for pay, earns about $35,000. Adult males living alone average about $20,000, and adult females living alone average about $15,000. More than 36 million people in the United States, including 14 million children, live below the official U.S. poverty line (about $15,000 per year for a family of four). Nearly one-fourth of all U.S. children under 6 years old live in families with incomes below that poverty line. While many highly educated and hard-working people earn below-average incomes, some sports stars, entertainers, and corporate executives earn millions of dollars each year.

This is the family's median income

Why are some people rich and others poor? Why do some people earn high salaries while others earn low wages? Why don't businesses or people who pay high salaries find people who are willing to work for less? Why have wages of unskilled workers stagnated for the last two decades while salaries of educated workers have risen? What can governments do about poverty?[3]

refer to ch. 17, 18, 21

PRICE CHANGES AND INFLATION

Some prices fall over time. The price of computing power (measured in millions of instructions per second, or MIPS) is only a tiny fraction of its level five years ago. Other prices rise over time. The average level of prices in the United States is now about 2.5 times as high as it was 20 years ago, and 6 times as high as in 1950. A rise in the average level of prices is called *inflation*. Inflation in the United States has averaged about 4 percent per year since 1980, down from 7.3 percent per year in the decade before that. Some episodes of inflation have been much higher. After World War I, inflation in Germany averaged 322 percent per *month*. More recently, inflation has reached 1,000 percent per year in Argentina, Bolivia, and Peru, and several hundred percent per year in Brazil and Israel.

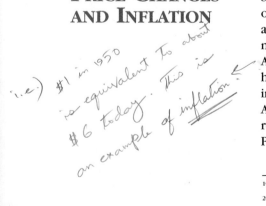

i.e.) $1 in 1950 is equivalent to about $6 today. This is an example of inflation

---

[1]These questions are the main topic of Chapter 26.

[2]This is their median income.

[3]These questions are discussed in Chapters 17, 18, and 21.

TABLE 1.1

HOW PEOPLE SPEND THEIR MONEY (AVERAGE ANNUAL SPENDING PER PERSON IN THE UNITED STATES)[a]

Type of Spending	Dollars Spent	Percentage of Total Spending
Food	$3,230	17.0%
Housing	3,040	16.0
Medical care	2,660	14.0
Household operations	1,140	6.0
Motor vehicles and parts	950	5.0
Gasoline and oil	475	2.5
Clothing	1,045	5.5
Furniture and household equipment	855	4.5
Other transportation	760	4.0
Other durable goods	380	2.5
Other nondurable goods	1,330	7.0
Other services (such as vacations, entertainment, haircuts, insurance, and education)	3,040	16.0

[a]Based on consumption spending per person of $19,000.

Why do some prices rise? Why do some prices fall? Why has the average price level risen? (It might seem easy to explain price increases by saying that sellers raise prices to earn more income. But that incomplete explanation does not address the questions of why sellers don't raise prices even higher or why sellers don't raise prices every year.) Why do prices rise more in some years than in others? Why is inflation higher in some countries than in others?[4] → ch. 4, 27, 32

WHERE THE MONEY GOES

What happens to the $28,000 per person in goods and services that the U.S. economy produces each year? Federal, state, and local governments buy about 18 percent of the economy's output, worth almost $5,000 per person. (Governments use tax dollars and borrow money to buy these goods for national defense, education, road maintenance, and other purposes.) This leaves about $23,000 worth of goods and services per person. About $4,000 of these remaining goods go for investment in new capital, that is, machinery, equipment, tools, buildings, and other manufactured items that can help produce more goods in the future. (The economy invests in new capital by producing this machinery and equipment. Some of the investment simply replaces old, worn-out equipment. The rest adds to the economy's capital.) Subtracting investment leaves goods worth about $19,000 for each person to buy in a year. **Table 1.1** shows what a typical person buys each year. About half of a typical person's spending goes to buy food, housing, and medical care.

What affects the amount of money that people spend on food, housing, and other goods and services? When gasoline prices rise, total spending

---

[4]Chapter 4 discusses prices. Chapters 27 and 32 focus on inflation.

TABLE 1.2

WHAT HAPPENS TO A DOLLAR SPENT AT A TYPICAL, LARGE SPECIALTY STORE

The Dollar Pays for:	Fraction of Each Dollar Spent
Cost of the goods that the store sells	59.5 cents
Operating costs	
Wages for store workers	15.7
Property rental or mortgage payment	7.1
Advertising (newspapers, radio, TV, and mail)	2.6
Depreciation (replacing worn-out equipment)	2.0
Services (lawyers, accountants, janitors)	2.0
Supplies (bags and receipt forms)	1.8
Fringe benefits for workers (insurance)	1.4
Taxes unrelated to profits (property and real estate taxes)	1.3
Insurance	0.6
Other expenses (telephone service, pensions, and bad debts)	4.0
Total operating costs	38.5
Profit before paying income taxes	2.0

on gasoline rises, but when fast-food restaurants raise their prices, total spending at those restaurants falls. What causes the difference? What happens to the economy when people decide to spend more money and save less, or to save more and spend less?[5]

What happens to the money you spend at a store? You pay $30 for a sweater that costs the store about $18, on average. The remaining $12 is the store's markup. **Table 1.2** shows what happens to each dollar spent at a typical, large specialty store (such as a clothing store or a sporting-goods store) in the United States. Out of every dollar spent in the store, about 59.5 cents covers the store's cost of buying the goods it sells. The other 40.5 cents—the markup—covers the store's net operating expenses (such as wages) and its profit. Expenses listed in Table 1.2 total 38.5 cents out of every dollar spent, so the store's total cost of goods and operating expenses are 98.0 cents of each dollar of sales. This leaves the typical store with 2.0 cents in profit from each dollar of sales. Some specialty stores earn additional income in other ways; for example, some record stores earn money by renting space to ticket agencies. This other income averages about 0.3 cents per dollar spent at the typical store. So the average specialty store ends up with a pretax profit of about 2.3 cents per dollar spent there.[6]

The numbers are similar at other kinds of stores. A fast-food restaurant, for example, has a markup of about 60 cents for every dollar spent. (The other 40 cents covers the restaurant's cost of food.) Operating expenses—wages and the other items listed in Table 1.2—are about 54 cents out of each dollar, leaving the fast-food restaurant a pretax profit of about 6 cents on each dollar spent. Only about 35 cents of every dollar you spend at a grocery store covers the direct cost of the food you buy.

---

[5]Chapters 5, 9, 24 to 26, and 29 to 31 discuss these and related issues.

[6]Smaller specialty stores have smaller profits than this, and larger stores average higher profits. These numbers change somewhat from year to year.

About 35 cents pays wages and benefits for workers, and about 27 cents covers other costs such as packaging, advertising, transportation, and utilities; this leaves the grocery store with a pretax profit of about 3 cents of each dollar you spend.

What determines the size of a business's profits? Why don't stores raise prices to increase their profits? What makes profits rise or fall? What affects business costs? What happens when business costs rise? How do business decisions affect workers and customers? How does foreign competition affect prices and profits? How does foreign competition affect the jobs available for people at home and their wages? What would happen if the government were to limit competition from foreign sellers?[7]

GOVERNMENT POLICIES

Most major political issues involve the economy. Some people argue that the government should play a more active role in the economy, perhaps spending more, levying higher taxes, and imposing more regulations on the economy. Others argue that the government should reduce its spending, cut taxes, and decrease the regulations that it imposes on the economy. Economic issues play key roles in almost every election, in the United States as well as most other countries.

How do government economic policies affect people's lives? How are people affected by taxes and government spending? Who benefits and who loses from government regulations? How will your life be affected by the government budget deficit and the national debt? How do economic events in Russia, China, Japan, Mexico, and other countries affect your life? What can the government do about unemployment, inflation, poverty, the environment, and other economic problems? What *should* it do?[8]

DEFINITIONS OF *ECONOMICS*

economics — the study of how a society uses its scarce resources to produce, trade, and consume goods and services; also, the study of people's incentives and choices and what happens to coordinate their decisions and activities

There is no perfect definition of economics. Roughly, economics is the study of the kinds of issues outlined above and discussed in this book. The most common definition states that:

Economics is the study of how a society uses its limited resources to produce, trade, and consume goods and services.

Another definition states that:

Economics is the study of people's incentives and choices and what happens to coordinate their decisions and activities.

The first definition emphasizes scarcity. Resources are scarce, or limited, so people cannot have everything they want. They have to make choices. People decide how to grow food with limited time and energy, and with limited land, tools, seeds, fertilizer, and rainfall. They decide how to divide their limited time

---

[7]Chapters 4 through 7, 10 through 14, 17, 25, and 35 discuss these issues.

[8]The government budget deficit is the amount of money that the government borrows from people because it spends more than it collects in taxes. The national debt is the amount of money that the government owes people because it has borrowed money in the past. Many chapters of this book discuss government policies that affect its deficit and debt.

between work and leisure. They decide whether to enjoy more consumption now or save more for the future. Each of the economic problems mentioned earlier arises from scarcity. Economic growth, poverty, price increases, and unemployment would not be problems if resources were not scarce. Real life involves scarcity, however, so it involves hard choices and tradeoffs. These are the subjects of economics.

The second definition emphasizes that people's decisions can conflict with one another, and that something must happen to make their decisions and activities fit together. Some people must choose to practice medicine, others to produce food, build houses, teach children, manufacture cars, push the frontiers of science, engineer new products, and entertain. The job choices that people make must fit together—they need coordination. A construction crew building a house may need supplies of wood, bricks, mortar, glass, electrical wire, and other materials. The right kinds of materials, in the right sizes and quantities, must arrive at the construction site at the right times. Hundreds of people around the country (or the world) work to produce and deliver these supplies; all of these workers' decisions and activities need coordination. Economics is about how the activities of many people are coordinated even though no one person plans and directs those activities. It is also about the results of this coordinated activity, how it affects people's lives, and how people change their decisions and activities when conditions change.

─────────────── **FOR REVIEW** ───────────────

1.1 State and explain two definitions of economics. *p. 7*

1.2 What is the total value of all of the goods and services produced in the world each year? How much is that per person? Repeat these questions for the U.S. production of goods and services.

1.3 Roughly how much has output of goods and services per person in the United States increased over the last 25 years? Roughly how much have prices in the United States increased (on average) since 1950? Roughly how large are the profits of a typical retail store per dollar spent at the store?

─────────────── **QUESTIONS** ───────────────

1.4 Consider this statement: "People were better off in the past than they are today because the prices of houses, cars, and most other goods were much lower in the past." Do you agree? Explain.

1.5 If the prices of textbooks increase, would your spending on textbooks rise or fall? An earlier section said that total spending at fast-food restaurants falls when those restaurants raise their prices. Explain how this could happen. Why might the textbook and fast-food cases differ?

SCARCITY AND CHOICE

goods — (also *goods and services*) things that people want

Goods (or goods and services) are products, services, and other things that people want.

A good is something that people want. It may be a tangible product like milk or a VCR, a service like a haircut, or something more abstract like leisure time or peace on earth. Economists say that a good is scarce (or limited) when people want

opportunity cost — the value of what someone must sacrifice or give up to get something

---

more than the total amount available. Obviously, most material goods are scarce and so are many other things. Space on earth is scarce; time is scarce. Things that are not scarce are free goods; air is a free good, though *clean* air can be scarce.

Scarcity requires people to make choices. How will you spend your limited income? How will you spend your time today? How will you spend your life?

SCARCITY AND OPPORTUNITY COST

Before reading further, get a pencil and paper (which you should always have handy while reading this book). List five things that you could be doing right now if you were not reading this book. When you complete your list, ask yourself which listed activity you would choose if this book were suddenly to vanish. You have just discovered an important economic truth: every scarce good has an opportunity cost.

The **opportunity cost** of something is the value of what someone must sacrifice or give up for it.

The opportunity cost of reading this book is the benefit you could have enjoyed from the activity that you chose above. Consequently, reading this book costs you something, even if you already own it. Your cost is the time that you could have spent doing something else. Of course, that other activity must be feasible (possible). Sailing on your private yacht might sound nice, but unless you can afford a yacht, it cannot be your opportunity cost of reading this book. This discussion implies an important principle of economics:

The cost of any decision or action is its opportunity cost.

EXAMPLES OF OPPORTUNITY COSTS

1. The opportunity cost of buying a T-shirt might be buying a compact disk. Perhaps your opportunity cost of becoming an economist is becoming a biologist.

2. Recycling often costs cities and towns more money than they would spend to dispose of the recycled materials in landfills. In 1993, studies showed that recycling plastic, glass, aluminum cans, and paper cost about $20 more per ton than disposal, not including the higher costs of collecting recyclables. Because local governments could have used that money for other purposes such as health care and education, the opportunity cost of recycling is higher government spending on these other services (or lower taxes).

3. The opportunity cost of buying a jacket includes not only the money you spend, but also includes the time you spend going to the store, making your decision, and waiting in line to pay. The time spent waiting in line can be a big part of the total cost of buying a good. In the Soviet Union, the average person routinely spent about one-fourth of her total time each day (excluding sleep) waiting in lines![9]

4. The opportunity cost of four years in college might be four years at Disney World, where you could work part-time waiting tables, learn about the amusement-park industry without paying tuition, and have a good time.

---

[9]People in many former socialist countries faced long lines at stores. Retired people often earned money by waiting in line for other people. The world energy crisis in the 1970s led to long lines to buy gasoline in the United States; some Los Angeles high-school students started businesses filling up other people's cars with gasoline.

DECISIONS AND INCENTIVES

Goods have opportunity costs because they are scarce, and these opportunity costs require people to make decisions. Is a pizza worth its opportunity cost? Is college worth its opportunity cost?

People make decisions every day. You must decide whether to watch more television or go to sleep, whether to eat dessert, whether and when to get married or have children, whether to put a hotel on Marvin Gardens or use the cash for another house on Boardwalk, whether to keep what you have or trade it for what's behind the curtain, whether to major in economics or engineering, and whether to keep reading this book.

Decisions are influenced by incentives—the expected benefits of each possible decision minus its opportunity cost.

incentive — the expected benefit of a decision minus its opportunity cost

> An **incentive** is the expected benefit of a decision minus its opportunity cost.

You have an incentive to do something if you expect its benefit to exceed its opportunity cost. You probably have an incentive to read this book because you want a good grade and because you expect economics to be useful to you in the future. If these benefits are worth more to you than the opportunity cost of reading this book (which you identified in the previous section), you have an incentive to continue reading. Incentives also affect business decisions such as how much to produce, how much to invest, and whether to fire or hire a worker. A business has an incentive to produce a good if it believes that customers are willing to pay a price higher than the cost of producing the good. A business has an incentive to hire a worker if the new employee would raise the value of its output by more than the firm would have to pay the worker. Government economic policies affect the economy partly through their effects on incentives. High sales taxes on a good, for example, discourage people from buying it.

Economics is partly the study of incentives and how laws, government policies, customs, advances in technology, and other forces affect incentives and influence decisions. It is also partly the study of how those incentives affect people's decisions, and how those decisions affect which goods and how many goods an economy produces, and who gets to consume those goods. This highlights the problem of coordinating people's decisions and activities.

IN THE NEWS

Increasingly, life and death issues become money matters

Medical care has always been a scarce resource, forcing decisions as to who will receive treatment and who will not. But the choices have come to seem more stark as public attention has been drawn to highly sophisticated techniques—treatments such as organ transplants and diagnostic methods such as nuclear magnetic resonance imaging—that are not available to everyone who needs them.

Scarcity of sophisticated equipment forces decisions about its use.

Source: "Increasingly, Life and Death Issues Become Money Matters," *New York Times,* March 20, 1988, p. E6.

FOR REVIEW

1.6 What is an opportunity cost? Give two examples.

1.7 What are incentives?

QUESTIONS

1.8 What is your opportunity cost of attending this economics course? What is your opportunity cost of attending college?

1.9 What choices have you made today? What incentives influenced your choices?

1.10 What are your incentives to study? How would these incentives change if your professors were to announce that they will give all *A*s in their courses? If you knew that the job market would be tight when you leave college? After you leave college, how will an increase in income taxes affect your incentive to work?

COORDINATION OF ECONOMIC DECISIONS AND ACTIVITIES

It is easy to take the coordination of our economy for granted. Every day, people buy corn from Iowa, clothes from New Jersey made from cotton grown in Texas, and televisions from Japan. They make products using parts from distant countries, and they ship their finished products across the country and around the world. People seldom stop to think how amazing this is. Although no one directs the economy, the activities of billions of people fit together.

What would life be like if you had to produce all of your own food, your own shelter, and all of the other goods you use? Even with access to every book ever published on modern technology, no single person could make many of the goods available in our economy. Millions of people would die if food, medical supplies, and energy for heat stopped flowing from around the world into the cities where they live. Few people ever pause to worry about this prospect, though. Most people never doubt that stores will continue to offer goods for sale. People buy all kinds of goods without knowing who made them or how. Meanwhile, people around the world are working right now to produce goods for people they have never met in places they will never go, for people who speak different languages and practice different cultures. How do all these people know which goods to produce and how much? How do they know where to ship the goods? The answers to these questions are the subjects of economics. Although the details vary across societies and situations, the answers almost always involve some form of competition for scarce resources, usually based on the market process.

COMPETITION

Not every team can win. Not everyone can be first in line, use the tennis court at noon, or live in a house on the ocean. When people, businesses, or sports teams try to get something that not all of them can have, they compete. Scarcity inspires competition.

competition — the process by which people attempt to acquire scarce goods for themselves

Competition is the process by which people attempt to acquire scarce goods for themselves.

Competition takes many forms. Sports teams compete for a scarce good— victory. Students compete for grades and honors, and later for good jobs. Workers compete for promotions. Stores compete for customers. Cities compete for tourists and new businesses. People compete for attention and affection from others.

You might think that competition for scarce resources would stop if the government were to allocate those resources, but whenever this has been tried, it has changed only the form of competition as people then compete for government favors. They may lobby the government (or even offer bribes) in pursuit of those favors.[10] When a local government chooses a cable-television company to serve a town, several companies are likely to compete, by lobbying, to be chosen. Business firms often compete for special favors from the government such as exemptions from regulations.

In a common form of competition, people or business firms compete for customers by trying to offer the most desirable good or service on the best terms (such as the lowest price or most flexible payment schedule). Colleges, for example, compete for students by trying to offer attractive campuses, strong academic

---

[10]Lobbying the government means trying to convince the government to do what you want, perhaps by presenting arguments for its merit, entertaining government officials, and trying to convince them that doing what you want raises their chances of reelection.

programs, interesting features of nonacademic life for students, and scholarships that reduce costs for students who might not otherwise attend. Restaurants compete by offering attractive combinations of price, food quality, selection, service, atmosphere, and convenience. Most of this book—indeed, most of economics—focuses on this form of competition, which employs the market process.

MARKET PROCESS

Most economic activity takes place in markets:

> A **market** is the activity of people buying and selling goods.

market — the activity of people buying and selling goods

Some people think of a market as a specific store or another place where people buy and sell, but economists use the term in a broader sense. For example, the real estate market is not a place; it is the actions of people trying to buy and sell houses and land. The incentives created by voluntary buying and selling coordinate the actions in a market. This process of coordination is the market process:

> The **market process** is the coordination of people's economic activities through voluntary trades. **Trading** means buying and selling.

market process — the coordination of people's economic activities through voluntary trades

trading — buying and selling

Adam Smith, an 18th-century philosopher who is regarded as the founder of modern economics, pointed out two important features of the market process:

1. When people trade voluntarily, all parties expect to benefit.
2. Because people trade, each person's actions affect other people. Even selfish actions often help other people.

The first point observes that people expect to benefit from a trade, or else they would not trade. This point is obvious, but it is still important to remember.

Smith's second point is more subtle. Think of a baker who cares only about his own income. The baker can spend his time baking either bread or cakes, but which should he bake? If his customers want bread, it would be foolish to bake mostly cakes; he could earn more money by baking bread. Even though he cares only about his own income, he has an incentive to bake the goods that customers want most, measured by how much those customers are willing to pay. Though the baker acts from a selfish motive, the market process gives him an incentive to help his customers by producing the goods that those customers want most.

In his landmark book, *The Wealth of Nations,* published in 1776, Adam Smith explained:

> It is not from the benevolence of the butcher, the brewer, or the baker that we expect our dinner, but from their regard to their own interest. We address ourselves not to their humanity but to their self-love and never talk to them of our own necessities but of their advantages.[11]

Through voluntary trades, each person helps others when she attempts to help herself. Even a person who acts selfishly is often "led by an invisible hand to promote an end which was no part of his intention." That unintended end is to help other people. Smith pointed out that, "By pursuing his own interest he frequently promotes that of society more effectually than when he really intends to promote it."

The market process coordinates people's economic actions by providing them with incentives to do things that benefit others. A story written as the auto-

---

[11]Adam Smith, *The Wealth of Nations* (1776; reprint, New York: Knopf, 1991).

biography of a pencil demonstrates the remarkable coordination of activities that arises from the market process.[12] A pencil is a simple good, but making one from scratch would be difficult. Pencils are made because the market process coordinates the activities of many people, fitting them together for a purpose. Some people grow trees and cut them for wood. They use saws, axes, motors, and ropes made by others. They transport the cut logs to a mill using equipment made by a third group of people. Other people convert the logs into slats at the mill, and still others ship the slats to pencil companies. Meanwhile, people in another country mine the graphite (the "lead") for the center of the pencil, and other people transport it to the country where it will be sold. Another group of people mine zinc and copper to manufacture the little piece of brass that holds the eraser at the top of the pencil. Still other people manufacture that eraser.

People from around the world work together to make the pencil. They do not know one another; few even know that they helped to make a pencil. The pencil was not made because any one person planned the whole operation and directed it from start to finish; the pencil was made because the market process coordinated the activities of many people who live in different lands with different languages, cultures, and religions. They may not understand or like each other. Most of them work mainly to serve their own self-interests. Still, the market process provides them with incentives and coordinates their actions to produce a pencil. The same process operates to produce nearly every good or service you can name.

It is this coordination of the activities of people who don't even know each other, let alone care about each other, that Adam Smith had in mind when he wrote of an "invisible hand" in the market process. The economist Friedrich Hayek has called this coordination a "spontaneous order" that is "the result of human action but not of human design."

PROPERTY RIGHTS

People must be able to own things to make the market process work; they must have private property.

ownership — the right to make decisions about a good

> **Ownership** means having the right to make decisions about a good; that good is the owner's **private property.**

private property — something that a person owns

Property rights are the legal recognition of ownership.[13]

property right — a person's legal right to decide whether and how to use a scarce resource or to sell it to someone else

> **Property rights** are people's legal rights to decide whether and how to use scarce resources or to sell them to others.

Owners have property rights in all kinds of goods, including land, various products, their bodies, and even their ideas. Property rights are related to freedom; people are free to choose what to do with their private property.

Laws and government regulations often limit property rights, restricting owners' choices about whether and how to use their property. Property rights are limited by laws that prohibit opening businesses in residential areas (on private land), taking illegal drugs (in one's own body), or selling medical advice (one's own ideas) without a license. Taxes on money that people earn also limit their property rights because they cannot keep all of the money for which they sell their labor services.

---

[12]Leonard E. Read, "I, Pencil: My Family Tree as Told to Leonard E. Read," *The Freeman,* December 1958.

[13]Some people use the term to refer to moral rights rather than legal rights.

Limitations on property rights (or uncertainty about them) can interfere with the market process. The market process needs property rights to provide people with incentives to do things that benefit others. Limits on property rights can interfere with these incentives. A baker may be willing to bake a cake if he can sell it for at least $6 to cover the cost of ingredients, the use of his oven, and his time and effort. If a customer is willing to pay $10 for a cake, then the baker will gladly bake it and collect the $4 profit. Suppose that the baker has only limited property rights in the cakes, however, because the government collects a $5 tax on each cake sold. If the baker were to sell a cake for $10, this would leave only $5 after paying the tax, not enough to cover the cost of the ingredients, the use of the oven, and the baker's time and effort. The baker would be willing to sell the cake for $11 (leaving $6 after paying the tax), but the customer may not be willing to pay $11 for the cake. The tax limits property rights and removes the baker's incentive to produce some of the goods that customers want.

Property rights also provide incentives for people to maintain and conserve scarce resources. When no one owns a lake or stream, few people have sufficient incentives to prevent its pollution. In contrast, the owner of a lake or stream that is private property has an incentive to care for it to maintain its value. Water pollution has not been a serious problem in Scotland because people own streams there. Forests around the world have been destroyed because no one owned the trees that were cut, so no one had an incentive to balance the gains from maintaining the forests with the gains from using the wood and replenishing the forests. Property rights are essential for the effective operation of the market process.

--- **FOR REVIEW** ---

1.11 What is competition? The market process?

1.12 Who wrote *The Wealth of Nations* and what important points did it make?

1.13 What are property rights?

--- **QUESTIONS** ---

1.14 Explain how someone can own a song. How can someone own information or an idea?

1.15 Explain how the market process can lead people who act out of selfish interests to do things that help others.

CONCLUSIONS

Some important issues in economics include:

▶ What causes economic growth?

▶ What causes differences in people's incomes?

▶ What affects the prices of goods and services?

▶ What affects the amounts of money that people spend and save, how they spend money, and the quantities of goods and services that the economy produces?

▶ What affects business costs, business profits, and job opportunities for workers?

▶ How do government policies affect the economy?

Clashing priorities: Cancer drug may save many human lives—at cost of rare trees

That angers conservationists, who say taxol extraction endangers the prized yew

Right now, medical researchers say, the only way to produce quickly all the taxol that is needed for treatment and testing would be to chop down tens of thousands of yews. And conservationists are successfully opposing any large-scale sacrificing of the tree, which grows in the ancient forests that are refuge to the endangered Northern spotted owl and other wildlife.

"This is the ultimate confrontation between medicine and the environment," says Bruce Chabner of the National Cancer Institute, sponsor of the studies. "It's the spotted owl vs. people. I love the spotted owl, but I love people more."

Opportunity costs can create political conflicts.

Source: "Clashing Priorities: Cancer Drug May Save Many Human Lives—At Cost of Rare Trees," *The Wall Street Journal*, April 9, 1991, p. A1.

DEFINITIONS OF *ECONOMICS*

The most common definition states that economics is the study of how a society uses its limited resources to produce, trade, and consume goods and services. Another definition states that economics is the study of people's incentives and choices, and what happens to coordinate their decisions and actions. These definitions are both correct; each emphasizes different aspects of economics.

SCARCITY AND CHOICE

Scarce goods have an opportunity cost, that is, people must sacrifice something for them. An incentive is the expected benefit of a decision minus its opportunity cost. Incentives affect decisions.

COMPETITION, THE MARKET PROCESS, AND PROPERTY RIGHTS

Competition is the process by which people attempt to acquire scarce goods for themselves. The market process is one form of competition that coordinates people's activities through voluntary trades. When people trade voluntarily, they expect to benefit. The market process can lead people pursuing only their own interests to do things that help others. Adam Smith described the market process in *The Wealth of Nations* with a metaphor: people acting in their own self-interest are "led by an invisible hand" to help others.

The market process operates well only when people have private property. A property right is a person's legal right to decide whether and how to use a scarce resource or whether to sell it to someone else. Limitations on property rights can interfere with incentives for voluntary trades and change the results of the market process.

LOOKING AHEAD

We will begin by studying the methods of economics in Chapter 2, and the gains from voluntary trades in Chapter 3. This will prepare you to delve more deeply into the principles of economics and its many applications.

This book is broadly divided into two parts covering macroeconomic issues, which involve the economy as a whole, and microeconomic issues, which involve the details of some part of the economy. **Table 1.3** shows some examples of macroeconomic and microeconomic issues. Sometimes an issue—such as unemployment—involves both microeconomics and macroeconomics. The main methods economists use are the same for microeconomics and macroeconomics, and the next chapter addresses these methods.

TABLE 1.3

MICROECONOMICS AND MACROECONOMICS

Microeconomic Issues	Macroeconomic Issues
Who works in which job?	Total employment and unemployment
Male/female or black/white wage differences	Average wages
Prices of computers and hamburgers	Average prices of all goods; inflation

KEY TERMS

economics

goods

opportunity cost

incentive

competition

market

market process

trading

ownership

private property

property right

QUESTIONS AND PROBLEMS

1.16 What is the opportunity cost of getting married?

1.17 Read the news article, "Clashing Priorities: Cancer Drug May Save Many Human Lives—At Cost of Rare Trees," and explain how it is related to scarcity and opportunity costs.

1.18 An auto dealer bought 300 new cars from the manufacturer in September for $12,000 each and 100 cars remained unsold by June. After selling the cars in July, the dealer complained, "My inventory costs of carrying those 100 cars from September to July were enormous." What did that mean? What is a business firm's opportunity cost of holding inventories?

1.19 Explain how a tax can interfere with the incentives of a seller to do things that benefit customers.

1.20 Explain how limitations on property rights can lead people to waste scarce resources.

INQUIRIES FOR FURTHER THOUGHT

1.21 Reread the news article from Problem 1.17. How do you think our society should make decisions on matters like this?

1.22 Do people always benefit from voluntary trades? Why might voluntary trades leave them worse off rather than better off?

1.23 Should the government prohibit people from trading some goods or services? Defend your answer.

1.24 Why do retail stores stay in business if they earn only a few cents profit per dollar spent in the store? What is the smallest profit that a retailer would be willing to accept rather than going out of business?

1.25 Do you think people respond to incentives? How would you find out if they do in some specific situation?

TAG SOFTWARE APPLICATIONS

TUTORIAL EXERCISES

▶ This module contains a review of the key terms in Chapter 1.

CHAPTER 2

SOLVING PUZZLES: THE METHODS OF ECONOMICS

WHAT THIS CHAPTER IS ABOUT

▶ Statements about what *is* versus what *should be*

▶ Economic models: logical thinking about economics

▶ Evidence in economics

▶ Logical fallacies

▶ Statistics and lying with statistics

A prominent economist recently told the U.S. Congress:

> Interest rates have risen due to higher government budget deficits. Congress should act promptly to reduce the deficit through tax increases and selective cuts in government spending.

Notice that the economist made two kinds of statements:

1. A statement of *fact:* that higher government budget deficits caused interest rates to rise.

2. A statement of *values:* that action "to reduce the deficit through tax increases and selective cuts in government spending" would be good (i.e., Congress *should* take such action).

The first statement is either true or false. It involves facts, not value judgements. It states what *is,* not what *should be.* The second statement is neither true or false. It represents a person's opinion about what *should be,* so it involves that person's value judgements. Economics is mostly about making statements of fact, though economists are often motivated by controversies over social and political issues raised by questions of economic policies and what *should be.*

POSITIVE AND NORMATIVE ECONOMICS

There are two kinds of statements, positive and normative.

Positive statements are statements of fact, of what *is* or what *would be* if something else were to happen. Positive statements are either true or false.

positive statement — a statement of fact, of what *is* or what *would be* if something else were to happen; such a statement is either true or false

[handwritten: Can be true or false]

normative statement — a statement that expresses a value judgement or says what *should be;* such a statement cannot be true or false

[handwritten: It's neither right or wrong]

Normative statements express value judgements; they state what *should be.* Normative statements cannot be true or false.

EXAMPLES

Positive Statements	Normative Statements
Drugs can affect your health.	Drugs should be illegal.
If drugs were legal, then more people would take drugs.	We need a stronger antidrug policy.
A reduction in the corporate income tax would raise investment, but it would also raise the budget deficit.	The corporate income tax should be cut.

Sometimes no one knows for sure whether a positive statement is true or false and opinions on it differ. For example, consider this positive statement: There are simple forms of life on other planets in our solar system. No one knows (yet) whether this statement is true or false, and scientists have different opinions about it. Someday, perhaps, we will learn who is right. On the other hand, consider this normative statement: Classical music is better than popular music. It is neither true or false. People disagree about it, but neither side is right or wrong.

Economics as a science involves positive statements about the economy. Knowledge about the economy gained by studying these positive statements can help people make more intelligent decisions. For example, positive statements about the effect of a tax increase on the economy can help us decide whether the government should raise taxes.

MODELS AND EVIDENCE

There are two ways to study almost any subject:

1. Think logically about it.
2. Gather evidence about it.

Economists use both methods. When economists think logically about an economic problem, they produce **economic models:**

economic model — a description of logical thinking about an economic issue stated in words, graphs, or mathematics

An **economic model** is a description of logical thinking about an economic issue. It may state its conclusions in words, graphs, or mathematics.

Logical thinking by itself is not sufficient to reach reliable conclusions about economics; logic needs the support of **evidence.**

evidence — any set of facts that helps to convince people that a positive statement is true or false

Economic **evidence** is any set of facts that helps convince economists that some positive statement about the economy is true or false.

Many sciences gather evidence through controlled experiments. Sometimes scientists also gather evidence simply by observing nature. Physicists learn about stars and galaxies by observing them and measuring their emissions of radiation; medical researchers learn about diseases by observing differences in their incidence in different societies and using statistical analysis to draw inferences about those observations.

statistical analysis — the use of mathematical probability theory to draw inferences in situations of uncertainty

Statistical analysis is the use of mathematical probability theory to draw inferences in situations of uncertainty.

Economists gather most of their evidence from observation followed by statistical analysis. An economist might examine inflation and interest rates in ten countries over the last 40 years (or the last century) to gather evidence about the connections between inflation and interest rates. This evidence could help the economist decide which of several economic models is best.

The rest of this chapter discusses economic models and evidence, logical fallacies and statistical fallacies, and how to interpret graphs. Much of the material in this chapter applies not only to economics but to other subjects as well.

ASSUMPTIONS AND CONCLUSIONS

Every economic model requires *assumptions* about how people behave. The model uses these assumptions to draw logical conclusions. These conclusions often take the form of "If . . . then . . . " statements that say what will happen *if* someone does something. These conclusions are the *predictions* of the model.[1]

Though you may not realize it, you use models in everyday life. Your models rely on assumptions and you use them to make predictions. Here are some examples of simple models:

EXAMPLES

1. All the other people who interview for the job will talk about their experiences and qualifications, but this company wants to find someone different, with innovative ideas. If I prepare a written summary of my goals on this job and give it to them at the interview, I will impress them. Then I'll probably get the job offer.

2. She would want me to kiss her if the time and place were right. She likes walks in the moonlight. If everything goes well tonight, I'll take her for a walk and then . . .

Figure 2.1 shows a model of a play in American football. The lines show where players on the offensive team are supposed to go on the play, and where that team *assumes* that the defensive players will go. If these assumptions are correct, the quarterback, can complete a pass to the wide receiver. This is the model's prediction. If the assumptions are wrong, then one of the defensive players may break up the play.

Each of these examples uses assumptions to derive a prediction or hypothesis. You can think of a model as a daydream based on logical reasoning.

GOOD AND BAD MODELS

A model is good if it achieves its purpose. The models in the previous examples are good if the actions that they suggest raise the chance of getting the job, the kiss, or the completed pass.

You might think it is easy to find out whether a model is good or bad: simply do what the model says and see what happens. But the predictions of a bad model might turn out to be true (someone might get the job, the kiss, or the completed pass) simply by luck. Also, the predictions of a good model might be wrong by chance (perhaps the quarterback throws a bad pass or the intended receiver drops the ball). So it is *not* easy to find out if a model is good or bad. However, a good

---

[1] A prediction, or the model that generated it, is sometimes called an *hypothesis*.

FIGURE 2.1

MODEL OF A PLAY IN AMERICAN FOOTBALL

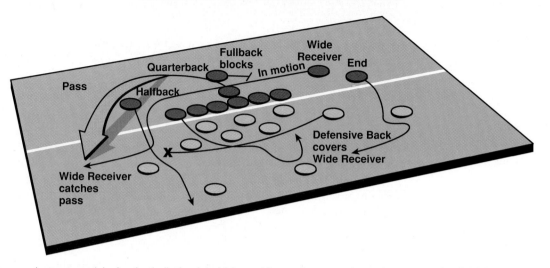

This diagram shows a model of a football play in which a wide receiver goes in motion across the field intending to fool the defensive back and break open to catch a pass.

model is more likely than a bad model to lead to a successful outcome. Therefore, economists use statistical analysis to control for luck and decide how good or bad their models are.

PURPOSES OF MODELS

Economic models have three purposes:

1. *Understanding.*   Models simplify an issue to help us understand it.
2. *Prediction.*   Models help us predict; they help us to answer questions like "What will happen . . . " and "What will happen *if* . . . " to resolve complicated, real-life issues.
3. *Interpretation.*   Models help us to interpret data as evidence about positive economic statements.

1.   MODELS SIMPLIFY AN ISSUE

Models are simpler than the real-life situations they represent. The limited abilities of human minds can make it hard to comprehend complicated real-life situations. Consequently, we create models—simplified versions of reality—to help us think logically about real life.[2] A model assumes that some features of an issue are important to think about while other features are unimportant enough to ignore.

---

[2]Models help us to economize on a scarce resource—our time and ability—and thereby make the search for knowledge more efficient.

EXAMPLES

Imagine explaining to someone how a car works. You might give a general explanation of how the engine works and ignore the details (such as the chemistry and physics of combustion). This simplified explanation, or model, may do the job. Similarly, suppose you are teaching a friend to play tennis. You cover the most important points about how to swing the racket, ignoring subtle details. Your *model* of tennis ignores these details to help focus your friend's attention on the most important aspects of the game; this model is useful because it helps your friend to understand the game and learn to play it.

2. MODELS HELP US TO PREDICT

Economists may want to predict next year's inflation rate or the effect of a cut in military spending on unemployment. *Unconditional predictions* answer questions of the form, "What will happen?" *Conditional predictions* answer questions of the form, "What will happen *if* . . . ?" (For example, how would unemployment change if the government cut military spending by $20 billion?) Conditional predictions are particularly important because they help people to make good decisions: they tell people the likely results of alternative choices. Economists use models for both conditional and unconditional predictions.

EXPLANATION

If you want to predict your grade in a course, you need a model. Your model might say that because you are smart and motivated to study, you are likely to receive a good grade. (This is an unconditional prediction.) You may be confident that your model is good because you have received good grades in the past when you have been motivated to study.[3] Economists use models to make unconditional predictions about matters such as next year's inflation rate or foreign trade.

Conditional predictions are necessary for good decisions. You need conditional predictions to make good decisions about how much to study for your courses. You must predict how your grades and future opportunities will change if you study more. You need a model based on logical thinking to make these conditional predictions. Your model might predict that your grade will rise by one letter, and your future salary by $1,000 per year, if you study an extra 30 minutes every day. You can use such conditional predictions to decide how much to study. Economists use models to make conditional predictions about issues such as how employment and prices would respond if the government changed its economic policies; predictions from models can help the government make policy decisions.

3. MODELS HELP US TO INTERPRET DATA AS EVIDENCE

Models can suggest which pieces of information to obtain as evidence—which statistical data are relevant for a particular economic issue. Models also indicate how to use data, clarifying questions like which numbers to add or multiply together to obtain a prediction. If a model makes accurate predictions about data, this accuracy is evidence that the model is good and that it gives reliable positive economic statements. Inaccurate predictions are evidence that the model is bad.

---

[3]A different model might say that grades are completely random. Your grade could then be anything, but would most likely be about average. You might believe that this is a bad model if your past experience shows that your grades are connected to your abilities and the amount of time you study. This would be evidence that the random grade model is a bad model.

Evidence can prove that a theory is false by contradicting the predictions of the theory. Evidence that is consistent with the predictions of a theory can increase our confidence that the theory is true, but evidence cannot conclusively prove a theory. No matter how much evidence supports a theory, a possibility always remains that new evidence will contradict it.

EXPLANATION

Models tell researchers which data are relevant and which are not. Medical researchers may want to explain why a disease is more common in one country than in other countries; they need a model to guide their data collection. The model involves logical thinking about the disease and indicates which kinds of information are relevant and which are not. The model might suggest collecting data on dietary intake of a particular substance and on family medical histories. It might indicate that other data (such as information on exercise, weight, or sleep habits) are not relevant for this disease.

Models also tell researchers how to *use* information. For example, the medical researchers' model might say that the disease is more likely only if dietary intake of a substance exceeds a threshold level, or only if diets also include an abundance of another substance. If the model accurately fits the data, scientific confidence in the model will rise. If the model does not accurately fit the data, scientists will search for ways to modify the model or think about alternative models.

Economic models help researchers to decide which economic data to collect and how to use those data. To explain why inflation is lower in Switzerland than in Italy, we need a model to tell us which features of the Swiss and Italian economies to compare. Should we gather data on differences in government policies (and which policies?) or interest rates, wage increases, business costs, foreign trade, or other factors? A model tells the economist which data are relevant to explain inflation and which data are not.

The model also tells the economist how to use the data. It may tell the economist to:

1. Note the amount of new money (Swiss francs or Italian lira) each country's government has printed in the previous two years

2. Divide by the total amount of money in the country

3. Subtract the country's economic growth rate (the increase in its output of goods and services) over the last two years

This would give the economist a number for each country. The model may predict that these numbers are roughly equal to the inflation rates in the two countries. If this prediction is accurate, it is evidence that the model is good; if not, it is evidence that economists need a different economic model to explain inflation.

EXAMPLE

Economists use an economic model called the *permanent income model* to explain how much money people spend and how much they save. The logical thinking in the model tells economists to collect data on a person's average income over many years to explain that person's spending in any particular month, say April 1996. The model says that two people who are the same age and have the same education and the same average income over many years will spend about the same amount of money in April 1996, even if one person earns more than the other in that month. (The theory says that income in April 1996 is not very relevant, but average income over many years before that month *is* relevant.)[4] Economists have found that the permanent income model gives reasonably accurate predictions, though certain inaccuracies have led economists to modify it slightly.

MODELS ARE ARTIFICIAL ECONOMIES

Imagine building 1,000 robots with computers inside them, programmed to direct the robot's behavior in various situations. You design each robot to produce a certain kind of toy, sell these toys to other robots, and use the money to buy other kinds of toys from other robots. You could program each robot to respond to changes in the conditions it faces; for example, you might program a robot to buy a certain toy only if its price were sufficiently low. If you put the robots together in a room and let them interact, you could watch an entire artificial economy made up of robots.

You could change the way the robots behave by changing the computer program and see what happens to inflation, unemployment, and interest rates in the robot economy. Or you could see what happens when you change taxes or government regulations in the robot economy. If the robot economy has features that are similar to our human economy, you might conclude that the robot economy is a good model of our real, human economy.

Building these robots would be expensive. Instead, you might use mathematics to describe the robot behavior and calculate what would happen in the robot economy. This is what economists do when they build models. Sometimes economists do the mathematics by hand, and sometimes they use computers. The mathematics that describe the robots' behavior and the results of their interactions is an economic model. Economic models are artificial economies that an economist invents and writes on paper or programs into a computer.[5]

MODELS OF BEHAVIOR

Economics deals with actions by real people, not robots, so economic models require assumptions about how people behave. Economists usually assume that people behave *rationally.* This term has a very specific meaning in economics.

rational behavior — the actions of people when they do the best they can, based on their own values and information, under the circumstances they face

> **Rational behavior** means that people do the best they can, *based on their own values and information,* under the circumstances they face.

In the words of a prominent economist, people may be "selfish, altruistic, loyal, spiteful, or masochistic," but they "try as best they can to anticipate the uncertain consequences of their actions" and "maximize their own welfare *as they conceive it.*"[6]

People who dislike your values may call you *irrational,* but there are no "rational" or "irrational" values according to our definition of rational behavior. Even criminals and thoroughly disgusting people may behave rationally. Rational behavior refers to the actions people take to further their own goals, whatever those

---

[4]This oversimplifies the permanent income model a bit. The person who earns a higher income in April may also be more likely to earn a higher average income in future years, so that person would spend more in April.

[5]Scientists in other disciplines such as physics and biology use similar methods.

[6]Gary Becker, Nobel Lecture, "The Economic Way of Looking at Behavior," *Journal of Political Economy,* June 1993, pp. 385–409.

goals are. A rational person's values need not be materialistic; they may involve caring about family, friends, and poor or oppressed people around the world.

People have limited information about the future results of their actions. How many times have you done something that seemed like a good idea at the time but that you later regretted? If you do what seems best to you at the time, based on your limited information, you are acting rationally, even if you later regret your actions.

People who behave rationally can make mistakes. Rational behavior does not preclude mistakes but it implies that a person does not make the same simple mistake repeatedly; rational behavior means that people learn from past mistakes. It also means that their beliefs about the future reflect whatever information they have.

Most economic models assume that people behave rationally. Economists usually make this assumption with confidence because it has been successful in the past; it is a key part of many good economic models. Some economic models, however, are based on other assumptions about behavior in cases where evidence may indicate departures from rationality. Economists continually look for new ways to improve their models to make them better tools for understanding, predicting, and interpreting real-life economies.

FOR REVIEW

2.1 What are positive statements? What are normative statements?

2.2 What is a model and what purpose does it serve?

2.3 What do economists mean by the term *rational behavior?*

QUESTIONS

2.4 Develop a model to explain the weather (such as why it rains some days and not others).
 a. Discuss how your model simplifies the real-world situation to make it more understandable.
 b. What are some assumptions of your model?
 c. Discuss how your model can help you to predict the weather in various circumstances.
 d. Discuss how your model can help you to interpret data as evidence for or against the model.

COMMON LOGICAL FALLACIES

Most of this book will discuss economic models. Because these models involve logical reasoning, you can apply them more effectively if you understand common logical fallacies. Unfortunately, logical fallacies are common in popular economic discussions in the news media and elsewhere. Awareness of these fallacies will help you to identify invalid arguments when you hear them (and help you to reason better).

FALLACY OF COMPOSITION

fallacy of composition — false reasoning that what is true for one person must be true for the economy as a whole

A **fallacy of composition** occurs when someone says that "what is true for one person must be true for the economy as a whole."

In fact, what is true for one person is *not* necessarily true for society as a whole.

EXAMPLES

Each of the following examples shows something that is true of an individual, but not true of a larger group:

1. When a professor grades exams on a curve, an individual student can increase her grade by studying more, but the class as a whole cannot increase its grades by studying more.

2. An individual at a sports event can see better by standing up, but spectators as a whole cannot see better if everyone stands up.

3. An individual can borrow money, but the world economy as a whole cannot borrow.

4. An individual farmer gains if good weather raises his output of wheat. But if good weather raises wheat output by *all* farmers, the price of wheat might fall so much that every farmer loses. (Each farmer may sell 10 percent more wheat than in a normal year, but at only half the price per bushel.)

POST-HOC FALLACY

post-hoc fallacy — false reasoning that because one event happened before another, the first event must have caused the second event

A **post-hoc fallacy** occurs when someone says that "one event happened before another, so the first event must have *caused* the second event."

In fact, there is no necessary relation between the timing of events and which event causes which.

EXAMPLES

1. Every year, Adrian sends Christmas cards to his friends before Christmas. But he would commit the post-hoc fallacy if he concluded that his cards *caused* Christmas.

2. It always gets dark soon after the street lights begin to shine. Some street lights have automatic timers that turn them on before dark. You commit the post-hoc fallacy if you concluded that it gets dark *because* the street lights shine.

3. Business firms often borrow money to expand their operations. A conclusion that increased borrowing *causes* business expansion would illustrate the post-hoc fallacy. Instead, the desire to expand causes business firms to borrow.

OTHER-CONDITIONS FALLACY

other-conditions fallacy — false reasoning that two events will always occur together in the future because they occurred together in the past

The **other-conditions fallacy** occurs when someone says that "if two events always occurred together in the past, they will always occur together in the future."

In fact, two events may occur together under some, but not all conditions. Even if these conditions have applied in the past, they may not apply in the future. Changes in conditions can change incentives. When incentives change, past behavior is not necessarily a reliable guide to future behavior.

EXAMPLES

1. All season long, a football team punts on fourth down when it has more than one yard to go for a first down. It would be wrong to conclude that the team will punt in this situation in the future, however, because conditions might be

different. If the team is losing by three points near the end of the championship game, it may pass the ball on fourth down with five yards to go. Why? Because conditions have changed: If it punts, it will lose the game, but if it passes the ball, it may win.

2. For many years, the government of a small country collected an extra billion dollars in tax revenue every time it raised the tax on business profits by 1 percent. Recently, the government increased the tax by 1 percent, but its tax revenue did not increase. Why? Because increases in world economic integration made it easier for business firms to move to other countries with lower taxes, and some firms responded to this tax increase by doing so.

STATISTICS

Economists use *statistical analysis* to draw inferences from economic data. We have already defined statistical analysis as the use of mathematical probability theory to draw inferences in situations of uncertainty. The application of statistical analysis to economic issues is called *econometrics* or *empirical economics.*

You may have heard that people can lie with statistics. It is important to understand some basic statistical fallacies so that you can identify invalid arguments and interpret statistical arguments correctly.

STATISTICAL FALLACIES

MISLEADING COMPARISONS

One important statistical fallacy involves misleading comparisons:

misleading comparison — a comparison of two or more things that does not reflect their true differences

Statistical fallacy

A **misleading comparison** occurs when someone compares two or more things in a way that does not reflect their true differences.

IMPORTANT EXAMPLE

FAILURE TO ADJUST FOR INFLATION People sometimes compare dollar amounts in different years without adjusting for inflation. Someone who tells you "When I was your age back in 1950, I was happy to work hard for $1 an hour!" may imply that you are lazy if you will not work for $4 an hour. But this may be a misleading comparison because of inflation: $1 in 1950 is equivalent to about $6 today. Similarly, politicians sometimes say a tax increase or tax cut is "the biggest in history"; this is often misleading because they fail to adjust for inflation.

Every few years someone claims that a new movie is the highest-grossing movie of all time (the one that has earned the most money); this is usually misleading because the person seldom adjusts for inflation. In fact, *Gone with the Wind* was the highest-grossing movie of all time after adjusting for inflation. When it was released in 1939, prices were much lower than they are today. Adjusted for inflation, *Gone with the Wind* earned about $500 million in today's dollars. The appendix to this chapter shows some misleading comparisons on graphs.

SELECTION BIAS

A second important statistical fallacy is selection bias:

selection bias — use of data that are not typical, but are selected in a way that biases results

Statistical fallacy

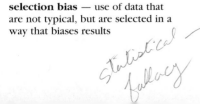

Selection bias occurs when people use data that are not *typical*, but *selected* in a way that biases their results.

EXAMPLES

1. Suppose you want to calculate the average income of rock musicians. If you use data on the average income of rock stars with hit videos on MTV, you would *not* get an accurate answer to your question. Your data would reflect only *successful* rock musicians with (on average) higher incomes. The data would not reflect the lower incomes of typical rock musicians without music videos on MTV. By looking only at the most successful performers, you cannot find out about the average income of all rock musicians.

2. Suppose you want to study the investment advice of stock analysts. You gather data on the results of investment advice given by all stock analysts who have been in business in your city for the last ten years. Did the analysts give good advice to their customers? You might find that the advice was good, on average: people who listened to these stock analysts may have earned more money on their investments (on average) than other people did. Does this mean that stock analysts give good advice, on average? Not necessarily. The problem is selection bias: you probably do not have data on those stock analysts who went out of business because they gave less successful advice. So it would be a fallacy to draw conclusions from your study about the average performance of investment advisors.

DISCUSSION

An illegal business scheme may help you to understand selection bias. First, buy a large mailing list (a list of potential customers and their addresses) and divide it into two parts. Write to people on the first part telling them that you are a stock-market expert and that you predict stock prices will *rise* next month. Write to the people on the second part of the list telling them that you are a stock-market expert and that you predict stock prices will *fall* next month. Next month, if stock prices have

---

IN THE NEWS

Data called misleading in rating contraceptives

Most methods can be effective, but bias clouds comparisons.

By Gina Kolata

The available data on the comparative effectiveness of different contraceptives is misleading and only marginally useful in helping people choose which method to use, according to a new study and a growing number of health experts.

'Selection Bias' Cited

A universal drawback of the contraception studies, the scientists said, is "selection bias." Women who are most anxious to avoid pregnancy will select methods they believe are most effective, so the group using pills, for example, is always more motivated to use the method correctly than those using contraceptive foams. Even if the foam were just as effective as the pill, more women using foam would become pregnant.

This bias is a problem "because it cannot be corrected in the analysis stage," Dr. Trussell and Dr. Kost reported.

Sample selection bias can occur in any kind of research.

Source: Gina Kolata, "Data Called Misleading in Rating Contraceptives," *New York Times,* December 1, 1987, p. C3.

fallen, your advice to people on the first part of the list was wrong, but your advice to people on the second part of the list was right. Throw away the first part of your list and keep the second part. Divide that list in two parts and repeat. After several months, you will have a small mailing list of people who have seen your predictions come true several times in a row, with no mistakes. You are now ready to charge them a high price for advice (unless they understand selection bias)!

only from one person

CORRELATIONS

When two variables (such as interest rates and inflation) tend to change together, we say they are correlated.

positive correlation — a relationship between variables that tend to rise or fall together

negative correlation — a relationship between variables that tend to move in opposite directions (inversely)

correlation — a measure of how closely two variables are related

> Two variables exhibit **positive correlation** if they tend to increase and decrease together. (They move in the same direction.) They exhibit **negative correlation** if one increases when the other decreases and vice versa. (They move in opposite directions.) The **correlation** of the variables is a number that measures how closely they are related.

EXAMPLES

Education level and income are positively correlated; people with more education tend to have higher incomes (see Figures 2A.4 and 2A.5 in the appendix to this chapter). Interest rates and inflation are positively correlated; they tend to rise and fall together. Automobile size and mileage per gallon of gasoline are negatively correlated; larger cars get fewer miles per gallon, on average.

INTERPRETING CORRELATIONS

Economists need models to interpret correlations. A correlation often has several possible interpretations. For example, many studies have found that married men earn higher wages than single men of the same age and race with the same education and experience. One interpretation is that married men work harder because they are more motivated. Another interpretation is that employers discriminate against single men; perhaps employers view married men as more reliable employees. Either of these interpretations might lead a man to believe that he could earn more money by getting married. This move might motivate him to earn more or persuade employers of his reliability. But there is a third interpretation of the correlation: perhaps women tend to marry men whose personal characteristics enable them to earn high wages. If the third interpretation is correct, a man would not be able to increase his earnings by getting married. No one knows which interpretation is correct. Until more evidence becomes available about the best model to explain this correlation, there is room for disagreement.

EVIDENCE IN ECONOMICS

Economists can gather data for statistical analyses from many sources, such as those discussed in the Economics Yellow Pages section at the end of this book. There are two main types of data. *Time series* are data on a single person, business, industry, or country over some period of time. For example, data on the average starting salary of college graduates over the last 20 years would be time-series data. *Cross sections* are data on many people, businesses, industries, or countries at one particular time. For example, data on last year's average starting salary for college graduates in each state would be cross-section data. Economists analyze time-series data to see which variables change together and how their changes are related. They analyze cross-section data to study how people or countries differ from one another and how these differences are related.

Most evidence in economics comes from nonexperimental data: data gathered by observation rather than controlled experiments, as in a science laboratory. Economics is not the only science that uses nonexperimental data. Scientists use nonexperimental data when they study stars and galaxies through telescopes or the behavior of animals in their natural environments. If economists could experiment with the economy, they could change government policies to examine the results, perhaps changing one policy at a time to isolate the separate effects of each policy. Since economists cannot do this, they usually rely on statistical analysis of nonexperimental data to produce evidence for their economic models.[7]

WHY ECONOMISTS DISAGREE

Impasse delays proposal to cut diet guidelines

By Robert Pear
Special to The New York Times

WASHINGTON, Oct. 7—In an unusual move, the National Academy of Sciences announced today that some of the nation's most eminent scientists were in an irreconcilable conflict over proposals to alter the recommended levels of certain vitamins and minerals in the human diet.

Despite "exhaustive deliberation," Dr. Press said, the experts were unable to agree on the interpretation of scientific data and the recommended allowances for several nutrients.

All sciences have areas in which experts disagree.

Source: Robert Pear, "Impasse Delays Proposal to Cut Diet Guidelines," *New York Times,* October 8, 1985, p. A14.

Economists do not always agree with each other about economic issues. Disagreements arise for two reasons:

1. Economists may disagree about the truth of positive economic statements. Sometimes the evidence for a model is mixed, with some evidence supporting the model and other evidence failing to support it. Sometimes there is simply not enough information, and the evidence is too weak to tell whether a model is good. Economists are not alone; scientists in every field have such disagreements. Disagreements over positive statements can be resolved only by accumulating more evidence.

2. Economists, like other people, disagree about values. Even if they agree about the truth of positive economic statements, they may disagree about normative statements such as what the government *should* do. Economists, like everyone else, want to convince people that they are smart and that their views on normative issues are correct, so economists who make public statements to the media are not always as honest as they should be. An economist who believes that the government should do something may exaggerate the evidence for positive economic statements that support this opinion. This exaggeration may be deliberate or unintentional, but it can create disagreements with economists who have other values.[8]

———————————————— FOR REVIEW ————————————————

2.5 Explain and give examples of:
  a. the fallacy of composition
  b. the post-hoc fallacy
  c. the other-conditions fallacy
  d. a misleading comparison
  e. selection bias

2.6 Why don't economists always agree with one another?

[7]Some evidence in economics does come from experiments. Economists create small, artificial economies and study their operation. For example, they may pay a group of students to participate in an artificial stock market to examine the behavior of stock prices in the experiment. The economist can manipulate conditions in the artificial economy to see what happens.

[8]Nobel laureate economist Robert Solow put the matter this way: economists "feel an apparently irresistible urge to push their science farther than it will go, to answer questions more delicate than our limited understanding of a complicated economy will allow. Some of the pressure comes from the outside. Your friendly financial journalist is frequently on the phone, and nobody likes to say 'I don't know,' or even 'nobody can know.' Some of the pressure comes from the inner drive to push against the frontiers of knowledge, to find answers. When the answer is very faint, you can hear what you want to hear." (*New York Times,* December 29, 1985, p. 2F.)

QUESTIONS

2.7 Develop a simple model to explain the spread of influenza (the flu). Contrast the problem of predicting exactly who catches influenza and when each victim catches it with the problem of predicting the average number of influenza cases in a month.

2.8 By age 30, the average college graduate earns about $10,000 more per year than the average high-school graduate. Does this imply that a person who did not attend college could have earned that much more if he had gone to college?

NOTE ON GRAPHS

Economists use many graphs, and you will need to use them to understand this book. The key point to remember is this: *every graph answers a question.* If you are not completely familiar with the use of graphs, you should read the appendix to this chapter.

CONCLUSIONS

POSITIVE AND NORMATIVE ECONOMICS
Positive statements are assertions about facts; normative statements express value judgements.

MODELS
Economic models are descriptions of logical thinking about economic issues: they are artificial economies written on paper or programmed into a computer. Evidence about economics is a set of facts that helps to convince economists that some positive statement about the economy is true or false. Statistical analysis is the use of mathematical probability theory to draw inferences in situations of uncertainty. Economic models can be used for understanding, predicting, or interpreting. Models may simplify an economic issue to help us understand it, help us make unconditional or conditional predictions about the economy, or help us interpret data as evidence about positive economic statements.

Economic models require assumptions about behavior. Economists usually assume that people behave rationally, which means they do the best they can, based on their own values and information, under the circumstances they face.

COMMON LOGICAL FALLACIES
Someone who reasons that what is true for one person must be true for the economy as a whole commits the fallacy of composition. Someone who reasons that because one event happened before another, the first event must have caused the second commits the post-hoc fallacy. Someone who reasons that two events that have always been related in the past will always be similarly related in the future commits the other-conditions fallacy.

STATISTICS
Economists use statistical analysis to draw inferences from economic data. Positively correlated variables tend to change in the same direction. Negatively correlated variables tend to change in opposite directions. Their correlation measures how closely the variables move together. Models are required to interpret correlations.

A misleading comparison occurs when someone compares two things in a way that does not reflect their true differences. A common misleading comparison involves comparing dollar amounts from different years without adjusting for inflation. Selection bias occurs when people use data that are not typical, but are selected in a way that biases the results.

WHY ECONOMISTS DISAGREE

Disagreements can arise among economists for two reasons. They may disagree about the truth of positive economic statements when they lack sufficient evidence to decide which of several economic models is best. They may also disagree about values, which can create disagreement about normative economic statements.

LOOKING AHEAD

Chapter 3 will use a model to explore the gains people may enjoy from voluntary trades and related issues. Chapter 4 will introduce the fundamental model of economics: the model of demand and supply. The rest of the book will use and extend these models to discuss issues that affect the world economy and that will influence your life.

KEY TERMS

positive statement	post-hoc fallacy
normative statement	other-conditions fallacy
economic model	misleading comparison
evidence	selection bias
statistical analysis	positive correlation
rational behavior	negative correlation
fallacy of composition	correlation

QUESTIONS AND PROBLEMS

2.9 Are the following quotes positive or normative statements?
  a. "The government budget deficit is too high and must be cut."
  b. "An increase in government regulations will make it harder for U.S. businesses to compete with foreign sellers."

2.10 According to the *Bill James Baseball Almanac,* professional baseball players lose ability to hit when they get older (their batting averages peak at age 27), yet the batting averages of older players are no worse than those of younger players. Bill James says that this illustrates selection bias.[9] Explain why.

2.11 To start a business, you make up a wild story about how to control whether a baby is male or female and you sell this advice to prospective parents. All customers pay you in advance, but you offer a money-back guarantee: if your procedure does not work, you refund their money.
  a. How is your business related to selection bias?
  b. Does your reasoning apply to businesses that sell advice on lottery numbers or sports betting?

---

[9]Bill James, *Bill James Baseball Almanac* (New York: Villard Books, 1987), pp. 60–64.

2.12 Develop a model to explain rain. How could you use statistical analysis to determine how good your model is?

2.13 Develop a model to explain the effects of diet on health. Why don't nutritionists always agree about the effects of vitamins and other nutrients on health?

2.14 Develop a model to explain:
- **a.** How the classes that college students choose affect their future salaries
- **b.** How the amounts of time college students study affect their future salaries
- **c.** How the crime rate is affected by the level of punishment for convicted criminals
- **d.** How gun controls affect crime
- **e.** The average birth rate in a country

In each case, discuss how you could use statistical data as evidence about the quality of your model.

INQUIRIES FOR FURTHER THOUGHT

2.15 This chapter suggested several possible theories of why married men earn higher incomes than single men. How would you use statistical evidence to find out which theory is correct? If you could do experiments, what experiments would you do to find out which theory is correct?

2.16 Do people behave rationally? How would you obtain evidence for or against your view?

TAG SOFTWARE APPLICATIONS

TUTORIAL **E**XERCISES
▶ This module reviews the key terms from Chapter 2.

ANALYTICAL **E**XERCISES
▶ The section covers how to calculate the slope of a straight line.

GRAPHING **E**XERCISES
▶ The module includes questions on how to illustrate relationships between variables graphically.

CHAPTER 2 APPENDIX — HOW TO USE GRAPHS IN LOGICAL THINKING

Every graph answers a question. You will understand a graph if you understand the question that it answers.

BASIC EXAMPLE

How much money has the average family in the United States earned in recent decades? The answer can be graphed, as in **Figure 2A.1.**[1] To find the answer to

---

[1]The graph shows *median family income,* meaning that half of all families earn more and half earn less.

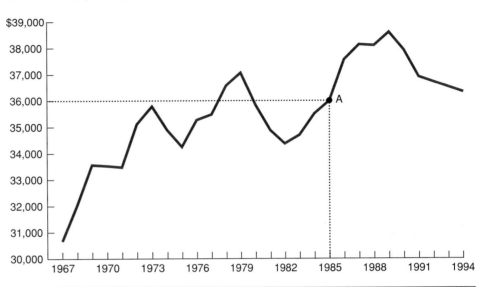

FIGURE 2A.1

MEDIAN FAMILY INCOME ADJUSTED FOR INFLATION

1. Find a year.
2. Go straight up until you hit the curve. Make a dot at that point (Point A).
3. Go left until you hit the Y-axis. Find the average family income for that year: about $36,000.

Source: Current Population Reports, Series P-60, No. 184.

---

the question on the graph, find a year on the horizontal axis, say 1985. Go straight up until you reach the curve, then straight left until you reach the vertical axis. The number on the vertical axis shows how much money an average family earned in 1985: about $36,000. You can do the same thing for other years.

Each point on the curve indicates two numbers, a year and an income. Point A in Figure 2A.1 indicates 1985 and $36,000. The two numbers allow each point to answer the question for a particular year.

The year and the income level are variables.

variable — name of a set of numbers analyzed with a graph (ranged along the horizontal and vertical axes) or with mathematical methods

> **Variables** are names for sets of numbers analyzed with a graph or with mathematics.

Every graph measures one variable along the horizontal axis and another variable along the vertical axis.

MISLEADING GRAPHS

The incomes in Figure 2A.1 have been adjusted for inflation to show how much money a family made in each year, measured in 1992 dollars. Adjusting for inflation prevents a misleading comparison; it allows accurate comparisons of family incomes in different years.

Figure 2A.2 shows a graph that makes a misleading comparison among different years because it does *not* adjust for inflation. **Figure 2A.3** shows that a typical good worth $10.00 in 1994 cost only about $5.50 in 1980 and only about $2.50 in 1970; prices have roughly quadrupled since 1970. Figure 2A.2 is misleading because

FIGURE 2A.2

MEDIAN FAMILY INCOME NOT ADJUSTED FOR INFLATION

Average family income measured in dollars has risen over time, but this diagram illustrates a misleading comparison. Prices of goods have also risen over time, so families have not become as rich as quickly as this graph implies.
Source: Current Population Reports, Series P-60, No. 184.

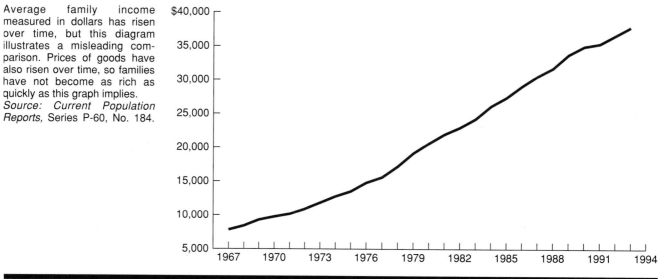

FIGURE 2A.3

TYPICAL PRICE OF A GOOD WORTH $10 IN 1994

A typical good that cost $10.00 in 1994 cost only about $5.50 in 1980 and only about $2.50 in 1970.

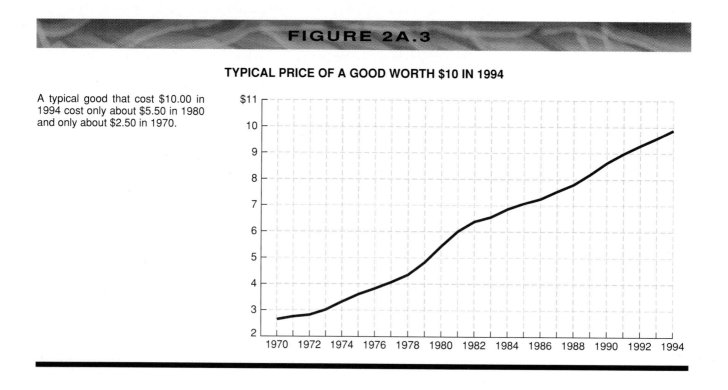

it fails to adjust for this inflation. Notice that the correct graph (Figure 2A.1) conveys a very different impression than the misleading message of Figure 2A.2.

A MORE SUBTLE POINT

Figure 2A.1 can also be misleading for another, more subtle reason: the typical family of today includes fewer people than families did in the past. Median income *per person* has risen faster than Figure 2A.1 suggests. If you remember to think critically about statistical evidence such as misleading graphs, you are less likely to make mistakes in personal and business decisions and you will be a more intelligent analyst of social and political issues.

MANY CURVES ON THE SAME GRAPH

When more than one curve appears on a single graph, each curve answers a different question.

EXAMPLE

Figure 2A.4 shows five curves. The highest curve answers the question, how much money can an average person with some graduate school education expect to earn at different ages? The second-highest curve answers the question, how much money can an average college graduate expect to earn at different ages? The other three curves repeat the question for people with some college, high-school graduates, and people with less education. The horizontal axis measures age and the vertical axis measures income, in thousands of dollars. Figure 2A.4 shows that

FIGURE 2A.4

EARNINGS OF FULL-TIME WORKERS

Each curve tracks income for a certain level of education.

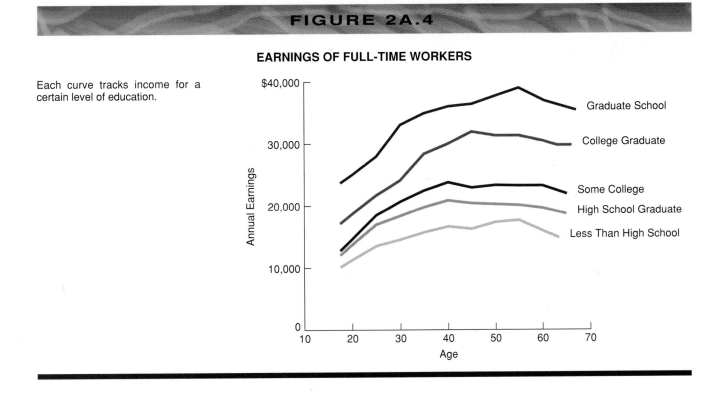

a person with a college education can expect her income to rise until around age 50, after which it falls slightly. The average high-school graduate earns more each year until around age 40, and income falls slightly after that. This graph is adjusted for inflation; you can expect inflation to raise your future *dollar* income above the numbers in the graph.

Figures 2A.5a and **2A.5b** show the same information separately for men and women. Compare these graphs to see that men earn, on average, more than women.

SHIFTING CURVES

shift — a change in the position of a curve on a graph

Logical thinking with graphs often requires us to shift curves.

A **shift** in a curve is a change in its position on a graph.

A curve on a graph shifts when a change in conditions changes the answer to the graph's question.

EXAMPLE

Consider a man who has just graduated from high school. The lower curve in **Figure 2A.6** shows the income that he can expect at various ages. Now suppose he goes to college. This raises his likely earnings at every age, so it shifts the curve in Figure 2A.6. The curve shifts because a change in conditions (more education) changes the answer to the question, what income can this man expect over his lifetime?

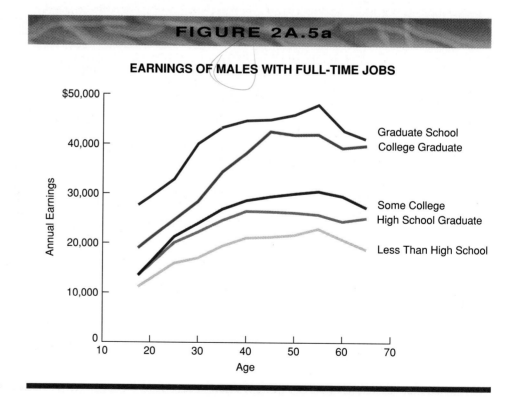

FIGURE 2A.5a

EARNINGS OF MALES WITH FULL-TIME JOBS

Graduate School
College Graduate

Some College
High School Graduate

Less Than High School

FIGURE 2A.5b

EARNINGS OF FEMALES WITH FULL-TIME JOBS

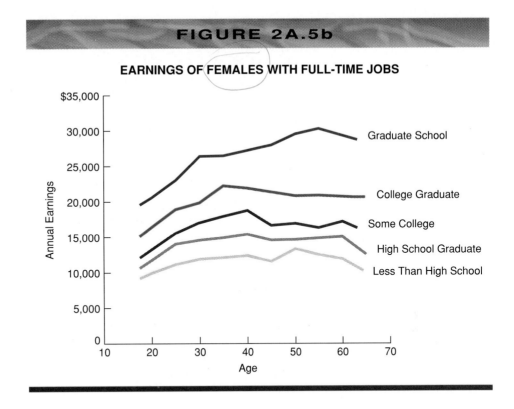

FIGURE 2A.6

THE EARNING CURVE SHIFTS WHEN A STUDENT GOES TO COLLEGE

The arrow shows the shift in the curve.

EXAMPLE

Figures 2A.5a and 2A.5b showed that women earn less (on average) than men of the same age with the same education. Many people blame part of this difference on discrimination against women. If this accusation is true, a fall in discrimination against women would shift the curves in Figure 2A.5b upward. **Figure 2A.7** shows the shift in one of these curves when a fall in discrimination changes the answer to the question, how does the likely annual income of a female high-school graduate vary with her age?

SLOPES OF CURVES

positive slope — the shape of a curve that runs upward and to the right

Figure 2A.8 shows the answer to the question of how a typical student's grade on a biology exam is affected by the amount of studying time. The figure shows a positive relation (or positive correlation) between the two variables, indicating that they move in the same direction; more studying corresponds to a higher grade. A curve showing a positive relation between two variables has a positive slope.

A **positive slope** refers to a shape that runs upward and to the right.

Figure 2A.9 answers the question, how does the time you have for watching television tonight depend on the amount of time you study? It shows a negative relation (negative correlation) between the two variables, indicating that they move in opposite directions. A curve showing a negative relation between two variables has a negative slope.

FIGURE 2A.7

SHIFTING A CURVE: IF REDUCED SEX DISCRIMINATION RAISES THE EARNINGS OF WOMEN

A fall in sex discrimination shifts the curve upward. (Both curves are drawn for a woman with a high-school education.)

FIGURE 2A.8

RELATION BETWEEN GRADE AND STUDYING TIME

The line has a positive slope.

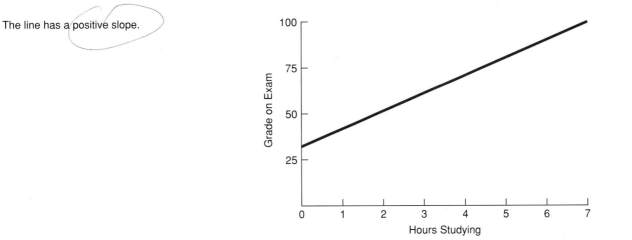

negative slope — the shape of a curve that runs downward and to the right

slope — a number that shows the distance by which a curve goes up or down as it moves one unit to the right

A **negative slope** refers to a shape that runs downward and to the right.

The slope of a curve is a number that measures its steepness:

The **slope** of a curve is the distance by which the curve goes up or down as it moves one unit to the right.

The slope measures how much the variable along the vertical axis changes as the variable along the horizontal axis increases by one unit. If the curve rises as it

FIGURE 2A.9

MORE STUDYING TIME LEAVES LESS TIME FOR TELEVISION

This line has a negative slope. How would you choose to spend your time?

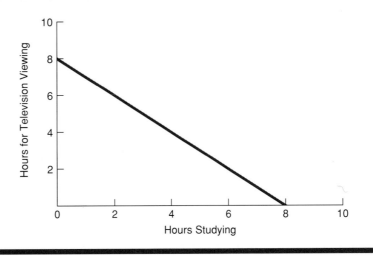

FIGURE 2A.10

CALCULATION OF SLOPE

As you study one more hour, your likely grade rises by 2 points. So the slope of the line is 2.

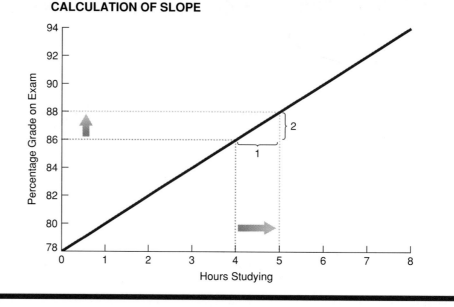

moves to the right, the slope is a positive number; if it falls as it moves to the right, the slope is a negative number. Higher numbers indicate steeper slopes.[2]

EXAMPLES

Figure 2A.10 shows a line with a slope of 2; by studying one more hour, your likely grade rises by two points. Figure 2A.9 showed a line with a slope of −1; spending one more hour studying leaves you one less hour for television.

The slopes of the curves in Figures 2A.5a and 2A.5b change at different ages. The curves are steeper for younger people than for older people. The slopes are positive at most ages: increases in age usually lead to increases in earnings. The slopes are negative for older people, though; at higher ages, further increases in age reduce earnings.

AREAS

area — a number that measures the size of some specific region in a graph

Logical thinking with graphs sometimes involves evaluating areas in graphs.

An **area** of some region in a graph is a number that measures the size of that region.

Here are two formulas to calculate areas:

1. If a region is a rectangle, as in **Figure 2A.11,** then the area of the rectangle equals its base times its height. In Figure 2A.11, the base of the shaded rectangle is 5 and the height is 6, so the area is 30 (5 times 6).

2. If the region is a triangle, as in **Figure 2A.12,** then follow these steps:
   a. Make a rectangle out of the triangle; one side of the triangle must become a side of the rectangle.

---

[2]Lines with slopes of 10 or −10 are steeper than lines with slopes of 3 or −3.

FIGURE 2A.11

AREA OF A RECTANGLE EQUALS THE BASE TIMES THE HEIGHT

The base of the shaded rectangle is 5 and the height of the rectangle is 6, so the area of the rectangle is 5 times 6 or 30.

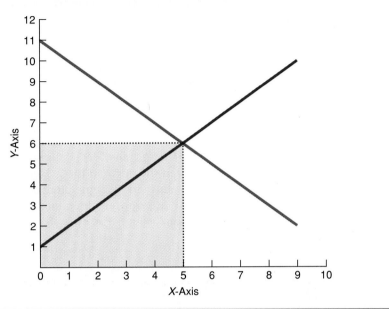

FIGURE 2A.12

AREA OF A TRIANGLE

To calculate the area of Triangle A:
First, make a rectangle out of Triangles A and B.
Second, find the area of Rectangle AB. Its base is 5 and its height is 5, so its area is 5 times 5, or 25.
Third, divide by 2 to get the area of Triangle A: $25/2 = 12\frac{1}{2}$.

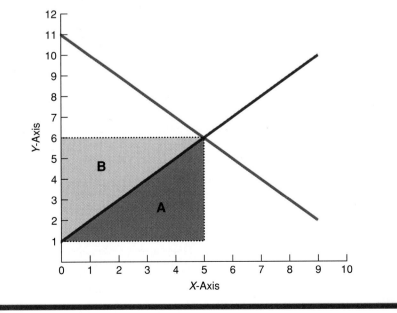

b. Calculate the area of the rectangle.

c. Divide by 2 to get the area of the triangle.

To find the area of Triangle B in Figure 2A.12, form the rectangle with areas A and B. This rectangle has a base of 5 and a height of 5, so the area of the rectangle is 25 (5 times 5). Dividing by 2 gives the answer $12\frac{1}{2}$ for the area of Triangle B.

You will use these formulas later in this book to calculate such things as how much money people pay in taxes and the losses in economic efficiency from restrictions on international trade.

CONCLUSION

Every graph answers a question. When a change in conditions changes that answer, the curve in the graph shifts. Curves with positive slopes show that variables move in the same direction. Curves with negative slopes show that variables move in opposite directions. Steeper curves have larger slopes (measured in absolute value). The area of a region in a graph measures the region's size.

KEY TERMS

variable	positive slope
shift	negative slope
slope	area

QUESTIONS AND PROBLEMS

2A.1 Draw a graph to show the profits that U.S. manufacturing businesses earned after taxes on each dollar's worth of goods they sold between 1974 and 1992.

	Profit after Taxes per Dollar of Sales
1974	5.5 cents
1975	4.6
1976	5.4
1977	5.3
1978	5.4
1979	5.7
1980	4.8
1981	4.7
1982	3.5
1983	4.1
1984	4.6
1985	3.8
1986	3.7
1987	4.9
1988	6.0
1989	5.0
1990	4.0
1991	2.5
1992	0.8

2A.2 What makes a curve in a graph shift?

2A.3 Draw graphs of curves with:
  a. Positive slope
  b. Negative slope
  c. Slope equal to 3
  d. Slope equal to -2
  e. A slope that changes

2A.4 *(Harder Problem)* How might you use data to analyze how much the curve in Figure 2A.7 would rise if discrimination against women were eliminated?

PART

2

FUNDAMENTAL TOOLS

CHAPTER 3

LET'S MAKE A DEAL: THE GAINS FROM TRADE

WHAT THIS CHAPTER IS ABOUT

▶ How people gain from trades
▶ How people share the gains from trade
▶ Different ideas of what is fair
▶ Economic efficiency
▶ How taxes cause economic inefficiency and reduce gains from trade

Economics is about trading—buying and selling. Without trading, our standard of living would have advanced little over the last thousand years. The progress of technology would hardly touch our lives if we could not trade. Knowledge of how to make antibiotics, televisions, plastics, cars, or computers would have little effect on people who were totally self-sufficient.

Historically, standards of living rose when people started to trade, and today trade plays a larger economic role than ever before. People in the United States now spend more on meals at restaurants than on meals at home; they trade their services as carpenters, accountants, lawyers, teachers, or doctors for meal preparation and cleanup, child care, and other goods and services that people once provided mainly for themselves. International trade is a growing fraction of world output as we continue to approach a single global economy.

Whenever two people trade voluntarily, they expect to gain. Some gains from trade are easy to understand: you want cookies and your friend wants an apple, but you have an apple and your friend has cookies, so you trade. The benefits of many trades are much less obvious, however, and this chapter explains them.

TWO-STUDENT EXAMPLE: A KEY EXAMPLE OF GAINS FROM TRADE

Two students, Lauren and Steve, moved into apartments next door to each other. The apartments are exactly alike, and each needs cleaning and repainting. The landlords provide paint and cleaning supplies, so the only cost of cleaning and painting is the time involved.

TABLE 3.1

TWO-STUDENT EXAMPLE OF GAINS FROM TRADE

Time Required to Get Work Done				Productivity of Each Person	
Time to:	Lauren	Steve		Lauren	Steve
Clean one apartment	3 hours	2 hours	Amount cleaned in one hour	$\frac{1}{3}$ apt.	$\frac{1}{2}$ apt.
Paint one apartment	1 hour	4 hours	Amount painted in one hour	1 apt.	$\frac{1}{4}$ apt.

Lauren would have to spend 3 hours to clean her apartment. It would also take her 3 hours to clean Steve's apartment. She could clean both apartments in 6 hours. It would take Lauren 1 hour to paint either apartment, or 2 hours to paint both.

Steve works differently. It would take him 2 hours to clean either apartment, or 4 hours to clean both. It would take Steve 4 hours to paint either apartment, or 8 hours to paint both. Lauren and Steve do equally good work, and neither prefers one job to the other.

The left side of **Table 3.1** shows the number of hours it would take Lauren and Steve to do each job in one apartment. The right side of the table shows the same information in a different form—it states how much work each person could complete in one hour, which is that person's productivity at that job.

GAINS FROM TRADE

Lauren and Steve can both gain from a trade. If Lauren cleans and paints her own apartment, she works 4 hours: 3 hours cleaning and 1 hour painting. If Steve cleans and paints his own apartment, he works 6 hours: 2 hours cleaning and 4 hours painting. Suppose that they trade so that Lauren agrees to paint Steve's apartment and he agrees to clean hers. Lauren paints both apartments and Steve cleans both apartments. All of the work gets done, but Lauren works only 2 hours (1 hour in each apartment) and Steve works only 4 hours (2 hours in each apartment). They *each gain two hours of leisure time* from the trade.

COMPARATIVE ADVANTAGE AND THE GAINS FROM TRADE

The general point of this example is that people gain from trade whenever they have different *relative* abilities to produce different goods. Economists measure relative abilities with the concept of comparative advantage:

> A person has a **comparative advantage** at producing a good if she can produce it at a lower opportunity cost than other people can.[1]

comparative advantage — a task at which a person has a lower opportunity cost than other people have

---

[1] Chapter 1 defined the *opportunity cost* of doing something as the value of what someone sacrifices to do it. In this example, Steve sacrifices four hours of time to paint an apartment; he could have used that time to clean two apartments, so his opportunity cost of painting one apartment is cleaning two apartments.

In the example, Lauren has a comparative advantage at painting and Steve has a comparative advantage at cleaning. In any situation like this, everyone has a comparative advantage at something. This is true even when one person has higher productivity at every job. (See Problem 3.16 at the end of the chapter.) People can gain from trades that allow them to spend more time on a task in which they have a comparative advantage and less time on other tasks.

EXPLANATION

Lauren has a comparative advantage at painting. Her opportunity cost of painting one apartment is cleaning $\frac{1}{3}$ of an apartment, that is, in the hour it takes her to paint an apartment, she could clean $\frac{1}{3}$ of an apartment. (It would take Lauren 3 hours to clean an entire apartment, so in 1 hour she could clean $\frac{1}{3}$ of an apartment.) Steve's opportunity cost of painting an apartment is cleaning 2 apartments. In the 4 hours it takes Steve to paint an apartment, he could finish cleaning 2 apartments. Since Lauren has a lower opportunity cost of painting than Steve, she has a comparative advantage.

Steve has a comparative advantage at cleaning. Steve's opportunity cost of cleaning an apartment is painting $\frac{1}{2}$ of an apartment, that is, in the 2 hours it takes him to clean an apartment, he could paint $\frac{1}{2}$ of an apartment. Lauren's opportunity cost of cleaning an apartment is painting 3 apartments. In the 3 hours it takes her to clean an apartment, she could finish painting 3 apartments. Steve has a lower opportunity cost of cleaning, so he has a comparative advantage at cleaning.

Everyone has a comparative advantage at something. Once we know that Lauren has a comparative advantage at painting, we know immediately that Steve has a comparative advantage at cleaning.

HINT ON FINDING COMPARATIVE ADVANTAGE

The left side of Table 3.1 shows costs of production. Those costs are stated in hours of leisure time, but they could be measured in dollars instead. If you have information on costs, you can identify comparative advantages in two steps. (1) Calculate each person's relative costs of doing the two jobs. It takes Lauren 3 times as long to clean as to paint (3 hours to clean divided by 1 hour to paint). It costs Steve only half as much time to clean as to paint. (2) The person with the lower relative cost of a job has the comparative advantage at that job. Steve has a lower relative cost of cleaning ($\frac{1}{2}$ is less than 3), so Steve has a comparative advantage at cleaning. Repeat this reasoning to find each person's relative cost of painting, and see why Lauren has a comparative advantage at painting.

The right side of Table 3.1 shows productivity. It indicates how much each person can produce in a certain amount of time. If you have information on productivity, two steps will tell you who has a comparative advantage at which job. (1) Calculate each person's relative productivity at each job. Lauren's productivity at cleaning ($\frac{1}{3}$ completed job per hour) is only $\frac{1}{3}$ of her productivity at painting (1 completed job per hour), so her relative productivity at cleaning is $\frac{1}{3}$. Steve's productivity at cleaning ($\frac{1}{2}$ completed job per hour) is twice his productivity at painting ($\frac{1}{4}$ completed job per hour), so his relative productivity at cleaning is 2. (2) The person with the higher relative productivity at a job has the comparative advantage at that job. Steve has a higher relative productivity at cleaning (2 is higher than Lauren's $\frac{1}{3}$), so Steve has a comparative advantage at cleaning. If you repeat this reasoning, you will find that Lauren has a comparative advantage at painting.

GAINS FROM TRADE AND POSITIVE-SUM GAMES

Some people believe that whenever one person gets richer, another person must become poorer. They think the economy is like a pie; if one person gets a bigger piece, less remains for other people. Those ideas are false. *Everyone* involved can gain from a voluntary trade, as the two-student example shows.

An environment in which one person's gain is another person's loss is called a **zero-sum game.**[2]

Dividing a cake between several people is a zero-sum game: a bigger piece for one person leaves a smaller piece for someone else. Most economic situations are *not* zero-sum games, though. They are positive-sum games.

An environment in which everyone can gain at the same time is called a **positive-sum game.**

People can all gain if they produce the same amount of goods with less effort or more goods with the same effort. They gain when each person produces goods at which he has a comparative advantage and then they all trade. The two-student example is a positive-sum game: both students gain from the trade. The world economy consists of billions of people like those two students, though the details of their lives differ in countless ways. The world economy is a positive-sum game.

The economy is a positive-sum game.

zero-sum game — environment in which one person's gain is another person's loss

positive-sum game — environment in which everyone can gain at the same time

ECONOMIC EFFICIENCY

The two-student example shows how people can gain from an increase in economic efficiency.

working well w/ little waste

A situation is **economically efficient** if there is no way to change it so that everyone gains or so that some people gain while no one else loses.

An economically efficient situation leaves no unexploited opportunities that can benefit everyone; people have *already* made use of every such opportunity.

A situation is **economically inefficient** if there is some way to change it so that everyone gains or so that someone gains while no one else loses.

A situation is economically inefficient when there are potential, *unrealized* gains from a change. It is economically inefficient to fail to exploit all the potential gains from trade.

economically efficient — a situation that cannot be changed so that someone gains unless someone else loses

economically inefficient — a situation that can be changed so that at least one person gains while no one else loses

EXAMPLES

1. Susie likes yogurt and Johnny likes peanut butter. If Susie has peanut butter and Johnny has yogurt, the situation is economically inefficient because a change could help them both: they could trade lunches. After they trade, Susie has yogurt and Johnny has peanut butter. That situation is economically efficient because any further change that would help one of them would hurt the other. (If Johnny takes some of Susie's yogurt, he gains and she loses.)

---

[2]The term means that if some people have positive gains, other people must have negative gains (i.e., losses) so that their gains sum to zero.

2. Glenn and Michelle make and sell tables and chairs. In one hour, Glenn can make either three chairs or one table. In one hour, Michelle can make either two chairs or one table. It is economically inefficient for Glenn to spend an hour making tables while Michelle spends an hour making chairs because they can switch jobs and produce more. If Glenn spends one less hour making tables and one more hour making chairs, he produces one less table and three more chairs. If Michelle spends one more hour making tables and one less hour making chairs, she produces one more table and two fewer chairs. By changing jobs for an hour, Glenn and Michelle can produce the same number of tables and one extra chair. They can both gain from this change, perhaps by selling the extra chair and sharing the money, so the *original* situation was economically inefficient.

3. In the two-student example, it would be economically inefficient for Lauren to clean and paint her own apartment while Steve cleaned and painted his because a change could help them both. That change is a trade in which Lauren paints both apartments and Steve cleans both. This trade creates an economically efficient situation in which no further change can help one person without hurting the other.

COMPARATIVE ADVANTAGE AND EFFICIENCY

Comparative advantage and economic efficiency are related. In an economically efficient situation, people tend to produce goods at which they have a comparative advantage. It is economically efficient for Steve to produce cleaning services, at which he has a comparative advantage, while Lauren produces painting services, at which she has a comparative advantage.

Sometimes, however, it is economically efficient for someone to produce a good at which he does not have a comparative advantage. It can be efficient for Lauren and Steve both to paint, even though Steve has a comparative advantage at cleaning, if painting is the main (or only) work that needs to be done (that is, if the apartments are already almost clean). It would *not* be economically efficient for Steve to paint while Lauren cleaned, though; they could both gain by switching jobs.[3]

People have incentives to trade when the trade can create economic efficiency because they can share the gains from changing an inefficient situation into an efficient one. Lauren and Steve have an incentive to trade and share the gains from creating efficiency in the two-student example. Such voluntary trades produce economic efficiency without anyone else directing them. In the example, the two parties share the gains from trade equally: each gets 2 extra hours of leisure time. We will soon discover other ways to share the gains from trade.

BARTER AND MONEY TRADES

The trade we have discussed is an example of barter: trading one good for another without exchanging money. Lauren trades her effort for Steve's effort. Most real-life trades involve money, however. People buy goods with money and sell other goods for money. So, it is useful to give the trade in the two-student example another interpretation. Lauren pays Steve $10 to clean her apartment and Steve pays Lauren $10 to paint his apartment, so the $10 payments cancel each other.

---

[3] The reasoning is the same as in the example of Glenn and Michelle above.

The real-life economy consists of millions of people like Lauren and Steve who trade voluntarily and share the gains from trade. We all trade our time for things we want. Most of us trade our time for money to buy these things and we get more if we trade than if we try to produce all these things ourselves. Lauren might pay Steve $10 for cleaning services while Steve pays Jim $10 for food, Jim pays Andrea $10 for medical care, and Andrea pays Lauren $10 for painting. Each voluntary trade allows people to produce goods at which they have comparative advantages. Money passes from person to person to make trading easier, with the same result as in the two-student example: each person gains from trading.[4]

──────────────── **FOR REVIEW** ────────────────

3.1 Explain why people can gain from voluntary trades.

3.2 What is comparative advantage?

3.3 When is a situation economically efficient? When is a situation economically inefficient?

──────────────── **QUESTIONS** ────────────────

3.4 Suppose that Argentina can produce 14 bottles of wine or 40 pounds of beef in one day, while Chile can produce 12 bottles of wine or 30 pounds of beef in one day. Which country has a comparative advantage in wine and which in beef?

3.5 Discuss: "If a situation is economically inefficient, everyone involved has an incentive to change it."

SHARING THE GAINS FROM TRADE

How do people share the gains from trade? In the two-student example, Lauren and Steve each gained two hours of leisure time from their trade. But there are many other trades they could have made, any of which would have helped them both. In fact, there are many economically efficient situations, each with a different distribution of income. Lauren would be better off in some of these situations, and Steve would be better off in others. The distribution of income refers to who gets how much of the available goods in an economy.

EXAMPLE: HOUR-FOR-HOUR TRADE

The trade in the two-student example, in which Lauren agrees to paint Steve's apartment and Steve agrees to clean Lauren's, leads to economic efficiency. However, Steve spends 2 hours cleaning Lauren's apartment, while she spends only 1 hour painting his. In other words, Lauren trades 1 hour of her time for 2 hours of Steve's time.

Suppose, instead, that Steve and Lauren agree to trade their time on an hour-for-hour basis: Steve will spend 1 hour cleaning Lauren's apartment and she will

───────────────────────

[4]This is not quite the same thing as saying that *everyone* gains. If people shop at Wal-Mart instead of K mart, Wal-Mart gains but K mart loses. Tape manufacturers lose when people buy more compact disks and fewer cassette tapes.

TABLE 3.2

HOUR-FOR-HOUR TRADE

Lauren	Steve
Paints her own apartment in 1 hour, completing the work	Cleans his own apartment in 2 hours, completing the work
Paints Steve's apartment in 1 hour, completing the work	Spends 1 hour cleaning Lauren's apartment, completing half of the work
Spends 90 minutes to finish cleaning her own apartment after Steve leaves	
Total work time: $3\frac{1}{2}$ hours	Total work time: 3 hours

spend 1 hour painting his apartment. In that 1 hour, Lauren will finish painting Steve's apartment, but Steve will not finish cleaning Lauren's apartment in 1 hour—that would take 2 hours. Steve will get half of the cleaning done in 1 hour, leaving the other half of the job for Lauren. Since Lauren can clean an apartment in 3 hours, it will take her $1\frac{1}{2}$ hours to finish the job. **Table 3.2** summarizes the work the students do when each trades an hour's time.

With the hour-for-hour trade, Lauren works $3\frac{1}{2}$ hours and Steve works 3 hours. Without any trade, Lauren would have worked 4 hours cleaning and painting her own apartment and Steve would have worked 6 hours in his. Each gains from the hour-for-hour trade; Lauren gains half an hour of leisure time, and Steve gains 3 hours. Although each gains, they do not share the gains from trade equally.

COMPARISON OF THE TWO TRADES

Table 3.3 compares these two trades. In the first trade, Lauren exchanges 1 hour of painting Steve's apartment for 2 hours of cleaning for her own. In the second trade, Lauren spends 1 hour painting Steve's apartment and he spends 1 hour

TABLE 3.3

COMPARISON OF THE TWO TRADES

No Trade	First Trade: One Hour for Two Hours	Second Trade: Hour for Hour
Economically inefficient	Economically efficient	Economically efficient
Lauren works 4 hours; Steve works 6 hours	Lauren works 2 hours; Steve works 4 hours	Lauren works $3\frac{1}{2}$ hours; Steve works 3 hours
	Compared with no trade: Lauren gains 2 hours of time; Steve gains 2 hours of time	Compared with no trade: Lauren gains $\frac{1}{2}$ hour of time; Steve gains 3 hours of time
	Lauren spends 1 hour working in Steve's apartment; Steve spends 2 hours working in Lauren's apartment	Lauren spends 1 hour working in Steve's apartment; Steve spends 1 hour working in Lauren's apartment

cleaning hers. Each trade leads to a different economically efficient situation. Lauren benefits from either trade, and so does Steve.

Lauren prefers the first trade (the 1-hour-for-2-hour trade) because it gives her 2 hours of leisure time, while she gains only 30 minutes of leisure time from the hour-for-hour trade. Steve prefers the hour-for-hour trade because it gains him 3 hours of leisure time, versus a gain of 2 hours from the first trade.

These trades produce two economically efficient situations with different distributions of income. The first trade earns Lauren an income of a cleaned, painted apartment and 2 extra hours of leisure time. Steve earns the same income from that trade. The hour-for-hour trade earns Lauren a cleaned, painted apartment and 30 extra minutes of leisure time, while Steve earns a cleaned, painted apartment and 3 extra hours of leisure time. In this way, the trades lead to different distributions of income.[5]

Lauren and Steve could also choose many other trades that would help them both and that would lead to economically efficient situations. Some are better for Lauren, and some are better for Steve. Each of the other economically efficient situations has a different distribution of income.

FAIRNESS, EQUITY, AND JUSTICE

Which trade is fairer? To answer this question, we would need to agree on what is fair. It might seem fair for Lauren and Steve to share the gains from the trade equally, so the 1-hour-for-2-hour trade might seem fair because Lauren and Steve each gain 2 hours of leisure time. It might also seem fair for Lauren to trade 1 hour of her time for 1 hour of Steve's time, so the hour-for-hour trade might seem fair.[6] Or you might believe that Lauren and Steve should have equal amounts of leisure time so they should spend equal amounts of time working. This would make *another* trade seem fair: one that would equalize the time they spend working.[7]

These three ideas of fairness conflict with each other. Each leads to a different conclusion about which trade is fair and which trades are unfair. Unfortunately, no definition of what is fair (or just or equitable) satisfies everyone. Many people use these words loosely without a clear, precise idea of what they mean. Even philosophers are unable to agree on what is fair. Consider some different ideas of fairness:

▶ There should be an equal distribution of income.

▶ People who need higher incomes for important purposes, such as medical expenses or to support large families, should have more.

▶ Incomes should not be equal, but no one should be too poor.

---

[5] Both trades create economically efficient situations, even though the total amount of time spent working is larger in the hour-for-hour trade ($6\frac{1}{2}$ hours) than in the first trade (6 hours).

[6] Since one interpretation of the example is that Lauren pays Steve $20 for his work and Steve pays Lauren $20 for her work, the hour-for-hour trade gives them equal wage rates.

[7] Lauren and Steve would work the same number of hours if Steve were to clean his own apartment (which would take him 2 hours) and spend 1 hour and 12 minutes cleaning Lauren's apartment. Since it would take Steve 2 hours to completely clean the apartment, he would get $\frac{3}{5}$ of the job done in 1 hour and 12 minutes. Lauren would do the remaining $\frac{2}{5}$ of the cleaning job in her own apartment, which takes her $(\frac{2}{5})(3$ hours), or $\frac{6}{5}$ hours (1 hour and 12 minutes). She also paints both apartments, which takes her 2 hours. Lauren and Steve each work for 3 hours and 12 minutes. This situation is economically efficient. (Notice that in this situation, Steve spends 1 hour and 12 minutes working in Lauren's apartment, while Lauren spends only 1 hour working in Steve's.)

▶ People who work harder should have higher incomes.

▶ People should get whatever incomes they can earn by working.

▶ There is no such thing as a fair distribution of income. Fairness applies only to *rules* (such as laws).

FAIRNESS AND RULES

Some people who believe that fairness applies only to rules say that rules are fair if everyone would agree on them in advance, not knowing whether they will be lucky or unlucky, beautiful or ugly, smart or dumb, talented or not, or born into a rich or poor family. Before an American football game, for example, the teams accept a coin toss to see who will receive the ball first. According to this view, it is neither fair or unfair that one team wins the coin toss. Outcomes are not fair or unfair. Only the rules that produce those outcomes can be fair or unfair.[8] In this case, the rule is the coin toss, which may be fair (or, if the coin is weighted to come up heads most of the time, unfair). Some people who believe that fairness applies only to rules say that rules are fair if they allow each person to keep her own property and make any desired peaceful, voluntary trades.[9]

Economics deals with positive statements (statements of fact); it does not say anything about fairness.[10] However, economics can help us understand the results of various laws, regulations, and government policies. This understanding helps people to apply their own ideas of fairness to decide what laws, regulations, and government policies they think are best.

─────────────── **FOR REVIEW** ───────────────

3.6 Discuss: "In voluntary trades, people share the gains from trade equally."

3.7 Briefly discuss alternative ideas of fairness.

3.8 Explain the idea that fairness applies only to rules, not to the distribution of income.

─────────────── **QUESTIONS** ───────────────

3.9 Explain why there are many economically efficient situations. How do they differ?

3.10 Discuss: "The hour-for-hour trade requires $6\frac{1}{2}$ total hours of work from Steve and Lauren, while the original trade required only 6 hours of work, so the hour-for-hour trade is economically inefficient."

───────────────────────────────

[8]In most real-life situations, we already know the outcomes: some people are born to rich families, others to poor families. Some are smarter, more talented, and more beautiful than others. We don't know what rules people would have accepted if they could have decided which rules were fair before knowing this outcome. We can only guess. This approach to fairness was pioneered by economist John Harsanyi in 1953 and by Harvard philosopher John Rawls in his book, *A Theory of Justice* (Cambridge, Mass.: Harvard University Press, 1971). Most of Rawls's book is about his guesses as to which rules people would say are fair before knowing these outcomes.

[9]This position grows out of a long tradition in philosophy asserting that people have natural rights. (The U.S. Declaration of Independence was influenced by this tradition.) For one statement of this libertarian position, see Robert Nozick, *Anarchy, State, and Utopia* (New York: Basic Books, 1974).

[10]See Chapter 2 for a discussion of positive statements.

COMPETITION AND THE GAINS FROM TRADE

Which trade would people like Lauren and Steve make in real life? When any one of several trades is possible, the trade people actually choose depends on their alternative opportunities. If one person has good opportunities for alternative trades, the other person faces strong competition for his services and has a weak bargaining position. The trades people choose depend on their relative bargaining positions, which depend on their alternative opportunities.

EXPLANATION

Table 3.3 compared two of the many possible trades that Lauren and Steve might have made. Each trade leads to a different economically efficient situation, with a different distribution of income. Lauren prefers some trades and Steve prefers others. The trade that they actually choose depends on their alternative opportunities, which affect each party's bargaining power. Steve might convince Lauren to trade time on an hour-for-hour basis by telling her that if she refuses, he will trade with Linda instead, who *will* agree to it. In that sense, Lauren would face competition from other potential painters. In the same way, Steve might agree to a trade that Lauren prefers because he faces competition from other potential cleaners.

COMPETITION AND PRICES

If Lauren and Steve agree that Lauren will paint both apartments and Steve will clean both, Steve works two hours in Lauren's apartment and Lauren works one hour in Steve's apartment, and Steve trades two hours of his time for one hour of Lauren's time. The price of one hour of Lauren's time is two hours of Steve's time.

price — the amount of something that a buyer trades away (pays) per unit of the good he receives

> The **price** of a good is the amount of something that a buyer trades away (pays) per unit of the good he receives.

Since Lauren trades away one hour of time for two hours of Steve's time, she buys two hours of his time. The price she pays for each hour of his time is a half hour of her own time.

If, instead, Lauren and Steve agree to the hour-for-hour trade, they each pay one hour of their own time for one hour of the other person's time. The price of Steve's time is one hour of Lauren's time, and the price of Lauren's time is one hour of Steve's time. The different trades involve different prices. Competition affects which trade they choose, so competition affects the price.

IS ECONOMIC EFFICIENCY GOOD?

Economics deals with statements of fact, not value judgements. Still, there is a sense in which economic efficiency is good, independent of individual values. Whenever a situation is economically inefficient, a change in the economy can help everyone to gain, or some people to gain while no one loses. Economic efficiency is good in the sense that waste is bad; eliminating inefficiencies makes people better off according to their own values. In an economically inefficient situation, people usually have incentives to make changes to achieve efficiency and share the gains.

Many people believe that the government should redistribute income to some degree from the rich to the poor. With this view of fairness or equity there is a tradeoff between equity and efficiency: to distribute income more equitably, the government usually must create economic inefficiencies. The government may tax people with high incomes and give the money to poorer people. The tax creates economic inefficiency by changing people's incentives to trade, as the next example will explain.

How Taxes Create Economic Inefficiency: An Example

Suppose that the government places a $5 tax on purchases of painting or cleaning services. Anyone who buys painting or cleaning services must pay $5 to the government. This tax can create an economically inefficient situation.

It is economically efficient for Steve to buy painting services from Lauren and for Lauren to buy cleaning services from Steve because each produces a good at which he or she has a comparative advantage. It would be economically inefficient for them not to trade. The tax may cause Lauren and Steve *not* to trade, however. If Lauren buys Steve's services, she gains leisure time but must pay the $5 tax. She may decide that the extra leisure time is not worth paying the tax. Steve faces the same decision. If the tax prevents the trade, it creates an economically inefficient situation. In addition, if Lauren and Steve do not trade, the government does not collect the tax revenue from them. The government collects tax revenue only from people who continue to buy painting and cleaning services despite the tax.

When a situation is economically inefficient, people usually have incentives to find voluntary trades that change the situation and make it efficient. They can then share the gains from eliminating the inefficiency. Taxes change this by altering incentives so that people do not always gain from eliminating inefficient situations. In this way, taxes create economic inefficiency.

A Tradeoff between Equity and Efficiency?

The government can use tax revenue to increase equity (at least according to some views of equity) at the cost of economic inefficiency. Economic inefficiency may be an opportunity cost of more equity (and vice versa). In other words, the economy may face a tradeoff between equity and economic efficiency. Many notions of equity, though not all, lead to conflicts with economic efficiency, at least in certain cases. It would be remarkable if a well-developed idea of fairness or equity never conflicted with economic efficiency.[11]

If economic efficiency and other values (including equity) conflict, people must choose whether to sacrifice equity or efficiency. Choosing involves value judgements about which people may differ, but it also involves economics. Economic analysis can help people understand how much economic inefficiency is required in order to achieve some other goal, thereby helping them to evaluate tradeoffs and to make more intelligent decisions.

A Note on International Trade

The two-student example showed how two people can each gain by trading. The same reasoning shows that nations can each gain from *international trades.* (Think, for instance, of two countries named Laurenland and Steveland producing fabric and food rather than engaging in cleaning and painting.) By producing

---

[11]For an attempt to create such a theory, see Richard Posner, *The Economics of Justice* (Cambridge, Mass.: Harvard University Press, 1983).

goods that they are able to produce at a comparative advantage and trading them with other countries, nations can obtain more goods and services than if they do not trade. The reason is simple: every trade between nations is really a trade between people living in those nations, so the lesson of the two-student example essentially applies to every trade. Some people compare international trade to a war, but that comparison is misleading because the world economy is a positive-sum game.

──────────────────── FOR REVIEW ────────────────────

3.11 In what sense is economic efficiency good?

3.12 Discuss the following statement: "There is a tradeoff between equity and economic efficiency."

──────────────────── QUESTION ────────────────────

3.13 How do taxes cause economic inefficiency?

CONCLUSIONS

THE TWO-STUDENT EXAMPLE: A KEY EXAMPLE OF THE GAINS FROM TRADE

People can gain from trades by producing goods that they are able to produce at a comparative advantage. A person has a comparative advantage of producing a good if he can produce it at a lower opportunity cost than can other people. Everyone possesses a comparative advantage at either producing or doing something. The economy is a positive-sum game: one person's gain is *not* another person's loss. Both participants gain in voluntary trades.

ECONOMIC EFFICIENCY

A situation is economically efficient if there is no way to change it so that everyone gains or so that people gain while no one else loses. Economic efficiency leaves no unexploited benefit opportunities; that is, people have already made use of all such opportunities. A situation is economically inefficient if there is some way to change it so that everyone gains or so that someone gains while no one else loses. In an economically inefficient situation there are potential but unrealized gains from a change.

In an economically efficient situation, people tend to produce goods that they can produce at comparative advantages. It is possible for everyone to share the gains from changing an economically inefficient situation into an efficient one.

SHARING THE GAINS FROM TRADE

There are many economically efficient situations, each with a different distribution of income. In any economically inefficient situation, people can choose from many mutually beneficial trades, each of which divides the gains from trade differently.

People have many different and conflicting ideas about fairness. Economics deals with positive statements and does not say anything about fairness. Both economic analysis and value judgements are required for intelligent decisions on public policy.

COMPETITION AND THE GAINS FROM TRADE

Alternative trading opportunities affect the trades that people choose. Better opportunities for alternative trades weaken the bargaining positions of potential trading partners by strengthening competition. In this way, alternative opportunities affect the prices at which people trade and the way they share the gains from trade.

IS ECONOMIC EFFICIENCY GOOD?

Economic efficiency is good in the sense that waste is bad. Eliminating inefficiencies benefits people according to their own values. Some ideas of equity imply an inverse relationship between equity and economic efficiency: the opportunity cost of greater equity is reduced economic efficiency, and the opportunity cost of greater economic efficiency is reduced equity. Taxes create economic inefficiency by changing people's incentives to trade.

INTERNATIONAL TRADE

Nations gain from international trade just as individuals gain from trade. The world economy is a positive-sum game.

LOOKING AHEAD

Chapter 4 explains the most important tools of economic analysis: supply and demand. That chapter will prepare you for the rest of your journey into economics.

KEY TERMS

comparative advantage

zero-sum game

positive-sum game

economically efficient

economically inefficient

price

QUESTIONS AND PROBLEMS

3.14 Explain why the economy is a positive-sum game.

3.15 Give an example of a situation that is economically inefficient and explain how to make the situation efficient.

3.16 Alter the two-student example as in Table 3.4.

    a. Who has a comparative advantage at cleaning? Why?

    b. Who has a comparative advantage at painting? Why?

    c. Find a trade that helps Steve and Lauren and creates economic efficiency. How much does Steve gain from the trade? How much does Lauren gain?

    d. How would your answers change if Lauren required 6 hours rather than 4 hours to clean an apartment?

3.17 Create your own example of the gains from trade, determine who has a comparative advantage producing which good, and show that there are gains from trade.

TABLE 3.4

ANOTHER TWO-STUDENT EXAMPLE OF GAINS FROM TRADE

Time Required to Get Work Done				Productivity of Each Person		
Time to:	**Lauren**	**Steve**			**Lauren**	**Steve**
Clean one apartment	4 hours	5 hours		Amount cleaned in one hour	$\frac{1}{4}$ apt.	$\frac{1}{5}$ apt.
Paint one apartment	3 hours	6 hours		Amount painted in one hour	$\frac{1}{3}$ apt.	$\frac{1}{6}$ apt.

INQUIRIES FOR FURTHER THOUGHT

3.18 Do you believe the distribution of income in our economy is equitable or inequitable, fair or unfair? What could be done about it? What should be done? What would be the opportunity cost?

3.19 Describe your own view of fairness or equity in as much detail as possible.

3.20 *(Harder Problem)* Some people have suggested that the government should guarantee equal pay for workers at different jobs if those jobs have "comparable worth"; that is, if they are equally important or require similar levels of education and skill. Suppose that the government were to decide that cleaning and painting are jobs of comparable worth. Consider the two-student example in Table 3.1. If Steve pays Lauren $10 to paint his apartment (which takes her 1 hour), and Lauren pays Steve $10 to clean her apartment (which takes him 2 hours), Lauren's wage is $10 per hour and Steve's wage is $5 per hour. What alternative trade could the government suggest to Steve and Lauren? Can the government suggest a trade with equal hourly pay for Steve and Lauren that Lauren would approve? Explain.

TAG SOFTWARE APPLICATIONS

TUTORIAL EXERCISES
▶ This module reviews the key terms from Chapter 3.

ANALYTICAL EXERCISES
▶ Questions on the calculation of the gains from trade are included.

GRAPHING EXERCISES
▶ This section tests the student's understanding of the production possibilities frontier.

CHAPTER 3 APPENDIX — PRODUCTION POSSIBILITIES FRONTIER

The production possibilities frontier is a graph showing how many goods the economy can produce with its available inputs and technology. This appendix discusses the production possibilities frontier and shows how it relates to opportunity costs and economic efficiency.

production possibilities frontier (PPF) — a graph of the combinations of various goods that an economy can produce with its current resources and technology

An economy's **production possibilities frontier,** or **PPF,** is a graph of the combinations of various goods that the economy can possibly produce with its resources and technology. It answers the question, how much of one good can the economy produce, with its current resources and technology, if it produces _____ units of another good?

To draw a PPF, fill in the blank in the question above with a number, answer the question, and plot that answer as a point on a graph. Repeat this procedure by filling in other numbers in the blank, and draw a curve to connect the points. That curve is the production possibilities frontier.

An example appears in **Figure 3A.1.** The goods marked *X* and *Y* (on the horizontal and vertical axes of the graph) could be food, houses, televisions, medical services, or any other goods. Figure 3A.1 shows that the economy can produce 50,000 units of good *Y* if it does not produce any of good *X*. It can produce 49,000

FIGURE 3A.1

A PRODUCTION POSSIBILITIES FRONTIER

The production possibilities frontier shows the possible combinations of goods that the economy can produce if it uses its resources and technology efficiently. This combination depends on the resources and technology available to the economy, so the PPF shifts when resource availability or technology changes.

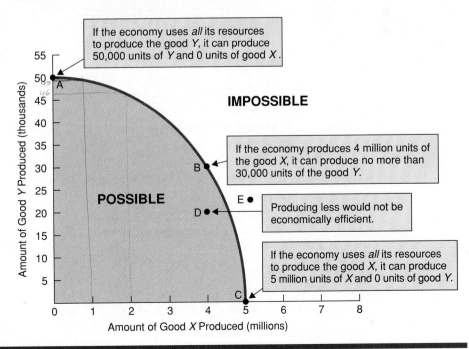

If the economy uses *all* its resources to produce the good *Y*, it can produce 50,000 units of *Y* and 0 units of good *X*.

IMPOSSIBLE

If the economy produces 4 million units of the good *X*, it can produce no more than 30,000 units of the good *Y*.

Producing less would not be economically efficient.

POSSIBLE

If the economy uses *all* its resources to produce the good *X*, it can produce 5 million units of *X* and 0 units of good *Y*.

Amount of Good *Y* Produced (thousands)

Amount of Good *X* Produced (millions)

units of Y if it produces 1 million units of X, 46,000 units of Y if it produces 2 million units of X, and so on. If the economy does not produce any Y, it can produce 5 million units of X. The answers to the PPF question give a list of numbers, each of which defines a dot on the graph; the PPF connects the dots. For Figure 3A.1, these numbers are the following:

Number of X-Goods Produced (thousands)	Number of Y-Goods Produced (millions)
0.0	50
1.0	49
2.0	46
3.0	40
4.0	30
4.5	22
5.0	0

MAIN FACTS ABOUT THE PPF

Production possibilities frontier (PPF)

technical efficiency — a situation in which an economy cannot produce more of one good without producing less of something else

technical inefficiency — a situation in which an economy could alter its use of resources so that it produces more output of some good without producing less of anything else

Several important facts guide understanding of an economy's production possibilities frontier:

1. The PPF shows the combinations of goods that an economy *can* produce with its current technology and resources. Each point on the PPF shows one combination of goods. All points under the PPF (such as Point D in Figure 3A.1) are also possible, but points above the PPF (such as Point E) are impossible.

2. Points on the PPF are technically efficient combinations of output.

   Technical efficiency means that it is impossible to produce more of one good without producing less of another. **Technical inefficiency** means that the economy could alter its use of resources so that it produces more output of some good without producing less of anything else.

   Technical efficiency means that the economy does not waste resources. Points A, B, and C are on the PPF in Figure 3A.1, so they are all technically efficient.

3. Points under the PPF (such as Point D) indicate technically inefficient production in which the economy could produce more of either good without reducing output of the other. (For example, it could produce more of good Y and the same amount of good X by moving to Point B.)

4. The PPF has a negative slope, which shows the tradeoff between producing the two goods. If the economy produces more of one good, it has fewer resources left to produce the other good. The absolute value of the slope of the PPF shows the opportunity cost of producing good X (the good on the X-axis).

EXPLANATION AND EXAMPLES

Alter the two-student example in Table 3.1 to assume that Steve and Lauren each own an apartment building with many apartments. Each apartment needs cleaning and painting. Suppose that Steve and Lauren are each willing to work 12 hours per day cleaning and painting apartments.

FIGURE 3A.2

STEVE'S PPF FOR CLEANING AND PAINTING APARTMENTS

The PPF's slope of $-\frac{1}{2}$ indicates that Steve's opportunity cost of cleaning 1 apartment is $\frac{1}{2}$ of a painted apartment.

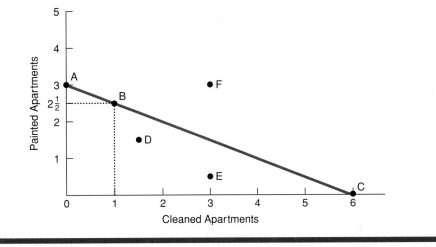

STEVE'S PPF

Figure 3A.2 shows Steve's PPF. It answers the question, how many apartments can Steve paint in one 12-hour working day if he cleans _____ apartments? To draw Steve's PPF:

1. Fill in the blank with a 0 and answer the question on the graph. If Steve cleans no apartments, he has 12 hours to paint. It takes him 4 hours to paint an apartment, so he can paint 3 apartments in one day. This is Point A on Steve's PPF.

2. Fill in the blank with a 1 and answer the question on the graph. It takes Steve 2 hours to clean 1 apartment, leaving him 10 hours to paint. Since it takes him 4 hours to paint each apartment, he can paint $2\frac{1}{2}$ apartments in those 10 hours. This is Point B on his PPF.

3. Continue drawing other points on his PPF. For example, suppose that Steve spends all 12 hours of his time cleaning so he paints no apartments. Since it takes Steve 2 hours to clean each apartment, he can clean 6 apartments. This is Point C on Steve's PPF.

4. Finally, connect the points to get Steve's PPF.

Steve's PPF shows the combinations of work that he can do in one day. He can paint 3 apartments and clean none (Point A) or clean 6 apartments and paint none. He can also choose some other combination of cleaning and painting on his PPF; for example, he can paint 1 apartment and clean 4.

Steve accomplishes less if he works inefficiently, however. If he cleans and paints only one apartment, the graph shows this combination as a point below his PPF. Points D and E indicate technically inefficient points. It is impossible for Steve to produce at a point above his PPF, such as Point F.

The slope of Steve's PPF is $-\frac{1}{2}$. For every extra apartment Steve cleans, he can paint one-half of an apartment _less._ Cleaning 1 apartment takes Steve 2 hours, and

FIGURE 3A.3

LAUREN'S PPF FOR CLEANING AND PAINTING APARTMENTS

The slope of Lauren's PPF, –3, indicates that her opportunity cost of cleaning 1 apartment is painting 3 apartments.

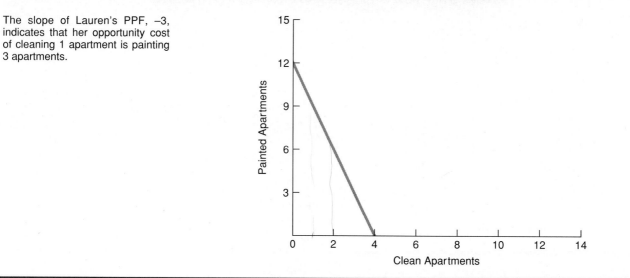

during this time he could paint half an apartment. The absolute value of the slope ($\frac{1}{2}$) is Steve's opportunity cost of cleaning an apartment.

LAUREN'S PPF

Lauren's PPF, drawn in the same way, appears in **Figure 3A.3.** Lauren can spend her 12 hours cleaning no apartments and painting 12, cleaning 4 apartments and painting none, or doing some other combination of work. Lauren's PPF shows what goods (painted and cleaned apartments) she can produce in one 12-hour day. The absolute value of the slope of Lauren's PPF is 3, which shows that Lauren's opportunity cost of cleaning 1 apartment is painting 3 apartments.

PPF FOR LAUREN AND STEVE TOGETHER

Steve's PPF and Lauren's PPF are straight lines, but the PPF in Figure 3A.1 (for a whole economy) was curved. To see why, consider a PPF for Lauren and Steve together. It answers the question, how many apartments can Lauren and Steve paint if they each work one 12-hour day and they clean _____ apartments? **Figure 3A.4** shows the PPF for Lauren and Steve together.

To derive the PPF in Figure 3A.4, begin, as before, by filling in the blank in the question above with the number 0 to determine how many apartments they can paint if they clean no apartments. Since both people have 12 hours for painting, Steve can paint 3 apartments and Lauren can paint 12. Together they can paint 15 apartments if they clean none. This is Point A in Figure 3A.4.

Suppose, instead, that they spend all their time cleaning. In 12 hours, Steve can clean 6 apartments and Lauren can clean 4. Together they would clean 10 apartments if they paint none, Point C on the PPF in Figure 3A.4.

FIGURE 3A.4

PRODUCTION POSSIBILITIES FRONTIER FOR STEVE AND LAUREN TOGETHER

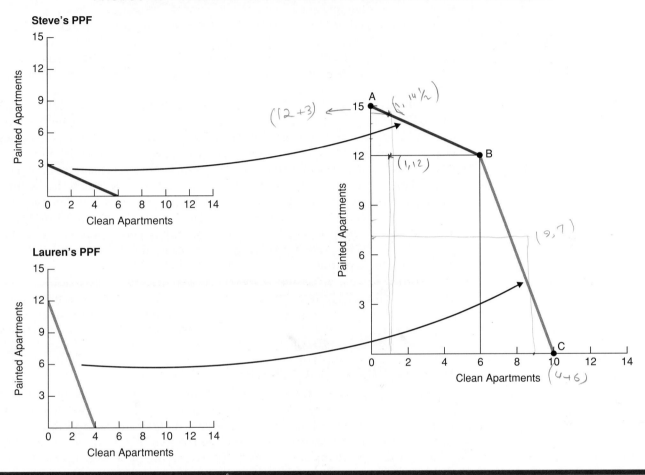

You might think that a straight line between Points A and C would define the PPF for Steve and Lauren together, but that would be wrong. As Figure 3A.4 shows, the PPF for Lauren and Steve together is not a straight line. The difference occurs because they have different opportunity costs of cleaning and painting.

Suppose that Steve spends his 12 hours cleaning and Lauren spends her 12 hours painting. Together they clean 6 apartments and paint 12, giving another point (Point B) on their joint PPF. Alternatively, Lauren and Steve might decide to clean just 1 apartment today and to spend the rest of their time painting. They would accomplish more if Steve were to clean the apartment and Lauren were to paint all day than if Lauren were to do any cleaning. Steve can clean 1 apartment in 2 hours, leaving him with 10 hours for painting. He can paint $2\frac{1}{2}$ apartments in that time and Lauren can paint 12 apartments in a full day, so together they can paint $14\frac{1}{2}$ apartments and clean 1. This is a point on the PPF for Steve and Lauren together.

It would be technically inefficient for Lauren to clean an apartment while Steve painted—they would produce at a point below their joint production possibilities frontier in Figure 3A.4. Suppose that they clean only one apartment and Lauren, rather than Steve, does this work. Because the cleaning takes her 3 hours, she has 9 hours left and she can paint 9 apartments. Meanwhile, Steve can paint 3 apartments. Together they can paint 12 apartments—$2\frac{1}{2}$ fewer than if Steve does the cleaning. Therefore, if they decide to clean 1 apartment, they get more painting done if Steve cleans it than if Lauren does. Because Steve has a comparative advantage in cleaning, production is technically efficient only if Steve cleans the apartment.

Similarly, suppose that Lauren and Steve decide to clean 2 apartments today and to spend the rest of their time painting. It is economically efficient for Steve to clean both apartments while Lauren paints. It would be economically inefficient for Lauren to clean either apartment.[1] This reasoning continues up to Point B, where Steve spends all his time cleaning and Lauren spends all her time painting. At Point B there is a kink in the PPF—it is not a straight line. If they want to clean more than 6 apartments, Lauren will have to spend some time cleaning, while Steve spends all of his time cleaning. For example, they can clean 7 apartments if Steve cleans 6 (which takes his whole day) and Lauren cleans 1. This leaves Lauren with 9 hours for painting, so she can paint 9 apartments. Together they can clean 7 apartments and paint 9.

Whenever people have different opportunity costs (as Lauren and Steve do), their joint PPF is *not* a straight line, but has a kink as at Point B in Figure 3A.4. The joint PPF for several people with different opportunity costs would have several kinks. If enough people in the economy have different opportunity costs, the PPF becomes the smooth curve in Figure 3A.1.

When Is the PPF a Straight Line?

The PPF is a straight line if the opportunity cost of producing each good is independent of its level of production. The opportunity cost of studying for one minute is one minute of television regardless of how much a person studies. Therefore, the PPF between study-time and television-time is a straight line. Similarly, the opportunity cost of one bushel of corn might be one bushel of wheat regardless of how much corn the economy produces: the PPF between wheat and corn likewise would be a straight line.

When Is the PPF Curved?

The PPF is curved as in Figure 3A.1 when the opportunity cost of producing each good in the graph depends on the amount produced. At each point on the PPF, the opportunity cost of X is the absolute value of the slope of the PPF at that point. Figure 3A.4 shows an example. If Steve and Lauren clean fewer than 6 apartments per day, the opportunity cost of cleaning an apartment is painting one-half of an apartment. If they clean more than 6 apartments per day, the opportunity cost of

---

[1] If Steve cleans both apartments, he spends 4 hours cleaning. This leaves him 8 hours to paint, so he can paint 2 apartments. Meanwhile, Lauren paints 12 apartments, so together they clean 2 apartments and paint 14. If Lauren were to clean both apartments, it would take her 6 hours, leaving her time to paint only 6 apartments. Steve can paint 3 apartments in 1 day, so together they would clean 2 apartments but paint only 9, 5 fewer than if Steve did the cleaning. Since Steve and Lauren together can clean 2 apartments and paint 14, this is another point on their joint PPF.

cleaning an apartment is painting 3 apartments. The difference in opportunity costs creates a kink in the PPF in Figure 3A.4.

More generally, suppose the economy produces a small amount of X and a large amount of Y. People who are relatively better at producing X—those with a comparative advantage at producing it—can produce all of the economy's X. If the economy produces more X (and less Y), it must use people who are less good at producing X (and better at producing Y). This boosts the opportunity cost of X as the economy produces more X, and the PPF curves.

A similar argument applies to other inputs, such as land and capital (equipment). Suppose that all of the land in a country is equally good for housing, but some land is better than other land for farming. If the economy produces only a small amount of farm products, it can use only the best farmland. To produce more farm products, the economy must bring some less fertile land into production. As the economy adds more acres of farmland, average output per acre falls because the economy begins using larger quantities of less productive land.

Figure 3A.5 illustrates an economy that can produce 40 million houses and no food (Point A) or 39 million houses and 1 million tons of food (Point B). As the economy moves from Point A to Point B, it gains 1 million tons of food and loses 1 million houses, so the opportunity cost of 1 million tons of food is 1 million houses.

The opportunity cost changes along the PPF in Figure 3A.5. If the economy moves from Point B to Point C, it raises output of food by 1 million tons per year (from 1 million to 2 million tons) while reducing output of houses by 2 million

---

FIGURE 3A.5

PRODUCTION POSSIBILITIES FRONTIER

The base of the triangle between Points E and F shows an increase in food output of 1 million tons (from 4 million to 5 million). The height of the triangle shows a fall in house production of 9 million houses (from 29 million to 20 million). This is the opportunity cost of producing 1 million more tons of food.

The negative slope of the PPF shows that as the economy produces more food, it can produce fewer houses. The curvature of the PPF shows that the opportunity cost of food rises when food output increases.

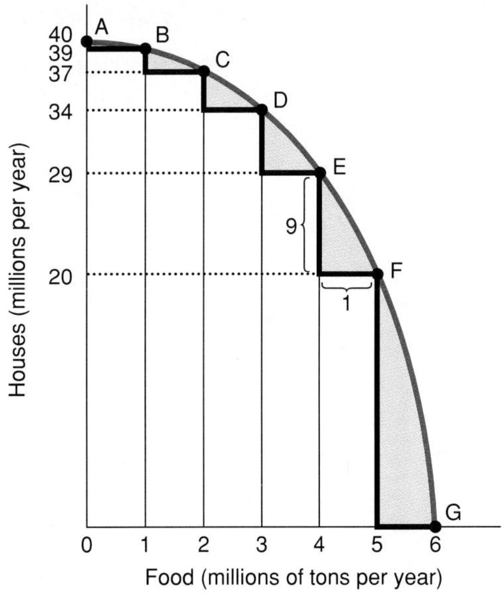

Case Study: Production Possibilities during World War II

During World War II, the U.S. government required the auto industry to convert from producing cars to producing military equipment. **Figure 3A.6** shows the automakers' production possibilities frontier between civilian automobiles and military equipment. In 1941, the auto industry produced and sold about 4 million cars and only a small amount of military equipment (Point A in the figure). During World War II, the U.S. government announced that the U.S. auto industry would convert to making military equipment. The government expected it to produce 117,000 tanks, 185,000 airplanes, and 28 million tons of merchant ships in 1942 and 1943 (Point G in Figure 3A.6).

The government underestimated the curvature of the industry's PPF, however, so Point G was impossible. Some conversion to military production was easy: producing a small amount of military equipment required only a small cut in auto production. Massive conversion was more difficult, though. For example, most of the auto industry's machine tools were not easy to convert to produce military equipment. The curvature of the economy's PPF meant that instead of producing at Point G, the U.S. economy produced at Point B: 56,000 tanks, 134,000 airplanes, and 27 million tons of merchant ships.

(from 39 million to 37 million). This means that the opportunity cost of the additional 1 million tons of food is 2 million houses. If the economy moves from Point C to Point D, the opportunity cost of 1 million tons of food rises to 3 million houses; if it moves from Point D to Point E, the opportunity cost of food reaches 5 million houses. Opportunity cost changes along a curved PPF. The opportunity cost of food rises as the economy produces larger quantities of food.

FIGURE 3A.6

U.S. PRODUCTION POSSIBILITIES FRONTIER DURING WORLD WAR II

In 1941, the U.S. auto industry produced at Point A. The government expected the auto industry to move to Point G in 1942 and 1943. Because the PPF was curved, however, the industry could produce only at Point B.

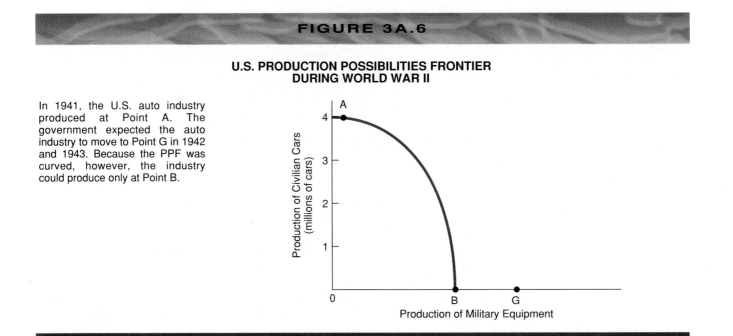

FIGURE 3A.7

SHIFTS IN A PPF

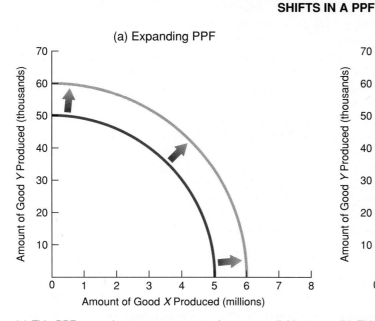

(a) Expanding PPF

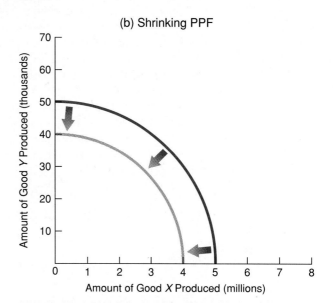

(b) Shrinking PPF

(a) This PPF expands as more resources become available to the economy or as technology improves.

(b) This PPF shrinks as the economy loses resources. This could occur if the economy failed to produce enough new machines and tools to replace those that became worn out. It could also result from an earthquake, a war, or another disaster that destroyed resources.

SHIFTS IN THE PPF

The PPF shifts whenever the economy's resources (labor, capital, land, or entrepreneurship) change, or when technology changes. More resources or better technology would expand the PPF, as in **Figure 3A.7a,** shifting the PPF upward and to the right. A loss of resources would shrink the PPF, as in Figure 3A.7b, shifting it downward and to the left. The opportunities open to economies change over time as their PPFs expand or shrink.

EXAMPLE: ECONOMIC GROWTH

Economic growth refers to an increase in the economy's output of goods and services per person. A growing economy's PPF expands faster than its population grows. Economic growth can occur because the economy either gains new resources or discovers better technologies.

The U.S. economy has grown for both reasons. In 1970, U.S. businesses owned about $3.3 trillion in capital (machines, tools, plants, equipment); this number is adjusted for inflation to avoid a misleading comparison with current conditions. People in the United States consumed some of the goods and services they produced over the next 25 years; they wore the clothes, drove the cars, ate the food, and listened to the music. People in the United States also invested some of the goods they produced; they built new machines, tools, plants, and other capital. By 1995, U.S. businesses owned about $6.3 trillion in capital. Business capital roughly doubled in the United States between 1970 and 1995, and this accounts for part of U.S. economic growth since 1970.

New technology also accounts for part of U.S. economic growth. In 1970, there were no personal computers, and even electronic calculators were large, expensive, and not very powerful. Major advances in medicine and biotechnology, space and satellite technology, fiber optics, lasers, and thousands of other technologies accompanied advances in microelectronics and computers to contribute to economic growth.

Figure 3A.8 represents economic growth in the United States over the century from 1890 to 1990. The figure shows how the U.S. PPF for consumption and investment has shifted every 20 years. Clearly, it has expanded rapidly over time. Growth in total output of goods and services in the United States and western Europe:

▶ Averaged less than 0.2 percent per year in the years 1500 to 1750

▶ Rose to about 1.0 percent per year by 1850

▶ Rose to between 1.0 and 1.5 percent per year between 1850 and 1950

FIGURE 3A.8

EXPANSION OF THE U.S. PPF, 1890–1990

The shifts in the U.S. production possibilities frontier show the expansion of total output per person in the United States, adjusted for inflation. Each PPF represents a different year. Over each 20-year period, the United States has experienced economic growth, raising output nearly six times the level of 100 years ago. It is now more than double the level of output in 1950, and will soon be 50 percent larger than the level in 1970.

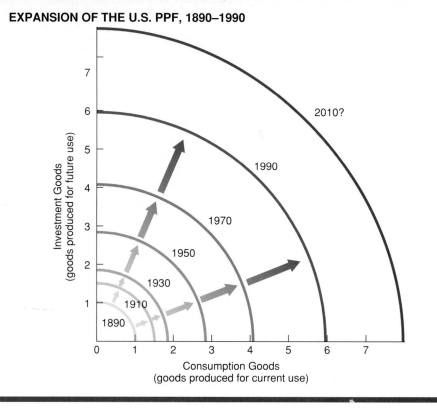

▶ Rose to about 1.8 percent per year since 1950 (faster before 1973 and slower since then)

There is a big difference between the annual economic growth of 0.2 percent long ago and the more recent growth of 1.8 percent per year. If the economy grows 1.8 percent per year, output doubles every 39 years; with 0.2 percent growth, output takes 350 years to double. Output per person in the United States has more than doubled since 1950. Unfortunately, a few countries have had negative economic growth since 1950, with shrinking PPFs.

KEY TERMS

production possibilities
frontier (PPF)

technical efficiency
technical inefficiency

QUESTIONS AND PROBLEMS

3A.1 Explain why the negative slope of a production possibilities frontier shows the opportunity cost of producing the good on the horizontal axis (*X*-axis). What is the opportunity cost of 1 million tons of food as the economy moves from Point F to Point G in Figure 3A.5?

3A.2 An old machine powered by natural gas can produce either 4,000 backpacks or 2,000 bicycles in a month. A newer machine that uses solar power can produce either 2,000 backpacks or 4,000 bicycles in a month. **Table 3A.1** shows the amount of each good that can be produced with a single machine of each type in a month.

a. Draw the production possibilities frontier for an economy with ten old, natural-gas-powered machines and no newer, solar-powered machines. What is the opportunity cost of backpacks? Of bicycles?

b. Draw the production possibilities frontier for an economy with no old, natural-gas-powered machines and ten newer, solar-powered machines. What is the opportunity cost of backpacks in this economy? Of bicycles?

c. Draw the production possibilities frontier for an economy with ten machines of each type available. What is the opportunity cost of backpacks? Of bicycles?

d. Suppose that buyers want the same number of backpacks as bicycles. How many months of each year would an economy with one natural-gas-powered machine spend producing backpacks to produce an equal num-

TABLE 3A.1

MONTHLY PRODUCTION FROM ONE MACHINE (THOUSANDS)

	Natural-Gas-Powered Machines	Solar-Powered Machines
Backpacks	4	2
Bicycles	2	4

ber of backpacks and bicycles? How many backpacks per year would it produce? What if the economy had one solar-powered machine instead?

e. Suppose that Country A has ten old, natural-gas-powered machines and no new, solar-powered machines while Country B has ten new, solar-powered machines and no old, natural-gas-powered machines. People still want the same number of backpacks as bicycles. Explain why the two countries would gain from trade. (*Hint:* Calculate the number of backpacks and bicycles the world economy can produce with international trade and compare your answer to the number each country can produce alone without international trade.)

CHAPTER 4

SUPPLY AND DEMAND

WHAT THIS CHAPTER IS ABOUT

▶ Prices

▶ The amount of a good people choose to buy

▶ The amount of a good producers choose to make and sell

▶ How buyers' and sellers' choices become coordinated in equilibrium

Why does a pair of shoes cost more than a compact disk? Why do entertainment stars earn more than mathematicians? Why do airline tickets cost more around holidays? Why have prices of personal computers and video equipment fallen?

What persuades farmers and manufacturers to produce all the food that people want to buy? What ensures that a city has enough apartments for people to rent? What prevents companies from making more watches than people want to buy?

Chapter 3 showed that people can gain from specialization and trade. This chapter explores which trades they choose and the prices they agree upon. The analytical tools in this chapter are the most important tools of economics: supply and demand.

INTRODUCTION TO DEMAND

How many movies will you see this month? Your answer depends on many conditions, such as:

▶ The price—How much do movie tickets cost?

▶ Your tastes—How much do you like movies?

▶ Your income—Do you have the money?

▶ Prices of other goods—How much does it cost to rent videos or attend a concert?

Other conditions also influence the choice, such as whether you have a video recorder, how many parties you could attend, what your friends want to do, and how much studying you have to do. How many movie tickets would you buy this month if each ticket cost $1? What if they cost $3, $5, or $10? Before you continue reading, briefly answer these questions based on your own tastes and circumstances. Write your answers as in **Table 4.1,** which shows *my* answers.

The table you made is your demand schedule for movie tickets this month. (A formal definition of this term appears in the next section.) Your demand schedule for a good lists the quantities you would buy at various possible prices. My demand schedule in Table 4.1 shows that my *quantity demanded* at a price of $1 is seven tickets and my quantity demanded at a price of $2 is six tickets. Look at your demand schedule: what is your quantity demanded at a price of $1?

TABLE 4.1

THE AUTHOR'S DEMAND SCHEDULE FOR TICKETS

Price of Tickets	Number I Would Buy
$1	7
2	6
3	4
4	3
5	2
6	1
7	0

FIGURE 4.1

MY DEMAND CURVE FOR MOVIE TICKETS

Each point is a row from Table 4.1.

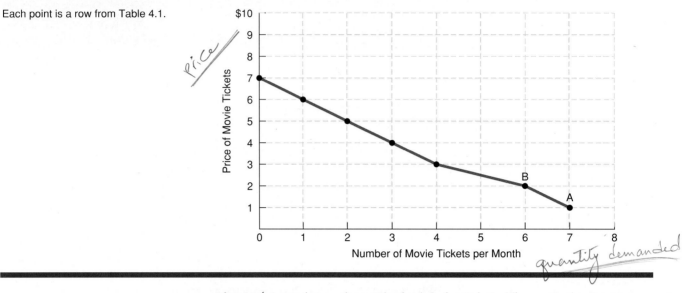

Figure 4.1 graphs my demand schedule for tickets. The vertical axis measures the price of tickets and the horizontal axis measures my quantity demanded at that price. If tickets cost $1 each, I would buy seven this month, Point A on the graph. If they cost $2 each, I would buy six, Point B. Each point on the graph shows a row from my demand schedule in Table 4.1. The curve that connects these points is my demand curve for tickets.

Now graph your demand schedule for tickets. Put the price on the vertical axis and your quantity demanded at that price on the horizontal axis. Each row of your demand schedule defines a point on your graph. Connect these points to draw your demand curve for movie tickets. Now that you have seen an example, we are ready for definitions.

DEMAND

quantity demanded (at a given price) — the amount of a good that a person would buy during a time period if she could buy as much as she wanted at that price

Roughly, a person's quantity demanded of some good is the amount she wants to buy.[1] More precisely:

> **A person's quantity demanded** of a good at some price is the amount of the good she would buy during some time period if she could buy as much as she wants at that price.

Notice three points about this definition. First, a person has many quantities demanded for any good: one for each possible price. Economists speak of "the quantity demanded *at a (particular) price.*" Second, a person's quantity demanded at each price is the amount she would buy at that price if possible, not the amount actually available or the amount sellers want to sell. Third, the quantity demanded at any price applies to a particular time period such as a month or year.

---

[1]Do not confuse the amount of a good you would like to *have* with quantity demanded (the amount you want to *buy*). You may want more of something, but it may not be worth the price. You may want more of almost everything, but this has nothing to do with your quantity demanded. Your quantity demanded shows the amount of a good you are willing to buy, given your limited budget.

demand schedule — a table that shows various possible prices and a person's quantity demanded at each price

demand curve — a graph of a demand schedule

A list of prices and quantities demanded at those prices is a demand schedule:

A person's **demand schedule** for a good is a table showing many hypothetical prices of the good and the person's quantity demanded at each price. *Table 4.1*

Table 4.1 shows an example of a demand schedule; the second column lists the quantity demanded at each price. Notice that a demand schedule lists hypothetical prices of the good. It does not say what price buyers actually pay; instead, it shows the quantity demanded if the price were $0.50, or if it were $1.00.[2]

Graphing a demand schedule gives a demand curve:

A person's **demand curve** for a good is a graph of his demand schedule.

Remember that every graph answers a question. For various possible prices, a person's demand curve answers the question, what is this person's quantity demanded at this price? Figure 4.1 shows an example.

CONDITIONS THAT AFFECT THE QUANTITY DEMANDED

The amount of a good you choose to buy depends on many conditions, including its price, your tastes (what you like and dislike), how useful it is (a coat is more useful in cold weather than warm weather), your income, the prices of other goods you could buy instead, and the time you have had to adjust to a past change in price. Later sections will discuss this list one condition at a time through thought experiments: what if *only* this condition changed and everything else stayed the same? How would this one change affect the quantity demanded? For example, the next section deals with price changes. For example, what happens to the quantity of T-shirts demanded if their prices change, holding constant people's tastes for wearing T-shirts, their incomes, the prices of sweat shirts, and the other conditions. This thought experiment gives the demand schedule for T-shirts, which holds constant all conditions except the price.

PRICE AND QUANTITY DEMANDED

An increase in the price of a good, with no change in the other conditions, generally reduces the quantity demanded. If the price of milk were to rise while the other conditions stayed the same, you would probably want to buy less milk— only rarely would anyone want to buy *more*. If the price were to rise enough, you would almost certainly buy less. Thousands of economic studies support the following generalization about the behavior of buyers:

When the price of a good rises, holding constant other conditions, the quantity demanded falls.

Sometimes economists call this the *law of demand*. To state it another way:

Demand curves have negative slopes.

Demand curves slope downward, as in Figure 4.1.[3]

Points A and B in Figure 4.1 both lie on my demand curve for movie tickets. My tastes (my likes and dislikes) are the same at Points A and B. I would buy more

---

[2]Because a person's demand schedule lists many hypothetical prices, that person may not know his demand schedule. For example, he may not know for sure how many shirts he would buy each year if shirts cost $1 each or $80 each. A person's quantity demanded at some price refers to the amount that the person would actually buy if that were the price. Unless shirts actually cost $1 or $80 each, however, the person might not know how he would behave under those conditions.

[3]Sometimes a price change does not affect the quantity demanded; then the demand curve is a vertical line.

FIGURE 4.2

INDIVIDUAL DEMANDS AND MARKET DEMAND

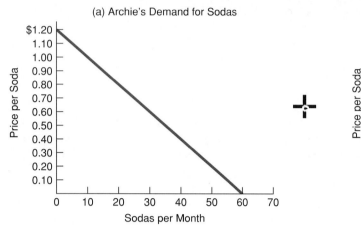

(a) Archie's Demand for Sodas

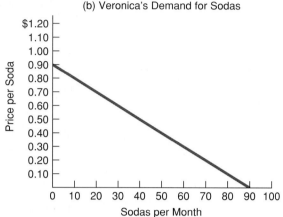

(b) Veronica's Demand for Sodas

Archie's Demand Schedule for Sodas (sodas per month)

Price per Soda	Quantity Demanded
$1.20	0
1.00	10
0.90	15
0.80	20
0.60	30
0.40	40
0.20	50
0.10	55

Veronica's Demand Schedule for Sodas (sodas per month)

Price per Soda	Quantity Demanded
$1.00	0
0.90	0
0.80	10
0.60	30
0.40	50
0.20	70
0.10	80

tickets at Point A than at Point B because the price is lower, not because my tastes are different. My income is also the same at Points A and B. The only difference in conditions between Points A and B is the lower price at Point A, so my quantity demanded is higher.

WHY DEMAND CURVES SLOPE DOWNWARD

Quantity demanded of a good falls when its price rises (holding constant other conditions) for two reasons. First, buyers can replace that good with some other, cheaper good. When a good's price rises, people tend to buy less of it and to substitute other goods in its place. If the price of corn rises, people tend to substitute broccoli and carrots for corn. The second reason is that people cannot afford to buy as much after a price increase. People must buy either less of the more expensive good or less of something else.[4] For both reasons, a price increase generally reduces the quantity demanded.

MARKET DEMAND

We add the quantities demanded by all buyers to obtain the market quantity demanded.

---

[4]They could save less, but they would then buy fewer goods in the future.

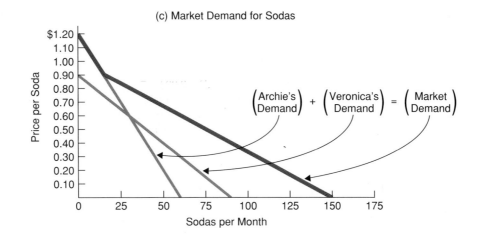

(c) Market Demand for Sodas

Market Demand Schedule for Sodas (sodas per month)

Price per Soda	Market Quantity Demanded
$1.20	0 (= 0 + 0)
1.00	10 (= 10 + 0)
0.90	15 (= 15 + 0)
0.80	30 (= 20 + 10)
0.60	60 (= 30 + 30)
0.40	90 (= 40 + 50)
0.20	120 (= 50 + 70)
0.10	135 (= 55 + 80)

market quantity demanded — the total amount of a good that *all buyers* in the economy would buy during a time period if they could buy as much as they wanted at a given price

The **market quantity demanded** of a good at some price is the total amount of the good that all buyers in the economy would buy during some time period if they could buy as much as they wanted at that price.

Similarly,

market demand schedule — a table of many hypothetical prices of a good and the quantity demanded by *all buyers* in the economy at each price

The **market demand schedule** for a good is a table of many hypothetical prices of the good and the quantity demanded by *all buyers* in the economy at each price.

market demand curve — a graph of the market demand schedule

The **market demand curve** for a good is a graph of its market demand schedule.

When economists talk about *the* demand curve for a good, they mean the market demand curve.

EXPLANATION AND EXAMPLE

Figure 4.2 shows how the market demand schedule and market demand curve relate to individuals' demand schedules and demand curves. Panel a shows Archie's demand schedule and demand curve for sodas. Panel b shows Veronica's demand schedule and demand curve for sodas. Panel c shows the market demand schedule and demand curve for sodas, assuming that Archie and Veronica are the only buyers. At a price of 80 cents, Archie wants to buy 20 sodas and Veronica wants to buy 10, so the total market quantity demanded is 30. At a price of 40 cents, Archie wants to buy 40 sodas and Veronica wants 50, so the market quantity demanded is 90.

CHANGES IN DEMAND

change in demand — a change in the numbers in the demand schedule and a shift in the demand curve. An increase in demand shifts the demand curve to the right; a decrease shifts it to the left

A **change in demand** means a change in the numbers in the demand schedule and a shift in the demand curve.

An increase (or rise) in demand increases the quantity demanded at each possible price and the demand curve shifts to the right as in **Figure 4.3,** from D_1 to D_2.

A decrease (or fall) in demand decreases the quantity demanded at each possible price and the demand curve shifts to the left as in **Figure 4.4,** from D_1 to D_2.

When demand changes, the distance by which the demand curve shifts left or right at each price shows the change in the quantity demanded at that price. Figures 4.3 and 4.4 show changes in demand.

CHANGES IN QUANTITY DEMANDED VERSUS CHANGES IN DEMAND

Economists distinguish between changes in the quantity demanded and changes in demand. A change in the quantity demanded occurs when the price changes, moving the economy from one row to another in the demand schedule. This is a movement along a demand curve, as from Point A to Point B in Figure 4.1.

A change in demand occurs when the numbers in the demand schedule change and the demand curve shifts, as in Figures 4.3 and 4.4. This happens when

---

FIGURE 4.3

INCREASE IN DEMAND

An increase in demand is a rise in the quantity demanded at each price. At each price, the new demand curve, D_2, shows a higher quantity demanded than the old demand curve, D_1.

Old Demand Schedule		New Demand Schedule	
Price	**Quantity Demanded**	**Price**	**Quantity Demanded**
$10	5	$10	8
9	6	9	10
8	8	8	12
7	10	7	15
6	14	6	18
5	20	5	24

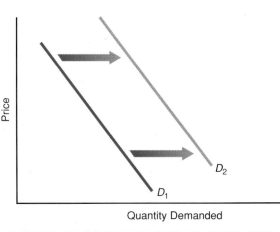

FIGURE 4.4

DECREASE IN DEMAND

A decrease in demand is a fall in the quantity demanded at each price. At each price, the new demand curve, D_2, shows a lower quantity demanded than the old demand curve, D_1.

Old Demand Schedule			New Demand Schedule	
Price	Quantity Demanded		Price	Quantity Demanded
$10	5		$10	2
9	6		9	3
8	8		8	4
7	10		7	6
6	14		6	9
5	20		5	15

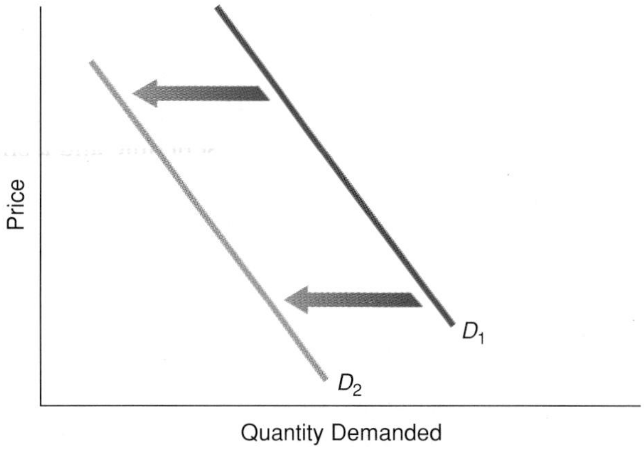

a change in conditions other than the price (such as a change in buyers' incomes) alters the demand schedule.

A change in price changes the quantity demanded. It does not change demand. A change in conditions *other than the price of a good* can change the demand for that good.

EXAMPLE
Six main conditions affect the demand for a good:

YOUR DEMAND FOR VIDEO RENTALS

Your Tastes	How much do you like watching videos?
Usefulness of the good	Do you have a VCR and a television?
Your Income and wealth	Do you have money to spend on videos?
Prices of other goods	How much does it cost to see a movie at a theater? How much does a VCR cost?
Adjustment time after a change	Have you found time to visit the new discount store to buy a VCR?
Number of potential buyers	How many people in the country might rent videos? The answer affects the *market* demand curve for video rentals.

Changes in these conditions can cause changes in demand (shifts in the demand curve). The next section will discuss changes in each condition separately, holding constant the other conditions.

FOR REVIEW

4.1 What is a demand schedule? What is the market demand schedule?

4.2 What is a demand curve? Why does it slope downward?

QUESTIONS

4.3 Draw graphs to explain the difference between an increase in demand and an increase in quantity demanded.

4.4 Draw a graph of your demand for leisure time. How can you buy leisure time?

4.5 Comment on the following quotation from a business owner: "We lowered our prices so the demand for our goods increased."

CHANGES IN CONDITIONS CAUSING CHANGES IN DEMAND

Table 4.2 summarizes the changes in conditions that can change demand. The following sections explain how each change affects demand, holding constant the other conditions.

1— TASTES

Tastes (or *preferences*) refer to people's underlying likes and dislikes. Economists do not explain why people have certain tastes or what makes these tastes change; that is a subject for psychologists. People's tastes affect their demands, though, and changes in tastes can cause changes in demand.

EXAMPLES

If your musical tastes change from rap to classical, your demand for classical music recordings rises, as in Figure 4.3, and your demand for rap recordings falls, as in Figure 4.4. The demand for chocolate candy increased in the United States after World War I: U.S. soldiers developed a taste for eating chocolate because the government gave soldiers chocolate bars during the war.

2— USEFULNESS

People often use goods they buy to create the products they really want. A good's usefulness is its benefit as an input into this process of household pro-

---

TABLE 4.2

EFFECTS ON DEMAND OF CHANGES IN CONDITIONS

Changes in Conditions That Increase Demand for a Good	Changes in Conditions That Decrease Demand for a Good
1. Change in tastes: people like the good more than before	1. Change in tastes: people like the good less than before
2. Increase in usefulness of the good	2. Decrease in usefulness of the good
3. Increases in buyers' income or wealth increase demand for a normal good; decreases in income or wealth increase demand for an inferior good	3. Decreases in buyers' income or wealth reduce demand for a normal good; increases in income or wealth reduce demand for an inferior good
4. Increase in the price of a substitute	4. Decrease in the price of a substitute
5. Decrease in the price of a complement	5. Increase in the price of a complement
6. Increase in adjustment time following a fall in the price	6. Increase in adjustment time following a rise in the price
7. Increase in the number of potential buyers	7. Decrease in the number of potential buyers

income — money received annually from all sources, measured as an amount per year

normal good — a good whose demand increases if income rises

inferior good — a good whose demand decreases if income rises

wealth — the value of accumulated past savings, including human wealth (the value of education and skills)

substitute — two goods are substitutes if an increase in the price of one raises demand for the other

Putting it mildly, more consumers prefer only products that are "pure," "natural"

Shift in Behavior

The trend represents a significant shift in consumer behavior. For years, consumers were motivated mainly by manufacturers' claims of convenience, performance, or prestige. Now, many people are avoiding products that contain harsh or unnecessary chemicals, especially in their homes.

The growing allure of pure products is paying off for marketers. Sales of Tom's of Maine natural toothpaste in supermarkets and drugstores soared 55 percent to $12.1 million during the 12 months ended Feb. 28.

Demand for "natural" products rises as consumers' tastes and beliefs about safety change.

Source: "Putting It Mildly, More Consumers Prefer Only Products that Are 'Pure,' 'Natural,'" *The Wall Street Journal,* May 11, 1993, p. B1.

duction. The demand for coats rises at the beginning of winter not because people's tastes change (people always want to be comfortable) but because coats are more useful in the winter: they help people to create comfort (the product that they really want). Similarly, ground beef is more useful if you have a stove to cook it.

Changes in usefulness cause changes in demand. The demand for Christmas cards rises in November and falls in January. The demand for air conditioners rises each summer. The demand for low-fat foods increased when people learned how these foods could help them to produce good health.

INCOME AND WEALTH

Changes in buyers' income or wealth cause changes in demand.

> **Income** is the amount of money a person earns each year from working, interest on savings, and other sources such as gifts.

Economists always measure income in units of money per year (or some other time period). Increases in income raise the demand for most goods, such as restaurant meals and vacations.

> If an increase in income raises the demand for a good, as in Figure 4.3, economists call it a **normal good.** If an increase in income decreases the demand for a good, as in Figure 4.4, economists call it an **inferior good.**

Economists use statistical analysis to identify normal goods and inferior goods. Normal goods include airline travel, big houses, and swimming pools. Long-distance bus travel and bologna are inferior goods. (When income rises, people tend to substitute other goods for bologna and bus travel.)

> **Wealth** is the value of a person's accumulated savings.

Wealth includes money in saving accounts, stocks and bonds, and the value of possessions like cars, houses, and record collections. Wealth also includes *human wealth:* the value of education and skills.[5] Economists measure wealth in money, *not* money *per year.* Changes in wealth have the same effects on demand as changes in income: an increase in wealth raises demand for normal goods and reduces demand for inferior goods.

PRICES OF OTHER GOODS

The demand for a particular good can change due to changes in prices of *other* goods. These other goods fall into two categories: substitutes and complements.

SUBSTITUTES

Goods are substitutes if they can be used in place of each other. Coke and Pepsi are substitutes, as are Fords and Chevys, or Wheaties and Cheerios. When the price of coffee rises, some people switch to tea or cocoa, so the demands for these substitutes rise. The general rule is:

> When the price of a good rises, the demands for its **substitutes** increase.

This rule defines the term *substitutes*. Similarly, demand for a good decreases when the price of a substitute falls.

---

[5]Human wealth is the value of all future income that a person's education and skills help create.

IN THE NEWS

Beef prices at record highs as cattle shortage continues

By Eben Shapiro

With barbecue season around the corner, a near 30-year low in the nation's cattle herd has resulted in the highest prices ever for steak, hamburger, and other cuts of beef.

Faced with the high meat prices, many grocers say they are promoting chicken breasts, which average $2.04 a pound, or less than half the price of a T-bone steak, and that more and more shoppers are choosing chicken.

Growing Popularity of Chicken

Last year, for the first time, Americans consumed more poultry than beef, an Agriculture Department survey found.

"Forget about nutrition; it is just plain old economics," said William Roenigk, vice pre-sident of the National Broiler Council in Washington.

Mr. Boehlje, the agriculture economist, said poultry would continue to gain market share at the expense of beef as meat prices rise. "The higher beef prices move, the more people are going to switch," he said. "We have seen substantial switching in the past and I think that is going to continue."

Chicken and beef are substitutes.

Source: Eben Shapiro, "Beef Prices at Record Highs as Cattle Shortage Continues," *New York Times,* April 16, 1991, p. A1.

COMPLEMENTS

Goods are complements if people tend to use them together. Cameras and film are complements, as are gasoline and cars, or compact disk players and compact disks.

> When the price of a good falls, the demands for its **complements** increase.

complement — two goods are complements if an increase in the price of one reduces demand for the other

This rule defines the term *complements.* Of course, when the price of a good rises, the demands for its complements decrease.

Economists use statistical analysis to identify pairs of goods that are substi-tutes, pairs that are complements, and pairs that are unrelated (neither substitutes or complements).

SUBSTITUTION OVER TIME

One substitute for buying a good now is to buy it later—a few days or a few months from now. You may postpone a vacation to take advantage of lower, off-season prices because a vacation later is a substitute for a vacation now. The cur-rent demand for a good falls when people expect its price to decline; they buy less now and plan to buy more later, when the price is lower. Similarly, the current demand for a good increases when people expect its price to rise; they buy now while the price is still low.

intertemporal substitution (sub-stitution over time) — a change in the current demand or supply of a good caused by a change in its expected future price

> **Intertemporal substitution** (substitution over time) occurs when a change in the expected future price of a good causes a change in the cur-rent demand for that good.

FIGURE 4.5

EFFECT OF A CHANGE IN ADJUSTMENT TIME ON DEMAND

When the price of a gallon of gasoline rose from 30¢ in 1973 to 44¢ in 1974, people bought less gasoline immediately—they went from Point A to Point B. As the adjustment time increased, people bought more fuel-efficient cars and the demand curve for gasoline shifted from D_1 to D_2.

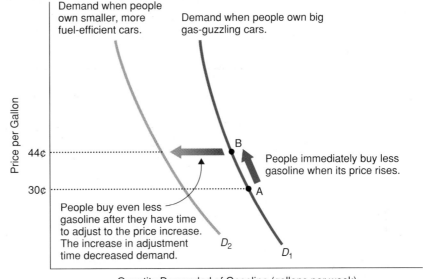

Quantity Demanded of Gasoline (gallons per week)

No one can predict future prices exactly, but people's guesses, or expectations, about future prices affect their demands.[6]

ADJUSTMENT TIME AFTER A PRICE CHANGE

Increases in adjustment time following a change in price cause changes in demand. The longer people have had to adjust, the bigger the change in demand.

EXAMPLE

The price of gasoline rose from 30 cents per gallon in 1973 to 44 cents per gallon in 1974. (Adjusted for inflation, this is about the same as a rise from $1.00 to $1.35 per gallon today.) **Figure 4.5** shows the effects. At first, people bought only slightly less gasoline. Many people had big cars with poor gas mileage, and they could use less gasoline only by driving less. Some people began using public transportation, walking, car pooling, driving to stores less often, and vacationing closer to home. The quantity of gasoline they demanded fell and people moved along the demand curve D_1 in Figure 4.5 from Point A to Point B. As months and years passed, people bought cars with better gas mileage and they demanded even less

---

[6]Other expectations also affect demand. If you expect your income to rise, your demand for new clothes or a vacation may increase. When you buy a food that you have never tried, you may expect to like it. Of course, expectations turn out sometimes to be right, and sometimes to be wrong.

gasoline. The increase in adjustment time decreased demand and shifted the curve from D_1 to D_2.

6 — NUMBER OF POTENTIAL BUYERS

Market demand curves shift when the number of potential buyers changes. Demographic changes, such as the fractions of the population in various age groups, can cause changes in demand.

EXAMPLES

The demand for children's books increased in the 1980s because a large number of children were born in the late 1970s and early 1980s to baby-boom generation parents, who were born from the end of World War II through the 1950s. Spending on children's books more than doubled in the 1980s. The U.S. Census Bureau projects that between now and 2020, the fraction of the U.S. population over 55 years old will rise from 21 percent to 31 percent, and the fraction over 75 will double (from 1.2 percent to 2.4 percent). This is likely to raise the demands for medical care, retirement properties, old-age homes, and other services that older people tend to buy more than younger people. World political changes have tended to allow increased international trade with Mexico and other Latin American countries, eastern European nations, China, and other countries. This may raise the number of potential buyers for U.S. products and thereby raise demands for those products.

INCOME EFFECTS AND SUBSTITUTION EFFECTS[7]

Price changes affect the quantity demanded in two logically separate ways, called the *income effect* and the *substitution effect* of a price change.

INCOME EFFECT

When a price rises, people cannot afford to buy all the goods they previously bought. They must buy less of something. (They could also save less, but lower savings would mean that they must buy fewer goods in the future.) Essentially, a price increase is like a fall in your income: it reduces the quantity of goods you can afford. The quantities demanded of normal goods fall; the quantities demanded of inferior goods rise.

income effect of a price change — the change in quantity demanded that results from a change in the amount of goods that buyers can afford

> The **income effect of a price change** is the change in quantity demanded that results from the change in the amount of goods that buyers can afford.

SUBSTITUTION EFFECT

When the price of a good rises, its opportunity cost increases. Buyers must sacrifice larger amounts of other goods (that they could have bought) for each unit of the good they buy at the higher price. The substitution effect of a price increase always reduces the quantity demanded.

substitution effect of a price change — the change in quantity demanded that results from a change in the opportunity cost of the good

> The **substitution effect of a price change** is the change in quantity demanded that results from the change in the opportunity cost of the good.

---

[7]The following section represents more difficult material.

SUBSTITUTION EFFECT EXAMPLE Suppose that you spend $2 on coffee every day to help stay awake and study. One day, the price of coffee doubles, so it costs $4 each day to buy as much coffee as before. You write to your parents:

Dear parents:

Help. The price of coffee has doubled. I drink coffee to stay up late and study. Coffee now costs $4 a day instead of $2 a day. Please send money.

If they send you an extra $14 per week for coffee, you can afford to buy exactly as much coffee as before without spending less on books, food, and entertainment. But *will you?* You can afford to buy the same goods as before because the extra money you receive cancels out the income effect of the price rise. Coffee is now twice as expensive compared to other goods you could buy instead. Every time you buy coffee you sacrifice more candy bars or magazines than before because the opportunity cost of coffee has risen. If you are like most people, you will probably not spend all the extra $2 a day on coffee. (You might even spend less on coffee than before.) Instead, you would spend some of the extra money on other goods and buy less coffee. This fall in the quantity demanded is the substitution effect of the price rise.

──────────────── **FOR REVIEW** ────────────────

4.6 What is a normal good? An inferior good?

4.7 What happens to the demand for a good if the price of a substitute for it rises?

4.8 What happens to the demand for a good if the price of a complement for it rises?

──────────────── **QUESTION** ────────────────

4.9 Draw a graph of your demand curve for vacation days on a beach in the Caribbean. What other conditions would affect your demand? How?

INTRODUCTION TO SUPPLY

TABLE 4.3

REBECCA'S PAINTING SERVICES SUPPLIED

Price per Room	Rooms Painted per Week
$ 80	0
100	1
120	2
140	3
160	4

Demand curves describe the behavior of buyers, summarizing the trades that buyers are willing to make. Similarly, supply curves summarize the behavior of sellers by describing the trades that they are willing to make.

Suppose that your college offers you a job painting dormitory rooms next week for $100 per room, with the condition that you provide your own paint and brushes. You may choose how many rooms to paint. What would you choose? How many rooms would you paint if the price were $80 per room, or $120, or $200? Your answer probably depends on conditions such as the cost of paint, your painting skills, how much you dislike painting, and how busy you are (the alternative uses of your time). Your answers form your supply schedule.

Table 4.3 shows Rebecca's supply schedule, that is, her quantity supplied of painting services at various prices. Rebecca is unwilling to paint for $80 per room. She will paint one room for a price of $100 per room, two rooms for $120 each, three rooms for $140 each, or four rooms for $160 each. **Figure 4.6** shows her supply curve of painting services. This curve graphs her supply schedule with the price on the vertical axis and her quantity supplied on the horizontal axis.

FIGURE 4.6

SUPPLY CURVE: REBECCA'S SUPPLY CURVE FOR PAINTING SERVICES

Each point is a row in Table 4.3.

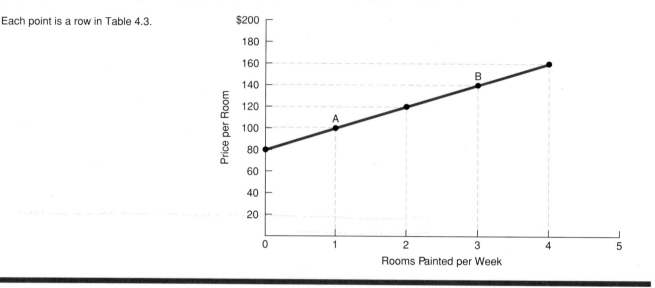

SUPPLY

quantity supplied (at some price) — the amount that a seller would offer to sell during some time period if she could sell as much as she wanted at that price

Stated roughly, a seller's quantity supplied of a good is the amount the seller wants to sell. More precisely:

> A seller's **quantity supplied** of a good at some price is the amount of the good she would sell during some time period if she could sell as much as she desired at that price.

Notice that the quantity supplied describes what *sellers* want to do; it is unrelated to the amount that buyers want to buy.

A table of various prices and the quantities supplied at those prices is a supply schedule:

supply schedule — a table that shows various possible prices and the quantity supplied at each price; the *market* supply schedule includes *all* sellers

> A seller's **supply schedule** for a good is a table showing many hypothetical prices of the good and the seller's quantity supplied at each price.

Table 4.3 shows an example of a supply schedule.

Graphing the supply schedule gives a seller's supply curve, as in Figure 4.6.

supply curve — a graph of a supply schedule

> A seller's **supply curve** for a good is a graph of her supply schedule.

The supply curve shows, for various possible prices, the seller's quantity supplied at each price.

The quantity supplied, like the quantity demanded, depends on several conditions, such as the cost of paint in the example. Changes in any of these conditions cause changes in the quantity supplied. The supply curve shows how a price change affects the quantity supplied, holding constant other conditions. For most goods, an increase in price raises the quantity supplied, so the supply curve has a positive slope as in Figure 4.6.

> When the price of a good rises, holding constant other conditions, the quantity supplied usually rises.

Sometimes economists call this the *law of supply.* Another way to say the same thing is:

> Supply curves usually have positive slopes. (They slope upward.)

Supply curves usually slope upward because a higher price raises the incentive to produce and sell the good.

MARKET SUPPLY

Market supply is the total supply of a good by all sellers in the economy.

market quantity supplied — at a given price, the total amount of a good that all sellers in the economy would sell during a time period if they could sell as much of the good as they wanted

> The **market quantity supplied** of a good at a given price is the total amount of a good that all sellers in the economy would sell during a time period if they could sell as much of the good as they wanted at that price.

Similarly,

market supply schedule — a table showing many hypothetical prices of a good and the quantity supplied at each price

> The **market supply schedule** for a good is a table showing many hypothetical prices of a good and the market quantity supplied at each price.

market supply curve — a curve graphing the market supply schedule

> The **market supply curve** for a good graphs the market supply schedule.

Market supply curves usually slope upward because each seller's supply curve slopes upward and because more potential sellers become actual sellers when the price rises.[8] When economists refer to *the* supply curve for a good, they mean the market supply curve.

EXAMPLE

Figure 4.7 shows Reebok's supply schedule for athletic shoes, Nike's supply schedule for athletic shoes, and the market supply curve if Reebok and Nike are the only potential sellers. The market quantity supplied is the total of the quantities supplied by Reebok and Nike.

CHANGES IN SUPPLY

change in supply — a change in the numbers in the supply schedule and a shift in the supply curve. An increase in supply shifts the supply curve to the right; a decrease shifts it to the left

> A **change in supply** means a change in the numbers in the supply schedule and a shift in the supply curve.

---

[8]For example, everyone with a ticket to a sold-out concert or football game is a potential seller—each could sell a ticket. More of these potential sellers become actual sellers if people offer to buy the tickets at high enough prices. Consequently, the market supply curve for tickets outside the stadium slopes upward, even though each seller has only one ticket to sell.

FIGURE 4.7

INDIVIDUAL SUPPLIES AND MARKET SUPPLY

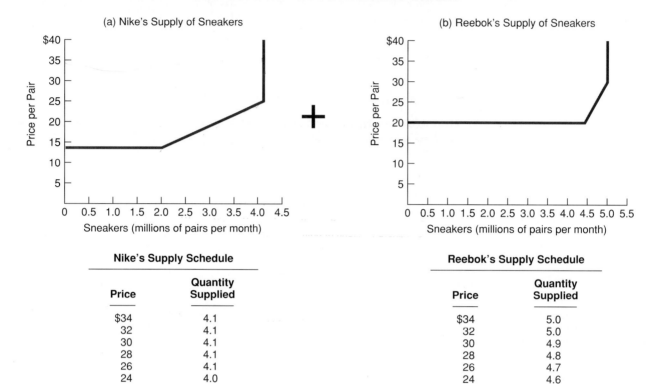

(a) Nike's Supply of Sneakers

(b) Reebok's Supply of Sneakers

Nike's Supply Schedule	
Price	Quantity Supplied
$34	4.1
32	4.1
30	4.1
28	4.1
26	4.1
24	4.0
22	3.6
20	3.2
18	2.8
16	2.4
14	2.0
12	0.0

Reebok's Supply Schedule	
Price	Quantity Supplied
$34	5.0
32	5.0
30	4.9
28	4.8
26	4.7
24	4.6
22	4.5
20	4.4
18	0.0
16	0.0
14	0.0
12	0.0

An increase (or rise) in supply is an increase in the quantity supplied at each possible price; the supply curve shifts to the right as in **Figure 4.8.**

A decrease (or fall) in supply is a decrease in the quantity supplied at each possible price; the supply curve shifts to the left as in **Figure 4.9.**

Figures 4.8 and 4.9 show examples. When supply changes, the distance by which the supply curve shifts left or right at each price shows the change in the quantity supplied at that price.

CHANGES IN QUANTITY SUPPLIED VERSUS CHANGES IN SUPPLY

The distinction between a change in supply and a change in the quantity supplied is the same as the distinction between changes in demand and changes in

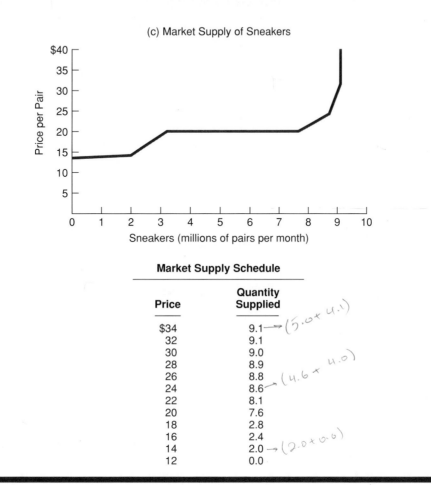

(c) Market Supply of Sneakers

Market Supply Schedule

Price	Quantity Supplied	
$34	9.1	→ (5.0 + 4.1)
32	9.1	
30	9.0	
28	8.9	
26	8.8	→ (4.6 + 4.0)
24	8.6	
22	8.1	
20	7.6	
18	2.8	
16	2.4	
14	2.0	→ (2.0 + 0.0)
12	0.0	

the quantity demanded. A change in the quantity supplied occurs when the price changes and the sellers move from one row to another in the supply schedule. This amounts to movement along a supply curve (as from Point A to Point B in Figure 4.6). A change in supply occurs when the numbers in the supply schedule change, which shifts the supply curve as in Figures 4.8 and 4.9. A change in supply occurs when a change in other conditions affects the supply schedule.

A change in price changes the quantity supplied, but it does not change supply.

A change in conditions other than price can change the supply of a good.

FIGURE 4.8

INCREASE IN SUPPLY

An increase in supply is a rise in the quantity supplied at each price. At each price, the new supply curve, S_2, shows a higher quantity supplied than the old supply curve, S_1.

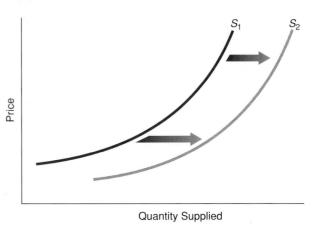

Old Supply Schedule		New Supply Schedule	
Price	Quantity Supplied	Price	Quantity Supplied
$7	70	$7	90
6	66	6	85
5	60	5	78
4	52	4	68
3	40	3	52
2	20	2	30

Five main conditions affect the supply of a good:

EXAMPLE: A FIRM'S SUPPLY OF T-SHIRTS

Prices of inputs	How much must the firm pay workers to make T-shirts? How much does cotton fabric cost? How much do sewing machines cost?
Technology	How many T-shirts per day can a worker produce?
Prices of other goods	How much do other cotton products (such as dresses) sell for?
Adjustment time after a change	How soon can the firm get new machinery delivered and installed?
Number of potential sellers	How many other firms could make and sell T-shirts? The answer affects the market supply of T-shirts.

Changes in these conditions can cause changes in supply, which produce shifts in the supply curve. Later sections will discuss changes in each condition separately, holding constant the other conditions.

CHANGES IN CONDITIONS CAUSING CHANGES IN SUPPLY

Table 4.4 summarizes the changes in conditions that change supply.

PRICES OF INPUTS

Increases in the prices of inputs (such as materials, equipment, labor, energy, and natural resources) can decrease supply as in Figure 4.9, by reducing the incentive to produce and sell the good. Similarly, a fall in input prices raises the incentive to produce and sell the good, increasing supply as in Figure 4.8.

FIGURE 4.9

DECREASE IN SUPPLY

A decrease in supply is a fall in the quantity supplied at each price. At each price, the new supply curve, S_2, shows a lower quantity supplied than the old supply curve, S_1.

Old Supply Schedule		New Supply Schedule	
Price	Quantity Supplied	Price	Quantity Supplied
$7	70	$7	50
6	66	6	46
5	60	5	40
4	52	4	32
3	40	3	22
2	20	2	5

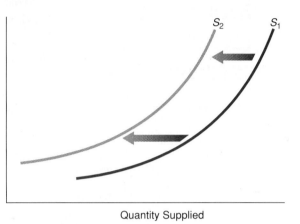

2 - TECHNOLOGY

If an advance in technology lowers the cost of producing a good, it raises the incentive to produce and sell it. In this way, advances in technology can increase supply, as in Figure 4.8.

3 - PRICES OF OTHER GOODS

A price change can change the supplies of *other* goods. For example, if a producer can use a machine to make either shirts or dresses, a rise in the price of dresses raises the opportunity cost of producing shirts. Therefore, a rise in dress prices decreases the supply of shirts. A different type of example involves goods that are jointly produced: an increase in the price of leather can raise the supply of beef because leather and beef are produced jointly from cattle.

TABLE 4.4

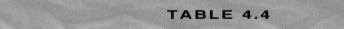

EFFECTS ON SUPPLY OF CHANGES IN CONDITIONS

Changes in Conditions That Increase Supply of a Good	Changes in Conditions That Decrease Supply of a Good
1. Fall in the price of an input	1. Rise in the price of an input
2. Improvement in technology that lowers the cost of production	2. Decrease in available technology (e.g., from a new law against using a certain technology)
3. Fall in the price of a good that sellers could produce *instead;* rise in the price of a jointly produced good	3. Rise in the price of a good that sellers could produce *instead;* or fall in the price of a jointly produced good
4. Increase in adjustment time following a rise in the price	4. Increase in adjustment time following a fall in the price
5. Increase in the number of potential sellers	5. Decrease in the number of potential sellers

INTERTEMPORAL SUBSTITUTION

One substitute for selling a good now is to wait and sell it in the future, when its price may be higher.

> Intertemporal substitution (substitution over time) affects supply when a change in the expected future price of a good causes a change in its current supply.

The supply of a good falls if its expected future price increases. Freezing weather in Florida may kill orange trees and raise the expected future price of orange juice; this decreases the current supply of orange juice as producers hold already-made juice off the market, waiting to sell it in the future at a higher price.

ADJUSTMENT TIME AFTER A PRICE CHANGE

Increases in adjustment time following a change in price cause changes in supply. The more time sellers have had to adjust, the larger the change in supply.

EXAMPLE

Production takes time. It takes time to build factories and offices. It takes 60 years to grow the trees used to make wooden baseball bats. An increase in the adjustment time available to auto producers following an increase in auto prices allows producers to add to their factories and raise their productive capacities, which increases the supply of automobiles.

NUMBER OF POTENTIAL SELLERS

Market supply increases when the number of potential sellers rises. For example, the supply of workers increased when the baby-boom generation graduated from high school and college in the 1960s and 1970s. The supply of mail-delivery services fell in 1845 when the U.S. government made it illegal for anyone except the government-operated post office to deliver first-class mail; this reduced the number of potential sellers. The supply of trucking services increased in 1980 when the U.S. government deregulated the trucking industry, which allowed people to start new trucking companies.

FOR REVIEW

4.10 What is a supply schedule? A market supply schedule?

4.11 What is a supply curve? Why does it usually slope upward?

QUESTION

4.12 Draw graphs to explain the difference between a change in supply and a change in the quantity supplied.

EQUILIBRIUM OF SUPPLY AND DEMAND

Demand curves summarize the behavior of buyers. They also summarize the opportunities available to sellers by showing the trades that buyers are willing to make. Supply curves summarize the behavior of sellers, and the opportunities available to buyers by showing the trades that sellers are willing to make. These

FIGURE 4.10

MARKET EQUILIBRIUM

Market equilibrium is a situation in which the quantity supplied equals the quantity demanded. This occurs where the supply and demand curves intersect. Point A is the equilibrium, P_1 is the equilibrium price, and Q_1 is the equilibrium quantity traded. At price P_1, the quantity supplied and quantity demanded both equal Q_1.

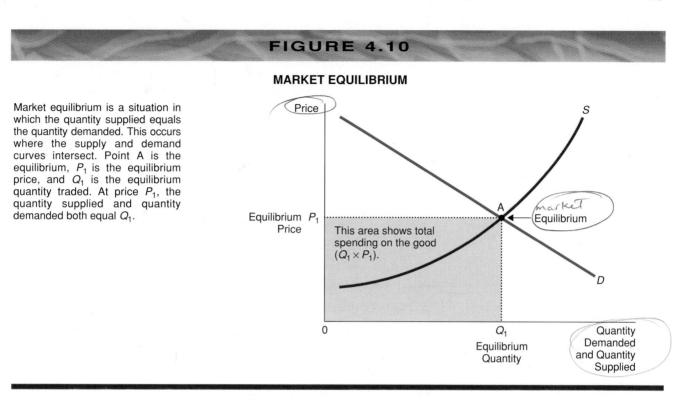

opportunities determine the trades people make—the amounts they buy and sell and the prices they pay or receive.

This section combines supply and demand to examine these issues. We begin with a definition of *equilibrium:*

> An **equilibrium** is a situation that has no tendency to change unless some underlying condition changes. A **market equilibrium** is a situation, described by a combination of price and quantity traded, in which the quantity supplied equals the quantity demanded. That price is the **equilibrium price** and that quantity is the **equilibrium quantity.**

Economists also use the term *market-clearing* for market equilibrium. They say that the equilibrium price "clears the market."

A market equilibrium appears on a graph as the point where the S (supply) and D (demand) curves intersect: Point A in **Figure 4.10.** The equilibrium price is P_1. The equilibrium quantity Q_1 shows the amount of the good bought and sold: the quantity traded. Buyers buy Q_1 units of the good from sellers, and pay P_1 dollars for each unit.[9]

Total spending on the good is the area of the shaded rectangle in Figure 4.10. This shaded area equals the quantity that people buy, Q_1, multiplied by the price per unit, P_1.[10] Of course, the area of this shaded rectangle also shows the total receipts of sellers since they collect the money that buyers spend.

equilibrium — a situation that has no tendency to change unless some underlying condition changes
market equilibrium — a situation, described by a combination of price and quantity traded, in which the quantity supplied equals the quantity demanded
equilibrium price — the price at which quantity supplied equals quantity demanded
equilibrium quantity — the quantity at which quantity supplied equals quantity demanded

---

[9]The X-axis of the graph now shows both the quantity demanded and the quantity supplied, so its label reads simply "quantity."

[10]The area equals the base of the rectangle times its height, or Q_1 times P_1.

WHY THE INTERSECTION OF THE CURVES SHOWS EQUILIBRIUM

The demand curve in Figure 4.10 shows that at a price of P_1, the quantity demanded is Q_1. The supply curve shows that at a price of P_1, the quantity supplied is Q_1. At a price of P_1, the quantity demanded equals the quantity supplied, that is, the amount that buyers want to buy equals the amount that sellers want to sell. Equilibrium occurs at Point A, where the supply and demand curves intersect.

At a price other than P_1, however, the quantity demanded does not equal the quantity supplied and the market is not in equilibrium. This is a disequilibrium situation.

disequilibrium — a situation in which the quantity demanded and the quantity supplied are not equal at the current price

> **Disequilibrium** is the absence of equilibrium; it occurs when the quantity demanded and the quantity supplied are not equal at the current price.

A disequilibrium situation has an inherent tendency for change. The price tends to change to move the economy toward equilibrium. There are two kinds of disequilibrium situations: excess demand and excess supply.

EXCESS DEMAND

Suppose that the price is P_0, below the equilibrium price of P_1 in **Figure 4.11.** The supply curve shows that the quantity supplied at the price P_0 is Q_0^s units of the good. The demand curve shows that the quantity demanded at the price P_0 is Q_0^d units of the good. So the quantity demanded exceeds the quantity supplied; at price P_0, buyers want to buy more than sellers want to sell. There is a shortage of the good.

FIGURE 4.11

EXCESS DEMAND

At a price, P_0, below the equilibrium price, buyers want to buy Q_0^d units of the good, and sellers want to sell only Q_0^s units, so there is a shortage or excess demand equal to $Q_0^d - Q_0^s$.

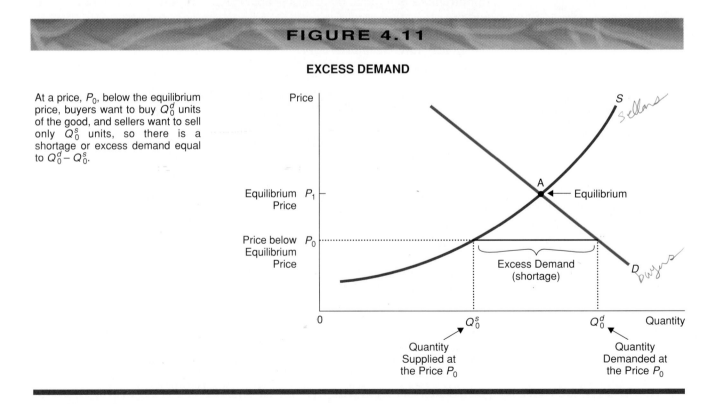

excess demand (shortage) — a situation in which the quantity demanded exceeds the quantity supplied

Excess demand, or a **shortage,** is a situation in which the quantity demanded exceeds the quantity supplied.

A shortage occurs when the price of a good is below its equilibrium price. The size of the shortage, or the amount of excess demand, equals the quantity demanded minus the quantity supplied. At a price of P_0, Figure 4.11 shows a shortage of $Q_0^d - Q_0^s$.

A shortage creates pressure for the price to rise. Some buyers cannot buy the good and stores run out of it. Sellers have an incentive to raise the price because enough buyers are willing to pay the higher price. The price tends to rise until it reaches the equilibrium price P_1 where the quantity demanded equals the quantity supplied.

> If the price is below the equilibrium price, there is a shortage and the price tends to rise toward the equilibrium.

The shortage shrinks when the price rises. When the price reaches the equilibrium level, the shortage vanishes for two reasons. First, the quantity supplied increases when the price rises, helping to eliminate the shortage. Second, the quantity demanded falls when the price rises, also helping to eliminate the shortage.

EXCESS SUPPLY

The second type of disequilibrium involves excess supply. Suppose that the price is P_2, above the equilibrium price of P_1 in **Figure 4.12.** The quantity supplied at the price P_2 is Q_2^s units of the good. The quantity demanded at the price P_2 is Q_2^d

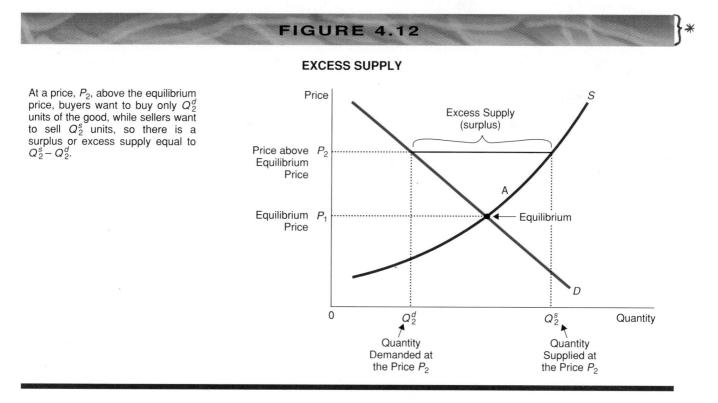

FIGURE 4.12

EXCESS SUPPLY

At a price, P_2, above the equilibrium price, buyers want to buy only Q_2^d units of the good, while sellers want to sell Q_2^s units, so there is a surplus or excess supply equal to $Q_2^s - Q_2^d$.

units of the good. So, the quantity demanded is less than the quantity supplied at the price P_2, that is, buyers want to buy less than sellers want to sell. There is a surplus of the good.

> **Excess supply,** or a **surplus,** is a situation in which the quantity supplied exceeds the quantity demanded.

excess supply (surplus) — a situation in which the quantity supplied exceeds the quantity demanded

A surplus occurs when the price of a good exceeds its equilibrium price. The size of the surplus, or the amount of excess supply, equals the quantity supplied minus the quantity demanded. At a price of P_2 in Figure 4.12, the surplus equals $Q_2^s - Q_2^d$.

A shortage creates pressure for the price to fall. Sellers have extra units that they cannot sell, and they would rather sell the goods at a lower price than not sell them at all. As sellers reduce the price to compete for customers, it tends to fall until it reaches the equilibrium price P_1 where the quantity supplied equals the quantity demanded.

> If the price is above the equilibrium price, there is a surplus and the price tends to fall toward the equilibrium.

A fall in the price of a good reduces a surplus in two ways: it decreases the quantity supplied and increases the quantity demanded. Sellers want to sell less while buyers want to buy more—both help to eliminate the surplus.

Surpluses of automobiles show up as rising inventories at car dealers. The dealers respond by lowering car prices, sometimes by giving rebates, low-interest financing, or free options. Surpluses of certain kinds of clothing occur when people don't buy the kinds of clothes that sellers expected them to buy. These surpluses lead stores to put the clothes on sale at lower prices.

SUMMARY OF EQUILIBRIUM

If the price is below the equilibrium price, there is a shortage and the price tends to rise. If the price is above equilibrium, there is a surplus and the price tends to fall. At the equilibrium price, the quantity supplied equals the quantity demanded; there is no shortage or surplus, and the price tends to remain constant unless supply or demand changes.

> At the equilibrium price, there is neither a shortage or a surplus, so the price shows no tendency to change, unless demand or supply changes.

EFFECTS OF CHANGES IN DEMAND OR SUPPLY

Changes in demand and supply cause changes in the equilibrium, as **Figures 4.13a** through **4.13d** show. In each figure, the original equilibrium price and quantity (before the change in demand or supply) are P_1 and Q_1. The new equilibrium price and quantity (after the change) are P_2 and Q_2. Always remember that demand and supply are distinct: demand describes buyer behavior and supply describes seller behavior. Some changes in conditions cause changes in demand, while other changes in conditions cause changes in supply.

INCREASE IN DEMAND

An increase in demand raises the equilibrium price and the equilibrium quantity, as in Figure 4.13a. At the original equilibrium, Point A, the original demand curve

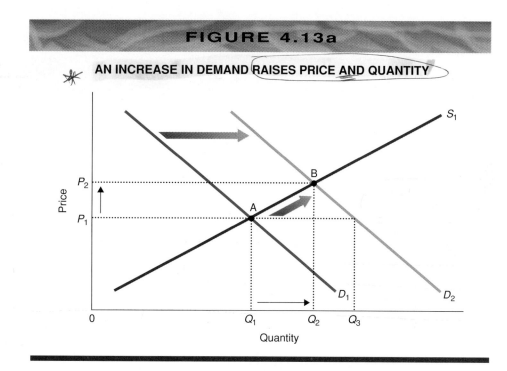

FIGURE 4.13a

AN INCREASE IN DEMAND RAISES PRICE AND QUANTITY

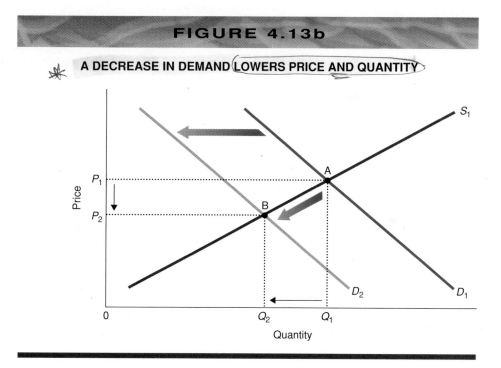

FIGURE 4.13b

A DECREASE IN DEMAND LOWERS PRICE AND QUANTITY

Source: The Far Side ©1987 Farworks, Inc. Distributed by Universal Press Syndicate. Reprinted with permission. All rights reserved.

FIGURE 4.13c

AN INCREASE IN SUPPLY LOWERS THE PRICE AND RAISES THE QUANTITY

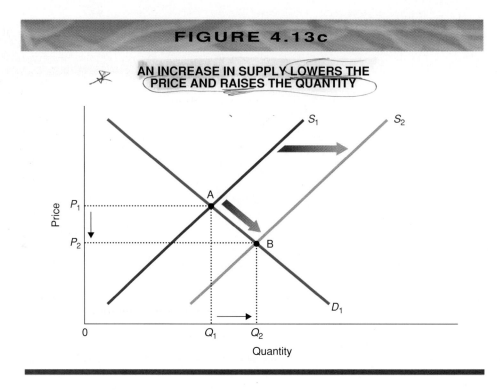

FIGURE 4.13d

A DECREASE IN SUPPLY RAISES THE PRICE AND LOWERS THE QUANTITY

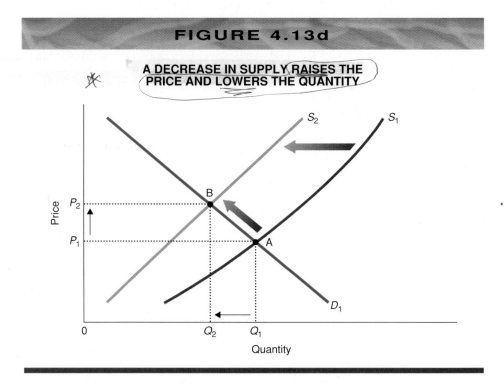

D_1 intersects the supply curve at an original equilibrium price of P_1 and an original equilibrium quantity of Q_1. At the new equilibrium, Point B, the new demand curve D_2 intersects the supply curve at a new equilibrium price of P_2 and a new equilibrium quantity of Q_2. The increase in demand raises both the price and the quantity that people buy and sell.

Notice that an increase in demand implies a shift in the demand curve *without* a shift in the supply curve. The supply curve stays at S_1 while the quantity supplied rises because the price increase from P_1 to P_2 causes movement along the supply curve from Point A to Point B.

The distance by which the demand curve shifts right shows the increase in the quantity demanded at each price. Look at Figure 4.13a: if the price stayed at P_1 (which it *doesn't*), people would want to buy Q_3 units of the good and a shortage would occur. Instead, the price rises to the new equilibrium level, P_2, at which the quantity demanded equals the quantity supplied.

Prices sometimes rise quickly; other times they rise slowly. Stores may learn that demand for a product has increased and raise its price only after a shortage develops or inventories of the good decline. A seller may raise the price only after receiving more orders for a product than expected. Sellers may use trial-and-error methods to find the new equilibrium price, but eventually the price will rise to P_2.

EXAMPLES

Concern over the spread of AIDS has increased the demand for both condoms and rubber gloves for health-care workers, leading to increases in quantities sold. The market demand for child-care centers increased when it became more common for both parents in families with children to work outside the home. This raised the number of child-care centers as well as the prices they charged.

DECREASE IN DEMAND

A decrease in demand lowers the equilibrium price and quantity, as in Figure 4.13b. The equilibrium point then moves from Point A and Point B. The equilibrium price falls from P_1 to P_2 and the equilibrium quantity traded falls from Q_1 to Q_2. The fall in price reduces the quantity supplied, causing movement along the supply curve from Point A to Point B.

EXAMPLE

The demand for fur coats decreased in the 1980s because of increased sensitivity to animal-rights issues. This reduced the prices of fur coats and the quantity bought and sold.

INCREASE IN SUPPLY

An increase in supply lowers the equilibrium price and raises the equilibrium quantity traded, as in Figure 4.13c. The increase in supply shifts the supply curve from S_1 to S_2 and moves the equilibrium from Point A to Point B. The equilibrium price falls from P_1 to P_2 and the equilibrium quantity rises from Q_1 to Q_2. Notice that an increase in supply means a shift in the supply curve *without* a shift in the demand curve, which stays at D_1. The fall in price from P_1 to P_2 raises the *quantity demanded,* that is, it causes movement along the demand curve from Point A to Point B.

EXAMPLE

An increase in the number of community recycling programs in the early 1990s increased the supplies of recyclable glass, plastic, and paper, and reduced their prices.

IN THE NEWS

With mandatory recycling programs in place in many areas of the country, materials brokers said, glass, aluminum, and plastic containers continue to pour into collection centers, regardless of demand. With excess supply chasing inadequate demand, prices took a beating.

The price paid by brokers for aluminum cans fell from almost 30 cents a pound at the beginning of the year to barely more than 20 cents by the end, according to the survey. The value of clear polyethylene terepthalate, which is used in large soda bottles, fell from almost 7.0 cents a pound to 1.2 cents.

An increase in supply lowers the price.

Source: New York Times, January 19, 1992, p. F8.

DECREASE IN SUPPLY

A decrease in supply raises the equilibrium price and lowers the equilibrium quantity traded, as in Figure 4.13d. The equilibrium moves from Point A to Point B as the equilibrium price rises from P_1 to P_2 and the equilibrium quantity falls from Q_1 to Q_2.

SIMULTANEOUS CHANGES IN DEMAND AND SUPPLY

Sometimes demand and supply change at the same time, as in **Figure 4.14.** If demand and supply both increase, as in Panel a, the quantity traded rises but the price might rise or fall, depending on the relative sizes of the increases in supply and demand. If demand increases while supply decreases, as in Panel b, the price rises but the quantity traded could rise or fall, depending on the relative sizes of the shifts in supply and demand.

――――――――――――― FOR REVIEW ―――――――――――――

4.13 What is an equilibrium? What is a market equilibrium?

4.14 Why does excess demand tend to raise the price, while excess supply reduces the price?

4.15 How does an increase in demand affect the equilibrium price and quantity traded? How does an increase in supply affect the equilibrium price and quantity traded?

――――――――――――― QUESTIONS ―――――――――――――

4.16 Use demand and supply curves to predict changes in the price of a rental car in Florida at different times of the year (winter, spring break, summer, Labor

FIGURE 4.14

WHEN DEMAND AND SUPPLY *BOTH* CHANGE

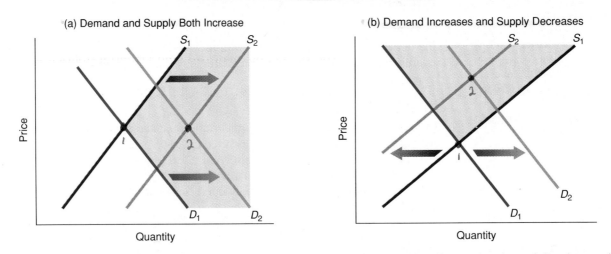

The new equilibrium price and quantity can be anywhere in the shaded areas, depending on the sizes of the changes in supply and demand.

Day, Christmas). Do the same analysis for motel rates at ski resorts in the Rocky Mountains.

4.17 Translate the following newspaper headlines into statements about supply and demand:

    a. Sweets Cost More Due to Sugar Price Rise
    b. Pork Prices Rise as Farmers Cut Output
    c. Profits from Popcorn Attract More Farmers

RELATIVE PRICES AND NOMINAL PRICES

nominal price — the money price of a good

relative price of one good in terms of another — the opportunity cost of the first good measured in units of the second good

Prices in the United States today are about 50 percent higher than prices ten years ago, on average, and about four times higher than prices in 1970. A typical good that cost $1.00 in 1970 cost about $3.75 in 1993. This rise in the average level of prices—inflation—makes it important to distinguish between two kinds of prices: nominal prices and relative prices.

The **nominal price** of a good is its money price.

Everyone is familiar with nominal prices: if a hamburger costs $2.50, that is its nominal price. Inflation is an increase in the average level of nominal prices.

The **relative price of one good in terms of another** good is its opportunity cost measured in units of that other good.

The rule to calculate the relative price between two goods is as follows:

If the nominal price of one good is P_1 and the nominal price of another good is P_2, the relative price of the first good in terms of the second good is P_1/P_2.

The relative price of a sweater in terms of candy bars is the number of candy bars you sacrifice each time you buy a sweater.

EXAMPLE

Suppose that a sweater costs $30.00 and a candy bar costs $0.50. (These are nominal prices.) The relative price of the sweater in terms of candy bars is 60 candy bars per sweater. You sacrifice 60 candy bars (and a monster stomach ache) when you buy the sweater.

The relative price is the ratio of the nominal prices:

$$\frac{\text{Relative price of a sweater}}{\text{in terms of candy bars}} = \frac{\text{Nominal price of a sweater}}{\text{Nominal price of candy bar}}$$

$$= \frac{\$30.00}{\$0.50} = 60 \text{ candy bars per sweater}$$

Similarly, the relative price of a candy bar in terms of sweaters is 1/60 of a sweater per candy bar.

WHICH PRICE IS ON THE GRAPH?

When economists use the term *relative price* without saying "in terms of" some other good, they mean the relative price in terms of all other goods in the economy. When a good's nominal price rises faster than the average of the nominal prices of other goods, its relative price rises. For example, the relative price of wooden furniture has increased in recent years, while the relative prices of computers and home electronics equipment (video and audio components) have fallen. If all nominal prices rise by the same percentage, relative prices do not change.

Which price—the nominal price or the relative price—is on the graph in a supply-and-demand diagram? It is the relative price.

not nominal price

The price on a graph of demand or supply is the good's relative price.

Demand is affected by the relative prices of substitutes and complements; supply is affected by the relative prices of inputs and other goods. Relative prices are inflation-adjusted prices. All analysis of demand and supply in this chapter applies to relative prices.

────────────── **FOR REVIEW** ──────────────

4.18 Which kind of price—a nominal or relative price—is on the vertical axis in a supply-and-demand graph?

────────────── **QUESTIONS** ──────────────

4.19 How is the relative price of tacos in terms of frisbees related to the nominal prices of tacos and frisbees?

4.20 If sneakers cost $30 and a hamburger costs $3, what is the relative price of sneakers in terms of hamburgers? What is the relative price of hamburgers in terms of sneakers?

CONCLUSIONS

DEMAND

A person's quantity demanded of a good at some price is the amount he would buy during some time period if he could buy as much as he wanted at that price. A person's demand schedule for a good is a table showing many hypothetical prices of the good and the person's quantity demanded at each price. A demand curve is a graph of a demand schedule.

The market quantity demanded at some price is the total amount that all buyers in the economy would buy during some time period if they could buy as much as they wanted at that price. The market demand schedule for a good is a table showing many hypothetical prices of the good and the market quantity demanded at each price. The market demand curve graphs the market demand schedule.

Demand curves have negative slopes because the quantity demanded falls when the price rises, holding constant the other conditions that affect the quantity demanded. Changes in these other conditions can cause changes in demand, displayed as shifts in the demand curve. Changes in price cause changes in the quantity demanded, but they do not cause changes in demand.

CHANGES IN CONDITIONS CAUSE CHANGES IN DEMAND

The six main conditions that affect demand are tastes, the usefulness of the good, buyers' income and wealth, the prices of substitutes and complements, the time buyers have had to adjust after past changes, and the number of potential buyers. An increase in income raises market demand for a normal good; an increase in income reduces market demand for an inferior good. Two goods are substitutes when an increase in the price of one increases demand for the other. Two goods are complements when an increase in the price of one decreases demand for the other.

A change in the price of a good affects the quantity demanded in two main ways. The substitution effect of a price change is the change in quantity demanded that results from the change in the opportunity cost of the good. The income effect of a price change is the change in quantity demanded that results from the change in the amount of goods buyers can afford.

SUPPLY

A seller's quantity supplied of a good at some price is the amount she would sell during some time period if she could sell as much as she wanted at that price. A seller's supply schedule for a good is a table showing many hypothetical prices of the good and the person's quantity supplied at each price. A supply curve is a graph of a supply schedule.

The market quantity supplied at some price is the total amount that all sellers in the economy would sell during some time period if they could sell as much as they wanted at that price. The market supply schedule for a good is a table showing many hypothetical prices of the good and the market quantity supplied at each price. The market supply curve graphs the market supply schedule. Supply curves usually have positive slopes because the quantity supplied usually rises when the price rises, holding constant other conditions.

CHANGES IN CONDITIONS CAUSE CHANGES IN SUPPLY

Five main conditions affect supply: prices of inputs, technology, prices of other goods, the time sellers have had to adjust after past changes, and the number of potential sellers. These conditions change supply, represented as shifts in the supply curve. A change in price changes the quantity supplied, but it does not change supply (that is, it does not shift the supply curve).

EQUILIBRIUM OF SUPPLY AND DEMAND

An equilibrium is a situation that has no tendency for change unless some underlying condition changes. Market equilibrium is a price and quantity traded at which the quantity supplied equals the quantity demanded. That price is the equilibrium price and that quantity is the equilibrium quantity. Market equilibrium occurs at the point where the supply and demand curves intersect. That point shows the equilibrium price and the equilibrium quantity.

If the price is *below* its equilibrium level, there is a shortage (excess demand), and the price tends to rise toward its equilibrium level. If the price is *above* its equilibrium level, there is a surplus (excess supply), and the price tends to fall toward the equilibrium. If the price is at its equilibrium level, there is no tendency for the price or the quantity traded to change unless demand or supply changes.

EFFECTS OF CHANGES IN DEMAND OR SUPPLY

Demand describes the behavior of buyers, and supply describes the behavior of sellers. Usually, a change in conditions affects either demand or supply, but not both. An increase in demand (a shift of the demand curve to the right) raises the equilibrium price and quantity. A decrease in demand lowers the equilibrium price and quantity. An increase in supply lowers the equilibrium price and raises the equilibrium quantity. A decrease in supply raises the equilibrium price and lowers the equilibrium quantity.

RELATIVE PRICES AND NOMINAL PRICES

The nominal price of a good is its money price. The relative price of a good in terms of another good is its opportunity cost measured in units of that other good. The relative price of a good is often expressed in terms of all goods produced in the economy. The price on the vertical axis of a supply or demand graph is a relative price.

LOOKING AHEAD

You now understand the model of supply and demand that plays a central role in most economic analysis. Chapter 5 will discuss quantitative measures of supply and demand and begin applying the model. After reading that chapter, you will be prepared to use supply-demand analysis to unravel the mysteries of our economy.

KEY TERMS

quantity demanded	quantity supplied
demand schedule	supply schedule
demand curve	supply curve
market quantity demanded	market quantity supplied
market demand schedule	market supply schedule
market demand curve	market supply curve
change in demand	change in supply
income	equilibrium
normal good	market equilibrium
inferior good	equilibrium price
wealth	equilibrium quantity
substitute	disequilibrium
complement	excess demand (shortage)
intertemporal substitution	excess supply (surplus)
income effect of a price change	nominal price
substitution effect of a price change	relative price of one good in terms of another

QUESTIONS AND PROBLEMS

4.21 Name six conditions that affect demand curves. Give examples of each.

4.22 Name five conditions that affect supply curves. Give examples of each.

4.23 A national newspaper reported: "Increased retail demand for roasted and ground coffee because of lower prices . . . has contributed to a higher price for coffee." What's wrong with this reasoning?

4.24 Suppose that three companies sell lawnmowers. Their supply schedules are:

If the Price Is	Alright Co. Wants to Sell	Better Co. Wants to Sell	Cut-It Co. Wants to Sell
$400	28	45	65
350	24	43	65
300	20	38	60
250	16	32	45
200	12	25	20
150	8	18	0
100	4	11	0
50	0	5	0

   a. Make a table of the market supply schedule.

   b. Draw the supply curve of each company and the market supply curve.

4.25 A change in the price of one good can affect demand and supply of other goods.

   a. How is an increase in the price of bologna likely to affect the price of peanut butter and the amount of peanut butter that people buy?

   b. How is an increase in the price of charcoal grills likely to affect the price of charcoal and the amount of charcoal that people buy?

4.26 Discuss this statement: "They're building too many hotels in this city. They think this town will become a big convention city. If they're wrong, we will have too many hotels and loads of empty rooms. It'll cost more to spend a night in a hotel here because the hotels will charge more to make up for all the empty rooms."

4.27 How would the following changes affect demand curves, supply curves, and equilibrium prices and quantities? (Discuss as many economic implications of these changes as you can imagine.)

   a. People learn that eating less fat is healthy.

   b. Global warming raises the average world temperature by 5 degrees.

   c. Scientists discover a cure for AIDS.

   d. The NCAA allows college athletes to collect salaries.

   e. A college improves its dormitories and makes dorm living more desirable.

   f. California legalizes gambling.

   g. Scientists perfect high-definition television (HDTV) and discover how to build a large-screen HDTV set for $300.

4.28 Suppose that a genetically engineered hormone were to raise the milk output of cows by 40 percent. How would this affect the price of milk, the quantity of milk produced, and the number of dairy farmers?

4.29 Read the following news headlines and excerpts and interpret them in terms of supply and demand:

   a. "Turning Back Time for Profit: Prices Soar as Antique Wristwatches Become Status Symbol"

   b. "Unexpected Strong Traffic Allows Airlines to Lift Fares"

   c. "Short Supply Causes Hotel Prices to Soar"

   d. "Crude Oil, Petroleum Product Prices Rise after Explosion at Large Shell Refinery"

   e. "Falling crude oil prices usually mean lower gasoline prices, but not this summer. What gives? Just this: Though crude oil is cheap and plentiful, gasoline isn't. Summer driving is up, demand for gasoline is unusually high, and prices reflect that.

'It's supply and demand,' says Ethel Hornbeck of the Petroleum Marketers Association. 'Refineries are producing like crazy,' but not enough to satisfy our gasoline appetite."

f. "A Troubling Picture for Fresh Mushrooms: Marketing Seasons Ending in August. "Demand is increasing moderately, but with yields per acre rising, farmers have seen little change in prices."

4.30 If the average price of goods rises **5** percent and the price of tortillas rises **8** percent, what happens to the relative price of tortillas?

INQUIRIES FOR FURTHER THOUGHT

4.31 Which relative prices do you believe will rise in the next 20 years? Which relative prices will fall? Explain why; what will cause the changes in demand or supply? Do your answers suggest that some types of businesses will become more profitable and expand, while others will become less profitable and shrink? How might you use these insights to make money?

4.32 How much would you be willing to pay to become more physically attractive? Translate this into a demand curve for physical attractiveness. What products would rise in price if the demand for physical attractiveness were to increase?

4.33 How could you obtain evidence to support or refute the law of demand?

TAG SOFTWARE APPLICATIONS

TUTORIAL EXERCISES
▶ This module reviews the key terms from Chapter 4.

ANALYTICAL EXERCISES
▶ Calculations of equilibrium price and quantity for given supply and demand equations are included.

GRAPHING EXERCISES
▶ The graphing section covers supply and demand curves.

CHAPTER 4 APPENDIX — ALGEBRA OF EQUILIBRIUM

We can write demand and supply schedules as equations. If the demand curve is a straight line, it can be expressed as:

negative slope

$$Q^d = a - bP \qquad \textit{Example: } Q^d = 10 - 2P$$

where Q^d is the quantity demanded, P is the price of the good, and a and b are positive numbers that depend on buyers' tastes, incomes, the prices of complements and substitutes, and the other conditions that affect demand. For example, a might be 10 and b might be 2.

The equation for the supply curve, if it is a straight line, can be written as:

Positive slope ← $Q^s = c + dP$ *Example:* $Q^s = -5 + 3P$

where Q^s is the quantity supplied, P is the price, and c and d are numbers that depend on technology, input costs, and the other conditions that affect supply. The number d is generally positive, which means that the supply curve slopes upward. The number c can be positive or negative. For example, c might be -5 and d might be 3.

The graphs show the equilibrium price and quantity as the intersection of the supply and demand curves. At the equilibrium price, P_1, we found that the quantity demanded equals the quantity supplied. In algebraic terms, that means:

$$Q^d = Q^s$$

Now substitute the two equations for Q^d and Q^s into this last equation (called the *equilibrium condition,* since it says that quantity supplied equals quantity demanded):

$a - bP = c + dP$ *Example:* $10 - 2P = -5 + 3P$

To solve for the equilibrium price, begin by adding bP to both sides:

$a = c + dP + bP$ *Example:* $10 = -5 + 5P$

Subtracting c from both sides:

$a - c = dP + bP$ *Example:* $15 = 5P$

Collect terms on the right-hand side:

$a - c = (b + d)P$

Divide both sides by the quantity $(b + d)$ and rearrange terms:

$P_1 = (a - c)/(b + d)$ *Example:* $P_1 = 3$

To find Q_1, the equilibrium quantity, substitute the solution for P_1 into either the demand curve equation or the supply curve equation. After simplifying the algebra, either equation gives the same answer for Q_1. For example, substituting the equilibrium price P_1 into the demand curve equation gives:

$Q_1^d = a - bP$ *Example:* $Q_1^d = 10 - (2 \times 3)$

$= a - b(a - c)/(b + d)$ *Example:* $Q_1^d = 4$

This is the formula for the equilibrium quantity.

Notice that changes in the numbers $a, b, c,$ and d affect the equilibrium price and equilibrium quantity. Those numbers change in response to changes in tastes, technology, or other conditions that affect demand and supply.

QUESTIONS AND PROBLEMS

4A.1 Suppose that the demand curve for rental cars is:

$$Q^d = 500 - 2P$$

(handwritten marginal work:)

$Q^d = 500 - 2P$

$Q^s = 100 + 6P$

$500 - 2P = 100 + 6P$

$500 - 2P = 100 + 6P$

$400 = 8P$

$P = \dfrac{400}{8} = 50$

$Q^s = 100 + 6(50) = 400$

or $Q^d = 500 - 2(50) = 400$

and the supply curve is

$$Q^s = 100 + 6P$$

where Q^d is the quantity demanded (in cars per day), Q^s is the quantity supplied, and P is the rental price per day. Find the equilibrium price and quantity. *400*   *50*

4.A.2 Suppose that the demand curve for movie tickets is:

$$Q^d = 250 - 20P$$

and the supply curve is

$$Q^s = 50 + 30P$$

where Q^d is the quantity demanded, Q^s is the quantity supplied, and P is the price. Find the equilibrium price and quantity.

CHAPTER 5

ELASTICITIES OF DEMAND AND SUPPLY

WHAT THIS CHAPTER IS ABOUT

▶ Measuring the effect of a price change on quantity demanded or supplied

▶ The effect of a change in supply on total spending on a good

▶ Measuring the effect of a change in demand or supply on a good's price

▶ Measuring the effect of a change in demand or supply on the quantity sold

▶ Special cases of demand and supply

S uppose that the government strengthens its fight against illegal drugs and the supply of illegal drugs falls. This reduces the quantity of drugs sold, but it raises the price. The government has evidence that total spending on illegal drugs affects the crime rate: higher spending leads to more robberies by people seeking money for drugs. If the government program reduces spending on illegal drugs, it will reduce crime; if it increases spending on drugs, it will increase crime. Does total spending on drugs and crime rise or fall due to the fight against drugs?

The Disney Corporation restricts the number of videotapes of its classic animated films that it sells. Unlike most sellers, who produce as many units of their products as they can sell, Disney strictly limits the number of its videos it produces, even when stores sell all available copies. Why might Disney's profits fall if it sold more videos?

These examples, like many real-life issues, involve *quantitative* analysis of supply and demand. They deal with the size of the change in quantity demanded or supplied when the price changes.

ELASTICITY OF DEMAND

Figure 5.1 shows how the shape of the demand curve determines whether total spending rises or falls when supply decreases. Recall from Chapter 4 that total spending on a good is shown by the area of a rectangle. The base of the rectangle is the number of units people buy, and the height of the rectangle is the price per unit, so the area of the rectangle represents total spending on the good. Roughly, an increase in supply raises total spending on a good if the demand curve is flat,

FIGURE 5.1

TOTAL SPENDING AND THE SHAPE OF THE DEMAND CURVE

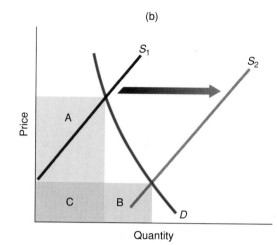

When supply is S_1, total spending on the good is the area of the Rectangles A and C. The height of the total rectangle shows the price that buyers pay for each unit, and the base of the rectangle shows the number of units they buy, so the area of the rectangle A + C shows total spending on the good. In

Panel a, the demand curve is flat and an increase in supply raises total spending on the good from Area A + C to Area B + C. In Panel b, the demand curve is steep and an increase in supply reduces total spending on the good from Area A + C to Area B + C.

as in Figure 5.1a; it reduces total spending if the demand curve is steep, as in Figure 5.1b.

The elasticity of demand measures the shape of a demand curve. *Elasticity* means responsiveness to a change in conditions. *Elasticity of demand* refers to the responsiveness of quantity demanded to a change in price. As we will see, the elasticity of demand is not the same as the slope of the demand curve. Before we formally define *elasticity,* we must define *percentage change.*

PERCENTAGE CHANGES

percentage change — 100 times the change in a number divided by the average (or midpoint) of the original number and the new number

The **percentage change** in a number is:

Percentage change in a number

$$= 100 \times \left(\frac{\text{Change in the number}}{\text{Average of the original number and the new number}} \right)$$

EXAMPLES

Suppose that a price rises from $1.00 to $1.50. The average or midpoint of the range between $1.00 and $1.50 is $1.25, so the price rises by 40 percent ($0.50/$1.25 × 100, or 50/1.25, which equals 40 percent). If a price falls from $1.50 to $1.00, the average or midpoint is again $1.25 and the price change is *minus* $0.50, so the percentage change in price is −40 percent.

A price increase from $5 to $10 is a $66\frac{2}{3}$ percent increase. (The midpoint is $7.50, so the percentage increase is 100 × $5.00/$7.50, or 500/7.5, which equals 66.67 percent.)

A price decrease from $10 to $9 is a 5.26 percent decrease because the midpoint is $9.50 and $100 \times 50/950$ equals 5.26.[1]

COMMENT

When a price rises from $1.00 to $1.50, some people say that the price rises by 50 percent. In fact, the price actually rises by 40 percent. The 50 percent figure is a common approximation, but not a strictly accurate one. To see why, suppose that the price later falls from $1.50 back to $1.00. Some people might say the price fell by $33\frac{1}{3}$ percent. The common approximation to percentage changes leads to the strange result that a price can rise 50 percent, and then fall only $33\frac{1}{3}$ percent to return to its original level. This strange result does not occur when percentage changes are measured correctly using the formula above.

ELASTICITY AND SLOPE

elasticity of demand (or supply) — the percentage change in the quantity demanded (or supplied) divided by the percentage change in price

The **elasticity of demand** is the percentage change in the quantity demanded divided by the percentage change in price:

$$\text{Elasticity of demand} = \frac{\text{Percentage change in quantity demanded}}{\text{Percentage change in price}}$$

Notice that the elasticity of demand is negative. An increase in price causes a decrease in quantity demanded. In other words, demand curves slope downward.

EXAMPLES

If a 5 percent fall in the price of shirts raises the quantity demanded by 10 percent, the elasticity of demand is $10/(-5)$, or -2. If a 20 percent increase in price lowers the quantity demanded by 5 percent, the elasticity of demand is $-\frac{5}{20}$, or $-\frac{1}{4}$.

ELASTICITY VERSUS SLOPE

The elasticity of demand is *not* the slope of the demand curve. Elasticity is measured as a percentage, while slope is not. Also, the elasticity of demand measures the percentage change along the horizontal axis (the quantity demanded) when the variable on the vertical axis (the price) changes by 1 percent. The slope, in contrast, measures the change along the vertical axis when the variable on the horizontal axis changes by 1 unit.

ELASTICITY AND THE SHAPE OF A DEMAND CURVE

The elasticity of demand *differs* at different points along a straight-line demand curve. **Figure 5.2** shows why. The demand curve shows that a price increase from $7 to $9 reduces the quantity demanded from 3 units to 1 unit per month. The price rises by 25 percent because it rises by $2 and the average of the two prices is $8, so the percentage rise is $100 \times 2/8$, or 25 percent). The quantity demanded falls by 100 percent when it falls from 3 units to 1 unit. (The quantity demanded falls by 2 units, and the midpoint of the two quantities is 2.) Therefore, the elasticity of demand around Point A, the midpoint of the change, is $-100/25$, or -4.

---

[1]This formula is actually an approximation. The exact way to calculate percentage changes is with natural logarithms. The percentage change in a number is the change in its natural logarithm. For example, if the price rises from $1.00 to $1.50, a calculator or computer gives the natural logarithm of 1, which is 0. The natural logarithm of 1.50 is 0.40547. Subtracting gives –0.40547 and multiplying by 100 gives the percentage change in price, which is –40.547 percent. The midpoint formula usually provides a close approximation.

FIGURE 5.2

ELASTICITIES ALONG A STRAIGHT-LINE DEMAND CURVE

The elasticity of demand is −4 at Point A, −1 at Point B, and −$\frac{1}{4}$ at Point C.

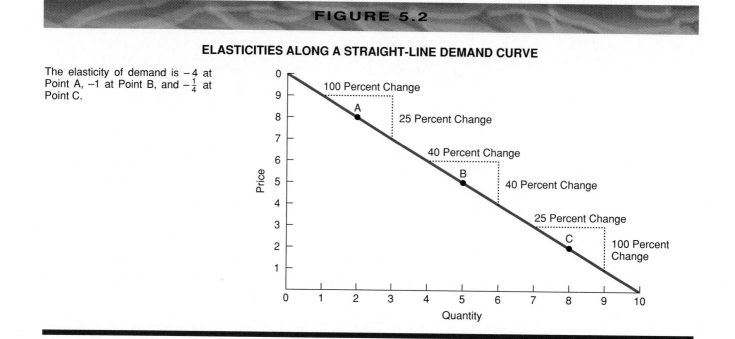

The demand curve in Figure 5.2 also shows that a price increase from $4 to $6 reduces the quantity demanded from 6 units to 4 units. A 40 percent increase in price produces a 40 percent decrease in quantity demanded, so the elasticity of demand around Point B, the midpoint of the change, is −40/40, or −1. Finally, the demand curve in Figure 5.2 shows that a 25 percent price increase from $1 to $3 reduces the quantity demanded by 100 percent, from 3 units to 1 unit, so the elasticity of demand around Point C, the midpoint of the change, is −25/100, or −0.25.

Notice that the absolute value of the elasticity of demand is higher at Point A than at Point B, and higher at Point B than at Point C. Whenever a demand curve is a straight line, the elasticity of demand differs at different points along the demand curve. However, not all demand curves are straight lines; many are curved as in **Figure 5.3.** The elasticity of demand is −3 at every point on the demand curve in Figure 5.3a. It is −$\frac{1}{3}$ at every point on the demand curve in Figure 5.3b. Finally, Figure 5.3c shows a demand curve with an elasticity of −1 at every point. When the elasticity of demand is −1, economists say that demand is *unit-elastic.*

unit-elastic demand (or supply) — elasticity with an absolute value equal to 1

Unit-elastic demand has an elasticity of demand of −1.

Economists say that demand is *elastic* or *inelastic* depending on whether the absolute value of the elasticity of demand is larger or smaller than 1.

elastic demand (or supply) — elasticity with an absolute value greater than 1

Elastic demand has an elasticity of demand with an absolute value larger than 1.

inelastic demand (or supply) — elasticity with an absolute value less than 1

Inelastic demand has an elasticity of demand with an absolute value less than 1.

FIGURE 5.3

ELASTIC VERSUS INELASTIC DEMAND CURVES

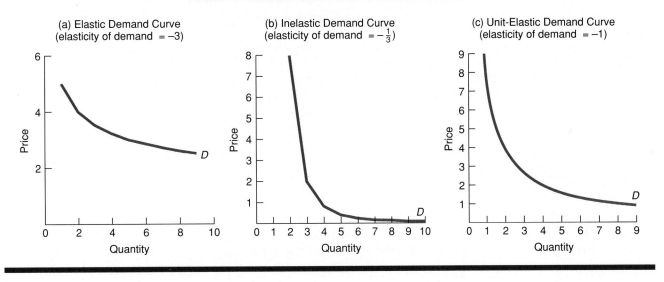

(a) Elastic Demand Curve
(elasticity of demand = −3)

(b) Inelastic Demand Curve
(elasticity of demand = −$\frac{1}{3}$)

(c) Unit-Elastic Demand Curve
(elasticity of demand = −1)

EXPLANATION AND EXAMPLES

Earlier discussion noted that elasticity of demand measures the responsiveness of quantity demanded to a price change. If a 4 percent increase in price causes a 20 percent drop in the quantity demanded, then the quantity demanded is very responsive to a change in price, that is, people buy much less at a higher price than they buy at a lower price. The elasticity of demand is −20/4, or −5. The absolute value of this elasticity (5) exceeds 1, so demand is elastic, as in Figure 5.3a. Statistical studies show that the demands for Chevy trucks, ski-lift tickets, and restaurant meals are elastic.

If a 15 percent increase in price lowers the quantity demanded by only 5 percent, the quantity demanded is not very responsive to a price increase; people buy almost as much at the higher price as they did at the lower price. The elasticity of demand is −$\frac{5}{15}$, or −$\frac{1}{3}$. The absolute value of this elasticity ($\frac{1}{3}$) is less than 1, so demand is inelastic, as in Figure 5.3b. Statistical analyses show that the demands for water, funeral and burial services, and opera tickets are inelastic. (Their quantities demanded do not respond much to changes in price.)

If a 10 percent increase in price lowers the quantity demanded by 10 percent, then the elasticity of demand is −1, so demand is unit-elastic. Statistical evidence shows that clothing, shoes, and electricity all have roughly unit-elastic demand.

As noted earlier, the elasticity of demand differs at different points along any straight-line demand curve. The straight-line demand curve in Figure 5.2 is elastic at Point A (where the absolute value of the elasticity of demand is 4), unit-elastic at Point B (where the absolute value of the elasticity of demand is 1), and inelastic at Point C (where the absolute value of the elasticity of demand is $\frac{1}{4}$).

perfectly inelastic demand (or supply) — elasticity equal to zero, illustrated by a demand (or supply) curve that is a vertical line

perfectly elastic demand (or supply) — infinite elasticity illustrated by a demand (or supply) curve that is a horizontal line

FIGURE 5.4

PERFECTLY INELASTIC DEMAND CURVE

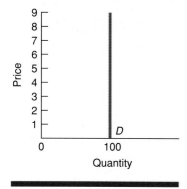

TWO SPECIAL CASES

Figure 5.4 shows a demand curve that is a vertical line. This curve shows a quantity demanded of 100 units per year regardless of the price. The quantity demanded does not respond to a change in the price.

> A vertical demand curve is **perfectly inelastic;** its elasticity is zero.

Perfectly inelastic demand means that people want to buy the same amount of a good even if its price rises or falls.[2]

Figure 5.5 shows a horizontal demand curve. The quantity demanded at the price of $4.99 per unit is *any amount up to 5,000 units per week,* but the quantity demanded at even a slightly higher price, such as $5.00 per unit, is zero. The demand curve is horizontal at the $4.99 price.

> A horizontal demand curve is **perfectly elastic;** its elasticity is infinite.

Perfectly elastic demand means that the quantity demanded is *very* responsive to a change in price; even a small increase in price reduces quantity demanded to zero.

EXPLANATION AND EXAMPLES

Cindy's demand for the textbook required in her course is perfectly inelastic at prices below $75. This means that she plans to buy one copy of the textbook regardless of its price, as long as the price is below $75. (Her demand for the textbook is not perfectly inelastic at prices above $75; she would share a textbook with friends in that case.)

Michael wants to buy one newspaper every day, no matter what its price (as long as it costs him $1.00 or less). His demand for newspapers is perfectly inelastic at prices below $1.00. His elasticity of demand is zero at these prices, because a change in price has no effect on his quantity demanded.

Ron and Susan have a farm. At $4.00 per bushel, they can sell as much wheat as they can grow, but if they try to charge more than $4.00, no one buys from them. (Instead, buyers get wheat from one of the other two million farmers in the United States or from farmers in other countries.) At prices above $4.00 per bushel, the quantity of wheat demanded from Ron and Susan's farm is zero, but they can sell as much wheat for $4.00 per bushel as they can grow on their farm. The demand for their wheat is perfectly elastic.

SPENDING AND ELASTICITY

The elasticity of demand for a good shows how much total spending rises or falls when its price changes.

> If demand is inelastic, buyers spend more on the good when its price is higher.

> If demand is elastic, buyers spend less on the good when its price is higher.

> If demand is unit-elastic, buyers spend the same amount on the good when its price is higher.

---

[2]If the price rises far enough (say, to $5,000 per unit), people must buy less because they cannot afford to buy as much as they would buy at a lower price. Consequently, the demand curve has a negative slope at some higher price; demand can be perfectly inelastic only for a limited range of prices.

FIGURE 5.5

PERFECTLY ELASTIC DEMAND CURVE

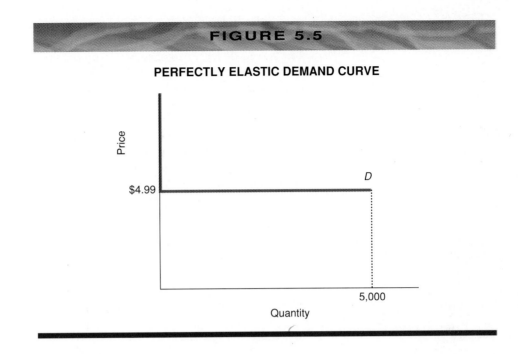

EXPLANATION AND EXAMPLES

With inelastic demand, an increase in price of a given percentage reduces quantity demanded by a smaller percentage, so total spending on the good rises. Suppose that people buy 100 flowers per day at a price of $1.00 per flower. After the price rises to $1.20, an 18.2 percent increase, people buy only 90 flowers per day, or 10.5 percent less. The elasticity of demand is $-10.5/18.2$, or -0.58, so demand is inelastic. The price increase raises total spending from $100 to $1.20 $\times$ 90, or $108 per day.

With elastic demand, a price increase causes a bigger percentage fall in the quantity demanded, so total spending on the good falls. For example, suppose that people buy 100 cans of paint per day at a price of $10.00 per can. After the price rises to $11.00 per can, a 9.5 percent increase, people buy only 80 cans per day, a 22.2 percent decrease. The elasticity of demand is $-22.2/9.5$, or -2.34, so demand is elastic. The price increase reduces total spending from $1,000 to ($11)(80), or $880 per day.

With unit-elastic demand, total spending on the good does not change when its price changes. An increase in price reduces the quantity demanded by just enough to keep spending on the good unchanged. (The lower quantity just offsets the higher price.) The unit-elastic demand curve in Figure 5.3c shows a quantity demanded of 1 unit per month at a price of $8.00 per unit, 2 units at a price of $4.00, 4 units at a price of $2.00, and 8 units at a price of $1.00. So, buyers spend $8.00 on the good regardless of the price. A ski club that has $50.00 to spend on beverages for its next party has a unit-elastic demand; if beverages cost $0.25 per can, the club will buy 200 cans; if the price is $0.50 per can, the club will buy 100 cans. Regardless of price, the club spends $50.00, so its demand is unit-elastic.

Total spending on a good differs at different points along a straight-line demand curve. Because the straight-line demand curve in Figure 5.2 is elastic at

Point A, a price increase from $7.00 to $9.00 reduces total spending from $21.00 to $9.00. Because the demand curve is unit-elastic at Point B, a price increase from $4.00 to $6.00 leaves total spending on the good unchanged at $24.00. Finally, the demand curve is inelastic at Point C, so a price increase from $1.00 to $3.00 raises total spending from $9.00 to $21.00.

APPLICATION TO DISNEY VIDEOS

The introduction to this chapter noted that the Disney Corporation restricts output of the videotapes of its classic animated films. Disney believes that additional sales of its videos would cause their prices to fall far enough that its profits would fall. Profits would fall if demand were inelastic because an increase in supply would reduce total spending. If Disney were to sell more videos, it would then lose profits in two ways: total spending on the videos would fall and Disney's costs would rise (as it produced more videos). If demand is inelastic, Disney gains by selling fewer videos at higher prices, rather than more at lower prices.

ELASTICITY OF SUPPLY

Recall that elasticity means responsiveness to a change in conditions. The elasticity of supply measures the shape of a supply curve; it refers to the responsiveness of quantity supplied to a change in price.

The elasticity of supply is the percentage change in the quantity supplied divided by the percentage change in price:

$$\text{Elasticity of supply} = \frac{\text{Percentage change in quantity supplied}}{\text{Percentage change in price}}$$

The elasticity of supply is usually positive because an increase in price usually raises the quantity supplied of a good. (Supply curves usually slope upward.) The definitions of other terms resemble those for elasticity of demand:

Supply is unit-elastic if the elasticity of supply is 1.

Supply is elastic if the elasticity of supply exceeds 1.

Supply is inelastic if the elasticity of supply is less than 1.

A horizontal supply curve is perfectly elastic: its elasticity is infinite.

A vertical supply curve is perfectly inelastic: its elasticity is zero.

Figure 5.6 shows a variety of supply curves with different elasticities. Panel a shows a perfectly inelastic supply curve. The quantity supplied is 6,000 units per day regardless of the price; sellers offer a fixed amount of the good for sale. In that sense, the quantity supplied is not responsive to price changes. Panel d shows a perfectly elastic supply curve. The quantity supplied at the price $0.10 per unit is *any amount up to 50,000 units per week.* But the quantity supplied at even a slightly lower price, such as $0.0999 per unit, is zero. The supply curve is horizontal at the price $0.10. With perfectly elastic supply, the quantity supplied is *extremely* responsive to a change in the price: even a small decrease in price reduces the quantity supplied to zero. Panels b and c show intermediate elasticities of supply.

FIGURE 5.6

INELASTIC, PERFECTLY INELASTIC, ELASTIC, AND PERFECTLY ELASTIC SUPPLY CURVES

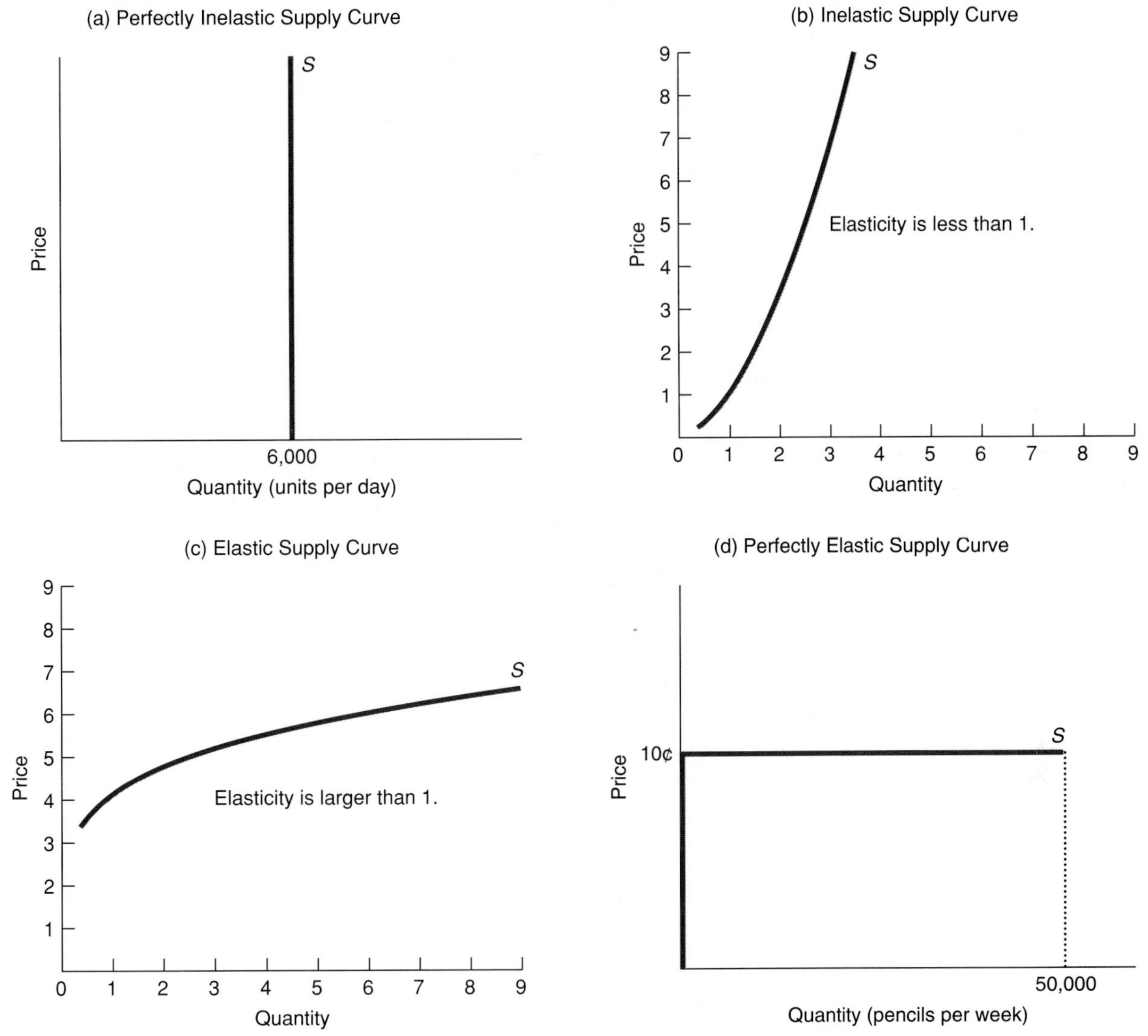
(a) Perfectly Inelastic Supply Curve
Price
S
6,000
Quantity (units per day)
(b) Inelastic Supply Curve
Price
S
Elasticity is less than 1.
0 1 2 3 4 5 6 7 8 9
Quantity
(c) Elastic Supply Curve
Price
S
Elasticity is larger than 1.
0 1 2 3 4 5 6 7 8 9
Quantity
(d) Perfectly Elastic Supply Curve
Price
10¢
S
50,000
Quantity (pencils per week)

FOR REVIEW

5.1 Define the term *elasticity of demand.*

5.2 What is an elastic demand curve? An inelastic demand curve? What is a perfectly elastic demand curve? A perfectly inelastic demand curve?

5.3 How does the elasticity of demand differ from the slope of the demand curve?

5.4 How is elasticity of demand related to total spending on a good?

QUESTIONS

5.5 If a price rises from $6.00 to $10.00, how large is the price increase in percentage terms?

5.6 If a 20 percent rise in the price of Frisbees reduces the quantity of Frisbees demanded by 10 percent, what is the elasticity of demand for Frisbees?

5.7 If a 10 percent fall in the price of pizzas reduces the quantity supplied by 30 percent, what is the elasticity of supply of pizzas?

CHANGES IN DEMAND OR SUPPLY

Elasticities of demand and supply play important roles in determining how changes in demand or supply affect equilibrium. First, recall that an increase in demand (or supply) means a rightward shift in the demand (or supply) curve. With perfectly elastic demand, this implies the following rule:

> With perfectly elastic demand, an increase (or decrease) in demand means that the demand curve shifts upward (or downward).

Figure 5.7a shows an increase in demand; the demand curve shifts upward. To understand why, draw a demand curve that is almost (but not quite) perfectly elastic. An increase in demand, which shifts any demand curve to the right, looks like an upward shift of the demand curve. In the extreme case of perfectly elastic demand, it *is* an upward shift. An increase in demand means that buyers are willing to pay higher prices; this means the demand curve shifts upward.

FIGURE 5.7

SHIFTS IN A PERFECTLY ELASTIC DEMAND CURVE

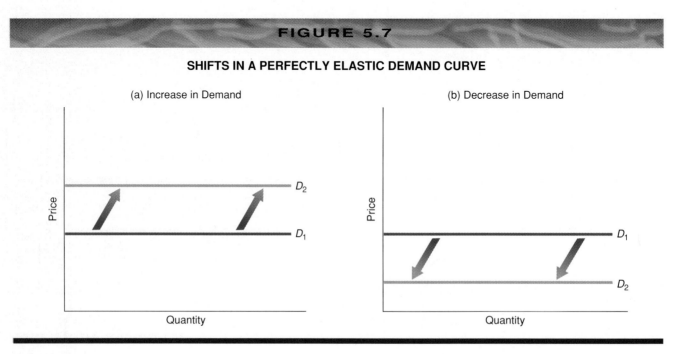

FIGURE 5.8

SHIFTS IN A PERFECTLY ELASTIC SUPPLY CURVE

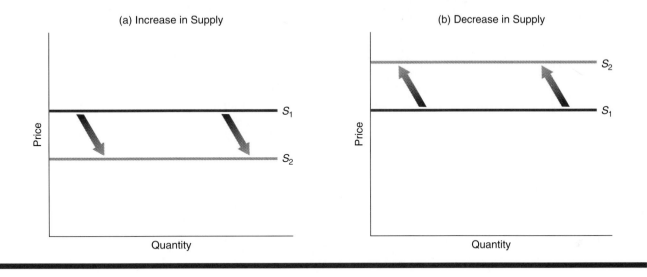

(a) Increase in Supply

(b) Decrease in Supply

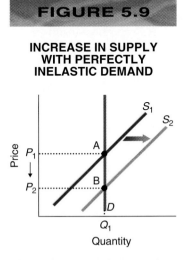

FIGURE 5.9

INCREASE IN SUPPLY WITH PERFECTLY INELASTIC DEMAND

With perfectly inelastic demand, an increase in supply lowers the price from P_1 to P_2, but the quantity remains unchanged at Q_1.

Similarly, a decrease in demand means the demand curve shifts downward, as in Figure 5.7b.

Figure 5.8 shows that an increase in supply shifts the supply curve downward. To understand why, draw a supply curve that is almost (but not quite) perfectly elastic; when it shifts to the right, it also appears to shift downward. In the extreme case of perfectly elastic supply, the curve *does* shift downward because an increase in supply means that sellers are willing to accept lower prices. Similarly, a decrease in supply means the supply curve shifts upward, as in Figure 5.8b.

> With perfectly elastic supply, an increase (or decrease) in supply means that the supply curve shifts downward (or upward).

Notice the difference between the shifts in Figures 5.7 and 5.8.

ELASTICITY AND CHANGES IN EQUILIBRIUM

Figures 5.9 and **5.10** show the effects of changes in demand or supply curves on the equilibrium when one of the curves is perfectly inelastic. In each case, the old equilibrium occurs at Point A and the new equilibrium occurs at Point B. Figure 5.9 shows that with perfectly inelastic demand, an increase in supply reduces the equilibrium price without changing the equilibrium quantity bought and sold. The quantity remains the same because buyers are totally unresponsive to a price change; they buy the same amount of the good regardless of its price. Similarly, with perfectly inelastic supply, as in Figure 5.10, an increase in demand raises the equilibrium price without affecting the equilibrium quantity, again because the quantity supplied is completely unresponsive to a price change. When one of the curves is perfectly inelastic, changes in the other curve do not affect the quantity traded.

FIGURE 5.10

**INCREASE IN DEMAND
WITH PERFECTLY
INELASTIC SUPPLY**

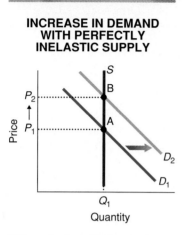

With perfectly inelastic supply, an increase in demand raises the price from P_1 to P_2, but the quantity remains unchanged at Q_1.

Figure 5.11 shows that with perfectly elastic demand, an increase in supply raises the equilibrium quantity without affecting the equilibrium price. Similarly, **Figure 5.12** shows that with perfectly elastic supply, an increase in demand raises the equilibrium quantity, but not the equilibrium price. When one of the curves is perfectly elastic, changes in the other curve do not affect the equilibrium price.

THE DRUGS-AND-CRIME EXAMPLE REVISITED

Let's return to the example of the fight against illegal drugs. Suppose that crime rises and falls with total spending on drugs. A government anti-drug program that reduces the supply of drugs increases crime (and spending on drugs) if the demand for drugs is inelastic; the program decreases crime if the demand for drugs is elastic. It leaves crime unchanged if demand is unit-elastic. Statistical studies of the demand for drugs show that the elasticity of demand differs between cities. One study found inelastic demand for heroin in Detroit, so a fall in supply would raise total spending on heroin there. Another study found elastic demand for heroin in New York City, so a fall in the supply there would reduce total spending on heroin, and perhaps crime, as well. (An effective government program to reduce the *demand* for drugs would reduce spending on drugs regardless of elasticities.)

TWO FACTORS THAT AFFECT ELASTICITIES

Two main factors affect elasticities of demand: the availability of substitutes and the fractions of their incomes that buyers spend on the good. The availability of substitute products also affects the elasticity of supply.

AVAILABILITY OF SUBSTITUTES

Demand for a good is more elastic (the absolute value of the elasticity of demand is larger) when close substitutes for it are available to buyers. Demand is less elastic when buyers cannot find close substitutes for a good. There are few substitutes for food, so the demand for food is inelastic. Food buyers can choose substitutes for beef (such as other meats and other types of food), so the demand for beef is more elastic than the demand for food. The demand for a specific brand of peanut butter is still more elastic, because consumers can easily find even better substitutes (other brands of peanut butter as well as other types of food).

The supply of a good is also more elastic (the elasticity is larger) when sellers could produce close substitutes for it. The supply of ground beef is more elastic than the supply of beef because butchers can sell cuts of beef either ground or whole; they can substitute one use of the beef for another.

FRACTION OF INCOME SPENT ON THE GOOD

As people spend higher fractions of their incomes on a good, their demand for the good becomes more elastic. As they spend smaller fractions of their income on the good, their demand for it becomes less elastic. The reason is somewhat subtle. Chapter 4 explained that a price increase reduces quantity demanded of a good for two reasons. The income effect of a price increase reduces the quantity demanded because buyers cannot afford as many goods. The substitution effect of a price increase has a similar effect because the price increase raises the good's opportunity cost, so buyers tend to buy less of it and substitute other, cheaper

FIGURE 5.11

**INCREASE IN SUPPLY
WITH PERFECTLY
ELASTIC DEMAND**

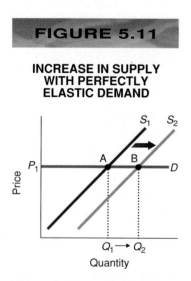

With perfectly elastic demand, an increase in supply raises the quantity from Q_1 to Q_2, but the price remains unchanged at P_1.

goods instead. As people spend more of their incomes on a good, the income effect of a change in its price becomes larger, so the quantity demanded falls more when the price rises. This helps to make demand elastic. On the other hand, the income effect is smaller for goods on which people spend less. If the price of shoelaces were to double, this would barely affect your budget. The tiny income effect tends to make the demand for shoelaces inelastic.

OTHER ELASTICITIES

cross-price elasticity of demand (or supply) — the percentage change in the quantity demanded (or supplied) of one good when the price of another good rises by 1 percent

Recall that elasticity measures responsiveness to changes in conditions. The elasticity of demand measures the responsiveness of the quantity demanded of a good to changes in its price. Economists also measure the responsiveness of the quantity demanded of a good to changes in *other* prices. This results in cross-price elasticities of demand.

> A **cross-price elasticity of demand (or supply)** is the percentage change in the quantity demanded (or supplied) of one good when the price of another good rises by 1 percent.

For example, a 10 percent increase in the price of potatoes may lead people to buy more rice instead. If the potato price increase raises the quantity of rice demanded by 5 percent, then the cross-price elasticity of the demand for rice with respect to the price of potatoes is 5/10, or $\frac{1}{2}$. Notice that cross-price elasticities of demand may be positive or negative; they are positive when goods are substitutes and negative when goods are complements.

Another elasticity measures the effect on demand of a change in income.

income elasticity of demand — the percentage increase in the quantity demanded of a good divided by the percentage change in buyers' incomes

> The **income elasticity of demand** is the percentage increase in quantity demanded divided by the percentage change in income.

An increase in the incomes of buyers raises the demand for a normal good; the income elasticity of demand measures the size of that increase in demand. Income elasticities of demand for normal goods are positive. Income elasticities for inferior goods are negative. Evidence shows that the income elasticity of demand for restaurant meals is about 2.0, while the income elasticity of demand for newspapers is about 0.4.

FIGURE 5.12

INCREASE IN DEMAND WITH PERFECTLY ELASTIC SUPPLY

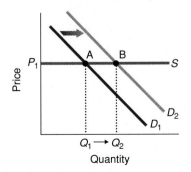

With perfectly elastic supply, an increase in demand raises the quantity from Q_1 to Q_2, but the price remains unchanged at P_1.

FOR REVIEW

5.8 Draw a perfectly elastic demand curve. Show a decrease in demand on your graph. Draw a perfectly elastic supply curve. Show a decrease in supply on your graph.

5.9 How does the availability of substitutes for a good affect its elasticity of demand? How does the fraction of their incomes that people spend on a good affect its elasticity of demand?

QUESTIONS

5.10 Suppose that the supply of bricks is perfectly elastic. What happens to the price of bricks and the quantity sold if the demand for bricks increases?

5.11 Suppose the demand for combs is perfectly inelastic. What happens to the price and quantity sold if the supply of combs increases?

5.12 If a 10 percent increase in income raises the demand for airline tickets by 30 percent, what is the income elasticity of the demand for airline tickets?

SHORT-RUN AND LONG-RUN DEMAND AND SUPPLY

long run — the time people need to fully adjust to a change

long-run demand (or supply) curve — a curve that shows prices and quantities demanded (or supplied) at each price after buyers (or sellers) have adjusted completely to a price change

Chapter 4 explained why the quantity demanded depends in part on the amount of time people have to adjust to a change in price. When the price of gasoline rises, the quantity demanded falls further after people have had time to replace cars with low fuel efficiency with higher-mileage cars. Economists call this a *long-run response* of demand.

Long run means "after people have fully adjusted to a change."

Notice that *long run* does not refer to a specific period of time, like two years or ten years; the length of time people need to adjust to a change varies from case to case. The term *long run* refers to the situation after all adjustments occur, regardless of calendar time.

Up to now we have discussed short-run demand curves, which shift after buyers have time to adjust to price changes. **Figure 5.13** shows the effects of a decrease in the supply of gasoline from S_1 to S_2.[3] In the short run, the equilibrium moved from Point A to Point B. The price of gasoline increased from $0.30 per gallon in 1973 to $0.44 per gallon in 1974 (roughly, from $1.00 to $1.35 per gallon in today's dollars) and the quantity demanded fell 7 percent, from Q_0 to Q_1. This was the short-run response to the fall in supply. During the next several years, people adjusted to the price increase by replacing their old cars with higher-mileage vehicles. This increase in adjustment time decreased demand further, as the short-run demand curve shifted from D_1 to D_2 and the equilibrium moved from Point B to Point C. The price fell from $0.44 cents to $0.39 cents per gallon and the quantity sold fell to Q_2, 21 percent below Q_1.

Drawing a curve through Points A and C in Figure 5.13 gives the long-run demand curve, D^{LR}.

The **long-run demand curve** shows prices and the quantity demanded at each price after buyers have adjusted completely to a price change.

Note that an increase in adjustment time does not shift the long-run demand curve. Instead, the equilibrium moves from one point to another *along* the long-run demand curve (such as the move from Point A to Point C in Figure 5.13). Because long-run demand curves do not shift with changes in adjustment time, they are convenient to use to examine the long-run effects of a change in supply.

SHORT-RUN AND LONG-RUN ELASTICITIES OF DEMAND

We can calculate long-run elasticities of demand just as we calculate short-run elasticities. Figure 5.13 shows that the price of gasoline rose 38 percent from 1973 to 1974 and the quantity demanded fell 7 percent (from Q_0 to Q_1). Accordingly, the short-run elasticity of gasoline demand was $-7/38 \times 100$, or about -0.2. Figure 5.13 also shows that the price of gasoline increased 26 percent (from $0.30 to $0.39 per gallon) in the long run and that quantity demanded fell 21 percent (from

---

[3]To keep matters simple, consider S_1 and S_2 to be both short-run and long-run supply curves.

FIGURE 5.13

LONG-RUN DEMAND CURVE

With the initial equilibrium at Point A, a decrease in supply from S_1 to S_2 moved the short-run equilibrium to Point B. The price rose 38 percent from $0.30 to $0.44, and quantity sold fell 7 percent, from Q_0 to Q_1. As time passed, people adjusted to the higher price and the short-run demand curve shifted from D_1 to D_2, moving the equilibrium from B to C. The price and the quantity sold both fell. Point C shows the *long-run equilibrium*. The *long-run demand curve*, D^{LR}, through Points A and C, shows what happens in the long run, after buyers adjust fully to a new price. The long-run effect of the decrease in supply was to raise the price 26 percent, from $0.30 to $0.39, and to reduce the quantity sold 21 percent. Notice that the price rose more in the short run than in the long run.

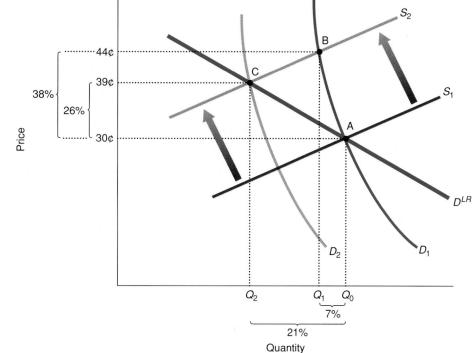

Q_0 to Q_2). So the long-run elasticity of gasoline demand was $-21/26 \times 100$, or about -0.8. Long-run demand is almost always more elastic than short-run demand (as in this example) because long-run demand shows the change in quantity demanded after people have fully adjusted to a price change.

Table 5.1 shows some short-run and long-run elasticities of demand. All of the elasticities in Table 5.1 are estimates from statistical analyses of people's past behavior. While evidence suggests that many elasticities stay nearly constant over time, behavior can change (in fact, all of the conditions that affect demand curves can change), so these elasticities can also change.

LONG-RUN SUPPLY

An increase in adjustment time affects the quantity supplied as well as the quantity demanded. Chapter 4 explained how an increase in adjustment time can cause a change in short-run supply. Many goods take time to produce, so a price increase has a stronger effect on the quantity supplied after producers have had time to expand factories, hire workers, and so on. The supply curves discussed so far are short-run supply curves, which can shift when adjustment time increases. Long-run supply curves, in contrast, show what happens after those shifts are completed.

TABLE 5.1

SOME SHORT-RUN AND LONG-RUN ELASTICITIES OF DEMAND

Good	Elasticity of Demand	
	Short Run	Long Run
Food	About 0.0	−0.7
Theater and opera	−0.2	−0.3
Gasoline	−0.2	−1.0
Toilet articles	−0.2	−3.0
Child care outside the home	−0.3	Not available
Jewelry and watches	−0.4	−0.7
Tobacco products	−0.5	−1.9
Radio and television repair	−0.5	−3.8
Flowers and potted plants	−0.8	−2.6
Movies	−0.9	−3.7
China, glassware, and utensils	−1.5	−2.5

The **long-run supply curve** shows prices and the quantity supplied at each price after sellers have adjusted completely to that price.

Long-run supply curves do not shift when sellers adjust to a price change, and long-run supply is more elastic than short-run supply. For example, the short-run supply of apartments in a city may be almost perfectly inelastic, as in **Figure 5.14,** but the long-run supply of apartments (after landlords have time to construct new apartment buildings) may be very elastic, as in **Figure 5.15.**

USING ELASTICITIES

BASIC CALCULATIONS

The definition of elasticity is stated in equation form as:

$$\text{Elasticity of demand} = \frac{\text{Percentage change in quantity demanded}}{\text{Percentage change in price}}$$

Multiplying both sides of this equation by the percentage change in price gives:

$$\text{Percentage change in quantity demanded} =$$
$$\text{Percentage change in price} \times \text{Elasticity of demand}$$

This equation shows how to calculate the change in quantity demanded if we know the change in price and the elasticity of demand. For example, suppose that you operate a catering business and you estimate the elasticity of demand for your services at −2. If you raise your price 20 percent (reducing your supply of catering services), your sales fall by 40 percent.

Dividing both sides of the last equation by the elasticity of demand gives:

$$\text{Percentage change in price} = \frac{\text{Percentage change in quantity demanded}}{\text{Elasticity of demand}}$$

In equilibrium, the quantity demanded equals the quantity supplied. Therefore, moving from one equilibrium point to another, the change in the quantity

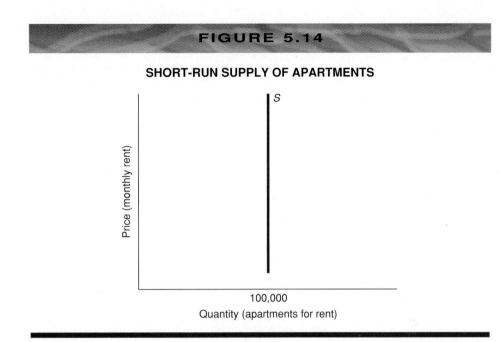

FIGURE 5.14

SHORT-RUN SUPPLY OF APARTMENTS

demanded equals the change in the quantity supplied, and both equal the change in the quantity traded. Substituting "change in quantity" for "change in quantity demanded" in the last equation, we get:

$$\text{Percentage change in price} = \frac{\text{Percentage change in quantity}}{\text{Elasticity of demand}}$$

This equation shows the relation between the change in the equilibrium quantity and the change in price when supply changes: the percentage change in the

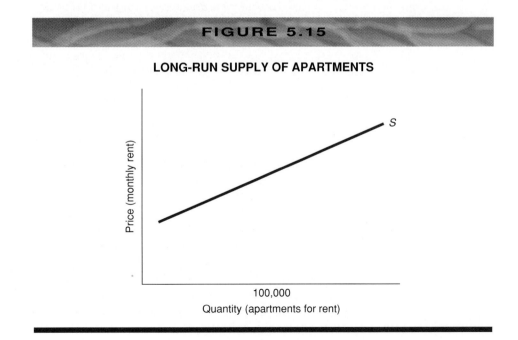

FIGURE 5.15

LONG-RUN SUPPLY OF APARTMENTS

FIGURE 5.16

EFFECT OF A U.S. DROUGHT ON THE WORLD WHEAT MARKET

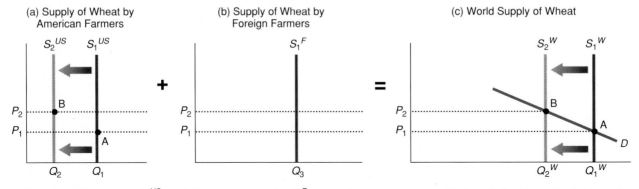

Adding the U.S. supply, S_1^{US}, and the foreign supply, S_1^F, gives the world market supply, S_1^W. A drought in the United States lowers the U.S. supply to S_2^{US}, and this lowers the world market supply to S_2^W. The old world equilibrium was at Point A, and the new world equilibrium is at Point B, so the price of wheat rises from P_1 to P_2.

American farmers sold Q_1 bushels at the price P_1 before the drought. After the drought, they sell Q_2 bushels at the price P_2. Foreign farmers, who sell their Q_3 units at P_2 instead of P_1, gain from the American drought. American farmers may gain or lose, depending on the elasticity of demand.

equilibrium price equals the percentage change in the equilibrium quantity divided by the elasticity of demand. For example, if the elasticity of demand for sneakers is $-\frac{1}{3}$ and an increase in supply raises the quantity sold by 5 percent, the price of sneakers must fall 15 percent. Similarly, the percentage change in the equilibrium quantity equals the percentage change in the equilibrium price multiplied by the elasticity of demand. Notice that when supply changes, the elasticity of demand measures movements along the demand curve.

Related formulas apply when demand changes. The percentage change in quantity supplied equals the elasticity of supply times the percentage change in price. So, the percentage change in price equals the percentage change in quantity divided by the elasticity of supply. For example, if the elasticity of supply of volleyballs is 4, then an increase in demand that raises volleyball purchases by 40 percent must raise the price of volleyballs by 10 percent (40/4). Similarly, when supply changes, the percentage change in the equilibrium quantity equals the percentage change in the equilibrium price multiplied by the elasticity of supply. Notice that when demand changes, the elasticity of supply measures movements along the supply curve.

APPLICATION: EFFECTS OF A DROUGHT

Suppose that a drought in the United States reduces the supply of wheat from American farms, leaving foreign farms unaffected. Because wheat trades on world markets, its equilibrium price is determined by total world supply and demand as in **Figure 5.16.** That figure shows three graphs that represent the supply of wheat from U.S. farmers, the supply from foreign farmers, and the world (market) supply of wheat.[4] The figure assumes that the supply of wheat from farms in each country is perfectly inelastic. The graph on the right also shows the world (market)

---

[4]Adding the American and foreign supplies gives the world market supply; see Chapter 4.

Dry days: Heat drought hurt many farmers, firms; but others are helped

Some crops wither, but gain in prices raises profits

Farm Prices Up

The increase in prices at the farm level, coupled with the varying severity of the drought itself, is likely to result in big gains and big losses to individual farmers. Farmers in states such as Illinois and Iowa, where the heat hasn't been so deadly, and farmers with irrigation will gain handsomely.

Says Robert Kadrmas, a Dickinson, N. Dak., farmer who will lose thousands of dollars this year when he plows under 90 percent of his wheat crop: "I guess some farmers are really benefiting at the expense of others. There are attractive prices out there, but I don't have anything to sell."

A drought creates both winners and losers.

Source: "Dry Days: Heat, Drought Hurt Many Farmers, Firms; But Others Are Helped," *The Wall Street Journal,* July 29, 1980, p. 1.

demand for wheat. The world equilibrium begins at Point A and the equilibrium world price of wheat begins at P_1. Total world production of wheat is Q_1^W, which equals American production, Q_1, plus foreign production, Q_3.

When a drought reduces supply by American farmers from S_1^{US} to S_2^{US}, the world market supply falls from S_1^W to S_2^W. The new equilibrium is at Point B; the price of wheat rises from P_1 to P_2 and world output falls from Q_1^W to Q_2^W. Foreign output remains the same, so foreign farmers can sell as much wheat as before at a higher price. The drought helps foreign farmers regardless of the elasticity of demand. American farmers also sell wheat at a higher price, but they have less to sell.

Do American farmers gain or lose from the drought? The answer depends on the elasticity of the world demand for wheat. If world demand is unit-elastic, buyers spend the same amount on wheat after its price rises. Because they spend more on wheat from foreign farms (since they buy the same amount, Q_3, but pay a higher price), they must spend less on wheat from American farms. Therefore, with unit-elastic world demand, the drought reduces farm income in the United States. Suppose, for example, that the drought reduces wheat supply by American farms from 100 bushels to 50 bushels per year—a 67 percent drop—and that foreign farms continue to sell 100 bushels per year. The drought reduces total world supply from 200 bushels to 150 bushels, a fall of 29 percent. Suppose that the equilibrium price of wheat was $3.00 per bushel before the drought. If the demand for wheat is unit-elastic, then the drought raises the price of wheat by 29 percent, from $3.00 to $4.02. Before the drought, American farms sold 100 bushels for $3.00 each, so they earned $300. After the drought, they sell 50 bushels for $4.02 each, so they earn only $201 and lose $99 from the drought.

American farmers can gain from the drought if world demand is sufficiently inelastic. Suppose, for example, that the elasticity of demand for wheat is $-\frac{1}{3}$ (rather than -1). Then the 29 percent fall in world supply raises the price by 87 percent:

$$\frac{29}{\frac{1}{3}} = 87 \text{ percent}$$

If the price of wheat is $3.00 per bushel before the drought, an 87 percent increase raises the price to $7.62. Before the drought, American farms sold 100 bushels for $3.00 each, so they earned $300. After the drought, they sell 50 bushels for $7.62 each, so they earn $381. Economists use elasticities of demand and supply to calculate the effects of changes in economic conditions on prices and to determine the other consequences of those changes.

You can use supply and demand to analyze the other effects of a drought. Grains such as wheat are inputs into the production of other goods, so higher grain prices reduce the supplies of those products and raise their prices. A drought would decrease supplies and raise the prices of breakfast cereals, beer, salad dressings, margarine and mayonnaise, pet foods, and rat poison. Economists estimate the sizes of these effects using elasticities of demand and supply.

FOR REVIEW

5.13 What is the long run?

5.14 What does a long-run demand curve or supply curve show?

5.15 Consider the example of the effects of a drought on wheat supply by American farmers. Explain why the drought reduced American farm income with unit-elastic world demand for wheat.

--- QUESTIONS ---

5.16 a. How does a 20 percent fall in the price of bumper stickers affect the quantity demanded if the elasticity of demand is $-\frac{1}{4}$?

b. An increase in the supply of donuts raises the quantity sold by 30 percent. If the elasticity of demand is -2, what happens to the price of donuts?

c. An increase in the demand for a computer game raises the quantity sold by 50 percent. If the elasticity of supply is 5, what happens to the price?

5.17 Consider the example of the effects of a drought on wheat supply by American farmers. Do American farmers gain or lose income if the elasticity of demand is $-\frac{1}{2}$?

CONCLUSIONS

TOTAL SPENDING AND ELASTICITY OF DEMAND

Elasticity refers to responsiveness to a change in conditions. It describes the shapes of demand and supply curves, but elasticity differs from the slope of the curve. The elasticity of demand (or supply) is the percentage change in quantity demanded (or supplied) divided by the percentage change in price.

Demand (or supply) is unit-elastic if the absolute value of its elasticity equals 1. Demand (or supply) is elastic if the absolute value of its elasticity exceeds 1, and it is inelastic if the absolute value of its elasticity is less than 1. When elasticity is zero, demand (or supply) is perfectly inelastic and the demand (or supply) curve is vertical. When elasticity is infinite, demand (or supply) is perfectly elastic and the curve is horizontal. A price increase raises spending on a good if its demand is inelastic and reduces spending if its demand is elastic.

CHANGES IN DEMAND OR SUPPLY

If demand is perfectly elastic, an increase in demand shifts the demand curve upward and a decrease in demand shifts the curve downward. If supply is perfectly elastic, an increase in supply shifts the supply curve downward and a decrease in supply shifts the curve upward. When the demand or supply curve is perfectly inelastic, changes in the other curve do not affect the quantity traded. When the demand or supply curve is perfectly elastic, changes in the other curve do not affect the equilibrium price.

TWO FACTORS THAT AFFECT ELASTICITIES

The elasticity of demand is larger when buyers can find close substitutes for a good and when buyers spend larger fractions of their incomes on the good. The elasticity of supply is larger when sellers can offer close substitutes.

OTHER ELASTICITIES

A cross-price elasticity of demand (or supply) is the percentage change in the quantity demanded (or supplied) of one good when the price of another good rises by 1 percent. The income elasticity of demand is the percentage change in quantity demanded divided by the percentage change in income.

SHORT-RUN AND LONG-RUN DEMAND AND SUPPLY

The long-run response of demand or supply to a change is the response after people have fully adjusted to the change. The long-run demand curve shows prices and the quantity demanded at each price after buyers have adjusted completely to that price. It does not shift as adjustment time increases. Similarly, the long-run supply curve shows prices and the quantity supplied at each price after sellers have adjusted completely to that price.

USING ELASTICITIES

When supply changes, the percentage change in the equilibrium quantity equals the percentage change in the equilibrium price multiplied by the elasticity of demand. Alternatively, the percentage change in the equilibrium price equals the percentage change in the equilibrium quantity divided by the elasticity of demand. Similarly, when demand changes, the percentage change in the equilibrium quantity equals the percentage change in the equilibrium price multiplied by the elasticity of supply. Alternatively, the percentage change in the equilibrium price equals the percentage change in the equilibrium quantity divided by the elasticity of supply.

LOOKING AHEAD

You now have the basic tools of economics that you will need to study a variety of economic problems. Glance through the other chapters of this book to get an idea of the topics we will cover. You are now ready to begin unraveling the complexities of our world economy.

KEY TERMS

percentage change

elasticity of demand (or supply)

unit-elastic demand (or supply)

elastic demand (or supply)

inelastic demand (or supply)

perfectly inelastic demand (or supply)

perfectly elastic demand (or supply)

cross-price elasticity of demand (or supply)

income elasticity of demand

long run

long-run demand (or supply) curve

QUESTIONS AND PROBLEMS

5.18 If the elasticity of demand for ice cream were $-\frac{1}{2}$, how much would the quantity demanded fall if the price were to rise 10 percent?

5.19 If the income elasticity of demand for steak were 2, how much would the quantity demanded increase if buyers' incomes were to rise 10 percent?

5.20 Which is likely to have a higher elasticity of demand:
  a. Ice cream or chocolate ice cream?

  b. Haircuts, or haircuts at the local Hair We Are outlet?

5.21 Comment: "Toothpaste is a necessity. Everyone has to brush his or her teeth, so the demand for toothpaste must be perfectly inelastic."

5.22 Suppose that the demand for Sam's Salami is perfectly elastic. Draw the demand curve, then show how to graph an increase in the demand for Sam's Salami.

5.23 It takes over 50 years to grow a new walnut tree to the size at which it can provide a profitable harvest. The demand for wood from walnut trees increased in recent years, causing the price of walnut to rise 20 percent. Use supply-and-demand analysis to show the effect of an increase in demand for walnut on its price and quantity sold in the short run and the long run.

5.24 Apply the elasticity-of-demand formulas to answer these questions:
a. An increase in demand for carrots raises the equilibrium quantity sold by 30 percent. If the elasticity of demand for carrots is −2 and the elasticity of supply is 3, how much does the price of carrots increase?
b. An increase in the supply of cellular phones reduces their price by 20 percent. If the elasticity of demand for cellular phones is −2 and the elasticity of supply is 1, how much do sales of cellular phones increase?

INQUIRIES FOR FURTHER THOUGHT

5.25 How would you try to measure the elasticity of demand for a good, such as pizzas or automobiles?

5.26 Why might a business firm be interested in knowing the elasticity of demand for its product?
a. If the demand for a firm's product were inelastic, would its profits rise or fall if it were to increase its price?
b. If the demand for a firm's product were elastic, would its profits rise or fall if it were to increase its price? What other information would you need to answer this question?

TAG SOFTWARE APPLICATIONS

TUTORIAL EXERCISES
▶ The module reviews the key terms from Chapter 5.

ANALYTICAL EXERCISES
▶ Calculations of the elasticity of demand are included.

GRAPHING EXERCISES
▶ The module examines how to illustrate special cases of elasticity of demand and supply.

CHAPTER 5 APPENDIX — ELASTICITIES AND SLOPES

Let Δ denote a change, and $\%\Delta$ a percentage change. The quantity demanded Q^d is a function of the price, so:

$$Q^d = f(P)$$

where P is the price. The function f describes the demand curve; a higher price P causes lower quantity demanded Q^d. The elasticity of demand is:

$$\text{Elasticity} = \frac{\%\Delta Q^d}{\%\Delta P} - \frac{\Delta Q^d}{\Delta P} \times \frac{P}{Q^d}$$

The slope differs from the elasticity. The slope of a demand curve is:

$$\text{Slope} = \frac{\Delta P}{\Delta Q^d}$$

APPLICATIONS OF SUPPLY AND DEMAND

APPLIED PRICE THEORY

WHAT THIS CHAPTER IS ABOUT

P. 133 - 146 (only)

▶ Government spending and budget deficits

▶ Government farm policies

▶ Time prices

▶ Economics of social pressures, illegal activities, and bribes

▶ Economics of risk and safety

▶ Economics of lifestyles and values

▶ Economics of dowries and children

▶ Responsibility for price increases

▶ Adjustment to equilibrium

Economic analysis applies to a wide range of subjects besides ordinary goods such as food, energy, and household products. Economics applies to health and safety, crime and punishment, marriage and divorce, family size and population growth, the legal system, fashions, and social norms.

This chapter introduces a few of these applications of microeconomics, or price theory. Each section of this chapter is independent of the others, and the sections can be read separately or in any order. Questions that follow each section pertain only to it. More difficult questions at the end of the chapter ask you to apply economic analysis to a few additional topics.

The first two sections of this chapter distinguish demand by the private sector of the economy from total market demand. Chapter 4 explained that market demand is the sum of all buyers' individual demands. When the government is one of the buyers, its demand is part of the market demand.

private demand — demand for a good by people and nongovernment businesses

market demand — demand for a good by all buyers, including the private sector and the government

Private demand refers to demand by the private sector, that is, people and nongovernment businesses.

The **market demand** for a good is the sum of government demand and private demand.

GOVERNMENT SPENDING AND BORROWING

Government spending on a good affects its price, its total production, and the amount that the private sector buys. Increases in government demand for a good drive up its price and reduce private purchases; decreases in government demand drive down a good's price and raise private purchases. The discussion here

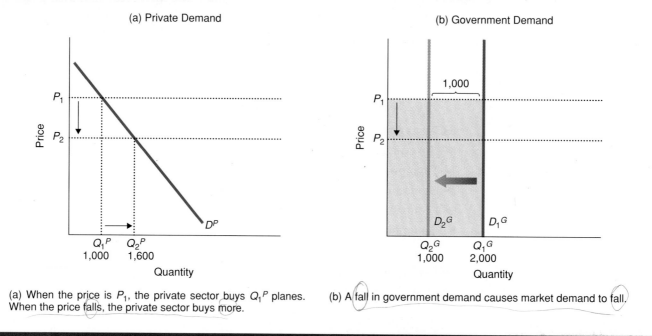

FIGURE 6.1

DECREASE IN GOVERNMENT DEMAND FOR AIRPLANES

(a) Private Demand

(b) Government Demand

(a) When the price is P_1, the private sector buys Q_1^P planes. When the price falls, the private sector buys more.

(b) A fall in government demand causes market demand to fall.

focuses on a fall in government demand; a problem at the end of this section asks you to discuss an increase in government demand.

Figure 6.1 shows the private demand, government demand, and market demand for airplanes. Private demand includes purchases by airline companies, other business firms, and individuals. The figure also shows the market supply curve for planes, labeled S. At the equilibrium (Point A on the graph in Panel c), the market demand and supply curves intersect. The equilibrium price is P_1 and the equilibrium quantity produced and sold is Q_1^M. (This analysis ignores differences among airplanes. A more sophisticated analysis would include different types of airplanes, but the reasoning and the conclusions would be similar.)

The graph in Panel a of the figure shows that the private sector buys Q_1^P planes (because the price is P_1). The graph in the middle shows that the government buys Q_1^G planes.[1] The area of the shaded rectangle shows government spending on planes. Total purchases of planes, Q_1^M, equal private purchases plus government purchases.

A FALL IN GOVERNMENT DEMAND

If the government decreases its demand for planes from D_1^G to D_2^G, as in Figure 6.1, the market demand falls from D_1^M to D_2^M. The *horizontal distance* that the market demand curve shifts equals the decrease in government demand.

---

[1]The graph shows a perfectly inelastic government demand for planes to simplify the discussion. The reader can show that the same reasoning applies in the more general case.

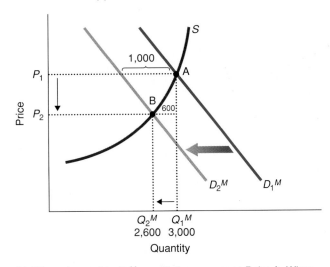

(c) Market Demand and Supply

(c) When demand is $D_1{}^M$, equilibrium occurs at Point A. When demand falls to $D_2{}^M$, the equilibrium moves to Point B, and both the price and the quantity traded fall.

The new equilibrium is at Point B. Total production of planes falls from $Q_2{}^M$ to $Q_1{}^M$ planes and the price falls from P_1 to P_2. The private sector now buys more planes than before ($Q_2{}^P$ rather than $Q_1{}^P$ planes) because the price is lower. Total production of planes falls by *less* than the decrease in government purchases because the private sector buys more.

EXAMPLE

Originally, the price is P_1 and 3,000 planes are sold each year; the private sector buys 1,000 and the government buys 2,000. The government then reduces its demand by 1,000 planes, so the market demand for planes decreases by 1,000. (The market demand curve shifts to the left by 1,000 planes.) Production of planes falls by 400, from 3,000 to 2,600 planes per year. The government buys 1,000 fewer planes, but the private sector buys 600 more because the price is lower.

TAXES

The government spends money that it gets from taxes, by borrowing, or by printing money. The next sections discuss the first two possibilities. First, suppose that the government increases spending on roads and bridges, and raises taxes to pay for the increased spending.

The increase in government spending raises the demands for concrete, steel, and other materials. The increase in taxes, however, leaves people and businesses with less after-tax income or profits, so people and businesses reduce spending. This decreases the demands for other goods.

If the tax increase causes people to spend less on new clothes and vacations, then the demands for clothes and vacations fall.[2] Therefore, increased government spending financed by higher taxes raises the demands for some goods and lowers the demands for other goods.[3]

> An increase in government spending financed by higher taxes raises demands for those goods that the government buys and lowers demands for the goods on which people reduce spending to pay the higher taxes.

GOVERNMENT BUDGET DEFICITS

The government can also raise money for higher spending by borrowing it. The amount of money the government borrows is the government budget deficit.

government budget deficit — the money that the government must borrow when it spends more money than it collects in taxes

> The **government budget deficit** is the amount of money that the government borrows each year when it spends more than it collects in taxes.

Changes in government borrowing affect the interest rate by changing the demand for loans.

DEMAND AND SUPPLY OF LOANS

Figure 6.2 shows the supply and demand for loans. Lenders (such as banks) supply loans by lending the money that people save. Borrowers demand loans. The interest rate is the price of a loan (per dollar loaned). The supply curve of loans slopes upward—an increase in the interest rate raises the incentive to lend money. The demand curve for loans slopes downward—a rise in the interest rate reduces the incentive to borrow.

GOVERNMENT BORROWING RAISES THE DEMAND FOR LOANS

An increase in the government budget deficit raises the demand for loans, as **Figure 6.3** shows. The demand curve D_1 shows the private demand for loans. If the government budget deficit is zero, then D_1 is also the market demand curve for loans. Then equilibrium occurs at Point A with an interest rate of i_1 and Q_1 dollars borrowed and lent each year.

Now suppose the government budget deficit rises to $100 billion per year. This raises the market demand for loans so the market demand curve shifts to the right by $100 billion. The new equilibrium is at Point B. The interest rate rises from i_1 to i_2 and total lending rises from Q_1 to Q_2. This rise in total lending is *less* than the $100 billion increase in government borrowing because the private sector borrows less; private borrowing falls from Q_1 to Q_0. For example, total lending might rise by $30 billion, and total private borrowing might fall by $70 billion. The original demand curve D_1 continues to show the private demand for loans, so the rise in the interest rate reduces the private sector's quantity demanded from Q_1 to Q_0. In this sense, government borrowing *crowds out* (reduces) private borrowing. Each dollar of government borrowing crowds out less than a dollar of private borrowing because the rise in the interest rate increases total lending.

Contractors must shrink with budgets

By David Craig
USA TODAY

The industry's problems can also be measured in human terms. McDonnell Douglas, which makes F-15 and F/A-18 fighter jets, slashed its work force 17,000, to 118,000 people last year—a 13 percent cut that is high even in this period of staff reductions in all industries. Northrop has slashed its work force 5,300, to 36,000—also a 13 percent cut. Grumman Corp., maker of the Navy's F-14 Tomcat and A-6E fighter jets, said in April that it will cut up to 1,900 of 25,600 jobs—a 7 percent decline.

A fall in government demand for defense items hurts their producers.

Source: David Craig, "Contractors Must Shrink with Budgets," *USA Today*, October 15, 1991, p. B1.

---

[2] Clothes and vacations are normal goods; a decrease in after-tax income raises demands for inferior goods. (See Chapter 4.)

[3] Taxes also affect incentives, so they cause other changes in supplies and demands. These will be discussed in Chapter 8 and later chapters.

FIGURE 6.2

DEMAND AND SUPPLY FOR LOANS

Some people save money and lend it to others (or put it in a bank account, in which case the bank lends it). These people supply loans. Other people, business firms, and governments borrow money. They demand loans. The supply and demand for loans determine the equilibrium interest rate, i_1.

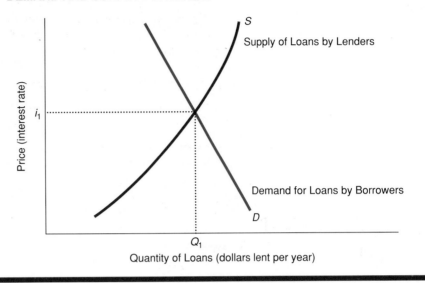

FIGURE 6.3

INCREASE IN GOVERNMENT BORROWING CROWDS OUT PRIVATE BORROWING AND RAISES THE INTEREST RATE

A $100 billion increase in government borrowing raises the demand for loans by $100 billion. This raises the interest rate from i_1 to i_2. It also raises total lending from Q_1 to Q_2 and lowers private-sector borrowing from Q_1 to Q_0.

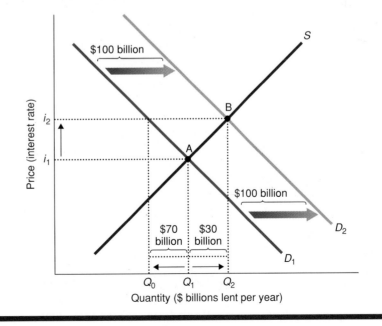

Big deficit cut could sharply reduce rates

Credit markets

By Constance Mitchell
Staff Reporter of the
Wall Street Journal

"The deficit is costing us significantly in terms of long-term interest rates," says David Wyss, an economist at Data Resources Inc., a Boston economic consulting firm. Allen Sinai, chief economist at Boston Co., agrees.

Data Resources, Boston Co., and WEFA Group in Bala Cynwyd, Pa.—three of the nation's leading economic consultants—each plugged hypothetical deficit cuts into the computer models they use to predict the behavior of the U.S. economy. All came to similar conclusions:

If the government cut the federal deficit by $100 billion, they say, the yield on the benchmark 30-year Treasury bond, now at 7.3 percent, would fall to between 6.4 percent and 6.6 percent.

Falling government borrowing would reduce the demand for loans and lower interest rates.

Source: Constance Mitchell, "Big Deficit Cut Could Sharply Reduce Rates," *The Wall Street Journal,* January 25, 1993, p. C1.

OTHER CONSEQUENCES

The government budget deficit has other consequences, as well. The decrease in private borrowing reduces the demands for houses, cars, vacations, and other goods that people would have bought with borrowed money. This reduces the equilibrium outputs of these goods. It also decreases the demands for new equipment and other goods that business firms would have bought with borrowed money, which reduces the equilibrium outputs of these goods as well.

Of course, a government budget deficit can result from either of two causes:

1. An increase in government spending, which raises demands for the goods the government buys

2. A decrease in taxes, which leaves taxpayers with more money to spend and raises demands for the goods they buy

An increase in the government budget deficit reduces demands for some goods and raises demands for others. Output falls in some parts of the economy and rises in other parts.

The deficit will also reduce future *supplies* of many goods because businesses that buy less equipment today will have less equipment available for future production than they would have had without the deficit. This reduces the economy's future output.

FOR REVIEW

6.1 What is a government budget deficit?

QUESTIONS

6.2 Draw graphs similar to Figure 6.1 to show the effects of an increase in government spending on office buildings. How would this increase affect total production of office buildings and the number bought by the private sector?

(Ignore the effects of higher taxes or government borrowing to pay for the increase in spending.)

6.3 Use graphs to show the effects of an increase in government spending financed by an increase in taxes, assuming that the government spends the money on schools and that the higher taxes lead people to eat at restaurants less often.

6.4 Suppose that the government raises its budget deficit by cutting taxes by $100 per person without reducing spending. Suppose that people use all their extra money from the tax cut to buy video games. What are the effects on:
  a. The interest rate
  b. Borrowing by the private sector
  c. Prices and output of video games

——————————— INQUIRIES FOR FURTHER THOUGHT ———————————

6.5 (*More difficult*) Repeat Question 6.3 but assume that people pay the higher taxes by saving less rather than spending less at restaurants. How does this affect the interest rate and the quantity of loans? (*Hint:* A fall in savings reduces the amount of money available for banks to lend, so it lowers the supply of loans.)

6.6 (*More difficult*) The government raises its budget deficit by cutting taxes by $100 per person without reducing spending.
  a. How does this affect the demand for loans? How far does the demand curve shift?
  b. Assume that people save all of the extra money that they get from the tax cut. (They put all this money into a bank account.) Also assume that banks want to lend this money. Show how this increase in saving affects the supply of loans.
  c. Combine parts a and b above. How does the tax cut affect the interest rate?

GOVERNMENT FARM POLICIES

Governments all over the world have programs to change the prices of farm products. Governments of most developed countries try to keep prices of farm products high; some less developed countries do the opposite. This section discusses U.S. government programs; many foreign programs are similar.

U.S. GOVERNMENT POLICIES THAT AFFECT DEMAND

The U.S. government buys farm products to help keep their prices high. The government began buying farm products in large quantities during the Great Depression of the 1930s. The Agricultural Adjustment Act of 1933 authorized the government to buy wheat, cotton, corn, dairy products, and other farm products to raise their prices. Sometimes the government stored the goods it bought, and sometimes it disposed of the goods in other ways. For example, the government bought and slaughtered pigs to reduce the total supply of pork.

The U.S. government keeps milk prices high by choosing a *support price* and then buying as much milk as dairy farmers want to sell at that price. For example, the U.S. support price for milk in 1993 was $10.10 per hundredweight (hundred pounds of milk). The U.S. government bought more than 10 billion pounds of milk in 1991, and about 7 billion pounds in each of the next several years. This kept milk prices high, helping dairy farmers to earn higher incomes at the expense of consumers and taxpayers.

Figure 6.4 shows the private demand, government demand, and market demand for milk. The government's demand for milk is perfectly elastic at the support price, as in the middle graph, so the market demand curve (in the right graph) never falls below the support price, $10.10. The equilibrium at Point A occurs at an equilibrium price of $10.10 and an equilibrium quantity of Q_1^M. The graph on the left shows that the private sector buys Q_1^P milk at the support price, and the government buys the rest (Q_1^G). If the government did not buy milk, the price of milk would be lower and the private sector would buy more.

Occasionally the government buys so many farm products that its storage facilities become full; then it either pays farmers to store more, or it destroys, sells, or gives away some of the goods. Selling the products, of course, raises their supplies and lowers their prices.

U.S. GOVERNMENT POLICIES THAT AFFECT SUPPLY

The U.S. government also started programs during the 1930s to keep prices of farm products high by reducing their supplies. The government paid farmers to destroy crops that they had already planted and to slaughter young pigs and pregnant sows. These programs reduced supplies of farm products such as pork and

FIGURE 6.4

GOVERNMENT PRICE SUPPORTS

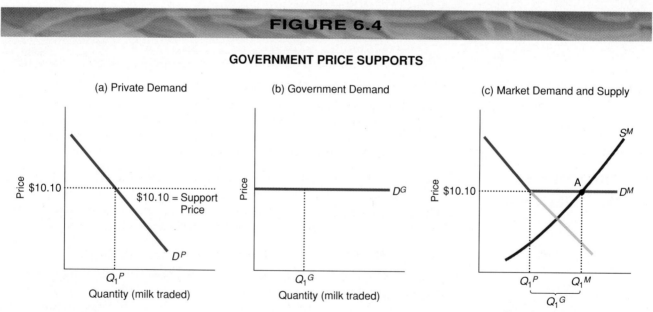

(a) Private Demand

(b) Government Demand

(c) Market Demand and Supply

(a) At a price of $10.10 per hundredweight, the private sector buys Q_1^P milk.

(b) The government's demand for milk is perfectly elastic at the support price of $10.10.

(c) At the support price, dairy farmers supply Q_1^M milk. The private sector buys Q_1^P, and the government buys the rest (Q_1^G). Without the price support, the equilibrium price would be lower.

IN THE NEWS

Continued fall in wheat prices is tied to U.S. program to reduce stockpiles

In November, the department launched a Friday wheat auction as part of its campaign to reduce a huge government-owned stockpile. While the long-term goal of the program is to boost prices by eliminating excess stockpiles, the infusions of government grain into the market depress prices.

When the government sells a good that it has held in storage, the increased supply lowers the good's price.

Source: "Continued Fall in Wheat Prices Is Tied to U.S. Program to Reduce Stockpiles," *The Wall Street Journal,* March 11, 1988, p. 34.

raised their prices. The government also began paying farmers not to plant crops on part of their land. This reduced supplies of farm products. (For example, cotton output fell 20 percent when these programs started.) These programs reduce the supplies of farm products by less than they reduce total acreage planted, however, because farmers naturally choose to stop producing on their least productive land, and they keep farming their most productive land. Farmers also increase their yields per acre in other ways, such as changing their use of fertilizer. When farmers began collecting money to grow less wheat, they grew more rice or soybeans instead (raising supplies of rice and soybeans and reducing their prices), so the government responded by changing the program to pay farmers to reduce their *total* acreage for all crops.

These programs have continued in recent years, and the government still pays farmers not to plant crops. In 1988, such programs took a record 78.4 million acres of farmland out of production. In recent years, U.S. government programs have removed about 50 million acres of farmland from production—about one-sixth of all U.S. farmland.

In administering supply-reduction programs, the government makes so-called *deficiency payments* to farmers. It pays farmers the difference between the equilibrium price of a commodity and a target price that the government sets. For example, the government has set a target price for wheat of $4.00 per bushel in recent years. If the equilibrium price of wheat is only $3.00 per bushel, the government pays farmers the extra $1.00 per bushel (up to a certain limit). The government also sets target prices for corn ($2.75 per bushel), rice ($10.71 per hundredweight), and cotton ($0.729 per pound). In addition, the government subsidizes loans to farmers who agree to reduce output. For example, the government sets a loan rate for soybeans at $5.02 per bushel. If a soybean farmer borrows money from the government in 1996 and the price of soybeans in 1997 turns out to be only $4.50, the farmer can repay the loan by giving the government only $4.50 for each $5.02 borrowed. Farmers must agree to produce less to qualify for these subsidies, reducing supplies of farm products and keeping their prices high.

Similar government programs work to reduce supplies of farm goods in other ways to keep prices high. For example, government marketing orders sometimes prohibit California farmers from selling all their fresh oranges. Political controversy resulted from a government program that required farmers to slaughter dairy cattle to reduce the supply of milk and raise its price. The slaughter raised the supply of beef and lowered its price, so angry cattle producers filed lawsuits to stop the program.[4] The government also subsidizes exports of farm products; as the United States exports more wheat, a smaller supply remains in this country and it commands a higher price.

QUESTIONS

6.7 Draw a graph to show the effect on the prices of farm products of government programs that pay farmers to reduce output.

6.8 Draw a graph like Figure 6.4 to show why the price of milk would fall if the government were to eliminate its price-support program.

6.9 Suppose that the supply of milk increases while the government support price remains at $10.10 per hundredweight. Draw a graph like Figure 6.4 to

---

[4]*The Wall Street Journal,* March 31, 1986 and April 9, 1986.

show how this affects the equilibrium price of milk, the quantity produced, the quantity purchased by the private sector, and the quantity purchased by the government.

INQUIRY FOR FURTHER THOUGHT

6.10 The government says that one purpose of its farm policies is to help small, family farms. Argue for or against the government continuing these programs.

a. Do you think the government should offer similar programs to help other small, family-run businesses? (It could pay motel owners not to rent all their rooms and pay grocers not to sell all their food.) What would be the effects?

b. Why do you think the government maintains farm-support programs, but not similar programs for most other industries?

TIME PRICES AND MONEY PRICES

You spend both time and money buying goods. You must travel to a store, find or choose what you want, pay for it, and go home. You also spend time using some of the goods you buy; you may have to assemble or prepare a good, read an instruction manual, or spend time learning how to use a good. It takes time to watch a movie, get a haircut, or cook a meal and clean the kitchen.

You pay two kinds of prices for many goods: a money price that you pay at the store, and a time price to buy, prepare, and enjoy the good.

time price — the time necessary to buy, prepare, and use a good

The **time price** of a good is the time required to buy, prepare, and use it.

Television shows, parties, and large, home-cooked meals have high time prices; fast food and home-delivered pizza have low time prices.

Time is valuable. Its opportunity cost is the extra after-tax income you could earn by working or by studying more (which could raise your future income), or the benefits you could enjoy from additional leisure time. The value of your time changes as your opportunities change: your time is probably more valuable during the week before final exams than the week after exams end.

We can measure time prices in units of time or in terms of dollars. Suppose that you attend a concert one evening when you could have worked for 3 hours instead, earning $5 per hour. Your time price of the concert is $15 because you could earn $15 in the time you spend at the concert; the value of your time is $5 per hour. Your money price of the concert is the price of your ticket, say $20, so the total price you pay for the concert is $35. (If you have the evening off from work, the opportunity cost of your time might be less than $5 per hour; you could measure it by the value of what you would have done if you had not gone to the concert.)

TIME PRICES AND CHANGES IN DEMAND

A change in the value of time changes the demands for goods with high time prices, such as parties and movies. The demand for movies rises on weekends and during school vacations when the value of time falls. The Chicago Cubs began playing night baseball on weekdays because the demand for night games is higher than the demand for day games, when many people work.

Figure 6.5 shows the demand and supply for haircuts. The price on the vertical axis is (as usual) the money price. Suppose that all buyers value their time at $8 per hour. If the time price of a haircut is 30 minutes, the demand curve is D_1 and the equilibrium money price is $10. Thus, the total price of a haircut (including the $4 value of the time price) is $14.

Now suppose that technology improves and reduces the time price by half because a haircut now takes 15 minutes instead of 30 minutes. Buyers value the 15 minutes they save at $2 (because each hour is worth $8 to them), so the demand curve shifts upward (vertically) by $2. The new demand curve, D_2, is $2 above the old demand curve, D_1. Buyers are willing to pay $2 more for the good because they pay $2 less in a time price. The equilibrium moves from Point A to Point B in Figure 6.5, but the equilibrium money price rises less than $2, from $10 to $11. Since buyers save $2 in the time price, the total price for haircuts falls by $1, from $14 ($10 money price plus $4 time price) to $13 ($11 money price plus $2 time price).

EQUILIBRIUM WITH DIFFERENT TYPES OF BUYERS

Sometimes buyers can choose either high time prices with low money prices or low time prices with high money prices. Convenience stores charge higher money prices than large grocery stores, but many buyers have lower time prices shopping at convenience stores. Similarly, your time price for clothes is lower at a store with a good selection of styles and sizes. The money price of clothes is often lower at a discount store than at a regular department store with a good selection, but the time price is usually higher at a discount store. Buyers can choose whether to save time and pay higher money prices, or spend more time and pay lower money prices. The choice depends on the value of a buyer's time at the moment. When a major university recently installed condom vending machines in dormitory bathrooms, some students complained that the money price was five times higher than prices at pharmacies. Nevertheless, some students used the vending machines because the time price was lower.

Figure 6.6 shows the demand and supply for a good at two types of stores: fast-service stores and slow-service stores. (It doesn't matter here why some stores provide faster service than others.) The demand curve at the fast-service stores is D^F; the demand curve at the slow-service stores is D^S. The equilibrium price is $25 at the fast-service stores and only $21 at the slow-service stores. If it takes 20 minutes longer to buy the good at the slow stores, then buyers who value their time higher than $12 an hour go to the fast stores and buyers who value their time lower than $12 an hour go to the slow stores. (The $12 an hour figure equals $4 for 20 minutes, the extra shopping time required at the slow stores.) People who value their time at exactly $12 an hour don't care where they shop; the money price is $4 lower at the slow stores, but their time price is $4 higher there.

People with a higher value of time are generally willing to pay higher money prices to save time. High-wage people use money-saving coupons less than low-wage people. Land prices are usually lower in suburbs farther from the center of a town or city than in closer suburbs because high-wage people are willing to pay more to live closer to the town. Apartments and houses at more convenient locations cost more than the same apartments and houses at less convenient locations; people with higher values of time tend to choose the more convenient locations.

FIGURE 6.5

EFFECTS OF A DECREASE IN A TIME PRICE

If the value of the time price of haircuts falls by $2, the demand curve shifts vertically by $2 and equilibrium moves from Point A to Point B. The money price of haircuts rises by an amount less than $2; it may rise by $1, from $10 to $11. The total price of haircuts, including the money and time prices, falls.

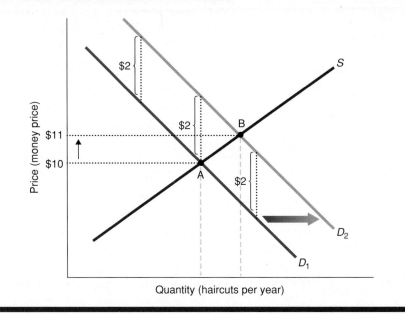

FIGURE 6.6

BUYERS' DIFFERENT TIME PRICES

(a) Fast-Service Stores

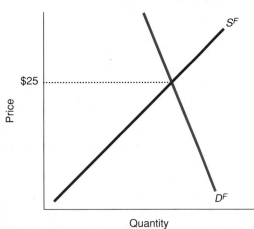

(b) Slow-Service Stores

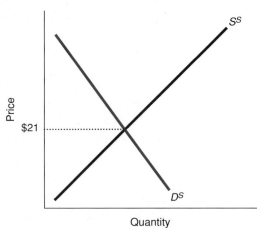

Goods might cost $4 more at fast stores, where shopping takes 20 minutes less than at slow stores. People whose value of time is more than $12 per hour shop at fast stores, and people whose value of time is less than $12 per hour shop at slow stores.

Demand for Sleep

Sleep has a high time price. If you sleep eight hours a night, you spend one-third of your lifetime asleep. Some evidence indicates that people with higher values of time sleep less. Holding wealth fixed, a 20 percent increase in wages reduces sleep by about 1 percent. This implies that a person who earns $40 an hour sleeps about half an hour less each night than a similar person who earns $10 an hour, but who has the same level of wealth, perhaps from an inheritance. (People work about 2,000 hours each year, so $10 an hour is about $20,000 per year.)

Evidence also indicates that employed people sleep about one hour less than unemployed people. Holding wages fixed, increases in wealth raise the demand for sleep. Therefore, despite higher average wages, people in rich countries sleep more than people in poor countries.

BUYING TIME

We can think of time as a good that people buy. People buy extra time when they buy time-saving goods or services. Microwave ovens, frozen dinners, and automatic dishwashers save time in meal preparation and cleanup. You can hire people to mow your lawn, clean your house, fix your meals, and even help you find appropriate friends or romantic partners.

QUESTIONS

6.11 People can reach the Island Restaurant only by boat. The round trip used to take one hour, but now it takes only 40 minutes. Draw a graph to show how this change affects the demand for meals at the Island Restaurant if all potential diners value their time at $12 per hour.

6.12 Figure 6.6 assumes that buyers spend 20 minutes longer at slow-service stores than at fast-service stores. Suppose that slow stores improve their service so that now buyers must spend only 10 minutes longer at those stores. Show on a graph how this change affects the equilibrium in Figure 6.6.

INQUIRIES FOR FURTHER THOUGHT

6.13 If you could save 15 minutes a day, every day, how much extra time would you have each year? How much would you be willing to pay for this time? What could you buy that would save you 15 minutes in an average day? How much would it cost?
  a. What is the value of your time? Does its value differ in the morning, afternoon, and evening? Do you expect its value to rise after you finish college? How much? Why?
  b. How long would you wait in line to save $10? How does your answer depend on what you can do while you wait in line?

6.14 Suppose that a business firm could save time for its customers by reorganizing the store, opening more checkout lines, or in some other way. Does the firm have an incentive to make the change? What factors affect the business firm's decision?

SOCIAL PRESSURES, ILLEGAL ACTIVITIES, AND BRIBES

SOCIAL PRESSURES

Some people feel social pressure not to buy certain products, such as the wrong kind of sneakers or car. Buying some goods (cigarettes, drugs, pornography, or the wrong kinds of clothes) can expose buyers to criticism and social ostracism. When buying a good involves social pressures, people pay both a money price and a nonmoney price: the nonmoney price is the criticism that the buyer endures. The buyer's total price is the sum of the money and nonmoney prices. People who are more sensitive than others to these social pressures (criticism or ostracism) pay higher total prices for the goods than other people pay.

CHANGES IN SOCIAL PRESSURES

An increase in social pressure not to buy a good raises its nonmoney price and reduces demand for it. **Figure 6.7a** shows the effects of an increase in social pressure not to buy a good: demand falls from D_1 to D_2, reducing the good's equilibrium price and quantity sold. Likewise, Figure 6.7b shows the effects of an increase in social pressure not to sell a good: supply falls from S_1 to S_2, which raises the money price of the good and reduces the quantity sold. An increase in social pressure not to buy or sell a good reduces both supply and demand. The quantity sold falls and the money price rises or falls depending on whether social pressure has a larger effect on supply or demand.

FIGURE 6.7

INCREASE IN SOCIAL PRESSURE

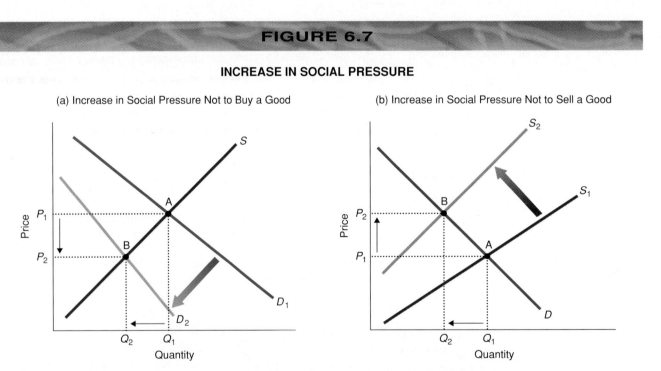

(a) Increase in Social Pressure Not to Buy a Good

(b) Increase in Social Pressure Not to Sell a Good

An increase in social pressure not to buy a good raises the nonmoney price that buyers pay, so it decreases their demand for the good.

An increase in social pressure not to sell a good raises the nonmoney price that sellers pay when they sell the good, so it reduces their supply of the good.

IN THE NEWS

Clean, not laundered

BERLIN — Corruption is common because the rusty machinery of international business calls out for lubrication. Corruption's beneficiaries are rich-country companies and officials of third-world—and, increasingly, East European—governments. The International Chamber of Commerce has had rules against bribery and extortion since 1977, but most people ignore them. America's antibribery law is more effective, though it is hardly fool-proof.

Still, most of the anticorruption drive has been directed at senior officials. Many say the biggest problem is at lower levels.

"They're probably too scared to attack it at the bottom because people don't make a living wage," said one shipping official. "So it's accepted that this subsidizes their income. But whenever it's accepted, it opens a Pandora's box, with the benefit to the smarter ones."

Bribes are common in some places.

Source: "Clean, Not Laundered," *Economist,* May 8, 1993; and *Journal of Commerce,* May 16, 1994, p. 3A.

ILLEGAL ACTIVITIES

Economic analysis applies to illegal as well as legal activities. Buyers or sellers of an illegal good face a threat of formal punishment that resembles the effects of social pressure. The buyer's total price includes a money price plus an expected-punishment price that reflects the buyer's risk of being caught and punished.[5]

EXPECTED-PUNISHMENT PRICE

The expected-punishment price for an illegal activity equals the chance of being caught times the money value of the punishment given that the person is caught. For example, suppose that the chance of being caught buying an illegal good is one-half and the punishment is a $100 fine. In this case, the expected-punishment price is $50. If the chance of being caught rises to three-fourths and the punishment stays at a $100 fine, the expected-punishment price increases to $75. If the law breaker faces a jail sentence rather than a fine, the expected-punishment price equals the chance of being caught times the money value of the jail sentence (the amount of money the criminal would be willing to pay to avoid jail).

The expected-punishment price rises if either the punishment or the chance of being caught increases. A rise in the expected-punishment price for buyers reduces demand for the illegal good, which lowers its price and quantity sold. An increase in the expected-punishment price for sellers reduces supply of the illegal good, which raises its price and quantity sold. Whether an increase in the expected-punishment price raises or lowers a good's price depends on whether it has a larger effect on the buyers' or sellers' expected-punishment price.

EXAMPLE Suppose that a person expects a one-tenth chance of being convicted of buying illegal firearms. Suppose also that the punishment for someone caught doing this rises from a $500 fine to a $1,000 fine. The criminal's expected-punishment price rises from $50 to $100, shifting the demand curve for illegal firearms downward by $50, as in **Figure 6.8.**[6] The equilibrium money price falls from P_1 to P_2. Notice that the money price falls by less than $50, so the total cost of the good (money price plus expected-punishment price) rises.

BRIBERY

A payola scandal rocked the popular-music industry in the 1950s when record companies bribed disk jockeys to play their records. (The record companies hoped that this would raise the demands for their records.) Bribes are a common part of business in some countries; sellers often obtain permits and licenses partly through bribes. Rumors circulate about bribery, particularly in certain occupations and cities where police and other local officials (such as health-and-safety inspectors) may ignore violations in exchange for bribes. In a burst of candor a few years ago, one politician complained that many friends who had contributed money to a successful presidential campaign "hadn't gotten anything" (such as government contracts and appointments) in return for their campaign contributions. Bribing ushers gets people better seats at theaters and ball games. Travel

---

[5]The total price that a seller receives, on the other hand, is the money price minus an expected-punishment price based on the seller's risk of punishment; the possibility of punishment subtracts from the seller's money price.

[6]This approximation ignores the buyer's dislike for risk; a later chapter will explore this question further.

FIGURE 6.8

EFFECT ON DEMAND OF A RISE IN THE EXPECTED-PUNISHMENT PRICE

If the expected-punishment price of buying an illegal firearm rises by $50, the demand curve shifts downward (vertically) by $50. The equilibrium price falls less than $50.

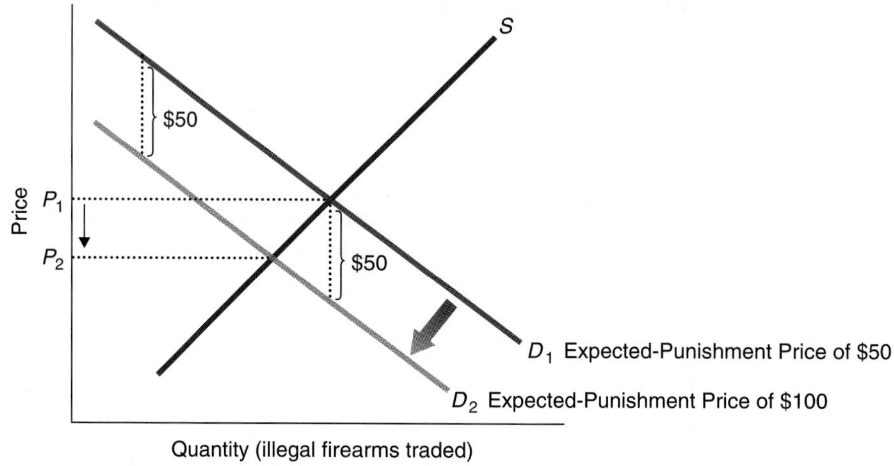

Quantity (illegal firearms traded)

Ambassadors: What price Monaco?

WASHINGTON, DC — "To the victor go the spoils" is an enduring political adage, and among the richest spoils of American politics are ambassadorships. New presidents treat glamorous postings like baubles to be handed out to friends and campaign contributors.

Bribes take many forms.

Source: "Ambassadors: What Price Monaco?" *Economist*, March 4, 1989.

writers often accept free airfare, hotel stays, and meals in return for writing favorably about resorts, airlines, hotels, or restaurants. The so-called *casting couch* was once (and may still be) a feature of Hollywood movie-making.

Supply-and-demand analysis can reveal the effects of bribes on equilibrium prices and quantities. The opportunity to collect bribes is a partial substitute for formal wage payments. The total payment for a job includes bribes, so an increase in the expected bribes in an occupation raises the supply of labor to that occupation. This increase in the supply of labor reduces the formal wage.

Figure 6.9 shows the supply and demand for disk-jockey services. The price axis measures the wage that ratio stations pay disk jockeys. At equilibrium (Point A), disk jockeys earn a wage of W_1 per week. When record companies begin paying bribes, disk jockeys get two kinds of income: wages and bribes. The supply of disk jockeys increases and the supply curve moves downward (vertically) by the average weekly bribe. The equilibrium moves from Point A to Point B and the formal wage for disk jockeys falls from W_1 to W_2. This fall in the wage is smaller than the average bribe, so disk jockeys earn higher total pay (including bribes). Honest disk jockeys who refuse to accept bribes earn a lower wage than before, so they may look for jobs in other professions.

QUESTIONS

6.15 Draw graphs to show the effects on money prices and quantities sold when:
  a. Social pressure to buy a good (such as a certain kind of sneakers) increases
  b. Social pressure to sell a good (such as environmentally friendly soap) increases

6.16 Make up a numerical example of the expected-punishment price of driving faster than the speed limit.

FIGURE 6.9

EFFECTS OF BRIBING DISK JOCKEYS

When bribery begins, the supply of disk-jockey services increases and the supply curve moves downward vertically, by the average bribe. The formal wage falls from W_1 to W_2, but this fall in the wage is smaller than the average bribe.

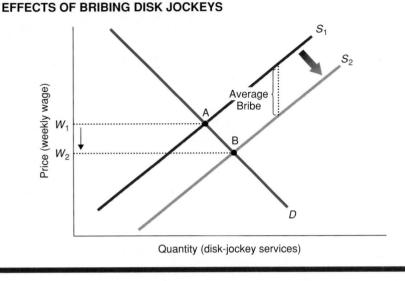

6.17 a. Suppose that a good that was formerly illegal to buy becomes legal, so the expected-punishment price falls from $100 to zero. Show (on a graph) how this change affects the money price of the good and its quantity sold.

b. Suppose that a good that was formerly illegal to sell becomes legal. Draw a graph to show the effects of legalizing the good on its money price and quantity sold.

6.18 A dishonest university president plans to grant one pizza vendor the right to sell pizzas in the new student activities building. Many pizza vendors have offered bribes to the president in return for that right. What will determine the equilibrium size of the winning bribe?

6.19 Read the article, "For Better Mets Seats, Pay an Usher." How would strict enforcement of the Mets policy against bribing ushers affect the equilibrium wages of ushers?

───────────── **INQUIRIES FOR FURTHER THOUGHT** ─────────────

6.20 Suppose that someone who works for a government regulatory agency for several years can expect to get a lucrative consulting job in later years with the industry that the agency regulates. How does this affect the supply of people to government regulatory jobs?

6.21 Some sports stars earn extra income by making television commercials. Explain how this opportunity affects average salaries in sports.

IN THE NEWS

For better Mets seats, pay an usher

By H. Eric Semler

Paying ushers for better seats is a time-honored practice at many ball parks around the country. But at Shea, it has evolved into a tightly organized and accepted ritual in the last few years, say stadium guards, ushers, and dozens of spectators.

Aware that many season-ticket holders will not show up at games, at least a dozen ushers in the field-level and loge sections, the two lowest levels, openly and aggressively try to sell the empty seats to wandering spectators, sometimes called "floppers."

Working in teams, the ushers share their finder's fees. Many command payments as high as $50 a seat at the most popular games, said some ushers, who said they were not involved in such deals. To get into the stadium, the floppers have to pay at least $6 for a ticket.

When a reporter was asked to show his ticket stub to a field-level usher at a game between the Mets and Cubs June 15, he was told to "come back and see me if you want a better view."

"What will it cost?" the reporter asked.

"Ten or 15 bucks," the usher said.

The Mets organization, which employs about 140 ushers for each game, said such hustling is only a minor problem at Shea.

Ushers working on the upper deck at Shea said their colleagues on the field level sometimes earn more than $200.00 in extra payments during a game. The Mets pay each usher $37.50 a game.

It is Mets policy to suspend or dismiss any usher who accepts money to seat people where they do not belong, said Robert Mandt, the team's director of operations.

Source: H. Eric Semler, "For Better Mets Seats, Pay an Usher," *New York Times,* June 26, 1989, p. B1.

RISK AND SAFETY

Safety is a good with a demand and a supply. Safety is not free—it also has a price. You buy safety when you drive carefully, use a seat belt, avoid smoking and dangerous substances, live in a safe neighborhood, eat healthy foods and exercise regularly, practice safe sex, and see your dentist twice a year.

We can measure safety as 1 minus the probability of death: a fall in the chance of injury amounts to an increase in safety. (We could, instead, measure safety as 1 minus the probability of injury; the discussion below would be similar.) **Figure 6.10** shows a person's demand for fire safety. The demand curve slopes downward as usual: when safety becomes more expensive, people buy less safety.

Safety can have a nonmoney price as well as a money price because risks sometimes lead people to avoid activities that they would enjoy. Higher enjoyment costs of safety lead people to choose less safety, just as higher money prices do.

EXAMPLES

Suppose that you face a choice between two kinds of acne medication. One kind costs $3.00 per tube and causes brain damage in 2 out of 1 million (2/1,000,000)

FIGURE 6.10

SUPPLY AND DEMAND FOR FIRE SAFETY

The price of safety is the price of a one one-millionth reduction in the chance of death this year.

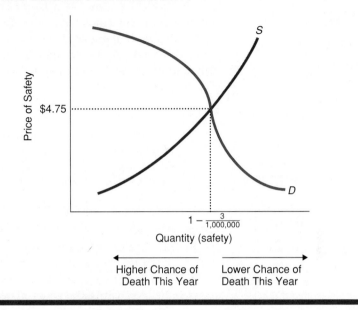

$1 - \frac{3}{1,000,000}$

Quantity (safety)

← Higher Chance of Death This Year   Lower Chance of Death This Year →

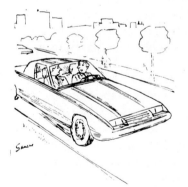

"Buying a $40,000 car made me a safer driver."

People buy more safety when they have more to lose.

Source: The Wall Street Journal, October 18, 1987.

people. The other kind costs $10.00 per tube and causes brain damage in only 1 out of 1 million (1/1,000,000) people. The medications are identical in all other ways.

You can buy safety in your choice of medication. A one one-millionth (0.000001) lower chance of injury costs $7. Many people would buy the additional safety at a cost of $7; fewer would buy the additional safety at a cost of $70. (The $7 price in this example reflects the amount that people pay, on average, to reduce the chance of death from accidents at work: evidence shows that, on average, people are willing to take riskier jobs if they are paid about $7 more per year for each one-millionth increase in the chance of death in a year.)[7]

Figure 6.10 shows the supply and demand for fire safety in an apartment building. Producing safety costs money. Improving safety requires smoke detectors and fire extinguishers, better fire-escape systems, building with less flammable materials, and so on. Builders are willing to produce safer apartment buildings if they can sell or rent them for higher prices to cover their higher costs. Therefore, the supply of safety slopes upward. The demand for safety slopes downward because people want to buy less safety as it becomes more expensive. The equilibrium occurs at Point A in Figure 6.10. At this equilibrium amount of safety, people in the example choose a 3/1,000,000 chance of death by fire at an equilibrium price of $4.75; it costs $4.75 to reduce the chance of death from fire by one one-millionth.

---

[7]Some estimates of the price that people are willing to pay for safety are as low as $0.80 for a one one-millionth reduction in the chance of death; other estimates are as high as $11. Most estimates fall between $4 and $8.

Genentech drug raises question on a life's value

By Marilyn Chase
Staff Reporter of
The Wall Street Journal

Health economists and cardiologists now have a sticky issue to consider: Is a human life worth $200,000?

The question has been raised because of the slim but surprising survival edge shown by Genentech Inc.'s heart drug, TPA, over its less-expensive rival, streptokinase, in a huge international study.

"You have to treat 100 patients with TPA to save one additional life, and the cost differential [between the drugs] is about $2,000," Dr. Parmley said. "So for $200,000, you've saved one life."

"This makes it difficult for managed care to make decisions," said Mark A. Hlatky, a Stanford University health policy expert. "It's very expensive for the amount of time it adds to people's life expectancy."

Doctors and other people must routinely decide whether additional safety is worth the price. People buy more safety when they have more to lose.

Source: Marilyn Chase, "Genentech Drug Raises Question on a Life's Value," *The Wall Street Journal,* May 3, 1993, p. B1.

EXPLANATION

People sometimes say, "You can't place a value on a human life." But people place money values on chances of death every day. They drive inexpensive, small cars when evidence shows that larger cars (which cost more) are safer. They live in houses without smoke and fire detectors. They drive cars on trips instead of spending more money to fly in airplanes, when passenger car travel exposes them to a death rate about 70 times larger than the death rate for airline travel.[8] Safety, like other goods, is amenable to economic analysis.[9]

QUESTION

6.22 Suppose that someone discovers that a chemical sprayed on apples is dangerous. Explain what happens to the price of apples. Does it make any difference whether the chemical is actually harmful? Will the same thing happen if people only *think* that it is harmful

INQUIRIES FOR FURTHER THOUGHT

6.23 What choices have you made recently that involve a decision about risk and safety? How much would you pay for a one one-millionth lower chance of death this year? (A 20-year-old in the United States has about a 1 in 1,000 chance of dying each year.) How much would you pay for a 1 in 2,000 lower chance? Translate your answers into your demand curve for a smaller chance of death.

6.24 The National Research Council (a branch of the National Academy of Sciences) decided in 1989 that the government should not require seat belts in school buses. The council argued that the additional safety would not be worth the cost because seat belts on large school buses would save (on average) one child's life per year at a cost of $40 million. (The council suggested making other changes in buses that would cost less and save more lives per year.) How *should* people make decisions about how much money to spend to save a life?

6.25 Airline travel would be safer if pilots had more training and more rest between flights, if planes were inspected more often and more thoroughly, and if older planes were scrapped. Each of these changes has a cost. How should people compare these costs with the additional safety that they would buy? How much training and rest should pilots get? How often and how thoroughly should planes be inspected? Could any general principles guide these decisions?

---

[8]The death rate for car travel in a recent year was 22 deaths per billion passenger miles, while the death rate for airline travel was about 0.3 deaths per billion passenger miles.

[9]Some surprising implications grow out of the observations that people routinely sacrifice safety for other values and that there is an equilibrium quantity of safety. For example, laws that require use of seat belts in cars lead people to drive less carefully. (If you doubt the truth of this, ask yourself whether you would try to drive even more carefully if your seat belt were broken; most people answer yes.) Lower speed limits, when enforced, have similar effects. As a result, seat belt laws and lower speed limits save fewer lives than they would without these changes in behavior.

Social and Economic Issues

Gaining from the Misfortunes of Others

Emergencies are inevitable. A fire, hurricane, flood, or earthquake may destroy homes or a whole city; a traffic accident or an assault may cause injuries that require immediate care. Some people benefit from each of these disasters. Construction companies—and their workers—gain from the added demand to rebuild houses destroyed by natural disasters and health-care workers earn their pay by treating medical problems. Mental-health professionals gain customers whose lives fall apart because of unemployment or other misfortune; companies benefit if their competitors go out of business.

Is it fair that some people gain from the misfortunes of others? Although economics cannot answer that question, it can shed light on the consequences of laws or regulations that would prevent people from gaining from others' misfortunes. This can help people decide whether any such law or regulation would be good or bad.

Suppose that a natural disaster destroys homes and raises the demand for shelter, clothing, beds, medical supplies, and other goods. The increases in demand for these goods raise their prices in the stricken area. These higher prices give sellers the incentive to raise the quantities of these goods that they supply to the area. (The higher prices make it in the self-interest of suppliers to provide the goods, so victims of the disaster do not have to rely on the altruism of others.) Sellers respond to the higher prices in two ways. They raise production of housing, beds, medical supplies, and other goods, and they divert supplies to the disaster area from outside that area. These decreases in supply in other areas area raise prices there, and these higher prices induce people who are not victims of the disaster to reduce their use of resources needed in the disaster area.

Decreased purchases by people outside the disaster area leave more resources available for disaster victims. For example, an increase in the cost of medical supplies leads hospitals in the rest of the country to use less where they can, freeing these supplies for sale to the disaster victims. Even buyers who are unaware of the disaster reduce their purchases of the goods that are in higher demand in the disaster area. Similarly, sellers who are unaware of the disaster also raise their quantities supplied to the stricken area because the higher prices make it profitable. Sellers benefit from the higher prices, but the victims of the disaster also benefit; they gain the opportunity to buy goods, albeit at higher prices, rather than doing without them.

Some people find it unfair that sellers benefit from higher prices when a disaster occurs. Critics suggest that the government prevent sellers from raising prices above "normal" levels in a disaster area, or that the government tax away the "excess" profits made by sellers who gain from the misfortunes of others without these steps. What would be the results of government programs like these? Without higher prices (or with higher prices offset by higher taxes) sellers would lack the self-interest incentive to raise the quantity of beds, medical supplies, and other goods they would supply to the disaster area. Altruism for disaster victims would no longer be assisted by help motivated by self-interest. Sellers would lack the financial incentive to produce more of the goods that the victims need, and buyers in other areas would lack the financial incentive to buy fewer of these goods.

The mere prospect that sellers can profit if a disaster strikes gives them an incentive to keep supplies readily available in the event of a disaster. This should not be surprising; after all, the mere prospect that someone might die keeps funeral businesses going even on days when no one dies, and the mere prospect that an ambulance might be needed keeps private ambulance companies in business on days without accidents. (The prospect of future demand induces these suppliers to buy ambulances and other equipment.) Similarly, the mere prospect of a disaster gives suppliers an incentive to make sure that they will be able to supply the goods that victims will need.

ECONOMICS OF EVERYDAY LIFE

IN THE NEWS

Former executive happily traded rat race for slow pace of Montana

By Dave Zelio
The Associated Press

CASCADE, Mont.—Pasquale, 53, can't help but smile whenever he talks about leaving the rat race in Washington, D.C., for a slower-paced life in rural Montana—something many executives only dream of doing.

He says only that his "substantially lower" salary is offset by other, greater rewards.

The lifestyle you want is for sale.

Source: Dave Zelio, "Former Executive Happily Traded Rat Race for Slow Pace of Montana," *Rochester Democrat and Chronicle*, January 31, 1993, p. 9F.

LIFESTYLES

You can buy a less stressful lifestyle by choosing a less stressful job; the price you pay is a lower wage. **Figure 6.11** shows the supply and demand for labor services in stressful jobs and peaceful jobs. The equilibrium wage for the stressful job is W_1^S and the equilibrium wage for the peaceful job is W_1^P. The stressful job pays a higher wage, and the difference in the wages $(W_1^S - W_1^P)$ is the price of the more peaceful lifestyle.

The same reasoning applies to other characteristics of jobs. People can buy increased job security, independence, schedule flexibility, or ability to take vacations or family leaves. Jobs with better characteristics usually pay lower wages than other jobs that require the same amount of education. The wage difference is the cost of the increased job security or other characteristic.

HONESTY AND OTHER VALUES

Honesty, fairness, compassion, patriotism, and other values also have prices, and their quantities demanded depend on their prices. People usually buy less honesty when its price rises; they tell more lies when they expect greater benefits from those lies. Athletes are more likely to cheat by using performance-enhancing drugs before important athletic events than unimportant events, and before events where they are less likely to be caught. Politicians are more likely to vote based on their beliefs on the merits of an issue when they are not tempted or pressured by lobbyists. Married people are more likely to cheat on their spouses when an attractive opportunity arises or when a marriage has deteriorated so that the benefits of remaining married to the same person have declined. The temptation to deal illegal drugs is high when a dealer can earn thousands of dollars a week; more people choose illegal jobs when earnings from those jobs are high. People are more willing to help others when helping costs less time, effort, or money.

People's willingness to choose more honesty when its price is lower explains why soft-drink vending machines and newspaper vending machines differ. Many newspaper dispensers open so that a buyer could take several newspapers after paying for only one. Soft-drink dispensers, on the other hand, prevent people from taking more than a single can at a time. The vending machines differ because people are unlikely to be dishonest when the benefits are small; few people want a second newspaper, but when the benefits of dishonesty are larger, as in the case of soft drinks, more people would choose dishonesty (if they could) by taking a second or third drink without paying.

These examples make two points. First, living according to certain values has an opportunity cost; people sacrifice something to be honest, fair, caring, or patriotic. Second, a change in the prices of these values can change behavior; people are less willing to live by these values when doing so entails larger sacrifices. When laws, customs, and social institutions make certain values more costly, fewer people adopt these values.

DOWRIES

In certain countries, such as India, marriage often involves an exchange of a *dowry*. When people marry, the woman (or her family) pays a dowry to the man. Marriages in some other countries, such as Egypt, often involve exchanges of *bride prices* paid by men to women. The size of the dowry or bride price is influ-

FIGURE 6.11

STRESSFUL AND PEACEFUL LIFESTYLES

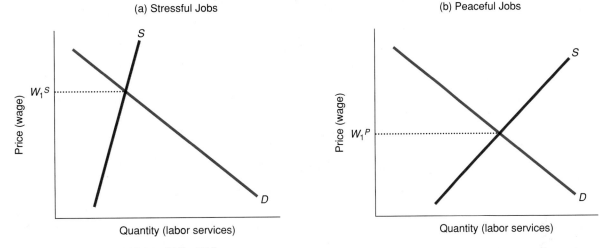

(a) Stressful Jobs

(b) Peaceful Jobs

The price of a more peaceful job is $W_1^S - W_1^P$.

Highway robbery! Aluminum thieves take metal and run

Current high price attracts pilferers to road signs, guardrails and light poles

By James P. Miller
Staff Reporter of The
Wall Street Journal

Don't look now, but robbers are dismantling America's highways.

Thieves are sweeping the USA, stealing traffic and road signs, guardrails, fire hydrant stems, even house siding, to cash in on scrap metal prices.

Increased prices for brass, copper and aluminum—up between 40 and 90 percent—are fueling the recent crime wave.

Psst, Got Any Extra Coke Cans?

It isn't just big-time crooks who are playing the metals game. The city of Mountain View, Calif., recently cracked down on "organized rings" stealing bags of aluminum soda cans left outside homes for recycling. And even awnings have become the object of larcenous desire. "People go on vacation and when they come back their aluminum patio covers have been stolen," says Detective Readhimer.

Criminals respond to incentives.

Source: James P. Miller, "Highway Robbery! Aluminum Thieves Take Metal and Run," *The Wall Street Journal*, September 22, 1988; and *USA Today*, January 23, 1989.

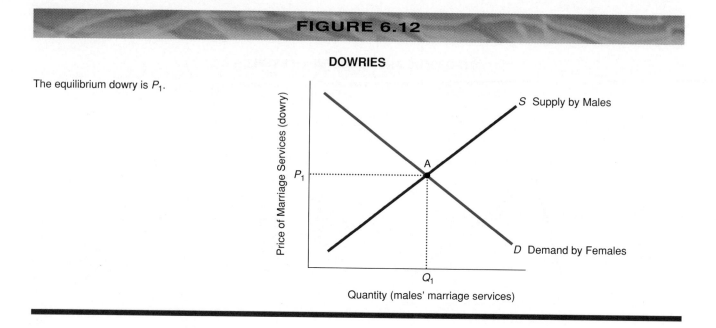

FIGURE 6.12

The equilibrium dowry is P_1.

DOWRIES

enced partly by culture and tradition, but also partly by economics. Think of a dowry as part of a price that a woman or her family pays to a man for his marriage services. **Figure 6.12** shows the supply of males' marriage services, S, and the demand for males' marriage services by females, D. At the equilibrium (Point A) the equilibrium dowry is P_1.

This analysis of dowries can combine with the earlier analysis of the price of quality. Indian women can marry men from higher social classes by paying larger dowries. In other words, they can buy higher-class husbands by paying higher prices.

CHILDREN

Although people do not (usually) buy children, raising children has a cost or price. Parents spend both money and time to raise children. The money price includes many items from prenatal medical expenses to food, clothing, a larger apartment or house, and the child's recreational expenses. The average money price of raising a child varies across families; estimates range from about $6,000 to $10,000 by the child's first birthday. The time price of children is also large, but some parents reduce it by buying child-care services or simply spending less time with their children.

Throughout most of history, the demand for children by farm families has exceeded the demand by city families. Food and housing were cheaper on farms than in cities, and farm children helped with work. These factors made the price of children lower for farm families than for city families. This price difference fell when farming became more mechanized because children could not help as much as they had. When the price difference fell, the difference in the average sizes of farm and city families also fell.

IN THE NEWS

Tens of thousands of Indian women, poor and rich alike, have undergone amniocentesis for the sole purpose of learning whether their fetus is a boy or girl. If it is a girl, they have an abortion; if it is a boy, they don't.

The reason for this strong preference for male babies is both traditional and economic. In many parts of India, boys are perceived as an economic benefit; girls are perceived as an economic burden. Although marriage dowries are technically illegal in India, they persist. And the price for marrying off a daughter can run as high as $10,000—the equivalent of a year's salary for a middle-class Indian. Several daughters and no sons can be a prescription for bankruptcy.

The Indian state of Maharashtra has opted for a law that bans any prenatal test to determine a fetus' sex. This has driven the testing underground or to other states with no such laws. The economic pressures are simply too great on families with several daughters.

Economic forces affect decisions about children, sometimes tragically.
Source: Rochester Democrat and Chronicle, August 15, 1988.

Sometimes the costs of raising boys and girls differ, and this affects demand. Rates of female infanticide and abortion of female fetuses (after medical tests to determine the sex of the fetus) are reported to be higher in northern India than in southern India. Stronger boys can provide more help raising wheat in the north, while girls are as valuable as boys for raising rice in the south. Because the cost of raising a child is lower when the child can help on a farm, the cost of girls is higher than the cost of boys in the north, while the costs are about the same in the south. This cost difference helps explain why the preference for boys over girls is less strong in southern India than in the north.

The demand for children falls when a woman's wage rises, because women usually provide the largest time-input into children for both biological and cultural reasons. The higher wage raises the price of children because it raises the opportunity cost of the woman's time. Economic forces also affect the timing of child-bearing; the demand for children is lower for those women in their teens and twenties who spend more time acquiring education. For this reason, expanded education programs for women tend to reduce population growth.

QUESTIONS

6.26 Suppose that people's tastes change and they want to switch from stressful to peaceful jobs. Draw graphs to show how this increase in demand for a peaceful job affects wages in stressful jobs and peaceful jobs.

6.27 Alan Dershowitz, a Harvard law professor, has argued that parents in some countries choose abortions or even infanticide for female babies because they prefer male babies due to tradition and to the high cost of dowries. His argument goes on, "If this is allowed to continue and expand, it could affect the natural balance between males and females. Throughout history, of course, there have been other factors that have skewed the proportion of males and females: wars, certain sex-linked illnesses, even crime."[10] Use supply-and-demand analysis to discuss the effect on the size of dowries if the number of females per male in the society were to decrease.

--------- INQUIRIES FOR FURTHER THOUGHT ---------

6.28 Some people claim that you cannot buy friends. Can you? What kind of nonmoney prices would you pay? What factors affect your demand for friends?

6.29 Can people find higher-quality romantic partners by paying higher prices? (The prices may not involve money; they may involve more time to search for the right person, to improve oneself, or to devote to a relationship.) Does romance implicitly involve a money price? Could someone find a higher-quality partner if he or she were richer and shared this weath with a partner?

ASSIGNING BLAME FOR PRICE INCREASES

When the demand for a good changes, it sets into motion a whole chain of events, which can have deceptive consequences. Suppose that the demand for beef rises. Grocers sell more beef, so they increase their orders from meat-packers. Meat-packers, in turn, increase their orders from cattle buyers, who increase their orders from cattle raisers. The increase in demand for cattle raises their price.

This price increase raises cattle buyers' costs. They pay more for cattle, so they charge higher prices to meat-packers. This raises meat-packers' costs, so they charge grocers higher prices for beef. This raises the grocer's costs, so grocers charge consumers higher prices for beef.

If you ask the grocer about the reason for the higher price for beef, she will explain that her costs have risen. She might say, "Beef prices rose because costs increased." And she is correct, but her statement is nevertheless deceptive. It would be wrong to blame "middlemen" (such as meat-packers) or cattle raisers for the higher price. They did not become greedier or more cunning than they had been. Grocers' costs increased because the demand for beef increased. The price of cattle affects the price of beef, but the price of beef also affects the price of cattle. Both respond to a change in the demand for beef. More generally, an increase in the demand for a product can raise both its price and its cost of production by raising the prices of the inputs used to produce it. In this way, a change in demand can change sellers' costs. A rise in costs might appear to cause a price increase when both actually result from a rise in demand. Appearances can be deceiving.

ADJUSTMENT TO EQUILIBRIUM

Market equilibrium is a situation in which quantity demanded equals quantity supplied. When a market is in equilibrium, the price and quantity traded tend to remain constant until supply or demand changes. When a market is in disequilibrium, the price tends to move toward the equilibrium price. The price tends to

---

[10]Alan Dershowitz, quoted in the *Rochester Democrat and Chronicle*, August 15, 1988.

rise to eliminate any shortage; the price tends to fall to eliminate any surplus. In either case, the price and quantity traded tend to move toward equilibrium. This adjustment to equilibrium follows any change in demand or supply that changes the equilibrium price and quantity.

Price adjustments take only a few seconds or minutes in some markets, such as the stock market and other financial markets. Prices in other markets may take much longer to adjust. Retail stores, for example, often put price tags on goods and then buyers make their choices. It can take time for a seller to recognize a surplus or shortage of a good at some price. Even then, it may take time to change price tags. Some sellers publish catalogs with prices and wait for buyers to place orders. In these cases, price changes may take days, weeks, or even months.

EXAMPLES

Clothing stores put price tags on their clothes and wait to see what customers buy. If the store develops a surplus of green shirts because fewer people bought them than the store manager expected, the store has a sale and lowers the price. This may take weeks, however, because the store may initially believe that low sales of the shirt are temporary and that sales will soon increase. Eventually, if sales remain low, the store will conclude that its price is above the equilibrium and it will reduce the price.

When a busload of people unexpectedly arrive at a fast-food restaurant, lines form to order burgers and fries. Demand rises for the restaurant's food, but the price does not increase immediately. Over a longer period of time, though, increases in demand at these restaurants raise their food prices.

—————————————————— FOR REVIEW ——————————————————

6.30 Explain why a price rise that may appear to result from an increase in costs actually results from an increase in demand.

6.31 Why does it take time (in some cases) for prices to adjust to new equilibrium levels after changes in demand?

KEY TERMS

private demand

market demand

government budget deficit

time price

QUESTIONS AND PROBLEMS

6.32 Do goods that last twice as long, or are twice as big, cost twice as much? Explain why or why not.

6.33 You can buy fame! Many colleges will name a building, classroom, or professorship after you for a price. Hospitals will name an operating room or patient's room after you. Sports facilities, gardens, and even seats at performing-arts centers have names for sale. What determines their prices?

6.34 Extend your imagination and develop a supply-and-demand analysis to predict the economic effects—the effects on the prices and quantities of various goods—of the following changes:
  a. The spread of AIDS
  b. A government anti-smoking campaign
  c. An increase in the average age of marriage
  d. An increase in the fraction of the population over age 65
  e. A new baby boom
  f. An increase in the number of women working outside the home
  g. A world-wide ban on products that harm the ozone layer
  h. A microelectronics revolution that makes supercomputers as cheap as shoes
  i. A major, conventional war in some part of the world
  j. A sudden and massive decrease in the demand for drugs

INQUIRIES FOR FURTHER THOUGHT

6.35 Single men in their twenties outnumber single women in their twenties in the United States by about a six-to-five ratio. (For every five women, there are six men.) A generation ago, the numbers were more equal. The ratio of men to women also varies across cities in the United States. What do you think are the results of the increase in the supply of men relative to the supply of women? What do you think are the effects of differences across cities? How might the economics of supply and demand apply to this situation?

IN THE NEWS

After first driving overland to Bulgaria, where the border guards refused him entry, he returned to Istanbul and eventually paid $300 to a man who promised to show him how to cross the frontier into Greece.

He cannot allow his real name to be used, so he asked to be called Ali. The lucky ones, he said, the ones who could pay $7,000 for a Canadian visa in Istanbul or buy a fake passport, or those with blood relatives in Frankfurt or London, have already gotten out.

Source: The Washington Post, March 15, 1989, p. A26.

6.36 Should the government limit the extent to which sellers profit from the misfortunes of others?

   a. If not, explain why not, then answer the following questions: Suppose that a woman sees a man about to drown. She yells to the drowning man, "I will save you if you give me your life savings!" The man yells "Okay, I promise!" and she saves him. Should the courts enforce his promise, or should the government limit profits made in this way from the misfortunes of others? Under what conditions, if any, should the government limit profits made from the misfortunes of others?

   b. If so, how? Does your argument suggest that the government should limit the incomes doctors earn by treating patients? Should it limit the gains of farmers from selling food to people who have the misfortune to be hungry? Doesn't a plumber gain from a person's misfortune to have clogged pipes? Doesn't every seller gain from the misfortune of buyers? How would you choose which gains to limit and which not to limit? What is your general principle for deciding?

6.37 It is possible to buy the right to immigrate to some countries; sometimes it is possible to buy citizenship in those countries. (Some of this trade is illegal.) What determines the price of immigration rights? Do you think that the United States should sell rights to immigrate to the highest bidders?

6.38 Do you think that the demand for democracy and freedom rises when people become richer? Does freedom ever have a price? Does democracy? For example, do countries ever sacrifice national security for freedom or democracy? (Perhaps national security could be improved by higher taxes to spend on defense, or by a military draft, or by permitting the police to search houses without search warrants.) Do countries ever sacrifice traditional cultures for freedom or democracy? What affects the demand for freedom? The demand for democracy?

TAG APPLICATION SOFTWARE

TUTORIAL EXERCISES
▶ This module reviews the key terms from Chapter 6.

GRAPHING EXERCISES
▶ Applications of supply and demand are reviewed.

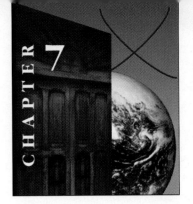

CHAPTER 7

INTERNATIONAL TRADE, ARBITRAGE, AND SPECULATION: APPLICATIONS OF SUPPLY AND DEMAND

P. 163 – 170 (only)

WHAT THIS CHAPTER IS ABOUT

▶ How supply and demand affect international trade (exports and imports)

▶ Arbitrage (buying goods to resell elsewhere)

▶ Speculation (buying goods to resell in the future)

▶ Winners and losers from international trade, arbitrage, and speculation

▶ International borrowing and lending

▶ Introduction to futures markets and the stock market

Y̲ou are part of a world economy. Events in distant countries touch your life, and your future will be affected by economic growth and government economic policies around the globe. The world economy is more integrated than ever before. Each year, people in the United States export goods and services worth nearly $3,000 per person—about one-tenth of total U.S. output—and import even more. This international trade has been growing, as well. In 1970, the United States exported only one-twentieth of its total output. More people's jobs involve producing goods for international trade than ever before. Changes in supplies and demands around the world affect economic conditions—prices, wages, employment—in every U.S. city and town.

163

Just as international trade links the economies of different nations, interregional trade between cities, towns, and states connects the economies of regions within a country. An earthquake in California affects prices, wages, and employment in Virginia. Economic changes in Michigan affect people in Texas.

Speculation creates economic links across time, between today and the future. People's expectations about the future affect today's economy. The prices people pay this week for food, houses, and other goods, and quantities of these goods supplied, depend on expectations about the future.

This chapter explains why the supply and demand for a good at any place or any time is related to the supplies and demands for the good at other locations and other times. It applies supply-and-demand analysis to three issues: international trade, interregional trade, and speculation. The same type of supply-demand diagram can illustrate all three issues.

INTERNATIONAL TRADE

The United States exports wheat, corn, cotton, chemicals, plastics, construction and industrial machinery, scientific equipment, computers, aircraft, and many other goods to foreign countries. It imports coffee, cocoa, crude oil, important raw materials (such as bauxite, cobalt, platinum, chromium, nickel, tin, and zinc), automobiles, clothing, toys, consumer electronic equipment such as televisions and audio equipment, and many other products.[1] Why does the U.S. economy export computers and import televisions rather than exporting televisions and importing computers? What economic factors affect a country's exports or imports of a good? How do changes in demand or supply in one country affect prices and outputs in other countries? Supply-and-demand analysis can illuminate these questions.

EQUILIBRIUM WITH INTERNATIONAL TRADE

Figure 7.1 shows how to graph international trade. Three side-by-side supply-and-demand diagrams illustrate markets in the United States, other countries, and the world as a whole. Without international trade, each country's curves would determine its equilibrium price and quantity traded. With international trade, world supply and demand determine the equilibrium price. The quantity supplied in each country at the equilibrium price shows the amount that each country produces. The quantity demanded in each country at the world equilibrium price shows the amount that each country consumes.

consumption of a good — the amount of a good people use for their current benefit (wearing, eating, driving, or watching the good, for example)

People consume a good when they use it to satisfy their wants; **consumption** is the total quantity consumed over some period of time.[2]

People consume a good when they wear it, eat it, drive it, or watch it.

export — a sale to a buyer in another country

import — a purchase from a seller in another country

A country **exports** a good when it sells the good to buyers in other countries. A country **imports** a good when it buys the good from foreign producers.

---

[1]Further discussion of international trade appears in a later chapter.

[2]Consumption does not include the use of a good to produce another good. (For example, the steel used to make an automobile is not part of consumption.)

FIGURE 7.1

INTERNATIONAL TRADE IN FILM

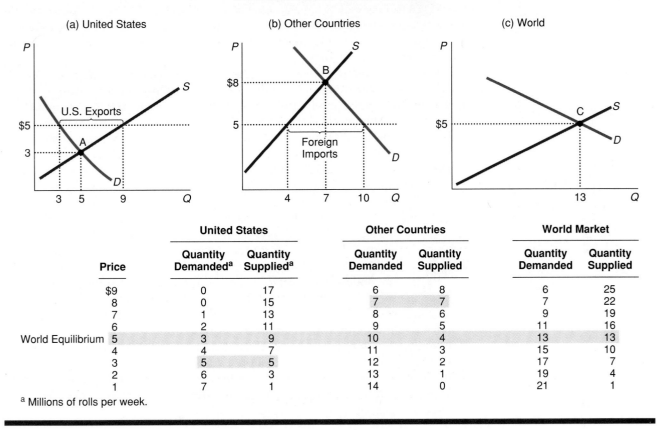

(a) United States

(b) Other Countries

(c) World

	United States		Other Countries		World Market	
Price	Quantity Demanded[a]	Quantity Supplied[a]	Quantity Demanded	Quantity Supplied	Quantity Demanded	Quantity Supplied
$9	0	17	6	8	6	25
8	0	15	7	7	7	22
7	1	13	8	6	9	19
6	2	11	9	5	11	16
World Equilibrium 5	3	9	10	4	13	13
4	4	7	11	3	15	10
3	5	5	12	2	17	7
2	6	3	13	1	19	4
1	7	1	14	0	21	1

[a] Millions of rolls per week.

A country exports a good if it produces more of that good than it consumes. (It exports the rest.) A country imports a good if it consumes more of that good than it produces.[3] One country's exports are another's imports.

EXPLANATION AND EXAMPLE

Figure 7.1a (labeled "United States") shows the supply and demand for film in the United States. The U.S. demand curve shows the quantities demanded at various prices by buyers in the United States. Similarly, the U.S. supply curve shows the quantities supplied at various prices by producers in the United States. Without international trade, equilibrium would occur at Point A at an equilibrium U.S. price of $3 and an equilibrium quantity of 5 million rolls of film per week.

Figure 7.1b (labeled "Other Countries") shows the demand and supply for film in all other countries. The foreign supply and demand curves refer to demand

---

[3]The discussion in this chapter applies to consumer goods (it abstracts from investment and uses of goods as inputs to produce other goods). A more complete analysis would replace the term *consumes* in the text with the phrase "consumes, invests, or uses as intermediate inputs."

by buyers in other countries and supply by foreign producers. Without international trade, the foreign equilibrium would occur at Point B at an equilibrium foreign price of film of $8 and an equilibrium quantity of 7 million rolls per week.[4]

Without international trade, the foreign equilibrium price exceeds the U.S. price. U.S. sellers would have an incentive to sell film in foreign countries at the higher price. Buyers in other countries would have an incentive to buy film from the United States at the lower price. The price difference creates incentives for international trade.

Figure 7.1c shows demand and supply by all buyers and sellers in the world.[5] World demand and supply determine the equilibrium price and quantity for an internationally traded good. At world equilibrium (Point C) the world equilibrium price is $5 and the world equilibrium quantity is 13 million rolls per week.

A horizontal line in Figure 7.1 shows the world equilibrium price of $5. At that price, the supply curves in the three panels show the quantities supplied in the United States, other countries, and the world market. The demand curves in the three panels show the quantity bought by people in the United States, other countries, and the world. At the equilibrium price of $5, the quantity of film demanded by U.S. buyers is 3 million rolls per week, as the U.S. demand curve shows. The quantity of film supplied by U.S. producers is 9 million rolls per week, as the U.S. supply curve shows. The United States produces and sells 9 million rolls per week, consumes 3 million, and exports 6 million.

Figure 7.1b shows that foreign countries import film from the United States. The foreign supply curve shows that foreign countries produce 4 million rolls per week; the foreign demand curve shows that they consume 10 million rolls. Foreign countries import 6 million rolls per week from the United States.

Notice that foreign imports equal U.S. exports. The horizontal distance between a country's demand and supply curves at the equilibrium price shows that country's equilibrium exports or imports. If a country's quantity supplied exceeds its quantity demanded, it exports the good; if its quantity demanded exceeds its quantity supplied, it imports the good.

ANOTHER WAY TO FIND THE EQUILIBRIUM PRICE

You do not need the graph in Figure 7.1c to find the equilibrium price. Instead, you can use trial-and-error to find the price at which one country's exports equal the other's imports. If you guess a price that is too high (above the equilibrium price of $5), the graph in Figure 7.1a will show U.S. exports of more than 6 million rolls per week (the horizontal distance between the supply and demand curves will exceed 6 million), and Figure 7.1b will show that other countries import less than 6 million rolls per week. This is not an equilibrium because U.S. exports do not equal foreign imports.

If, instead, you guess a price that is too low (below the equilibrium price of $5), Figure 7.1a will show U.S. exports of less than 6 million rolls per week, while Figure 7.1b will show other countries importing more than 6 million rolls. Again,

---

[4]Foreign prices are usually quoted in a foreign money such as yen, francs, or pesos. The $8 price refers to the dollar value of the foreign price.

[5]Chapter 4 showed how to derive the market demand curve from the demand curves of individual buyers. Figure 7.1 derives the world market demand curve from the demand curves of individual countries. It then repeats this procedure for supply.

this is not an equilibrium because U.S. exports do not equal foreign imports. Only at the equilibrium price ($5) do U.S. exports of the good equal foreign imports. (The horizontal distance by which U.S. supply exceeds U.S. demand equals the horizontal distance by which demand exceeds supply in other countries.)

WINNERS AND LOSERS FROM INTERNATIONAL TRADE

Some people gain from international trade while others lose. Without international trade, the U.S. price of film would be $3 and the foreign price would be $8. International trade moves the price to $5 in all countries. U.S. film buyers lose from international trade in film because it raises the price they pay. U.S. film manufacturers gain from international trade because they can sell film at a higher price, and they choose to sell more film as a result (9 million rolls rather than 5 million rolls per week). Foreign buyers gain from international trade in film because it reduces the price they pay from $8 to $5 per roll. Foreign sellers lose from international trade in film because it reduces the price at which they can sell their film.

Chapter 11 will show how to compare the sizes of these gains and losses, concluding that the winners from international trade gain more than the losers lose; U.S. sellers gain more from international trade than U.S. buyers lose, and foreign buyers gain more than foreign sellers lose. As a result, international trade is economically efficient.

CHANGES IN SUPPLY AND DEMAND IN INTERNATIONAL TRADE

International trade brings reactions from an economy to changes in foreign demand or supply. Questions at the end of this chapter ask you to evaluate changes in U.S. demand or supply.

IN THE NEWS

U.S. drought a reprieve to South American farmers

Los Angeles Times

BUENOS AIRES, Argentina — This summer's drought may be devastating for North American farmers, but it has handed a multibillion dollar bonanza to grain growers in Argentina and Brazil, generating a glimmer of optimism in an otherwise desperate economic climate.

Argentina expects a windfall of up to $2 billion in extra revenue from agricultural exports because of higher prices this year, government officials said.

Nearly half the bonus is attributed directly to the drought in the United States and Canada.

In Brazil, too, agriculture ministry officials predicted an increase in farm exports of $1.2 billion this year, thanks to the extra price surge caused by the drought.

"I am sorry for the Americans, but I am happy for our own farmers, who have suffered for years," said Fernando Miguez, 37, a Buenos Aires agronomist who also is co-owner of a 340-acre farm in Rojas, near Buenos Aires.

A fall in U.S. supply raises both the world price and U.S. imports.

Source: "U.S. Drought a Reprieve to S. American Farmers," *Rochester Democrat and Chronicle*, August 14, 1988.

FIGURE 7.2

EFFECTS OF A RISE IN FOREIGN DEMAND

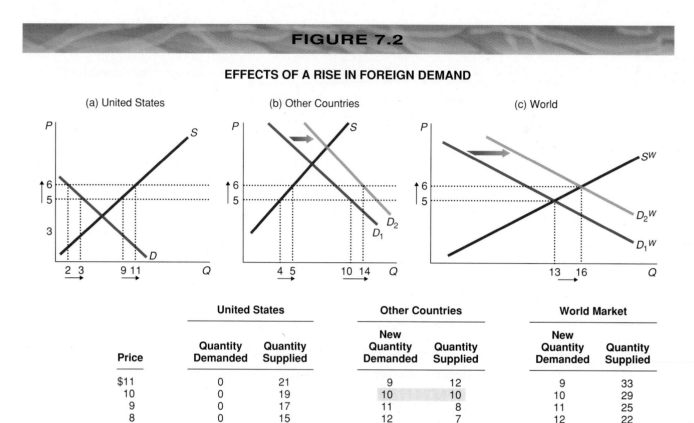

(a) United States   (b) Other Countries   (c) World

	United States		Other Countries		World Market	
Price	Quantity Demanded	Quantity Supplied	New Quantity Demanded	Quantity Supplied	New Quantity Demanded	Quantity Supplied
$11	0	21	9	12	9	33
10	0	19	10	10	10	29
9	0	17	11	8	11	25
8	0	15	12	7	12	22
7	1	13	13	6	14	19
New Equilibrium 6	2	11	14	5	16	16
Old Equilibrium → 5	3	9	15	4	18	13
Price (Figure 7.1) 4	4	7	16	3	20	10
3	5	5	17	2	22	7
2	6	3	18	1	24	4

RISE IN FOREIGN DEMAND

Figure 7.2 shows how a rise in foreign demand for film affects its price, output in each country, consumption in each country, and international trade. If foreign demand rises by 5 million rolls of film per week, the foreign demand curve shifts to the right by that amount. This raises world market demand and shifts the world market demand curve to the right by 5 million rolls. The equilibrium price rises from $5 to $6 and the equilibrium quantity rises from 13 million to 16 million rolls per week.

Output of film rises in each country, because the price increase raises the quantity supplied. U.S. film output rises from 9 million to 11 million rolls per week; output in other countries rises from 4 million to 5 million. Altogether, total world output of film rises from 13 million to 16 million. The higher price reduces U.S. consumption of film from 3 million to 2 million rolls per week. Film consumption in other countries rises from 10 million to 14 million rolls per week. (Notice that foreign consumption rises by 4 million rolls even though foreign demand increased by 5 million rolls. Foreign consumption rises by less than the increase in demand because the price increase reduces the foreign quantity demanded from 15 million to 14 million rolls.) U.S. film exports rise from 6 million to 9 million rolls per week because the United States produces more film and consumes less; foreign film imports also rise from 6 million to 9 million.

RISE IN FOREIGN SUPPLY

Figure 7.3 shows that a rise in the foreign supply of film by 5 million rolls per week reduces the world equilibrium price from $5 to $4 and raises the world quantity traded from 13 million to 15 million rolls per week.

U.S. output of film falls from 9 million to 7 million rolls per week, and U.S. film consumption rises from 3 million to 4 million rolls, so U.S. exports of film fall from 6 million to 3 million rolls per week. Foreign output of film rises from 4 million to 8 million rolls and foreign film consumption rises from 10 million to 11 million, so foreign imports fall from 6 million to 3 million rolls per week.

--- FOR REVIEW ---

7.1 Define *consumption, exports,* and *imports.*

7.2 Draw three graphs side by side to show equilibrium in the world market for corn, U.S. exports of corn, and foreign imports of corn.

FIGURE 7.3

EFFECTS OF AN INCREASE IN FOREIGN SUPPLY

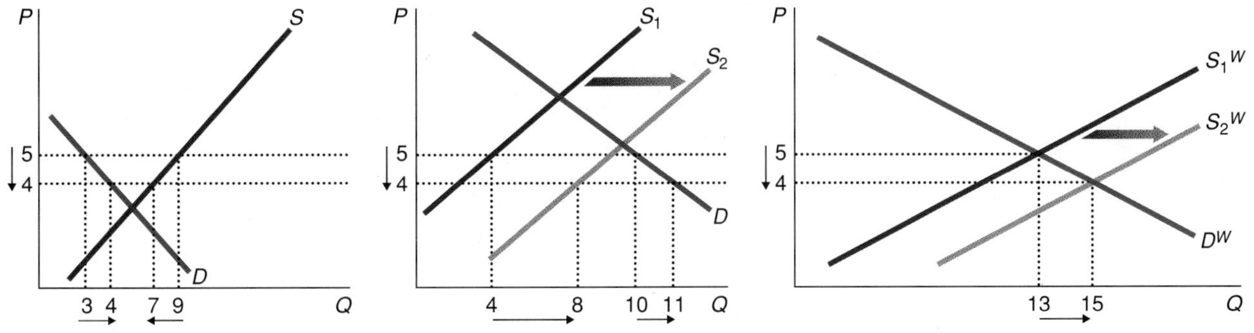

(a) United States   (b) Other Countries   (c) World

	United States		Other Countries		World Market	
Price	Quantity Demanded	Quantity Supplied	Quantity Demanded	New Quantity Supplied	Quantity Demanded	New Quantity Supplied
$9	0	17	6	13	6	30
8	0	15	7	12	7	27
Old Equilibrium 7	1	13	8	11	9	24
Price (Figure 7.1) 6	2	11	9	10	11	21
→ 5	3	9	10	9	13	18
New Equilibrium 4	4	7	11	8	15	15
3	5	5	12	7	17	12
2	6	3	13	6	19	9
1	7	1	14	5	21	6

─────────────────────── **QUESTIONS** ───────────────────────

7.3 Who would gain and who would lose if foreign governments were to prohibit imports of film from the United States?

7.4 Explain why an increase in the foreign supply of film reduces output of film in the United States.

ARBITRAGE

arbitrage — buying a good at a place where its price is low and selling it where its price is higher

The price of lobsters does not vary much between cities near ocean ports and cities far from the ocean. The price of corn does not vary much between America's heartland and Boston or San Francisco. Prices of many goods tend to be about the same in different places. This results from arbitrage.

> **Arbitrage** is the process of buying something at a place where its price is low, and selling it where its price is higher.

If a good sells at a much higher price in one place than another, people arbitrage—they buy it in the low-price place and resell it in the high-price place. This raises the price in the low-price location and lowers the price in the high-price location, which tends to equalize prices in the two places.

price differential — a difference between the prices of identical goods in two different locations

> A **price differential** is a difference between the prices of identical goods in two different locations.

Arbitrage tends to eliminate price differentials.

Anyone can arbitrage. Producers arbitrage when they decide to sell more goods where the price is high and fewer where the price is low. Other people arbitrage by buying and then reselling goods. Some people have full-time jobs arbitraging financial markets, such as stock markets; they spend their days checking financial prices in different locations, looking for price differentials to eliminate.[6]

Arbitrage has a cost. The arbitrager must identify the price differential, go to the low-price location, buy the goods, ship them to the higher-price location, and find buyers there. If the price differential across locations is small, people will not find it worthwhile (profitable) to arbitrage. For this reason, the cost of arbitrage puts an upper bound on price differentials.

arbitrage opportunity — a recognized price differential that exceeds the costs of arbitrage

> You have an **arbitrage opportunity** if you know about a price differential that exceeds your costs of arbitrage.

It is hard to find real-life arbitrage opportunities because they disappear quickly as people take advantage of them. In equilibrium, they vanish:

> In equilibrium, there are no arbitrage opportunities.

When people have arbitrage opportunities, they can profit by additional arbitrage. This additional arbitrage reduces the price differential until the arbitrage opportunity disappears.

─────────────────────

[6]These people work for big banks and other financial institutions.

FIGURE 7.4

PRICE DIFFERENTIAL AND THE EFFECTS OF ARBITRAGE

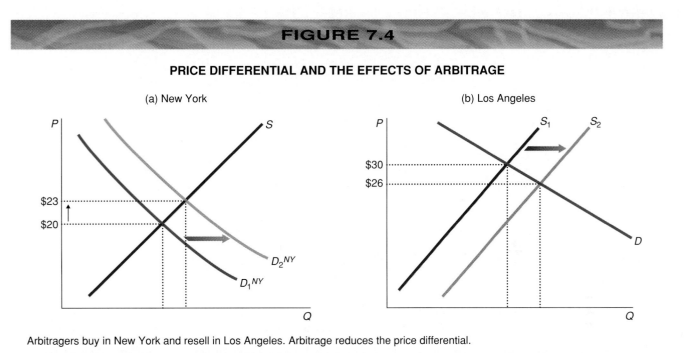

Arbitragers buy in New York and resell in Los Angeles. Arbitrage reduces the price differential.

EFFECTS OF ARBITRAGE

Figure 7.4 shows the effect of an arbitrage opportunity. People buy goods in New York and resell them at a higher price in Los Angeles. The increased demand in New York raises the price there from $20 to $23; the increase in supply in Los Angeles lowers the price there from $30 to $26. Arbitrage reduces the price differential.

The demand curve D_2^{NY} shows the demand in New York by everyone, including arbitragers, while D_1^{NY} shows the demand by everyone in New York *except* the arbitragers. Because arbitrage raises the price in New York, it raises production and reduces consumption of the good there. Because it lowers the price in Los Angeles, arbitrage reduces production and raises consumption of the good there.

Figure 7.4 shows an equilibrium if a $3 price differential does not provide people with an incentive to arbitrage more, by shipping a larger quantity of the good from New York to Los Angeles. If the costs of arbitrage are less than the new $3 price differential, however, people have an incentive for additional arbitrage. This raises the question, how much will arbitragers buy and resell? The following sections first discuss the simplest case which includes no costs of arbitrage.

EQUILIBRIUM WITH NO COSTS OF ARBITRAGE

When arbitrage costs nothing, the equilibrium price differential is zero. Any price differential creates an arbitrage opportunity, so all price differentials must disappear in equilibrium.

FIGURE 7.5

EQUILIBRIUM WITH NO-COST ARBITRAGE

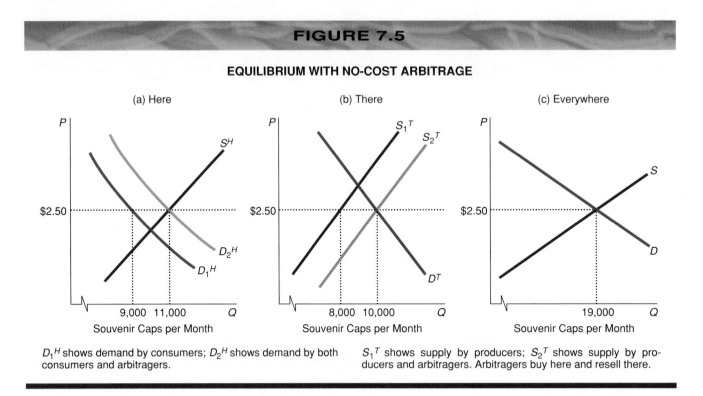

$D_1{}^H$ shows demand by consumers; $D_2{}^H$ shows demand by both consumers and arbitragers.

$S_1{}^T$ shows supply by producers; $S_2{}^T$ shows supply by producers and arbitragers. Arbitragers buy here and resell there.

Figure 7.5 shows an equilibrium with no costs of arbitrage.[7] Figure 7.5a, labeled "Here," shows supply and demand in one place; Figure 7.5b, labeled "There," shows supply and demand for the same good in another place. Figure 7.5c, labeled "Everywhere," shows the total market supply and demand. Figure 7.5 resembles Figure 7.1, but it applies to different cities rather than different countries. Without arbitrage, the supply and demand in each place determine the equilibrium in that place. With costless arbitrage, however, the equilibrium is determined by the supply and demand everywhere; the equilibrium price is $2.50 in both places.

The demand curve $D_1{}^H$ shows demand by everyone here except arbitragers, with equilibrium consumption here of 9,000 souvenir caps per month. The demand curve $D_2{}^H$ shows demand by all buyers here, including arbitragers. The supply curve shows supply by all producers here, so equilibrium production here is 11,000 caps per month. Arbitragers buy 2,000 per month here and resell them there. The supply curve $S_1{}^T$ shows supply by everyone there except arbitragers, so equilibrium production there is 8,000. The supply curve $S_2{}^T$ shows supply by everyone there, including arbitragers. Equilibrium consumption there is 10,000.

Figure 7.5 shows an equilibrium because the quantity supplied equals the quantity demanded, and no one has an incentive to change the amount of arbitrage from its current level of 2,000 units per month. If arbitrage were less than 2,000 caps per month, the price here would be lower than the price there, creating an

---

[7]In some real-life situations, such as financial markets, the costs of arbitrage are very small and the assumption no-cost arbitrage is a good approximation.

incentive to arbitrage more. That would not be an equilibrium. Similarly, if arbitrage were more than 2,000 caps per month, the price here would be above the price there, creating an incentive to arbitrage less. That would not be an equilibrium, either. The only equilibrium occurs when arbitrage is 2,000 caps per month.

Notice that arbitragers do *not* earn profits in equilibrium, because the price differential is zero. The best way to understand this is to think of a very small price differential that creates a profit just large enough to provide people with an incentive to buy and resell the goods.

HINT ON THINKING ABOUT ECONOMICS

Two of the most important questions economists ask themselves are:

▶ In this situation, what will people do to make themselves better off?

▶ When people do it, how will the situation change?

Asking these questions can help people think more clearly about economics. For example, suppose that the price of bandages in New Orleans is below the price in Columbus. What will people do to make themselves better off? They will buy bandages at the low price in New Orleans and resell them in Columbus.[8] Alternatively, bandage-makers might arbitrage by shipping fewer bandages to New Orleans and more to Columbus. Equilibrium occurs when people are *already* doing whatever is best for themselves; there is nothing else they can do (in this market) to make themselves better off.

WINNERS AND LOSERS FROM ARBITRAGE

Arbitrage, like international trade, creates winners and losers. Arbitrage raises the price of a good in one location and reduces it somewhere else. Sellers gain and buyers lose in the location where the price rises. Sellers lose and buyers gain in the location where the price falls. Chapter 11 will show that, because the winners gain more than the buyers lose, arbitrage (like international trade) is economically efficient.

EQUILIBRIUM WITH COSTLY ARBITRAGE

Now consider cases in which arbitrage has a cost. This cost can include money and time costs of purchasing goods in one place, transporting them to another place, and reselling them. Suppose that arbitrage costs total $2 per unit of the good. Arbitrage is profitable only if the price differential exceeds $2. If the good costs $12 here and $13 there, arbitrage is not profitable. If it costs $12 here and $15 there, however, arbitragers earn profits. Any price differential that exceeds $2 creates an arbitrage opportunity. Since equilibrium allows no arbitrage opportunities, the equilibrium price differential is $2 or less.

Figure 7.6 shows an equilibrium with costly arbitrage. The per-unit cost of arbitrage, $2, means that arbitragers must pay $2 to buy, ship, and resell each unit of the good. The price in Boston, $14, exceeds the price in Minneapolis, $12, by the cost of arbitrage. Output in Minneapolis is 200 units, consumption in Minneapolis is only 160 units, and arbitragers buy 40 units of the good in Minneapolis for resale in Boston. Consumption in Boston is 180 units and production is 140 units. Consumption exceeds production in Boston because arbitragers sell the goods they bought in Minneapolis, so Boston effectively imports 40 units from Minneapolis. In this way, arbitrage creates interregional trade.

---

[8]They would arbitrage as long as the price differential exceeded the cost of arbitrage.

FIGURE 7.6

EQUILIBRIUM WITH COSTLY ARBITRAGE

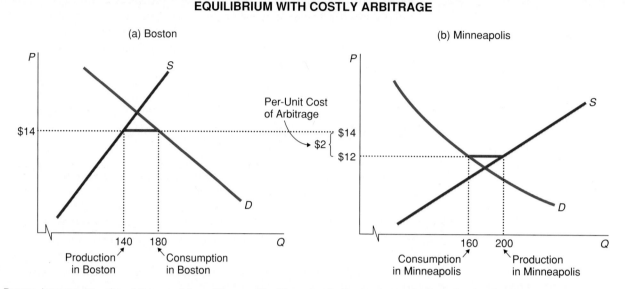

Boston imports 40 units of the good from Minneapolis. The price in Boston exceeds the price in Minnneapolis by the per-unit arbitrage cost, $2.

A price differential can occur in equilibrium when arbitrage is costly. You probably know many examples of goods that cost more in one place than another. These differentials occur because arbitrage is costly. Otherwise, everyone would buy in the low-price place, or some would buy in the low-price place and profit by reselling in the high-price place. The per-unit costs of arbitrage limit the sizes of price differentials.

Some goods have low costs of arbitrage and therefore have roughly the same prices in different cities. You can buy a stock, bond, or other financial asset for the same price in any city. The costs of arbitrage are very low because people can buy financial assets over the phone, through the mail, or by computer. Low arbitrage costs keep the prices of soap, paper, pencils, books, baseballs, light bulbs, plastic cups, and comic books roughly the same everywhere. Other goods have high costs of arbitrage, and their prices can differ substantially across locations. Costly arbitrage allows the prices of land, houses, auto repairs, and haircuts to differ from city to city. Land and houses cannot be transported cheaply from one city to another, nor can services such as auto repairs and haircuts. The supply and demand in each city determine the equilibrium in that city, as long as the price differential is smaller than the per-unit cost of arbitrage.

FOR REVIEW

7.5 What is arbitrage? What is an arbitrage opportunity?

7.6 Explain why equilibrium allows no arbitrage opportunities.

QUESTIONS

7.7 Suppose that arbitrage is costless. Explain why the equilibrium price differential is zero.

7.8 Who gains and who loses from arbitrage?

SPECULATION

speculation — buying a good when its price is low and storing it to sell in the future when its price might be higher

Speculators have a bad reputation. Many people think of speculation as an ethically questionable activity pursued by people seeking quick profits for little work effort. Most speculation, however, is rather mundane.

> **Speculation** is the process of buying something at a time when its price is low and storing it to sell later when its price might be higher (or storing it to use later).

The discussion in this section considers only storable goods such as lumber, rather than nonstorable goods such as fresh fish.

Speculation works like arbitrage or international trade across time rather than between locations or countries. Storing goods is like exporting them from the present to the future; using or selling stored goods is like importing them from the past.

Speculation differs from arbitrage or international trade in that the future is uncertain. Speculators risk the chance that the future price might be lower rather than higher. Whenever people plan for the future, whether speculating or planning a picnic, they base their plans on their beliefs or expectations about the future. Speculators expect to profit from speculation if they expect the prices of their goods to rise so that they can resell them at the higher, future prices. To avoid unnecessary complications, this discussion will consider only cases in which every speculator has the same expectations about the future.[9]

If people expect the price of a good to be much higher in the future than it is today, they speculate. They buy and store the good, planning to sell it at a higher price in the future. This activity raises the price today and reduces the expected future price, so it tends to make the expected future price equal to the price today.

Speculation, like arbitrage, may have a cost. If the expected future price increase is smaller than this cost, then speculation is not profitable. The cost of speculation puts an upper bound on the expected rise in the equilibrium price of a storable good. With costless speculation, a good's expected future price cannot exceed its current price.

EQUILIBRIUM WITH NO-COST SPECULATION

Figure 7.7 shows an equilibrium with speculation when there are no costs of speculating. Figure 7.7a shows supply and demand now. Figure 7.7b shows expected supply and demand next year. Figure 7.7 resembles Figures 7.1 and 7.5 except that it represents different times rather than different nations or regions.

---

[9]If people's expectations differ, those people who expect a high future price are likely to be the speculators, just as people who expect good weather are more likely to plan picnics than people who expect bad weather.

FIGURE 7.7

EQUILIBRIUM WITH COSTLESS SPECULATION

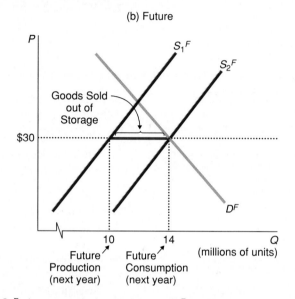

(a) Now

(b) Future

D_1^N shows demand by consumers; D_2^N shows demand by both consumers and speculators.

S_1^F shows supply by producers; S_2^F shows supply by both producers and speculators.

Without speculation, the expected future price exceeds today's price, creating an incentive for speculators to buy the good now, store it, and resell it in the future. Speculation raises current demand, and future supply [10]

With costless speculation, the equilibrium price now equals the expected future price, as in Figure 7.7. The reasoning is the same as in the discussion of arbitrage; if costs of arbitrage are zero, the equilibrium price is the same in both locations. Here the equilibrium price is the same in both time periods if speculation costs nothing.

The demand curve D_1^N shows current demand by everyone *except* speculators. Equilibrium consumption now is 8 units of the good. The demand curve labeled D_2^N shows the current demand by everyone, including speculators. Equilibrium output now is 12 units of the good; people consume 8 units, and speculators buy 4 to store for the future. The expected future demand curve is D^F. The expected future supply curve by everyone *except* speculators is S_1^F, and the expected future supply curve by everyone, including speculators, is S_2^F.

---

[10]The opposite would happen if speculators were to expect a future price below the current price. Speculators would try to profit by selling more of the good now and storing less for the future. This would raise current supply and reduce the current price, and it would decrease future supply and raise the expected future price. In equilibrium, the expected future price equals the current price. The situation becomes more complicated if the amount of the good that people store falls to zero because it becomes impossible to store less for the future. In that case, the current price can be above the expected future price, and speculators can do nothing to profit from the situation.

PERSONAL DECISION MAKING

Profiting from Differences in People's Expectations

When expectations about the future differ, people can gain from trade. Suppose that your friends expect your college football team to win its game against Rival State, and you know people at Rival State who expect *their* team to win. You can profit by arranging for these people to trade.

You issue an *asset* (or IOU) by writing on a piece of paper "I will pay the owner of this IOU $1 if our team wins." Call this the *home-team asset*. You then issue another asset: a piece of paper that says "I will pay the owner of this IOU $1 if Rival State wins." Call this the *Rival State asset*. You then *sell* these assets in equal numbers. (You must sell the same number of each kind of asset.)

People who expect your college's team to win will probably be willing to pay more than 50 cents for a home-team asset, which will pay $1 if your team wins. Someone who estimates your school's chances of winning at three out of four may be willing to pay up to 75 cents for this asset. This person will expect to *profit* by paying anything less than 75 cents. Suppose you sell this asset to the person for 60 cents.

Similarly, people who expect Rival State to win will probably be willing to pay more than 50 cents for the Rival State asset, which pays them $1 if Rival State wins. Someone who estimates the chance that Rival State will win at 60 percent may be willing to pay up to 60 cents, and this person will expect to profit by paying anything less. Suppose you sell the Rival State asset to this person for 55 cents.

You collect more than a dollar ($1.15) by selling these two assets. After the game, you will have to pay $1 to one person or the other, depending on which team wins, and you will keep 15 cents in profit. Obviously, the size of your profit depends on how many pairs of assets you sell, as well as the prices people are willing to pay for them. This idea generalizes to any difference in expectations about the future:

> When people have different expectations about the future, they can gain from trade.

Each person with whom you trade gains from the trade, regardless of who wins the football game. These gains are similar to the benefits people get from purchasing fire insurance, even if they are lucky and a fire never erupts in their home. When they purchase insurance, people are uncertain about the future, so they gain by buying the insurance. Similarly, people gain from buying your assets because they are uncertain about the outcome of the football game.

Many sophisticated financial assets (such as options and futures contracts) function like the assets described above, and they are traded every day in major cities around the world. These real-life financial assets create trades between people with different expectations about the future. Financial institutions such as banks and the New York Stock Exchange play the role that you played in the football example; they profit by bringing together people with differing expectations who expect to gain by buying these assets.

Note: The general rule is this: a person who estimates the chance that your team will win at p percent (such as 55 percent) will expect to break even by paying p cents for the home-team asset. Someone who estimates the chance of winning at 75 out of 100 will expect to break even by paying 75 cents for the asset. By paying any price less than 75 cents, this person will expect to profit from the home-team asset.

Speculators expect a future price of $30, future consumption of 14 units, and future output of 10. They plan to sell 4 units out of storage in the future.

Speculators, like arbitragers, earn zero expected profits in equilibrium. Positive expected profits would create incentives for people to increase the amount of speculation. Negative expected profits would create incentives to reduce the amount of speculation. Neither of those situations could be an equilibrium because both create tendencies for change. As in the discussion of arbitrage, the best way to understand this is to think of a very small expected price increase that would give speculators a profit just large enough to create an incentive to buy and store the goods for later resale.

Although expected profits are zero, the actual situation may eventually differ from what people expected. The figure shows the actual future price, output, and consumption if speculators' expectations are accurate. If speculators turn out to be wrong and the future price is below $30, speculators lose money. If the price turns out to be above $30, speculators profit. No matter what happens, future consumption is higher than future output because speculators sell the goods they have stored.

EQUILIBRIUM WITH COSTLY SPECULATION

Costly speculation alters this analysis slightly. Speculation can be costly for several reasons. First, speculators must pay to buy a good now, but they do not collect anything from selling goods until later, so a speculator ties up money in the speculation. Speculation has an opportunity cost equal to the interest income that the money could have earned in another investment or in a savings account. A speculator's opportunity cost (per dollar of speculation) is the interest rate.

IN THE NEWS

The speculator as hero

By Victor Niederhoffer

I am a speculator. I own seats on the Chicago Board of Trade and Chicago Mercantile Exchange. . . .

Like hundreds of thousands of other traders, I try to predict the prices of common goods a day or two or a few months in the future. If I think the price of an item will go up, I buy today and sell later. If I think the price is going down, I'll sell at today's higher price. The miracle is that in taking care of ourselves, we speculators somehow ensure that producers all over the world will provide the right quantity and quality of goods at the proper time, without undue waste, and that this meshes with what people want and the money they have available.

When a harvest is too small to satisfy consumption at its normal rate, speculators come in, hoping to profit from the scarcity by buying. Their purchases raise the price, thereby checking consumption so that the smaller supply will last longer. Producers encouraged by the high price further lessen the shortage by growing or importing to reduce the shortage. On the other side, when the price is higher than the speculators think the facts warrant, they sell. This reduces prices, encouraging consumption and exports and helping to reduce the surplus.

Of course, speculators aren't always correct. When they are wrong, their actions contribute to shortages or gluts. Manias such as the Tulipomania, the South Sea Bubble, the Mississippi Bubble, gold panics, stock market crashes, and violent swings in the value of the dollar are frequently cited as examples of occasions when speculators contributed to instability and imbalance. But who could do the job better?

A speculator describes his job.

Source: Victor Niederhoffer, "The Speculator as Hero," *The Wall Street Journal,* February 10, 1989.

FIGURE 7.8

EQUILIBRIUM WITH COSTLY SPECULATION

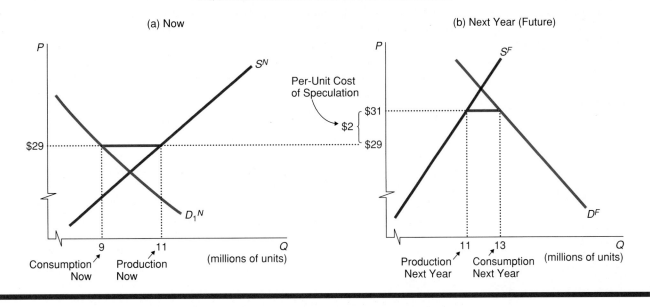

(a) Now

(b) Next Year (Future)

A second cost of speculation is risk. A speculator profits by selling a good later at a higher price than the purchase price now. This person loses money if the price later turns out to be below the price now. Most people do not like taking risks like this, so people are willing to speculate only if they expect, on average, to earn enough money to compensate them for taking risks. A payment for bearing risk is a second cost of speculation.

A third cost of speculation involves storage costs and depreciation of goods in storage. Speculators must pay storage costs to keep goods in a warehouse or some similar place until a future time. Depreciation is the loss in value of goods because of spoilage or other wear and tear due to storage. Depreciation occurs each year as rats eat a certain fraction of the wheat stored in silos. Depreciation also occurs if only nine out of every ten goods a speculator puts into storage will remain in good condition for future sale. Storage costs and depreciation are additional costs of speculation.

Figure 7.8 shows an equilibrium with costs of speculation. Figure 7.8 resembles Figure 7.6 except that it applies to speculation over time rather than arbitrage across locations. The per-unit cost of speculation, $2 in Figure 7.8, includes foregone interest, risk, storage costs, and depreciation. People are willing to speculate only if the price is expected to increase by at least $2. In Figure 7.8, the equilibrium current price is $29 and the equilibrium expected future price is $31. The expected future price exceeds the current price by the per-unit cost of speculation, $2. Equilibrium production today is 11 million units of the goods. People consume 9 million units and speculators buy the other 2 million to store for the future. Expected future production is 11 million units and expected future

IN THE NEWS

Drop in soybean, wheat, and corn prices continues as chances increase for rain

Current prices fall when changes in expectations for rain cause expectations of future supplies to rise.

Source: "Drop in Soybean, Wheat, and Corn Prices Continues and Chances Increase for Rain," *The Wall Street Journal*, May 27, 1988.

consumption is 13 million, which exceeds expected future production by the 2 million units that speculators will sell out of their inventories.

WHO ARE SPECULATORS?

A speculator can be a producer who stores goods rather than selling them now in expectation of selling for a higher price in the future. A speculator can also be a buyer who avoids an expected price increase by buying extra goods now (to store for future use) while the price is still low. A speculator can also be a third party who believes that a good's price will rise and attempts to profit by buying now with plans to resell in the future. People speculate when they buy art or real estate that they plan to sell in the future.

WINNERS AND LOSERS FROM SPECULATION

Speculation, like arbitrage and international trade, creates winners and losers. Speculation raises a good's price at times when it would otherwise be unusually low, so buyers lose and sellers gain at those times. Speculation also lowers the price (as speculators sell goods) at times when the price would otherwise be unusually high, so buyers gain and sellers lose at those times.

Chapter 11 will show that, at each point in time, the gains from speculation are larger than the losses if speculators have reasonably accurate expectations about the future. In that case, speculation (like international trade and arbitrage) is economically efficient.

EFFECTS OF CHANGES IN EXPECTATIONS

Suppose that people's expectations about the future change and that people expect an increase in future demand for mouthwash. **Figure 7.9** shows that an increase in expected future demand from D_1^F to D_2^F raises the expected future price. This creates an incentive for speculators to store more bottles of mouthwash for future resale. The increased demand by speculators raises current demand from D_1^N to D_2^N, which raises the current price from $2.00 to $2.40. Expected future supply rises from S_1^F to S_2^F as speculators will sell their stored goods.

If the costs of speculation are close to zero, the equilibrium price today and the expected future price both rise from $2.00 to $2.40. Current output rises from 100,000 to 115,000 bottles per week, current consumption falls from 100,000 to 90,000, and speculators store 25,000 bottles. Expected future output rises from 100,000 to 130,000 bottles, and, since speculators will sell 25,000, expected future consumption rises from 100,000 to 155,000 bottles. Notice that the change in beliefs about the future affects prices, output, and consumption now. This is an important point:

> **Economic conditions now depend partly on what people expect about the future.**

Changes in expectations about the future affect the economy now.

INTERTEMPORAL SUBSTITUTION

Suppose that you want to buy a computer, but you expect computer prices to fall next month. You might choose to wait until next month to make the purchase. Similarly, you might take a vacation during an off-season when prices are lower, or buy your textbooks early or late when the lines at the bookstore are shorter.

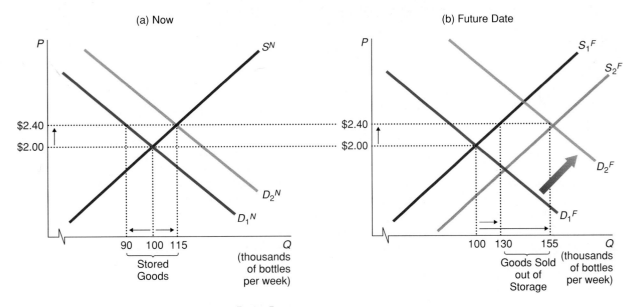

FIGURE 7.9

INCREASE IN EXPECTED FUTURE DEMAND

An increase in expected future demand, from D_1^F to D_2^F:

- Raises the price from $2.00 to $2.40
- Raises current output from 100,000 to 115,000
- Lowers current consumption from 100,000 to 90,000
- Raises future (expected) output from 100,000 to 130,000
- Raises future (expected) consumption from 100,000 to 155,000

How often have you waited for an item to go on sale at a lower price before buying it, or bought a good sooner than you planned because its price was low? You may have waited for a book to come out in paperback or a movie to come out on video. These are examples of intertemporal substitution, or substitution over time.

Chapter 4 defined intertemporal substitution as a change in current demand or supply of a good caused by a change in its expected future price. People often choose when to buy or sell a good to take advantage of expected price changes. You might wait to buy something later because you expect the price to fall, or you might buy now because you think that the price might soon rise. A change in the expected future price of a good causes a change in its current demand.

Intertemporal substitution resembles speculation, except it can affect even nonstorable goods. You can get a haircut today or next week or go to the beach this year or next, but haircuts and beach vacations are not storable goods. If people expect the price of a good to rise, they can buy it now. If it is storable, they can save it to use later. If it is not storable, they may be able to use it now instead of later. If people expect the price of a good to fall, they may wait until later to buy and use it.

IN THE NEWS

Foreign buying of U.S. Treasurys helps keep interest rates down

By Thomas T. Vogel Jr.
Staff Reporter of
The Wall Street Journal

NEW YORK — One reason U.S. interest rates are so low now is a surge of foreign buying of U.S. Treasurys during the fourth quarter of last year and the first quarter of this year.

Foreign lending to the United States ("Buying of U.S. Treasury Securities") lowers U.S. interest rates, as in Figure 7.10.

Source: Reprinted from Thomas T. Vogel, Jr., "Foreign Buying of U.S. Treasurys Helps Keep Interest Rates Down," *The Wall Street Journal,* July 12, 1993, p. C16.

IN THE NEWS

Brazil's frost puts chill on coffee prices

Wholesalers have raised prices almost $1.00 a pound in the past month and the consumer, who had been paying about $3.69 a pound for preground coffee beans in markets, has seen the price go to $4.69.

Beans that were selling at about $1.30 a pound wholesale three months ago rose to more than $2.70 a pound this week.

The initial reason for the increases, according to Donald Schoenholt, founding chairman of the Specialty Coffee Association of America, a trade group of small specialty coffee shops and roasters, is "the nervous, frightening climate" in the coffee-growing world caused by news that frost in Brazil killed more than 40 percent of that country's coffee crop for sale in 1987. Brazil supplies one-third of all the coffee sold in the world.

Supplies of coffee are plentiful now, but the prospect of a shortage next year has caused wild speculation on contracts for future purchases in the New York Coffee, Sugar and Cocoa Exchange, the commodity market whose transactions ultimately determine prices. This speculation has driven up the prices for the coffee beans called Arabica.

Prices rise today when new information reduces expected future supplies.

Source: "Brazil's Frost Puts Chill on Coffee Prices," *Rochester Democrat and Chronicle,* January 19, 1986, p. 17A.

FOR REVIEW

7.9 What is speculation?

7.10 What are the costs of speculation?

QUESTIONS

7.11 Suppose that speculation costs nothing. How is today's equilibrium price related to the expected future price? Explain why.

7.12 What happens to the current price of a storable good if its expected future demand rises?

OTHER APPLICATIONS

INTERNATIONAL BORROWING AND LENDING

From the end of World War II until the 1980s, the United States was a lender in markets for international loans.[11] Since then, the United States has borrowed from the rest of the world.

> International borrowing or lending occurs whenever people in one country lend to or borrow from people in another country; it is international trade in loans.

---

[11]This refers to total net lending by people, business firms, and governments. Some Americans borrowed from people in other countries, but as a whole the United States was a lender.

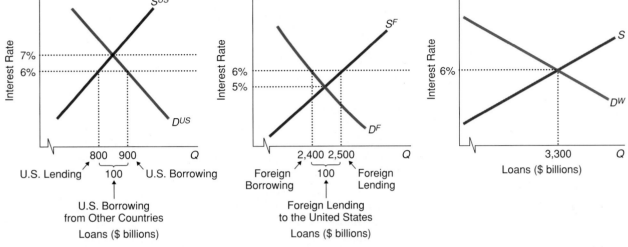

INTERNATIONAL BORROWING AND LENDING

International trade in loans resembles international trade in goods. People supply loans when they lend money, and they demand loans when they borrow money. The quantity of loans supplied is the amount of money that people are willing to lend, and the quantity demanded is the amount of money that people want to borrow. The price of a loan per dollar loaned is the interest rate. Increases in the interest rate raise the incentive to lend money, so the supply curve for loans slopes upward, as in **Figure 7.10.** Increases in the interest rate reduce the incentive to borrow money, so the demand curve for loans slopes downward.

Figure 7.10 shows an equilibrium in the international trade in loans. Figure 7.10 resembles Figure 7.1, except it applies to loans. The equilibrium world interest rate is 6 percent per year in this example, and total world loans are $3,300 billion. The supply of loans in the United States, S^{US}, represents lending by people in the United States. The demand for loans in the United States, D^{US}, represents borrowing by people in the United States. At the equilibrium interest rate of 6 percent, U.S. lenders lend $800 billion, while U.S. borrowers borrow $900 billion. People in the United States borrow $100 billion from people in other countries. Figure 7.10b shows the foreign supply of loans, S^F, and foreign demand for loans, D^F, which represent lending and borrowing by people in foreign countries. At the equilibrium interest rate of 6 percent, foreign borrowers borrow $2,400 billion, while foreign lenders lend $2,500 billion, so foreign lenders lend $100 billion to borrowers in the United States.

What would happen if foreign countries could not lend to the United States? (Suppose, for example, that foreign governments prohibited lending to the United States.) Then the interest rate in the United States would be determined by U.S.

supply and demand for loans (the curves in Figure 7.10a). The equilibrium U.S. interest rate would be 7 percent instead of 6 percent, and the foreign interest rate would be 5 percent. This shows how foreign lending to the United States keeps the U.S. interest rate lower than it would otherwise be.

EFFECTS OF HIGHER U.S. GOVERNMENT BORROWING

The government borrows money when it has a budget deficit—when it spends more money than it receives in tax revenues.

government budget deficit — the amount of money that the government borrows each year when it spends more than it collects in taxes

> The **government budget deficit** is the amount of money that the government borrows each year when it spends more than it collects in taxes.

Changes in government borrowing affect the interest rate by changing the demand for loans. A $100 billion increase in the U.S. government budget deficit raises the U.S. demand for loans by $100 billion, from D_1^{US} to D_2^{US} in **Figure 7.11.** This raises the world demand for loans, which raises the world interest rate from 6.0 percent to 6.5 percent. The interest-rate increase raises U.S. lending from $800 billion to $820 billion, while U.S. borrowing rises from $900 billion to $980 billion. The interest-rate increase also raises foreign lending from $2,500 billion to $2,530 billion, while foreign borrowing falls from $2,400 billion to $2,370 billion. Before the increase in the U.S. government budget deficit, the United States borrowed $100 billion from foreigners each year. After the increase, the United States borrows $160 billion from foreigners each year. Higher government budget deficits increase equilibrium borrowing from foreign countries.

FIGURE 7.11

EFFECTS OF HIGHER U.S. GOVERNMENT BORROWING

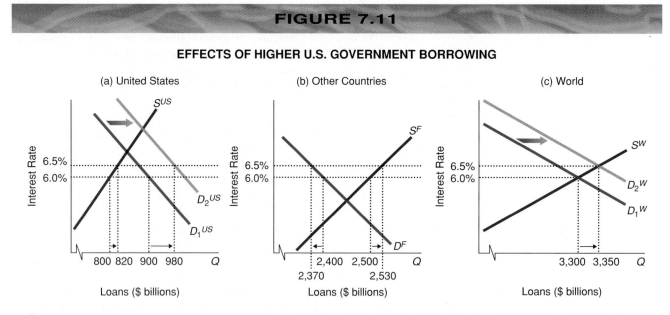

The interest rate starts out at 6 percent. An increase in U.S. government borrowing raises U.S. demand for loans from D_1^{US} to D_2^{US} and the world market demand rises from D_1^W to D_2^W. This raises the world interest rate from 6.0 percent to 6.5 percent. U.S. lending rises to $820 billion and U.S. borrowing rises to $980 billion. Foreign lending rises to $2,530 billion and foreign borrowing falls to $2,370 billion. U.S. borrowing from other countries rises from $100 billion to $160 billion.

The interest-rate increase from 6.0 percent to 6.5 percent also reduces borrowing by the private sector in the United States (that is, by people and business firms). Total borrowing from foreign countries by people, business firms, and the government in the United States rises by $80 billion (from $900 billion to $980 billion), but total *government* borrowing rises by $100 billion. Thus, total borrowing by the private sector falls by $20 billion per year.

FUTURES MARKETS

When you buy a sweater at a store, you get it right away and take it home with you. When you order a shirt from a catalog or a custom-made bike, however, you get your goods at a future time.

> **Futures markets** are markets in which people buy and sell goods for future delivery. **Future prices** are prices of goods for delivery at future dates.

Some futures markets, such as the Chicago Mercantile Exchange, are formal organizations. Financial pages of newspapers list futures prices of corn, wheat, barley, cattle, cocoa, cotton, orange juice, gold, silver, gasoline, lumber, and many other goods. Futures prices differ from spot prices:

> **Spot prices** are the prices of goods for current delivery (delivery now).[12]

Spot prices are prices as people normally think of them.

> Speculation creates a link between today's futures price and the spot price that people expect in the future:

> The equilibrium futures price equals the expected future spot price.[13]

EXPLANATION AND EXAMPLE

Suppose that you expect the spot price of wheat next April 1 to be $5.00 per bushel. If the futures price is $4.70, you would expect to profit from buying wheat futures. Suppose that you buy 5,000 bushels of wheat on the futures market at a cost of $4.70 per bushel; the wheat will be delivered to you on April 1, and you can sell it then. If your expectations turn out to be right and the future spot price is $5, you make a profit of $0.30 per bushel (or $1,500 on the 5,000 bushels). If the future spot price turns out to be less than $4.70, you lose money because you sell the wheat for less than the $4.70 you paid for it. (Like other speculators, you would not wait until April 1 to sell the wheat. You would sell it before April 1 to avoid having the wheat actually delivered to you.)

If you expect the price of wheat next April 1 to be $5.00 and the futures price is $5.25, then you can sell wheat futures. Suppose that you sell 5,000 bushels of wheat on the futures market at a cost of $5.25 per bushel. (If you don't have any wheat to sell, you can borrow wheat and sell it; you can buy wheat later to repay the loan.) The sale obligates you to deliver 5,000 bushels of wheat to someone on April 1. If your expectations turn out to be right and the spot price is $5.00 on April 1, you make a profit of $0.25 per bushel because you bought the wheat for

futures market — a market in which people buy and sell goods for future delivery

futures price — the price of a good for delivery at a future date

spot price — the price of a good for current delivery

---

[12]Actually, it can take one or two days to get delivery of some goods on spot markets, which, in principle, offer on-the-spot delivery.

[13]Because people dislike risk (see Chapter 19), this conclusion is an approximation that applies closely in most, but not all, futures markets.

$5.00 and you deliver it to another buyer, who pays you $5.25. If the price turns out to be more than $5.25, you lose money.

If the futures price of wheat is below the expected future spot price of wheat, then people buy wheat futures. This raises the demand for wheat futures, and it raises the futures price of wheat. This speculation continues until the futures price equals the expected future spot price. At that point the market reaches equilibrium. If, instead, the futures price of wheat exceeds the expected future spot price, people sell wheat futures, raising the supply of wheat futures and lowering the futures price. This continues until the futures price equals the expected future spot price.

The futures price changes whenever expectations about the future spot price change. Rainfall in Brazil changes the futures price of coffee. Frost in Florida raises the futures price of orange juice.

STOCK PRICES

Every night, people watch television news reports on the stock market, yet few viewers know much about it.

> **Shares of stock** are legal rights of ownership in business firms. The stock market is an organized system for trading shares of stock. The prices of these shares are **stock prices.**

The costs of speculating on the stock market are small, so Figure 7.7 (which shows an equilibrium with no-cost speculation) approximates the stock market. This has an important implication:

> The equilibrium stock price today equals (approximately) the expected future stock price.

EXPLANATION

If the expected future price exceeded the price today, people could profit by buying stock now and selling it later. If the expected future price were lower than the current price, people could profit by selling the stock now and buying it back later at a lower price.[14] With costless speculation on the stock market, the equilibrium current price and expected future price are equal.

STOCK PRICES TAKE A RANDOM WALK

In equilibrium, the expected future price of a stock approximately equals its current price. People know that the stock price might rise or might fall, but, on average, they expect it to stay at about the same level.

> A price follows a **random walk** if it is equally likely to rise or fall by the same amount, so, on average, it will stay about where it is.

Stock prices follow random walks (approximately).

COSTS OF STOCK-MARKET SPECULATION

The costs of speculating on the stock market are not *exactly* zero. The opportunity cost of buying stock equals the interest you could have earned by putting the same money in a bank or lending it. Another cost of buying stock is risk; the stock invest-

share of stock — legal right of ownership in a business firm, traded on a stock market

stock price — price of a share of stock

random walk — a price that is equally likely to rise or fall by the same amount, so, on average, people do not expect it to change

---

[14]Anyone who does not own stock can borrow it to sell. Organized financial markets accommodate this kind of activity, called short selling. Later, you buy the stock and use it to repay the loan.

IN THE NEWS

Soybean prices surge as radio report on plant disease incites speculators

By Scott Kilman
Staff Reporter of The
Wall Street Journal

Soybean prices jumped yesterday after speculators heard Chicago radio commentator Paul Harvey rehash old news about a mysterious disease that suddenly kills soybean plants.

Grain brokers were stunned when Mr. Harvey's noon broadcast about "sudden death syndrome in the soybean fields" helped fuel a buying binge in the last 10 minutes of trading, apparently on speculation that the disease could wipe out part of the crop.

Futures prices respond quickly to any new information that people believe is important.

Source: Scott Kilman, "Soybean Prices Surge as Radio Report on Plant Disease Incites Speculators," *The Wall Street Journal*, February 18, 1988, p. 34.

ment may lose money rather than make money. In real life, these costs are small enough that, from day to day, stock prices follow random walks very closely.

Many investment advisors deny that stock prices are approximately random walks. They claim to be able to tell you when to buy and sell certain stocks to make large profits. Maybe they can, but it is fair to ask them, "If you're so smart, why aren't you rich?" If these investment advisors knew which stock prices were likely to rise or fall, they would probably stop working and vacation for the rest of their lives! (They could also use their knowledge to earn large sums of money to donate to charity.) Of course, a few investors earn high profits in the stock market by chance. These lucky investors are usually willing to tell you about their investment skills, but you are less likely to hear from the people who lose money by chance.

Some people have privileged information about certain companies and may be able to earn high profits in the stock market by trading based on that information. Most people do not have this kind of special information, though. In equilibrium—and in real life—stock prices come close to random walks. To make large profits, you must have better luck, better information, or better skills at using information than most other people.

FOR REVIEW

7.13 What is a futures price? A spot price?

7.14 How is the equilibrium futures price of lumber related to the spot price that people expect for a future date?

7.15 Explain why stock prices follow a random walk.

QUESTIONS

7.16 Would the U.S. interest rate rise or fall if the government were to prohibit borrowing from people in foreign countries? Explain why.

7.17 Would the United States borrow more or less from people in other countries if people in the United States saved more? Explain why.

CONCLUSIONS

INTERNATIONAL TRADE

The price of an internationally traded good is determined on the world market. The quantity supplied in each country at the world equilibrium price shows that country's output of the good, while the quantity demanded at that price in each country shows its consumption. If a country's quantity supplied at the world equilibrium price exceeds its quantity demanded, the difference is that country's exports. If a country's quantity demanded at the world equilibrium price exceeds its quantity supplied, the difference is its imports.

An increase in demand in any country raises the world equilibrium price, which lowers consumption in other countries and raises output in all countries. An increase in supply of the good in any country lowers the world equilibrium price, which lowers output in other countries and raises consumption in all countries.

Arbitrage

Arbitrage means buying a good at a place where its price is low and selling it where its price is higher. Like international trade, arbitrage tends to reduce or eliminate price differentials. As arbitragers buy in low-price locations to resell in higher-price locations, the price rises in the low-price place and falls in the high-price place. An arbitrage opportunity arises when someone knows of a price differential that exceeds the costs of arbitrage. Equilibrium allows no arbitrage opportunities. If the cost of arbitrage is zero, the equilibrium price is the same in both locations. More generally, the equilibrium price differential can be no larger than the per-unit cost of arbitrage.

Speculation

Speculation means buying a storable good when its price is low and reselling it at a later time when its price may be higher. Speculation is like arbitrage across time, rather than across regions or between countries. If speculation costs nothing, the equilibrium price of a good today equals its expected future price. When speculation has a cost, the expected future price can be no higher than equilibrium price today plus the per-unit cost of speculation. The total cost of speculation includes the interest rate (which is the opportunity cost of using money for speculation), the cost of bearing risk, storage costs, and depreciation. While international trade and arbitrage tend to make prices the same in different places, speculation tends to make expected prices the same in different months or years. Because of speculation, a fall in the expected future supply of a product raises its price today. Intertemporal substitution resembles speculation: people time their buying or selling to take advantage of temporarily low or high prices.

Other Applications

International trade in loans resembles international trade in goods. Some countries lend (or export loans), while other countries borrow (or import loans). The price of a loan is the interest rate, and the world equilibrium interest rate determines international trade in loans. Changes in the supply or demand for loans in any country affect the world interest rate. An increase in the government budget deficit in some country can raise that country's demand for loans, which raises the world interest rate and the amount that the country borrows on world markets.

People buy and sell goods for future delivery on futures markets. The equilibrium futures price of a good equals its expected future spot price. People buy and sell shares of stock on stock markets. The costs of speculating on the stock market are low, so it is a good approximation to say that the equilibrium price of a stock equals its expected future price. We summarize this by saying that stock prices follow a random walk.

Looking Ahead

Chapter 8 applies supply-and-demand analysis to taxes and government control of prices. Chapters 9 and 10 then turn to more detailed discussions of the conditions that affect demand and supply, and the factors that affect the decisions of buyers and producers.

KEY TERMS

consumption of a good

cxport

import

arbitrage

price differential

arbitrage opportunity

speculation

government budget deficit

futures market

futures price

spot price

share of stock

stock price

random walk

QUESTIONS AND PROBLEMS

7.18 Refer to the accompanying table to answer the following questions:
   a. Fill in the rest of the table. What is the world market demand for radios? What is the world market supply?
   b. Find the world equilibrium price and quantity.
   c. Draw graphs of the U.S. demand and supply, the rest of the world's demand and supply, and the world market demand and supply.
   d. Does the United States export or import radios in this example? How much does it export or import? What is the money value of these exports or imports? Does the rest of the world export or import radios? How much do other countries import?

	United States		Other Countries		World Market	
Price	Quantity Demanded	Quantity Supplied	Quantity Demanded	Quantity Supplied	Quantity Demanded	Quantity Supplied
$12	2	13	5	25		
11	4	12	6	22		
10	6	11	7	19		
9	10	10	8	17		
8	11	9	9	15		
7	12	8	10	14		
6	14	6	11	13		
5	16	0	12	12		
4	18	0	13	9		
3	20	0	14	0		
2	22	0	15	0		

7.19 Refer to the table from Problem 7.18 and answer each of the following questions separately:
   a. Suppose that the U.S. demand for radios increases by 4 units at every price. (Add 4 to all numbers in the U.S. Quantity Demanded column, so the United States demands 6 if the price is $12, 8 if the price is $11, and so on.) Find the new world equilibrium price and quantity. How much does the United States produce now? How much does it consume? How much does it export or import? How much does the rest of the world produce, consume, and export or import?
   b. Suppose that the foreign demand for radios increases by 4 units at every price. Find the new world equilibrium price and quantity. How much

does the United States produce, consume, and export or import? How much does the rest of the world produce, consume, and export or import?

c. Suppose that the U.S. supply of radios increases by 6 units at every price. Find the new world equilibrium price and quantity. How much does the United States produce, consume, and export or import? How much does the rest of the world produce, consume, and export or import?

d. Suppose that the foreign supply of radios increases by 6 units at every price. Find the new world equilibrium price and quantity. How much does the United States produce, consume, and export or import? How much does the rest of the world produce, consume, and export or import?

7.20 Start with the equilibrium in Figure 7.1. Use graphs similar to Figures 7.2 and 7.3 to show what happens to output, consumption, and exports or imports of film by the United States and other countries when:
a. U.S. demand for film increases
b. U.S. supply of film increases

7.21 Begin with the equilibrium in Figure 7.1. Show in a diagram what would happen to prices, production, and consumption of film in each country if the U.S. government were to prohibit international trade in film.

7.22 A drought in North America reduces output of oats in the United States. Use graphs to help explain why this increases U.S. imports of oats from Argentina.

7.23 Begin with the equilibrium in Figure 7.5 (which represents trade between here and there). Draw graphs to show what happens to the equilibrium price and equilibrium output and consumption in each place if:
a. Demand for souvenir caps increases there
b. Supply of souvenir caps increases there

7.24 Explain why the equilibrium price differential cannot exceed the cost of arbitraging one more unit of a good.

7.25 Use a graph like Figure 7.6 to show how a fall in the cost of arbitrage affects (a) the price at each location, (b) output at each location, and (c) consumption at each location.

7.26 When the price of crude oil increases, gasoline prices rise immediately, even for gasoline that sellers already had in storage and that was produced from older, cheaper crude oil. Use graphs to explain why.

7.27 Snow in Florida reduces the number of oranges that will be available in the future. Comment on the following statement: "The price of orange juice may rise in the future, but the current price does not change because the weather in Florida does not change the amount of orange juice already in stores."

7.28 Draw diagrams to show the effects of an increase in the expected future demand for a product next year on today's (a) price of the good, (b) quantity produced, and (c) quantity consumed. Also show the amount of the good (d) produced next year and (e) consumed next year, along with (f) the price next year.

Sudden impact: invasion of Kuwait sends U.S. gasoline prices soaring

Gasoline prices have shot up as much as 15 cents a gallon in the wake of Iraq's invasion of Kuwait and are likely to go higher despite outcries from motorists, politicians and consumer groups.

Only hours after news of the hostilities broke, prices were being raised all along America's gasoline supply chain, from refineries to the corner service station. "I've never seen it happen so quickly," said Bill Dodd, a harried staff member at the Florida branch of the Automobile Association of America in Orlando. Pump prices in that state jumped two to 15 cents on Friday and "indications are they are going up higher," he said. "As we're speaking, the price is going up."

Increases across the Nation
Public irritation over the speedy price increases could cause unexpected results. Most troublesome is the possibility that the fear and furor—all by itself—could fuel further price increases.

Gasoline demand may jump sharply and stay unusually high in coming weeks simply because motorists, trying to beat the next price rise or worried about shortages, may insist on filling up their tanks and keeping them full. Normally, they might drive around on half a tank most of the time.

"If you put another quarter of a tank [of gasoline] in every car in the U.S., Western Europe and Japan, it makes a huge difference," said Bryan Jacoboski, an oil analyst at PaineWebber Inc. in New York.

Gasoline prices in the United States rose suddenly when Iraq invaded Kuwait in 1990. (See Problem 7.26.)

Source: "Sudden Impact: Invasion of Kuwait Sends U.S. Gasoline Prices Soaring," *The Wall Street Journal,* August 6, 1990, p. B1.

7.29 Use a graph like Figure 7.7 to show what happens to equilibrium production and consumption now and later, and to the equilibrium price, when:
a. Demand for the good now increases
b. Supply of the good now increases
c. The expected future supply decreases

7.30 On the day that U.S. forces started fighting Iraqis in 1991, the price of crude oil produced in the Middle East fell from about $31 to $21 per barrel, a record single-day fall. Use the economic principles from this chapter to suggest a reason why.

7.31 What can you do to try to profit if the futures price of eggs differs from the spot price of eggs that you expect next month?

7.32 Comment on this claim made by a well-known financial consulting firm: "Our stock analysts can help you pick the winners and avoid the losers, and our track record over the last year proves it."

7.33 Suppose that the U.S. government's budget deficit increases, raising the government's demand for loans. Assume in your answer that the supply and demand curves for loans by the private sector (everyone except the government) do not change.

a. Draw a graph to show the effect of the higher budget deficit on total U.S. borrowing from the rest of the world and on the interest rate.

b. Does U.S. borrowing from the rest of the world rise as much as the government's borrowing increases?

c. Do people and businesses in the United States borrow more or less than they did before the budget deficit increase?

d. Does the U.S. interest rate rise more or less than it would without international borrowing and lending?

7.34 Use graphs to help explain the economics of the following newspaper headlines:

a. Soybean Prices Fall as Exporters in South America Prepare to Sell Big Harvests

b. Cocoa Prices Climb on Rumors of Strikes at Ports in Nigeria

c. Soybean Prices Rise Amid Speculation that U.S. Will Restrict Planting

d. Cattle Futures Prices Fall as Traders See Possibility of Ranchers Sending Big Supply to Slaughter

7.35 Suppose that traders must pay the costs of transporting a good across the ocean from one country to another. Treat this cost of shipping goods internationally like a cost of arbitrage and draw a graph to show how the equilibrium price(s), outputs, and consumption of the good are determined for each country.

INQUIRIES FOR FURTHER THOUGHT

7.36 Do you have any arbitrage opportunities? What price differentials do you know about? What would be your costs of arbitrage?

7.37 On what goods could you speculate? What would be your costs of speculation? Under what conditions would you profit or lose money?

7.38 Do you think that profiting from speculation is due more to luck or to skill? How could you tell?

7.39 Sunville and Dismaland are two cities in different parts of the United States. Sunville has good weather and opportunities for outdoor activities. Dismaland has terrible weather and little to offer in recreational activities. Comment on the differences in (a) the prices of food, books, clothing, and other goods in the two cities, (b) wages in the two cities, and (c) the prices of land in the two cities. In your comments, discuss whether any economic forces tend to make prices of food, books, clothing, and other goods equal in the two cities. Do the same forces affect wages and land prices?

TAG SOFTWARE APPLICATIONS

TUTORIAL EXERCISES

▶ This module reviews the key terms from Chapter 7.

GRAPHING EXERCISES

▶ This section covers the impact of trade on equilibrium prices and quantities and how to measure a country's imports or exports.

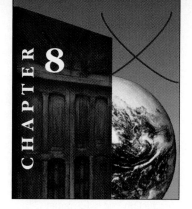

PRICE CONTROLS AND TAXES

P. 193-203 only

WHAT THIS CHAPTER IS ABOUT

▶ The effects of maximum legal prices (such as rent controls)

▶ The effects of minimum legal prices (such as the minimum wage)

▶ How taxes or subsidies affect prices and output

▶ The effects of taxes on imports and other restrictions on international trade

General George Washington and his Continental Army troops spent the winter at Valley Forge, Pennsylvania, in 1777 and nearly starved to death. They could not buy enough food because the government had put price controls on many goods, including food, and farmers were not willing to produce and sell food at the low, government-set prices. Governments throughout history have tried to keep prices low by making it illegal to charge prices above some level. But laws cannot repeal the forces of supply and demand, so price controls have unintended consequences.

Like price controls, taxes affect incentives to buy, sell, and produce. Taxes even affected the development of popular music. In the 1940s, a 20 percent tax on live vocal music in New York City nightclubs led those clubs to switch from vocal acts to bands playing instrumental music; this hindered the development of vocal jazz and encouraged instrumental jazz. Jazz musician Max Roach said, "That 20 percent tax was the most important thing," for American musical development in the mid-20th century.

PRICE CONTROLS: MAXIMUM LEGAL PRICES

maximum legal price (or price ceiling) — the highest price at which the government allows people to buy or sell a good

Governments all over the world try to keep prices low by setting maximum legal prices. These price controls cause long lines and shortages and reduce production. **Figure 8.1** shows what happens when the government places a maximum legal price on a good.

A **maximum legal price** (or price ceiling) is the highest price at which the government allows people to buy or sell a good.

The following discussion deals only with a maximum legal price *below* the equilibrium price.

193

FIGURE 8.1

MAXIMUM LEGAL PRICE

A maximum legal price, $\overline{P}$ below the equilibrium price causes a shortage of $Q^D - Q^S$. Actual production and sales equal Q^S.

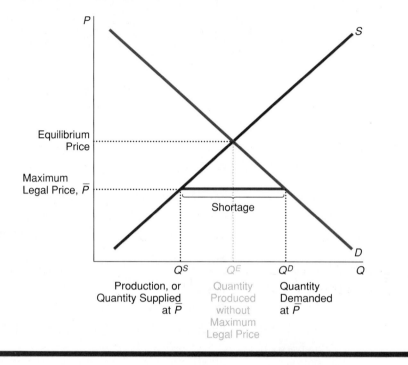

In Figure 8.1, the maximum legal price, $\overline{P}$, is below the equilibrium price. A maximum legal price causes a shortage and reduces output.

shortage — a situation in which the quantity demanded exceeds the quantity supplied at the current price

A **shortage** is a situation in which the quantity demanded exceeds the quantity supplied at the current price.

The maximum legal price reduces the quantity supplied from Q^E to Q^S and raises the quantity demanded from Q^E to Q^D. The shortage equals the quantity demanded minus the quantity supplied, $Q^D - Q^S$. Output falls (along with the quantity supplied) from Q^E to Q^S; although consumers would like to buy more, sellers are willing to sell only Q^S. Chapter 4 explained that a shortage usually causes the price to rise, but the price cannot rise if the government enforces the maximum legal price law.

NONPRICE RATIONING

When there is a shortage, not all buyers can buy as many goods as they want at the current price.

nonprice rationing — a system for choosing who gets how many goods in a shortage

Nonprice rationing is a system for choosing who gets how many goods when there is a shortage.

The many types of nonprice rationing include rationing by waiting, rationing by coupons, and bribery.

After hours in a queue, due to price controls in Eastern Europe, a jubilant women is lucky enough to purchase a pair of Italian boots.
Source: New York Times, July 28, 1989.

RATIONING BY WAITING

Rationing by waiting occurs when people toward the front of a line can buy the good, but people further back in line cannot. Goods are allocated by a first-come, first-served method. Rationing by waiting is also called *queuing* and the line is called a *queue.* The people who buy the good (those who get in line first) are the people who are willing to spend the most time to buy it. These people either value the good more than others or place a lower value on their time.

Rationing by waiting sometimes leads buyers to hire other people with lower time values to wait in line for them. This was common in the former socialist economies of Eastern Europe and the former Soviet Union, where rationing by waiting was a daily experience. Retired people worked part-time waiting in long lines at stores to buy goods for other people. Buyers hired them on the streets in front of the stores. When the United States put a maximum legal price on gasoline in the 1970s, high-school students in the Los Angeles area earned money waiting in queues to buy gasoline for other people. They picked up cars in the morning, waited in line at gas stations, and returned the cars with the tanks filled to their owners.

Rationing by waiting forces buyers to pay more than the money price, $\bar{P}$; they also pay a time price equal to the value of the time they spend waiting in line. The total cost of the good includes this time price plus the money price.

Sometimes buyers can choose either to wait in line or to pay a higher money price. If you pay someone to wait in line and buy a good for you, you pay a higher money price and a lower time price. Some former socialist economies allowed people to sell some of the goods they produced. This gave buyers a choice between government-owned stores with prices below equilibrium, but long queues, and the risk that the store would run out while the buyer waited in line, and private sellers with higher prices, but without queues.

COUPON RATIONING

Rationing by coupons occurs when the government provides certain buyers with legal rights to buy a good. To do this, the government prints and distributes coupons that buyers must exchange along with money to buy the good. Each coupon lets a person buy one unit of the good at the maximum legal price of $\overline{P}$. Buyers give the coupon to the store along with the $\overline{P}$ dollars when they buy the good.

Soon after Japan bombed Pearl Harbor in 1941, the U.S. government set up the Office of Price Administration (OPA) with power to set maximum legal prices on eight million types of goods and to ration those goods. The OPA rationed goods by issuing books of colored stamps (coupons). Each stamp represented the right, valid until a certain date, to buy a certain good such as butter, beef, or sugar. A buyer gave the stamp to the store along with the price $\overline{P}$ for the good. People needed stickers on their cars to buy gasoline. (Many politicians got X stickers that allowed them to buy unlimited amounts.) The U.S. government eliminated the OPA in 1947.

SELLABLE COUPONS   The government does not usually allow people to buy, sell, or trade rationing coupons, so the people who can buy the rationed goods are those who receive the coupons from the government. When people can buy and sell the coupons, however, the goods go to those who are willing to pay most. **Figure 8.2** shows an example with seven potential buyers:

▶ Alice is willing to pay up to $10 to buy a chocolate cake.

▶ Bill is willing to pay up to $9.

▶ Carol is willing to pay up to $8.

▶ Dave is willing to pay up to $7.

▶ Elaine is willing to pay up to $6.

▶ Fred is willing to pay up to $5.

▶ Geoff is willing to pay up to $4.

Without a maximum legal price, the equilibrium price is $6 per cake and 5 cakes are bought and sold. Alice, Bill, Carol, Dave, and Elaine buy cakes; Fred and Geoff do not. With a maximum legal price of $3, only 3 cakes are sold because bakers are willing to sell no more at a price of $3.

Who gets these 3 cakes? To answer this question, suppose that the government prints up exactly 3 coupons that state:

> This coupon allows the owner to buy one chocolate cake at a price of $3. This coupon can be bought and sold.

Suppose also that the government *sells* these coupons. The supply of coupons is perfectly inelastic at a quantity of 3 as in Figure 8.2b.[1] To find the demand for

---

[1] If the government prints only 2 coupons, then only 2 people can buy the cakes. If it prints 4 coupons, then not everyone with a coupon will be able to buy a cake, and some other form of rationing (such as rationing by waiting) will occur.

FIGURE 8.2

COUPON RATIONING WITH SELLABLE COUPONS

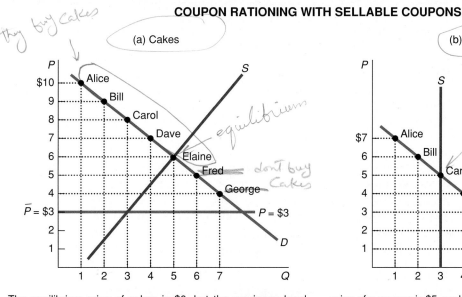

(a) Cakes

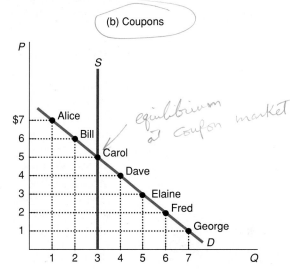

(b) Coupons

The equilibrium price of cakes is $6, but the maximum legal price is $3. At equilibrium in coupon market, the equilibrium

price of a coupon is $5, and Alice, Bill, and Carol buy coupons.

coupons, ask how much money each person would be willing to pay for a coupon. Alice is willing to pay up to $10 for a cake, so she is willing to pay up to $7 for a coupon. (If she pays $7 for a coupon and $3 at the store, the cake costs her $10.) Similarly, Bill is willing to pay up to $6 for a coupon, Carol is willing to pay up to $5, Dave is willing to pay up to $4, Elaine is willing to pay up to $3, and so on. These points trace out the demand for coupons in Figure 8.2b. At the $5 equilibrium price of coupons, Alice, Bill, and Carol each purchase a coupon, so only they buy chocolate cakes.

Notice that Alice, Bill, and Carol each pay $5 for a coupon and $3 at the store, so each pays $8 for a cake. Although the maximum legal price of cakes is $3 (below the equilibrium price of $6), the true cost to buyers, $8 per cake, exceeds the cost without the maximum legal price. Instead of lowering the cost of cakes to buyers, the maximum legal price with rationing by sellable coupons *raises* the cost to buyers.

The result is similar if the government *gives* coupons to Alice, Bill, and Carol. If Alice already has a coupon, she has an opportunity cost of using it. Because Alice is willing to pay up to $10 for a cake and the price at the store is $3, she is willing to sacrifice up to $7 to keep the coupon; the lowest price at which she would be willing to sell the coupon is $7. If someone were to offer Alice $5 for the coupon, she would reason:

> I could sell the coupon for $5 and not get the cake, or I could use the coupon and $3 of my money to buy the cake. So, buying the cake really costs me $8—$3 out of my wallet plus the $5 I could have earned by selling the coupon. I would rather have the cake than the $8.

Another 'shadow economy'

Private medical practice has long flourished illegally in the Soviet Union, creating what has been called a "shadow medical economy." Influential people use connections and gifts to get appointments with hard-to-see specialists. State doctors are bribed with money and lavish presents to open their offices after hours. Nurses demand candy, flowers, or liquor to give basic hospital care to patients. These practices are so common that people consider them part of everyday life.

Maximum legal prices led to bribery in the former Soviet Union.

Source: "Another 'Shadow Economy,'" *New York Times,* March 5, 1989, p. 3.

---

tie-in sale — a sale in which a seller sells only to buyers who also agree to buy some other product

On the other hand, if someone were to offer Alice $9 for the coupon, she would reason:

> I could sell the coupon for $9 and not get the cake, or I could use the coupon and $3 to buy the cake. So, the cake really costs me $12—$3 out of my wallet and $9 that I could have earned by selling the coupon. I would rather have the $12 than the cake.

And she would sell the coupon.

With the equilibrium price of coupons at $5, Alice's cost for a cake is $8, even if she already has a coupon. Coupons cost $5, so she gives up $5 by using the coupon instead of selling it. She also has to pay $3 at the store to buy the cake, so the cake costs her $8.

Finally, the result is similar if the government gives the coupons to other people. For example, suppose that the government gives all three coupons to Dave. Alice, Bill, and Carol then buy the coupons for $5 from Dave, who is willing to sell the coupons because he prefers to have $8 (the $5 he gets from selling the coupon plus the $3 he would have spent at the store for the cake) than to have a cake. In other words, the opportunity cost of a cake is $8, but he is willing to spend only $7, so he does not buy a cake, he sells the coupons.

RATIONING BY BRIBERY

Bribery is another method for rationing with maximum legal prices. Sellers provide goods to their friends, to people who do favors for them, or to people who give them gifts or money. Buyers pay more than the explicit money price, P; they also pay the cost of the bribe.

TIE-IN SALES

Sometimes people avoid laws on maximum legal prices through tie-in sales.

> **Tie-in sales** occur when a seller sells only to buyers who also agree to buy some other product. (like renting furniture along w/ the apartment)

When the government limits rents on apartments (setting a maximum legal price for shelter), landlords sometimes require renters to rent furniture along with the apartment. By agreeing to a high rent for the furniture, a landlord and a renter essentially evade the maximum legal price on apartment rental. If, for example, the equilibrium rent is $300 per month and the maximum legal price is $200 per month, landlords might charge an extra $100 per month for the furniture. Or they might require renters to pay them an extra $100 per month for cleaning services.

EXAMPLES OF MAXIMUM LEGAL PRICES

The United States imposed price controls during World Wars I and II. More recently, President Nixon imposed temporary price controls in 1971. The United States imposed maximum legal prices on gasoline in 1974 when the world price of oil quadrupled. These price controls caused long queues for gasoline in many parts of the country, and in the late 1970s, the government printed coupons planning for possible rationing. The government never distributed the coupons and later destroyed them.

Price controls have a long history, dating from about 2350 B.C. in ancient Sumeria. Later, Hammurabi's code of law for Babylon (around 1750 B.C.) set legal prices for medical services and other labor services. The Roman emperor

Politics, as well as weather, also continues to play a significant role. The aftereffects of civil war in Sudan, Somalia, and Mozambique have left agriculture in disarray. In Angola, renewed civil war has affected food production and prevented relief distribution. New refugees in Rwanda, displaced by civil war, need food assistance. And in Kenya, politics has added a new twist to planting. With the government maintaining the price of cereals an artificially low level while fertilizer prices have skyrocketed, many farmers are refusing to plant maize and wheat and are growing only enough food for themselves.

Maximum legal prices keep food production low in many poor countries.

Source: New York Times International, April 23, 1993.

Diocletian set maximum legal prices for many products in 301 A.D., and violators faced the death penalty. The Roman price controls caused shortages and riots, and they were abandoned when Diocletian abdicated four years later.

Despite this ancient experience, price controls have remained common throughout history. Governments of former socialist countries controlled prices on most goods and sold many goods in government-owned stores. Even in nonsocialist countries, governments often control prices of food, grain, houses, and many other goods and services. Price controls are a major reason for the low supplies of food in many—less-developed countries because governments keep prices so low that farmers don't bother to produce much food beyond what their families eat. Governments of many African countries have required farmers to sell their food output to the government, which pays them less than one-half, and sometimes less than one-fourth, of the world equilibrium price. African per-capita food production fell by about one-fourth from 1960 to 1985 as more governments imposed maximum legal prices and other regulations. Some countries have changed these policies in the last decade. Ghana, for example, once paid farmers about one-fifth of the value of their output; when the government abolished maximum legal prices on food in 1987, corn production tripled.[2]

RENT CONTROL

Rent control is common in many cities around the world. About 200 U.S. cities impose some form of rent control, with apartments rationed by queues, bribes, and tie-in sales. In many former socialist countries, people had to sign up years, even decades, in advance to get apartments. As a result, many young, married couples lived with one set of parents for years as they waited for an apartment to become available. Queuing is the usual method for rationing apartments with rent control, though bribery is also common. Tie-in sales are less common because the government can outlaw them.

About one million New York City apartments—nearly half of all apartments in the city—are subject to some kind of rent control. Rent control in New York began in 1943 as a temporary law and it is still legally temporary. Many celebrities, including a former New York mayor, have lived in rent-controlled apartments in New York City, paying only a fraction (often only one-tenth to one-fourth) of the monthly rent of similar apartments without rent control.

The short-run effects of rent control differ from its long-run effects. The supply of apartments is very inelastic in the short run. If it were perfectly inelastic, as in **Figure 8.3,** a maximum legal price would reduce apartment rents, but the available quantity would not increase. A shortage would occur because more people would want apartments, and people would want larger apartments, at the lower rent. In the longer run, rent controls reduce incentives to build new apartments and to repair and maintain existing ones, so fewer new apartments appear and landlords let old apartments deteriorate. In this way, rent controls have caused serious urban decay in the form of disrepaired or abandoned buildings. Rent controls also create incentives for landlords to convert rental buildings to condominiums or other uses. In the longer run, this decreases both the quality and number of available apartments and makes the shortage worsen.

---

[2]Chapter 18 discusses connections between price controls and world poverty.

FIGURE 8.3

RENT CONTROL: SHORT-RUN AND LONG-RUN EFFECTS

In the short run, rent control may not affect the number of available apartments, but in the long run, rent control reduces available apartment space to Q^{LR}.

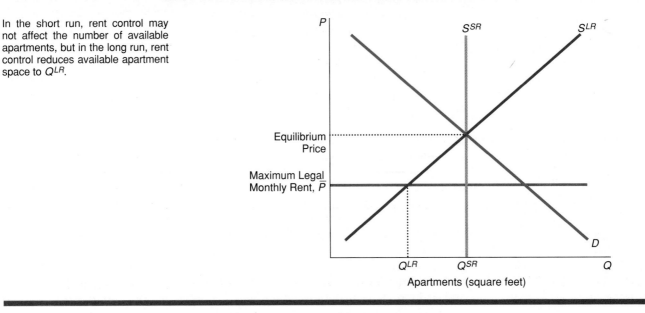

MAXIMUM LEGAL PRICES OF ZERO

Sometimes the government sets maximum legal prices at zero by allowing people to give things away free, but prohibiting them from charging prices. One example of such a good is human organs. Medical advances have made organ transplants common. Doctors transplant kidneys, for example, because a person can donate one of two kidneys and stay alive with the other one. Doctors also transplant hearts, livers, and other organs from people who have recently died. Most countries do not allow people to sell their organs, however, either while they are alive or at death; they allow people only to donate their organs without collecting payment. This reduces the number of organs available for transplant.

Other examples of goods with maximum prices of zero include blood for transfusions (which people can donate, but not sell in most places), babies (adoption is legal, but baby-selling is not), and sexual services. The NCAA sets a maximum price of zero on the services of college athletes by prohibiting member colleges from paying athletes explicitly. This causes a shortage and leads to subtle, indirect ways of paying college athletes.

BLACK MARKETS

When people buy or sell an illegal good, or sell a good at an illegal price, they trade on the black market.

black market — an illegal market

Black markets are illegal markets.

Some goods are illegal to trade at any price, such as certain drugs, alcohol during prohibition, abortions before 1973, and certain weapons. Other goods are legal, but the government controls their prices. By preventing people from making voluntary, mutually beneficial trades, price controls give people incentives to find ways to avoid them and trade illegally. Black markets are common wherever governments impose price controls or prohibit trade. Of course, people who buy or sell goods on black markets risk being caught and punished, and this risk of punishment affects demands and supplies.

MAXIMUM LEGAL PRICES ON INPUTS

It might seem that the government could reduce the cost of producing a good by putting a maximum legal price on its inputs. In fact, however, a maximum legal price on an input *raises* the price of the final good.

EXPLANATION

Figure 8.4 shows the supplies and demands for peanuts and peanut butter. Suppose that each jar of peanut butter requires 1 cup of peanuts. Without a maximum legal price on peanuts, the equilibrium quantity of peanuts is 100 million cups per year. The supply of peanut butter is S_1^{PB}, so the equilibrium quantity of peanut butter is 80 million jars per year and the equilibrium price is $3. Production of peanut butter uses 80 million cups of peanuts per year, and people eat the other 20 million as nuts.

A maximum legal price on peanuts reduces output of peanuts from 100 million to 50 million cups (the quantity supplied at the maximum legal price). Because fewer peanuts are available for peanut butter (or anything else), the supply of peanut butter falls from S_1^{PB} to S_2^{PB}. Since each jar of peanut butter requires 1 cup of peanuts, it is impossible to produce more than 50 million jars of peanut butter each year.[3] The fall in supply raises the price of peanut butter from $3 to $4 per jar.

PRICE CONTROLS: MINIMUM LEGAL PRICES

minimum legal price (or price floor) — the lowest price at which the government allows people to buy or sell a good

surplus — a situation in which the quantity demanded is less than the quantity supplied at the current price

Governments sometimes impose price controls to keep prices *high*. For many years, the U.S. government kept airline and trucking prices high; airlines, for example, were not permitted to cut fares without government permission. Today, the best-known minimum legal price is the minimum wage.

A **minimum legal price** (or price floor) is the lowest price at which the government allows people to buy or sell a good.

Figure 8.5 shows the effects of a minimum legal price on a good, assuming that the minimum legal price exceeds the equilibrium price. In Figure 8.5, the minimum legal price, $\underline{P}$ is above the equilibrium price. A minimum legal price causes a surplus and reduces output of the good.

A **surplus** is a situation in which the quantity demanded is less than the quantity supplied at the current price.

With a surplus, sellers cannot sell all the goods they would like to sell at the minimum legal price. The minimum legal price reduces the quantity demanded from

---

[3]The supply of peanut butter may be less than 50 million jars because people may buy some of the 50 million cups of peanuts to eat. This depends on how peanuts are rationed. Figure 8.4 assumes that peanut-butter producers get all the peanuts.

FIGURE 8.4

MAXIMUM LEGAL PRICE ON AN INPUT

A maximum legal price on peanuts reduces output of peanuts from 100 million to 50 million cups, which reduces the supply of peanut butter, raising its price.

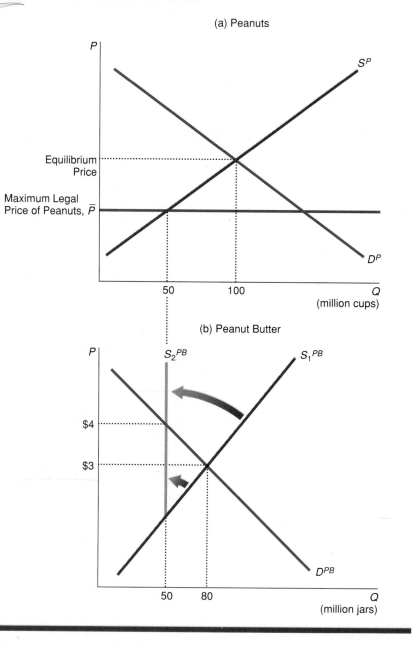

(a) Peanuts

(b) Peanut Butter

Q^E to Q^D and raises the quantity supplied from Q^E to Q^S. The surplus equals the quantity supplied minus the quantity demanded, $Q^S - Q^D$. Output falls, along with the quantity demanded, from Q^E to Q^D. Producers would like to produce and sell more, but buyers are not willing to buy more than Q^D, so producers reduce output rather than accumulate goods they cannot sell. Chapter 4 explained that a

P max P min

FIGURE 8.5

MINIMUM LEGAL PRICE

A minimum legal price of *P*, above the equilibrium price, creates a surplus of $Q^S - Q^D$. Sellers reduce production to Q^D rather than produce goods they cannot sell.

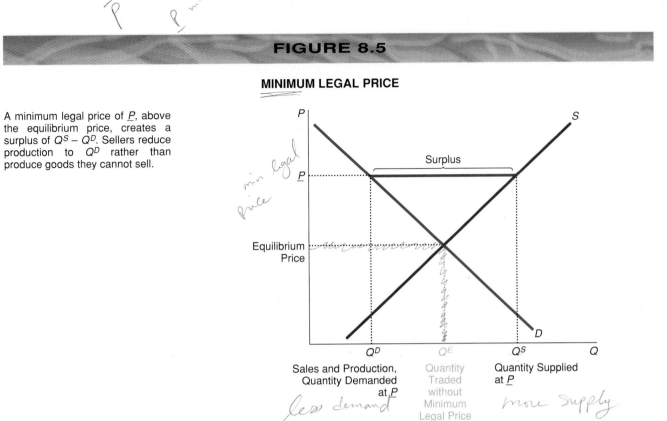

surplus usually causes the price to fall, but the minimum legal price prevents the price from falling.

MINIMUM WAGE

The minimum wage is a minimum legal price of labor services. Minimum–wage laws began in New Zealand in 1894 and England in 1909. The U.S. federal government imposed a minimum wage in 1938 with the Fair Labor Standards Act, which set 25 cents per hour as a minimum wage for some workers. This was 40 percent of the average wage in manufacturing industries at the time. By 1995, the U.S. federal minimum wage was $4.25 per hour, 37 percent of the average wage in manufacturing (about $11.75 per hour). A person who works 8 hours per day, 5 days a week, 50 weeks a year (with 2 weeks vacation) works 2,000 hours per year. (U.S. full-time workers average about 1,800 hours per year.) A worker earning the $4.25 per hour minimum wage for 2,000 hours per year earns $8,700 annually, which is below the official government definition of poverty for a family of three.

About 5 million Americans earn the minimum wage, two-thirds of them part-time workers. Five percent of all men and 10 percent of all women in jobs with hourly wages (1 out of 20 full-time workers and 1 out of 5 part-time workers) earn the minimum wage. Of these workers, 2 million are older than 25, and 1 million live in families with incomes below the government's poverty line. Nearly 1 out of 3 working teenagers—but fewer than 1 out of 20 workers over age 25—earn the minimum wage. About half of minimum-wage earners work in retail trade, most as sales clerks.

The minimum wage causes a surplus of labor services (unemployment) when it exceeds the equilibrium wage. It lowers the quantity of labor services demanded from Q^E to Q^D in **Figure 8.6.** Although more people want jobs, employers are willing to hire only Q^D workers, so the minimum wage reduces employment.

The effect of a minimum wage on employment is easier to understand if you think like an employer and ask yourself, "If I have to pay $4.25 an hour plus legally required fringe benefits (such as workers' compensation insurance or retirement plans), is it profitable to hire a worker who produces only $4.00 worth of output each hour?" A minimum wage reduces employment both by making fewer jobs available and by turning full-time jobs into part-time jobs.

EVIDENCE

Statistical evidence shows that the minimum wage has a stronger effect on employment of teenagers than on employment of adults. A 10 percent rise in the minimum wage reduces employment of teenagers by about 1 to 3 percent (probably closer to 1 percent). This means that an increase in the U.S. minimum wage from $4.25 to $4.70 an hour would eliminate about 80,000 teenage jobs. The effect of a minimum wage on adult employment is much smaller. Most evidence indicates that blacks and females lose more jobs as a result of a minimum wage than do whites and males.

The minimum wage helps some workers and hurts others. The winners include unskilled workers who keep their jobs and receive higher wages than they would earn without the minimum wage along with more skilled workers who

---

FIGURE 8.6

MINIMUM WAGE

A minimum wage reduces employment from Q^E to Q^D.

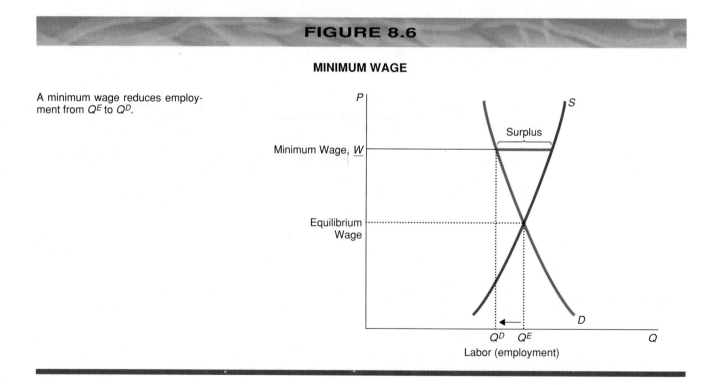

(along with machinery) replace less-skilled workers because of the minimum wage. The losers are unskilled workers who lose their jobs, who never find jobs, or who get only part-time jobs because of the minimum wage.

FOR REVIEW

8.1 Draw a graph to show how a maximum legal price below the equilibrium price affects output. Why does it cause a shortage? Draw a graph to show how a minimum legal price above the equilibrium price affects output. Why does it cause a surplus?

8.2 Which buyers obtain goods with rationing by waiting?

8.3 How does a maximum legal price on an input affect the price of the final good (the good that the input helps to produce)?

8.4 Discuss the effects of a minimum–wage law.

QUESTIONS

8.5 A usury law establishes a maximum legal interest rate (the price of a loan). Discuss the effects of a usury law with a maximum legal interest rate below the equilibrium interest rate.

8.6 Suppose that landlords avoid rent controls with tie-in sales by requiring renters to rent furniture from them. (Renters must pay separately for the furniture.) Use a graph of supply and demand to show the equilibrium rental price of furniture. What would happen to the rental price for furniture if rent controls on apartments were eliminated?

TAXES

There is no known civilization that did not tax. The first civilization we know anything about began 6,000 years ago in Sumer, a fertile plain in modern Iraq. The dawn of history, and tax history, is recorded on clay cones excavated at Lagash, in Sumer. The people of Lagash instituted heavy taxation during a terrible war, but when the war ended, the tax men refused to give up their taxing powers. From one end of the land to the other, these clay cones say "there were the tax collectors." Everything was taxed. Even the dead could not be buried unless a tax was paid. The story ends when a good king, named Urukagina, "established the freedom" of the people, and once again, "There were no tax collectors." This may not have been a wise policy because shortly thereafter the city was destroyed by foreign invaders.[4]

PRICES TO BUYERS VERSUS PRICES TO SELLERS

Most state governments in the United States charge sales taxes. When you buy a good with a price of $10, you pay $10 *plus* the sales tax. These taxes are often expressed as tax rates.

tax rate — the per-unit tax on a good, expressed as a percentage of its price

The **tax rate** on a good is its per-unit tax, expressed as a percentage of its price.

---

[4]Charles Adams, *Fight, Flight, Fraud: The Story of Taxation* (Buffalo, N.Y.: Euro-Dutch Publishers), pp. 9–10.

A tax might be expressed as a fixed amount of money, such as 12 cents per gallon of gasoline, or as a percentage of the price, such as a 5 percent sales tax or a 28 percent income tax. When you buy a $5.00 good with a 5 percent sales tax, you pay $5.25 to the store. The store keeps $5.00 and sends $0.25 to the government. The tax creates a gap between two prices: the *price buyers pay* ($5.25) and the *price sellers receive* after the government gets its money ($5.00). The difference between these prices is the per-unit tax ($0.25).

EXAMPLES

The federal government charges a tax of 14.1 cents per gallon of gasoline. This tax is included in the prices displayed on signs at gas stations. If you pay $1.259 per gallon for gasoline (the price to you, the buyer), the price the seller receives is $1.118, which is $1.259 minus $0.141.

Zach works for General Utilities, which pays him $14.00 per hour. He pays one-fourth of his income to the government as income taxes: his tax rate is 25 percent. Think of Zach as a seller of labor services, which his employer buys. The buyer pays a price of $14 per hour, but the seller (Zach) receives a price of $10.50 per hour. The per-unit tax is $3.50 per hour.

EQUILIBRIUM WITH A TAX

Figure 8.7 shows equilibrium with a tax on sales. The price buyers pay (including tax) is P_B. The price sellers receive (net of tax) is P_S. The difference, $P_B - P_S$, equals the per-unit tax. The equilibrium quantity bought and sold is Q_1. The equilibrium with a tax satisfies two conditions: the price buyers pay (including tax) exceeds the price sellers receive (net of tax) by the per-unit tax, and the quantity supplied equals the quantity demanded.

FIGURE 8.7

SUPPLY AND DEMAND WITH A TAX

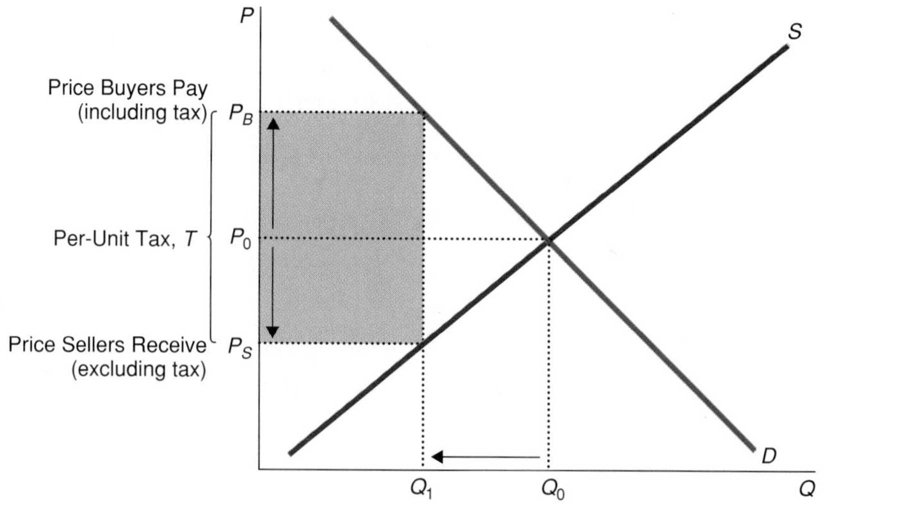

Buyers pay P_B dollars per unit of the good. Sellers keep P_S dollars after taxes, while T dollars per unit go to the government as taxes. The tax per unit, T, separates the price buyers pay and the price sellers receive net of taxes: $P_B = P_S + T$. The tax reduces the equilibrium quantity from Q_0 to Q_1. The area of the shaded rectangle shows total tax payments.

Without a tax, the equilibrium price would be P_0 and the equilibrium quantity traded would be Q_0. (See Figure 8.7.) A tax raises the price to buyers from P_0 to P_B, lowers the price to sellers from P_0 to P_S, and lowers the quantity bought and sold from Q_0 to Q_1.

EXPLANATION
The price buyers pay (including tax) is relevant for demand. The demand curve in Figure 8.7 shows a quantity demanded of Q_1 if buyers pay the price P_B. The price sellers receive (net of tax) is relevant for supply. The supply curve shows a quantity supplied of Q_1 units if sellers receive the price P_S. The price buyers pay, P_B, equals the price sellers receive, P_S, plus the per-unit tax, T. Since the quantity demanded equals the quantity supplied, this is the equilibrium.

EXAMPLE
Figure 8.8 shows the supply and demand for tapes. The demand curve shows that buyers want to buy 7 million tapes if the price they pay (including tax) is $10.50. The supply curve shows that sellers want to sell 7 million tapes if the price they receive (net of tax) is $10.00. The two conditions for an equilibrium are met: the price buyers pay exceeds the price sellers receive by the 50-cent-per-tape tax, and the quantity demanded equals the quantity supplied. Figure 8.8 shows the equilibrium. The figure also shows that, without the tax, the equilibrium price would be $10.20 and 8 million tapes would be bought and sold.

DRAWING THE EQUILIBRIUM
Figure 8.9 shows how to find the equilibrium with a tax in a graph. Fit a line with a height equal to the per-unit tax into the supply-demand diagram until its top

FIGURE 8.8

TAX ON SALES OF TAPES

A 50-cent-per-unit tax on tapes raises the price that buyers pay, including tax, from $10.20 to $10.50, and it reduces the price sellers receive, excluding tax, from $10.20 to $10.00. The tax reduces the number of tapes sold from 8 million to 7 million. The area of the shaded rectangle shows total tax payments of $3.5 million (50 cents each on 7 million tapes).

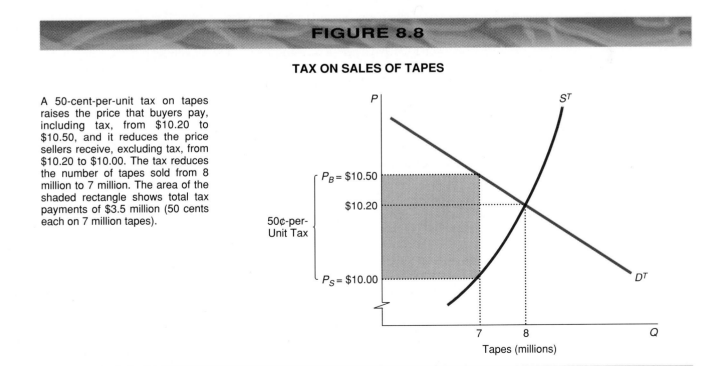

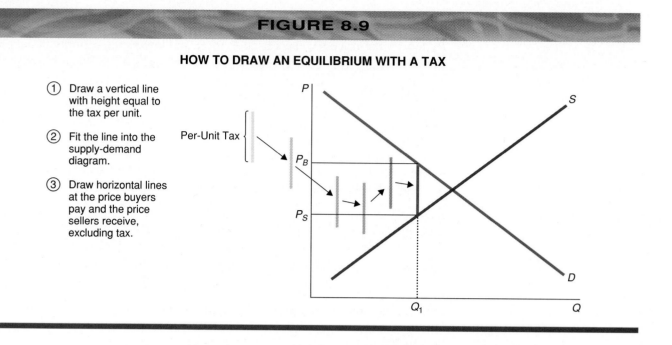

FIGURE 8.9

HOW TO DRAW AN EQUILIBRIUM WITH A TAX

① Draw a vertical line with height equal to the tax per unit.

② Fit the line into the supply-demand diagram.

③ Draw horizontal lines at the price buyers pay and the price sellers receive, excluding tax.

touches the demand curve and its bottom touches the supply curve. The top of the line shows the price that buyers pay, including tax; the bottom of the line shows the price that sellers receive, excluding the tax.

TOTAL TAX PAYMENTS

The area of the shaded rectangle in Figure 8.7 shows total tax payments from the tax example, that is, the total amount of money that buyers or sellers pay the government. Total tax payments equal the per-unit tax multiplied by the number of units of the good that people buy. The height of the shaded rectangle shows the per-unit tax (T) and the base of the rectangle shows the number of units sold (Q_1), so total tax payments equal the area of the rectangle (T times Q_1). Of course, total tax payments equal the government's tax revenue, or its total receipt of money from the tax, so the shaded rectangle also shows the government's tax revenue. The area of the shaded rectangle in the example in Figure 8.8 is $3.5 million, which equals the rectangle's height (50 cents per unit) times its base (7 million units).

HOW BUYERS AND SELLERS SHARE THE TAX PAYMENT

Buyers and sellers each pay part of the tax on production or sales of a good. The price that buyers pay (including tax) rises by less than the amount of the tax, and the price that sellers receive (net of tax) falls by less than the amount of the tax. Sellers pass on part of a tax increase to consumers in the form of a higher price, but they pay the rest of the tax. As **Figure 8.10** shows, the price to buyers rises a lot when demand is very inelastic or supply is very elastic. The price to buyers rises only a little when demand is very elastic or supply is very inelastic.

EXAMPLE

The 50-cent tax on tapes in Figure 8.8 raises the price that buyers pay (including tax) by 30 cents, from $10.20 to $10.50, so buyers pay 30 cents of the 50-cent tax.

The tax reduces the price that sellers receive (excluding tax) by 20 cents, from $10.20 to $10.00, so sellers pay 20 cents of the tax. If the demand for tapes is more inelastic or the supply is more elastic, as in Figure 8.10a, the price to buyers rises more and buyers pay a larger fraction of the tax. (Buyers pay 45 cents of the 50-cent tax in the figure, and sellers pay only 5 cents.) If the demand for tapes is more elastic or the supply is more inelastic, as in Figure 8.10b, the price to buyers rises less and buyers pay a smaller fraction of the tax. Buyers pay 10 cents of the 50-cent tax in the figure, and sellers pay 40 cents.

WHY DON'T BUYERS PAY THE WHOLE TAX?

Sellers choose not to raise the price to buyers by the full amount of the 50-cent tax in Figure 8.8. If they raised the price by 50 cents per tape, the price to buyers would rise to $10.70 and buyers would want fewer than 7 million tapes. Since the price to sellers would remain at $10.20, sellers would want to sell 8 million tapes. This would create a surplus, and the price would fall toward the equilibrium ($10.50 to buyers and $10.00 to sellers). So, in equilibrium, sellers do not pass the entire tax on to consumers; buyers and sellers share the tax payments. Precisely how they share the payments depends on the elasticities of supply and demand.

TAXING BUYERS VERSUS TAXING SELLERS

The price to buyers, including tax, does *not* depend on who is responsible (buyers or sellers) for sending the tax money to the government. Similarly, the price to sellers, net of tax, does not depend on who must send the tax money to the government. Buyers and sellers share the tax in the same way regardless of whether the government requires buyers or sellers to pay the tax.

FIGURE 8.10

HOW BUYERS AND SELLERS SHARE A TAX PAYMENT

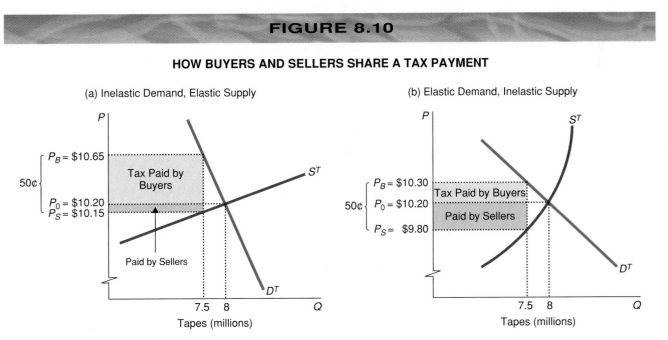

(a) Inelastic Demand, Elastic Supply

(b) Elastic Demand, Inelastic Supply

(a) More inelastic demand and more elastic supply shifts more of the tax to buyers.

(b) More elastic demand and more inelastic supply shifts more of the tax to sellers.

EXPLANATION

Suppose that the government imposes a tax on sales of a good. Figure 8.7 shows that if the tax is T per unit, buyers pay the price P_B and sellers receive the price P_S. If the government requires sellers to send in the tax money (as is typical with sales taxes in the United States), buyers pay P_B dollars at the store, and sellers send T dollars to the government and keep the remaining P_S dollars. If, instead, the government requires buyers to send in the tax money, buyers pay the price P_B in two parts. They pay P_S dollars to the store and T dollars to the government. Since $P_S + T = P_B$, buyers pay the same total price regardless of who must send the tax money to the government. Sellers keep P_S dollars (net of taxes) in either case. Who sends the tax money to the government does not matter because buyers pay the government either directly or indirectly by giving sellers the money to send to the government.

EXAMPLES

If sellers are responsible for paying the tax money in Figure 8.8 to the government, buyers pay $10.50 to the store for a tape and the store sends 50 cents to the government and keeps $10.00. If, instead, buyers are responsible for paying the tax money to the government, buyers pay only $10.00 to the store for a tape, but they also pay 50 cents to the government. Either way, tapes cost buyers $10.50 each and sellers get $10.00, net of the tax.

The Social Security tax in the United States has two parts: an employer's part and an employee's part. If you earn $20,000 per year, your employer pays $1,530, 7.65 percent of your salary, in Social Security taxes. You pay an additional 7.65 percent for Social Security tax, which is deducted from your salary. You are the seller of labor services and your employer is the buyer in this analysis. The price that the buyer pays for your labor services is $21,530 per year; the price that you, the seller, receive, net of the tax, is $18,470 (which is your $20,000 salary minus the $1,530 you pay directly in Social Security taxes). So:

$$\left. \begin{array}{l} \text{Price to buyer} = \$21,530 \\[2em] \text{Price to seller} = \$18,470 \end{array} \right\} \$3,060 \; tax$$

If the law changes so that your employer must pay the entire $3,060 tax to the government, the equilibrium price of your labor services (your salary) falls from $20,000 to $18,470 per year. This makes no difference either to you or to your employer, who still pays $21,530 per year while you still get $18,470. If the law changes so that *you* must pay the entire $3,060 tax to the government, the equilibrium price of your labor services (your salary) rises to $21,530 per year. Again, neither you or your employer will care about the change: your employer still pays $21,530 per year and you still get $18,470. Buyers and sellers share the tax the same way regardless of who pays the money to the government.

–––––––––––––––––––––– **FOR REVIEW** ––––––––––––––––––––––

8.7 Explain the difference between the price that buyers pay, including tax, and the price that sellers receive, net of tax.

8.8 Draw a graph to show how a sales tax affects (a) output; (b) the price that buyers pay, including tax; (c) the price that sellers receive, net of tax; and (d) total tax payments.

8.9 In what sense do buyers and sellers share the payment of a sales tax?

———————————————— Questions ————————————————

8.10 Suppose that the tax law changes so that buyers, rather than sellers, must pay sales tax to the government. Would sellers benefit from this change? Explain.

8.11 Draw a graph of the supply and demand for loans to show the effects of a tax on interest income earned by lenders.

WHY TAXES REDUCE THE QUANTITY TRADED

A tax reduces the quantity of a good bought and sold because the gains from some trades are smaller than the per-unit tax.[5] People stop making those trades because of the tax. People make only those trades that create a total gain (to buyers and sellers) that exceeds the tax.

EXAMPLE

Shelley wants to trade her car for Jake's stereo system. Jake agrees because the car is worth $800 to him and the stereo is worth only $700 to him. The car is worth only $750 to Shelley, but the stereo is worth $800 to her. They both benefit if they trade: the value of Shelley's gain is $50, and the value of Jake's gain is $100. Their total gain from the trade is $150.

If the government puts a $200 tax on this trade, Shelley and Jake choose not to trade. By not trading, they avoid paying the tax. Shelley would trade only if the tax she would have to pay were less than her $50 gain from the trade; Jake would trade only if the tax he would have to pay were less than his $100 gain from the trade. If the tax on their trade totaled less than $150, they would trade because the total gains from the trade would exceed the tax, so they could share the net gain. But the tax on their trade exceeds $150, so they choose not to trade.

When there are many traders like Shelley and Jake, a tax on trade usually prevents some, but not all of the trades. A tax prevents trades with gains smaller than the tax, but trades that create larger gains occur even with the tax. This is why a tax reduces the equilibrium quantity traded.

SPECIAL CASES OF ELASTICITIES

Figure 8.11 shows four special cases of elasticities. These special cases are important because some real-life situations approach these extreme cases closely. You should compare the effects of taxes in these special cases with the general case in Figure 8.7.

PERFECTLY INELASTIC DEMAND

Figure 8.11 shows how to draw supply-and-demand graphs with taxes in four special cases of elasticities of supply and demand. Panel a shows the effect of a tax when the demand curve is perfectly inelastic. A tax raises the price that buyers pay, including tax, but it does not change the price that sellers receive, net of tax, nor does it change the quantity bought and sold. Because the price paid by buy-

———————————————————

[5]Chapter 3 discussed gains from trades.

FIGURE 8.11

TAXES WITH SPECIAL CASES OF ELASTICITIES

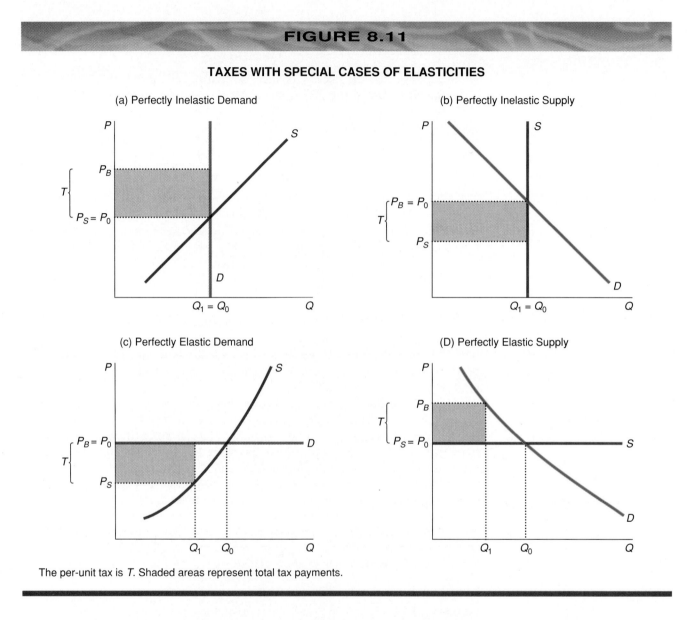

The per-unit tax is *T*. Shaded areas represent total tax payments.

ers rises by the amount of the tax, buyers pay all the tax in this case. The shaded rectangle in the figure shows total tax payments.

EXPLANATION

Perfectly inelastic demand means that the quantity demanded is Q_0 regardless of the price. People want to buy as much when the price is P_B as when it is P_0. Sellers, however, are willing to sell the same amount only if the price they receive, net of tax, stays at P_0. So the price to sellers stays at P_0 and the price to buyers rises to P_B.

PERFECTLY INELASTIC SUPPLY

Panel b of Figure 8.11 shows the effects of a tax if supply is perfectly inelastic. The tax lowers the price that sellers receive, net of tax, and leaves the price that buy-

Sawmill closings were caused by tax on lumber: Lawmakers

OTTAWA (CP) — Five Northern Ontario sawmills have shut down and more closures are imminent because of Ottawa's 15 percent surtax on softwood lumber, says a task force of Liberal MPs from the region.

The MPs, who held hearings in six Northern Ontario communities in mid-February, said yesterday the region has lost 900 jobs so far due to a sharp decline in softwood exports to the United States.

"A lot of companies are losing money that never lost money before," said Maurice Foster, MP for Algoma and chairman of the group, at a news conference. "A lot of companies are operating one shift rather than three shifts."

Source: "Sawmill Closings Were Caused by Tax on Lumber: Lawmakers," *Montréal Gazette,* March 10, 1989, p. E1.

ers pay, including tax, unchanged. Sellers pay the full amount of the tax and the tax does not change the equilibrium quantity bought and sold. The shaded rectangle shows total tax payments.

EXPLANATION

Perfectly inelastic supply means that the quantity supplied is Q_0 regardless of the price. The amount of the good for sale is fixed. If the price that buyers pay were higher than P_0, people would buy less, which would create a surplus. Therefore, in equilibrium the price that buyers pay, including tax, remains at P_0. The price that sellers receive falls by the full amount of the tax, and the quantity traded remains at the fixed amount that sellers have for sale.

PERFECTLY ELASTIC DEMAND OR SUPPLY

Panel c of Figure 8.11 shows the effects of a tax when demand is perfectly elastic. A tax lowers the price that sellers receive while leaving the price that buyers pay unchanged and reducing the equilibrium quantity. Panel d shows the effects of a tax when supply is perfectly elastic. A tax raises the price that buyers pay while leaving the price that sellers receive unchanged and reducing the equilibrium quantity.

The taxes [in 19th-century England] were important not only because of the bite they put on people but because of their individual social consequences. Until repealed in 1861, for example, the tax on paper helped to keep books scarce and expensive. Soap was taxed until 1853 with the consequence of the poor personal hygiene which may have contributed to some of the epi-demics of typhus and other diseases that periodically dev-astated elements of the popu-lation. (In fact, a black market sprang up in soap, and it was smuggled in from Ireland, where there was no tax, to the western shore of England.) The tax on win-dows mentioned in [Jane Austen's] Mansfield Park was perhaps the most pernicious one, since even a hole cut in a wall for ventilation was counted as a window, mak-ing, among other things, for dark houses for the poor. The fact that a family was taxed £2.8s. for each male servant in 1812 (bachelors £4.8s.) helped to steer people toward womenservants—both this and the tax on carriages were based on the government's (correct) assumption that these were two of the leading ways to get revenues from the wealthy.

A tax on any good reduces its production and sales.

Source: Daniel Pool, "What Jane Austen Ate and Charles Dickens Knew" (New York: Simon & Schuster, 1993).

EXPLANATION

If demand is perfectly inelastic, a tax cannot raise the price that buyers pay because the quantity demanded would fall to zero because no buyer is willing to pay a higher price. So the price that buyers pay, including tax, remains the same and the price that sellers receive, net of tax, falls by the full amount of the tax. This reduces both the quantity supplied and output.

The perfectly elastic supply curve means that sellers would not be willing to produce and sell the good at all at a price below P_0, so the price received by sellers does not fall. Instead, the price paid by buyers rises by the amount of the tax. Buyers, however, do not want as much at the higher price, so a tax reduces the equilibrium quantity bought and sold.

TAX RATES AND TOTAL TAX PAYMENTS

You might expect an increase in the per-unit tax on production, sales, or purchases of a good to raise total tax payments. An increase can *reduce* total tax payments, however, if it reduces the quantity traded sufficiently.

Figure 8.12a shows the usual case, in which a higher tax rate raises total tax payments and government revenue from the tax. The area of the rectangle shows total tax payments; that area is larger with the higher tax rate, T_2, than with the lower tax rate, T_1.

Figure 8.12b shows that a higher tax rate can reduce total tax payments and government revenue. The area of the taller, thinner rectangle shows total tax payments with the higher tax rate, T_2. That area is smaller with the higher tax rate than with the lower tax rate, T_1. When the tax rate rises from T_1 to T_2, people pay

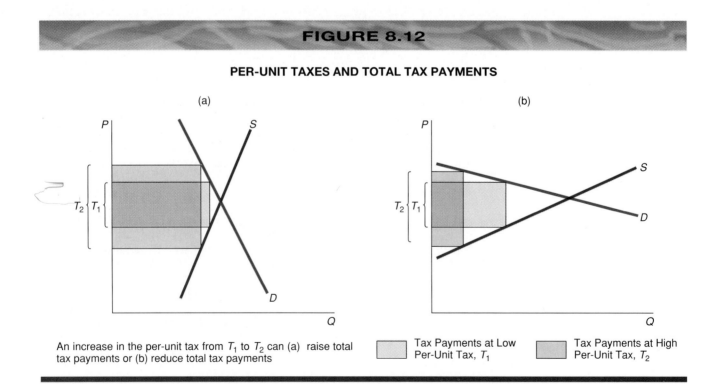

FIGURE 8.12

PER-UNIT TAXES AND TOTAL TAX PAYMENTS

(a)

(b)

An increase in the per-unit tax from T_1 to T_2 can (a) raise total tax payments or (b) reduce total tax payments

Tax Payments at Low Per-Unit Tax, T_1

Tax Payments at High Per-Unit Tax, T_2

FIGURE 8.13

A LAFFER CURVE

If the tax rate is below T^*, a tax rate increase raises total tax payments. If the tax rate is above T^*, a tax rate increase reduces total tax payments.

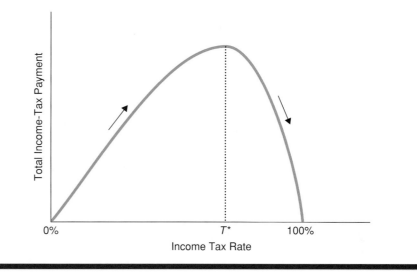

a higher tax on each unit they buy and sell, but the amount that they buy and sell falls so much that total tax payments fall.

The idea that higher tax rates can reduce government tax revenue is sometimes captured in a graph called a *Laffer curve,* like the one in **Figure 8.13.** If the income tax rate were zero, no one would pay income taxes. If the income tax rate were 100 percent, no one would bother working to earn taxable income and total tax payments would again be zero. For this reason, very low or very high tax rates create very low tax payments. Total tax payments are higher at intermediate tax rates, such as 40 percent. Figure 8.13 shows the general relation between the tax rate and total tax payments. If the tax rate is less than T^* (a particular intermediate tax rate), then an increase in the tax rate raises total tax payments as in Figure 8.12a. If the tax rate exceeds T^*, a further increase in the tax rate reduces total tax payments as in Figure 8.12b. In that case, the government could increase its tax revenue by lowering the tax rate.[6]

Statistical evidence shows that most real-life tax rates are below T^*. Some evidence does indicate, however, that tax payments in the United States increased as a result of cuts in the highest income tax rates from 70 percent to 50 percent and then to 33 percent in the 1980s.[7] Some evidence also suggests that government tax revenue falls from increases in the tax rate on certain investment income.

---

[6]The tax rate T^* maximizes total tax payments. This does not imply that T^* is in any sense a bad or good tax rate, but it implies that tax rates higher than T^* are economically inefficient because some lower tax rate would raise just as much tax revenue for the government.

[7]See *The Growth Experiment* by Lawrence Lindsay, an economist who is now a governor of the Federal Reserve System (New York: Basic Books, 1988).

SUBSIDIES

Subsidies work like negative taxes. The price that buyers pay (net of the subsidy) is less than the price that sellers receive (including the subsidy). The difference is the per-unit subsidy.

The U.S. government subsidizes production of many goods with direct payments to producers, special tax breaks, loan guarantees, or other programs. **Figure 8.14** shows the equilibrium when the government subsidizes production of a good. The price that sellers receive including the subsidy, P_S, exceeds the price that buyers pay, P_B, by the per-unit subsidy, Y. The subsidy raises the price that sellers receive from P_0 to P_S, reduces the price buyers pay from P_0 to P_B, and raises the quantity traded from Q_0 to Q_1. The area of the shaded rectangle shows the total cost of the subsidy to the government. The height of the rectangle is the subsidy per unit, Y, and the base is the number of units subsidized, Q_1. The subsidy costs the government Y times Q_1.

Buyers and sellers share the benefits of the subsidy because the subsidy raises the price that sellers receive and lowers the price that buyers pay. Neither the price to buyers or the price to sellers depends on which group (buyers or sellers) gets the subsidy from the government. Buyers and sellers share the subsidy in the same way, regardless of whether the government pays the subsidy to buyers or to sellers.

FOR REVIEW

8.12 Draw graphs to show the effects of a tax on sales when (a) demand is perfectly inelastic, (b) supply is perfectly inelastic, (c) demand is perfectly elastic, and (d) supply is perfectly elastic.

8.13 Draw a graph to show why an increase in the tax rate can reduce government tax revenue. Explain in words why this can happen.

FIGURE 8.14

SUPPLY AND DEMAND WITH A SUBSIDY

A subsidy creates a gap between the price that sellers receive and the price that buyers pay. The price that sellers receive, including the subsidy, P_S, exceeds the price that buyers pay, P_B, by the per-unit subsidy, Y. That is, $P_S = P_B + Y$. The subsidy raises the equilibrium quantity from Q_0 to Q_1. The area of the shaded rectangle shows the cost of the subsidy to the government.

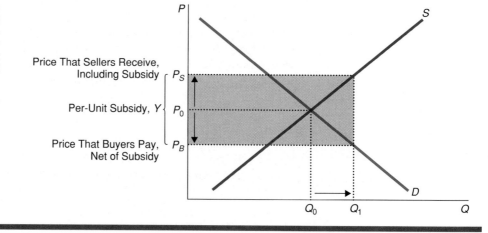

8.14 Draw a graph to show how subsidizing production of a good affects (a) its output, (b) the price that buyers pay, and (c) the price that sellers receive. (d) Use your graph to show the total cost of the subsidy to the government.

──────────────────── QUESTIONS ────────────────────

8.15 Comment on this statement: "An increase in the tax rate on a good leads to a larger increase in tax revenue to the government when the demand and supply curves are more inelastic."

8.16 State governments subsidize education at many state colleges and universities. Draw a graph to help explain how these subsidies affect (a) college tuition, (b) college revenue per student, and (c) the total number of students at these institutions. (d) How does subsidized education at state colleges and universities affect tuition and financial aid at private colleges?

TAXES AND OTHER RESTRICTIONS ON INTERNATIONAL TRADE

This section builds on the discussion of international trade in Chapter 7, adding taxes and government controls to that discussion.

TARIFFS

Almost all governments tax imports from other countries. To do this, they impose taxes called *tariffs*.

tariff — a tax on an import

> A **tariff** is a tax on an import.

The United States has set tariffs on many products, from televisions to pasta. The largest American tariffs are on imports of textiles and clothing, steel, automobiles, and sugar. The North American Free Trade Agreement (NAFTA) is phasing out all tariffs on trade between the United States, Canada, and Mexico.

Figure 8.15 shows the effects of a tariff. Panel a shows the equilibrium without a tariff; this graph resembles Figure 7.1. Panel b shows the equilibrium with a tariff. This graph resembles Figure 7.6 because the tariff works like a cost of arbitrage.

Without international trade, the U.S. price is $300 and the foreign price is $200. With international trade and no tariff (as in Panel a), the world price is $260 and the U.S. imports the good from other countries. In Panel b, the $50 tariff raises the price to the buyer country (the United States) from $260 to $280 and lowers the price to the foreign seller from $260 to $230. The tariff reduces international trade as U.S. imports and foreign exports fall from 180 units of the good per month (Panel a) to 100 units per month (Panel b).

EXPLANATION

An American who buys from a foreign seller must pay the U.S. government a tariff of $50, so the price that American buyers pay, $280, exceeds the price that foreign sellers receive, $230, by the $50 tariff. Since Americans can buy from foreign sellers, American sellers cannot charge more than $280. (If they did, no one would buy from them.) Therefore, the good's U.S. price is $280 with the tariff. When an American buyer buys from an American seller, no one pays a tariff. The tariff is a tax only on imports.

FIGURE 8.15

EFFECTS ON A TARIFF OR QUOTA ON IMPORTS

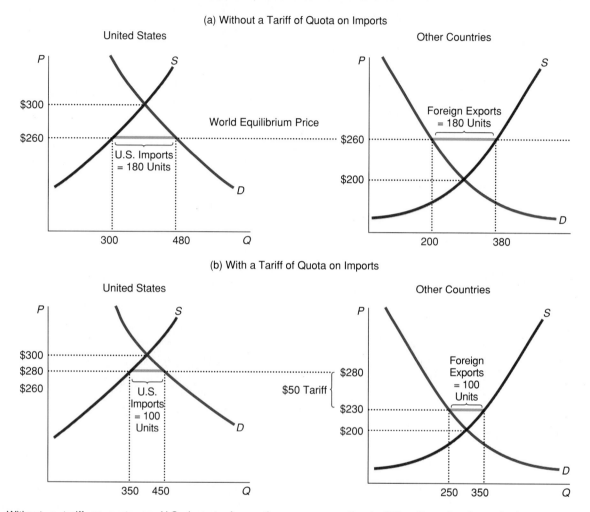

(a) Without a Tariff of Quota on Imports

(b) With a Tariff of Quota on Imports

(a) Without a tariff or quota on U.S. imports from other countries, the world equilibrium price is $260. The United States consumes 480 units and produces only 300, so it imports 180 units. Other countries produce 380 units and consume only 200; they export 180 units.

(b) With a $50-per-unit tariff on U.S. imports from other countries, the U.S. price, $280, exceeds the price in other countries, $230, by the per-unit tariff. The tariff reduces U.S. consumption to 450 units and raises U.S. output to 350 units, so U.S. imports fall to 100 units. The tariff raises foreign consumption to 250 units and reduces foreign output to 350 units, so foreign exports fall to 100 units.

An import quota that restricts U.S. imports to 100 units raises the U.S. price to $280, raises U.S. output to 350 units, and lowers U.S. consumption to 450 units. The U.S. import quota limits foreign exports to 100 units, so it lowers the foreign price to $230, raises foreign consumption to 250 units, and reduces foreign output to 350. The effects of a quota are the same as the effects of a tariff, except that the U.S. government collects revenue from a tariff but none from a quota.

Buyers and sellers share the tariff payment. The tariff hurts American buyers because it raises the price that they pay for the good and it reduces the amount that they buy. It helps American sellers because it raises the price that they receive. The American tariff hurts foreign sellers because the price that they receive falls from $260 to $230. It helps foreign buyers by reducing the price that they pay.

Higher tax hits utility truck imports

By Jim Freschi and James R. Healey, USA Today

The U.S. government just added up to $3,000 to the price of some imported trucks.

The Treasury Department said Thursday that imported sport-utility vehicles with only two doors are meant for hauling cargo, not people, so must pay the truck tax—a tariff equal to 25 percent of what the truck costs its American importer.

A tariff on imports raises prices to consumers.
Source: Jim Freschi and James R. Healey, "Higher Tax Hits Utility Truck Imports," *USA Today*, December 17, 1989, p. B1.

import quota — a limit on the quantity of imports of a good

Group seeks phase-out of steel-import quotas

The program is linked to high prices and shortages

By Jonathan P. Hicks

An association of steel importers pitted itself against the nation's major steelmakers yesterday, calling for the Government to modify the program that limits steel imports.

"We are opposed to any effort to renew steel quotas or to broaden them," said William C. Lane, a trade specialist with Caterpillar Inc., the large machinery manufacturer based in Peoria, Ill. "Quota-induced shortages of steel have hurt our efforts to meet export demand."

Import quotas, like tariffs, raise prices in the importing country.
Source: "Group Seeks Phase-out of Steel-Import Quotas," *New York Times*, December 6, 1988, p. D7.

QUOTAS ON IMPORTS

Most countries impose legal limits on imports of certain goods, or import quotas.

An **import quota** is a limit on the quantity of imports of a good.

Figure 8.15 can also show the effects of an import quota, which are similar to the effects of a tariff. Without a quota, the world price is $260 as in Panel a, the United States produces 300 units of the good each month, and U.S. consumption is 480 units per month. Therefore, the United States imports 180 units of the good each month.

Panel b shows the effects of an import quota of 100 units per month. The horizontal distance between the U.S. supply and demand curves (which shows U.S. imports) falls to 100 units. The U.S. price rises from $260 to $280, U.S. consumption falls from 480 units to 450 units, and U.S. production rises to 350 units. The foreign price falls from $260 to $230, foreign consumption rises to 250 units, and foreign production falls to 350 units.

The import quota, like a tariff, raises the good's price in the United States. The quota differs from a tariff in one important way: the government collects tax revenue from a tariff, but not from a quota. A quota raises the price that U.S. buyers pay, but the extra money goes to foreign sellers who export goods to the United States.

The quota hurts American buyers because it raises the price that they pay. It helps American sellers because it raises the price that they can charge. It helps foreign buyers because it lowers the foreign price. It has mixed effects on foreign sellers. The import quota helps foreign sellers who are lucky enough to export to the United States because those sellers charge a higher price than they would charge without the quota; it hurts foreign sellers who cannot export to the United States because the quota limits U.S. imports.[8]

---

[8]Chapter 11 discusses the sizes of these gains and losses.

SOCIAL AND ECONOMIC ISSUES

Government Milk and Sugar Programs

Milk

The U.S. government has come to own a large amount of milk and cheese through its milk program. The government sets minimum legal prices above the equilibrium (called *support prices*) on three classes of grade-A milk and grade-B milk, and buys all the surplus milk at those prices. The government helps keep the cost of buying milk down by paying farmers not to produce milk, to slaughter cows, to get out of the dairy business for five years, and through various other programs. The government has also taxed milk to try to reduce output.

The milk support price exceeds the world equilibrium price, so foreign producers try to export their milk to the United States. To prevent people from importing cheaper milk from other countries, the government imposes import quotas.

U.S. dairy programs began in 1922 when the government exempted dairy-marketing organizations from antitrust laws. (See Chapter 14.) The government began a formal program to keep milk prices high in 1937, setting minimum milk prices above equilibrium prices and promising to buy milk to keep prices above this level. The government added import quotas in 1953.

Most estimates (including the government's own) suggest that these programs roughly double the price of milk. In a recent and typical year, these programs raised the cost of milk to consumers by about $10 billion and cost taxpayers about $2 billion. Of course, the higher milk prices benefit producers.

Sugar

Sugar costs more in the United States than in the rest of the world. In a typical recent year, the world wholesale price of sugar was 14 cents per pound, but the U.S. price was 24 cents per pound. This is the result of the U.S. government sugar program, which sets a support price for sugar in the United States. The government keeps the price high with import quotas that keep imports at less than 10 percent of U.S. sugar consumption.

The U.S. government imposed a tariff on sugar imports in 1796, and a large tariff on sugar continued for most of the 19th century. The government raised the U.S. price far above the world price only in the 20th century, however. In 1981, the U.S. government began setting a support price for sugar and established a tariff equal to 50 percent of the world sugar price, adding import quotas in 1982. The high price of sugar has led U.S. buyers to substitute other sweeteners such as high-fructose corn syrup, honey, and maple syrup. Soft-drink companies, for example, replaced sugar with high-fructose corn syrup. (Coke Classic does not really follow the original Coca-Cola formula, which was sweetened with sugar.)

Because U.S. import quotas prevent foreign farmers from exporting sugar to the United States, those farmers often raise other crops, including marijuana and coca. The average person in the United States consumes about 60 pounds of sugar and about the same amount of other nondiet sweeteners such as honey and corn syrup. This amounts to 7 million or 8 million tons of sugar per year for the whole United States, or 15 million tons of sugar and other nondiet sweeteners, which is about 15 billion pounds of sugar per year. At a U.S. price 10 cents above the world price, the level of recent years, the quotas cost U.S. consumers about $1.5 billion. In addition, people would buy lower-price sugar instead of higher-price corn syrup and other sweeteners without the quotas, so this figure underestimates the cost of the quota to consumers. Estimates of the total cost to consumers range from $1.5 billion to $3 billion per year.

FOR REVIEW

8.17 Draw a graph to show the equilibrium with a tariff on imports. Show (a) output in each country, (b) consumption in each country, (c) the price in each country, (d) the per-unit tariff, and (e) total tariff (tax) payments.

8.18 Draw a graph to illustrate the effects of an import quota. How do the effects of a quota differ from the effects of a tariff?

QUESTION

8.19 Who gains and who loses from the elimination of a tariff or quota on imports? What groups might be expected to favor eliminating a tariff and what groups might be expected to oppose it?

CONCLUSIONS

PRICE CONTROLS: MAXIMUM LEGAL PRICES

A maximum legal price below the equilibrium price causes a shortage by reducing the quantity supplied and raising the quantity demanded. It reduces production of the good and causes nonprice rationing based on some formal or informal system for choosing which buyers can buy goods and how much each can buy. This nonprice rationing may occur through queuing (rationing by waiting), rationing by coupons, or bribery. With rationing by coupons, the demand and supply for coupons determines their price.

Rent control is an example of a maximum legal price. It reduces the number of apartments available and creates a shortage. Price controls often lead to black markets where transactions take place at illegal prices. A maximum legal price on an input raises the price of the goods produced with that input.

PRICE CONTROLS: MINIMUM LEGAL PRICES

A minimum legal price above the equilibrium price causes a surplus by reducing the quantity demanded and raising the quantity supplied. It lowers output of the good (along with the quantity demanded) because producers can sell only as many goods as people are willing to buy at the minimum legal price. One minimum legal price, the minimum wage, reduces employment (particularly of teenagers).

TAXES

A tax on sales or production of a good creates a gap between the price that buyers pay, including tax, and the price that sellers receive, net of tax; the difference is the per-unit tax. A tax raises the price to buyers, lowers the price to sellers, and lowers the quantity bought and sold. Buyers and sellers share the tax payment since buyers pay more than they would pay without the tax and sellers receive less (net of tax). Neither the price buyers pay or the price sellers receive depends on who is legally responsible for paying the tax to the government, so neither buyers or sellers care who must legally pay the tax. A tax reduces output because the gains from some trades are smaller than the tax that people would have to pay if they made those trades. An increase in the tax rate (the tax expressed as a fraction of the price) usually raises total tax payments and government tax revenue, but it can lower total tax payments and government revenue if it reduces the quantity traded sufficiently.

When demand is perfectly inelastic, a tax raises the price to buyers without changing the price to sellers or the quantity traded. When supply is perfectly inelastic, a tax lowers the price to sellers without changing the price to buyers or the quantity traded. When demand is perfectly elastic, a tax does not affect the price to buyers; when supply is perfectly elastic, a tax does not affect the price to sellers.

SUBSIDIES

Subsidies work like negative taxes. Subsidizing sales or production of a good lowers the price that buyers pay (net of the subsidy), raises the price that sellers receive (including the subsidy), and raises the quantity bought and sold. The government pays the cost of the subsidy, and buyers and sellers share the benefits of the subsidy. Neither the price buyers pay or the price sellers receive depends on which group (buyers or sellers) gets the subsidy, so it does not matter whether the government subsidizes buyers or sellers.

TAXES AND RESTRICTIONS ON INTERNATIONAL TRADE

A tariff (a tax on imports) raises the price of a good to the importing country and lowers the price to the exporting country; the difference is the tariff (the per-unit tax). The tariff raises output and reduces consumption in the importing country, and lowers output and raises consumption in the exporting country. It also reduces international trade. A quota on imports has the same effects, except that the government collects revenue from a tariff but none from a quota. Instead, a quota raises the price that foreign exporters receive, so they get the money that the government would have collected with a tariff.

LOOKING AHEAD

Chapters 9 and 10 discuss the choices that buyers and sellers make that influence the shapes and positions of demand and supply curves. These chapters show how to measure buyers' and sellers' gains from trades. Chapter 11 then returns to applications of demand and supply to apply the results of Chapters 9 and 10 to issues of economic efficiency. Chapter 11 shows how to measure and compare the gains and losses to various people from international trade, speculation, arbitrage, price controls, taxes, and restrictions on international trade.

KEY TERMS

maximum legal price (or price ceiling)	minimum legal price (or price floor)
shortage	surplus
nonprice rationing	tax rate
tie-in sale	tariff
black market	import quota

QUESTIONS AND PROBLEMS

8.20 Waiting in line (queuing) is part of the price that buyers pay when a maximum legal price leads to rationing by waiting. What determines the equilibrium length of a line?

8.21 Comment on this statement: "An effective way to keep the price of clothing down would be to put price controls on fabric; this would reduce the costs of making clothing and reduce clothing prices."

8.22 Suppose that maximum legal prices on food lead to rationing by waiting. What would happen to the lengths of lines at stores today if people expected the government to raise maximum legal prices on food next week?

8.23 Suppose that the government prohibited selling shoes for more than a maximum legal price of $30 a pair, spurring development of a black market in shoes. Use supply-and-demand analysis to discuss what determines the equilibrium price of shoes on the black market. How would that price change if the government were to crack down harder on black-market sellers?

8.24 What would happen if the government were to raise the minimum wage to $50,000 per year for all workers? What if the government were to raise the minimum wage for college graduates to $100,000 per year?

8.25 **a.** Use a graph to show how a 50-cent-per-gallon tax on gasoline would affect the quantity sold and the price. Also show on your graph the revenue that the government would collect from this tax.
  b. Suppose that the supply of gasoline is perfectly inelastic and repeat your analysis.
  c. Suppose that the supply of gasoline is perfectly elastic and repeat your analysis.

8.26 At a well-known prep school, freshmen who buy candy from machines in the dorms are "required" to give part of their candy bars to seniors. Why do seniors require freshmen to give only *part* of each candy bar instead of the whole thing? How should seniors decide how large of a part to ask for if they want to maximize the amount of candy they collect?

8.27 Read the excerpt on the next page from the *New York Times* article, "Affluent Urged to Buy and Avoid New Tax." One representative in Congress stated that sellers are "only stealing future business from themselves" when they advise customers to buy before the tax takes effect; he could not understand why sellers would do this. Use economic analysis to help explain why sellers want consumers to buy before the tax takes effect.

INQUIRIES FOR FURTHER THOUGHT

8.28 Comment on this statement from the chair of a federal government commission: "A subminimum wage is inequitable. It would violate the requirements of social justice and ought to be rejected as a policy option even if we thought that it would substantially reduce youth unemployment."

8.29 Should the government set a minimum wage? How high should it be?

8.30 Many colleges keep the rental prices of dormitory space below the equilibrium prices. As a result, dorms often cannot accommodate all the students who want to live in them. Do you think that colleges should raise dormitory rental prices to the equilibrium levels? If not, how should they ration space? How would raising the prices of dorms affect off-campus rents?

8.31 Discuss the two news reports on markets for human organs (page 225). If you favor allowing people to sell their organs, explain how you think that market would operate. If you oppose sales of organs, explain why you think a market for organs differs from a market for food or clothing, and how you

---

IN THE NEWS

Affluent urged to buy and avoid new tax

By Robert Pear
Special to The New York Times

WASHINGTON, Nov. 25—Retailers are urging affluent consumers to buy expensive cars, boats, jewelry, and furs before the new Federal "luxury tax" takes effect on Jan. 1. And many consumers appear to be accepting the advice, with some retailers of luxury goods reporting a surge in sales.

"Nobody wants to pay a tax they can legally avoid," said Morton J. Zetlin, a general partner in the American Service Center in Virginia. He said he was receiving telephone calls every day from people who say: "This is the car I want. Can you get it for me before the first of the year?"

Numerous car dealers and boat brokers are publicizing the tax in an effort to stimulate business in the remaining five weeks of the year. So are the Neiman Marcus Company department stores. And jewelers like Cartier Inc. and Van Cleef & Arpels Inc. say they expect a brief upturn in business.

"Beat the 10 percent Luxury Tax," says an advertisement by Staten Island Boat Sales in New York, which offers yachts from $185,000 to $900,000. In Santa Monica, Calif., an auto dealer's ad urges customers: "Buy Now Before Luxury Tax." And the American Service Center in Arlington, Va., advises readers of its advertisement: "This is the optimum time to purchase the ultimate motor car—a Rolls-Royce or Bentley—before the new luxury tax becomes effective January 1, 1991."

Note: Congress repealed this luxury tax in 1993 because it reduced sales of the affected goods enough to reduce government revenue from the tax payments.

Source: Robert Pear, "Affluent Urged to Buy and Avoid New Tax," *New York Times*, November 26, 1990.

---

think organs should be rationed. (How would you determine which patients get the organs and which do not?)

8.32 The maximum legal price on sales of children is zero. It is legal to adopt children, but not to pay for them. What are the effects of this maximum legal price of zero? Are the effects good or bad? Should married couples who are medically unable to have children be legally allowed to pay adoption agencies to speed up adoptions? Should they be allowed to pay adoption agencies to find children for them? Should they be allowed to pay biological parents for children? Should they be allowed to pay women for surrogate mother services using sperm from either the father or a sperm bank? What would be the effects of eliminating the maximum legal price of zero?

8.33 A letter to a New York newspaper claimed that abolishing rent control would "turn New York City into a complete Yuppie City," with "no poor and no middle class." What really would happen? How could the poor afford to stay in New York without rent control? Discuss.

8.34 People who live in rent-controlled apartments benefit from the lower rents. Is it fair to make the owners of the rent-controlled buildings pay for their benefits, or should taxpayers pay for such benefits through taxes? Is rent control an unconstitutional taking of property without fair compensation

Trying to cure shortage of organ donors

By Glenn Ruffenach
Staff Reporter of The Wall Street Journal

A rapidly growing gap between the number of people waiting for organ transplants and the supply of organs has educators and researchers searching for ways to increase organ donations.

Some studies suggest that the timing of a physician's or nurse's request to surviving family members can raise consent rates substantially. Other proposals call for some type of federal tax benefit to a donor's estate or assis-tance with funeral expenses. A physician writing in today's *Journal of the American Medical Association* broaches the once-heretical notion of paying families outright—say, $1,000—for an organ donation.

Though physicians, medical ethicists and patients differ, sometimes sharply, over the effectiveness of these strategies, there is little dispute about the need for added measures to procure organs.

Higher Success Rates
More people are being recommended for transplants, reflecting soaring success rates for these operations, but organ donations "haven't kept up with demand," says Wanda Bond, a spokeswoman for the United Network for Organ Sharing, a national clearinghouse that maintains the waiting list for organs and matches organs with recipients.

Source: Glenn Ruffenach, "Trying to Cure Shortage of Organ Donors," *The Wall Street Journal,* March 13, 1991, p. B3.

Ethical debate over selling body organs

By Jeff Kleinhuizen
USA Today

Paying for the kidneys, livers, hearts, and lungs of brain-dead patients might help those awaiting organ transplants, two surgeons say. But a medical ethicist says the proposal could create a black market for body organs.

Writing in today's *Journal of the American Medical Association,* Dr. Thomas Peters, Jacksonville, Fla., says that, despite public awareness programs, 1,878 people died awaiting organ transplants in 1989.

He suggests pilot programs offering $1,000 as a death benefit to the consenting next-of-kin. State and federal laws now prohibit buying and selling organs.

Ethicist Dr. Edmund Pellegrino, Georgetown University, Washington, D.C., writes that payments would subject the poor "to more duress and manipulation than the well-to-do, and this is discriminatory."

Transplant surgeon Dr. Jimmy Light, Washington Hospital Center, Washington, D.C., says blacks make up 35 percent of those on transplant waiting lists, but only 8 percent of donors. Nearly 2,400 people died last year awaiting transplants, he says.

"If education and altruism aren't working," asks Light, "is it more unethical to let people die waiting for transplants, or to offer some kind of incentive to stimulate donations?"

But Pellegrino says paying donors would replace altruism with selfishness.

"The body is not an object to be scavenged even for good purposes," he says.

Source: Jeff Kleinhuizen, "Ethical Debate over Selling Body Organs," *USA Today,* March 31, 1991, p. D1.

(as the 5th amendment to the U.S. Constitution requires)? If not, how does it differ from taking of property? By forcing landlords to give benefits to tenants, does rent control violate the equal protection clause of the 14th amendment?

8.35 Comment on this quote:

> Take filet mignon and chuck steak. Assume that consumers, holding all else constant, prefer filet mignon to chuck steak, a not too unrealistic assumption. The question is: Why is it, in spite of consumer preferences, chuck steak sells at all? The actual fact of business is that chuck steak outsells (is more employed than) filet mignon! How does something less liked compete with something more liked?
>
> It offers compensating differences. In other words, as you wheel your shopping cart down the aisle, chuck steak, in effect, says to you, "I don't look as nice as filet mignon; I'm not as tender and tasty; but I'm not as expensive either." . . .
>
> What would be the effect of a minimum steak [price] law . . . ? Again, put yourself in the position of the shopper wheeling the shopping cart down the aisle. Chuck steak says to you, "I don't look as nice as filet mignon, I'm not as tender and tasty, and I sell for the *same* price as filet mignon. Buy me." Such a message would fall on deaf ears. . . . The lower the price of discriminating, the more of it will be done.[9]

8.36 Discuss these statements.

  a. "A large tax on printers and photocopying machines would violate the right of free speech."

  b. "Applying the income tax to churches, or to businesses they own, would violate the separation of church and state."

  c. "A large tax on guns would violate the second amendment to the Constitution."

8.37 Do you think that the government should set taxes and subsidies to achieve some social goals, such as discouraging smoking or drinking, encouraging exercise or family farms, or promoting "family values"?

8.38 The government often assists people whose houses are destroyed by natural disasters. In what sense is this a subsidy? What is the government subsidizing? What are the effects of this kind of program?

8.39 The government of Italy subsidizes its steel industry. Italy also exports steel to the United States. How does Italy's subsidy affect U.S. consumers? How does it affect U.S. steel producers? Some people say that, in cases like this, the United States should impose an import quota or tariff on Italian steel. Do you agree? If so, how big should the quotas or tariffs be, and who would gain and lose from them?

---

[9] Walter Williams, *The State against Blacks*, pp.40–41.

TAG SOFTWARE APPLICATIONS

TUTORIAL EXERCISE

This module reviews the key terms from Chapter 8.

GRAPHICAL EXERCISE

The module contains questions analyzing the impact of price controls and taxes on markets.

CHAPTER 8 APPENDIX—ALGEBRA OF EQUILIBRIUM WITH TAXES

The appendix builds on the Chapter 4 Appendix on the algebra of equilibrium. The demand and supply curves are straight lines represented by equations. The demand curve is:

$$Q^d = a - bP_B \qquad Example: Q^d = 10 - 2P_B$$

where Q^d is the quantity demanded (in millions of units per year) and P_B is the price that buyers pay.

The supply curve is:

$$Q^s = c + dP_S \qquad Example: Q^s = -5 + 3P_S$$

where Q^s is the quantity supplied (in millions of units per year).

The price to buyers exceeds the price to sellers by the per-unit tax, T:

$$P_B = P_S + T \qquad Example: P_B = P_S + 1$$

Substitute this last equation into the equation for the demand curve to eliminate the variable P_B. This gives a new equation for the demand curve:

$$Q^d = a - b(P_S + T) \qquad Example: Q^d = 10 - 2(P_S + 1)$$

To find the equilibrium, where the quantity demanded (Q^d) equals the quantity supplied (Q^s), set the equations for Q^d and Q^s equal:

$$a - b(P_S + T) = c + dP_S \qquad Example: 10 - 2(P_S + 1) = -5 + 3P_S$$

$$or \quad 10 - 2P_S - 2 = -5 + 3P_S$$

Solve for the equilibrium price to sellers:

$$P_S = (a - bT - c)/(b + d) \qquad Example: P_S = 13/5 = \$2.60$$

The equilibrium price to buyers exceeds this price by the per-unit tax, so:

$$P_B = (a - bT - c)/(b + d) + T \qquad Example: P_B = \$3.60$$

Now substitute the solution for the price to sellers into the supply curve equation, or substitute the price to buyers into the demand curve equation, to solve for the equilibrium quantity:

$$Q = c + d(a - bT - c)/(b + d) \qquad Example: Q = 2.80 \text{ million units per year}$$

Total tax payments equal the per-unit tax times the quantity sold:

$$T[c + d(a - bT - c)/(b + d)] \qquad Example: \$2.80 \text{ million per year}$$

QUESTIONS AND PROBLEMS

8A.1 Suppose that the demand curve for rental cars is:

$$Q^d = 500 - 2P_B$$

The supply curve is:

$$Q^s = 100 + 6P_S$$

Q^d is the quantity demanded (in cars per day), Q^s is the quantity supplied, P_B is the price per day paid by renters (including tax), and P_S is the price per day received by sellers (excluding tax). Suppose that the government taxes car rentals at \$8 per day. Find the equilibrium prices to buyers (including tax) and to sellers (excluding tax), the equilibrium quantity, and total tax payments to the government.

8A.2 Suppose that the demand curve for a product is:

$$x^d = 1,000 - 120p$$

where x^d is the quantity demanded and p is the price (measured in dollars). Suppose that the supply curve for the product, with x^s as the quantity supplied, is:

$$x^s = 200 + 40p$$

a. Find the equilibrium price and quantity.
b. Suppose that the government imposes a per-unit tax of \$4 on the product. Find the new equilibrium quantity, price paid by buyers (including tax), price received by sellers (net of tax), and total tax payments to the government.

8A.3 Repeat Question 8A.2, but suppose that the government offers subsidy of \$4 per unit instead of imposing a tax. Find the equilibrium quantity, the price paid by buyers (net of the subsidy), the price received by sellers (including the subsidy), and the cost of the subsidy to the government.

CHOICES AND THEIR IMPLICATIONS

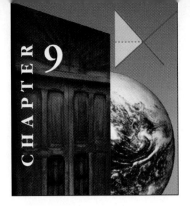

CHAPTER 9

CHOICES AND DEMAND

WHAT THIS CHAPTER IS ABOUT

▶ The benefit that people get from buying a good

▶ How opportunities and tastes affect choices

▶ The logic of rational choice

▶ The relationship of demand curves to buyers' opportunities and tastes

If you had a million dollars, how would you spend it? How would you make your decisions? Would you decide rationally or would you waste the money? How much happier would you be than you were before you got the money? With less money to spend, how do you make your decisions?

A useful logic governs rational choice. That logic appears in new technologies that allow computers to help people make decisions. It also appears in most economic models. The logic of rational choice helps economists determine how people and businesses are likely to respond to new economic situations when they cannot rely on past experience as a direct guide. It helps economists determine how the economy is likely to respond to new government programs.

You could not have bought video recorders 30 years ago, nor compact disks, computers, cable television service, or other goods that many people now take for granted. How much do you benefit from these goods? The logic of rational choice gives economists a way to measure the gains to people from these goods, not by endorsing or criticizing people's tastes and values, but by using their tastes to measure their gains.

Are your decisions usually rational? Would someone else—someone who knew your tastes and values thoroughly and invariably decided rationally—be able to make your everyday decisions much better than you do? If not, the logic of rational choice may describe (at least approximately) your decisions.

CONSUMER SURPLUS

You have finished exercising and you're thirsty. You would pay several dollars, if you had to, for a drink. Fortunately, you find a water fountain nearby. How much do you gain from access to that free water? If you could not find a water fountain, how much would you benefit from access to a machine that would sell soft drinks for 75 cents?

Economists measure a buyer's gain from a trade by that person's consumer surplus.

231

consumer surplus — the benefit to a consumer of the chance to buy a good at the equilibrium price, rather than being unable to buy the good at all

Consumer surplus is the benefit to a consumer of being able to buy a good at the equilibrium price, as opposed to being unable to buy the good at all.

Figure 9.1 shows consumer surplus as the area under the demand curve, above the equilibrium price (P^*), and between the quantity zero and the equilibrium quantity (Q^*).

Consumer surplus measures the gain to buyers based on their own tastes and values, as revealed by their willingness to pay. If Valerie values a product more than Bruce, indicated by her willingness to pay more for it, then Valerie gets higher consumer surplus than Bruce. Economists evaluate consumer surplus by using statistical analysis to estimate the highest prices that people would be willing to pay, that is, the height of the demand curve.

EXPLANATION AND EXAMPLE

You're thirsty and you would pay up to $3.00 for a soft drink. A machine offers them for 75 cents each. You buy one and you are not thirsty enough for another. Your consumer surplus is $2.25. If you were less thirsty, the highest price you would pay might be only $1.90 and your consumer surplus would then be $1.15. If the highest price you would pay were only $0.80, your consumer surplus would be only $0.05.

The height of the market demand curve shows consumers' willingness to pay. The demand curve shows the highest prices that buyers would pay, *if they had to,* for each unit of the good. They actually pay the equilibrium price, and the dif-

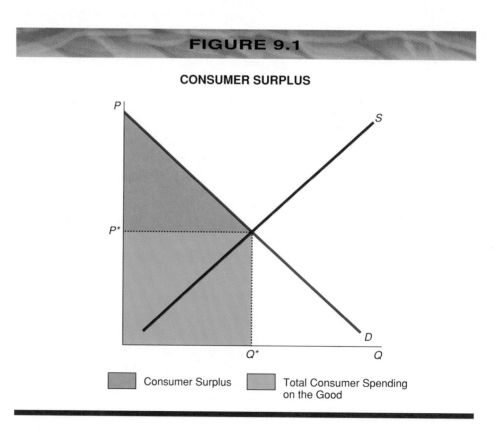

FIGURE 9.1

CONSUMER SURPLUS

Consumer Surplus

Total Consumer Spending on the Good

ference is consumer surplus. Consumer surplus measures the benefit consumers get when they buy the good at the equilibrium price. The consumer surplus on each unit purchased is the vertical distance between the demand curve and a line showing the equilibrium price, as in **Figure 9.2a.** Adding these vertical distances on all the units purchased gives the area that shows total consumer surplus as in Figure 9.1 or Figure 9.2b. Figure 9.2 also shows total spending on the product.

WILLINGNESS TO PAY

Your willingness to pay for a good, minus the price you actually pay, measures your benefit from buying the good. If you like a good more, compared to other goods, you are willing to pay more, and your consumer surplus increases. In this sense, your consumer surplus is based on your own tastes or values.

Your willingness to pay also depends on your ability to pay, that is, how rich you are. Adding together the consumer surpluses of different buyers gives total consumer surplus, as in the example above. This amounts to adding your willingness to pay to someone else's willingness to pay. You might be willing to pay more for a good because you are richer than someone else, but you might not get more happiness from the good than that poorer person. Consumer surplus does not measure the happiness or enjoyment that consumers get from goods. (There is probably no way to measure this.) It measures the total benefit to consumers based on their tastes or values and on their abilities to pay (how rich or poor they are). The consumer surplus measurement reflects the current distribution of income and wealth across people.

FIGURE 9.2

CONSUMER SURPLUS

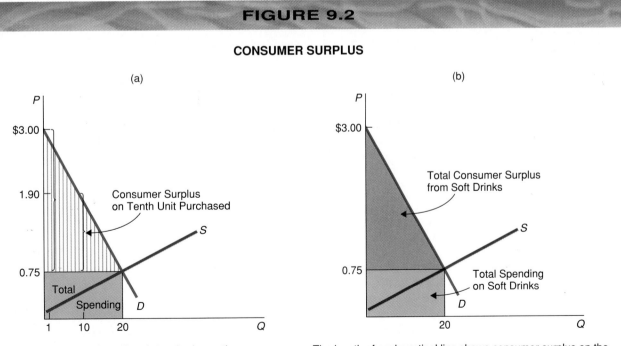

(a)

The vertical line at a quantity of 1 unit shows the consumer surplus on the first unit purchased ($3.00 − $0.75 = $2.25).

(b)

The length of each vertical line shows consumer surplus on the nth unit purchased.

FIGURE 9.3

WATER AND DIAMONDS

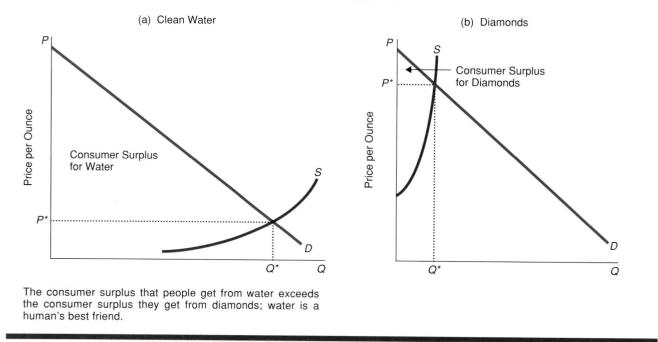

The consumer surplus that people get from water exceeds the consumer surplus they get from diamonds; water is a human's best friend.

VALUE AND PRICE: COMMON CONFUSIONS

Many intelligent people have been confused by the fact that important goods like air and water are free or inexpensive, while less important goods like diamonds are expensive. They wonder why an important good like an ounce of water could cost less than an unimportant good like an ounce of diamonds. They are confused because they do not understand that the equilibrium price of a good does not measure its importance to people. **Figure 9.3** shows the supplies and demands for clean water and diamonds. Clearly, the equilibrium price of diamonds (per ounce) exceeds the equilibrium price of clean water (per ounce). Consumer surplus for water, however, is much larger than consumer surplus for diamonds; in that sense, water is more valuable.

CHOICES AND CONSUMER BEHAVIOR

The effects of taxes, foreign competition, new products, and other changes in conditions depend on consumer behavior. How do consumers respond to changes in conditions? If economists could devise simple ways to describe consumer behavior (such as "people spend one-tenth of their income on restaurant meals"), they could use those rules to study the economy. Simple descriptions of consumer behavior are often inaccurate, however, particularly in new economic situations when consumers must respond to changes that have never happened before. For example, how would consumer spending change if the government were to replace the income tax with a tax on total spending, so that people would not pay taxes on money that they saved? A simple rule such as "consumers always save 10 percent of their income" would probably fail; consumers would probably save more after the change in tax law. To avoid this problem with simple rules, economists have developed models of consumer behavior that describe it more accurately.

EXAMPLE

Consider a simple rule that describes the behavior of a National Football League team: "the team punts on fourth down when the goal line is over 40 yards away." This rule may accurately predict the team's behavior most of the time. Now suppose that a new situation arises: the league changes the rules to give teams five downs rather than four. The change causes the simple description of behavior to fail. A new description of behavior, stated as "the team punts on fifth down . . ." would be accurate most of the time. This new description of behavior would be obvious to any football fan because the fan knows the reasons for the team's decision to punt. A person who understands *why* the team punts can better predict how the team will respond to a change in circumstances.

BUDGET LINES

Economists distinguish between a person's opportunities, tastes, and choices. A budget set lists a person's opportunities; a budget line shows those opportunities on a graph.

budget set — a person's opportunities or feasible choices

budget line — a graph of a budget set

> A **budget set** describes a person's opportunities or feasible choices. A **budget line** graphs a budget set.

Your budget line shows the various combinations of goods that you can afford to buy with your budget, as in **Figure 9.4.** You can afford any point on or below your budget line, such as Points A, B, or C. You cannot afford points above your budget line, such as Points D or E. Your choice of what to buy appears as a point

---

FIGURE 9.4

BUDGET LINE

You can afford to buy one of the combinations of Goods *X* and *Y* shown by Points A, B, and C. You cannot afford the combinations at Points D or E.

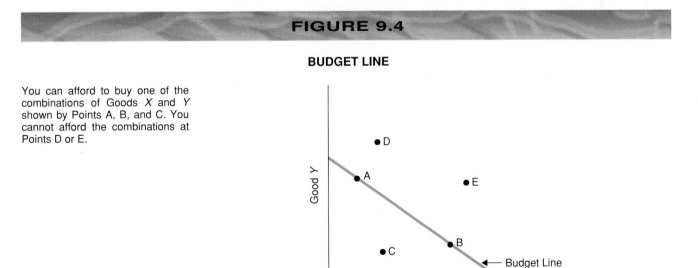

on the graph. You must choose a point that is on or below your budget line (like Points A, B, or C). Which point you choose depends on your tastes.

EXAMPLE

You have $10.00 to spend. You can rent tapes for $1.00 each or play video games for $0.25 each. If you spend all $10.00 on tapes, you can rent 10 tapes. If you spend all $10.00 on video games, you can play 40 games. **Figure 9.5** shows your budget line, which defines the combinations of tape rentals and video games that you can afford. (Point A, for example, shows that you can afford to rent 4 tapes and play 24 games.) Perhaps you prefer Point B, where you rent 7 tapes and play 12 video games, to the other points in your budget set.

SLOPE OF A BUDGET LINE

The absolute value of the slope of the budget line is the relative price of the good on the horizontal axis of the graph in terms of the good on the vertical axis. Chapter 4 defined the relative price of a good in terms of another good as the opportunity cost of the first good, measured in units of the second. If P_A is the nominal price of apples, and P_B is the nominal price of bananas, then the relative price of apples in terms of bananas is P_A/P_B.

FIGURE 9.5

BUDGET LINE BETWEEN TAPES AND VIDEO GAMES

You can afford 40 video games and no tapes, 10 tapes and no video games, or other combinations along the budget line such as 4 tapes and 24 video games.

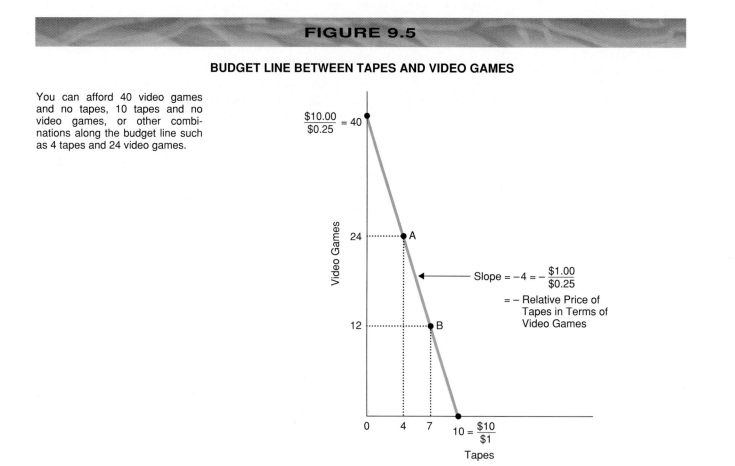

EXAMPLE   The nominal price of a tape rental is $1.00 and the nominal price of a video game is $0.25, so the relative price of tape rentals in terms of video games is 4. Each time you rent a tape for $1.00, you sacrifice playing 4 video games for $0.25 each. So the absolute value of the slope of the budget line in Figure 9.5 is 4.

CHANGES IN OPPORTUNITIES

Your budget line shifts in response to a change in your income or a price. An increase in income shifts your budget line outward (upward and to the right) as in **Figure 9.6;** its slope remains the same. The change in position shows that you are richer so you can afford to buy more. Similarly, a decrease in income shifts your budget line inward (downward and to the left).

Price changes rotate your budget line. An increase in the price of the good on the horizontal axis rotates your budget line as in **Figure 9.7a.** An increase in the price of the good on the vertical axis rotates your budget line as in Figure 9.7b. A decrease in a price rotates your budget line in the opposite direction.

EXAMPLES   You still have $10.00 to spend, but the price of renting a tape rises from $1.00 to $2.00. Video games still cost $0.25 each. If you spend all $10.00 renting tapes, you can now afford to rent only 5 tapes. You can still spend all $10.00 on 40 video games. The rise in the price of tapes, the good on the horizontal axis, rotates the budget line as in Figure 9.7a. The new budget line shows all the new combinations from which you can choose.

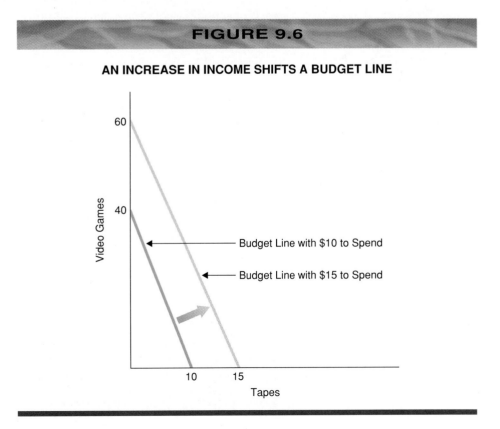

FIGURE 9.6

AN INCREASE IN INCOME SHIFTS A BUDGET LINE

FIGURE 9.7

A PRICE CHANGE ROTATES A BUDGET LINE

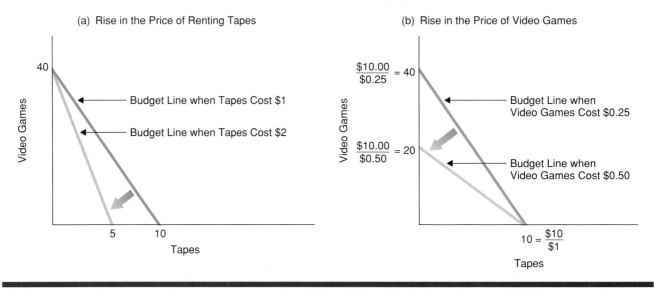

(a) Rise in the Price of Renting Tapes

(b) Rise in the Price of Video Games

If the price of playing video games were to rise from $0.25 to $0.50 while the price of renting a tape remained at $1.00, your budget line would rotate as in Figure 9.7b. Spending all $10.00 playing video games, you could afford to play only 20 games, or you could spend all $10.00 to rent 10 tapes. The new budget line shows all the possible combinations from which you can choose.

BUDGET LINE FOR TIME

Budget lines can apply to time as well as money. Suppose that you have an evening class tonight from 6:00 to 8:00 and that you always go to bed at midnight. This leaves you four hours of free time outside class tonight; you might spend this time at a party or watching television. Your budget line is the lower line in **Figure 9.8,** and you can choose any point on the line. For example, you might watch television for one hour and party for three hours (Point A).

If your class tonight were canceled, you would have six hours of free time. Your budget line would shift outward to the higher line in Figure 9.8. You might then choose Point B: watch 3 hours of television and spend 3 hours partying. Of course, you might choose another point; your actual choice depends on your tastes.

TASTES AND OPPORTUNITIES

Your budget line shows your opportunities (what you are able to buy). Your tastes determine which choice you make (what you are willing to buy), that is, which point on your budget line you choose. Appendix A to this chapter discusses indifference curves, with which economists graph people's tastes. The main point to remember is that each person chooses the point on her budget line that she likes best.

When your budget line changes, as in Figures 9.6 to 9.8, your choice changes. (For example, you might move from Point A to Point B in Figure 9.8. (This is not

FIGURE 9.8

Budget lines can indicate ways to spend time as well as money. When you have more time to spend, your budget line is higher.

A BUDGET LINE FOR TIME

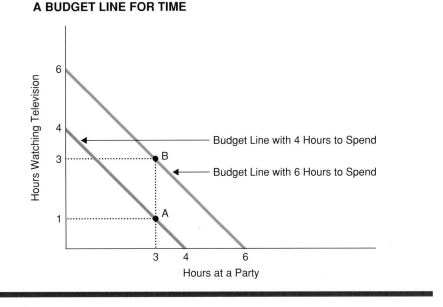

a change in tastes; it is simply a change in opportunities that affects your choice. A graph would represent a change in tastes by a change in your choice of points on a stable budget line (such as a shift from Point A to Point C in Figure 9.10).

EXAMPLE

Robert has $100 that he can either spend on karate lessons or donate to charity. Suppose that he spends $70 on karate lessons and donates $30 to charity. This is Point A on Robert's budget line in **Figure 9.9**—the point that he likes best.

If the price of karate lessons were to rise from $10 to $15 per lesson, he might choose Point B instead of Point A and take fewer karate lessons. Robert's choice changes because his opportunities change, not because his tastes change.

Of course, Robert's tastes could change. Suppose that his tastes do change and he decides to spend less on karate lessons and give more to charity. His opportunities stay the same (his budget line does not move), but his choices and demands change. He moves from Point A to Point C in **Figure 9.10.**

A change in the *information* on which Robert bases his decision can also change his choice. Perhaps a television show about poor people in another country would cause him to switch from Point A to Point C in Figure 9.10. His tastes would remain the same, but the change in information about living conditions in a poor country might change his choice.

--- FOR REVIEW ---

9.1 Define the term *consumer surplus* and show it on a graph.

9.2 Draw a budget line, explain what it means, and what its slope shows. Show how it would change if income were to increase or a price were to increase.

FIGURE 9.9

A CHANGE IN PRICE CHANGES OPPORTUNITIES TO BUY

An increase in the price of karate lessons reduces the number purchased from 7 to 5. This change in the choice of how many lessons to buy results from a change in opportunities to buy, not from a change in tastes.

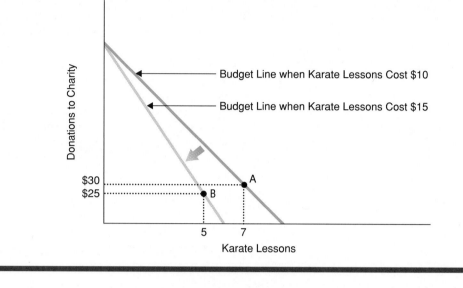

FIGURE 9.10

CHANGES IN TASTES OR INFORMATION

Karate Lessons

If Robert chose Point A before seeing the television show, and Point C after the show, then the show changed his information, altering his decisions. A change in tastes could have a similar effect on his choices.

QUESTIONS

9.3 Use a graph of supply and demand to show how consumer surplus is affected by:
  a. An increase in supply
  b. An increase in demand

9.4 Bill is willing to pay up to $2.00 (but not more) for one roller-coaster ride. He would be willing to pay up to $1.50 for a second ride, $1.25 for a third ride, $1.00 for a fourth ride, and up to $0.75 for each additional ride. Elaine is willing to pay up to $1.75 (but not more) for one ride, up to $1.75 for a second ride, up to $1.25 for a third ride, and up to $0.90 for each additional ride. Roller-coaster rides cost $1.00 each, so Bill chooses four rides and Elaine chooses three rides. How much consumer surplus does Bill get from roller-coaster rides? How much consumer surplus does Elaine get?

9.5 Pedro has $100 to spend on tapes and T-shirts. Tapes cost $5 each and T-shirts cost $10 each.
  a. Draw Pedro's budget line.
  b. Show how his budget line changes if the price of tapes rises to $10.

RATIONAL CHOICE

rational choice — the choice in your budget set that you most prefer

Economic models of consumer choice often assume that consumers choose rationally.

A **rational choice** is the choice in your budget set that you most prefer.

Your choice is rational if you do not prefer any other choice in your budget set, given your own tastes and values. A rational choice is the best choice from your point of view. This is not a judgement about your tastes, values, or goals.

DISCUSSION

Sometimes people confuse the idea of rational choice with their judgements of good and bad choices. Someone might accuse you of having irrational tastes (for example, saying "buying a sports car is irrational") when what they should say is that they disagree with your tastes. Rationality does not refer to whether a person's tastes are good or bad in some sense, but whether people do what is best based on their own tastes.

Rational choices are not necessarily selfish choices. People may be altruistic and make choices out of concern for other people or for animals or the environment. They may risk their lives to help other people or give anonymous gifts with no tangible returns. These choices may be rational based on their own values, tastes, and goals.

LOGIC OF RATIONAL CHOICE

Rational choice follows a basic rule of logic:

> It is rational to do something until its marginal benefit equals its marginal cost.

(*Marginal benefit* and *marginal cost* are defined below.) This logical rule plays a central role in economic analysis and it is one of the most important points for you to understand. The rule applies to any action, from how many socks you buy to how much food you eat; it applies to how long you study for an exam and how many friendships you cultivate. The next chapter will apply this rule to the decisions of business firms and the rest of this book will use the rule extensively. The following sections give definitions of the terms and an important caveat.

MARGINAL BENEFIT

You seek to obtain some benefit (money, happiness, pleasure, fulfillment) from your actions. Your total benefit represents all the benefit you obtain from doing something. Your marginal benefit is the extra benefit you get from doing it once more.

> The **marginal benefit** of doing something is the increase in total benefit from doing it once more.[1]

marginal benefit — the increase in total benefit from doing something once more

EXAMPLE

Figure 9.11 shows an example. The first time you do something (hold a bake sale, listen to a compact disk) your benefit is 100 units (measured in dollars or some unit of happiness). The second time you do it your benefit is 90, the third time your benefit is 80, and so on. Panel a shows a total benefit of 100 if you do it once, 190 if you do it twice, 270 if you do it three times, and so on. Figure 9.11b shows your marginal benefit. The marginal benefit of doing something the second time is 90, the marginal benefit of the third time is 80, the marginal benefit of the fourth time is 70, and so on.

---

[1]Readers who know calculus will recognize marginal benefit as the derivative of total benefit from doing something with respect to the number of times you do it.

FIGURE 9.11

TOTAL AND MARGINAL BENEFIT AND COST

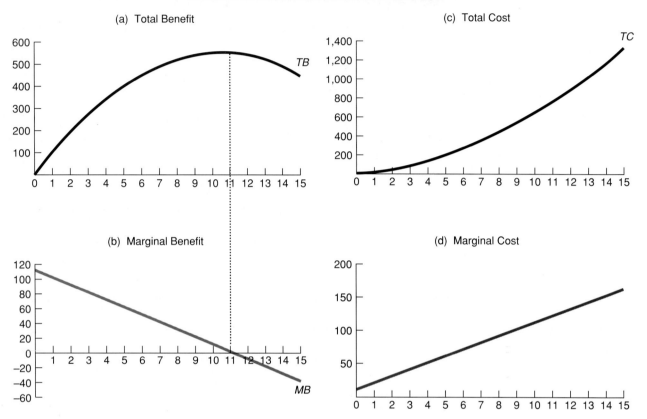

DISCUSSION

Some actions, such as holding bake sales or listening to compact disks, occur sequentially, so it makes sense to talk about the first time or the fourth time. In such a case, the marginal benefit of doing something is the additional benefit from doing it another time. Other actions are not sequential; you choose a small, medium, or large drink, or you choose between televisions with 13-inch, 19-inch, or larger screens. You get some total benefit from a drink or television screen of a certain size. The marginal benefit of a bigger television screen is the extra enjoyment you get from viewing the larger screen rather than the smaller one.

MARGINAL COST

Every action has an opportunity cost in money, happiness, and so forth, equal to the value of what you sacrifice or give up for it. Your total cost refers to the entire

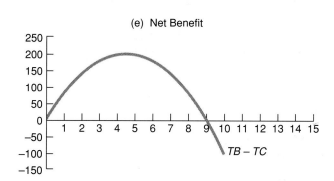

(e) Net Benefit

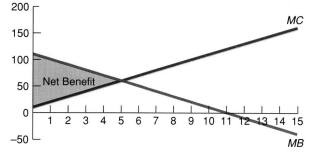

(f) Do Something until Marginal Benefit Equals Marginal Cost

Panel e shows the net benefit (profit) at various quantities. The net benefit of doing something once is 80, the net benefit of doing it twice is 140, and so on. The net benefit is maximized at a quantity of 5, and the highest possible net benefit is 200. The area under the marginal benefit curve and above the marginal cost curve represents the net benefit or profit. To maximize net benefit, choose a quantity so that marginal benefit equals marginal cost; in this case, choose to do the activity five times.

In Panel f, the net benefit of the first time is 100 minus 20, or 80. The net benefit of the second time is 90 minus 30, or 60, and so on. The net benefits of the third and fourth times are 40 and 20. The net benefit of the fifth time is zero. The total net benefit of doing it five times is 200 (80 + 60 + 40 + 20 + 0).

Number of Times	Total Benefit	Marginal Benefit	Total Cost	Marginal Cost	Net Benefit	MB–MC
1	100	100	20	20	80	80
2	190	90	50	30	140	60
3	270	80	90	40	180	40
4	340	70	140	50	200	20
5	**400**	**60**	**200**	**60**	**200**	**0**
6	450	50	270	70	180	−20
7	490	40	350	80	140	−40
8	520	30	440	90	80	−60
9	540	20	540	100	0	−80
10	550	10	650	110	−100	−100
11	550	0	770	120	−220	−120
12	540	−10	900	130	−360	−140
13	520	−20	1,040	140	−520	−160
14	490	−30	1,190	150	−700	−180
15	450	−40	1,350	160	−900	−200

cost that you pay to do something. Your marginal cost refers to the extra cost you pay to do it more.

marginal cost — the increase in total cost from doing something once more

The **marginal cost** of doing something is the increase in total cost from doing it once more.[2]

EXAMPLE

Suppose that the cost of doing something once is 20, the cost of doing it a second time is 30, the cost of a third time is 40, and so on. The total cost of doing it once is then 20, the total cost of doing it twice is 50, the total cost of doing it three

---

[2]Readers who know calculus will see that marginal cost is the derivative of total cost with respect to the number of times you do something.

times is 90, and so on. Figure 9.11c shows the total cost. Panel d shows the marginal cost; the marginal cost of doing it a second time is 30, the marginal cost of a third time is 40, and so on.

NET BENEFIT

The net benefit of an action equals the amount by which its total benefit exceeds its total cost:

> The **net benefit** or **profit** from doing something is the total benefit minus the total cost of doing it.

net benefit (or **profit**) — total benefit minus total cost

EXAMPLE

In Figure 9.11, the net benefit or profit from doing something once is 80 (dollars or units of happiness) because the total benefit is 100 and the total cost is 20. The net benefit of doing it twice is 140. Figure 9.11e shows that the highest possible net benefit is 200 from doing it four or five times. (The fifth time does not change the net benefit.) The net benefit falls below 200 if you do it more than five times, and the net benefit is actually negative if you do it ten or more times. At that point, the total cost exceeds the total benefit.

MAXIMIZING NET BENEFIT (PROFIT)

You make a rational choice when you maximize your net benefit from an action. To maximize net benefit, you do something until its marginal benefit equals its marginal cost. This is the logical rule stated at the beginning of this section.[3]

EXAMPLE   Figure 9.11f shows marginal benefit and marginal cost on the same graph. Marginal cost equals marginal benefit when you do something five times. At that point, the marginal benefit and the marginal cost both equal 60 and the net benefit or profit is 200. Doing it more or less cannot produce a higher profit (net benefit).[4] The figure also shows that the net benefit equals the area above the marginal cost curve and below the marginal benefit curve.

DISCUSSION   Net benefit (profit) rises as you do something one more time if the marginal benefit exceeds the marginal cost. In that case, the extra benefit from the additional action exceeds the extra cost of that action. When the marginal benefit exceeds the marginal cost (at any number of times less than five in the last example), you raise your net benefit by expanding your action (doing it once more). Similarly, net benefit *falls* as you do something one more time *if the marginal benefit is smaller than the marginal cost.* The extra benefit from the additional action is smaller than the extra cost in that case (at any number of times above five in the last example). In Figure 9.11, the marginal benefit exceeds the marginal cost when the number of times is three because the marginal benefit of the third time is 80 and the marginal cost is only 40. Doing something a third time raises the

---

[3]This basic logical rule states that it is rational to do something until its marginal benefit equals its marginal cost. This applies to any action with decreasing or constant marginal benefits and increasing or constant marginal costs. With a decreasing (or constant) marginal benefit, the marginal benefit of an action gets smaller (or stays the same) as you do it more. With increasing (or constant) marginal costs, the marginal cost of an action gets larger (or stays the same) as you do it more. These conditions apply to almost all economic decisions.

[4]You could also get a profit of 200 by choosing a quantity of four, but you could not do better.

PERSONAL DECISION MAKING

"Anything Worth Doing Is Worth Doing Well"—True or False?

You've heard the old saying, "Anything worth doing is worth doing well." Is it true? The logic of rational choice shows that sometimes it is worthwhile not to do something well. Rational choice suggests doing something until the marginal benefit of doing more equals the marginal cost. Sometimes that means doing the job well. Other times it means doing only an adequate or passable job.

Examples are everywhere. Some people say that athletes should always give 100 percent of their energy to a game, but an athlete who works as hard as possible every minute of a game tires earlier than an athlete who conserves energy for the most impor-

tant times. Suppose that you are in a hurry to go somewhere important, but you are also hungry. Should you cook dinner only if you will do a good job of cooking? Not necessarily: perhaps you should spend only enough time to fix a quick, but mediocre dinner. Should you take a course only if you intend to do well in it? Not necessarily, if the bulk of your time would be better spent on other courses or other activities. The old saying should be modified:

> Anything worth doing is worth doing until the marginal benefit equals the marginal cost.

net benefit from 140 to 180. Doing it a fourth time raises your net benefit further because the marginal benefit of doing it the fourth time (70) exceeds the marginal cost (50). Doing it a fifth time does not affect your net benefit.

When the marginal benefit of doing something is smaller than its marginal cost, you raise your net benefit by doing it less. In Figure 9.11, the marginal benefit of the sixth time is 50, but the marginal cost is 70. Thus, the net benefit *falls* by 20, from 200 to 180, if you do it a sixth time. If the marginal benefit of doing something is smaller than the marginal cost, it is better to do it less.

APPLICATION TO DEMAND

The marginal cost of buying a candy bar is its price. The marginal benefit of an additional candy bar is the dollar value of the extra enjoyment it gives you during one day (or some other period of time). Your marginal benefit of candy bars probably decreases; you probably get less enjoyment during one day from a second candy bar than you get from the first, and you probably get even less from a fifth or sixth candy bar.[5] To maximize your net benefit, you would choose to buy a quantity that would set the marginal cost equal to the marginal benefit.

> A rational consumer chooses a quantity demanded of a good that sets its marginal benefit equal to its marginal cost (its price). A person's demand curve for a good is that person's marginal benefit curve.

---

[5]Even if you enjoy your 100th candy bar in a day as much as your first, the dollar value of your enjoyment is likely to fall as you buy more candy bars. As you spend more on candy bars, you can spend less on other goods and the value of a dollar to spend on them increases. This means that the dollar value of your enjoyment from candy falls. To see why, think about an extreme case. Suppose that you spent almost all your money on candy, so you had almost nothing else—no healthy food, few clothes, and so on. Then an extra dollar's worth of good food or other goods would probably be worth a lot to you. This means that a dollar is worth a lot to you, so the dollar value of your enjoyment from a candy bar is smaller than if a dollar were not worth so much to you.

EXAMPLE

Figure 9.12 shows Mike's marginal cost and marginal benefit of candy bars. At a price of $0.50, he maximizes his net benefit by eating 3 candy bars per day. If the price rises from $0.50 to $1.00, he reduces his quantity demanded to 2 candy bars a day. The figure also shows Mike's demand curve. Point A shows his choice of 3 candy bars when they cost $0.50 each; Point B shows his choice of 2 candy bars when they cost $1.00 each. Notice that Mike's demand curve is the same as his marginal benefit curve. Also notice that Mike's demand for candy is inelastic; he spends more on candy when its price rises. If he were to buy only 1 candy bar per day when its price rose to $1.00, his demand would be elastic; he would spend less on candy when its price is higher.

OPPORTUNITY COST AND DEMAND

The marginal cost of buying any good equals whatever you sacrifice to buy one more unit of it. If you buy an issue of *Sports Illustrated,* you sacrifice benefits you would have obtained if you had bought an issue of *Ms.* magazine. The marginal benefit of watching television is the benefit you get from an extra half-hour show; the marginal cost may be the benefit you could have obtained by going to bed 30 minutes earlier and getting more sleep. The marginal cost of a restaurant meal is the enjoyment from other goods that you sacrifice if you buy another meal at a restaurant. You maximize your net benefit if you choose a quantity demanded that sets your marginal benefit equal to your marginal cost.

EXAMPLE

Jane has $24 to spend on posters, which cost $2 each, and snack-packs, which cost $2 each. Each row of **Table 9.1** shows a combination of goods that Jane can afford (a point on her budget line in **Figure 9.13**). For example, she can afford 1

FIGURE 9.12

MARGINAL BENEFIT AND DEMAND

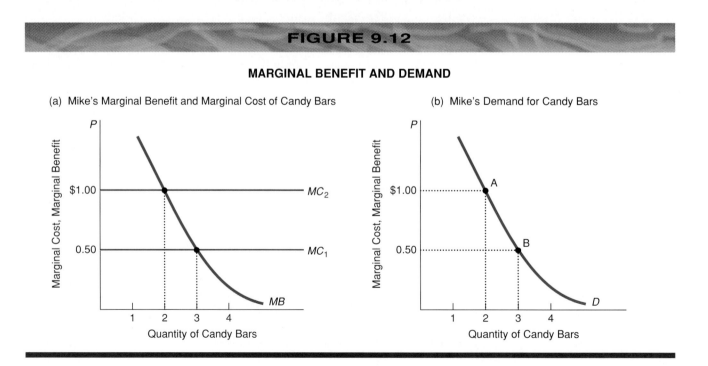

(a) Mike's Marginal Benefit and Marginal Cost of Candy Bars

(b) Mike's Demand for Candy Bars

TABLE 9.1

JANE'S RATIONAL CHOICE OF QUANTITIES DEMANDED

Number of Posters	Total Benefit of Posters	Marginal Benefit of Posters[a]	Number of Snack-Packs	Total Benefit of Snack-Packs	Marginal Benefit of Snack-Packs[b]
0	0		12	234	4
1	24	24	11	230	8
2	44	20	10	222	10
3	60	16	9	212	12
4	74	14	8	210	14
5	86	12	7	196	16
6	96	10	6	180	20
7	104	8	5	160	24
8	110	6	4	136	28
9	115	5	3	108	32
10	119	4	2	76	36
11	122	3	1	40	40
12	124	2	0	0	

[a]Equals the marginal opportunity cost of snack-packs.
[b]Equals the marginal opportunity cost of posters.

FIGURE 9.13

RATIONAL CHOICE OF A POINT ALONG A BUDGET LINE

The numbers in Table 9.1 show that Jane's rational choice is Point A.

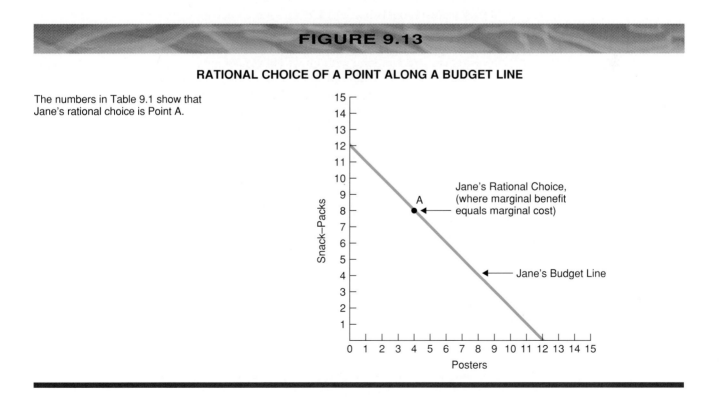

Jane's Rational Choice, (where marginal benefit equals marginal cost)

Jane's Budget Line

Snack-Packs

Posters

poster and 11 snack-packs, or 3 posters and 9 snack-packs. The table also shows Jane's total and marginal benefits from each possible level of consumption of each good. For example, her marginal benefit of buying a third poster is 16, and her marginal benefit of a ninth snack-pack is 12. Because posters and snack-packs each cost $2, *the marginal cost of a poster is the marginal benefit of the snack-pack that Jane sacrifices to buy it,* and the marginal cost of a snack-pack is the marginal benefit of the poster that she sacrifices to buy the snack-pack.

Jane maximizes her net benefit by choosing quantities demanded that set her marginal benefit equal to her marginal cost for each good. Jane chooses 4 posters and 8 snack-packs. Her marginal benefit from a poster is then 14, which equals her marginal cost of a poster (her marginal benefit of a snack-pack). This is Point A on Jane's budget line in Figure 9.13.

RATIONAL AND IRRATIONAL CHOICES

A large body of evidence on a wide range of economic issues supports the assumption made in most economic models that people make most economic decisions rationally, or close to rationally. While people's responses to surveys and questionnaires sometimes appear irrational, evidence indicates that people's actions are more rational than their words.

Obviously, people do not consciously and formally calculate marginal benefits and marginal costs when they make decisions. That would be too difficult and time-consuming. Still, people's choices, at least in common situations, can match the choices that they would make if they were to calculate marginal costs and benefits and choose quantities that would equate the two. In that sense, people act *as if* they were rational. (Many experiments show that even animals often behave as if they made rational choices!) The rational choice model is a reasonably good predictor of actual economic decisions.

Some rational choices can appear to be irrational. For example, a rational choice made by someone with limited information may appear irrational to someone with more information. A person may buy a product for a high price at one store when another store nearby sells the same product for less. This may appear irrational, but the buyer may not know that the price is lower at the other store, or the trip to the other store may not seem worth the additional time involved to the buyer. Information is not free; buyers must spend time and sometimes money to obtain it. They must spend time to understand, digest, and remember information (such as the information in this book).

Sometimes rational choices appear irrational for other reasons. You may say to yourself, "This term I'm going to study more," but as each day arrives, you find something else to do. You may decide to diet, but every day an ice cream sundae forces its way into your mouth. Are your actions rational? They might be. It can be rational to plan to do something, decide later not to do it, and even to regret your decision afterward.[6]

Although evidence suggests that much economic behavior is rational, experiments reveal that people sometimes make irrational choices. Experiments have

---

[6]If you behave this way, economists say that you have time-inconsistent tastes. It is rational for you to commit (if you can) to your plan of action. You might commit not to do something (such as drinking) by avoiding certain situations (such as parties with alcohol). It is usually difficult or impossible to commit completely, but sometimes you can commit partially to a future action. For example, some people avoid carrying credit cards to make it more difficult for them to spend more than they had planned.

PERSONAL DECISION MAKING

Economics of Personal Improvement

Many books and articles that give advice for personal improvement or self-help rely on basic economic principles. These books often warn that many people do not spend their time efficiently, spending too much time doing unimportant things and too little time doing important things. The books do not use the language of economics, but they remind people of opportunity costs—the time spent on one task could be spent doing something else. Although these books and articles use less precise language, they tell people to spend time on any project until its marginal benefit equals its marginal cost. They often suggest methods to calculate these costs and benefits. They tell you to list your goals, review the way you spend your time, and regularly examine whether your actions are helping you to achieve those goals. These techniques try to help people equate the marginal costs and marginal benefits of their actions.

Books and articles on personal improvement also emphasize that rational decisions ignore sunk costs. Without using the terms of economics, they tell people not to dwell on past misfortunes, mistakes, or failures, but instead to concentrate on the future. Ignoring sunk costs can be psychologically difficult, so the articles often suggest techniques to help. These techniques include positive thinking, visualizing results, and concentrating on goals. They are designed to help you make choices that equate marginal benefits with marginal costs.

uncovered two main kinds of irrationalities. First, people sometimes ignore opportunity costs and instead take into account only direct payments.[7] Second, people sometimes act irrationally by not ignoring sunk costs.

sunk cost — a cost that you have already paid and cannot recover

Sunk costs are costs that you have already paid and cannot recover.

Rational choices ignore sunk costs. Bygones are bygones; it is too late now to undo the past. Rational choices equate the marginal benefit and marginal cost of taking some action. The cost of that action is the best opportunity that you sacrifice when you take that action. The cost of the action does not include payments made in the past that you cannot now recover. For example, suppose that you paid $5 to see a movie. After 20 minutes, you realize that you made a mistake; the movie is terrible. Should you leave now, or should you stay and watch the rest of the movie because you paid $5 to see it? A rational choice would ignore the $5 because it is a sunk cost. You have already paid the $5 and you cannot get your money back. Your decision to stay or leave should compare the benefits and time cost of staying. If you have something better to do, you should leave. Experimental evidence suggests, however, that people do not always ignore sunk costs.

Although people sometimes behave irrationally, evidence indicates that they learn. Their choices become more rational when they face a situation repeatedly. People learn to ignore sunk costs and not to ignore opportunity costs; they learn to choose in a way that is approximately rational.[8]

---

[7]This is clearly irrational! You are not paying anyone to read this book right now. If you thought only about direct payments, you would think that reading this book was free. Reading has an obvious opportunity cost, though, because you could be doing something else right now.

[8]A summary of some of this evidence appears in an article by experimental economist Vernon Smith, "Theory, Experiments, and Economics," *Journal of Economic Perspectives* vol. 3, Winter 1989, pp. 151–169.

Even when people behave irrationally, many of the conclusions of standard economic models remain the same as if people were rational. For example, demand curves are likely to slope downward. If you randomly choose how much to buy, a rise in the price of a good is likely to reduce your quantity demanded because you cannot afford to buy as much of the good at a higher price (unless your random spending on other goods falls sufficiently). Demand curves are likely to slope downward whether people behave rationally or randomly.

Most economic theories assume that people make rational choices, though some consider the consequences of people making certain decisions irrationally.[9] Economists have even applied the logic of rational choice to behaviors that many people consider irrational, such as crime. Evidence shows that criminal behavior responds to incentives. Higher punishments and higher chances of being caught and punished reduce crime.[10]

FOR REVIEW

9.6 What is marginal benefit? What is marginal cost?

9.7 State and explain the basic rule of rational choice.

9.8 What is a sunk cost? Why do rational decisions ignore sunk costs?

QUESTIONS

9.9 Suppose that the marginal cost in Figure 9.11 increases by 20 (changing from 20, 30, 40, . . . , 160 to 40, 50, 60, . . . , 180).
   a. Show this increase in marginal cost on a graph.
   b. How does this increase in marginal cost affect the rational choice of the number of times to take the action in Figure 9.11?

9.10 Suppose that the marginal benefit in Figure 9.11 increases by 20 (changing from 100, 90, 80, . . . , −40 to 120, 110, 100, . . . , −20).
   a. Show this increase in marginal benefit on a graph.
   b. How does this increase in marginal benefit affect the rational choice of the number of times to take the action in Figure 9.11?

CONCLUSIONS

CONSUMER SURPLUS
Consumer surplus measures a buyer's gain from a trade, based on the buyer's own tastes and values. It is represented by the area under the demand curve and above the price between the zero quantity and the equilibrium quantity.

CHOICES AND CONSUMER BEHAVIOR
A budget line shows a person's opportunities (feasible choices). The absolute value of the budget line's slope equals the relative price of the good on the horizontal axis in terms of the good on the vertical axis. Changes in income shift the

---

[9]These include certain models of irrational speculation on the stock market and other financial markets.

[10]Two interesting experiments focused on basketball. The Atlantic Coast Conference raised the number of referees for its basketball tournament from two to three per game in 1979. This increased the chance that a player who committed a foul would be caught, and the number of fouls per game dropped by one-third. Similarly, a lower punishment for fouls raised the number of fouls. Before 1963, fouled defensive players got free throws; after 1963, an offensive foul only cost possession of the ball. This reduction in punishment raised the number of fouls committed.

budget line without changing its slope; changes in relative price rotate the budget line. Each person chooses the point on his budget line that he likes best.

RATIONAL CHOICE

Rational choice means choosing what you most prefer among your alternatives. Rational choices may be good or bad from another person's point of view. Rational choices are not necessarily selfish; they can be altruistic. The basic rule of rational choice is to do something until its marginal benefit equals its marginal cost. Marginal benefit is the increase in total benefit from doing something once more; marginal cost is the increase in total cost from doing it once more. Doing something until its marginal benefit equals its marginal cost maximizes net benefit. Applied to demand, the basic rule of rational choice means that a rational consumer chooses a quantity demanded of a good that sets its marginal benefit equal to its marginal cost (its price).

RATIONAL AND IRRATIONAL CHOICES

Considerable evidence indicates that people make most economic decisions rationally, or almost rationally. People are more rational in what they do than in what they say. Though people do not consciously calculate marginal benefits and marginal costs to make decisions, evidence suggests that they often act as if they did. Rational choices sometimes appear (incorrectly) to be irrational to people with more information.

Although much economic behavior is rational, experimental evidence indicates that people sometimes make irrational decisions by ignoring opportunity costs or not ignoring sunk costs, which are costs that have already been paid and cannot be recovered. Rational decisions ignore sunk costs. The evidence also shows, however, that people learn. When people face a situation repeatedly, they learn to ignore sunk costs and not to ignore opportunity costs, so their decisions become more rational.

LOOKING AHEAD

Chapter 10 applies the logic of rational choice to business decisions, and it introduces producer surplus to measure the gain to sellers from selling goods. Chapter 11 shows how to measure gains and losses from international trade, speculation, and taxes using consumer and producer surplus, and discusses economic efficiency.

Many choices in life involve risk. Driving, sports, sex, marriage, and career choices all involve risk; so does buying a product that you might not like. Chapter 19 returns to the logic of rational choice and extends it to situations of uncertainty and risk.

KEY TERMS

consumer surplus

budget set

budget line

rational choice

marginal benefit

marginal cost

net benefit (or profit)

sunk cost

QUESTIONS AND PROBLEMS

9.11 Draw a budget line and show how it changes if:
  a. Income falls
  b. The price of the good on the horizontal axis falls
  c. The price of the good on the vertical axis falls

9.12 Suppose that the nominal prices of deodorant and soap both double. What happens to the relative price of deodorant in terms of soap? How does a budget line between them shift?

a. Suppose that your money income doubles along with the nominal prices of all the goods you buy. What happens to your budget line? Do you change what you buy? Explain.

b. If your tastes do not change in Question 9.12a, what happens to your quantities demanded?

9.13 Judy has midterm exams today in molecular biology and quantum physics. She has only one more hour to study and she wants to maximize the total number of points she gets on the two exams added together. She expects the following scores depending on how much she studies each subject:

Minutes Studying Biology	Expected Score in Biology	Minutes Studying Physics	Expected Score in Physics
0	70	0	55
10	77	10	65
20	83	20	73
30	88	30	80
40	92	40	85
50	95	50	90
60	97	60	93

a. Create two new columns to show Judy's marginal benefit and marginal cost from studying biology for 10 more minutes.

b. How much time should she spend studying for each exam? Explain why.

c. Draw Judy's budget line between points on the biology exam and points on the physics exam. Show in your diagram which point on the budget line she should choose.

d. Suppose that Judy has 70 rather than 60 minutes to study. How does this change affect her budget line? How long does she study biology? How long does she study physics? How many additional points could she expect to get by studying the extra 10 minutes?

9.14 You organize a used-book exchange to buy used textbooks for half of their original prices and resell them for $1 more than you paid for them. This takes several hours during which you could be working at a local store earning $5 per hour. You also have other costs (such as advertising). You calculate that your total benefits and total costs of working on this book exchange are:

Hours Worked	Total Benefit	Total Cost
1	$ 20	$ 8
2	40	15
3	58	22
4	73	29
5	85	36
6	96	44
7	105	53
8	113	63
9	119	74

Calculate the marginal benefit and the marginal cost of hours worked. How many hours should you work to maximize your net benefit?

9.15 Explain the economic principle behind the comic strip.

Source: Plain Dealer, August 25, 1985.

INQUIRIES FOR FURTHER THOUGHT

9.16 Think of a good you recently bought. How much did you pay for it? How much more would you have been willing to pay for it? What was your consumer surplus?

9.17 An article in a magazine says, "the pleasures of music are incalculable, either in wattage or in money." Do you agree? Can you think of a way to calculate a person's pleasure from music in terms of money?

9.18 You are a doctor in a city where an earthquake injured thousands of people yesterday. Your medical supplies are limited, though new supplies will arrive tomorrow. You must decide which victims get medical attention and supplies today (and how much) and who must wait. How would you make your decision? Express your answer in terms of marginal benefits and costs.

9.19 People leave tips at restaurants even if they never plan to return to the restaurant. Is this rational? Is it rational to cooperate with other people? To be courteous, polite, and honest?

9.20 Are opportunities and choices the same as freedom? Nobel-laureate economist George Stigler once argued that wealth is the same as freedom. He argued that more wealth means the ability to buy or do more things, just as freedom does. Do you agree? If not, what is the difference between wealth and freedom?

9.21 Discuss this statement: "People do not choose rationally. They buy some products they don't need and other products (like cigarettes) that are harmful. They underestimate important risks, such as the risk of injury in automobile accidents without a seat belt. People would be better off if the government would make more decisions for them."

TAG SOFTWARE APPLICATIONS

TUTORIAL EXERCISES
▶ The module contains a review of the key terms from Chapter 9.

ANALYTICAL EXERCISES
▶ The numerical appendix includes calculations of marginal costs and benefits.

GRAPHING EXERCISES
▶ The graphing module includes questions on budget lines, the measurement of consumer surplus, and marginal cost and marginal benefit analysis. The graphical appendix to this chapter examines indifference curves.

CHAPTER 9 APPENDIX A — INDIFFERENCE CURVES

Economists graph people's tastes with indifference curves.

indifference curve — a graph of combinations of goods between which a person is indifferent

> A person is indifferent between two combinations of goods if she does not prefer one to the other. An **indifference curve** shows combinations of goods between which a person is indifferent.

Each point on an indifference curve represents a combination of goods. A person is indifferent between the various points on her indifference curve: she does not care which combination of goods she consumes.

EXAMPLE

Figure 9A.1 shows one of Lee's indifference curves. Lee does not care whether he consumes 5 hamburgers and 40 hot dogs per month, or 8 hamburgers and 25 hot dogs, or 10 hamburgers and 20 hot dogs, or 20 hamburgers and 10 hot dogs, or 40 hamburgers and 5 hot dogs. He does not prefer any of these combinations to any of the others.

MANY INDIFFERENCE CURVES

Combinations of goods that do not lie on one indifference curve lie on other indifference curves, and it takes many indifference curves to describe a person's tastes. Every possible combination of goods is a point on *some* indifference curve. As long as you want more of both of a pair of goods, you prefer combinations of goods on higher indifference curves.

Figure 9A.2 shows several of Lee's indifference curves. He prefers points on higher indifference curves to points on lower indifference curves. For example, he is indifferent between Point A (16 hamburgers and 25 hot dogs) and Point B (20 of each), but he prefers both Point A and Point B to Point C (8 hamburgers and 25 hot dogs) and to other points on lower indifference curves.

The indifference curves of a rational person never cross. If they did, as in **Figure 9A.3,** the person would be indifferent between Points A and B, and indifferent between Points B and C. That would make this person indifferent between Points A and C, though Point A represents more of both goods than Point C. Point A represents eight pairs of shorts and six concert tickets while Point C represents only six pairs of shorts and four concert tickets. Whenever a person prefers more goods to fewer goods, that person's indifference curves cannot cross.

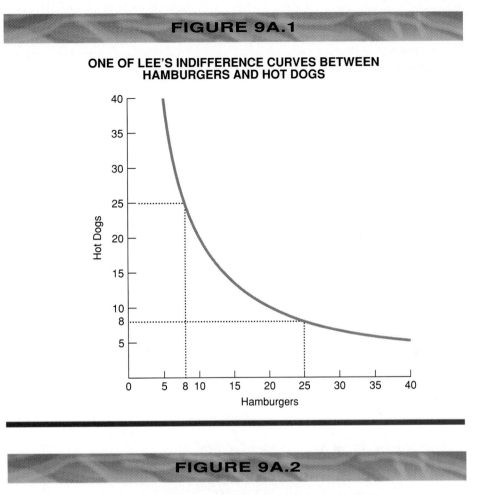

FIGURE 9A.1

ONE OF LEE'S INDIFFERENCE CURVES BETWEEN HAMBURGERS AND HOT DOGS

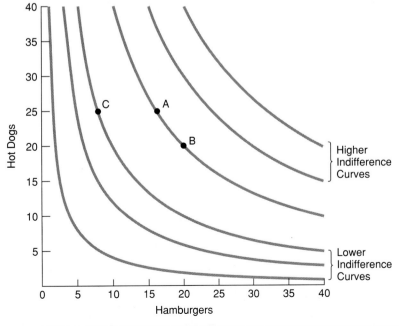

FIGURE 9A.2

MORE OF LEE'S INDIFFERENCE CURVES BETWEEN HAMBURGERS AND HOT DOGS

FIGURE 9A.3

A RATIONAL PERSON'S INDIFFERENCE CURVES CANNOT CROSS

This person is indifferent between Point A (eight pairs of shorts and six tickets) and Point B (four pairs of shorts and eight tickets). He is also indifferent between Point B and Point C (six pairs of shorts and four tickets), so he must be indifferent between Points A and C, which does not make sense if he likes shorts and tickets.

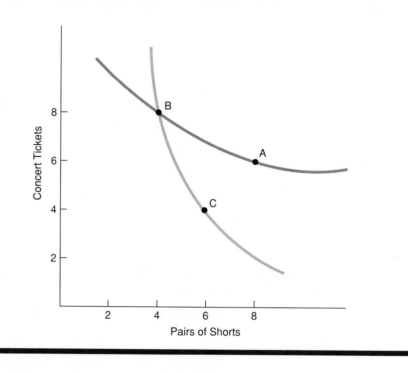

QUESTIONS

9A.1 Choose two goods, such as pizza and ice cream, and graph one of your own indifference curves between them.

9A.2 Draw another of your indifference curves on the same graph.

SLOPES OF INDIFFERENCE CURVES

Indifference curves usually slope downward. If you get fewer hot dogs in one situation than in another, you need more hamburgers to compensate and make you indifferent between the two situations.[1] The number of hamburgers you need to compensate for the loss of one hot dog is your marginal rate of substitution between hot dogs and hamburgers.

marginal rate of substitution — the largest amount of one good that you would be willing to trade away for one unit of another

Your **marginal rate of substitution** between Goods A and B is the largest amount of B that you would be willing to trade away for one unit of A.

Your marginal rate of substitution between books and socks depends on your *willingness to pay* for an extra book, measured by the number of socks you would give up for it. Your marginal rate of substitution between vacation days and money shows the amount of money that you would be willing to pay for an extra vacation day.

Your marginal rate of substitution is the absolute value of the slope of your indifference curve for two goods, such as Goods X and Y in **Figure 9A.4.**

---

[1]Indifference curves slope upward if you like one of the goods, but dislike the other.

FIGURE 9A.4

MARGINAL RATES OF SUBSTITUTION

Your marginal rate of substitution is the absolute value of the slope of your indifference curve. This value depends on how much you consume.

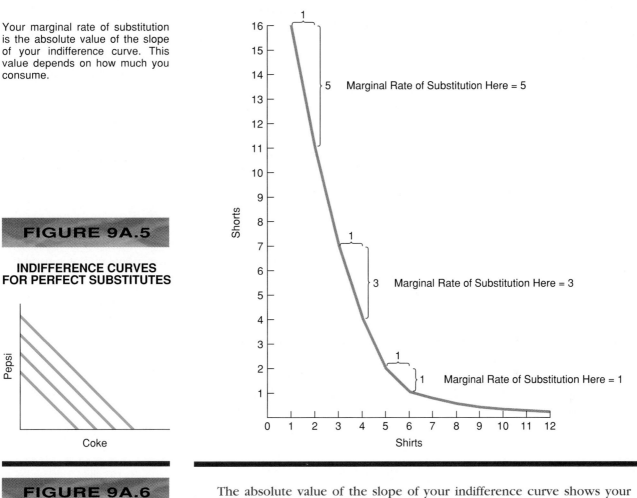

FIGURE 9A.5

INDIFFERENCE CURVES FOR PERFECT SUBSTITUTES

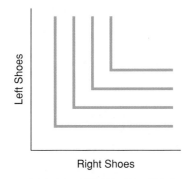

FIGURE 9A.6

INDIFFERENCE CURVES FOR PERFECT COMPLEMENTS

The absolute value of the slope of your indifference curve shows your marginal rate of substitution between two goods.

The absolute value of your indifference curve's slope shows the amount of Y you would be willing to trade for one X. Indifference curves usually look something like the ones in Figure 9A.2, but if two products are very good substitutes for each other, then you may not care whether you have five of one and ten of the other or vice versa. If you care only about the total amount of cola you drink, but you don't care whether you drink Coke or Pepsi, then those drinks are perfect substitutes to you. In this case, your marginal rate of substitution between the goods is constant and equal to 1 because you want one can of Pepsi as compensation for losing one can of Coke. Your indifference curves look like those in **Figure 9A.5.**

By contrast, if two products are very strong complements for each other, like left shoes and right shoes, then you benefit from extra units of one only if you also have extra units of the other. Goods are perfect complements if one is useless to you without the other; your indifference curves for such goods would look like those in **Figure 9A.6.**

RATIONAL CHOICE WITH INDIFFERENCE CURVES

Rational choice means reaching the highest possible indifference curve by choosing the feasible consumption combination that a person most prefers. A budget line shows opportunities, so a rational decision would choose the highest indifference curve that a person's budget line could reach. The rational choice in **Figure 9A.7** is Point A, where the budget line just touches the highest indifference curve that it can reach. (The indifference curve is tangent to the budget line at Point A.) Any other point that you can afford (such as Points B and C) are on lower indifference curves than Point A. Point A shows the combination of goods that you prefer to all other combinations that you can afford.

The slope of the indifference curve at Point A equals the slope of the budget line. Since the absolute value of the slope of the indifference curve is the marginal rate of substitution between X and Y, and the absolute value of the slope of the budget line is the relative price of X in terms of Y, this means that:

At Point A, the marginal rate of substitution equals the relative price.

This rule governs rational choice (the effort to reach the highest possible indifference curve): buy quantities of products that set your marginal rate of substitution between a pair of products equal to their relative price.

FIGURE 9A.7

RATIONAL CHOICE WITH INDIFFERENCE CURVES

The rational choice is Point A, where your budget line reaches the highest possible indifference curve.

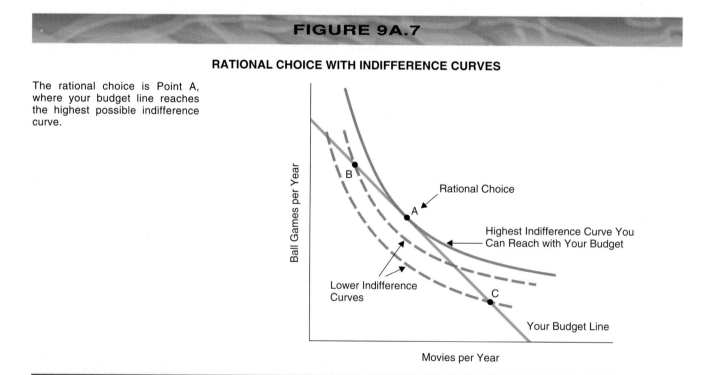

FIGURE 9A.8

DERIVING A DEMAND CURVE FROM BUDGET LINES AND INDIFFERENCE CURVES

(a) Elee's Budget Lines and Indifference Curves

(b) Elee's Demand Curve

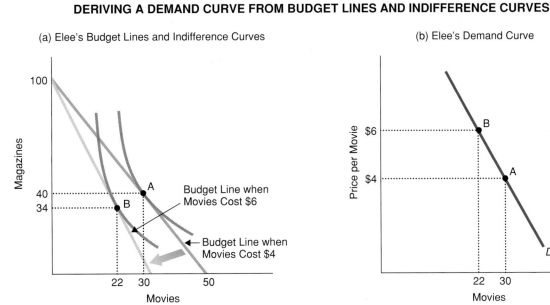

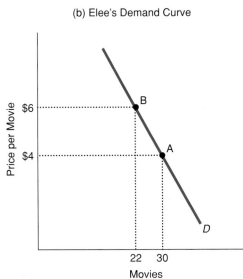

Elee's budget line rotates when the price of movies rises from $4 to $6 and her rational choice changes from Point A to Point

B. Plotting the movie prices and her quantities demanded on a graph gives her demand curve for movies.

--- QUESTIONS ---

9A.3 Explain why the absolute value of the slope of an indifference curve shows a person's marginal rate of substitution between two goods.

9A.4 Draw a graph with a budget line and indifference curves.
a. Show the person's rational choice on your graph.
b. Explain your graph. Why is this the rational choice?

DEMAND CURVES AND INDIFFERENCE CURVES

When a budget line rotates in response to a price change, this changes the rational choice. **Figure 9A.8** shows an example. Elee has $200 per year to spend on movies and magazines. When movies cost $4 and magazines cost $2, she sees 30 movies and buys 40 magazines each year (Point A in the figure). When the price of seeing a movie rises to $6, her budget line rotates and she chooses Point B, where she sees 22 movies and buys 34 magazines, instead of Point A.[2]

These two choices are two points on Elee's demand curve for movies. When movies cost $4, she sees 30 movies, so Point A on her original budget line defines Point A on her demand curve. When movies cost $6, she sees 22 movies, and

---

[2]If her indifference curves were different (because her tastes were different), she would have made another choice. For example, she might have chosen 20 movies and 40 magazines.

Point B on her new budget line defines Point B on her demand curve. As the price changes, the new budget line and the indifference curves give new rational choices that define new points on the demand curve.[3]

KEY TERMS

indifference curve   marginal rate of substitution

QUESTIONS AND PROBLEMS

9A.5 Use a graph with budget lines and indifference curves to show how to derive a demand curve. Find the rational choices at several prices and graph them as points on a demand curve.

CHAPTER 9 APPENDIX B — UTILITY AND CHOICE

UTILITY

utility — the benefit people get from the goods that they buy

util — a unit of utility

Economists often use utility theory to analyze the choices that people make and to study how choices would change if conditions were to change.

Utility is a name for the benefit people get from consuming goods and services, or from other actions. **Utils** are units of utility.

Your utility from a good is whatever pleasure, happiness, or fulfillment it gives you. You might get 10 utils from staying in bed an extra hour, 27 utils from eating lunch, and 140 utils from your activities on Friday night. You might get 30 utils from listening to music that gives someone else *minus* 10 utils. Utility is subjective rather than objective in the sense that a person's utility depends on that person's tastes and values. No one can objectively measure utility.

Nevertheless, the logic of utility theory implies much about consumer behavior that matches the evidence about real-life behavior reasonably well. As a result, utility theory can be a useful model of behavior even though rigorous measurement of utils is impossible and the very concept of utility vastly oversimplifies the complexities of human psychology.

Rational people, by definition, maximize utility. People get utility from many goods, and they choose the combination of goods that gives them the highest possible utility. The concept of marginal utility resembles marginal benefit.

marginal utility — the increase in total utility that you gain from an additional unit of a good

Your **marginal utility** of a good is the increase in total utility that you gain from an additional unit of the good.

A general rule guides the choice of quantities of goods to maximize utility:

To maximize utility, choose quantities of goods that give you the same marginal utility per dollar on each good you buy.

---

[3]Notice that these changes in choice result from changes in opportunities (indicated by changes in the budget line), not from changes in tastes. A change in tastes would shift the indifference curves.

Let *MU*(pizzas) be the marginal utility of pizzas, *P*(pizzas) be the price of pizzas, *MU*(videos) be the marginal utility of videos, *P*(videos) be the price of videos, and so on. Mathematically, the general rule is:

$$\frac{MU(\text{pizzas})}{P(\text{pizzas})} = \frac{MU(\text{videos})}{P(\text{videos})} = \frac{MU(\text{T-shirts})}{P(\text{T-shirts})} = \ldots$$

The marginal utility per dollar—marginal utility divided by price—should be the same for all the products that a person buys.

EXPLANATION AND EXAMPLE

Suppose that donuts cost $0.50 each and brownies cost $1.00 each. You have $3.50 to spend. Panels a and b of **Figure 9B.1** show your total and marginal utility from donuts. Eating one donut gives you 10 utils of utility, a second donut gives you 9 more utils, a third gives you 7 more, a fourth gives you 4 more, a fifth gives

---

FIGURE 9B.1

TOTAL UTILITY AND MARGINAL UTILITY

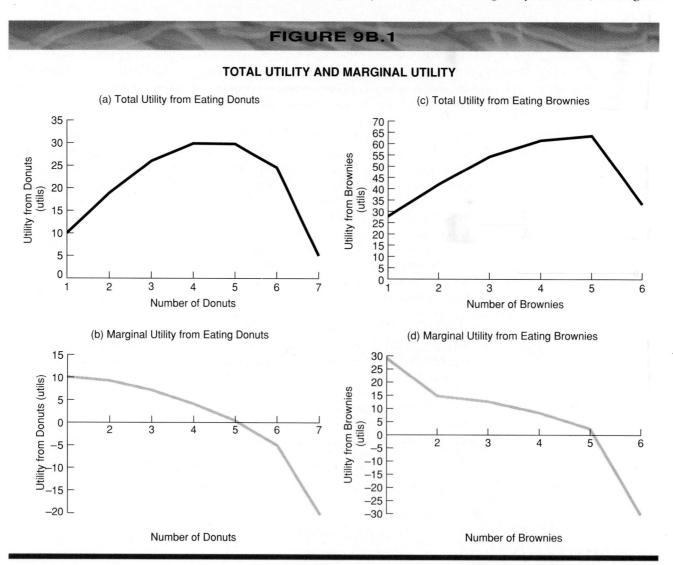

(a) Total Utility from Eating Donuts

(b) Marginal Utility from Eating Donuts

(c) Total Utility from Eating Brownies

(d) Marginal Utility from Eating Brownies

you no additional utility (you are indifferent between eating it or not), and a sixth donut reduces your utility by 10 utils (perhaps by making you sick).

Panels c and d of Figure 9B.1 show your total utility and marginal utility of brownies. Eating one brownie gives you 28 utils, a second brownie gives you 14 more utils, a third brownie gives you 12 more, a fourth gives you 8 more, a fifth gives you 2 more utils, and a sixth brownie reduces your utility by 30 utils.

You maximize utility if you buy three donuts and two brownies. The marginal utility of the third donut is 7 utils. Since donuts cost $0.50, your marginal utility per dollar spent on donuts is:

$$MU(\text{donuts})/P(\text{donuts}) = 7/\$0.50 = 14 \text{ utils per dollar}$$

The marginal utility of the second brownie is 14 utils. Since brownies cost $1.00, the marginal utility per dollar spent on brownies is:

$$MU(\text{brownies})/P(\text{brownies}) = 14/\$1.00 = 14 \text{ utils per dollar}$$

The marginal utility per dollar spent on donuts and brownies is the same:

$$\frac{MU(\text{donuts})}{P(\text{donuts})} = \frac{7}{\$0.50} = \frac{14}{\$1.00} = \frac{MU(\text{brownies})}{P(\text{brownies})}$$

Your total utility from donuts and brownies together is 68 utils (26 utils from three donuts and 42 utils from two brownies). This is the highest utility you can get with $3.50. If you were to buy one less brownie, you could use that dollar to buy two more donuts, but you would lose the 14 utils from that second brownie and gain only 4 utils from the fourth and fifth donuts. Your total utility of eating one brownie and five donuts would be only 58 utils. You could also buy three brownies and only one donut, but then you would get only 64 utils. You would maximize utility by choosing quantities that give the same marginal utility per dollar for both goods.

The rule for maximizing utility comes from the rule for maximizing net benefit: do something until its marginal benefit equals its marginal cost. Notice that when you buy two brownies, the marginal utility of the dollar spent on the second brownie is 14 utils. The marginal cost of that second brownie is its opportunity cost because you could have spent that dollar on two donuts. Because the marginal utility of donuts is 7 utils when you buy three, you give up 14 utils to buy a brownie. The marginal cost of the brownie, 14 utils, equals its marginal benefit.

APPLICATION: TAKING AN EXAM

When you take an exam, you must choose how much time to spend on each question. Think of utility as your grade on the exam. To maximize it, you must allocate your time so that you get the same marginal utility per minute spent on each question. (In this example, you spend time instead of money, and you equate marginal utilities per minute rather than marginal utilities per dollar.) If you could spend a minute on a question that would add 2 points to your score or on another question that would add 3 points to your score, you should spend the minute on the latter question.

UTILITY AND MARGINAL RATE OF SUBSTITUTION

Another way to state the rule for maximizing utility is:

$$\frac{MU(A)}{MU(B)} = \frac{P(A)}{P(B)} \qquad \text{for all goods A and B that you buy}$$

The ratio *MU(A)/MU(B)* equals the marginal rate of substitution between Goods A and B.

> The marginal rate of substitution between Goods A and B is the largest amount of B you would be willing to trade away for one unit of A. This equals the marginal utility of Good A divided by the marginal utility of Good B.

Your marginal rate of substitution between books and socks is your willingness to pay for an extra book, measured by the number of socks you would exchange for it.

The equation above has an important implication:

> To maximize utility, choose quantities of goods so that the marginal rate of substitution between any pair of goods equals their relative price.

In other words, buy an amount of each good so that your willingness to pay for another unit of the good equals its price. The height of your demand curve for a good shows the amount you are willing to pay for another unit; whatever the price, you maximize utility when you buy the quantity on your demand curve.

EXAMPLE

Your marginal rate of substitution between donuts and brownies is the amount of brownies you are willing to trade for one donut. The relative price shows the number of brownies you *can* trade for one donut (by buying fewer brownies and more donuts). The relative price of donuts in terms of brownies is \$0.50/\$1.00, or $\frac{1}{2}$. You maximize utility by buying two brownies and three donuts because this sets your marginal rate of substitution at $\frac{1}{2}$:

$$\frac{MU(\text{donuts})}{MU(\text{brownies})} = \frac{7}{14} = \frac{\$0.50}{\$1.00} = \frac{P(\text{donuts})}{P(\text{brownies})}$$

COMMENT

Utility theory is not intended to describe human psychology. It does not say that anyone actually feels utility or calculates marginal utility before buying goods. Instead, utility theory describes behavior in a way that economists can use in models intended to represent features of real-life economies. Utility theory describes how the rational actors *in the model* behave. If people make approximately rational choices in real life, even if they do not calculate marginal utilities or consciously equate marginal rates of substitution with relative prices, then the model can approximately mimic the real-life economy.[1]

KEY TERMS

utility	marginal utility
utils	

---

[1]Similarly, biologists have found that animals and even plants often behave as if they were maximizing something called fitness. The assumption about animal and plant behavior is not intended to describe what animals consciously do; it does not mean that animals and plants feel fitness or do calculations to maximize it (or even that they could do those calculations).

QUESTIONS AND PROBLEMS

9B.1 State the general rule for choosing quantities demanded to maximize utility.

9B.2 Look at Table 9.1 in the chapter text and interpret the term *benefit* as *utility*. What is Jane's marginal rate of substitution between posters and snack-packs if she chooses 4 posters and 8 snack-packs?

9B.3 **Table 9B.1** shows the combinations of goods that Jane can afford if she has $24, X costs $2, and Y costs $4. (This table resembles Table 9.1, except the price of Y is twice as high, and the term *utility* replaces the term *benefit*.)

  a. Find the quantities demanded of X and Y that maximize utility.

  b. Show that your answer to Part a satisfies the general rule for maximizing utility.

  c. Use the data from Tables 9.1 and 9B.1 to graph two points on Jane's demand curve for Y.

  d. Use your answer to Part c to calculate Jane's elasticity of demand for Y.

TABLE 9B.1

WHAT IS JANE'S RATIONAL CHOICE?

Amount of X	Total Utility of X	Marginal Utility of X	Amount of Y	Total Utility of Y	Marginal Utility of Y
0	0		6	180	20
2	44	20	5	160	24
4	**74**	**14**	**4**	**136**	**28**
6	96	10	3	108	32
8	110	6	2	76	36
10	119	4	1	40	40
12	124	2	0	0	

CHAPTER 9 APPENDIX C — ALGEBRA OF CONSUMER SURPLUS

Consider the straight-line demand and supply curves represented by these two equations:

$$Q^d = a - bP \qquad \textit{Example: } Q^d = 10 - 2P$$

$$Q^s = c + dP \qquad \textit{Example: } Q^s = -5 + 3P$$

where Q^d is the quantity demanded, Q^s is the quantity supplied, P is the price of the good, and *a, b, c,* and *d* are numbers.

The Chapter 4 Appendix showed that the equilibrium price is:

$$P_1 = (a - c)/(b + d) \qquad \textit{Example: } P_1 = 3$$

The equilibrium quantity is:

$$Q_1 = a - b(a - c)/(b + d) \qquad \text{\textit{Example:} } Q_1^d = 4$$

Figure 9C.1 illustrates these equations. Because the demand curve is a straight line, consumer surplus is the area of the triangle in Figure 9C.1. The height of the triangle is:

$$H = a/b - P_1 \qquad \text{\textit{Example:} } 5 - 3$$

$$= a/b - (a - c)/(b + d) \qquad \text{\textit{Example:} } 2$$

The base of the triangle is the equilibrium quantity, so the area of the triangle, consumer surplus, is half the area of the base times the height:

$$CS = (H)(Q_1)/2 \qquad \text{\textit{Example:} } (2)(4)/2 = 4$$

QUESTIONS AND PROBLEMS

9C.1 Suppose that the demand curve is:

$$Q^d = 30 - P$$

and the supply curve is:

$$Q^s = 2P$$

   a. Calculate the equilibrium quantity and price.
   b. Show the equilibrium on a graph.
   c. Calculate consumer surplus. Your answer should be a number. (*Hint:* Look at your graph and use the formula for the area of a triangle.)

FIGURE 9C.1

CALCULATING CONSUMER SURPLUS

Consumer surplus is the area of the shaded triangle, which is
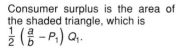

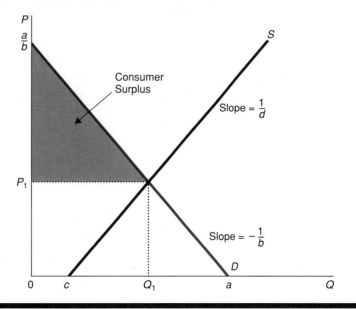

CHAPTER 9 APPENDIX D — MATHEMATICS OF RATIONAL CHOICE*

Your total benefit from doing something depends on how much you do it. Your benefit is a function of the amount you do. Let B denote the total benefit from doing something Q times. B is a function of Q:

$$B = f(Q)$$

Your marginal benefit, MB, is the derivative of total benefit with respect to Q:

$$MB = f'(Q)$$
$$= dB/dQ$$

The total cost is also a function of Q. Let C be your total cost of doing something Q times. C is a function of Q:

$$C = g(Q)$$

Your marginal cost, MC, is the derivative of total cost with respect to Q:

$$MC = g'(Q)$$
$$= dC/dQ$$

Your net benefit is your total benefit minus your total cost, so your net benefit is also a function of Q:

$$\text{Net benefit} = f(Q) - g(Q)$$

To maximize your net benefit, take its derivative with respect to Q and set the derivative equal to zero:

$$f'(Q) - g'(Q) = 0$$
$$f'(Q) = g'(Q)$$
$$MB = MC$$

To maximize net benefit, choose a quantity Q so that marginal benefit equals marginal cost.

QUESTIONS AND PROBLEMS

9D.1 Suppose that the total benefit of doing something Q times is:

$$60 Q - Q^2$$

and the total cost of doing something Q times is:

$$20 + Q^2$$

a. Calculate the marginal benefit and marginal cost.
b. Which choice of Q maximizes net benefit?
c. When you choose Q to maximize net benefit, how large is your net benefit?

*Note: This appendix requires knowledge of calculus. It uses derivatives.

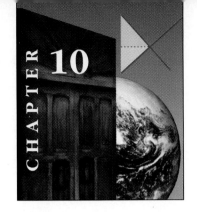

CHAPTER 10

BUSINESS DECISIONS AND SUPPLY

WHAT THIS CHAPTER IS ABOUT

▶ Types of business firms

▶ The logic behind business decisions

▶ Connections between costs of production, supply decisions, and profit

▶ The gain to producers from selling a good

Business decisions mystify most people. Everyone knows that the cost of producing an item affects it price, but few people understand how costs affect the decisions of business firms to use plastic or metal parts, to use sucrose or fructose as sweeteners, to hire workers and raise output or reduce employment and production, to launch new enterprises, to stop producing products, or to go out of business entirely. This chapter discusses the fundamental logic of business decisions. That logic shows connections between supply curves and profits.

BUSINESS FIRMS

The United States has nearly 20 million business firms, about one for every eight adults. Japan has about 22 million firms, about one for every four adults. Most U.S. firms are small; about 60 percent of them generate annual revenues less than $25,000. A few large firms (about 4 percent of all firms) generate annual revenues of more than $1 million.

firm — an organization that coordinates the activities of workers, managers, owners, lenders, and other participants to produce and sell a good or service

A **firm** is an organization that coordinates the activities of workers, managers, owners, lenders, and other participants to produce and sell a good or service.

A firm or business organization consists of the network of contracts between owners, workers, and other people that state each party's obligations, rights, and payoffs in various situations. Some of these contracts are explicit, stated in formal documents, and others are informal or implicit. Firms borrow money, hire workers, buy materials, and rent equipment. The contracts specify who gets any money left over from selling the goods produced by workers with the firm's equipment and materials.

TYPES OF FIRMS

There are three main types of firms:

1. Sole proprietorships
2. Partnerships
3. Corporations

A sole proprietorship is a firm owned by one person, such as a small store. Anyone can start a sole proprietorship and relatively few government regulations apply to them. They do not pay corporate income taxes; instead, the owner pays personal income tax on the firm's revenue. The owner is personally responsible for all the debts of a sole proprietorship. Sole proprietorships rely mainly on owners' personal funds and personal loans from banks or other financial institutions to finance their operations. Almost three-quarters of all U.S. firms are sole proprietorships, but most of them are small firms; together, they receive only about 6 percent of the total revenue (income) of all U.S. firms.

A partnership resembles a sole proprietorship, except two or more people share ownership through a written contract or an informal agreement. The owners divide the firm's revenue and pay personal income taxes on it; they pay no corporate income tax. All partners bear responsibility for all the firm's debts, and the firm relies mainly on personal loans to finance its operations. Fewer than 10 percent of U.S. firms operate as partnerships, but they are larger, on average, than sole proprietorships. Partnerships receive about 4 percent of the total revenue of all U.S. firms.

A corporation is a firm with special legal rights:

1. The law treats it as an artificial person that lives on even if its owners change.
2. The owners, called *stockholders,* have limited liability that shields them from personal responsibility for the firm's debts.[1] If the firm goes bankrupt and does not repay all its loans, the lenders cannot legally force the owners (stockholders) to pay them.

One person or a few people own some corporations. Others issue shares of stock that trade publicly on stock markets such as the New York Stock Exchange or NASDAQ. Stockholders, who own the firm, receive residual income, which means that they collect the firm's profit. Although they own the firm, they usually do not make its management decisions directly; instead, stockholders vote to hire (or fire) managers to run their firm. The top manager is usually called the *CEO,* for *chief executive officer.* Corporations operate under special laws and government regulations.

Corporate income is taxed twice. First, the firm pays the corporate tax on its income. Second, the stockholders pay tax on distributions of the firm's income that they receive. The owners receive the firm's income partly in the form of dividends, which are direct payments from the firm to its stockholders. They may also earn capital gains from increases in the price of the stock. Owners pay personal income tax on dividends, and either personal income tax or a special capital gains tax on any capital gains that they realize when they sell stock.

Corporations often borrow money from banks and other financial institutions. They also borrow money directly from investors by selling IOUs called corporate

---

[1]This separation between the obligations of the corporation and those of its owners is sometimes called the *corporate veil.* Court decisions have sometimes *pierced the corporate veil* by ruling that corporate owners must personally fulfill certain corporate obligations.

bonds in financial markets. Bondholders loan money to the firm in exchange for IOUs on which they will collect in the future. About 20 percent of U.S. firms are corporations. Because many are large, they receive 90 percent of the total revenue of all U.S. firms.

TWO CRITICAL BUSINESS DECISIONS

Every producer must make two critical decisions: *how* to produce its good or service and *how much* to produce. These are not separate decisions. A firm may use different kinds of equipment and production methods to produce 10,000 lamp shades than it would use to produce a few hundred. Still, it is useful to separate the questions to discuss the logic of business decisions.

EXAMPLE

A furniture business must decide:

1. How to make furniture (Hire more workers using hand saws or fewer workers using power saws?)
2. How many tables to make this year (10? 100? 1,000?)

The following sections discuss the logic of each decision.

DECIDING HOW TO PRODUCE

technically efficient method of production — a method that does not waste any inputs, so the firm cannot produce the same amount of output using less of any input without using more of other inputs

A business firm's decision of how to produce includes three logical steps:

1. Choose a hypothetical quantity to produce and list all the technically efficient methods of producing that quantity.
2. Choose the economically efficient (lowest-cost) method of producing that quantity.
3. Repeat Steps 1 and 2 for all other possible quantities.

STEP 1: LIST ALL TECHNICALLY EFFICIENT METHODS

A method of production is **technically efficient** if it does not waste any inputs (i.e., if the firm could not produce the same amount using less of any one input without using more of the other inputs).

Firms can identify many technically efficient methods to produce most goods. Some methods use many workers and less equipment; others use more equipment and fewer workers. A firm can use high-technology equipment or older equipment, more experienced or less experienced workers, rubber or plastic, sugar or corn syrup, and so on. A production function summarizes the technically efficient methods of production.

A production function is a description of technically efficient ways to combine inputs to produce various amounts of output (final product).

A production function summarizes the state of technical knowledge in a form like a collection of recipes or blueprints. It might tell a firm how to combine flour, yeast, an oven, and other inputs to make bread, or how to combine iron ore and other inputs to make steel. The production function changes if a scientist discovers a new, technically efficient way to produce a good. Farmers needed 3 pounds of feed to grow each pound of chicken in 1960, for example, but subsequent advances in animal science reduced the required input to under 2 pounds of feed.

economically efficient method of production — the technically efficient method with the lowest cost

STEP 2: CHOOSE THE ECONOMICALLY EFFICIENT METHOD

The **economically efficient method of production** is the technically efficient method with the lowest cost.

While a firm can identify many technically efficient ways to produce, usually only one of them is economically efficient, that is, only one minimizes the costs of production.[2]

EXAMPLE

It may be technically efficient for a worker to cut five cords of wood in 10 hours using an axe or in 1 hour using a chain saw. Which method is economically efficient? The answer depends on the costs of workers, axes, and chain saws. Suppose that a worker costs $5 per hour, an axe costs $10, and a chain saw costs $50. The axe method costs $60 for 10 hours of work and one axe, but the chain saw method costs only $55 for 1 hour of work and a saw. The economically efficient method of cutting the wood is with a chain saw. If chain saws cost $60, however, then it is cheaper to cut the wood with an axe, even though it takes 10 hours of work.

The economically efficient method of production may depend on how much the firm produces. To cut one cord of wood rather than five, it is economically efficient to use an axe because 2 hours of labor plus one axe costs $20, which is less than the chain saw method costs. The economically efficient way to cut 50 cords of wood, however, is with a chain saw.

NOTE ON QUALITY

The discussion here applies to some fixed level of quality. The economically efficient method of producing a good is not a method that cuts costs by reducing quality; it is the lowest-cost method of producing a good with some particular level of quality. Think of high-quality goods and low-quality goods as different products. Producers decide which product (which quality level) to make, and then they determine its economically efficient method of production.

STEP 3: REPEAT STEPS 1 AND 2 FOR ALL OTHER POSSIBLE QUANTITIES

These three steps give a firm the economically efficient method of producing each possible quantity of the good. After the firm knows how to produce each possible quantity in an economically efficient way, it can decide how much to produce.

──────────────── FOR REVIEW ────────────────

10.1 Discuss the differences between sole proprietorships, partnerships, and corporations.

10.2 What is a technically efficient method of production? What is an economically efficient method?

──────────────── QUESTION ────────────────

10.3 Explain why some technically efficient methods of production are not economically efficient.

IN THE NEWS

A [representative] for PepsiCo Inc. said: "We have no immediate plans to go to sucrose. However, Pepsi is always exploring different, more economic ways to sweeten our drinks. If the price of sucrose becomes competitive with high fructose corn syrup, we'd consider our options." Sucrose is a sugar extracted from sugar cane or sugar beets.

A beverage firm chooses the lowest-cost (economically efficient) method of production by calculating whether it is cheaper to use sucrose or high-fructose corn syrup to sweeten its product.

Source: The Wall Street Journal, June 28, 1988, p. 47.

─────────────────

[2]Chapter 16 discusses the rules of rational choice for choosing the combination of inputs to produce at the lowest cost.

DECIDING HOW MUCH TO PRODUCE

total revenue — total receipts from selling a good

profit — total revenue minus total cost

marginal revenue — the increase in total revenue as the quantity produced rises by 1 unit

The general rule for rational choice discussed in Chapter 9 applies to the choice of how much to produce. If a firm decides to produce at all, it maximizes its net benefit by producing a quantity for which its marginal benefit equals its marginal cost.

BENEFITS AND REVENUES

A firm's net benefit from producing a good has two parts: profit and nonmonetary rewards. Profit is total revenue minus total cost.

Total revenue means the total receipts from selling a good.

Profit is total revenue minus total cost.

If you sell 200 yearbooks at $10 each, your total revenue is $2,000. If your costs to produce the yearbooks totaled $1,800, then your profit is $200.

Nonmonetary rewards are benefits other than profit from producing and selling a good, such as a sense of accomplishment, a feeling of power, respect, fame, an air-conditioned office, or good feelings from helping other people or contributing to the community. Producers face tradeoffs between profits and nonmonetary rewards. Better working conditions provide nonmonetary rewards, but they also add to costs. A producer who is concerned about the environment might choose lower profits and a more costly but more environmentally friendly method of production. Another producer might choose higher profits with the lower-cost production method and contribute more money to an environmental cause.

Most of this chapter will focus on cases in which nonmonetary rewards are small compared to profits, so the net benefit of producing a good can be approximated by the producer's profit. Then the total benefit from producing a good is simply the total revenue it creates, and the marginal benefit is the marginal revenue.

Marginal revenue is the increase in total revenue from producing another unit of a good.[3]

Table 10.1 shows an example. If a firm charges $16, it sells 1 unit and its total revenue is $16. If it charges $15, it sells 2 units for total revenue of $30. The marginal revenue of the second unit is the increase in total revenue from selling it, or $14. The table also shows the firm's total cost of producing goods and its marginal cost (the increase in total cost from producing another unit). In summary, if a producer cares only about profit and ignores nonmonetary rewards, then:

▶ Total benefit is total revenue.

▶ Marginal benefit is marginal revenue.

▶ Net benefit is profit.

The basic logic of rational behavior from Chapter 9 now applies directly to a firm's decision of how much to produce. One new issue arises: a firm might shut down its operations (produce zero output) rather than earn negative profit (suffer a loss). The basic rule of rational behavior states that, if a firm produces at all, it maximizes profit by equating marginal revenue with marginal cost. To examine the logic that governs when a firm should shut down, the following sections

---

[3]Readers who know calculus will recognize marginal revenue as the derivative of total revenue with respect to the quantity produced. See the appendix to this chapter.

TABLE 10.1

CHOOSING A QUANTITY TO PRODUCE

Quantity (Q)	Price (P)	Total Revenue (TR)	Marginal Revenue (MR)	Total Cost (TC)	Marginal Cost (MC)	Profit
1	16	16	16	28	28	−12
2	15	30	14	42	14	−12
3	14	42	12	44	2	−2
4	13	52	10	46	2	6
5	12	60	8	48	2	12
6	11	66	6	51	3	15
7	**10**	**70**	**4**	**55**	**4**	**15**
8	9	72	2	60	5	12
9	8	72	0	66	6	6
10	7	70	−2	73	7	−3
11	6	66	−4	81	8	−15
12	5	60	−6	90	9	−30

distinguish between the short run and the long run. The long-run case is simpler, so the next section discusses it first.

PROFIT MAXIMIZATION IN THE LONG RUN

Chapter 4 discussed differences between short-run and long-run demand and supply. When people have a longer time to adjust to a change, the quantity supplied (or demanded) reacts more strongly to a change in the price. It takes time to build new factories and offices or to grow trees or corn. Chapter 4 defined the long run as a period of time over which people can fully adjust to a change.

> The **long run** refers to a period of time over which people fully adjust their behavior to a change in conditions. Applied to a business firm, the long run refers to a period of time over which the firm can change the quantities of all its inputs.

In the long run, a firm maximizes profit by choosing its level of production in three steps. First, it finds the level of output for which marginal revenue equals marginal cost, with marginal cost rising or constant. It then calculates total revenue and total cost at that level of output. Finally, it chooses whether to shut down or to produce the chosen level of output.

long run — a period of time over which people fully adjust their behavior to a change in conditions; a period of time over which a firm can change the quantities of all its inputs

STEP 1

Find the level of output at which two statements are true:

1. Marginal revenue equals marginal cost

2. Marginal cost is rising or constant[4]

Marginal cost is rising when the marginal cost curve slopes upward so that marginal cost rises as output rises. Marginal cost is constant when the marginal cost curve is flat so that marginal cost remains constant as output rises.

---

[4]Technically, a firm can also maximize profit by producing a quantity at which marginal revenue equals marginal cost and marginal cost is falling, if marginal cost falls more slowly than marginal revenue as output rises.

Figure 10.1a shows an example of Step 1, using the numbers from Table 10.1. Marginal cost equals marginal revenue at both Point A where output is 7 units and Point B where output is 2 units. Marginal cost is rising at Point A (the *MC* curve slopes upward there), but marginal cost is falling (not rising or constant) at Point B. Step 1 says to choose Point A, with output equal to 7 units. **Figure 10.2** shows an example with constant marginal cost that also implies a level of output from Step 1 of 7 units (Point A).

FIGURE 10.1

LONG-RUN PROFIT MAXIMIZATION WITH RISING MARGINAL COST

Step 1 in the profit-maximization decision identifies the quantity at Point A, 7 units per year.

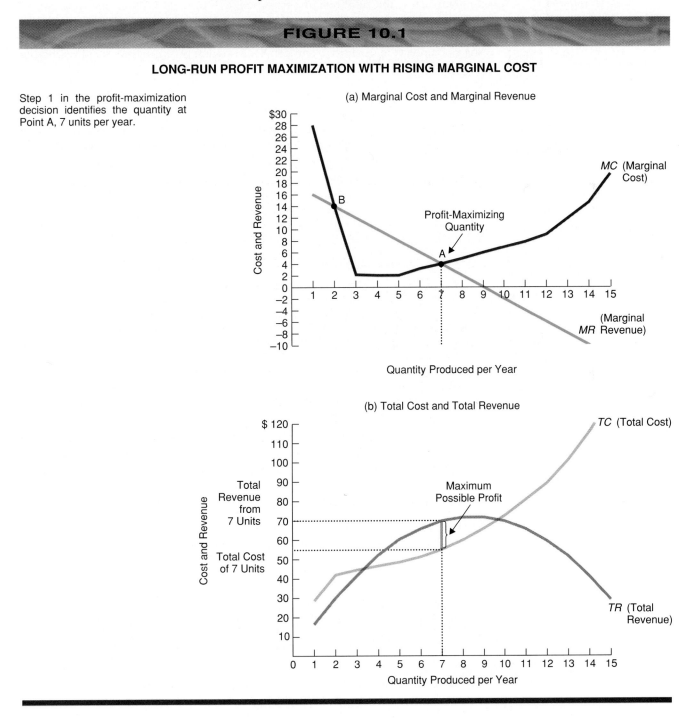

FIGURE 10.2

LONG-RUN PROFIT MAXIMIZATION WITH CONSTANT MARGINAL COST

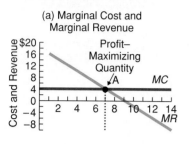

(a) Marginal Cost and Marginal Revenue

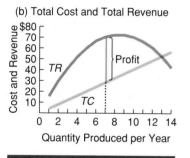

(b) Total Cost and Total Revenue

Step 1 shows the quantity that the firm will produce to maximize profit if it does not shut down. The next two steps determine whether or not the firm should shut down. The second step calculates total revenue and total cost at the level of output from Step 1.

STEP 2

Calculate total revenue (*TR*) and total cost (*TC*) at the level of output from Step 1. In Figure 10.1, the total revenue from selling 7 units is $70 and the total cost of producing them is $55. Figure 10.1b shows the total revenue and total cost figures for various levels of output. The highest possible profit occurs when the firm produces 7 units (the quantity from Step 1). Knowing this, the firm decides whether to produce or shut down.

STEP 3

If total revenue is smaller than total cost at the level of output from Step 1, so that profit would be negative (the firm would suffer a loss), then the firm should shut down (not produce anything). Shutting down would prevent the loss because the firm would have zero revenue, zero cost, and zero profit. If total revenue equals or exceeds total cost, so that profit would be zero or positive, then the firm should produce the level of output from Step 1.

Step 3 says that a profit-maximizing firm stays in business in the long run if its total revenue covers its total cost; otherwise, it shuts down to avoid losing money. To summarize Step 3 mathematically, *in the long run:*

1. If *TR* < *TC,* then shut down.

2. If *TR* > *TC,* then produce the quantity from Step 1, and earn a profit equal to *TR* − *TC.*

In Figure 10.1 (and Table 10.1), total revenue ($70) exceeds total cost ($55), so the firm produces the quantity from Step 1 (7 units) to earn a profit of $15. Figure 10.1b shows that the firm gets the highest possible profit, $15, when it produces 7 units. At this quantity, total revenue exceeds total cost by $15.

Figure 10.3 shows an example in which a firm would shut down in the long run because total revenue falls short of total cost. Step 1 tells the firm to produce 7 units of output (Point A), because marginal cost equals marginal revenue and marginal cost is rising at that point.[5] Step 2 tells the firm to calculate total cost and total revenue at that quantity; the total cost of producing 7 units is $75 and the total revenue from selling those 7 units is $70. Step 3 tells the firm to shut down in the long run, because total revenue is smaller than total cost. If the firm were to produce 7 units, it would lose $5; by shutting down, the firm avoids the loss.

EXPLANATION If marginal revenue exceeds marginal cost, the firm raises its profit by producing more. The extra revenue from an additional unit of output exceeds the cost of that additional unit, so profit rises. In Table 10.1, for example, the firm earns $6 profit if it produces 4 units of the good. The marginal revenue from a fifth unit ($8) exceeds the marginal cost of a fifth unit ($2) by $6, so producing a fifth unit raises the firm's profit by $6 (from $6 to $12).

Similarly, if marginal revenue is less than marginal cost, the firm raises its profit by producing less. If the firm produces 8 units, its profit is $12. Since the

---

[5]Marginal cost is not rising at Point B, so Step 1 does not choose that point.

FIGURE 10.3

A FIRM THAT SHUTS DOWN IN THE LONG RUN

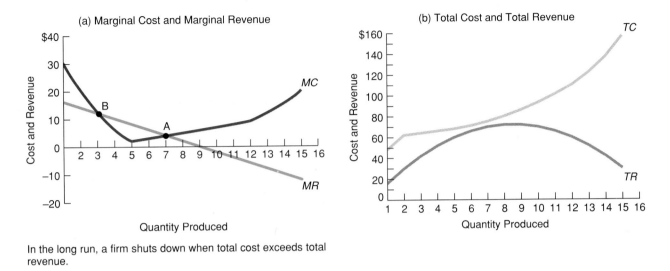

In the long run, a firm shuts down when total cost exceeds total revenue.

marginal revenue of the eighth unit is only $2 while its marginal cost is $5, producing the eighth unit reduces the firm's profits by $3 (from $15 to $12). In that case, the firm can raise its profit by reducing output from 8 units to 7. The firm earns the highest possible profit by producing the quantity for which marginal revenue equals marginal cost, when marginal cost is rising or constant. If this highest possible profit is *negative* so that the firm would suffer a loss by producing, then the firm shuts down to avoid that loss.

PROFIT MAXIMIZATION IN THE SHORT RUN

The long run is a period of time over which people can fully adjust to a change, but many adjustments take time. It takes time to build new factories, new offices, or new equipment or to grow crops. The short run is a period of time over which people cannot fully adjust to a change.

short run — a period of time over which people cannot fully adjust their behavior to a change in conditions; a period of time over which a firm cannot vary the quantities of all its inputs

The **short run** refers to a period of time over which people cannot fully adjust their behavior to a change in conditions. Applied to a business firm, the short run refers to a period of time over which the firm cannot vary the quantities of all of its inputs, though it may be able to change the quantities of some inputs.[6]

---

[6]More precisely, the cost of adjusting quickly to a change in conditions is sometimes higher than the cost of adjusting slowly. The short run is the period of time before a complete adjustment occurs when people or firms choose their speed of adjustment. For example, suppose that a person wants to sell a house. She can sell it in *one day* if she is willing to accept a low enough price. But if she is willing to wait, she is likely to find a buyer who is willing to pay more than she could get in a shorter period of time. Her *cost* of selling the house quickly is higher (it brings a lower price) than if she sells the house over a longer period of time. The short run, then, refers to the time before the owner chooses to sell the house; the long run refers to later times.

Over the short run, the firm has some fixed inputs whose quantities it cannot change.

fixed input — an input whose quantity a firm cannot change in the short run

Fixed inputs are those whose quantities a firm cannot change in the short run. All other inputs are **variable inputs,** those whose quantities the firm can change in the short run.

variable input — an input whose quantity a firm can change in the short run

Short-run costs differ from long-run costs because in the short run, a firm faces an extra constraint or limit on its choices: it cannot change the quantities of its fixed inputs over the short run.[7] The firm is constrained by the quantities of fixed inputs that it chose in the past. (This constraint disappears in the long run when the firm can vary all of its inputs.) In the short run, a law firm may be stuck with the office space it currently rents, an auto-maker with a fixed number of machines, and a medical lab with a certain amount of equipment. Some firms might not use all of their equipment or office space, but they have already paid for those inputs. This constraint implies that in the short run, a firm's average cost may include some fixed costs.

fixed cost — an unavoidable cost of a fixed input

Fixed costs are costs of fixed inputs (those whose quantities are fixed in the short run).

variable cost — an avoidable cost of a variable input

Variable costs are costs of variable inputs (those whose quantities the firm can vary in the short run).

Total fixed cost is the sum of all fixed costs. Total variable cost is the sum of all variable costs.

Total cost equals total fixed cost, also called *overhead cost,* plus total variable cost. The firm has already paid (or agreed to pay) for machinery, equipment, or office space; these payments are fixed (overhead) costs. Fixed costs are unavoidable in the short run; a firm can avoid variable costs by producing less. All costs that the firm can avoid in the short run are variable costs.

EXAMPLES

If a firm has signed a lease for office space and cannot terminate the lease, its payment for office space is a fixed cost. If the firm has the right to terminate the lease without penalty, then its payment for office space is a variable cost. The cost of electricity to operate the firm's machinery is a variable cost—it can change quickly. **Table 10.2** adds a $10 total fixed cost to the example presented in Table 10.1, so the total cost now exceeds total variable cost by $10.

HOW SHORT IS THE SHORT RUN?

The terms *short run* and *long run* do not refer to fixed amounts of calendar time. The short run may be measured in minutes in some situations and in years in other situations. The long run for a travel bureau may be only a few days (the time required to buy and set up phones and desks); the long run for another firm may be decades (the time to grow trees for certain types of wood). Economists make these distinctions precise in the context of individual issues.

---

[7]More precisely, it is more costly to obtain more of these inputs quickly. The distinction between the short run and the long run really involves the costs of changing inputs over various periods of time. The short-run constraint arises from the higher cost of changing inputs quickly. See the previous footnote.

TABLE 10.2

REVENUES AND COSTS WITH $10 TOTAL FIXED COST

Quantity (Q)	Price (P)	Total Revenue (TR)	Marginal Revenue (MR)	Total Cost (TC)	Total Variable Cost (TVC)	Marginal Cost (MC)	Profit	
1	16	16	16	38	28	28	−22	
2	15	30	14	52	42	14	−22	
3	14	42	12	54	44	2	−12	
4	13	52	10	56	46	2	−4	
5	12	60	8	58	48	2	2	
6	11	66	6	61	51	3	5	
7	10	70	4	65	55	4	5	MC = MR
8	9	72	2	70	60	5	2	
9	8	72	0	76	66	6	−4	
10	7	70	−2	83	73	7	−13	
11	6	66	−4	91	81	8	−25	
12	5	60	−6	100	90	9	−40	

WHY MARGINAL COST RISES AT HIGH LEVELS OF OUTPUT

Notice that marginal cost rises as output increases beyond 5 units in Table 10.2. Marginal cost rises partly because, in the short run, the firm is limited by its existing fixed inputs, those that it chose in the past. To raise output above a certain quantity, it must either use the fixed inputs more intensively (operate machinery at a faster speed, for example) or switch to other, more expensive methods of production. Marginal cost also rises because increases in production raise the costs of managing the firm. These costs include keeping track of the work of various people in the firm, coordinating decisions in various parts of the firm, and maintaining control of the parts of the firm.

STEP-BY-STEP PROCEDURE FOR CHOOSING SHORT-RUN OUTPUT

In the short run, a firm maximizes profit by choosing its level of production in three steps. The first step is the same as in the long-run decision: find the level of output for which marginal revenue equals marginal cost, with marginal cost rising or constant. In the second step, the firm calculates total revenue and total variable cost. In the third step, the firm decides whether to shut down or produce.

STEP 1

Find the level of output at which two statements are true:

1. Marginal revenue equals marginal cost
2. Marginal cost is rising or constant[8]

---

[8]Technically, a firm can also maximize profit by producing a quantity at which marginal revenue equals marginal cost and marginal cost is falling, if marginal cost falls more slowly than marginal revenue as output rises.

STEP 2

The second step is slightly different in the short-run than in the long-run decision. Calculate total revenue (*TR*) and total variable cost (*TVC*) at the level of output from Step 1.

STEP 3

Finally, the firm decides whether to produce or shut down.

1. If total revenue is smaller than total variable cost at the level of output from Step 1, then shut down the firm (produce nothing). In this case, the firm takes a loss equal to its total fixed cost.

2. If total revenue equals or exceeds total variable cost, then produce the level of output from Step 1. This case leaves two possibilities:
   a. If total revenue equals or exceeds total cost, then the difference is the firm's profit.
   b. If total revenue falls short of total cost, then the firm produces while suffering a loss equal to its total cost minus its total revenue. In this case, the firm suffers a smaller loss if it produces than if it shuts down.

To summarize Step 3 mathematically:

1. If $TR < TVC$, then shut down and lose *TFC* (total fixed cost).
2. If $TR \geq TVC$, then produce the quantity from Step 1:
   a. If $TR > TC$, earn a profit of $TR - TC$.
   b. If $TR < TC$, lose $TC - TR$.

The following table summarizes the three situations:

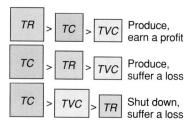

TR > TC > TVC   Produce, earn a profit

TC > TR > TVC   Produce, suffer a loss

TC > TVC > TR   Shut down, suffer a loss

Situation	Action
(a) Total revenue > Total cost > Total variable cost	Produce, earn a profit
(b) Total cost > Total revenue > Total variable cost	Produce, suffer a loss
(c) Total cost > Total variable cost > Total revenue	Shut down, suffer a loss equal to fixed costs

In Situations a and b, the firm maximizes its profit (or minimizes its loss) by producing the quantity at which marginal cost equals marginal revenue. In Situation c, the firm minimizes its loss by producing zero output. (Note that a firm may shut down temporarily without going out of business permanently.)

Notice that with fixed costs, the benefit to the firm from staying in business and producing the good rather than shutting down is not measured solely by its profit. If the firm shuts down, it suffers a loss equal to its fixed cost, so its benefit from staying in business is its profit plus its total fixed cost. This is also called *producer surplus,* as a later section of this chapter explains. Suppose, for example, that a firm with a fixed cost of $10 earns a profit of $5. If it were to shut down, it would take a $10 loss, so its gain from producing rather than shutting down is $15; that is its producer surplus.

Figure 10.4 shows the profit-maximizing level of output in each of the situations outlined above. In Panel a, the firm produces and earns a profit because total revenue exceeds total cost at the quantity of output from Step 1. In Panel b, the firm produces, but suffers a loss. At the quantity from Step 1, the firm's total revenue exceeds its total variable cost, but its large fixed cost pushes total cost above total revenues. The firm produces at a loss because its loss would be even larger if it were to shut down. In Panel c, the firm minimizes its loss by shutting down because its total variable cost exceeds its total revenue at every level of output.

FIGURE 10.4

SHORT-RUN PROFIT MAXIMIZATION WITH FIXED COSTS

(a) The firm has a total fixed cost of $5, so its total cost exceeds its total variable cost by $5. When total revenue exceeds total cost, the firm earns a profit. (b) The firm has a total fixed cost of $25, so its total cost exceeds its total variable cost by $25. When total revenue exceeds total variable cost, but falls short of total cost, the firm produces and suffers a loss. (c) When total variable cost exceeds total revenue, the firm shuts down in the short run.

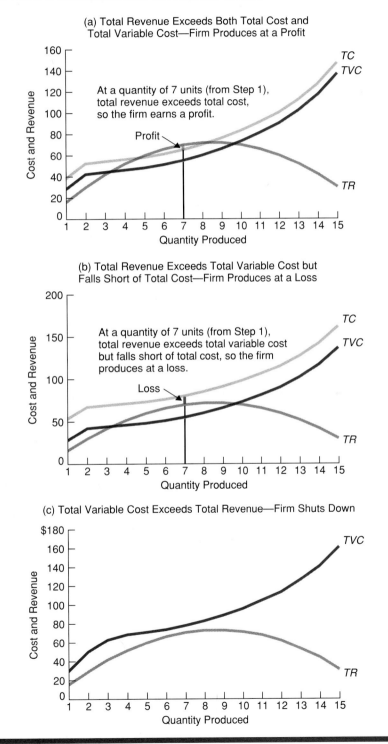

(a) Total Revenue Exceeds Both Total Cost and Total Variable Cost—Firm Produces at a Profit

At a quantity of 7 units (from Step 1), total revenue exceeds total cost, so the firm earns a profit.

Profit

(b) Total Revenue Exceeds Total Variable Cost but Falls Short of Total Cost—Firm Produces at a Loss

At a quantity of 7 units (from Step 1), total revenue exceeds total variable cost but falls short of total cost, so the firm produces at a loss.

Loss

(c) Total Variable Cost Exceeds Total Revenue—Firm Shuts Down

EXAMPLES   A firm produces 200 cans of beans per day to maximize its profit. (This is the quantity at which marginal cost equals marginal revenue.) It has a fixed cost of $100 and a variable cost of $200, so its total cost is $300. The firm can face three possible situations. (a) If its total revenue is $350, the firm earns a $50 profit and stays in business. (b) If its total revenue is $250, it takes a $50 loss. This is smaller than the $100 loss the firm would have if it shut down (losing its entire fixed cost), so the firm stays in business and produces at a loss. (c) If its total revenue is only $150, the firm would suffer a $150 loss if it produced, so it shuts down to reduce its loss to $100.

EXPLANATION   Economists distinguish between variable cost and total cost because each serves a different purpose. Total cost helps analysts to evaluate the outcomes of decisions made in the past. To answer the question, "Has the firm been profitable?" we must subtract all costs—both fixed and variable costs—from total revenue. However, only variable cost is relevant to any current decision of the firm. The firm cannot avoid its fixed costs, which it has already either paid or agreed to pay. It cannot avoid paying these fixed costs or get its money back. In the language of Chapter 9, fixed costs are sunk costs. As Chapter 9 explained, rational choices ignore sunk costs for current decisions, such as whether to stay in business or shut down. Therefore, to answer the question, "Should the firm produce or shut down (produce zero output)?" we compare total revenue with total variable cost.

> If a firm's total variable cost is larger than its total revenue, the firm suffers a loss which it can minimize by producing zero output, that is, by shutting down (at least temporarily).

A firm might suffer a loss even if its total revenue exceeds its total variable cost because its total cost (including its fixed cost) may exceed its total revenue. In this case, the firm can reduce its loss by producing instead of shutting down.

> If total revenue exceeds total variable cost, the firm minimizes its loss by producing the quantity at which marginal revenue equals marginal cost.

FOR REVIEW

10.4 What is marginal revenue?

10.5 What is the long run? What is the short run?

10.6 What are fixed inputs? What are variable inputs? Give examples of each.

10.7 What are fixed costs? What are variable costs?

QUESTIONS

10.8 What are the three steps by which a firm chooses its output to maximize profit in the long run?

10.9 What are the three steps by which a firm chooses its output to maximize profit in the short run?

10.10 Under what conditions does a firm minimize its loss by shutting down? Under what conditions does it minimize its loss by staying in business and producing output at a loss? Explain.

TABLE 10.3

AVERAGE COSTS WITH A $10 FIXED COST

Quantity (Q)	Total Cost (TC)	Average Cost (AC)	Total Variable Cost (TVC)	Average Variable Cost (AVC)	Average Fixed Cost (AFC)
1	38	38	28	28	10
2	52	26	42	21	5
3	54	18	44	$14\frac{2}{3}$	$3\frac{1}{3}$
4	56	14	46	$11\frac{1}{2}$	$2\frac{1}{2}$
5	58	$11\frac{3}{5}$	48	$9\frac{3}{5}$	2
6	61	$10\frac{1}{6}$	51	$8\frac{1}{2}$	$1\frac{2}{3}$
7	65	$9\frac{2}{7}$	55	$7\frac{6}{7}$	$1\frac{3}{7}$
8	70	$8\frac{3}{4}$	60	$7\frac{1}{2}$	$1\frac{1}{4}$
9	76	$8\frac{4}{9}$	66	$7\frac{1}{3}$	$1\frac{1}{9}$
10	83	$8\frac{3}{10}$	73	$7\frac{3}{10}$	1
11	91	$8\frac{3}{11}$	81	$7\frac{4}{11}$	$\frac{5}{6}$
12	100	$8\frac{1}{3}$	90	$7\frac{1}{2}$	$\frac{5}{6}$

AVERAGE COST AND AVERAGE REVENUE

average revenue — total revenue divided by the quantity produced

average cost — total cost divided by the quantity produced

average variable cost — total variable cost divided by the quantity produced

The steps for maximizing profit can be restated in terms of average costs and revenues.

Average revenue (or per-unit revenue) is total revenue divided by the quantity produced.

Average cost (or per-unit cost) is total cost divided by the quantity produced.

Average variable cost (*AVC*) is total variable cost divided by the quantity produced. Average fixed cost (*AFC*) is total fixed cost divided by the quantity produced.

Average cost includes fixed cost, but average variable cost does not, so average cost exceeds average variable cost. Average fixed cost falls as output rises because the higher production spreads the fixed cost over more units of output.

EXAMPLES

If a store sells 1,000 televisions at $300 each, it earns total revenue of $300,000, so its average revenue (revenue per unit sold) equals $300. Whenever a firm charges the same price to all its customers (rather than giving student discounts, for example), its average revenue is simply the price of its good or service.[9] **Table 10.3** shows average cost, average variable cost, and average fixed cost for the data from Table 10.2 with a $10 total fixed cost.

STEP-BY-STEP PROFIT-MAXIMIZATION PROCEDURE USING AVERAGE COST AND REVENUE

This section restates the three-step procedure for choosing short-run output in terms of average revenues and costs.

---

[9]If a seller gives student discounts, its average revenue is less than its official (nondiscounted) price.

STEP 1

Find the level of output at which two statements are true:

1. Marginal revenue equals marginal cost

2. Marginal cost is rising or constant

STEP 2

Calculate average revenue (*AR*) and average variable cost (*AVC*) at the level of output from Step 1.

STEP 3

Decide whether to produce the quantity from Step 1 or shut down.

1. If average revenue falls short of average variable cost at the level of output from Step 1, then shut down the firm. In this case, the firm takes a per-unit loss equal to its average fixed cost.

2. If average revenue equals or exceeds average variable cost, produce the level of output from Step 1. This case leaves two possibilities; in this case:
   a. If average revenue equals or exceeds average cost, then the difference is the firm's per-unit profit.
   b. If average revenue falls short of average cost, then the firm produces at a per-unit loss that equals its average cost minus its average revenue.

Again, to summarize Step 3 mathematically:

1. If $AR < AVC$, then shut down and take a per-unit loss equal to *AFC* (average fixed cost).

2. If $AR \geq AVC$, then produce the quantity from Step 1:
   a. If $AR > AC$, earn a per-unit profit of $AR - AC$.
   b. If $AR < AC$, take a per-unit loss of $AC - AR$.

The following table summarizes the three situations:

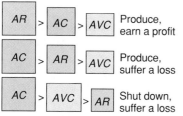

	Situation	Action
(a)	Average revenue > Average cost > Average variable cost	Produce, earn a profit
(b)	Average cost > Average revenue > Average variable cost	Produce, suffer a loss
(c)	Average cost > Average variable cost > Average revenue	Shut down, suffer a loss

MARGINAL COST PULLS ALONG AVERAGE COST

Marginal and average cost are related in a simple way: marginal cost pulls along average cost.

▶ When $MC > AC$, marginal cost pulls the average upward.

▶ When $MC < AC$, marginal cost pulls the average downward.

▶ When $MC = AC$, average cost does not change.

These statements apply both to average cost and average *variable* cost.

AN ANALOGY

A baseball analogy makes this easy to understand. A player's batting average is his *average* hitting record. It shows the fraction of total at-bats in which the player gets a hit. A player with a batting average of .250 gets a hit, on average, one-fourth of the time. A player who gets three hits in four chances on a particular day compiles a marginal hitting record on that day of three out of four, or .750. Since this

FIGURE 10.5

MARGINAL COST PULLS ALONG AVERAGE COST

When *MC* is below *AC*, *AC* falls with an increase in output. When *MC* is above *AC*, *AC* rises with an increase in output.

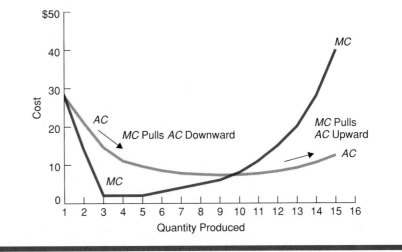

marginal hitting record exceeds the player's average, that average rises. A player who gets only one hit in five chances on a particular day compiles a marginal hitting record of one out of five, or .200; since this marginal hitting record is less than the player's average, that average falls.

EXAMPLE

Figure 10.5 shows that when marginal cost is below average cost (at quantities up to 9 units), average cost falls as output rises. When marginal cost exceeds average cost (at quantities of 10 or more units), average cost rises as output rises. Notice that the marginal cost curve intersects the average cost curve at its lowest point (at the bottom of the *AC* curve).

CAPACITY OUTPUT

The quantity at which average cost reaches its lowest point is called *capacity output.*

capacity output — the level of output that minimizes average cost

> **Capacity output** is the level of output that minimizes average cost.

Capacity output is (loosely) the quantity that a factory was built to produce. A firm can produce more than its capacity output, but doing so raises its average cost. A firm can also produce at less than its capacity, which also raises its average cost because it does not fully utilize its fixed inputs. **Figure 10.6** shows a firm's capacity output.

COSTS IN THE LONG RUN AND THE SHORT RUN

In the long run, all inputs are variable; firms have no fixed inputs, and so there are no fixed costs. Therefore, average cost and average variable cost are the same in the long run. **Figure 10.7** shows three common shapes for long-run average cost and marginal cost curves. Panel a shows a case of constant costs in which all units of output cost the same regardless of how much the firm produces.

FIGURE 10.6

CAPACITY OUTPUT

Capacity output is the quantity that minimizes average cost.

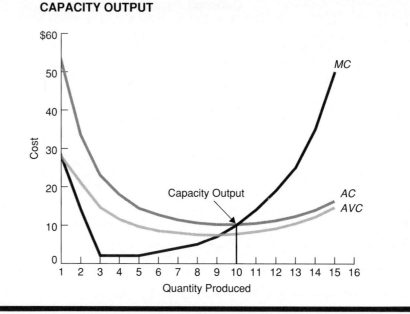

---

constant costs — long-run marginal cost and long-run average cost that do not change with the level of output

A firm has **constant costs** if its long-run marginal cost and average cost are the same and equal for all levels of output.[10]

Panel b shows a case of *increasing costs* at high levels of production: average cost rises as output rises.

increasing costs — long-run marginal cost and long-run average cost that rise with an increase in output

A firm has **increasing costs** if its long-run marginal cost and average cost rise with increases in output.

Average cost rises when marginal cost exceeds average cost. As firms become larger and produce more, they face several challenges:

▶ More complex problems of organizing and coordinating the activities of employees

▶ Increased difficulty in managing internal information flows

▶ Higher costs of monitoring employees to make sure they do their jobs properly

These forces cause marginal cost and average cost to increase along with output.

Panel c shows a U-shaped long-run average cost curve. At high levels of output, the firm has increasing costs (as in Panel b). At low levels of output, the firm has decreasing costs: the average cost of producing the good falls as the firm produces larger quantities.

decreasing costs — long-run marginal cost and long-run average cost that fall with an increase in output

A firm has **decreasing costs** if its long-run marginal cost and average cost fall with increases in output.

---

[10]This is closely related to a concept called *constant returns to scale,* which means that the firm could double its output by doubling all its inputs (or raise output by 20 percent by raising all its inputs by 20 percent). If a firm has constant returns to scale and the prices of its inputs do not depend on how many units of input it buys, then the firm has constant costs.

FIGURE 10.7

THREE COMMON SHAPES FOR LONG-RUN AVERAGE COST CURVES

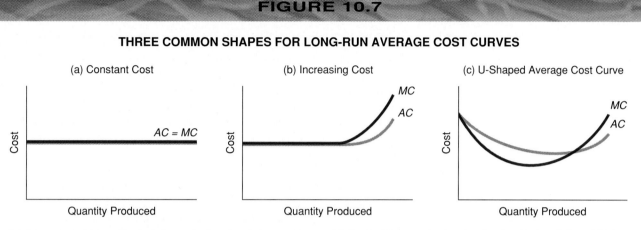

(a) Constant Cost (b) Increasing Cost (c) U-Shaped Average Cost Curve

(a) Average cost is constant, and marginal cost equals average cost. (b) Costs increase for sufficiently high levels of output. (c) Costs decrease for low levels of output and rise at higher levels.

Average cost may decrease as output expands for several reasons:

▶ Some inputs (such as certain machines) have minimum sizes. A firm that produces a small quantity of output does not make full use of these inputs, so its average cost is higher than if it were to produce a larger quantity. If a firm produces a large enough quantity, it may find an economically efficient method of production with a lower average cost.

▶ Employees of larger firms can specialize more in the activities at which they have comparative advantages. (See Chapter 3.) This specialization can reduce average cost.

▶ Higher output can have a smaller average cost for technical reasons. A firm may build a pipe to transport water to a desert. A pipe with a 2-inch radius carries four times as much water as a pipe with a 1-inch radius, but it costs only twice as much to make because the material required to make the pipe rises with the radius of the pipe while its capacity rises with the square of the radius. The larger pipe reduces average cost. Similarly, a large retail store can cost less per

---

IN THE NEWS

Is your company too big?

Even as they argue that size is necessary to compete against global rivals, executives at many big companies are trying to mimic smaller firms. One corporate Goliath after another is trying to act like the Davids of the business world, creating smaller, highly decentralized business units and giving managers greater flexibility and freedom with less staff review.

To accomplish such aims, . . . corporate leaders are hacking away at bureaucracy by axing management layers, pushing down decision making, and shortcutting the approval process.

Costs of production may rise if a firm is either too large or too small.

Source: "Is Your Company Too Big?" *Business Week,* March 27, 1989, p. 84.

square foot to operate than a small retail store. A similar argument also applies to trucks, boxes, and other products.

CONNECTIONS BETWEEN SHORT-RUN AND LONG-RUN COSTS

At any quantity, a firm can produce that output at lower cost (or the same cost) in the long run than in the short run, when its choices are constrained by fixed inputs. For this reason, short-run average cost curves are always above or the same as (but never below) long-run average cost curves.

Figure 10.8 shows a firm's short-run and long-run average cost curves. A firm has many short-run average cost curves, such as $SRAC_1$, $SRAC_2$, and $SRAC_3$, each pertaining to a different quantity of fixed inputs (such as a different factory size). $SRAC_1$ shows a firm's short-run average cost if it has a small quantity of fixed inputs, giving it a capacity of 20,000 units per year. $SRAC_2$ shows the firm's short-run average cost with a slightly larger quantity of fixed inputs that boost capacity to 25,000 units per year. $SRAC_3$ shows the firm's short-run average cost if still more fixed inputs give it a capacity of 50,000 units per year. The long-run average cost curve just touches each of the short-run average cost curves.

EXPLANATION

Recall that short-run costs reflect costs when a firm is constrained (limited) by the quantity of fixed inputs that it chose in the past. Long-run costs reflect costs free from such constraints. The constraints limit the firm's choices and prevent it from changing its fixed inputs to reduce its costs. The firm can only gain, not lose, when the constraint disappears in the long run.

A firm with a small factory has the short-run average cost curve $SRAC_1$ in Figure 10.8. The firm's capacity output is 20,000 units per year, and its average cost of producing that quantity is $10 per unit. In the short run, its average cost

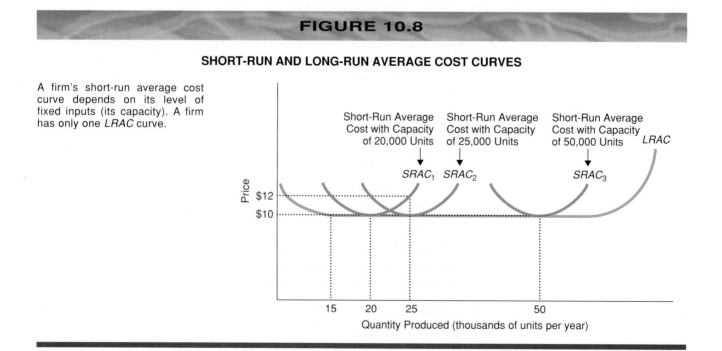

FIGURE 10.8

SHORT-RUN AND LONG-RUN AVERAGE COST CURVES

A firm's short-run average cost curve depends on its level of fixed inputs (its capacity). A firm has only one *LRAC* curve.

Short-Run Average Cost with Capacity of 20,000 Units $SRAC_1$

Short-Run Average Cost with Capacity of 25,000 Units $SRAC_2$

Short-Run Average Cost with Capacity of 50,000 Units $SRAC_3$ LRAC

Price

$12

$10

15   20   25   50

Quantity Produced (thousands of units per year)

rises to $12 if it raises output to 25,000 units per year because the factory was built to handle only 20,000 units per year. In the long run, the firm can replace its factory with a larger one designed to handle the higher output, so in the long run, the firm's average cost of producing 25,000 units per year is only $10 per unit. If the firm were to build a much larger factory with a capacity of 50,000 units per year, its short-run average cost curve would be $SRAC_3$.

Similarly, if a firm with a capacity of 20,000 units per year reduces output to 15,000 units per year, its short-run average cost rises to $12 per unit because the firm's costs include extra capacity (a larger factory than it needs to produce 15,000 units per year). In the long run, the firm could replace its factory with a smaller one designed to produce 15,000 units per year, so in the long run, the firm's average cost of producing 15,000 units per year is $10 per unit.

FOR REVIEW

10.11 What are average revenue, average cost, and average variable cost?

10.12 What is capacity output?

QUESTIONS

10.13 Explain why a firm maximizes its profit (or minimizes its loss) by shutting down if average variable cost exceeds average revenue.

10.14 If marginal cost exceeds average cost, is average cost likely to rise or fall as the firm raises output? Explain why.

10.15 Why is a firm's long-run average cost always less than or equal to its short-run average cost?

DISCOUNTED PRESENT VALUE AND THE VALUE OF A FIRM

value of a firm — the discounted present value of the firm's expected future profits

A firm can raise its current profit by cutting its spending on research and development, but this might reduce its future profits. Obviously, a firm's owners may not want to raise this year's profit by $100 if it would reduce next year's profit by $500. This example illustrates an important point: the owners of a firm do not want to maximize the firm's profit, they want to maximize its value.

> The **value of a firm** is the discounted present value of its expected future profits.

INTEREST RATES

Economists use the interest rate to calculate a discounted present value.

interest rate — the price of a loan, expressed as a percentage of the loaned amount per year

> The **interest rate** is the price of a loan, expressed as a percentage of the loaned amount per year.

EXAMPLES

If you borrow $100 for 1 year at an interest rate of 12 percent per year, you owe $112 at the end of the year. The price of the loan is the extra $12 that you must pay next year when you repay the loan. This is 12 percent of the $100 loan. Similarly, if you borrow $200 for 1 year at an interest rate of 12 percent, you owe $224 at the end of the year. The price of the loan is the $24 you must pay at the end of the year when you repay the loan. Expressed as a percentage, this $24 price is 12 percent of the $200 loan.

If you borrow \$100 from a bank for 2 years at an interest rate of 10 percent per year, you owe the bank \$121 at the end of two years. The bank charges you 10 percent per year *each* year. After one year, your debt to the bank is \$110. This increases another 10 percent (\$11) to \$121 at the end of the second year. The price of the loan is \$21 paid two years from now, when you repay the money you borrowed. This \$21 is 10 percent of your loan per year.

More generally, if you borrow X dollars for 1 year, you must pay back $X(1 + i)$ dollars the next year, where the number i is the interest rate on the loan, stated as a decimal so that a 5 percent interest rate means that i equals 0.05, a 10 percent interest rate means that i equals 0.10, and so on.

DISCOUNTED PRESENT VALUE

One of the most useful formulas you will learn in economics is the formula to calculate a *discounted present value* of some future amount of money. Interest rates and discounted-present-value formulas are important for understanding any economic decisions that involve time.

discounted present value (of a future amount of money) — the money you would need to save and invest now to end up with that specific amount of money in the future

> The **discounted present value** of a future amount of money is the money you would need to save and invest now to end up with that specific amount of money in the future. It is the value today (at the present time) of receiving that money in the future.

Present value is based on a simple main idea: it is better to receive money today than in the future because you can save money that you have today and earn interest. You might put it in a bank or some other investment. If you have \$100 today and the interest rate is 5 percent per year, you can turn your money into \$105 next year. This makes a dollar today more valuable than a dollar in the future.

EXAMPLES

Suppose that you have \$100 now and the interest rate is 6 percent per year. If you invest your money for 1 year, you will have \$106 next year, so the discounted present value of \$106 next year is \$100 now. This means that \$106 next year has the same value as \$100 today when the interest rate is 6 percent per year. Since they have the same value, you can trade one amount for the other. If you have \$100 now, you can trade it for \$106 next year by lending your money or putting it in a bank account. If someone is going to pay you \$106 next year, you can trade that money for \$100 now by borrowing \$100 and using the \$106 you receive next year to repay the loan with interest.

If the interest rate is 10 percent per year, the discounted present value of \$121 paid 2 years from now is \$100. Again, \$121 two years from now and \$100 now have the same value when the interest rate is 10 percent per year. People can trade one for the other by borrowing or lending \$100 for 2 years.

GENERAL FORMULA

The general formula for discounted present value is:

The discounted present value of X dollars payable

$$\text{1 year from now} = \frac{X}{1 + i} \text{ dollars now}$$

where i is the interest rate stated as a decimal, so a 12 percent interest rate is the number 0.12. You are likely to use this formula many times in your future personal and business decisions. You should remember both the formula and the main idea: a dollar today is worth more than a dollar in the future because you can save the dollar today and earn interest.

Explanation   This formula is not hard to understand. If you had $X/(1 + i)$ dollars now, you could save it (put it in the bank or make another investment) and earn interest. Next year you would have

$$\frac{X}{1 + i} \, (1 + i) = X \text{ dollars}$$

The value *now,* the *present value,* of the X dollars next year is $X/(1 + i)$ dollars. You can turn $X/(1 + i)$ dollars now into X dollars next year, and you can turn X dollars next year into $X/(1 + i)$ dollars now.[11] This means that X dollars next year and $X/(1 + i)$ dollars now have the same value.[12]

Using the Formula

Examples   Suppose that you want to find the discounted present value of $20,000.00 to be received next year. Replace X in the formula with $20,000.00. If the interest rate is 8 percent, then 1 plus i is 1.08. Divide $20,000.00 by 1.08 and get $18,518.52. This is the discounted present value of $20,000.00 next year when the interest rate is 8 percent. If you had $18,518.52 this year, and you put it in a bank and earned 8 percent interest, you would have $20,000.00 next year.

Suppose that you will receive $100.00 one year from now. If the interest rate is 10 percent per year, the discounted present value of the $100.00 next year is $100.00/(1.10), or about $91.91. If you had $91.91 now, and you could save it and earn a 10 percent interest rate for a year, you could have $100.00 next year.

To find the discounted present value of $1,000 two years from now, apply the general formula twice. Suppose that in 1996 the interest rate is 10 percent per year. Someone has promised to pay you $1,000.00 in 1998. You can find the discounted present value, in 1996, of that money in two steps. First, apply the formula to find out how much $1,000.00 payable in 1998 is worth in 1997. The formula gives a 1997 value of $1,000/(1.10), or $909.09. You then apply the formula again to find the 1996 value of $909.09 in 1997. (This time, substitute $909.09 for X in the formula.) The formula shows that it is worth $909.09/(1.10), or $826.45. The discounted present value of $1,000.00 paid 2 years from now is $826.45 if the interest rate is 10 percent per year.

To find the discounted present value of $1,000.00 N years from now, apply the general formula N times. The formula for the discounted present value of X dollars paid N years from now is:

$$X \text{ dollars payable after } N \text{ years} = \frac{X}{(1 + i)^N} \text{ dollars now}$$

where i is the interest rate per year. That is, the discounted present value of X dollars paid N years from now is $X/(1 + i)^N$. For example, if the interest rate is 10

---

[11]You can do this by borrowing X dollars now and repaying $X/(1 + i)$ dollars next year.

[12]Notice that the term *discounted present value* refers to the fact that X dollars in the future have the same economic value as $X/(1 + i)$ dollars at the present time.

percent per year, the discounted present value of $2,000.00 paid 2 years from now is $2,000.00/(1.10)^2$, or $2,000.00/1.21, which is $1,652.89.

USING THE FORMULA FOR REPEATED PAYMENTS

To calculate the value of a firm, we take the discounted present value of all its future profits, including its profits next year, the year after, the year after that, and so on. Repeated application of the general present–value formula implies the following results:

> The discounted present value of X_1 dollars paid 1 year from now and X_2 dollars paid 2 years from now and X_3 dollars paid 3 years from now, and so on, is:

$$\frac{X_1}{(1 + i)} + \frac{X_2}{(1 + i)^2} + \frac{X_3}{(1 + i)^3} + \ldots$$

The sum goes on until some ending date, or it may go on forever.

> The discounted present value of X dollars paid every year forever is:

$$\frac{\$X}{i}$$

EXAMPLE   Suppose that the interest rate is 10 percent per year and a firm earns $2,000 per year, every year, for 4 years. The discounted present value of these profits is:

$$\frac{\$2,000}{(1.10)} + \frac{\$2,000}{(1.10)^2} + \frac{\$2,000}{(1.10)^3} + \frac{\$2,000}{(1.10)^4} = \$6,340$$

If the firm earns $2,000 in profits every year forever, then the discounted present value of its profits is $2,000/0.10, or $20,000.

COMMENTS

1. The future is uncertain; the value of a firm is the discounted present value of its *expected* future profits.[13]

2. The formula for the discounted present value of X dollars paid every year forever, X/i, is a rough approximation to the discounted present value of X dollars paid every year for N years if N is 30 years or more. You can verify this by using a calculator or computer to solve for these discounted present values.

3. A firm's owners generally want to maximize its value, so they are willing to sacrifice $100 in profits this year to gain future profits with a discounted present value of more than $100. They are willing to sacrifice future profits for current profits if the discounted present value of the lost future profits is smaller than the value of the profits they could gain today.

> A firm's owners usually seek to maximize the value of the firm.

4. It is common to use the phrase *maximizing profit* in place of the more precise phrase *maximizing value.* Often they imply the same result, and this imprecise terminology does little harm. This book will adopt the usual term *profit maximization,* except when the distinction is important for some issue.

---

[13]See Chapter 19.

Do Firms Make Rational Decisions?

Do business firms make rational decisions? More precisely, do the people associated with firms make rational decisions and have they organized their firms and chosen the terms of the contracts that define their organizations rationally? Everyone associated with a firm—the owners, workers, managers, creditors—have personal interests. The personal interests of different parties often conflict with each other.

The firm's owners usually want to maximize the value of the firm, while the managers and workers often prefer to sacrifice some profits and firm value for better working conditions for themselves, better relations with co-workers, and so on. The personal interests of creditors such as bondholders (investors who have loaned money to the firm) also differ from the interests of the owners.

The owner of a small firm may make all its decisions. Owners of larger firms hire managers to make most decisions. Owners try to design managers' contracts to give them incentives to act *in the owner's interests.* Many details of the structures and organizations of business firms were designed by owners to provide the incentives for other people in the firm to act in the owners' interests (to make their goals correspond to the owners' goals). It is not easy to make these goals coincide, however, so owners design firms' structures and their contracts with others to make those goals coincide partly but not completely. There is a separation of ownership and control: owners do not completely control the firm. As a result, a firm may not maximize its value even though its owners want to do so and even if every person associated with the firm makes rational decisions.

Nevertheless, most decisions of most firms are well-approximated by an economic model that assumes firms maximize their values. If the people in a firm make irrational choices repeatedly, competitors are likely to drive the firm out of business. Irrational firms tend not to survive competition. If a firm's owners fail to create incentives that lead the firm approximately to maximize its value, another person may buy the firm when its value is low and change the way the firm is run (replace the management, alter incentives for managers and workers, and so on) so that the firm maximizes its value. The new owner then profits from the increase in the value of the firm.

--------------------------- **For Review** ---------------------------

10.16 What is the value of a firm?

10.17 What is a discounted present value?

--------------------------- **Questions** ---------------------------

10.18 Explain in words why $100 today is worth more than $100 in the future, even if prices are the same in the future.

10.19 Complete the following discounted-present-value calculations.
  a. If the interest rate is 10 percent per year, what is the discounted present value of $200 to be paid 1 year from now? What if the interest is 5 percent?
  b. Suppose that the interest rate is 10 percent per year. Find the discounted present value of $20,000 to be paid 2 years from now.

c. Suppose that the interest rate is 10 percent per year. What is the discounted present value of $10,000 to be paid 1 year from now along with $10,000 two years from now?

10.20 What is the general formula for the discounted present value of X_1 dollars to be paid 1 year from now, *and* X_2 dollars to be paid 2 years from now, X_3 dollars to be paid 3 years from now, and so on?

10.21 What is the general formula for the discounted present value of X dollars paid every year forever?

10.22 If people expect a firm to earn profits of $100,000 per year, every year, forever, and the interest rate is 5 percent per year, what is the value of the firm?

SUPPLY CURVES

price taker — a firm that faces a perfectly elastic demand for its product

A firm's supply decisions are related to its costs and revenues. This section considers the important case of firms that cannot significantly affect the prices that their customers are willing to pay.

A firm is a **price taker** if it faces a perfectly elastic demand for its product.

A price taker that tried to raise its price would lose all its customers, so it takes the price as given (as something that it cannot affect). Many firms are approximately price takers, and economic models of price takers provide good approximations to their behavior. The supply decisions of these firms are related to their costs in a simple way:

> The supply curve of a price-taking firm is the portion of its marginal cost curve that lies above its average variable cost curve.

EXAMPLES OF PRICE TAKERS

The elasticity of the market demand for wheat is about $-\frac{1}{2}$, but the demand for the wheat that Willard grows on his farm is perfectly elastic. Willard's farm is a price taker. When the market price of wheat is $4.50 per bushel, Willard cannot sell any wheat for a higher price than that. If he tries to charge more, his customers will buy from other farmers instead. Willard can sell as much wheat for $4.50 per bushel as he can grow; he does not need to reduce his price to attract more customers. **Figure 10.9** shows the perfectly elastic demand for the wheat Willard grows on his farm. Notice that Willard's average revenue is simply the price per bushel, $4.50, which is also his marginal revenue.

Peerless Pete's Pizza, a carry-out pizza store, also approximates a price taker. If it raised its price many of its customers would switch to other, nearby pizza stores. Peerless Pete's gets as many customers as it can handle on most days, so it has little incentive to reduce its price. **Figure 10.10** shows the demand for pizza at Peerless Pete's. With an elasticity of -10, this demand is not perfectly elastic, but it is close enough for most purposes of economic analysis. Peerless Pete's is not exactly a price taker, but a model that assumes that it is a price taker is good enough for most purposes.

MARGINAL COST AND SUPPLY CURVES

If a firm is a price taker, its average revenue equals its price. For example, if Willard sells each bushel of wheat for $4.50, his average revenue is $4.50 per

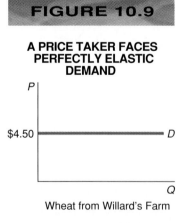

FIGURE 10.9

A PRICE TAKER FACES PERFECTLY ELASTIC DEMAND

The demand for wheat from Willard's farm is perfectly elastic, so the farm is a price taker.

FIGURE 10.10

ALMOST PERFECTLY ELASTIC DEMAND

Pizzas from Peerless Pete's

The demand for pizzas from Peerless Pete's Pizza is almost perfectly elastic, so it approximates a price taker.

bushel. Because a firm shuts down in the short run if average revenue falls short of average variable cost, a price-taking firm shuts down if the price is less than its average variable cost. If, on the other hand, the price equals or exceeds the firm's average variable cost, it produces the quantity from Step 1, discussed earlier.

If a firm is a price taker, its marginal revenue equals its price. For example, if Willard sells one additional bushel of wheat for $4.50, his total revenue rises by $4.50; this means that his marginal revenue is also $4.50. The marginal revenue curve of a price taker is a horizontal line at the price of its product, as in **Figure 10.11,** which shows price, marginal revenue, and marginal cost for a price taker. If the price exceeds a firm's average variable cost, then it maximizes its profit (and its value) by producing a quantity at which marginal cost equals marginal revenue. Because marginal revenue equals price:

> A price taker maximizes its profit (and firm value) by producing a quantity at which price equals marginal cost, or by shutting down if the price is less than average variable cost.

The firm maximizes profit (and firm value) by producing the quantity Q_1 in Figure 10.11.

All of this yields an important result:

> The part of a price-taking firm's marginal cost curve that lies above its *AVC* curve is its supply curve.

The supply curve of a price taker is the portion of its marginal cost curve that lies above its average variable cost curve. If the price is below the firm's average variable cost, the firm shuts down. For any price above its average variable cost, the

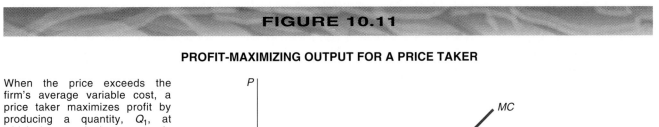

FIGURE 10.11

PROFIT-MAXIMIZING OUTPUT FOR A PRICE TAKER

When the price exceeds the firm's average variable cost, a price taker maximizes profit by producing a quantity, Q_1, at which its marginal cost equals the price.

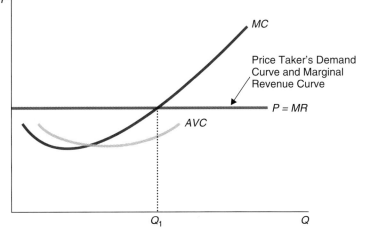

FIGURE 10.12

MARGINAL COST AND SUPPLY CURVE OF A PRICE TAKER

The supply curve of a price-taking firm is the portion of its marginal cost *(MC)* curve that lies above its average variable cost curve. At lower prices, the firm shuts down.

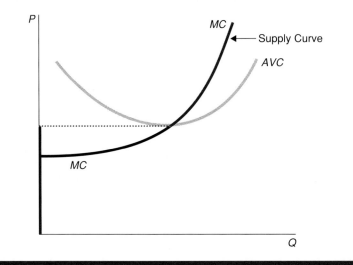

marginal cost curve and supply curve of a price-taking firm are identical, as in **Figure 10.12.**[14]

PRODUCER SURPLUS

producer surplus — the benefit to a producer from being able to sell goods at the equilibrium price, rather than being unable to sell them at all

Economists measure a seller's gain from trade by evaluating producer surplus.

> **Producer surplus** is the benefit to a producer of being able to sell goods at the equilibrium price, rather than being unable to sell them at all.

Producer surplus resembles consumer surplus, but it applies to sellers rather than buyers. **Figure 10.13** shows the producer surplus of a price-taking firm as *the area above the supply curve and below the price,* between the quantity zero and the quantity that the firm produces. Producer surplus is the darkly shaded area in the figure.

The lightly shaded area under the marginal cost curve shows the firm's total variable cost of producing Q_1 goods.

> The area under the marginal cost curve, between zero and any quantity, represents the total variable cost of producing that quantity.

The area of the rectangle made by both shaded areas together represents the firm's total revenue:

> A firm's total revenue appears as the area of the rectangle with its height equal to the price and its base equal to the quantity sold.

---

[14]Chapters 13 through 15 discuss production decisions by firms other than price takers.

FIGURE 10.13

PRODUCER SURPLUS

Producer surplus equals profit plus fixed (unavoidable) costs, represented by the darkly shaded area in the graph. The lightly shaded area shows total variable cost, and both areas together show total revenue.

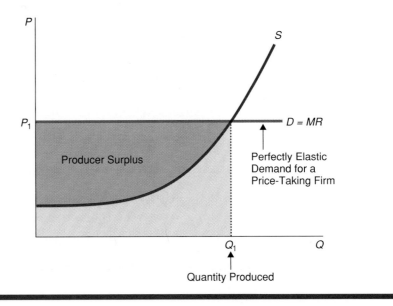

Because the shaded areas together show total revenue, and the lightly shaded area shows total variable cost, the darkly shaded area, producer surplus, shows total revenue minus total variable cost.[15] Producer surplus, then, equals the firm's profit plus its fixed cost. Since the firm cannot avoid the fixed cost (it is an unavoidable sunk cost), the firm maximizes profit if its maximizes producer surplus. Since the firm has no fixed cost in the long run, long-run producer surplus is the firm's profit and are identical in the long run.

Producer surplus is profit plus fixed (unavoidable) costs.

Producer surplus is total revenue minus total variable costs, the only costs that are not already sunk.

EXPLANATION

The height of the supply curve shows the lowest price at which a firm is willing to sell another unit of the good, that is, the lowest price that the firm would accept for each unit of the good. The difference between the price that the firm actually receives and the lowest price that it would accept is its producer surplus on each unit of the good. Therefore, the price minus the height of the supply curve shows the producer surplus on that unit. Summing the producer surplus on each unit gives the firm's total producer surplus, the darkly shaded area in Figure 10.13.

---

[15]This is exactly accurate for a firm whose marginal cost curve does not slope downward for small quantities; otherwise, this statement requires a minor correction that does not affect the main points of the discussion.

EXAMPLE

Figure 10.14 shows the marginal cost curve of a price-taking firm with a $10 fixed cost. The price is $5, and the firm maximizes its profit by producing 7 units of its good. The firm earns a profit of $5. Its producer surplus is $15.

The firm obtains $3 producer surplus on the first unit it sells because the marginal cost of producing that unit (the lowest price that the firm is willing to accept for it) is only $2, while it gets a price of $5. The firm gets another $3 producer surplus on each of the second, third, and fourth units. It gets $2 producer surplus on the fifth unit, $5 minus the $3 marginal cost of producing that unit (which is the lowest price it would accept to produce that unit). It gets $1 producer surplus on the sixth unit and no producer surplus on the seventh, so its total producer surplus is $15, which equals its profit, $5, plus its fixed cost, $10.

--------- FOR REVIEW ---------

10.23 What is a price taker?

10.24 What is the connection between a price-taking firm's marginal cost curve and its supply curve?

10.25 Define *producer surplus* and show it on a graph.

10.26 What is the connection between producer surplus and profit?

FIGURE 10.14

PRODUCER SURPLUS AND PROFIT

The firm earns a $15 producer surplus. It has a $5 profit and a $10 fixed cost.

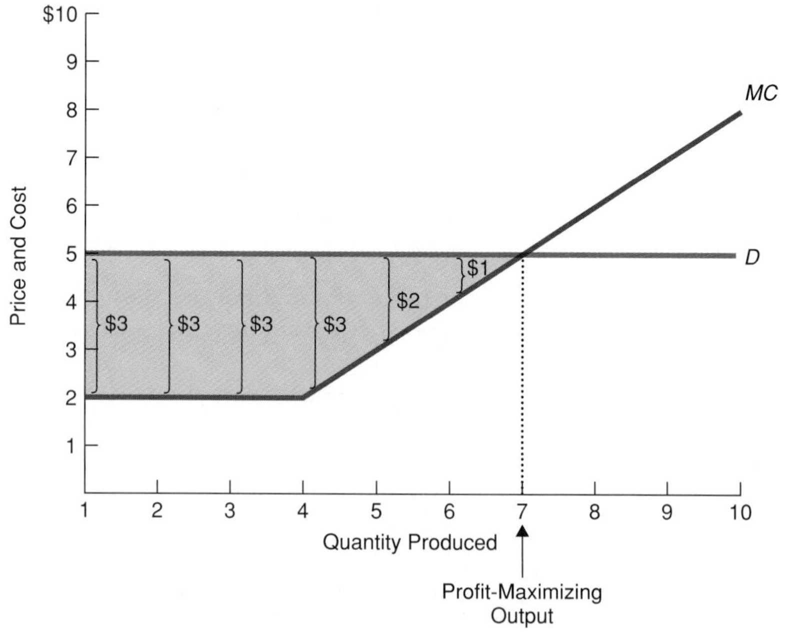

10.27 On Figure 10.14, suppose that the price were $6 per unit instead of $5. How much would the firm produce? How large would its producer surplus be?

10.28 What does the area under a firm's marginal cost curve represent? Explain why.

CONCLUSIONS

BUSINESS FIRMS

A firm is an organization that coordinates the activities of workers, managers, owners, lenders, and other participants to produce and sell a good or service. Most firms in the United States are sole proprietorships, which tend to be small, and some others are partnerships, which tend to be larger. About one-fifth of U.S. firms are corporations, which tend to be even larger.

DECIDING HOW TO PRODUCE

A business firm's decision of how to produce its good or service follows three logical steps. First, choose a hypothetical quantity to produce and list all the technically efficient methods to produce that quantity. From that list, choose the economically efficient (lowest-cost) method of production. The economically efficient method is the technically efficient method with the lowest cost for producing that quantity. Finally, repeat this procedure for all other possible quantities.

DECIDING HOW MUCH TO PRODUCE

The *long run* refers to a period of time over which people fully adjust their behavior to a change in conditions. For a firm, the long run is the time when it can change the quantities of all its inputs. A firm maximizes long-run profit by choosing its level of production in three steps. First, it finds the level of output for which marginal revenue equals marginal cost, while marginal cost is rising or constant. The firm produces this quantity if it does not shut down. Second, the firm calculates total revenue and total cost at this level of output. Third, the firm shuts down if total cost exceeds total revenue.

The *short run* refers to a period of time over which people can make only incomplete adjustments. A firm cannot change the quantities of its fixed inputs in the short run, though it can change the quantities of its variable inputs. In the short run, a firm has fixed costs, unavoidable (sunk) costs of its fixed inputs. The firm can avoid its variable costs (the costs of its variable inputs) by reducing the quantity that it produces and use of variable inputs. In the long run, all fixed costs become variable costs because a firm can vary the quantities of all its inputs. In the short run, the firm first finds the level of output for which marginal revenue equals marginal cost, while marginal cost is rising or constant. It produces this quantity if it does not shut down. The firm decides whether to shut down or produce by calculating its total revenue and total variable cost at this level of output. If total variable cost exceeds total revenue, the firm shuts down.

AVERAGE COST AND AVERAGE REVENUE

A firm's decision of whether to produce or shut down can be restated in terms of average costs and revenues. In the long run, a firm shuts down if its average cost exceeds its average revenue. In the short run, a firm shuts down if its average *variable* cost exceeds its average revenue.

Marginal cost and average cost are related. When marginal cost exceeds average cost, average cost rises as output increases. When marginal cost is less than average cost, average cost falls as output increases. When marginal cost equals average cost, average cost does not change as output increases.

COSTS IN THE LONG RUN AND SHORT RUN

Firms have no fixed costs in the long run because all inputs are variable in the long run. Therefore, average cost and average variable cost are the same in the long run. A firm has constant costs if its long-run marginal cost and long-run average cost are the same and equal for all levels of output; it has increasing costs if its long-run marginal cost and average cost rise with increases in output, and decreasing costs if its long-run marginal cost and average cost fall with increases in output.

A firm can always produce at the same or a lower cost in the long run than in the short run, so short-run average cost curves always lie *above or at the levels of* (but never below) long-run average cost curves. The long-run average cost curve just touches each of the short-run average cost curves.

VALUE OF A FIRM

A firm's owners usually want to maximize its value. The value of a firm is the discounted present value of its expected future profits. The discounted present value of a future amount of money is the money that you would need to save and invest now to end up with that specific amount of money in the future. The discounted present value of X dollars to be paid 1 year from now is $X/(1+i)$ where i is the interest rate. The profit-maximization rules in this chapter also apply to value maximization.

SUPPLY CURVES

A firm is a price taker if it faces a perfectly elastic demand for its product. If a firm is a price taker, its marginal revenue equals its price. In that case, it maximizes profit (and firm value) by producing a quantity at which the price equals its marginal cost (or by shutting down if the price is less than its average variable cost). As a result, the supply curve of a price-taking firm is the portion of its marginal cost curve that lies above its average variable cost curve.

PRODUCER SURPLUS

Producer surplus is the benefit to producers from selling goods at the equilibrium price (rather than being unable to sell them at all). It resembles consumer surplus, but applies to sellers rather than buyers. On a graph, producer surplus is the area above the supply curve and below the price, between the quantity zero and the quantity that the firm produces. Because the area under the marginal cost curve, between zero and any quantity, is the total variable cost of producing that quantity, producer surplus equals profit plus fixed (unavoidable) costs.

LOOKING AHEAD

Chapter 11 shows how economists use producer and consumer surplus to measure the gains from trades and the effects on economic efficiency of taxes, restrictions on international trade, and various changes in economic conditions. Chapter 12 then discusses competition among price-taking firms. Chapters 13 through 15 discuss competition among firms other than price takers and how costs, demand, and other factors affect the decisions of those firms. Chapter 16 examines in greater detail firms' decisions about methods of production and which inputs to use. It also discusses why some firms are large and others are small, and why some production activities occur entirely within a single firm and others occur through the actions of many different firms. These discussions will lead to more advanced topics of microeconomics.

KEY TERMS

firm

technically efficient method of
   production

economically efficient method of
   production

total revenue

profit

marginal revenue

long run

short run

fixed input

variable input

fixed cost

variable cost

average revenue

average cost

average variable cost

capacity output

constant costs

increasing costs

decreasing cost

value of a firm

interest rate

discounted present value

price taker

producer surplus

QUESTIONS AND PROBLEMS

10.29 Can a technically inefficient method of production be economically efficient? Can an economically inefficient method of production be technically efficient?

10.30 Explain why a firm can raise its profits by producing less if marginal cost exceeds marginal revenue.

10.31 Explain this statement: "Fixed costs are unavoidable in the short run."

10.32 Discuss this statement: "A rational firm might decide to produce in the short run, but shut down in the long run, even if the demand for its product and its costs do not change."

10.33 Comment on this statement: "A good businessperson never sells a product for less than the cost of producing it."

10.34 Table 10.1 applies to a firm with no fixed cost.
   a. Suppose, instead, that the firm in Table 10.1 has a fixed cost of $10. How does this change the marginal cost and profit numbers in the table? What quantity maximizes the firm's profit in this case? How much profit does the firm make when it maximizes profit?
   b. Repeat Question 10.34a for a fixed cost of $20 instead of $10.

10.35 Change the numbers in Table 10.1 so that marginal cost is 4 for every quantity (every number in the *MC* column is 4) and total cost is 4 times the quantity.
   a. What is the profit-maximizing quantity of output? How large is the firm's profit in this case?
   b. Repeat Question 10.35a assuming a marginal cost of 6 for every quantity.

10.36 Change the numbers in Table 10.1 to make the firm a price taker by assuming that the price is 8 for every quantity (every number in the Price column is 8). Notice that marginal revenue also becomes 8 for every quantity. What is the profit-maximizing quantity of output? How large is the firm's profit in this case?

10.37 How does an increase in a firm's fixed cost affect:
   a. Its profit-maximizing short–run level of output?
   b. Its short–run profit?
   c. Its decision to stay in business or shut down in the short run?

10.38 Your history professor gives five quizzes this term, each worth 10 points. You get 6 points on the first quiz, 7 on the second, 3 on the third, 5 on the fourth, and 8 on the fifth. Calculate your marginal and average scores. Explain why your marginal score pulls along your average score.

10.39 How is the supply curve of a price-taking firm related to its costs of production? Explain the connection in as much detail as you can.

INQUIRIES FOR FURTHER THOUGHT

10.40 Why might the price of a share of stock be related to the discounted present value of the dividends that it will pay in the future?

10.41 You own a fast-food restaurant where you can package your food and drinks in biodegradable containers or in cheaper, nonbiodegradable containers. Your business could sacrifice profit to spend more for biodegradable containers that would be better for the environment. You want to make a profit for yourself and you also want to help the environment. How would you decide between:

▶ Earning lower profits using biodegradable containers
▶ Earning higher profits using nonbiodegradable containers, and donating part of your profit to help a worthy cause

Under what conditions would you want your firm to maximize profit?

10.42 Do firms have a social responsibility to sacrifice profit to help the poor, improve the environment, and help other worthy causes, or should they maximize profit and leave these other goals to individual people (including the firms' owners, private charities, and the government)? Who pays for a social program that a firm promotes at the expense of profit?

10.43 Do nonprofit firms (such as most colleges, hospitals, and charitable organizations) earn profits or losses? What do you think these firms maximize?

TAG SOFTWARE APPLICATIONS

TUTORIAL EXERCISES
▶ The module contains a review of the key terms from Chapter 10.

ANALYTICAL EXERCISES
▶ The analytical section looks at how to calculate total costs, average costs, marginal costs, and marginal revenues.

GRAPHING EXERCISES

▶ The graphing section covers cost and revenue curves, the identification of profit maximization for a price taker, and producer surplus.

CHAPTER 10 APPENDIX — MATHEMATICS OF CHOOSING HOW MUCH TO PRODUCE*

A firm wants to maximize its profit from selling swimming pools. First, summarize the demand for pools with a function $d(Q)$. To sell quantity Q, the highest price the firm can charge is P. This price is a function of the quantity that the firm sells, Q, so:

$$P = d(Q)$$

The demand curve slopes downward, so the derivative of d with respect to Q is negative: $d'(Q) < 0$. This means that the firm must reduce its price to sell more pools.

The firm's total revenue, TR, is the quantity that it sells multiplied by the price:

$$TR = QP$$

Rewrite this as:

$$TR = Qd(Q)$$
$$= f(Q)$$

This defines the function $f(Q)$ and shows that the firm's total revenue is a function of the quantity that it sells.

Marginal revenue is the derivative of total revenue with respect to Q:

$$MR = f'(Q)$$

The firm's total cost of producing pools, TC, is also a function of the quantity:

$$TC = g(Q)$$

Marginal cost is the derivative of total cost with respect to quantity, so:

$$MC = g'(Q)$$

The firm's profit equals total revenue minus total cost:

$$\text{Profit} = TR - TC$$
$$= f(Q) - g(Q)$$

To maximize profit, set its derivative (with respect to Q) equal to zero. This gives:

$$f'(Q) - g'(Q) = 0$$
$$f'(Q) = g'(Q)$$

Note: This appendix requires knowledge of calculus.

which says that marginal revenue equals marginal cost. The firm maximizes its profit by choosing to produce a quantity at which marginal revenue equals marginal cost.

PRICE TAKERS

A special case occurs when firms are price takers. A price taker faces perfectly elastic demand. (A price-taking firm cannot raise its price without losing all its customers.) This means that the function $d(Q)$ is a constant; it does not depend on Q. Therefore, $P = d$, where d is some number. (Price does not depend on Q.) Total revenue becomes:

$$f(Q) = Qd$$

so marginal revenue is:

$$f'(Q) = d$$
$$= P$$

This says that marginal revenue equals price for a price-taking firm. The firm maximizes profit by choosing a quantity so that:

$$P = g'(Q)$$

which says that marginal cost equals price.

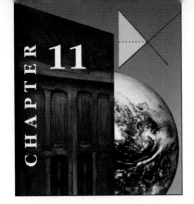

CHAPTER 11

ECONOMIC EFFICIENCY AND THE GAINS FROM TRADE

WHAT THIS CHAPTER IS ABOUT

▶ Economic efficiency: What it is and how it affects people

▶ Who gains and who loses—and how much—from international trade

▶ Who gains and who loses—and how much—from taxes, government subsidies, and price controls

What *should* an economy do? How many houses, video recorders, taxi rides, and french fries should it produce? How many people should be doctors, lawyers, plumbers, scientists, and accountants? What economic policies should the government adopt? Economics does not answer questions about what should be, but it can help people make informed and intelligent judgements about these issues. It cannot answer questions such as "Should we permit people to import foreign cars?" It can, however, help provide answers about who would gain and who would lose from economic changes or from changes in government policies.

When Supreme Court Justice Anthony Kennedy faced senators' questions during his confirmation hearings, one senator urged him "not simply to weigh economic efficiency" but also to consider how his decisions would affect consumers. What is economic efficiency? Why does anyone care about it? How does it affect consumers? How might it help to answer questions about which economic policies the government should follow? This chapter addresses these issues.

GAINS FROM TRADE

Consumer surplus is the benefit that people get from buying goods at equilibrium prices (see Chapter 9). Producer surplus is the benefit that producers get from selling goods at equilibrium prices—their profit plus fixed costs (see Chapter 10). **Figure 11.1** shows:

1. Consumer surplus—area *CS* under the demand curve above the equilibrium price, between the quantity zero and the equilibrium quantity

FIGURE 11.1

GAINS FROM TRADE

Buyers and sellers share the gains from trade; buyers get the consumer surplus and sellers get the producer surplus.

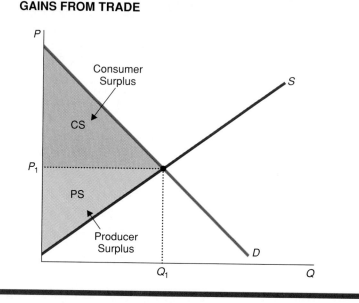

2. Producer surplus—area *PS* above the supply curve and below the equilibrium price, between the quantity zero and the equilibrium quantity

total gain from trade — the sum of consumer and producer surplus

The **total gain from trade** in some good equals the consumer and producer surplus that buyers and sellers receive from that good.

The total gain from trade is the sum of areas *CS* and *PS* in Figure 11.1. It equals the good's total benefit to buyers from the good minus the total variable cost of producing the good.

EXPLANATION

The shaded area under the demand curve in **Figure 11.2a** shows the benefit to consumers from drinking 3 million quarts of root beer each month; the shaded area under the supply curve in Figure 11.2b shows the total cost of producing that root beer (minus the fixed cost). The difference—the shaded area in Figure 11.2c—shows the gain to consumers from 3 million quarts of root beer per month minus the variable cost of producing the root beer.

SHARING THE GAINS FROM TRADE

Buyers and sellers share the gains from trade. Buyers get consumer surplus and sellers get producer surplus. **Figure 11.3** shows that the shapes and positions of demand and supply curves determine whether buyers or sellers get most of the gains. Panel a shows two demand curves, with D_2 more elastic than D_1. With the demand curve D_1, consumer surplus is the sum of Areas A and B. With the demand curve D_2, consumer surplus is only Area A. Consumer surplus is larger when demand is less elastic. (Area *PS* is producer surplus.)

Panel b shows two supply curves, with S_2 more elastic than S_1. With the supply curve S_1, producer surplus is the sum of Areas A and B. With the more elastic

FIGURE 11.2

TOTAL GAIN FROM TRADE: ANOTHER VIEW

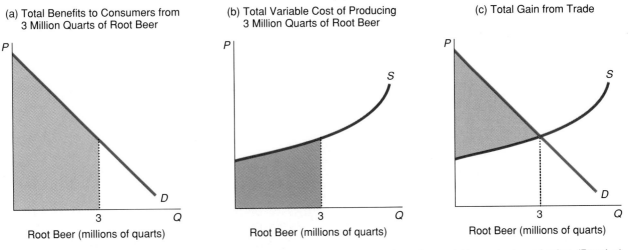

(a) Total Benefits to Consumers from 3 Million Quarts of Root Beer

(b) Total Variable Cost of Producing 3 Million Quarts of Root Beer

(c) Total Gain from Trade

Root Beer (millions of quarts)

Root Beer (millions of quarts)

Root Beer (millions of quarts)

The total gain from trade equals the total benefit to consumers from producing a good (Panel a) minus the total variable cost of producing the good (Panel b). All together the benefit to consumers minus the variable cost of production (Panel c) equals the gain from trade.

supply curve S_2, producer surplus is only Area A. Producer surplus is larger when supply is less elastic. (Area CS is consumer surplus.)

PARETO IMPROVEMENTS AND ECONOMIC EFFICIENCY

Pareto improvement — a change that helps at least one person without hurting anyone

A change in the economy is a **Pareto improvement** if at least one person gains and no one loses.

(*Pareto* is pronounced "par ā′ tō.")

EXAMPLE

Suppose that Jeremy eats a piece of pie that Amy was going to throw away. Eating the pie is Pareto improving because Jeremy gains and Amy does not lose.

potential Pareto improvement — a change that could allow the winners to compensate the losers to make the change a Pareto improvement

A change in the economy is a **potential Pareto improvement** if it could allow the winners to compensate (pay) the losers to make the change a Pareto improvement.

EXAMPLE

Suppose that Jeremy eats a piece of pie that Amy was going to eat, but that Jeremy could bake cookies for Amy, which she would like just as well or better than the pie. It is potentially Pareto improving for Jeremy to eat the pie if he could compensate Amy by baking cookies that Amy would like just as well or better. Jeremy would gain because he prefers the pie and Amy would not lose. It is a *potential* Pareto improvement for Jeremy to eat the cookie, even if he does not compensate Amy. (It actually becomes a Pareto improvement if and when he bakes the cookies for her.)

FIGURE 11.3

CONSUMER SURPLUS IS LARGER WHEN DEMAND IS LESS ELASTIC

(a) The size of consumer surplus depends on the elasticity of demand. If demand is D_1, consumer surplus is the sum of Areas A and B. If demand is D_2, consumer surplus is only Area A. (b) The size of producer surplus depends on the elasticity of supply. If supply is S_1, producer surplus is the sum of Areas A and B. If supply is S_2, producer surplus is only Area A.

(a) Consumer Surplus and Elasticity of Demand

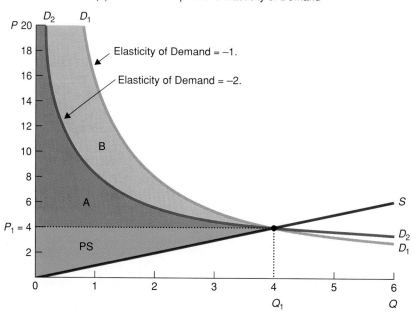

(b) Producer Surplus and Elasticity of Supply

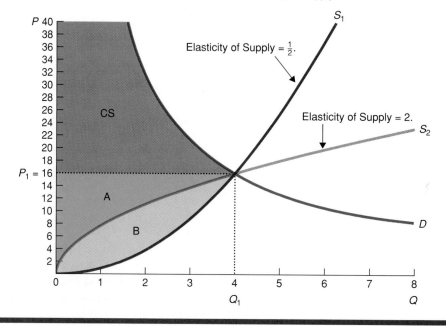

A change in the economy is potentially Pareto improving if the winners gain more than the losers lose. The winners could then compensate the losers (pay them enough to keep them from losing). The winners might not actually compensate the losers, but the winners gain enough that they could.

increase in economic efficiency — a change that is a potential Pareto improvement

A change causes an **increase in economic efficiency** if it is a potential Pareto improvement.

Note that every actual Pareto improvement is also a potential Pareto improvement (in which no compensation is necessary). But not all potential Pareto improvements are actual Pareto improvements.

EXAMPLES

Many people have gained from the technological developments that led to calculators and personal computers, but these changes harmed hundreds of people who worked at firms that produced slide rules and mechanical adding machines or whose jobs were tied in other ways to older technologies. The development of calculators and personal computers was not an actual Pareto improvement because, although most people gained, some people lost. The change was potentially Pareto improving, however, because the winners from these technological developments gained more than the losers lost, in the sense that the winners could have compensated the losers enough to keep the losers from actually losing. The technological developments of calculators and personal computers raised economic efficiency. Virtually every new product that displaces an older product creates a change that is potentially Pareto improving, but not actually Pareto improving. Although these changes hurt some people, they raise economic efficiency.

ECONOMIC EFFICIENCY

Most changes in the economy help some people, but hurt others; there are very few actual Pareto-improving changes.

economically efficient (or Pareto efficient) situation — a situation that allows no potentially Pareto-improving change

A situation is **economically efficient**—or **Pareto efficient**—if there is no potentially Pareto-improving change.

economically inefficient (or Pareto inefficient) situation — a situation that is not economically efficient, so a potentially Pareto-improving change *could* be made

A situation is **economically inefficient**—or **Pareto inefficient**—if it is not economically efficient, that is, if there are potentially Pareto-improving changes in that situation.

If it is possible to make a potentially Pareto-improving change in a situation, then (before that change is made) that situation is economically inefficient. After the change, of course, the new situation may be economically efficient. There are many economically efficient situations, each with a different distribution of income.

EXAMPLE Chapter 3 discussed the gains from trade between two students who have apartments to clean and paint. **Table 11.1** reproduces the two-student example. Lauren could clean either apartment in 3 hours, or both in 6 hours. She could paint either apartment in 1 hour, or both in 2 hours. It would take Steve 2 hours to clean either apartment (4 hours to clean both), and it would take him 4 hours to paint either apartment (8 hours to paint both). The left side of Table 11.1 shows the number of hours each person would need to do each job in one apartment; the right side shows how much work each person could do in one hour (each person's productivity at each job).

TABLE 11.1

TWO-STUDENT EXAMPLE OF GAINS FROM TRADE

Time Required for Work			Productivity of Each Person		
Job	Lauren's Time	Steve's Time	Job	Lauren's Time	Steve's Time
Clean one apartment	3 hours	2 hours	Amount cleaned in 1 hour	$\frac{1}{3}$ apt.	$\frac{1}{2}$ apt.
Paint one apartment	1 hour	4 hours	Amount painted in 1 hour	1 apt.	$\frac{1}{4}$ apt.

Chapter 3 showed that it would be economically inefficient for each person to clean and paint his or her own apartment because that situation would leave a potential Pareto-improving change: have Steve clean both apartments while Lauren paints both apartments. *Each* person gains 2 hours of leisure time from this change. This new situation is economically efficient.

Chapter 3 showed that another economically efficient situation would have Lauren paint both apartments and clean half of her own apartment while Steve would clean his own apartment and half of Lauren's apartment. This is a Pareto improvement over the situation in which each person does all the work in his or her own apartment because Lauren gains 30 minutes and Steve gains 3 hours of leisure time compared to that situation.[1] Many other economically efficient situations would have Steve working more and Lauren working less, or Lauren working more and Steve working less.

IS ECONOMIC EFFICIENCY GOOD?

It is easy to argue that Pareto-improving changes are good since no one loses and some people gain (based on their own values). People may disagree about whether a particular change is actually Pareto-improving in real life, but few argue that Pareto improvements are bad.[2]

People often disagree about whether a *potential* Pareto improvement is good or bad. Nearly every innovation in technology throughout history has hurt some people, while benefiting millions of others. A cure for cancer would obviously help millions of people, but some people would lose their jobs. The development of a cheap way to harness solar energy would help many people, but it would throw coal miners out of work. Radial tires last several times as long as older, bias-ply tires, so their development caused people to buy new tires less often. This fall in the demand for tires eliminated 40 percent of the jobs in the U.S. tire industry within a decade.

---

[1] This results from the hour-for-hour trade discussed in Chapter 3.

[2] There is usually room for disagreement about whether a change is actually a Pareto improvement. Suppose, for example, that Andy and Pat each have $100, then someone gives Andy $100 more. Most people would say that this is a Pareto improvement because Andy gains and Pat does not lose. However, one could argue that Pat loses because he now feels envious of Andy. Similarly, suppose that the government were to repeal the laws that prevent under-age purchases of alcoholic beverages. Some people would say that they gain from being able to buy these drinks, while others would argue that the people who abuse alcohol as a result are actually worse off, though they may erroneously believe that they gain. Whether you think this is a Pareto improvement depends on whether you think people know and act in their own interests.

SOCIAL AND ECONOMIC ISSUES

Tradeoff between Economic Efficiency and Equity?

Government policies on international trade often provoke loud public debate, and the debate on the North American Free Trade Agreement (NAFTA) was no exception. Some people claimed that NAFTA would raise economic efficiency, reduce prices to U.S. consumers, and help improve the political climate in Mexico by boosting the Mexican economy. Others claimed that NAFTA would cost U.S. jobs as U.S. firms relocated to Mexico to gain access to cheaper labor, and that it would reduce wages in the United States. Virtually every economic study of NAFTA indicated that it would raise economic efficiency, but that some people (such as unskilled workers in many U.S. industries) would lose.

The NAFTA debate centered on the question of whether a potential Pareto improvement is good or bad. NAFTA would raise economic efficiency (it would be potentially Pareto improving) because the winners in each country would gain more than the losers would lose. Still, no provision in NAFTA would compensate the losers. Is a policy like this good or bad? Some people say that the losses to some people make the policy bad. Others say that the policy is good because the losses are outweighed by benefits to other people.

Nearly every change in government economic policies hurts some people. Should the government follow policies that promote economic inefficiency to prevent some people from losing from a policy change? Should the government adopt policies to promote economic efficiency even if some people lose from the policy changes? Economics alone cannot answer these questions; the answers require value judgements. You implicitly answer these questions nearly every time you express an opinion about government policies.

The development of radial tires was not a Pareto improvement because it hurt some people (workers who lost their jobs). Like nearly every technical innovation, however, it was a *potential* Pareto improvement.[3] Are technical innovations good? The answer depends on how you compare the gains to the winners with the smaller losses to the losers. Someone who does not care about the distribution of wealth among people would say that all potential Pareto improvements are good. Someone who cares about the distribution of wealth would say that many potential Pareto improvements are good, but some are not. Even if the winners win more than the losers lose, a change can be bad because it can be unfair to the losers.

COMPETITIVE EQUILIBRIUM IS ECONOMICALLY EFFICIENT

The equilibrium quantity Q_1 in Figure 11.1, with competition between price-taking firms, is an economically efficient level of production.[4] The equilibrium quantity Q_1 maximizes the total gain from trade. The demand curve for a good shows its marginal benefit to buyers, measured by their willingness to pay for it. The supply

---

[3]Consumers could have compensated tire workers by paying them the same wages as before while they quit making tires and produced other goods instead. Then the workers would not have lost, and consumers would have gained (consumers would have had both their radial tires *and* these other goods). Therefore, the development of radial tires, like virtually all technical innovations, was a potential Pareto improvement.

[4]Chapter 10 defined a price taker; also see Chapter 12. This conclusion that the competitive equilibrium quantity is economically efficient assumes that no externalities complicate the analysis; see Chapter 20.

curve shows the marginal cost to firms of producing the good. The equilibrium quantity Q_1 is the quantity at which the *marginal benefit of the good to consumers equals its marginal cost to producers,* and both equal the equilibrium price.

EXAMPLE AND DISCUSSION

Suppose that firms were to produce *less* than the equilibrium quantity. If firms produced only 500 cans of soup per week in **Figure 11.4,** buyers and sellers would both gain from an increase in the quantity of soup. The height of the demand curve at the quantity 501 shows the benefit to buyers of the 501st can, indicating that some buyer is willing to pay 78 cents for a 501st can of soup. The height of the supply curve shows the marginal cost of producing the 501st can, indicating that a firm can produce the 501st can for only 61 cents. Because the demand curve lies above the supply curve at the quantity 501, buyers and sellers can share the gains from production of the 501st can of soup. Figure 11.4 shows a gain from the 501st can of 17 cents (78 cents minus 61 cents). Whenever output is less than the equilibrium quantity Q_1, output is economically inefficient, and buyers and sellers can share the gain from an increase in output.

Similar reasoning applies if output exceeds Q_1. The supply curve lies above the demand curve, so buyers and sellers can both gain by reducing output. If it costs 94 cents to produce the 1,321st can of soup and buyers are willing to pay only 30 cents for it, then buyers and sellers jointly lose 64 cents on that can of soup. Buyers and sellers can share the 64-cent gain from not producing it.

FIGURE 11.4

EQUILIBRIUM QUANTITY AND ECONOMIC EFFICIENCY

The equilibrium quantity, Q_1, is economically efficient. Higher or lower quantities would be economically inefficient.

Cans of Soup per Week

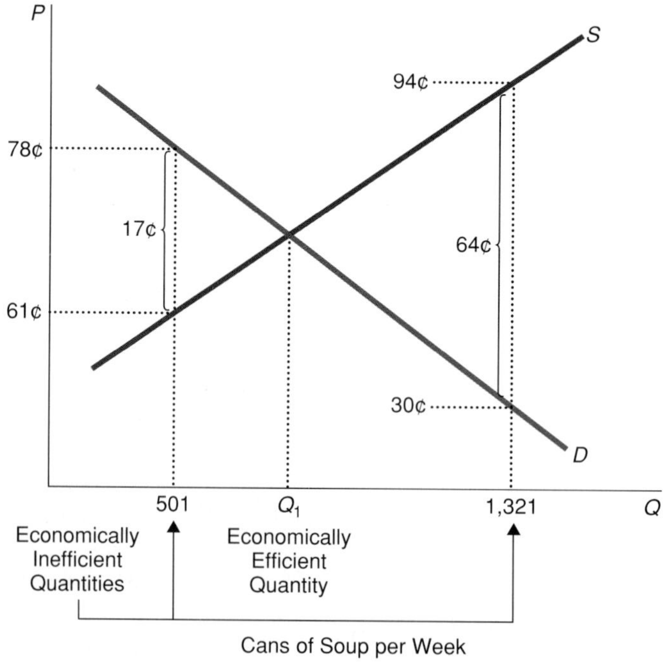

FIGURE 11.5

DEADWEIGHT SOCIAL LOSS

Deadweight social loss measures the size of the economic inefficiency at an output other than Q_1.

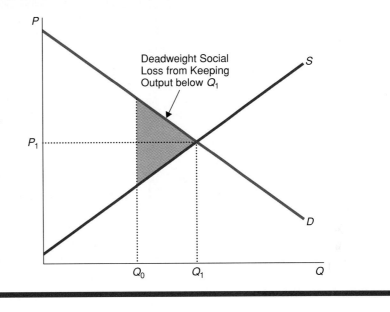

DEADWEIGHT SOCIAL LOSSES

This discussion suggests a way to measure the loss from an economically inefficient situation.

deadweight social loss — the amount that people would be willing to pay to eliminate an inefficiency

> The **deadweight social loss** from an economically inefficient situation is the amount that people would be willing to pay to eliminate the inefficiency.[5]

Roughly, a deadweight social loss is a loss to some people that is not a gain to anyone else. The shaded area in **Figure 11.5** represents the deadweight social loss from a restriction that keeps output at Q_0, below the equilibrium quantity.

EXPLANATION

Suppose that the government were to limit output of a good to 10 units when the equilibrium quantity was 15, as in **Figure 11.6.** The marginal cost of producing an 11th unit would be $8, but the marginal benefit to buyers would be $12. If the government were to allow production of an 11th unit, the buyer and seller could share the $4 gain from trade on that unit, so they would be willing to pay up to $4 to eliminate the prohibition on the 11th unit. (For example, if they were to pay the government $3 to eliminate the prohibition, they could still share the remaining $1 gain from trade.) This means that the deadweight social loss from not having the 11th unit traded would be $4.

---

[5]This definition applies to small inefficiencies; for larger inefficiencies, it is only an approximation. Further discussion is beyond the scope of this book.

FIGURE 11.6

DEADWEIGHT SOCIAL LOSS OCCURS WHEN MARGINAL BENEFIT DOES NOT EQUAL MARGINAL COST

The deadweight social loss from limiting output to 10 units equals the gains from trade that people would have had if they had traded the 11th, 12th, 13th, 14th, and 15th units. In this case, the deadweight social loss is $10.

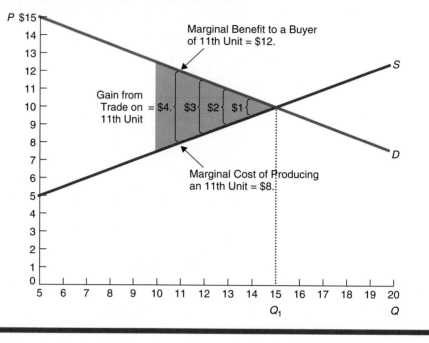

Similarly, the deadweight social loss from prohibiting the 12th unit would be $3, and the deadweight social losses from prohibiting the 13th and 14th units would be $2 and $1. The prohibition of the 15th unit creates no deadweight social loss, so the total deadweight social loss from limiting output to 10 units would be $10, represented by the shaded area in the figure ($4 plus $3 plus $2 plus $1).

Chapter 3 introduced deadweight social loss without using that term. In the two-student example, each student gains 1 hour of free time by trading. The deadweight social loss from prohibiting trade would be 2 hours of free time.

───────────── FOR REVIEW ─────────────

11.1 What is a Pareto improvement? What is a potential Pareto improvement?

11.2 What is an economically efficient situation?

11.3 What is a deadweight social loss?

───────────── QUESTIONS ─────────────

11.4 Why is it economically inefficient to produce less than the equilibrium quantity of a good?

11.5 Explain why the shaded area in Figure 11.5 represents the deadweight social loss from limiting output of a good to Q_0.

APPLICATIONS

Economists use the concepts discussed in this chapter to measure the gains and losses from changes in underlying economic conditions. The following sections discuss some specific applications.

INCREASE IN SUPPLY

Advances in computer technology will someday make it possible for computers to understand normal human speech. Computers will then be able to do many jobs that currently require humans such as selling products by telephone or answering students' questions about economics or history. These technological advances will reduce the marginal costs of many services, causing increases in their supplies. (Does this sound far-fetched? It isn't; computers have already eliminated many middle-management jobs, just as technical innovations in farm machinery eliminated many farm jobs years ago.)

Figure 11.7 shows the effect of a technological advance that would replace professors with computers that can lecture and answer student questions. This change would reduce the marginal cost and raise the supply of college-education services. The price would fall from P_1 to P_2 and the equilibrium quantity would rise from Q_1 to Q_2. Consumer surplus would increase from Area A to Area A + B + C, and producer surplus would change from Area B + D to Area D + E. The total gain from trade would increase from Area A + B + D to Area A + B + C + D + E. The technological innovation would boost the total gain from trade by the Area C + E. While this could be a Pareto improvement, it would more likely be only a potential Pareto improvement; consumers would gain, some people would lose (such

FIGURE 11.7

INCREASE IN SUPPLY

Before supply increases, consumer surplus is Area A and producer surplus is Area B + D. After supply increases, consumer surplus is Area A + B + C and producer surplus is Area D + E. The net gain is Area C + E.

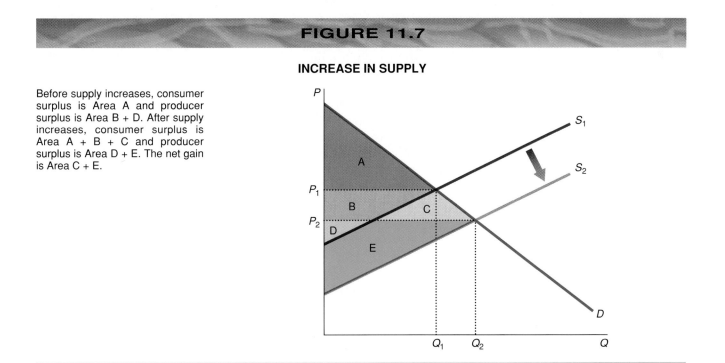

FIGURE 11.8

POTENTIAL PARETO IMPROVEMENT FROM INTERNATIONAL TRADE

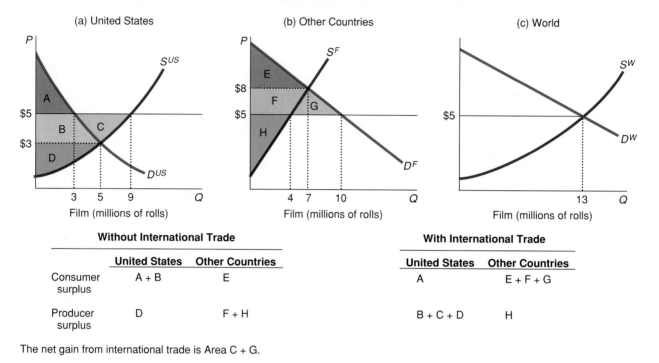

(a) United States   (b) Other Countries   (c) World

Film (millions of rolls)   Film (millions of rolls)   Film (millions of rolls)

Without International Trade

	United States	Other Countries
Consumer surplus	A + B	E
Producer surplus	D	F + H

With International Trade

	United States	Other Countries
Consumer surplus	A	E + F + G
Producer surplus	B + C + D	H

The net gain from international trade is Area C + G.

---

as professors who would lose their jobs to computers or take pay cuts), but the gains to winners would exceed the losses to losers.[6]

INTERNATIONAL TRADE

Figure 11.8 shows the effects of international trade. (This figure resembles Figure 7.1 in Chapter 7.) Without international trade, the U.S. price is $3, and the foreign price is $8. The United States produces and consumes 5 million rolls of film and foreign countries produce and consume 7 million rolls.

Without international trade:

▶ U.S. consumer surplus is the sum of Areas A and B.

▶ U.S. producer surplus is Area D.

▶ Foreign consumer surplus is Area E.

▶ Foreign producer surplus is the sum of Areas F and H.

The equilibrium without international trade is not economically efficient. The marginal benefit of film to foreign buyers is $8, so some foreign buyer would be

---

[6]Recall that the statement "the gains to winners exceed the losses to losers" means that the winners gain enough that they could fully compensate the losers.

willing to pay $8 for an additional roll of film. The marginal cost of producing film in the United States is only $3, so a U.S. manufacturer could produce an extra roll of film for only $3. The marginal benefit of an additional roll of film is larger than its marginal cost, and buyers and sellers in each country could share the $5 gain from producing one more roll of film in the United States and providing it to a foreign buyer. Since this change would be potentially Pareto improving, the equilibrium without international trade is economically inefficient.

With international trade, the world price is $5. The United States produces and sells 9 million rolls per week, consumes 3 million rolls, and exports 6 million rolls. Foreign countries produce 4 million rolls per week, consume 10 million rolls, and import 6 million rolls from the United States.

With international trade:

▶ U.S. consumer surplus is Area A.

▶ U.S. producer surplus is the sum of Areas B, C, and D.

▶ Foreign consumer surplus is the sum of Areas E, F, and G.

▶ Foreign producer surplus is Area H.

Notice that international trade is a potential Pareto improvement over no trade, but not a Pareto improvement.

International trade affects different people differently:

▶ U.S. consumers lose Area B.

▶ U.S. producers gain Areas B and C.

▶ Foreign consumers gain Areas F and G.

▶ Foreign producers lose Area F.

Notice that *U.S. producers gain more than U.S. consumers lose,* and *foreign consumers gain more than foreign producers lose.* So, each country gains from international trade in the sense that the winners in each country win more than the losers lose. Area C represents the net gain to the United States and foreign countries gain Area G. This implies that the deadweight social loss from prohibiting international trade would be the sum of Areas C and G. The equilibrium with international trade is economically efficient, leaving no potentially Pareto-improving changes because the marginal benefit of an additional film in each country equals its marginal cost in each country.

This logical demonstration that international trade is economically efficient and that prohibitions on international trade are economically inefficient is one of the most famous results in economics. It is the basis for the near-universal support of free international trade among economists. Similar arguments apply to the effects of arbitrage and speculation.

TAXES

Figure 11.9 (like Figure 8.7) shows the effects of a tax. Without the tax, the equilibrium price and quantity are P_1 and Q_1, and consumer surplus is the sum of Areas A, B, and C. Producer surplus is the sum of Areas D, E, and F. The equilibrium without a tax is economically efficient.

A per-unit tax of T dollars raises the price that buyers pay to P_B (including tax), while sellers receive the price P_S (net of the tax), which is T dollars less

FIGURE 11.9

EFFECT OF A TAX

With no tax, the equilibrium price and quantity are P_1 and Q_1, consumer surplus is A + B + C, and producer surplus is D + E + F. With a per-unit tax, T, buyers pay P_B, sellers keep P_S, and Q_2 units are traded. Consumer surplus is A, producer surplus is F, government tax revenue is B + D, and the deadweight social loss is C + E.

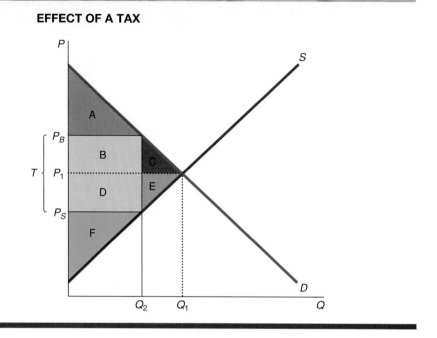

than P_B. Output with the tax is Q_2, consumer surplus is Area A, and producer surplus is Area F. The sum of Areas B and D shows total tax payments, which the government collects as tax revenue. The sum of Areas C and E is a deadweight social loss.

▶ Consumers lose Areas B and C from the tax.

▶ Producers lose Areas D and E from the tax.

▶ The government gains Areas B and D from the tax.

▶ Areas C and E show the deadweight social loss from the tax.

EXPLANATION AND EXAMPLE

A tax causes a deadweight social loss because it prevents some mutually advantageous trades. Chapter 3 first introduced this idea in the section, *How Taxes Create Economic Inefficiency: An Example.* (You may want to reread that section now.) **Figure 11.10** shows that a $1 tax on haircuts causes a deadweight social loss. Without the tax, haircuts cost $10, and people in the United States get 1 billion haircuts per year. With the tax, haircuts cost $10.50; the government gets $1.00 and barbers get $9.50. With the tax, people get only 950 million haircuts per year. The figure shows that someone would be willing to pay $10.25 for haircut number 975 million and a barber would be willing to provide that haircut for $9.75. They could share the $0.50 gain from trade by agreeing on any price between $9.75 and $10.25, but they choose not to trade because the gain from this trade, $0.50 is smaller than the per-unit tax ($1) that they would have to pay. The tax causes a deadweight social loss because it prevents some mutually beneficial trades.

FIGURE 11.10

DEADWEIGHT SOCIAL LOSS FROM A TAX

A tax of $1 reduces the number of haircuts traded per year to 950 million. Some buyer is willing to pay up to $10.25 for haircut number 975 million, and some seller is willing to provide that haircut for $9.75. The tax prevents this trade, however, causing a deadweight social loss.

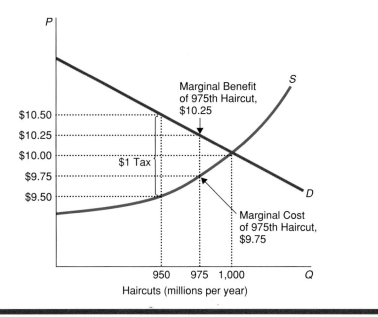

SPECIAL CASES OF ELASTICITIES

If the supply of a good is perfectly inelastic, a tax on that good does not cause a deadweight social loss. **Figure 11.11** shows that without a tax the price is $5 and the quantity sold is 120 per week; consumer surplus is Area A and producer surplus is the sum of Areas B and C. A $1 per-unit tax leaves the price that buyers pay (including tax) at $5 and the price that sellers receive (net of tax) falls to $4; consumer surplus is Area A, producer surplus is Area C, and the government gains Area B in tax revenue. The total gain from trade to everyone, including the government, does not change; it remains the sum of Areas A, B, and C. A similar argument applies when the demand for a product is perfectly inelastic to show that a tax on that product does not cause a deadweight social loss (see Question 11.12 at the end of the chapter).

COMMENT

This discussion has ignored the cost of calculating and paying taxes. The time and expense that people and business firms spend to fill out forms, calculate, and pay their taxes is an additional source of deadweight social loss from the tax that does not appear in these diagrams. (This deadweight social loss occurs even when supply or demand is perfectly inelastic.) This additional deadweight social loss can be large; the cost of filing personal and business income taxes in the United States each year is roughly 1 percent of the economy's total output.[7]

---

[7]Government programs have benefits, of course, and it is probably impossible for the government to obtain enough revenue to finance its operation without taxes that cause deadweight social losses. The government can, however, choose its mix of taxes to minimize the deadweight social losses they cause; see Chapter 21.

FIGURE 11.11

EFFECTS OF A TAX WITH PERFECTLY INELASTIC SUPPLY

Without a tax, consumer surplus is Area A and producer surplus is Area B + C. With a tax, consumer surplus is Area A, producer surplus is Area C, and the government collects Area B. Because supply is perfectly inelastic, the tax does not cause a deadweight social loss.

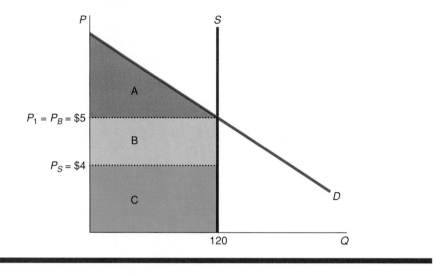

SUBSIDIES

Taxes cause deadweight social losses, but do subsidies provide social gains? The answer is no—subsidies also cause deadweight social losses. **Figure 11.12** shows the effects of a $20 per-unit subsidy to production of waterbeds. Without the subsidy, waterbeds cost $140 and 360,000 are sold each year. Consumer surplus is the sum of Areas A and B, and producer surplus is the sum of Areas F and G. The equilibrium without a subsidy is economically efficient.

With a per-unit subsidy of $20 buyers pay $125 (net of the subsidy), sellers receive $145 (including the subsidy), and 420,000 waterbeds are sold each year. Consumer surplus is the sum of Areas A, B, E, and F. Producer surplus is the sum of Areas B, C, F, and G. Consumers gain Area E + F from the subsidy and producers gain Area B + C. Who loses? The government loses because it provides the subsidy (that is, taxpayers lose). The subsidy costs the government $20 on each of the 420,000 waterbeds sold each year, so it loses the sum of Areas B, C, D, E, and F. The loss to the government is larger than the total gain to consumers and producers. The difference, Area D, is the deadweight social loss due to the subsidy. In summary:

▶ Consumers gain Areas E and F from the subsidy.

▶ Producers gain Areas B and C from the subsidy.

▶ The government loses Areas B, C, D, E, and F from the subsidy.

▶ Area D shows the deadweight social loss from the subsidy.

PRICE CONTROLS

Figure 11.13 (like Figure 8.2) shows the effects of a maximum legal price with rationing by sellable coupons. Without the maximum legal price, the equilibrium

FIGURE 11.12

EFFECTS OF A SUBSIDY

Without a subsidy, consumer surplus is Area A + B and producer surplus is Area F + G. With a subsidy, consumer surplus is Area A + B + E + F, producer surplus is Area B + C + F + G, the government pays Area B + C + D + E + F, and the deadweight social loss is Area D.

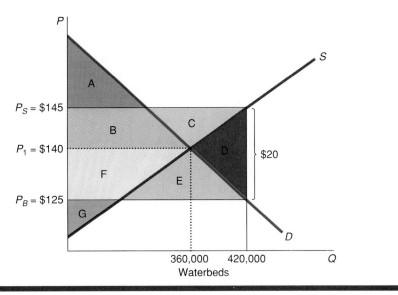

FIGURE 11.13

MAXIMUM LEGAL PRICE WITH RATIONING BY SELLABLE COUPONS

A maximum legal price of $\overline{P}$ with rationing by sellable coupons changes consumer surplus from A + B + C to A + B + D, and it lowers producer surplus from D + E + F to F. The deadweight social loss is Area C + E.

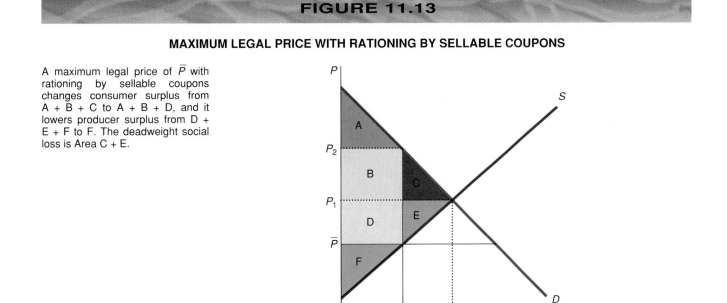

price and quantity are P_1 and Q_1. Consumer surplus is the sum of Areas A, B, and C; producer surplus is the sum of Areas D, E, and F. This equilibrium without price controls is economically efficient. With a maximum legal price and rationing with sellable coupons, consumer surplus is the sum of Areas A, B, and D, and producer surplus is Area F. The maximum legal price is economically inefficient because it causes a deadweight social loss equal to the sum of Areas C and E.[8]

The deadweight social loss from a maximum legal price is higher with rationing by waiting than with rationing by sellable coupons for two reasons. First, some people who value the good highly cannot buy it because they are near the end of the line, while other people who value the good less are able to buy it because they are near the front of the line. Second, rationing by waiting adds to the deadweight social loss because people could use the time that they spend in line to do something else. Generally, people with a comparative advantage at obtaining goods with some rationing system (such as people with a lot of free time to wait in a line) gain from price controls with that rationing system, and other people lose. Experiments in economics have shown that the size of the deadweight social loss due to a price control often exceeds C plus E; the exact amount of the loss depends on the type of rationing system.

EXAMPLE: DEADWEIGHT SOCIAL LOSS FROM SELECTIVE PRICE CONTROLS ON GASOLINE

In spring 1980, the government required Chevron gas stations in California to reduce their prices, for about two months, to levels 16 to 21 cents per gallon below prices at other stations. This caused lines for gasoline at the Chevron stations, while other stations had no lines but higher prices. The wait to buy gas at a Chevron station averaged about 15 minutes.

If you wait 15 extra minutes to buy 10 gallons of gas and you save $0.20 per gallon, you effectively earn $2.00 in 15 minutes, which amounts to a wage of $8 per hour. More precisely, it is an after-tax wage of $8 per hour, because you don't pay any tax on the money you save by waiting in line to buy at a low price. Some California buyers, particularly people whose time was worth less than $8 an hour, waited in lines at Chevron stations. Other buyers, particularly those with a higher value of time, avoided the lines by going elsewhere.

The size of the deadweight social loss from waiting in line depends partly on how much people dislike waiting in line. A line did not bother some people who listened to their car radios or talked to friends as they waited; these people tended to go to the Chevron stations. Others, who disliked the lines more, tended to buy their gasoline elsewhere.

The average customer bought about 10 gallons of gas. Chevron customers paid about $0.20 per gallon less by waiting in line so they saved about $2.00 per 10-gallon fill-up. A study showed that the typical Chevron customer would have been willing to spend $1 to avoid waiting in the line, so an average Chevron customer had a net gain of $1.00 for each 10-gallon fill-up. Chevron stations, though, lost $2.00 on each 10-gallon fill-up. The difference between a *buyer's gain of $1.00* and a *Chevron station's loss of $2.00* was a deadweight social loss. This loss was $1.00 for each 10-gallon fill-up, so the deadweight social loss at each Chevron

---

[8]The deadweight social loss is larger than Areas C and E if the coupons are not sellable because people who want to buy the good but lack coupons cannot buy, while other people who have coupons gain less from buying the good than they would from selling the coupons.

station that sold 20,000 gallons of gasoline per month was about $2,000 per month.

———————————————— QUESTIONS ————————————————

11.6 Use a graph to show how an increase in supply changes consumer and producer surplus.

11.7 Draw a graph like Figure 11.8 and use it to show consumer and producer surplus:
a. Without international trade
b. With international trade

11.8 Draw a graph to show consumer and producer surplus:
a. Without a tax
b. With a tax on production of a good (Also show the deadweight social loss.)

11.9 Draw a graph to show consumer and producer surplus:
a. Without a subsidy
b. With a subsidy for the production of a good (Also show the deadweight social loss.)

11.10 Draw a graph to help explain why a tax does not cause a deadweight social loss if supply is perfectly inelastic.

CONCLUSIONS

GAINS FROM TRADE

The total gain from trade in some good is the sum of consumer and producer surplus from that good. This sum equals the total benefit to buyers minus the total variable cost of production. A change in the economy is a Pareto improvement if at least one person gains and no one loses. A change is a potential Pareto improvement if the winners gain more than the losers lose, so that it would be *possible* for the winners to compensate the losers enough that the change would not hurt them. A potential Pareto improvement is also called an increase in economic efficiency.

A situation is economically efficient if there is no potentially Pareto-improving change that could be made in that situation. Otherwise, a situation is economically inefficient and some potential Pareto-improving change could be made. The equilibrium quantity is economically efficient because the marginal benefit of the good to buyers equals the marginal cost to producers. Deadweight social loss measures the size of the loss from an economic inefficiency.

APPLICATIONS

An advancement in technology that raises the supply of a product is a potential Pareto improvement, but not necessarily a Pareto improvement. International trade is a potential Pareto improvement over a situation without trade. International trade helps consumers and hurts producers in the country where the price would have been higher without international trade, but consumers gain more than producers lose in that country. International trade hurts consumers and helps producers in the country where the price would have been lower without international trade, but producers' gains exceed the consumers' losses in that country. For these reasons, international trade is economically efficient. The same argument applies to arbitrage and speculation.

Taxes cause economic inefficiencies. The government revenue from a tax is smaller than the losses that it causes in consumer and producer surplus (except when either supply or demand is perfectly inelastic). The difference is the deadweight social loss from the tax. Subsidies, like taxes, are economically inefficient. The cost of a subsidy to the government exceeds the gains to buyers and sellers, and the difference is a deadweight social loss. Price controls are also economically inefficient and cause deadweight social losses.

LOOKING AHEAD

Chapters 12 through 15 discuss competition and its results under various conditions using the concepts developed in this chapter. Chapter 12 discusses competition among price-taking firms; Chapters 13 through 15 discuss competition among firms that are not price takers.

KEY TERMS

total gain from trade	economically efficient (or Pareto efficient) situation
Pareto improvement	
potential Pareto improvement	economically inefficient (or Pareto inefficient) situation
increase in economic efficiency	deadweight social loss

QUESTIONS AND PROBLEMS

11.11 Use a graph to show how an increase in demand affects consumer and producer surplus.

11.12 Use diagrams to show the effect of a tax on consumer and producer surplus, and to show the deadweight social loss from the tax, when:
  a. The demand curve is perfectly inelastic
  b. The supply curve is perfectly inelastic
  c. The demand curve is perfectly elastic
  d. The supply curve is perfectly elastic
  Also explain your results in words.

11.13 Draw a diagram to illustrate the effects of a subsidy for the production of candy. Show the effects on (a) output of candy, (b) the prices paid by buyers and received by sellers, (c) consumer surplus, and (d) producer surplus. Also show (e) the cost of the subsidy to the government and (f) the social gain or loss from the subsidy.

11.14 Comment on these statements:
  a. "Economists say that taxes cause a deadweight social loss, but this is misleading. Obviously, when one person *pays* money in taxes, another person *collects* money in taxes, so there is no loss to society as a whole."
  b. "A tax causes a deadweight social loss to the extent that people change their behavior so that they don't have to pay it."

11.15 Draw a diagram that shows equilibrium with international trade. Suppose that foreign demand rises. How much do U.S. consumers gain or lose? What about U.S. producers, foreign consumers, and foreign producers?

11.16 Draw a diagram that shows equilibrium with international trade. Suppose that foreign supply rises. How much do U.S. consumers gain or lose? What about U.S. producers, foreign consumers, and foreign producers?

11.17 Suppose that a foreign country puts a tariff on imports of U.S. beef. Use a diagram to discuss the effects of the tariff. Who gains and who loses? How much?

11.18 Explain why not every potential Pareto improvement is a Pareto improvement.

11.19 Complete the following exercises to continue a problem from Chapter 7.
  a. Use the table below to find equilibrium prices, quantities produced, and quantities consumed with international trade.
  b. Repeat Question 11.19a *without* international trade.
  c. Calculate the gains or losses to consumers and producers in each country and the deadweight social loss from a law prohibiting international trade. (*Hint:* Use the table below to draw a graph of demand and supply in each country to help you calculate consumer and producer surplus.)

| | United States | | Foreign Countries | | World Market | |
Price	Demand	Supply	Demand	Supply	Demand	Supply
$12	2	13	5	25	7	38
11	4	12	6	22	10	33
10	6	11	7	19	13	30
9	10	10	8	17	18	27
8	11	9	9	15	20	24
7	12	8	10	14	22	22
6	14	6	11	13	25	19
5	16	0	12	12	28	12
4	18	0	13	9	31	9
3	20	0	14	0	34	0
2	22	0	15	0	37	0

INQUIRIES FOR FURTHER THOUGHT

11.20 Do you think that the economy faces a tradeoff between equity and economic efficiency?
  a. If so, give examples of increases in economic efficiency that are unfair or inequitable. Should government policies promote equity even at the cost of economic efficiency? What general principles should guide the government's decision whether to promote equity or efficiency?
  b. If not, explain the general principles behind your concept of equity. Can equity ever conflict with efficiency? Why or why not? If a conflict were to arise, how should the government decide whether to promote equity or efficiency?

11.21 When Supreme Court Justice Anthony Kennedy was questioned in the U.S. Senate during his confirmation hearing, one senator urged him "not simply to weigh economic efficiency" but also "to consider the impact on consumers" of his decisions. Did the senator's comment make sense? Discuss it.

IN THE NEWS

Since most teenagers are sensitive to the disincentive effects of high tobacco taxes, a tax hike could be deemed "economically efficient" on the grounds that it might prevent many from starting to smoke in the first place—something they would have done if they were fully aware of the risks.

Is it economically efficient for the government to use taxes to prevent decisions that it views as irrational?

Source: Business Week, June 5, 1989, p. 27.

11.22 People risk death to flee bad economic conditions or oppressive governments in many countries. U.S. immigration policy limits the number of foreigners that can come to live in the United States. Think of the right to come to the United States as a good that could be bought and sold. The U.S. government imposes a maximum legal price of zero on this good and then rations it. (The government chooses who gets to buy this good at the legal price of zero.)

    a. Discuss the effects of this maximum legal price on consumer and producer surplus.

    b. Suppose that the U.S. government were to decide to allow more immigration. Who would gain and who would lose? How much? What would be the effects on consumer surplus?

    c. What should U.S. immigration policy be? Why?

11.23 Discuss this statement: "People often make irrational choices, such as smoking despite the health risks. The government should tax goods such as cigarettes and alcohol to make the economy more efficient. A higher tax on cigarettes could reduce smoking; it would force people to make rational decisions."

11.24 Consider these issues that arise in relation to international trade.

    a. When the United States chooses its international trade policies, should it design policies to benefit only U.S. citizens or should it also take into account the effects on people in other countries?

    b. Suppose that U.S. residents would gain $100 and foreigners would lose $150 from some U.S. government policy, and that foreign residents would gain $100 and U.S. residents would lose $150 from a foreign government's policy. Should the government of each country take into account only the effects on its own residents? What else might they do?

11.25 Farm wages rose when tighter immigration laws reduced the supply of labor. Who would gain and who would lose, and how much, if the U.S. government were to allow more immigrant workers into the United States?

TAG SOFTWARE APPLICATIONS

TUTORIAL EXERCISES
▶ The module contains a review of the key terms from Chapter 11.

GRAPHING EXERCISES
▶ The graphing module examines consumer surplus and deadweight loss.

CHAPTER 11 APPENDIX — CALCULATING THE DEADWEIGHT SOCIAL LOSS FROM TAXES

This appendix builds on the Chapter 4 and Chapter 8 Appendixes. Suppose that the demand curve is:

$$Q^d = 10 - 2P_B$$

where Q^d is the quantity demanded, in millions, and P_B is the price that buyers pay. The supply curve is:

$$Q^s = -5 + 3P_S$$

where Q^s is the quantity supplied, in millions, and P_S is the price that sellers receive. Without a tax, P_B and P_S are the same; the equilibrium price is $3 and the equilibrium quantity is 4 million units. (See the Chapter 4 Appendix.)

The Chapter 8 Appendix showed that a tax of $1 per unit reduces the equilibrium price to sellers to $2.60, raises the equilibrium price to buyers to $3.60, and drops the equilibrium quantity to 2.8 million. The deadweight social loss is represented by Area A in **Figure 11A.1.** This region is a triangle, so its area is one-half of its base times its height. The base of the triangle is the change in quantity because of the tax. The quantity falls from 4.0 million to 2.8 million, so the base

FIGURE 11A.1

CALCULATING DEADWEIGHT SOCIAL LOSS

Area A is a triangle with a base of 1.2 million goods, and a height of $1 per unit, so its area represents $600,000.

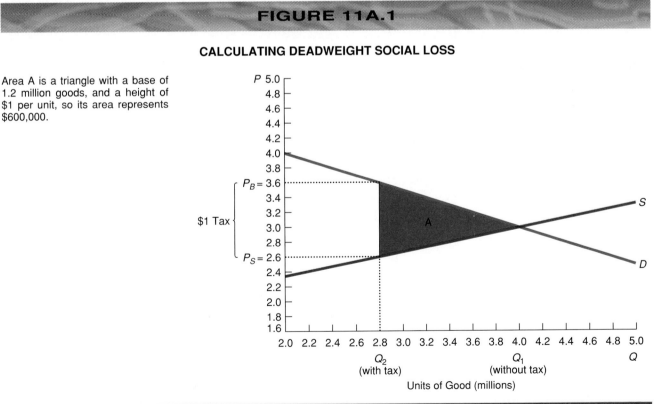

Units of Good (millions)

of the triangle is 1.2 million. The height of the triangle is the per-unit tax, which is $1. This gives an area for the triangle—the deadweight social loss—of:

$$(\tfrac{1}{2})(1.2 \text{ million})(\$1) = \$600,000$$

QUESTIONS AND PROBLEMS

11A.1 (Follow-up to Question 8A.1 in the Chapter 8 Appendix) Suppose that the demand curve for rental cars is:

$$Q^d = 500 - 2P_B$$

and the supply curve is:

$$Q^s = 100 + 6P_S$$

where Q^d is the quantity demanded (in cars per day), Q^s is the quantity supplied, P_B is the price per day paid by renters, including taxes, and P_S is the price per day received by sellers, excluding taxes. Suppose that the government taxes car rentals at $8 per day. Find the effects of this tax on consumer surplus and producer surplus, and find the deadweight social loss from this tax.

11A.2 (Follow-up to Question 8A.2 in the Chapter 8 Appendix) Suppose that the demand curve for a product is:

$$x^d = 1,000 - 120p$$

where x^d is the quantity demanded and p is the price (measured in dollars). Suppose that the supply curve for the product, with x^s as the quantity supplied, is:

$$x^s = 200 + 40p$$

Suppose also that a per-unit tax of $4 is placed on the product. Find the effects of this tax on consumer surplus and producer surplus, and find the deadweight social loss from this tax.

11A.3 (Follow-up to Question 8A.3 in the Chapter 8 Appendix) Reconsider Question 8A.2 for a subsidy of $4 per unit instead of a tax. Find the effects of this subsidy on consumer surplus and producer surplus, and find the deadweight social loss from this subsidy.

11A.4 Suppose that the demand curve for a good is:

$$x^d = 1,000 - 6p$$

and the supply curve is:

$$x^s = 4p$$

Suppose that the government places a tax of $30 per unit sold on this product. Find the equilibrium quantity, the price paid by buyers, the price paid by sellers, and the deadweight social loss from the tax.

COMPETITION AND STRATEGIC INTERACTIONS

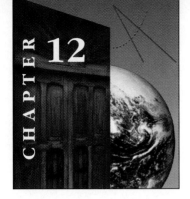

CHAPTER 12

PERFECT COMPETITION

WHAT THIS CHAPTER IS ABOUT

▶ What happens when firms compete for customers

▶ How competition leads to economic efficiency

▶ How costs and profits differ from the measures reported on accounting statements

▶ Why competition is a dynamic process in which some firms expand and other firms go out of business

Everyone participates in some form of competition. Children compete for attention and toys; as people grow older, they compete for friends, for use of the family television and car, for victory in games and sports, for college admission, for good jobs, and for good spouses. Gas stations compete for customers, airlines compete for passengers, television networks compete for viewers, and colleges compete for students. Firms compete for customers by trying to offer lower prices, better quality, more selection or convenience, or other things that they think people want. The firms that best anticipate and satisfy the desires of customers at the lowest cost earn profits and survive the process of competition; other firms suffer losses and may go out of business.

Some people mistakenly believe that competition is the opposite of cooperation, and because cooperation is good, competition must be bad. The next few chapters will illustrate the confusions in that idea. Competition gives sellers an incentive to cooperate with buyers by providing the products that buyers want at the lowest possible prices. Competition does not replace cooperation; it channels and directs cooperation.

This chapter discusses the form of competition that characterizes (approximately) many farms and small businesses, pizza parlors, gas stations, retail stores, computer and software vendors, decorator firms, stock brokers, investment firms, and so on. Competition promotes economic efficiency and its results are often dramatic. Countries around the world where competition flourishes have high standards of living, while countries whose governments interfere with the process of competition, often to protect domestic firms from foreign competition, tend to be poor.

IN THE NEWS

Pizza makers slug it out for share of growing eat-at-home market

Competition forces firms to try to provide the goods and services that customers want at the lowest price.

Source: "Pizza Makers Slug It Out for Share of Growing Eat-at-Home Market," *The Wall Street Journal*, January 12, 1988.

PRICE TAKERS

Chapter 10 defined a price taker as a firm that faces a perfectly elastic demand curve for its output. A price-taking firm can sell as much as it wants at the equilibrium price, but it loses all its customers if it raises its price. For a price-taking firm, marginal revenue equals price. As a result, the portion of the firm's marginal cost curve above its average variable cost of production becomes its supply curve.

ELASTICITY OF DEMAND FOR A FIRM'S OUTPUT

Many individual firms face more elastic demand for their output than the elasticity of market demand for the product. **Figure 12.1** shows the market demand curve for tomatoes (Panel c) and the almost-perfectly-elastic demand curves facing two firms in that industry. Because each firm produces only a small fraction of total industry output, and because buyers do not care which firm's product they buy (the products from different producers are perfect substitutes), each firm is approximately a price taker.

EXAMPLE

The elasticity of market demand for tomatoes is about $-\frac{1}{2}$, as Figure 12.1c shows. World output of tomatoes is about 20 million tons per year, grown on about 1 million acres of land. Sunny's 1,000-acre farm produces 20 tons of tomatoes per year (see Panel a of the figure), which is one millionth of world output. Suppose that Sunny's farm doubles its output of tomatoes; this is a 67 percent increase in Sunny's output, using the formula from Chapter 5. This raises world output by 0.0001 percent, from 20,000,000 tons to 20,000,020 tons. Since the elasticity of demand is $-\frac{1}{2}$, the equilibrium price falls by (0.0001/0.5)%, or 0.0002 percent, from $144.6000 per ton to $144.5997 per ton. Because the 67 percent increase in output on Sunny's farm reduces the price by only 0.0002 percent, the elasticity of demand for the tomatoes from Sunny's farm is $-67/0.0002$, or $-335,000$; the demand is almost perfectly elastic.

Dan's larger 100,000-acre farm produces 2,000 tons of tomatoes each year (see Figure 12.1b), or 1/10,000 of world output. If Dan's farm doubles its output (a 67 percent increase), world output rises by 0.01 percent. Since the market elasticity of demand is $-\frac{1}{2}$, the equilibrium price falls by (0.01/0.5)%, or 0.02 percent, or $0.0289 per ton. Dan's farm faces an elasticity of demand of $-67/0.02$, or $-3,350$, which is also nearly perfectly elastic.

PRICE TAKING IN THE SHORT RUN AND THE LONG RUN

A firm may be a price taker in the long run, but not in the short run. In the early days of personal computers, for example, only a few firms manufactured and sold them. Each firm could raise its price without losing a large share of its customers; these firms were not price takers at the time. Since then, hundreds of firms have started manufacturing and selling personal computers, and most of these firms are now approximately price takers.

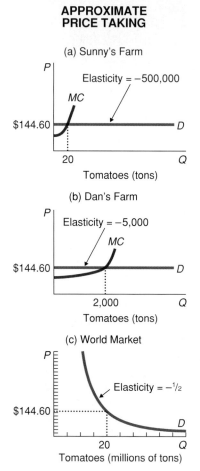

FIGURE 12.1

APPROXIMATE PRICE TAKING

(a) Sunny's Farm

Elasticity = −500,000

(b) Dan's Farm

Elasticity = −5,000

(c) World Market

Elasticity = −¹/₂

The elasticity of market demand is $-\frac{1}{2}$. Sunny's farm produces 1 millionth of world output, so it faces an elasticity of demand of around −500,000. Dan's farm produces 1/10,000 of world output, so the elasticity of demand facing Dan's farm is around −5,000. Sunny and Dan are approximately price takers.

PERFECT COMPETITION

Competition is a process. Competition gives people incentives to innovate to achieve their goals. For example, two people competing for the same job promotion both have incentives to find new and better ways to do their jobs in the hope of getting promoted. Firms compete for customers by trying to provide the goods and services that people want at low prices and by looking for new ways to satisfy customers. This is the process of competition.

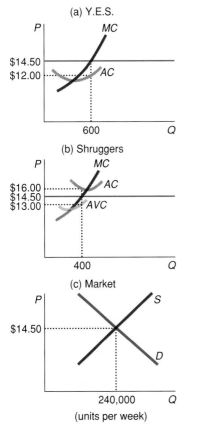

FIGURE 12.2

SHORT-RUN EQUILIBRIUM WITH PERFECT COMPETITION

(a) Y.E.S.

(b) Shruggers

(c) Market

(units per week)

(a) Y.E.S. earns a $2.50 profit margin, and it maximizes its profit by producing 600 units. Its average cost of producing 600 units is $12.00, and it sells them for $14.50. (b) Shruggers takes a $1.50 loss on each unit it sells. It minimizes its loss by producing 400 units. Its average cost is then $16.00, while the price is only $14.50. Shruggers stays in business because the price exceeds its average variable cost of $13.00.

perfect competition — competition among price-taking sellers

short-run equilibrium — an equilibrium with a fixed number of firms

long-run equilibrium — an equilibrium over a time long enough to allow firms to enter or exit the industry

markup (or profit margin) — price minus average cost

This chapter will focus on the results of this process, that is, the equilibrium toward which this process of competition carries buyers and sellers. We begin by considering competition among price taking firms.

Perfect competition is competition among price-taking sellers.

The model of perfect competition (the logical reasoning about it) applies approximately when sellers are approximately price takers.

SHORT-RUN EQUILIBRIUM WITH PERFECT COMPETITION

Figure 12.2 shows a short-run equilibrium with perfect competition. The figure shows the market demand and supply and the costs and outputs of two typical firms in the industry.

The **short run,** when applied to equilibrium, refers to a period over which the number of firms is fixed (though firms may temporarily shut down). The **long run,** applied to equilibrium, refers to a period over which the number of firms can change.

Figure 12.2c shows a market equilibrium price of $14.50 and a market equilibrium quantity of 240,000 units per week. Each firm takes the $14.50 price as given; it faces a perfectly elastic demand curve at that price. Each firm chooses output to maximize profit, so it produces the quantity at which its marginal cost equals its marginal revenue. Since marginal revenue equals the price, it chooses the quantity at which its marginal cost equals the price. For any price above the firm's average variable cost, its marginal cost curve is its supply curve.

The firm in Panel a, Y.E.S., produces 600 units per week (1/400 of total industry output).[1] Its average cost of producing 600 units per week is $12.00, so it earns $2.50 profit on each unit. Its markup or profit margin is $2.50.

A firm's **markup** or **profit margin** is its price minus its average cost.

Since Y.E.S. sells 600 units per week at a $2.50 markup per unit, its total profit is $1,500.00 per week.

The firm in Panel b, Shruggers, has higher costs of production than Y.E.S. It minimizes its loss by producing 400 units per week (1/600 of industry output), but its average cost is $16.00, so it loses $1.50 on each unit it sells. Still, its average *variable* cost is only $13.00 because its total cost of production is $6,400.00, its total variable cost is $5,200.00, and its total fixed cost is $1,200.00. If Shruggers were to shut down, it would lose $1,200.00 (its fixed cost); by producing 400 units per week, it loses only $600.00 per week ($1.50 per unit times 400 units). The price is higher than Shruggers' average variable cost, so it does not shut down.

ENTREPRENEURS

Why do some firms, like Y.E.S., earn profits while other firms, like Shruggers, lose money? Frequently, the difference is better entrepreneurial ability of some firms than others.

---

[1] If the elasticity of the market demand curve is −1, this implies that Y.E.S. faces an elasticity of demand of about −270, so this firm is approximately a price taker.

entrepreneur — a person who conceives and acts on a new business idea and takes the risk of its success or failure

An **entrepreneur** is a person who conceives and acts on a new business idea and takes the risk of its success or failure.

Profit is easier to study than to acquire. Costs of production and revenues from sales are not data that an owner or manager can find in a book. Firms must estimate costs and revenues under changing conditions and make decisions on what, how, and how much to produce, taking the risk that their estimates will be wrong. Based on their guesses, entrepreneurs choose how and when to start a firm, expand it, or shut it down. Some people perform these tasks better than others. Entrepreneurship involves not only discovering or inventing ideas, but also implementing them—not just dreaming, but also doing. In return for their work and the risks they take, entrepreneurs receive their firms' profits (or suffer their losses).

The entrepreneur is easy to identify in a small company. It is usually the person who starts and runs the business. A larger company may include many entrepreneurs. The owners (stockholders) may act as entrepreneurs, since they get the firm's profit or loss and are responsible for choosing the managers who run the company on a daily basis. Managers and other workers may also be entrepreneurs, though. Their pay may depend on the firm's profit or loss, and the firm's fortune may depend on their ideas and their implementation of those ideas.

IN THE NEWS

Valentines came to this country as early as 1847, when a Worcester, Mass., woman, Esther Howland, became aware of her British cousin's use of Saint Valentine's Day as a commercial-printing bonanza.

In short order Howland set up an assembly line to produce Valentine cards. One of her staff glued paper flowers on the cards, another added lace. By 1850 Howland was doing a $100,000-a-year business.

The rest is history.

Entrepreneurship is risky. Some projects succeed—and some fail.

Not every invention is that successful, of course. Some are just plain wacky. Others are entirely practical but either aren't marketable or are ahead of their time.

Bathrooms seem to preoccupy many inventors. In Atlanta, Walter Hibbs's ex-wife used to complain that he didn't put down the seat after using the toilet. So he developed Seat Down, a hydraulic device that is attached to the seat of the toilet. Lifting the seat activates a timer that slowly closes the seat over two minutes, which Mr. Hibbs says is four times longer than the average man needs. The couple got a divorce anyway.

Sources: San Francisco Chronicle, February 10, 1989, p. C2; and The Wall Street Journal, June 10, 1988, p. R18.

IN THE NEWS

Day-care business lures entrepreneurs

Market growth, fragmentation spur ventures

By Lawrence Ingrassia
Staff Reporter of
The Wall Street Journal

Day care is hot. Entrepreneurs, who once flocked into frozen yogurt or computer software, are now catering to kids. A half-dozen venture-capital firms have financed child-care start-ups recently.

And despite the presence of a few major child-care chains—led by Kinder-Care Inc. and La Petite Academy Inc.—no one dominates the business. There are an estimated 60,000 to 70,000 day-care centers nationwide. But only about a dozen companies operate more than 20 centers, and 90 percent of all for-profit companies in the field have fewer than five centers, according to Roger Neugebauer, publisher of Child Care Information Exchange, an industry magazine.

"It's very simple. You can make money where there's a market niche and growing demand," says an accountant who recently started a day-care center but doesn't want to be identified. Though the industry may be fragmented, competition is stiff because there are many nonprofit centers that charge lower fees. Start-up costs are steep—typically $150,000 to $300,000 per center. And salaries account for more than half of operating costs, but can't be cut much if things go wrong because of state rules setting maximum numbers of children per employee.

"Day care runs on a tight margin," says Cheri L. Sheridan, a day-care consultant in Silver Spring, Md.

Source: Lawrence Ingrassia, "Day-Care Business Lures Entrepreneurs," The Wall Street Journal, June 3, 1988, p. 21.

Economic Costs and Accounting Measures

The cost of any decision or action is the value of what you sacrifice or give up for it. It is the value of your best foregone opportunity. Accounting statements show measures of a firm's costs, but they do not necessarily measure a firm's true costs. A firm's profit is its total revenue minus its total cost. Because accounting measures of cost can inaccurately measure true costs, accounting measures of profit can inaccurately measure true profit. This section discusses the reasons why.

Why Accounting Measures of Costs Can Be Inaccurate

Accounting measures omit some of a firm's costs, and they state other costs inaccurately.[2] The main differences arise from:

1. Use of historical costs to measure the costs of inputs
2. Omission of some costs

Historical Costs of Inputs

historical cost — a price paid for something in the past

The **historical cost** of an input is the price that a firm paid for it in the past.

The historical cost of an input does not necessarily equal a firm's cost of using that input now. A firm's cost of using an input, the value of what the firm gives up to use it, equals its historical cost *if* the firm uses the input soon after buying it, before its price changes. Examples include electricity to operate machinery and fresh foods to prepare and serve at a restaurant. If much time passes between when the firm buys the input and when it uses the input, however, or if the input price changes between those dates, then the cost of the input differs from its historical cost. This is particularly important for inputs such as buildings, machinery, and equipment.

The cost of an input purchased in the past may differ from the accounting measure of its cost for two main reasons: price changes and implicit costs of depreciation and interest.

Sometimes firms hold inventories of inputs that they have purchased at various prices.

inventories — goods that a firm owns, including raw materials or other inputs, partially finished goods (goods in process), and finished goods that the firm has not yet sold

Inventories are goods that a firm owns, including raw materials or other inputs, partially finished goods (goods in process), and finished goods that the firm has not yet sold.

Suppose that a firm purchased 1,000 barrels of oil 6 months ago at $15 per barrel and 800 more barrels last month at $18 per barrel. If the firm could now resell the oil for $20 per barrel, then the opportunity cost of using any of this oil now is $20 per barrel rather than either historical cost. One accounting measure, the FIFO (first-in, first-out) method, values inventory at historical costs and supposes that the firm uses its $15 oil first, then its $18 oil. Another accounting measure, the LIFO (last-in, first-out) method, values inventory at historical costs and supposes that the firm uses the oil that it purchased most recently first.

---

[2]This is not a dispute between economists and accountants. Everyone agrees on these issues, and firms have reasons, such as tax laws, to use accounting measures of costs.

Even if input prices do not change, historical costs fail to measure true costs. They do not accurately measure implicit rental rates on capital goods such as machinery, equipment, tools, and buildings.

capital good — an input that a firm can use repeatedly to produce other goods

> **Capital goods** are inputs that firms can use repeatedly to produce other goods.

A firm's cost of using a capital good is called the *implicit rental rate* on the capital good.

implicit rental price — the cost of owning and using a capital good over some period of time

> The **implicit rental price** on a capital good is the cost of owning and using it over some period of time.

An implicit rental rate is the sum of two costs:

1. Depreciation—the fall in the value (price) of the capital good because of its age and accumulated use
2. The *interest cost* of owning the capital good

depreciation — the fall in the value of a capital good over time

> **Depreciation** is the fall in the value of a capital good over some period of time.

Suppose that a firm buys a machine at the beginning of the year for $100,000 when the interest rate is 6 percent per year. If the firm borrows money to buy the machine, it pays 6 percent of $100,000 in interest, or $6,000, during the first year it owns the machine. (If the firm uses its own money to buy the machine, it still has a $6,000 *opportunity cost* of using the machine, because if it had not bought the machine, it could have loaned that money and earned 6 percent interest.) If the value of the machine remains at $100,000 through the end of the year (the firm could sell the machine at that time for $100,000), then the firm's only cost of using the machine during the year is its $6,000 interest cost.

It is likely, though, that the machine will lose value with use and age, that is, that the machine will depreciate.[3] If the resale value of the machine at the end of the year is only $80,000, then the machine costs the firm $20,000 in depreciation in addition to the $6,000 interest cost. This gives an implicit rental price for the machine of $26,000 for the year. The resale value of the machine at the end of the year might depend only on its age, or it might depend on how much the firm uses the machine during the year. For this reason, the implicit rental price for the machine might depend on the machine's use.

Accounting measures of depreciation usually do not accurately measure the actual depreciation of a capital good (that is, the fall in its value). A good measure of depreciation would reflect the resale price of the capital good, information that is not always easy to obtain. Accounting measures of depreciation follow rules that are intended to approximate the correct values on average, or to meet the requirements of tax laws.

OMISSION OF COSTS FROM ACCOUNTING STATEMENTS

In addition to distortion by historical costs, accounting measures can state true costs inaccurately if they omit some relevant costs. A firm's costs include some opportunity costs that are not direct payments for inputs. (We have already dis-

---

[3]If inflation is high enough, its money value may actually rise, but its inflation-adjusted value is likely to fall.

implicit cost — a cost that does not require any direct payment; solely an opportunity cost

explicit cost — a cost that requires some direct payment

economic costs — all of a firm's costs, explicit and implicit

economic profit — total revenue minus total economic cost

accounting profit — total revenue minus total cost as measured on accounting statements

IN THE NEWS

The Weyerhaeuser example

The Weyerhaeuser Company illustrates the point. This highly profitable wood and paper-products company reported a net income of $276.7 million last year.

That profit, however, represented only a 5.8 percent return on the billions of dollars the company had spent to build or purchase its network of paper mills and sawmills, its vast array of high-technology machinery, its forests, and its many other assets.

At this rate of return, Weyerhaeuser could have earned more money if it had sold off all those holdings and invested the proceeds in Treasury notes or bonds, which paid above 7 percent last year.

The opportunity cost of investing in new capital, such as paper mills, sawmills, machinery, and forests, is the interest that a firm could have earned on other investments. This is part of the firm's implicit costs. In this case, Weyerhaeuser had an accounting profit, but an economic loss because it could have earned more money investing in Treasury notes, which paid 7 percent.

Source: New York Times, November 30, 1987, p. A1.

cussed one of these costs—a firm that buys a capital good with its own money pays an implicit cost equal to the amount of interest that the firm could have earned if it had loaned the money.)

Implicit costs are costs that do not require direct payments; they are solely opportunity costs.

Explicit costs are costs that require direct payments.

Accounting statements do not include all implicit costs.

The most important implicit cost is the opportunity cost that a firm must pay to its owners for providing capital and entrepreneurial services to the firm, including generating and implementing new ideas, providing money to buy the firm's capital goods, and taking risks. An entrepreneur who starts a printing firm, a restaurant, or a landscape business could have spent her time and energy on something else; she could have put her money into a bank account or another investment instead of using it to start the firm, avoiding the risk that it would fail. The opportunity cost of her time and money is an implicit cost to the firm. The same is true of the stockholders of a large corporation; these owners invest their money in the corporation and take the risk that they will lose that money. The firm's implicit cost of their money is the interest that the owners could have earned by investing their money elsewhere. The stockholders also choose the firm's managers, and the cost of this responsibility is an implicit cost.

Another implicit cost is associated with intangible assets such as brand names and trademarks ("Coca Cola," "Disney," "McDonald's," and so on). Firms face opportunity costs of not using intangible assets by selling or licensing them (just as the firm has an opportunity cost of not using some equipment that it owns, because it sacrifices revenue that it could have earned by using that equipment). A sports team sacrifices income if it does not sell or lease the right to use its name and logo (intangible assets) on clothing and other items; an entertainment firm like the Walt Disney Company could raise revenue by allowing more firms to use its name on various products, but overuse of a brand name or trademark also has a cost: depreciation. Depreciation of an intangible asset is an implicit cost. Many public figures, such as entertainment or sports stars, earn extra income by endorsing products or appearing in commercials. If a celebrity loses those opportunities because of a public scandal, that person pays an implicit cost in depreciation of the person's "brand name." Similarly, a firm's brand name can lose value due to overuse or if the firm puts its name on poor-quality products and loses its reputation for high quality.

Implicit costs are hard to estimate. How much must an entrepreneur be paid to start and invest in a risky firm? Still, these are real costs because they are opportunity costs to a firm's owners.

PROFIT AND ACCOUNTING MEASURES OF PROFIT

Rational decisions must take into account *all* costs.

Economic costs are all costs, explicit and implicit. Economic costs are the correct measure of costs for a firm's decisions.

Economic profit is total revenue minus total economic cost.

Accounting profit is total revenue minus total cost as measured on accounting statements.

Economic profit differs from accounting profit because accounting statements do not accurately measure economic costs. As explained above, accounting statements use historical costs and they omit some implicit costs. As a result, accounting measures of profit usually overstate economic profit because they count some opportunity costs as profit.

Firms often report their accounting profits as rates of return on investment (profits expressed as percentages of investment) or as rates of return on equity (profits as percentages of the total value of the firm, measured by the total market value of all of the firm's stock).

--------- FOR REVIEW ---------

12.1 What is perfect competition?

12.2 What is an entrepreneur and how does an entrepreneur collect payment?

12.3 What is economic profit and why does it differ from accounting profit?

--------- QUESTIONS ---------

12.4 Explain why any one firm may face demand that is more elastic than the market demand for the product. How can a firm such as Y.E.S. in Figure 12.2 be approximately a price taker when the market demand curve slopes downward?

12.5 Explain two reasons why historical costs differ from opportunity costs.

12.6 Explain two reasons why accounting statements do not accurately measure economic costs.

LONG-RUN EQUILIBRIUM WITH PERFECT COMPETITION

entry — when a firm begins producing and selling a product

exit — when a firm stops selling a product

free entry or exit — entry or exit opportunities with no legal barriers

In the long run, firms that continually suffer losses go out of business or drop their unprofitable products; they exit the industry that produces those losses. New firms enter an industry to capture potential profits, sometimes replacing other firms that, while they generate profits in the short run, have higher costs and cannot compete profitably in the long run.

> **Entry** into an industry means that a firm begins producing and selling that product; **exit** from an industry means that a firm stops selling that product.

Economic profit or loss, not the accounting measures of profit or loss, guide firms' decisions on entry and exit. The transition from short-run equilibrium to long-run equilibrium is a dynamic process. Many old firms may die and be replaced by new firms with lower costs. This process requires free entry and exit.

> **Free entry** means that no legal barriers prevent a firm from entering an industry. **Free exit** means that no legal barriers prevent a firm from exiting the industry.

Many industries in the United States and other developed countries offer free entry. Laws or government regulations prevent free entry in some industries, however, such as first-class mail delivery, taxi-cab services, and cable television.

When new firms enter an industry, the goods that they produce add to the total quantity supplied and shift the short-run market supply curve to the right as in **Figure 12.3a.** This reduces the equilibrium price from P_1 to P_2, which reduces the profits that all producers earn. Positive economic profits give new firms an incentive to enter, tending to reduce profits. Similarly, when firms exit an indus-

IN THE NEWS

Dental hygienists seek to start practices on their own—raising the ire of dentists

By Rhonda L. Rundle
Staff Reporter of The
Wall Street Journal

Judy Boothby, a dental hygienist in Sacramento, Calif., invested $10,000 in a van and portable equipment so she could make house calls as part of an experimental state project begun earlier this year.

But the van is now parked and locked. By raising questions about the legality of the service, she says, some local dentists are scaring away her clients, many of which are nursing homes.

Mrs. Boothby's venture is mired in a struggle over the proper role of hygienists in

dental care. Besides cleaning teeth, hygienists often take X-rays and give fluoride treatments. They usually work for dentists, but some of them—like Mrs. Boothby—want to go into business for themselves. The idea has dentists gnashing their teeth.

Restrictions sometimes hinder attempts to enter an industry.

Source: Rhonda L. Rundle, "Dental Hygienists Seek to Start Practices on Their Own—Raising the Ire of Dentists," *The Wall Street Journal,* April 24, 1987.

try, the total quantity supplied falls. The short-run market supply curve shifts to the left as in Figure 12.3b, and this raises the equilibrium price from P_1 to P_2, which raises the profits of remaining firms. Negative economic profits give firms an incentive to exit the industry, tending to raise profits.

Entry and exit create a tendency for economic profits to fall when they are positive, and to rise when they are negative. In long-run equilibrium, economic profits are zero.

FIGURE 12.3

EFFECTS OF ENTRY AND EXIT

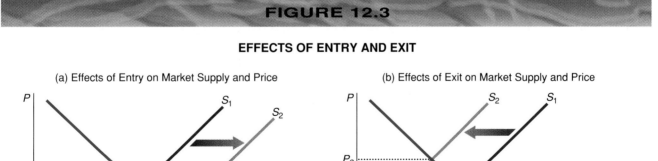

(a) Effects of Entry on Market Supply and Price

(b) Effects of Exit on Market Supply and Price

(a) As new firms enter an industry, short-run market supply increases and the price falls.

(b) As firms exit an industry, short-run market supply decreases and the price rises.

long-run equilibrium — a situation in which entry or exit has adjusted the market until each firm earns zero economic profit

Long-run equilibrium is a situation in which entry or exit has adjusted the market until each firm earns zero economic profit.

Long-run equilibrium with perfect competition requires free entry and exit, because entry and exit are the forces that drive economic profits to zero in the long run.

Why do firms with zero economic profits stay in business? A firm that earns zero economic profit pays its owners their opportunity costs. The owners would not gain by shutting down the firm and doing something else; they cannot do better than to keep the firm in business.

Figure 12.4 shows a long-run equilibrium with perfect competition. Panel d shows the market equilibrium price, $11.00, and the market equilibrium quantity,

FIGURE 12.4

LONG-RUN EQUILIBRIUM WITH PERFECT COMPETITION

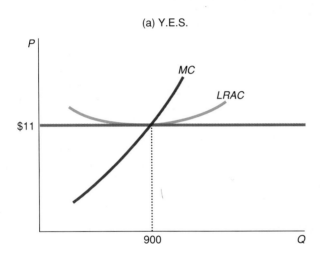

(a) Y.E.S.

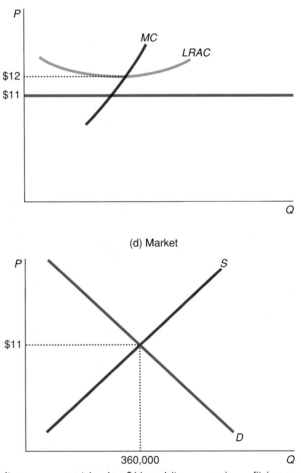

(b) Shruggers

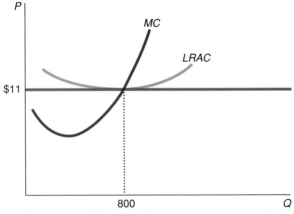

(c) LOUD!

(d) Market

Y.E.S. produces 900 units of the good in long-run equilibrium. Its average cost of $11 equals the price, so Y.E.S. earns zero economic profit. A new firm named LOUD! has entered the industry and produces 800 units in long-run equilibrium.

Its average cost is also $11 and its economic profit is zero. Shruggers has exited the industry because its lowest average cost of $12 exceeds the $11 long-run equilibrium price.

360,000 units per week. Each individual firm faces a perfectly elastic demand curve at the $11.00 equilibrium price, and chooses output to maximize its profit by producing the quantity at which its marginal cost equals the price.

Figure 12.4a shows that Y.E.S. has survived competition and produces 900 units of the good per week in long-run equilibrium. At its average cost of $11.00, it earns zero profit. Its accounting statement might show a positive profit of $2,700 per week (a profit margin of $3 on each of the 900 units it sells), but that $2,700 is accounting profit, not economic profit. Accounting profit is a payment to the firm's owners to cover the opportunity costs of their time, money, and willingness to bear risk. Since Y.E.S. has zero economic profit, it earns a normal (accounting) profit.

normal (accounting) profit — the level of accounting profit required for a zero economic profit

A **normal (accounting) profit** is the level of accounting profit required for a zero economic profit.

A firm earns a normal accounting profit if its economic profit is zero.

Figure 12.4b shows that Shruggers has exited the industry. Shruggers was unprofitable because its average cost exceeded the $11 long-run equilibrium price no matter how much it produced. Less efficient firms like Shruggers (firms with higher costs than their competitors) do not always survive competition in the long run.

Panel c shows a new firm named LOUD! that has entered the industry. LOUD! maximizes profit by producing 800 units per week. Its average cost of $11 gives it an economic profit of zero. LOUD! may report a higher (or lower) accounting profit than Y.E.S. if its accounting statements show lower (or higher) costs, but this means that its implicit costs are higher (or lower) than those at Y.E.S.

Figure 12.5 shows the short-run and long-run cost curves for Y.E.S. In the short-run equilibrium (see Figure 12.2), Y.E.S. produced 600 units per week. Its average cost curve was $SRAC_1$ in Figure 12.5 and its average cost of production was $12. In the long run, Y.E.S. expanded its operation. It built a larger factory,

FIGURE 12.5

Y.E.S. EXPANDS IN THE LONG RUN

Y.E.S. builds a larger factory, shifting its short-run average cost curve from $SRAC_1$ to $SRAC_2$, and reducing its average cost to $11.

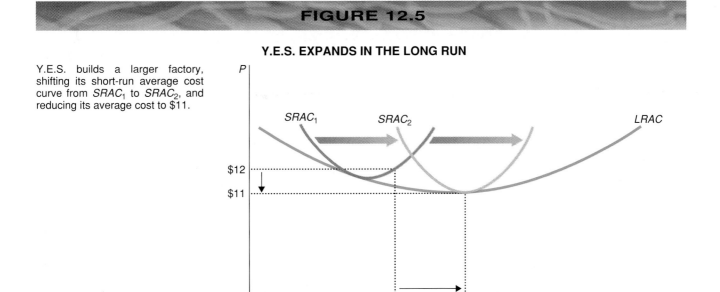

purchased additional machinery and equipment, and hired and trained more workers. This shifted its short-run average cost curve to $SRAC_2$. Y.E.S. had to expand to survive competition because new entry into the industry reduced the price from \$14.50 to \$11.00. In the long run, Y.E.S. produces 900 units per week, which minimizes its long-run average cost at \$11.

Not every firm that suffers a short-run loss (as Shruggers did) exits the industry in the long run. Some firms may have short-run losses because they are too large or too small to reduce their average costs of production enough to earn short-run profits. In the long run, however, these firms can expand by acquiring new machinery and equipment and hiring and training new workers, or they can shrink by selling machinery and equipment and making other changes to reduce costs. **Figure 12.6** shows another firm, Wetlands, that suffered a loss in the short run, but managed to reduce its average cost in the long run by expanding, as Y.E.S. did. Unlike Shruggers, Wetlands was able to reduce its cost enough (to \$11 or less) to stay in business in the long run.

ECONOMIC RENTS

As Figure 12.6 shows, Wetlands reduced its long-run average cost of production below \$11 by producing more efficiently than other firms. In long-run equilibrium, Wetlands produces 1,000 units at an average cost of \$10. In Figure 12.6, Wetlands *appears* to earn a \$1-per-unit economic profit in long-run equilibrium. What makes Wetlands more efficient than other firms? Perhaps its owner-manager motivates workers more effectively than do managers at other firms or organizes the firm more efficiently. Perhaps Wetlands owns some land or equipment that is more efficient than the land or equipment of other firms in a way that other firms cannot duplicate.[4] One of Wetlands' costs of production is a payment for this especially useful input; this payment is part of Wetlands' implicit costs. If, for example, Wetlands does not pay enough to keep this owner-manager, that person will sell her management services to other firms such as Y.E.S., LOUD!, or even Shruggers. So what *appears* to be Wetlands' profit is actually an implicit cost of production, the cost of the special input that enables the firm to produce more efficiently than any other firms. Economists call this implicit cost an *economic rent.*[5]

In long-run equilibrium,

1. No firm can raise its profit by increasing or decreasing its output

2. No firm has an incentive to enter or exit the industry

3. Every firm earns zero economic profit *if we properly count economic rent as one of its costs*[6]

—————————————————— FOR REVIEW ——————————————————

12.7 What happens to the price of a good when new firms enter an industry? Why?

12.8 What is normal accounting profit?

—————————————

[4]Other firms would duplicate this land or equipment (if they could) to reduce their own costs and earn higher profits. If they could, market supply would increase and the price would fall as other firms copied Wetlands to reduce their own marginal costs. In long-run equilibrium, any duplications that can take place have already taken place.

[5]See Chapter 16 for further discussion of economic rent.

[6]When we include economic rent as a cost (as we should), every firm produces at the lowest possible average cost in long-run equilibrium. No firm could reduce its average cost by raising or lowering its output.

FIGURE 12.6

WETLANDS EXPANDS AND ELIMINATES ITS SHORT-RUN LOSS

In the original short-run equilibrium, Wetlands' short-run average cost curve is $SRAC_1$ and its marginal cost curve is MC_1. It produces 200 units in the short run at a price of $14.50. Its average cost is $16.00, so it takes a $1.50 loss on each good it produces. Wetlands expands in the long run so its new short-run average cost curve is $SRAC_2$ and its new marginal cost curve is MC_2. In long-run equilibrium, it produces 1,000 units and it appears to earn a $1 profit. The cost curves in this figure do not include economic rent, though. Including economic rent in Wetlands' costs shows that it earns zero economic profit in long-run equilibrium.

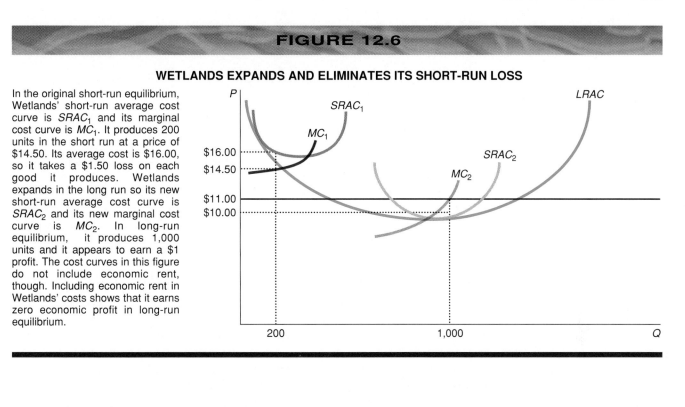

QUESTIONS

12.9 Explain why firms earn zero economic profit in long-run equilibrium with perfect competition. Why does a firm with zero economic profit stay in business?

12.10 Explain why economic rent is an implicit cost.-

LONG-RUN SUPPLY CURVES

Figures 12.7 and 12.8 show two possible shapes for long-run market supply curves: perfectly elastic curves or rising curves.

PERFECTLY ELASTIC LONG-RUN SUPPLY

The long-run supply curve is perfectly elastic, as in **Figure 12.7,** if many firms have the same cost of producing the good in the long run and their costs do not depend on the total output of the industry. In this situation, an increase in demand raises the number of firms in the industry, but does not change the price or the quantity that each firm produces.

EXAMPLE

Suppose that many firms can produce flashlights at an average cost of $3 each if they produce 10,000 flashlights per month, so that many firms have the long-run average cost curve in Figure 12.7. Even though each firm has an upward-sloping supply (marginal cost) curve, as shows the figure, the long-run market supply of flashlights is perfectly elastic at the price $3. If the price is higher than $3, flashlight producers earn positive economic profits and new firms enter the flashlight

FIGURE 12.7

PERFECTLY ELASTIC LONG-RUN MARKET SUPPLY: A CONSTANT-COST INDUSTRY

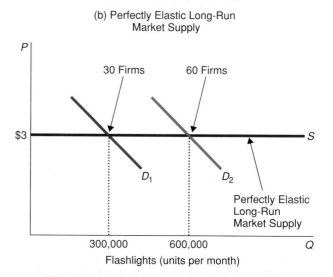

(a) Long-Run Average and Marginal Cost
for Each Firm in the Industry

(b) Perfectly Elastic Long-Run
Market Supply

Many firms have the long-run average and marginal cost curves shown above. In long-run equilibrium, the price is $3 per flashlight and each firm earns zero economic profit by producing 10,000 flashlights per month. Even though each firm has an upward-sloping supply (marginal cost) curve, the long-run market supply of flashlights is perfectly elastic at the price $3. The number of firms in the industry depends on demand. If demand is D_1, the industry includes 30 firms in long-run equilibrium. If demand is D_2, the industry includes 60 firms.

industry. This new entry raises the quantity supplied and reduces the price back to $3 in long-run equilibrium. If the price is lower than $3, losses lead some firms to exit the industry, which reduces the quantity supplied and raises the price back to $3. In long-run equilibrium, each firm produces 10,000 flashlights per month and the number of firms in the industry depends on demand. If the demand curve is D_1, with a quantity demanded at the $3 equilibrium price of 300,000 flashlights per month, then in long-run equilibrium the industry includes 30 firms. If the demand curve is D_2, with a quantity demanded at the $3 price of 600,000 units per month, then the industry includes 60 firms. Entry and exit keep the long-run supply curve perfectly elastic. Industries like this are called *constant-cost industries.*

constant-cost industry — an industry with a perfectly elastic long-run supply curve

A **constant-cost industry** is an industry with a perfectly elastic long-run supply curve.

RISING LONG-RUN SUPPLY

In an increasing-cost industry, the long-run market supply curve slopes upward, as in **Figure 12.8.** An industry may have increasing costs for two reasons. First, each firm's average cost may depend on total output in the industry. Every ocean-front hotel requires ocean-front property as an input, but only a fixed quantity of ocean-front property is available. As more firms enter the ocean-front hotel industry, the demand for ocean-front land rises, which drives up its price. This raises the cost of producing an ocean-front hotel. Since the average cost of producing

FIGURE 12.8

UPWARD-SLOPING LONG-RUN MARKET SUPPLY: AN INCREASING-COST INDUSTRY

In an increasing-cost industry, the long-run market supply slopes upward. In long-run equilibrium, the number of firms depends on demand. If the demand curve is D_1, the industry includes 20 firms. If the demand curve is D_2, it includes 35 firms.

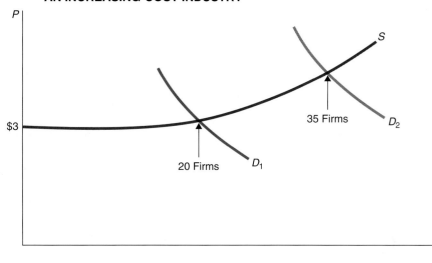

an ocean-front hotel rises with total output, the long-run market supply curve slopes upward. The equilibrium number of firms in an increasing-cost industry depends on demand. If the demand curve is D_1, in Figure 12.8, the industry includes 20 firms in long-run equilibrium. If the demand curve is D_2, the industry includes 35 firms.

increasing-cost industry — an industry with an upward-sloping long-run market supply curve

> An **increasing-cost industry** is an industry with an upward-sloping long-run market supply curve.

The second reason for increasing costs is that some firms may operate more efficiently than others. In **Figure 12.9a,** some firms can produce flashlights at an average cost of $3.00 each if they produce 10,000 flashlights per month. Suppose that only a few firms have costs this low, while other firms have higher costs; the firm in Panel b has an average cost of $3.25 (minimized by producing 9,000 flashlights per month), and the firm in Panel c has an average cost of $3.50 (minimized by producing 11,000 per month). As total industry output expands, the new firms that enter the industry operate less efficiently, so they have higher average costs. In this case, the long-run supply curve slopes upward and the inputs that make some firms more efficient than others earn economic rents in long-run equilibrium.

GOING FROM THE SHORT RUN TO THE LONG RUN

FALL IN DEMAND

If an industry has constant costs, its long-run supply curve is perfectly elastic, so a fall in demand reduces the quantity, but not the price. If each firm has a U-shaped average cost curve, as in Figure 12.7, the long-run fall in quantity results entirely from a fall in the number of firms in the industry, without any change in output

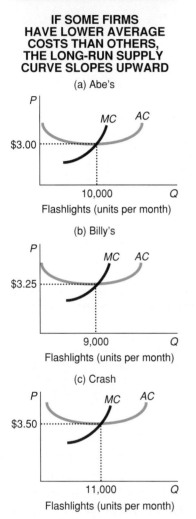

FIGURE 12.9

IF SOME FIRMS HAVE LOWER AVERAGE COSTS THAN OTHERS, THE LONG-RUN SUPPLY CURVE SLOPES UPWARD

(a) Abe's

Flashlights (units per month)

(b) Billy's

Flashlights (units per month)

(c) Crash

Flashlights (units per month)

If the equilibrium price is $3.00, only firms like Abe's are in the industry. If the price is $3.25, firms like Billy's are also in the industry, and some inputs at firms like Abe's earn economic rents. If the equilibrium price is $3.50, firms like Crash also enter the industry and certain inputs at firms like Abe's and Billy's earn economic rents.

per firm. Each firm continues to produce the quantity at the lowest point on its long-run average cost curve.

If the industry has increasing costs, then a fall in demand reduces both the quantity and the price. In the long run, the fall in quantity results from both a fall in the number of firms in the industry and a fall in output per firm. **Figure 12.10** shows the effect of a fall in demand in an increasing-cost industry. In the short run, the price falls from $10 to $6 and all firms reduce output (Point B). Some firms, those whose average variable costs exceed $6, shut down immediately. Other firms may continue to produce, but suffer losses. The most efficient firms, those that earned economic rents to certain inputs that made them more efficient, may earn less economic rent on those inputs, but continue to earn zero economic profits. In the long run, more firms go out of business and equilibrium moves to Point C. The quantity supplied falls, and the price rises from $6 to $8. This helps some of the firms that suffered losses in the short run (at the $6 price) to earn zero economic profits in the long run at the $8 price. Firms that go out of business are those that would suffer losses even at a price of $8, that is, the firms whose lowest average costs exceed $8 in the long run. Firms that stay in business are the more efficient ones that can earn zero economic profits at a price of $8, that is, firms whose lowest average costs are less than or equal to $8 in the long run.

LIFE CYCLE OF AN INDUSTRY

Some industries change in a sequence like the one shown in **Figure 12.11.**

1. Technical change allows firms to produce a new product or an existing product at a lower cost as in Figure 12.11a. Average cost and marginal cost both fall.

2. The fall in marginal cost means an increase in supply, which lowers the equilibrium price and raises the equilibrium quantity, as in Panel b.

3. Firms in the industry earn short-run profits, as in Panel c, which shows a profit of $1 per unit.

4. Profits lure new firms into the industry, further reducing the price and increasing the quantity, as in Panel d.

5. In some industries, Panel d may show the new long-run equilibrium. In other industries, however, demand eventually falls, as in Panel e. Sometimes, as for durable goods like video recorders (VCRs) or compact disc (CD) players, demand soars as people buy goods for the first time. Once many people own VCRs or CD players, however, demand falls. Some people buy newer models, or they buy new VCRs to replace old ones that break, but total demand may decline as the market becomes saturated with the good. In either case, the fall in demand in Panel e lowers the price, causing producers to suffer losses.

6. Losses caused by the fall in demand reduce the number of firms in the industry, as in Panel f. As firms exit the industry, the fall in short-run market supply raises the price until losses disappear and firms earn zero economic profits in the new long-run equilibrium (Panels f and g). Panel f shows market supply and demand, and Panel g shows costs and demand for a typical price-taking firm in the new equilibrium.

The producers of hard-disk drives for computers experienced some of these changes. This industry developed between the mid-1950s and the mid-1980s. Technical change reduced costs enormously during this period, and the potential for profits attracted more than 138 firms to enter the industry. Industry capacity

FIGURE 12.10

EFFECTS OF A FALL IN DEMAND

The fall in demand moves the equilibrium from Point A to Point B in the short run and to Point C in the long run.

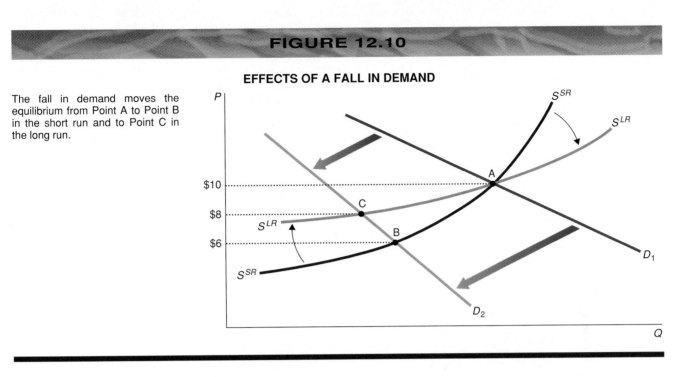

expanded much more quickly than demand, prices fell enough to create losses at the less efficient firms, and eventually 103 of those 138 firms exited the industry.

─────────────── **FOR REVIEW** ───────────────

12.11 What is a constant-cost industry? What is an increasing-cost industry?

─────────────── **QUESTIONS** ───────────────

12.12 Explain how a fall in demand affects the price, total output, and number of firms in an increasing-cost industry.

12.13 Suppose that technical change reduces costs of production, as in Figure 12.11a. Explain how this may affect the equilibrium price and quantity traded in the short run and in the long run.

WHAT IS PERFECT ABOUT PERFECT COMPETITION?[7]

The equilibrium quantity with perfect competition is economically efficient (that is, any other quantity creates a deadweight social loss) under certain conditions. The most important condition is that there are no externalities. This means that the producer of a good pays *all* the costs of producing it and the people who buy the good receive *all* of its benefits. Externalities might include, for example, a steel manufacturer polluting the air; this would force people who suffered harm from the pollution to pay part of the cost of producing steel. (They would not pay a money price, but rather a price measured in unpleasantness or ill health.) Similarly, externalities can emerge when a pharmaceutical company discovers a

───────────────

[7]This section requires the first section of Chapter 11, "Gains from Trade," as background.

FIGURE 12.11

LIFE CYCLE OF AN INDUSTRY

(a)

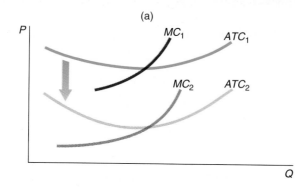

(b)

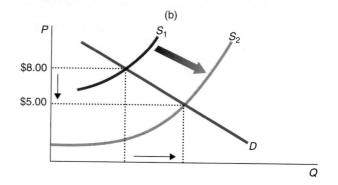

(c)

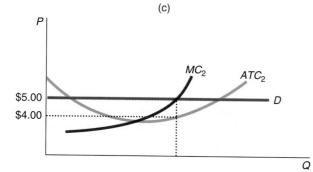

(d)

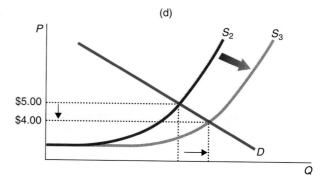

(e)

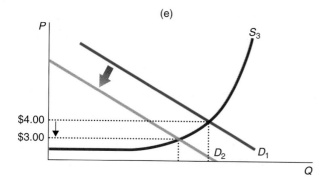

(f)

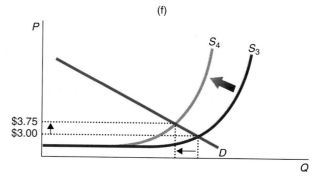

(g)

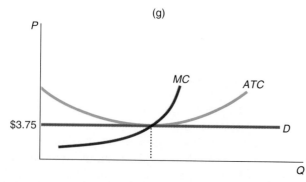

A technical improvement reduces costs (a) and increases supply (b). Profits (c) lead new firms to enter the industry (d). If demand later falls (e), losses eventually cause firms to exit the industry, reducing supply and raising the price (f) until each firm earns zero economic profit (g).

The drop in demand and price has taken a severe toll throughout the industry. Ranchers have slashed cattle herds to 105 million head from 132 million in 1975. Heavy losses have caused tens of thousands of ranchers to abandon cattle raising altogether, devastating rural communities from Texas to North Dakota. Even now, with the market firming a bit, many ranchers are just breaking even.

The number of slaughterhouses has plummeted, too, by 35 percent in a decade. In meatpacking, the number of employees has fallen to 148,500, from 168,000 in 1975. Labor-management relations remain tense as the packers push for wage concessions as a buffer against weak demand. Despite union resistance—epitomized by the protracted Hormel strike in Austin, Minn.—labor has taken a beating, with packing wages down to $8.50 or less an hour in many houses, from about $10.50.

A fall in demand causes losses that lead some firms to exit the industry.

Source: New York Times, September 28, 1986.

new medicine; the people who buy that medicine are not its only beneficiaries because the discovery creates knowledge that may help other scientists to solve their own problems, leading to new discoveries.

Chapter 20 discusses externalities in greater detail; the remaining discussion in this section applies to situations without externalities. For example, the insurance and textile industries probably include no externalities. Insurers and clothing manufacturers pay all costs of producing insurance policies and clothing, and buyers receive all the benefits. In cases like these (with a few technical conditions that fall outside the scope of this book), equilibrium with perfect competition is economically efficient.

Equilibrium may seem obviously economically efficient whenever people trade voluntarily. After all, if a situation is not economically efficient, there are potentially Pareto-improving changes that can be made in that situation. People could get together and find some way to trade so that some would gain and no one would lose. People would voluntarily do this, so you might think that voluntary trading always creates an economically efficient situation.

In fact, things are not quite this simple. For example, many small retail stores have gone out of business in recent years because they could not compete with Wal-Mart and various wholesale clubs. The voluntary trades between Wal-Mart and its customers suggest that each side expects to gain. How do we know that the gains to Wal-Mart and its customers exceed the losses to the small stores that went out of business? Remarkably, perfect competition leads to an economically efficient equilibrium. Perfect competition among sellers for customers creates losers, but their losses are always smaller than the gains to successful sellers and to buyers.[8]

Equilibrium with perfect competition is economically efficient because it equates the marginal benefit of a good to the economy with its marginal cost. Each equals the good's price. The economy faces tradeoffs between producing food and cars, health care and video games, education and houses. People also face tradeoffs between buying these goods; they can spend more money on food and less on cars, or vice versa.

> In equilibrium with perfect competition, the economy makes the tradeoffs that consumers want to make, as revealed by their willingness to pay for various goods.

Figure 12.12 shows the economy's tradeoff between producing T-shirts and hamburgers. This is the economy's production possibilities frontier for these goods, as discussed in the Chapter 3 Appendix. This curve forms a sort of budget constraint for the economy. The economy can produce any combination of goods on the curve, such as 40 million T-shirts and 600 million hamburgers per month (Point A) or 90 million T-shirts and 300 million hamburgers per month (Point B). The economy cannot produce combinations of goods such as Point C because it does not have enough inputs (with current technology) to produce this much. Points on the curve (such as Points A and B) are technically efficient combinations of production of hamburgers and T-shirts. Points below the curve, such as Point D, are technically inefficient levels of production; the economy could make more hamburgers without sacrificing any T-shirts or more T-shirts without sacrificing any hamburgers.

---

[9] The proof of this fact is actually a deep mathematical theorem that far exceeds the scope of this book. Chapter 13 and 14 will discuss conditions of competition in which outcomes are not economically efficient

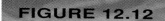

FIGURE 12.12

PERFECT COMPETITION IS ECONOMICALLY EFFICIENT

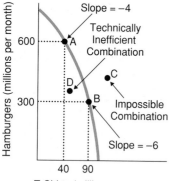

The economy's production possibilities frontier shows possible combinations of output. In equilibrium with perfect competition, the economy produces the combination that consumers prefer most.

The absolute value of the slope of this curve shows the economy's tradeoff between producing T-shirts and hamburgers. It shows the economy's opportunity cost of producing T-shirts, measured in terms of hamburgers. If the economy produces the combination of goods at Point A, the production tradeoff is 4 hamburgers per T-shirt; it can produce 1 additional T-shirt per month by producing 4 fewer hamburgers. If, on the other hand, the economy produces the combination of goods at Point B, the production tradeoff is 6 hamburgers per T-shirt; if the economy produces 6 fewer hamburgers, it can produce 1 more T-shirt.

The production tradeoff between T-shirts and hamburgers is the marginal cost of producing T-shirts, measured in numbers of hamburgers. Perfect competition leads firms to produce quantities that set a good's marginal cost equal to its price, so producers choose Point A if the relative price of T-shirts is 4 hamburgers per T-shirt, and they choose Point B if the relative price is 6 hamburgers per T-shirt.

Suppose that consumers prefer the combination of hamburgers and T-shirts shown by Point A to all other possible combinations. This makes Point A the single, economically efficient point. It is also the equilibrium with perfect competition. At Point A, the tradeoff between production of T-shirts and hamburgers is exactly the tradeoff that consumers want to make. In contrast, at Point B (or any other point on the curve) consumers' and producers' tradeoffs differ. At Point B, the producers' tradeoff (6 hamburgers for 1 T-shirt) is higher than the tradeoff that consumers want to make. Buyers may be willing to sacrifice up to 4 hamburgers for 1 T-shirt, but at Point B the economy sacrifices 6 hamburgers for each T-shirt it produces. At Point B, the economy would produce too many T-shirts and too few hamburgers. Similarly, at a point on the curve above Point A, the economy would produce too few T-shirts and too many hamburgers.

The prices that consumers are willing to pay provide information to producers about the tradeoffs that consumers want to make. At Point A in Figure 12.12, the relative price of T-shirts equals the rate at which buyers are willing to trade off hamburgers for T-shirts. Firms choose levels of output at which the relative price of T-shirts equals the marginal cost of producing them. Relative prices guarantee that the economy makes the production tradeoffs that consumers want.

In equilibrium with perfect competition:

▶ The relative price of each good equals the tradeoff that consumers are willing to make to buy that good.

▶ The relative price of each good also equals the tradeoff in production, that is, the marginal cost of producing the good, measured in terms of other goods.

▶ The tradeoff that consumers want to make equals the tradeoff that the economy can make to produce the goods.

This discussion raises an important question: Why is the tradeoff that consumers are *willing* to make equal to the tradeoff that the economy *can* make? To answer this question, suppose that these tradeoffs are *not equal.* This situation is not economically efficient because it allows a potentially Pareto-improving change. For example, suppose that people are willing to trade 1 T-shirt for 4 hamburgers, but the economy's actual tradeoff in production is 1 T-shirt for 6 hamburgers, as at Point B in Figure 12.12. What potentially Pareto-improving change could the economy make? It would be potentially Pareto improving to change the quantities of production so that the economy produces 6 more hamburgers and 1 less T-shirt. Consumers would give up that T-shirt in return for 4 hamburgers, so they would be no better off and no worse off if they were to receive 1 less T-shirt and 4 more hamburgers. This leaves 2 extra hamburgers, so someone can gain from the change without hurting anyone else. Whenever the tradeoff that the economy *can* make does not equal the tradeoff that consumers *want* to make, there are potentially Pareto-improving changes that could be made in the economy. Equilibrium with perfect competition is economically efficient because it sets these two tradeoffs equal to each other.

The economic efficiency of equilibrium under perfect competition is a formal statement of the proposition advanced by Adam Smith in 1776 in *The Wealth of Nations* that competition and voluntary exchange in free markets automatically coordinate people's activities to promote general welfare:

> Every individual . . . neither intends to promote the general interest, nor knows how much he is promoting it. He intends only his own security, his own gain. And he is in this led by an invisible hand to promote an end which was no part of his intention. By pursuing his own interest he frequently promotes that of society more effectually than when he really intends to promote it.[9]

Economists in the 20th century have proved a very strong version of Smith's *invisible hand* proposition: not only do people "frequently promote" the interests of society when they pursue their own gain through trade in free markets, but (under certain conditions) perfect competition leads to an equilibrium in which no potentially Pareto-improving change is possible—an economically efficient equilibrium.

─────────────── **FOR REVIEW** ───────────────

12.14 How does Figure 12.12 show the economy's opportunity cost of producing T-shirts?

12.15 What was the name of Adam Smith's famous book? What did Smith say about the idea that an equilibrium is economically efficient?

─────────────── **QUESTIONS** ───────────────

12.16 Explain why equilibrium with perfect competition equates the tradeoff that consumers want to make between any two goods and the tradeoff that the economy can make in producing those goods.

12.17 Explain why equilibrium with perfect competition is economically efficient.

CONCLUSIONS

PRICE TAKERS
Price-taking firms, those that face perfectly elastic demand curves for their output, have marginal revenue equal to the price. The supply curves of these firms are the portions of their marginal cost curves above their average variable cost curves. A firm that produces a small fraction of total industry output, when consumers do not care which firm produces the good, is approximately a price taker.

PERFECT COMPETITION
Perfect competition is competition between price-taking firms. Short-run equilibrium with perfect competition refers to equilibrium with a fixed number of firms in the industry. Long-run equilibrium with perfect competition refers to equilibrium when the number of firms can change. In short-run equilibrium, some firms

---

[9]Adam Smith, *The Wealth of Nations* (Chicago: University of Chicago Press, 1976), pp. 477–478.

may have lower costs and higher profits than other firms. Costs differ across firms for many reasons. One reason is that some firms have better entrepreneurial abilities than others. Entrepreneurs are people who conceive and act on a new business idea, taking the risk that it will succeed or fail.

ECONOMIC COSTS AND ACCOUNTING MEASURES

The cost of any decision or action is its opportunity cost. Accounting measures of cost do not necessarily measure true economic costs accurately for two reasons: (1) they measure the costs of inventories and inputs such as capital equipment at their historical costs, rather than their current opportunity costs, and (2) accounting measures do not include implicit costs, costs that are solely opportunity costs that require no direct payments. A firm's most important implicit costs are the opportunity costs to the firm's owners of providing money to buy the firm's capital goods, generating and implementing new ideas, and taking risks.

Economic costs (the sum of all explicit and implicit costs) are the correct measures of costs for a firm's decisions. Because accounting measures of cost do not equal economic costs, accounting measures of profit do not equal economic profits (total revenue minus total economic costs).

LONG-RUN EQUILIBRIUM WITH PERFECT COMPETITION

Firms with negative economic profits (losses) eventually exit an industry. Long-run equilibrium with perfect competition occurs after unprofitable firms have left an industry and new firms have had the opportunity to enter. Entry and exit create a tendency for positive economic profits to fall or for negative economic profits to rise. In long-run equilibrium, economic profits are zero. Firms earn a normal accounting profit, that is, the accounting profit that reflects a zero economic profit.

In long-run equilibrium, some firms have some special resources (such as particularly good entrepreneurs or plots of land) that keep their average costs below other firms' costs. These special resources earn economic rents, which are profits that some firms earn in long-run equilibrium because their inputs enable them to produce more efficiently than other firms. In long-run equilibrium, no firm can raise its profit by increasing or decreasing its output, no firm has an incentive to enter or exit the industry, and every firm earns zero economic profit, counting economic rent as a cost.

LONG-RUN SUPPLY CURVES

A constant-cost industry is an industry with a perfectly elastic long-run supply curve. Each firm in an industry may have an upward-sloping supply curve, but the industry supply curve is perfectly elastic if all firms have the same average cost curve and each firm's average cost does not depend on total industry output. Total output in a constant-cost industry rises or falls with changes in the number of firms, each of which produces the quantity that minimizes its average cost. If firms do not have the same average cost curve or each firm's average cost depends on total industry output, then the long-run supply curve may slope upward and the industry has increasing costs.

GOING FROM THE SHORT RUN TO THE LONG RUN

In the long run, a fall in demand in a constant-cost industry reduces output and the number of firms in the industry without changing the price or output at each firm. In the short run, the price may fall and firms may incur losses, leading some firms to exit the industry. A fall in demand in an increasing-cost industry reduces the price, which reduces economic rent at some firms, creates losses at other firms, and leads some firms to exit the industry. In the long run, output falls through a combination of a smaller number of firms in the industry and a fall in output per firm. More efficient (lower-cost) firms survive, while higher-cost firms exit.

Some industries go through predictable life cycles in which costs of production fall, raising output, lowering the price, and attracting new firms to enter the industry. The new entries further raise supply and reduce the price. Demand eventually falls, reducing the price and creating losses at some firms. Some unprofitable firms exit the industry, reducing (short-run) market supply and raising the price until losses disappear and firms earn zero economic profits in the new long-run equilibrium.

WHAT IS PERFECT ABOUT PERFECT COMPETITION?

Under certain conditions, the equilibrium quantity with perfect competition (and *only* that quantity) is economically efficient. The most important condition requires an absence of externalities, which means that the producer of a good pays all costs of production and buyers receive all its benefits. (See Chapter 20.) Equilibrium with perfect competition is economically efficient because it equates the marginal benefit of a good to the economy with its marginal cost; each equals the price. This means that the economy makes the production tradeoffs that consumers want to make, as revealed by their willingness to pay. In equilibrium with perfect competition, the relative price of each good equals both the tradeoff that consumers are willing to make when they buy the good and the marginal cost of producing the good. Whenever the tradeoff the economy can make differs from the tradeoff that consumers want to make, the situation is economically inefficient. Equilibrium with perfect competition is economically efficient because it equates these two tradeoffs.

LOOKING AHEAD

This chapter discussed competition between price-taking firms. The next three chapters discuss competition among firms that are not price takers. Chapter 13 begins with the extreme case of monopolies, then Chapters 14 and 15 discuss intermediate situations and the strategies by which such firms compete for customers.

KEY TERMS

perfect competition	implicit rental price
short-run equilibrium	depreciation
long-run equilibrium	implicit cost
markup (or profit margin)	explicit cost
entrepreneur	economic costs
historical cost	economic profit
inventories	accounting profit
capital good	entry

exit

free entry or exit

long-run equilibrium

normal (accounting) profit

constant-cost industry

increasing-cost industry

QUESTIONS AND PROBLEMS

12.18 Suppose that the elasticity of market demand for computers is -1 and Cool Technologies produces 1 of every 1,000 computers. Cool Technologies then doubles its output of computers (a 67 percent increase in its output), which raises industry output by about 0.1 percent. Assume that all computers are alike, regardless of who produces them.
  a. By what percentage will the price of computers fall?
  b. What is the elasticity of demand for computers produced by Cool Technologies?

12.19 Suppose that new firms enter a perfectly competitive industry. Draw a graph to show the effects on the market supply curve, the price, the demand curve facing each firm, and the output of a typical firm. Repeat for a situation in which firms exit an industry.

12.20 Discuss two reasons why an industry can have increasing costs.

12.21 What are a firm's economic costs of these actions?
  a. Holding inventories
  b. Owning a machine
  c. Taking a risk by producing a new product that might succeed or fail

12.22 Draw a graph to help discuss the short-run and long-run effects on the price, total industry output, and the number of firms in the industry of:
  a. An increase in demand in a constant-cost industry
  b. An increase in demand in an increasing-cost industry

12.23 Suppose that the government forces all firms that were in an industry at the beginning of the current year to pay a one-time, $10,000 fine. How does this fine affect industry output, the price, and the number of firms? Explain.

INQUIRIES FOR FURTHER THOUGHT

12.24 In which of the following industries do you think sellers are approximately price takers? Why?
  a. Aspirin and other pain relievers
  b. Ice
  c. Valentine cards
  d. Gasoline
  e. Donuts
  f. Movies
  g. Jeans
  h. Antiques
  i. Videotape rentals
  j. Houses
  k. Auto repair
  l. Candy
  m. Breakfast cereals

12.25 The government restricts entry into some industries, sometimes by laws and regulations that directly prevent entry and other times by requiring sellers to pay certain costs (such as license fees) to enter.
  a. How do restrictions on entry into an industry affect the price, total output of the good, and output per firm?
  b. What would be the effects of restricting entry into the fast-food industry?
  c. What would be the effects of removing restrictions on entry into the prescription-drug dispensing industry?

IN THE NEWS

Doctors stir controversy by selling drugs directly to their patients . . .

By Rhonda L. Rundle
Staff Reporter of The
Wall Street Journal

The $20-billion market in prescription-drug sales has some new players, a group of competitors that pharmacists are finding impossible to ignore.

Although the practice is still unusual, increasing numbers of doctors are selling drugs directly to patients.

The trend alarms many pharmacists.

Benefits for Patients
For patients, the change appears to offer several immediate benefits. Buying drugs from a doctor might mean fewer trips to the pharmacy and less standing in line for prescriptions. Patients might also save money.

Arguments about doctors dispensing drugs are usually couched in terms of patient care, but there is no doubt that the economic stakes are high. At some walk-in care centers with large staffs of doctors, annual profits from drug sales can run into six figures.

See Question 12.25.

Source: Rhonda L. Rundle, "Doctors Stir Controversy by Selling Drugs Directly to Their Patients," *The Wall Street Journal,* September 29, 1988, p. 45.

TAG SOFTWARE APPLICATIONS

TUTORIAL EXERCISES
▶ The module contains a review of the key terms from Chapter 12.

GRAPHING EXERCISES
▶ The graphing section contains questions on profit maximization, increasing-cost industries, and responses to technological change.

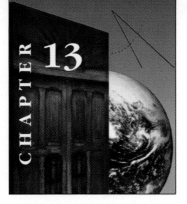

CHAPTER 13

MONOPOLY

WHAT THIS CHAPTER IS ABOUT

▶ Why a firm can profit by reducing its output and sales

▶ How sellers other than price takers choose their prices

▶ How sellers collude to raise prices and why this collusion often fails

▶ Why some sellers profit by charging different prices to different customers

▶ Why monopolies create economic inefficiency

Monopoly. The word connotes power and its abuse, a failure of competition, rich corporations exploiting workers and buyers. Many years ago, the U.S. government passed laws to tame monopolies, limit their powers, or break them up into smaller firms. What are monopolies and what do they do? What logic drives their behavior?

INTRODUCTION TO MONOPOLIES

monopoly — a firm that faces a downward-sloping demand curve for its product and makes decisions without considering the reactions of other firms

Loosely, a monopoly is the only seller of some product. More precisely:

> A firm is a **monopoly** if (a) it faces a downward-sloping demand curve for its product, and (b) it makes decisions without considering the reactions of other firms, perhaps because the effects of those reactions are small.

The first condition means that a monopoly is not a price taker; it can raise its price without losing all its customers, and it must reduce its price to sell more. The second condition means that the monopoly can ignore the possibility that its decisions will cause some other firm that sells a similar product to change its price in a way that shifts the demand curve facing the monopoly firm. (See Chapters 14 and 15 for further discussion of this point.)

EXAMPLES

The post office and most local telephone, gas, electric, and water companies are approximately monopolies. Dolby has a near monopoly on its noise-reduction system for tapes and movies. Other firms have had monopolies on products they invented such as aluminum foil, photocopying machines, and various medications.

KEY EXAMPLE

Loretta catches fish and sells them on a street corner in town. Today she has eight fish to sell, and she is the only person in town who sells fish. **Figure 13.1** shows the

FIGURE 13.1

LORETTA'S DEMAND AND MARGINAL REVENUE

Loretta maximizes revenue by selling five fish at $4 each. Since her marginal cost is zero, this is the quantity at which marginal revenue equals marginal cost.

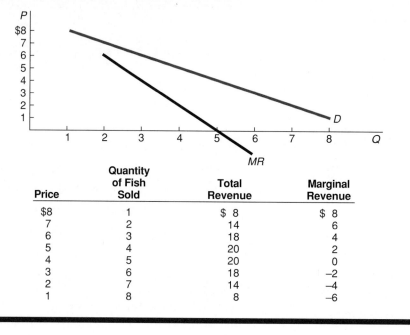

Price	Quantity of Fish Sold	Total Revenue	Marginal Revenue
$8	1	$ 8	$ 8
7	2	14	6
6	3	18	4
5	4	20	2
4	5	20	0
3	6	18	−2
2	7	14	−4
1	8	8	−6

IN THE NEWS

In free rein of cable TV, fees are up

Moreover, most areas that have cable television are served by only one company, so there is no direct competition to restrain prices.

'Pricing Like Monopolies'
"In a monopoly situation, they are pricing like monopolies," said Nicholas Miller, a partner in the law firm of Miller, Young & Holbrook, which represents many municipalities on cable issues.

Most local cable television companies are monopolies.

Source: "In Free Rein of Cable TV, Fees Are Up," *New York Times,* December 11, 1988, p. 1.

demand curve for her fish. She can sell all eight fish if she charges $1 per fish, seven fish if she charges $2 per fish, and so on. If she charges $8, she sells only one fish.

Does Loretta maximize her profit by selling all eight fish? Figure 13.1 shows that selling all eight fish at a price of $1 gives her total revenue of only $8. In contrast, she earns total revenue of $20 by charging $4 or $5 per fish, in which case people buy only five or four of her eight fish. She is actually better off throwing out the other fish than selling them.

Since she has *already* caught the fish, Loretta's marginal cost is *zero* (ignoring the time she spends on the street corner). The time she spent at the lake catching the fish is now a *sunk cost* that does not affect her rational choice about how many fish to sell today, though it will affect her choice of how many fish to catch tomorrow, as a later discussion will explain. Figure 13.1 also shows Loretta's marginal revenue. She maximizes profit by choosing the quantity (five fish) at which her marginal revenue equals her marginal cost (zero).

Loretta sells one fish if she charges $8 each and two fish if she charges $7 each. Why is her marginal revenue of selling the second fish only $6? The answer is important: *to sell to another customer, a seller usually must lower the price to* ALL *customers.* If Loretta charges $8, one customer buys a fish. To sell two fish, she must reduce the price to $7. She then gains $7 by selling the second fish, but loses $1 that she could have earned on the first fish (because she charges only $7 instead of $8). Therefore, her marginal revenue from selling the second fish, only $6, is less than the $7 price.

The same argument applies to larger quantities. To sell three fish, Loretta must charge only $6, so she gains $6 from the sale of the third fish but loses $2

FIGURE 13.2

WHY MARGINAL REVENUE IS LESS THAN PRICE

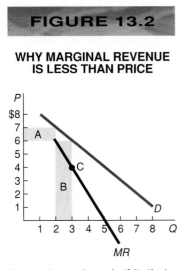

Loretta loses Area A ($2) if she reduces the price from $7 to $6 to sell a third fish, but her revenue rises by Area B ($6). The $2 loss and $6 gain mean that the marginal revenue of selling three fish is $4 (Point C).

because she sells the first two fish for only $6 each rather than $7 each. Therefore, her marginal revenue is only $4, less than the $6 price. **Figure 13.2** shows how selling another unit causes both an increase in revenue equal to the price and a loss in revenue from lowering the price to buyers who would other-wise have paid more. Loretta earns a higher profit by charging $4, selling five fish, and throwing out three fish, than by selling all her fish because if she sold more than five, she would have to lower the price and earn a lower profit on the first five fish.

What if Loretta could charge different prices to different customers? She might charge $4 and sell five fish to the customers who would pay that much, and *then* reduce the price so that *other* customers would buy her other fish. Instead of throwing out the last three fish, she could sell them for $1 each and raise her profit by $3. If she were to try this, however, her customers might wait until she reduced the price before buying their fish, so she might not sell any fish at the $4 price. *Most of this chapter will assume that she must charge the same price to all of her customers.*[1] In this case, she maximizes profit by selling five fish and throwing out the other three.

Throwing away fish is wasteful. It creates a deadweight social loss (a loss to the economy) of three fish. Some buyer would be willing to pay $3 for one of those fish. (Loretta could sell an additional fish by reducing the price to $3.) Another buyer would be willing to pay $2 for one of those wasted fish, and a third buyer would pay $1 for the last fish. The prices that people are willing to pay mea-sure the values that they place on these fish. Since the three fish that Loretta

FIGURE 13.3

DEADWEIGHT SOCIAL LOSS BECAUSE LORETTA SELLS ONLY FIVE FISH

The deadweight social loss is $6 ($3 + $2 + $1).

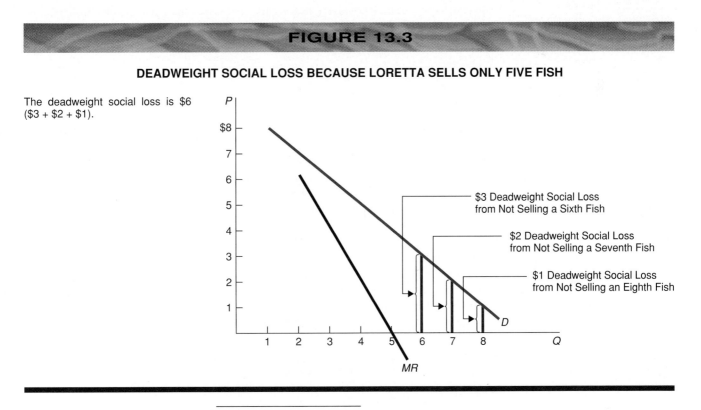

throws out are worth $3, $2, and $1 to buyers, the value of the deadweight social loss is $6. **Figure 13.3** shows the deadweight social loss graphically.

Price takers would never throw away fish. They would sell all their fish because they would not have to reduce the price to sell more. Sellers who face downward-sloping demand curves for their goods can sell more, however, only by reducing the price. If reducing the price would reduce their profits, they don't reduce the price. Instead, they choose to sell less.

If Loretta catches fish regularly, she will choose to catch fewer than eight fish rather than catching them and throwing them out—she will reduce her output. Even if catching fish is costless, she maximizes her profit by catching and selling only five fish per day. This causes a $6 deadweight social loss because people would like to have three more fish, and they would be willing to pay $6 in total for those fish ($3 for the first one, $2 for another, and $1 for the last), but Loretta doesn't provide them.

This situation seems peculiar. Catching fish is costless, and some people would like to buy more fish, but the only seller in town declines to provide them. Why doesn't someone else compete with Loretta by catching fish and selling them to these potential buyers? Another seller could sell two fish for $2 each and earn $4. If other sellers enter the business, then Loretta will lose her monopoly on selling fish in the town. She can maintain her monopoly only if some barriers to entry stop potential competitors. Such barriers might take several forms:

▶ Perhaps no one else can legally sell fish in the town.

▶ Perhaps Loretta owns the only nearby stream with fish, and the town has no other source of fresh fish.

▶ Perhaps Loretta's costs of catching fish are lower than anyone else's costs. If no one else can profit by selling fish for $5 or less, no other sellers will enter the business.

You should look for features from this example in the general discussion below.

SHORT-RUN EQUILIBRIUM WITH A MONOPOLY

A monopoly faces a downward-sloping demand curve, as in **Figure 13.4.** If it charges the price P_1, it can sell the quantity Q_1; if it charges P_2, it can sell Q_2, and so on. A monopoly chooses which price to charge, recognizing that its choice affects the quantity that it sells. A monopoly has no supply curve.[2] It chooses the price–quantity combination along its demand curve (such as Point A, B, or C in Figure 13.4) that maximizes its profit.

A monopoly maximizes its profit by choosing its quantity so that its *marginal cost* equals its *marginal revenue,* and selling that quantity for the highest price that buyers will pay (the price on the demand curve at the quantity).

Figure 13.5 shows the logic of profit maximization for a monopoly. The marginal revenue curve, *MR,* differs from the demand curve, *D.* The monopoly chooses the quantity, Q_M, at which marginal cost (*MC*) equals marginal revenue

---

[2]The supply curve of a perfectly competitive firm (as in Chapter 12) is the portion of its marginal cost curve above its average variable cost curve. That supply curve is independent of the demand curve; changes in demand do not change supply. In contrast, it is impossible to define a supply curve for a monopoly because the quantity supplied at any one price depends on demand.

FIGURE 13.4

DEMAND CURVE FOR A MONOPOLY'S PRODUCT

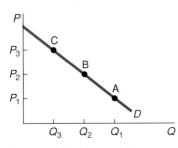

A monopoly faces a downward-sloping demand curve. If it charges the price P_1, it can sell the quantity Q_1 (Point A). If it charges P_2, it can sell Q_2 (Point B). If it charges P_3, it can sell Q_3 (Point C). A monopoly chooses the point on its demand curve (such as A, B, or C) that maximizes its profit.

FIGURE 13.5

MONOPOLY PRICE AND OUTPUT

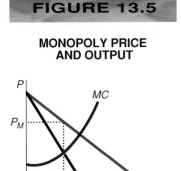

A monopoly maximizes its profit by choosing the quantity, Q_M, at which its marginal cost (MC) equals its marginal revenue (MR). It charges the price P_M and sells the quantity Q_M.

(where the curves intersect), and charges the highest price at which it can sell this quantity, P_M.

EXPLANATION AND EXAMPLE

The marginal revenue curve (MR) differs from the demand curve (D) because the firm must reduce its price to all customers to raise the quantity that it sells. The first two columns of the table in **Figure 13.6** show a demand schedule; the third and fourth columns show total and marginal revenue; the remaining columns show total, marginal, and average cost, and the firm's profit. Figure 13.6 graphs the demand curve, the marginal revenue curve, and the marginal and average cost curves. If the firm charges a $12 price, it can sell 5 units of the good per week for a total revenue of $60 per week. The firm could sell 6 units per week only by reducing the price to $11. This would raise its total revenue to $66 per week, so the marginal revenue of a 6th unit per week is $6. The difference between the demand and marginal revenue curves is the difference between the second and fourth columns of the table.

In words, marginal revenue is less than price for a monopoly because to sell one more unit of the good, the monopoly must reduce its price to all customers. Its marginal revenue from selling a 10th unit equals the gain in revenue from selling that 10th unit, which is the price, minus the loss in revenue from selling the other 9 units at a lower price. (See also Figure 13.2.)

A firm maximizes its profit by choosing a quantity that sets marginal revenue equal to marginal cost. (See Chapter 10.) The monopoly described in Figure 13.6 maximizes profit by producing 7 units per week and charging $10 per unit (the price at which the quantity demanded equals 7). It earns a $48 profit, and cannot raise its profit by charging more and selling less or charging less and selling more.

MONOPOLY PROFIT

Figure 13.7 shows the monopoly profit for a monopoly without fixed costs.[3] People buy Q_M units of the good and pay P_M for each unit, so the area of the rectangle with height P_M and base Q_M shows the monopoly's total revenue from its sales. The area under the marginal cost curve shows the variable cost of producing the good, so the remainder of the rectangle shows the monopoly's profit.

Figure 13.8 graphs monopoly profit in a second way. The monopoly's profit equals its markup (price minus average cost) times the number of goods that it sells. This is the area of the rectangle in Figure 13.8. These two ways to show monopoly profit in a graph are equivalent.

DEADWEIGHT SOCIAL LOSS FROM A MONOPOLY

Monopolies cause economic inefficiency. Figures 13.7 and 13.8 both show the deadweight social loss from a monopoly. As in the fish example (Figure 13.3), the deadweight social loss occurs because the monopoly sells less than the economically efficient quantity.

The economically efficient quantity is the quantity at which the producer's marginal cost of the good equals buyers' marginal benefit, which is the height of the demand curve. The economically efficient quantity is the quantity where the marginal cost curve and the demand curve intersect, the quantity Q^E in **Figure**

---

[3]If the monopoly has a fixed cost, its profit is smaller than this area by its fixed cost. The area under the marginal cost curve equals the variable cost of producing the good.

FIGURE 13.6

AN EXAMPLE OF MONOPOLY DECISION MAKING

In this example, the monopoly maximizes its profit by producing 7 units per week and charging $10 per unit. Its profit is $48.

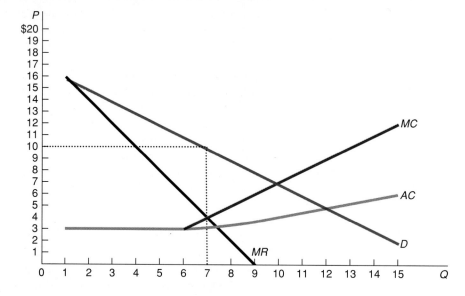

Quantity per Week (Q)	Price (P)	Total Revenue (TR)	Marginal Revenue (MR)	Total Cost (TC)	Marginal Cost (MC)	Average Cost (AC)	Profit
1	$16	$16	$16	$ 3	$ 3	$3.000	$13
2	15	30	14	6	3	3.000	24
3	14	42	12	9	3	3.000	33
4	13	52	10	12	3	3.000	40
5	12	60	8	15	3	3.000	45
6	11	66	6	18	3	3.000	48
7[a]	10	70	4	22	4	3.143	48
8	9	72	2	27	5	3.375	45
9	8	72	0	33	6	3.667	39
10	7	70	-2	40	7	4.000	30
11	6	66	-4	48	8	4.364	18
12	5	60	-6	57	9	4.750	3
13	4	52	-8	67	10	5.154	-15
14	3	42	-10	78	11	5.571	-36
15	2	30	-12	90	12	6.000	-60
16	1	16	-14	103	13	6.437	-87

[a]$MC = MR$ here.

13.9. Panel b shows the total gain from trade (total consumer and producer surplus) when the economically efficient quantity is produced and traded. Panel a shows the gain from trade (total consumer and producer surplus) with a monopoly. The gain from trade in Panel a is smaller than that in Panel b. The difference, Area A in Panel a, is the deadweight social loss due to the monopoly.

The deadweight social loss occurs because the monopoly charges a price above its marginal cost. At this higher price, people buy only Q_M rather than Q^E units. The deadweight social loss represents the potential gains from the trades that do not occur because of the monopoly. It results from a monopoly's choice

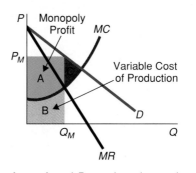

FIGURE 13.7

MONOPOLY PROFIT AND DEADWEIGHT SOCIAL LOSS[a]

Areas A and B together give total spending on the monopoly's product (total revenue for the monopoly). Area C gives the deadweight social loss.

[a] For a monopoly without fixed costs.

not to sell additional units of the good even though some people are willing to pay more than the cost of producing the additional units. The firm chooses not to sell to these potential customers because if it did, it would have to lower the price to all of its customers, even those who would willingly pay more.

EXAMPLE

Ralph has two candy bars to sell. (He does not want to eat them.) Luke is willing to pay up to 50 cents for one; Violet is willing to pay up to 20 cents. Neither Luke or Violet wants two candy bars. Suppose that Ralph must charge the same price to both Luke and Violet. He maximizes his profit by selling only to Luke, for 50 cents, and throwing out the other candy bar. (If he were to sell both candy bars, he could charge only 20 cents each, so he would earn only 40 cents for both.) This is economically inefficient because Ralph throws out something that Violet is willing to buy. The potential trade with Violet, which would be economically efficient, does not occur because it would reduce Ralph's total profit. The deadweight social loss from Ralph's monopoly in this example is 20 cents (the value of the candy to Violet).

COMPARING MONOPOLIES AND PERFECT COMPETITION

An industry with perfect competition produces the economically efficient quantity and charges a price equal to marginal cost. A monopoly produces less than that quantity and charges a price above marginal cost. **Figure 13.10** contrasts a monopoly with perfect competition, assuming that marginal cost is the same in both cases.

FIGURE 13.8

MONOPOLY PROFIT: ANOTHER WAY TO GRAPH IT

Area A shows monopoly profit (markup times Q_M). Area B shows the deadweight social loss.

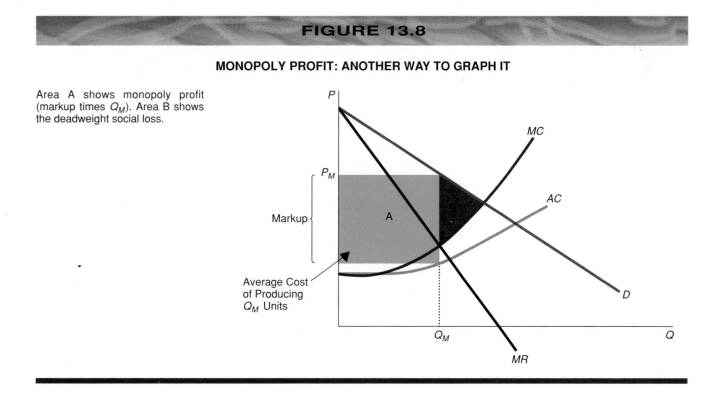

FIGURE 13.9

GAINS FROM TRADE (CONSUMER AND PRODUCER SURPLUS) WITH THE MONOPOLY QUANTITY AND THE ECONOMICALLY EFFICIENT QUANTITY

Total consumer and producer surplus is smaller with the monopoly quantity, Q_M, than with the economically efficient quantity, Q^E. The difference, Area A, is the deadweight social loss from the monopoly.

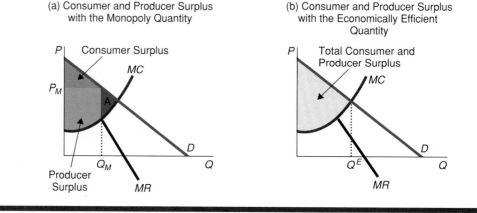

(a) Consumer and Producer Surplus with the Monopoly Quantity

(b) Consumer and Producer Surplus with the Economically Efficient Quantity

FIGURE 13.10

MONOPOLY VERSUS PERFECT COMPETITION

Total consumer and producer surplus is smaller with a monopoly than with perfect competition, which is economically efficient. The difference, Area A, is the deadweight social loss from a monopoly.

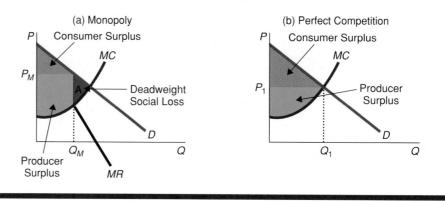

(a) Monopoly

(b) Perfect Competition

Suppose that the market supply curve with perfect competition is the *MC* curve in Figure 13.10.[4] Industry output with perfect competition is then Q_1, the economically efficient quantity, while monopoly output, Q_M, is smaller. The monopoly charges a higher price (P_M instead of P_1) and earns a higher profit. (Producer surplus is larger with the monopoly.) Consumer surplus with a monopoly is smaller for two reasons: buyers pay more for each good, and they buy less.

These conclusions apply only if a monopoly has the same costs of production as a perfectly competitive industry. In some cases, however, a monopoly may have

---

[4]The supply curve of each firm under perfect competition is the portion of its marginal cost curve above its average variable cost, so the market supply curve is the industry marginal cost curve, *MC* in the figure.

lower costs of production than a perfectly competitive industry. In fact, a firm might become a monopoly *because* its costs are much lower than those of any potential competitors.[5] The later section titled "Natural Monopoly" discusses a related situation.

FOR REVIEW

13.1 Draw a graph to show:
  a. Monopoly output
  b. Monopoly price
  c. Monopoly profit (with no fixed costs)
  d. Deadweight social loss from a monopoly

13.2 Contrast the prices and quantities produced by a monopoly and a perfectly competitive industry.

QUESTIONS

13.3 Why is a monopoly's marginal revenue less than its price?

13.4 Why does a monopoly produce less than the economically efficient quantity?

LONG-RUN EQUILIBRIUM AND BARRIERS TO ENTRY

barrier to entry — a cost high enough to prevent potential competitors from entering an industry

Monopoly profits tempt other firms to enter the industry. If enough new firms enter, the industry may reach perfect competition (and zero economic profits) in the long run. If only a few firms enter, the industry may become an oligopoly, which is the subject of Chapter 14. A firm can remain a monopoly in the long run only if some barriers to entry keep other firms out.

> **Barriers to entry** are costs high enough to prevent potential competitors from entering an industry.

Barriers to entry may be *natural,* resulting from lower costs of production at the monopoly firm, or *artificial,* resulting from laws or government regulations.

EXAMPLES

Laws and regulations sometimes prohibit new firms from entering an industry. No firm other than the U.S. Postal Service can legally deliver first-class mail in the United States. Legal barriers to entry do not fully protect monopolies from competition because potential competitors can often produce substitute products. The Postal Service, for example, competes with private overnight-delivery companies, parcel carriers, fax machines, and electronic (computer-based) mail. Advertising inserts in newspapers were invented in the 1960s as a way to compete with the Postal Service by substituting newspaper delivery for mail delivery.[6]

Most countries prohibit new firms from competing with their government-owned airlines. The U.S. government prohibited new firms from entering the

---

[5]In this case, the economically efficient situation would be for the monopoly to produce the good (since it has low costs), but at a quantity of Q^E in Figure 13.9 rather than Q_M. The monopoly would not voluntarily produce this higher quantity, of course.

[6]Although the post office is a government agency, it hires private firms to transport and deliver some of its mail, particularly in rural areas. This practice has a long tradition; King William III of Britain contracted the first colonial postal service to Thomas Neale in 1692; in 1785, the U.S. Congress authorized the postmaster general to hire private stagecoaches to carry mail.

SOCIAL AND ECONOMIC ISSUES

Should the Post Office Have a Monopoly?

The U.S. Postal Service has a legal monopoly on delivery of first-class mail in the United States; the government prohibits entry by other firms. Other companies can compete in delivery of packages, overnight mail, magazines, and so on, but not first-class mail.

People who believe that the government should permit competition with the Postal Service in delivery of first-class mail argue that competition would lower prices and raise the quality of service. People who favor continuing the prohibition say that other firms would deliver mail only on the most profitable mail routes and leave the government Postal Service with the unprofitable routes. They say that this would raise prices for people who live in out-of-the-way places. Currently, the Postal Service charges everyone the same price, so it makes profits on low-cost routes and suffers losses on high-cost routes.

Those who favor allowing competition reply that mail delivery to out-of-the-way places may become more expensive, but that it is unfair for the government to force everyone else to subsidize mail delivery to those places. People in those places, they say, should have to pay the higher costs of living there. (To keep their costs lower, they might choose to pick up their mail at the post office instead of buying home delivery, or they might take only weekly delivery.) Opponents of postal competition also argue that mail delivery is a natural monopoly; if many firms were to deliver mail they may all have higher average costs, and this could make mail delivery more expensive. Supporters of postal competition argue that mail delivery is not a natural monopoly, but that even if it were, competition would keep prices down and raise incentives for efficient service.

trucking industry for several decades. Many state governments operate lotteries, but prohibit private firms from operating competing lotteries. State governments often limit the number of restaurants and gas stations along toll roads. In the former Soviet Union (and many other socialist countries), the government had a monopoly on production and sales of most goods, and it prohibited competition. Until recently, a national law in Japan prevented large retail stores from competing with smaller, "mama-papa" stores. It was illegal for a store of more than about 5,000 square feet in size to open in any town without permission from the community's store owners with whom it would compete.

License requirements are another form of artificial barrier to entry. The U.S. government requires radio and television stations to have licenses, and historically, it has used this requirement to limit the number of stations. Governments require people to obtain licenses to become doctors, pharmacists, lawyers, barbers, and hairdressers; to operate stores and restaurants; and to stage rock concerts.

Patents and copyrights (which protect rights to intellectual property) are also artificial barriers to entry. A patent is the legal right to produce and sell a product you have created. Polaroid patented the instant-picture cameras that it invented. The patent prevented other companies from producing and selling such cameras without Polaroid's permission. A copyright resembles a patent, but it protects rights to works of art, books, music, movies, television programs, and paintings. This book is copyrighted, as are most songs. (Even the song "Happy Birthday" is copyrighted; you are legally required to pay the copyright owner if you perform it for pay, though singing it at a party, without pay, is legal!) Patents and copyrights raise the incentive to invent new products and create new intellectual property and works of art, but they also create barriers to entry.

Some barriers to entry result from natural cost advantages. A firm that owns the only spring in a desert may be a monopoly in the long run because no other firm can provide water there at a sufficiently low cost. More than 90 percent of the world's output of boron, which is used in bleach, glass, ceramics, electronics, and other products, comes from just two mines, one in California and another in Turkey, both owned by the same company, RTZ Borax. A Canadian company once owned almost all the world's nickel reserves. The Louvre is the only museum in the world with the Mona Lisa; it has a monopoly on showing that painting because it owns the only original.

NATURAL MONOPOLY

One type of natural barrier to entry occurs when the average cost of producing a good falls with quantity. In that case, it may be cheaper for one firm to produce all of the industry output than for many small firms to produce portions of that output. This is a situation of natural monopoly.

increasing returns to scale — a situation in which average cost of production decreases with higher output

There are **increasing returns to scale** if the average cost of production decreases with higher output.

Figure 13.11 shows increasing returns to scale as the downward slope of the average cost curve, *AC*.

FIGURE 13.11

NATURAL MONOPOLY

The natural monopoly maximizes profit by producing 8,000 units (the quantity at which *MC* = *MR*) and charging $18 (Point A). The average cost of producing 8,000 units is $13 per unit (Point B). The average cost of producing fewer than 8,000 units is higher than $13. The quantity demanded at the price $4 is 26,000 units per year and the marginal cost of producing this quantity is $4 (Point C), but average cost is almost $5. The quantity demanded at the price $5 is 24,000 units per year and the average cost of producing 24,000 units is $5 (Point D), but the marginal cost is below $5.

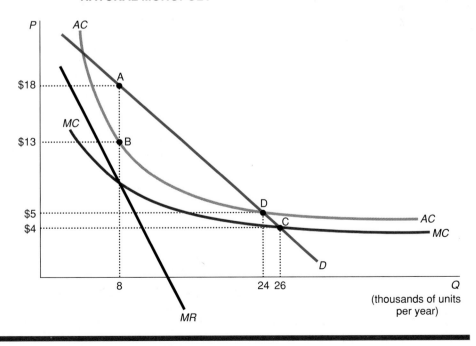

natural monopoly — an industry with increasing returns to scale over sufficiently large quantities

Another monopoly bites the dust

By Seth Lubove

Anthony Tortoriello, a blunt-talking Chicago car dealer and industrial oil seller, has a hot deal for you: 1,400 megawatts of electricity, enough to power 40 small towns. Asking price: at least 15 percent to 20 percent lower than you're likely to get from your local electric monopoly.

Interested? For now, you can buy Tortoriello's electricity only if you're another utility. But Tortoriello anticipates the end of the local electric companies' monopoly privileges—a day, not far off, when electric consumers can buy power from whomever they want, much as they now choose their long distance carriers.

Local electric monopolies in the high-tax states fear that they'll be stuck with billions of dollars' worth of excess capacity, or "stranded investment," if their big customers are allowed to shop around for cheaper power. Says Goodman of Howell, "If you don't hear the fear in the utility executives' voices, you're not listening carefully."

Public utilities, traditionally protected by government on the grounds that they are natural monopolies, will face increasing competition in the years ahead.

Source: Seth Lubove, "Another Monopoly Bites the Dust," *Forbes,* May 23, 1994, p. 42.

An industry with increasing returns to scale over sufficiently large quantities is a **natural monopoly.**

The phrase "sufficiently large quantities" refers to all quantities demanded at prices high enough to cover the firm's average cost.[7]

A natural monopoly may occur if production requires high fixed costs. The monopoly is natural because it is more efficient for one firm, rather than several firms, to produce all units of the good. Dividing output among several firms would give each a higher average cost than a single firm would have. Figure 13.11 shows an example. If one firm produces 24,000 units per year, its average cost is $5; if three firms produce 8,000 units each, then each has an average cost of $13. One firm can produce all of the industry output more efficiently than three firms can.

Public utilities such as local telephone companies; cable-television companies; and electric, gas, and water companies are often cited as natural monopolies. In recent years, however, competition in these areas has begun to flourish, raising questions as to whether these industries really *are* natural monopolies.[8]

Why might a public utility be a natural monopoly? It may be more efficient to have a single gas line (or telephone line) on a street than to have several (one for each of several firms). While a few cities have permitted competition between more than one cable-television firm, few neighborhoods have more than one set of cable lines; each cable company avoided installing lines where the other company had already installed them. If CableRight has already wired a neighborhood, it is not likely to be profitable for CableFamily to install its own, separate wires in the same neighborhood. Natural monopoly is a natural barrier to entry that makes it unprofitable for new firms to enter the industry and compete with an entrenched firm.

Though natural monopoly makes it efficient to have a single producer, the monopoly level of output is not economically efficient. A natural monopoly, like any other monopoly, chooses its quantity to equate marginal cost and marginal revenue. The natural monopoly in Figure 13.11 produces 8,000 units per year and charges a price of $18. Its average cost is $13, so its markup is $5. The economically efficient level of output is 26,000 units, indicated by the point where the demand curve intersects the marginal cost curve; this quantity equates the marginal cost of producing the good with its marginal benefit to buyers (measured by their willingness to pay for it).

Can government regulation force a natural monopoly to produce the economically efficient quantity? If the government knew the economically efficient quantity (which would require knowledge of the demand curve and costs of production), it could try to force the natural monopoly in Figure 13.11 to produce 26,000 units. This would create a problem, though: to sell 26,000 units per year, the firm could not charge a price higher than $4, but its average cost would be almost $5. The firm would lose nearly $1 per unit, or $26,000 per year. Unable to cover its costs, it would go out of business.

---

[7]A firm with a U-shaped average cost curve (as in Figure 12.5) has increasing returns to scale at low levels of output, but not at higher levels. Such a firm is not a natural monopoly unless market demand for its product is low enough to intersect the average cost curve at a point where that curve slopes downward.

[8]Cable-television firms and phone companies have competed in the market for local phone service in Great Britain since 1991; similar competition is now starting in some areas of the United States, beginning with a 1994 agreement in Rochester, New York. Similar competition has also begun in the gas and electricity industries. Most of the monopolies in these industries have been specifically created by government. For example, in 1984, the U.S. federal government banned local telephone companies from providing cable service in their regions.

Can a natural monopoly sell the economically efficient quantity without taking a loss? It can, if it can charge a multipart price.

multipart price — a price with several components

A **multipart price** is a price composed of several parts, such as a startup fee, a monthly fee, and a per-use fee.

A telephone company typically charges both a monthly fee and a fee per telephone call; this is a multipart price. Cable-television firms often charge one-time hookup fees in addition to monthly fees, and many also offer pay-per-view programming. If, for example, a cable-television firm has a fixed cost of $20 to wire a house for cable, it can charge a $20 hookup fee to cover this cost. It can then charge a monthly fee equal to its marginal cost of providing cable service each month, say $12. Since the monthly price of cable service equals its marginal cost, people will buy the economically efficient amount of cable service. A multipart price allows the firm to charge separately for various components of its product (such as cable hookup and monthly cable service). This price structure recognizes that the firm provides two services: initial hookup and subsequent delivery of programming. If the firm charges the marginal cost for each separate service, such as $20 for initial hookup and $12 for subsequent delivery of programming, people will buy the economically efficient quantities. In Figure 13.11, the natural monopoly could charge $4 per unit in addition to an annual fee high enough to eliminate the loss it would otherwise suffer. People would then buy the economically efficient quantity of the good.

Without a multipart price, the government could force the natural monopoly to produce 24,000 units per year at a price equal to its average cost (assuming that the government had the relevant information and authority). The firm would then earn zero profit, and although the quantity would not be economically efficient, it might approximate efficiency.

HOW DO MONOPOLIES START?

How does a firm become a monopoly? How do monopolies begin? Some monopolies begin under the protection of government regulations or laws that create artificial barriers to entry. A firm may also become a monopoly by acquiring most or all of a unique input that is necessary to produce a good (such as the boron mines mentioned earlier). Other firms become monopolies when they invent and obtain patents on new products. Some firms become monopolies by reducing their costs of production enough that other firms cannot profitably compete with them. Without other barriers to entry, monopolies based on patents end when those patents expire, and monopolies based on low costs of production end after other firms copy the lower-cost production methods. Consequently, monopolies that result from new or improved products, or from new technology that reduces costs, are usually only temporary. The monopoly power that results from an entrepreneur's success can provide an incentive (much like the incentive from a patent or copyright) for people to try to create new and better products that customers will want to buy. Monopolies may also begin with mergers or with implicit agreements among firms to stop competing and cooperate to act as if they were all part of one monopoly firm. These cartels are the subject of the next section.

─────────────────── **FOR REVIEW** ───────────────────

13.5 What happens to a monopoly in the long run if no barriers to entry deter potential competitors? State three examples of barriers to entry.

13.6 What is a natural monopoly?

QUESTION

13.7 Discuss this statement: "If an industry is a natural monopoly, it is economically efficient to have a monopoly in that industry."

CARTELS

People of the same trade seldom meet together, even for merriment and diversion, but the conversation ends in a conspiracy against the public, or in some contrivance to raise prices.—Adam Smith, *The Wealth of Nations,* 1776.

If a monopoly does not already exist, competitors can profit by forming one. They could form a monopoly through a merger (in which two firms legally become one) or an acquisition (in which one firm buys another). Sometimes firms collude (make joint decisions) without merging. Laws in many countries, including the United States, prohibit mergers to form a monopoly and certain kinds of collusion. When firms collude and agree to act jointly as a monopoly, they form a cartel.

cartel — a group of firms that try to collude to act as a monopoly

A **cartel** is a group of firms (which become members of the cartel) that try to collude to act like a monopoly and share the monopoly profit.

A successful cartel works like any other monopoly, producing the monopoly level of output and charging the monopoly price. Cartels are illegal in most countries.

PROBLEMS FACING CARTELS

A cartel faces special problems that a single-firm monopoly does not. The cartel must convince its members to reduce output to the monopoly level, it must

---

IN THE NEWS

OPEC set to discuss output cut

By Youssef M. Ibrahim
Special to The New York Times

PARIS, Feb. 9—The president of the Organization of Petroleum Exporting Countries said today that he would press for a significant cut in oil production to prop up sagging prices, which have dropped by 20 percent since November.

OPEC, the oil cartel, reduces output to raise the price of oil and its profit.

Source: Youssef M. Ibrahim, "OPEC Set to Discuss Output Cut," *New York Times,* February 10, 1992, p. D1.

IN THE NEWS

Cola sellers may have bottled up their competition

Agreements on pricing and marketing of Coke and Pepsi are alleged

---

By Andy Pasztor and Larry Reibstein
Staff Reporters of The Wall Street Journal

When four executives of local Coca Cola and Pepsi Cola bottling companies gathered at a popular, late-night restaurant in Norfolk, Va., four years ago, they did more than share a meal.

By the end of the meeting, the executives allegedly established a single wholesale price—$5.50 a case—for cans of Coke and Pepsi sold in much of Virginia, according to sworn testimony, government filings, and other federal court documents in Norfolk. The participants also agreed on the sizes and timing of future price increases for both cans and bottles, Justice Department prosecutors and government witnesses allege.

Over the next year and a half, executives of the two area bottlers conspired to share confidential price and marketing information at meetings in such places as hotel bathrooms and lounges, parking lots, fast-food outlets, and an airport coffee shop, according to prosecutors and the testimony, filings, and other court documents.

The result, prosecutors charge, was to inflate soft-drink prices paid by consumers.

Adam Smith's observation is as true today as it was 2 centuries ago.

Source: Andy Pasztor and Larry Reibstein, "Cola Sellers May Have Bottled Up Their Competition," *The Wall Street Journal,* December 9, 1987, p. 6.

decide how to divide and share the monopoly profit among its members, and it must prevent members from cheating on the cartel agreement by reducing their prices to sell more.

Suppose that ten firms in a perfectly competitive industry each produce 20 units of a good per month, so that industry output is 200 units per month. These firms' cost curves appear in **Figure 13.12.** At the $12 equilibrium price, each firm earns zero economic profit. If the firms form a cartel, they can maximize the cartel's profit by reducing industry output to 120 units per month and raising the price to $18.

The cartel's first problem is how to divide production and profit among firms. The amount of output that each firm is supposed to produce is called its output *quota.* In this example, each firm's quota might be 12 units. (In real life, cartel members may find it difficult to agree on the quotas as larger firms want larger quotas.) A related problem is how to share the cartel profit (monopoly profit) among the members; they might share the profit equally, in proportion to output, or in some other way.

FIGURE 13.12

FORMING A CARTEL

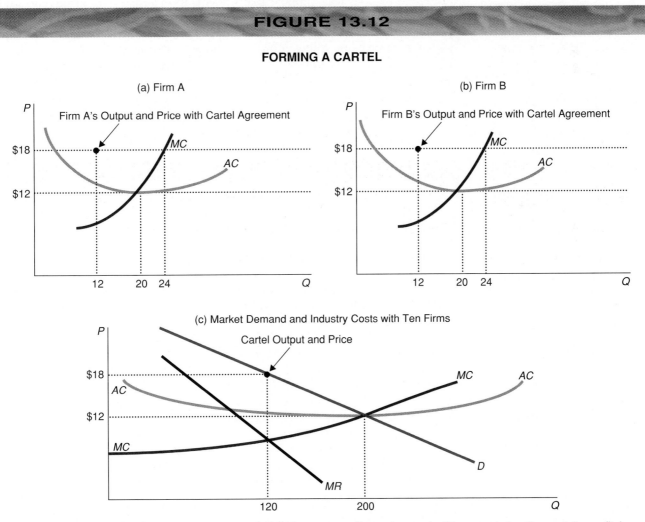

Under perfect competition, the equilibrium price is $12 and ten firms produce 20 units each per month, so industry equilibrium output is 200 units per month. If the firms form a cartel, they act like a monopoly. They maximize the cartel's profit by reducing industry output to 120 units per month (so that each firm produces 12 units per month) and raising the price to $18.

Dutch government moves to curb cartels' influence

Special to The Wall Street Journal

THE HAGUE—After years of benign neglect, the Dutch government began a campaign to rein in price-fixing and market-sharing by cartels allowed to flourish in nearly all sectors of the economy in the Netherlands.

At issue are longstanding antitrust rules in the Netherlands that allow companies to form cartels, carve up markets, and fix prices freely as long as the Economics Ministry is kept abreast of what is happening. Licensing or government approval of the cartels generally isn't required, officials said.

Cartels are legal in some countries and illegal in others.

Source: "Dutch Government Moves to Curb Cartels' Influence," *The Wall Street Journal,* June 22, 1988, p. 20.

Another problem for a cartel is how to prevent member firms from cheating on the cartel agreement by producing more. Cartel members rarely rely on contracts that are enforceable in courts because most cartel agreements are illegal. In the example, each firm can raise its profit by producing more than 12 units. As long as the other firms restrict output to keep the price at $18, Firm A can maximize its profit by producing the quantity at which marginal cost equals $18, that is, 24 units.[9] **Figure 13.13** shows the extra profit that Firm A can earn by cheating on the agreement if other firms honor it.

Every individual member of the cartel has an incentive to cheat by producing more than its quota. If many firms begin cheating, however, the increase in output reduces the price below $18 and the cartel falls apart. Except where cartels are legal (so that quota agreements can be enforced in courts), the incentive to cheat tends to make cartels unstable.

To understand the incentive to cheat in a cartel, imagine that your professor grades on a curve. Each student can get the same grade with less studying if everyone agrees to study less. Suppose that students form a cartel and all agree to study only 15 minutes for an exam. Each student has an incentive to cheat on this agreement because, if other students study only 15 minutes, a cheater can raise his grade substantially by studying for a few hours. Of course, if everyone cheats on the agreement, the entire cartel breaks down. The incentive to cheat is even stronger if cartel members think that others might cheat; if other people study for a few hours and one person studies for only 15 minutes, that person is likely to fail the exam. Without some outside enforcement mechanism, it is difficult to prevent cheating and the cartel becomes unstable.

Cartels can operate for long periods of time when the government helps to prevent cheating. In 1931, Texas and other oil-producing states made it illegal for any firm to produce more than a certain amount of oil. The purpose of these laws was to reduce oil production, and therefore to raise the price of oil and the profits of oil producers, that is, to establish a cartel. The U.S. government helped by raising the tax on imported oil, protecting the cartel from foreign competition.

International oil companies had never formed a successful cartel on their own, but in 1970 the government of Libya began to suggest that countries restrict their oil output. By 1973, the OPEC members—national governments—had formed a cartel agreement and quadrupled the price of oil. Even before the OPEC cartel, firms in other industries had tried—and often failed—to form successful cartels. Cartels have been attempted in the tin, nickel, cocoa, coffee, potash, bauxite, natural rubber, nutmeg, and banana industries (though the Organization of Banana-Exporting Countries never achieved OPEC's fame or success). The International Tin Council (ITC) cartel collapsed in 1985. Many member countries of the International Coffee Organization (ICO) cartel cheated on the cartel agreement by producing more coffee than their quotas and selling it for less than the ICO price; the cartel then collapsed in 1989 and the wholesale price of coffee fell from $1.25 to about $0.50 a pound. After that, seven Latin American countries formed a new group, the Association of Coffee Producing Countries, as the basis for a new cartel. A bauxite cartel lasted for only a few years. Governments of the United States, Canada, Australia, Russia, and the 12-nation European Union set up

---

[9]If Firm A cheats by producing more than 12 units and other members of the cartel produce their quotas, total industry output rises so the price falls slightly below $18; the example ignores this effect for simplicity. It does not change the conclusion that each firm has an incentive to cheat.

FIGURE 13.13

INCENTIVE TO CHEAT ON A CARTEL AGREEMENT

The cartel agreement may require that each firm restrict output to 12 units per month and charge $18. Each firm has an incentive to cheat on this agreement. Firm A's marginal cost of producing a 13th good is only $8, but it can sell the good by charging just under $18 and stealing customers from other members of the cartel. The shaded area shows the extra profit that Firm A can earn by cheating on the cartel (if the other firms don't cheat).

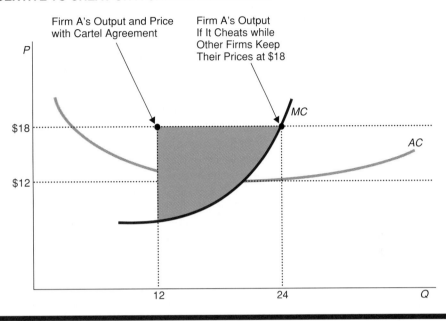

Firm A's Output and Price with Cartel Agreement

Firm A's Output If It Cheats while Other Firms Keep Their Prices at $18

Collusion in the Classroom

A classic classroom experiment shows why it is hard for a cartel to prevent cheating. Each of 15 students in a class secretly writes the number 1 or 2 on a sheet of paper and gives it to the professor. The professor pays students depending on what they write, as in the following table:

If This Many Students Write 1	Then Each Student Who Wrote 1 Gets	And Each Student Who Wrote 2 Gets
0	$0.00	$0.45
1	0.05	0.50
2	0.10	0.55
3	0.15	0.60
4	0.20	0.65
5	0.25	0.70
6	0.30	0.75
7	0.35	0.80
8	0.40	0.85
9	0.45	0.90
10	0.50	0.95
11	0.55	1.00
12	0.60	1.05
13	0.65	1.10
14	0.70	1.15
15	0.75	1.20

If everyone writes 1, then everyone gets $0.75. If everyone writes 2 (and no one writes 1), then everyone gets only $0.45. You might think that everyone would write 1, but if everyone else writes 1 and you write 2, you get $1.15 and everyone else gets $0.70. If students in the class can collude, they will all write 1, but every student has an incentive to cheat by writing 2.

Experiments show that if students are not allowed to talk to each other before choosing a number, then most students write 2. If students are allowed to talk to each other first, they usually try to form a cartel by agreeing that they will all write 1. If you think that most people would honor this kind of agreement, you will be disappointed in the result. Time after time, when this experiment is performed in classrooms, many students write 2 after agreeing to write 1. Cheating is a persistent problem for cartels.

an informal aluminum cartel in 1994, agreeing to reduce output of aluminum by about 10 percent to raise its price.

ANTITRUST LAW

antitrust law — a law that prohibits monopolies and cartels or monopoly-like behaviors

Governments, when they are not forming or assisting monopolies and cartels, often fight them with antitrust laws.

Antitrust laws are laws that prohibit monopolies and cartels or monopoly-like behaviors.

In the United States, the Sherman Act of 1890 declared illegal any "contract, combination, . . . or conspiracy, in restraint of trade or commerce" or any action to "monopolize, or attempt to monopolize, or combine or conspire with any other person or persons, to monopolize" any "trade or commerce." If this language seems hard to understand, you are not alone. (What exactly does "restraint of trade or commerce" mean?) The U.S. Supreme Court also had difficulty understanding the Sherman Act, and finally decided that restraining trade or monopolizing an industry meant "unreasonable conduct." The court described a rule of reason stating that the Sherman Act made "unreasonable conduct" illegal, but did not apply to "reasonable" conduct even if a seller had a monopoly.[10] In 1911, the court applied this rule of reason in two famous cases and found the Standard Oil Company and the American Tobacco Company guilty of violating the Sherman Act. The court ruled that the Standard Oil Company (which controlled more than 90 percent of the refining business in the United States) violated the Sherman Act in several ways, including the use of predatory pricing.

predatory pricing — selling goods at prices below their average costs to try to drive a competitor out of busines

Predatory pricing occurs when a seller charges less than its average cost to try to drive a competitor out of business.

Predatory pricing is rare for a good reason: the predator loses money in the process. You might expect that a large predator firm with more resources could outlast a small victim firm with less money. That would be true if each firm were to lose the same amount of money each week from predatory pricing, but a predator with twice the sales of a victim (and with the same costs and price) loses twice as much money as the victim firm.[11] (If each firm loses $1 on each sale, a firm with 1,000 sales per week loses $1,000 per week, while a firm with 100 sales per week loses only $100 per week.) Economists disagree about whether Standard Oil actually tried predatory pricing, though no one doubts that the oil giant threatened to do so. It told a small firm, Cornplanter Oil, to stop cutting into Standard Oil's business. Otherwise, Standard Oil said, it would reduce its price below cost and drive Cornplanter out of business. Cornplanter Oil stood up to this threat, though, as its manager testified in court about his reply to the Standard Oil manager:

> Well, I say, "Mr. Moffet, I am very glad you put it that way, because if it is up to you the only way you can get it [the business] is to cut the market [reduce the price], and if you cut the market I will cut you for 200 miles around, and I will

OPEC members agree to reduce output but must decide who cuts by how much

All cartels face the problem of agreeing how to divide output and profits.

Source: "OPEC Members Agree to Reduce Output But Must Decide Who Cuts by How Much," *The Wall Street Journal,* February 14, 1992, p. A2.

---

[10]Chief Justice White said that the rule of reason was required because Congress did not write into the Sherman Act "any direct prohibition against monopoly" and only made certain actions illegal.

[11]A victim of predatory pricing may be able to reduce its short-run loss by shutting down temporarily, while remaining ready to produce again when the predatory pricing stops. A monopoly that understands this may have little incentive to try predatory pricing.

IN THE NEWS

Fighting quotas: Independent farmers oppose rules letting cartels decide output

Fruit, nut growers challenge depression-era legacy; Will almond butter sell? Repealing curb on grapefruit

By Marj Charlier
Staff Reporter of
The Wall Street Journal

SANGER, Calif.—Inside a big metal building on the Riverbend International Corp. farm here, shiny oranges bounce jauntily along conveyor belts and down chutes, automatically joining like-sized fruit in boxes bound for Pacific Rim markets.

But outside, in orchards that stretch across the San Joaquin Valley, oranges just as fine plop off trees and rot in the scorching heat. Perry Walker, Riverbend's vice president, says that the fruit wouldn't be going to waste if it weren't for restrictions imposed by a government-backed cartel.

Rotting fruit and lost profits have become a cause.

Fifty-year-old federal regulations allow farmers to form cartels to control supplies, share marketing efforts, and allocate production rights through "marketing orders" approved and enforced by the U.S. Agriculture Department.

The government enforces some cartel agreements.

Source: Marj Charlier, "Fighting Quotas: Independent Farmers Oppose Rules Letting Cartels Decide Output," *The Wall Street Journal,* June 17, 1987, p. 1.

IN THE NEWS

The ostrich cartel could be staring at disaster

By Bill Keller
Special to The
New York Times

OUDTSHOORN, South Africa —Smirk, if you like, at the ostrich-egg lamps and ostrich jerky on sale in the curio shops, the ostrich jockeys at the Safari tourist farm, the South African flag composed of ostrich feathers, the ubiquitous, low-cholesterol ostrich steak platter, the ostrich crossing sign posted on Langenhoven Street.

Go ahead, roll your eyes at the Feather Inn, the Early Bird television repair shop, and Chez L'Austriche. But he advised that in Oudtshoorn, which bills itself without exaggeration as the world's ostrich capital, they take their ostriches seriously.

Almost somberly, in fact, these days. For after nearly 50 years of controlling the world's supply of this comical but lucrative commodity, the Oudtshoorn ostrich cartel faces an alarming threat: competition.

With two new rival ostrich associations beginning to challenge from inside South Africa, and smugglers spiriting breeding stock away to ranchers overseas, farmers here fear that the days of the $500 ostrich-hide handbag may be numbered.

The government of South Africa successfully protected the ostrich cartel from competition from 1945 until recently. Every cartel faces potential competition unless governments limit it by restricting entry.

Source: Bill Keller, "The Ostrich Cartel Could Be Staring at Disaster," *New York Times International,* September 15, 1993.

IN THE NEWS

OPEC is reining in runaway output despite some cheating by its members

By James Tanner
Staff Reporter of The
Wall Street Journal

The Organization of Petroleum Exporting Countries has reined in runaway oil production despite cheating by some members on their March quotas.

The OPEC oil cartel, like all cartels, faces the problem of members cheating on the agreement.

Source: James Tanner, "OPEC Is Reining in Runaway Output Despite Some Cheating by Its Members," *The Wall Street Journal*, March 24, 1993.

make you sell the stuff," and I says, "I don't want a bigger picnic than that; sell it if you want to," and I bid him good day and left.[12]

Standard Oil never carried out its threat against Cornplanter, but for other actions, the Supreme Court found Standard Oil guilty of violating the Sherman Act and the government split the firm into several smaller firms.[13] In the 1946 American Tobacco case, the court ruled that an informal cartel violates the Sherman Act.

The Supreme Court changed its mind about the rule of reason in the 1945 Alcoa case. A U.S. court acting for the Supreme Court found Alcoa guilty of violating the Sherman Act because it had a monopoly in raw aluminum (selling more than 90 percent of all aluminum) rather than because of its actions. Justice Learned Hand, the most famous U.S. judge of the 20th century, said that the law should consider a firm to be a monopoly if it has 90 percent of industry sales, though not necessarily if it has two-thirds or less of industry sales. Nevertheless, the court ruled in 1975 that Xerox had a monopoly of photocopying equipment because it sold 65 percent of all such equipment. The court required Xerox to increase competition by allowing some of its competitors to produce its patented products.

The second main U.S. antitrust law, the 1914 Clayton Act, made three specific actions illegal if they helped to create a monopoly or reduce competition:[14]

▶ Tie-in sales (offers to sell products only to people who also buy other products)

▶ Mergers (two firms joining together to form one firm)

▶ Price discrimination (See the next section.)

Countries differ in their antitrust laws and policies. Cartels operate legally in some countries such as Switzerland and, in some cases, Japan. Antitrust law in Japan and many European countries is considerably less restrictive than U.S. law, in the sense that those countries prohibit fewer actions.

──────────── **FOR REVIEW** ────────────

13.8 Why can firms benefit by forming a cartel?

──────────── **QUESTIONS** ────────────

13.9 Why do members of a cartel have an incentive to cheat?

13.10 Why is predatory pricing rare?

PRICE DISCRIMINATION

price discrimination — charging different prices to different buyers for the same good

An earlier section raised the possibility of a monopoly charging different prices to different buyers. It could charge a high price to buyers who would willingly pay a lot and lower prices to others who would not buy the product at the high price. A monopoly can raise its profit through price discrimination.

> **Price discrimination** means charging different prices to different buyers for the same good.

──────────────────────────────

[12]Cited in John S. McGee, "Predatory Price Cutting: the Standard Oil Case," *Journal of Law and Economics* I (October 1958), p. 155.

[13]The court also found American Tobacco guilty.

[14]The law has been revised several times to prohibit other actions, as well.

IN THE NEWS

Wal-Mart on trial on 'predatory pricing' charges

By Kathryn Jones

Wal-Mart Stores Inc. and its pricing practices went on trial yesterday in an Arkansas courtroom, where three independent pharmacies are trying to prove that the nation's largest retailer sold merchandise below its costs in an effort to drive competitors out of business.

The retail druggists in Conway, Ark., north of Little Rock, contend that their business suffered from Wal-Mart's "predatory prices" on a range of items, from toothpaste to mouthwash to over-the-counter drugs, sold at its Conway supercenter store. The drugstores charge that Wal-Mart violated the Arkansas Unfair Practices Act, which forbids selling merchandise below cost "for the purpose of injuring com-

petitors and destroying competition." They are seeking $1.1 million in damages.

In court filings, Wal-Mart has acknowledged selling some products for less than they cost, but insists that the policy has not damaged competition in the Conway area.

"It would be better if you could make a profit on everything you sell, but in the real world, that isn't possible," David Glass, Wal-Mart's president and chief executive officer, testified yesterday in Faulkner County Chancery Court in Conway. "That's the principal reason why we do it."

The sheer size of Wal-Mart, with $55.5 billion in revenues last year and more than 2,300 discount stores and warehouse-club outlets, allows it to buy in volume

and offer "everyday low prices." But smaller merchants, especially those in small towns, have complained that they cannot match Wal-Mart's prices and are often forced out of business when one of the megastores moves into their markets.

The Supreme Court in June rejected predatory pricing charges by the Brooke Group Ltd. and its Liggett unit against a rival cigarette manufacturer, the Brown & Williamson Tobacco Corporation. The court upheld lower-court decisions against Liggett, saying it believed predatory pricing was generally impractical, since a company would have to endure long-term losses to drive competitors out of business.

Is Wal-Mart guilty of predatory pricing, or does it charge lower prices simply because its costs are lower?

Source: Kathryn Jones, "Wal-Mart on Trial on 'Predatory Pricing' Charges," *New York Times*, August 24, 1993.

Two goods are not the same if their costs of production differ, so selling them for different prices would not constitute price discrimination. For example, it costs more to deliver a piano to a fourth-floor, walk-up apartment than to a ground-level apartment, so a music store does not practice price discrimination if it charges more for delivery to the fourth floor; piano delivery to a fourth-floor apartment is a different good than piano delivery to a ground-level apartment.

EXAMPLES

Pharmacies sometimes charge senior citizens lower prices than younger people for the same prescription medicines. Theaters and airlines sometimes charge less for children than for adults. Some stores and theaters give student discounts. Antique stores quote higher prices to well-dressed customers who look wealthy or show particular interest in an item than to customers who look poorer or only mildly interested. These may all be cases of price discrimination.

PERFECT PRICE DISCRIMINATION

perfect price discrimination — charging each customer the highest price that that customer is willing to pay

Perfect price discrimination occurs when a seller charges each customer the highest price that she is willing to pay.

Figure 13.14 illustrates perfect price discrimination. The monopoly seller produces the economically efficient quantity, Q_1 (the same quantity it would produce under perfect competition). A monopoly that practices perfect price discrimination creates no deadweight social loss. The monopoly captures all the gains from trade; consumer surplus is zero and producer surplus is the shaded area in Figure 13.14.

EXPLANATION

The height of the demand curve shows the highest prices that buyers are willing to pay. As long as the demand curve lies above the marginal cost curve, some buyer is willing to pay more for another unit of the product than it costs to produce, so the seller profits by producing and selling that extra unit. The seller maximizes profit by selling to every buyer who is willing to pay more for a good than it costs to produce, so the seller maximizes profit by producing and selling Q_1 units of the good in Figure 13.14. This is the same quantity that would result from perfect competition. Since this is the economically efficient quantity, there is no deadweight social loss. The seller charges $20 to a buyer who is willing to pay up to $20, $19 to a buyer who is willing to pay up to $19, and so on. Because the seller charges the highest price that each buyer is willing to pay, no buyer gets any consumer surplus. The perfectly price-discriminating monopoly captures all the gains from trade.

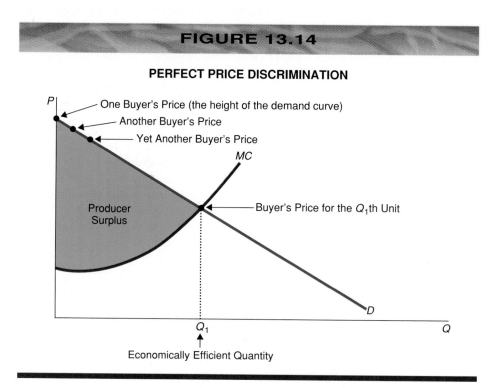

FIGURE 13.14

PERFECT PRICE DISCRIMINATION

EXAMPLES

Ralph has two candy bars to sell. (He does not want to eat them.) Luke is willing to pay up to 50 cents for one; Violet is willing to pay up to 20 cents. Neither Luke or Violet wants two candy bars. An earlier example in this chapter showed that if Ralph must charge the same price to both Luke and Violet, he maximizes his profit by selling only to Luke, for 50 cents, and throwing out the other candy bar. This economically inefficient result gives Ralph a profit of 50 cents.

If Ralph can perfectly price-discriminate, however, he charges Luke 50 cents for one candy bar and charges Violet 20 cents for the other. Notice that neither Luke nor Violet gets any consumer surplus in this case, but Ralph's profit is 70 cents, and this solution is economically efficient. Perfect price discrimination eliminates the deadweight social loss from a monopoly and raises the monopoly's profit.

Figure 13.1 showed the demand for Loretta's eight fish. Recall that if she must charge the same price to all buyers, she maximizes profit at $20 by charging $4, selling five fish, and throwing out the other three fish. If Loretta can perfectly price-discriminate, however, she sells one fish for $8 to the buyer who is willing to pay that much, another fish for $7 to the buyer who is willing to pay $7, another for $6, a fourth for $5, a fifth for $4, and the sixth, seventh, and eighth for $3, $2, and $1. She earns more profit—$36—and she doesn't throw out any fish. This situation is economically efficient.

DIFFICULTIES WITH PERFECT PRICE DISCRIMINATION

Perfect price discrimination creates two problems. First, the seller must know the highest price that each buyer is willing to pay; sellers seldom know this, and buyers have no incentive to tell them. Second, the seller must prevent buyers from reselling their goods. Otherwise Violet may buy a candy bar for 20 cents and resell it to Luke for 50 cents. A theater that gives student discounts must be able to prevent students from buying discounted tickets and reselling them to non-students. When a seller has trouble preventing resale, it has trouble price-discriminating.

IMPERFECT PRICE DISCRIMINATION

Often, sellers can price-discriminate only imperfectly, charging higher prices to some groups of buyers than to others. A firm can increase its profit if it can charge a higher price to people in a group that, on average, is willing to pay more, and a lower price to people in a group that, on average, is not willing to pay as much. The seller must determine which people are willing to pay which price, and it must prevent resale.

"$200 for a loaf of bread! I told you never to go shopping in uniform!"

Source: *The Wall Street Journal*, May 20, 1988.

EXAMPLES

On average, students will not pay as much for theater tickets as people with full-time jobs will pay. By giving student discounts, a seller can charge a higher price to people who, on average, are willing to pay more, and a lower price to people who are, on average, unwilling to pay as much. By requiring students to present IDs to receive the discount, the seller can discriminate between the two groups.

Airlines charge lower round-trip air fares to people who stay over a Saturday night on trips. This is imperfect price discrimination between business travelers, who are usually willing to pay more but not to stay over a Saturday night, and personal travelers who are usually not willing to pay as much and who are more likely to stay over a Saturday night.

Discount coupons permit sellers to charge lower prices to people who spend the time to clip, sort, and use the coupons than to people who don't. On average, people who don't use discount coupons are willing to pay higher prices than people who do. (A person who does not bother to use discount coupons is not likely to bother with comparison shopping and searching for the lowest price.) In this way, discount coupons allow sellers to price-discriminate by charging more to people who, on average, are willing to pay more, and less to people who, on average, are not willing to pay as much.

Some stores promise to sell products for the lowest prices, and to give rebates to customers who later see lower advertised prices at other stores. This is a method of imperfect price discrimination because some customers search through advertisements after buying a product to try to find a lower price and collect the rebate, while other customers don't bother. This allows the seller to charge higher prices to customers who are less concerned with price than to customers who are more concerned with price.

APPLICATIONS OF MONOPOLY

INCREASE IN COSTS

Although monopolies charge prices above their marginal costs, they do not fully pass on all cost increases to their consumers. **Figure 13.15** shows why. The figure illustrates the effect of a $2 increase in a monopoly's marginal cost (from $8 to $10) with a straight-line demand curve. The monopoly maximizes profit by raising its price by only $1, from $16 to $17.

FIGURE 13.15

EFFECTS OF AN INCREASE IN A MONOPOLY'S MARGINAL COST

A $2 increase in marginal cost raises the monopoly's price by $1 and reduces its quantity supplied.

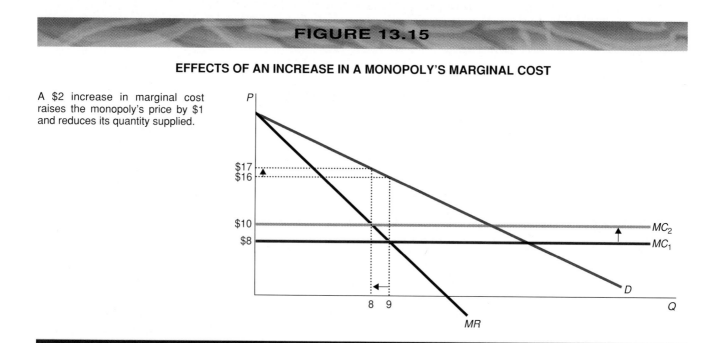

Monopolies' Incentives for Cost Reduction and Innovation

Monopolies, like perfectly competitive firms, have an incentive to produce at the lowest possible cost to earn the highest possible profits. Some people argue that a monopoly may feel a weaker incentive than a perfectly competitive firm because the owners of a monopoly might become complacent and fail to control costs or produce efficiently. On the other hand, monopolies sometimes have lower costs than perfectly competitive firms would have. After all, monopolies can result from successful innovations that allow a firm to produce at a lower cost than other firms.

Some economists have argued that the same weakness in incentives for monopolies to keep costs down can reduce their success in research and innovation. Others have argued the opposite, reasoning that a monopoly or cartel is more likely to succeed at research and development, partly because it can use its monopoly profit to finance large-scale research projects. Perfectly competitive firms may face difficulty convincing lenders to fund a risky research project; a monopoly may be able to use its internal funds and avoid this difficulty. The evidence on this issue is mixed.

Product Durability

Do monopolies benefit by making their products fall apart quickly or become obsolete?[15] A company once advertised that its roach-killer product would permanently rid a home of roaches, and that the product was available only by mail because stores refused to sell it fearing that it would work so effectively that customers would never have to buy roach killers again! This argument makes no sense. Although planned obsolescence may seem likely to raise profits by making sure that people buy the product more often, this argument ignores the effect of obsolescence on price. People are willing to pay more for products that last longer or work more effectively. Most people are willing to pay about twice as much for a gallon of milk as for a half-gallon or for a box of cereal that is twice as large as another. They are willing to pay about twice as much for a 1-year health-club membership as for a 6-month membership. Similarly, people are willing to pay about twice as much for an alarm clock that will last 2 years as for one that will last only 1 year. Since clothing styles change over time, people are not willing to pay twice as much for clothes that will last twice as long. Every good has some optimal durability that takes into account style changes, costs of producing goods that last longer, and other relevant factors. A seller, even a monopoly, has no incentive to make products wear out more quickly than is optimal.

Competition to Become a Monopoly

Honeoye Falls is a rural community without cable television. Several cable-television firms want to serve the town and each has asked the town government to make it the only legal cable company there. The firms point out that most U.S. cities have given monopoly rights to single cable-television companies. The town government has decided to grant monopoly cable rights to whichever company

---

[15]This idea was immortalized in an old movie, *The Man in the White Suit* (1952, with Alec Guiness). A man invents a fabric that never gets dirty and never wears out. Garment producers set out to suppress the invention because they believe that their profits will fall since people will never have to replace their clothing. You should be able to see what is wrong with the economics in this movie plot.

pays the town the most money. This forces the companies to compete for the right to be the monopoly seller.

How much would a firm be willing to pay to become a monopoly? The highest price it would pay is the discounted present value (see Chapter 10) of all its future monopoly profits. If the town government sells the right to become the monopoly and many firms bid for that right, they are likely to outbid each other until the winner pays that discounted present value. This reduces the winner's economic profit to zero and the government collects a fee equal to the discounted present value of the monopoly profit that the firm would have earned.

Competition to become a monopoly also occurs when television networks bid for the monopoly right to broadcast a special event such as the Super Bowl or the Olympics. The highest price that a television network is willing to pay the National Football League or the Olympic Committee for broadcast rights is the discounted present value of its expected monopoly profit from broadcasting the special event. When the networks bid against each other for the monopoly broadcasting rights, the equilibrium price is usually close to that discounted present value.[16] The National Football League and the Olympic Committee capture most of the monopoly profits from these broadcasts.

RENT SEEKING

When firms compete for rights to a legal monopoly or to obtain other special favors from the government, their actions can create a deadweight social loss because they spend time and other resources arguing about the division of the economy's wealth rather than creating new wealth. This activity, which economists call *rent seeking,* can create economic inefficiency.

rent seeking — competition for favors from the government

Rent seeking is competition for favors from the government.

People or firms engage in rent-seeking behavior when they try to obtain or keep special status from the government. Many firms and special-interest groups lobby the government; they hire lobbyists to wine, dine, and entertain government officials, and to try to convince them to do things that benefit those firms or special-interest groups. Lobbying wastes resources because the lobbyists could be producing goods rather than spending resources haggling over how to divide existing resources (trying to get the government to do favors for *them* rather than others).

If monopolies had to spend all of their profits on rent seeking to keep their monopolies, then Figures 13.7 through 13.10 would change. The deadweight social losses would become bigger because all the areas marked "Monopoly Profit" or "Producer Surplus" would become part of the deadweight social loss.[17] Estimates of the total deadweight social loss from monopoly in the United States range from 0.1 percent of the country's annual output to more than 5 percent when rent seeking is included.

---

[16]This would not be the case if the networks could collude to keep their bids down.

[17]If monopolies simply bribed government officials, then you might think that there would be no deadweight social loss (just a redistribution of resources) because when a firm pays a $1 million bribe, a government official collects that $1 million bribe. But there is a deadweight social loss from the competition among people to be the government officials who can collect such bribes!

A well-known New York madame of the 1920s, Polly Adler, wrote in her book, *A House Is Not a Home,* that her "house" (and others like it) were much less profitable than they seemed to outsiders, because madames had to make large payoffs to the police and politicians. Competition among corrupt police and politicians takes wasteful forms well known to viewers of gangster movies.

MONOPSONY

monopsony — a buyer that faces an upward-sloping supply curve and makes decisions without considering the reactions of other buyers

A monopoly is a seller that reduces output to keep its price high; a monopsony is a buyer (or cartel of buyers) that reduces purchases to keep the price low. Loosely, a monopsony is the only buyer of some product. More precisely:

> A buyer is a **monopsony** if (a) it faces an upward-sloping supply curve, and (b) it makes decisions without considering the reactions of other firms or buyers (perhaps because those reactions have small effects).

EXAMPLE

The company that runs a one-company mining town has a monopsony on labor—it is the only employer in town. It keeps its wages lower and its profit higher than those of a perfectly competitive industry by hiring fewer workers. It would have to raise wages to attract more workers, so it maximizes profit by keeping wages low and employing only workers who are willing to work for the low wages.

Figure 13.16 illustrates the basic characteristics of a monopsony. Curve *MB* shows the buyer's marginal benefit of the good. Curve *S* is the seller's supply curve. To keep the price low, the monopsony must keep its quantity demanded low. (To buy more, it must pay a higher price.) Curve *MCM* shows the *marginal cost to the monopsony* of buying the good. The marginal cost to the monopsony is higher than the price because if the monopsony buys another unit of the good, it raises the price of all of the units it buys.

The monopsony maximizes its profit by buying a quantity that sets its marginal benefit equal to its marginal cost and paying the lowest price at which

FIGURE 13.16

MONOPSONY

Curve *MB* is the buyer's marginal benefit of the good. Curve *S* is the seller's supply curve. To keep the price low, the monopsony buyer keeps its quantity demanded low. Curve *MCM* shows the marginal cost to the monopsony of buying the good. The monopsony buyer maximizes its profit by buying a quantity where its marginal benefit equals its marginal cost: the monopsony buys 5 units at $5 each. The shaded area shows the deadweight social loss due to the monopsony.

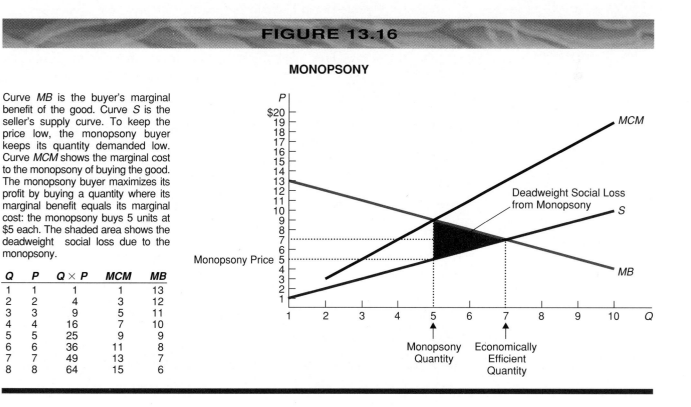

Q	P	Q × P	MCM	MB
1	1	1	1	13
2	2	4	3	12
3	3	9	5	11
4	4	16	7	10
5	5	25	9	9
6	6	36	11	8
7	7	49	13	7
8	8	64	15	6

N.F.L.'s free-agency system is found unfair by U.S. jury

By Thomas George
Special to The
New York Times

MINNEAPOLIS, Sept. 10— The National Football League's system of free agency, under which teams retain the rights to their best players, was rendered illegal today by an eight-women jury in an antitrust lawsuit brought by eight players.

After deliberating for 16 hours over two days, the Federal jury found for the players and awarded damages totaling $540,000 to four of the plaintiffs. Under antitrust law, that figure is tripled.

The court ruled that NFL teams were illegal monopsonies.

Source: Thomas George, "N.F.L.'s Free-Agency System Is Found Unfair by U.S. Jury," *New York Times,* September 11, 1992.

sellers will sell that quantity (the price on the supply curve at that quantity). Because the monopsony buys less than the economically efficient quantity, it causes a deadweight social loss.

EXAMPLE

Figure 13.16 shows the supply curve for a product and the marginal benefit of the good to buyers. With perfect competition, the buyers' marginal benefit curve is the demand curve, so the equilibrium quantity is 7 units of the good and the equilibrium price is $7. The third column shows the total cost of the good to buyers.

The fourth column shows the marginal cost of the good to a monopsony (given by the change in the total cost from the third column). The monopsony maximizes its profit by buying only 5 units so that its marginal benefit equals its marginal cost. By forming a monopsony, the profit to buyers rises from $21 to $30.

SOME FAMILIAR MONOPSONIES

The de Beers diamond cartel (a South African company that buys diamonds from mines in most parts of the world) has been the only major buyer of diamonds in the world market for most of the 20th century; it uses its monopsony power to reduce the price that it pays for diamonds.[18]

The NCAA, in combination with professional sports leagues, exercises monopsony power to keep payments to college and high-school athletes low. Top college players probably would command high salaries if the NCAA and professional leagues would permit it.[19] Payments-in-kind to top college athletes such as loans that can be repaid after signing professional contracts, or gifts of various kinds, are attempts to avoid the NCAA rules.

Before U.S. professional baseball and football adopted free agency systems, each team was a monopsony buyer of the services of its players. The players could not offer their services to other teams in the league. This monopsony power kept players' salaries low. Free agency reduced the teams' monopsony power and vastly increased players' salaries.

─────────────── **FOR REVIEW** ───────────────

13.11 What is price discrimination? Cite an example.

13.12 Discuss this statement: "If a monopoly's marginal cost of production rises by $5, the monopoly raises the price by $5."

13.13 What happens when many firms compete for the legal right to operate as a monopoly?

─────────────── **QUESTIONS** ───────────────

13.14 How large is the deadweight social loss if a monopoly perfectly price-discriminates? Explain your answer.

─────────────────────

[18]It is also approximately a monopoly; it sells more than 80 percent of all diamonds sold in the world. It produces about one-third of the world's diamonds, and buys the others to resell. As a buyer and reseller, it coordinates a cartel.

[19]Colleges have an incentive to keep payments to athletes low. They gain from low-cost sports on campus that help attract students, help raise money from alumni, and provide free advertising for the college in the sports news. Also, professional sports players may benefit from the reduction in competition from college athletes.

13.15 Explain why rent seeking can cause a deadweight social loss.

13.16 Draw a graph to show (a) the quantity purchased by a monopsony, (b) the price it pays, and (c) the deadweight social loss from the monopsony.

CONCLUSIONS

INTRODUCTION TO MONOPOLIES
A monopoly faces a downward-sloping demand curve for its product and makes its decisions independently of the reactions of other firms.

SHORT-RUN EQUILIBRIUM WITH A MONOPOLY
A monopoly chooses a price–quantity combination that lies along its demand curve. To maximize profit, it chooses the quantity at which marginal cost equals marginal revenue and it charges the highest price at which it can sell that quantity. A monopoly earns a higher profit than a firm in a perfectly competitive industry would earn with the same costs of production. But consumer surplus is lower with a monopoly than in a perfectly competitive industry. Monopolies cause economic inefficiency because they produce less than the economically efficient quantity. The deadweight social loss represents the potential gains from the trades that do not occur because the monopoly charges a price higher than its marginal cost.

LONG-RUN EQUILIBRIUM AND BARRIERS TO ENTRY
Monopoly profit tempts other firms to enter an industry. A monopoly can persist in the long run only if barriers to entry keep other firms out. These barriers to entry may be natural (resulting from lower costs of production at the monopoly firm) or artificial (resulting from laws or government regulations).

One type of natural barrier to entry results from increasing returns to scale (average cost that falls with output). A natural monopoly is a firm with increasing returns to scale over sufficiently large quantities.

CARTELS
A cartel is a group of firms that try to collude to act like a monopoly and share the profits. Cartels face special problems. They must decide which firms produce the goods and how the firms share the monopoly profits. They must also prevent member firms from cheating on the cartel agreement by reducing their prices and selling more, which is profitable for each firm individually but not for all firms jointly.

ANTITRUST
Antitrust laws make monopolies, cartels, and monopoly-like behaviors illegal.

PRICE DISCRIMINATION
Price discrimination occurs when a seller charges different prices to different buyers for the same good. Sellers can raise profits by price-discriminating. The extreme case is perfect price discrimination in which a seller charges each customer the highest price that the customer is willing to pay. In that case, the seller maximizes profit by producing the economically efficient quantity, although the seller gets all the gains from trade so consumer surplus is zero. In the less extreme case of imperfect price discrimination, a seller charges higher prices to some groups of buyers than to other groups.

APPLICATIONS OF MONOPOLY

Although monopolies charge prices higher than their marginal costs, they do not pass on all increases in their costs to consumers in the form of higher prices. Although monopolies create economic inefficiency, they generally have no incentive to produce inferior products or products that become obsolete.

Firms sometimes compete against each other for the right to operate as a monopoly. The process of competition can reduce the winner's monopoly profit to zero. This is a special case of rent seeking (competition for favors from the government), which can create a deadweight social loss because firms spend time and other resources fighting about how to divide the economy's wealth rather than creating new wealth.

MONOPSONY

A monopsony is a monopoly buyer, that is, a buyer that faces an upward-sloping supply curve and makes decisions independently of the reactions of other buyers. A monopsony chooses a quantity to buy that sets its marginal cost equal to its marginal benefit; it then pays the lowest price at which it can buy that quantity. Monopsonies, like monopolies, cause economic inefficiencies by reducing the quantity traded.

LOOKING AHEAD

Chapter 14 discusses two situations in which nonmonopoly firms face downward-sloping demand curves. One situation involves firms that produce products that differ slightly from the products of their competitors. The other situation involves firms that act strategically by taking the reactions of other firms into account when they choose their prices and outputs. Chapter 15 develops this theme further by discussing the general theory of strategic behavior—game theory—and its applications.

KEY TERMS

monopoly	antitrust law
barrier to entry	predatory pricing
increasing returns to scale	price discrimination
natural monopoly	perfect price discrimination
multipart price	rent seeking
cartel	monopsony

QUESTIONS AND PROBLEMS

13.17 Rebecca can produce lemonade for $1 per gallon. (Her marginal cost and average cost both equal $1 per gallon.) She faces the demand schedule in **Table 13.1.**

a. How much should she produce and what price should she charge to maximize her profit?

b. How big is her profit?

c. How much consumer surplus do her customers get?

d. How big is the deadweight social loss from Rebecca's monopoly?

e. Repeat Questions 13.17a through 13.17d assuming that Rebecca can perfectly price-discriminate.

TABLE 13.1

Price	Quantity Demanded
$7.00	1
6.00	2
5.00	3
4.00	4
3.00	5
2.00	6
1.00	7
0.50	8

13.18 Explain why colleges often charge higher tuition (perhaps full tuition, without rebates or any other form of financial aid) to students with government scholarships.

13.19 Discuss this statement: "A natural monopoly would lose money if it were to charge a price equal to its marginal cost, unless it charged a multipart price."

13.20 Why does the phone company charge a flat monthly fee plus another fee based on the number of calls you make?

13.21 Comment on this statement: "Producers could raise their profits by making their products fall apart or go out of style faster."

13.22 Who benefits and who loses if a monopoly uses predatory pricing to try to put a competitor out of business? Does predatory pricing increase or decrease the deadweight social loss from a monopoly?

13.23 The city of Santa Barbara, California, passed a law to prevent any new hookups to the city's water supply. Discuss the effects of this law on the value of houses in Santa Barbara.

13.24 Hot-Time Amusement Park does not allow people to bring their own food into the park. The park sells food at concession stands and charges prices twice as high as those at restaurants outside the park. The park charges an admission fee for entrance.
  a. Suppose that everyone who comes to the park buys exactly one hamburger and one soft drink. How would the price of an admission ticket to the park that maximizes the park's profit change if the park lowered the price of food? Would the amusement park gain by charging a high price for food in this case?
  b. Suppose that people have different demands for food at the amusement park. Some people are willing to pay much more than others. Some people would pay very high prices for food at the park, while others prefer to eat before going there and not buy any food inside. Explain why the park could maximize its profits by charging a high price for food.

13.25 Explain the news article at the top of the next page using the economic concepts introduced in this chapter.

INQUIRIES FOR FURTHER THOUGHT

13.26 Do you think that cable television is a natural monopoly? Should local governments allow more than one cable-television company to serve a single area? What would be the results of cable competition? Should governments regulate or control cable-television companies? If so, how?

13.27 U.S. colleges and universities share information about tuition increases. In 1989, the U.S. government charged some private colleges with forming a cartel to keep tuition high. Do you think that colleges have a cartel? What evidence would you want if you were to argue this case before the Supreme Court?

13.28 U.S. drug manufacturers have asked the government for an exemption from antitrust laws on the grounds that collaboration may reduce their costs of developing new treatments for AIDS and other diseases. Opponents of this idea believe that the exemption would simply allow the companies to form a cartel and raise prices. What should the government do? Why?

IN THE NEWS

Home sellers profit by banding together and selling to commercial developers

By Robert Johnson
Staff Reporter of
The Wall Street Journal

It's a beautiful day in the neighborhood. Homeowners joining together for the benefit of all. Neighbor helping neighbor.

The goal: to destroy the neighborhood.

In growing numbers, homeowners are signing pacts with each other to sell entire subdivisions at a shot. The owners are getting prices more than twice the individual appraisals on their homes by selling to commercial developers. Such joint ventures—called assemblages—allow homeowners to profit when encroaching office-building complexes and shopping centers threaten their life styles and the values of their homes.

The deals aren't easy to put together, however. Among the problems: getting all the homeowners in a neighborhood to agree to sell, keeping them from backing out once they do, and then putting up with the long wait while a buyer is found and local officials decide whether to rezone the tract for commercial use.

Perhaps the biggest problem is the initial one: getting the neighbors to join in a group sale. . . . One deal in Atlanta nearly came undone when a homeowner suddenly demanded a larger share of the prospective sale's proceeds.

Source: Robert Johnson, "Home Sellers Profit by Banding Together and Selling to Commercial Developers," *The Wall Street Journal,* December 7, 1988, p. B1.

13.29 Should major-league baseball be exempt from antitrust laws, as it was when this book went to press? What would happen to player salaries and to other features of the business if antitrust laws applied to baseball?

13.30 A news clipping in this chapter reported charges that Wal-Mart has engaged in predatory pricing. If you were a judge, how would you decide whether Wal-Mart is guilty? What should the law say about the prices that business firms charge? Should certain kinds of pricing decisions be illegal? If so, which ones and why? If not, why not?

13.31 Should the NCAA eliminate its rule that prevents colleges from paying college athletes for their services? What would be the effects?

13.32 Discuss this statement: "U.S. immigration laws create a cartel of U.S. workers and keep U.S. wages high by limiting the number of foreigners that can enter the U.S. labor market."

13.33 Name three firms that you think are monopolies. How did they get to be monopolies? Why don't other firms enter their industries and compete with them?

13.34 After Adam Smith's famous quote on collusion cited in this chapter, Smith went on to write, *"It is impossible, indeed, to prevent such meetings, by any law which either could be executed, or would be consistent with liberty and justice."* Do you agree or disagree? Why? What (if anything) should the government do about monopolies?

13.35 Discuss this statement: "Monopolies are good because the potential to earn a monopoly profit provides a strong incentive for people to create new products and patent them."

13.36 Many towns have laws and regulations to limit growth by prohibiting or raising the costs of building new houses and apartment buildings. Who gains from these restrictions?

13.37 How much should an inventor be allowed to patent? How long should the patent last? Should Nintendo have been able to prevent Atari from making games for Nintendo systems?[20] Should the author of an encyclopedia of trivia have been able to prevent the inventors of Trivial Pursuit from selling that game, as one author tried to do? Should researchers in genetic engineering be permitted to patent new forms of life, such as bacteria that would aid farmers or new kinds of farm animals (such as geeps, combinations of goats and sheep)?

If patents and copyrights create valuable incentives for new products and ideas, but result in economically inefficient monopolies, what should the government do? How would you make decisions on these matters?

13.38 Should the United States allow firms to collude so that they can better cope with foreign competition?

TAG SOFTWARE APPLICATIONS

TUTORIAL **E**XERCISES

▶ The module contains a review of the key terms from Chapter 13.

ANALYTICAL **E**XERCISES

▶ The analytical section includes questions on the calculation of monopoly profits.

GRAPHING **E**XERCISES

▶ The graphing segment contains questions on monopolies' profit maximization and deadweight losses and the taxing and subsidization of monopolies.

---

[20]This case arose in the early 1990s. Another issue involves why Nintendo would care. You might think that Nintendo would want to keep Atari from making the games so that Nintendo could sell more games instead, but if Atari makes any games that people want—because they are either better or cheaper—then more people will buy the Nintendo system to play those games and the ability to play those other games raises the price that Nintendo can charge for its machines. Nintendo would benefit by allowing other firms to make games for its machines. The reasons why Nintendo did not want Atari to make games for its machines are more complicated and beyond the scope of this book.

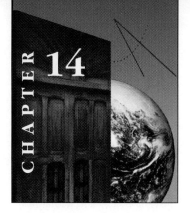

CHAPTER 14

MONOPOLISTIC COMPETITION AND OLIGOPOLY

WHAT THIS CHAPTER IS ABOUT

▶ Situations that lie between perfect competition and monopoly

▶ How firms compete through quality levels and images as well as price

▶ Tradeoffs between efficient production and product variety

▶ Advertising

▶ Measuring competition

▶ Business strategies—what happens when firms anticipate how their competitors will react to their price changes, and how this affects output and prices

Many real-life industries are neither monopolies or perfectly competitive. Burger King can raise the price of a Whopper without losing all of its customers to Wendy's or Hardees, so it is not a price taker. A perfectly competitive firm would not advertise to try to attract customers because it could sell as much as it wanted to sell at the equilibrium price, but fast-food restaurants advertise to convince people that they have the best food and offer unique products (such as salad bars or the best prizes in children's meals). Yet no one in the industry has a monopoly, and, as in a perfectly competitive industry, entry is free; virtually anyone can start a fast-food restaurant. This chapter discusses competition in industries that lie between perfect competition and monopoly.

MONOPOLISTIC COMPETITION

differentiated product — a product that buyers consider to be a good, but not perfect, substitute for another

Restaurants are not all alike. They produce differentiated products.

> Firms produce **differentiated products** if buyers consider the products to be good, but not perfect, substitutes.

If buyers view each seller's product as slightly different than the products of other sellers, these firms produce differentiated products. The products may differ in appearance, design, quality, location, image, or in other ways. The difference can be real or merely perceived. Advertising may differentiate products by creating a unique image for each one. Other differentiated products include hair salons, cars, and colleges.

When many firms in an industry produce differentiated products, there is monopolistic competition.

> **Monopolistic competition** means that (1) each firm sells a differentiated product, (2) the industry has enough firms that when one cuts its price, every other firm loses only a small quantity of its sales, and (3) the industry has free entry.

Monopolistic competition requires all three conditions. The first condition implies that firms in monopolistic competition are *not* price takers. Each faces a downward-sloping demand curve like that of a monopolist. If a firm raises its price, it loses some, but not all its customers; some customers continue to buy from the firm because they would rather pay the higher price than switch to other firms' slightly different products.

The second condition means that the actions of any one firm have only small effects on sales by any other firm. Like a monopoly, each firm acts independently, making decisions without considering the reactions of other firms. To understand this condition, think about a situation in which firms do not act independently. Suppose that three gas stations compete near an exit along a divided highway, each serving 100 customers per hour. If one station cuts its price by 2 cents per gallon it gains 20 customers per hour, 10 from each of the other stations. The other stations, seeing 10 percent losses in business, cut their prices by 2 cents per gallon to regain their customers. Each station then has a lower price, but the same number of customers as before. If the first gas station knows that other stations will react to its actions, it may choose not to lower its price. Such a firm does not act independently, because it takes account of the reactions of its competitors when it chooses its price.

If 21 gas stations compete near the same exit, however, and one gains 20 customers by cutting its price by 2 cents, each other station loses only about *one* customer. Because this loss is so small, the other firms may not react to the price cut; they may keep their prices unchanged. In this case, the firm acts independently because it does not need to take into account the reactions of its competitors. (The later section on "Oligopoly" returns to this issue.)

The third condition for monopolistic competition guarantees that new firms enter the industry in the long run if it offers positive economic profits, and some firms exit the industry if they suffer losses. This implies that monopolistic competition generates zero economic profits in the long-run equilibrium, just as perfect competition does.

EXAMPLES

The credit-card market is an example of monopolistic competition. Many banks issue credit cards such as Visa and Mastercard. Each bank tries to differentiate its product by giving its credit card a better picture, a higher credit line, a lower interest rate or annual fee, or by providing prizes or other services.

The restaurant industry is monopolistically competitive, with many different types of restaurants offering different atmospheres and types of food. Some people prefer some types of restaurants; other people prefer other types. As a result, most restaurants are not price takers—they face downward-sloping demand curves. Nevertheless, enough restaurants compete to ensure that changes in

---

monopolistic competition — an industry in which (1) each firm sells a differentiated product, (2) the industry has enough firms that when one cuts its price, every other firm loses only a small quantity of its sales, and (3) the industry has free entry.

IN THE NEWS

Beefpackers are trying to win back consumers by selling leaner cuts, brand names, and convenience

The packers are hoping that the brand-name approach could do for beef sales what designer labels did for blue jeans and Frank Perdue did for chicken: create distinctions where none existed—and do so at higher prices and, presumably, higher profits. If the industry's innovators have their way, a steak will no longer be a steak; it will be a steak by Excel or IBP.

Differentiating a product

Source: "Beefpackers Are Trying to Win Back Consumers by Selling Leaner Cuts, Brand Names, and Convenience," *New York Times,* September 28, 1986, p. F1.

FIGURE 14.1

ONE FIRM UNDER MONOPOLISTIC COMPETITION

A monopolistically competitive firm chooses a quantity that equates marginal revenue and marginal cost. It then charges the highest price at which it can sell that quantity. In the short run, the firm can earn a positive economic profit. In this example, the firm's average cost is $5 and the price is $8, so it earns a $600 profit ($3 on each of 200 units sold).

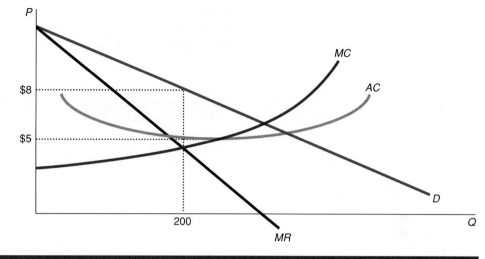

prices at any one restaurant have only a small effect on business at any other particular restaurant. Each restaurant acts independently without having to consider the reactions of other restaurants to its decisions. Finally, potential competitors can enter freely into the restaurant business. Other examples of monopolistic competition include clothing, soaps and detergents, movies, pain relievers, sneakers, and music.

Product differentiation does not guarantee success, though. Duncan Hines once tried to sell cookies that it advertised as crispy on the outside and soft on the inside. This differentiated product failed; customers did not buy them because, according to an industry consultant, "the package tasted better than the product."[1]

SHORT-RUN EQUILIBRIUM WITH MONOPOLISTIC COMPETITION

Each firm in a monopolistically competitive industry faces a downward-sloping demand curve, so its marginal revenue curve lies below its demand curve, as in **Figure 14.1.** Like a monopoly, it chooses a combination of price and output along its demand curve. It maximizes profit by choosing a quantity that gives a marginal cost equal to its marginal revenue and charging the highest price at which it can sell that quantity. Figure 14.1 shows the profit-maximizing output and price for a monopolistically competitive firm: 200 units at a price of $8 per unit.

Figure 14.1 also shows the firm's average cost curve, which indicates that the average cost of producing 200 units equals $5. The firm charges $8, so it earns a $3 profit on each unit it sells. (It has a $3 markup.) In the short run, with a fixed number of firms, monopolistic competition resembles monopoly, and Figure 14.1 looks like the basic graph for a monopoly.

---

[1]*New York Times,* August 15, 1987.

LONG-RUN EQUILIBRIUM WITH MONOPOLISTIC COMPETITION

In the long run, positive economic profits induce new firms to enter the industry and produce products that are good substitutes for the products of the older firms. As more firms share the industry's customers, the demand for each firm's output falls. **Figure 14.2** shows that entry of new firms reduces demand for the product of a firm that already competes in the industry. This new entry shifts the demand curve for the existing firm's product to the left. As demand shifts from D_1 (a short-

FIGURE 14.2

EFFECTS OF ENTRY IN A MONOPOLISTICALLY COMPETITIVE INDUSTRY

(a) If existing competitors earn profits in the short run, new firms enter the industry, reducing demand for the products of old firms. Each firm's marginal revenue curve shifts downward along with the demand curve for each differentiated product. (b) Long-run equilibrium occurs when the demand curve shifts far enough that each firm earns zero economic profit when it produces the quantity at which marginal revenue equals marginal cost. A firm earns zero economic profit when the demand curve is tangent to the average cost curve (so average cost equals price).

(a) Entry of New Firms with Monopolistic Competition

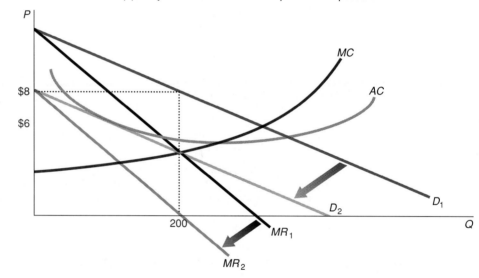

(b) Long-Run Equilibrium with Monopolistic Competition

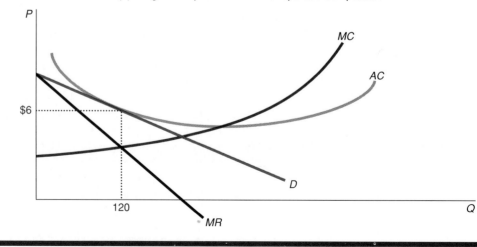

run equilibrium) to D_2 (the long-run equilibrium), the marginal revenue curve shifts to MR_2 from MR_1.

Long-run equilibrium occurs when new firms see no further incentives to enter the industry and old firms see no reason to exit, that is, when economic profits are zero. Figure 14.2b shows long-run equilibrium with monopolistic competition. Each firm maximizes profit by producing 120 units of the good (the quantity at which marginal revenue equals marginal cost) and charging a price of $6 per unit. This price equals average cost, so each firm earns zero economic profit. Long-run equilibrium occurs when entry of new firms has reduced demand sufficiently to position the demand curve tangent to (just touching) the firm's average cost curve.

It firms lose money in short-run equilibrium, then some exit the industry in the long run. This raises demand for the products of the remaining firms. The demand curves shift to the right until the industry reaches a long-run equilibrium with zero economic profit, as in Figure 14.2b.

EXPLANATION

Why does demand for each firm's output fall, as in Figure 14.2, when new firms enter the industry? Consider competition among ice-cream stands along a beach. **Figure 14.3** shows a short-run situation with three ice-cream stands. They all sell the same kinds of ice cream, but their products are differentiated by their locations. The sellers are not perfectly competitive because they face downward-sloping demand curves. If they all charge the same price, a person closest to Joanne's stand goes there. Joanne could raise her price somewhat without losing all of her customers because people close enough to her stand would still buy from her rather than walk farther to other stands. For this reason, Joanne faces a downward-sloping demand curve. Donna and Linda face downward-sloping demand curves for the same reason. These ice-cream stands are monopolistic competitors.

If enough people on the beach buy ice cream, then each stand earns positive economic profits and in the long run new firms enter the industry. **Figure 14.4**

FIGURE 14.3

SHORT-RUN EQUILIBRIUM ON THE BEACH WITH MONOPOLISTIC COMPETITION

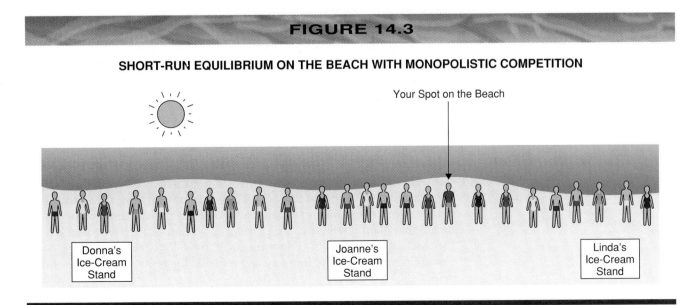

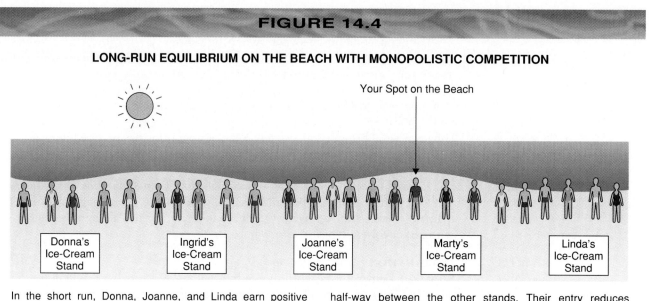

FIGURE 14.4

LONG-RUN EQUILIBRIUM ON THE BEACH WITH MONOPOLISTIC COMPETITION

In the short run, Donna, Joanne, and Linda earn positive economic profits. This leads Marty and Ingrid to enter the industry by setting up their own ice-cream stands. They locate their stands where they can attract the most customers: half-way between the other stands. Their entry reduces demands for ice cream at the three original stands, and in the long-run equilibrium, each seller earns zero economic profit.

shows the long-run equilibrium. Two new firms, Ingrid's Ice Cream and Marty's Ice Cream, have entered the industry and now compete with Donna, Joanne, and Linda. The new firms have located their stands to attract the largest number of customers, and some people who would previously have bought from Donna, Joanne, or Linda now buy ice cream from Ingrid or Marty. The demands for Donna's, Joanne's, and Linda's ice cream have fallen, so the demand curves for their ice cream have shifted leftward, as in Figure 14.2. New entry occurs until firms earn zero economic profits, as in Figure 14.2b.

FOR REVIEW

14.1 What three conditions characterize a monopolistically competitive industry?

14.2 Why don't monopolistically competitive firms earn economic profits in long-run equilibrium?

14.3 How does entry by new firms shift the demand curve for the product sold by a firm already in the industry?

QUESTION

14.4 Consider the beach example in Figure 14.3, in which each of three sellers earns a profit in the short run. (a) Draw a graph showing the demand for Joanne's ice cream, Joanne's marginal and average costs, the quantity of ice cream that Joanne sells, and the price of ice cream. (b) Draw similar graphs for the long run, after two new firms (Marty's Ice Cream and Ingrid's Ice Cream) have entered the industry and reduced long-run economic profits to zero.

A Firm in Monopolistic Competition: McDonald's

The fast-food industry is monopolistically competitive. Burger King, Hardees, Wendy's, McDonald's, and many other fast-food restaurants differentiate their products and face downward-sloping demand curves. They tend to act independently of other firms because they are numerous enough that, when one cuts it price, the loss in customers to each other restaurant is small. Also, there is free entry into the fast-food business. The table shows estimated sales and costs at a typical McDonald's franchise.

Over 2,000 people apply each year to start McDonald's franchises. The firm accepts only about one applicant out of twenty. Each accepted franchisee (franchise owner) spends about $310,000 to open a McDonald's and about $500,000 more a few years later. Most of these payments cover equipment; they also include a franchise fee and a security deposit. The franchisee must also spend about 2,000 hours in training (working and attending Hamburger University without pay) before being allowed to open the franchise.

The $97,084 net revenue to the franchise owner equals the sum of:

▶ The opportunity cost of the owner's time and effort running the franchise

ESTIMATED SALES, COSTS, AND PROFIT OF A TYPICAL McDONALD'S RESTAURANT

Sales	$1,760,000
Costs	1,579,396
Costs of food and paper	646,034
food costs	569,786
paper costs	76,248
Crew labor costs	291,414
Management labor costs	106,669
Advertising and promotion	110,989
Utilities	61,813
Royalties/rent	202,400 (set by McDonald's at 11.5% of sales)
Other expenses	160,077
Operating profit	180,604 (Accounting profit)
Cost of capital	83,520 (Interest and depreciation)
Pretax net revenue to franchisee	$ 97,084 (See below.)

▶ Partial payment toward the owner's opportunity cost of the 2,000 hours of training

▶ A payment to the owner for bearing risk

▶ Economic profit (or economic rent to the owner for entrepreneurial services)

Source: Table data are based on estimates reported in Patrick Kaufmann and Francine Lafontaine, "Costs of Control: the Sources of Rents for McDonald's Franchises," working paper, Georgia State University and University of Michigan, 1992, adjusted and transformed to 1995 dollars by the author.

EXCESS CAPACITY AND PRODUCT VARIETY

Monopolistically competitive firms have excess capacity in long-run equilibrium.

excess capacity — the opportunity for a firm to reduce its average cost by raising its output

A firm has **excess capacity** if it could reduce its average cost by raising its output.

Recall from Chapter 10 that a firm's capacity output is the quantity that minimizes its average cost. A firm has excess capacity if it produces less than its capacity output. Firms in an industry with monopolistic competition would reduce their average costs if they were to produce more, but they don't because doing so would reduce their profits.

EXPLANATION AND EXAMPLE

The connection between average cost and excess capacity is easy to understand. Suppose that a person moves from one apartment to another and rents a larger truck than she needs because a smaller truck is not available. The extra space in the truck is excess capacity. Suppose that the truck costs $40 for the day and it can hold 200 boxes. If the person moves 100 boxes, the average cost of moving a box is 40 cents. If she had moved 200 boxes, the average cost would have been 20 cents. Excess capacity implies that average cost is lower with a larger quantity.

Figure 14.2b shows a firm in long-run equilibrium with monopolistic competition that produces 120 units of its product. Its capacity output is larger than 120 units, so it could reduce its average cost by producing more. Why doesn't the firm produce more to reduce its average cost? The answer is that the firm would have to lower its price to sell more, and the price cut would reduce profit, even though it would also reduce average cost. For example, the firm in Figure 14.2b might reduce its average cost from $6 to $5 by raising output to 150 units per month, but to sell 150 units the price would have to fall from $6 to $4. In that case, the firm would lose $150 (a $1 loss per unit on 150 units) each month. Instead, the firm chooses to produce 120 units and earn an economic profit of zero.

IS MONOPOLISTIC COMPETITION INEFFICIENT?

Sometimes people argue that excess capacity is economically inefficient. In long-run equilibrium, the price is higher than marginal cost (as in Figure 14.2) and firms could reduce their average costs by producing more. When price exceeds marginal cost, some buyer is willing to pay more for an additional unit of the good than the supplier would spend to produce that unit. As Chapter 13 explained, this makes monopolies economically inefficient. Before you conclude that monopolistic competition is also economically inefficient, however, notice that it differs from monopoly because it provides buyers with differentiated products, or product variety.

Firms face a tradeoff between reducing their average costs and providing product variety. Average cost would be lower if there were fewer firms in the industry because each firm would produce more, but there would be less product variety. The lower average cost would be good, but the smaller variety of products might be bad. Buyers might enjoy a larger variety of products because each buyer could choose the type of product he likes best. In a sense, the excess capacity in monopolistic competition is the price that people pay for more product diversity and choice.

MONOPOLISTIC COMPETITION VERSUS PERFECT COMPETITION AND MONOPOLY

Monopolistic competition resembles perfect competition in two important ways:

▶ Each firm acts independently, without regard to the responses of its competitors.
▶ Free entry guarantees that firms earn zero economic profits in long-run equilibrium.

Monopolistic competition also differs from perfect competition in two ways:

▶ Each firm faces a downward-sloping demand curve because each produces a differentiated product; monopolistic competitors are not price takers.
▶ The firm's equilibrium price exceeds its marginal cost (see Figure 14.2), and firms have excess capacity in long-run equilibrium.

The difference between monopolistic competition and perfect competition vanishes as demand becomes large enough to accommodate many firms in the industry in long-run equilibrium. More firms increase the similarity between one firm's product and the products of its closest competitors, so products are less differentiated. For example, as more ice-cream stands open on the beach, the distance between the *closest* and *second-closest* stands declines and the demand curve facing each firm becomes more elastic. If the number of firms in the industry grows very large, each firm becomes a price taker and monopolistic competition turns into perfect competition.

The main difference between monopolistic competition and monopoly is that monopolistic competition applies to situations with free entry in the long run. Free entry guarantees that economic profit in long-run equilibrium is zero.

NONPRICE COMPETITION

Firms in a monopolistically competitive industry engage in nonprice competition to raise demands for their products.

> **nonprice competition** — competitive rivalry based on better-quality products or product characteristics designed to match the preferences of specific groups of consumers

> **Nonprice competition** occurs when firms compete by providing better-quality products or product characteristics designed to match the preferences of specific groups of consumers.

Better-quality products might provide faster or friendlier service, longer warranties, quicker delivery, and so on. Firms match product characteristics with the preferences of certain groups of consumers when they produce products tailored to the demands of those consumers, such as baby strollers for twins and triplets, mango soda, or designer hearing aids.

Sometimes nonprice competition involves location, as in Figure 14.3. Suppose that Joanne opens the first ice-cream stand on the beach and locates it in the middle of the beach. When Donna establishes a competing ice-cream stand, she will probably not choose the location in Figure 14.3 because she can attract more customers by locating closer to Joanne, as in **Figure 14.5.** That way, Donna can be

FIGURE 14.5

DONNA'S PROFIT-MAXIMIZING LOCATION DECISION

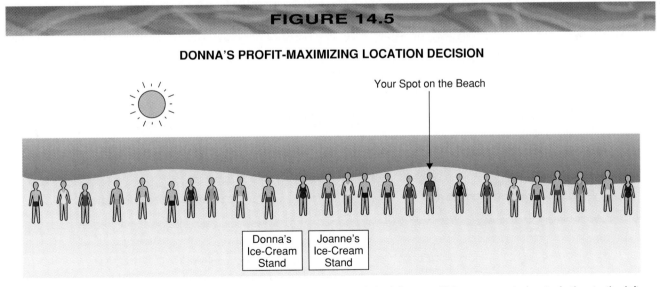

Your Spot on the Beach

Donna's Ice-Cream Stand

Joanne's Ice-Cream Stand

Joanne's ice-cream stand sits in the middle of the beach before Donna enters the business. To attract the most customers, Donna sets up her stand as close to Joanne's stand as possible. That way, Donna attracts the business of everyone to the left of Joanne. (If Donna were to locate farther to the left, some people between the two stands would be closer to, and buy from, Joanne's stand.)

the closest seller to everyone on one side of the beach. (Donna will locate close to Joanne because a location farther to the left would leave some customers on the left part of the beach closer to Joanne than to her.) In this case, competition results in only a small amount of product differentiation. You are probably familiar with many examples of this, such as several gas stations located close to each other, often at the same intersection.

Similar reasoning applies to many features of goods. Suppose that an organization on your campus earns a large profit by selling brownies, and your club decides to go into the brownie business, too. Brownies range from very soft to very chewy, as **Figure 14.6** illustrates, with many in-between varieties. Suppose that equal numbers of people like each possible type of brownie and the other organization sells an in-between type (not too soft and not too chewy). Your club is likely to maximize its profit by selling brownies that are only *slightly* softer or *slightly* chewier than those sold by your competitor. (If your brownies were *very* soft or *very* chewy, fewer people would buy them.) By making your product only slightly different from the product of your competitor, you maximize the number of your customers.

COMPETITION AMONG CITIES AND STATES

Cities compete against each other for new businesses, sports franchises, and tourists. Monopolistic competition describes this situation well. Many cities freely enter this competition and cities' differing characteristics create product differentiation. Cities compete vigorously to induce major-league football and baseball teams to move from elsewhere or to obtain new teams when leagues expand by offering tax breaks, new stadiums, and other services that the teams desire. Similarly, cities compete to attract other types of businesses by offering low tax rates or special tax exemptions along with other benefits. States and countries compete in this way for tourists and residents, as well as businesses. Warm-weather states compete for retirees by offering free fishing licenses, free college tuition, retail discounts, and other benefits. France and Spain competed for Disney's European theme park; France won partly because it offered more tax breaks and other assistance. All of these examples share an important feature: despite product

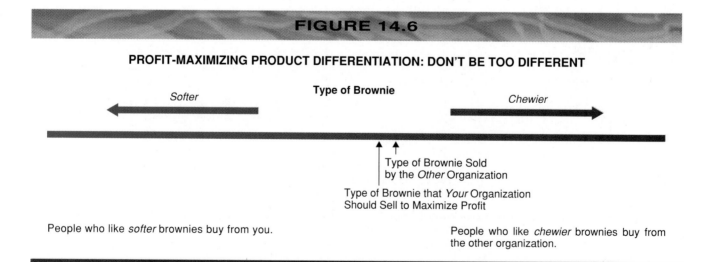

FIGURE 14.6

PROFIT-MAXIMIZING PRODUCT DIFFERENTIATION: DON'T BE TOO DIFFERENT

Softer **Type of Brownie** *Chewier*

Type of Brownie Sold
by the *Other* Organization

Type of Brownie that *Your* Organization
Should Sell to Maximize Profit

People who like *softer* brownies buy from you.

People who like *chewier* brownies buy from the other organization.

differentiation, new players can freely enter the competitions. The logic of monopolistic competition suggests that cities, states, and countries earn zero economic profits in the long run from these activities.

─────────────────────── **FOR REVIEW** ───────────────────────

14.5 What is excess capacity and why does long-run equilibrium with monopolistic competition exhibit excess capacity?

14.6 What is nonprice competition?

14.7 How does monopolistic competition resemble perfect competition and how does it differ? How does it resemble monopoly and how does it differ?

─────────────────────── **QUESTIONS** ───────────────────────

14.8 Why do competing firms often locate near each other? Why do they often sell products that differ only slightly from the products of their competitors?

14.9 Use the economic analysis in this chapter to explain why politicians often take middle-of-the-road positions on issues in public, even if they are privately more liberal or conservative than their public positions indicate.

OLIGOPOLY

oligopoly — an industry in which (1) firms are not price takers (each faces a downward-sloping demand curve), and (2) each firm acts strategically, taking into account its competitors' likely reactions to its decisions and how it will be affected by their reactions

If American Airlines cuts ticket prices, United Airlines may cut its prices, too. American would gain more new business if United would keep its prices constant. When an airline decides whether to cut prices, it must take into account how its competitors will respond. The airline industry is an oligopoly.

Roughly, an oligopoly is competition among a small number of sellers. More precisely:

> **Oligopoly** occurs when (1) firms are not price takers (each faces a downward-sloping demand curve), and (2) each firm acts strategically, taking into account its competitors' likely reactions to its decisions and how it will be affected by their reactions.

An oligopolist reasons as follows: "What *I* do affects what *they* will do, and what *they* do affects *me*." Each firm anticipates its competitors' reactions to its own actions when it decides what to do; firms interact strategically.

STRATEGIC INTERACTION

Strategic interaction takes many forms. When a company builds a new hotel in a resort area, it must take into account how its rivals will respond. Will they react by building even more hotels or by canceling their expansion plans? Industries with perfect competition have no strategic interaction because they encompass so many firms that, when one firm sells more, the loss in sales at each of its competitors is small enough to be insignificant. For example, suppose that 100 firms compete in an industry, each selling 100 units per month. When one firm doubles its output to 200 units per month, each of its competitors loses only about one sale per month, so it is unlikely to react to the change. The same reasoning applies to a monopolistically competitive industry, so perfectly competitive and monopolistically competitive industries exhibit no strategic interaction.

If, however, only five firms compete in the industry and one firm doubles output from 100 to 200 units per month, each of the other four firms may lose 25 sales per month (25 percent of its business). These competitors are likely to react. Knowing that its competitors will react in this case, each firm anticipates these likely reactions in its decision making. This process leads oligopolistic firms to act strategically. **Table 14.1** contrasts oligopoly with monopolistic competition and perfect competition.

EXAMPLES OF STRATEGIC INTERACTION

Governments evaluate the likely reactions of allies and adversaries in their foreign-policy decisions. Personal decisions (particularly regarding romantic issues) often take into account the reactions of other people and the likely effects of those reactions. Candidates for public office consider their opponents' reactions to public statements, positions, and political advertisements. Each of these cases illustrates a strategic interaction—the actions of each decision maker take into account the reactions of others.

SOME FAMILIAR OLIGOPOLIES

The video-game industry is an oligopoly that is currently dominated by Nintendo and Sega. Automobile production was once a classic example of oligopoly before increased competition from foreign cars, particularly Japanese cars, raised the number of firms in the industry and made the market more competitive; nevertheless, the auto industry still demonstrates many features of an oligopoly. Other oligopolistic industries include airlines, television broadcasting (despite increased competition from cable networks), breakfast cereals (in which Kelloggs and General Mills share about two-thirds of total industry sales), meat packing (in which three firms account for about two-thirds of all sales), and the soft-drink industry (which Coca Cola and PepsiCo dominate).

TABLE 14.1

DIFFERENCES BETWEEN MONOPOLISTIC COMPETITION, OLIGOPOLY, AND PERFECT COMPETITION

Monopolistic Competition	Oligopoly	Perfect Competition
Many firms produce closely related products	Few firms produce closely related products	Many firms produce the same product
When one firm lowers its price, it gains sales. *Each* other firm loses only a few sales because so many other firms compete. When one firm changes its output or price, other firms *do not react.*	When one firm lowers its price, it gains sales. *Each* other firm loses a significant amount of sales because only a few other firms compete. Those firms react, perhaps by lowering their prices. Each firm knows that other firms will react to its decisions, and it anticipates these reactions when making its decisions.	Any firm can sell more without reducing its price. With many firms, the loss in sales to each other firm is very small. When one firm changes its output, other firms *do not react.*

BARRIERS TO ENTRY

Oligopolistic firms, like monopolies, can earn positive economic profits in the long run only if barriers to entry protect them from competition. Otherwise, new firms enter and the industry becomes perfectly competitive or monopolistically competitive. Barriers to entry (costs high enough to prevent new firms from entering an industry) can take many forms. Artificial barriers to entry include laws against new firms in an industry, license requirements or other government regulations that hinder entry, and patents or copyrights. Natural barriers to entry include the fixed costs of starting a firm, increasing returns to scale (average costs that fall with a rising scale of production), and the cost advantages of established firms that either own unique inputs that new firms cannot obtain or operate more efficiently than new firms, perhaps due to their experience in the industry.

PRODUCT DIFFERENTIATION BY OLIGOPOLIES

The logic of oligopoly sometimes applies to industries with *many* firms and differentiated products. If only a few firms out of many in an industry produce close substitutes for the product of HighLite Corporation, then HighLite and those few firms may strategically interact as an oligopoly. Figure 14.4 shows an example. Ingrid's ice cream is a closer substitute for Donna's and Joanne's ice cream than for Marty's or Linda's, because Donna's ice-cream stand is farther away. This could give rise to strategic interaction between sellers; if Ingrid reduces her price, she attracts most of her new customers from Donna and Joanne. These two sellers may react to changes in Ingrid's price, and Ingrid may take these possible reactions into account when she chooses her price. In such a case, the logic of oligopoly better describes competition among these firms than the logic of monopolistic competition does.

Similarly, although many firms compete in the real-life ice-cream industry, some brands are closer substitutes than others. For example, Breyer's may be a closer substitute for Baskin-Robbins than for generic ice cream or Discount Village's store brand ice cream. Kellogg's Raisin Bran and Post Raisin Bran are closer substitutes for each other than either is for Batman or Lucky Charms cereal. Even in an industry with many firms, if only a few sell close substitutes, those firms may strategically interact with each other.

MEASURING COMPETITION IN AN OLIGOPOLY

A concentration ratio roughly indicates the amount of competition in an industry.

n-firm concentration ratio — the total sales of the largest *n* firms in an industry as a percentage of total industry sales

> The ***n*-firm concentration ratio** in an industry is the total sales of the largest *n* firms as a percentage of total industry sales.

For example, in a recent year, nine firms competed in the U.S. chewing-gum industry and the four-firm concentration ratio was 95, which means that the four largest firms sold 95 percent of all chewing gum in the United States. Industries with high three-firm or four-firm concentration ratios are sometimes called *concentrated industries.* On the other hand, 4,161 firms operated in the U.S. ready-mixed cement industry in a recent year; the four-firm concentration ratio was 6 and the eight-firm concentration ratio was 9. Together, the eight largest cement firms sold only 9 percent of all U.S. cement. This industry is quite unconcentrated.

Most industries lie somewhere between these examples. One study found that metropolitan-area four-firm concentration ratios in U.S. retail food stores ranged from 26 in Charleston, North Carolina, to 81 in Cedar Rapids, Iowa, with an average of 52. **Table 14.2** shows concentration ratios in the United States for several other industries. Part B of the table shows that, for most industries, the four largest firms generate between 20 percent and 60 percent of industry sales.

The fraction of U.S. industries with four-firm concentration ratios above 50 has not changed much over time, indicating that the United States has about the same number of oligopolies and monopolies as it had in the past. U.S. concentration ratios are smaller, on average, than those in most other countries. Smaller countries, measured by the sizes of their economies, such as Canada, Sweden, and Korea tend to have higher concentration ratios than larger countries such as the United States, Germany, and Japan. The average concentration ratio in Japan is slightly lower than the U.S. average, but its interpretation is complicated by the fact that many Japanese companies are part of *keiretsu* family groups that resemble larger companies.

TABLE 14.2

CONCENTRATION IN THE U.S. ECONOMY

A. Concentration Ratios for Some Industries

Industry	Four-Firm Concentration Ratio	Eight-Firm Concentration Ratio	Number of Firms
Passenger cars	97	99	*
Chewing gum	95	99	9
Refrigerators, etc.	94	98	39
Electric lamps	91	96	113
Breakfast cereals	86	99	32
Zippers	70	81	*
Tires and inner tubes	66	86	108
Aircraft	64	81	139
Soap and detergent	60	63	642
Farm machinery	53	62	1,787
Games and toys	39	55	*
Women's shoes	38	47	209
Bread and cake	34	47	1,869
Paints and allied products	24	36	1,170
Men's dress shirts	19	29	535
Plastic products	7	24	10,152
Women's dresses	6	10	5,489
Ready-mix concrete	6	9	4,161

B. Overview of Industry Concentration Ratios, 1982

Four-Firm Concentration Ratio Range	Percentage of All Industries
0–19	19.2%
20–39	36.4
40–59	26.8
60–79	12.5
80–100	5.1

*Indicates that no data are available.

Source: U.S. Bureau of the Census, *1982 Census of Manufacturers,* Table 6, "Concentration Ratios in Manufacturing," MC82-S-7, April 1986 and various studies surveyed by Richard Schmalensee, "Inter-Industry Studies of Structure and Performance," and Timothy Bresnahan, "Empirical Studies of Industries with Market Power," in R. Schmalensee and R. Willig, eds., *Handbook of Industrial Organization* (Amsterdam: North-Holland, 1989).

Concentration ratios ignore foreign competitors. If only two U.S. firms produce motorcycles, the two-firm concentration ratio is 100, but those U.S. firms may face strong foreign competition that this figure ignores.

In some cases, concentration ratios are useful as rough summaries of the degree of competition in an industry, but they are not sophisticated measures of competition. Concentration ratios are not closely related to costs of production or economic efficiency.

PRICES AND PROFITS IN THE U.S. ECONOMY

Price equals marginal cost in perfectly competitive industries. Price exceeds marginal cost in industries with oligopoly, monopoly, or monopolistic competition. Evidence suggests that price exceeds marginal cost in many U.S. industries, and some evidence finds a larger average difference between price and marginal cost in more concentrated industries. Some estimates indicate that, in American industry, marginal cost averages between half and two-thirds of price.[2]

Evidence also suggests that prices in more concentrated industries change less often and by smaller amounts than other prices. More concentrated industries have more price rigidity.

price rigidity — slow adjustments of prices to changes in costs or demand

> **Price rigidity** refers to slow adjustments of prices to changes in costs or demand.

Prices of magazines at newsstands, like prices of tickets to rock concerts or major sporting events, tend to show some price rigidity. Economists do not yet fully understand the reasons for price rigidity and its variation across industries. Nevertheless, evidence indicates that prices change more often in some industries than in others, and they tend to change less often in more concentrated industries. Wholesale prices are fixed for 6 to 18 months on average, depending on the industry. For example, the average length of time between price changes is about 6 months for household appliances and plywood, 1 year for glass and paper, and 18 months for cement, steel, and chemicals.

Firms earn higher profits (on average) in more concentrated industries. There are two possible interpretations of this fact. First, higher concentration may mean less competition, higher prices, and higher profits. In such a case, profits are high because the industry is concentrated. Second, firms that succeed in earning high profits (perhaps because they successfully reduce their costs) tend to expand, raising the concentration ratios in their industries. In such a case, the industry becomes concentrated because some firms have earned high profits.

Firms often report their accounting profits as rates of return.

rate of return on investment — a firm's accounting profit per dollar of its previous investments, expressed as a percentage per year

> A firm's **rate of return on investment** is its accounting profit per dollar of its previous investments, expressed as a percentage per year.

The after-tax rate of return on investment in American industries, adjusted for inflation, averaged about 8 percent per year from the end of World War II until the mid-1970s. Since that time, the after-tax rate of return on investment in American industries, adjusted for inflation, has averaged less than 2 percent per year. Rates of return differ across industries, and highly concentrated industries tend to have higher rates of return.

---

[2] These estimates are somewhat controversial. Some economists believe that the evidence indicates that marginal cost is a much larger fraction of price than these estimates suggest.

EQUILIBRIUM WITH OLIGOPOLY

Each firm in an oligopoly must anticipate other firms' likely reactions to its actions. The equilibrium in an oligopoly depends on *what firms believe* about the likely reactions of their competitors. Each type of belief leads to a different model of oligopoly. The remainder of this chapter discusses the main types of oligopoly models.[3]

NASH EQUILIBRIUM

The logic of strategic interactions is based on the concept of a Nash equilibrium, which says that each firm's action is optimal *given* the actions of the other firms. More precisely:

> A firm's **best response** to a situation is the action that maximizes its profit, given the actions of its rivals.

> A **Nash equilibrium** is a situation in which each firm makes its best response.

In other words, a Nash equilibrium is a situation in which each firm's action maximizes its profit, given the actions of rival firms. In a Nash equilibrium, each firm's action is a best response to its competitors' actions, and no firm has an incentive to change its actions. The following sections apply this concept to several models of oligopoly. In each model, firms produce identical (not differentiated) products unless stated otherwise.

BERTRAND MODEL

The Bertrand model is one model of oligopoly.

> In the **Bertrand model,** each firm believes that other firms will react to its decisions by changing the quantities they sell to keep their prices fixed.

If firms have constant marginal costs (horizontal marginal cost curves), then the Nash equilibrium price in the Bertrand model equals marginal cost.

EXPLANATION OF THE BERTRAND MODEL

The equilibrium with Bertrand competition is easiest to understand by beginning with a situation, as in **Figure 14.7,** that is *not* a Nash equilibrium. Suppose that two firms in an industry each have a constant marginal cost of $10.00 per unit; both charge the monopoly price, $20.00, and sell 50 units. Each firm earns $500.00 profit ($10.00 per unit on 50 units sold).

This is not a Nash equilibrium. Since each firm believes the other will keep its price constant, each believes that it could raise its profit by lowering its price a small amount and taking all of the other firm's customers away. Each firm believes that it would attract all 101 buyers if it cut its price to $19.75; it would then earn a profit of $9.75 per unit on 101 units, or $984.75. Therefore, charging a $20.00 price does not maximize the firm's profit; it is not a best response to the other firm's action (of keeping its price constant), and it is not a Nash equilibrium.

This logic applies whenever the price exceeds marginal cost, which is $10.00 in the figure. Therefore, no price above marginal cost is a Nash equilibrium price in this example.[4] Nash equilibrium in the Bertrand model occurs when price

---

best response — the action that maximizes a firm's profit, given the actions of rivals

Nash equilibrium — a situation in which each firm makes its best response, i.e., maximizes its profit, given the actions of rival firms

Bertrand model — a model of oligopoly in which each firm believes that other firms will react to its decisions by changing the quantities they sell to keep their prices fixed

FIGURE 14.7

NOT A NASH EQUILIBRIUM WITH BERTRAND COMPETITION

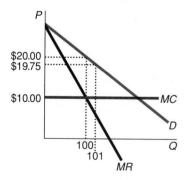

The monopoly or cartel price of $20.00 is *not* a Nash equilibrium with Bertrand competition (in which each seller believes that other sellers will keep their prices fixed) because any *one* firm could raise its profit by reducing its price. A firm that reduced its price to $19.75 would sell 101 units and raise its profits.

---

[3]Chapter 15 discusses the general theory of strategic interactions—game theory—and its application.

[4]If the price exceeds marginal cost and each firm believes that other firms will keep their prices fixed, then each firm has an incentive to cut its own price to steal customers away from other firms to raise its profit.

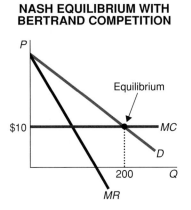

FIGURE 14.8

NASH EQUILIBRIUM WITH BERTRAND COMPETITION

In a Nash equilibrium in the Bertrand model with constant marginal cost, the equilibrium price equals marginal cost and the equilibrium quantity is economically efficient.

equals marginal cost. At that point, each firm makes its best response and no firm has an incentive to change its price. **Figure 14.8** shows the Nash equilibrium with Bertrand competition. The equilibrium quantity of 200 is the quantity demanded at the $10.00 price. (The 200 units sold are arbitrarily divided between the firms.) Each firm maximizes its own profit. Since each believes that its rivals will keep their prices equal to marginal cost, each firm maximizes profit by charging a price equal to marginal cost. If it charges more, it loses all of its customers; if it charges less, it takes a loss because it sells below cost. For this reason, it has no incentive to change its price.

COMMENTS ON THE BERTRAND MODEL

The Nash equilibrium with Bertrand competition is economically efficient. Price equals marginal cost, as in perfect competition, even if only two firms operate in the industry. Evidence suggests that real life is more complicated than the Bertrand model suggests. With only two firms, the price tends to be higher than marginal cost, but below the monopoly price, and the price tends to be closer to marginal cost when more than two firms compete in the industry.

The Bertrand model can apply only to cases *without* product differentiation.[5] The Bertrand model does not apply if firms have steeply rising marginal cost curves. **Figure 14.9** shows why. Each of the two firms in the industry has a capacity constraint of 50 units per month; neither firm can produce more than that.[6] If each firm charges $20, the quantity demanded is 100 and each firm can sell 50 units and earn a $500 profit. The capacity constraint eliminates both firms' incentives to reduce price because each firm already sells all that it can produce, so it cannot serve additional customers. The monopoly price, $20, is a Nash

FIGURE 14.9

NASH EQUILIBRIUM WITH BERTRAND COMPETITION AND CAPACITY CONSTRAINTS

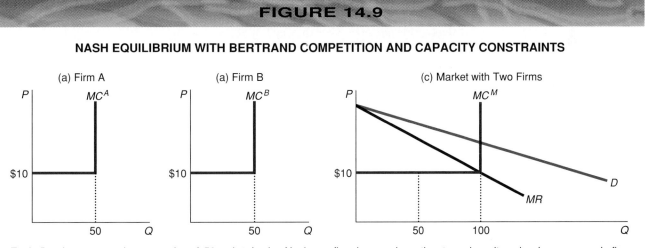

Each firm has a capacity constraint of 50 units. In the Nash equilibrium, each firm charges $20 and sells 50 units. Neither firm has an incentive to reduce its price because each firm already sells as much as it can produce.

---

[5]If firms sell differentiated products, then a firm that cuts its price does not take away all of the customers from other firms. It may not choose to reduce its price to gain only a few customers, and the Nash equilibrium price may exceed marginal cost.

[6]This is an extreme case of steeply rising marginal cost.

equilibrium. This example shows why the Bertrand model does not apply to situations with capacity constraints; similar reasoning applies to less extreme cases of rising marginal cost.

COURNOT MODEL

The Cournot model is another model of oligopoly.

> In the **Cournot model,** each firm believes that other firms will react to its decisions by changing their prices to keep their levels of output and sales fixed.

In Nash equilibrium with the Cournot model, price exceeds marginal cost, but is less than the monopoly price.

EXPLANATION OF THE COURNOT MODEL

It is easiest to understand Nash equilibrium with Cournot competition by beginning with two situations that are not Nash equilibria. First, think about a cartel that charges the monopoly price. If a firm were to believe that other firms would keep their outputs constant, then it would have an incentive to cheat on the cartel by raising its own output. (See Chapter 13.) Therefore, the cartel solution is not a Nash equilibrium in the Cournot model.

Next, suppose that price equals marginal cost (the Nash equilibrium with Bertrand competition). This is not a Nash equilibrium in the Cournot model because each firm would have an incentive to raise its price. To see why, suppose that two firms compete in an industry, Kiwi Computer and Mango Computer. Each has a constant marginal cost of $1,000 per computer. If each firm charges a price of $1,000, each sells 3,000 computers per month. If, however, each firm believes that the other firm will keep its output constant, the owner of Kiwi Computer would reason, "Mango, our competitor, will always change their price to sell 3,000 computers. The demand for *our* computers is whatever consumer demand is *left over* after they sell 3,000, so we can maximize our profit by acting like a monopoly for this *left-over demand*. We will choose the quantity at which marginal revenue equals marginal cost."

Figure 14.10a shows what Kiwi will do in this situation. The figure shows the market demand for computers, D^{Mkt}, and D^K, the left-over demand for Kiwi computers after Mango sells 3,000 computers. With Kiwi's marginal revenue curve, MR^K, it maximizes profit by producing a quantity where marginal cost equals marginal revenue, 1,500 computers, and charging the highest price at which it can sell that quantity, $2,500.

This is not the whole story, however. Mango now sees that Kiwi is selling 1,500 computers. Mango thinks, "Kiwi, our competitor, will always change their price so that they sell 1,500 computers. The demand for *our* computers is the consumer demand that remains after they sell 1,500. We can maximize our profit by acting like a monopoly for this left-over demand. We will choose the quantity at which marginal revenue equals marginal cost." Mango finds that it maximizes its profit by selling fewer than 3,000 computers, say 2,200 computers. Kiwi then repeats the same reasoning, thinking that Mango will sell 2,200 computers.

Kiwi and Mango keep reacting to each other until they reach a Nash equilibrium, as in Figure 14.10b. In this Nash equilibrium, Kiwi and Mango each sell 2,000 computers for $3,000 each. Each firm looks at the left-over demand, assuming that the other firm will sell 2,000 computers, and each firm maximizes profit

Cournot model — a model of oligopoly in which each firm believes that other firms will react to its decisions by changing their prices to keep their levels of output and sales fixed

FIGURE 14.10

COURNOT COMPETITION

(a) Kiwi Maximizes Profit

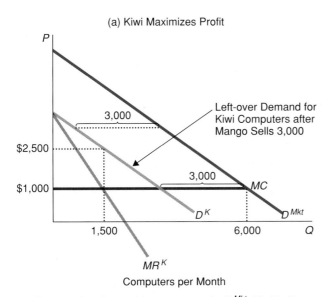

(b) Nash Equilibrium

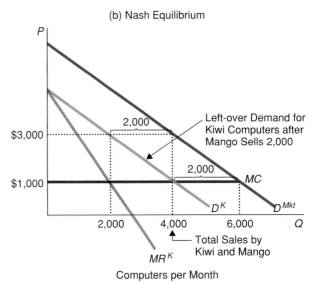

Computers per Month

(a) Total market demand for computers is D^{Mkt}. Kiwi believes that Mango will always change its price to sell 3,000 computers, so the demand for Kiwi computers is market demand minus 3,000; this is the demand curve D^K. The curve MR^K shows Kiwi's marginal revenue. Kiwi maximizes profit by producing a quantity at which its marginal revenue equals its marginal cost, so it produces 1,500 computers and sells them for $2,500 each.

(b) In the Nash equilibrium with Cournot competition, each firm believes that the other will sell 2,000 computers (which it does), and its best response is to sell 2,000 computers, because that is the quantity at which marginal revenue equals marginal cost. Each firm sells 2,000 computers and charges $3,000 each.

by choosing to produce 2,000 computers because that is the quantity at which marginal revenue equals marginal cost. Each firm charges the highest price at which it can sell its 2,000 computers, which is $3,000. Notice that in the Nash equilibrium with Cournot competition, the price exceeds marginal cost. The equilibrium price is closer to marginal cost when more firms compete in the industry.

COMMENTS ON THE COURNOT MODEL

The Cournot model applies to situations in which each firm expects other firms to react to its actions by keeping their levels of output constant, possibly varying their prices. In some real-life situations, this is not a reasonable assumption because other firms have no incentive to react in this way. The Cournot model applies in *some* real-life situations, though. For example, firms sometimes choose their production or capacity levels before they know what prices will be. The Cournot model applies in many such cases, particularly if production or capacity is fixed for a long period of time. Evidence from economic experiments also shows that the Cournot model describes situations of duopoly (oligopoly with two firms) well. The Cournot model is also consistent with the observation that more concentrated industries generate higher profits, while the Bertrand model cannot easily explain this evidence.

BUSINESS DECISION MAKING

Business Strategies in Oligopoly

Business strategies in an oligopolistic market take many forms and involve complex issues, including commitment to flexible or inflexible technologies, inventory decisions, industrial secrecy, product differentiation, and investments in experience.

Flexible and Inflexible Technologies

Some firms can choose between relatively flexible or inflexible technologies for producing their goods. Suppose that a firm could use either of two technologies with average costs as in **Figure 14.11.** Curve AC_1 shows the average cost curve with one technology and Curve AC_2 shows the average cost curve with a second technology. Technology 1 is the lowest-cost method of producing 100 units per month, but Technology 2 is more flexible; it is the lowest-cost way to produce most other levels of output. The average cost of production using Technology 2 does not change much if the firm changes its output, so the

firm has flexibility. Technology 1, in contrast, gives the firm little flexibility in the sense that average cost is much higher at any output that differs much from 100 units per month.

Flexibility helps a firm that is uncertain about the demand for its product. It can also help a firm to raise or lower output in response to the actions of another firm. Inflexibility can also provide benefits, though. If potential competitors are aware of a firm's inflexible technology, they may be less likely to begin competing with that firm than if they believe that the firm's flexible technology would allow it to reduce its output more easily. Because choosing an inflexible technology can help deter entry, it can be an advantageous business strategy in an oligopolistic market.

An inflexible technology can also help a cartel to prevent cheating by its members. If firms in the cartel rely on inflexible technologies designed to produce the quantities that the cartel has set, each firm has less incentive to cheat by raising output because its average cost would also rise.

Inventories

Firms in an oligopoly can sometimes deter new firms from entering the industry by holding large stocks of inventories. A firm can threaten to sell these inventories to reduce the price if a new competitor enters. If potential competitors are aware of these inventories, they may choose not to enter the industry. Holding inventories has the same effects as using a flexible technology: it allows a firm to increase supply quickly without a large increase in costs of production. Of course, a firm can deter entry by threatening price reductions only if it produces at lower

---

FIGURE 14.11

FLEXIBLE AND INFLEXIBLE TECHNOLOGIES

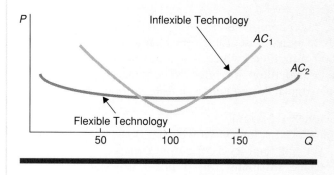

DOMINANT-FIRM MODEL

Some industries have one large, *dominant firm* and many smaller firms. One firm may become dominant because it enters the industry first and learns about cost-reducing techniques or grows to a size that gives it the lowest average cost. A firm may be dominant because it once had a patent on a product and remains larger than newer competitors who entered the industry after the patent expired. Even with free entry, industries sometimes have dominant firms. The Cheerleader Supply Company, for example, sells more than half of all cheerleaders' products

costs than potential competitors do. Otherwise, the firm would take a loss if it were to reduce the price enough to force a loss on the new competitor; knowing this, new firms enter the industry.

Information

A firm can deter entry into its industry if it can make other firms *believe* that its costs are lower than theirs would be, so they would expect to lose money if they were to enter the industry. This gives firms an incentive to keep their costs secret and make potential competitors believe that they produce at particularly low costs. Of course, potential competitors know that an entrenched firm has an incentive to deceive them about costs. Potential competitors may try to obtain information on the firm's true costs in various ways. (This is one motive for industrial espionage.)

Product Differentiation

Studies show that if a dominant firm operates in an industry, a new firm cannot usually enter successfully unless it has lower costs than the dominant firm or a differentiated product that consumers want. [See, for example, Michael Porter, *Competitive Strategies* (New York: Free Press, 1985). Porter studied hundreds of industries and summarized his results in this book.] The new entrant must also overcome other advantages of the dominant firm and prevent a strong reaction from that firm. A new entrant has the best chance of succeeding if it produces a differentiated product that the dominant firm could produce only at a higher cost.

Japanese car makers, for example, successfully challenged the three big American car makers in the 1970s by producing small, fuel-efficient cars at a time when most American cars were big. They saw an opportune moment to enter the American market because the price of gasoline had risen dramatically at about the same time, giving consumers an incentive to buy smaller cars with better fuel efficiency. American car makers could not quickly switch to making good, small cars because of the time required to design, test, and produce them. After succeeding in that portion of the car market, Japanese firms later expanded to larger and more expensive cars.

Another example of successful entry because of a cost advantage is Federal Express, which successfully entered the freight business, competing with United Parcel Service (UPS) and other such firms by inventing a new kind of delivery system with a single hub (in Memphis, Tennessee) that allowed it to provide reliable overnight delivery at a lower cost. The hub technology was later copied by other firms in the industry.

Experience

Experience can affect the cost of producing a good. A more experienced firm with better trained workers often has lower costs of production. If learning by doing can reduce costs sufficiently, then the first firm in an industry has an incentive to charge a low price rather than the monopoly price, even if it loses money in the short run! By keeping the price low, it sells more and gains more experience, reducing future costs. These lower future costs can help deter future entry by potential rivals who lack this experience. The firm trades off a lower price and losses in the short run for lower costs, less competition, and higher profits in the long run.

sold in the United States, even though free entry has allowed many other firms to enter the industry.

A dominant firm acts like a monopoly that faces the demand curve left over after the smaller firms have sold their outputs. From this remaining demand, the dominant firm chooses the quantity at which its marginal revenue equals its marginal cost, and it charges the highest price at which it can sell that quantity.

Unless a dominant firm can keep its costs lower than those of its competitors, it will not remain dominant in the long run. Often a dominant firm can earn profits only temporarily, before other firms enter the industry. Apple and IBM, for example, were the first major producers of personal computers and earned higher profits before many new firms entered that industry than they earned after competitors appeared. U.S. Steel had a 66 percent market share when it was formed by merger in 1901, but its market share and profits fell over time as new steel producers appeared. Harley Davidson had the entire U.S. motorcycle market in 1962, but only 36 percent of the market 20 years later; Xerox saw its market share of photocopying machines fall from 100 percent to 42 percent over the same period.

--------- FOR REVIEW ---------

14.10 What is an oligopoly? What is strategic interaction?

14.11 What is a Nash equilibrium?

14.12 How do firms expect rivals to react to their actions in the Bertrand model? In the Cournot model?

--------- QUESTIONS ---------

14.13 Assume constant marginal cost and compare the equilibrium prices in the Bertrand model and the Cournot model.

14.14 Suppose that a dominant firm operates in an industry. Draw a graph to show the connection between market demand and demand for the product of the dominant firm; also show the dominant firm's marginal cost and profit-maximizing level of output.

SUMMARY OF MARKET BEHAVIOR

Experimental evidence on prices and quantities is generally consistent with these conclusions:

1. The monopoly model applies when there is only one firm in an industry.

2. The Cournot model applies when two firms compete.

3. If the same people make price and output decisions repeatedly in an oligopoly, the monopoly (cartel) model eventually applies best.

4. Otherwise, perfect competition begins when three or more firms compete.

Table 14.3 summarizes both the difference between price and marginal cost and economic profit in long-run equilibrium with perfect competition, monopolistic competition, oligopoly, and monopoly. With perfect competition, price equals marginal cost and firms earn zero profits in the long run. With monopolistic competition, price exceeds marginal cost in the long run and firms earn zero profits. With oligopoly or monopoly, price exceeds marginal cost and firms are likely to earn positive profits. The difference between oligopoly and monopoly is mainly in the size of the profit and the markup of price above marginal cost. Monopolies usually charge higher prices than oligopolies with the same marginal cost. Short-run profits can be positive or negative in any of these cases. Positive profits create incentives for entry, and negative profits lead firms to exit the industry. Whether an industry has a monopoly, a cartel, or an oligopoly in the short run, perfect competition or monopolistic competition can prevail in the long run if no barriers to entry deter potential competitors.

TABLE 14.3

LONG-RUN PRICES AND PROFITS WITH DIFFERENT KINDS OF MARKETS

Structure of Competition	Markup of Price over Marginal Cost	Economic Profit
Perfect competition Many sellers, no entry barriers, identical products	0	0
Monopolistic competition Many sellers, no entry barriers, differentiated products	+	0
Oligopoly Few sellers, possible entry barriers, identical or differentiated products	+	+ or 0
Cartel Few sellers, entry barriers, identical or differentiated products	+	+ or 0
Monopoly One seller, entry barriers, one product	+	+ or 0

CONCLUSIONS

MONOPOLISTIC COMPETITION

In monopolistic competition, many firms in an industry produce differentiated products and act independently. Entry is free. Each firm faces a downward-sloping demand curve and produces a quantity at which its marginal revenue equals its marginal cost. Free entry guarantees that firms earn zero economic profits in long-run equilibrium. Firms have excess capacity in long-run equilibrium. Each firm could reduce its average cost by increasing output, but doing so would reduce its price and cause the firm to lose money. Although monopolistic competition does not minimize the average cost of production, it provides customers with product variety. Nonprice competition is common in monopolistically competitive industries. To maximize their profits, firms often have incentives to produce products that are different, but not *too* different, from the products of their competitors.

OLIGOPOLY

An industry is an oligopoly if a small number of firms interact strategically. In strategic interaction, each firm's decisions take into account the reactions of other firms and the effects of those reactions. In the short run, oligopolies may earn economic profits, but new firms enter in the long run and reduce economic profits to zero unless barriers to entry prevent this.

A concentration ratio is a rough indicator of the amount of competition in an industry, though such ratios have important limitations. Profits tend to be higher in more concentrated industries, perhaps because concentrated industries tend to be oligopolies or perhaps because industries become more concentrated when a small number of firms succeed in raising their profits by reducing costs or improving their products.

SOCIAL AND ECONOMIC ISSUES

Is Advertising Good or Bad?

Advertising. It bombards people daily in newspapers and magazines, on television and radio, by direct mail, and even by telephone, fax, and electronic mail. Advertising is a major industry that accounts for more than 2 percent of U.S. gross domestic product (the total value of all goods and services produced in the United States). Firms advertise to gain customers; some of these new customers may come at the expense of other firms in the industry and some may come as a result of higher product demand due to advertising.

Some People Say . . .

Some people say that advertising is socially wasteful. It tries to convince people to buy things that they don't want or need. It tries to mold people's tastes and values, and it diverts their attention from the important things in life toward whatever raises advertisers' profits. Because of advertising, firms do not provide the goods that people really want; instead, it induces people to want whatever firms supply.

Advertising is mostly image-making. Most advertising provides little information about products; instead, it creates images without any basis in reality. Advertising is socially wasteful because it encourages the wrong kind of competition. Customers lose when sellers compete with images rather than lower prices and higher-quality goods, better services, or more socially responsible business practices.

Advertising raises prices. Advertisements by any *one* car dealer may add to that dealer's sales, but mainly at the expense of other car dealers. When *all* car dealers in a city advertise, the advertisements tend to neutralize each other, so advertising wastes money. Each seller gets about as many customers as it would get without advertising, but consumers pay the costs of advertising. By raising the cost of selling products, advertising raises prices.

Advertising discourages competition by raising the cost of new entry into an industry. To compete successfully with entrenched firms, a new firm needs enough money to launch a major advertising campaign.

Advertising creates wasteful product differentiation. People don't really need 100 kinds of laundry detergent, each of which is really about the same, or 20 brands of toilet paper. Advertising all these brands is economically inefficient.

Other People Say . . .

Advertising is socially useful. It provides valuable information about a product's availability, what it does, how much it costs, and who sells it. It reminds people of their opportunities.

Advertising cannot influence people to continue to buy things they don't really want. Of course, advertising creates images. People *like* images and

EQUILIBRIUM WITH OLIGOPOLY

A firm's best response to a situation is the action that maximizes its profit, given the actions of its rivals. In a Nash equilibrium, each firm follows its best response, that is, each firm's action maximizes its profit, given the actions of rival firms. The equilibrium in an oligopoly depends on what firms believe about the likely reactions of their rivals; different sets of beliefs lead to different models of oligopoly, such as the Bertrand model or the Cournot model. In the Bertrand model, each firm believes that other firms will react to its decisions by changing the quantities they sell to keep their prices fixed. Unless firms have steeply rising marginal cost curves, such as capacity constraints, price equals marginal cost in a Nash equilibrium with the Bertrand model and output is economically efficient. In the Cournot model, each firm believes that other firms will react to its decisions by changing their prices to keep their levels of output fixed. Price exceeds marginal cost in a Nash equilibrium with Cournot competition. If an industry has a dominant firm, it

advertising must entertain to catch and hold people's attention. Entertainment is the best way to provide (or to get people to seek) information about a product; few people would watch a commercial that sounded like a dry, college lecture. Celebrities, jingles, and entertainment help people to remember the commercial, so it helps them to remember the product. Sellers of arcane goods such as aluminum ingots and special industrial parts advertise in trade journals that are read mainly by hard-headed businesspeople, and even these advertisements try to be entertaining and eye-catching to get their information across to readers.

Advertising does not discourage competition; it encourages competition because it provides information about the availability of alternative products. Without advertising, some buyers might not realize that there are good alternatives to the products they usually buy. Advertising helps new firms to enter an industry and compete by providing them with a forum in which to tell potential customers about their products. Evidence shows that advertising makes demand curves more elastic by increasing the willingness of customers to switch to the products of new firms.

Other evidence shows that advertising increases competition. A famous study compared the prices of eyeglasses in states that allowed advertising of eyeglasses against prices where such ads were prohibited. It found that eyeglasses cost 28 percent more in states that prohibited advertising. Advertising reduced the price by making it easier for sellers to compete with each other and attract customers through lower prices. Evidence also indicates that other goods, such as toys and prescription drugs, are cheaper when advertising is allowed than when it is prohibited.

Even if advertising sometimes raises prices, consumers must want the advertising. If people preferred lower-priced, unadvertised products (or goods with less advertising), firms would have an incentive to sell them. A firm could reduce its price and raise its profit by reducing advertising costs. (If a firm could save $1.00 per unit by reducing its advertising, it could reduce its price by 90 cents and still increase its profit by 10 cents per unit.) If customers preferred less advertising and lower prices, firms would not advertise. They advertise because people want (and are willing to pay for) that advertising.

Advertising gives firms an incentive to serve customers better. Advertising creates consumer recognition of brand names that helps to make these brand names valuable to firms. This raises the incentives of firms to protect their brand names by providing quality goods and services.

acts like a monopoly that faces the demand left over after other, smaller firms have sold their outputs.

SUMMARY OF MARKET BEHAVIOR

Experimental evidence suggests that the monopoly model applies when only one firm operates in an industry, the Cournot model applies when two firms compete, and perfect competition is a good approximation when three or more firms compete. However, when the same people or firms act repeatedly in an industry with only a few firms, the monopoly (cartel) model applies best.

LOOKING AHEAD

Chapter 15 will discuss a general theory of strategic interactions: game theory. Game theory has many applications to oligopolies and other areas of economics, political science, biology, psychology, and sociology.

Key Terms

differentiated product	price rigidity
monopolistic competition	rate of return on investment
excess capacity	best response
nonprice competition	Nash equilibrium
oligopoly	Bertrand model
n-firm concentration ratio	Cournot model

Questions and Problems

IN THE NEWS

If the battle continues much longer, many fast-food businesses will close or merge, predicts Vincent Morrissey, who owns a string of Kentucky Fried Chicken stores in the Midwest. "The industry is overbuilt," he says. "Fast-food franchisers have managed to squeeze in stores into every corner available."

Is there excess capacity in the fast-food industry?

Source: *The Wall Street Journal*, August 23, 1989, p. B1.

14.15 Draw a graph of a short-run equilibrium with monopolistic competition in which firms suffer losses, then explain what happens in the long run and draw a graph of the long-run equilibrium.

14.16 Suppose that marginal cost is constant, as in Figure 14.8. Explain why the Nash equilibrium price in the Bertrand model equals marginal cost. Why doesn't a firm raise its price above marginal cost in that model? Why does the Nash equilibrium price in the Cournot model exceed marginal cost?

14.17 Suppose that firms have capacity constraints and draw a graph to show the Nash equilibrium in the Bertrand model.

14.18 Summarize the experimental evidence on oligopoly.

14.19 Summarize the main facts about concentration ratios, prices, and rates of return on investment in U.S. industries.

14.20 Over 100,000 fast-food restaurants operate in the United States. Some people say that these restaurants have been overbuilt, that the industry has excess capacity. Can this be a long-run equilibrium? Explain.

14.21 Summarize arguments that advertising is economically inefficient or bad in some way, and then summarize arguments against this view.

Inquiries For Further Thought

14.22 Do people like variety? Is it good or bad to have many choices of products? Does variety cause wasteful duplication?

14.23 What markets do you think are monopolistically competitive? Why? Do you see too much or too little variety in these markets? Why?

14.24 Suppose that consumers value standardization of a product (e.g., people want all camcorders and video games to be compatible rather than running in different, incompatible formats). Can the economy standardize products without letting companies collude (which risks monopoly or oligopoly)? Do free markets choose the best standard? Discuss.

14.25 A high concentration ratio does not insulate a firm from competition. Nike had a large share of the sports shoe market until Reebok expanded rapidly in the 1980s and surpassed Nike's sales in 1987. Can you think of other examples of firms that had large shares of their industries' sales until new firms entered and eventually surpassed the old leaders?

14.26 a. Suppose that advertising misleads some people to view Brand X as the best cleaner, when scientific evidence proves other brands more effective. Is the advertising bad if people believe that they have the best product? Do people benefit if advertising convinces them that a product makes them sexier? Would they be better off if the government were to ban such advertising? What should the government do if it could identify a case like this? Do you think it could identify a case like this?

b. Similarly, placebos are pills that people falsely believe to contain medicine. Medical researchers have documented a strong placebo effect, proving that placebos have actual, physical effects and can help sick people get well. (They reduce headaches in about half of the population, for example.) Might advertising have a placebo effect? If so, is this good or bad?

Tag Software Applications

Tutorial Exercises

▶ The module contains a review of the key terms from Chapter 14.

Graphing Exercises

▶ The graphing segment contains questions on short-run and long-run profit maximization in monopolistic competition and questions about the various models of oligopolistic behavior.

GAME THEORY

CHAPTER 15

WHAT THIS CHAPTER IS ABOUT

▶ Strategic interaction between people, firms, and nations

▶ Strategic planning and strategies for decision making

▶ Connections between individual incentives and socially desirable outcomes

▶ Commitments and reputations

▶ Designing institutions for efficient and fair outcomes

In a simple child's game, two players place five sticks on the ground. The players take turns picking up either one or two sticks, and the player who picks up the last stick loses. If you can leave your opponent with only one stick to pick up, you win. You can do this if two or three sticks remain on the ground when you start your last turn. You can guarantee this if you take the first turn and you pick up one stick. With four sticks remaining, your opponent must leave you with either two or three at the end of his turn. When both players understand this game, the first player wins. If the game starts with seven sticks, on the other hand, the second player wins.

The logic of games like this extends beyond entertainment; it applies when two stores compete for customers, when three employees compete for a promotion, when governments conduct foreign policy, and when U.S. senators trade votes on bills in Congress. It applies to economic situations like the oligopolies discussed in Chapter 14 and to personal interactions in many areas of life. Firms employ highly paid executives whose jobs consist largely of strategic planning: making decisions for the firm after considering the likely reactions of competitors, consumers, and suppliers. Most people recognize how other people will react to their decisions, and they take these reactions into account in their decisions. You can apply game theory to any situation in which your actions affect other people, and their actions affect you.

BASIC IDEAS OF GAME THEORY

game theory — the general theory of strategic behavior

The general logic of strategic behavior is known as *game theory*.

Game theory is the general theory of strategic behavior.

Game theory was developed by the mathematician John von Neumann around 1928 and extended by von Neumann and an economist, Oskar Morgenstern, in

417

their 1944 book, *The Theory of Games and Economic Behavior.*[1] The theory is usually written in mathematical form and plays an important role in modern economics; it also has applications in biology, political science, psychology, military planning, and other disciplines.

Most games involve strategic interaction among the players. As each player decides what to do, she must consider how her actions will affect the actions of other players. What she does affects what others do, and what they do affects her. Each player takes into account the actions of other players and their reactions to their actions. Chapter 14 presented some examples of strategic behavior in the context of an oligopoly.

RULES, STRATEGIES, PAYOFFS, AND EQUILIBRIUM

When economists use game theory, they think of an economic situation as a game. To do this, you must think carefully about:

▶ The rules of the game
▶ Possible strategies for each player
▶ The players' payoffs

Then you can choose the players' *best* strategies and find an *equilibrium* of the game, that is, a prediction of what is likely to happen in this economic situation.

The rules of the game describe its economic, legal, and social environment.

rules of a game — statements of who can do what, and when

The **rules of a game** say who can do what, and when they can do it.

Suppose that two aircraft firms bid for a government contract. The rules might say that each firm must submit a price at the same time, without seeing the price that the other firm submits. The government then chooses the lowest price and the winning firm must sell ten planes to the government at that price.

strategy — a plan for actions in each possible situation in a game

A player's **strategy** is a plan for actions in each possible situation in the game.

You might ask a friend to go to a movie, planning to go if the answer is "yes" and stay home if the answer is "no." That is a strategy of a simple game; other possible strategies might include going to the movie alone or asking someone else if the first person says "no." The strategies available to bidders on a government contract involve the prices they could charge.

The next step is to list the payoffs to the players in the game: what they would win or lose in various situations.

payoff — the amount that a player wins or loses in a particular situation in a game

A player's **payoff** is the amount that the player wins or loses in a particular situation in a game.

The payoffs in a game might state the profits or losses of the bidders on a government contract or the utility (happiness) of family members deciding how to spend their holiday.

Once you know the rules, possible strategies, and payoffs, you can find the players' *best strategies* or *best responses.* A player's best strategy often depends on what other players do. Your best strategy in the 50-yard dash may be simply to

[1]John von Neumann and Oskar Morgenstern, *The Theory of Games and Economic Behavior* (Princeton, N.J.: Princeton University Press, 1944).

run as fast as you can, but your best strategy in chess or football depends on how your opponents play. If a player's best strategy does not depend on what other players do, it is called a *dominant strategy*.

dominant strategy — a strategy that is best regardless of what other players do

A player has a **dominant strategy** if that player's best strategy does not depend on what other players do.

NASH EQUILIBRIUM

A Nash equilibrium occurs when each player's strategy is optimal, given the strategies of the other players. Recall the more precise definitions from Chapter 14:

best response (or best strategy) — the strategy that maximizes a player's payoff given the strategies of other players

A player's **best response (or best strategy)** is the strategy that maximizes that player's payoff, given the strategies of other players.

Nash equilibrium — a situation in which each player makes her best response

A **Nash equilibrium** is a situation in which each player makes her best response.

In a Nash equilibrium, each player's strategy is a best response to other players' strategies, so no player has an incentive to change strategies. Examples of rules, strategies, payoffs, and Nash equilibria will appear throughout this chapter.

PRISONER'S DILEMMA

A famous example in game theory called the *prisoner's dilemma* has many applications. The police catch two people, Bonnie and Clyde, and charge them with a crime. The police take them into separate rooms, where each prisoner must decide either to confess or not to confess without knowing what the other prisoner will do. The police tell each prisoner that they have collected enough evidence to send both to prison for 3 years. If only one prisoner confesses and testifies against the other, that prisoner will get only 1 year and the other will get 8 years. If both confess, each will get 4 years. **Table 15.1** summarizes these payoffs to Bonnie and Clyde for each possible choice. Bonnie chooses a row of the table (top or bottom). In the top row, she confesses; in the bottom row, she does not confess. Clyde chooses a column of the table (left or right). In the left column, he confesses; in the right column, he does not confess.

What is each prisoner's best strategy when neither knows what the other will do? **Figure 15.1** graphs Bonnie's choices in a *decision tree* with two parts. If Clyde confesses, Bonnie can:

▶ Confess and serve 4 years in prison

▶ Not confess and serve 8 years

TABLE 15.1

PRISONER'S DILEMMA

		Clyde	
		Confess	Not Confess
Bonnie	**Confess**	4 years each	1 year for Bonnie and 8 years for Clyde
	Not Confess	8 years for Bonnie and 1 year for Clyde	3 years each

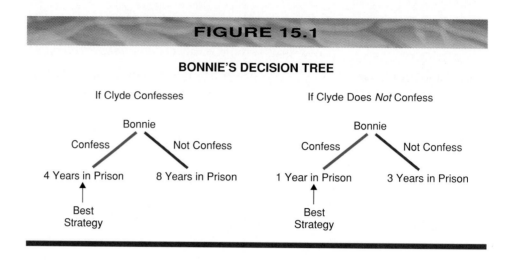

FIGURE 15.1

BONNIE'S DECISION TREE

Her best strategy in this situation is to confess. If Clyde does not confess, Bonnie can:

▶ Confess and serve 1 year in prison

▶ Not confess and serve 3 years

Again, her best strategy is to confess. No matter what Clyde does, Bonnie gains by confessing. This makes confessing a dominant strategy for Bonnie. By the same reasoning, Clyde concludes that he should confess regardless of what Bonnie does, so confessing is also a dominant strategy for Clyde.[2]

Since each player's best response is to confess, the Nash equilibrium of the prisoner's dilemma game is for both players to confess, and each gets a 4-year prison term. The dilemma is that both would fare better if neither were to confess, but they lack the proper incentives to achieve this better outcome.

FOR REVIEW

15.1 What is a strategy in a game?

15.2 What is a Nash equilibrium?

QUESTIONS

15.3 Draw a decision tree for Clyde in the example from Table 15.1 and indicate his best strategy.

15.4 The police charge Rat and Skunk with shoplifting. If both plead *not guilty*, each will get a $300 fine. If both plead *guilty*, each will get a $500 fine. If Rat pleads guilty and implicates Skunk (who pleads not guilty), Rat will go free and Skunk will get a $1,000 fine. Skunk faces the same choice if Rat pleads not guilty. Draw a table to summarize the *payoffs* in this game and find each player's best response. What is the Nash equilibrium of this game?

---

[2]This ignores issues of what either might do to the other after both leave prison; that question would complicate the game, but it would not change the main ideas.

A Hint on Studying Games

It often helps to write down a table with payoffs (as in Table 15.1) and draw arrows to show the best responses of each player. The vertical arrows show Bonnie's best strategy in the prisoner's dilemma game. They point from the worse outcome to the better outcome for Bonnie for each possible situation. The horizontal arrows show Clyde's best strategy; they point toward his preferred outcome in each situation.

When two arrows point to the same place (such as the upper, left-hand corner, where each player confesses to the crime), this point is a Nash equilibrium.

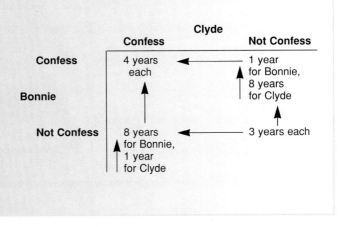

ECONOMIC APPLICATIONS OF GAME THEORY

This section considers three applications of the prisoner's dilemma game to economics: cheating on a cartel, an international-trade war, and advertising. In each of these examples, the players have dominant strategies. This section then discusses a fourth example of a game in which the players have no dominant strategies.

CHEATING ON A CARTEL

Suppose that the Coca Cola Company and PepsiCo form a cartel, agreeing to charge the monopoly price and split profits equally. Chapter 13 explained that firms have incentives to cheat on cartel agreements because each firm could raise its own profit by charging a slightly lower price and taking customers away from the other cartel members. Each firm must choose its own price without knowing which price others choose. Each firm in a two-firm soft-drink cartel has two possible strategies: it can either charge the monopoly price or charge a low price.[3]

Table 15.2 shows the payoffs. Coca Cola chooses a row of the table, and PepsiCo chooses a column. If Coke and Pepsi both charge the monopoly price (Coke chooses the bottom row and Pepsi chooses the right column), each earns a $6 million profit. If Coke cheats on the cartel by charging a low price (the top row) while Pepsi charges the monopoly price (the right column), Coca Cola earns $8 million and Pepsi earns only $2 million. The reverse is true if Pepsi charges a low price and Coca Cola does not. If both charge a low price (Coke chooses the top row and Pepsi chooses the left column), each earns only $3 million.

Figure 15.2 graphs Coke's decision tree. If Pepsi charges the monopoly price, Coke can either charge the low price and earn $3 million or charge the monopoly price and earn $2 million. Coke's best strategy in this situation is obviously to charge the lower price. If Pepsi charges the monopoly price, Coke earns $8 million if it charges the low price and $6 million if it charges the monopoly price, so Coke's best strategy is again to charge the low price. No matter what PepsiCo

---

[3]The assumption that each could charge only one possible low price simplifies the analysis. The analysis is more complicated, but the main point is the same, when the firms could choose from *many* low prices.

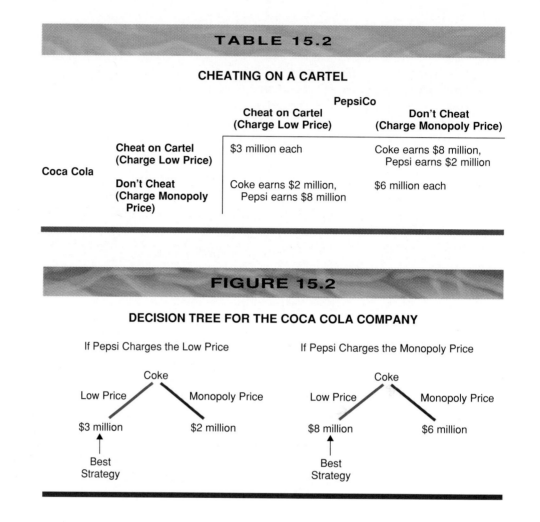

TABLE 15.2

CHEATING ON A CARTEL

		PepsiCo	
		Cheat on Cartel (Charge Low Price)	Don't Cheat (Charge Monopoly Price)
Coca Cola	Cheat on Cartel (Charge Low Price)	$3 million each	Coke earns $8 million, Pepsi earns $2 million
	Don't Cheat (Charge Monopoly Price)	Coke earns $2 million, Pepsi earns $8 million	$6 million each

FIGURE 15.2

DECISION TREE FOR THE COCA COLA COMPANY

If Pepsi Charges the Low Price

Coke

Low Price   Monopoly Price

$3 million $2 million

Best Strategy

If Pepsi Charges the Monopoly Price

Coke

Low Price   Monopoly Price

$8 million $6 million

Best Strategy

does, Coca Cola gains by charging the low price, and no matter what Coke does, Pepsi gains by charging the low price. Both companies have dominant strategies: charge the low price. As a result, in the Nash equilibrium of this game, both companies charge the low price and earn only $3 million profit each.

TRADE WARS BETWEEN COUNTRIES

Suppose that two countries, the United States and Japan, trade internationally. The United States produces only food and Japan produces only televisions. The United States exports food and imports televisions; Japan exports televisions and imports food. Assume also that food and television production are perfectly competitive industries.[4]

The United States can gain by imposing a *tariff* on Japanese televisions, that is, by taxing imports of televisions. **Figure 15.3** shows the effects of this tax. The U.S. government collects revenue from this tax represented by Areas A and B. The tax raises the price to U.S. buyers from $300 to $350, so U.S. consumer surplus

---

[4]Similar reasoning applies for monopoly, monopolistic competition, or oligopoly.

FIGURE 15.3

In this example, the United States imports all of its televisions from Japan. Without a tariff, the equilibrium price is $300 per television. A $100 tariff raises the price to buyers to $350 and reduces the price to sellers to $250. U.S. consumer surplus falls by the sum of Areas A and C, but the U.S. government gains the sum of Areas A and B. (The government could give this money back to U.S. consumers.) Net U.S. gains are Area B minus Area C. As long as Area B is larger than Area C, the United States as a whole gains from the tariff. (Japan loses the sum of Areas B and E in producer surplus. The world as a whole loses Areas C and E from the tariff.)

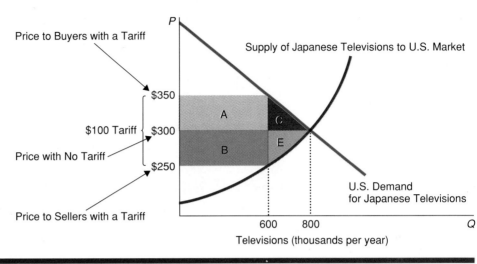

EFFECTS OF A TARIFF ON JAPANESE TELEVISIONS

Price to Buyers with a Tariff

Supply of Japanese Televisions to U.S. Market

$350

$100 Tariff $300

Price with No Tariff

$250

A

C

B

E

U.S. Demand for Japanese Televisions

Price to Sellers with a Tariff

600   800   Q

Televisions (thousands per year)

falls by Areas A and C. Therefore, the United States gains Area B minus Area C from the tariff. (The government could give the money in Area A + B to consumers, which would more than offset their loss.) Of course, the tariff hurts Japanese producers, who lose Areas B and E in producer surplus. The U.S. gains B − C, but Japan loses B + E, so the tariff causes a deadweight social loss of Areas C and E.

The same logic applies to Japanese imports of American food. Japan can gain by imposing a tariff on imports of American food, but its gain would be smaller than the loss of producer surplus to the United States.

Table 15.3 shows the payoffs in this application of the prisoner's dilemma game. If *neither* country adopts a tariff (both maintain *free trade*), then each country gains $8 million in consumer and producer surplus. If either country imposes a tariff on its imports while the other does not, it gains $9 million and the other country gains only $4 million.[5] If both countries put tariffs on imports, each country gains only $5 million from trade.

Figure 15.4, a decision tree for the United States, shows that regardless of what Japan does, the United States has an incentive to put a tariff on television imports. The same argument applies to Japan; it gains from a tariff on food regardless of U.S. policy. Imposing a tariff on imports is a dominant strategy for each country, so each country imposes a tariff in the Nash equilibrium of this game, and each country gains only $5 million from trade. The Nash equilibrium is economically inefficient because both countries would gain from free trade.

---

[5]Total producer and consumer surplus in the world without tariffs is $16 million ($8 million in each country). If the United States puts a tariff on televisions, total world producer and consumer surplus falls to $13 million ($9 million for the United States and $4 million for Japan). The difference—the $3 million fall in total world consumer and producer surplus—is the sum of Areas C and E in Figure 15.3.

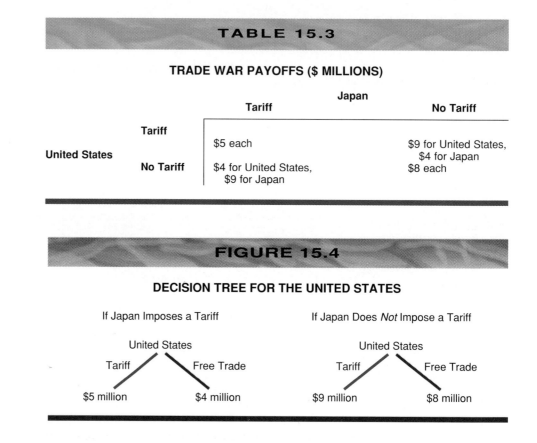

TABLE 15.3

TRADE WAR PAYOFFS ($ MILLIONS)

		Japan	
		Tariff	No Tariff
United States	**Tariff**	$5 each	$9 for United States, $4 for Japan
	No Tariff	$4 for United States, $9 for Japan	$8 each

FIGURE 15.4

DECISION TREE FOR THE UNITED STATES

If Japan Imposes a Tariff	If Japan Does *Not* Impose a Tariff
United States	United States
Tariff · Free Trade	Tariff · Free Trade
$5 million · $4 million	$9 million · $8 million

ADVERTISING

The prisoner's dilemma also applies to advertising. Folger's advertisements take away business from Maxwell House, and Maxwell House advertisements take away business from Folger's. Suppose that advertising does not change the total amount of coffee that people buy; it affects only which brand people buy. If neither seller advertises, each firm earns $1 million profit. If either firm spends $1 million on advertising while the other firm does not advertise, the advertiser gains $5 million in revenue, or a $4 million profit, and the other firm loses $5 million. If *each* firm spends $1 million on advertising, their advertisements cancel out and neither firm gains revenues, meaning that each firm earns zero economic profit. (The $1 million in advertising costs eliminate each firm's profit.) **Table 15.4** shows the payoffs. If each firm must decide at the same time whether to advertise, then in the Nash equilibrium, *both* firms advertise, even though each would gain if neither were to advertise.

GAMES WITHOUT DOMINANT STRATEGIES

In the previous examples, each player had a dominant strategy. In many games, however, players have no dominant strategies; a player's best strategy often depends on the strategies of other players. **Table 15.5** shows an example for the noted gangsters, Ma and Pa. The police have caught them and, like Bonnie and Clyde, taken them into separate rooms, where each prisoner must decide either to confess or not to confess without knowing what the other prisoner does. If both confess, Ma (the mastermind of their crimes) gets 6 years in prison and Pa

TABLE 15.4

ADVERTISING PAYOFFS ($ MILLIONS)

Folger's		Maxwell House Advertise	Don't Advertise
	Advertise	$0 each	$4 for Folger's, −$5 for Maxwell House
	Don't Advertise	−$5 for Folger's, $4 for Maxwell House	$1 each

TABLE 15.5

A GAME WITH NO DOMINANT STRATEGY

Ma		Pa Confess	Not Confess
	Confess	6 years for Ma, 1 year for Pa	5 years for Ma, 3 years for Pa
	Not Confess	8 years for Ma, 0 years for Pa	4 years for Ma, 2 years for Pa

gets 1 year. If neither confesses, Ma gets 4 years in prison and Pa gets 2 years. If only Ma confesses, she gets 5 years in prison and Pa gets 3 years. If only Pa confesses, Ma gets 8 years in prison and he goes free. Table 15.5 shows the results in each case; Ma chooses a row of the table (showing whether she confesses or not) and Pa chooses a column.

What is each prisoner's best strategy when neither knows what the other will do? **Figure 15.5** shows Ma's decision tree. If Pa confesses, Ma gains by confessing, but if Pa does not confess, Ma gains by not confessing. Ma's best strategy depends on what Pa does, so she has no dominant strategy. Pa, on the other hand, has a dominant strategy: confess. Because Pa confesses, Ma confesses also. Ma and Pa both confess in the Nash equilibrium of this game.

MULTIPLE EQUILIBRIA

Every game discussed so far has a single Nash equilibrium. Some games, however, have more than one Nash equilibrium: they have multiple (Nash) equilibria.[6] When a game has multiple equilibria, the game theorist requires some extra information (information that is not part of the game itself) to predict what will happen when people actually play the game.[7]

[6]Some economists believe that multiple equilibria occur in the stock market and the foreign-exchange market. Multiple equilibria may also play important roles in business cycles and unemployment.
[7]This information might include culture, history, or other things that influence behavior.

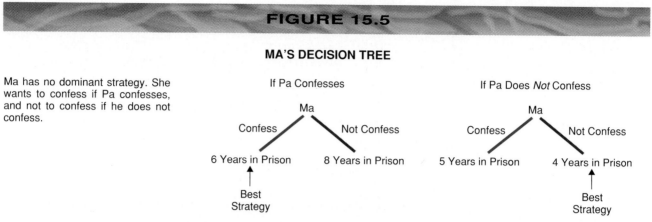

FIGURE 15.5

MA'S DECISION TREE

Ma has no dominant strategy. She wants to confess if Pa confesses, and not to confess if he does not confess.

If Pa Confesses

Ma

Confess   Not Confess

6 Years in Prison   8 Years in Prison

↑

Best Strategy

If Pa Does *Not* Confess

Ma

Confess   Not Confess

5 Years in Prison   4 Years in Prison

↑

Best Strategy

EXAMPLE

A famous example in game theory with multiple equilibria involves two friends, Carolyn and Mark, who plan to go out tonight. They have two choices: a party or a movie. Carolyn wants to go to the party; Mark wants to see a movie. Most important to both of them, however, is that they do something together. **Table 15.6** shows the happiness that each person would get from each activity.

If they go to a party, Carolyn gets 2 units of enjoyment and Mark gets 1 unit. The reverse occurs if they go to a movie. If they do different things, each loses 2 units of enjoyment. This game has *two Nash equilibria,* one in which both go to a movie, and one in which both go to a party.

--- FOR REVIEW ---

15.5 What does it mean for a player to have no dominant strategy?

15.6 Explain why it is a Nash equilibrium in Table 15.6 for Carolyn and Mark to go to:
 a. A party
 b. A movie

--- QUESTIONS ---

15.7 Draw decision trees for Folger's and Maxwell House in the example from Table 15.4.

15.8 Draw a decision tree for Pa in the example from Table 15.5.

TABLE 15.6

PAYOFFS IN A GAME WITH MULTIPLE EQUILIBRIA (UNITS OF UTILITY)

		Mark	
		Party	**Movie**
Carolyn	**Party**	Carolyn gets 2 units, Mark gets 1 unit	Each loses 2 units
	Movie	Each loses 2 units	Carolyn gets 1 unit, Mark gets 2 units

Ad spending: Growing market share

By James C. Schroer

Most of the time, competitors are in a state of equilibrium where the leaders' market shares remain stable despite marginal changes in their ad expenditures. Competitors that understand the spending game will establish this equilibrium at a level so high that no upstart can afford the extra sustained investment needed to increase its share.

A competitor with an aggressive ad spending strategy will keep up the attack only so long as it is adding to market share. By pouring in enough dollars to convince this aggressor that the market has returned to stalemate, the combatants can force a return to share equilibrium levels.

Conventional analysis suggests that the market leader's share of ad spending (SOV) can be less than its share of market (SOM). I agree. The leader enjoys a scale advantage enabling it to outspend the followers at a lower per-unit cost.

Conventional wisdom also suggests that smaller players overspend, taking a share of voice greater than share of market. I disagree. This logic leads to a spending war that the smaller players cannot hope to win. A smaller competitor trying to exploit a differentiated niche should not try to grow beyond narrow limits. It would be folly to launch an ad offensive on the leaders.

Offense and Defense

Rational competitors halt their ad offensives when they cease to produce share gains and equilibrium reigns once again. The implication for defense is clear: spend to deter attack. Assailants must recognize the signs and be prepared to back off.

If I yell loud and you yell loud, the audience will hear both of us. But if I start yelling louder when you are quieter, the audience will hear only me.

Market leaders have this problem. Spending at levels loud enough to be heard, they are in a zero-sum jousting match. For either company #1 or company #2, cutting share of voice too much can be a disaster. The share of voice effect takes hold, and the "quieter" competitor loses share while the "louder" competitor gains. Similarly, an obvious run at an SOV advantage is likely to spark an unprofitable war as both players spend to maintain equilibrium.

The shrewd marketer, therefore, picks its attacks carefully, targeting markets wisely, aiming at markets for share gain where the competitor is vulnerable, markets where that competitor is (perhaps knowingly) underspending, markets where a voice can be raised without breaking the budget.

Before marketers decide to aim for leadership in a particular market, they should consider if they are ready for a long war and indeed whether they want one. To start one, they need a high ad budget backed by large volume and a low cost structure. They may be better off modifying their ambitions and looking for market niches outside the spending wars.

Good business strategists must understand game theory.

Source: James C. Schroer, "Ad Spending: Growing Market Share," *Harvard Business Review,* January–February 1990.

SEQUENTIAL GAMES AND CREDIBILITY

sequential game — a game in which players make decisions at different times

Some games are *sequential,* that is, players take turns making moves.

A **sequential game** is a game in which players make at least some of their decisions at different times.

It is useful to draw a diagram like **Figure 15.6** for a sequential game. The figure shows a game with two players, a monopoly and a new firm.[8] This diagram combines the

---

[8]The diagram is called the *extensive form* of the game.

FIGURE 15.6

A SEQUENTIAL GAME

This sequential game has two steps. First, a new firm decides either to enter or not enter the industry and compete with the monopoly. Second, the monopoly chooses whether to charge a high price or a low price. The monopoly's *four possible strategies* are: high price if new firm enters, low price otherwise; low price if new firm enters, high price otherwise; high price in either case; and low price in either case.

There are three Nash equilibria in this game: the monopoly charges a high price in either case and the new firm enters; the monopoly charges a high price if the new firm enters and a low price otherwise, and the new firm enters; and the monopoly charges a low price if the new firm enters and a high price otherwise, and the new firm enters.

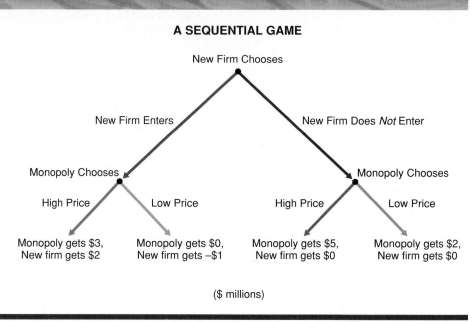

decision trees of the two players. Each small circle shows a point at which someone makes a decision; arrows show the possible decisions and point to the payoffs.

We begin at the top of the diagram (at the point labeled "New Firm Chooses"). The new firm must decide whether to enter or not enter the industry and compete with the monopoly. If the firm enters, we move down the arrow on the left side of the decision tree to the circle labeled "Monopoly Chooses." If the new firm does not enter, we move down the arrow on the right side of the decision tree. Next, the monopoly chooses whether to charge a high price or a low price. If it chooses a high price, we move down the corresponding arrow to the left; if it chooses a low price, we move down the arrow to the right. At the bottom of the decision tree are the payoffs, which also appear in **Table 15.7.**

The bottom half of Figure 15.6 (below the "Monopoly Chooses" circles), which describes the second half of the game, looks like some decision trees dis-

TABLE 15.7

PAYOFFS IN A SEQUENTIAL GAME OF ENTRY ($ MILLIONS)

| | | New Firm (N) | |
		Enter	Do Not Enter
Monopoly	**High Price**	Monopoly gets $3, New firm gets $2	Monopoly gets $5, New firm gets $0
	Low Price	Monopoly gets $0, New firm gets –$1	Monopoly gets $2, New firm gets $0

IN THE NEWS

S till, some analysts doubt that soft-drink makers are seriously considering a switch to refined sugar from high-fructose corn syrup, and suggested the reports could be a ploy to frighten corn processors into keeping a lid on syrup prices.

Business firms routinely behave strategically, but their threats are not always credible. Do these firms *really* have an incentive to switch sweeteners, or is the threat just a ploy?

Source: The Wall Street Journal, June 28, 1988.

subgame perfect Nash equilibrium — a Nash equilibrium in which every player's strategy is credible

cussed earlier. In the second half of the game, the monopoly has a dominant strategy: charge a high price. Knowing that the monopoly will choose a high price, it is reasonable to expect the new firm to enter the industry. (The new firm earns $2 million if it enters and the monopoly charges a high price, and it earns nothing if it does not enter.) In fact, this is a Nash equilibrium of the game: the new firm enters, and the monopoly charges a high price.

This equilibrium, in which the monopoly chooses a high price regardless of what the new firm does, and the new firm chooses to enter, is called the *subgame perfect Nash equilibrium* of this game.

A **subgame perfect Nash equilibrium** is a Nash equilibrium in which every player's strategy is credible (no player makes incredible threats).[9]

A strategy is credible if a player would have an incentive to carry out that strategy.

This new idea of a subgame perfect equilibrium is important because the monopoly would like to tell the new firm, "If you enter, we'll cut our price and you'll lose $1 million, so don't enter!" This threat is not credible, however, because once the new firm enters, the monopoly has no incentive to carry out the threat. For this reason, the only subgame perfect Nash equilibrium of the game in Figure 15.6 is for the monopoly to charge a high price in either case and for the new firm to enter. The monopoly then earns $3 million and the new firm earns $2 million.[10]

In some real-life games, one player may *not know* whether another player's strategy is credible. The player with incomplete information must make decisions based on his beliefs about the credibility of the other player's threats. This gives players an incentive to seek information about the strategies and incentives of other players.

FOR REVIEW

15.9 What is a sequential game?

15.10 What is a subgame perfect Nash equilibrium?

[9]More precisely, a subgame perfect Nash equilibrium is a Nash equilibrium in which each player's strategy is consistent with what that player would do in a Nash equilibrium in every part of the game (every subgame). Suppose that the new firm enters the industry, and think about the second part of the game in Figure 15.6 after the new firm has already decided this. The monopoly's best response is to charge a high price, so the only Nash equilibrium of this subgame is for the monopoly to charge a high price. So, a subgame perfect Nash equilibrium of the original game in Figure 15.6 requires that the monopoly choose a high price if the new firm enters. The same logic applies if the new firm chooses not to enter, so a subgame perfect Nash equilibrium of the original game requires that the monopoly follow its dominant strategy: choose a high price no matter what the new firm does. This means that the only subgame perfect Nash equilibrium of the game in Figure 15.6 is for the monopoly to charge a high price in either case and for the new firm to enter.

[10]As mentioned in Figure 15.6, this game has two other Nash equilibria, but the others are not subgame perfect. The first is for the monopoly to threaten to charge a low price if the new firm enters and charge a high price if it doesn't, and for the new firm therefore not to enter. This is a Nash equilibrium because (a) the monopoly earns $5 million and cannot do any better by changing its strategy, given that the new firm does not enter, and (b) the new firm cannot do any better by changing its strategy (to enter the industry) given that the monopoly would then charge a low price. Of course, the monopoly does not actually have an incentive to charge a low price if the new firm enters (it would lose $3 million by charging a low price instead of a high price). That is why this Nash equilibrium is not subgame perfect.

The other Nash equilibrium that is not subgame perfect is for the monopoly to charge a high price if the new firm enters and threaten a low price if the new firm does not enter, and for the new firm to enter. It may seem silly for the monopoly to do this, because the monopoly would have no incentive to charge a low price if the new firm failed to enter. That is why this is not a subgame perfect Nash equilibrium, but it is a Nash equilibrium.

───────────────────────── QUESTIONS ─────────────────────────

15.11 Give examples of a credible threat and an incredible threat.

15.12 Consider the example of Carolyn and Mark in Table 15.6, but suppose that they play a *sequential game.* First, Carolyn chooses whether she will go to the party or the movie, then Mark chooses where he will go.

 a. Draw a diagram like Figure 15.6 to describe this game.

 b. Find the subgame perfect Nash equilibrium of the game.

COMMITMENTS

Commitments are valuable. Although it may seem paradoxical, people can benefit by committing even though it limits their future choices.

> People can benefit from being able to limit their future actions so that they cannot do what they would want to do in the future.

Commitments allow people to limit their future actions in beneficial ways.

commitment to a future action — doing something now to create a future incentive to take that action

> A person **commits to a future action** if she does something now to limit her future options or change her future incentives so that she will have an incentive to take that action in the future.

A person commits not to take a future action by doing something to make that action either impossible or against her own future interest. Commitments can provide valuable benefits by restricting future choices in a way that changes other people's actions to one's own benefit.

EXAMPLES

Many governments try to commit *not* to bargain with kidnappers or terrorists. If potential terrorists know that governments cannot bargain, they are less likely to conduct terrorist attacks. People try to commit to romantic relationships by getting married; this limits the options of each partner, but each may gain from the commitment of the other. People try to commit to diets by avoiding places with candy machines or eating before shopping for groceries. The phrase "burning your bridges behind you" comes from an important military application of commitment—an advancing army may literally burn bridges behind it to prevent a future retreat and commit the soldiers, seeing no escape, to fight hard instead.

COMMITMENT MECHANISMS

It is often difficult or impossible to commit to a future action. Governments may proclaim that they will not deal with terrorists, but they may back down when terrorists hold hostages. Marriage does not perfectly commit people to relationships. Sometimes, however, people can commit by using the legal system to enforce explicit contracts. Other times people commit by relying on social pressure and etiquette to enforce promises; in many cultures honor plays this role. The next example illustrates one of many other ways to commit.

EXAMPLE: EXCESS CAPACITY

Consider a game like the one in Figure 15.6, but suppose that a monopoly can choose whether to invest in extra capacity by adding new machines and equip-

FIGURE 15.7

The monopoly and the new firm play this game if the monopoly decides to invest in additional capacity (equipment). (If not, they play the game in Figure 15.6.) This game is exactly like the game in Figure 15.6 except the payoffs differ in the situations where the monopoly charges a low price.

This game (a subgame of the complete game) has only one subgame perfect Nash equilibrium: the monopoly charges a low price if the new firm enters and a high price otherwise while the new firm chooses not to enter. The monopoly then earns $5 million and the new firm earns nothing.

The monopoly earns a higher payoff than in the subgame perfect Nash equilibrium of the game in Figure 15.6, so the monopoly will choose to invest in new capacity. This commits the monopoly to charge the low price if the new firm enters. Knowing this, the new firm does not enter and the monopoly charges the high price. Investing in additional capacity allows the monopoly to earn a higher profit by committing to a future action.

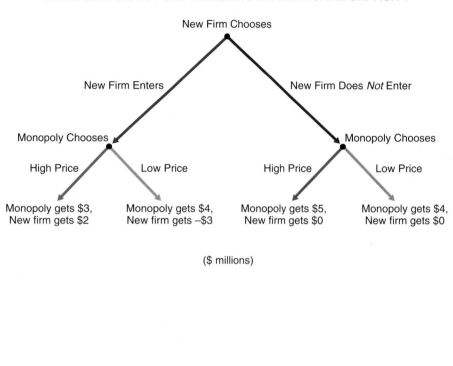

GAME WITH MONOPOLY INVESTING IN ADDITIONAL CAPACITY

New Firm Chooses

New Firm Enters — New Firm Does *Not* Enter

Monopoly Chooses — Monopoly Chooses

High Price — Low Price — High Price — Low Price

Monopoly gets $3, New firm gets $2

Monopoly gets $4, New firm gets –$3

Monopoly gets $5, New firm gets $0

Monopoly gets $4, New firm gets $0

($ millions)

ment before playing the game. Extra capacity reduces the monopoly's marginal cost of increasing its output, so it raises the profit that the monopoly would earn by reducing its price and selling more.

If the monopoly does *not* invest in extra capacity, then it and the new entrant play the game in Figure 15.6. If the monopoly invests, they play the game in **Figure 15.7.** The only difference between these games is the payoff when the monopoly charges a low price. The games in Figures 15.6 and 15.7 are parts (or subgames) of the complete game that includes the monopoly's decision of whether to invest in extra capacity.

The game in Figure 15.7 has only one subgame perfect Nash equilibrium in which the monopoly charges a low price if the new firm enters the industry and a high price otherwise, while the new firm chooses not to enter.[11] The

---

[11]To see why this is the only subgame perfect Nash equilibrium in Figure 15.7, begin at the bottom of the figure and suppose that the new firm enters the industry. The monopoly then earns $3 million if it charges the high price and $4 million if it charges the low price. This gives it an incentive to charge the low price. Now suppose that the new firm does not enter the industry. The monopoly then earns a higher profit if it charges a high price than if it charges a low price, so the monopoly would charge a low price if the new firm were to enter and a high price otherwise. The new firm, knowing this, realizes that it will lose $3 million if it enters the industry, and it will earn zero otherwise, so the new firm chooses not to enter. The monopoly then charges the high price and earns a $5 million profit.

monopoly's threat to charge a low price if the new firm enters is credible because the monopoly would have an incentive to do this if the new firm entered. The monopoly's investment in extra capacity makes the threat credible because it allows the monopoly to commit to a future action. Because of this commitment, the new firm chooses not to enter and the monopoly never has to carry out its threat to cut the price.

Now consider the complete game, which begins with the monopoly's decision to invest. If the monopoly invests in added capacity, it will play the game in Figure 15.7 and end up earning a $5 million profit. If the monopoly does not invest, it will play the game in Figure 15.6 and earn only a $3 million profit. Therefore, the subgame perfect Nash equilibrium is for the monopoly to invest in new capacity, the new firm not to enter, and the monopoly to charge a high price.

Notice that *the monopoly never uses its extra capacity* in equilibrium because it charges the high price and keeps output low. The monopoly benefits from investing in new equipment *even though it knows that it will never use the equipment.* The sole benefit of the equipment is to make its threat credible. This is similar to the idea behind deterrence in national defense: if one country has enough weapons and it can make the other side believe that it will use them if attacked, then the other side has an incentive not to attack, and the weapons go unused.[12]

COMMITMENT IN OTHER GAMES

The ability to commit would help the criminals in the prisoner's dilemma game. If *both* prisoners could commit not to confess, both would gain. (However, if only one prisoner could commit not to confess, the other still would have an incentive to confess.)

By limiting their capacity to produce, firms may commit not to cheat on a cartel. If a firm sells all that it can produce when it charges a high price, it has no incentive to cut its price. (Chapter 14 discussed a related example of capacity constraints with Bertrand competition.) Firms sometimes commit to future actions by convincing the government to regulate them; the government can then require them to take the actions to which they want to commit. For example, the government may prevent firms from reducing prices, as it did in the trucking and airline industries for many years.

REPEATED GAMES

People and firms face many real-life situations repeatedly. Understanding the logic of these situations requires an analysis of repeated games.

> A **repeated game** is a game that the same players play more than once.

repeated game — a game that the same players play more than once

Repeated games differ from one-shot (nonrepeated) games because people's current actions can depend on the past behavior of other players. In the prisoner's dilemma, neither prisoner can punish the other for confessing, but in a repeated game, players can punish other players at a later time for bad behavior in previous

---

[12]Commitment to massive retaliation to any attack was an important part of nuclear deterrence. Similarly, incumbent politicians sometimes prevent serious opposition in elections by amassing large "warchests" of money before their campaigns begin. This deters opponents from challenging incumbents because they know that the campaigns would be very expensive, and without serious opponents, incumbents get reelected without spending all the money in their warchests, saving it for future campaigns to deter entry again.

Oil ultimatum: Saudis plan to pump all the crude they can sell if OPEC can't agree on new quotas

Outside the kingdom, it is assumed that the Saudis' recent opening of the oil spigot is aimed at lowering prices to punish other exporters for their excesses. One widely held theory says that the kingdom wants to teach them a lesson so they will return to the OPEC bargaining table chastened.

_____

In repeated games, players can threaten each other with future punishment for bad current behavior.

Source: "Oil Ultimatum: Saudis Plan to Pump All the Crude They Can Sell if OPEC Can't Agree on New Quotas," *The Wall Street Journal*, November 17, 1988, p. A10.

tit-for-tat — a strategy in which players cooperate unless one of them fails to cooperate in some round of the game, in which case others do in the next round what the uncooperative player did in the current round, then rturn to cooperation

rounds of the game. One-shot games also differ from repeated games when players have limited information about other players' incentives. In repeated games, each player can learn from experience what other players are likely to do in various situations.

Repeated games encourage cooperative behavior more than one-shot games do. Experimental evidence shows, for example, that the equilibrium in an oligopoly tends to be closer to the monopoly (cartel) solution if the same firms compete repeatedly than if they compete only once.

Think about repeating the game in Table 15.2 (the Pepsi–Coke example) many times. If this game is played once, the only Nash equilibrium is for both players to charge the low price. If this game is repeated indefinitely, it has other subgame perfect Nash equilibria.[13] In equilibrium, each firm says, "We will charge a high price, but if some other firm ever charges a low price, we will punish that firm by charging a low price the next time. We will then go back to charging a high price." This strategy is called tit-for-tat, that is, doing to others what they did to you.

> In the **tit-for-tat** strategy, players cooperate unless one of them fails to cooperate in some round of the game, in which case the others do in the next round what the uncooperative player did in the current round, then return to cooperation.

One Nash equilibrium of the repeated prisoner's dilemma is for players to adopt this strategy. Unless the players care very little about the future, no prisoner ever confesses. Similarly, firms in the indefinitely repeated Pepsi–Coke game always charge the high price. Each firm believes that if it were to charge a low current price, the other firm would reduce its price in the future. The first firm would gain $2 million currently (its profit would rise from $6 million to $8 million), but it would lose $3 million in the next round of the game (its profit would fall from $6 million to $3 million), when the other firm would reduce its price. If the discounted present value of this $3 million loss exceeds the $2 million gain from reducing the price, then the firm will not reduce its price. Of course, in this case no firm faces punishment because every firm charges a high price every round of the game. The threat of punishment prevents the need to carry out punishment. Experimental evidence confirms that repeated games tend to produce cooperative behavior.

EXPERIMENTAL EVIDENCE ON TIT-FOR-TAT

Political scientist Robert Axelrod reported on his studies of a repeated prisoner's dilemma in his book, *The Evolution of Cooperation*.[14] Axelrod invited economists, political scientists, and others to submit strategies for playing a prisoner's dilemma game. Some players chose very complicated strategies. After repeating the game many times, Axelrod found that the winning strategy was tit-for-tat. He announced this result and held another game to allow players to devise strategies to beat tit-for-tat. Again, the best strategy turned out to be tit-for-tat.

This result surprised most game theorists, because tit-for-tat is not an aggressive strategy. It says to cooperate, never be the first one to cheat, always punish with "an-eye-for-an-eye," then forgive and cooperate again. Axelrod speculates that the success of the tit-for-tat strategy lies behind our social customs and etiquette.[15]

_____

[13]This is the result if the game never stops or if some *chance* always remains that the game will continue.

[14]Robert Axelrod, *The Evolution of Cooperation* (New York: Basic Books, 1985).

[15]It turns out that animals sometimes seem to play strategies like tit-for-tat in natural game situations.

IN THE NEWS

Nice guys finish first

When dealing with your neighbor, a business rival, or the Soviet Union, the way to get ahead is to get along.

By William F. Allman

Captain J. R. Wilton, an officer in the British Army, was having tea with his fellow soldiers in the mud near Armenières, France. It was August 1915, and World War I had become a trench-lined struggle for barren stretches of countryside. Wilton's teatime was suddenly disrupted when an artillery shell arced into the camp and exploded. The British soldiers quickly got into their trenches, readying their weapons and swearing at the Germans.

Then from across no-man's-land, writes Wilton in his diary, a German soldier appeared above his trenches. "We are very sorry about that," the soldier shouted. "We hope no one was hurt. It is not our fault, it is that damned Prussian artillery."

Enemy soldiers might seem like the last people on Earth who would cooperate with each other, but they did. Despite exhortations to fight and threats of reprisals from their commanders if they didn't, peace often broke out among the German and English infantry. Sometimes there were truces arranged through formal agreements, but many times the soldiers simply stopped shooting at each other, or at least shot where it would do no harm. According to an account by one German soldier, for example, the English battalion across the way would fire a round of artillery at the same spot every evening at seven, "so regularly you could set your watch by it. There were even some inquisitive fellows who crawled out a little before seven to watch it burst."

The World War I trench soldiers' tacit cooperation arose because, unlike most wars, the troops were stationed so that the enemies faced each other day after day; they knew that the same people they shot at one day would be shooting at them the next. According to one soldier, "It would be child's play to shell the road behind the enemy's trenches . . . but on the whole there is silence. After all, if you prevent your enemy from drawing his rations, his remedy is simple: He will prevent you from drawing yours."

Even soldiers in wartime have discovered the benefits of cooperating by playing tit-for-tat.

Source: William F. Allman, "Nice Guys Finish First," *Science '84,* October 1984.

FOR REVIEW

15.13 Explain, with an example, why people can benefit from commitments.

15.14 Explain how a firm can deter entry by investing in excess capacity.

15.15 Explain why repeated games can have different Nash equilibria than one-shot games.

15.16 Explain the tit-for-tat strategy. What evidence suggests that it is a good strategy in some games?

CONCLUSIONS

BASIC IDEAS OF GAME THEORY

Game theory is the general theory of strategic behavior. A game is described by its rules, strategies, and payoffs. A Nash equilibrium of a game is a situation in which each player's strategy is a best response to other players' strategies.

The prisoner's dilemma is a famous example of a two-person game. Each player gains by deviating from the cooperative solution regardless of what the other player does, so both players deviate and end up receiving lower payoffs than they would with the cooperative solution.

ECONOMIC APPLICATIONS

The prisoner's dilemma applies to many situations such as cheating on a cartel, trade wars between countries, and advertising wars. A player has a dominant strategy when that player's best strategy does not depend on other players' actions. In some games, players have dominant strategies; in other games, they do not.

MULTIPLE EQUILIBRIA

Some games have multiple Nash equilibria. The coordination game is an example of a game with two Nash equilibria.

SEQUENTIAL GAMES AND CREDIBILITY

Players make decisions at different times in a sequential game. A subgame perfect Nash equilibrium is a Nash equilibrium in which every player's strategy is credible, that is, when players have incentives to carry out their strategies.

COMMITMENTS

A person commits to a future action by doing something to limit his future options or change his future incentive to take that action. People can gain from commitments, even though they limit future choices, because they affect the actions of other people.

REPEATED GAMES

A repeated game is a game that the same players play more than once. Players' actions can depend on the past behavior of other players, so they can punish other players for bad behavior in the past. Players can also learn from experience about the strategies and incentives of other players. Games that are repeated indefinitely can have more Nash equilibria than one-shot games. These other equilibria may involve more cooperation between players than in a one-shot game (as in the repeated prisoner's dilemma). One strategy that has widespread success in repeated games is tit-for-tat, in which players cooperate unless one of them fails to cooperate in some round of the game, in which case the others do in the next round whatever the uncooperative player did in the current round, and then return to cooperation.

LOOKING AHEAD

The ideas of game theory will provide useful insight into the issues of the economics of information in Chapter 19. Game theory will also help to clarify the discussion in Chapter 20 of issues such as pollution, the discussion in Chapter 21 of government regulations and taxes, and the discussion in Chapter 22 of the economics of the law. You may find game theory useful long after you finish studying economics; it has many applications for business strategies and personal issues that involve formal or informal negotiations or bargaining.

KEY TERMS

game theory	sequential game
rules of a game	subgame perfect Nash equilibrium
strategy	commitment to a future action
payoff	repeated game
dominant strategy	tit-for-tat

15.17 What is the Nash equilibrium of the following game?

| | | Player 2 | |
		Heads	Tails
Player 1	**Heads**	$5 each	$0 for Player 1, $9 for Player 2
	Tails	$10 for Player 1, $1 for Player 2	$2 each

15.18 Explain how the prisoner's dilemma may apply to:
   a. Picnickers in a park with competing boom boxes
   b. The nuclear arms race
   c. The Bertrand model of oligopoly in Chapter 15
   d. Children sharing a birthday cake or friends sharing a pizza

15.19 Make up an example of a game with multiple equilibria.

15.20 Think of a real-life example of a repeated game.

15.21 Find all the multiple equilibria in the following game. Two cars drive toward each other on a road. If both drive on the left-hand side (as in England) or on the right-hand side (as in most other countries), they pass each other safely. If one drives on the left and the other on the right, however, they crash.

| | | Boris | |
		Drive on Left	Drive on Right
Natasha	**Drive on Left**	Each gets 1	Each loses 2
	Drive on Right	Each loses 2	Each gets 1

15.22 Explain how a monopoly might deter entry of new competitors by accumulating large inventories of goods. (*Hint:* Review the example in which a monopoly invests in extra capacity to deter entry and follow a similar logic.)

15.23 Comment on this statement: "Committing is never a good idea because it takes away your flexibility to respond to a situation in whatever way is best at the time."

15.24 Comment on this statement: "Nuclear deterrence is most effective if the government is willing to respond to a nuclear attack by completely destroying the other country, even if such destruction would be pointless because it would be too late to prevent damage from the initial attack."

15.25 What are the subgame perfect Nash equilibria of the game in **Figure 15.8?**

15.26 A Stanford professor of education and psychology, Robert Calfee, recommends teaching tit-for-tat in grade school. "It's a technology . . . [for] how to deal with others in society. What do you do when you're mad at someone you love? Nothing in our schools teaches that."[16]

---
[16]Quoted in William F. Allman, "Nice Guys Finish First," *Science '84*, October 1984.

How can you apply the tit-for-tat strategy in everyday situations? Discuss examples and likely results. Is tit-for-tat an effective way to behave in these situations? Is it a fair or moral way to behave? Would other behaviors be better in some way (more likely to produce good results or more ethical)? Be as specific as possible. Is tit-for-tat a *bad* strategy in any situation?

15.27 In what recent real-life situation has your strategy for behavior depended on the strategies or behavior of other people? Can you analyze the situation using game theory?

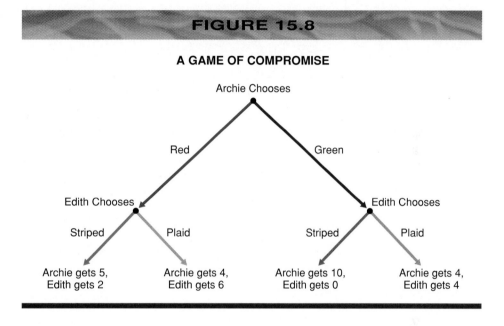

FIGURE 15.8

A GAME OF COMPROMISE

Archie Chooses

Red   Green

Edith Chooses   Edith Chooses

Striped   Plaid   Striped   Plaid

Archie gets 5,   Archie gets 4,   Archie gets 10,   Archie gets 4,
Edith gets 2   Edith gets 6   Edith gets 0   Edith gets 4

TAG SOFTWARE APPLICATIONS

TUTORIAL EXERCISES
▶ The module contains a review of the key terms from Chapter 15.

PART

6

INPUTS AND THEIR EARNINGS

ECONOMICS OF INPUT MARKETS

WHAT THIS CHAPTER IS ABOUT

▶ Economically efficient uses of inputs by firms

▶ Connections between prices of inputs and prices of final products

▶ Connections between the productivity of inputs and their prices

Is Coca-Cola Classic really the original formula? The answer depends on when you ask the question, because soft-drink producers change the type of sugar they use (and sometimes other ingredients) in response to changes in the prices of these inputs. (Coca-Cola switches between fructose and sucrose, depending on the cost.) In fact, most producers alter their use of inputs when input prices change. Sophisticated machinery and equipment such as computers have replaced low-skilled labor at many firms as technical progress has reduced the cost of that equipment. This is one reason why U.S. manufacturing output has increased about 40 percent since 1980 while employment in manufacturing has decreased about 15 percent.

The economics of input markets may sound arcane and far-removed from the concerns of your life, but remember that every worker sells an input: labor. Your life will be significantly influenced by the price of that input (your wage or salary). The economics of input markets affect people through their employment opportunities as well as their wages. This chapter introduces the basic economics of input markets; Chapter 17 then discusses labor markets in more detail.

PRODUCTIVITY AND DIMINISHING RETURNS

Firms buy inputs, also called *factors of production,* to produce final products, so the demand for inputs is related to their productivity. Economists consider two important measures of productivity.

average product — a firm's total output divided by the quantity of an input

marginal product — the increase in a firm's total output when it adds one more unit of an input while keeping the quantities of other inputs fixed

The **average product** of an input is a firm's total output divided by the quantity of that input.

The **marginal product** of an input is the increase in a firm's total output when it adds one more unit of the input while keeping quantities of other inputs fixed.

TABLE 16.1

AN EXAMPLE OF DIMINISHING RETURNS TO LABOR

Input of Labor	Output (thousands of units)	Marginal Product of Labor (thousand units per worker)	Average Product of Labor (thousand units per worker)	Value of the Marginal Product of Labor[a] ($ thousands) per year)
0	0	—	0.0	—
1	50	50	50.0	$25.0
2	120	70	60.0	35.0
3	180	60	60.0	30.0
4	230	50	57.5	25.0
5	270	40	54.0	20.0
6	300	30	50.0	15.0
7	320	20	47.1	10.0
8	330	10	41.2	5.0
9	332	2	36.9	1.0
10	333	1	33.3	0.5

[a]The numbers for the value of the marginal product assume a product price of $0.50 each.

EXAMPLES

The average product of land where a farmer grows corn is the number of bushels of corn divided by the number of acres of land. The marginal product of this land is the increase in corn that the farmer could produce by planting one more acre, but using no more seed, fertilizer, labor services, or other inputs. The average product of labor to repair transmissions is the number of repairs per worker-hour. The marginal product of labor to repair transmissions is the number of additional repairs per day if the shop hires one more worker, but uses the same tools and other equipment. A numerical example appears in **Table 16.1.**

DIMINISHING RETURNS

The law of diminishing returns summarizes the simple idea that a tenth person does not add much to a floor cleaning crew that has only one mop.

> The **law of diminishing returns** states that raising the quantity of an input eventually reduces its marginal product, if the quantity of another input remains fixed.

law of diminishing returns — the generalization that raising the quantity of an input eventually reduces its marginal product, if the quantity of another input remains fixed

Many firms use some inputs whose quantities are fixed in the short run, such as the sizes of factories or the quantities of specialized machines. When these firms increase the quantities of their variable inputs, those inputs eventually generate diminishing returns.[1] For example, an auto repair shop can double the number of cars it repairs each week if it doubles the number of mechanics it employs, the quantity of equipment, and the size of the repair shop. If it doubles the number of mechanics without changing the quantity of equipment or the size of the shop, however, the number of cars it can repair each week less than doubles. The shop

---

[1]Variable inputs are inputs whose quantities a firm can change in the short run. (See Chapter 10.)

FIGURE 16.1

MARGINAL AND AVERAGE PRODUCT OF LABOR FROM TABLE 16.1

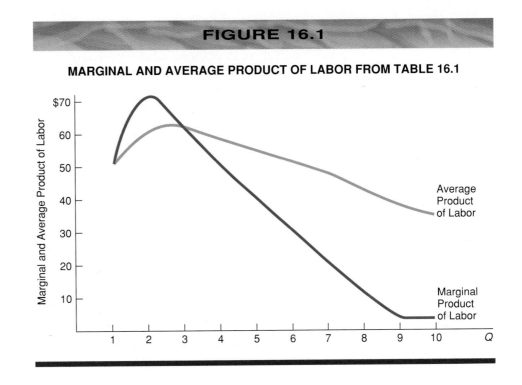

experiences diminishing returns to adding more mechanics while keeping other inputs (the quantity of equipment and shop size) fixed.

EXAMPLE

Table 16.1 shows the marginal and average products of labor for a firm with two machines. If the firm employs one full-time worker, it produces 50,000 plastic containers per year. With two workers, it produces 120,000 containers per year; with three workers, it produces 180,000. The firm's output increases as it adds more workers, but if it still has only two machines, its output increases more slowly as the number of workers rises. Increases in the quantity of labor, holding the number of machines fixed, eventually reduces the marginal product of labor. The marginal product of labor falls from 70,000 containers per year with two workers to 50,000 containers per year with four workers, to less than 10,000 containers per year with more than eight workers. The firm faces diminishing returns to adding labor, holding the number of machines fixed.

Notice that the average product of labor rises when the marginal product exceeds the average product and falls when the marginal product is smaller than the average product.[2] **Figure 16.1** graphs the marginal product of labor, MPL, and the average product of labor, APL. (Ignore the last column of the table for now.)

DIMINISHING RETURNS AND COSTS

Short-run marginal cost and average variable cost rise with increasing output, at least after output reaches a certain level, because of the law of diminishing

---

[2]Chapter 10 discussed a related result; a firm's average cost rises with increasing output when marginal cost exceeds average cost, and falls with increasing output when marginal cost is less than average cost.

returns. **Figure 16.2** shows the marginal and average variable cost curves for the firm in Table 16.1, assuming that workers earn $25,000 per year. The marginal cost curve slopes upward after output reaches 120,000 units per year; the average variable cost curve begins to slope upward when output exceeds 200,000 units per year. These cost curves begin sloping upward at higher quantities because the firm has some fixed inputs (its two machines), so it encounters diminishing returns as it raises the quantity of its labor input.

Calculating marginal and average costs for Table 16.1 illustrates why the curves slope upward. Assume that workers earn $25,000 per year. The firm in Table 16.1 has a total variable cost of $75,000 if it hires three workers and $100,000 per year if it hires four workers. It produces 180,000 containers with three workers and 230,000 containers with four workers. By spending the extra $25,000 for a fourth worker, the firm increases its production by 50,000 containers. The firm's marginal cost when it hires four workers and produces 230,000 containers becomes $25,000/50,000 containers, or $0.50 per container.

FIGURE 16.2

MARGINAL COST AND AVERAGE VARIABLE COST FROM TABLE 16.1

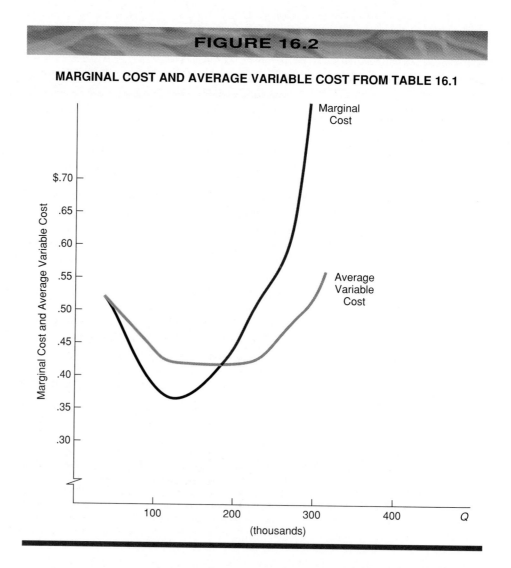

Now consider the firm's marginal cost when it hires eight workers. It produces an extra 10,000 containers by hiring the eighth worker, that is, by spending $200,000 rather than $175,000. This gives an extra cost for those extra 10,000 containers of $25,000. The firm's marginal cost when it hires eight workers and produces 330,000 containers is $25,000/10,000 containers, or $2.50 per container. This shows how diminishing returns make the firm's marginal cost rise with increasing output after output reaches a certain level, as in Figure 16.2.

Now consider the average variable cost of the firm in Table 16.1. Workers earn $25,000 per year, so hiring four workers gives it a total variable cost of $100,000 per year. Because it produces 230,000 containers per year with four workers, its average variable cost is $0.435 per container ($100,000/230,000). If, however, it hires eight workers, its total variable cost rises to $200,000 and it produces 330,000 containers, so its average variable cost is $0.606 per container ($200,000/330,000). This shows how diminishing returns make the firm's average variable cost rise with increasing output after output reaches a certain level, as in Figure 16.2.

VALUE OF THE MARGINAL PRODUCT

The marginal product of an input refers to the increase in the number of goods that a firm produces by adding one more unit of that input holding other inputs fixed. In contrast, the value of the marginal product of an input refers to the increase in the value of those goods.

value of the marginal product — the increase in the money value of a firm's output when it adds one more unit of an input, keeping the quantities of other inputs fixed

The **value of the marginal product** of an input is the increase in the money value of a firm's output when it adds one more unit of the input, keeping the quantities of other inputs fixed.

If a firm operates in an industry with perfect competition, the value of the marginal product of an input equals its marginal product multiplied by the price of the final product. For example, suppose that adding one more full-time worker raises a firm's output by 20 shirts per week, and each shirt sells for $10. The marginal product of labor at the firm is 20 shirts per week, and the value of the marginal product of labor is $200.[3] The last column in Table 16.1 shows the value of the marginal product in that example, assuming that the containers sell for $0.50 each.

─────────────────────── FOR REVIEW ───────────────────────

16.1 What is the marginal product of an input? What is the value of an input's marginal product?

16.2 Explain the law of diminishing returns.

─────────────────────── QUESTIONS ───────────────────────

16.3 How would the numbers in the last column of Table 16.1 (which show the value of the marginal product of labor) change if the product price were $2.00 each instead of $0.50 each?

─────────────────────────────

[3]For a firm, such as a monopoly, that faces a downward-sloping demand curve, the value of the marginal product of an input is *less* than its marginal product times the price of the final product. Suppose that the marginal product of a worker is 20 shirts per week. If the monopoly sells 180 shirts per week, the price of shirts is $10.00 each; if it sells 200 shirts per week, the price is only $9.50. In this case, hiring an additional worker to raise output from 180 to 200 shirts per week raises the total value of output from $1,800 (180 shirts at $10.00 each) to $1,900 (200 shirts at $9.50 each) per week. This gives a value of the marginal product of labor of $100 per week.

16.4 Suppose that the firm in Table 16.1 hires six workers who earn $30,000 per year. What is its marginal cost of producing containers?

DEMAND FOR NONDURABLE INPUTS

nondurable input — an input that a firm uses soon after acquiring it and can use only once to produce a product

price taker in an input market — a firm that faces a perfectly elastic supply of an input

The rule for rational decisions from Chapters 9 and 10 applies to inputs: a firm maximizes its value (the discounted present value of its profits) by choosing a quantity of each input that equates its marginal benefit and its marginal cost. This section considers nondurable inputs (such as fresh fish to produce a meal at a restaurant), or inputs that firms use soon after buying and that have no value after being used. For example, suppose that a firm buys cotton and makes shirts out of it soon afterward; the cotton becomes part of the shirts and so cannot be used again. (In contrast, a sewing machine used to produce shirts is a durable input; it can be reused in the future.) All such nonreusable inputs are nondurable inputs.

A **nondurable input** is an input that a firm uses soon after acquiring it and can use only once to produce a product.

The marginal benefit of a nondurable input is the value of its marginal product. Most firms are price takers in input markets.

A firm is a **price taker in an input market** if it faces a perfectly elastic supply of that input.

In other words, the firm cannot reduce the price it pays for the input by buying less, and the input price will not rise if the firm buys more. (Chapter 10 discussed price takers in output markets.)

A firm is a price taker in the input market when it buys such a small fraction of total sales of an input that changes in its demand have little or no effect on the input price. A typical fast-food restaurant, for example, cannot reduce the costs of its inputs such as labor, ground beef, potatoes, and electricity by reducing its demands for those inputs, and it can buy more of those inputs without raising their prices; the restaurant is a price taker in input markets. Most firms are price takers in most input markets.

If a firm is a price taker in an input market, the marginal cost of an input is its price.[4] In this case, the rule equating marginal benefit and marginal cost says:

A firm maximizes its profit by choosing a quantity of each nondurable input so that the value of the input's marginal product equals its price.

A firm raises its profit when it buys a nondurable input that costs less than the value of its marginal product. A firm's profit falls when it buys a nondurable input that costs more than the value of its marginal product. For these reasons:

A firm's demand curve for a nondurable input graphs the value of the marginal product of the input.

In other words, the demand curve for a nondurable input is its value-of-marginal-product curve. To obtain the market demand for a nondurable input, add the

FIGURE 16.3

DEMAND FOR LABOR AT A GROCERY

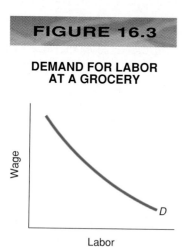

The demand curve slopes downward because the firm receives diminishing returns to labor. The height of the demand curve shows the value of the marginal product of labor at the grocery.

---

[4]If a firm is not a price taker in some input market (if it faces an upward-sloping supply curve for the input), then the firm has monopsony power in the market for that input. (See Chapter 13 for a discussion of monopsony.) In this case, the marginal cost of the input exceeds its price because the input price rises as the firm buys more.

quantities demanded by all firms, just as you obtained the market demands for final products by adding quantities demanded by all buyers. (See Chapter 4.)

EXAMPLE

Figure 16.3 shows the demand for labor (a very important input) by a grocery. The curve slopes downward because of the law of diminishing returns. The store can sell more groceries by hiring more cashiers to keep lines short and more workers to stock shelves, assist customers, unload new shipments of food, and so on. Some inputs (such as the size of the store) are fixed in the short run, however, so the marginal product of labor falls as the grocery hires more workers.[5] The height of the demand curve in Figure 16.3 shows the value of the marginal product of labor at the grocery.

CHANGES IN INPUT DEMANDS

A firm's demands for inputs change when the demand for its final product changes, when technology changes (raising or lowering marginal products), and when the prices of other inputs change. An increase in demand for a product raises the demand for inputs to produce it, as in **Figure 16.4.** The increase in demand for the final product raises its price, which raises the value of the marginal product of each input. This raises demands for the inputs.

EXAMPLES

A cereal maker needs two scoops of raisins for a box of Raisin Bran cereal. If an increase in the demand for Raisin Bran cereal raises the equilibrium quantity by 100,000 boxes per year, it raises the demand for raisins by 200,000 scoops per year. Similarly, an increase in the demand for peanut butter may raise its price from $2 to $4 per jar. Although the marginal product of peanuts to produce peanut butter has not changed, the value of the marginal product has doubled because the price has doubled. The increase in the value of the marginal product of peanuts is an increase in the demand for peanuts.

CHANGES IN TECHNOLOGY

A change in technology can increase or decrease the demand for an input. Suppose that a change in technology raises the marginal product of an input. If the price of the final product remains unchanged, then the value of the marginal product of the input rises, raising the demand for the input. The change in technology may also reduce the marginal cost of producing the final product, though, raising the supply of that product and reducing its price. This fall in the price of the final product lowers the value of the marginal product of the input. In this way, a change in technology may raise the demand for an input by raising the value of its marginal product, or the change may reduce demand for the input by reducing the value of its marginal product.

EXAMPLES A technical change improves the machinery to make sneakers, doubling the number that a worker can produce in one hour so that the marginal product of labor rises from two to four pairs of sneakers per hour. This increases the supply of sneakers and lowers the price. If the price of sneakers falls from $40 to $30 per pair, then the value of the marginal product of labor rises from $80 per

---

FIGURE 16.4

INCREASE IN DEMAND FOR A FINAL PRODUCT AND DEMAND FOR AN INPUT

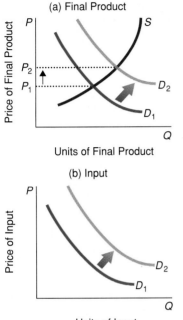

(a) Final Product

(b) Input

An increase in demand for a final product raises its price from P_1 to P_2. This raises the value of the marginal product of the input, and therefore the demand for the input.

---

[5]Some inputs, such as the manager's skills, may be fixed even in the long run, so the grocery's long-run demand curve for labor may also slope downward.

hour (two pairs at $40 each) to $120 (four pairs at $30 each). This raises the demand for labor. If the price of sneakers falls from $40 to $20 per pair, then the value of the marginal product of labor stays at $80 per hour (four pairs at $20 each). In this case, the demand for labor does not change. If, however, the price of sneakers falls from $40 to $10 per pair, then the value of the marginal product of labor falls from $80 per hour to $40 (four pairs at $10 each), reducing the demand for labor. The actual size of the fall in the price of sneakers depends on the elasticity of demand for sneakers; more elastic demand causes a smaller fall in price. In this way, a technical change can either increase or decrease the demand for an input (such as labor).

CHANGES IN INPUT PRICES

substitute inputs — two inputs for which an increase in the price of one raises demand for the other

Complement inputs — two inputs for which an increase in the price of one raises demand for the other

Two inputs are **substitute inputs** if an increase in the price of one input raises demand for the other. Two inputs are **complement inputs** if an increase in the price of one input lowers demand for the other.

Some inputs are substitutes for each other, such as sucrose and fructose (two types of sugar) as sweeteners in soft drinks. An increase in the price of one sweetener leads soft-drink manufacturers to switch to the other, increasing the demand for that other sweetener. Similarly, some types of machinery have replaced workers in certain jobs. Computerized switching equipment, for example, has largely replaced people as telephone operators. An increase in wages leads firms to switch from labor toward automated machinery, raising the demand for that machinery.

Many inputs, however, are complements. Trucks and drivers are complements; a fall in the prices of trucks may lead a firm to buy more trucks, raising the marginal product of drivers and the firm's demand for drivers. Equipment and labor tend to be complementary inputs, which is one reason that wages have increased over the last century. Technical change has reduced the prices of machinery and equipment, increasing the demand for workers and raising the equilibrium wage (which is the price of labor).

TIME TO ADJUST

The effects on input demand of changes in product demand, technology, or the prices of other inputs depend partly on the amount of time available to adjust to the change. Firms need time to change their methods of production, to adopt new technologies, replace machinery and equipment, and hire or retrain workers. As a result, the demand for inputs is more elastic in the long run than in the short run. When the price of oil rises 10 percent, firms may demand 5 percent less oil as an input in the short run. In the long run, they may replace oil-fueled equipment with gas-fueled equipment, further reducing the quantity of oil demanded and making input demand more elastic in the long run than in the short run.

————————————————— FOR REVIEW —————————————————

16.5 How does a profit-maximizing firm determine the quantity of an input to buy?

16.6 How is the demand curve for an input related to the value of its marginal product?

16.7 How is the demand for an input affected by an increase in the demand for the final product?

16.8 Suppose that a technical change doubles the amount of orange juice that can be squeezed from an orange. How does this affect the price of orange juice? How does it affect the demand for oranges to produce juice?

DEMAND FOR DURABLE INPUTS: INVESTMENT DEMAND

durable input — an input that a firm buys for future use or one that the firm can use repeatedly

net present value of a durable input — the discounted present value of the future values of the input's marginal product minus the discounted present value of its cost

The logical rule, "choose a quantity of each input so that its marginal benefit equals its marginal cost," also applies to durable inputs. The discussion in this section applies to firms that are price takers in input markets.[6]

A **durable input** is an input that a firm buys for future use or one that the firm can use repeatedly.

Offices, factories, machinery, equipment, land, and knowledge are durable inputs. The marginal benefit of a durable input is the discounted present value of the value of its marginal product.[7] The height of a firm's demand curve for a durable input indicates the discounted present value of the future values of the marginal product of that input.

Chapter 10 defined the value of a firm as the discounted present value of the firm's expected future profits. Although economists frequently speak of "maximizing profits" they really mean "maximizing the value of the firm," or the discounted present value of all its expected future profits. To do this, a firm follows a simple rule: buy any durable input with a positive net present value.

The **net present value of a durable input** is the discounted present value of the future values of its marginal product minus the discounted present value of its cost (including its price and future maintenance expenses).[8]

If the net present value of a durable input is positive, a firm maximizes the discounted present value of its profits (the value of the firm) by buying that input.

If a firm can lease or rent a durable input for a year, the logic of nondurable inputs applies, because leasing a durable input is like buying a nondurable input. A firm chooses the quantity of the durable input to lease so that the value of its marginal product equals the price of leasing it.

EXPLANATION AND EXAMPLE

When a firm buys a machine, or any other durable input, it gets the use of that machine repeatedly over some period of time (until it wears out or the firm sells it). Suppose that a machine lasts 3 years and the value of its marginal product is $400,000 at the end of the first year, $400,000 more at the end of the second year, and $300,000 at the end of the third year.[9] The firm wants to know the discounted

[6]The analysis is only slightly different, but somewhat more complicated, for firms that are not price takers in input markets.

[7]Chapter 10 discussed discounted present values.

[8]The cost of the durable input also includes all opportunity costs.

[9]You can imagine, for example, that if the machine begins operation on June 1, 1997, it produces 400,000 units of a good worth $1 each on June 1, 1998, 400,000 more units worth $1 each on June 1, 1999, and 300,000 more units worth $1 each on June 1, 2000.

present value of these future benefits that it expects from the machine. If the interest rate is 5 percent per year, the discounted present value of the future value of the machine's marginal product is $1,002,915:

$$\frac{\$400,000}{1.05} + \frac{\$400,000}{1.05^2} + \frac{\$300,000}{1.05^3} = \$1,002,915$$

This is the highest price that the firm is willing to pay for the machine.

Now suppose that the machine costs $800,000 and requires $150,000 worth of maintenance at the end of the first year and no upkeep after that. If the interest rate is 5 percent per year, the discounted present value of the cost of the machine is $942,857:

$$\$800,000 + \frac{\$150,000}{1.05} = \$942,857$$

The *net present value* of the machine is then $1,002,915 minus $942,857, or $60,058.

$$-\$800,000 + \frac{\$400,000 - \$150,000}{1.05} + \frac{\$400,000}{1.05^2} + \frac{\$300,000}{1.05^3} = \$60,058$$

Because the net present value is positive if the interest rate is 5 percent per year, buying the machine is profitable in that case—it raises the value of the firm. The firm maximizes its value, the discounted present value of its profits, if it buys all durable inputs for which it calculates positive net present values (taking into account all opportunity costs of the input).

Notice that a higher interest rate could make the net present value of the machine negative. At an interest rate of 10 percent per year, the net present value of the machine would equal:

$$-\$800,000 + \frac{\$400,000 - \$150,000}{1.10} + \frac{\$400,000}{1.10^2} + \frac{\$300,000}{1.10^3} = -\$16,754$$

In this case, buying the machine would *not* be profitable.

OPTIMAL INVESTMENT DECISIONS

Durable inputs are also called *capital.*

capital stock — the quantity of durable inputs

> The quantity of durable inputs at a firm (or in the economy) is its **capital stock.**

investment — an increase in the capital stock

> **Investment** is an increase in the capital stock.

The discussion about durable inputs implies a rule for optimal investment decisions:

> Invest in any project with a positive net present value.

─────────────── FOR REVIEW ───────────────

16.9 What is net present value? How is it related to the logical rule for buying durable inputs?

─────────────── QUESTION ───────────────

16.10 Suppose that the value of the marginal product of a machine is $1,000 this year and $1,000 next year. (a) If the interest rate is 10 percent per year, what is the discounted present value of the future values of the marginal product of the machine? (b) If the machine costs $1,800 this year and has no maintenance costs, what is its net present value? (c) Would a firm profit by buying this machine?

EQUILIBRIUM IN INPUT MARKETS

Input markets and output markets are connected—each affects the other. These connections lead to three main conclusions. In equilibrium, each input goes to its most highly valued use. Changes in supplies of inputs affect the prices of final goods. Finally, changes in demand for a final good cause changes in the prices of inputs.

INPUTS GO TO THEIR MOST HIGHLY VALUED USES

Inputs, like most goods, are scarce. In equilibrium, the firms that actually buy and use an input are those that are willing to pay the highest prices for it. The highest price that a firm is willing to pay for an input is the value of the input's marginal product to that firm, so every input moves toward the firms for which it has the highest value of marginal product.

Inputs go to their most highly valued uses.

EXAMPLES

Near a lake lies fertile land that can be used for farmland or houses. A farmer values the land at $32,000 per acre, the discounted present value of the future value of its marginal product as farmland. A housing developer values the land at $30,000 per acre. (Although other land in the area sells for $18,000 an acre, house buyers are willing to pay an extra $12,000 per acre for a house by the lake.) Because the farmer values the land more than the developer, in equilibrium this land will be used for farming.

Suppose that a technical change raises the supply of food, reducing food prices. The value of the marginal product of this land to the farmer falls to $26,000, so housing becomes the highest-valued use of the land. The owner then finds it profitable to sell the land to a housing developer. Again, the land goes to its most highly valued use.

Oil is an input that firms use for heating and producing gasoline. **Figure 16.5** shows the market for oil. Equilibrium output is 60,000 barrels, 30,000 barrels to produce heat and 30,000 to produce gasoline. Suppose that a bad winter storm raises the demand for oil to produce heat, and therefore the demand for oil. This increases the equilibrium price of oil and the equilibrium quantity produced rises from 60,000 to 70,000 barrels. It reduces the amount of oil used to produce gasoline from 30,000 to 25,000 barrels. Because the input becomes temporarily more valuable in one use (heating), the input goes from a less valuable use (gasoline production) to a more valuable use (heating). In equilibrium, the value of the marginal product of oil in each use is equal, and it equals the price of oil.[10]

ECONOMIC RENT

Sometimes the equilibrium price of an input is higher than necessary to move the input toward its most highly valued use. For example, a baseball star earning $3

---

[10]It should not be surprising that the value of the input's marginal product is the same in both uses. Each industry chooses a quantity of the input so that the value of its marginal product equals the price of the input. Because they both equal the price, they also equal each other.

FIGURE 16.5

AN INCREASE IN DEMAND FOR A FINAL PRODUCT RAISES DEMAND FOR INPUTS

The total demand for oil equals the demand for oil to produce heat plus the demand for oil to produce gasoline. The equilibrium price is $15 per barrel, and 30,000 barrels of oil are used for each purpose. (See Panel a.) A winter storm raises the demand for oil to produce heat (Panel b), raising the price of oil to $18. In the new equilibrium, oil goes to its most highly valued use and the value of the marginal product of oil is $18 in every industry that uses oil as an input.

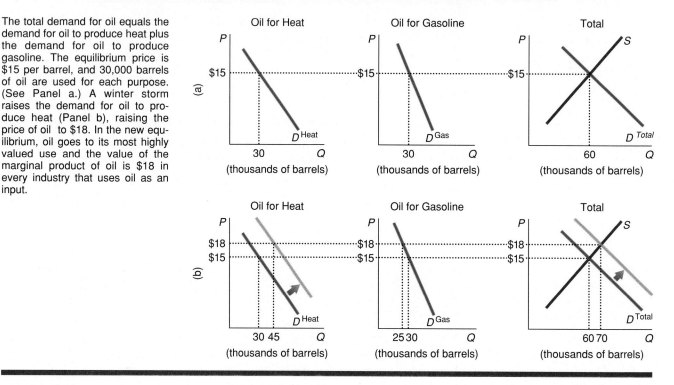

million per year might be willing to play baseball for only $50,000 per year. (The player's best alternative job might be as a sportscaster earning $50,000 per year.) The player earns an economic rent of $3 million minus $50,000, or $2,950,000 per year. This idea extends to all resources; if any resource sells for a price that is higher than its opportunity cost, the difference is its economic rent.[11]

economic rent — the price of an input minus its opportunity cost

An **economic rent** is the price of a resource minus its opportunity cost.

Do not become confused by economic jargon. The term *economic rent* has nothing to do with renting an apartment or leasing a car; the meaning of *rent* here is completely different.

Figure 16.6 shows demand and supply for original Rembrandt paintings. The supply is perfectly inelastic because there is a fixed number of these paintings. The opportunity cost of a Rembrandt painting is zero because they already exist and they have no valuable use except as art. When a resource has a perfectly inelastic supply as in Figure 16.6a, its opportunity cost is zero and economists say that it earns *pure economic rent*. When someone buys an original Rembrandt painting, the price is pure economic rent. More generally, a graph of a resource's economic

---

[11]The sportscasting job might pay $60,000 per year, but the player might still play baseball for $50,000 because of a preference for playing over announcing; the player's economic rent in this case is still $2,950,000 per year.

FIGURE 16.6

ECONOMIC RENT

(a)

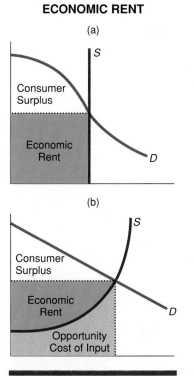

(b)

rent can show it as the producer surplus earned by its owner, as in Figure 16.6b. That figure shows the supply and demand for an input, the consumer surplus earned by input buyers (firms), and the producer surplus or economic rent earned by input sellers. The area under the supply curve shows the opportunity cost of the input.

INPUT MARKETS AFFECT OUTPUT MARKETS AND VICE VERSA

Input markets affect output markets and vice versa. Firms produce quarter-pound hamburgers with inputs such as a quarter-pound of ground beef, a grill to cook it, a person to cook it, a bun, and perhaps some mustard. To see why input markets affect output markets, suppose that the supply of beef decreases, as in **Figure 16.7.** This raises the price of beef and the marginal cost of producing hamburgers, decreasing the supply of hamburgers and raising their price. More generally, a decrease in the supply of an input raises the prices of final goods that use that input in their production.

To see why output markets affect input markets, suppose that the demand for hamburgers increases, as in **Figure 16.8.** This raises the price of hamburgers and the value of the marginal product of ground beef, increasing the demand for beef. This increase in the demand for beef raises its price. More generally, an increase in the demand for a good raises the prices of inputs that firms use to produce it.

It is a common mistake to think that the cost of producing a product is determined by the prices of its inputs. This is an example of the fallacy of composition discussed in Chapter 2. It is true for one seller, but not for the economy as a whole. Prices of an input and a final product are jointly determined by supply and

FIGURE 16.7

A FALL IN THE SUPPLY OF AN INPUT RAISES THE PRICE OF THE FINAL PRODUCT

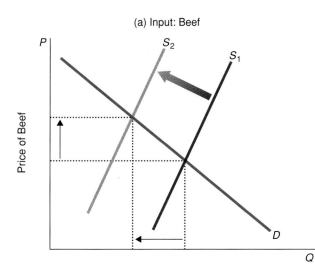

(a) Input: Beef

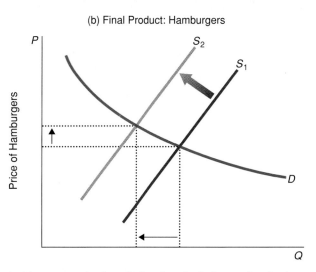

(b) Final Product: Hamburgers

A fall in the supply of beef (an input into the production of hamburgers) raises the price of beef, which raises the marginal cost of producing hamburgers. This decreases the supply of

hamburgers and raises their price. In that way, input prices affect the prices of final products.

FIGURE 16.8

AN INCREASE IN DEMAND FOR A FINAL PRODUCT RAISES THE PRICE OF INPUTS USED TO PRODUCE IT

(a) Input: Beef

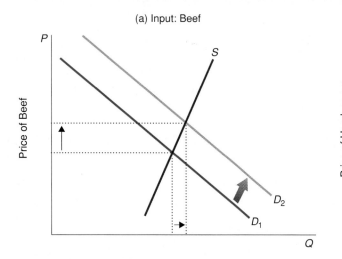

(b) Final Product: Hamburgers

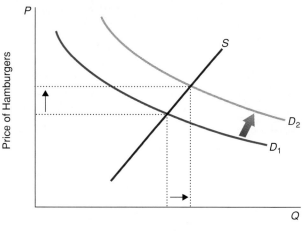

A rise in the demand for hamburgers raises their price. This raises the value of the marginal product of beef, and therefore the demand for beef. The rise in the demand for beef increases its price. In this way, the prices of final products affect the prices of inputs.

demand in each market. Both respond to changes in the supplies of inputs, technology, and the demand for final products.

DISTRIBUTION OF INCOME

Prices of inputs have two roles: they *allocate resources* and *distribute income.* Input prices allocate resources by ensuring that inputs go to their most highly valued uses and by providing incentives for firms to create more inputs by investing in capital when the benefits exceed the costs. Input prices distribute income because workers receive wages and owners of other inputs (such as land and equipment) earn income from selling their services. These two roles of input prices are intimately related; if input prices did not affect the distribution of income, they could not allocate resources efficiently. Prices allocate resources by affecting the incentives to use those resources in various ways. They affect incentives by affecting the distribution of income.

With one exception, owners of inputs must receive the income from those inputs to assure that they will be allocated to their most highly valued uses. The exception involves economic rents; inputs go to their most highly valued uses even when their owners do not receive the economic rents earned by those inputs. The use of an input, for example, would not be affected by a tax that reduced its economic rent. Aside from this exception, input prices must affect the distribution of income for the economy to use inputs efficiently.

This connection between economic efficiency and the distribution of income raises the issue of fairness. Some people believe it is unjust for the owner of an

TABLE 16.2

PRODUCTION OF NOTEBOOKS

Number of Workers	Output per Hour	Marginal Product	Value of Marginal Product
0	0	—	—
1	5	5	$15
2	9	4	12
3	12	3	9
4	14	2	6
5	15	1	3

input to receive income equal to the value of its marginal product; they believe that the government should distribute income in some other way. Chapter 3 discussed some differing ideas of fairness.[12] To understand the issues better, think about the following question:

> If firms pay workers the value of their marginal products, why do the firms have any money left over for profit?

Suppose, for example, that a firm uses labor and one machine to produce notebooks, which it sells for $3 each. **Table 16.2** shows the number of notebooks the firm produces with various quantities of labor. If the firm hires two workers, it produces 9 notebooks per hour and the marginal product of labor is 4 notebooks per hour. Because notebooks sell for $3 each, the value of the marginal product of labor is $12 per hour in this case. If, instead, the firm hires four workers, it produces 14 notebooks per hour. The marginal product of labor is 2 notebooks per hour and the value of the marginal product of labor is $6 per hour. Notice that because the firm has only one machine, the law of diminishing returns makes the marginal product of labor fall as it hires more workers.

The firm chooses the number of workers so that the value of the marginal product of labor equals the wage. If workers cost $6 per hour, the firm hires four of them. Total wages are $24 per hour and total revenue is $42 per hour (14 notebooks per hour at $3 each), so profit is $18 per hour. The firm's owners, those who own the machine, collect this profit. The firm pays each worker the value of her marginal product, and still makes a profit.

Is this fair? Does the firm exploit workers? The answer depends on the meanings of the words *fair* and *exploit*. Whatever your opinion, you should notice three points. First, each worker receives all of the extra money that the firm earns by employing him (rather than employing one fewer worker). With three workers, the firm would produce 12 notebooks per hour and its total revenue would be $36 per hour; a fourth worker adds $6 per hour to the firm's revenue, and this is what the firm pays the workers. Second, workers and the firm share the gains from trade; the firm's $18 profit is its consumer surplus from buying the labor services. Third, the machine is valuable (because the workers would produce less

---

[12]Also see Chapter 18.

without it) and its owners must earn the opportunity cost of the machine to give them an incentive to provide it to the firm.

The owners of the machine might receive more than its opportunity cost, that is, the machine might earn economic rent. Suppose that the machine's owners receive $18 per hour in profit, but the machine costs only $15 per hour. (Perhaps the machine operates 1,000 hours at a cost of $15,000.) In this case, the machine earns economic rent of $3 per hour. Such an economic rent seldom lasts long. New firms buy additional machines and enter the industry to take advantage of the opportunity to earn rents. As they enter, the supply of notebooks rises and the price falls. In long-run equilibrium, the machine earns zero economic rent. A resource earns a long-run economic rent only if it cannot be replicated, as most machines can; examples may include a unique piece of land, a uniquely talented entertainer, or a uniquely savvy businessperson. Whether it is fair that such a resource earns economic rent depends on your views about fairness. Chapter 18 returns to the distribution of income.

SCOPE OF A FIRM

Some construction firms employ their own bricklayers, carpenters, electricians, painters, and plumbers. They pay their workers annual salaries and order them to perform various jobs. Other construction firms hire freelance bricklayers, carpenters, electricians, painters, and plumbers, who are independent contractors in business for themselves, on a per-job basis; they negotiate a wage for each job separately. The firm may hire different freelance workers at different times.

Why do these firms make different choices? Why do some firms employ their own lawyers while other firms hire lawyers in private practice as needed? Why do some firms set up their own computer networks while other firms hire outside companies to set up and manage their computer networks? In other words, what determines the scope of activities within a firm?

There are two ways to coordinate the activities of inputs so they work jointly to produce a good. One way is through the market; a person who wants to build a house can hire workers individually for each particular task and arrange for them to work together. The second way to coordinate inputs is through a command system within a firm; the firm employs its own workers and tells them that this month they will build a house. The workers are employees rather than independent contractors; they agree to let the firm dictate (within certain guidelines) what work they will do, and they do not negotiate separate agreements with the firm for each job.

If people always used markets to coordinate inputs, there would be no firms. People create firms when it becomes less costly to organize inputs within a firm than through markets. Firms can reduce transactions costs.

transactions costs — the costs of finding people with whom to trade, and the costs of buying, selling, or negotiating agreements, paying for products or services, and enforcing contracts

> **Transactions costs** are the costs of finding people with whom to trade, and the costs of buying, selling, or negotiating agreements, paying for products or services, and enforcing contracts.

Organizing inputs through markets can have high transactions costs. It may take time and money to negotiate agreements with every worker to build a house and with suppliers to provide materials at the right times. A firm may be able to organize inputs more cheaply by ordering its workers to perform certain tasks at certain times. The firm need not negotiate a new contract with each worker for each new job; instead, it simply hires the worker and then directs the work. This reduces the number of agreements that the parties must negotiate and it lowers the transactions costs required to coordinate inputs.

Imagine if the inputs into your education were organized through markets rather than through a firm (your college). You and every other student would each have to negotiate a separate agreement with each professor to provide lectures, reading assignments, office hours, and grades. If each student has 40 professors over the course of a college career, a college with 10,000 students would require 400,000 contracts. The college is a firm that reduces such transactions costs by hiring professors on long-term contracts and then requiring them to perform various services. Each student negotiates one contract with the college and each professor negotiates one contract with the college. This eliminates the need for each student to negotiate a separate contract with each professor.

Production costs may also be lower when firms, rather than markets, coordinate certain activities. This occurs when a firm can produce a million standard windows in a factory and then store them until they are needed more cheaply than producing a few thousand windows every week as the market needs them. Team production can also reduce costs. When the same employees work together over a long period of time, they may learn to work more productively as a team than separately on different jobs at different times.[13] Generally, people create firms to organize inputs when it is more efficient than organizing inputs through markets.

FOR REVIEW

16.11 Explain why inputs go to their most highly valued uses.

16.12 Define *economic rent* and show it on a graph of the supply and demand for an input.

16.13 Explain how an increase in demand for a product affects the prices of its inputs.

QUESTIONS

16.14 Why do firms have any money left over for profit after they pay workers the values of their marginal products?

16.15 Explain why it is sometimes more efficient for firms to organize inputs than for markets to organize inputs.

CONCLUSIONS

PRODUCTIVITY AND DIMINISHING RETURNS

The marginal product of an input is the increase in a firm's total output when it adds one more unit of the input, keeping the quantities of other inputs fixed. The law of diminishing returns states that raising the quantity of an input eventually reduces its marginal product, if the quantity of some other input remains fixed. Diminishing returns imply that short-run marginal cost and average variable cost

---

[13]Firms can also reduce the cost of financing the organization of inputs, taking advantage of economies of scale in borrowing money for labor costs and equipment, and borrowing money at lower interest rates than individuals can arrange.

rise with increasing output. The value of the marginal product of an input is the increase in the value of a firm's output when it adds one unit of the input, keeping the quantities of other inputs fixed. With perfect competition, the value of the marginal product of an input equals its marginal product multiplied by the price of the final product.

DEMAND FOR NONDURABLE INPUTS

The rule for rational decisions states that a firm maximizes its value by choosing a quantity of each input so that its marginal benefit equals its marginal cost. A price taker in input markets chooses quantities of each nondurable input so that the value of each input's marginal product equals its price. A firm's demand curve for a nondurable input shows the value of the marginal product of that input.

An increase in the demand for a product raises the demands for inputs that firms use to produce it. A change in technology can raise the demand for an input by raising the value of its marginal product, or reduce the demand for the input by reducing the value of its marginal product. An increase in the price of an input can affect the demands for other inputs, raising the demands for substitute inputs and lowering the demands for complementary inputs.

DEMAND FOR DURABLE INPUTS: INVESTMENT DEMAND

The net present value of a durable input is the discounted present value of the future values of its marginal product minus the discounted present value of its cost. A firm maximizes the discounted present value of its profits (the value of the firm) by buying any durable input that has a positive net present value.

EQUILIBRIUM IN INPUT MARKETS

Changes in the supplies of inputs affect the prices of final goods, and changes in demands for final goods cause changes in the prices of inputs. In equilibrium, each input goes to its most highly valued use, that is, to firms at which the value of the input's marginal product is highest. An economic rent is the price of a resource minus its opportunity cost. If the equilibrium price of an input exceeds the price necessary to give that input an incentive to go to its most highly valued use, then the input earns economic rent. Input markets affect output markets and vice versa. A decrease in the supply of an input raises the prices of final goods that use that input in their production. An increase in demand for a product raises the prices of inputs that firms use to produce it.

DISTRIBUTION OF INCOME

Input prices allocate resources by ensuring that inputs go to their most highly valued uses and by providing incentives for firms to create more inputs when the benefits exceed the costs. Input prices also distribute income. These two roles of input prices are intimately related, and this relationship raises issues of fairness about the distribution of income.

SCOPE OF A FIRM

Inputs can be coordinated by the market or by command within firms. People establish firms to coordinate inputs when doing so reduces transactions costs, which are the costs of finding people with whom to trade, and the costs of buying, selling, or negotiating agreements, paying for products or services, and enforcing contracts.

LOOKING AHEAD

Chapter 17 discusses the economics of an extremely important input: labor services. Chapter 18 discusses the distribution of income, poverty, and discrimination. Later chapters discuss special topics in microeconomics.

KEY TERMS

average product

marginal product

law of diminishing returns

value of the marginal product

nondurable input

price taker in an input market

complement inputs

substitute inputs

durable input

net present value of a durable input

capital stock

investment

economic rent

transactions costs

QUESTIONS AND PROBLEMS

16.16 **Table 16.3** shows the marginal and average products of labor for a firm with two machines. Suppose that the firm sells its final product for $3 and its labor costs $9 per hour. How many hours of labor services should the firm buy to maximize its value? How would the answer change if the price of the final product were $4.50?

16.17 How does an increase in the interest rate affect investment? Explain why.

16.18 Someone invents a machine that turns industrial waste into hamburgers. The industrial waste is available at zero cost. The machine churns the waste for exactly 1 year and then emits 3,000 hamburgers at the end of the year. The machine continues to churn for a second year and emits 2,000 more hamburgers at the end of that year, after which the machine falls apart and is worthless. Suppose that hamburgers sell for $3 each and everyone expects the price to stay at that level over the next several years. The interest rate is 5 percent per year.

TABLE 16.3

PRODUCTION AT A FIRM WITH TWO MACHINES

(Variable) Input of Labor	Output per Hour	Marginal Product of Labor	Average Product of Labor
1	5	5	$5.00
2	12	7	6.00
3	18	6	6.00
4	23	5	5.75
5	27	4	5.40
6	30	3	5.00
7	32	2	4.71
8	33	1	4.12

a. What is the discounted present value of the value of the marginal product of the machine?

b. What is the net present value of the machine?

c. Suppose that everyone expects the price of hamburgers to rise by 3 percent per year, to $3.09 after 1 year and $3.18 after 2 years. How does this affect the net present value of the machine?

d. Repeat Question 16.18c assuming that the interest rate is 8.125 percent per year instead of 5.000 percent per year. Compare your answer to the result of Question 16.18b.

16.19 Suppose that the demand for popped popcorn is perfectly inelastic at the quantity 1,000 pounds. Unpopped popcorn is an input in making popped popcorn. Peter Popper proposes a procedure to pop practically all of the kernels in the pot. Suppose that this doubles the quantity of popped popcorn from a given quantity of unpopped popcorn. How does this affect the demand for the input (unpopped popcorn)? (How many pounds of unpopped popcorn do people purchase to pop?)

16.20 Comment on a newspaper article's claim that "steak prices have risen because beef prices are up." Under what circumstances would this claim be correct? Explain how the newspaper might have the economics backward.

INQUIRIES FOR FURTHER THOUGHT

16.21 Is it fair for firms to pay workers the value of the marginal products of their labor?

16.22 You produce goods and services such as parties, your education, good impressions on other people, and good health. What inputs do you use to produce them? How do your input demands respond to changes in input prices and technology?

16.23 A popular entertainer earns several million dollars a year from concerts, videos, and recordings. Do you think that this entertainer earns economic rent? Is he or she paid more than the value of his or her marginal product? Is this fair? If not, what changes would you propose?

TAG SOFTWARE APPLICATIONS

TUTORIAL EXERCISES
▶ The module contains a review of the key terms from Chapter 16.

ANALYTICAL EXERCISES
▶ The analytical section contains questions of the calculation of marginal and average product.

GRAPHING EXERCISES
▶ The graphing segment examines marginal product, average product, the demand for the supply of inputs, the determination of input prices, and the calculation of economic rent. The graphing appendix to this chapter looks at isoquants and isocost lines, which are discussed next in the chapter appendix.

CHAPTER 16 APPENDIX — ISOQUANTS

This appendix describes a graphical approach to choosing inputs to maximize the value of a firm. It introduces *isoquants,* which are like indifference curves applied to production decisions. (The Chapter 9 Appendix discusses indifference curves.) Indifference curves show combinations of two goods that give a person equal utility; isoquants show combinations of two inputs that give a firm equal output.

> Isoquants graph technically efficient combinations of inputs that give the same amount of output.

Each isoquant applies to one level of output; higher isoquants indicate higher levels of output.

Figure 16A.1 shows examples of isoquants. Panel a shows an extreme example in which inputs are perfect complements; a firm must use exactly one unit of labor and one unit of capital to make one unit of output (think of cars, drivers, and taxi services). With the isoquants in Panel a, extra labor produces nothing unless the firm also provides extra capital, and extra capital produces nothing unless the firm hires extra labor. Panel b shows another extreme case in which labor and capital are perfect substitutes in producing output; a firm produces the same amount with four workers and no machine as with no workers and two machines. Only the total amount of machines and pairs of workers affects total production. Panel c shows the usual shape of isoquants; the firm can produce the same amount of output with less capital and more labor, or vice versa, but the inputs are *not* perfect complements or substitutes.

Isoquants resemble indifference curves, with two exceptions:

▶ Each isoquant shows a certain quantity of output instead of a certain amount of utility.

FIGURE 16A.1

ISOQUANTS

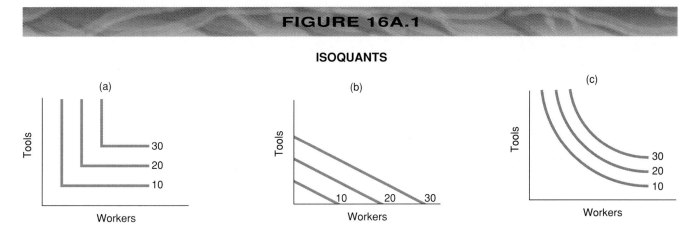

Each graph shows three isoquants; one for producing 10 goods per day, one for producing 20 goods per day, and one for producing 30 goods per day. In Panel a, one worker and one tool can produce one unit of output; tools and workers are perfect complements. In Panel b, total output equals the number of tools plus twice the number of workers; tools and workers are perfect substitutes. In Panel c, the normal case, tools and workers are neither perfect complements or perfect substitutes.

▶ Isoquants show technical possibilities for production instead of a person's tastes.

Whatever quantity of goods a firm chooses to produce, it wants to produce at the lowest possible cost to maximize its profit. Suppose that the firm wants to produce 75 units of a good per hour and that labor costs $10 per hour and tools rent for $5 per hour. The isoquant for 75 units of output in **Figure 16A.2** shows the various combinations of workers and tools with which the firm can produce that quantity. To find the lowest-cost method of production, draw an *isocost* line (similar to a budget line from Chapter 9) with a slope equal to the negative of the relative price of labor in terms of tools. In the figure, the relative price of labor in terms of tools is two tools per worker, so the slope of the line is –2. Now find the lowest isocost line (which represents the lowest possible level of spending on inputs) that touches the 75-good isoquant. In the figure, that line touches the isoquant at Point A where the firm produces 75 units of output using six workers and eight tools, which costs the firm $100. This is the lowest-cost way to produce 75 goods. Any other combination of workers and tools to produce 75 units would cost more.

The slope of an isoquant equals the negative of the *marginal rate of substitution in production* between labor and tools, which is the ratio of their marginal products. The firm minimizes its cost of production by choosing combinations of inputs so that the marginal rate of substitution in production equals the relative price of the inputs. This occurs at Point A in Figure 16A.2, where the slope of the line equals the slope of the isoquant. Changes in input prices cause changes in the

FIGURE 16A.2

ECONOMICALLY EFFICIENT CHOICES OF INPUTS

The straight line shows combinations of inputs that the firm can buy for $100. The slope of the line is the negative of the relative price of labor in terms of tools.

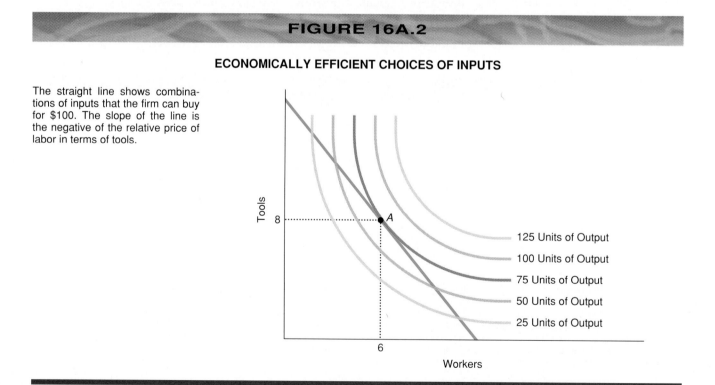

slope of the straight line in the figure. For example, an increase in wages would make the line steeper, which would lead the firm to use less labor and more tools in production.

Questions and Problems

16A.1 Explain why isoquants cannot cross each other.

16A.2 How would isoquants between machines and workers change in response to these events:

    a. Technical progress allows each machine to replace a larger number of workers.

    b. The price of machines rises.

    c. The average and marginal products of machines and workers all increase by 10 percent.

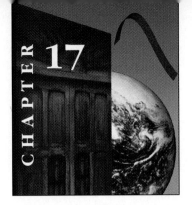

CHAPTER 17

LABOR MARKETS

WHAT THIS CHAPTER IS ABOUT

▶ Why some jobs pay higher wages than others

▶ Why people earn higher wages if they

Have more education

Are older or have more seniority at a firm

Are members of unions

Are white males

▶ Why there is unemployment

▶ Why workers pay for some kinds of training and firms pay for other kinds

▶ Why some firms pay higher wages than necessary to attract workers

In 1931, Babe Ruth earned more than the president of the United States. When asked about this fact, Ruth, perhaps the most talented baseball player of all time, is said to have responded, "Why not? I had a better year than he did." (Ruth hit .373 with 46 home runs; President Herbert Hoover contended with the Great Depression.) Why have Madonna and Michael Jordan earned more than scientists doing research on cancer or AIDS? Why do some people work overtime while others struggle with unemployment? These are some of the issues of labor economics.

LABOR SUPPLY AND DEMAND

Labor markets differ from markets for goods like shoes or pizzas for two reasons. First, people earn most of their incomes by working, that is, by selling their services in labor markets. In the United States and most other developed countries, people earn about three-fourths of their income from selling labor. (The other one-fourth of income comes from investments, that is, from owning capital.) In 1994, for example, the total income of everyone in the United States amounted to $6.7 trillion; $4.5 trillion of this income came from selling labor.

Labor markets differ from other markets for a second reason—labor services are physically connected to the worker. Machines don't care where they work, but people do. People care about their work environments, their fellow workers, flexibility of hours, the risk of injury on the job, and other job characteristics.

Not all labor is alike. People differ in their abilities, education, and experience. The supply and demand for labor always refer to particular types of labor. They can also refer to particular geographical areas or local labor markets. A different set of supply and demand curves, and a different equilibrium, characterize every type of labor and each labor market. One can, for example, apply supply–demand analysis to the markets for unskilled labor in Philadelphia, dental hygienists in Dallas, or airline pilots in the entire country. Local labor markets are related in the long run—if wages in one city exceed wages in another city (adjusted for differences in housing prices and each city's amenities), people may eventually move to the high-wage city or employers may move to the low-wage city.

LABOR SUPPLY

A person's labor supply decisions include whether to work, what occupation to choose, which job offer to take (or whether to operate an independent business), and how many hours to work each year. Economists say that a person *works in the market* if someone pays the person to work or if that person is self-employed. A person works in the home if that work brings no explicit pay (caring for children, volunteering, and so on). Although most of the discussion in this chapter concerns work in the market, work in the home is also valuable. Economists estimate that the average value of work in the home (caring for a family) is about $30,000 per year, and nearly $40,000 if the person cares for children under age 6.

labor force — all the people who work in the market or who are looking for a job in the market

A person is in the **labor force** if he or she works in the market or is looking for a job in the market.

In 1900, almost nine out of ten men, but only two out of ten women, were in the labor force. By 1995, about three-fourths of men over age 16 were in the labor force, as were about six out of every ten women. A person is more likely to participate in the labor force if the opportunity cost is low (e.g., the value of time in the home is small because the person has no children or child-care costs are low) or the benefit is high (e.g., the family has no other source of income).[1]

Occupation choice, another labor-supply decision, depends on a person's job preferences and opportunities. Wages, possibilities for advancement, flexibility, job security, and location affect the decision. A person's job opportunities depend partly on her abilities, training, and experience. In 1900, more than one-third of U.S. workers worked on farms; by 1995, farm jobs amounted to only 3 percent of total jobs. In 1900, only about two out of every ten U.S. jobs were in a service industry; today, about six out of ten U.S. jobs are in service industries (counting government workers), while about three out of every ten jobs are in industries that produce goods. Only one out of five U.S. jobs was white-collar work in 1900; by 1995, more than half were white-collar jobs.

Occupation choice responds to changes in costs and benefits. People choose more flexible, mobile occupations if their spouses' jobs require frequent moves. In China, illiterate manual laborers earn more than college graduates; this pay differential increased in the last decade, leading more students to drop out of school and fewer to enter college.

Self-employed workers usually have some choice about the number of hours they work. Other workers also have some choice because they can find jobs that require more or fewer hours per week or that offer options to work overtime. Some people work additional hours to raise their chances of advancement in a firm; some increase their work hours by taking second jobs. At the beginning of

---

[1]Higher wages frequently lead people to postpone retirement.

the 20th century, workers in U.S. manufacturing industries averaged 55 hours per week; today their average work week is about 35 hours.

LABOR SUPPLY CURVES

Figure 17.1 shows two possible shapes for a labor supply curve. The quantity of labor supplied—the number of hours per week (or per year) a person chooses to work—depends on the wage. The labor supply curve may slope upward, as in Panel a, or it may bend backward, as in Panel b.

> A **backward-bending labor supply curve** is a labor supply curve that has a negatively sloped portion.

Labor supply curves can have either shape because rising wages may lead people to work either more *or* less. The substitution effect of a higher wage makes people want to work more; the income effect of a higher wage makes them want to work less.[2]

SUBSTITUTION AND INCOME EFFECTS OF A WAGE INCREASE

The substitution effect of a wage increase makes people want to work more because, at the higher wage, the worker sacrifices more for each hour *not* spent working. The wage rate is the opportunity cost of leisure time. When this cost rises, people buy less leisure time by working more.

The income effect of a wage increase makes people want to work less because a wage increase raises the worker's income, and most workers want to spend some of this increased income on more leisure time (that is, leisure is a normal good).

The income effect of a permanent increase in wages is larger than the income effect of a temporary increase. An extreme example shows why. You would not be much richer if your wage were to double for one day; your wealth would rise much more if your wage were to double permanently. You are more likely to want to buy additional leisure time by working less in the latter case. For this reason, labor supply curves are more likely to bend backward when a wage increase is permanent than when it is temporary.

EXAMPLE If you work 40 hours per week and earn $10.00 per hour, you earn $400.00 per week. If your wage were to rise to $12.50 per hour, you could:

▶ Work 8 hours less each week (only 32 hours per week) and still earn $400; in this case, your labor supply curve is backward-bending (as in Figure 17.1b).

▶ Work 4 hours less each week (only 36 hours per week) and earn $450 per week; in this case, your labor supply curve is backward-bending (as in Figure 17.1b).

▶ Continue to work 40 hours per week and earn $500 per week; in this case, your labor supply curve is perfectly inelastic.

▶ Work 4 hours more each week (44 hours per week) and earn $550; in this case, your labor supply curve is upward-sloping (as in Figure 17.1a).

EVIDENCE ON LABOR SUPPLY

Statistical evidence indicates that most adult males and unmarried females who work full time have labor supply curves that bend backward but that are close to

---

FIGURE 17.1

LABOR SUPPLY CURVES

(a) Upward-sloping Labor Supply

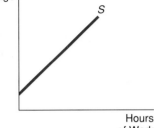

(b) Backward-bending Labor Supply

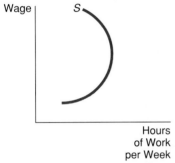

backward-bending labor supply curve — a labor supply curve with a negatively sloped portion

---

[2]You may want to review the discussion of substitution effects and income effects in Chapter 4.

perfectly inelastic. A permanent 10 percent wage increase appears to reduce the quantity of labor supplied by about 1 or 2 percent. On the other hand, labor supply curves slope upward when wage changes last only a few days or a few months. Evidence indicates that labor supply curves of married females slope upward even when wage changes are permanent.[3] Teenagers and older workers also tend to have upward-sloping labor supply curves.

CHANGES IN LABOR SUPPLY

Labor supply increases when the nonpay features of a job improve (when the work environment improves, stress or risk of injury fall, the work becomes more interesting, and so on) or when family income from other sources decreases (perhaps because another family member loses a job). Labor supply decreases when the nonpay features of a job become less attractive, when family income from other sources rises (a spouse gets a big raise), or when the opportunity cost of working rises (as with the birth of a child).

MARKET SUPPLY OF LABOR

The market supply of labor refers to the supply to a particular occupation or industry by people with the requisite skills. Even if each person has a backward-bending or vertical labor supply curve, the market supply of a labor to a particular occupation may slope upward because an increase in wages in that occupation may lead more people to choose that kind of work. Wage increases in one occupation or industry induce workers to switch from other occupations or industries. The market supply of labor to any particular occupation depends partly on the number of people with the required skills, their preferences for different types of work, and the wages they could earn in other occupations or industries.

Similarly, economists speak of the market supply of labor in a particular city, which depends partly on wages in other cities. An increase in the demand for labor in Texas raises wages there and leads workers to move from other states, raising the quantity of labor supplied in Texas.

LABOR DEMAND

As Chapter 16 explained, the demand for labor reflects the value of its marginal product. A firm's demand for labor increases when the marginal physical product of labor rises, making labor more productive. A firm's demand for labor also rises when the relative price of the firm's good rises, increasing the value of the marginal product of labor. Workers may become more productive by acquiring more education or training, by gaining experience, by working with more capital equipment, by utilizing improved technologies, or by improving coordination between the activities of a team of workers.

The demand for a certain type of labor falls, however, when technical change reduces the value of its marginal product. For example, the invention of the plow reduced the demand for farm workers not because they became less productive (the plow raised their productivity) but because the plow raised farm output, reducing food prices and decreasing the value of the marginal product of farm

---

[3]Historically, the income effects of wage changes have been smaller for married females than for unmarried females because married females have obtained income from their spouses; the difference between married females and married males apparently reflects the facts that females earned (and still earn) less on average than males and that fewer males were willing to work in the home. Whether these differences will continue in the future remains to be seen.

workers' labor. Advances in computer technology in the last decade have led firms to replace middle management, white-collar workers with computers. If robot technology continues to improve, prices of industrial robots may fall and reduce the demands for certain types of manual labor.

EVIDENCE ON THE ELASTICITY OF LABOR DEMAND

Evidence suggests that the long-run elasticity of demand for labor for the entire U.S. economy is between −0.15 and −0.50. Therefore, a 10 percent wage increase would reduce the quantity of labor demanded by between 1.5 percent and 5.0 percent. The short-run demand for labor (before firms can adjust fully to a change in the wage) is even more inelastic. The long-run demand for labor in manufacturing industries is between −0.1 and −0.6, which is also inelastic. On the other hand, the long-run demand for unskilled teenage labor is very elastic; the elasticity of demand is about −8.0.

LABOR MARKET EQUILIBRIUM

nominal (money) wage — the wage rate measured in money (such as dollars, yen, or pesos)

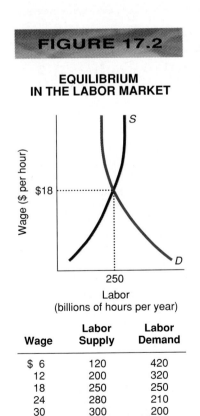

FIGURE 17.2

EQUILIBRIUM IN THE LABOR MARKET

Wage	Labor Supply	Labor Demand
$ 6	120	420
12	200	320
18	250	250
24	280	210
30	300	200

Figure 17.2 shows equilibrium in the labor market. The United States has about 125 million workers and about 5 million employers. In equilibrium, people work about 250 billion hours per year and receive an average hourly wage of about $18 per hour.[4]

EMPLOYMENT AND HOURS IN EQUILIBRIUM

Equilibrium of supply and demand for labor determines total labor hours. But what determines whether a firm using 1,400 hours of labor per week employs 35 people each working 40 hours per week, or 40 people each working 35 hours per week? Will the firm offer 40 jobs or only 35 jobs? The answer depends on the costs and benefits of more employees versus more hours per employee.

A firm hires fewer employees and each employee works more hours if:

▶ Hiring and training costs are high, allowing a firm to reduce total training costs by hiring fewer workers each working more hours.

▶ Fewer employees working longer hours make the firm more productive. For example, each worker may require some setup time at the beginning of each work day, so fewer employees require less setup time, or employees may require time to exchange information on the job, which takes less time with fewer employees.

▶ Laws and regulations make it cheaper to have fewer employees. For example, some taxes and government regulations are tied to the number of employees.

▶ Employees want to work long hours. They may prefer long hours or they may face fixed costs of commuting to work or fixed costs of arranging child care.

REAL AND NOMINAL WAGES

Figure 17.3 shows average real and nominal wages in the United States since 1914.

The **nominal (money) wage** is the wage rate measured in money (such as dollars, yen, or pesos).

---

[4]The average wage for nonsupervisory workers is about $12 per hour; see Figures 17.3 and 17.4.

FIGURE 17.3

NOMINAL AND REAL WAGES IN THE UNITED STATES, 1914–1995 (NONSUPERVISORY WORKERS)

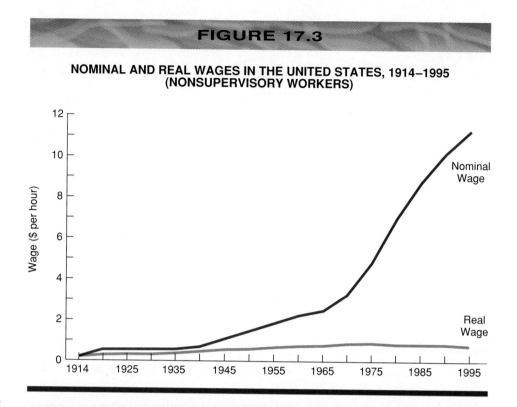

IN THE NEWS

Fewer jobs filled as factories rely on overtime pay

Hiring is 'a last choice'

By Louis Uchitelle

For decades, overtime encouraged hiring. Companies found it cheaper to hire a new worker rather than assign more hours to existing employees, who have to be paid a 50 percent premium for the extra work.

But particularly in the last two years, the cost of a new employee—recruiting, training, and ever-more-costly health insurance—has made overtime the less expensive choice.

Heavy Demand for Product
"You almost always hire people now only as a last choice," said Robert Cizik, chairman of Cooper Industries and also of the National Association of Manufacturers.

When Cooper had a surge in orders for the computer cables it makes, more than 2,000 workers were asked to work an additional two hours a day, on overtime pay. Only as a last resort has Cooper recently begun to hire. "People got tired of working 10-hour days," Mr. Cizik said.

The Costs of Hiring
The overtime phenomenon is most evident in manufacturing. Factory workers, who represent 17 percent of the nation's employees, are generally skilled and well paid, and they usually work full time because factory shifts require full timers. Each new worker, as a result, means a considerable investment not only in benefits but also in recruiting and training.

The number of new jobs in equilibrium depends partly on the costs of adding employees versus the costs of increasing hours per employee.

Source: Louis Uchitelle, "Fewer Jobs Filled as Factories Rely on Overtime Pay," *New York Times*, May 16, 1993, p. A1.

real wage — the wage rate adjusted for inflation, that is, measured in purchasing power units

The **real wage** is the wage rate adjusted for inflation, that is, the wage measured in purchasing power units.

The real wage, rather than the nominal wage, guides the decisions of workers and firms because it measures the amount of goods that a person can buy with her wages. While the average nominal wage in the United States has risen, on average, about 5.5 percent per year since 1914, the average real wage has risen about 2 percent per year. Figure 17.4a shows the average real wage and average real (inflation-adjusted) weekly earnings for U.S. workers since 1914. Weekly earnings have risen less than real wages because people have worked fewer hours per week over time.

Figure 17.4b shows the average real wage of U.S. nonsupervisory workers in recent decades. This graph demonstrates the striking fact that the average real wage has fallen since 1973. While the figure makes it appear that the average real wage has fallen back to its 1964 level, this conclusion is misleading. Much of the fall in the average real wage since 1973 reflects a change in the composition of the labor force. Holding fixed a person's education, experience, and gender, the average hourly real wage has increased about 20 percent since 1964. The wage had increased more than 20 percent before 1973 and has fallen slightly since then. Nearly all of this fall in the average real wage since 1973 has affected workers with less than five years' job experience, and most of it has affected less-educated workers. The average wage of educated, experienced workers has changed little over that period.

Another part of the fall in the average real wage since 1973 reflects an increase in the number of women in the labor force. The average wage of women has increased since 1973 (holding fixed education and experience), while the average wage of men has fallen. The overall average has fallen because women earn a lower average wage than men, so an increase in the number of women in the labor force places a greater weight on women's wages.[5]

--- **FOR REVIEW** ---

17.1 What affects a person's decision to be in the labor force?

17.2 What affects a firm's decision to hire 200 full-time workers or 300 part-time workers?

17.3 Explain the difference between real and nominal wages.

--- **QUESTIONS** ---

17.4 Why might a labor supply curve bend backward? What would make it slope upward?

17.5 Explain how a permanent improvement in technology is likely to affect real wages and employment. How would the effects differ if the improvement in technology were to raise productivity for only a few months?

---

[5]Suppose that the labor force includes two men each earning $10.00 per hour and one woman earning $7.00 per hour. The overall average wage is $9.00 per hour. Now suppose that a second woman enters the labor force and earns $7.00 per hour. The overall average wage falls to $8.50 per hour. The average would fall even if the average wage of women were to increase from $7.00 to $7.50 per hour.

FIGURE 17.4

REAL WAGES AND EARNINGS IN THE UNITED STATES

Weekly earnings rose less than wages because people started working fewer hours.

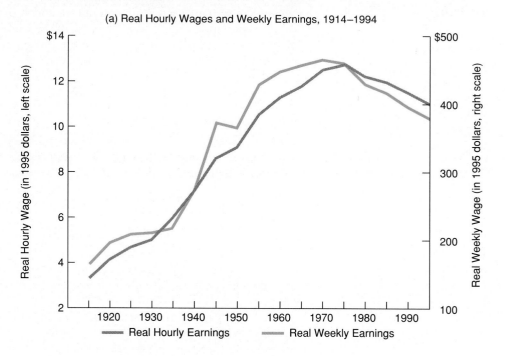

(a) Real Hourly Wages and Weekly Earnings, 1914–1994

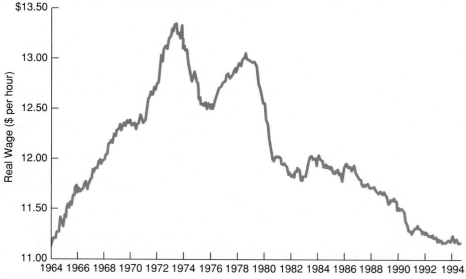

(b) Average U.S. Real Wage, 1964–1995 (Production and Nonsupervisory Workers)

FEATURES OF EQUILIBRIUM IN LABOR MARKETS

COMPENSATING DIFFERENTIALS

Why do different occupations, and even different jobs in the same occupation, pay different wages? One reason is to compensate people for differences in nonpay features of jobs. Compare a tedious job and a relatively fun job that require the same skills and experience. Since workers prefer the relatively fun job, the supply of labor for it is greater than the supply of labor for the tedious job. If the demand for labor is the same for each job, as in **Figure 17.5,** then in equilibrium the tedious job pays a higher wage. Firms must pay higher wages to persuade people to take more tedious jobs; they can hire workers for relatively fun jobs at lower wages. In equilibrium, no worker in either job is tempted to quit and try to obtain the other type of job. The wage in the tedious job is high enough to compensate for the tedium.

compensating differential — a difference in wages that offsets differences in nonpay features of jobs

> A **compensating differential** is a difference in wages that offsets differences in the nonpay features of two jobs.

Some occupations expose workers to more risk than others. Workers in a riskier job have a higher chance of injury or death. Riskier jobs pay compensating differentials if workers are aware of the risks. Studies have found compensating differentials ranging from $30 to $500 per year if the chance of being killed on the job in one year rises by 1 in 10,000. This means that a firm with 1,000 workers could save between $3,000 and $50,000 in wage costs every year by investing in safety equipment that would, on average, prevent one death every ten years. When workers are unaware of a job's risks (as people were unaware of risks from asbestos and lead), the risks do not affect labor supply and the wage for the job does not include a compensating differential.

FIGURE 17.5

COMPENSATING DIFFERENTIALS

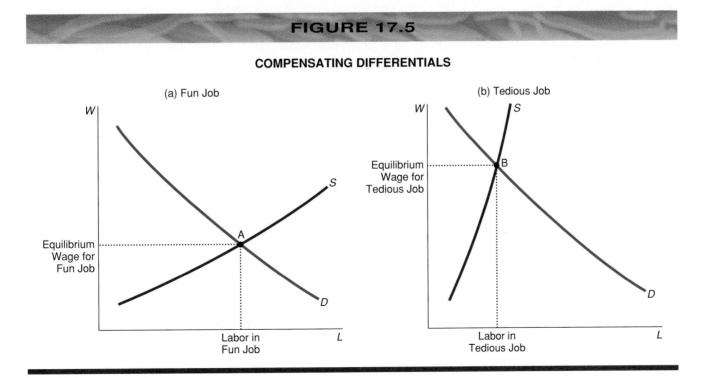

IN THE NEWS

Jersey cows face uncertain future

ST. JOHN, JERSEY—The realities of modern farming are intruding upon the cozy world of the Channel Islands where men and women lovingly raise real Jersey and Guernsey cows.

Every evening at about 7, Philip Romeril goes out to the field behind his 18th-century farmhouse to check on his 60 Jerseys.

Their golden brown hides glow in the soft, receding summer light. Their tails swish and their round, brown eyes blink. They have names like Carol and Marie, and they ooze contentment.

Romeril scratches the tops of a few heads, tugs at a floppy ear here and there, runs his hand over a pregnant cow's bulge.

And then he has a chat with them.

"People think I'm crazy because I talk to my cows,"

Romeril said. "But it's important. A cow that runs away from you is not a happy cow."

Explained Anne Perchard, another Jersey dairy farmer, who serves as chairman of the World Jersey Cattle Bureau, "There has to be a tremendous feeling towards the cow itself, otherwise there are easier ways of making a living."

Compensating differentials: The nonpay benefits of certain jobs lead people to take them despite low pay.

Source: "Jersey Cows Face Uncertain Future," *Rochester Democrat and Chronicle,* September 25, 1989.

HUMAN CAPITAL

Wages differ across occupations mainly because some occupations require higher levels of skill and training, that is, human capital, than others.

human capital — the skills, knowledge, and abilities of people

Human capital means the skills, knowledge, and abilities of people.

Human capital can be created by education and experience. The value of a person's human capital is the discounted present value of the wages that the person can receive with it. As Chapter 10 explained, the discounted present value of W_1 dollars paid one year from now and W_2 dollars paid two years from now and W_3 dollars paid three years from now, and so on, is

$$\frac{W_1}{(1 + i)} + \frac{W_2}{(1 + i)^2} + \frac{W_3}{(1 + i)^3} + \ldots$$

where i is the interest rate, measured so that $i = 0.06$ indicates an interest rate of 6 percent per year, and the sum goes on until some ending date (or forever).

EXAMPLE

Consider a 22-year-old worker with sufficient human capital to earn an annual salary that starts at \$25,000 per year, rises 8 percent per year until age 50, and then stays the same until retirement at age 65. If the interest rate is 5 percent per year, the value of this person's human capital is

$$\$25,000 + \$\frac{(25,000)(1.08)}{1.05} + \$\frac{(25,000)(1.08)^2}{1.05^2} + \ldots + \$\frac{(25,000)(1.08)^{28}}{1.05^{28}}$$

$$+ \$\frac{(25,000)(1.08)^{28}}{1.05^{29}} + \ldots + \$\frac{(25,000)(1.08)^{28}}{1.05^{43}}$$

$$= \$1,944,730$$

INVESTMENTS IN HUMAN CAPITAL

People invest in human capital through education, on-the-job training, and experience. Human capital in the United States is worth about $25 trillion to $30 trillion, or about half of total U.S. wealth (which is about $50 trillion to $60 trillion).[6] This is about $120,000 of human capital for each person (including children) in the United States, or about one-quarter of a million dollars of human capital per worker in the U.S. labor force.

WAGES AND HUMAN CAPITAL

The graphs in the Chapter 2 Appendix showed that people with more education earn higher wages throughout their lives. On average, they are more productive, so the demand for their labor is higher and their equilibrium wages are higher.

Employers must pay higher wages for jobs that require more education to compensate people for the costs of this additional education. Otherwise, people would not acquire that additional education. If these jobs were to overcompensate people for the education costs, more people would acquire the education, and the supply of labor to these jobs would rise. Wages at these jobs would fall until workers were just compensated for the additional education costs. In equilibrium, the difference in the discounted present values of wages in two jobs equals the discounted present value of the difference in the required education costs.

The two main costs of investing in human capital through education are direct expenditures for school, such as tuition and supplies, and the opportunity cost of time in school, such as the income a person could earn by working instead. People in the United States spend about 10 percent of GDP (the nation's total output of goods and services) on education, including the opportunity costs of high school and college students (the wages they sacrifice by staying in school instead of working). The rate of return on investment on human capital in the United States, which is roughly the interest rate a worker receives on an investment in education, averages about 5 to 15 percent per year, adjusted for inflation. It has risen over time.[7]

A worker's wages usually rise with age, partly due to gains in experience which increase the person's human capital and productivity, thereby raising the demand for her labor. Wages in most occupations rise until some time between ages 40 and 55, then remain the same or fall slightly as the worker gets older. Wages stop rising around ages 40 to 55 because the value of additional experience becomes small, so a worker's productivity stops rising. In addition, a worker may actually lose human capital through depreciation as skills start becoming old and obsolete; the worker's human capital may not keep up with changes in technology.

Younger workers have higher marginal benefits of investing in human capital than older workers with fewer working years ahead of them. A person also expects a higher marginal benefit of investing in human capital if he plans to stay in the labor force for a long time. In the past, women worked in the market fewer years on average than men, so on average women invested less in human capital

---

[6]A trillion is 10^{12}, or 1,000 billion.

[7]The estimated rate of return is imprecise because people differ. People who are particularly good at academic work tend to stay in school longer than other people. Their rate of return from education may be higher than the rate of return that others get. The rate of return on human capital is higher than the figures quoted above before the adjustment for inflation.

than men. (More precisely, they invested less in the kinds of human capital that are useful for market work.) These facts have been changing in recent years.

GENERAL AND SPECIFIC HUMAN CAPITAL

Some kinds of human capital, such as the ability to read, write, understand interest rates, and use computers, are useful at many jobs. *General human capital* includes knowledge and skills that workers will find useful regardless of where they work in the future. When on-the-job training gives workers general human capital, workers pay many of the costs of this training by accepting lower wages while they are being trained. Workers are willing to take lower wages in return for this kind of training because it will help them earn higher wages in the future regardless of where they work. Workers can view this training as part of their overall pay.

Other kinds of human capital are useful mainly in one industry, one occupation, or at one firm. This *specific human capital* is useful only at a particular firm or in a particular industry. Workers are less willing to pay for training that will not benefit them if they leave the firm, so the firm cannot use the prospect of training to lure workers at lower wages. When on-the-job training gives workers human capital that is specific to a firm (useful only at that firm), the firm must pay most of the costs of training.

After a firm has provided a worker with firm-specific training, the firm has a strong incentive to keep the worker—to persuade her not to quit and not to fire her—so that it does not have to repeat the training with another worker. Consequently, workers benefit from firm-specific training, and firm-specific human capital induces firms to promote from within. Promoting from within is easier and more common in large firms than small firms, which can choose from fewer employees. Large firms are usually more willing to invest in specific training for their workers because these workers are more likely to stay with those firms. The specific training also makes the workers more productive, raising their wages. As a result, quit rates at large firms are less than half of those at small firms, and larger firms pay higher wages than smaller firms. Manufacturing firms with more than 500 workers pay about 10 percent more than firms with fewer than 100 workers.

Workers with more seniority (those who have been with the firm longer) often receive higher wages than workers with less seniority. To help keep workers with firm-specific human capital from quitting, firms can pay them less than the values of their marginal products when they are young, and compensate by paying them more than the values of their marginal products when they are older (partly through pension plans), so that the discounted present value of wage payments remains unaffected. This is one reason why wages rise with age and seniority. This also gives workers an incentive to stay with the firm, so workers are likely to be more productive and less likely to misbehave or take actions that could jeopardize their jobs.

LIFE-CYCLE EARNINGS

A lawyer may bill clients and receive payment months after providing services. Each month, the lawyer's earnings differ from the value of her marginal product, but they average out over time. Similarly, any worker's annual wage may differ from the value of that worker's marginal product that year. The important thing—for both the firm and the worker—is that the differences average out, so that the discounted present value of wages equals the discounted present value of the worker's marginal product.

SIGNALING

Some firms hire workers only with a certain level of education even for jobs that are unrelated to anything that the workers studied in school. Firms sometimes use education as a signal that the person will be a good employee. Someone with the motivation and ability to acquire an education or do well in school, they reason, is likely to be a good employee. Firms also use other signals such as how a person dresses and speaks, whether a resume is neat and well-written, conduct during an interview, and so on. Age and marital status may also be signals.

Education has limited use as a signal because it is expensive. If a person can convince a firm in some other way that he will be a good employee, he can save the costs of education beyond that required to obtain the necessary human capital. For example, a person might work for the firm on a trial basis.

FOR REVIEW

17.6 How and why does human capital affect wages?

17.7 What happens to a typical worker's wage over that worker's lifetime? Why?

QUESTIONS

17.8 Make some guesses about your future wages and use a calculator or computer to calculate the value of your human capital. (Choose an interest rate for your calculation from a newspaper or the television news. How does your choice of an interest rate affect your answer?)

17.9 What factors are likely to affect the investments in human capital that people choose?

17.10 Who pays for most investments in general human capital? Why? Who pays for most investments in human capital that is specific to a firm? Why?

NONWAGE LABOR COSTS

Firms pay more than wages for workers. Total worker compensation averaged about $16.14 per hour in U.S. industry in 1992. Wages accounted for only $11.58 of this amount. The remaining $4.55 was nonwage compensation including $1.12 per hour for insurance, $0.54 for paid vacations, $0.37 for paid holidays, $0.14 for paid sick days and other paid leave, $0.39 for extra pay, $0.46 for pensions and other savings plans for employees, $0.96 for Social Security payments, $0.36 for workers' compensation insurance to cover job-related injuries, and $0.13 for unemployment benefits.[8]

Firms' nonwage labor costs also include the costs of hiring and training workers. Hiring costs include advertising job openings, testing and evaluating job applicants, and filling out government-required forms to comply with tax laws and other regulations. Hiring and training costs in the U.S. economy typically total more than $1,000 (and sometimes several thousand dollars) per employee. Because hiring and training costs depend on the number of workers a firm

---

IN THE NEWS

Rising costs of benefits may hold down wages

Firms' job expenses go far beyond take-home pay

▲

The reluctance to begin rehiring

'The guy who earns $1,000 really costs $1,400.'

Changes in nonwage labor costs affect equilibrium wages.

Sources: "Rising Costs of Benefits May Hold Down Wages," *Washington Post,* July 14, 1991, p. H3; and "The Reluctance to Begin Rehiring," *New York Times,* March 10, 1993.

[8]Firms sometimes reduce nonwage labor costs by outsourcing work, that is, by hiring people who are not permanent employees of the firm to do certain jobs.

employs rather than the number of hours worked, it is usually more expensive to employ ten part-time workers than five full-time workers.

TYPES OF PAY

Most workers collect hourly wages or weekly or monthly salaries; they are paid based on the time they spend at work. About 15 percent of U.S. workers collect piece-rate pay based on how much they produce. Some workers receive commissions (shares of total sales) or shares of a firm's accounting profit in a profit-sharing program.

PIECE RATES

Piece-rate pay gives workers an incentive to work quickly and not to shirk, but it can also give them an incentive to sacrifice quality for larger quantities. As a result, piece-rate pay is common mainly in industries in which quality is unimportant or easy to judge (so the firm can easily enforce a minimum quality standard).

TIME RATES

Hourly wages give workers less incentive than piece-rate pay to work hard, but they avoid creating an incentive to sacrifice quality for quantity. Time-rate pay is more common in industries in which it is easy to judge quantity, but hard to determine quality. A second reason for time-rate pay is that piece-rate pay can be risky for workers. A worker's productivity may depend partly on circumstances beyond that single worker's control, such as changes in weather or equipment problems. These random factors do not affect the incomes of workers who receive time-rate pay, but they create risks for workers who receive piece-rate pay. Most workers prefer the more predictable incomes they receive with time-rate pay. Firms have an incentive to provide pay in a form that workers like because if they provide pay in some other way, they may have to pay more on average to attract good workers.

When the quality of work is observable and luck plays only a small role, time-rate pay (such as monthly salaries) can create nearly the same incentives as piece-rate pay. For example, consider the salaries of professional baseball players. Although they receive annual salaries, one study found that those salaries closely approximate piece-rate pay (with a one-year delay) in which a player receives $9,000 for each additional home run, $6,000 for each run scored or run batted in, and, for pitchers, $3,000 per inning pitched, $38,000 for each victory, and $16,000 per save.

PROFIT SHARING

Some workers, particularly top executives, receive at least part of their pay through profit sharing plans in which they collect part of the firm's accounting profit. Their pay falls automatically when the demand for a firm's product falls, causing its profits to fall, and rises automatically in the opposite situation. The automatic fall in pay when profits are low gives the firm less incentive to lay off workers when demand is low. For this reason, some analysts believe that more firms should use profit sharing and pay less time-rate pay.[9] Although profit sharing reduces the risk of being laid off, it can be riskier for workers than time-rate pay because it makes a worker's pay unpredictable and allows it to vary substantially from one year to the next.

---

[9]See Martin Weitzman, *The Share Economy* (Cambridge, Mass.: Harvard University Press, 1984). Professor Weitzman is an economist at the Massachusetts Institute of Technology.

Profit sharing gives workers an incentive to maximize the firm's profit. Workers also have an incentive to watch each other to make sure that everyone contributes to that profit because everyone's pay depends on it. This incentive is strongest if a group of workers can have a large effect on the firm's profit, and weaker if their actions have little effect on profit.

Profit sharing is not common in the United States, though it may be growing. Few U.S. firms have profit-sharing programs for all employees, though many have them for top executives. In contrast, most workers in Japan receive bonuses based on their firms' profits; these bonuses comprise about one-fourth of Japanese workers' total pay.

TOURNAMENTS

When the demand for taxi rides or computers rises, the quantity supplied can rise only if more people become taxi drivers or computer makers. However, when the demand to watch the evening news or read a spy novel rises, the quantity supplied can rise without any increase in the number of newscasters or spy novelists. Instead, more people can watch the same news show or read the same spy novel. If Connie is a slightly better newscaster than Berta, a television network will prefer to hire Connie as a newscaster and pay her the value of her marginal product. Even though Berta is almost as good as Connie, Berta will not get the newscaster job and may have to settle for another type of job with a much lower wage. In equilibrium, a person who is 10 percent (or even 1 percent) better at a job than the next best person may earn a much higher wage. Differences among the abilities of the best actors, musicians, and sports performers may be small; the best performers may be only slightly better than the next best performers, but in equilibrium, the best performers may be superstars earning enormous salaries, while the next best performers, the "almost-contenders," may be relegated to driving taxis or flipping burgers. These are examples of job tournaments in which the person who gets a job earns a much higher wage for only slightly higher productivity.

The same reasoning applies to executive positions at business firms. The person who gets a top executive job may receive triple the salary of people who did not get the job, despite being much less than three times as productive as the other candidates would have been. Firms use tournaments to motivate workers—the *chance* of winning the good job motivates workers to perform well at their current jobs. Of course, a worker who does not get the good job and feels overlooked or unappreciated may then perform poorly. Firms often use early retirement bonuses to get rid of these "deadwood" workers. In the past, many firms also had mandatory retirement rules that required people to retire at a certain age. More recently, however, the federal government has outlawed these rules.

EXECUTIVE COMPENSATION

Executives of large corporations receive high levels of pay. The average (median) compensation of chief executive officers (CEOs) of the 100 largest U.S. corporations exceeds $1 million per year. This is about three times higher than the average salary of top executives in Japan, although perks—nonmoney wage payments such as access to company yachts, country estates, home entertainment, and longer vacations—are much larger in Japan. The average pay for all CEOs in the United States is about $200,000 to $250,000. Average CEO salaries in Germany, France, and the United Kingdom are smaller (about $100,000 to $150,000), but

Perks

Perks often include health insurance and health care, paid vacations, paid sick leave, discounts from a company store, and child care. Top executives sometimes get perks such as chauffeur service; company cars or airplanes; free memberships in country clubs, health clubs, and other clubs; and home security systems. A small scandal developed in 1993 when a U.S. automobile manufacturer hired a new chief executive officer who had relied on the perk of a free car for so long that he couldn't remember the last time he had bought or even owned a car.

firms in those countries also provide CEOs with more perks. Economists disagree about whether executive pay results from tournaments and allocates resources efficiently or whether corporate laws and regulations create an economically inefficient situation that keeps executive pay artificially high.[10]

LABOR TURNOVER

Even in equilibrium, the labor market constantly changes. Every year some people finish school and look for jobs while other people retire. Still others enter or leave the labor force, quit their jobs to take or look for other jobs, or get fired or laid off.

labor turnover — the continuing flows of people into and out of the labor force, employment and unemployment, and various jobs

> **Labor turnover** refers to the continuing flows of people into and out of the labor force, employment and unemployment, and various jobs.

Figure 17.6 shows an overall picture of U.S. labor turnover. The quit rate in manufacturing is 1 to 2 percent per month, or 12 to 24 percent per year. Every month, about 3 percent of workers in manufacturing industries have just been hired less than 1 month earlier. The median that a U.S. worker spends 3.6 years in one job (this means that half of all workers have spent less than 3.6 years in their current jobs and half have spent more than 3.6 years).[11] While three-fifths of all jobs last less than one year, nearly half of all adult workers eventually find a job at which they work for more than 20 years.

People change occupations as well as jobs. Each year nearly one-tenth of U.S. workers change their occupations, moving among categories such as salesperson, lawyer, teacher, or physician. Younger workers are more likely to change occupations than older workers.

The amount of labor turnover in equilibrium depends on:

▶ Labor mobility, determined by factors such as how easily people can move to a new city to find a new job, family preferences, and the number of two-career households

▶ How much information workers have about other job opportunities

▶ How much information firms have about workers before hiring them, and how much information people have about firms before taking jobs. (More information creates better matches and less turnover.)

---

[10]A related disagreement among economists concerns the extent to which executives' pay provides them with the proper incentives. Executives often receive various types of pay based on their firms' performance levels (profits, stock-market values, sales, and so on) that are designed partly to affect their incentives.

[11]The mean is about 4 years.

FIGURE 17.6

YEARLY LABOR TURNOVER IN THE UNITED STATES (MILLIONS OF PEOPLE)

Source: Employment and Earnings, U.S. Department of Commerce Bureau of Labor Statistics, January 1995, p. 26, Table A-11.

▶ The extent of underlying economic change. (How much do changes in technology, tastes, demographics, government policies, and other factors affect demands and supplies for goods, so that some firms expand and other firms go out of business? More volatile economic conditions increase labor turnover.)

UNEMPLOYMENT

unemployed person — someone who wants a job, but does not have one

underemployed person — someone who does not have a job that makes full use of his or her training and skills, but wants one

A person is **unemployed** if that person does not have a job, but wants one.

A person is **underemployed** if that person does not have a job that makes use of his or her training and skills, but wants one.

These definitions are somewhat vague because of the phrase *wants one.* The federal government measures unemployment in the United States through a monthly survey called the *Current Population Survey,* conducted by the Bureau of Labor Statistics (BLS), an agency in the U.S. Department of Labor.[12] The BLS randomly chooses about 58,000 households to survey; it counts people as unemployed if they:

1. Are not working, but have actively looked for work in the last month, or
2. Were laid off from their previous jobs and are waiting to be recalled by the same firms, or
3. Are waiting to start new jobs within the next month

The measurement of the unemployment rate is imperfect for at least three reasons. First, it does not count people as unemployed who have become so

---

[12]Nations differ in how they measure unemployment; Japan and Canada also use surveys, while most European countries measure it by the number of people collecting unemployment compensation.

SOCIAL AND ECONOMIC ISSUES

Mommy Track

An article in the *Harvard Business Review* argued that firms should offer two types of career opportunities, one for "career-primary" women and men who would plan to devote most of their time to their careers and another for "career/family" women and men who wanted to play larger roles in raising their children and who would be willing to sacrifice some career growth and salary for the freedom and flexibility to do so. Pundits soon dubbed the career/family track the *mommy track,* although *daddy track* would do as well in principle.

The proposal advocated allowing workers to choose career options. Workers themselves, not their employers, would make these decisions. Workers in the so-called *mommy track* would (on average) get less pay and fewer promotions, and they would accumulate less human capital, but they would also work fewer hours and gain flexibility in hours and employment choices, perhaps choosing to stop working or work part-time for several years to raise children.

Proponents argued that this would give workers more control over their own lifestyles. Opponents argued that firms would use the idea as an excuse to discriminate against women and not permit true choice. Some also argued that the mommy track would reinforce undesirable social customs where women rather than men bear most of the responsibility for raising children. (Recall from the chapter on game theory that people can sometimes gain from committing themselves and limiting their own options. If no mommy track is available, women can commit to choose either the regular career track or no career at all. Faced with this choice for their wives, men might choose to take a greater role in raising children.) Other people argued that the mommy-track idea did not go far enough, that firms should permit greater flexibility in career paths for all workers, with each worker choosing his or her own commitment to career versus other aspects of life.

Questions

1. How much of a personal or family life must people sacrifice to advance to the top of a business? Do you think the sacrifice is worth it?

2. Would women work more or less it firms were to offer a mommy track? How would the mommy track affect the wages of men and women in the career-primary track?

3. What kinds of jobs are best-suited for a mommy or daddy track? What kinds are least well-suited?

4. Should firms offer a mommy track? Defend your position, then argue against it.

5. Why don't firms permit more choice and flexibility in careers now? Does flexibility have a cost?

Source: See Felice Schwartz, "Management Women and the New Facts of Life," *Harvard Business Review,* January–February 1989. Schwartz is president of Catalyst, an advisory group on women's leadership.

---

discouraged that they have stopped looking for jobs. Instead, the survey classifies these people as not in the labor force, rather than as unemployed. Second, it counts underemployed workers (mathematicians driving cabs, and so on) as employed. Also, it counts people who work part-time as employed, though they may want full-time jobs. Third, it counts people as unemployed if they say they looked for work within the previous month, even if they did not look seriously or were unwilling to accept a job at a realistic wage. Due to the first two problems, unemployment is higher than the BLS measures it; the third problem has the opposite effect. **Figure 17.7** shows the rate of unemployment in the United States since 1948. **Table 17.1** shows the composition of unemployment in a typical month.

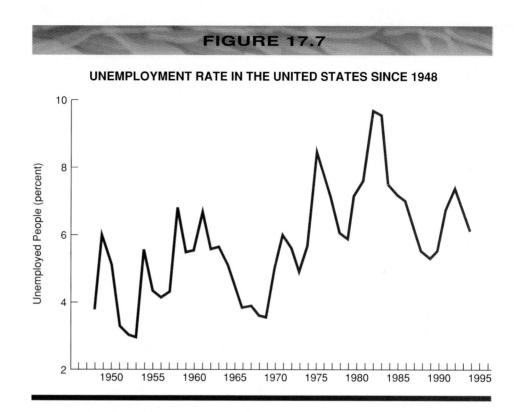

FIGURE 17.7

UNEMPLOYMENT RATE IN THE UNITED STATES SINCE 1948

Most newly unemployed people find jobs within 1 or 2 months. While most spells of unemployment end within 1 month, some drag on much longer. As a result, most unemployed people have been unemployed for several months or more. As a person remains unemployed longer, the likelihood that he will find a job declines, as does the wage at an eventual job. People lose their skills when

TABLE 17.1

UNEMPLOYMENT IN THE UNITED STATES—JANUARY 1995

Total labor force	130.4 million people
Civilian labor force[a]	124.6
Employed	117.1
Unemployed	7.5
Unemployed more than 15 weeks	2.3
Unemployment rate	6.3%
Men age 20 and over	5.0
Women age 20 and over	4.9
Teenagers (both sexes age 16 to 19)	16.7
Whites	4.8
Blacks	10.1
Hispanics	9.0

[a]Labor force except armed forces.
Source: Survey of Current Business.

FIGURE 17.8

UNEMPLOYMENT WITH THE WAGE ABOVE EQUILIBRIUM

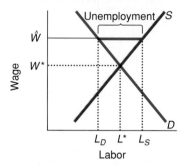

The equilibrium wage is W^* and the equilibrium quantity of labor is L^*. If the wage is $\hat{W}$, which is above the equilibrium wage, the quantity of labor demanded is only L_D, which is smaller than the equilibrium quantity. Therefore, only L_D hours of labor are actually employed (only that many people actually get jobs at the wage $\hat{W}$), while the quantity of labor supplied is L_S. Unemployment is L_S minus L_D.

unemployed, so they become less productive. Also, firms use unemployment as a signal that the person may not be a good worker.

WHY UNEMPLOYMENT?

Unemployment can occur if the wage is above the equilibrium wage, as in **Figure 17.8**. Ordinarily, the wage falls toward its equilibrium level in this situation, just as any price above its equilibrium level falls toward that level. The wage may exceed its equilibrium level, however, for any of several reasons:

1. It *takes time* for the wage to fall to its equilibrium level, creating temporary unemployment
2. Government regulations and minimum wage laws prevent the wage from falling
3. Unions prevent the wage from falling
4. Firms set wages above the equilibrium level for other reasons

Unions might prevent the wage from falling because union workers who currently have jobs at the higher wage do not want the wage to fall, and they have more influence on union decisions than currently unemployed people who would obtain jobs if the union allowed the wage to fall. Firms may set wages above the equilibrium level for reasons discussed in the later section on efficiency wages.

Labor turnover can create unemployment even if the wage is at its equilibrium level. Some workers who leave jobs through quits or layoffs are unemployed before finding other jobs, though most job changes do not involve unemployment. Some people are also unemployed after leaving school and before finding jobs. It takes time to find the right match between employers and employees, so firms commonly have job vacancies while unemployed people look for work. Even with the wage at the equilibrium level for every worker with a job, unemployment may occur because some people and firms have not yet found the right matches, as in **Figure 17.9.** Continual labor turnover as new people enter the labor force, some firms expand, and others go out of business may keep the economy in this situation indefinitely, with equilibrium unemployment.

FOR REVIEW

17.11 Name some advantages and disadvantages of:
  a. Piece-rate pay
  b. Time-rate (e.g., hourly or weekly) pay
  c. Profit sharing

17.12 What affects the degree of labor turnover?

17.13 How does the U.S. government measure the unemployment rate?

17.14 Discuss some reasons for unemployment.

QUESTIONS

17.15 How is an increase in hiring costs likely to affect wages, employment, and hours worked per week for an average worker?

17.16 Suppose that an increase in government regulations makes it more difficult for firms to fire workers. How is this likely to affect wages, employment, and hours worked per week for an average worker?

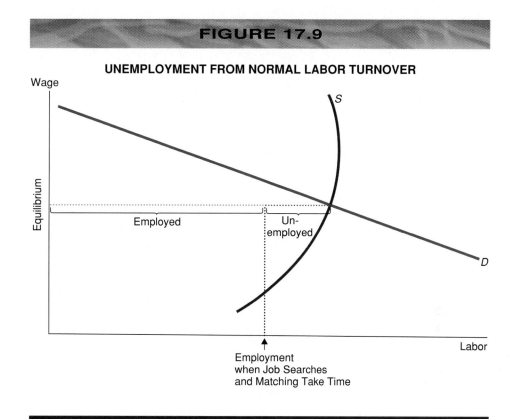

FIGURE 17.9

UNEMPLOYMENT FROM NORMAL LABOR TURNOVER

EFFECTS OF CHANGES IN LABOR SUPPLY AND DEMAND

POPULATION CHANGES

Increases in population through increases in birth rates, lower death rates, or immigration raise the supply of labor. Unless corresponding increases in technology or other inputs such as land and capital raise the marginal product of labor sufficiently, population increases reduce the equilibrium wage. (This reflects the law of diminishing returns, as discussed in Chapter 16.) When the black plague killed between 17 percent and 40 percent of the population of England and about one-third of the entire European population in 1347 through 1351, the resulting fall in labor supply raised wages by 30 percent to 100 percent. Recall that economists estimate the elasticity of labor demand in the United States at between 0.15 and 0.50; this suggests that each 1 percent increase in labor supply would reduce the equilibrium wage by between 2 percent and 7 percent. Of course, real-life population increases are not independent of investments in capital (including human capital) and advances in technology.

BABY BOOM

People born in the 1950s and early 1960s, when U.S. couples had many more babies than usual, are part of the so-called *baby-boom* generation. By 1980, for example, 44 percent more 22 year olds were looking for work than had been searching two decades earlier. This raised the supply of labor by young, inexperienced workers in the late 1970s, reducing their wages by about 12 percent to 15 percent.

The effects of the baby boom on wages continue to this day. By 2000, the baby boom generation will have about 20 to 25 years of work experience, which will raise the supply of workers with that level of experience and reduce their wages. Members of the baby-boom generation are likely to receive lower wages throughout their lives than they would have received if their generation had not been so large.

ADVANCES IN TECHNOLOGY

Improvements in technology raise the marginal products of labor in industries that use new technologies, often raising the demand for labor. This raises equilibrium wages and employment in those industries. The wage increase spreads to other industries because people leave those industries to seek employment in the higher-wage industries, which reduces the supply of labor in the other industries and raises wages throughout the economy.

CHANGES IN TASTES

If consumers decide to buy less of one good and more of another, the demand for the first falls and demand for the second increases. This reduces the price of the first good and raises the price of the second good, lowering the value of the marginal product of labor in the first industry and raising it in the second industry. This decreases the demand for labor in the first industry, reducing wages and employment in that industry, and increases the demand for labor in the second industry, raising wages and employment there. In this way, changes in demands for goods affect jobs and wages. This labor turnover may also create temporary unemployment as workers shift from the first industry to the second.

"He may be a highly paid anchorman but I have the power to zap him away."

Source: *The Wall Street Journal,* August 12, 1993.

REAL-LIFE COMPLICATIONS

OVERPAID AND UNDERPAID WORKERS

Workers can be called *overpaid* if their wages exceed the equilibrium wages for their jobs. These situations arise when an excess supply of labor leads to rationing of available jobs. New York City, for example, once paid its sanitation workers 60 percent more than the New York area average for similar jobs; the city employed about 11,000 sanitation workers, but at one point the waiting list for those jobs included 36,849 names. Similarly, workers are underpaid if firms face a shortage of workers for a job. The United States military draft (eliminated in 1973) required selected young men to work in the military for two years; the government drafted people because its military employees were underpaid. When the government eliminated the draft, it raised military wages to a level high enough to attract the employees that it wanted.

LABOR UNIONS

Labor unions are organizations of workers intended to represent their interests in bargaining with firms over wages and working conditions and to provide other services.

labor union — an organization of workers intended to improve the working conditions and pay of its members

> **Labor unions** are organizations of workers designed to improve the working conditions and pay of their members and to provide other services.

Labor unions are also social and political institutions that help to represent their members in the political arena and to provide social support of many kinds, from parties to college scholarship funds.

Industrial unions like the United Auto Workers usually cover workers with different occupations who work for the same firm or in the same industry. Craft unions (such as an electrician's union) typically cover workers in some occupation regardless of the industry in which they work. Most U.S. unions are members of the AFL–CIO, the American Federation of Labor–Congress of Industrial Organizations, which is roughly a union of unions. Some occupational organizations, such as the American Medical Association and the American Bar Association, share many features of unions but are not legally considered unions in the United States.

Unions play roles in several scenarios. People can work at a firm with an open shop without being union members. A closed shop, made illegal in the United States in 1947 by the Taft-Hartley Act, required every worker to be a union member. In a union shop, a firm can hire nonunion workers, but those workers must join the union after a short period of time. A right-to-work law is a state law that makes union shops illegal or requires open shops; about 20 states have these laws. *Collective bargaining* refers to negotiations between firms and unions about labor contracts. A strike occurs when a group of workers (usually a union) refuses to work until the firm meets certain conditions in collective bargaining. A lockout occurs when a firm refuses to allow employees to work until their union meets certain conditions in collective bargaining.

UNIONS AS MONOPOLY SELLERS OF LABOR

Unions can raise the wages of their members by acting as monopoly sellers of labor. Workers sell labor services, and unions are essentially legal cartels of workers that restrict the number of workers in an industry to raise wages.[13] **Figure 17.10** shows a labor market equilibrium when a union is a monopoly seller of labor to an industry. Without the union, the marginal cost of working curve would define the supply of labor. The equilibrium wage with no union would be W^N and equilibrium employment would be L^N. Members of a union can gain by restricting the quantity of labor supplied just as any monopoly restricts its quantity. Figure 17.10 shows the marginal revenue curve, *MR,* associated with the industry demand for labor, *D.* The union maximizes its profit (total wage payments minus the opportunity cost of working) by raising the wage to W^U, which it can do by restricting employment or hours per worker to L^U.

The reasoning is the same as for any monopoly or cartel. The union can divide the gains among its member workers. As in any monopoly situation, the gain to the (monopoly) union is smaller than the loss to buyers (employers), so the union's actions cause a deadweight social loss, indicated by the shaded area in Figure 17.10.

Evidence suggests that some unions do even better than this. When a union and firms in an industry sit down to negotiate, they have an incentive to reduce the deadweight social loss and share the gain in some way. This can allow unions to obtain higher benefits for their members than Figure 17.10 shows while firms lose less than the figure indicates. Unions also attempt to raise the demand for labor through their support of government policies that restrict competing imports from other countries or that promote industry sales in other ways.

Economists estimate that unions raise wages about 10 percent to 20 percent, on average. They estimate the deadweight social loss from union monopoly power

---

[13]Chapter 13 discusses cartels.

FIGURE 17.10

UNIONS AS MONOPOLY SELLERS OF LABOR

The marginal cost of working curve would be the supply curve of labor with no union, and Point A would be the equilibrium point. With a union, equilibrium occurs at Point B.

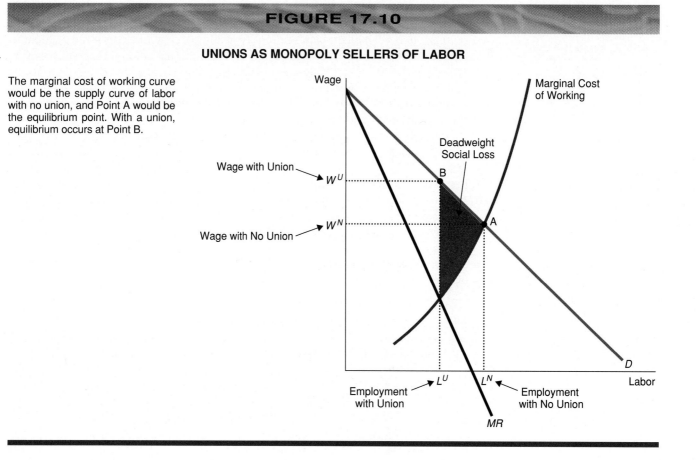

and from strikes to be about 0.8 percent to 1 percent of the economy's total output (GNP) each year.[14]

About one-fifth of all nonfarm workers are union members in the United States today. This rate is lower than the rate earlier in the 20th century and the rates in most European countries.[15]

---

[14]Some evidence indicates that unions also raise productivity by improving worker–firm relations and reducing quit rates. Lower quit rates induce firms to invest in more specific human capital (as discussed above). Unions may also raise productivity by raising morale and worker motivation.

[15]Union membership in the United States may have declined because fewer people now work in industries that have traditionally been unionized, such as manufacturing, construction, and transportation. Employment in those industries has fallen from one-half of the labor force in the mid-20th century to one-third of the labor force today. More people now work in service industries, which tend not to be unionized because the elasticity of demand for their products is high, so unions cannot raise wages much without large decreases in employment. With smaller gains from unionization, workers in these industries have not tended to form unions. However, union membership in Canada increased over the same recent decades as membership has declined in the United States despite the fact that the Canadian economy experienced many of the same kinds of changes as did the U.S. economy over that period. This suggests that some or much of the decline in union membership in the United States may be the result of U.S. government policies or greater employer opposition to unions in the United States.

EXPLICIT AND IMPLICIT CONTRACTS

In unionized industries, firms and workers usually agree to detailed, formal labor contracts. The contracts usually set wages, procedures for deciding details of issues such as layoffs and filling job vacancies, and other issues. Many employees without these formal, explicit contracts have implicit labor contracts with their firms.

implicit labor contract — an informal agreement or understanding about the terms of employment

> An **implicit labor contract** is an informal agreement or understanding about the terms of employment.

While courts cannot enforce implicit labor contracts because the terms are not explicitly written down and signed, competition among firms to maintain good reputations helps to enforce the informal agreements. A firm would risk losing its good reputation if it were to renege on an implicit contract. Firms value good reputations because they can help firms to hire better workers without paying higher wages because workers prefer to work for firms that have histories of treating employees fairly and living up to their implicit agreements.

EFFICIENCY WAGES

An earlier section noted that after a firm has provided firm-specific training to a worker, it has a strong incentive to keep that worker employed. Recall also that unemployment may result from firms keeping wages above the equilibrium level. These observations are related: sometimes a firm has an incentive to pay workers more than the value of their marginal product to keep them from quitting.

A firm can also increase employees' incentives to do high-quality work by paying a higher wage than the employees could get at similar jobs elsewhere. This gives employees more to lose from being fired. A worker with a particularly good job has a stronger incentive to keep it than a worker who could easily get a similar job at another firm. A worker with a stronger incentive to keep a job is likely to do higher-quality work and be more productive. By paying unusually high wages, firms can give employees incentives not to shirk to help keep their jobs. In this way, higher wages can substitute for more active supervision of workers, reducing a firm's supervision costs. Finally, some people argue that a high wage raises productivity by raising morale and providing a sense of fair treatment.[16]

When Henry Ford started the Ford Motor Company, he had very high quit rates among his employees. (Also, he frequently fired workers.) The company's employee turnover rate was 370 percent in 1913; Ford had to hire 370 people each year just to keep 100 jobs filled. On an average day, more than 10 percent of workers failed to show up at work. Despite worker unhappiness, Ford could choose among long lines of people who wanted to work there, so it could easily hire new workers. Nevertheless, Ford decided in January 1914 to double its wage from $2.50 to $5.00 per hour (in today's dollars). The $2.50 wage was an equilibrium wage. (If it had been below equilibrium, Ford would not have been able to hire new employees so easily.) As a result of the new wage above the equilibrium level, the quit rate fell 87 percent and absenteeism fell 75 percent. Workers performed better, and firings fell 90 percent.[17]

---

[16]Studies show that in very poor countries, increasing the wage can make workers more productive because workers can then afford to eat more food, which gives them more energy.

[17]On the other hand, a 1947 U.S. government study noted that higher wages gave some workers an incentive to raise their absenteeism. One worker said he had had several "very good weeks" of work, and that he and his "old lady" would take a "little trip for most of the next week."

efficiency wage — a wage above equilibrium intended to raise worker productivity

When firms pay wages above equilibrium to try to raise worker productivity, economists say they pay **efficiency wages.**

Efficiency wages can cause unemployment. To see why, ask yourself what happens if all firms try to pay unusually high wages, wages above the levels at other firms. Of course, this cannot happen. As all firms try to pay more than other firms, however, wages rise above the equilibrium level, which causes unemployment, as in Figure 17.8. The incentive effects of the higher wages still operate, but in a different way—now a worker who shirks responsibility and loses a job risks unemployment.

─────────────────── **For Review** ───────────────────

17.17 How can unions affect wages?

17.18 Why might firms pay efficiency wages? What are the likely results?

─────────────────── **Questions** ───────────────────

17.19 Explain how an improvement in technology might hurt unskilled workers.

17.20 If workers in half of the industries in the economy formed new unions to increase their wages, how would this affect wages and employment in other, nonunionized industries?

Conclusions

Labor Supply and Demand
People decide whether to be in the labor force (to look for work in the market), what occupation to choose, which job offer to take, whether to operate their own businesses, and how many hours to work. Labor supply curves may slope upward (if the substitution effect of a wage increase outweighs the income effect) or bend backward (if the income effect of a wage increase outweighs the substitution effect). The demand for labor reflects the value of its marginal product. A firm's demand for labor rises when the marginal (physical) product of labor rises or the relative price of the firm's good rises. The marginal product of labor may rise if workers acquire additional education or training, gain experience, work with more capital or a better technology, or have their activities better coordinated with activities of other workers.

Labor Market Equilibrium
Labor market equilibrium consists of an equilibrium real wage and an equilibrium number of hours worked for each type of labor. Other factors, such as hiring and training costs, laws and regulations, fixed costs of working, and workers' preferences, determine how a firm chooses its number of employees and hours per employee to achieve its equilibrium total hours worked. The real wage is the wage measured in purchasing power, that is, the nominal (money) wage adjusted for inflation.

Features of Equilibrium in Labor Markets
Wages differ across occupations partly because nonpay aspects of occupations or jobs differ. Compensating differentials are differences in wages that offset these

differences in nonpay features of jobs. Wages also differ because some occupations or jobs require higher levels of human capital (education, skills, knowledge, experience, and ability) than others. People invest in human capital through education, on-the-job training, and experience. When a wage difference compensates people for a difference in education required by two jobs, the equilibrium difference in the discounted present value of wages equals the discounted present value of the difference in education costs. Wages usually rise with age and experience up to a certain point as a worker's human capital increases, then wages begin to fall slightly as human capital depreciates.

Workers are willing to accept lower wages in jobs that provide them with general human capital, which they can use at other jobs. However, a firm must pay most of the costs of training that gives workers human capital that is specific to the firm and has little value elsewhere.

Firms may pay workers based on the time they work (a time rate), the quantity they produce (a piece rate), or the firm's profits (profit sharing). Each type of pay creates different incentives. Firms also have nonwage costs of employment such as insurance, pension plans, and taxes based on employment.

Job tournaments occur when the person who gets a job receives a much higher wage than rivals get even though one worker's productivity is only slightly higher than others'. Firms use tournaments to motivate workers. Tournaments may help to explain high levels of executive compensation.

Labor turnover occurs constantly as people finish school and look for jobs, retire, enter or leave the labor force, quit their jobs to take or look for other jobs, or get fired or laid off. The amount of labor turnover in equilibrium depends on factors such as the degree of labor mobility, the amount of information that workers and firms have about their opportunities, and the extent of underlying changes in the economy. Constant labor turnover is one reason for unemployment. A person is unemployed if she wants a job but does not have one; someone is underemployed if she wants a job that makes use of her training and skills but does not have one. The U.S. government measures unemployment through a monthly survey. While labor turnover is one reason for unemployment, unemployment also occurs if wages are kept above their equilibrium levels.

REAL-LIFE COMPLICATIONS

Labor unions can raise the wages of their members by acting as monopoly sellers of labor that restrict the number of workers in an industry. Members gain even more if their union does not choose the standard monopoly/cartel solution, but bargains with industry representatives to reduce the deadweight social loss and divide it between the firms and the union. Implicit labor contracts are informal agreements between firms and employees about the terms of employment. While courts cannot enforce implicit labor contracts, firms have some incentive to honor them to maintain valuable reputations. Firms may pay wages above equilibrium (efficiency wages) to retain workers with firm-specific training, provide workers with incentives to work effectively and not to shirk, or to raise worker productivity.

LOOKING AHEAD

Labor income comprises most of the incomes of most people. Chapter 18 discusses the extents of wealth and poverty—the distributions of income and wealth—in the United States and the world. It also discusses related issues such as discrimination, government programs to fight poverty, and alternative views of fairness and justice. Chapters 19 through 22 discuss advanced topics in microeconomics such as the economics of information, pollution, the economics of government regulation, and the incentive effects of laws.

KEY TERMS

labor force

backward-bending labor supply curve

nominal (money) wage

real wage

compensating differential

human capital

labor turnover

unemployed person

underemployed person

labor union

implicit labor contract

efficiency wage

QUESTIONS AND PROBLEMS

17.21 If wages differ because of compensating differentials, why do business executives earn more money and have nicer working conditions than garbage collectors?

17.22 Why do rock stars get such high pay? Is this an equilibrium wage for them? Explain.

17.23 Explain why a worker may be willing to sacrifice a higher wage this year in return for a higher discounted present value of future wages.

17.24 What are some deficiencies of the official measure of unemployment?

17.25 How large is total wealth in the United States?
   a. How much of this is human capital?
   b. Roughly how large is the rate of return on human capital?

17.26 Comment on this statement: "Workers with more seniority receive higher wages because they are more likely to have families and need more income." Why do firms pay more to workers with more seniority?

17.27 A college dean said in a speech that colleges will see fewer students in the coming decade because there will be fewer people of college age. He said that colleges will lower tuitions to compete with each other for students, and that this creates a problem because professors' salaries have been rising. How would you expect a fall in the demand for college admission to affect professors' salaries?

17.28 How would wages, employment, and average weekly hours per worker be affected by:
   a. A change in tastes so that people want to work more
   b. An earthquake that destroys much of a city
   c. A law that requires firms to buy health insurance for workers
   d. Worsening traffic problems that raise the time it takes a person to get to work

17.29 Suppose that people irrationally believe that a job is safer or more dangerous than it really is. Does this irrational belief affect wages? Explain.

INQUIRIES FOR FURTHER THOUGHT

17.30 Why do people buy and sell labor services? Why don't all workers work for themselves as many doctors, lawyers, accountants, plumbers, artisans, and farmers do, rather than working as employees of business firms?

17.31 Why are people unemployed? If someone wants a job and cannot find one, why doesn't this person say to a firm, "Look, calculate the value of what I can produce for your firm, and then pay me less than that. Then you will profit from hiring me and we'll both be better off"? Alternatively, why doesn't this person start an independent business?

17.32 Is unemployment involuntary or voluntary?

17.33 What should the government do about unemployment, if anything?
   a. Do you think that the government should be involved in job training? What incentives do workers and firms have to provide this training?
   b. Should the government subsidize moves by people in areas with high unemployment to areas with more job opportunities? What would be the results of such a subsidy?
   c. Should the government require job sharing to try to reduce unemployment?
   d. Should the government subsidize companies to employ more workers? Would this reduce unemployment?

17.34 How would increased immigration affect U.S. employment and wages?
   a. Should the United States permit more immigration or unlimited immigration so that anyone who wants to immigrate can do so?
   b. Should immigrants be eligible for welfare? Should they be eligible to vote?
   c. Should the United States sell immigration rights to the highest bidders?
   d. Should a country give priority in immigration to political refugees (those who are subject to punishment in their home countries for their political views)? What about people who want to immigrate to the United States to avoid poverty in their home countries?

17.35 In *The Wealth of Nations,* Adam Smith wrote, "We trust our health to the physician; our fortune and sometimes our life and reputation to the lawyer and attorney. Such confidence could not safely be reposed in people of a very mean or low condition. Their reward must be such, therefore, as may give them that rank in society which so important a trust requires."[18] Do you agree? What does this argument have to do with efficiency wages?

17.36 Do top executives deserve the pay they get? How about sports figures, musicians, and actors?

17.37 How are technical progress and economic growth (an increase in per-person income and output of goods and services in the economy) likely to affect peoples' willingness to work hard?

17.38 The number of hours that an average person spends working each year is higher in Japan than in the United States, and higher in the United States than in most European countries.
   a. Why might countries differ in this way?
   b. Comment on the following claim: "Profit-driven employers will always seek to encourage longer working hours."

---

[18]Adam Smith, *The Wealth of Nations* (1776; reprint, New York: Knopf, 1991).

TAG SOFTWARE APPLICATIONS

TUTORIAL EXERCISES
▶ The module contains a review of the key terms from Chapter 17.

GRAPHING EXERCISES
▶ The graphing segment contains questions on the supply of the labor curve, the effects of a wage increase on the budget line, and the determination of unemployment.

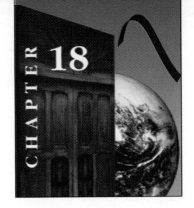
RICH AND POOR: INCOME DISTRIBUTION, POVERTY, AND DISCRIMINATION

WHAT THIS CHAPTER IS ABOUT

▶ The distribution of income
▶ Poverty and wealth
▶ Justice
▶ Discrimination

The distribution of income is one of the most volatile subjects of public discussion, and it runs like an undercurrent through many political debates. Are the poor getting poorer while the rich get richer? How poor are the poor? How rich are the rich? Are economic conditions becoming better or worse for the average family? How does poverty in the United States compare to poverty in the rest of the world? How large are the income differences between men and women, different racial groups, or people in different countries? What are the effects of or remedies for discrimination?

DISTRIBUTION OF INCOME IN THE UNITED STATES

income — the value of money and goods that a person receives during some time period

wealth — the value of accumulated savings plus the discounted present value of expected future labor income

PRELIMINARY DEFINITIONS

Income is the value of money and goods that a person receives during some time period.

People earn income from working, as returns on investments, or as gifts or inheritances.

Wealth is the total value of a person's accumulated savings plus the discounted present value of that person's expected future labor income.

The accumulated-savings portion of wealth is called *nonhuman wealth;* the discounted present value of expected future income is called *human wealth* (the value of human capital). Economists measure wealth in dollars; they measure income in dollars per year.

495

The terms *distribution of income* or *wealth* refer to comparisons of income or wealth across people or families.

median income — the income level at which half of the people have more income and half have less

> **Median income** is the income level at which half of the people have more income and half have less.

mean income — total income divided by the number of people

> **Mean income** is total income divided by the number of people.

If one person earns $10, another person earns $20, and a third earns $60, their median income is $20. This is the income level of the person in the middle; one person earns more and one person earns less. Their mean income is $30 = (10 + 20 + 60)/3.

money income - before-tax income including transfer payments, excluding noncash transfers and noncash benefits paid by employers

Money income, as reported in government statistics, refers to income:

▶ Including transfer payments of money from the government (sometimes called *entitlements*), such as Social Security and unemployment compensation

▶ Excluding noncash transfers from the government, such as food stamps, health benefits like Medicare and Medicaid, and subsidized housing

▶ Excluding noncash benefits paid by employers such as free housing for farm workers, employee medical care, and health insurance

▶ Before taxes (before the person pays income taxes and Social Security taxes)

Unless the text states otherwise, all statistics for the United States in this chapter use this definition of *money income.* Notice that this definition overstates poverty somewhat because it does not include nonmoney income such as food stamps. Similarly, all numbers in this chapter are measured in 1995 dollars unless otherwise noted. They are adjusted for inflation so that the analysis can compare different years properly.

Figure 18.1 shows the distribution of household income in the United States. Because the distribution is skewed (one side of the hill is steeper than the other side), median household income (about $34,000) is less than mean household income (which was about $44,000).

> The top fifth of the income distribution refers to the 20 percent of households or people with the highest incomes; the bottom fifth of the income distribution refers to the 20 percent of households or people with the lowest incomes.

Similarly, we can speak of the second-highest fifth, the middle fifth, and the second-lowest fifth of the income distribution.

The U.S. government reports income data for families and for households separately:

family — people living with others to whom they are related by nature or marriage

household — family or an individual living alone

> **Families** are people living with others to whom they are related by nature or marriage; **households** are families plus individuals living alone.

About 90 million households live in the United States, of which about two-thirds (about 60 million) are families by this definition.

MAIN FACTS OF INCOME DISTRIBUTION

This section discusses the main facts of the distribution of income in the United States (details appear below). A list can summarize these facts:

1. Median household income in the United States has doubled since the middle of the 20th century.

FIGURE 18.1

SKEWED INCOME DISTRIBUTION

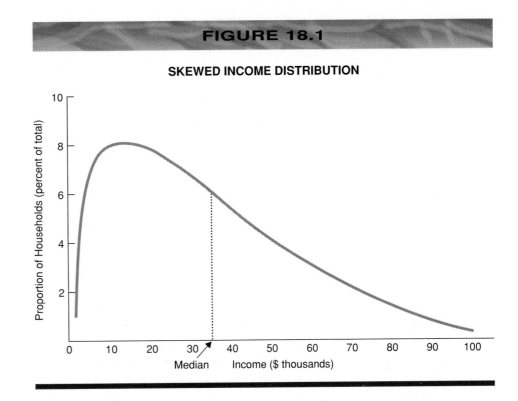

2. Each year, households in the top fifth of the U.S. income distribution collect just under one-half of all U.S. income, and households in the bottom fifth get only about 4 percent, down from close to 5 percent two decades ago.

3. Family income inequality in the United States is roughly the same as it was half a century ago. Inequality fell in the third quarter of the 20th century, but increased in the last quarter of the century. The number of households with two incomes and the number with no earned income have increased in the last quarter-century. More recently, wage differences between skilled and unskilled workers have increased along with rapid changes in technology. Government programs have helped to mitigate increases in income inequality resulting from these changes, though the average income of people in the bottom fifth of the income distribution has fallen in the last two decades.

4. Poverty is higher among women, children, blacks, and Hispanics than among other groups.

5. People in the United States are economically mobile; a low income in one year does not rule out a higher income in future years, and a high income in one year does not guarantee high incomes in future years. About half of all people with incomes in the bottom fifth of the income distribution move to higher fifths of the distribution within seven years.

6. About 10 percent to 15 percent of the U.S. population lives in households with incomes below the official poverty line. About 2 percent of the population stays below the poverty line for many years.

TABLE 18.1

PERCENTAGES OF HOUSEHOLDS IN EACH INCOME RANGE (IN 1990 DOLLARS)

	Under $10,000	$10,000–$15,000	$15,000–$25,000	$25,000–$35,000	$35,000–$50,000	$50,000–$75,000	Over $75,000	Median Household Income
1970	15.6%	8.7%	17.6%	18.6%	20.0%	13.8%	5.6%	$29,421
1980	16.3	9.7	18.9	16.6	18.6	13.6	6.4	28,091
1990	14.9	9.5	17.7	15.8	17.5	14.9	9.7	29,943
1993	14.3	9.4	17.1	15.6	17.4	15.1	11.1	29,969

Source: Statistical Abstract of the United States (Washington, D.C.: U.S. Bureau of the Census, 1992), Table No. 695. Data for 1993 provided by Bureau of the Census.

EXPLANATION AND DATA

Table 18.1 shows the percentages of households with incomes in various ranges in 1970, 1980, 1990, and 1993. In 1993, 14.3 percent of households had incomes below $10,000; in 1970, this figure was 15.6 percent. Another 9.4 percent of households had incomes between $10,000 and $15,000, which is lower than the percentage in 1980 but higher than that in 1970. Over one-fourth of households had incomes above $50,000 in 1993 (15.1 percent plus 11.1 percent), while only one-fifth had incomes that high in 1970 or 1980. (Recall that all incomes have been adjusted for inflation to avoid misleading comparisons, as discussed in Chapter 2, so differences between years do not reflect inflation.)[1]

Table 18.1 reveals a striking fact: median household income rose only 1.8 percent between 1970 and 1993. **Figure 18.2** shows the percentage increase in median household income since 1975. Together, this table and figure seem to imply that people have made almost no material progress in the last two or three decades, but total U.S. output of goods and services increased from $18,127 per person in 1970 to $25,716 per person in 1993.[2] Why the apparent contradiction?

There are several explanations. First, the income figures in the table and the figure, from surveys conducted by the government, do *not* include noncash income provided by the government or employers, and this income has risen over time.[3] Second, median income differs from mean income. When the distribution of income becomes more unequal (as it has since 1970), the median income per person rises more slowly than the mean. Third, the average household size has fallen over time. The United States also has many more two-income households than it did two or three decades ago, and, many more households consist of a female, her children, and no adult male; these households are often poor.[4]

These changes have increased the inequality in the distribution of money income (pretax income excluding noncash transfers). The distribution of after-tax

[1]This means that actual money incomes from earlier years (such as 1970) were smaller than the figures in the table; the actual median income in 1970 was $8,734, but prices were (on average) 3.37 times higher in 1990 than in 1970, so an income of $8,734 in 1970 was equivalent to an income of $29,421 in 1990.

[2]These figures are adjusted for inflation to avoid a misleading comparison as discussed in Chapter 2.

[3]The surveys are conducted annually by the Bureau of the Census and reported in *Current Population Reports* as series P-60.

[4]See Table 18.4.

FIGURE 18.2

PERCENTAGE CHANGES IN MEDIAN HOUSEHOLD INCOME ADJUSTED FOR INFLATION

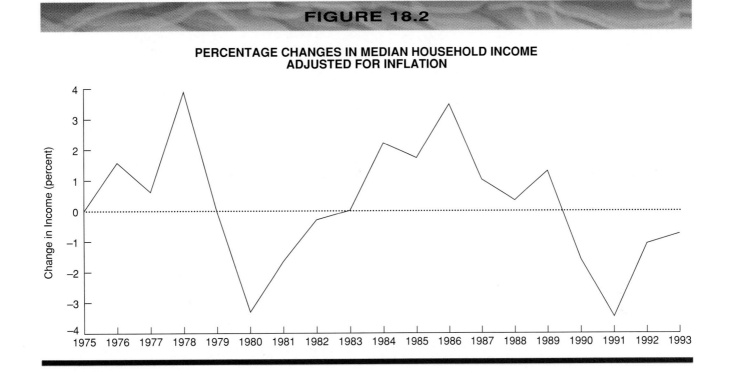

income including noncash transfers, however, is roughly the same as it was in 1970. This broader measure of after-tax income shows less increase in inequality in recent decades than the narrower measure shows.[5]

Many households with incomes under $10,000 consist of females with children and no male adult. The median income of these families is only about one-third of the overall median income. This illustrates the fact that poverty in the United States falls more heavily on females and children.

Median *household* income in 1993 was $33,115 (in 1995 dollars), but median *family* income was $39,176. Median family income has doubled since 1947 (when it was $20,720 in 1995 dollars, after rising from $16,547 in 1929, just before the Great Depression). This doubling since 1947 understates the increase in material living standards because many goods we now take for granted had not even been invented in 1947, and the quality of many goods has increased since then.[6] Further, in 1947, white males accounted for two-thirds of the labor force; opportunities for blacks and women were much more restricted than they are today.

Table 18.2 presents data like those in Table 18.1 for family incomes. The differences between the two tables reflect two facts. Families tend to have higher incomes than individuals living alone and the compositions of households have changed over time.

---

[5]Table 18.3 shows the difference in these measures.

[6]Even pollution was worse then in many respects, such as the amount of lead in the air and in various products.

TABLE 18.2

PERCENTAGES OF FAMILIES IN EACH INCOME RANGE (IN 1990 DOLLARS)

	Under $10,000	$10,000– $15,000	$15,000– $25,000	$25,000– $35,000	$35,000– $50,000	$50,000– $75,000	Over $75,000	Median Income
1970	8.7%	7.5%	17.6%	20.3%	23.1%	16.2%	6.5%	$33,238
1980	9.5	8.0	17.9	17.9	21.9	16.8	7.9	33,346
1990	9.4	7.5	16.4	16.2	20.1	18.2	12.3	35,353
1993	9.6	7.2	15.5	15.8	18.9	19.4	13.5	35,410

Source: Statistical Abstract of the United States (Washington, D.C.: U.S. Bureau of the Census, 1992), Table No. 702. Data for 1993 provided by Bureau of the Census.

Incomes differ substantially across different types of households. **Table 18.3** shows the median incomes of several household types in 1993. The first four rows of the table show median incomes of four types of families while the last two rows apply to individuals living alone. **Table 18.4** shows the percentages of whites, blacks, and Hispanics with incomes in various ranges in 1993.

Table 18.5 compares the distribution of money income with the distribution of a broader measure of income that includes noncash transfers and noncash payments from employers after subtracting income taxes and Social Security taxes. This table shows the percentage of *total* income that various groups receive. This broader concept of income finds slightly more income going to poorer households and less to richer households; taxes and government welfare and transfer programs make incomes slightly more equal. The overall picture of the distribution is the same and has not changed much over time. Using the broader definition of income, the percentage of all income earned by households in each fifth of the income distribution is about the same as it was in the middle of the 20th century.

TABLE 18.3

TYPES OF HOUSEHOLDS AND THEIR MEDIAN INCOMES, 1993

Type of Household	Median Income (1993 dollars)
Married-couple family with both spouses in labor force	$51,204
Married-couple family with only one spouse in labor force	30,218
Male adult (no female adult) living with children or other related people	29,849
Female adult (no male adult) living with children or other related people	18,545
Male living alone	24,728
Female living alone	14,883

Source: Income, Poverty, and Valuation of Noncash Benefits: 1993 (Washington, D.C.: U.S. Bureau of the Census, 1995), Tables No. 1 and 3.

TABLE 18.4

PERCENTAGE OF HOUSEHOLDS IN EACH INCOME RANGE, 1993

Race	Under $10,000	$10,000–$15,000	$15,000–$25,000	$25,000–$35,000	$35,000–$50,000	$50,000–$75,000	Over $75,000	Median Income
White	12.7%	8.9%	16.6	14.9%	17.0%	17.0%	13.4%	$32,960
Black	29.0	11.8	19.2	13.8	12.0	9.3	4.9	19,533
Hispanic	20.0	12.4	21.5	16.5	13.3	10.8	5.5	22,866

Source: Income, Poverty, and Valuation, of Noncash Benefits: 1993 (Washington, D.C.: U.S. Bureau of the Census, 1993), Table No. 2.

Some people have claimed that the middle class is vanishing and that people are polarizing into two groups, the rich and the poor, with few people left in the middle. Table 18.5 shows, however, that the middle class, defined as the middle 60 percent of the income distribution, gets about half of total U.S. income, only slightly less than the amount half a century ago.

POVERTY

Table 18.6 shows the official poverty level for a family of four, as defined by the U.S. government. The government specifies other official poverty levels for other family sizes. The official poverty lines rise over time to keep up with inflation. These lines were originally intended to equal three times estimated basic minimum food costs, based on a survey of food consumption.

Besides the poverty line, the table also shows the percentages of people in different groups living in U.S. households with incomes below the poverty levels defined for their family sizes. The fraction of people living in poverty fell from about 30 percent of the U.S. population in 1950 to about 12 percent in 1975, but the proportion has increased since then.

Figure 18.3 shows the percentage of people with incomes below the poverty line since 1959. Table 18.6 and Figure 18.3 both measure poverty using money income. Based on the broader definition of income (after-tax income including noncash transfers and benefits), 15 percent of the population lived below the poverty line in 1993.

TABLE 18.5

PERCENTAGE OF TOTAL INCOME EARNED BY HOUSEHOLDS IN EACH INCOME RANGE, 1990

	Lowest Fifth	Second-Lowest Fifth	Middle Fifth	Second-Highest Fifth	Highest Fifth	Median Income
Money income before taxes and including cash transfers, but excluding noncash transfers and benefits	3.5%	9.1%	15.1%	23.7%	48.6%	$31,241
After-tax income including noncash transfers from the government	4.8	10.7	16.1	23.6	44.8	30,395

Source: Income, Poverty, and Valuation of Noncash Benefits: 1993 (Washington, D.C.: U.S. Bureau of the Census, 1995, Table G.

TABLE 18.6

PERCENTAGES OF PEOPLE BELOW THE OFFICIAL U.S. POVERTY LEVEL

	All Races	White	Black	Hispanic	Official Poverty Level (Family of Four)[a]
1959	22.4%	18.1%	55.1%	N.A.	$ 2,973
1966	14.7	12.2	41.8	N.A.	3,317
1970	12.6	9.9	33.5	N.A.	3,968
1975	12.3	9.7	31.3	26.9%	5,500
1980	13.0	10.2	32.5	25.7	8,414
1985	14.0	11.4	31.3	29.0	10,989
1990	13.5	10.7	31.9	28.1	13,359
1993	15.1	12.2	33.1	30.6	14,763

[a]The poverty level in the last column of this table is not adjusted for inflation.
N.A. = data are not available.
Source: U.S. Bureau of the Census.

FIGURE 18.3

PERSONS BELOW THE POVERTY LEVEL: 1959 TO 1993

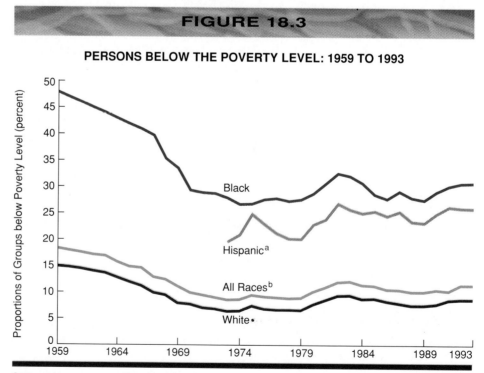

[a] Hispanic persons may be of any race.
[b] Includes other races not shown separately.
Source: U.S. Bureau of the Census.

To keep the magnitude of the U.S. poverty level in perspective, it is useful to compare it with average world output of goods and services per person. The U.S. government's official poverty level for a person living alone in 1993, $7,363 per year, was about 34 percent above average world output per person. (World output per person is about $5,200.) The official U.S. poverty level in 1993 for a four-person family was $14,763, meaning that each family member would get roughly two-thirds of average world output per person.

Poverty has struck children particularly painfully. **Table 18.7** shows the percentage of children in the United States who live below the official poverty level. Overall, the fraction of children living in households with incomes below the poverty line rose from 14.9 percent in 1970 to 21.0 percent in 1993. This group included more than 14 million children. The fraction is even higher for children under age 6; in 1993, nearly one-fourth of all children under that age reportedly lived in households with incomes below the federal poverty line. Studies show that children who grow up in poverty generally get less education and have higher chances of being poor as adults. Much of the increase in the fraction of children living in poverty in recent decades has been associated with increases in the number of teenage mothers living in households without fathers and in the number of young, two-parent households with low incomes.

MEASURING INEQUALITY

Economists measure inequality of income in many ways. Two common ways are with a picture called a Lorenz curve and a number called a Gini coefficient.

LORENZ CURVE

Figure 18.4 shows a Lorenz curve for the United States.

Lorenz curve — a graph that shows percentages of the population on the horizontal axis and percentages of income that they receive on the vertical axis

> A **Lorenz curve** is a graphical representation of the income distribution in an economy. It shows the percentage of the economy's total income that is received by people below a given level in the income distribution.

The Lorenz curve shows the percentage of total income that goes to the poorest 1 percent of people, the poorest 5 percent, and so on. It graphs percentages of the population on the horizontal axis and percentages of income on the vertical axis. If everyone had exactly the same income, the Lorenz curve would be a straight, 45-degree line. More curvature in the Lorenz curve indicates more inequality of incomes. Therefore, a larger shaded area in the graph represents more inequality.

TABLE 18.7

PERCENTAGE OF CHILDREN BELOW THE OFFICIAL U.S. POVERTY LEVEL

	All Races	White	Black	Hispanic
1970	14.9%	10.5%	41.5%	N.A.
1980	17.9	13.4	42.1	33.0%
1990	19.9	15.1	44.2	39.7
1993	21.0	16.2	44.0	37.9

N.A. = data are not available.
Source: Statistical Abstract of the United States (Washington, D.C.: U.S. Bureau of the Census, 1994), Table No. 728. Data for 1993 from Bureau of the Census.

FIGURE 18.4

LORENZ CURVE FOR THE UNITED STATES

Point A shows that the lowest 80 percent of all families in the United States receive 55 percent of total U.S. income, while the top 20 percent of families receive the other 45 percent. The area of the shaded region is about 0.20. This equals half of the Gini coefficient for the United States, which is about 0.40.

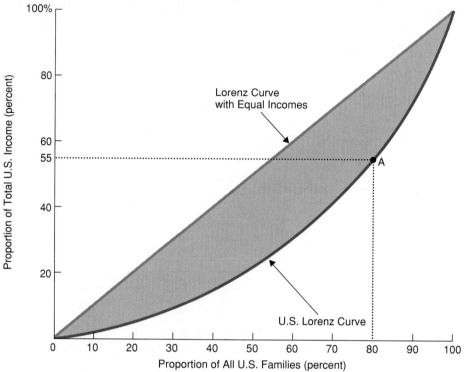

GINI COEFFICIENT

The Gini coefficient is a number between 0 and 1 that summarizes inequality in the income distribution.

Gini coefficient — a summary of income inequality equal to twice the shaded area enclosed in a Lorenz curve graph

The **Gini coefficient** is a one-number summary of the income distribution equal to twice the area of the shaded region in the Lorenz curve graph, as in Figure 18.4.

If everyone had the same income, the size of the shaded area would be zero and the Gini coefficient would be 0. The Gini coefficient would equal 1 if all of the income in the economy went to one person and everyone else got nothing. (In that case, the Lorenz curve forms a backwards *L* that lies along the horizontal axis and goes up the vertical axis; the shaded area equals 0.5, so the Gini coefficient equals 1.)

The Gini coefficient for U.S. family income is about 0.40, about the same as in the first half of the 20th century. Although the Gini coefficient fell to about 0.35 after the middle of the century, it has risen for the last third of the century. The Gini coefficient for individuals living alone in the United States has fallen in the last half-century and now stands at about 0.45.

UPWARD (AND DOWNWARD) MOBILITY IN THE INCOME DISTRIBUTION

People seldom stay in one place in the U.S. income distribution; they often move upward or downward. Evidence suggests that a family in the top fifth of the income distribution has a one-half chance of remaining in the top fifth for seven years. It has a 30 percent chance of moving down to the second-highest fifth within seven years, and a 20 percent chance of falling somewhere below that. A family in the bottom fifth of the income distribution has a one-half chance of moving out of that bottom fifth, and a 6 percent chance of reaching the top fifth, within seven years. Families in the middle fifth of the income distribution have about a one-third chance of remaining there seven years later, a one-third chance of rising, and a one-third chance of falling.

About half of all people with incomes below the official poverty level in any year remain there for a year, while the rest rise above it. Many fewer people continue to live in poverty for several years. While about one-fourth of the U.S. population receive help from government welfare programs at some time over the course of a decade, only a few percent depend on welfare over a long period. This explains why households in the bottom fifth of the income distribution spent, on average, almost twice as much as their incomes. They can spend more than their incomes because many of these people suffer low incomes only temporarily; they borrow money or dig into their savings to spend more than they earn during their temporary, low-income years.

These facts do not imply that poverty is not a problem. They show that the poverty problem is more serious for a small part of the population than for the many people who experience temporary poverty. They also show that temporary receipt of welfare from the government does not automatically create a dependence on welfare and a large, permanent class of welfare recipients. There is, however, a strong connection between the average incomes of parents and the average incomes of their children when those children become adults. One study found that parents with 10 percent higher incomes over many years have children who earn 8 percent more as adults. While economic mobility is common in the United States, the children of the poor are more likely to be poor as adults, and the children of the rich are more likely to be rich.

WAGES

Average wages have fallen in the last two decades. Hourly wages (in 1995 dollars) averaged $12.70 in 1970, $12.35 in 1980, and $11.44 in 1993.[7] Average weekly earnings fell 8 percent from 1970 to 1980 and 7 percent more from 1980 to 1993. Wages for college graduates rose, but wages for workers with less education fell.

This fall in wages appears to have resulted from a combination of factors. First, the much-discussed shift of workers to low-wage, service industries reduced the average wage. Second, wages fell because advances in technology have reduced the demand for low-skilled workers, who are often replaced by equipment that exploits technological advances, and raised the demand for highly skilled "knowledge workers." Third, increased world economic integration, by raising international trade, may have contributed to the fall in wages in the United

---

[7]This refers to production workers, excluding supervisors and agricultural workers, and includes overtime.

States. The decline of unions may also have played a role in reducing the average wage.

Although wages have fallen, total labor income has not. Instead, more people have worked and total payments to workers have increased along with the economy's total output. While hourly wages among males became more unequal in the last two decades, hourly wages among females did not.

DISTRIBUTION OF WEALTH

Wealth is distributed less equally than income. In the United States, the richest 2 percent of the population own about one-fourth of all household assets (nonhuman wealth). The richest 25 percent own about three-fourths of all household assets.

The distribution of wealth has gradually become more equal throughout most of the 20th century in the only three countries for which long-term data on the distribution of wealth are available: the United States, the United Kingdom, and Sweden. In 1922, the richest 0.5 percent of the U.S. population owned 30 percent of all household wealth. This figure fell to 21 percent by mid-century and to under 15 percent by 1975. It has increased since then, though. The Gini coefficient for the distribution of wealth in the United States is about 0.7, well above the Gini coefficient for the income distribution, but below its level earlier in the century.

The difference between the average wealth of blacks and whites in the United States is much larger than the difference between their incomes. Measuring nonhuman wealth by financial assets minus debts, plus the value of real estate and motor vehicles, the median nonhuman wealth of white households is about $75,000, but for black and Hispanic households, it is only about $5,000. Married couples have much more nonhuman wealth than individuals living alone. Families headed by white, married couples have a median nonhuman wealth of about $80,000, while those headed by white women with no spouses present have a median wealth of about $30,000, and those headed by white men with no spouses present have a median wealth of about $22,000. Households headed by black, married couples have a median wealth of about $23,000; those headed by black women with no spouses present have a median wealth of only about $1,000, and those headed by black men with no spouses present have a median wealth of only about $2,000. The figures for Hispanics are about the same as those for blacks. Even blacks with the same incomes as whites are (on average) less wealthy; the average wealth of black families with incomes above $30,000 per year (roughly the richest third) is only one-third the average wealth of white families with the same incomes.

How did the very rich get that way? Of the 400 people on the *Forbes* magazine list of the richest people in America (with an average wealth of about $500 million dollars), about one-third got rich through inheritance. The other two-thirds got rich through working, starting their own businesses, inventing new products, and so on.

────────────────────── **FOR REVIEW** ──────────────────────

18.1 List the main facts about the distribution of income in the United States.

18.2 What is a Lorenz curve? Explain it. What is a Gini coefficient? How would you represent it on a graph?

18.3 Draw a Lorenz curve and calculate the Gini coefficient assuming that people in the richest one-fourth of the population have equal incomes and get one-half of all income in the economy, while people in the other three-fourths of the population have equal incomes and share the other half of the economy's income.

18.4 What is the connection between an economy's production of goods and services and its income? Why has median household income remained roughly constant in the last quarter-century while the economy's output of goods and services has risen by about one-third?

DISTRIBUTION OF INCOME IN THE WORLD

purchasing power parity method — a method of comparing incomes in different areas by adjusting for price differences between those areas

An effort to look at the *world* distribution of income encounters the problem of differences in the prices of goods and services across countries and another problem with differences in the goods and services available.[8] Some comparisons of incomes across countries ignore these differences. Other studies attempt to adjust for the differences in prices across countries. This adjustment is known as the *purchasing power parity method.*[9]

The **purchasing power parity method** of comparing incomes in different areas adjusts for differences in prices in those areas.

Table 18.8 compares the per-capita incomes of many countries using the purchasing power parity method. The table ranks the countries by per-capita income in U.S. dollars (adjusted for differences in the prices of goods across countries).

The distribution of income across countries is much less equal than the distribution within the United States. The poorest fifth of the countries in the world get only 2.3 percent of the world's income; the second-poorest fifth get 4.8 percent, and the middle fifth get just 11.2 percent. Together, the poorest 60 percent of the world's countries get less than 20 percent of its income. The richest 20 percent of the countries get 58 percent of the world's income, and the richest 5 percent get 18 percent of the world's income. The Gini coefficient of per-capita income across countries is 0.54.

Table 18.9 compares how countries differ in their distributions of income across people. The table shows the fractions of national income received by the highest and lowest fifths of the populations in ten countries.

---

[8]Prices also differ across states in the United States, but the differences are smaller so the problem is less important.

[9]Suppose, for example, that someone wants to compare real income per person in New York City and Peoria, Illinois. Average dollar income in New York City is higher than in Peoria, so one could say that people in New York have more real income. The purchasing power parity method would, however, adjust for the fact that prices are higher in New York. Looking at prices for comparable housing and other goods in the two cities, one could use these prices to compare real income (purchasing power).

TABLE 18.8

DISTRIBUTION OF INCOME ACROSS COUNTRIES

	Country	Average Income per Person		Country	Average Income per Person
1	United States	$25,390	49	Tunisia	5,250
2	Switzerland	24,400	50	Botswana	5,250
3	Germany	22,140	51	Modlova	5,200
4	Japan	21,720	52	Armenia	5,160
5	Canada	21,640	53	Poland	5,040
6	Hong Kong	20,740	54	Kazakhstan	5,030
7	France	20,640	55	Slovakia	5,030
8	Denmark	20,030	56	Ecuador	4,640
9	Austria	19,810	57	Georgia	4,110
10	Belgium	19,610	58	Jamaica	4,110
11	Sweden	19,590	59	Azerbaijan	4,100
12	Norway	19,230	60	Egypt	4,030
13	Italy	19,080	61	Turkmenistan	3,960
14	Netherlands	18,840	62	Paraguay	3,830
15	Australia	18,680	63	Morocco	3,740
16	United Kingdom	18,300	64	Kyrgyzstan	3,670
17	Finland	18,040	65	Guatemala	3,560
18	Singapore	17,650	66	Peru	3,480
19	New Zealand	15,650	67	Dominican Republic	3,450
20	Israel	15,080	68	Congo	3,140
21	Spain	14,190	69	Uzbekistan	3,120
22	Ireland	12,800	70	Indonesia	3,060
23	Mauritius	12,520	71	Sri Lanka	2,970
24	Czech Republic	11,650	72	Philippines	2,730
25	Portugal	10,580	73	Cameroon	2,690
26	South Korea	9,320	74	Tajikistan	2,440
27	Venezuela	9,090	75	Bolivia	2,430
28	Estonia	9,060	76	Zimbabwe	2,420
29	Greece	8,600	77	El Salvador	2,360
30	Latvia	8,440	78	Pakistan	2,210
31	Malaysia	8,290	79	Honduras	2,040
32	Mexico	8,030	80	China	1,890
33	Chile	7,910	81	Senegal	1,880
34	Russia	7,760	82	Cote d'Ivoire	1,750
35	Romania	7,730	83	Benin	1,680
36	Belarus	7,670	84	Nigeria	1,520
37	Uruguay	7,470	85	Kenya	1,500
38	Hungary	6,810	86	Bangladesh	1,300
39	Columbia	6,120	87	India	1,290
40	Lithuania	6,060	88	Zambia	1,130
41	Thailand	5,900	89	Malawi	900
42	Brazil	5,870	90	Sierra Leone	900
43	Syria	5,850	91	Madagascar	800
44	Ukraine	5,800	92	Rwanda	760
45	Argentina	5,730	93	Tanzania	640
46	Costa Rica	5,710	94	Mali	540
47	Panama	5,500	95	Ethiopia	410
48	Turkey	5,420			

Source: World Bank, *World Development Report 1993,* Table 30, from the International Comparison Project, updated and coverted to 1995 dollars by author.

TABLE 18.9

INCOME DISTRIBUTIONS IN TEN COUNTRIES

Country	Percentage of National Income Received by	
	Lowest Fifth of Population	Highest Fifth of Population
Mexico	2.9%	57.7%
Singapore	5.1	48.9
Hong Kong	5.4	47.0
United States	4.7	41.9
India	8.1	41.4
United Kingdom	5.8	39.5
Bangladesh	10.0	37.2
Germany	6.8	38.7
Japan	8.7	37.5
Sweden	8.0	36.9

Source: *World Development Report,* World Bank (various issues).

Table 18.10 shows the fraction of people living in absolute poverty, defined by the United Nations as the income level below which a person cannot afford a nutritionally adequate diet and nonfood requirements. The United Nations estimates this income to be $525 per year in 1995 U.S. dollars adjusted for price differences across countries. Using this definition, about 1 billion people—nearly one-fifth of the world's population—live in absolute poverty. Two-thirds of those people live on less than $400 per year. About half of the people living in absolute poverty live in South Asia. Sub-Saharan Africa is another area with a large fraction of people in absolute poverty. While these numbers overstate world poverty because measured incomes do not include some sources of food, the extent of world poverty is clearly enormous.

Poverty in America is bad enough, but no words written here can impart to most readers the full impact of poverty among one-fifth of the world's population. One should remember that *people* live behind these statistics. Even when these people can get enough calories to survive under normal conditions, most of them lack even the most basic medications for sickness. Infant mortality rates, mortality rates of children under age 5, and death rates of mothers during childbirth are orders of magnitude higher than in richer countries.

Table 18.10 also shows relative poverty, the ratio of the income received by the highest fifth of the population to the income received by the lowest fifth. This table states three clear lessons. First, many people live in absolute poverty under conditions that probably defy the imaginations of readers of this textbook. Second, when countries become richer, absolute poverty declines. Third, relative poverty differs in rich and poor countries;[10] income tends to be more equal within richer countries.

---

[10]Compare, for example, the OECD countries with sub-Saharan Africa or South Asia.

TABLE 18.10

POVERTY RATES AROUND THE WORLD

OECD	Urban	Rural	Income Ratio[a]
Australia			8.7
Belgium			4.6
Canada			7.5
Denmark			7.2
Finland			6.0
France			7.7
Germany			5.0
Ireland			5.5
Italy			7.1
Japan			4.3
Netherlands			4.4
New Zealand			8.8
Norway			6.4
Portugal			9.4
Spain			5.8
Sweden			5.6
Switzerland			5.8
Turkey			16.3
United Kingdom			5.7
United States			7.5
Asia			
Hong Kong			8.7
Indonesia	26	44	7.3
South Korea	18	11	6.8
Malaysia	13	38	14.4
Papua New Guinea	10	75	
Philippines	50	64	10.3
Thailand	15	34	8.8
China		10	

South Asia	Urban	Rural	Income Ratio[a]
Bangladesh	86	86	7.2
India	40	51	7.0
Nepal	55	61	
Pakistan	32	29	
Sri Lanka			8.3
Sub-Saharan Africa			
Benin		65	
Botswana	40	55	
Burundi	55	85	
Cameroon	15	40	
Central African Republic		91	
Chad	30	56	
Côte d'Ivoire	30	26	25.6
Ethiopia	60	65	
Ghana	59	37	
Kenya	10	55	25.0
Lesotho	50	55	
Liberia		23	
Madagascar	50	50	
Malawi	25	85	
Mali	27	48	
Mauritius	12	12	15.0
Niger		35	
Rwanda	30	90	
Sierra Leone		65	
Somalia	40	70	
Sudan		85	
Togo	42		
Zaire		80	
Zambia	25		19.0

Middle East/North Africa	Urban	Rural	Income Ratio[a]
Algeria	20		
Egypt	21	25	8.5
Israel			6.7
Jordan	14	17	
Morocco	28	45	
Syria			15.8
Tunisia	20	15	
South Yemen		20	
Latin America/Caribbean			
Argentina			11.3
Bolivia		85	
Brazil			33.7
Chile	27		
Colombia	32		
Dominican Republic	45	43	
Ecuador	40	65	
El Salvador	20	32	8.5
Guatemala	66	74	
Haiti	65	80	
Honduras	14	55	
Jamaica		80	
Mexico			19.6
Nicaragua	21	19	
Panama	21	30	31.5
Paraguay	19	50	
Peru	49		32.0
Trinidad and Tobago		39	
Uruguay	22		
Venezuela			18.2

[a]Ratio of income received by highest fifth of population to income received by lowest fifth.
Source: Economist Book of Vital World Statistics (New York: Random House, 1990), p. 229.

PERSPECTIVE

In 1993 dollars, the U.S. poverty level for a family of four was $14,763, or about $3,691 per person, which is about 7 times the absolute poverty income defined above and more than half of world output per person. If total world income were distributed equally (assuming that this redistribution did not affect the total), each person in the world would have an income about 10 times the absolute poverty level.[11]

---

[11]Any attempt to redistribute income on this scale would cause a massive fall in the total.

The poverty of economic policy that is driving black Africa deeper into poverty

It will take 40 years for the region to reach the level of wealth of 20 years ago, says the World Bank

By Michael Holman, Africa Editor

Unless sub-Saharan Africa's "poor" economic policies improve, it will be 40 years before the region returns to its per-capita income of the mid-1970s, warns a World Bank report on the region published tomorrow.

Even Ghana, rated the best of Africa's reforming countries which has achieved real growth of about 5 percent a year, is still among the world's poorest countries: "At this growth rate, the average Ghanaian will not cross the poverty line for another 50 years," says the report.

The economic policies of governments in sub-Saharan Africa have contributed to a fall in per-capita output in the last two decades.

Source: Michael Holman, "The Poverty of Economic Policy that Is Driving Black Africa Deeper into Poverty," *Financial Times*, March 12–13, 1994, p. 3.

Report by World Bank sees poverty lessening by 2000 except in Africa

A fifth of the world's people are now too poor to obtain the necessities.

By Clyde H. Farnsworth Special to The New York Times

WASHINGTON, July 14—The first major study of the world's poor in a decade says that poverty is likely to decline by the year 2000, except in sub-Saharan Africa.

There, the number of impoverished people is expected to rise by 85 million and to continue to account for more than 40 percent of the region's population.

The report, being issued on Monday by the World Bank, the largest provider of aid to developing countries, found that 1.1 billion people—a fifth of the world's population—still live with annual incomes of less than $370 a year. The bank draws its poverty line at that amount, below which people are deemed unable to buy adequate food, shelter, and other necessities.

But the report foresees a decline by nearly a third in the number of the world's poor in the next 10 years. It bases its forecast on the World Bank's projections of somewhat faster economic growth in developing countries, a continuation of historical trends of moderate growth in industrial countries, declining interest rates, and slowly improving commodity prices.

Fewer of the Very Poor

The report said that if those projections hold up, there would be 825 million people living in poverty in the year 2000, down by 300 million from 1985. Put another way, 18 percent of the world's population would live in poverty, a decline from 32.7 percent in 1985.

Many economists expect world poverty to decline in the coming years. Will they be right?

Source: Clyde H. Farnsworth, "Report by World Bank Sees Poverty Lessening by 2000 Except in Africa," *New York Times*, July 16, 1990, p. A3.

TRENDS IN WORLD POVERTY

Overall, world poverty is declining. It declined through most of the 19th and 20th centuries, and the poorest fifth of the world's population is less poor now than it was a century ago or even two decades ago. World food production per person has risen despite government policies in most developed countries that reduce food production by paying farmers not to grow food and government policies in many developing countries that discourage food production by placing maximum legal prices on food. The prices reduce the quantities supplied, create shortages, and leads to dependence on higher-priced food imported from developed countries. Consumption of food, however, has risen more slowly in poorer countries than in advanced countries.

Occasional setbacks occur in the general trend toward less world poverty. Income per person in sub-Saharan Africa has remained stagnant or even fallen in the last quarter-century. Progress has not stopped in many other parts of the world, though. Income per person in South Asia (which has the largest concentration of the world's absolute poverty) rose 3.2 percent in the decade of the 1980s, more than double its increase in the previous two decades. Most studies predict that economic growth and development will continue to reduce world poverty in the years ahead.

EVALUATING POVERTY AND WEALTH

WHAT AFFECTS INEQUALITY AND POVERTY?

About three-fourths of personal income in the United States comes from working (selling labor services). The other one-fourth comes from income on investments (stocks, bonds, real estate, and so on). People's incomes differ because they differ in:

▶ Education

▶ Experience

▶ Ability (intelligence, creativity, talents, and so on)

▶ Effort (Some people work harder than others.)

▶ Luck (fortunate investments; being born at a certain time, in a certain country, into a certain type of family environment, or with certain abilities)

▶ Inheritance

▶ Discrimination encountered (in education, employment, and other opportunities)

▶ Willingness to take risks (People who take risks earn more, on average.)

▶ Past savings (People earn income on money they have saved in the past.)

Some people also earn higher money incomes than others because of the compensating differentials discussed in Chapter 17; other things being equal, people earn less at more pleasant or desirable jobs.

What affects inequality in a society? What affects poverty? A poor society could have little inequality, but much poverty while a rich enough society could have poverty, but considerable inequality. On average, however, richer countries have more equal distributions of income, and less poverty.

Several other factors affect poverty and inequality. A more equal distribution of education, skills, and talents among people in a society makes for a more equal distribution of income. Countries whose governments permit people to succeed and fail economically without large redistributions of income from the winners to the losers tend to have higher inequality. Countries that redistribute more income from rich to poor (or rich to middle class), or whose laws and regulations make higher incomes more difficult to obtain, tend to have more equal distributions of income.

Two factors have combined to raise inequality in the United States in recent decades. First, technical change has increased the wages of more educated, skilled workers compared to less-educated, less-skilled workers. Nothing guarantees that technical change must favor more educated workers. One could imagine technical change favoring less-educated workers, just as the development of farm machinery such as tractors favored less-strong farm workers. In practice, however, recent technical change has greatly increased the return to education. Wage differences between skilled and unskilled workers have increased significantly in the last two decades.

The second cause of higher inequality comes from expanded international trade. Competition from producers in countries with lower average wages has increased inequality in the United States by reducing the demand for less-skilled workers in the United States (since they tend to produce goods that U.S. consumers can import from abroad at lower cost). Trade has also raised the demand for skilled workers, who tend to produce goods that the United States exports.

Societies whose cultures, laws, or regulations limit economic mobility may have more or less inequality than societies with fewer limits on economic mobility. Cultural and legal limitations may raise inequality by preserving traditional differences and limiting opportunities for the poorer segments of the society that would reduce inequality. These same restrictions, however, may also limit new inequalities that would occur as some people became wealthy through business successes or by exploiting their unique talents in entertainment, sports, or other areas.

Economic growth tends to reduce both poverty and inequality; wealthier countries have less of each, and both have generally fallen over the last century as economies have grown. Currently, people whose incomes place them in the lowest fifth of the U.S. population, for example, spend more per person than the per-capita income of the median U.S. household of half a century ago.

WHAT IS JUST?

Opinions differ about what is fair, equitable, or just. Questions of fairness or justice arise whenever people make judgements about the distributions of income or wealth or the desirability of any government economic policies.

EGALITARIANISM

egalitarianism — the view that fairness requires equal results

Egalitarianism is the view that fairness requires equal results.

A simple version of egalitarianism says that fairness requires everyone to have the same income. Another version of egalitarianism says that fairness requires that some people get more income than others to compensate them for other differences. Perhaps a handicapped person or a person with greater medical needs should get more income than other people. Perhaps a person who is physically unattractive should get more income than a popular, good-looking person. Perhaps a person whose job is unpleasant should get more income than a person with a personally satisfying job (such as an artist). Another version of egalitarianism "From each according to his abilities, to each according to his needs," was advocated by Karl Marx. Egalitarianism in some form has obvious appeal to many people. It is, after all, one reason for giving every person one vote in an election.

Problems arise, however, when one tries to decide which version of egalitarianism is best or to design policies that would create an egalitarian society. The main problem is that egalitarian policies reduce incentives to work. If egalitarianism is desirable for its own sake, it may be worth sacrificing some economic efficiency to achieve a more equal distribution (of whatever one wants to equalize). These issues raise many questions. What is the best tradeoff between equality and efficiency? Which is better, a society in which half of the people have 100 and half have 200, or an egalitarian society in which everyone has 100? What if everyone could have 120 or 140 instead? Is it just to punish a poor person who robs from a rich person, or does the robbery contribute to justice? Should socially valuable behavior, such as curing a disease or producing a good that people want, be rewarded with extra income? Should esteem (bestowed by other people) be distributed equally like income? Can it be? Should people with more esteem get less income? That is, should people with less esteem receive more income as compensation? Can people give material or physical tokens of esteem in an egalitarian world, or do these tokens count as income?

Another set of issues arises when people become unequal through their actions. Suppose that two people have the same wealth at age 20, but one saves more than the other. In later years, the saver will have investment income that the other person will lack. Is this just? Is it consistent with egalitarianism?

One need not be an egalitarian to favor a more equal distribution of wealth. Nor need one be an egalitarian to believe that, regardless of the degree of income inequality, government policies should try to reduce poverty. These views can be deduced from other views of justice considered in the following sections.

UTILITARIANISM

utilitarianism — the view that justice consists of maximizing the total amount of human happiness

Utilitarianism is the view that justice consists of maximizing the total amount of human happiness.[12]

Only total happiness matters to a utilitarian, not who is happy and who is not. In this sense, utilitarianism differs strongly from egalitarianism, which argues that distribution is important and should be equal.

Despite this concentration on total happiness rather than its distribution, utilitarianism can provide an argument for redistributing income from the rich to the poor. Some utilitarians argue that if you take a dollar from a rich person and give it to a poor person, the loss in happiness to the rich person is smaller than the gain in happiness to the poor person. The poor person, according to this argument, values money more than the rich person because he has less of it. The marginal utility (benefit) of the money is larger for the poor person than for the rich person, so redistributing income from the rich to the poor raises total utility (happiness).[13]

Critics of this argument say that it requires an impossible *interpersonal comparison of utility,* that is, no one can compare one person's happiness with another person's. For all we know, according to this criticism, redistributing income from the rich to the poor might actually reduce total happiness. A utilitarian might reply that while one can never be sure of these comparisons, it seems reasonable that poor people gain more happiness from an extra $10 than rich people lose when they give up $10. Indeed, a utilitarian might say, people make interpersonal comparisons of utility regularly when they decide to give money to charities.

Critics of utilitarianism have advanced numerous arguments against it. Many people object to utilitarianism because it treats the *distribution* of happiness as unimportant. A utilitarian would prefer a situation in which Jeremy has 10 units of happiness and John has 1 unit to a situation in which Jeremy and John each have 5 units of happiness; an egalitarian would prefer the latter situation.

A second criticism of utilitarianism is that it ignores people's fundamental rights. If someone needs an emergency kidney transplant to stay alive and no one offers to donate a kidney, a utilitarian might say that the government should force someone to donate, because the gain in happiness to the recipient exceeds the loss in happiness to the donor, who can live with her remaining kidney. Some critics of utilitarianism say that, while the situation is unfortunate, forcing someone to

---

[12]Some versions of utilitarianism may also include animals. Utilitarianism was developed largely by the English philosophers Jeremy Bentham and John Stuart Mill.

[13]See Abba Lerner, *The Economics of Control: Principles of Welfare Economics:* (1944; reprint 1970, New York: Augustus M. Kelley Publications).

donate a body part would violate that person's rights. Many philosophers believe that utilitarianism has "morally monstrous" implications.[14]

JUSTICE AS AN IMPLICIT CONTRACT

Before you play a game with a friend, you agree on rules. Football teams agree on rules before they know the outcome of the coin toss that determines which team will receive the first kickoff.

Suppose that people could meet with each other and agree on the *rules of life* before the toss of a coin (that is, luck) turns them into unique individuals living in diverse circumstances around the world. One can imagine that people meet together before they are born, before they find out if they will be smart or dumb, beautiful or ugly, lucky or unlucky, whether they will have rich or poor parents, tastes for material goods or for spiritual fulfillment, and so on.[15] This is called meeting in the *original position* or *behind the veil of ignorance.*[16]

At this meeting, people would choose the legal rules and government policies that would affect their lives. They would decide whether the government should redistribute income from rich people to poor people and how much it should transfer. They would decide what rights and obligations everyone would have. Because people would not yet know their own individual circumstances when they made these decisions, they would not be able to make rules to give themselves special benefits. Instead, they would presumably choose rules that would benefit the whole society in some sense; in that sense, the rules that they choose would be fair and would give meaning to the concept of justice.

According to one view of justice, only rules can be fair or just, not outcomes like who wins a game or how equally income is distributed. Rules are fair or just if everyone would agree to them at this magical meeting behind the veil of ignorance. Because this meeting is impossible to arrange, however, no one knows for sure what rules would command agreement. In his book *A Theory of Justice,* John Rawls guessed that people would choose a system of rules that would involve considerable redistribution from the lucky to the unlucky—from the rich to the poor—to make certain that no one would fall below a certain level of income. Justice would then amount to enforcement of this agreement. Other proponents of the idea that justice is an implicit contract have other guesses about what rules people would choose.

NATURAL RIGHTS

Some philosophers have argued that people "are endowed by their Creator with certain inalienable rights . . . " Justice, in the natural-rights view, consists of enforcing these rights. Some people believe that these rights come from God; others,

---

[14]As one critic put it, "It might well be the case that more good and less evil would result from your painlessly and undetectedly murdering your malicious, old, and unhappy grandfather than from your forebearing to do so: he would be freed from his wretched existence; his children would be rejoiced by their inheritances and would no longer suffer from his mischief. . . . Nobody seriously doubts that a position with such a consequence is monstrous."—Alan Donagan, "Is There a Credible Form of Utilitarianism?" in Michael D. Bayles, ed., *Contemporary Utilitarianism* (Magnolia, Mass.: Peter Smith Publications, 1968), p. 187–188.

[15]All generations—and everyone in each generation—would have to attend this meeting.

[16]This idea was developed by economist John C. Harsanyi and later by philosopher John Rawls. See John C. Harsanyi, "Cardinal Utility in Welfare Economics and the Theory of Risk-Taking," *Journal of Political Economy* 61 (1953); and John Rawls, *A Theory of Justice* (Cambridge, Mass.: Harvard University Press, 1971).

such as the English philosopher John Locke, believe that rights can be deduced from human nature. Perhaps in the original position behind the veil of ignorance, people would choose a society that would guarantee a set of fundamental rights, and perhaps this choice is the source of human rights.[17] The main shortcoming of the natural-rights argument comes from a disagreement about precisely what those rights consist of. Some people may claim that everyone has a right to a minimum amount of food, health care, and so on. Others may claim that one has rights to one's own body and property, and that government-enforced redistribution, however needy the recipient, violates those rights. Some alleged rights obligate other people to perform specific tasks. For example, a right to health care would require someone else to provide that care, yet forcing someone else to do so might violate that person's rights. Whether a natural-rights proponent views the distribution of income or a government policy of redistribution as just or unjust will depend on the specific natural rights in which the person believes.

FOR REVIEW

18.5 Explain the purchasing power parity method of comparing incomes across countries.

18.6 How does the United Nations define absolute poverty? Compare the absolute poverty level, the official U.S. government poverty level, and average per-person income in the world.

QUESTION

18.7 What evidence would you gather to decide why one person earns a higher income than another?

GOVERNMENT PROGRAMS AND POVERTY

Governments of many developed countries pursue antipoverty programs. Some countries, such as Sweden, have much more comprehensive welfare systems than the United States. The effects of welfare programs are controversial. Many people believe that welfare programs reduce poverty and human misery, and that, while some people may receive support over a long period of time and a few may abuse the system, most recipients receive welfare only temporarily when bad luck strikes their lives. Critics of the welfare system argue that it discourages people from seeking productive work and fosters a culture of welfare dependency, sometimes creating perverse incentives to break up families or avoid employment. Some critics have argued that the system of U.S. government programs has failed to eliminate poverty and has even caused some poverty.[18] Other scholars dispute this claim, but economists generally agree that government welfare programs have had some perverse effects on incentives that have contributed to the problems of

---

[17]This is sometimes called *rule-utilitarianism,* because it involves a choice of rules (laws and government policies) made in the original position, behind the veil of ignorance, that people in that original position think will maximize their happiness.

[18]Charles Murray, *Losing Ground* (New York: Basic Books, 1984).

the poor.[19] They disagree mainly on the sizes of these effects and on their importance compared to the benefits of welfare programs.

The primary U.S. antipoverty programs include:

▶ Aid to Families with Dependent Children (AFDC), which provides money to families with children, low incomes, and few assets (often families made up of a woman, her young children, and no adult male)

▶ Supplemental Security Income (SSI), which pays money to very poor elderly people with few or no assets

▶ Food stamps, which recipients buy at subsidized prices and exchange at groceries for food (or sell illegally for cash in the black market)

▶ Medicare and Medicaid, which are noncash transfers that provide health care and hospitalization for low-income people (Medicaid) and health insurance for elderly and disabled people (Medicare)

▶ Unemployment compensation, which provides payments to workers for limited periods of time (usually 20 weeks) when they are fired or laid off from jobs at which they have worked for certain periods of time

Total social welfare spending by the U.S. federal government in 1994 (excluding Social Security, Medicare, education, and veterans' programs) was about $260 billion.

Medicaid, AFDC, SSI, and food stamps are means-tested programs; only people with low incomes can collect benefits. The largest transfer program in the United States is the Social Security system. U.S. government spending on Social Security in 1994 was about $500 billion. Social Security and Medicare differ from welfare programs because they are not means-tested, that is, people receive benefits regardless of their incomes or wealth. Through the old-age and survivors' insurance (OASI) program, a smaller program of disability insurance, and the Medicare program, Social Security pays money to retired workers, their families when affected workers die, and disabled workers and their dependents. The retirement portion of Social Security, OASI, resembles a pension fund. The government requires most people in the country to participate in the Social Security system, which means that workers must pay a Social Security tax (called *FICA* on pay stubs), and their employers must also pay a tax. In 1994, workers and employers each paid a 7.65 percent tax on wages and salaries up to $60,600 for a total Social Security tax rate of 15.30 percent.

Some economists have proposed replacing the welfare system with a negative income tax.[20] In this system, people with very low incomes would pay negative taxes, that is, they would receive money from the government. A person with no income might, for example, get $5,000 per year in negative income taxes, and this payment might fall by 50 cents for each dollar of income earned; exact figures differ across proposals. While the incentive to work may appear small if a person keeps only half of each dollar earned, most studies indicate that the current welfare system allows people to keep much less of any income they earn because they lose welfare payments. Currently, people on welfare can often keep only 10 cents to 35 cents of each extra dollar they earn, so a negative income tax might raise

---

[19]Frank Levy, *Dollars and Dreams: The Changing American Income Distribution* (Ithaca, N.Y: Russell Sage Foundation, 1987).

[20]See, for example, Milton Friedman, *Capitalism and Freedom* (Chicago: University of Chicago Press, 1961).

their incentive to work. Proponents also argue that a negative income tax would be more efficient because it would reduce the government welfare bureaucracy.

Severe poverty in less-developed countries often results from government policies and wars.[21] Many government policies create poverty. Maximum legal prices for food reduce food production by making it unprofitable. High taxes, regulations, and threats of confiscation weaken incentives to produce food and other products. They also reduce the incentive for foreign investment that would provide capital equipment to raise the productivity of local labor and improve living standards. Like a tax, the need to bribe local officials in order to conduct normal business operations in many countries prevents businesses from operating in these countries or investing there. Civil wars, attempts by dictators to expand or maintain their power, and corruption in the military and civil branches of government all help to create poverty. While famines and other natural disasters contribute to world poverty, persistent poverty is not caused by famines. People would not stay in an area of persistent poverty if they had the opportunity to leave. Without government policies that keep people from leaving some countries and entering others, most people would not continue to live in places where they found it continually impossible to grow food or earn income in some other way.

Technology is now sufficiently advanced, and the world's capital stock is large enough, that everyone in the world (even people without skills) could produce enough goods and earn enough income to stay well above the absolute poverty level. To do this, however, people need access to technology and capital equipment or natural resources. Owners of capital equipment would provide it to poor people if it were profitable to do so, and this would be profitable (because wages would be low, though high enough to prevent absolute poverty) if government policies did not prevent it. In this sense, government policies are largely responsible for absolute poverty in the modern world. Policies prevent people from making use of current world technology and capital and receiving the higher incomes they could then earn.[22]

DISCRIMINATION

Some income inequality has resulted from discrimination against minorities and women. Discrimination may reduce a person's job opportunities or make it difficult for a person to buy a house in a certain neighborhood or join some organization. Victims of discrimination face higher costs for their actions because they suffer negative reactions from other people. Discrimination can also have indirect effects; a business may refuse to hire minorities, not because its owner is prejudiced, but because the business would lose sales to prejudiced customers if it did.[23] Discrimination in employment can result from the prejudices of employers, other workers, or customers.

DISCRIMINATION IN LABOR MARKETS

One decade ago, the average black man's weekly earnings were only 66 percent of the average white man's. At the same time, the average woman's weekly earnings

---

[21]The developing countries of the world spend about five times as much on armed forces as they receive in foreign aid.

[22]For an interesting case study (of Biafra), see Dan Jacobs, *The Brutality of Nations* (New York: Alfred A. Knopf, 1990). Ethiopia in the 1970s and 1980s is another clear example. A good summary of other cases is contained in Karl Zinsmeister, "All the Hungry People," *Reason,* June 1988, pp. 22–30.

[23]Of course, a prejudiced employer could falsely claim that the business would lose customers.

were only 62 percent of the average man's, and the average black woman earned only 88 percent as much as the average white woman. The average hourly wage for women was 65.1 percent of that for men, though the fraction varied by age. Women ages 20 to 24 earned hourly wages that were 86 percent of men's; women 25 to 34 had hourly wages that were 75 percent of men's; women over 35 had hourly wages that were only 56 percent of men's. These numbers have changed little in recent years.[24] Economists generally agree that the wage differences between these groups are due in part to factors other than discrimination; they disagree on the extent to which discrimination explains the remaining differences.

WAGE DIFFERENCES BETWEEN WOMEN AND MEN

The hourly wage of women has averaged about 60 percent of that of men since World War II (and, scarce data suggest, long before that).[25] Recently, women's average hourly wages have risen to about 65 percent of men's, up from 60 percent a decade earlier.[26] Relatively young women have made the largest wage gains.

Women and minorities earn less than white men for at least three reasons: they face discrimination in labor markets, they have less human capital on average (possibly due to discrimination earlier in life and lower-quality educational opportunities), and they take lower-paying jobs on average (partly due to discrimination and below-average human capital).[27]

Wages of women have actually risen more quickly than the 65 percent figure indicates. The growth of the average wage for women relative to that for men understates improvements in economic opportunities for women due to changes in education and experience. Today, the education and experience of the average woman in the labor force, compared to that of the average man, is lower than in the past. This does not imply that women have become less educated; in fact, women have become more educated relative to men. The average education of women in the labor force has fallen, however, because relatively more low-skilled women have entered the labor force. To understand why, suppose that Anna has graduated from medical school, Betty has graduated from college, and Carol has only a high-school education. If Anna and Betty are in the labor force and Carol is not, then the average education of women in the labor force exceeds a college education, but if Carol enters the labor force, the average education of women in the labor force falls. This entry of more low-skilled women has reduced the growth rate of the average wage of women relative to that of men.[28] Thus, one study concludes that "Women's wages are rising more rapidly than commonly

---

[24]Sources: James P. Smith and Michael Ward, "Women in the Labor Market and in the Family," *Journal of Economic Perspectives* 3, no. 1 (Winter 1989); Victor Fuchs, "Women's Quest for Economic Equality," ibid.; Barbara Bergmann, "Does the Market for Women's Labor Need Fixing?" ibid.; and Jonathan Leonard, "Women and Affirmative Action," ibid.

[25]This 60 percent figure may date to biblical times. Leviticus 27 (verses 1–4) indicates that women may have earned only 60 percent of the wages of men.

[26]The average woman's weekly earnings are still only about 62 percent of the average man's, reflecting the fact that women work in the market (for pay) fewer hours per week.

[27]Chapter 17 discussed human capital.

[28]A typical, 30-year-old, college-educated woman earned 12 percent more in 1986 ($22,429) than in 1973, while a typical, 30-year-old, college-educated man earned 2 percent less in 1986 ($30,257) than in 1973. The same is true of women with only high-school educations. The average wage of women as a fraction of the average wage of men remained about the same because more relatively less-educated women entered the labor force over this period, pulling down the average. This trend has continued in more recent years.

IN THE NEWS

Studies link subtle sex bias in schools with women's behavior in the workplace

By Sharon E. Epperson
Staff Reporter of The
Wall Street Journal

What's holding women back as they climb the success ladder?

Classrooms may be partly to blame.

Overt discrimination it isn't, for schools are increasingly offering equal opportunities to girls and boys in both formal courses and extracurricular activities, including sports. But several studies suggest that, from first grade through college, female students are the victims of subtle biases. As a result, they are often given less nurturing attention than males.

Researchers maintain that a chilly climate for women in the classroom undermines self-esteem and damages morale. They believe, too, that some of these patterns of student-teacher interaction may help set the stage for expectations and interactions later in the workplace.

Past discrimination can affect a woman's wage (even without current discrimination) by affecting her human capital.

Source: Sharon E. Epperson, "Studies Link Subtle Sex Bias in Schools with Women's Behavior in the Workplace," *The Wall Street Journal,* September 16, 1988, p. 27.

believed, but they are also lower relative to men's than is commonly believed."[29] At least half of the male/female wage difference is due to measurable differences in education and experience.

Some part of the male/female wage difference may also reflect the typical division of child-rearing responsibilities in our society. Sex (or race, or any other feature of a person) may help to predict other characteristics of that person. As a result, the race or sex of a job applicant may affect a firm's willingness to hire the applicant, even if race and sex are otherwise irrelevant to its decision (that is, even if neither the firm or its customers are prejudiced).

statistical discrimination — using the fact that a person is a member of a certain group to make predictions about that person

Statistical discrimination involves using the fact that a person is a member of a certain group to make predictions about that person.

Insurance companies use statistical discrimination when they charge higher prices for life insurance to older people than to younger people; on average, younger people are less likely to die soon. They also use statistical discrimination when they charge lower prices for women than for men, because women are statistically likely to live longer than men.

Statistical discrimination may explain part of the male/female wage differential. Inequality in hourly wages between women and men is larger, adjusted for education, than inequality between blacks and whites. One reason for this may be that females in our society usually bear more child-rearing and housework respon-

---

[29]Claudia Goldin, "Development of the American Economy," *NBER Reporter,* Winter 1989/1990. Economists can measure some differences in education, such as the number of years of school, but other differences in education, such as quality of education, may defy measurement.

sibilities than men.[30] This division of child-rearing responsibilities implies that women, on average, have less time to acquire education, work at a formal job, or work overtime. It also implies that women have less experience than men, on average, if they leave their jobs for a few years to raise children. Finally, because women are more likely to leave jobs to raise children, employers are less willing to hire women and invest in training them.

These forces reduce the average wage of women relative to that of men. Childless women earn about 20 percent less than men, while overall women earn 35 to 40 percent less than men. This could mean that about half of the wage difference between men and women is due to children and the greater child-raising roles of women. Of course, even childless women may earn less, on average, than men because they might have children at some future time and employers practice statistical discrimination. This makes an employer less willing to invest money in training that it would lose if a woman were to quit.[31]

Job segregation is another result of discrimination. Employers may place minorities or women in lower-level jobs or jobs in different locations than other workers. Some studies indicate that about half of the education-adjusted wage difference between men and women results from placement of women in lower-level jobs than equivalent men.

WAGE DIFFERENCES BETWEEN BLACKS AND WHITES

Median weekly wages of black men fell from 77 percent of white men's wages in 1974 to 74 percent in 1993. Wages of black women are about 87 percent of those of white women, lower than as in the mid-1970s. Blacks have made large gains over longer periods of time. In 1940, black men earned only 43 percent of what white men earned; in 1950, this figure was 55 percent.

About half of the difference in the black/white wage differential is due to measurable differences in average education. Adjusted for measured differences in education, black men earn 85 percent of the average wage of white men. The remaining 15 percent wage differential may reflect discrimination or other factors such as unmeasured differences in education. (Pertinent studies measure the number of years of schooling, but not the quality of education, which might be expected to be lower among blacks partly because, on average, they grow up in lower-income areas that spend less on schooling.)

Discrimination may also play a larger role. The fact that black men average less education than white men may partly reflect discrimination in educational opportunities. It may also reflect past job discrimination that reduced the education of black children by adversely affecting home and family life. Some human capital is acquired in the home through interaction with parents in an environment that promotes education. As a result, the effects on wages of past racial discrimination may last for generations because parents with low levels of human

---

[30]This fact may reflect discrimination in a larger sense as traditional social roles may persist partly because of discrimination in the form of social pressures, differences in education and socialization of boys and girls, and so on. Of course, it could also result from choices that males and females tend to make differently.

[31]Because most of these women would not expect to be childless, they would make the same education choices as other women. They would also be subject, on average, to the same discrimination in education as other women. Earlier in this century, when unmarried women were less likely to bear children than they are today, many firms had so-called *marriage bars;* they refused to hire married women and they fired single women who married.

IN THE NEWS

Blacks found lagging despite gains

By Julie Johnson
Special to The New York Times

WASHINGTON, July 27— Although blacks have made important economic and social gains over the last five decades, they still lag significantly behind whites, a new study concludes, to the point that a "great gulf" separates the two races.

"If all racial discrimina- tion were abolished today, the life prospects facing many poor blacks would still constitute major challenges for public policy," said the report by the council, an arm of the National Academy of Sciences and Engineering.

"We have really two major findings one positive, the other negative: by any calibration other than that of an unrepentant segregationist, race relations and blacks' status are remarkably improved since the World War II era," said Mr. Jaynes, who is also a scholar in Yale's African and African-American studies department. "However the major fraction of this improvement was in place by 1970. Since then, material measures of status relative to whites have not improved and many have deteriorated."

Experts disagree on the causes of the continuing gap in the average wages and incomes of white Americans and African Americans.

Source: Julie Johnson, "Blacks Found Lagging Despite Gains," *New York Times,* July 28, 1989.

capital due to discrimination are likely to have children with below-average levels of human capital.

A TYPICAL DISCRIMINATION STUDY

A typical discrimination study uses statistical techniques to explain differences in the wages of women and men, or blacks and whites, by differences in their education, experience, and other economically relevant characteristics. The typical study then attributes all unexplained differences to discrimination. It is easy to see a potential problem with this technique. Imagine a study that tries to explain individual intelligence with measures of a person's environment and then attributes any unexplained differences in intelligence to genetics. This study would overstate the role of genetics because it would fail to measure some differences in environment. Studies of discrimination may overstate its effect on wages for the same reason: factors that such studies do not include or properly measure may explain part of the differences in wages.[32] On the other hand, the usual studies understate the effect of discrimination on wages to the extent that lower education and experience levels result from past discrimination.

EQUILIBRIUM WITH DISCRIMINATION

A person who discriminates pays a price; as a result, prejudiced people do not always discriminate. Consider a business owner who is prejudiced against blacks and women. This person wants both high profits and to hire only white males. If only a few business firms were to discriminate against blacks and women, then in equilibrium blacks and women would work at other firms that did not discrimi-

---

[32]For example, the fact that men die seven years earlier than women, on average, does not indicate that doctors discriminate against men. Instead, other (currently unknown) differences in men and women (possibly environmental as well as genetic) presumably explain this difference in life expectancy.

nate and the discrimination would not affect their wages. If, however, many firms were to discriminate against blacks and women, then discrimination would reduce the demand for labor by blacks and women, lowering their equilibrium wages. In this equilibrium, white men would earn higher wages than equally skilled women and blacks. Each firm that discriminated by hiring white males would pay for this discrimination by sacrificing the higher profits it could earn by hiring lower-wage women and blacks with equally good skills. (Unless its customers were prejudiced, the firm could not raise its price to cover its higher costs. Even prejudiced customers may not be willing to pay higher prices to buy from a firm that employed only white males.) In this situation, the least prejudiced firms might choose not to discriminate in hiring decisions because they would not be willing to pay this price.

Now suppose that prejudiced customers want to buy from a firm that does not employ blacks. Customers seldom know whether blacks or whites, or men or women, produce the goods that they buy. However, for some goods and most services (such as haircuts), buyers have direct contact with workers. Because blacks earn lower average wages than whites, firms that employ only whites have higher marginal costs, so buyers must pay higher prices to buy from these firms. The higher product prices represent a cost of discrimination to buyers.[33]

The fact that discrimination has a price explains why laws have often *forced* people to discriminate. In the 19th century, public transportation was not racially segregated in southern U.S. cities (including Montgomery, Alabama, the site of Rev. Martin Luther King's famous boycott). Laws requiring segregation in these cities were passed around 1900.[34] Many streetcar companies, which had voluntarily segregated smokers and nonsmokers into different parts of their streetcars, opposed laws requiring segregation by race because discrimination had a price and racial segregation reduced their profits.

Many countries have had laws requiring discrimination. South African mining companies opposed laws requiring them to hire white workers rather than black workers, because white workers cost more.[35] Businesses in South Africa often tried to evade the laws that limited hiring of blacks, not necessarily because the business owners wanted to be fair to blacks, but because discrimination forced them to pay the cost of higher wages.[36] Similarly, immigration laws in many countries arose from attempts to prevent foreigners from competing for jobs by offering to work at lower wages; immigration laws force employers to discriminate against foreigners by not allowing them to work in the country. Even a firm that is prejudiced against foreigners has an incentive to hire them if they will work for lower wages. White neighborhoods that want to exclude blacks can often do so only with regulations, because even a prejudiced homeowner who wants to sell a house is unlikely to refuse a good offer from a black buyer.[37]

---

[33]Baseball cards of nonwhite players sell for about 10 percent less in used-card markets than cards of white players with comparable accomplishments, suggesting customer discrimination. In his 1987 *Bill James Baseball Abstract* (New York: Villard, 1987), pp. 68–71, Bill James also finds evidence of discrimination against blacks.

[34]See Thomas Sowell, *Preferential Policies* (New York: William Morrow & Co, 1991).

[35]After the Rand Rebellion, the new government subsidized the mining companies by enacting tariffs to protect them from foreign competition. This helped to offset the higher cost of white labor.

[36]Some of the strongest proponents of these laws were white workers with few skills who relied mainly on being white to find employment.

[37]Blacks were able to buy land after the Civil War despite organized attempts of whites to prevent the sales. The price of discrimination was too high to stop the land sales.

REMEDIES FOR DISCRIMINATION IN THE UNITED STATES

Before the Equal Pay Act of 1963, many U.S. states' laws limited the job opportunities of women, their hours of work, and work during pregnancy. The federal Equal Pay Act overturned these laws. The following year, Congress passed the Civil Rights Act of 1964, which outlawed many forms of discrimination (such as discrimination in hiring and promotions) based on "race, color, religion, sex, or national origin." The law also established the Equal Employment Opportunities Commission. When firms claim to be "equal-opportunity employers" they are complying with this law.

In 1965, the U.S. federal government began requiring firms with large government contracts to take "affirmative action" to employ more women and minorities, or to risk losing their government contracts.[38] The government expanded the requirements for affirmative action (actions to redress imbalances in employment, whether due to discrimination or other causes) in the 1970s. Affirmative action plans usually required firms to prove that they were taking actions to employ more women and minorities, particularly in cases where they employed fewer than seemed appropriate to the government or to courts.

Opponents of affirmative action claim that it creates reverse discrimination against white males or other people not in the favored groups. They also claim that affirmative action makes firms guilty until proven innocent and that some firms employ fewer minorities by chance (while others employ more), and that such chance events do not imply discrimination against women or minorities. Finally, opponents argue that affirmative action weakens incentives because people in the favored group have less incentive to acquire skills if the affirmative-action policy can guarantee a job, while people in the disfavored group have less incentive to acquire skills if they believe that affirmative action reduces the value of those skills. Affirmative action, according to its critics, is unfair and economically inefficient.[39]

Proponents of affirmative action argue that discrimination is usually (even if not always) the cause of large differences in employment, promotions, and wages of different groups. They also argue that even a firm that is not guilty of discrimination should be required to try to remedy the past discrimination of others by making efforts to hire more women and minorities. They argue that affirmative action promotes diversity, mixing people from different groups, and that this diversity and mixing has (in the language of Chapter 20) a positive externality; it creates benefits for society as a whole by raising tolerance of differences, creating the habit of associating with members of other groups, and reducing social and economic barriers. Affirmative action and other proposed remedies for discrimination remain nearly as controversial in public discussions as discrimination itself.

--- FOR REVIEW ---

18.8 How large are black/white and male/female wage differentials? What reasons other than current employer discrimination may create these wage differentials?

---

[38]The term comes from an executive order by President Kennedy requiring equal treatment of all job applicants, "without regard to race, creed, color, or national origin." The meaning of the term is now different, since it requires employers to pay specific attention to those characteristics and try to hire and promote people from under-represented groups.

[39]In Malaysia, the government has required universities to adjust grades to achieve "ethnic balance." See Gordon P. Means, "Ethnic Preference Policies in Malaysia," in Neil Nevitte and Charles H. Kennedy, eds., *Ethnic Preference and Public Policy in Developing States* (Boulder: Lynne Reinner, 1986), p. 108.

18.9 Describe a typical study of discrimination and discuss its limitations.

18.10 What is statistical discrimination? Why might it reduce the wages of women relative to wages of men?

––––––––––––––––––––––– QUESTIONS –––––––––––––––––––––––

18.11 How would a decrease in discrimination affect the equilibrium price of discrimination?

18.12 Suppose that many firms discriminate against hiring blacks. What happens if one firm in a perfectly competitive industry decides not to discriminate?

CONCLUSIONS

DISTRIBUTION OF INCOME IN THE UNITED STATES

The term *distribution of income* refers to comparisons of incomes across people or families. The median income in the United States has doubled since the middle of the 20th century. Households in the top fifth of the income distribution get almost one-half of all of the nation's income, and households in the bottom fifth get about 5 percent. Family income inequality has stayed about the same in the last half-century, partly because of government programs. The average income of people in the bottom fifth of the income distribution fell in the last two decades as the difference between the wages of skilled and unskilled workers rose.

Poverty in the United States occurs mainly among blacks, Hispanics, women, and children. There is, however, some degree of economic mobility in the United States. A family in the bottom fifth of the income distribution has a one-half chance of moving out of that bottom fifth within seven years. While 10 percent to 15 percent of the population live in households with incomes below the poverty line, about 2 percent remain below the poverty line for many years. A Lorenz curve represents income inequality on a graph; a Gini coefficient summarizes it in a single number.

Average hourly wages in the United States have fallen in the last two decades, but total labor income has increased because more people are employed. Economists have not found a complete explanation for this fall in wages.

Wealth is distributed much less equally than income. In the United States, the richest 2 percent of the population own about one-fourth of all household assets, and the richest 25 percent own about three-fourths. Black families have, on average, about one-tenth as much household assets as white families. Despite these inequalities, the distribution of wealth has gradually become more equal throughout the 20th century.

DISTRIBUTION OF INCOME IN THE WORLD

The distribution of income in the world is more unequal than in the United States. About one-fifth of the world's people—1 billion people—live in absolute poverty, with incomes of less than $525 per person per year. The official U.S. poverty level is about 7 times higher than this absolute poverty income. If all the income in the world were distributed equally with no effect on the total, each person would have an income about twice the U.S. poverty level and about 10 times the absolute poverty level. World poverty declined through most of the 19th and 20th centuries, and it has declined further in the last several decades.

Wars and government policies are major reasons for absolute poverty in the modern world.

EVALUATING POVERTY AND WEALTH

Luck, effort, and other factors are among the many reasons why some people are poor while others are rich. Opinions about what is fair, just or equitable differ, though questions of fairness and justice arise whenever people make judgements about government economic policies. Egalitarianism is the view that every person's wealth (or some measure of happiness) should be equal. Utilitarianism is the view that government policies should maximize total happiness, regardless of its distribution. Another view holds that justice applies only to rules, and rules are just if people would choose them in a fictional original position, behind a veil of ignorance. Still another view holds that people have natural rights that government policies should not violate. Good arguments can be made for and against each of these views.

GOVERNMENT ANTIPOVERTY PROGRAMS

Governments have developed many programs designed to reduce poverty; policy analysts disagree about their effects and desirable changes in policies. Some disagreements occur because people disagree about justice and fairness; other disagreements occur because evidence about the effects of various government policies remains inconclusive. Economists agree that some government policies have disastrous effects and contribute to the plight of the 1 billion people living in absolute poverty.

DISCRIMINATION

One reason for income inequality has been discrimination against minorities and women. Discrimination in the labor market affects wages, creating an equilibrium price of discrimination. This price takes the form of lower profits for firms that discriminate. About half of male/female and black/white wage differences can be explained by measured differences in education and experience (though differences in education and experience may themselves reflect results of past discrimination). The remainder of the wage differences may result from current discrimination in labor markets, from other unmeasured factors such as quality of education, or from statistical discrimination.

LOOKING AHEAD

People differ not only in incomes and job opportunities, but also in the information on which they base economic decisions. Chapter 19 discusses the economics of situations in which some people have more information than others about product prices or about how healthy they are or how hard they work.

KEY TERMS

income

wealth

median income

mean income

money income

family

household

Lorenz curve

Gini coefficient

purchasing power parity method

egalitarianism

utilitarianism

statistical discrimination

QUESTIONS AND PROBLEMS

18.13 How has average household income changed in the last quarter-century?

    a. About how large is the difference in average nonhuman wealth (measured by household assets) between white families and black or Hispanic families?

    b. Roughly how many people in the world live below the United Nations' absolute poverty line?

    c. On average, is there more or less poverty in richer countries? More or less income inequality?

18.14 Define *egalitarianism,* then argue (a) for it, and (b) against it.

18.15 Define *utilitarianism,* then argue (a) for it, and (b) against it.

18.16 Explain the view that justice is an implicit contract, then argue (a) for it, and (b) against it.

18.17 Would a fall in discrimination against hiring women raise the wages that women earn or reduce the wages that men earn, or both? Explain, using supply and demand analysis.

18.18 Who gains from laws that require firms to discriminate in their hiring? Explain why.

INQUIRIES FOR FURTHER THOUGHT

18.19 A song from the 1960s said, "What the world needs now is love, sweet love. It's the only thing that there's just too little of." A commentator recently said, "That song is wrong. Many people lack food to eat, basic health care, and any opportunity or hope for the future." Discuss these two claims.

18.20 Are some people richer than others mainly because of luck or because they work harder? How would you find data to support your claim?

18.21 Comment on this statement: "Income differences are all due to luck; even differences in effort are due to luck, because some people are lucky enough to have the motivation to educate themselves and work hard."

18.22 Is the distribution of income in the market system equitable or inequitable, moral or immoral? What could be done about it? What should be done? What would be the costs?

18.23 Should uglier people get to pay lower taxes as compensation for being uglier? Should handicapped people get similar benefits? People with less physical ability than others? People with less mental ability?

18.24 Would people rather live (a) in a society that offers many opportunities, but also much risk (so that one could end up rich, but at the risk of ending up poor) or (b) in a society with the same average income, but no chance of being either rich or poor?

18.25 Discuss alternative concepts of justice. What, in your opinion, is justice?

18.26 Comment on the implications for justice of the following statements. In each case, what would be the effects of a government policy to implement this view of justice?

    a. The government should distribute income equally.

    b. People who work harder should have higher incomes.

    c. People who need higher incomes for medical expenses should have higher incomes.

    d. People who have larger families to support should have higher incomes.

    e. Everyone should be made equally happy.

    f. From each according to her abilities, to each according to her needs.

    g. More virtuous people should get more income.

18.27 What government policies and laws would you choose behind the veil of ignorance?

18.28 Does a rich person have a moral obligation to give money to poor people? How much money?

18.29 Does a rich country have a moral obligation to give money to poor countries? How much money?

18.30 Discuss these statements and questions:

    a. It is unjust not to help a poor person, even if you did not cause his poverty.

    b. It is unjust not to help a person who is injured, even if you did not cause the injury.

    c. If justice requires people to help in either (a) or (b), how much help does it require? Should failing to help in either case be illegal?

    d. Is it important to distinguish between harming a person and failing to help her?

18.31 A utilitarian argues that people get less happiness from watching sports events than the poor people could get if the money were used instead to buy food, housing, and medical care for them. The utilitarian convinces the government to outlaw sports events. Discuss whether this is just or unjust, and why.

18.32 Should the government redistribute income to increase equality? To what extent should it redistribute income? How much should it take from whom and how much should it give to whom?

18.33 Is it just for the U.S. government to redistribute wealth from rich Americans to poor Americans if most of the poor Americans are already richer than 1 billion other people in the world? Should redistribution include only people who live in the United States or everyone in the world? Why?

18.34 Is it fair to take wealth away from people who are wealthier because they worked harder? Would (or does) this affect how hard people work?

18.35 Should sports and entertainment figures be permitted to make as much money as they do? What would happen if the government were to limit their incomes?

18.36 Argue for a negative income tax to replace existing welfare programs. Argue against it.

18.37 Evaluate the claim that government welfare programs perpetuate dependence and poverty. Comment on this summary of government welfare programs since the late 1960s: "We tried to provide more for the poor and produced more poor instead."[40]

---

[40]Charles Murray, *Losing Ground* (New York: Basic Books, 1984), p. 9.

18.38 The fifth amendment to the U.S. Constitution requires the government to pay just compensation when it takes a person's property. Does the government violate this requirement when it taxes people?

18.39 Should people with higher incomes pay higher percentages of their incomes in taxes?

18.40 Should the government replace an income tax with a tax on wealth? What would be the effects?

18.41 Should the government tax inheritances? How much? What would be the effects of a 100 percent tax on inheritances? Would a smaller tax be better for any reason? What should determine the size of this tax?

18.42 Should wealthy countries forgive the foreign debts of poor countries? If private lenders have loaned the money, should governments compensate those lenders? What would be the effects on poverty? Why don't the poor countries just refuse to pay?

18.43 Argue both sides of the following issue:

> The government should compensate people who are members of groups that were victims of discrimination or slavery in the past, such as African Americans, Native Americans, and Japanese Americans (for internment during World War II). Even though many of the actual victims are dead, their children, grandchildren, and great-grandchildren suffer because of that past discrimination; they live in poorer families, get poorer educations, have fewer opportunities and less stable families, and face poorer prospects for their children. The effects of discrimination do not die with the victims. While compensation cannot undo the effects of past discrimination, it can and should help remedy the lingering effects.

18.44 Discuss: "[E]conomic studies have consistently shown that rising female wages encourage work and inhibit fertility, and that, more directly, marriages where women earn more are likely to dissolve. . . . As a result, one price of the very labor market success women have enjoyed may well be a less stable American family."[41]

18.45 A disproportionately large number of National Merit Scholarship finalists and people listed in *Who's Who* are first-born children.
   a. Does this suggest discrimination against nonfirst-born children? Discuss alternative explanations. (Note: This result is not likely to be due to chance.)
   b. Should the government adopt policies to help nonfirst-born children, perhaps taxing them at a lower rate later in life?

18.46 Should discrimination on the basis of race or sex be illegal? What would be the effects?

18.47 Women live about seven years longer than men, on average. Suppose that a firm has a pension program for its workers. It pays the same amount of money into the pension program for every worker, male or female. If a man and a woman both work at the firm for the same number of years, the firm has saved the same amount of money in the pension program for each of them.
   a. Suppose that the firm gives each worker all of the pension money that it saves for the worker over the years on the day the worker retires.

---

[41]Smith and Ward, "Women in the Labor Market and in the Family," p. 22.

IN THE NEWS

Proposals for equal insurance fees for men and women spark battle

Insurance companies, almost unanimously, say that the two sexes should pay different rates because their claims patterns are different. "It's a basic issue of fairness," says Sean Mooney, a senior vice president and economist with the Insurance Information Institute, a trade group. "The price should reflect the risks involved. If I'm a maker of fireworks I should pay more for insurance than a garment maker does."

Charges of Discrimination

Logical as all that seems to insurers, the current system is blatant sex discrimination in the eyes of many people. Says a spokeswoman for the National Organization for Women: "There's no compelling reason to divide the human race in that fashion."

Unisex insurance pricing is controversial wherever the issue is raised. Indeed, beset by complaints—many from parents whose daughters' auto-insurance rates had soared—Montana lawmakers voted this year to repeal the law. But Democratic Gov. Ted Schwinden vetoed their action, and an override attempt failed by a few votes.

Source: "Proposals for Equal Insurance Fees for Men and Women Spark Battle," *The Wall Street Journal,* August 27, 1987.

Since women live longer on average, the same amount of money at retirement means that women have less money to spend per year (on average) after retirement. Is this fair? Is this discrimination?

b. Suppose that the firm does not give the worker all of the pension money on the day the worker retires. Instead, the firm pays the worker a certain amount of money each month. Since women live longer than men on average, the firm pays women retirees less per month than men. Is this fair? Is it discrimination?[42]

c. Suppose the firm gives workers monthly payments, but it gives male and female retirees the same monthly pensions. To do this, the firm must save more money in the pension fund for each female employee than for each male employee, so the firm finds male employees are cheaper if it pays equal wages. As a result, it wants either to hire men instead of women, or pay women less than men. Would this be fair? Would it be discrimination?

18.48 When a firm must pay more to provide life insurance to men than to women (because men will die sooner, on average), or when men must pay more for auto insurance than women (because men—particularly young men—drive more recklessly, on average), is it discrimination to charge different prices to men and women for insurance?[43] Is it fair?

18.49 Discuss the issue of discrimination raised in the news item about the auto dealer's "Christian Plan." Should this be legal or illegal? What would be the economic effects of either decision?

---

[42]The U.S. Supreme Court ruled that this is illegal discrimination under U.S. law.

[43]At most ages, a woman has a 40 percent lower chance of dying within a year than a man does.

IN THE NEWS

Auto dealer's 'Christian plan' is called bias

Special to The New York Times

FAIRFAX, Va., May 26—One night last August the letters C, M, B and P popped into Freddy (Action) Jackson's head. Business at his car dealership has never been the same since.

The next morning, he said, he had it: "Christian Members Buying Plan." Christians would buy cars at bargain prices and a percent-age of his profit would go to their church.

The American Civil Liberties Union and the Anti-Defamation League of B'nai B'rith say Brown Lincoln-Mercury discriminates against non-Christians.

A lawyer for the A.C.L.U., Victor Glasberg, told the Federal Trade Commission this month that the policy violated equal-opportunity credit laws.

Three years ago, the Anti-Defamation League was involved in a similar dispute in Pensacola, Fla., where Jerry Harrison, an Exxon station owner, had put up a sign reading, "For Christians Only: 10 percent discount on labor."

"We are sick and tired of Christians and Christian values being expunged from every area of public life," he said. "This isn't separation of church and state; this is a private merchant."

Source: "Auto Dealer's `Christian Plan' Is Called Bias," New York Times, May 27, 1990.

18.50 Do you think that a country sacrifices long-run economic growth if it adopts policies to reduce inequality? Why or why not? How would you measure the effects of such policies on long-run economic growth?

TAG SOFTWARE APPLICATIONS

TUTORIAL EXERCISES
▶ The module contains a review of the key terms from Chapter 18.

GRAPHING EXERCISES
▶ The graphing segment examines the Lorenz curve.

ADVANCED TOPICS IN MICROECONOMICS

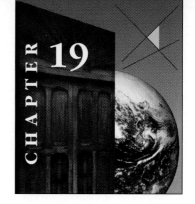

CHAPTER 19

ECONOMICS OF INFORMATION

WHAT THIS CHAPTER IS ABOUT

▶ The economic effects of imperfect information and situations in which some people have information advantages

▶ Why prices differ between stores

▶ Why tourists pay higher prices than local residents

▶ Why stores put products on sale at reduced prices

▶ Why low-quality products can drive out high-quality products (why the quality level of the average used car bought and sold is lower than that of the average used car)

▶ Why some products have guarantees and others don't, and why guarantees don't cover everything

▶ Why interest rates on credit cards are so high

Our time has been called the *information age.* Technical advances have made information easier to obtain, transfer, manipulate, and utilize than ever before. Firms spend billions of dollars obtaining and processing information. Consumers are increasingly bombarded with information from the media, the government, and the labels on products they buy. Yet useful information often remains costly to obtain, difficult to understand, and hard to remember. Information is not always accurate, and this accuracy can be difficult or costly to verify. The facts that information is limited and imperfect, and that some people may have better information than others and attempt to exploit their information advantages, have economic consequences.

EXPECTATIONS ABOUT THE FUTURE

expected value — an average of numbers weighted by the probabilities (chances) that they will occur

EXPECTED VALUES

People often guess at numbers they don't know, such as the score of tomorrow's ball game or their incomes after ten years. Under certain conditions, a rational guess is the expected value.[1]

> An **expected value** is an average of the sum of every possible number, weighted by the probabilities (chances) that they will occur.

---

[1]The expected value is also called the *mean* of a distribution of numbers.

We calculate an expected value in three steps:

1. List the number (e.g., the score or the income) in each possible situation.
2. Multiply each number by its probability or chance of occurring.
3. Add the results from Step 2.

EXAMPLES

1. Consider the expected number of points that a team will score in the last 20 seconds of a basketball game. If the team has a one-third chance of scoring 0 points, a one-third chance of scoring 2 points, and a one-third chance of scoring 4 points, the expected value of the score (or expected score) is:

$$(1/3)(0) + (1/3)(2) + (1/3)(4) = 2 \text{ points}$$

2. Suppose you have a 9/10 chance of earning $50,000 per year ten years from now and a 1/10 chance of earning $300,000. Then your expected salary is:

$$(9/10)(\$50,000) + (1/10)(\$300,000) = \$75,000$$

LIMITED INFORMATION ABOUT PRICES

With perfect competition, firms are price takers. If one firm raises its price above the equilibrium price, it loses *all* of its customers. In many markets, however, buyers have limited information. When a store raises its price, many buyers may not realize that the product is cheaper elsewhere, so it may lose only some of its customers. When a store reduces its price, many people may continue to buy from higher-priced competitors because they have not learned about the price cut. Firms face downward-sloping demand curves when buyers have limited information about prices.

SEARCH COSTS

A buyer with limited information may search for the best price. This search for a lower price or better product has costs (of travel, phone calls, and so on).

search cost — the time and money cost of obtaining information about a price or a product

> **Search costs** are the time and money costs of obtaining information about prices and products.

The optimal amount of search occurs when the expected marginal benefit of searching (the expected benefit from trying one more store) equals its expected marginal cost.[2]

EXAMPLE

Suppose that four stores sell a product that a buyer wants. The average price is $40, but some stores charge more and others charge less. **Table 19.1** shows that two stores charge $40, one store charges $35, and one store charges $45.

The buyer is willing to pay up to $50 for the product, and knows that one store charges $35, two stores charge $40, and one store charges $45, but does not know which store is which. Choosing a store at random, the buyer has a one-

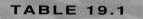

TABLE 19.1

A SEARCH EXAMPLE

Number of Stores	Price
1	$35
2	40
1	45

---

[2]This statement abstracts from risk; it applies strictly to consumers who are risk-neutral. A later section discusses risk neutrality.

fourth chance of choosing the low-price store and buying the product for $35. The buyer also has a one-fourth chance of choosing the high-price ($45) store and a one-half chance of choosing a store that charges $40. If the first store charges $40 or $45, the buyer must decide whether to go to another store to look for a lower price.

Suppose that the first store charges $40, and the buyer decides to go to one, and only one, other store. This person has a one-third chance of visiting a store that charges $35 and a one-third chance of visiting a store that charges $40; in either case, the buyer would buy the product. There is also a one-third chance that the second store will charge $45, in which case the buyer would return to the original store and pay $40.[3] In summary, if the first store charges $40, a buyer who tries one more store has a one-third chance of saving $5 and a two-thirds chance of not saving any money. The expected marginal benefit of search at the second store is:

$$(1/3)(\$5) + (2/3)(\$0) = \text{about } \$1.67$$

If this expected marginal benefit exceeds the expected marginal cost of going to the second store, then the buyer expects to gain from searching. If not, it is then rational to stop searching.

Similarly, if the first store charges $45, the buyer must compare the expected marginal benefit of searching with its expected marginal cost. If this person visits one more store, there is a two-thirds chance that it will charge $40 and a one-third chance that it will charge $35. The expected marginal benefit from search is:

$$(2/3)(\$5) + (1/3)(\$10) = \text{about } \$6.67$$

If this exceeds the expected marginal cost of the search, the buyer gains by trying another store; if not, it is rational to stop.

In most situations, people do not know how many stores charge which prices. They must learn from experience and from other sources, such as advertising and talking with friends, about the expected benefits of searching.

Price Differences between Stores

Some buyers know more about prices than others. Tourists, for example, usually have less information than local residents about which stores charge high prices. For that reason, tourists are more likely to buy products at high-priced stores.

When some customers have better information than others, a distribution of prices can exist in equilibrium.

distribution of prices — a situation in which some sellers charge higher prices than others

A **distribution of prices** means that some sellers charge higher prices than others.

Informed consumers go to low-price stores. Some uninformed consumers go to the low-price stores by chance, but others buy from high-price stores because they don't know that other stores offer lower prices.

When most consumers are well-informed, all stores charge low prices (equal to marginal cost, as in perfect competition). Any store that tried to charge a higher

---

[3]In this example, the buyer could also try a third store at random. That third store would charge either $35 or $40, so the buyer could do *at least as well* as going back to the original store. To keep the discussion from becoming too complex, we ignore this possibility (which seldom arises in real life because buyers usually face many more than four possible stores).

price would lose enough customers to make it unprofitable. For this reason, when most consumers are well-informed, the perfect competition model applies. When many consumers are poorly informed and have high search costs, however, they can face a distribution of prices in equilibrium. Some stores have an incentive to charge high prices while others charge low prices. The high-price stores sell less, but earn higher profits on each item sold; the lower-price stores earn less per item, but sell more.

Some firms sell a single good under different brand names at different prices. Some firms operate more than one store (perhaps one at each of several shopping malls), and charge more for a single good at some stores than at others. Informed consumers buy the cheaper brand or go to the low-price store. Many uninformed consumers buy the high-price brand or buy from the high-price store, so the firm earns a higher profit on sales to them. These are methods by which firms price-discriminate (see Chapter 13) by charging higher prices to some, less-informed buyers.

BETTER INFORMATION REDUCES PRICES

As consumers get better information about prices, they pay lower average prices. With better information, more buyers go to low-price stores and fewer to high-price stores, which gives high-price stores incentives to reduce their prices. Better information can reduce prices even if all consumers are equally well-informed because the information improves their guesses about which stores charge lower prices.

EXAMPLE   Two stores, Prescott's and Summers', sell the same game, but Prescott's charges $20 and Summers' charges $21. Suppose that all consumers are uninformed; half think that Prescott's charges $19 and the other half think that Prescott's charges $21. Half think that Summers' charges $20 and half think that Summers' charges $22. One-fourth of all consumers think that Prescott's charges $21 *and* Summers' charges $20, so they buy the game from Summers'. The other three-fourths buy from Prescott's.

Suppose that consumers become better informed and everyone's guess gets closer to the actual price. Now half of all consumers think that Prescott's charges $19.75, and half think that it charges $20.25. Half think that Summers' charges $20.75, and half think that it charges $21.25. In this case, all consumers would buy from Prescott's. Consumers have become better informed, and they pay a lower average price even though neither store changed its price.[4]

SEARCHING FOR A GOOD MATCH

Products as well as prices differ between stores. Buyers search not only for the best price, but also for the type of product they want. Some people prefer a record store with a good selection of rock music; others look for a good selection of vintage jazz. This kind of search is often more costly than searching for the lowest price, which may take only a phone call.

EXAMPLES

Search is important in labor markets. People want jobs with good wages, but they also search for jobs that suit them best—they search for the best match between

---

[4]Of course, Summers' would have an incentive to reduce its price in this situation, but this does not change the conclusion about better information.

jobs and workers. Firms also search for workers who match their needs well. Similarly, people search for good matches when they look for husbands or wives. Romantic notions aside, some people get married not because they have found the perfect match, but because they have found a satisfactory match and the costs (especially the time costs) of continuing the search are not worth the expected benefits. Even though they might find someone who matches them better if they were to search more, the chance is small so the expected marginal benefit from search is less than its cost, and they stop searching. (In these cases, divorce may result from the additional information that comes free with everyday life.)

APPLICATIONS OF SEARCH THEORY

Many aspects of life involve imperfect information and search. A fair number of college students don't know whether they want to major in economics, physics, history, engineering, or some other field of study. Most students take classes in various disciplines, partly to learn which disciplines they find most interesting. The cost of search involves time (the opportunity cost of taking other classes or working) and direct payments of money (tuition). The benefit involves a better match between a student's interests and that student's ultimate field of concentration and career.

Adults have noted that younger generations often "revolt" against their lifestyles, experimenting with new or different lifestyles. Perhaps this tendency to revolt (which has been noted throughout history) involves rational searching for the lifestyle that best matches each person's interests. Young people may sample alternative lifestyles not becaue they dislike their parents' lifestyles but because they are searching to see if any alternative better matches their values and interests. Many people already have some information about how well their parents' lifestyles might satisfy their desires for fulfillment in life. By experimenting with alternative lifestyles, they learn how well those alternatives satisfy their desires. People search and experiment more when they are young than when they are older because the benefits of the information are larger for younger people (who have more years left to live their lives and make use of that information).

FIRMS HAVE LIMITED INFORMATION ABOUT DEMAND

Firms have limited information about the prices that buyers are willing to pay, so they must learn in some way about the demand curves they face. They may learn by trial and error, charging different prices at different times. Putting a product on sale can help a firm learn about the demand curve because it can observe how much consumers buy at the lower price. A firm with limited information about demand often profits by charging a high price at first, then reducing the price over time and putting the good on sale if it does not sell well enough. (Some retail stores carry nothing but goods that have previously sold at higher prices elsewhere.) The firm benefits from this pricing strategy because it charges more to buyers who are willing to pay more. The strategy has two costs. First, some consumers would pay the high price if necessary, but expect the price to fall and postpone buying until the firm reduces the price. Also, the firm sells goods more slowly than it would with a low initial price, so it has higher inventory costs.

EXPLANATION

Suppose that all buyers are the same; each is willing to pay (at most) P dollars for one unit of the good, and no buyer wants more than one unit. Sellers, though, do

PERSONAL DECISION MAKING

Some Information that Sellers Try to Hide

Sometimes stores don't sell designer clothes after a normal period of time. If they were simply to cut the prices, consumers would realize that they could eventually buy the clothes at still lower prices. To prevent consumers from learning this, and to keep less-informed consumers more willing to pay the high initial prices, stores cut off designers' labels.

Informed consumers may know this, and some can even determine who made a product because federal law requires labels to carry *RN* or *WPL* numbers that identify manufacturers. (You can find out which companies have which numbers by consulting a directory in your local library.) Less-informed consumers pay higher prices.

not know P; they know only that P is between $10 and $20. Suppose that a seller's best guess of P (its expected value) is $15; if the seller charges $15, there is a one-half chance that people will buy the good.

The seller could charge less than $15 to raise the chance of selling the good, but would sacrifice profit if people were actually willing to pay more. To avoid this, a seller might initially charge $19 or $20, then reduce the price slowly over time if people did not buy the good. This method may allow the seller to charge people the highest price that they are willing to pay. Of course, if buyers believe that the seller will reduce the price further, they may wait for lower prices before buying. The seller cannot then sell at the highest price that buyers are willing to pay. If buyers differ in the prices they are willing to pay, some might pay a higher price to buy the good now rather than waiting for a lower price.

FOR REVIEW

19.1 Give an example of an expected value.

19.2 What is a distribution of prices? Why can a distribution of prices exist in equilibrium?

19.3 Why do firms charge high prices for new products, then later put them on sale at reduced prices?

19.4 Why do tourists often pay more than local residents for the same good?

QUESTIONS

19.5 Calculate expected values in two situations:

   a. You bought a raffle ticket. The chance is 999/1,000 that your ticket will not win anything, and 1/1,000 that it will win a stereo system valued at $500. What is the expected benefit from your raffle ticket?

   b. There is a one-half chance that you will lose $100 on an investment, a one-quarter chance that you will break even (your profit will be zero), and a one-quarter chance that your profit will be $400. What is the expected profit on your investment?

19.6 You are shopping for a television set and you learn the price at a local store. You could visit other stores, with a 1/10 chance that the next store you visit will charge $25 less for the same television set, and a 9/10 chance it will charge the same price as the current store. What is your expected benefit from visiting the other store to check the price?

RISK

Some situations, investments, businesses, and jobs are riskier than others. Economists have developed a complicated mathematical theory of risk and economic equilibrium in risky situations, but the basic ideas do not require complicated mathematics. Most people have a general idea of which situations are riskier than others.[5]

Consider the following investments; which are riskier, those in Column A or those in Column B?

A	B
1. Certainty of no gain and no loss	One-half chance of gaining $10 and one-half chance of losing $10
2. One-half chance of gaining $10 and one-half chance of losing $5	One-half chance of gaining $1,000 and one-half chance of losing $500
3. Buying fire insurance	Buying no fire insurance
4. 999/1,000 chance of losing $100, and 1/1,000 chance of losing zero	999/1,000 chance of losing zero, and 1/1,000 chance of losing $99,900

Most people would say that in every case, Column B is riskier. In Case 1, the expected gain is zero for both columns, but Column A involves no risk while B involves risk. In Case 2, the expected gains are $2.50 in Column A and $250 in Column B, but B involves more risk; you could win more, but you could also lose more. Cases 3 and 4 are similar. If you have a house worth $99,900 that has a 1/1,000 chance of burning down, and fire insurance costs $100, whether or not you buy fire insurance, your expected loss is $99.90. Insurance reduces your risk, however, by paying you if something bad happens.

DIVERSIFICATION

An old adage, "Don't put all your eggs in one basket," is usually the best investment advice you can get. People can reduce the risks of their investments by diversifying.

diversification — spreading risks across many different, unrelated investments

Diversification refers to spreading risks across many different, unrelated investments.

The following example shows the benefits of diversification.

EXAMPLE

Beth has $100 to invest and can buy stock in either of two companies: the Romer Corporation or the Solow Corporation. Romer is on the verge of inventing a new medical-research technology that may replace one sold by Solow. The new technology has a flaw, however, and Romer has a one-half chance of correcting the flaw. A share of stock in either company sells for $50, so Beth can buy 2 shares. She must decide whether to buy 2 shares of Romer and no Solow, 2 shares of Solow and no Romer, or 1 share of each.

---

[5]Some more complicated situations require a careful definition of risk.

PERSONAL DECISION MAKING

Diversifying Risks

The key to diversifying risks is to choose investments whose returns move in opposite directions. An investor is better diversified if some of that person's investments provide high returns in those situations where her other investments provide low returns. This protects the investor, rather like insurance, because at least some of her investments are likely to do well. With some doing well, it matters less if others do poorly.

The example in the preceding section is a special case. The two investments (Romer and Solow stock) move in opposite directions perfectly consistently. Few real-life investments move so perfectly in opposite directions, but optimal diversification requires choosing investments to approximate this kind of situation. In the stock market, an investor gains by choosing stocks that perform out of step. Some should provide their highest returns at times when others provide low returns, and vice versa.

A homeowner with a variable-rate mortgage must make higher payments when interest rates rise and can make lower payments when interest rates fall. That homeowner can diversify by choosing investments that pay higher returns when interest rates rise and lower returns when interest rates fall. If interest rates rise, the higher returns on the investments help with the higher mortgage payments; if interest rates fall, the investments pay less, but the mortgage payments are also lower.

Similarly, a person with a risky job can partly diversify the income risk from that job by choosing investments that are likely to have their highest returns when income from the job will turn out to be low.

If Romer corrects the technical flaw, the price of Romer stock will rise to $80 and the price of Solow stock will fall to $30. In this case, Beth will gain $30 on each share of Romer stock and lose $20 on each share of Solow stock. If the flaw remains uncorrected, the price of Romer stock will fall to $30 and the price of Solow stock will rise to $80. In that case, Beth will lose $20 on each share of Romer stock and gain $30 on each share of Solow stock.

If she buys either 2 shares of Romer stock or 2 shares of Solow stock, Beth has a one-half chance of gaining $60 and a one-half chance of losing $40. Her expected profit is $10:

$$(1/2)(\$60) + (1/2)(-\$40) = \$30 - \$20 = \$10$$

If she diversifies by buying 1 share of stock in each firm, Beth gains $30 on one of the stocks and loses $20 on the other, so her profit is $10 and is not risky. Whether or not she diversifies, Beth's expected profit is $10. However, diversifying reduces her risk—she earns $10 with certainty rather than taking a one-half chance of earning $60 and a one-half chance of losing $40.

RISK AVERSION

Diversification is valuable to most people because they dislike risk; that is, they are risk averse.

risk averse — a preference for a less risky income, holding fixed the expected value of the income

A person is **risk averse** if he prefers a less risky income, holding fixed its expected value.[6]

---

[6]More precisely, a person is risk averse if she would dislike an increase in the standard deviation of her future wealth, holding fixed its expected value.

IN THE NEWS

Portfolios tango the best when they're out of step

Your money matters

By Barbara Donnelly
Staff Reporter of The
Wall Street Journal

When it comes to building an investment portfolio, there's a crucial distinction between true diversification and simply holding a hodgepodge of securities.

An investor could hold dozens of small-company stocks, for instance, and still be ravaged by the special per-ils that affect this volatile sector. Even if the holdings comprised many small-company mutual funds, which themselves are diversified, the investor's portfolio would still be vulnerable.

The real secret of portfolio diversification, investment professionals say, is to mix investments that don't move in tandem—then regularly readjust the mix to maintain its original proportions.

The basic objective is always to have at least some investments that do well, to offset others that are lagging.

Right Place at Right Time
In effect, diversification insures that at least part of the portfolio will always be in the right place at the right time. Consequently, it makes money for investors through a series of base hits, rather than home runs—a feature that could seem disappointing to some individuals who crave more action.

The basics of diversification.

Source: Barbara Donnelly, "Portfolios Tango the Best When They're Out of Step," *The Wall Street Journal,* September 1, 1989, p. C1.

Risk averse people prefer to avoid risks unless the risks carry with them sufficiently large expected gains; risk averse people would diversify in the example above. In fact, risk averse people would choose the less risky investment even if it had a slightly smaller expected profit; they are willing to sacrifice some expected profit in order to eliminate some risk. However, risk averse people will take risks if the expected profits are high enough to make risk taking worthwhile.

risk neutral — indifference toward risk

A **risk neutral** person does not care about risk.

Risk neutral people would not care whether they invest in Solow stock or Romer stock, or both, in the example; diversifying provides no gain to them. A person who likes risk would not buy insurance or diversify investments. Such a person would be willing to pay to take chances. While many people pay to take certain risks—they buy lottery tickets and vacation at gambling resorts—these activities involve entertainment. Most of the people who gamble also buy insurance against big risks such as fire, theft, and accidents; their behavior shows that (at least for large gambles) they are risk averse. Evidence from financial markets, where risky investments must pay higher expected returns to induce people to buy them, also shows that most people are risk averse.

MORAL HAZARD

People often lack important information about others' actions. Firms may not know how hard their employees work; a person with a house for sale may not know how hard a real-estate agent tries to sell it. These are examples of hidden action or moral hazard. We begin with definitions of important terms.

principal — a person who hires someone else to do something

agent — the person hired to do something for a principal

A **principal** is a person who hires someone else, an **agent,** to do something.

A home seller is a principal; a real-estate broker is an agent. The owner of a firm is a principal; an employee is an agent. A principal sets goals for the agent to achieve for the principal's benefit, such as high profits or a well-built house. Whether or not the agent succeeds depends on both the amount of effort the agent exerts and luck. Interesting economic issues arise when the principal can observe the outcome, but not the agent's actions or the effect of luck on the outcome. While the principal can observe the outcome, knowledge about how much credit or blame for the outcome should go to the agent (and how much to luck) remains elusive. If the outcome turns out well because of luck, the agent can try to take credit for it. If the outcome is bad because the agent shirks, the agent can blame bad luck.

moral hazard — a situation in which a principal cannot observe the actions of an agent who lacks an incentive to act in the best interests of the principal

Moral hazard occurs when an agent lacks an incentive to act in the best interests of the principal and the principal cannot observe the actions of the agent.

OPTIMAL CONTRACTS

In any moral hazard situation, the principal is likely to recognize an incentive for the agent not to act in the principal's interests. The principal can give the agent an incentive to try hard by paying more for good results than for bad results. If the principal were to pay the agent enough of a bonus for good results, the agent would have a reason to act in the principal's interest. A contract between a principal and an agent is an agreement that states how the agent's pay depends on the results.

optimal contract — an agreement that maximizes the principal's profit while providing an incentive for the agent to participate in the agreement

An **optimal contract** between a principal and an agent is an agreement that maximizes the principal's profit while providing an incentive for the agent to participate in the agreement.

In a moral hazard problem, the optimal contract is a compromise between the benefit to the agent of a flat salary (low risk), and the incentive to act in the principal's interest that comes from a higher salary for a better outcome. The optimal contract determines the sensitivity of the agent's pay to the results by setting the marginal benefit of additional sensitivity equal to the marginal cost. The marginal benefit of additional sensitivity is the incentive it provides for the agent to try harder. The marginal cost of additional sensitivity is the additional effect of luck on the agent's pay, which makes the agent bear more risk and raises the expected salary that the principal must pay to attract an agent to the job. The optimal contract makes the marginal benefit of better incentives equal to their marginal cost.

EXAMPLE

"Naughty or nice? You mean you'll just take my word for it?"

Incomplete information about an agent's actions creates moral hazard.

Source: The Wall Street Journal, December 22, 1989.

A business owner (the principal) hires a salesperson (the agent) to sell new, biodegradable food containers. The amount the agent sells depends on both the agent's effort and luck. The principal knows only the firm's profit. Suppose that this profit equals either $300,000 or zero. The chance of earning $300,000 depends on the agent's effort, as in **Table 19.2.** If the agent tries hard, the firm has a two-thirds chance of getting $300,000 and a one-third chance of getting nothing; the expected profit is $200,000. If the agent shirks, the chance of a $300,000 profit is only one-third and the expected profit is only $100,000.

TABLE 19.2

CHANCE OF A HIGH PROFIT DEPENDS ON THE AGENT'S ACTION

	Agent's Action	
	Try Hard	Shirk
$300,000 profit	2/3	1/3
No profit	1/3	2/3

A $30,000 salary would give the agent an incentive to shirk. It would be easier than trying hard, and the principal will never know. If the firm earns a zero profit, the agent can falsely claim that, despite vigorous effort, the poor profit resulted from bad luck.

Now consider some alternative payment schemes to the $30,000 salary.

CASE 1   Suppose that the agent receives nothing if the firm earns zero profits, and $45,000 if it earns $300,000. This gives an expected salary if the agent shirks of:

$$(1/3)(\$45,000) + (2/3)(\$0) = \$15,000$$

The expected salary if the agent tries hard is:

$$(2/3)(\$45,000) + (1/3)(\$0) = \$30,000$$

The agent has an incentive to try hard because effort can raise the expected salary from $15,000 to $30,000.

The problem with this payment scheme is that the agent may not like bearing the risk of earning a zero salary. A risk neutral agent would not care about the risk. A risk averse agent, like most people, would prefer to take another job that would guarantee a $30,000 salary. To attract a worker to this job, the firm must pay a higher expected salary to compensate the worker for the risk of a zero salary. Of course, the firm could also reduce the worker's risk by paying more than zero, even if its profit were zero.

CASE 2   Suppose that the agent receives $32,000 if the firm earns a profit of $300,000 and $29,000 if it earns zero. An agent who shirks can expect a salary of:

$$(1/3)(\$32,000) + (2/3)(\$29,000) = \$30,000$$

An agent who tries hard can expect a salary of:

$$(2/3)(\$32,000) + (1/3)(\$29,000) = \$31,000$$

The agent bears much less risk than in Case 1, so a worker might prefer this risky job to a job that would guarantee $30,000. The expected salary rises by $1,000 if the agent tries hard instead of shirking. Whether this gives the agent an incentive to try hard depends on how much expected salary the agent is willing to sacrifice in order to shirk. If the agent enjoys shirking sufficiently, this $1,000 difference in expected salary will not be enough to induce hard work. Now consider a payment scheme between Case 1 and Case 2.

CASE 3   Suppose that the agent would be willing to try hard if effort would increase the expected salary by $3,000. The firm could pay the agent $37,000 if it were to earn a profit of $300,000 and $28,000 if it were to earn zero. An agent who shirks could expect a salary of:

$$(1/3)(\$37{,}000) + (2/3)(\$28{,}000) = \$31{,}000$$

An agent who tries hard could expect a salary of:

$$(2/3)(\$37{,}000) + (1/3)(\$28{,}000) = \$34{,}000$$

Now the agent is willing to try hard. The agent bears less risk than in Case 1, but more than in Case 2. The agent may be willing to take this risk, however, for the expected salary of $34,000, which is $4,000 more than other jobs would pay. (If the firm paid only $36,000 for a high profit and $27,000 for a zero profit, the agent's expected salary from working hard, $33,000, may not be enough to make the job attractive.)

Case 4   Suppose that the agent is not willing to take the job (because of the risk) even for expected pay of $34,000, as in Case 3. Perhaps the agent could try a little, however, as a compromise between shirking and trying hard. (See **Table 19.3**.)

If the agent tries a little, the firm has a one-half chance of a $300,000 profit and a one-half chance of nothing for an expected profit of $150,000. (Expected profit is $100,000 if the agent shirks, and $200,000 if the agent tries hard.) This suggests another payment scheme.

Suppose that the agent receives $35,000 for a $300,000 profit and $29,000 if the profit is zero. The agent's expected salary for shirking is $31,000, $32,000 for trying a little, and $33,000 for trying hard. In this case, the agent may be willing to try a little to earn an expected salary of $32,000 rather than $31,000, but unwilling to try hard just to raise the expected salary by another $1,000.

An optimal contract may give the agent an incentive to try a little, but not to try hard. The agent may try hard only if the pay for a $300,000 profit is much higher. That may raise the expected salary more than it raises the principal's expected profit, though, so the principal would be unwilling to pay enough to make the agent work hard.

TABLE 19.3

CHANCE OF A HIGH PROFIT AND THREE POSSIBLE AGENT ACTIONS

	Agent's Action		
	Try Hard	Try a Little	Shirk
$300,000 profit	2/3	1/2	1/3
No profit	1/3	1/2	2/3

MONITORING

In many moral hazard situations, the principal can obtain some information about the agent's actions by monitoring the agent.

monitoring — obtaining information about an agent's actions (perhaps by watching)

Monitoring an agent means obtaining information about that person's actions (perhaps by watching).

Perfect monitoring—learning *exactly* what an agent does—is usually too costly for a principal. (Sometimes it is impossible.) Imperfect monitoring—getting some indication of the agent's actions—can be less costly, though. A principal may not be able to tell exactly how hard an engineer is working to come up with a new design for a complex product, but some indication of the engineer's effort exists in the volume and nature of research reports, performance at staff meetings, hours of work, and so on. James Ritty, a bar owner in the 1870s, invented the cash register to help prevent bartenders from dipping their fingers in the till—stealing money. The cash register recorded every sale, so at the end of a day Ritty could see how much money it should contain. He later sold his bar to a person who added a bell to the cash register, so a store owner could hear when a sale was made and help prevent a cashier from selling something and pocketing the money without ever putting it in the register.

Monitoring has costs because the principal must either spend time watching the agent or hire someone else to do so.[7] Owners of firms employ accountants and auditors to monitor company managers. The owners want to make sure that managers are trying hard to maximize profits.

A principal can choose the degree to which he monitors an agent. Principals monitor agents until the expected marginal cost of monitoring equals the expected marginal benefit. Sometimes firms ask employees to monitor each other. Employees who work together in small groups may easily observe how hard other employees work. By paying each worker a wage that depends on the group's output, each member of the group loses if any worker shirks. Employees who fail to work hard feel pressure from the rest of the group to do better.

Firms have tried innovative methods of monitoring. One firm, whose employees were prone to go fishing rather than show up at work, gave workers points for showing up at work that they could redeem for prizes. The firm gave the points to the workers' spouses rather than directly to the workers, which gave spouses an extra incentive to monitor the workers.

On the other hand, some firms benefit by creating new ways for agents to cheat on principals. The frequent-flyer plans of airlines encourage employees to take actions that oppose the interests of their employers. Many firms allow their employees to use frequent-flyer miles they collect during business travel for personal travel. This gives employees an incentive to take more business trips than necessary to acquire frequent-flyer miles for personal use.

APPLICATIONS OF MORAL HAZARD

INSURANCE

Insurance is a classic example of moral hazard. Insurance protection reduces a person's incentive to prevent a loss. The insurance company (the principal) does not know if the policy holder (the agent) is doing everything possible to prevent a loss. The optimal insurance contract sets up a compromise between incentives and risk, so insurance companies sell only incomplete insurance. For example, insurance policies may pay only 80 percent of a loss or only the part of a loss above a certain amount called a *deductible*. Incomplete insurance provides the policy holder with an incentive to prevent a loss while still reducing risk.

PRODUCT GUARANTEES

Like insurance, a product guarantee reduces an owner's incentive to take proper care of a product. If a car company guarantees that your car will operate perfectly for the first 60,000 miles, you will have little incentive to care for it properly. A

---

[7]Workers may also dislike being watched, so another cost of monitoring may be the extra wages required to attract workers who will be monitored.

THE LOCKHORNS HOEST

"Since we took out that million-dollar insurance policy, I notice you don't remind me to use my seat belt anymore."

Insurance creates problems of moral hazard.
Source: Washington Post, November 22, 1988.

guarantee does not create a moral hazard problem if the principal can tell whether a problem results from a defect or poor care by the owner. Moral hazard arises, however, when the principal cannot tell why a problem occurs.

The optimal contract again involves a compromise between a complete guarantee (which would eliminate a consumer's risk) and no guarantee (which would give the consumer a strong incentive to care for the good properly). In the compromise, people have reduced risk, but retain an incentive to take good care of what they own. For example, guarantees that pay for new parts but not for labor reduce the risks of owning a product while maintaining an incentive to take care of it to avoid the labor costs of repairs.

Some sellers offer service contracts under which they agree to repair products without charge if they ever break. Service contracts are subject to moral hazard because they reduce people's incentive to properly care for and use products, so products break more often when people buy service contracts. One study found that a 10 percent increase in the number of service contracts leads to a 5 percent increase in the number of product repairs.

EXECUTIVE COMPENSATION

The interests of top corporate executives can differ from the interests of a firm's owners, who want to maximize the value of the firm. Because the owners cannot closely monitor an executive's activities and any monitoring would be costly, executive employment involves moral hazard. This problem is sometimes called the *separation of ownership and control* of a firm: the firm's owners—its stockholders—are the principals, and the managers or executives are the agents.

The optimal contract between a firm's owners and managers equates the expected marginal benefit and the marginal cost of making managers' pay more sensitive to the value of the firm. The contract provides some incentives for managers to act in the owners' interest by maximizing the firm's value while not making managers' pay overly risky. Evidence suggests that the chief executive officer (CEO) of a typical American corporation gets only $325 in additional salary and other forms of compensation when the value of the firm rises $100,000. Many economists believe that $325 per $100,000 in firm value does not provide a sufficiently strong incentive for a typical CEO to maximize a firm's value. Suppose, for example, that a CEO can undertake a pet project worth $1,000 to him or her personally (perhaps in extra prestige) that costs the firm $100,000. The CEO would expect to lose $325 in compensation from the project, so the CEO's net gain would be $675 ($1,000 minus $325). The CEO would choose to undertake the project, though it would be contrary to the interests of stockholders because it would reduce the value of the firm.

Economists disagree about the reasons for the apparent shortfall in incentives for CEOs to maximize profits. Perhaps stockholders can monitor CEOs well enough that the moral hazard problem is not important for executive compensation, or perhaps executives have little control over profits (which would also make the moral hazard problem unimportant for executive compensation). Other economists believe that social pressures prevent firms from paying CEOs much more when profits rise. Evidence that profits rise when CEO compensation is more closely tied to firm performance suggests that the moral hazard problem *is* important for executive compensation. In fact, some economists argue that CEO pay is optimal, that the situation is analogous to the earlier example in which an optimal contract paid an agent to try a little rather than to try hard.

INTEREST RATES ON PERSONAL LOANS

Most borrowers repay their loans, but some default and declare bankruptcy (a legal procedure in which the debtor gives up all but a small amount of personal property and the court liquidates the rest of the person's property to eliminate debts).[8] Firms can also declare bankruptcy. The possibility of declaring bankruptcy creates a moral hazard problem by reducing borrowers' incentives to try hard to earn enough money to repay their debts and by giving borrowers incentives to choose risky actions that raise their chances of bankruptcy.

EXAMPLE   Derek is $5,000 in debt. He has assets worth $6,000 and no other source of income. He meets someone who offers him a double-or-nothing bet on a football game; the chance of winning the bet is one-half. If Derek refuses the bet, he has $1,000 in assets after paying his debt. If Derek bets and wins, he has $12,000, or $7,000 after paying his debts. If he bets and loses, he has no assets and declares bankruptcy, which wipes out his debt. The bet gives Derek a one-half

---

[8]The precise amount of personal property that escapes liquidation varies across states in the United States. The bankruptcy court uses the property it takes from the person to pay creditors in part.

IN THE NEWS

Marriott to revise terms of split

By Paul Farhi
Washington Post
Staff Writer

Marriott Corp. agreed yesterday to change some of the terms of its plan to split into two companies, backing down in the face of a challenge from bondholders angered by the restructuring.

"We were surprised by how hurt and angry [the bondholders] were when we first announced the restructuring," said Stephen F. Bollenbach, Marriott's chief financial officer. "So what we did was change it."

———

The interests of stockholders and bondholders can conflict. When the Marriott Corporation split into two companies in 1993, stockholders tried to say that one of the companies, Host Marriott, would owe most of Marriott's debts, while the other company, Marriott International, would be relatively free of debts. This would raise the chance that Host Marriott would go bankrupt and bondholders would lose. Meanwhile, stockholders would gain because the other company would be relatively debt-free. Bondholders filed lawsuits to prevent the original plan from going into effect.

Source: Paul Farhi, "Marriott to Revise Terms of Split," *Washington Post*, March 12, 1993, p. F3.

chance of winning $6,000 and a one-half chance of losing only $1,000; his expected profit from the bet is:

$$(1/2)(\$6,000) + (1/2)(-\$1,000) = \$2,500$$

Derek dislikes risk, but the expected profit on the bet is high enough that he takes the risk.

The lender would want Derek to refuse to bet. If he bets and loses, he does not repay the loan. The bet exposes the lender to risk with no chance of gain. This moral hazard problem reduces the willingness of lenders to lend money, raising the interest rates that they charge on loans. To prevent borrowers from doing things that jeopardize loan repayment, lenders often require them to pledge property (such as a car or house) as collateral, which the lender can take if the borrower defaults on the loan.

BONDHOLDERS AND STOCKHOLDERS

Stockholders own firms. *Bondholders* are a firm's creditors—people who have loaned money to it. A person who lends money to a firm and becomes a bondholder knows that there is some chance that the firm will go bankrupt and not repay the loan. After the firm has already borrowed the money, stockholders would like the firm to choose riskier investments because they keep the gains if a risky investment pays off and they can force some of the loss onto bondholders (by declaring bankruptcy) if the risky investment does not pay off. The logic is precisely the same as in the personal loan example; the agent (the firm) has an incentive to engage in risky actions that raise the chance of bankruptcy, and the principal (the bondholder) cannot perfectly observe the firm's actions. The principal sees only the results (repayment of the loan or bankruptcy). For this reason, stockholders and bondholders frequently disagree about a firm's optimal business strategies. Stockholders prefer riskier business activities (such as investments in new product lines) than bondholders.

———— **FOR REVIEW** ————

19.7 Explain how diversification can reduce risk.

19.8 Explain moral hazard and present an example, identifying the principal and the agent.

———— **QUESTIONS** ————

19.9 Explain why a person's incentive to shirk depends on how the person is paid.

19.10 With an optimal contract in a moral hazard situation, do agents have an incentive to try as hard as the principal would like? Why or why not?

ADVERSE SELECTION

Moral hazard occurs when a person (the principal) has imperfect information about an agent's actions. Sometimes people lack relevant information about the reasons for the actions of others with whom they interact. A potential buyer knows that you are selling your car, but not whether you are selling it because it is a bad car or simply because you want a newer model. This is an example of hidden information or adverse selection.

adverse selection — a situation in which two people might trade with each other and one person has relevant information about some aspect of the product's quality that the other person lacks

Adverse selection occurs when two people might trade with each other and one person has relevant information about some aspect of the product's quality that the other person lacks.

The market for used cars is the classic example of adverse selection. Someone who sells a car knows something about its quality that a buyer does not know: how well the car worked in the past. The car might be reliable or it might be faulty. Because most buyers cannot tell if a car is faulty, good used cars and faulty ones sell for the same price. In a sense, buyers overpay for faulty cars and underpay for good ones. If they had better information, buyers would not be willing to pay as much for the faulty cars, but they would be willing to pay more for the good cars. Because good cars are underpriced, people who own good cars are less likely to sell them and more likely to keep them. Because faulty cars are overpriced, people who own them are more likely to sell them. For this reason, good cars are underrepresented in the used-car market and faulty cars are overrepresented. The term *adverse selection* refers to this result. The cars that people offer in the used-car market tend to be those of lower-than-average quality. The low-quality cars offered for sale tend to drive the higher-quality cars out of the used-car market.

Moral hazard differs from adverse selection. Moral hazard occurs when one person does not know what another person is doing; a principal cannot see whether an agent is acting in the principal's best interest. Adverse selection occurs when people know what an agent is doing, but not *why*.

EXAMPLE Suppose that good cars are worth $1,000, faulty cars are worth $500, and each car has a one-half chance of being good or being faulty. Also suppose that people are risk neutral. Buyers would be willing to pay $1,000 for a car if they could be certain that it was good, and only $500 for a car if they were certain that it was faulty. Buyers do not know if a car is faulty, however, so the expected value of a particular car is:

$$(1/2)(\$1,000) + (1/2)(\$500) = \$750$$

Buyers are willing to pay $750 for a car that might turn out to be either good or faulty. Buyers pay a price equal to the expected value of the car and take their chances. They end up overpaying for faulty cars by $250, and underpaying for good cars by $250.

Most people with good cars (worth $1,000) will not choose to sell them for $750, and some people who would keep their faulty cars if they could fetch only $500 choose instead to sell them for $750. In the extreme case, if every owner of a good used car were to value it at $1,000 and every owner of a faulty car were to value it at $500, no one would ever want to sell a good used car for $750 and every owner of a faulty car would want to sell it. All used cars offered for sale would be faulty! Knowing this, buyers would not be willing to pay $750 for used cars. Because all used cars would be faulty, they would be willing to pay only $500. This would push the equilibrium price down to $500 and low-quality cars would drive all high-quality cars out of the used-car market.

In a less extreme case, owners would place different values on their cars. If some owners of good cars were willing to sell them for less than $1,000, then some good cars might be sold in equilibrium and the equilibrium price might be above $500. Perhaps some owners of good cars would be willing to sell them for $600, though all buyers value good cars at $1,000 and faulty cars at $500. This could create an equilibrium in which the price of a used car would be $600, one-fifth of all used cars for sale would be good, and four-fifths would be faulty. This gives an expected value of a car to a buyer of:

$$(4/5)(\$500) + (1/5)(\$1,000) = \$600$$

which is the equilibrium price. In this case, low-quality products would tend to drive out high-quality products, but not completely.

EXAMPLES OF ADVERSE SELECTION

MEDICAL INSURANCE

Adverse selection applies to many kinds of insurance, and insurance professionals understand the economic issues well. Someone with a high risk of medical problems is more likely to buy medical insurance, and to buy a more comprehensive policy, than someone with a lower risk of medical problems. The same argument applies to life insurance.

People may know about their risks from family histories, health habits, and their own health histories. Insurance companies try to obtain this information, but they cannot do so with perfect certainty, so they end up selling relatively more insurance to high-risk people than to low-risk people. The price of insurance reflects an average of the costs of providing insurance to both types of people, so low-risk people overpay for insurance and high-risk people underpay. The price of insurance to a low-risk person is higher than it would be if insurance companies had more information.

LABOR MARKETS

Adverse selection is also important in labor markets. A job applicant usually knows more about the quality of her labor than prospective employers know. Whatever wage a firm offers to pay, it will get many applicants with worse alternative jobs, but few job applicants with better alternative jobs. Firms try to obtain information on the quality of job applicants, but the information is never perfect. In response they hire people for low-level jobs and then, after learning more about the quality of their labor, promote the high-quality people and not the low-quality people. Firms may also offer higher wages to attract higher quality job applicants.

CREDIT CARDS

Because some people do not pay their bills, banks take risks when they issue credit cards. Banks spend money on lawyers and collection agencies and still never collect payments from some people. Banks also incur interest costs and collection costs on the many late payments that they receive. Banks have limited information on which to judge who is a good credit risk. If they could separate high-risk people from low-risk people, they would charge a higher interest rate to the high-risk people. Limited information prevents this, so banks charge an interest rate that reflects the average credit risks of their customers. This creates adverse selection because low-risk (creditworthy) people overpay interest and high-risk people underpay. This encourages a larger number of relatively high-risk people to apply for credit cards, further raising the interest rates that banks must charge to earn zero profits in equilibrium.

LIMITS ON ADVERSE SELECTION PROBLEMS

GUARANTEES

Firms that sell high-quality goods can try to limit the adverse selection problem by guaranteeing high quality to buyers. For example, a firm might give a money-back guarantee to buyers or offer free repairs or replacement for products with defects. Guarantees can communicate information about quality to buyers because a firm selling high-quality products will not hesitate to offer a guarantee, expecting few of its products to be returned or to need repair. Firms selling low-quality products must pay high costs to honor guarantees, however, so they provide guarantees less frequently. Buyers, therefore, properly view a good guarantee as a signal of a high-quality product. Guarantees reduce the problem of adverse selection by allowing producers of higher-quality products to sell those products for higher prices than the lower-quality products of other firms.

Guarantees cannot completely eliminate adverse selection problems because a guarantee provides information to buyers only if it is enforceable. Firms that make low-quality products may issue guarantees and then go out of business; a buyer may not trust a guarantee offered by a stranger selling a used car. A firm that sells a low-quality product may try later to escape responsibility for its guarantee.

Moral hazard problems also limit the use of guarantees. A buyer may not take proper care of a product with a guarantee, but a seller who cannot show that a problem arose from misuse or poor care may be stuck paying for repairs or replacement. This moral hazard problem leads sellers to tend to guarantee only products that buyers cannot ruin though negligence or for which sellers can monitor buyers' care. This is why automobile guarantees require regular servicing of cars.

Adverse selection is a less serious problem when the buyers and sellers deal with each other repeatedly. In this case, sellers can develop reputations for high-quality goods. Because these reputations allow them to charge higher prices, good reputations are valuable and provide firms with incentives not to reduce quality.

When buyers do not deal repeatedly with the same sellers, franchising can help to reduce the adverse selection problem by providing a signal of quality. Franchising gives sellers a way to buy reputations. Consumers are more willing to trust a store with a franchise name that they trust from past experience, such as McDonald's, The Limited, or The Gap. Franchises charge fees to allow stores to use the franchises' names and they monitor stores' quality levels to prevent losses in the reputation of the franchises.[9]

PRODUCT REVIEWS

Consumers can sometimes buy information from product reviewers such as movie and book reviewers, auto magazines, stereo magazines, or publications like *Consumer Reports.* The information provided in these reviews can help to limit adverse selection problems, but the amount of information that consumers can buy in this way is limited because people who sell information cannot make sure that buyers pay for it. If someone spends time and money to investigate a product's quality and then sells that information to one group of people, it is hard to keep it from others who have not paid for it. This limits the incentive to provide information and reduces the amount of product information provided in equilibrium.

SEPARATING EQUILIBRIUM

Sometimes innovative price and product schemes can reduce adverse selection problems. Suppose that an insurance company sees two types of people: high-risk

---

[9]About one-half million franchised stores operate in the United States, generating more than one-third of all U.S. retail sales.

SOCIAL AND ECONOMIC ISSUES

Limited Consumer Information and the Role of Government

Liability laws and government regulations can limit adverse selection problems. The government can reduce sales of low-quality goods by requiring firms to sell only products that meet minimum quality levels.

Some people argue that guarantees issued by sellers are better than government regulations. Some consumers may prefer to pay lower prices for lower-quality products, rather than buying higher-quality products at higher prices. Firms selling higher-quality products can issue guarantees to help consumers to identify high-quality products, leaving them free to choose which levels of quality they want to purchase. Those who favor government regulations and liability laws argue that private guarantees are insufficient because some people mistakenly buy lower-quality products than they want and some people have limited information about quality differences. Government regulations, they argue, help to protect people from making bad choices.

Some people believe that the government should license only high-quality sellers when consumers have limited information about product quality. Of course, the government may face the same problems as consumers in obtaining information about product quality. If the government can obtain better information about product quality than consumers can obtain, perhaps the government should provide that information to consumers rather than licensing sellers or regulating product quality. The government could either provide information about product quality directly or require sellers to provide the information on product labels.

Licensing has another disadvantage in that it restricts the number of sellers and thereby reduces competition. Although consumers may benefit from higher-quality goods, they may lose from reduced competition among sellers. Like government regulations on product quality, licensing also prevents consumers who want lower-quality products at lower prices from being able to buy them.

Some argue for licensing or regulation instead of government-provided information or labeling laws, claiming that consumers may not always obtain the information or read the labels and they may not understand the information that they receive. In that case, people might make choices they would later regret and that government regulations or licensing could prevent.

people and low-risk people. It is more costly for the company to insure high-risk people because they have higher chances of accidents. If an insurance company offers only one type of insurance policy, some of its customers will be high-risk people and others will be low-risk people. If the insurance company cannot identify high-risk customers, it must charge the same price to every customer. Low-risk people then overpay for insurance and high-risk people underpay, compared to the prices that each would pay if firms could charge high-risk people more.

Suppose, however, that the insurance company offers people a choice of two kinds of policies. One policy provides basic insurance with limited coverage and limits on payments. The other provides more comprehensive insurance that pays a larger amount in case of an accident. If the insurance company were to allow people to buy only one of these policies, low-risk people might be satisfied with the basic insurance policy. Higher-risk people, however, would prefer the more comprehensive insurance. The insurance company could then identify or separate the high-risk and low-risk people by the choices they made. The firm could set the price for each type of policy based on the knowledge that only low-risk people would buy the limited, basic policy, while everyone who bought the more comprehensive policy would be a high-risk person.

IN THE NEWS

How much should patients be told?

As with most medical procedures, a person considering genetic testing must give "informed consent"—not just agreeing to take the test but understanding just what the test shows and how reliably, the stresses of coping with a positive result, possible treatments, and the stresses that might result from not taking the test.

Explaining all this is demanding. The Johns Hopkins Huntington's program, for example, gives people extensive counseling before even asking for a decision on whether they want to take the test.

"Informed consent is an enormous problem," says Joan Marks, who oversees a Sarah Lawrence College program training graduate students to be genetic counselors. "If a patient doesn't understand what he is being told, how can he give informed consent? And many physicians are just not that great at communicating."

What about Doctors Who Are Ill-Informed?
Some see a strong role for government in this area, to make sure that biotechnology firms don't oversell their tests' abilities and to ensure a high standard of laboratory work.

Do these information problems create a role for government policy? What role?

Source: *The Wall Street Journal*, September 14, 1987, p. 27.

FOR REVIEW

19.11 Explain adverse selection and present an example of it. Explain how adverse selection differs from moral hazard.

19.12 Why can't guarantees completely solve adverse selection problems? Explain how moral hazard limits the use of guarantees.

QUESTIONS

19.13 Discuss this statement: "Adverse selection means that all products will be of the lowest possible quality."

19.14 Firms that sell medical insurance try to judge the risks of applicants by investigating their current health indicators (such as their blood pressure readings), family medical histories (to look for diseases that might run in a family), and personal habits (such as smoking). The firms charge higher prices to insure higher-risk applicants. Suppose that the government requires firms to offer everyone who lives in a community the same price, based on the average risks of people in that community. How would this affect the decisions of people to buy medical insurance?

CONCLUSIONS

EXPECTATIONS ABOUT THE FUTURE

An expected value is an average of numbers weighted by the probabilities (chances) that each will occur. Under certain conditions, the expected value of a number is a rational guess of that number.

Limited Information about Prices

When consumers have limited information about prices and they incur costs of searching for the lowest price, sellers face downward-sloping demand curves. The optimal amount of search occurs when the expected marginal benefit of search (the expected benefit from trying one more store) equals its expected marginal cost.

When some customers have better information than others, a distribution of prices can exist in equilibrium. Some sellers charge higher prices than others and better-informed consumers buy from lower-price sellers. High-price stores sell less than low-price stores, but earn higher profits on each item they sell; lower-price stores earn less per item, but sell more. A firm can price-discriminate between well-informed and poorly informed buyers by operating several stores that charge different prices or by selling essentially the same product under different brand names at different prices. Poorly informed consumers are more likely to buy at the higher-price stores or to buy the higher-priced brands. As consumers get better information, the distribution of prices narrows and the average prices they pay fall.

Firms with limited information about demand can learn about the demand curves they face by trial and error. They may put products on sale at reduced prices to learn about demand. They may also put goods on sale to price-discriminate by charging higher prices to buyers who are willing to pay more to buy goods without waiting for sales.

Risk

Diversification—spreading risks across many different, unrelated investments—can reduce risk. This is valuable to people who are risk averse.

Moral Hazard

When a principal has imperfect information about the actions of an agent, that agent may not have an incentive to act in the best interests of the principal. This is a problem of moral hazard. To give the agent an incentive to take actions more consistent with the principal's interests, the principal wants to pay the agent for good results, even those due to good luck. As the agent's pay becomes more sensitive to outcomes that can be affected by luck, the agent's income becomes riskier. Agents who are risk averse (as most people are) dislike this risk, so the principal must pay a higher expected income to attract agents. An optimal contract between a principal and an agent compromises between the benefit to the agent of a flat salary (low risk) and the incentive to act in the principal's interest that results from higher pay for better outcomes. It sets the marginal benefit of better incentives equal to their marginal costs. Principals can often obtain some information about an agent's actions by monitoring the agent, though obtaining perfect information is often too costly, or even impossible. Moral hazard problems arise in insurance, product guarantees, executive compensation, interest rates on personal loans, and conflicts between bondholders and stockholders.

Adverse Selection

Adverse selection occurs when two people might trade with each other and one person has important information about product quality that the other person lacks. It occurs when people lack relevant information about the reasons for the actions of people with whom they interact. A classic example involves used cars. Buyers do not know whether a person selling a car does so because it is faulty (a bad car) or for other reasons. When buyers lack information about quality, high-quality products and low-quality products sell for the same price. In this case, sellers offer mainly low-quality products because they cannot charge higher prices for higher-quality products. Low-quality products tend to drive high-quality products out of the market under adverse selection. Adverse selection applies to insurance, labor markets, interest rates on credit cards, and other situations. Firms can reduce the problem of adverse selection by offering guarantees. The problem is also less severe when buyers and sellers deal repeatedly with each other or when people can buy information about quality.

LOOKING AHEAD

Chapter 20 discusses the economics of pollution and related issues. The problems of limited information and pollution are often cited as reasons for government regulation of the economy. Chapter 21 studies government regulation and taxes. The study of government and the legal system continues in Chapter 22 on the economics of law.

KEY TERMS

expected value	principal
search cost	agent
distribution of prices	moral hazard
diversification	optimal contract
risk averse	monitoring
risk neutral	adverse selection

QUESTIONS AND PROBLEMS

19.15 A new business has a one-tenth chance of succeeding and earning a profit with a discounted present value of $500,000. It has a nine-tenths chance of failing and incurring a loss with a discounted present value of $40,000. What is the discounted present value of the expected profit from starting this business? What would it be if the $40,000 loss were to change to $60,000?

19.16 Explain two ways that firms price-discriminate when some consumers are uninformed. Why does more consumer information lead to lower prices?

19.17 Why do moral hazard problems not arise when monitoring costs are very low?

19.18 Explain how adverse selection applies to:
   a. Medical and life insurance
   b. Firms hiring workers
   c. Credit cards

19.19 Real-estate agents earn sales commissions when they sell houses. Does this give a real-estate agent the same incentives as the owners of the house? Explain how agents' incentives might differ, and why it might be hard to improve their incentives.

19.20 Describe the incentives of an investment advisor who earns a fraction of the profits of recommended investments. How does your answer depend on whether the advisor has to pay for part of any losses from those investments?

19.21 Suppose people were to pay doctors every week that they remain well and stop the payments when they became sick. How would this affect doctors' incentives? Why aren't doctors paid this way?

19.22 Explain why the average used car offered for sale has lower quality than the average used car not offered for sale.

19.23 Discuss the following quotations and situations.

a. "Do you really want to pay $100 for that 'oil well'? If it's such a great deal, why isn't everyone trying to buy it? Why are they so anxious to sell it to *you?* Maybe you have overestimated its value."

b. "Whoever bids the most either knows more than everyone else, or has bid too much!"

c. "I wouldn't join any club that would have me."

d. Mary has applied for jobs at five firms. Each firm has limited information about the quality of her labor and each makes a different guess about its quality. Discuss the following quotation.

> The firm with the highest guess of Mary's labor quality probably overestimates it, just as the firm with the lowest guess underestimates it. The firm with the highest guess will offer the highest wage, and she will take that job. That firm will end up overpaying her because it will have overestimated the quality of her labor. The same argument applies to sports teams that hire players; the team that outbids others for a player is the one that most overestimates the player's ability, and then overpays the most. In situations like this, every employee is paid more than he or she is worth.

19.24 Monte Carlo, where Cooley sells ice cream on the beach, has hot days and normal days. On a hot day, he earns a $1,000 profit. On a normal day, he earns a $200 profit. He always faces a one-half chance that tomorrow will be a hot day.

a. What is Cooley's expected profit from selling ice cream tomorrow?

b. Suppose that the casino at Monte Carlo starts a new weather gambling game. Every day, the casino sells weather tickets for $100 each. If the next day is normal, the weather ticket pays $200. If the next day is hot, the weather ticket pays zero. What is the expected profit from buying a weather ticket?

c. Suppose that Cooley buys one weather ticket every day. What is his net profit on a normal day after selling ice cream and buying a weather ticket? What is his net profit on a hot day?

d. Could Cooley eliminate all risk by buying weather tickets? How many tickets would he have to buy each day to eliminate all of his risk? What would his income be?

INQUIRIES FOR FURTHER THOUGHT

19.25 To what extent can the government increase consumer information about quality or prices? How? Should it do so? What other policies should the government follow to deal with problems of limited consumer information?

19.26 If information is costly to produce, disseminate, and remember, how much information is it economically efficient to produce? Can an economy produce this information without government regulations? What might the government do?

19.27 Why can't or don't people buy insurance from private insurance companies against being unemployed? (The insurance might pay people when they are unemployed, just as fire insurance pays them if their houses burn down.) Should the government provide this kind of insurance? How should the program be run? Should the government require unemployment insurance or make it voluntary? If the government requires it, should the government provide the insurance itself or require that people buy unemployment insurance from private insurance companies? What problems of moral hazard or adverse selection might emerge?

19.28 Discuss these statements.

    a. "Economists see an adverse selection problem with health insurance that would be solved if insurance companies could gather more information about people. If insurance companies had more information, however, that might create a new problem. Some people are born with medical problems. If an insurance company knows about the problem, it will charge that person a high price for insurance. If the company does not know about the problem, then people with and without such problems will pay the same price for insurance. It is better that insurance companies do not have this information, so people can insure against such pre-existing conditions."

    b. "The government should require insurance companies to issue health insurance without a test for HIV (the AIDS virus)."

19.29 Is more information always better? Would you want information about how long you will live or that you have some disease that might be treatable if you could act promptly? Information about your birthday gifts next month or about what someone else thinks of you? What factors affect the demand for information? What factors affect its supply?

19.30 Does competition in the creation and dissemination of information provide the economically efficient amount of information? If not, does competition produce too little or too much? Explain your answer.

TAG SOFTWARE APPLICATIONS

TUTORIAL EXERCISES

▶ The module contains a review of the key terms from Chapter 19.

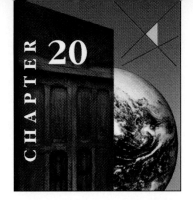

CHAPTER 20

ENVIRONMENTAL ECONOMICS AND PUBLIC GOODS

WHAT THIS CHAPTER IS ABOUT

▶ How private costs and social costs differ

▶ Economics of pollution

▶ Incentives to overuse or conserve resources

▶ Production of public goods such as knowledge, music, and national defense

Pollution, destruction of rain forests and the ozone layer, extinction and annihilation of biodiversity: all of these problems involve economics. Economics addresses incentives to pollute the air and water, incentives to conserve or destroy natural resources, and incentives to conduct economic activities that affect ecological systems and could eradicate entire species. What are the appropriate economic solutions? A complete answer cannot be found in this chapter, or anywhere else, but this chapter discusses the fundamental economic analysis of these problems, on which people must someday build an answer.

EXTERNALITIES

Pollution and similar problems occur when people do not bear all of the costs of their actions. They force polluted air or water on the rest of society; they overuse or destroy natural resources. Analysis of these problems must begin by making a careful distinction between the private costs and social costs of human actions.

DEFINITIONS AND EXAMPLES

Economists distinguish between private and social costs. The private cost of producing a good is the cost to firms that produce it.

private cost — the cost paid by a firm to produce and sell a good

The **private cost** of producing a good is the cost paid by the firm that produces and sells it.

Sometimes producing a good creates costs for other people as well, as when a factory causes air pollution that harms people who live nearby. The cost to other

561

people of producing a good is the value of the harm it creates for those people, measured by the amount of money they would be willing to pay to eliminate the harm. Consumption of some goods may also impose costs on other people, as when driving a car (consuming the car's services) pollutes the air. The social cost of producing a good is the total private cost plus the total cost to other people from producing various quantities of the good.

social cost — the total cost of a good to everyone in society

> The **social cost** of a good is its cost to everyone in the society, including people who do not produce or consume it. The social cost of producing a good equals the private cost of producing it plus the cost to other people.

Private and social costs differ whenever production or use of a good directly affects people who do not buy or sell it. When a factory pollutes the air, the social cost of the good produced includes the harm to other people from that pollution. Similarly, the social cost of driving a car includes the harm to other people from the pollution that it causes.

Economists distinguish between private benefits and social benefits in the same way.

private benefit — the benefit to people who buy and consume a good

> The **private benefit** of consuming a good is its benefit to the people who buy and consume it.

social benefit — the total benefit of a good to everyone in society

> The **social benefit** of consuming a good is its total benefit to everyone in the society.

If a scientist discovers a better medicine to treat a disease, her gains (and her firm's profits) from selling this medicine are private benefits. The gains to people who use the medicine are also private benefits. The social benefits of the new medicine include these private benefits plus gains to other people, perhaps because the scientist's discovery provides new ideas that help other scientists working on other problems. Similarly, the private benefit from planting a tree may be its beauty or shade; the social benefit includes the enrichment of the atmosphere from the oxygen that the tree produces.

externality — a difference between the private and social costs or benefits

> An **externality** occurs when the private cost or benefit of a good differs from its social cost or benefit.

When economic activity produces externalities, economists sometimes call this a *market failure.*

negative externality — the result of a social cost of a good in excess of its private cost

positive externality — the result of a social benefit of a good in excess of its private benefit

> A **negative** (or harmful) **externality** occurs when the social cost of a good exceeds its private cost. A **positive** (or beneficial) **externality** occurs when the social benefit exceeds the private benefit.[1]

Negative externalities harm other people; positive externalities help them. Most of this chapter concentrates on negative externalities. Pollution is not the only example of a negative externality; negative externalities result from poor

---

[1]Something can have both positive and negative externalities if it helps some people and hurts others. For example, some people may like to hear the music from a loud rock concert near their neighborhood, while other people may dislike it. The Eiffel Tower had both positive and negative externalities in Paris when it was first built—some people liked it and others hated it. Strictly, a negative externality occurs when the social cost minus the social benefit is larger than the private cost minus the private benefit. A positive externality occurs when the social benefit minus the social cost is larger than the private benefit minus the private cost.

Examples of Externalities

▶ Driving a car that uses leaded gasoline

▶ Dumping waste into a river that kills fish

▶ Spreading flu germs by sneezing

▶ Planting a beautiful garden

▶ Using dangerous chemicals that might spread through the ecosystem

▶ Using a product that may damage the ozone layer

health practices that raise other people's chances of contracting contagious diseases. Negative externalities arise from the installation of security systems on houses and cars because these devices frequently redirect burglars to other, nearby houses or cars. Similarly, increased law enforcement in one area of a city may move crime to other areas.

EQUILIBRIUM AND ECONOMIC EFFICIENCY

Figure 20.1 shows the basic demand and supply graph with a negative externality. The graph shows the demand for a product, its marginal private cost, *MPC*, and its marginal social cost, *MSC*. The marginal private cost of producing a good is the increase in total private cost from producing one more unit. The marginal cost to other people is the increase in total cost to other people from producing one more unit. The marginal social cost of producing a good, *MSC*, is the increase in the total social cost from producing one more unit.

The marginal social cost curve lies above the marginal private cost curve, and the difference shows the negative externality (such as the harm from pollution) from producing or using one more unit. The vertical difference between the *MSC* and *MPC* curves represents the marginal cost to other people.

With perfect competition, the marginal private cost curve is the industry supply curve. Therefore, equilibrium with perfect competition occurs at Point A with equilibrium quantity Q_A and equilibrium price P_A. The economically efficient quantity, however, is Q_B. The quantity Q_B is economically efficient because the marginal social cost equals the marginal social benefit at that quantity.[2]

> A negative externality creates an economically inefficient equilibrium quantity that exceeds the economically efficient quantity.

EXPLANATION

Output of a good is economically efficient if its marginal social benefit equals its marginal social cost, as at Point B in Figure 20.1. Equilibrium with perfect competition, Point A, is economically inefficient because the marginal social cost of the good exceeds its marginal social benefit.

Chapter 11 discussed the gains from trade, economic efficiency, and deadweight social losses. People buy and sell goods voluntarily because they expect to gain from trades. Buyers and sellers share the gains as consumer surplus and

---

[2]The situation becomes somewhat more complicated when the cost to other people from producing a good can be alleviated without reducing production of the good such as by use of more pollution-abatement devices. Still, the main lessons of the analysis continue to apply. Similarly, the situation becomes more complicated if the marginal social benefit and the marginal private benefit differ. A later section discusses differences in social and private benefits.

FIGURE 20.1

EQUILIBRIUM WITH A NEGATIVE EXTERNALITY

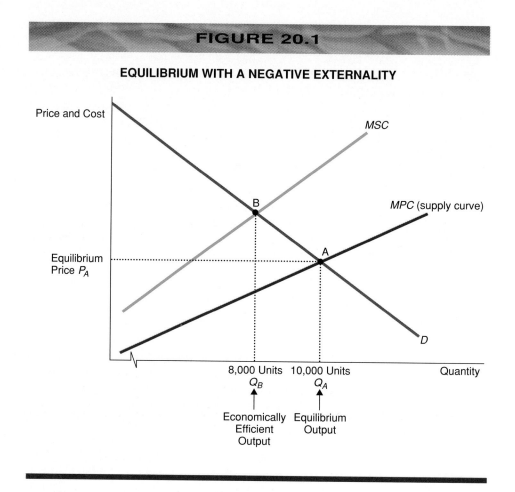

producer surplus; the total gain from trade is the sum of consumer and producer surplus. With externalities, producing or using a good affects people other than the buyers and sellers, so the total gain from trade must include their gains (or subtract their losses).

The quantity of a product is not economically efficient if its marginal social benefit exceeds its marginal social cost, as in **Figure 20.2.** If the quantity produced is 5,000 units, the marginal social benefit of the good is $210 and the marginal social cost is $90. In this case, society can gain $210 minus $90, or $120, by producing one more unit of the good. The total gain from trade rises with higher output, and people can share this gain. (By the same reasoning, Chapter 11 showed that a tax causes economic inefficiency.) Equilibrium output might fall short of Q_B, due to a high tax on output of the good or government regulations that limit its production.

Similarly, the quantity of a product is not economically efficient if its marginal social benefit is less than its marginal social cost, as in Figure 20.1 and **Figure 20.3,** where output is 10,000 units and the marginal social benefit of the good is $100, but its marginal social cost is $180. This means that the social cost of the 10,000th unit exceeds that unit's social benefit by $80, so society could gain $80 by producing one unit less of the good.

FIGURE 20.2

EQUILIBRIUM OUTPUT BELOW Q_B IS ECONOMICALLY INEFFICIENT

Producing less than Q_B is economically inefficient. At output of only 5,000 units, the marginal social benefit of another unit of output is $210, while the marginal social cost is only $90. Society as a whole would gain $120 from producing another unit of the good.

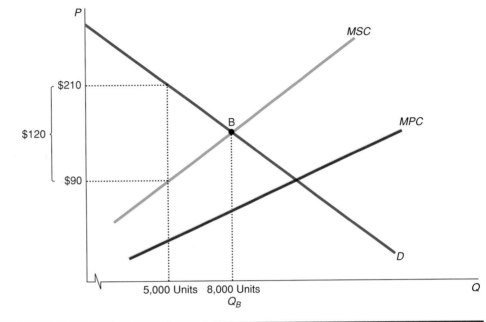

Point B in each figure represents an economically efficient quantity because the marginal social benefit of the product equals its marginal social cost. The height of the demand curve shows the good's marginal benefit to society, that is, society's gain from one more unit of the product; the height of the marginal social cost curve shows what society sacrifices to produce that unit. That sacrifice includes both the private cost of producing the good and the cost to other people, such as the harm they suffer due to pollution from producing or using the good.

DEADWEIGHT SOCIAL LOSSES FROM EXTERNALITIES

Figure 20.3 shows the deadweight social loss from a negative externality. At the equilibrium, Point A, the quantity is 10,000 units and the price is $100. In equilibrium, the marginal private cost of the good equals its price, which is $100. The marginal social cost of the good is $180, however, because the marginal cost to other people is $80. The shaded area of the graph shows the deadweight social loss from the externality.

Notice that people would buy the economically efficient quantity of the product if its price were P_B, but the equilibrium price, P_A, is less than P_B, so people buy too much of the product in equilibrium; they buy more than the economically efficient quantity (Q_B). Also notice that the economically efficient quantity of the good is positive, not zero. Applying this analysis to pollution, we find that *it would not be economically efficient to eliminate pollution* completely. This would require doing without the product entirely. Some pollution would result even if firms were to produce the economically efficient quantity of the product.

FIGURE 20.3

EQUILIBRIUM AND ECONOMIC INEFFICIENCY WITH A NEGATIVE EXTERNALITY

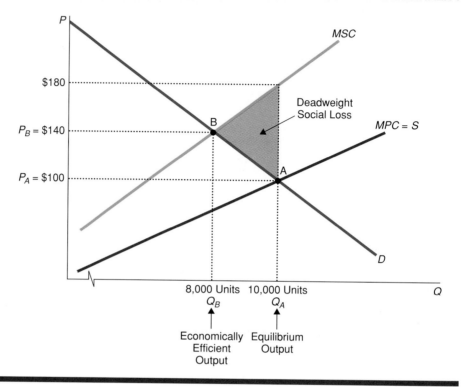

The economically efficient level of pollution is not zero.

The economically efficient level of pollution occurs when the marginal benefit of reducing it equals the marginal cost of reducing it.[3]

As an example, people pollute the air whenever they drive cars. If polluting the air were completely illegal, no one could drive cars. On the other hand, if any amount of pollution were legal, then the equilibrium use of cars would exceed its economically efficient level, as at Point A in **Figure 20.4.** The curves in this graph show the marginal cost per mile of driving a car, which differs from the average cost per mile due to fixed costs such as insurance. Requiring cars to use unleaded gasoline and emission-reducing equipment raises the cost per mile of driving cars. This shifts the marginal private cost curve upward from MPC_1 to MPC_2 in Figure 20.4, reducing the equilibrium use of cars to 2,000 billion miles per year. It also reduces the marginal social cost of driving from MSC^* TO MSC^{**}. If the marginal

[3]Reducing pollution has a cost because people must sacrifice other things they want. People could reduce air pollution by driving less or doing without CFC-based air conditioners. Air pollution from burning oil or other fossil fuels would also be lower if people used more efficient cars, trucks, light bulbs, and electric generators that recover more useable energy from the same amount of fuel. Making these products more energy efficient would create costs, however, and the people who pay these costs would sacrifice other things of value.

FIGURE 20.4

INCREASE IN THE MARGINAL COST OF DRIVING CARS

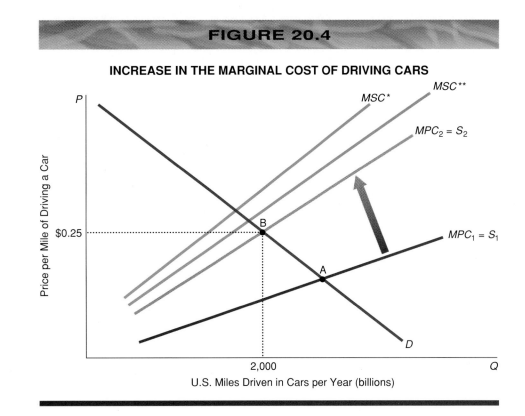

social cost of driving continues to exceed the marginal private cost, as in Figure 20.4, then economic efficiency would require a further rise in the marginal private cost curve to make it identical to the marginal social cost curve, eliminating any discrepancy between private and social costs. It would also require reduction of pollution in the least-cost manner.[4] In that case, automobile use and pollution from automobiles would be at their economically efficient levels.

FOR REVIEW

20.1 Explain the distinction between private costs and social costs.

20.2 Explain in words why an equilibrium with a negative externality is not economically efficient.

20.3 Draw the basic demand and supply diagram with a negative externality. Show (a) the marginal private cost of the good, (b) the marginal social cost of the good, (c) the marginal cost to others from the good, (d) the marginal private benefit and marginal social benefit of the good, (e) the economically efficient quantity of the good, (f) the equilibrium quantity, (g) the equilibrium price, and (h) the deadweight social loss from the externality.

---

[4]Economic efficiency requires that total pollution from *all* sources be reduced with the lowest-cost method. This may imply that it is economically efficient to reduce pollution caused by some activities (in which the cost of reducing pollution is relatively low) without reducing pollution caused by other activities (in which the cost of reducing pollution is relatively high).

QUESTIONS

20.4 Explain how an analyst might determine the economically efficient level of pollution.

20.5 Why do factories dump chemicals into the air and water and not on people's lawns or in their houses or cars? What does your answer suggest about ways to tackle problems of pollution?

INTERNALIZING EXTERNALITIES

internalizing an externality — changing the private costs or benefits so that they equal social costs or benefits; making people responsible for all the costs to other people of their own actions

A negative externality occurs when people do not pay all the costs of their own actions, that is, when other people bear some of the costs. An externality is *internalized* when people are made responsible for all of the costs of their own actions.

> **Internalizing an externality** means changing private costs or benefits so that they equal social costs or benefits.

Internalizing an externality eliminates the deadweight social loss from the externality. For this reason, internalizing an externality is economically efficient. One way to internalize externalities is with *side payments*.

SIDE PAYMENTS

People can make side payments to other people or firms in return for specified actions. (You can think of a side payment as a kind of bribe.) In some cases, people can internalize externalities with side payments. People who suffer harm from a factory's pollution may offer to pay the polluter to stop. This may seem unfair, but it could be effective. This offer of a side payment creates an opportunity cost for the factory, because it sacrifices the side payment if it keeps polluting. The offer of a side payment raises the factory's private cost of producing. A side payment of the right size would equalize the factory's private costs with its social costs, internalizing the externality.

EXAMPLES

For many years, a small factory has dumped wastes into a lake a few miles away through a pipe running from the factory to the lake. Twelve families build cottages around the lake and ask the factory to stop dumping wastes in the lake. The factory refuses, so the families offer to pay the factory $600 each year ($50 per family) to stop. The factory stops polluting and uses its $600 annual side payment to pay for waste treatment.

Similar payments occur in many situations. A store in a gang-infested area or in a city with corrupt police may pay protection money to prevent destruction of the store. People say to their roommates, "Look, the noise you're making is bothering me while I'm trying to study (or sleep); please quiet down and I'll return the favor some time."

In 1990, the Unocal Corporation paid people in Los Angeles to turn in old cars that caused pollution. (The company presumably did this as a public service gesture that would also generate good publicity.) Unocal paid $700 each for the first 7,000 old cars. In the same year, the city of St. Paul, Minnesota, paid a sex-oriented business $1.8 million to leave town and not come back.

DENNIS THE MENACE

"Let's call it a 'divorce.' You stay in your yard and I'll give you ten cents a week."

Side payments can internalize externalities.
Source: San Francisco Chronicle, February 10, 1989.

WILLINGNESS TO MAKE AND ACCEPT SIDE PAYMENTS

The highest price that a person would be willing to pay to reduce pollution is the value of the harm that the pollution causes that person. If pollution causes someone $500 worth of harm (including health costs, cleaning costs, unpleasantness, and all other types of harm), he would be willing to pay up to $500 to eliminate the pollution. If a person were to place a value of $120 per year on a 10 percent reduction in pollution from a factory, he would be willing to pay up to $120 per year to reduce pollution by 10 percent. The harm that people suffer from additional pollution when the production of a good rises by one unit, the marginal cost of that good to other people, equals the highest side payment that people would be willing to make to prevent that increase in pollution.

Consider a firm that usually produces 1,000 tons of steel per month and that can reduce pollution only by reducing output. Suppose that people offer to pay the firm $10 for each ton it does not produce up to 1,000 tons per month. In this case, the firm could collect $2,000 per month in side payments by reducing output to 800 tons per month. The offer of a side payment would raise the marginal private cost by $10 per ton. The firm would then choose its level of output to maximize its profit, taking into account all of its costs, including the opportunity cost of losing side payments if it were to produce more.

SIDE PAYMENTS CAN INTERNALIZE AN EXTERNALITY

To internalize an externality, the marginal private cost must equal the marginal social cost of the product. This occurs if the marginal private cost rises by the marginal cost to other people. This happens if people offer to pay polluting firms, for each unit they do not produce (up to some level), an amount of money equal to the marginal cost to other people. These side payments would internalize the externality. The marginal private cost (*MPC*) curve in Figure 20.3 shifts upward so that it becomes the same curve as the marginal social cost (*MSC*) curve, with equilibrium output of Q_B, as in **Figure 20.5**. This equilibrium is economically efficient.

SIDE PAYMENTS IN REVERSE

Side payments can also work in reverse. For example, if it is illegal for a firm to pollute, it might pay people to allow the pollution, that is, pay them not to bring lawsuits to enforce the law against pollution. The largest side payment that the firm would be willing to make would equal the extra profit that it would earn if it could pollute. The smallest side payment that people would accept to allow the pollution would equal the harm that they would suffer from that pollution. These side payments could produce economic efficiency; instead of producing zero output to create zero pollution, the firm would produce the economically efficient quantity, Q_B.

EXPLANATION   Suppose that it is impossible to produce a product without causing pollution. Completely outlawing pollution would mean outlawing the product. This may not be economically efficient, however, because people may want the product so much that they would pay a high price for it, enough to allow producers to compensate others to tolerate the pollution. When firms must compensate people for the effects of pollution, private costs become the same as social costs, and the marginal private cost curve shifts upward, as in Figure 20.5. As a result of this compensation, firms choose the economically efficient level of output, QB. This shows why reverse side payments from a polluter to people harmed by the pollution lead to economic efficiency, if the required side payments equal the marginal cost of the pollution to other people.

FIGURE 20.5

SIDE PAYMENTS TO INTERNALIZE AN EXTERNALITY

The offer of side payments equal to the marginal cost to other people raises the marginal private cost to equal the marginal social cost.

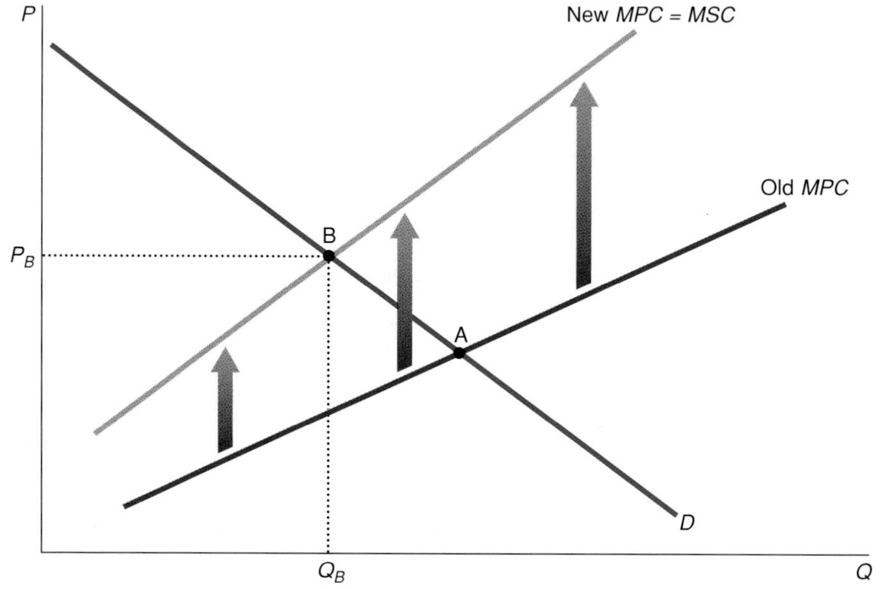

Economic efficiency can result from side payments in either direction. If pollution is legal, people can pay the polluter to reduce pollution to the economically efficient level. If pollution is illegal, firms can pay people to accept the pollution. (In essence, they can buy the right to pollute.) Obviously, the polluter prefers legal pollution, and other people favor illegal pollution. Still, side payments in either direction can result in the same, economically efficient level of output, Q_B.

EXAMPLE   Quantum Corporation builds a new research facility, but its electronic equipment interferes with television reception at a nearby hotel. Without good television reception, the discounted present value of the hotel's profit falls by $20,000. Quantum could eliminate the interference by modifying its equipment at a cost of $50,000. The hotel could eliminate the interference by replacing its televisions at a cost of $12,000.

It is economically efficient to eliminate the interference at the lowest possible cost, so economic efficiency suggests spending $12,000 to replace the televisions rather than $50,000 to modify Quantum's equipment. This does not settle the matter of who should pay this $12,000 cost, though. Perhaps the hotel should pay; perhaps Quantum should pay. Replacing the televisions is economically efficient regardless of who pays.

If Quantum Corporation has a legal right to use its equipment despite the problems at the hotel, then the hotel will pay $12,000 to replace the televisions. It has an incentive to spend the money to replace the televisions because its profits will rise by $20,000, which exceeds the cost of the replacements. If Quantum has no legal right to cause this problem for the hotel, then Quantum maximizes its profit by paying the hotel to replace its televisions rather than spending $50,000 to modify its equipment. Quantum gains as long as it pays the hotel less than $50,000; the hotel gains (and is willing to replace its televisions) as long as it receives at least the cost of the replacements, $12,000. We can expect Quantum Corporation and the hotel to reach a voluntary agreement that helps them both. Quantum pays the hotel some amount of money between $12,000 and $50,000, the hotel replaces its televisions, and Quantum continues using its research equipment.

This example shows that the same outcome (replacement of the televisions) occurs regardless of whether the law permits Quantum to create the interference. The economically efficient outcome can result from side payments in either direction. The law determines the direction of the side payments, so it affects the *distribution of income* (who pays whom) but not the *allocation of resources* (actual production and modification or replacement of equipment).

FOR REVIEW

20.6 What does the phrase *internalize an externality* mean?

20.7 Explain how side payments can internalize an externality.

20.8 What determines who makes side payments to whom (i.e., the direction of side payments)?

QUESTION

20.9 Alter the Quantum Corporation example so that Quantum could eliminate the television interference at the hotel by spending only $4,000.
   a. What happens if Quantum Corporation has a legal right to use its equipment despite the reception problems it causes at the hotel?
   b. What happens if Quantum has no legal right to cause this problem for the hotel?

PROBLEMS WITH SIDE PAYMENTS

In reality, side payments do not internalize all externalities. People harmed by pollution may find it impractical to get together, identify polluters, agree on the side payments and on how to share their costs, make the offers, and make sure that polluters honor the agreements. To say this another way, transactions costs may be too high.

TRANSACTIONS COSTS

transactions cost — a cost of trading (buying and selling)

Transactions costs are the costs of trading (buying and selling).

Transactions costs include the time and money that a person spends to go to a store or arrange an appointment, obtain information, bargain with people, wait in a line, transport products, and so on.

Side payments can internalize externalities if transactions costs are sufficiently low. Low transactions costs give people incentives to arrange side payments to eliminate economic inefficiencies and share the gains from creating economic efficiency. Laws and property rights determine who makes side payments to whom in equilibrium.

If transactions costs are too high, side payments are impractical because arranging them is too expensive. It may simply be too difficult or costly to bring

"Oh, we're not having a party. That noise is the tape of the party you gave last night."

Early negotiations about future side payments.
Source: The Wall Street Journal.

people together, bargain and agree on side payments, and enforce an agreement. In that case, an equilibrium may be economically inefficient as in Figure 20.3; high transactions costs prevent side payments that could create efficiency. Laws and property rights (for example, laws regarding the amount of pollution a firm can generate) affect marginal private costs, so they affect equilibrium prices and quantities produced.

The Coase theorem summarizes these results:[5]

> Coase theorem: If transactions costs are sufficiently low, the equilibrium is economically efficient regardless of whether firms have the right to pollute, though the law affects who makes side payments to whom. With high transactions costs, however, laws and property rights affect the equilibrium quantity, and the equilibrium may not be economically efficient.

EXAMPLE: LOW TRANSACTIONS COSTS Railroad tracks run by a farm, and sparks from passing trains damage crops near the tracks. A farmer loses $50 from the sparks, and the railroad could prevent sparks by spending $100. It is economically efficient for the railroad to emit sparks because the social cost of preventing the sparks ($100) exceeds the social benefit from preventing them ($50). The transactions costs are low because the farmer and the railroad can fairly easily discuss the situation; for simplicity, suppose that the costs are zero.

If the farmer has the legal right not to suffer crop damage, the railroad will offer a side payment to the farmer to buy the right to emit sparks. The railroad is willing to pay up to $100 for this right; the farmer is willing to sell the right for any price above $50. The railroad and farmer will agree on a voluntary trade in which the railroad will pay the farmer some amount between $50 and $100 and its trains will continue to emit sparks.

Suppose, instead, that the railroad has the legal right to emit sparks. The highest price that the farmer will offer the railroad to prevent the damage is $50, but the railroad will not accept this payment because it would have to spend $100 to prevent sparks. The railroad and farmer will not agree on any side payments, and the trains will continue to emit sparks.

This example shows that the result is economically efficient (the railroad emits sparks) regardless of how the law assigns property rights. The law does affect the distribution of income, though. The railroad benefits if it has the legal right to emit sparks because it does not have to make side payments to the farmer; the farmer benefits if the law does not give the railroad the right to emit sparks because in that case the railroad will pay for that right.

EXAMPLE: HIGH TRANSACTIONS COSTS Suppose that Quantum Corporation's research equipment interferes with television reception in 1,000 nearby houses, each with one television. (The hotel from the earlier example has gone out of business.) It would cost $60 per house to modify the televisions to prevent the interference for a total cost of $60,000. Quantum, however, could modify its equipment for $50,000 to prevent interference. The transactions costs are higher in this example than in the example with the hotel because it might be quite costly for Quantum to negotiate separately with each of 1,000 house-

---

[5]This theorem is named for Ronald Coase, a recipient of the Nobel Memorial Prize in Economic Science.

holds. For simplicity, assume that such negotiation would be prohibitively expensive.

Assume also that good television reception is worth more than $60 to each homeowner. Each homeowner would prefer to pay $60, if necessary, to modify her television to avoid suffering from the interference. In the economically efficient outcome, Quantum will modify its equipment because this is the cheapest way to stop the interference. This solution is economically efficient because the benefit of good reception exceeds its cost ($50,000).

Suppose that Quantum Corporation has the legal right to use its equipment, even if it causes interference. If transactions costs were sufficiently low, people would get together and pay Quantum to modify its equipment. High transactions costs will prevent this, though. Instead, Quantum will go on using its equipment, and each homeowner will prefer to spend $60 rather than suffer the interference, so 1,000 homeowners will spend $60 each. This result is economically inefficient because it would be cheaper to modify Quantum's equipment.

If, on the other hand, Quantum has no legal right to interfere with television reception, then Quantum will spend $50,000 to modify its equipment and stop the interference. This is the economically efficient outcome. This example shows that when transactions costs are high, the law affects the economic efficiency of the outcome.

GOVERNMENT POLICIES

When transactions costs are high and the equilibrium is not economically efficient, the government may, in principle, be able to improve the situation. It may create a more efficient situation by imposing taxes or regulations or by issuing sellable rights to pollute. Whether government actions will actually create a more efficient situation depends on the political forces that determine government policies. (Chapters 21 and 22 discuss influences on government policies.)

TAXES AND REGULATIONS

The government can internalize an externality by taxing or fining firms that pollute. The tax or fine raises the private cost of production. If the tax for each additional amount of pollution equals the marginal cost to other people of that pollution, then the tax equalizes the private and social costs and internalizes the externality.

We must distinguish between the *total tax*—the total amount of money that a firm must pay to the government if it pollutes—and the *marginal tax*—the extra amount that the firm must pay if it pollutes *more*. If the marginal tax equals the marginal cost to other people from the pollution, then the tax internalizes the externality. **Figure 20.6** shows the equilibrium at Point B, where buyers pay the price P_B (including tax), sellers receive the price P_S (net of tax), and equilibrium output is Q_B, the economically efficient quantity.

The government can impose the tax in Figure 20.6 only if it has sufficient information to calculate the marginal cost to other people so it can set the appropriate level of the tax and change the tax when the marginal cost to other people changes. An alternative to such a tax or fine is a government regulation. The government may be able to require industry output at the economically efficient level, Q_B. Regulations can be effective, however, only if the government also has

FIGURE 20.6

TAX ON POLLUTION

A per-unit tax on a good, equal to its marginal cost to other people, causes equilibrium production to fall to Q_B, the economically efficient level.

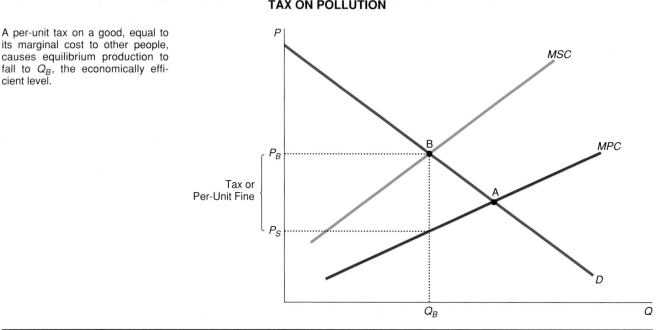

reliable, up-to-date information about the economically efficient quantity and if it can impose that quantity on firms in an efficient manner.

Taxes can provide better incentives than regulations. For example, suppose that the government wants to limit the total amount of pollution from an industry. If it does so through regulation, a firm that learns of a new method to reduce pollution may have no incentive to adopt that method. However, if the government limits pollution by taxing it, the firm may be able to reduce its taxes and raise its profits by adopting the new method. Taxes can provide firms with more effective incentives to use new, lower-cost methods of reducing pollution than regulations can provide.[6]

Taxes have a second benefit over regulations to internalize externalities. They generate revenue for the government, allowing reductions in other taxes. If the government were to receive $100 billion from taxes on pollution, for example, it could reduce income taxes by that amount, lowering the deadweight social losses from both income taxes and pollution.

SELLABLE RIGHTS TO POLLUTE

The government can limit the total amount of pollution at the lowest possible cost by issuing sellable rights to pollute, as the U.S. government began doing on a limited scale in 1991. The government might limit total pollution of a certain type to

---

[6]If the government could always learn about a new method at the same time that firms learn about it, the government could change its regulations. If firms sometimes obtain technical information that the government lacks, however, then taxes create stronger incentives to adopt new methods.

Taxes fail to cover drinking's costs, study finds

By Gina Kolata

Taxes on cigarettes cover the costs imposed on society by smoking, but taxes on alcohol do not pay for the costs of drinking, a new study reports.

The findings published in today's issue of The Journal of the American Medical Association, reflected the fact that smokers tend to die sooner than nonsmokers, saving society the cost of their pensions and other benefits. This saving would offset the extra costs of smoking, like the cost of days lost from work and extra medical care.

Taxes on alcohol, in contrast, did not reimburse society for the cost of drinking because the costs of drunken driving were so high, the researchers found.

Although there have been numerous discussions in Congress about raising the taxes on cigarettes and alcohol, legislators have considered raising these taxes to alleviate the budget deficit, not to repay society for the costs of smoking and drinking.

Looking for Cost of Bad Habits

"What we were looking at was economic reasons for not wanting to subsidize bad health habits," said Willard G. Manning of the University of Michigan in Ann Arbor, an author of the study.

The state and federal taxes on a pack of cigarettes averaged 37 cents. The researchers calculated that the cost to society of smoking was about 15 cents per pack of cigarettes, but if they also included the cost of fires and the health effects of passive smoking on other family members, the cost to society of smoking was 38 cents a pack.

The average taxes on an ounce of alcohol were about 23 cents per ounce. But the researchers found that the cost to society of drinking was about 48 cents per ounce of alcohol consumed.

The researchers calculated that from the age of 20 a smoker lost 137 minutes of life expectancy for every pack of cigarettes smoked. They said a heavy drinker lost 20 minutes of life expectancy for every ounce of pure alcohol consumed in excess of 2.3 ounces a day, or approximately five drinks.

The study distinguished between the external costs tobacco and alcohol abusers inflict on others and the internal costs they and their families pay. The researchers said the study, which considered only the external costs, was the first to compare those costs to tax revenues from tobacco and alcohol sales.

Results Were Not Expected

The research was financed by the National Center for Health Services Research and was conducted by Dr. Manning and Ennett B. Keeler of the Rand Corporation, a private research organization in Santa Monica, Calif.

Dr. Manning said that the group decided to look at the costs of smoking and drinking because "there's a sense that smokers don't pay their own way." He and his colleagues strongly suspected that when they added up the costs of medical care, time lost from work, and other expenses, they would find that society was subsidizing smokers.

"It is true that smokers use more resources, but they also die early," he said. "They don't get to collect on the Social Security and Medicare services that they have paid for. The net result is that the differences between smokers and nonsmokers are not as great as we thought."

With drinking, Dr. Manning said, "drunk driving is the principal cost." Drunken driving each year kills 7,400 people who were not drinking, Dr. Manning said. The researchers calculated a value to society of $1.6 million for each life lost. "That's the dominant figure in the calculation," he said.

Dr. Manning added that there are other reasons besides economic costs to think of increasing taxes on cigarettes and alcohol. Some studies have found that when cigarettes cost more, teenagers are less likely to start smoking. Other studies have found that when beer costs more, young adults drink less.

The researchers said that there were strong reasons to increase federal taxes on beer and wine, which are taxed at a much lower rate than distilled spirits.

"Higher beer taxes would make particular sense," Dr. Manning said in a statement, "because it's the drug of choice for teens and young adults who drive when they're drunk."

Taxes and the Externalities of Alcohol: What policies would you recommend to the government on the basis of this study?

Source: Gina Kolata, "Taxes Fail to Cover Drinking's Costs, Study Finds," *New York Times*, March 17, 1989, p. A13.

---

3 million units per year (measured in terms of tons of particulates, gases, etc.). It could then issue 300,000 pollution certificates, each of which would give the owner the legal right to emit 10 units of that type of pollution each year. The government would prohibit polluting without a certificate. The government could sell these pollution certificates to the highest bidders, allowing owners to buy or

A new commodity to be traded: government permits for pollution

In a departure from traditional regulatory practices, Congress gave polluters the right to meet sulfur emissions standards by buying and selling allowances that the Environmental Protection Agency will allot to individual plants.

One company may find that it pays to install smokestack scrubbers on aging coal-fired boilers, bringing its emissions below the require-ments, and then sell the surplus allowances. Another may leave untouched a heavy sulfur polluter that is otherwise efficient, and will buy allowances to cover the excess emissions. Still another may subsidize customers' purchases of energy-efficient appliances and lighting equipment, thereby cutting electricity demand and permitting it to shut down its offending boilers.

Could Serve as a Model

Many environmental analysts say, moreover, that the new market could serve as a model for least-cost controls on other pollutants—notably the smog-producing chemicals that bedevil most American cities. And it could presage a far more ambitious effort to limit emissions of gases that are widely thought to be warming the earth's atmosphere.

Sellable rights to pollute the air.

Source: "A New Commodity to Be Traded: Government Permits for Pollution," *New York Times,* July 17, 1991, p. A1.

sell the certificates at any time. Firms with the highest costs of reducing pollution would have incentives to pay the highest prices for these certificates; firms with lower costs of reducing pollution would have incentives to reduce pollution rather than to buy the certificates.

This system has an important economic advantage: it leads to the lowest-cost method of reducing pollution to the specified level. Suppose that the steel and rubber industries cause the same kind of pollution. If the government taxes both industries, both will respond by reducing pollution. It may be cheaper, however, to reduce pollution in the rubber industry than in the steel industry. In that case, it would be economically efficient to allow the steel industry to pollute more and to concentrate pollution-reduction efforts on the rubber industry, where it is cheaper. It is difficult to create taxes and regulations that match these incentives, particularly when economic conditions (demand and supply in each industry and technologies to reduce pollution) change continually. Pollution certificates could accomplish the goal of economically efficient reduction of pollution. Firms in the steel industry would outbid firms in the rubber industry for the certificates. This method would give firms with the lowest-cost methods of reducing pollution the incentive to do so, while allowing pollution by firms that face high costs of reducing it.

For Review

20.10   Explain the Coase theorem.

20.11   Explain why an equilibrium with externalities and high transactions costs can be economically inefficient.

20.12 Draw a graph to show how taxes can internalize externalities with high transactions costs.

---   QUESTION   ---

20.13 What would be the effect on the amount of chocolate sold and the price of chocolate if chocolate manufacturers were made legally liable for increases in dental bills as a result of consumption of chocolate? (Assume that it is easy to figure out how much of each dental bill is due to eating chocolate, and assume that the law does not affect the frequency of tooth brushing or flossing.)

EXTERNALITIES AND PROPERTY RIGHTS

Many externalities occur because no one in particular owns some resources. When no one owns a resource, no one is likely to protect it from misuse. Throughout history, people have destroyed forests because they were unowned, used farming methods that destroyed soil on unowned land and moved on to other land, and polluted unowned lakes and streams. No one owns the ozone layer; no one owns the upper atmosphere of the earth.

Some externalities would not occur if all resources were owned and property rights were clearly defined and well-enforced. No one, for example, would permit pollution of a lake on her land without adequate compensation. The requirement that a polluter must compensate the owner raises the polluter's costs so that the private costs of his actions equal the social costs; it eliminates the externality. While it is easy to define and enforce property rights in some resources, it is much harder in others, such as the air outside a person's house or the ozone layer.

When transactions costs are low, well-enforced property rights in all relevant resources eliminate externalities because side payments can equate private and social costs. In this case, the assignment of property rights (the decision of who owns what resources) affects only the distribution of income. When transactions costs are high, however, the assignment of property rights can determine whether the resulting equilibrium is economically efficient or inefficient. In the earlier Quantum Corporation example, ownership of the right to create electromagnetic radiation within several miles of the factory versus the right of freedom from that radiation determines whether Quantum will modify its equipment to prevent the radiation (the economically efficient equilibrium in the example) or whether each family will modify its television (the economically inefficient equilibrium).

PRIVATE OWNERSHIP AND COMMON RESOURCES

property right — a legal right to decide the use of a scarce resource or to sell the resource to someone else

private ownership — a property right held by one person or a small group of people

A **property right** is a legal right to decide the use of a scarce resource or to sell the resource to someone else.

Private ownership means that one person (or a small group of people) has a property right to use or sell a resource.

Most people privately own their clothes, cars, stereo equipment, and other personal goods. People also privately own businesses or shares of stock in corporations.

If a resource is not privately owned, it may be unowned or it may legally belong to society as a whole.

common resource — a resource that belongs to no one or to society as a whole

A **common resource** is something that belongs to no one or to society as a whole.

Legally, property rights are matters of degree rather than being all-or-nothing. An owner has the legal right to do certain things with his property, but not other things. Zoning laws, for example, can prevent a homeowner from establishing a business in his home or painting his house fluorescent orange. Restrictive covenants control uses of some land. These legal restrictions prevent an owner from doing certain things with property, such as cutting down trees or constructing a building.[7]

Owners of private property have incentives to protect their properties' values. Logging on private land reduces the value of that land by removing valuable trees, so owners of private land allow logging only if loggers pay the owners an amount that exceeds the fall in the value of the land. Loggers will pay this amount only if someone values the wood highly enough to pay a price that will cover this cost. Nothing similar prevents people from destroying rain forests, however, or other valuable lands that are common resources. Property rights put decision making in the hands of accountable people who want to protect the values of their properties.

Because everyone has the right to use common resources, they are overused. No one has a strong incentive to use less or conserve a common resource; each person wants to be a free rider and let other people work to protect the resource. This is called the *tragedy of the commons.*[8]

tragedy of the commons — the overuse of a common resource relative to its economically efficient use

The **tragedy of the commons** is the overuse of a common resource relative to its economically efficient use.

Examples

There are many examples of common resources. Throughout history, wilderness has usually been a common resource. Many species of life are endangered because, as common resources, they are overhunted. Rain forests and other valuable lands are overused and destroyed. Roads and highways, public parks, and beaches are often overcrowded. Lakes and oceans are overfished. For example, cod, once plentiful off the New England coast, is now scarce; deep-sea fish may be next.

The problem is not new. Wood was the major source of energy and an important construction material for houses, ships, furniture, tools, and carriages in 15th-century to 18th-century Europe. The forests destroyed in the process of cutting wood were common resources and were not replaced. As historian Fernad Braudel puts it, "Common land was the enemy of the forest." By the beginning of the 18th century a much smaller supply of wood was available because of deforestation in the earlier centuries, and the price of wood rose dramatically. This led people to substitute to coal as a major source of fuel.[9] The tragedy of the commons

---

[7]Some environmental groups, such as the Nature Conservancy, protect wildlife by buying restrictive covenants. For example, a firm may own land with a forest that is home to a rare species of bird. The group may pay the firm for a restrictive covenant that would prevent the owner from doing things to the land that might harm the birds. Even if the company were to sell the land, the restrictive covenant would remain and prevent the new owner of the land from doing those things.

[8]The term comes from the classic paper by biologist Garrett Hardin, "The Tragedy of the Commons," *Science* 162 (December 13, 1968), p. 1,244.

[9]Fernad Braudel, in *The Structures of Everyday Life*, vol. 1 of *Civilization and Capitalism, 15th–18th Century* (New York: Harper & Row, 1986), pp. 363–367.

IN THE NEWS

U.N. talks combat threat to fishery

Seek to control overfishing that is said to be wiping out several species

By David E. Pitt
Special to The New
York Times

UNITED NATIONS, July 23— In a basement conference room a world away from the klieg-lighted talks upstairs on Bosnia, Iraq, and Haiti, more than 150 diplomats here have been grappling with what most agree is a grave but less photogenic crisis: the threat to the earth's fisheries.

Alarmed by evidence that cod, tuna, mackerel, pollack, and scores of other valuable species are being wiped out by overfishing, the United Nations opened a three-week conference on July 12 to try to lay the groundwork for a global system to manage and repropagate the fish that are still left.

"Fish are a common property resource," Ross Reid, Canada's newly installed Minister of Fishing and Oceans, said at the conference last week. "There is a natural tendency for each fishing vessel, and each fishing country, to try to take as much as it can from the common resource. The result is as predictable as it is disastrous."

The tragedy of the commons.
Source: David E. Pitt, "U.N. Talks Combat Threat to Fishery," *New York Times,* July 25, 1993, p. 13.

also led to overgrazing of medieval pastures, air pollution associated with the industrial revolution, and the destruction of prairies through overgrazing in the early United States. In the Middle East, people cut trees for firewood, destroying forests and expanding the desert.

The tragedy of the commons afflicts many common resources including public parks and beaches, highways, air and water, the so-called *electronic superhighway* (the Internet), and endangered species of life. Traffic jams in Los Angeles alone have been estimated to cost $10 billion per year in lost output. If drivers had to pay the social cost of their road use, they would drive at different times to reduce traffic jams at peak hours, switch to less congested roads, car pool more, and drive less. For several years, Singapore has charged drivers to use certain roads at peak hours by requiring badges on cars. Newer technologies will allow electronic monitoring and billing for road use, reducing the costs of collecting tolls.

NUMERICAL EXAMPLE: LAKE NESS

Lake Ness is a common resource with many fish that can be sold for $2 each. One person fishing on Lake Ness can catch 400 fish on an average day. Two people fishing on the lake can expect to catch 350 fish each on an average day. **Table 20.1** shows how the number of fish caught per person depends on the number of people fishing. The opportunity cost of each person's time working at another job is $200 per day, and the other job is exactly as much fun as fishing. The marginal private cost and marginal social cost of fishing are equal; both are $200 per day.

Because Lake Ness is a common resource, it is overused. To see why, think about the private incentives to fish. A person has an incentive to fish if he can expect to catch at least 100 fish per day, earning at least $200. Otherwise, he will

TABLE 20.1

FISHING ON LAKE NESS

Number of People Fishing	Number of Fish Caught per Person	Total	Marginal Private Benefit	Total Value of Fish Caught	Marginal Social Benefit
1	400	(400)	$800	$ 800	$ 800
2	350	(700)	700	1,400	600
3	300	(900)	600	1,800	400
4	250	(1,000)	500	2,000	200
5	200	(1,000)	400	2,000	0
6	150	(900)	300	1,800	−200
7	100	(700)	200	1,400	−400
8	50	(400)	100	800	−600

take the other job for $200 per day. If fewer than seven people were to fish on the lake, then someone else would have an incentive to join them, until seven people were fishing on the lake. No one would choose to be the eighth person fishing on the lake, however, because that person would earn only $100 from fishing, less than the $200 that the other job would pay. Equilibrium occurs when the marginal private benefit from fishing equals the marginal private cost ($200), so the equilibrium number of people fishing is seven.

It is economically inefficient, however, for seven people to fish on the lake. Each of seven people would catch 100 fish, so their total catch is 700 fish worth $1,400. If only six people were to fish the lake, each person would catch 150 fish for a total catch of 900 fish; six people catch more fish than seven people. That is

IN THE NEWS

The new range war has the desert as foe

Hundreds of millions of acres are being lost

By Myra Klockenbrink

Before the era of great cattle drives, bison, bear, and other wildlife were abundant. Giant trees paved the mountain sides and commanded flood plains and grasses grew as high as a horse's belly.

"Now it's hard to find anything growing that would scratch a horse's ankles," said Norbert Riedy of the Wilderness Society. "The natural grasslands are all but gone."

Chief among the expensive habits that have depleted the land in the West is overgrazing. The cattle industry began with millions of acres of free and unrestricted pasturage. Though much of the damage was done in the great cattle drives of the late 1800s, the number of cattle on the land has reached an all-time high of more than 19 million head in the 11 western states today.

The number of cattle and the long periods they are kept in one area are what lead to overgrazing, and repeated overgrazing undermines tissue reserves until the plant grows weak and dies.

Overuse of a common resource.

Source: Myra Klockenbrink, "The New Range War Has the Desert as Foe, *New York Times*, August 20, 1991, p. C4.

Experts say space junk may create peril by 2000

By William J. Broad

Unless concerted action is soon taken, low orbits around the Earth could become so clogged with space junk by the turn of the century that they will be too dangerous for satellites and manned spacecraft to use, federal experts said yesterday.

Space is overused because it is unowned.

Source: William J. Broad, "Experts Say Space Junk May Create Peril by 2000," *New York Times,* October 12, 1990, p. A13.

not the only reason to have six rather than seven people fishing, though. If a seventh person fishes, the economy loses the productivity of that person at the other job (paying $200 per day). The economy's loss from the seventh person fishing equals 200 fish worth $400 plus $200 worth of work that the seventh person could have done at the other job. A similar argument shows that the economy suffers a loss if six or five people fish on the lake.

It is economically efficient for four people to fish. To see why, think about the marginal social benefit from fishing (the last column in the table). The marginal social benefit is the value of the extra fish that society obtains if one more person fishes. The marginal social benefit of a fourth person, $200, equals the marginal social cost (the value of the person's work at the other job). Adding a fifth person would be economically inefficient because it would not add to the total value of fish caught in the lake and it would reduce the value of output at the other job by $200. It is economically efficient to have only four people fishing on the lake.[10]

When the lake is a common resource, people indulge in overfishing. The equilibrium amount of fishing exceeds the economically efficient amount. In this example, each person creates an externality by reducing the number of fish that other people catch. This negative externality causes overfishing, just as negative externalities from pollution cause overproduction of products that cause pollution.[11] In many real-life cases, overfishing a lake also causes a fall in the fish population that reduces the number of fish that people will catch in the future.

Figure 20.7 graphs the tragedy of the commons on Lake Ness. The marginal private benefit of fishing is the value of the fish that one additional person would catch by fishing. The marginal social benefit of fishing is the value of the increase in the total number of fish that would be caught if one more person fishes. There is an externality because the marginal social benefit is smaller than the marginal private benefit. For example, suppose four people fish in Lake Ness. Table 20.1 shows that if a fifth person fishes, she catches 200 fish worth $2 each, so the marginal private benefit of fishing is $400. But the marginal social benefit of fishing (the last column) is *zero*. Figure 20.7 shows that the equilibrium quantity is seven people while the economically efficient quantity is four, so there is overfishing.

DISCUSSION

The problem of overfishing led the United States to extend its claim on off-shore ocean waters from the traditional 3 miles to 200 miles. Though this reduced fishing by foreigners, it did not reduce overfishing by Americans. Despite government attempts to limit overfishing through limits on nets, catches, and the length of the fishing season, overfishing continues. Private ownership of harvesting rights would provide a solution, as success in Canada, Alaska, and Delaware shows. Some policy analysts have suggested that the government auction off these rights, as it does mineral rights.

Excessive logging in forests, a similar problem, generally occurs on government lands. Sweden has considerable forest land, mostly privately owned, yet Sweden imports wood because land owners do not want to cut their trees down fast enough. The situation in Finland was similar until the Finnish government

[10]It would *also* be economically efficient for three people to fish in this example. If a fourth person fishes, the value of fish output rises by $200 (from $1,800 to $2,000), but the value of other output in the economy (the goods that the fourth person could have produced at the other job) falls by $200.

[11]Negative externalities cause output of those goods to exceed the economically efficient level.

FIGURE 20.7

TRAGEDY OF THE COMMONS: OVERUSE OF A COMMON RESOURCE

Q_A shows the equilibrium quantity with a common resource. Q_B shows the economically efficient quantity. $Q_A - Q_B$ gives the amount of overuse of the common resource (overfishing in the example).

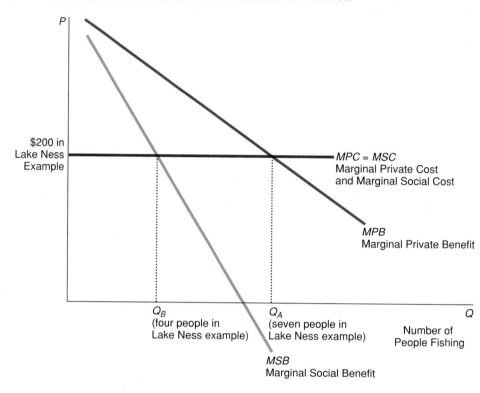

tried to encourage more cutting by taxing land owners on the value of the timber they could have cut. Governments of third-world countries frequently subsidize cutting forests. In the decade of the 1980s alone, for example, the government of Brazil subsidized deforestation of an area larger than France in the Amazon basin. In the decade of the 1990s, deforestation may occur on common-resource land around the world in an area twice this size, mostly in poorer countries where burning wood is a main source of energy and woodlands are not privately owned.

PRIVATE OWNERSHIP TO INTERNALIZE EXTERNALITIES

Private ownership of a resource can internalize externalities and eliminate the tragedy of the commons. Property rights give an owner an incentive to care for property by preventing its overuse. Private ownership shifts the marginal private benefit curve in Figure 20.7 downward so that it equals the marginal social benefit curve, creating an economically efficient equilibrium.

EXAMPLE: LAKE NESS CONTINUED

Suppose that someone owns Lake Ness so it is no longer a common resource and the owner can charge people to fish on her lake. She maximizes her profit by allowing only four people (the economically efficient number) to fish on the lake.

World's whales worth more alive than dead

International Whaling Commission meeting

*By Bronwen Maddox
Environment
Correspondent*

Whales are worth more alive than dead, UK and US officials will argue when they meet in Mexico tomorrow ahead of the annual meeting of the International Whaling Commission.

Potential revenues from whale watching—an increasingly popular form of tourism—could soon reach several hundred million pounds worldwide.

Can whales be saved from extinction by private property rights?

Source: Bronwen Maddox, "World's Whales Worth More Alive than Dead," *Financial Times*, May 16, 1994, p. 6.

To see why, think about the fees that she can charge people to fish on the lake. If she charges a fishing fee of $300 per day, four people will fish, each catching 250 fish and selling them for $500. After paying the $300 fee, each person has $200 left over. These people earn as much fishing as at the other job ($200 per day), so they are willing to pay the fee and fish. The owner of the lake earns a profit of $1,200 ($300 from each of the four fishermen).[12]

The $1,200 profit is the highest profit that the owner can obtain. If she were to charge a higher fishing fee, fewer people would be willing to fish and her profit would be lower. For example, if she were to charge $350, only three people would fish.[13] If she were to charge a lower fishing fee, more people may fish, but her profit would be lower. For example, a $200 fee would generate a profit of only $1,000 because five people would pay the fee and fish, each catching 200 fish, selling them for $400, paying the $200 fee, and keeping $200. Private property rights create an incentive for the owner to set fees for use of the property in a way that makes its use economically efficient. In this way, private ownership of the common resource eliminates the tragedy of the commons.

OTHER EXAMPLES

Many private game farms charge fees for hunting. Like the owner of Lake Ness, they have incentives not to permit overhunting. The National Wildlife Sanctuary manages thousands of acres of wildlife preserves for the benefit of birds. It charges fees for people to watch the birds and for cattle to graze on the land. Private ownership prevented extinction of abalone; when the price of abalone rose far enough, preservation became profitable. Similarly, private turtle farms have helped prevent extinction of sea turtles. In Scotland, water pollution of streams has not been a serious problem because people have private property rights to streams.

Indigenous peoples living in the Labrador Peninsula developed private property rights to reduce externalities in the fur trade. In the mid-1600s, before fur trade was an important business, people hunted mainly for food and clothing. Though animals were a common resource, they were plentiful and the externalities were small. In the 1700s, however, increasing demand for fur by European settlers raised its price and increased hunting. This increased the externalities from common ownership. The indigenous groups solved this problem by establishing private property rights that gave families ownership of hunting land to the exclusion of other families. Poaching (illegal hunting) of animals continues to be a problem throughout the world.

SAVING RESOURCES FOR FUTURE GENERATIONS

The overuse of a common resource frequently leads to its depletion, so common resources are usually used up more rapidly than is economically efficient, leaving fewer resources for future generations than would be economically efficient.[14] Private ownership can eliminate this problem and provide owners with incentives to conserve resources for future generations. A person who owns a resource has

---

[12]If it makes the example easier to understand, think of the fishing fee as $299 rather than $300, giving four people an incentive to choose fishing over the alternative job.

[13]She can also earn a $1,200 profit by charging a $400 fishing fee. In that case, three people pay the fee and fish. This is also economically efficient, as footnote 10 explained.

[14]How many resources is it economically efficient to save for future generations? That is a subject of controversy; a brief discussion of this topic appears in Chapter 21 in the section on cost–benefit analysis.

SOCIAL AND ECONOMIC ISSUES

Externalities, Actions That Hurt Other People, and the Role of Government

Consider the following ("libertarian") idea:

> People have the right to do whatever they want with themselves and their own property as long as they do not hurt other people.

Some opponents of this view believe it creates problems, including how to decide what actions hurt other people. Suppose, for example, that some people feel seriously offended because other people use drugs, alcohol, or pornography; listen to songs with offensive lyrics; act in rude and ill-mannered ways; dress offensively; or advocate offensive government policies. Knowledge of these actions may cause people moral anguish, and the psychological feelings may even contribute to physical health problems. If a person is clearly affected badly by these actions, do (or should) other people have a right to continue these behaviors, or do they have no such right because their behaviors hurt other people? Should the government limit these behaviors?

What is the difference between harm caused by pollution and harm caused by knowledge or a belief about what another person is doing? Some people claim that there is no difference, and that the govern-ment is as justified in using taxes and regulations to reduce use of pornography or songs with offensive lyrics as to reduce air pollution. In this view, both pollution and these other behaviors have negative exter-nalities that justify government actions.

Other people see a difference between the phys-ical harm people suffer from polluted air and the moral or psychological harm, and even the physical harm, that results from knowing that other people engage in offensive behaviors. They make at least two arguments. First, some people argue for a dis-tinction between a physical invasion of property, such as polluting someone's water or air, and other harms (such as moral or psychological distress from private behaviors of other people) that do not result from physical invasions. Pollution is a physical inva-sion of property because the polluter causes actual physical particles to go into someone's water or air. (Presumably sound waves count as a physical inva-sion for this purpose, also.)

At least two problems complicate this view. First, it is not clear why anyone should care about this dis-tinction between physical invasion and other harm. Psychological and moral distress can be just as harm-ful to a person's well-being as many physical inva-

an incentive to conserve it for the future because conservation raises its value, that is, it raises the price at which the owner can sell the resource to someone who plans to use it in the future. That is why people take care of their own property; why firms invest in new machinery, equipment, or research and development; and why mining companies limit the rates at which they extract minerals from the earth.

DRAWBACKS OF PRIVATE PROPERTY RIGHTS

Though private property rights can provide a powerful way to internalize exter-nalities, three main drawbacks complicate this kind of solution to the problems of externalities. First, costs of defining or enforcing property rights in some resources may be high. For example, it is hard to define and enforce property rights in the air because the wind blows and air moves. How could anyone know whose air is whose? This drawback makes private property rights nearly impossi-ble in some cases, though technology provides a solution to the problem in other cases. For example, when grazing lands in the American West became crowded in

sions, or more harmful. (One response is that the harm from a physical invasion of property is clearly caused by the invader, while psychological harm may result as much from the beliefs and psychological makeup of the person who claims harm as the person he blames for offensive behavior.) Second, it may be hard to distinguish between a physical invasion and a psychological invasion. If Bob paints his house bright orange, and his neighbor Ray finds the color offensive, is this merely a psychological harm rather than a physical invasion? After all, photons of light travel from Bob's house into Ray's eyes; these photons may constitute a physical invasion. The same is true of sound waves from Bob's stereo, or from his mouth when he advocates some action that is morally offensive to Ray.

A second argument for distinguishing physical invasion of property from other cases is that people may have natural rights to their property that are violated by physical invasions such as pollution, but not by their own mental or psychological responses to other peoples' actions. This argument is subject to many of the same problems as the first argument. In addition, this view must explain the source of these natural rights, and why those rights are violated in one case but not the other.

Even if people were to agree that only a physical invasion of someone's property is an externality, additional problems arise. Anyone who breathes exhales carbon dioxide particles that spread to other people's property. (What if someone has bad breath?) Is this a physical invasion of property? Obviously, the government cannot stop people from exhaling. Should government policy distinguish between a situation in which a person lights a candle or flashlight at night and slightly illuminates her neighbor's property, and a situation in which she shines a very bright light on her neighbor's property at night? Perhaps you can just hear your neighbor's television if you listen closely; is this an externality that calls for the same government policy response as if your neighbor were to play loud music at full volume all night, every night, or open an explosives-testing business in his backyard?

In one sense, the idea of externalities is straightforward and this chapter discusses the main issues associated with them. On a deeper level, however, the idea of externalities involves rather complex issues on which people have fundamental disagreements, despite the immediate importance for real-life government policies.

the mid-19th century, people found it difficult to keep their cattle separate and it became hard to enforce property rights in cattle. Fences might have helped, but wood to make fences was too expensive. A solution emerged from two new ideas: branding cattle and barbed-wire fencing, which was cheaper than wood. More recently, it has become possible to "brand" whales by recording genetic prints and tracking the animals by satellite, making it cheaper to define and enforce private property rights in whales. It may soon be profitable to establish property rights in many endangered species; if those species generate profitable sales for their owners, the establishment of property rights could prevent their extinction.

A second drawback of private property rights is the potentially high transactions costs of charging people to use the property. Streets, for example, are common resources. Anyone can drive on them, so they become overcrowded, particularly at certain times of day. Each person who uses a street adds to its congestion and creates a negative externality for other drivers and passengers. If streets were privately owned, owners could charge tolls for their use (as in the Lake Ness example). Streets would be less crowded, and driving times and accident rates would be lower, but toll booths are costly to set up and operate.[15] When transactions costs are high, costs of government regulation are also likely to be high; in some cases, the only relevant choice may be between overuse and no use of a resource.

If transactions costs are high, correct assignment of property rights is important for the reasons discussed earlier in the chapter. In an earlier example, Quantum Corporation had property rights to use its equipment despite creating electromagnetic radiation that interfered with reception for nearby televisions. High transactions costs led homeowners to modify their televisions, which was economically inefficient.

FOR REVIEW

20.14 Explain the tragedy of the commons and why private property rights prevent it.

20.15 What difficulties arise in preventing the tragedy of the commons with private property rights?

QUESTIONS

20.16 a. Consider the Lake Ness example in the text. Recall that a private owner of the lake earned a $1,200 profit by choosing a $300 fee, which made use of the lake economically efficient (four people fished). Show that the owner's profits would be lower if she charged a fee of $200, or $500, or $600. (In each case, use Table 20.1 to find the number of people who would pay the fee and fish, and then calculate the owner's profit.)
b. Rework the Lake Ness example assuming fish sell for $1.00 each.

20.17 Many of the world's rain forests are common resources. If governments were to make the rain forests private property and give private property rights to certain people, who would gain and who would lose? Would it be possible to compensate any losers so that everyone would gain from creating private property rights in the rain forests?

POSITIVE EXTERNALITIES AND PUBLIC GOODS

Positive externalities generate less attention in political discussions than negative externalities, but they can be quite important. Many economists believe that scientific research and production of knowledge have positive externalities that play major roles in long-term economic growth. The development of cities as dynamic centers of business and culture may reflect positive externalities, and it may also have promoted economic growth. Culture itself is a product of positive externalities from the creation of music, art, and literature. Education and manners have positive externalities that enhance social interactions.

EQUILIBRIUM AND ECONOMIC EFFICIENCY WITH POSITIVE EXTERNALITIES

Figure 20.8 shows the basic graph of an equilibrium with a positive externality. The marginal private cost equals the marginal social cost; there is no marginal cost

---

[15]New electronic devices to monitor road use can automatically recognize a sticker on a car and mail a bill to its owner, but these devices are also costly.

FIGURE 20.8

POSITIVE EXTERNALITY

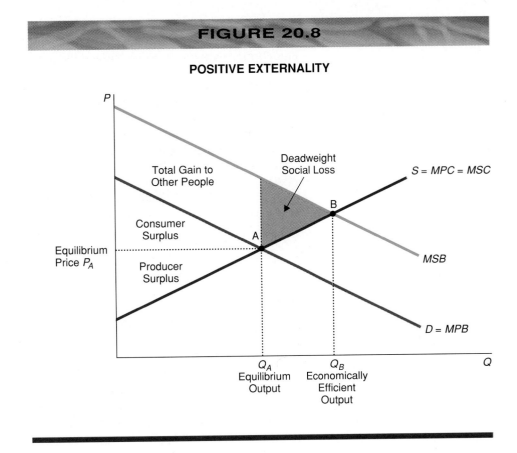

to other people. Others enjoy a marginal benefit, though, so the marginal social benefit (*MSB*) exceeds the marginal private benefit (*MPB*). The marginal private benefit curve is the demand curve; the marginal private cost curve is the supply curve.

If high transactions costs prevent people from making side payments, the equilibrium with perfect competition is at Point A, where the demand and supply curves cross, with equilibrium quantity Q_A. The economically efficient quantity, however, is Q_B, where the marginal social cost equals the marginal social benefit. The positive externality creates underproduction in which the equilibrium quantity is less than the economically efficient quantity. Underproduction occurs because people who buy and sell the good ignore its benefits to other people. The area of the shaded triangle shows the deadweight social loss from the underproduction. The figure also shows the producer surplus, consumer surplus, and total gain to other people in equilibrium.

With high transactions costs, the government could raise equilibrium output to the economically efficient level by doing the opposite of what it would do for a negative externality. It could, for example, subsidize production of goods with positive externalities. Just as a tax can create economic efficiency with negative externalities, so can a subsidy can create economic efficiency with positive externalities.[16] If transactions costs are sufficiently low, side payments can internalize positive externalities just as they internalize negative externalities, and the equilibrium (without subsidies) is economically efficient (Point B).

EXAMPLE: SIDE PAYMENTS

One example of side payments to internalize positive externalities occurs among apple growers and beekeepers. Apple trees have a positive externality for nearby beekeepers because apple blossoms provide nectar from which bees make honey. Beekeepers sometimes make side payments to apple growers to increase the number of apple trees to the economically efficient level (from Q_A to Q_B in Figure 20.8). Interestingly, beekeeping also has a positive externality for apple production, because bees pollinate apple blossoms. So apple growers sometimes make side payments to beekeepers rather than the reverse.

PUBLIC GOODS

Positive externalities are particularly important for certain types of goods, such as information, television broadcasting, and national defense.

NONRIVAL GOODS

If you eat an apple, one less apple remains for other people. If you watch a television show, however, you do not reduce the number of other people who can watch that show on their own televisions. When a farmer uses 100 acres of land to grow wheat, that land becomes unavailable for other people's use. But when a scientist or engineer uses technical knowledge to create new insights into biology or new types of computer chips, that technical knowledge remains available for other people to use.

nonrival good — a good for which the quantity available to other people does not fall when someone consumes it

> A good is **nonrival** if the quantity available for other people does not fall when someone consumes it.

Nonrival goods are not used up or depleted when people consume them.

EXAMPLES   Knowledge is an important nonrival good. One person's knowledge of science, technical formulas, computer algorithms, product designs, or methods for operating business firms does not reduce the amount of knowledge available to other people. Similarly, songs and music, stories, national defense, television and radio broadcasts, and (to some extent) police protection are nonrival goods.

NONEXCLUDABLE GOODS

nonexcludable good — a good that is prohibitively costly to provide only to people who pay for it while excluding other people from obtaining it

> A good is **nonexcludable** if it is prohibitively costly to provide the good only to people who pay for it (and prevent or exclude other people from obtaining it).

EXAMPLES   It may be prohibitively costly for a television station, such as a Public Broadcasting Service affiliate, to require that only people who send money to the station can watch its shows. Unless it scrambles its broadcast signals and sells

---

[16]Governments of many countries subsidize the arts—painting, music, theater, literature, and so on. A rationale for these subsidies is that the arts have a positive externality for society, and the subsidies prevent underproduction of paintings, music, theater, and literature. The subsidies could raise output from Q_A to Q_B in Figure 20.8. A more likely reason for these subsidies, however, is that they benefit consumers (patrons) of the arts, who comprise the main political constituency for these subsidies.

descrambling services, anyone with a television can watch its show. Its broadcasts are nonexcludable if descrambling is prohibitively costly. National defense is also a nonexcludable good; it is hard to exclude a few houses or isolated people when an army defends a city from a foreign aggressor.

PROBLEMS OF PUBLIC GOODS

public good — a nonrival and nonexcludable good

A **public good** is a nonrival and nonexcludable good.

Public goods present a unique economic problem because firms have little incentive to produce them. Few buyers willingly pay for nonexcludable goods because they can get them free. (Some people do pay for nonexcludable goods, as when people voluntarily contribute to PBS fund drives, but these payments are usually insufficient to cover costs.) A consumer might be willing to pay $100 for a public good if he had to pay to get the good, but he might prefer to be a *free rider* and let other people pay for the good. However, if everyone tries to be a free rider, then no one pays for the good and no firm is willing to produce it. Even if a few people choose to pay, their total payments may not be enough to make it profitable for firms to produce the good, or the small revenues may make it profitable for firms to produce the good only on a limited scale. For example, a television station may limit its broadcast hours or broadcast only less expensive shows.

The free-rider problem holds the equilibrium quantity of a public good below the economically efficient quantity.

In the extreme case, the equilibrium quantity of a public good is zero. No firm is willing to produce the good because no one pays for it; though people may value the good at more than its cost, they all try to be free riders. This equilibrium is economically inefficient. Suppose, for example, that 5,000 people would be willing to pay up to $1 each for a public good that costs $2,000 to produce. It would be economically efficient to produce the good because its value to buyers exceeds its cost of production. However, if fewer than 2,000 people resist the chance to be free riders and pay $1 each, no firm will produce the good.

Potential buyers of a public good might try to join together and share the payment for a public good. Even if low transactions costs would allow them to join together, however, many potential buyers would try to be free riders. They would falsely deny that they really wanted the public good or understate their willingness to pay for it, secretly hoping that other people would pay more and give them a free ride. As the number of people in the group increases, so does the free-rider problem.[17]

PRIVATE SUPPLY OF PUBLIC GOODS

Firms have devised methods to reduce the free-rider problem enough to make it profitable to produce certain public goods. For example, television broadcasts are public goods, but private firms in the United States produce them by combining them with advertising so that advertisers, rather than viewers, pay for the broadcasts. This method may become less effective in the future as more people watch previously taped shows and fast-forward through commercials. Advertisers try to avoid this problem sometimes by placing commercials within shows or movies by having characters conspicuously use products. Some cable and satellite broadcasters achieve

---

[17]Economists have devised complex methods to give people incentives to tell the truth about their willingness to pay for goods, but these methods have not yet found widespread use (and for some problems, they are not practical).

Copied software now common

Although the industry remains hugely profitable and competitive, some experts say the amount of theft reduces the incentives that developers have to create programs. But software creators are trying to fight back.

Last year, the Software Publishers Association, a trade group, conducted 75 raids, sent 561 warning letters, and filed 33 lawsuits against organizations and individuals it suspected of software piracy.

The problem will only get worse, industry executives say, as each new technology makes it easier to copy digital information.

Many in the industry feel that finding a way to protect copyrights is essential for the industry to avoid a crisis.

Private firms produce software, despite its public-good features, though the inability to exclude nonpayers may reduce incentives for innovation.

Source: "Copied Software Now Common," *New York Times,* July 27, 1992, p. D3.

excludability by scrambling their broadcasts. Some computer software is copy protected to achieve excludability; software firms achieve partial excludability by providing technical support only to registered users. A higher cost of achieving excludability reduces the incentive for firms to develop and produce new products.

ROLE FOR GOVERNMENT

The free-rider problem associated with public goods provides a fundamental rationale for government to provide certain public goods. The government may produce a public good, such as national defense, and require people to pay for the good through taxes. In a previous example, the government might tax 5,000 people 20 cents each to obtain $2,000 in tax revenue that it could use to pay for the public good. Government coercion can solve the free-rider problem. The government need not actually produce the public good; the key role of the government is to eliminate free riders. The government could raise the funds for the public good through taxes and then buy the public good from the private firm that would produce it at the lowest cost.

Government provision of public goods has two main drawbacks. First, the government lacks information about the amount of money that various people are willing to pay for any particular public good. This creates two more problems: the government cannot calculate the economically efficient level of the public good, and it may tax some people more and others less than they are willing to pay for the public good. The counter-argument to this objection states that the government may at least get closer to the economically efficient level of the public good than the free market would. Government provision of a public good has a second main drawback because actual government programs may reflect political pressures to benefit special-interest groups rather than considerations of economic efficiency.

Governments help provide excludability through patents and copyrights that provide limited-time property rights in ideas, product designs, and artistic creations. Patents increase scientists' incentives to produce new knowledge by giving them temporary property rights that (if enforced) help them to achieve excludability in the use of the new idea. Similarly, copyrights help artists to achieve excludability for their artistic creations such as stories and songs.

SOCIAL RESPONSIBILITY

If it were possible to change human behavior, the problems of externalities could be solved. Education and propaganda may be part of a socializing process in which people adopt certain values or learn to behave in certain ways. Clearly, it is sometimes possible to convince people to behave in ways that reduce externalities; people recycle, practice good manners, and contribute to charities. Experimental evidence suggests that people do not always free ride when given the opportunity; they often cooperate with other people, particularly when they interact with other people repeatedly in the same kind of situation. Evidence also suggests that persuasion can affect the level of charitable contributions. Whatever the chances for changes in human behavior in the future, however, externalities remain a problem in today's world.

FOR REVIEW

20.18 Draw a graph of an equilibrium with a positive externality. Show the equilibrium quantity, the economically efficient quantity, and the deadweight social loss.

20.19 What is a public good and what special problem does it present?

IN THE NEWS

Equations patented; Some see a danger

By Edmund L. Andrews
Special to The New
York Times

WASHINGTON, Feb. 14— Encouraged by a new attitude in the courts and at the Patent and Trademark Office, universities and corporations are rushing to stake patent claims in a whole new arena of intellectual property: mathematical equations.

The equations, known more technically as algorithms, use mathematics to solve such problems as how an airline can most efficiently schedule its planes or how a computer should handle data to operate as fast as possible.

But the growing number of the patents is causing concern among some mathemati-

cians that basic research and the free exchange of information could be inhibited.

"We face the real prospect that mathematics will become poorer as mathematicians become richer," said John Barwise, a mathematician and philosopher at Stanford University's Center for the Study of Language and Information. "If you suddenly create barriers so that people are not able to freely use the results of others, you're changing the rules that mathematicians have used for centuries."

Other scientists, university officials, and patent attorneys, however, say the patents are necessary to provide incentives for future research.

Ronald Bracewell, a profes-

sor of electrical engineering at Stanford who developed a new way to calculate what is known among mathematicians as a Fast Fourier Transform, said that without patent protection future research would be inhibited.

"By the time you've spent six months writing 10,000 lines of computer code, you know darn well it isn't something nature put there," he said. "The world of industry is demanding protection for what they very well know is proprietary information. Without the protection of patents, the incentive to get into the hard work of development would be lost."

To what degree should the government use patents to encourage the production of knowledge?

Source: Edmund L. Andrews, "Equations Patented; Some See a Danger," *New York Times,* February 18, 1987.

QUESTIONS

20.20 Well-attended parties are more fun than poorly attended parties. Explain what this observation has to do with this chapter.

20.21 A movie company sues people who made and sold pirated (unauthorized) copies of a movie on videotape. The movie originally cost $2 million to make and appeared at theaters last year. Draw a graph to show the marginal cost and average cost of providing the movie to a person on videotape. Would it be economically efficient for courts to allow people to make copies of videotapes (a) for their own use, (b) to lend to their friends, (c) to sell? How is this problem related to natural monopoly?

CONCLUSIONS

EXTERNALITIES

A negative externality occurs when the social costs of an action exceed its private costs. A negative externality raises the equilibrium quantity above the economically efficient quantity. The economically efficient quantity of pollution is not zero. The economically efficient level of pollution occurs when the social marginal benefit of reducing it equals the social marginal cost of reducing it.

INTERNALIZING EXTERNALITIES

Negative externalities occur when people do not pay all of the costs of their own actions so that other people bear some of the costs. Internalizing an externality makes people responsible for all of the costs of their own actions so that private and social costs are equal. When an externality is internalized, the equilibrium is economically efficient.

If transactions costs are low, side payments can internalize externalities and make an equilibrium economically efficient regardless of whether the law gives firms the right to pollute. The law determines only who makes side payments to whom.

If transactions costs are high, side payments do not occur. In this case, laws and property rights affect the equilibrium quantity, and the equilibrium may not be economically efficient. The government may be able to create a more efficient situation with taxes or regulations or by issuing sellable rights to pollute.

EXTERNALITIES AND PROPERTY RIGHTS

A property right is a legal right to decide the use of a scarce resource or to sell the resource to someone else. Private ownership of a resource gives one person or a small group of people a property right to use or sell that resource. A common resource is something that belongs to no one or to society as a whole.

Owners of private property have incentives to protect its value. But common resources are overused because no one has an incentive and legal right to prevent their overuse. Private ownership of a resource can eliminate this *tragedy of the commons* by giving the owner an incentive to care for the resource and prevent its overuse. The main drawbacks to this solution are the costs of establishing and enforcing property rights and the problems of economic inefficiency that high transactions costs may create.

POSITIVE EXTERNALITIES AND PUBLIC GOODS

A positive externality occurs when the social benefits of an action exceed its private benefits. With a positive externality, the equilibrium quantity is lower than the economically efficient quantity. Underproduction occurs because people who buy and sell a good ignore its benefits to other people. Low transactions costs allow side payments to internalize positive externalities. When transactions costs are high, the government may be able to raise equilibrium output to the economically efficient level through subsidies or regulation.

The quantity of a nonrival good available for other people does not fall when someone consumes it. It is prohibitively costly to provide a nonexcludable good only to people who pay for it and prevent or exclude other people from obtaining it. A public good is a nonrival and nonexcludable good.

Public goods present problems because firms have little incentive to produce them. Most buyers are unwilling to pay for nonexcludable goods because they can get them free; they prefer to be free riders and let other people pay. When everyone tries to free ride, no one pays for the good and no firm produces it. The free-rider problem reduces the equilibrium quantity of a public good below the economically efficient quantity. Firms have devised methods to reduce the free-rider problem enough to make it profitable to produce certain public goods, but a higher cost of excludability creates a smaller incentive for firms to develop and produce new products. The free-rider problem provides a fundamental rationale for government financing of public goods.

LOOKING AHEAD

This chapter suggested some important roles for government in the economy to reduce the deadweight social losses from externalities and to help provide public goods. The next two chapters turn to government policies. Chapter 21 discusses government regulations and taxes; Chapter 22 discusses the economics of law and public choice.

KEY TERMS

private cost	transactions cost
social cost	property right
private benefit	private ownership
social benefit	common resource
externality	tragedy of the commons
negative externality	nonrival good
positive externality	nonexcludable good
internalizing an externality	public good

QUESTIONS AND PROBLEMS

20.22 Governments usually limit the hunting seasons for most animals. What does this have to do with common resources?

20.23 Explain, with a graph, why subsidizing the production of goods with a positive externality can eliminate a deadweight social loss and create economic efficiency if transactions costs are high.

20.24 Suppose that the owners of a company have no legal liability for paying hospital bills, sick-leave, and so on, for their employees who are injured on the job. Do the owners have an incentive to invest in equipment and programs that reduce the probability and severity of accidents on the job?

20.25 A dentist and a writer live next door to each other, and each has her office at home. Screams of pain from the patients in the dentist's office interfere with the writer's creativity, causing her to write inferior novels and lose $800 per year in income. It would cost $600 for the dentist to install sound-absorbing material on her office walls, and this material would have to be replaced each year. (It is a rowdy dentist office.) The writer sues the dentist. The court can rule in favor of the author and require the dentist to soundproof her walls, or it can rule in favor of the dentist and dismiss the case. Explain what would happen under each ruling if:

    a. The dentist and the writer are on speaking terms (small transactions costs, ignoring court fees).

    b. They are not speaking to each other under any circumstances (large transactions costs).

20.26 Turkeys run wild on Turkey Island. The island is not the property of anyone in particular, and people are free to hunt turkeys there and sell them to food wholesalers. Turkey Island is fairly small, though, and several hunters at once tend to scare away the turkeys, leaving fewer to shoot. One hunter alone can shoot 20 turkeys on an average day, and two hunters hunting at once can each get 15 turkeys, on average. If three hunters are on the island at once, each will get 12 turkeys, on average. Each of four hunters will get 9 turkeys on an average day. With more than four hunters, no one gets any turkeys. All of the people who live in the vicinity of Turkey Island (those who might come to the island to hunt) could earn $80 in a day if they were not turkey hunting. (Of course, this $80 reflects the social value of the goods they would produce if they were not hunting turkeys.) If they go turkey hunting, they can sell the turkeys that they shoot for $10 each. Assume that turkeys reproduce adequately to eliminate any danger of extinction, and that all of the numbers stated above stay the same over time.

a. In long-run equilibrium, how many people would hunt turkeys on Turkey Island when anyone could freely do so? Why?

b. What is the economically efficient number of hunters on the island? Why? Does the island have overhunting, underhunting, or the economically efficient amount of hunting?

c. Suppose that the island were owned by someone interested in earning the largest profit possible. What is the maximum price that someone would be willing to pay to hunt turkeys on the island for a day if he were the only hunter allowed? What is the maximum price per day that someone would pay to hunt on the island if one other person were also allowed to hunt? What is the maximum price per day a person would pay if two other hunters were allowed on the island? Three others?

d. How many hunters would an owner of the island allow to maximize his own profits from owning the island? How much profit would he make? If the island were owned, would overhunting, underhunting, or the economically efficient amount of hunting occur?

20.27 A geneticist who specializes in recombinant DNA research invents a new bacteria that is harmless and unnoticeable to humans, but obnoxious to insects that feed on farm crops. The bacteria can be easily spread on farmland along with seed. The scientist obtains a patent on this new bacteria and sets up a company to sell it to farmers. The research that led to the discovery cost thousands of dollars, but enough bacteria to protect one acre of farmland costs only 3¢ now that the scientist has perfected the technique. The scientist's company is the only company allowed to sell the product, because of the patent.

a. Draw a graph to illustrate the forces that determine the equilibrium price and quantity sold of the bacteria.

b. Illustrate on your graph the economically efficient amount of bacteria to be produced and sold, now that it has been invented.

c. If the government were to force the scientist's company to produce and sell the economically efficient amount of the product (assuming that the government could determine this number exactly), would the company make a profit or suffer a loss?

d. Does a conflict emerge between the economically efficient use of a product that has already been invented and the economically efficient amount of research on new inventions and discoveries?

20.28 Suppose that someone builds a house near an airport and later complains about noise from the planes. Does an externality arise in this case? Does it matter if the homeowner was aware of the airport before building the house?

20.29 Many, though not all, scientists believe that carbon dioxide emissions will lead to global warming, with average temperatures rising 2 to 9 degrees Farenheit within the next century. Assume that this possibility could be prevented by reducing carbon dioxide emissions. How would an economist determine whether it would be more economically efficient to reduce the emissions (at a cost that the U.S. government calculates to be in excess of $100 billion per year) or to spend the resources on irrigation, dikes, and air conditioning to help reduce negative effects of global warming?

INQUIRIES FOR FURTHER THOUGHT

20.30 Do you think that social costs or benefits differ from private costs or benefits for the goods or activities on the following list? Explain why in each case. For each externality that you identify, explain what, if anything, you think the government (or someone else) should do about the externality.
   a. Drug use
   b. Pornography
   c. Violence on television or in the movies
   d. Rock lyrics advocating violence, drugs, sex, or suicide
   e. Fast driving on a freeway
   f. Abortions
   g. Births and world population growth
   h. Social customs
   i. Celebrations of holidays
   j. Good manners and etiquette
   k. Physically fit, well-dressed, and attractive people
   l. Well-educated people
   m. Nearby hazardous waste sites or nuclear reactors
   n. Someone lights a candle, and the photons of light shine on the house next door.
   o. Someone turns on a 1,000-watt searchlight, which shines on the house next door.
   p. Jane plans to marry Peter until Dick comes along, then Jane dumps Peter for Dick.

20.31 a. How bad is pollution relative to its level 20 years ago? 100 years ago? 500 years ago? 2,000 years ago? Justify your answer with as many facts and as much evidence as possible.
   b. Comment on this statement: "People live much longer now than they did in the past. This indicates that externalities pose a less serious problem now than in the past."

20.32 Does culture have a positive externality? Art? Music? Plays? Sports? Is this a good reason for the government to subsidize any of these activities (such as paying grants to support the arts or constructing new sports facilities)?

20.33 Do cultural diversity and racial diversity have positive externalities? Discuss them. Does an externality result from the spread of English-language music, television, and movies and American culture around the world? (Some countries refer to this as U.S. *cultural imperialism*.)

20.34 Does a neighborhood have externalities for the people who live in it? Do cities?

20.35 Does trash disposal involve externalities? How would you estimate the benefits of recycling? How would you estimate the costs? Should governments require people to recycle? What alternative policies might governments adopt?

20.36 Suppose that people have an irrational fear of something like contracting AIDS through casual contact or believing falsely that use of some technology is harmful. Suppose that the fear permeates peoples' lives, perhaps even causing ulcers, heart attacks, alcoholism, and behavior problems. Does an externality arise from the object of the irrational fear? In a situation like this, should the government do something such as taxing or regulating that object?

20.37 Suppose that business development brings jobs and more people to a small, quaint town and begins to change its character. Do externalities arise?

20.38 When a pregnant woman drinks a significant amount of alcohol or uses a drug that is dangerous to her fetus, does she create an externality? What if only a chance of a long-term problem to a baby exists if the mother uses some product? How big does that chance have to be before an externality arises?

20.39 Discuss this statement:

> Animals have rights. The concept of economic efficiency that economists use is flawed because it ignores animal rights and considers only the welfare of humans by looking at consumer and producer surplus and the benefits or costs of actions to other humans. This is fine for inanimate objects, but not for animals. A better concept of economic efficiency would include the benefits and costs to animals from human actions. For example, the usual approach to economic efficiency would consider it economically efficient for people to raise cattle for slaughter or raise animals for human entertainment in zoos. The humans who own the animals maximize their own profits, and sometimes this involves treating the animals very poorly. If we take the welfare of animals as well as humans into account, as we should, we find that perfect competition on free markets with private property rights in animals is economically inefficient. We need government to solve this problem by protecting the rights of animals.

If you agree with the statement, what would you propose as a better concept of economic efficiency and how could a society achieve your concept of economic efficiency?

20.40 Most people would feel guilty after stealing a videotape or almost anything else. Many fewer people seem to feel guilty when they take public goods without paying by copying computer software, music tapes, movies on video, or by receiving cable television without paying for it. Is this stealing? Is it as bad as stealing an ordinary, nonpublic good? Explain why or why not. Why do people feel less guilty about these crimes? What, if anything, should the government do to enforce property rights in computer software, audio and video materials, and similar products?

20.41 **a.** Discuss this statement: "An externality arises every time a child is born. The world must share its limited resources with one more person. It will feed her, clothe her, and educate her at public expense. It will provide her with highways, police protection, and other public services. Each new person imposes a burden on the limited resources such as water, clean air, fossil fuels, and even space on the ground. Each person has a negative externality."

b. Which would be better, a world with 5 trillion people and a $6,000 per-person average annual income, or a world with 3 trillion people and a $10,000 per-person average annual income?

c. Which would be better, a world with 5 trillion people and a $6,000 per-person average annual income, or a world with 3 trillion people earning $9,000 per person and 2 trillion people earning $1,500 per person? Discuss how your answer to this question compares with your answer to Question 20.41b.

20.42 The U.S. government bans smoking on all domestic, commercial airline flights; some cities have banned smoking in all restaurants. Are bans of this sort necessary to internalize externalities from second-hand smoke? Are they economically efficient? Are they good public policy?

20.43 The United States spends over 2.0 percent of its total output (about $150 billion) each year on controlling pollution and cleaning up the environment.

a. How much *should* the U.S. economy spend? On what basis should this decision be made? Who should make the decision?

b. A study has estimated that environmental regulations in place prior to the 1990 Clean Air Act reduced U.S. economic growth by 0.2 percent per year from 1973 to 1985, and that this will amount to a permanent 2.6 percent reduction in GDP (about $180 billion per year in 1995 dollars) after 1995. (Note that any estimate of this effect is subject to considerable uncertainty.) How much economic growth should a country sacrifice to improve the environment? On what basis should this decision be made? Who should make the decision?

20.44 How should the government choose its policies when genuine scientific uncertainty surrounds some possible environmental disaster?

20.45 In 1965, the Supreme Court decided the case of *Griswold* v. *Connecticut,* striking down a law that made it a crime, even for married couples, to use contraceptive devices. In a 1971 article in the *Indiana Law Journal* criticizing the court's reasoning, Judge Robert Bork wrote,

> In Griswold a husband and wife assert that they wish to have sexual relations without fear of unwanted children. The law impairs their sexual gratification. . . . The majority finds use of contraceptives immoral. *Knowledge that it takes place* and that the State makes no effort to inhibit it *causes the majority anguish,* impairs their gratifications. Neither case is covered . . . in the Constitution. . . . Why is sexual gratification more worthy than moral gratification? . . . Courts must accept any value the legislature makes unless it clearly runs contrary to a choice made in the framing of the Constitution. (Emphasis added.)

Does the knowledge or belief that other people engage in certain sexual acts of which some people disapprove constitute an externality? If government policies should deal with externalities, is this a rationale to overturn the *Griswold* decision, as Judge Bork favored?

20.46 In what ways would global warming (a possible effect of carbon dioxide emissions) be good or bad for people? How would you estimate the effects on human health and productivity? Compare your answers with the 1991 study by the U.S. National Academy of Sciences, available through your library.

TAG SOFTWARE APPLICATIONS

TUTORIAL EXERCISES

▶ The module contains a review of the key terms from Chapter 20.

ANALYTICAL EXERCISES

▶ The analytical section contains a question on the calculation of total social cost, marginal social cost, and marginal social benefit.

GRAPHING EXERCISES

▶ The graphing segment contains questions on the measurement of *MSC*, the determination of efficient output in the presence of externalities, and the calculation of deadweight social loss.

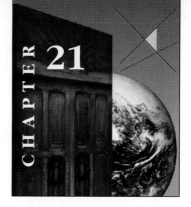

CHAPTER 21

GOVERNMENT REGULATIONS AND TAXES

WHAT THIS CHAPTER IS ABOUT

▶ Purposes of government regulations

▶ Results of regulations

▶ Optimal taxation

People face government regulations and taxes every day. You wake up on a mattress with a tag printed with, "Do not remove this tag under penalty of law," and shower in water sold by the local government in a bathtub made to satisfy government-approved specifications.[1] You dress in clothes with labels required by the government, eat breakfast foods made from government-subsidized grains by firms subject to long lists of government regulations. You may take a prescription medicine that has been approved for sale by the government and which you can buy only if a doctor with a government license writes a prescription filled by a licensed pharmacist. When you leave your house, built to conform to government regulations and purchased from a government-licensed real-estate broker, you drive a government-licensed car with government-required safety and emissions features on a government-owned road. Your driver's license shows that the government has given you permission to drive. Your work place must meet government health and safety regulations; your employer spends money to fill out papers required by government regulatory agencies and may employ lawyers to deal with these regulations. If you are a manager, you may meet with the personnel department to discuss compliance with government hiring regulations. Your business travel will probably involve taking a government-licensed taxi to a government-owned or government-regulated airport.

Your paycheck shows deductions for income taxes and Social Security taxes. You may stop on the way home at the government-regulated store where you pay sales taxes on most of your purchases and buy gasoline for your car at a price that is about one-third taxes. When you return home, you check the mail that the government has delivered, mow your lawn with a government-approved lawn mower, or watch a television program from a network with a government-issued broadcast license or from a government-regulated cable company.

---

[1] It is legal to remove the tag after you buy the mattress.

Governments are heavily involved in our lives. They raise money through taxes, buy goods, make direct payments of money (transfer payments such as Social Security payments and unemployment compensation), produce goods and sell them or provide them free (such as roads, education, and national defense), and regulate many aspects of the economy and the society.[2] Regulations serve varied purposes: to protect the environment, limit the power of monopolies, guarantee minimum standards of safety, or achieve other results. Criticisms of regulation are also varied; critics claim that regulations create economic inefficiencies, reduce competition, and stifle innovation and economic growth.

Taxes and regulations are alike in many ways. Both represent government-imposed limits on private property rights, restricting either the use of property or the proceeds from some use. Both serve similar goals. Taxes raise revenue for the government, encourage or discourage production or purchases of certain products, and affect the distribution of income. If the government wants to transfer income from one group to another, it may tax one group and give the money to another group, or it may impose minimum-wage laws, rent controls, requirements that firms provide certain benefits for their employees, and so on. If the government wants to discourage consumption of certain goods (such as alcoholic beverages or cigarettes), it may raise taxes on these goods or impose regulations to reduce their use. Government mandates require most firms to provide employees with a type of insurance called worker's compensation; evidence shows that it operates like a tax on employment, with 85 percent of its costs paid by employees in the form of lower wages.

Different combinations of taxes can create the same total revenue for the government while having different effects on economic efficiency. This chapter discusses how a government can choose a combination of taxes to raise revenue or achieve its other goals with the lowest possible deadweight social loss from economic inefficiency.

REGULATION

government regulation — a limit or restriction on the actions of people or firms, or a required action

Government regulations are limits or restrictions on the actions of people or firms, or actions that the government requires of them.

Some government regulations result from legislation; other regulations are created by the regulatory agencies themselves, such as the Food and Drug Administration or Environmental Protection Agency.

PURPOSES OF GOVERNMENT REGULATIONS

Most government regulations are intended to serve one of the following purposes:

Examples

1. *Protect the environment* by internalizing externalities (in the language of Chapter 20) when transactions costs are high

   Government regulations limit industrial emissions that would pollute the air, require preparation of environmental impact statements for certain activities, and restrict disposal of hazardous waste materials.

2. *Reduce economic inefficiencies* that may result from monopolies, oligopolies, or imperfect information of consumers

   Government regulations control prices charged by cable-television companies, insurance companies, and utilities (electricity, gas, and water suppliers). Regulations also require sellers to provide certain types of information about their products.

---

[2]Governments also perform other tasks such as setting rules for publicly owned resources (speed limits and fees at government parks) and dealing with foreign governments.

3. *Increase fairness* (by some view of fairness) or *redistribute income*	Government regulations require firms to provide working conditions that meet certain health and safety standards and to provide certain benefits for their employees. Regulations also help to prevent discrimination against minorities, women, and people with disabilities.
4. *Protect people from making bad decisions* (by some view of those decisions)	Government regulations require people to use seat belts and to buy cars with air bags. They prevent people from buying drugs without prescriptions from licensed physicians or from using unproven or experimental drugs. They also prevent people from buying or selling certain products deemed to be harmful or immoral, and from trading with hairdressers, insurance agents, or real-estate brokers who have not obtained licenses.
5. *Improve products*	U.S. government regulations prevent the use of certain chemicals in food, require cars to meet minimum levels of fuel efficiency, ban all food additives that induce cancer in humans or animals (no matter how large the doses required to do so), require minimum standards for doctors, and require building materials and other products to meet certain standards.
6. *Set rules for the use of common resources*	Government agencies set rules for the use of public parks and speed limits on roads.

Regulations do not always accomplish their intended purposes, as this chapter and the next will show. The actual outcome of a regulation depends on the equilibrium of a political environment in which interest groups compete and in which political forces and institutions shape the incentives facing the people who make and carry out regulations. As a result, regulations may serve other purposes such as helping certain groups with political power. Indeed, this is the primary purpose of some regulations, such as those that prohibit or restrict entry into various industries and those that prevent firms from reducing their prices.

SCOPE OF REGULATION IN THE UNITED STATES

Government regulations have a long history. The first big, independent regulatory agency in the United States, the Interstate Commerce Commission, was created in 1887. Regulation in the United States grew rapidly after that, increasing dramatically during World War I (when the U.S. government nationalized the railroads and telephone lines, regulated prices, and controlled production and distribution of many goods) and again during the Great Depression in the 1930s and World War II.[3] In the last several decades, U.S. government regulation has increased in some areas (such as environmental regulation) but decreased in others, with active deregulation in certain industries, including the airline, trucking, petroleum, and natural gas, and financial services industries. The same mix of increased regulation in certain areas and deregulation in others also characterizes many other countries.

deregulation — a decrease in government regulations

Deregulation is a decrease in government regulations.

---

[3]World War I served as a period of training in regulation for many officials in the U.S. government. They put their training to use later in the Great Depression of the 1930s and World War II, when regulation again rose dramatically. See Robert Higgs, *Crisis and Leviathan* (Oxford, U.K.: Oxford University Press, 1987); and Paul Johnson, *Modern Times* (New York: Harper & Row, 1983).

Source: Los Angeles Times, July 8, 1991, p. E5.

Estimates of the total costs of complying with U.S. federal government regulations vary widely, from about $100 billion to $500 billion per year, or about $400 to $2,000 for every person in the country each year. **Table 21.1** lists some of the main U.S. regulatory agencies and **Table 21.2** gives a few examples of regulations. All regulations have costs and benefits. Most economists believe that some regulations are reasonable and justified for one or more of the reasons listed earlier, while others create economic inefficiencies primarily to benefit certain special-interest groups at the expense of others.

EXAMPLES

Regulations that restrict pollution may be justified as attempts to reduce the economic inefficiencies created by externalities, as discussed in Chapter 20. Speed limits on public roads are rules for use of common resources that may raise their value. Prohibiting discrimination on the basis of race or sex responds to widely shared notions of fairness. Government-required health warnings and label requirements may be justified as providing a public good—information—that might raise economic efficiency. Whether any specific regulation actually raises or reduces economic efficiency, however, depends on its costs as well as its benefits. Some government regulations appear mainly to benefit certain groups at the expense of everyone else. These include restrictions on the quantities of goods that consumers can buy from foreign sellers, regulations that restrict the hours that stores are allowed to be open, and farm programs such as the U.S. government's milk and sugar programs. (See Chapter 8.)[4]

---

[4]While U.S. stores now face few restrictions on hours of operation, these regulations remain common in other countries. Japan began in the first half of the 1990s to ease regulations that prevented large stores from opening and competing with existing, small stores. Many countries, including Japan and Germany, have regulations that prevent stores from remaining open after a certain time (such as 5 or 8 p.m.) or from opening on certain days. These regulations help the industry by reducing competition while allowing each firm to reduce costs by operating fewer hours. The losers are customers who face less choice of hours in which to shop.

TABLE 21.1

SOME U.S. REGULATORY AGENCIES

Interstate Commerce Commission (ICC)	Regulates the operations of railroads, trucks, buses, and water carriers
Consumer Product Safety Commission (CPSC)	Regulates the design, use, and labeling of products to reduce injuries
Food and Drug Administration (FDA)	Regulates the manufacture, sale, and labeling of foods and drugs
Environmental Protection Agency (EPA)	Deals with regulations on pollution and other environmental issues
Occupational Safety and Health Administration (OSHA)	Regulates the health and safety conditions at firms
National Highway Traffic Safety Administration (NHTSA)	Regulates vehicles to reduce traffic accidents
Nuclear Regulatory Commission (NRC)	Regulates nuclear power facilities
Federal Aviation Administration (FAA)	Regulates the airline industry
Federal Communications Commission (FCC)	Controls licenses for television and radio and regulates telephone service
Federal Energy Regulatory Commission	Regulates energy industries
Federal Maritime Commission	Regulates ocean freight
Federal Trade Commission (FTC)	Regulates advertising to prevent deceptive advertisements
Securities and Exchange Commission (SEC)	Regulates stock exchanges and other financial markets
Commodity Futures Trading Commission (CFTC)	Regulates futures markets (See Chapter 7.)
National Labor Relations Board (NLRB)	Regulates labor issues and collective bargaining
Equal Employment Opportunity Commission (EEOC)	Investigates and enforces laws against discrimination in employment
Antitrust Division of the Justice Department	Enforces antitrust laws (See Chapter 14.)
Federal Reserve System, or Fed	Regulates banks
Federal Deposit Insurance Corporation (FDIC)	Regulates banks and insures bank deposits

See the Economics Yellow Pages in the back of this book for more information.

TABLE 21.2

EXAMPLES OF REGULATIONS IN THE UNITED STATES

Limits on the number of people who can immigrate from other countries

Ban on all food additives that have been found to induce cancer in humans or animals, no matter how large the doses required to do so (See the 1958 Delaney Amendment to the Food, Drug, and Cosmetic Act.)

Occupational licensure (requirements for people to have government-issued licenses before practicing some professions, such as doctors, real-estate agents, barbers, and so on)

Regulations on toxic waste disposal

Emission standards for automobiles

Fuel-economy requirements for automobiles

Rent controls

Minimum-wage rates

Regulations of public utilities such as electricity, gas, and water suppliers

Regulations of cable-TV providers and prohibitions on new competitors in the industry

Regulation of broadcast television and radio, licensing of stations, restrictions on commercials, and equal-time rules for political messages

Affirmative action rules on hiring and other antidiscrimination rules

Dumping regulations that penalize foreign companies for selling in the United States at low prices

Health regulations

Safety regulations for homes, schools, stores, cars (seat belts, airbags), hotels, and firms, and regulations affecting the construction of many consumer products

Zoning regulations that state what kinds of houses or businesses can locate on certain property

Compulsory schooling requirements

Child labor laws that limit the number of hours worked

Building codes that require certain kinds and qualities of materials, certain types of construction, and work by government-licensed workers

Regulations on investments by banks and other financial institutions, on interest rates they can charge, and interest rates they can pay; also, regulations requiring them to hold certain assets

Regulations preventing people from buying drugs without doctors' prescriptions, and preventing sales of prescription drugs without clear evidence that drugs are both safe and effective

Food regulations outlawing certain food additives, restricting the uses of others, and requiring labels with specified information

Required health warnings on products such as cigarettes and alcohol

Mandatory bottle deposits

Regulations on what insurance companies can charge and the types of policies they can offer customers

Medical regulations

Regulation of day-care centers and old-age homes

State laws making takeovers of firms more difficult or impossible

Laws against smoking on airlines or requiring restaurants to set aside nonsmoking areas

Laws making certain products illegal such as drugs, prostitution, etc.

Laws prohibiting *sales* of certain goods that are legal to possess such as babies, surrogacy services, human organs, etc.

Laws on possession or registration of guns

Laws requiring people to participate in the Social Security system

EVALUATING REGULATIONS: COST–BENEFIT ANALYSIS

cost–benefit analysis — the process of finding and comparing the costs and benefits of a regulation, tax, or other policy

Economists use cost–benefit analysis to compare benefits and opportunity costs of a regulation or tax.

> **Cost–benefit analysis** is the process of finding and comparing the costs and benefits of a regulation, tax, or other policy.

Economists measure the costs and benefits of a regulation or tax by the changes in consumer surplus and producer surplus and the effects on people of externalities such as pollution.

As Chapter 11 explained, a change in the economy is a Pareto improvement if at least one person gains while no one loses. A change in the economy is a potential Pareto improvement, or increase in economic efficiency, if it would be possible for the winners to compensate the losers to make the change a Pareto improvement. Cost-benefit analysis makes use of these ideas. If the benefits of a regulation exceed its costs, then the regulation is a potential Pareto improvement, though not necessarily an actual Pareto improvement because some people may lose from the regulation. If a regulation is a potential Pareto improvement, the people who would gain from the regulation could compensate those who would lose so that no one would end up losing. Cost-benefit analysis can help settle the question of which regulations and taxes are economically efficient and which are not.

The costs or benefits of a regulation or tax are sometimes intangible, such as the benefits of a lower chance of accidental death or a neighborhood without airplane noise. In these cases, economists measure the benefits by the amounts of money that people are willing to pay for a lower chance of death or a quiet neighborhood.

UNCERTAIN COSTS AND BENEFITS

The costs and benefits of most government policies are uncertain when the policies are adopted. In some cases, costs and benefits extend far into the future, so economists compare the expected values of benefits and the expected values of costs. The expected value of a benefit or cost is an average of each possible benefit or cost, weighted by the chance that it will occur.[5] For example, if there is a one-half chance that the benefit of a regulation will be $1 million and a one-half chance it will be $2 million, the expected benefit is:

$$(1/2)(\$1 \text{ million}) + (1/2)(\$2 \text{ million}) = \$1.5 \text{ million}$$

Expected costs can be calculated in the same way.

USING COST–BENEFIT ANALYSIS: AN EXAMPLE

A higher tax on alcoholic beverages, or tighter regulations on their use, would reduce consumption of alcohol and reduce deaths from traffic accidents caused by drunk drivers.[6] This is the benefit of the potential tax or regulation. It would have two costs. First, the tax or regulation would hurt consumers who wanted alcohol and would drink responsibly; a tax would raise the price and reduce their

---

[5]See Chapter 19.

[6]A tax would also raise revenue for the government, but this would not benefit society as a whole because consumers would lose the tax money that the government would gain.

FIGURE 21.1

COST–BENEFIT ANALYSIS OF A 30 PERCENT TAX ON BEER

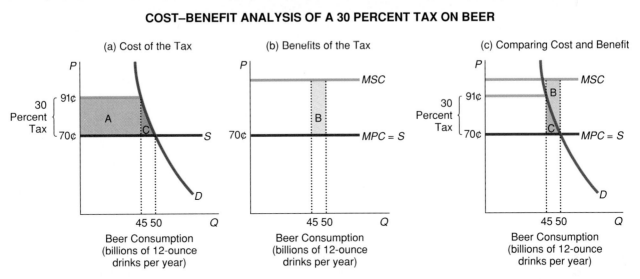

(a) Cost of the Tax   (b) Benefits of the Tax   (c) Comparing Cost and Benefit

Panel a: Consumers would lose Areas A and C from a 30 percent tax on beer. The government would gain revenue equal to Area A from the tax. Therefore, the cost of the tax would be Area C. This is approximately the area of a triangle: (5 billion)(21¢)/2, or $525 million. *Panel b:* The marginal private cost of beer, *MPC*, is its price, 70¢ before the tax. The marginal social cost of beer, *MSC*, is higher because of externalities from drunk drivers. Area B shows the value of the benefit of fewer highway deaths from drunk drivers if the equilibrium quantity of beer falls from 50 billion to 45 billion drinks per year. Estimates show that Area B is at least $1,752 million per year, and probably closer to $14,600 million per year. *Panel c:* Area C shows the cost of the tax, and the portion of Area B that does not overlap Area C shows the net benefit of the tax. In this case, cost–benefit analysis shows that the benefits of the tax would exceed its costs.

consumer surplus, and a regulation might raise the price or limit access. The second cost of a tax or regulation is the loss in producer surplus.

Consider a 30 percent tax on beer. We can measure its costs by estimating the elasticities of demand and supply. The elasticity of demand for beer is about $-\frac{1}{3}$.[7] Suppose that supply is perfectly elastic (which is a good approximation to the actual elasticity).[8] **Figure 21.1a** shows the cost of the tax, which is the deadweight social loss from the tax, *ignoring* the externality (traffic accidents) from alcohol consumption. The tax would reduce consumer surplus, with consumers losing Areas A and C. The government would gain Area A, so the cost of the tax would be Area C.

How large is this cost? With perfectly elastic supply, a 30 percent tax would raise the price by the full amount of the tax, so the price of 12 ounces of beer would rise from about 70 cents to about 91 cents, as in the figure. With an elasticity of demand of $-\frac{1}{3}$, the quantity demanded falls by one-third of 30 percent, or 10 percent, roughly from 50 billion to 45 billion 12-ounce drinks per year. The base of Area C in Figure 21.1a (the cost of the tax) is 5 billion beers per year, and

[7]Stanley I. Ornstein, "Control of Alcohol through Price Increases," *Journal of Studies on Alcohol* 41 (1980), pp. 807–818.

[8]This discussion follows the analysis in a study by Charles E. Phelps, "Death and Taxes: An Opportunity for Substitution," (unpublished paper, University of Rochester, 1987).

the height of the triangle is 21 cents. The area of the triangle is one-half of the base times the height:

$$(0.5)(5 \text{ billion})(\$0.21) = \$525 \text{ million per year}$$

This gives the cost of the tax.[9]

Would the benefit of fewer deaths from traffic accidents outweigh this cost? Figure 21.1b shows the marginal social cost of alcohol consumption. It lies above the supply curve (the marginal private cost curve) by a distance equal to the marginal cost to other people of the externality (traffic accidents), as discussed in Chapter 20. The benefit of the tax, Area B in the figure, would be the fall in costs to other people when the equilibrium quantity falls from 50 billion drinks per year to 45 billion. One study has estimated that this would save 2,920 lives per year by reducing traffic accidents from drunk drivers.[10] About 1,650 of these lives would be the drunk drivers, and about 1,270 would be lives of other people. This does not say whose lives would be saved, only that the chance of death would fall for many people.

To measure the dollar value of this lower chance of death, economists ask, "How much are people willing to pay to reduce the chance of death in some situation by 1 percent?" To answer this question, they look at how much money people are willing to pay for safety equipment at home or in their cars, how much higher a person's wage must be to make work at a riskier job attractive, and so on. Estimates of this price vary from around $0.60 to $8.00 for a one-millionth reduction in the chance of death. This implies that people are willing to pay somewhere between $600,000 and $8 million to save one life, probably around $5 million. Even with the lowest figure, $600,000, a savings of 2,920 lives per year would be worth:

$$(2,920)(\$600,000) = \$1,752 \text{ million per year,}$$

This is more than three times the estimated cost of the tax.[11] The $5 million per-life estimate would give a benefit from the tax of $14,600 million per year, 28 times the estimated cost of the tax. The benefit of the tax would actually be higher than this estimate indicates because the tax would also reduce injuries and property damage from accidents. Clearly, cost–benefit analysis indicates that the benefits to society of this tax would outweigh its costs.

Figure 21.1c graphs these costs and benefits of the tax together. Area C shows the cost of the tax, while the portion of Area B that does not overlap Area C shows its net benefit. The figure indicates that an even larger tax would be required to eliminate the deadweight social loss from the externalities associated with alcohol consumption; the optimal tax would lead to an equilibrium quantity where the marginal social cost curve would intersect the demand curve. (See Chapter 20.)

---

[9]The procedure for estimating the cost of a regulation would be similar. A more thorough analysis would also include the costs of paying the tax (including recordkeeping by sellers) and collecting the tax (an increase in government bureaucracy), or the costs of operating the government regulatory agency.

[10]Phelps, "Death and Taxes." For several reasons, this estimate is probably too low.

[11]This calculation of the benefit assumes that the analysis should value the lives of the drinkers. One might argue that drinkers know they have a higher chance of death and choose to drink anyway, so they must think the benefits they get from drinking outweigh their higher chances of death. In that case, perhaps the analysis should count only the deaths of the other 1,270 people whose lives would be saved each year by the tax. This would give a benefit between (1,270)($600,000), or $762 million and (1,270)($5 million), or $6,350 million per year; even the lowest figure still exceeds the cost of the tax.

CRITICISMS OF COST–BENEFIT ANALYSIS

Sometimes people criticize cost-benefit analysis by claiming that costs are less important than benefits, that money expenditures are less important than human values. The beer-tax example shows the error in this criticism. That example measures costs, including human lives, and benefits, including human enjoyment. More generally, this criticism shows a misunderstanding of costs. *Costs are foregone values.* If a regulation costs $100 million, that is $100 million less that people have for food, housing, health care, or video games.

Similarly, some people criticize cost-benefit analysis because, they say, human lives and certain other values cannot be measured in money terms. This criticism ignores the fact that people do sometimes choose higher chances of death or injury in return for more money. For example, they buy smaller, cheaper cars that are, on average, less safe in accidents than larger, more expensive cars. They spend money on curtains rather than smoke detectors; they take riskier jobs for higher pay. These choices allow economists to measure the amount of money that people are willing to accept in return for a higher chance of death. In this sense, a lower chance of death does have a money value. The beer-tax example made use of the money value of a reduced chance of death.

A third criticism of cost-benefit analysis charges that it ignores people's rights and the distribution of costs and benefits. This criticism is more substantial. Cost-benefit analysis finds the *total* benefits and costs of a regulation, but the people who pay the costs and the people who get the benefits may differ.[12] If the benefits of a regulation exceed its costs, then the regulation is a potential Pareto improvement, but not necessarily an actual Pareto improvement. The winners *could* compensate the losers, but in reality they usually do not. For this reason, cost-benefit analysis cannot determine whether a tax or regulation would be a good policy. Something that increases economic efficiency may be unfair to some people or violate their rights.

To use cost-benefit analysis properly, analysts should consider the costs and benefits of alternative solutions to a problem, and choose the solution with the greatest excess of benefits over costs. For example, one alternative to a higher tax on beer would be a higher penalty for drunk driving. This solution would not penalize people who consume beer but do not drive drunk. A cost-benefit analysis of this solution would have to consider the costs of catching drunk drivers, prosecuting them, and punishing them (including the costs of enforcing punishments such as suspended licenses, so that such people would not drive without licenses). It would also have to estimate the size of the incentive effects of punishment. (How much less drunk driving would a higher penalty induce?) If the incentive effects are large, then the costs of prosecuting and punishing drunk drivers are small because few people would drive drunk; if the incentive effects are small, the costs may become important.

FUTURE COSTS AND BENEFITS

A regulation or tax may have benefits now and costs in the future, or vice versa. In such a situation, economists compare the discounted present values of the costs and benefits.

---

[12]In the beer-tax example, responsible drinkers might lose more than they gain, while people who do not drink beer (and do not pay the beer tax) gain from the fall in traffic accidents.

EXAMPLE

Suppose that consumers are willing to pay $20 billion this year to build a giant, virtual-reality amusement park. The park would permanently destroy a beautiful forest that people value at $2 billion per year, every year. The discounted present value of the benefit from the project is $20 billion; the discounted present value of the cost of the project is the discounted present value of $2 billion per year, every year, forever:

$$\frac{2}{1 + i} + \frac{2}{(1 + i)^2} + \frac{2}{(1 + i)^3} + \frac{2}{(1 + i)^4} + \frac{2}{(1 + i)^5} + \cdots$$

This cost is measured in billions of dollars, where i is the interest rate (measured so that 0.05 means a 5 percent per year interest rate) and where the sum goes on forever. It turns out that this formula can be simplified to

$$\frac{2}{i}$$

So if the interest rate is 10 percent per year, the discounted present value of the costs equals ($2 billion)/(0.10), or $20 billion. If the interest rate is 5 percent per year, the discounted present value of the costs equals $40 billion, while if the interest rate is $12\frac{1}{2}$ percent per year, the discounted present value of the costs is $16 billion. The benefits of the virtual-reality park exceed its costs if the interest rate is higher than 10 percent per year and fall short of its costs if the interest rate is below 10 percent per year.

ANOTHER CRITICISM OF COST–BENEFIT ANALYSIS

Another criticism of cost-benefit analysis involves the use of discounted present values when some people affected by a policy are not yet born. According to this criticism, discounted present values improperly give less weight to costs and benefits borne by future generations than to people currently alive. This happens because discounted present values divide future benefits or costs by an interest rate. For example, with an interest rate of 10 percent per year, cost-benefit analysis using discounted present values would suggest adopting a regulation that would prevent the death of one infant today even if that regulation would cause the deaths of 100 infants 50 years from now. Some critics advocate calculating discounted present values differently so that effects on future generations carry greater weight; they propose using a smaller interest rate for intergenerational calculations.

CHOOSING AMONG ALTERNATIVE POLICIES WITH COST–BENEFIT ANALYSIS

Table 21.3 shows 18 proposed, rejected, or actual government regulations that were intended to reduce people's risk of accidental death. The table shows the year each regulation was proposed but not yet adopted (*P*), rejected (*R*), or adopted (*F* for final rule), along with the regulatory agency involved. It also shows the risk per year before the regulation was adopted, the estimated lives saved per year from the regulation (estimated by the regulatory agency at the time of the decision), and the cost per life saved. The costs of saving a life vary greatly, from $150,000 per life to $106 billion per life in 1995 dollars.

Notice that, overall, regulators have adopted the more cost-effective regulations. Most lives saved from regulations like these have come from NHTSA regu-

TABLE 21.3

COST OF VARIOUS RISK-REDUCING REGULATIONS PER LIFE SAVED

Regulation	Year	Agency	Status[a]	Annual Lives Saved	Cost per Life Saved (1995 $000)[b]
Steering column protection	1967	NHTSA	F	1,300.000	$ 150
Unvented space heaters	1980	CPSC	F	63.000	150
Oil and gas well service	1983	OSHA-S	P	50.000	150
Cabin fire protection	1985	FAA	F	15.000	300
Passive restraints/belts	1984	NHTSA	F	1,850.000	440
Fuel system integrity	1975	NHTSA	F	400.000	440
Trihalomethanes	1979	EPA	F	322.000	440
Underground construction	1983	OSHA-S	P	8.100	440
Alcohol and drug control	1985	FRA	F	4.200	730
Servicing wheel rims	1984	OSHA-S	F	2.300	730
Radionuclides/DOE facilities	1984	EPA	R	0.001	300,000
Radionuclides/elemental phosphorous	1984	EPA	R	0.046	400,000
Benzene/ethylbenzenol styrene	1984	EPA	R	0.006	710,000
Arsenic/low-arsenic copper	1986	EPA	R	0.090	1,123,000
Benzene/maleic anhydride	1984	EPA	R	0.029	1,205,000
Land disposal	1986	EPA	P	2.520	5,145,000
EDB	1983	OSHA-H	P	0.002	22,900,000
Formaldehyde	1985	OSHA-H	P	0.010	106,000,000

[a]Proposed, rejected, or final rule.
[b]Updated by author.
Source: Regulation, November/December 1986, p. 30.

lations on motor vehicles—the collapsible steering column requirement, the passive restraint (seat belt or airbag) rule, the fuel system rule, and a regulation on side-door strength. Overall, evidence suggests that health regulations are much more expensive per life saved than safety regulations. On average, regulations intended to prevent cancer cost much more per life saved than safety regulations. Many proposed regulations cost more than $5 million per life saved, so with estimated value of saving a life of about $5 million (based on the average prices people are actually willing to pay to avoid risks), the benefits of those regulations would not be worth their costs.

A Harvard School of Public Health life-saving study of 587 government regulations and health-care practices concluded that medical care tends to save lives at a much lower cost than regulations on workplace safety or environmental conditions. The study concluded that the costs of alleviating very minor cancer risks are often enormous. For example, each year of life saved by a heart transplant costs, on average, $104,000, but each year of life saved by preventing factories from releasing carcinogens costs over $2.5 million. The study also concluded that the U.S. government could prevent 60,000 deaths per year by using cost–benefit analysis to reallocate the roughly $20 billion per year it spends on about 200 major life-saving programs. Similarly, cost–benefit analysis of health-care spending could save about $31 billion per year without increasing the death rate. Childhood immunizations, drug and alcohol treatment programs, and prenatal health care are among the lowest-cost methods of saving lives, while the most expensive are government regulations on chloroform (a carcinogen) at pulp mills, which cost nearly $100 billion for each year of life saved.

EXAMPLES

The government proposed a regulation to require infants traveling in airplanes to sit in approved infant safety seats. Parents had been allowed to carry small infants on their laps on airplanes. Everyone agrees that infant seats would help save lives of infants in airline accidents. The cost may appear to be limited to the extra money that parents would pay for additional airline seats for infants. However, because the regulation would raise the cost of airline travel for families with infants, it would make them more likely to drive rather than fly on vacations. But the death rate in passenger cars is about 22 deaths per billion passenger miles, which is about 70 times larger than the death rate for airline travel (about 0.3 deaths per billion passenger miles). If enough people were to switch from flying to driving because of the regulation, the death rate could rise rather than fall.[13] Perhaps because of this calculation, the regulation has not been adopted.

Government regulations called CAFE (for *corporate average fuel economy*) standards are intended to help the environment by reducing gasoline use. CAFE standards require auto manufacturers to achieve a certain minimum level of fuel efficiency measured in miles per gallon averaged over all of the cars they produce. They can produce some cars with lower fuel efficiency ratings as long as they produce others with higher ratings. Critics of CAFE standards argue that these regulations cause thousands of deaths in auto accidents because they force manufacturers to produce more small cars which are both more fuel efficient and more dangerous. Studies indicate that CAFE standards have reduced the average weight of an automobile by about 500 pounds, which translates into about 3,000 deaths and 15,000 injuries every year. Supporters of CAFE standards argue that auto manufacturers should be forced to meet the fuel-efficiency requirements with alternative technologies rather than lower average car sizes and that, when firms reduce car sizes, they should be required to add other safety features. Critics respond that these additional regulations would raise car prices and that, even after adding other safety features to cars, the safety costs of CAFE standards exceed the benefits of fuel efficiency.

FOR REVIEW

21.1 List six government regulatory agencies and what they do. List ten government regulations and state their intended purposes.

21.2 Explain cost–benefit analysis and the main criticisms of it.

21.3 Explain how economists measure the value of saving lives in terms of money.

QUESTIONS

21.4 Suppose that the government were to require all colleges to find or provide jobs for their graduates and that the jobs must pay at least three-quarters of the average wages for new graduates in those occupations. What would be the costs and benefits of this regulation?

21.5 How would you calculate the costs and benefits of reducing the maximum speed on highways to 40 miles per hour? Raising it to 80 miles per hour?

---

[13]Estimates of the substitution between flying and driving show that enough people would probably switch to cars that the death rate would probably rise. Because the death rate is about 70 times larger in cars, even a small substitution to driving could raise the overall death rate.

IN THE NEWS

Clearly wrong on eyeglasses

Q: What's the difference between $60 reading glasses prescribed by an optometrist in New York and a $12 pair from Woolworth's in New Jersey?

A: $48.

Most people eventually need reading glasses, and many can meet their needs with mass-produced eyewear from a five-and-dime counter display. Forty-eight states permit the sale of simple magnifying glasses without a prescription. Only New York and Rhode Island deny access to cheap, safe eyewear. The $48 question is whether Albany can be nudged to reform.

Natural aging of the eye makes it difficult for most people over 50 to read news-paper-size print. The problem can generally be remedied with magnifying lenses. Do-it-yourself fitting works for people without complicated vision impairment.

According to Dr. Calvin Roberts, associate professor of ophthalmology at Cornell Medical College, the only loss from a misfitting is the purchase price; the wrong lenses won't damage the eyes. Why, then, does New York bar sales without a prescription from a physician or optometrist?

The prescription eyeglass lobby argues, lamely, that the prohibition forces those afflicted with reading problems to have eye exams. That makes it possible for doctors to catch glaucoma and other degenerative eye diseases before sight is irreparably damaged.

In fact, there is no evidence that the ban has made New Yorkers more conscientious about eye care than residents of other states. By the same logic, aspirin would only be dispensed by prescription because anyone who feels a pain might benefit from seeing a doctor.

The opticians' lobby packs a solid financial punch in Albany. Senator Joseph Bruno and Assemblyman Richard Gottfried, sponsors of the repeal bill, deserve the help of every citizen who can see the larger public interest more clearly.

As this *New York Times* editorial notes, regulations that restrict advertising usually raise prices and benefit producers.

Source: "Clearly Wrong on Eyeglasses," *New York Times,* May 16, 1988.

PROBLEMS WITH REGULATION

While some regulations are intended to save lives, protect the environment, reduce inefficiencies, and so on, other government regulations seem mainly to benefit special-interest groups. For example, for a long time, government regulations prevented both fare reductions by existing airlines and entry into the industries by new airlines. Regulations also kept prices of trucking services high by preventing any existing firm from reducing its price or any new firm from entering the industry. Government regulations have also prevented firms from reducing the prices of many other goods, such as natural gas.

Since deregulation of the airline industry in the late 1970s and early 1980s, the average price per mile flown (adjusted for inflation) has fallen, the number of flights has increased, the number of passengers has increased, and the number of towns served by more than one airline has increased. Deregulation has saved consumers several billion dollars per year; the average fare per passenger mile (adjusted for inflation) fell roughly by half, despite increased monopoly power of certain airlines at hub cities such as Chicago, Pittsburgh, and Atlanta. Despite increased air traffic, deregulation did not increase the death rate. Deregulation in the trucking industry also reduced prices and has saved consumers about $50 billion per year.

Critics of government regulations contend that the actual effects of regulations frequently differ from their intended effects. There are three main views of regulation.

public-interest view of regulation — the view that government regulations serve the public interest

The **public-interest view of regulation** says that regulations serve the public interest.

According to the public-interest view, politicians do what most voters want in order to be reelected; politicians establish and operate regulations to serve the majority of voters.

special-interest view of regulation — the view that government regulations serve special-interest groups

The **special-interest view of regulation** says that government regulations serve special-interest groups.

According to this view, special-interest groups have enough political power to convince the government to create and operate regulations for their benefit, even if the regulations reduce economic efficiency and harm most people.

capture view of regulation — the view that regulatory agencies originally established to serve the general public interest end up serving the special interests of the industries they were intended to regulate

The **capture view of regulation** says that regulatory agencies originally established to serve the general public interest end up serving the special interests of the industries they were intended to regulate.

According to the capture view, regulated industries often convince regulatory agencies to formulate and enforce rules that benefit the industries, even if the rules are economically inefficient and contradict the public interest. According to this view, regulations help industries to maximize their producer surplus at the expense of other groups. The main idea of the capture view is that an industry or occupation with enough political power to influence the government will try to control entry into that industry or occupation. Proponents of this view argue that many government regulations benefit the special interests of firms in the regulated industries at the expense of consumers.

DIFFUSE AND CONCENTRATED INTERESTS

Proponents of the special-interest and capture views of regulation argue that the political power of concentrated interests exceeds that of equal-sized diffuse interests.

concentrated interest — a benefit to a small group of people or firms

diffuse interest — a benefit that is spread across many people

A **concentrated interest** is a benefit to a small group of people or firms; a **diffuse interest** is a benefit that is spread across many people.

For example, 200 million people might gain 10¢ each if the government were to abolish some regulation. While the gain might total $20 million, the gain to each individual would be small. As a result, the potential beneficiaries have little incentive to learn about or study the regulation, or to put pressure on the government to abolish it. The $20 million cost of the regulation is too diffuse, spread among too many people, for them to exert strong political pressure to abolish it. On the other hand, the benefits of the regulation may be concentrated. If a small number of firms, say, five firms, gain $1 million each from the regulation, then each firm has an incentive to spend time and money to support it politically. In a case like this, the government might adopt a regulation even though its total costs ($20 million) exceed its total benefits ($5 million).

Similarly, the government may not regulate or tax an industry if the costs of the regulation or tax are concentrated while the benefits are more diffuse. For example, the cost–benefit analysis earlier in this chapter suggested that the benefits of a higher tax on beer would exceed the costs. The costs tend to be more con-

IN THE NEWS

Higher-cost gasoline

Clean air is not cheap, as many motorists will soon discover. On Jan. 1, gas stations serving 30 percent of the national market will start selling a cleaner-burning fuel that costs 3 cents to 8 cents more per gallon than conventional gasoline.

Motorists in the affected area—the Northeast and mid-Atlantic states, and parts of the Midwest, Texas, and California—will have no choice but to buy it. But as they learn more about the new, reformulated gasoline, they may well wonder why drivers, as opposed to other polluters, must pay so much of the bill for cleaning up urban smog.

Motorists, however, are responsible for less than one-third of overall emissions in major cities; factories, refineries, and power plants, along with other mobile sources such as trucks and buses, are bigger polluters. So why were drivers stuck with most of the bill for keeping the air clean? The American Automobile Association, the drivers' lobby, says the reasons have more to do with politics than with science or economics. AAA suggests, plausibly enough, that local and state officials decided to spread the costs widely among the driving public rather than concentrate them in specific, politically influential industries.

Concentrated interests usually have more political power than diffuse interests have.

Source: "Higher-Cost Gasoline," *Journal of Commerce,* November 21, 1994, p. 10A.

centrated than the potential benefits because a relatively small number of firms that produce and sell the product can organize opposition to higher taxes on behalf of their customers.

The argument behind the special-interest and capture views of regulation is that the government is more likely to establish regulations with concentrated benefits and diffuse costs. Firms in a regulated industry usually have a more concentrated interest than consumers, so regulations are more likely to serve the interests of those firms than the interests of consumers or general public interests such as economic efficiency. Even if a regulation is originally designed to help consumers, the more concentrated interests of producers may soon capture the regulatory agency, changing regulations and their enforcement for the benefit of producers. The airline and trucking industry regulations mentioned earlier are examples.

Why would regulators allow their agencies to be captured by these interest groups? Critics believe that many regulators intend to promote the public interest, but they also care about their own careers and families. A person who works as a regulator learns about the regulated industry, acquiring knowledge and skills that have particular value within that industry. A regulator who leaves government service can often become a valuable employee or consultant for that industry. Bureaucrats have incentives not to jeopardize these opportunities by alienating the firms in the industries they regulate; instead, their incentives may lead them to formulate and enforce regulations in ways that benefit the industries.

More generally, understanding government regulations requires understanding the incentives of regulators. While regulators may have incentives to do their jobs by carrying out the intentions of regulations, considerable evidence indicates that regulators generally act in their own interests. The important question then

SOCIAL AND ECONOMIC ISSUES

Slippery-Slope Hypothesis

Does one regulation lead to another? Does any amount or type of censorship threaten freedom of speech for everyone? Do a few steps in the wrong direction lead people down a *slippery slope* to a place they do not intend to go? This *slippery-slope argument* has many applications. Political conservatives often make the slippery-slope argument when they discuss government regulation of the economy; they argue that a regulation is bad partly because it creates a slippery slope leading to other bad policies. Political liberals often make the slippery-slope argument when they discuss freedom of speech; they argue that any restriction on freedom of speech is bad partly because it creates a slippery slope leading to threats against all freedom of speech. Libertarians often make slippery-slope arguments in both cases.

In *The Road to Serfdom* (Chicago: University of Chicago Press, 1944), economist Friedrich Hayek, who later won a Nobel Memorial Prize in Economic Science, argued that increased regulation and central planning of the economy eventually lead to complete government control, that increased government in the economy sets into motion a process that, through political pressures, tends to create other government regulations. For example, the U.S. government sets a minimum price for milk above the equilibrium price and buys all the milk required to keep the price high. This created political pressures to reduce government spending on the program by paying farmers not to produce milk, to slaughter cows, and to get out of the dairy business. It also led the government to limit the amount of milk that Americans can import from countries where the price of milk is lower. Programs like this raise the prices of milk and milk products. This in turn creates political pressures to help poor people

buy milk products. Governments then create programs to redistribute income through the tax system, and so on.

One argument against the slippery-slope hypothesis is that the United States and many other countries have had some degree of government regulation for a long time, and it has not yet led to complete government control. Similarly, governments in the United States have long had some control over free speech and engaged in various kinds of censorship, but these restrictions have not yet led to complete control over speech. Of course, *yet* may be a key word here, though complete government control does not appear to be a near-term threat in the United States. Nevertheless, the size of government in the United States has expanded over time more rapidly than the U.S. economy, so this argument against the slippery-slope hypothesis may be inconclusive.

Another argument against the slippery-slope hypothesis postulates an equilibrium amount of regulation, so that some regulations do not necessarily lead to others. While some special-interest groups have enough power to create government regulations that help them, they cannot get everything they want from those regulations, nor can all special-interest groups obtain the regulations they desire. (Just because some people can get away with robbing you doesn't mean that everyone can.) An equilibrium amount of regulation may emerge from the balance of political powers. Changes in political forces may raise the equilibrium amount of regulation, but that increase in regulation does not automatically lead to further increases. The same argument may apply to restrictions on free speech.

focuses on where those interests lie; what political and institutional forces affect the incentives of regulators? Evidence suggests, for example, that regulators lose more from clearly visible mistakes, such as allowing sales of harmful products, than from less visible mistakes, such as keeping valuable products off the market. The incentives to avoid clearly visible mistakes may lead regulators to permit less innovation and risk taking than would be economically efficient. Critics of regulation suggest that this better-safe-than-sorry incentive is particularly important in food and drug regulations, resulting in overregulation that keeps useful medicines off the market because of excessive concern with safety. Another important incentive facing a regulator relates to the desire to obtain a good job when the regulatory job ends, creating the incentives mentioned earlier to cooperate with industry interests.[14]

RENT SEEKING

The mere possibility that the government will help producers through its regulations gives producers an incentive to spend resources trying to obtain beneficial regulations. *Rent seeking,* or competition for favors from the government, occurs when these producers spend time, money, and other resources seeking regulations that benefit them. Rent seeking is economically inefficient because it consumes resources to fight over how to divide the economy's wealth rather than to create new wealth.

--- **QUESTIONS** ---

21.6 Discuss this statement:

> Opium and morphine are certainly dangerous, habit-forming drugs. But once the principle is admitted that it is the duty of the government to protect the individual against his own foolishness, no serious objections can be made against further encroachments. A good case can be made out in favor of prohibition of alcohol and nicotine. And why limit the government's benevolent providence to the protection of the individual's body only? Is not the harm a man can inflict on his mind and soul even more dangerous than bodily evils? Why not prevent him from reading bad books and seeing bad plays, from looking at bad paintings and statues, and from hearing bad music? The mischief done by bad ideologies, surely, is much more pernicious, both for the individual and for the whole society, than that done by narcotic drugs.... If one abolishes man's freedom to determine his own consumption, one takes away all freedoms. (Ludwig von Mises, *Human Action* [New Haven, Conn.: Yale University Press, 1949])

21.7 Does one regulation lead to another? Does one restriction on free speech lead to another?

REGULATIONS AND THEIR ALTERNATIVES

The effects of regulations, and the alternatives to regulations suggested by policy analysts, differ from case to case depending on the details of the regulation and the situation. This section considers a few examples.

OCCUPATIONAL LICENSURE

Governments require people to hold government licenses to work as doctors, lawyers, real-estate agents, hair stylists, and so on. Occupational licensure reduces competition by creating a barrier to entry. The main argument for occupational licensure is that it guarantees a minimum level of quality in the licensed occupation. The main economic arguments against occupational licensure state that it raises prices to consumers, by restricting competition, and creates economic inef-

---

[14]In his book *Breaking the Vicious Circle* (Cambridge, Mass.: Harvard University Press, 1994), Stephen Breyer, now a justice on the U.S. Supreme Court, argues that government regulators do not face the proper incentives to use reasonable procedures for calculating the costs and benefits of government regulations.

ficiencies by preventing people from choosing lower-quality goods or services at lower prices.

Proponents of licensure argue that licenses provide people with information about quality; opponents argue that the government could provide that information directly to consumers.[15] As an alternative, it could license high-quality suppliers, but allow other people to enter professions without licenses, as governments do in some occupations such as plumbing.[16] Proponents of licensure argue that the license requirements prevent people from making mistakes; a person might not realize she is seeing a low-quality doctor, for example. Opponents of occupational licensure argue that this prevents people who want to buy lower-quality services and pay lower prices from doing so. They also argue that licensure does not protect people from mistakes about quality, it only shifts the possibility of mistakes to the licensure process, and that the cost of licensure in reduced competition and higher prices is not worth the benefits from preventing mistakes.

REGULATING A NATURAL MONOPOLY

Chapter 13 defined a natural monopoly as a firm with a downward-sloping average cost curve. Local telephone service is an example; the large fixed cost of setting up the equipment and the telephone lines, along with a small marginal cost, creates a downward-sloping average cost curve, as in **Figure 21.2.**

An unregulated monopoly chooses output to equate marginal cost with marginal revenue, as in Figure 21.2. At the economically efficient level of output, Point B, marginal cost equals demand. The monopolist produces less than the economically efficient quantity. People would buy the economically efficient quantity at a price of P_B, but an unregulated monopoly charges a higher price, P_A.

Government regulation cannot force the firm to charge the price P_B because the firm would lose money and go out of business. Its average cost would be AC_B, so the firm would lose AC_B minus P_B on each unit it would sell. (It would sell Q_B units.) Government regulation could require average-cost pricing, though, in which the government would force the firm to charge P_C. The firm would then maximize its profit by producing the amount Q_C. Although this is not the economically efficient quantity, it is closer than the quantity produced by an unregulated natural monopoly. Alternatively, government regulation could require the firm to charge a two-part price, perhaps made up of a fixed monthly fee for electric service plus a fee based on the amount of electricity used that month. Suppose that the government requires the firm to charge two prices, a price P_B for each kilowatt-hour of electricity use and a monthly fee large enough to prevent the firm from incurring a loss: $(AC_B - P_B)(Q_B)$. The firm then maximizes its profit by producing the economically efficient quantity, Q_B, and it earns zero economic profit. The fixed monthly fee covers the natural monopoly's fixed costs and prevents it from losing money.

Real-life regulation of natural monopolies (and other firms) does not often work out this simply. The regulations result from a political process in which the

---

[15]Do consumers need government licenses to provide this information? *Consumers Reports* regularly rates products; Underwriter's Laboratory (UL) sets standards for electrical equipment; *Motor Trend, Audio,* and other magazines regularly rate specialty products such as automobiles and hi-fi equipment; newspapers, magazines, and television carry reviews of books and movies. Could similar arrangements work for doctors, lawyers, barbers, and so on?

[16]The government would still enforce laws on fraud, so an unlicensed person could not legally claim to hold a license.

FIGURE 21.2

REGULATING A NATURAL MONOPOLY

An unregulated monopoly would produce Q_A (where $MC = MR$) and charge P_A. The economically efficient quantity is Q_B. The government could not force a firm to charge P_B, so that people would buy Q_B, because the firm would lose $AC_B - P_B$ on each unit sold. The government could, however, require the firm to charge P_C, in which case it would sell Q_C units and break even, or the government could require a two-part price.

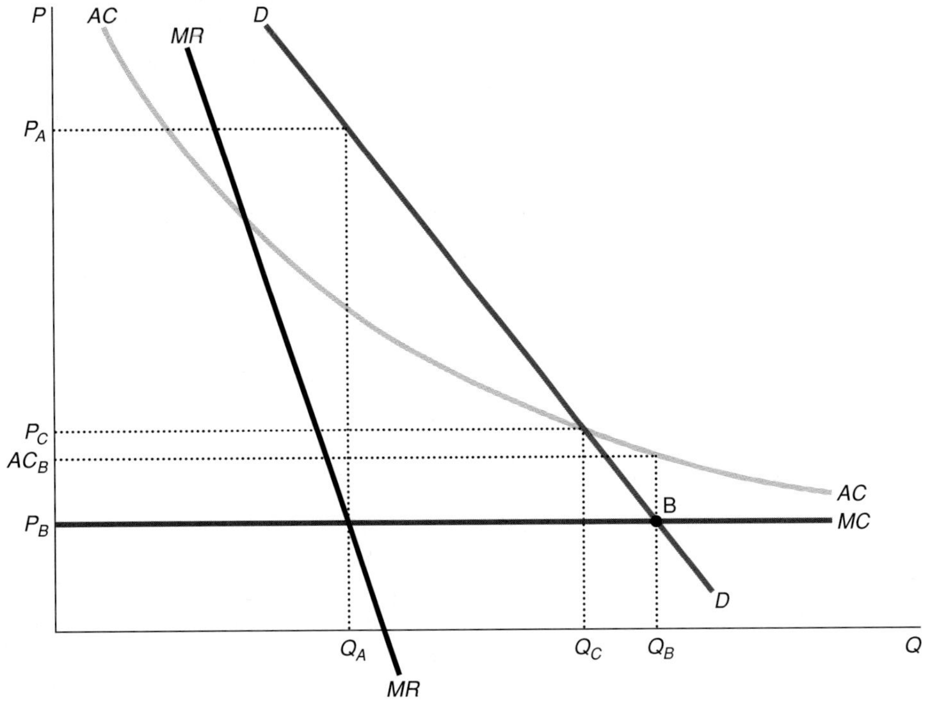

interests of the producer are more concentrated than those of consumers. Consider, for example, limits on prices and profits. Regulators often impose rate-of-return regulations that limit firms' accounting profits as percentages of their costs. Regulators calculate an individual firm's total cost, then add an allowable profit based on profits in other industries and use this figure to calculate the maximum price that the firm can charge.

Rate-of-return regulation gives the firm an incentive to raise its costs in certain ways. It may raise wages to make employees happier or provide its executives with luxurious offices, corporate jets, cars, premium tickets to sports events, first-class business trips to vacation resorts, entertainment, and so on. These expenses raise the firm's costs, so the regulators permit price increases to cover them. Without regulation, the firm might prefer to spend less money on these items and earn higher profits instead. Because rate-of-return regulation limits profits, however, firms take nonmoney forms of benefits that show up as costs rather than profits. Opponents of government regulation of natural monopolies argue that the government regulates many firms that are not natural monopolies and that, in practice, regulation results in higher prices and greater economic inefficiency than unregulated natural monopolies would produce on their own because, in practice, regulations benefit regulated firms.

IN THE NEWS

How children's safety can be put in jeopardy by day-care personnel

Human tragedy

Ashley Snead, 10 months old, died in the home of sitter with child-abuse record

The crusade for regulations

By Cathy Trost
Staff Reporter of
The Wall Street Journal

The quality of care ranges from "absolutely excellent to

absolutely awful," says Yale University child-care expert Edward Zigler. "You knock on one door and it may be wonderful. You knock on another door and your kid may be dead that night."

Should a 'mother down the block' be regulated as day-care provider?

By Cathy Trost
Staff Reporter of The Wall Street Journal

Many providers of child care go unregulated under a hodge-podge of state laws, while a controversial proposal to impose federal child-care standards recently met defeat.

Children's advocacy groups intend to press their case in the next Congress. Marian Wright Edelman, president of the Children's Defense Fund, says she questions the judgment of a nation that has "no qualms" about licensing hairdressers, restaurants, and plumbers but not the people who care for children.

Standards are no guarantee of safety, says DeAnn Lineberry, an official of Virginia's Department of Social Services. But she says regulated care is still "much less risky" because it gives child-care providers rules to follow and gives parents more resources to deal with problems.

Others, however, argue that burdensome regulation would force many day-care providers out of business, while the survivors would have to increase their prices

beyond the reach of many parents. Moreover, says Robert Rector, policy analyst for the conservative Heritage Foundation, unlicensed child-care "is far from being the onerous type of dangerous cesspool facility." He adds, "It's one mother down the block who has a preschooler of her own, and is taking care of one other preschooler. . . . All the scientific evidence we have," shows that informal, unlicensed day-care is as safe as regulated care.

Should the government license child-care services? Try to argue both sides.

Source: Cathy Trost, "How Children's Safety Can Be Put in Jeopardy by Day-Care Personnel," and "Should a 'Mother Down the Block' Be Regulated as Day-Care Provider?" *The Wall Street Journal,* October 18, 1988.

TELEVISION AND RADIO BROADCASTING

The government licenses television and radio broadcasters and assigns them frequencies at which they can legally broadcast. This gives the government greater power over the broadcast media than it has over printed media such as newspapers and magazines. Occasionally, the government has exercised this control in controversial ways. Some argue in favor of regulation of broadcasting because

IN THE NEWS

Anti-acne drug faulted in birth defects

By Gina Kolata

Government officials estimate that the popular anti-acne drug Accutane has caused hundreds, perhaps more than 1,000, babies to be born with severe birth defects in the past six years.

Officials say they are seriously considering removing the drug from the market or asking the maker to severely limit its distribution.

Despite clear warnings that the drug can cause devastating and sometimes fatal deformities if taken by preg-

nant women, experts estimate that thousands of women have taken Accutane in their pregnancies.

Although Dr. Oakley suggests that it might be best to remove the drug from the market, some dermatologists disagree.

'Extremely Important Drug'
Dr. Robert Stern, a dermatologist at the Harvard Medical School, agreed that the situation "is a serious problem," but he said Accutane is the

only treatment available for many patients with disfiguring acne.

"Accutane is an extremely important drug," he said. "There are thousands—perhaps tens of thousands of patients a year—for whom this drug really changes their lives. There is no alternative that is anywhere near as effective." He stressed that severe acne, left uncontrolled, "scars patients both physically and psychologically."

Safety regulations cannot always prevent dangerous products.

Source: Gina Kolata, "Anti-Acne Drug Faulted in Birth Defects," *New York Times,* April 22, 1988.

radio and television can use only a limited number of broadcast frequencies. However, scarcity of a resource does not imply that unregulated market forces create economic inefficiencies; land, food, and original Picasso paintings are also scarce. Free markets could operate for broadcasts just as they operate for land and other goods if people had private property rights in broadcast frequencies, so that someone owned the right to a particular frequency band in a particular region.[17] In fact, the government has created private property rights in certain other frequency bands (for use with cellular phone and paging technologies).

FOOD AND DRUG REGULATIONS

Current U.S. regulations require sellers to prove that foods are safe for humans and that drugs are both safe and effective. Critics of regulations that require clinical trials to prove a drug's effectiveness argue that the regulations cause long delays in bringing valuable new drugs to the market.

One alternative to health regulations, such as regulations that prevent sales of certain foods and drugs, is to abolish the regulations and let people buy and sell what they want. The government would still enforce laws against fraud; if a producer were to claim falsely that a drug was safe, consumers could sue the producer for damages and compensation. One problem with this method of

---

[17]The government could sell property rights in broadcast frequencies through an auction, as it has done with other parts of the electromagnetic spectrum. One argument against this move is that rich people might buy up all of the broadcast frequencies. The counterargument says that this would not occur; rich people do not buy all of the other goods in the economy. (Of course, rich people own most of the luxury yachts and private mansions; do you think that ownership of television and radio broadcasting frequencies would be different?)

guaranteeing safety is that producers often have limited liability, which means that a court can force a producer to pay only limited amounts because the producer may declare bankruptcy. One possible solution to this problem would be to change the laws on limited liability and make producers fully liable (completely responsible for the results of their own actions) in certain cases.

Another alternative to current regulations would be for the government to provide information about food and drug items, but not to prohibit their sale or purchase. The government might require producers to distribute information (on labels or in pamphlets distributed with products). Still another alternative would require proof of safety, but not proof of effectiveness. This would reduce the length of time before a producer could sell a drug, and people would be free to buy any safe medicine. If a drug were to turn out to be effective, this change would bring benefits because the drug could save lives. If a drug were to turn out to be ineffective, some people would have wasted their money. Critics of this idea argue that ineffective drugs may give people with serious diseases false hopes. They also argue that people might take ineffective medications rather than seeking more promising professional help.

NATIONALIZED INDUSTRIES AND PRIVATIZATION

nationalized firm — a firm that the government owns

privatization — creation of private property rights in a nationalized firm so that it becomes privately owned

An extreme case of regulation and taxation occurs when the government makes all of the decisions of a firm or industry and takes all of its profits—it nationalizes the firm or industry.

A **nationalized firm** is a firm that the government owns.[18]

Nationalization occurs when a government acquires a firm, either by buying it or (more often) by confiscating it from its previous owners. Confiscation may take the form of forcing owners to sell to the government at a low price.

Privatization occurs when a previously nationalized firm becomes private property.

Governments privatize by selling or giving away nationalized firms and creating private property rights to those firms. Privatization has played a major role in the transformation of the economies of Russia and other eastern European countries since 1990 from socialism to free-market economies. A number of other countries, such as Great Britain and Mexico, have also privatized many firms in recent years.

DECISIONS OF NATIONALIZED INDUSTRIES

A privately owned firm seeks to maximize the discounted present value of its profits—the value of the firm. If the manager of a firm makes poor decisions, someone else has an incentive to buy the firm, operate it more efficiently, and raise its value. For example, suppose that Pickens owns and operates a firm with a value (measured by the discounted present value of expected future profits) of $200,000. If you believe that you could raise the firm's value to $300,000 by operating the firm more efficiently, you would be willing to pay up to $300,000 to buy it. Pickens would be willing to accept any offer above $200,000, so you and Pickens could find a mutually beneficial, voluntary trade in which you would buy

---

[18]The government may completely own the firm, or it may own most of the firm's stock.

the firm (perhaps for $250,000). You would *take over* the firm. The incentive for someone to take over a firm, if that firm does not maximize its value, helps to create a tendency for efficient operation of privately owned firms.

Nationalized firms, in contrast, have little incentive to maximize the discounted present value of the firm's profits. No potential for takeovers exists to create a tendency for efficient operation. The managers of a nationalized firm, like managers of firms under rate-of-return regulation, may have incentives to increase their costs in ways that provide benefits to themselves (luxurious offices, company cars, and other perks). Because the incentive to maximize firm value is weak, nationalized firms often have low incentives to provide products or services that customers want at the lowest possible prices, to improve quality standards, or to innovate. Most nationalized firms are also legal monopolies. Their incentives to maximize value would increase if they faced competition and could not rely on government subsidies to cover losses.

One argument against allowing private firms to compete with nationalized firms is the cream-skimming argument. This argument says that private firms would take away all the customers whose business would provide easy profits and leave the nationalized firm with the customers that generate losses. For example, if private firms were to compete with the government in delivering first-class mail, they would take away the business of delivering letters from one office to another in the same city and mail delivery between major cities. They would leave the government to deliver mail between small towns or remote areas of Texas and Alaska. As a counterargument, note that cream-skimming can occur only if the nationalized firm subsidizes some customers at the expense of others, perhaps by charging the same price to all customers despite higher costs of serving some customers than others. For example, the U.S. Postal Service subsidizes mail delivery to people in remote areas by charging them no more than it charges people who send letters between Los Angeles and San Francisco; it takes a loss on the remote customers and earns a profit on the more popular routes. If the nationalized firm were to charge each customer a price equal to its cost of serving that customer, cream-skimming could not occur when the government allowed private firms to compete with nationalized firms.

PRIVATE SUPPLY OR GOVERNMENT SUPPLY?

Governments provide many goods and services that private firms could (and sometimes do) provide, such as collecting garbage, operating airports, delivering mail, running schools, and selling unemployment insurance. Private garbage-collection firms, airports, and schools also perform these services. Private postal companies have operated (until the government shut them down) and several private firms deliver overnight letters and packages. Private firms sell many kinds of insurance; presumably, they could sell unemployment insurance also. (Governor Franklin Roosevelt of New York State, before he became president, signed a state law making it illegal for private insurance companies to sell unemployment insurance.) When a government provides goods and services, the political process determines quantities supplied, quality levels, prices, and methods of production. Sometimes a low quantity supplied or low quality level induces private firms to enter the industry and provide supplementary goods and services. For example, some people and businesses hire private police and security guards to protect themselves or their property; this is a substitute for government-provided, public police services. Some firms use private courts and

IN THE NEWS

Public services found more efficient if private companies compete

By Louis Uchitelle

'It's the Competition'

In Florida, the commissioners of Bay County, dissatisfied with the way the sheriff's office ran the county jail, invited outsiders to bid for the job. The Corrections Corporation of America won with an offer of $26 a day per prisoner. The sheriff's best offer was $36.

The Tallahassee, Fla., fire department tried to raise the fees it charged to respond to alarms in surrounding Leon County. But when the county commissioners sought bids from the Rural/Metro Corporation, the department lowered its rate increase and expanded its services.

"It isn't that the private sector or the public sector is better; it's the competition between the two of them that works," said John D. Donahue, a public policy expert at the Kennedy School of Government at Harvard.

Geoffrey Bogart, an official of the International City Management Association, an organization of appointed officials, added, "Contracting, in many cases, is turning out to be a useful tool in providing cost-effective services."

So far, the experience with privatization has been mostly in contracting services from business at the county and municipal levels. The next big step could be giving to families some state funds now used for public school education or to build public housing. Under this scenario, parents would pick what they considered the best school for their child, public or private. That school would get their state money. In housing, state money would go toward rental of a home anywhere in a city.

Privatization might never get this far. But it has clearly gained a foothold after a decade of experimentation. While garbage collection is the service most opened up to competition, the private sector has become involved in many others in hundreds of cities. These include data processing, fire fighting, vehicle maintenance, street light repair, hospital management, and park maintenance.

Competition tends to improve the efficiency of production of public services.

Source: Louis Uchitelle, "Public Services Found More Efficient if Private Companies Compete," *New York Times,* April 26, 1988.

arbitrators in legal disputes; they sign contracts that specify arbitrators to handle any disputes that later arise.[19] Even private prisons and jails operate in the United States.

As an alternative to supplying a good itself or allowing private firms to supply it, government can finance private production. For example, governments of some communities pay for garbage collection out of tax revenues without actually operating garbage-collection services; instead, they hire private companies to collect garbage. This system gives firms incentives to provide goods at low prices (assuming that governments want to buy from the lowest-cost suppliers) but requires everyone to pay for the goods through taxes. Some analysts have suggested this scheme for other goods and services. For example, the government could use tax revenues to pay for education without actually operating schools by hiring private firms to operate schools. It could also provide people

---

[19]You may be familiar with examples of arbitration from professional sports.

with education vouchers and let the recipients use the vouchers to buy education services at the schools of their choice or any government-approved schools.

Many proposals for privately supplying products or services that are currently supplied mainly by governments, including schools, prisons, fire fighting, and health care services in many countries are controversial. The main argument for private supply is that private firms can provide higher-quality products or services at lower prices than the government. The main argument against private supply is that government supply can ensure uniform quality standards. Other arguments on both sides appear on a case-by-case basis.

FOR REVIEW

21.8 Explain the public-interest view, special-interest view, and capture view of regulation.

21.9 Explain diffuse and concentrated interests and how the difference between them may affect regulations.

21.10 Discuss arguments for and against occupational licensure (license requirements to work in certain occupations).

21.11 Discuss arguments for and against current U.S. food and drug regulations.

QUESTIONS

21.12 What are the effects of regulations that require restaurants to provide no-smoking sections? How do these regulations affect prices at the restaurants, profits in the restaurant industry, lines at restaurants, and so on? Without these regulations, would a restaurant have an incentive to offer a no-smoking section to customers who wanted it? Why or why not? (Note that no-smoking sections became common at about the same time that laws began to require them.) Who gains and who loses from these regulations?

21.13 Some textile workers work in factories, and others work in their homes. The union in the textile industry wants the government to prohibit work at home, as it did for about four decades in the middle of the century. They argue that work at home can violate workplace fire and safety regulations, maximum-hours laws, child labor laws, and other regulations. The industry says that allowing work at home gives workers flexibility, and that the union wants to restrict competition from people who work at home in order to raise wages. Who would gain and who would lose from a regulation banning textile work in the home?

TAXES

Taxes, like regulations, serve several purposes. Governments use taxes to fund their programs, redistribute wealth, and achieve other social goals like discouraging or encouraging activities such as smoking, driving, polluting the air, buying imported goods, saving money, or spending money. Most taxes create economic inefficiencies. As a result, different combinations of taxes can provide the same revenue to the government while creating different amounts of economic inefficiency and having different effects on the government's goals.

How can the government choose a combination of taxes that best meets its objectives? This section begins with a discussion of how a government can choose a combination of taxes to raise a certain amount of revenue with the lowest possible cost in economic inefficiency.

OPTIMAL TAXATION: MINIMIZING THE DEADWEIGHT SOCIAL LOSS

Chapter 11 explained that taxes create economic inefficiency; the deadweight social loss from a tax consists of the gains from trade that it prevents. A tax on a good reduces the quantity traded, so people who choose not to trade because of the tax lose consumer and producer surplus on these foregone trades.

The size of the deadweight social loss from a tax depends on the elasticities of supply and demand. **Figure 21.3** shows several cases. If either demand or supply is perfectly inelastic, then the tax causes no deadweight social loss because it does not change the quantity traded. As supply and demand become more elastic, the deadweight social loss from a tax increases.

By placing high tax rates on goods with low elasticities of demand and supply and low tax rates on goods with high elasticities of demand and supply, the government can minimize the economic inefficiency of collecting any amount of total tax revenue. This is optimal taxation.

FIGURE 21.3

BIGGER DEADWEIGHT SOCIAL LOSS FROM A TAX WITH MORE ELASTIC DEMAND AND SUPPLY

Panels a and d show no deadweight social losses. Shaded areas in the other panels show deadweight social losses.

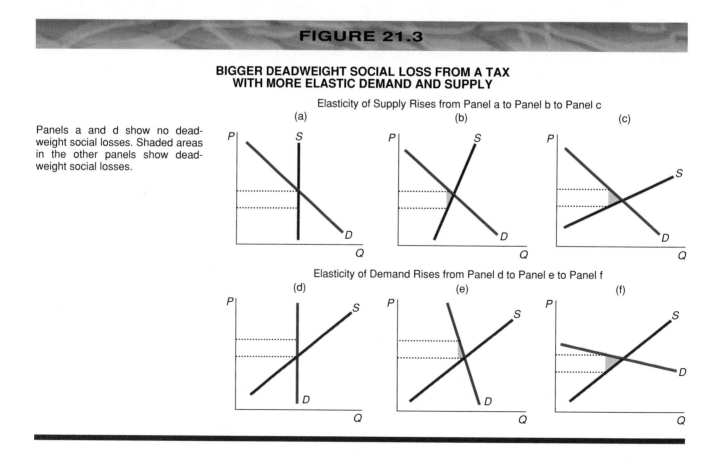

Elasticity of Supply Rises from Panel a to Panel b to Panel c

Elasticity of Demand Rises from Panel d to Panel e to Panel f

optimal taxation — a system of tax rates that minimizes the total deadweight social loss from taxes while raising a certain amount of revenue for the government

Optimal taxation minimizes the total deadweight social loss from taxes that raise a certain amount of revenue for the government.

Optimal taxation sets tax rates that minimize the total deadweight social loss required to raise a fixed amount of revenue. One set of optimal taxes would raise $500 billion for the government; another set would raise $800 billion, and so on.

The example in **Table 21.4** shows the main idea. Suppose that the government wants to raise $4,000 in tax revenue. It could do this in many ways. It could tax labor income at 20 percent and collect $4,000 with a deadweight social loss of $800, or it could tax investment income at 40 percent and raise $4,000 with a deadweight social loss of $1,600. However, the government can do even better by combining the taxes. If it taxes labor income at 10 percent and investment income at 20 percent, it raises $2,000 from each tax, for a total of $4,000, with a total deadweight social loss of only $600 ($200 from the tax on labor income and $400 from the tax on investment income). Even better, it could tax labor income at 15 percent and investment income at 10 percent to raise $4,000 with a total deadweight social loss of only $550 ($450 from the tax on labor income and $100 from the tax on investment income). These are the optimal tax rates when the government wants to raise $4,000 in revenue. Other optimal tax rates would apply to raise other levels of revenue.

An implication of this logic is that the government can minimize the economic inefficiency from its taxes by taxing only goods with perfectly inelastic demands or supplies, if it can identify any such goods and if taxes on these goods alone would raise sufficient revenue. Some people have argued that land has a perfectly inelastic supply, so taxes on land would not create economic inefficiency. However, real-life taxes on land are partly taxes on improvements to the land (such as buildings on it, care for its soil or plant life, cultivation, and so on), and the supply of improvements is not perfectly inelastic. Another suggestion is a head tax in which everyone pays a fixed amount of money. This is tax on live people, and the number of live people is close to perfectly inelastic (although a head tax would affect the number of births).

CRITICISMS

While taxes on goods with perfectly inelastic demands or supplies would be the most economically efficient way for the government to collect a certain amount of revenue, many people may regard them as unfair. Most people believe that the

TABLE 21.4

EXAMPLE OF OPTIMAL TAXATION

Tax on Labor Income			Tax on Investment Income		
Tax Rate	Tax Revenue	Deadweight Social Loss	Tax Rate	Tax Revenue	Deadweight Social Loss
5	$1,000	$ 50	5	$ 500	$ 25
10	2,000	200	**10**	**1,000**	**100**
15	**3,000**	**450**	15	1,500	225
20	4,000	800	20	2,000	400
25	5,000	1,250	25	2,500	625
30	6,000	1,800	30	3,000	900
35	7,000	2,450	35	3,500	1,225
40	8,000	3,200	40	4,000	1,600

government should choose tax rates partly on the basis of fairness or equity. Therefore, the government may choose to sacrifice economic efficiency to increase fairness or equity. Great Britain replaced property taxes with a head tax (called a *poll tax*) in 1988; despite some rebates for poor people, the public viewed the head tax as unfair and it was soon repealed.

To see the tradeoff between economic efficiency and fairness, suppose again that the government wants to raise $4,000 in tax revenue from the taxes in Table 21.4. It could minimize economic inefficiency by choosing a 15 percent tax on labor income and a 10 percent tax on investment income for a deadweight social loss of $550. Some people may regard these taxes as unfair, however; they may want higher taxes on investment income and lower taxes on labor income or the reverse. The consideration of fairness may lead the government to tax labor income at 10 percent and investment income at 20 percent, even though the deadweight social loss, $600, would be higher. Obviously, the conclusions about whom to tax depend on one's ideas of equity and fairness. People may disagree on principles of equity; economic analysis alone cannot settle these issues.

Of course, actual government tax policies may be guided more by the political power of various groups than by actual considerations of either economic efficiency or fairness. If investors' political power were strong enough, for example, the government might choose to tax labor income at a 20 percent rate and not tax investment income at all; this would raise the total deadweight social loss to $800.

Economists distinguish between two dimensions of fairness in taxes: *horizontal equity* and *vertical equity*. Horizontal equity is the principle that people with the same characteristics should be treated equally. Applied to taxes, it says that people in equal conditions should pay equal taxes. This suggests, for example, that men and women should not be taxed differently. Vertical equity is the principle that people in unequal conditions should be treated differently. For example, taxes should be based partly on the ability to pay.

TAX AVOIDANCE

The term *tax avoidance* refers to choices that help reduce taxes. (Tax avoidance differs from illegal tax evasion.) People find many ways to exploit "loopholes" and other features of the tax laws to reduce their taxes. The most obvious way for people to avoid taxes is to cut back on activities that the government taxes. Taxes affect many decisions such as labor supply (how much to work), choice of occupation, whether to get married, the number of children to have, choice of residence (high-tax areas versus low-tax areas), which goods to buy, how much money to save for the future, and which investments to choose.

Consider the effect of marriage on income taxes. Each of two single persons who earned $30,000 per year in 1994 and took the standard deduction paid $3,700 in U.S. federal income taxes, for a total income tax of $7,400. (Each person also paid $2,295 in Social Security taxes.) If they had married and filed a joint return, they would have paid an income tax of $8,717. Getting married would have raised their federal income tax by $1,317 per year. (Marriage would not have affected their Social Security taxes.) In some well-publicized cases several years ago, people got divorced each year to file their taxes, then remarried. Although the government declared this illegal, taxes clearly affect the marriage decisions of some people.

The deadweight social losses caused by taxes are actually much larger than the shaded areas in Figure 21.3 due to changes in behavior induced by taxes. Evidence suggests the deadweight social loss from raising all income taxes would be about $200 for each $1.00 in extra tax revenue for the government.

TAXES IN THE UNITED STATES

Table 21.5 shows U.S. federal income taxes and self-employment taxes (which are the Social Security taxes paid by a self-employed person) for various income levels in 1994. **Figure 21.4** shows average tax rates and the marginal tax rates.

A person's **average tax rate** equals her tax obligation divided by her income.

A person's **marginal tax rate** equals the increase in taxes she would pay if her income were to rise by $1.

The relationship between marginal and average tax rates resembles the relation between marginal and average costs discussed in Chapter 10. A person's average tax rate rises when her marginal tax rate exceeds her average tax rate, and falls when her marginal tax rate is less than her average.

Taxes often apply only to part of a person's income. For example, people are allowed to deduct certain charitable contributions from their incomes. *Taxable income* refers to the part of income that the government taxes (income minus allowed deductions).

Table 21.5 shows that a single, self-employed person, who earned $30,000 of income in 1994 and took the standard deduction on her taxes, paid $7,483 in federal and self-employment taxes. Her average tax rate, therefore, was 25 percent, and her *marginal* tax rate was 28 percent—if she had earned another $100, she would have paid an extra $28 in federal taxes.

The U.S. federal income tax began in 1913 with a maximum tax rate on personal income of 7 percent that applied only to the richest 2 percent of people in the country.[20] The top rate was raised to 15 percent in 1916 and to 77 percent during World War I, then it fell to 25 percent after the war. It increased again to 55 percent in 1931 (during the Great Depression) and to 77 percent during World War II. By the early 1960s, the highest federal income tax rate was 91 percent. The government then reduced it to 70 percent, then to 50 percent in 1982, and to 33 percent in 1987, before raising it again.

GRADUATED TAX RATES

If everyone were to pay the same percentage of income in taxes, people with high incomes would pay more than people with low incomes. A *flat-rate tax system* requires the same percentage for everyone. However, most countries, including the United States, have *graduated* income tax rates in which tax rates rise with income, so people with higher incomes pay higher income tax percentages of income as taxes. Figure 21.4 shows that average tax rates in the United States rise with income.

Some people have proposed replacing the graduated income tax system with a modified flat-rate tax. One such proposal would place a 20 percent tax on all income above a certain level, such as $20,000 earned per person, with no deductions allowed. Under this proposal, people earning less than $20,000 per year would pay no income tax, and people earning more than $20,000 would pay 20 percent of their income in excess of that amount. For example, a person earning

average tax rate — a person's tax payment as a fraction of income

marginal tax rate — the increase in a person's tax payment due to a $1 increase in income

TABLE 21.5

U.S. FEDERAL INCOME TAXES AND SELF-EMPLOYMENT TAXES FOR A SINGLE, SELF-EMPLOYED PERSON, 1994

Gross Income	Total Tax[a]
$ 10,000	$ 1,867 (28%, 19%)
20,000	4,675 (28%, 23%)
30,000	7,483 (28%, 25%)
40,000	11,354 (41%, 28%)
50,000	15,371 (39%, 31%)
60,000	19,388 (39%, 32%)
80,000	26,413 (34%, 33%)
100,000	33,071 (32%, 33%)
150,000	51,074 (40%, 34%)
250,000	89,923 (38%, 36%)
500,000	193,900 (42%, 39%)
1,000,000	402,640 (42%, 40%)

Note: Figures in parentheses are marginal and average tax rates (marginal rate, average rate).

[a]The tax figures assume that the taxpayer takes one exemption and the standard deduction.

[20]An income tax was proposed in the United States, but never passed, during the War of 1812. The U.S. government began collecting income taxes, with rates rising to 10 percent, during the Civil War; this tax lasted only until 1872.

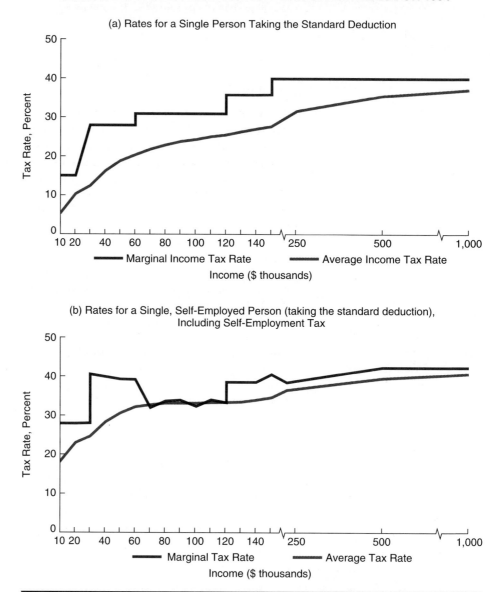

FIGURE 21.4

MARGINAL AND AVERAGE FEDERAL INCOME TAX RATES FOR 1994

(a) Rates for a Single Person Taking the Standard Deduction

(b) Rates for a Single, Self-Employed Person (taking the standard deduction),
Including Self-Employment Tax

$30,000 would pay 20 percent of $10,000, or $2,000 in federal income tax. This proposal, which would probably raise about the same amount of government revenue as the current tax system does, has two main advantages over the current system—simplicity (which would reduce the time that people must spend to calculate their taxes) and lower marginal tax rates (which would raise people's incentives to work).

The main argument against a flat-rate tax centers on fairness. Critics of a flat-rate tax believe that higher-income people should pay higher percentages of their incomes in taxes. The modified flat-rate proposal that calls for a tax only on

TABLE 21.6

GOVERNMENT TAX REVENUES, 1993 ($ BILLIONS)

Source	Federal Revenues	State and Local Revenues[a]	Total Government Revenues
Personal taxes (mainly income taxes)	$ 566	$177	$ 743
Social insurance (mainly Social Security)	555	71	626
Corporate taxes	170	36	206
Excise taxes, sales taxes, and import taxes	175	226	301
Property taxes	—	191	191
Other taxes	16	46	62
Total	$1,382	$748	$2,130

[a]State and local government receipts exceeded this number because those receipts included grants from the federal government of $198 billion in 1994.
Source: Survey of Current Business 75, no. 1 (January 1995), Tables 3.2 and 3.3.

incomes above a certain level, such as $20,000 per year, attempts to remedy this problem. With a 20 percent flat-rate tax on income above $20,000 per year, people who earn $30,000 annually would pay income taxes of $2,000, or 6.7 percent of their income, while people who earned $100,000 annually would pay 16 percent of their income. In this way, the average tax rate would rise with income.

SOURCES OF GOVERNMENT TAX REVENUE

Table 21.6 shows the main types of taxes in the United States, and the amounts of money that units of government collect from them. Federal, state, and local governments collected $2.130 trillion ($2,130,000,000) in taxes in 1994, which amounted to 31 percent of the country's GDP (the total output of all final goods and services in the economy).

TAXES ON CORPORATIONS

Table 21.6 shows that the corporate income tax provides the federal government with slightly more than 10 percent of its total tax revenue. Where do corporations obtain the money to pay corporate income taxes? Do the owners of corporations— the stockholders—pay the tax by receiving lower profits? Or do corporations' customers pay the tax in the form of higher prices for the products that they buy? Or do workers bear the burden of the corporate income tax in the form of lower wages?

Owners, customers, and workers share payment of corporate income taxes in a way that reflects the alternative opportunities available to each group. The better the alternative opportunities of workers, that is, the better their job opportunities outside of corporations, the less corporate income tax the workers will pay and the more owners and customers will pay.[21] The better the alternative opportunities of customers, that is, the better their opportunities to buy products from

---

[21]It is easy to understand this if you think about elasticities of demand and supply. Suppose, for example, that workers have very good job opportunities at firms that are not subject to the corporate income tax, making the supply of labor to corporations very elastic. In such a case, corporations could not reduce wages without losing a large number of workers to noncorporate jobs, so they could not shift the burden of a corporate income tax increase to their workers by paying lower wages.

firms not subject to corporate taxes (such as partnerships or sole proprietorships, which do not pay the corporate income tax), the less corporate income tax that customers will pay and the more owners and workers will pay. Finally, the better the alternative investment opportunities of the firm's owners, the less they will pay and the more workers and customers will pay. It is very difficult to calculate precisely who actually pays corporate income taxes. However, current evidence, although weak, suggests that most of the corporate income tax is paid by the owners (stockholders) of corporations.

Many economists favor abolition of the corporate income tax on grounds of efficiency and equity. The efficiency argument for eliminating the corporate tax notes that some corporate income is taxed twice. First, corporations pay taxes on their profits; second, people who receive those profits in the form of stock dividends or capital gains pay personal income taxes on it again. This raises the overall tax rate on savings and investment, which may reduce the level of overall output and decrease the rate of economic growth.

Taxes on business firms, like taxes on individuals, can require extensive recordkeeping and other costs. The costs of obeying corporate income tax laws is particularly high. For example, nine out of ten U.S. corporations have assets of less than $1 million; each dollar of corporate income taxes that such a firm pays costs it more than $3 because of the costs of recordkeeping, filling out and submitting required forms, and other related costs.

The equity argument for abolishing the corporate income tax notes that corporate profits are taxed at the same rate regardless of whether they are paid to high-income owners or low-income owners. The argument says that low-income people who own stock in a corporation should pay lower tax rates on their shares of the corporation's profits than higher-income people should pay; this would occur if the corporate tax were abolished and everyone were to pay only individual income taxes on the income they received from corporate profits.

─────────────── **FOR REVIEW** ───────────────

21.14 What is optimal taxation?

21.15 What is the average tax rate? The marginal tax rate?

21.16 Roughly how large is the combined federal income tax rate and Social Security tax rate on most people in the United States?

─────────────── **QUESTIONS** ───────────────

21.17 Explain why the burden of the corporate income tax may fall on customers, workers or owners. What determines how they share the burden of the tax?

21.18 Who would gain and who would lose if the corporate income tax were eliminated? How would elimination of this tax affect economic efficiency?

CONCLUSIONS

REGULATION

Government regulations restrict the actions of people and firms, and they require people and firms to do certain things. Government regulations are intended to protect the environment, reduce economic inefficiency, increase fairness, protect people from their own bad decisions, improve products, or set rules for using common resources. Some regulations are intended mainly to benefit certain special-interest groups at the expense of other people.

EVALUATING REGULATIONS: COST–BENEFIT ANALYSIS

Economists use cost–benefit analysis to compare the benefits and costs of regulations, taxes, and other government policies. The cost of a regulation results from an increase in economic inefficiency (lost consumer and producer surplus and costs to other people from externalities such as pollution). Economists measure costs and benefits of intangibles (such as safety) by the amount of money that people are willing to pay for that intangible in other situations. When a regulation or tax has future costs or benefits, economists compare the discounted present values of the costs and benefits. When the costs or benefits are uncertain, economists compare the discounted present values of the expected values of costs and benefits. One criticism of cost–benefit analysis is that the winners and losers from a regulation or tax may differ, and cost–benefit analysis shows only whether it would be a potential Pareto improvement, but not whether it would be an actual Pareto improvement. A second criticism is that the use of discounted present values causes cost–benefit analysis to place lower weight on the effects on future generations than some critics deem appropriate.

PROBLEMS WITH REGULATION

Critics of government regulations contend that the actual effects of regulations frequently differ from their intended effects. The three main economic views of regulation are the public-interest view (that regulations serve the public interest), the special-interest view (that regulations serve special-interest groups), and the capture view (that regulatory agencies originally established to serve the general public interest end up serving the special interests of the industries they were intended to regulate). The special-interest and capture views are based on the argument that the political power of concentrated interests exceeds that of equal-sized diffuse interests, so regulations tend to benefit groups with concentrated interests such as firms in the regulated industries. The possibility that government will help producers through regulation gives them an incentive to spend resources to obtain beneficial regulations; this rent seeking is economically inefficient.

NATIONALIZED INDUSTRIES AND PRIVATIZATION

Nationalized firms (those owned by the government) have different incentives than privately owned firms. Nationalized firms have weaker incentives to maximize value, partly because nationalized firms face no potential takeovers. Many nationalized firms are legal monopolies that would have stronger incentives to maximize value if they faced competition and did not receive government subsidies. One argument against allowing private firms to compete with nationalized firms, the cream-skimming argument, states that private firms would take away only profitable customers. The counterargument is that cream-skimming occurs only when nationalized firms subsidize some customers at the expense of others; competition would prevent this. Private firms could supply many products and services that governments supply; an alternative method of supply is for the government to pay for a good with tax revenues and to hire the lowest-cost private supplier to produce it.

TAXES

Taxes, like regulation, have several purposes: they fund government programs, redistribute income, and achieve other social goals. Because most taxes create economic inefficiencies, different combinations of taxes that give the government the same amount of revenue can create different amounts of economic inefficiency. Optimal taxation sets tax rates that minimize the total deadweight social loss from taxes while raising a certain amount of tax revenue for the government. Optimal tax rates are higher on goods with more inelastic supplies and demands and lower on goods with more elastic supplies and demands. If the government can identify goods with perfectly inelastic supplies or demands, it is optimal to tax only those goods. Other considerations, such as fairness, may suggest that the government should not choose tax rates solely to minimize economic inefficiency. Economists distinguish between horizontal equity (the principle that people who have the same characteristics should be treated equally) and vertical equity (the principle that people in unequal conditions should be treated differently). Actual taxes, like regulations, are determined partly by political forces rather than economic considerations.

A person's average tax rate equals his tax payment divided by his income. His marginal tax rate is the increase in taxes he would pay if his income were $1 higher. The average tax rate rises when the marginal tax rate exceeds the average and falls when the marginal rate is below the average. Most countries set graduated income tax rates rather than flat rates. Corporate taxes are paid partly by employees (in the form of lower wages), customers (in the form of higher prices), and owners (in the form of lower after-tax returns on their investments). Evidence suggests that owners probably pay the largest share of corporate taxes.

LOOKING AHEAD

Chapter 22 continues the discussion of government. It applies economic analysis to laws and the way governments make decisions.

KEY TERMS

government regulation	diffuse interest
deregulation	nationalized firm
cost–benefit analysis	privatization
public-interest view of regulation	optimal taxation
special-interest view of regulation	average tax rate
capture view of regulation	marginal tax rate
concentrated interest	

QUESTIONS AND PROBLEMS

21.19 Suppose that a regulation has benefits of $250,000 every year forever, and a one-half chance of costs of $2 million and a one-half chance of costs of $6 million. In either case, all costs are paid this year, and no future costs will arise. Use cost-benefit analysis to evaluate this regulation, assuming an interest rate of 5 percent per year.

21.20 A proposed regulation would raise prices so consumers would pay $10 million more for a product, and sellers' profits would rise by $10 million. Is the $10 million a cost of the regulation or a benefit of the regulation? Explain.

21.21 Why do regulated firms have incentives to raise their costs?

21.22 Explain why a military draft is like a tax. Who pays the tax?

INQUIRIES FOR FURTHER THOUGHT

21.23 Should the government try to protect adults from their own, possibly bad decisions, or should people be free to make their own mistakes?

21.24 The government restricts smoking and taxes cigarettes partly to protect the health of smokers. The government requires seat belts and airbags to raise safety in cars. Should the government also regulate weight, exercise, sleep, and high-cholesterol foods? Should it tax people based on how healthy they are? What would be the effects on quantities and prices of such taxes or regulations? How far should the government go to protect people from their own bad choices? Should the government require people to buy health insurance? To save for retirement? To do other good things? (Which things and why?)

21.25 Discuss this statement: "If people want more energy-efficient refrigerators and other appliances, better gas mileage in their cars, and so on, they can freely buy these products without any need for government regulation. If people were willing to pay enough to cover the cost of the greater energy efficiency, producers would make these products because they could raise their profits by doing so. There is no justification for government regulations of energy standards."

21.26 Suppose that a government regulation saves one life in our country, but kills two people in a distant country. Suppose that another government regulation saves one life today, but destroys two lives in the distant future. Are the costs and benefits the same or different in these two cases? Should cost–benefit analysis take discounted present values of the losses in the future, but not current losses in other countries?

21.27 Several government regulations make it difficult for firms to fire employees. Should regulations ever prevent a firm from firing an employee? Under what circumstances?

21.28 Some people claim that regulations in the United States hurt U.S. businesses that compete with foreign sellers. Should the government take this into account in forming its regulations? If so, how? How could foreign competition affect the cost–benefit analysis of government regulations?

21.29 Should the government regulate product quality or safety? Is higher quality or greater safety always better, even if it costs more? How should the government decide on quality and safety regulations? Who gains and who loses from government regulations on minimum quality or safety? Apply this analysis to the quality of (a) medical care, (b) schools, and (c) food and drugs.

21.30 U.S. government regulations require drug makers to prove their products both safe and effective. What are the likely effects of these regulations?

21.31 Suppose that two people are identical, except that one person has saved more and spent less in the past than the other. Should the government tax them at the same rate or different rates? Should it tax the interest income received by the person who saved money? What incentives are created by taxing (or not taxing) interest income?

21.32 Being as specific as possible, argue for and against:
   a. Graduated income tax rates
   b. A flat-rate income tax
   c. A head tax

21.33 Discuss this statement: "Horizontal equity does not suggest that men and women should be taxed at the same rates because women live longer than men, so they are likely to collect Social Security income longer. Therefore, women should pay higher Social Security taxes than men."

21.34 The U.S. government has occasionally bailed out a large company that was about to go bankrupt by giving the company enough money to stay in business. Should the government do this? Why or why not? If so, which companies should it bail out and which should it allow to fail?

TAG SOFTWARE APPLICATIONS

TUTORIAL EXERCISES
▶ The module contains a review of the key terms from Chapter 21.

GRAPHING EXERCISES
▶ The graphing segment contains questions on regulating natural monopolies and questions on the calculation of deadweight social loss from taxation.

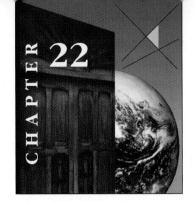
ECONOMICS OF PUBLIC CHOICE AND LAW

WHAT THIS CHAPTER IS ABOUT

▶ Economics of voting

▶ Political pressure and special-interest groups

▶ Roles of justice and economic efficiency in law

▶ Economically efficient laws and court decisions

▶ Accident and product-liability law

▶ Economics of theft and criminal law

Political markets differ from markets for most products. In the market for cars, several firms compete with each other and each consumer buys the car he wants. Production is determined by consumer demands, based on ability to pay. In political markets, production is often determined by a majority vote and all customers get a single type of product or service that results from this vote. (All share the same type of school, fire protection, or national-defense system.) In the markets for most products, firms can survive by selling goods to small market niches; a politician competing in political markets must appeal to a broad enough set of voters to survive competition from opponents.

How do people in government positions make decisions? How are their decisions related to the preferences of voters? Are the results of competition in the political arena economically efficient? This chapter examines these and other questions of public choice. It then turns to the economic analysis of law. Economic analysis of law began with Ronald Coase's insights on the role of property rights when transactions costs are high. (See the discussion of the Coase theorem in Chapter 20.) Since that time, the economic analysis of law has blossomed and spread from property law into contract law, tort (accident) law, product-liability law, and criminal law. This chapter explains how economic analysis can determine which laws and legal rules promote economic efficiency and which do not.

PUBLIC CHOICE

People often speak of government decisions as if the government were a single decision maker like a person or a small committee. The government consists of many parts, however, each staffed by people with different interests, views,

635

information, and powers. These different parts do not always cooperate with each other, so government actions often result from competition and compromise within the branches and agencies of government.

Similarly, people often think that the government has more information about the economy and the effects of its policies than it actually has. In fact, government officials frequently lack important information that is relevant to their policy decisions. They lack much of the knowledge they need to manage economies effectively because that kind of information is scattered throughout society. Some people know how to produce better refrigerators, some know how to produce spare parts for medical devices or farm equipment; some people know how to run successful restaurants, others know how to repair automobiles or how to manage research in new technologies for home electronics or health-care products. A government cannot possibly acquire all of this information, because it is spread among people in the society and it changes too fast.[1]

Finally, people often think of government officials as motivated by the desire to follow policies that serve the national interest. Government decisions are made by people, though. These people care about their own careers, salaries, prestige, families, and friends. Despite deep concern about promoting justice, helping the needy, defending the country, and pursuing the perceived national interest, even dedicated public servants are subject to personal pressures, and their perceptions of the national interest may change. Most people are motivated by wide-ranging desires that sometimes conflict, and people in government are no exceptions. When the views of elected officials conflict with those of the majority of the people who elected them, their desires to follow the policies that seem best to them can conflict with their desires to be reelected. A similar conflict arises when an elected official has the opportunity to receive campaign contributions from a group that favors certain policies along with the chance that those contributions will go to his opponent if he does not support the contributors' policies. The conflicting motivations and pressures facing a government official may lead to a political equilibrium that determines the final decision.

political equilibrium — a situation, characterized by peoples' votes and campaign contributions, the positions and strategies of candidates for office, and the decisions and actions of government officials, that shows no tendency for a change unless some underlying condition changes

A **political equilibrium** is a situation, characterized by peoples' votes and campaign contributions, the positions and strategies of candidates for office, and the decisions and actions of government officials, that shows no tendency for a change unless some underlying condition changes.

When someone suggests that the government should do something, such as appoint a commission to find and eliminate wasteful government spending, one can evaluate the suggestion in two ways. The traditional way is to assume that the government will carefully follow the suggested policy; a commission will identify waste in certain areas (such as overpaying for computers or duplicating tasks in two different agencies) and eliminate it. The alternative, public-choice analysis, would ask what the government would actually do in a political equilibrium if it were to adopt the suggested policy. For example, public-choice analysis might suggest that political forces would, in equilibrium, maintain much of the wasteful spending that the commission would identify. Public-choice analysis takes into account some of the forces that affect the political equilibrium when evaluating a proposed policy.

---

[1]This information problem was a key reason for the poor performance of socialism (centralized government planning of the economy) as an economic system.

IMPLICIT MARKETS FOR VOTES

Voters supply votes; politicians demand votes. Because votes cannot (usually) be explicitly bought and sold, the price of a vote is not a dollar amount. Instead, politicians acquire, or buy, votes through their positions on various government policies and the impressions they convey to voters about their general philosophies, competence levels, and other characteristics. People supply votes to politicians who support the policies that they want most or who have other characteristics that they like.

A politician who is interested mainly in votes (rather than good policies) can choose political positions to reflect those of voters, trying to match the views of a majority of voters better than other candidates. On the other hand, a politician with strong views on good policies can succeed only if those views match the views of voters more closely than the views of other candidates. Politicians can also try to obtain votes by changing voters' views, suggesting new arguments and new policy ideas that voters find attractive.

MEDIAN-VOTER THEOREM

The median-voter theorem is a logical result about equilibrium in political markets (under certain conditions). To define the term *median voter,* recall that the median of any distribution is the number with half of the distribution below it and half of the distribution above it. For example, in the list of numbers {1, 4, 10}, the median is 4, although the average, or mean, is 15/3, or 5. In a class of four students, if three students get *A*s while one fails, the median grade is an *A,* but the mean is lower than an *A.*

> The **median voter** is the voter whose views on a policy issue are in the middle of the spectrum; half of the other voters are on one side of this voter's views, and half are on the other side.

> The **median-voter theorem** states that, under certain conditions, the equilibrium government policy chosen in political markets is the policy favored by the median voter.

EXPLANATION AND EXAMPLE

Suppose that five voters disagree about the level of government spending on roads. Voter A wants the government to spend $10, Voter B wants it to spend $20, Voter C wants it to spend $30, Voter D wants it to spend $40, and Voter E wants it to spend $100. The median voter is C because two people want the government to spend more and two people want it to spend less.

The median voter can swing an election. Suppose that Smith and Jones are running for Congress. If Smith promises to support $20 in road spending, Jones can win the election by promising to spend $30 because Voters C, D, and E will prefer that position to Smith's. The winner will be the candidate who supports the policy favored by Voter C, the median voter.

Smith, knowing that a promise to spend $20 would give the election to Jones, may instead promise to spend $30 (as Voter C favors). In that case, Jones faces losing the election by choosing any other position, so both candidates will choose the policy favored by the median voter. (Politicians do commonly try to appeal to middle-of-the-road voters.) In that case, both candidates have the same views and whether Smith or Jones wins the election is then determined by some other issue, personal characteristics, or chance.

median voter — the voter whose views on a policy issue are in the middle of the spectrum, with half of the other voters on one side and half on the other side

median-voter theorem — the proposition that, under certain conditions, the equilibrium government policy chosen in political markets is the policy favored by the median voter

More generally, if only one issue (such as the level of defense spending) determines the outcome and an analyst can list all voters in order of their preference on this issue (from the person who wants the most spending to the person who wants the least), the median voter is in the middle of the list. If one of two candidates for office advocates the policy favored by the median voter, that person will receive more votes than an opponent who advocates a different policy.[2] According to the median-voter theorem, in such a situation, both politicians are likely to choose the same political position—a middle-of-the-road position favored by the median voter. In real life, of course, politicians are usually uncertain of the positions held by the median voter and do not all take the same middle-of-the-road positions. Still, the median-voter theorem explains the tendency for politicians to take middle-of-the-road positions.

LIMITATIONS OF THE MEDIAN-VOTER THEOREM

Government policies in reality often appear to differ (sometimes substantially) from the policies favored by the median voter. In fact, the median-voter theorem has several limitations. It does not apply to certain situations with more than two candidates or more than one issue, nor does it apply to certain situations in which voters prefer either high spending or low spending to a more moderate level of spending. (Some voters, for example, might want either high levels of spending on a public park or no spending at all, rather than some moderate amount of spending.)

Finally, the median-voter theorem does not apply to certain situations in which voters' choices are limited because someone has previously established an agenda for voters. Suppose, for example, that a local school board wants the highest possible spending on schools, while all voters want spending as close to $10 million as possible. If current spending on schools is $8 million, the school board may propose a $3.9 million increase in spending, so voters must decide between spending $11.9 million or the status quo spending level of $8 million. Because the school board's proposal is closer to the $10 million level that voters prefer, they vote for the spending increase. In this case, spending is higher than the level preferred by the median voter (who, like all voters, prefers to spend $10 million). Of course, in the long run, voters might choose a school board that would better represent their preferences. In the short run, however, evidence suggests that this model explains spending on local schools better than the median-voter model. School boards generally propose higher spending than the median voter wants and require voters to choose between that high level and a lower level of spending that most voters like even less. This indicates that spending on local public schools exceeds the level desired by the median voter.

PARADOX OF VOTING

While some political situations have equilibria like the one described in the median-voter model, other political situations are more complicated. Some may have no equilibrium or many possible equilibria; the results then depend on factors outside of the economic model.

Suppose that three voters will evaluate three possible government actions, as in **Table 22.1.** Alan favors Policy A, considers Policy B second best, and thinks

---

[2]The results may differ, and the logic becomes much more complicated, for situations with more than two candidates. It also becomes more complicated when many issues are at stake in the same election.

TABLE 22.1

PARADOX OF VOTING

Person	First-Choice Policy	Second-Choice Policy	Last-Choice Policy
Alan	A	B	C
Bill	B	C	A
Cindy	C	A	B

Policy C is the worst policy. Bill favors Policy B, thinks Policy C is second best, and thinks Policy A is worst. Cindy thinks that Policy C is best, Policy A is second best, and Policy B is worst. If they vote on Policy A versus Policy B, Policy A wins because Alan and Cindy vote for A over B, and only Bill votes for B over A. Policy A beats Policy B in an election. If, instead, they vote on Policy B versus Policy C, Policy B wins because Alan and Bill vote for C and only Cindy votes for Policy C. Policy B beats Policy C in an election.

You might think that Policy A would beat Policy C in an election because A beats B, and B beats C. This is not true, however. If they vote between Policies A and C, Policy C wins! Bill and Cindy vote for C and only Alan votes for A. Such an election produces strange results: A beats B, B beats C, and C beats A! Even if every voter is rational in the sense that each has a clearly defined first, second, and third choice, still, no clearly defined first, second, or third choice emerges from voting for society as a whole. This is an example of the Arrow impossibility theorem.

Arrow impossibility theorem — under very general conditions, the results of voting can be inconsistent (in the sense that A can beat B in an election while B beats C, but A does not beat C) even if all voters make consistent choices

The **Arrow impossibility theorem** states that, under very general conditions, the results of voting can be inconsistent (in the sense that A can beat B in an election while B beats C, but A does not beat C) even if all voters make consistent choices.

If a majority of voters prefer Policy A to either Policy B or Policy C (or any other policy), then it may seem that Policy A is, in one sense, in the public interest. The Arrow impossibility theorem shows that it is usually impossible to define the public interest in this way. One generally cannot combine the preferences of individual people, expressed by voting, into a consistent set of preferences for society as a whole.

This result also shows the importance of setting an agenda for voting. The outcome of voting between several alternatives can depend on the order in which people consider those alternatives. If people must choose *first* between A and B, and *then* between C and the winner in the first election, Policy C wins. If people first choose between B and C, then choose between A and the winner in that election, Policy A wins. If people first choose between A and C, then between B and the winner in that election, Policy B wins. This example illustrates that a political equilibrium can depend crucially on factors other than the views or preferences of voters.

INTENSITY OF PREFERENCES AND LOGROLLING

Simple majority voting allows people to vote only yes or no on an issue, so no one can express intensities of her views. Nevertheless, the intensities of people's views can matter in a political equilibrium, in one way, by affecting the prices at which people are willing to trade votes. While ordinary voters seldom trade votes, legislators frequently do. Legislator A might promise to vote for a bill that Legislator B favors in return for B's vote on a bill that A favors. This informal vote trading, or *logrolling,* provides a way for a minority that feels strongly about some issue to obtain majority support on that issue in return for changing votes on other issues that the minority considers less important.

To see how logrolling works, consider a town with three people, as in **Table 22.2.** The government would have to spend $9 to build a new park, and the cost would be split evenly among the three people; each would pay $3 more in taxes. Pat would gain $11 from the new park, so she wants the local government to build it, giving her a net gain of $8. Liz and Jean oppose the park, which would give them benefits of $1 each, so they would suffer a net loss of $2 each. Society as a whole—the three people—would gain from the park because Pat's net gain of $8 would exceed the $4 net loss to Liz and Jean; the net gain to society from the park would be $4. (In other words, it is potentially Pareto improving to build the park.) If the decision to build the park were made by majority rule, however, it would lose by a vote of two to one. Majority rule does not take into account the intensity of preferences.

To see why the intensity of preferences matters when people can trade votes, suppose that the same three people would evenly share the $15 cost of building a new library; each would pay $5 more in taxes. Suppose that Liz values the library at $14, so her net gain from it would be $9, while Pat and Jean each value the library at $1, so they would each suffer a net loss of $4. Society as a whole would gain $1 from the library because the $9 gain to Liz would exceed the $8 loss to Pat and Jean. Again, however, the majority would vote not to build the library because majority voting does not take into account the intensity of preferences. Now suppose that Pat offers to support a new library in return for Liz's support of a new park. Pat would gain $8 from the park and lose only $4 from the library, so she is willing to support the library in return for support on the park. Liz would gain $9 from the library and lose only $2 from the park, so she is willing to support the park in return for support on the library. Pat and Liz outvote Jean on each issue, and the local government builds both a new park and a new library.

If the decision to build the park were left to individuals rather than decided by majority vote, Pat would choose to spend her own money to build the park. The park would cost $9 and she would personally gain $11 from it. If the decision to build the library were left to individuals, however, Liz would not spend her

TABLE 22.2

OPPORTUNITY FOR LOGROLLING

	Net Gain (or loss) from Each Policy	
Person	New Park	New Library
Pat	$8	−$4
Liz	−2	9
Jean	−2	−4
Society as a whole	4	1

Constituent service is pivotal to way Congress works, and ethical line is fuzzy

WASHINGTON—Nobody is groaning louder about the federal farm-spending cuts than wheat growers. But once they look a little deeper into the 1990 farm bill, they're apt to change their tune.

Hidden in the legislation is a perk tailor-made for them, a provision that pays them for idling their wheat fields while allowing them to profit from the sale of another crop grown on the same acreage.

It's all part of the congressional rite for making winners out of losers when agriculture spending is on the line. Take a few bursts of legislative creativity, add raw political power, and act quickly—preferably late at night. Tag teams of lobbyists, working almost round-the-clock in the waning days of budget reconciliation, succeeded in taking much of the sting from the $13.6 billion in five-year subsidy cuts for their commodity-group clients.

Lobbyists for groups with concentrated interests frequently influence legislation.

Sources: "Constituent Service Is Pivotal to Way Congress Works, and Ethical Line Is Fuzzy," *The Wall Street Journal,* January 10, 1991, p. A1; and *The Wall Street Journal,* January 19, 1990, p. A16.

---

own money for it; the library would cost $15, which exceeds her personal benefit from it ($14). The rationale for government to provide the library in a case like this is that it may be too costly for Liz to negotiate with Pat and Jean to get them to contribute to the library. In this example, the political system requires logrolling to accomplish this task.

INFORMATION COSTS AND ORGANIZING COSTS

Information is costly, as are organizing, bargaining, and trading. As a result, the political power of a group with a concentrated interest, in which a benefit or cost affects a small group, may exceed the political power of a group with diffuse interests, in which benefits or costs are spread across many people. Ten people may gain $1 million each from some government policy that also wastes $5 million, while the total $15 million cost of the policy is spread across 250 million other people, each of whom loses only 6 cents from the policy. Although the policy is economically inefficient (it creates a deadweight social loss of $5 million), none of the 250 million losers from the government policy may find it worthwhile to bother spending time and money to learn about the policy, think about it and evaluate its benefits and costs, or do anything about it. Without knowledge of the issue, a person may not even know how a policy affects her or what policy she prefers.

Many people are each affected only slightly by certain government policies. For example, the U.S. government sugar program raises prices to consumers, but few individual consumers lose enough money to make it worthwhile for them to learn about that program. As a whole, the loss to consumers is large, but the cost is diffused over many people. Without costs of information or organizing, the losers would find out about this policy and organize political pressure to stop it. With costs of information and organization, however, the government may adopt the policy in the political equilibrium.

WHY VOTE?

Why does anyone vote? The cost of voting is a few minutes of time, which may seem small, but the benefit appears to be even smaller. In an election with millions of voters, the chance that one vote will change the outcome is minuscule. Even in local elections with only thousands of voters, it is extremely unlikely that an election will turn out differently if you do not vote. Of course, if no one else were to vote, then any one person could determine the outcome by voting. If only a few people were to vote, the outcome might be affected by one vote. When many other people vote, however, the benefits to any one voter appear much smaller than the costs.

Many people do vote, however, so they must have reasons for voting other than the chance of affecting the outcome of the election. People may vote because they enjoy voting for (or against) certain people or issues on the ballot, or because they feel a duty to vote; they may view it as a responsibility that goes with citizenship. The chance of affecting the outcome appears to matter, however. Studies have shown that people are more likely to vote in elections that they expect to be close than in elections that are not expected to be close.

SOME CONSEQUENCES

Because any one person's vote is unlikely to affect the outcome of an election, each person has less incentive to study government policies and stay informed than if her vote were more likely to affect those policies. This may increase the political power of groups with concentrated interests because people with diffuse interests are less likely to be informed. It also raises campaign costs for politicians who try to create winning coalitions by informing voters about policies. Higher campaign costs make these politicians more susceptible to offers of campaign contributions from special-interest groups. Also, as the typical voter becomes less informed, the likely cost to a politician who supports policies favored by special-interest groups diminishes.

As the typical voter becomes less informed, politicians have stronger incentives to favor policies with short-run benefits and long-run costs. Similarly, politicians have stronger incentives to inform voters about short-run benefits while ignoring longer-term costs when voters are less informed. After all, a politician may be out of office by the time the costs of policies become large. One check on this incentive is the endorsement of a political party. Even though a politician may have a limited term in office, a political party has an incentive to maintain its reputation; that reputation may suffer in the long run if its elected officials ignore the longer-run costs of the policies they adopt.

BUREAUCRATS

Many government decisions are made, not by elected officials, but by bureaucrats: unelected government workers, such as the heads of government regulatory agencies. Bureaucrats, like elected politicians, have a variety of interests. Because their productivity is hard to measure, their pay seldom reflects the efficiency with which they provide services to their customers. A bureaucrat may gain personal influence, power, and prestige by increasing an agency's budget and number of employees. A bureaucrat who is honestly concerned about doing a good job may also prefer a larger budget and more employees to do that job better; a higher budget would bring more power over resources to spend to advance the bureaucrat's view of society's interests, as well as the personal benefits that go with influence and power. Bureaucrats try to increase the sizes of their agencies by influencing elected politicians; this leads them to exaggerate their own importance (the Defense Department exaggerates the need for more defense spending, and so on).

——————————————— **FOR REVIEW** ———————————————

22.1 Explain the median-voter theorem. What are its limitations?

22.2 Explain why information costs and organization costs increase the political power of groups with concentrated interests relative to groups with diffuse interests.

——————————————— **QUESTIONS** ———————————————

22.3 Make up an example to illustrate the Arrow impossibility theorem.

22.4 Make up an example to show how logrolling can help make the outcome of a vote economically efficient.

ECONOMIC ANALYSIS OF LAW

What does economics have to do with law? Laws affect incentives. A law against doing something raises its price by creating the risk of a punishment. Laws affect incentives to take precautions against accidents, to make safe products, and to invest. Laws, and procedures to enforce them, can strongly affect a society's overall economic performance. Economies that lack clear, enforceable laws on property rights and contracts tend to have lower levels of output and economic efficiency. Deficiencies in such laws added to the difficulties of the transition to free markets in formerly socialist countries such as Russia. Economic efficiency is promoted by laws that create incentives to solve problems in the cheapest, most economically efficient way, and that minimize transactions costs so that people can settle disputes cheaply (for example, without always going to court to settle disputes). This section explores the incentives created by laws and their effects on economic efficiency.

Some economic analyses of law try to explain why laws developed as they did, why court decisions and other laws change over time, and why they differ across countries. Most law in the United States comes from English common law, which grew out of court decisions based on customary practices, historical legal systems, and judges' ideas of good public policy. Some economists and legal theorists, such as Judge Richard Posner, have argued that common law developed in a way that makes it economically efficient.[3]

Other economic analyses of law try to determine which legal rules are economically efficient. For example, laws on product liability determine whether a firm is responsible when someone is injured while using its product; liability laws affect incentives for producers to make safe products, for consumers to use products carefully, and for both sides to settle disputes efficiently. Liability laws affect the costs of production, so they affect equilibrium prices and quantities. Some laws promote economic efficiency, while others cause inefficiencies.

———————————————

[3] See Richard Posner's *Economic Analysis of Law* (New York: Little, Brown & Co., 1986), and *Economics of Justice* (Cambridge, Mass.: Harvard University Press, 1981). This theory is controversial; for a contrary view, see Ronald M. Dworkin, *Taking Rights Seriously* (Cambridge, Mass.: Harvard University Press, 1977).

PRECEDENTS, INCENTIVES, AND JUSTICE

Suppose that Carston suffers an injury while using a defective product made by the Jones Corporation and takes Jones to court. The court must decide how much money Jones should pay Carston as compensation for the injury. One important question for the court to answer is, "What is fair or just?" Another important question at stake is how the outcome of the case will affect future incentives. The outcome may establish a legal precedent that will affect decisions in similar cases in the future; such a precedent affects incentives.

Carston's accident has already happened, so the harm that Carston has suffered is a sunk cost; the court cannot undo that harm, it can only transfer resources from Jones to try to compensate Carston. This does not undo the harm, it merely redistributes wealth. It shifts some of the harm to Jones. The incentives created by the court decision can affect future behavior, however, along with the total amount of future harm in similar cases. The incentives can affect the number of similar accidents in the future, the severity of those accidents, and the methods by which people try to avoid future accidents. The court's decision has costs and benefits associated with the incentives that it creates.

Suppose that the court requires Jones to pay Carston enough money to compensate for all of Carston's costs from the accident, including the court's estimate of psychological costs. With complete compensation, Jones would pay Carston enough money that Carston would no longer care that the accident happened. What incentives would this decision create? Jones Corporation, and other, similar firms, would have an incentive to avoid future cases like this, either by making its product very safe or discontinuing the product entirely. On the other hand, buyers would have no incentive to use the product carefully if they could rely on complete compensation in any future accident. Because Jones knows that buyers have little incentive to use the product carefully, Jones must make the product essentially foolproof.

Is this economically efficient? The answer depends on the relative costs to producers and consumers of safety. If it is cheaper for Jones to make very safe products than for customers to avoid accidents through careful use, then this court decision may be economically efficient. It would lead to production of safety by the person who could produce it at the lowest cost. On the other hand, it may be impossible to make the product completely safe, but relatively easy for users to take precautions. The court decision would then create economic inefficiency by failing to give users the incentive to use precautions. The economically efficient court decision would be to require users to take care and not to require Jones to compensate Carston, assuming that Jones had made the product as safe as possible.

More generally, the economically efficient court decision would provide incentives to everyone who might help prevent a future accident. It would give users incentives to take precautions up to the point at which the marginal social cost of additional precautions would equal the marginal social benefit of those precautions in reducing accidents. This might involve requiring a firm like the Jones Corporation to pay part, but not all, of the cost of an accident, or to pay only if it were negligent (that is, if it had failed to take reasonable measures to produce a safe good). Perhaps a decision might allow Jones to avoid paying if Carston was negligent (careless) in using the good. Sometimes the economically efficient court decision may correspond to a person's sense of justice; other times the two may conflict.

CONTRACTS

Contract law deals with agreements between people. These agreements or contracts can be explicit (formally printed and signed legal documents) or implicit (informal or even verbal agreements). Whenever you buy a good, you make a contract with the seller. An implicit contract says that the cereal box you take home contains the amount and kind of cereal specified on the label with the ingredients listed on that label. These terms of the contract are enforceable in a court of law.

Should courts always enforce contracts, or should people sometimes be able to get out of contracts they have signed? What would happen to incentives and equilibrium prices and quantities in either case? What should a court do when someone breaks a contract? Should it require that person to honor the contract? What if that is impossible? Should it require a person who breaks a contract to pay compensation to the other people involved? If so, how much? What are the economic effects of alternative laws and court decisions on contracts?

LEGAL REMEDIES FOR BREACH OF CONTRACT

Suppose that the Epstein Corporation and the Carlton Corporation signed a contract last year, and now Carlton wants to break the contract (get out of the agreement). Legally, this is called a *breach of contract.* Courts seldom require anyone to honor a contract. Instead, they usually require the person or firm that breaks the contract to pay damages or compensation to the other person or firm. The economically efficient level of damage payments is the level that creates incentives for people to honor contracts when doing so is economically efficient and to break contracts when that is economically efficient.

Courts have used two types of general rules to decide levels of damage payments. One rule says that damages should be based on expectations; Carlton should pay damages to Epstein sufficient to make Epstein as wealthy as it could have expected to be if Carlton had honored the contract.

> Expectations damages: The person who breaks the contract should pay enough money to make the other people as wealthy as they could have expected to be if the contract had been honored.

The second rule bases damages on the fact that Epstein relied on Carlton to honor the contract; Carlton should pay enough money to make Epstein as wealthy as it would have been if it had never signed the contract.

> Reliance damages: The person who breaks the contract should pay enough money to make the other people as wealthy as they would have been if the contract had never been signed.

Which rule is economically efficient? To examine this issue, fill in some details. The contract said that Carlton would produce and deliver new machines to Epstein's factory and that Epstein would pay $10 million for these machines. Epstein spent $2 million to train its workers to operate the new machines. Epstein expected to increase its gross revenue by $15 million (in discounted present value terms), so it expected to earn a $3 million profit by obtaining the new machines ($15 million in revenue minus the $10 million cost of machines minus the $2 million training costs).

Suppose that Carlton breaks the contract because the Landes Corporation offers to pay more than $10 million for the machines, so Carlton sells the machines

Expectations Damages versus Reliance Damages: An Example

A very rich man marries a very poor woman, who quits her job to travel full-time with her husband. After a few years, the man breaks the marriage contract and leaves his wife. She takes him to court and asks for damages (alimony) for breaking the contract. The rule based on expectations says that the man should pay the woman enough money to make her as wealthy as she would have been if he had not broken the marriage contract, which would make her quite rich. The rule based on reliance costs says that the man should pay the woman enough money to make her as wealthy as she would have been if she had never married him and quit her job, which would leave her quite poor.

to Landes. Epstein takes Carlton to court. How much money should the court require Carlton to pay Epstein? According to the rule of expectations damages, Carlton should pay $5 million to Epstein. This is the revenue that Epstein could have expected to earn if Carlton had honored the contract. Epstein's profit would then be $3 million, the same as if Carlton had honored the contract. According to the reliance rule, Carlton should pay Epstein only $2 million to reimburse Epstein for the money it spent because it relied on Carlton to honor the contract.

In this case, the expectations damages rule is economically efficient, and the reliance damages rule is not. It is economically efficient for Carlton to break the contract and sell the machines to Landes if (and only if) Landes values them more than Epstein does. If transactions costs were low, voluntary exchanges would guarantee economic efficiency because if Epstein had the machines and Landes valued them more than Epstein, Landes would have an incentive to buy them from Epstein, and vice versa. With high transactions costs, however, Landes and Epstein may not trade. In that case, economic efficiency requires that Carlton provide the machines to whichever firm values them most.

Who values the machines most? Epstein's gross revenue would rise by $15 million if it were to get the machines, so the highest price that Epstein would be willing to pay for the machines, if it had to, is now $15 million. This is the value to the Epstein Corporation of the machines.[4]

If Landes is not willing to pay at least $15 million for the machines, then it is economically efficient for Carlton to sell the machines to Epstein and not to break the contract. On the other hand, if Landes is willing to pay more than $15 million for the machines, then it is economically efficient for Carlton to break the contract and sell the machines to Landes. Carlton's incentives are consistent with economic efficiency if (and only if) the court uses the expectations damages rule, which says that Carlton must pay Epstein $5 million to break the contract. In this case, Carlton gets $10 million if it sells to Epstein and it must pay Epstein $5 million if it breaks the contract, so it has an incentive to break the contract and sell to Landes if (and only if) Landes is willing to pay more than $15 million. In this way, the expectations damages rule is economically efficient. Any other amount of damages would be economically inefficient because it would not always give

---

[4]Notice that Epstein would not have been willing to pay this much for the machines originally, before it spent $2 million on retraining workers; it would have been willing to pay no more than $13 million for the machines at that time. Now that the $2 million expenditure is a sunk cost and no longer enters into any rational decision, Epstein would be willing to pay up to $15 million for the machines because that is how much they would add to its revenue.

firms like Carlton the incentive to break contracts if and only if doing so would be economically efficient.

While the expectations damages rule is economically efficient in this example, certain real-life complications can change this conclusion; the reasoning of the example shows only how economists approach these problems.

Courts may be concerned with values other than economic efficiency, such as fairness and justice. Scholars hold differing views on fairness and justice, and they also attach differing relative importance to the law's concern with economic efficiency and fairness, if and when these concepts conflict. Chapter 18 discussed alternative views of fairness.

─────────────── **FOR REVIEW** ───────────────

22.5 In what ways can a law promote economic efficiency?

22.6 What is a legal precedent? Explain how it can be economically efficient or inefficient.

─────────────── **QUESTIONS** ───────────────

22.7 Suppose that a wealthy person promises to pay for your college education. Elated, you quit your part-time job and enroll in college full-time. The wealthy person then refuses to pay. It is too late to get your job back—you have relied on what you regarded as a promise. How much would the court make the person pay based on (a) reliance damages? (b) Expectations damages?

22.8 Explain why damages for breach of contract based on the expectations damages rule are economically efficient in the Epstein–Carlton example. Explain why damages based on the reliance damages rule are not economically efficient in this example.

TORTS

Tort law deals with accidents.

> **Torts** are acts that injure other people either intentionally or by accident.

tort — an act that injures other people, either intentionally or by accident

Common tort cases focus on auto accidents, airline accidents, dog-bite cases, libel, defamation of character, and medical malpractice. The law can adopt various liability rules to resolve tort cases.

> A **liability rule** is a legal statement of who is responsible under what conditions for injuries or other harms in a tort.

liability rule — a legal statement of who is responsible under what conditions for injuries or other harms in a tort

In a typical tort case, such as an automobile accident, two or more people could have taken precautions that would have prevented or reduced the chance of an accident, or reduced the severity of an accident. An economically efficient liability rule would give each person the incentive to exercise the economically efficient amount of care or precautions. Because two or more people are involved, the economically efficient amount of care for each person depends on how careful other people are. The general rule for the economically efficient amount of care is to set the marginal cost of care equal to its marginal benefit. Each person's marginal cost and marginal benefit depend on what she expects others to do and on the liability rule.

Suppose that Gary and George are involved in a joint scientific experiment that involves dangerous materials. Each could take several levels of precautions to reduce the chance or severity of an accident. Increasing levels of precaution involve safer but more expensive procedures and equipment. Precautions are costly, so the liability rule should set the economically efficient level of precautions for each person. **Table 22.3a** shows the total and marginal costs of precautions by Gary and George. If Gary exercises five levels of precautions, his total cost is $10 and his marginal cost of precautions is $2. If George exercises four levels of precautions, his total cost of precautions is $16 and his marginal cost of precautions is $6. Table 22.3b shows the expected total and marginal benefits of precautions. The benefits depend only on the total amount of precautions that Gary and George take, not on who takes the precautions.

The rule for economic efficiency says that the marginal cost of precautions by each person must equal the marginal benefit of those precautions. In this example, it is economically efficient for Gary to exercise seven levels of precautions while George exercises two levels of precautions. Then the marginal cost of precautions to each person is $4. Together they exercise nine levels of precautions, so the marginal benefit of precautions is also $4. This is economically efficient

TABLE 22.3

EFFICIENCY IN TORT CASES

a.   Costs of Precautions

Gary's Precaution Levels	Gary's Total Cost	Gary's Marginal Cost	George's Precaution Levels	George's Total Cost	George's Marginal Cost
0	0	—	0	0	—
1	2	2	1	1	1
2	4	2	2	5	4
3	6	2	3	10	5
4	8	2	4	16	6
5	10	2	5	24	8
6	13	3	6	34	10
7	17	4	7	46	12
8	22	5	8	60	14

b.   Benefits of Precautions

Total Levels of Precautions by Gary and George	Expected Total Benefit of Precautions	Expected Marginal Benefit of Precautions
0	0	
1	100	100
2	180	80
3	230	50
4	260	30
5	280	20
6	290	10
7	298	8
8	304	6
9	308	4
10	311	3
11	313	2
12	314	1

IN THE NEWS

Failure to wear seat belts can cut crash-suit awards

By Paul M. Barrett
Staff Reporter of The
Wall Street Journal

A drunk driver slams into a car idling at a stop light. The victimized driver isn't wearing a seat belt. Should a jury in a subsequent lawsuit reduce the victim's award if failure to buckle up contributed to the victim's injuries?

An increasing number of state appellate courts are saying yes, and that has plaintiffs' lawyers worried. These attorneys fear that the seat-belt defense will distract juries from the cause of an accident—whether it is driver negligence or a defective car part—and shift the blame to the injured person.

Supporters of the trend applaud the courts' creation of incentives for drivers to use seat belts. The legal decisions "do have a deterrent effect, especially when the cases get a lot of publicity," says David A. Westenberg, a Boston, Mass., lawyer who has written academic articles on the issue.

Tort law usually gives everyone an incentive to take the economically efficient level of precautions.

Source: Paul M. Barrett, "Failure to Wear Seat Belts Can Cut Crash-Suit Awards," *The Wall Street Journal*, October 27, 1988, p. B1.

because the marginal benefit of precautions by each person equals their marginal cost. It would not be economically efficient to take additional precautions because their cost would exceed their expected benefit. Society's total gain from precautions—the total benefits net of total costs—would fall if either person were to take more precautions. Similarly, it would be economically inefficient to take fewer than nine levels of precautions.

DISCUSSION

Some economists believe that the government and courts should choose and interpret laws to maximize economic efficiency. If one person has a lower cost of taking precautions than another, they believe that the law should require that person to take most of the precautions. They believe that judges should compare the economically efficient level of precautions with the actual precautions that people take in order to judge whether any person has taken proper care or been negligent; they also believe that the main purpose of liability rules is to induce people to take the economically efficient levels of precautions. While courts cannot usually measure precautions as accurately as in the example, they can loosely measure the levels of precautions that people take.

Economists have developed detailed analyses of liability rules to evaluate the economic efficiency of rules such as strict liability (which says that whoever causes an accident bears total responsibility for it) or negligence (which says that the person who causes an accident bears responsibility only if he did not take enough precautions to prevent it).[5]

---

[5]Many accidents result from joint actions of two or more people; in such a case, no single person may have caused the accident.

For example, suppose that a fire begins in Hans's Print Shop and spreads to Henryck's Bakery, doing $10,000 worth of damage. The rule of strict liability would make Hans liable for paying for all of the damage.[6] With the rule of negligence, the court would ask, "Did Hans take all cost-justified precautions to prevent an accident (such as a fire) and damage to nearby shops?" The court must decide what precautions Hans could have taken that would have reduced the expected loss from an accident. This involves deciding the chance that an accident would occur and how this chance, or the loss in the event of an accident, would be affected by various possible precautions. The court must also determine the costs of these precautions and which were cost-justified. The court would then have to find out if Hans failed to take any of these precautions, perhaps by overloading an electrical system or failing to inspect his machinery properly. If so, the court would find Hans negligent and make him pay damages. If Hans took all cost-justified precautions, he would not be negligent or liable.

Other people criticize the idea that liability rules should maximize economic efficiency on the grounds that it ignores fairness or justice by concentrating solely on economic efficiency and not on the distribution of wealth. For example, some people might find it unfair for the law to require one person to take more precautions than another.

One feature of an economically efficient legal system is that it does not overuse resources such as lawyers and courts to settle disputes. It may be better to settle a dispute quickly and cheaply while getting results (and incentives) *approximately* right rather than to spend more resources settling a dispute and getting results that are closer to ideal. The improvement in results may not be worth the expenditure for lawyers and other legal resources. This suggests that good legal rules do not require a court to obtain information that is very costly to obtain, even if that information would have some value to the court in making its decision. This is the main argument for no-fault automobile insurance laws in which insurance companies share costs and do not even try to determine who is at fault in an auto accident, except in a serious case. Although this reduces the incentive to drive carefully because an accident might raise a person's payments for auto insurance, it reduces the information costs of determining the facts of the accident, and reduces transactions costs of bargaining (over who should pay how much money to whom) by so much that it is worth the reduction in incentives for better driving.

When an accident involves injuries or death, the court must decide how to measure damages in terms of money. It is impossible to give back an arm, let alone a life. Earlier chapters have already introduced the idea that people constantly choose not to be as safe as possible because safety has a price. By observing how much people are willing, or unwilling, to pay to avoid risks of injuries, courts can determine how much people, on average, value their health, limbs, and lives. Courts frequently use these estimates to set damage payments in personal injury or death cases. In addition, courts usually use other criteria, such as the discounted present value of lost wages, the amount of pain and suffering, and, more recently, the reduced ability to enjoy life.

---

[6]You may wonder about insurance. If Hans and Henryck have insurance with no deductible, then the statement, "Hans is liable" would amount to, "Hans's insurance company is liable." In real life, most insurance policies cover losses only above certain (deductible) levels. Hans, and not his insurance company, would be liable for damages up to that level.

Liability insurance needs rise with jury awards

Can you afford a dog that bites or icy walks?

When it comes to snow, however, New Yorkers face a dilemma. If they fail to shovel, they face a $25 fine. If they clear a path, they become liable to any passerby who slips on a stray icy patch and decides to sue. Many lawyers advise that if you don't want to be sued, don't shovel. "It may be ridiculous, but it's the law," Sullivan said.

Tort law and jury awards of damages affect a wide variety of everyday activities.

Source: "Liability Insurance Needs Rise with Jury Awards," *Rochester Democrat and Chronicle*, September 7, 1987, p. 12D.

TORT LAW AND CONTRACTS

Suppose that people involved in an accident could get together before the accident occurs to decide on the precautions that each person should take, penalties for failing to take those precautions, and who must pay whom how much money if an accident occurs anyway. This would amount to signing a contract to resolve the issues usually covered by tort law. If they faced no costs of negotiating this contract, the people involved would choose the economically efficient levels of precautions. They would never choose inefficient levels of precautions, except by mistake, because they could share the gains of eliminating the inefficiency and agreeing to efficient precaution levels. Of course, getting people together to negotiate these contracts prior to accidents is impossible in many real-life situations, but economically efficient tort law can try to duplicate the contracts that people would have chosen if they had been able to meet in advance. Therefore, some people argue, tort law should require economically efficient levels of precautions.

Some analysts believe that contracts should replace tort law in cases where it is easy and inexpensive for people to negotiate contracts, such as product-liability cases.

PRODUCT LIABILITY

Product-liability law is law related to accidents in which a person who suffers an injury while using a product seeks damages from the seller or manufacturer of the product. Someone who is injured while using a product sometimes sues the firm that made it. Suppose that courts hold firms responsible for injuries that people suffer while using their products, even if the firms take reasonable (economically efficient) levels of precautions. This *strict liability rule* essentially requires a firm to provide an implicit *insurance* policy to people who use its product; if an accident happens, and the user was not negligent or reckless in using the product, the firm pays for the injuries from the accident.

This implicit insurance policy is not free. It raises prices because it raises firms' marginal costs. A higher price reflects the cost to the firm of providing the implicit insurance. The cost of this implicit insurance accounts for 30 percent of the price of a stepladder, 95 percent of the price of childhood vaccines, and one-third of the price of a small airplane. It adds more to the price of a football helmet than the cost of making the helmet itself. It adds about $300 to the price of delivering a baby and prevents certain drugs, even ones certified as safe and effective by the Food and Drug Administration, from being produced in the United States.[7]

Product liability is part of tort law, though some people argue that it should be part of contract law. This relates to an important difference between an accident involving use of a product and an auto accident (a classic example of a tort). In the product-liability case, the buyer and seller already had a contract to pay for and deliver a product or service. That contract could state how the buyer and seller will divide the costs of any accident and what levels of precautions each side must take. A firm might offer to sell a product on the condition that it accepts no liability whatsoever for injuries that people might receive while using it, or it might offer to sell a product on the condition that it is liable only if the product is defective or does not meet certain standards, but not otherwise. A firm might offer full insurance to buyers as in the strict liability case.

---

[7]See Peter W. Huber, *Liability: The Legal Revolution and Its Consequences* (New York: Basic Books, 1988).

Business struggles to adapt as insurance crisis spreads

Price increases and profit cuts are common; some drop products, exercise greater caution

A Wall Street Journal News Roundup

The soaring cost and worsening shortage of liability insurance are taking their toll on businesses, professionals, and local governments across the country. The crisis is forcing companies to raise prices or accept smaller profits, change their operations, and eliminate products and services.

Day-care centers, hotels, restaurants, bars, ski resorts, ice-skating rinks, and other service businesses face sharply higher premiums or a lack of liability coverage. While some smaller operations are closing up, others are trying to make themselves less vulnerable to lawsuits or are passing higher costs to their customers.

The insurance crisis is also making life difficult for many professionals. While the rising cost of medical malpractice insurance has dominated the headlines, malpractice premiums for architects, engineers, and accountants are rising even more sharply.

For big companies, which can more easily absorb higher insurance costs, the most serious problem is the lack of coverage at any price in such areas as directors' and officers' liability, pollution liability, and product liability.

Product-liability laws affect prices and production levels of various products as well as research on new products.

Source: "Business Struggles to Adapt as Insurance Crisis Spreads," *The Wall Street Journal,* January 21, 1986, p. B1.

Some economists argue that courts should enforce whichever contract buyers and sellers enter into voluntarily. Until recently, the law in the United States enforced whatever contracts to which buyers and sellers agreed. In situations with no contractual agreement on liability, the law served as a standard contract and standard tort law applied. Laws in many countries still enforce contracts when they exist, but modern tort law in the United States does *not* enforce these contracts; instead, it often imposes a strict liability rule (or some variant of this rule) for nearly all product-liability cases. The chance that the *plaintiff* (the person who brings the lawsuit against the firm) will win a product-liability suit and the size of the damage payment to the winner have increased substantially in recent years. This has led some people to speak of a *liability crisis* in the United States. The Social and Economic Issues box discusses the question of whether courts should enforce contracts entered into by firms and customers that determine liability in case of accidents.

LAW OF PROPERTY RIGHTS AND ECONOMIC EFFICIENCY

The economically efficient level of property rights enforcement occurs when the marginal cost of enforcing rights equals the marginal benefit. It would be economically inefficient (and perhaps impossible) to enforce property rights perfectly because it would cost more than the benefit would be worth.[8]

---

[8]This discussion presumes throughout that the government enforces property rights and ignores issues associated with private police, courts, and so on. For a discussion of these issues, see David Friedman, *The Machinery of Freedom,* 2d ed. (La Salle, Ill.: Open Court, 1989). Also see Gary S. Becker and George J. Stigler, "Law Enforcement, Malfeasance, and Compensation of Enforcers," *Journal of Legal Studies* 3, January 1974; and David D. Friedman, "Efficient Institutions for the Private Enforcement of Law, *Journal of Legal Studies* 13, June 1984.

SOCIAL AND ECONOMIC ISSUES

Product-Liability Crisis

Should firms and customers be permitted to sign contracts that determine liability in the case of accidents? Should courts overrule such contracts and impose another liability rule?

Arguments for Enforcing Contracts That Determine Liability

▶ It is economically efficient to enforce mutually voluntary contracts when no externalities exist. People can then share risks as they choose. Enforcing contracts allows freedom of choice. Buyers and sellers can freely agree on liability rules for products.

▶ Buyers and sellers can determine the economically efficient way to share liabilities better than courts can. For example, it might be cheaper for an insurance company rather than a product manufacturer to sell accident insurance to people, because the insurance company may be able to pool the risks better than the manufacturer. [Critics reply that, in such cases, manufacturers can always buy liability insurance.]

▶ Competition among sellers helps to achieve economically efficient contracts. It would not be economically efficient to overrule the contract and apply some other liability rule.

▶ The court system works poorly for product liability because juries award such high damage payments to victims that they distort incentives. Manufacturers spend too much on safety and decline to produce some products at all, even though many people want them. These problems would be reduced if courts were to enforce contracts that determine liability.

▶ The court system also works poorly because, with many different lawsuits, the same manufacturer may pay punitive damages repeatedly. The punitive damages can sum to economically inefficient levels, resulting in products that are too safe in the sense that the extra safety is not worth the higher price. Excessive punitive damages also result in some good products being withdrawn from the market entirely, as has happened, for example, with some childrens' vaccines.

Arguments for Imposing Strict Liability and Not Enforcing Contracts

▶ People do not always act in their own best interests. The law must protect people from their own bad decisions.

▶ People underestimate the risks they take with some products, so contracts will not result in economic efficiency because people will take more risks than they should.

▶ People do not buy enough insurance on their own. They are better off if the law forces them to buy it through product-liability laws.

▶ Society will not let the people who fail to buy insurance suffer big losses; society will pay for them through the welfare system. To reduce welfare costs, people should be required to buy insurance through the product-liability laws, even if they don't want it.

▶ Even if people were to act in their own best interests, information is costly. The law should protect people who don't read the small print or don't understand the complexities of a contract that includes liability clauses.

▶ People are better off if they don't have to bother reading all the fine print and worrying about different liability rules in different contracts, and they don't have to bother if the law sets a product-liability rule that applies to all products.

▶ Sellers can insure risk more cheaply than buyers, so imposing strict liability divides risk in an efficient way. [But, replies the other side, if this were true, then people would choose contracts in which the seller provides insurance for accidents; the law would not have to impose it. The usual responses to this are the arguments made above—that people do not act in their own best interests and would not buy this insurance, and that they are better off if the government forces them to buy it.]

Most theft is economically inefficient. The possibility of theft leads people to spend money, time, and energy to protect their property from thieves. This is economically inefficient because people could use their time and energy to produce more goods rather than fighting over the distribution of existing goods. If Chip steals $100 from Susan, Chip's private benefit is $100, but the social benefit is zero because Chip's gain equals Susan's loss. In essence, Chip imposes a $100 negative externality on Susan. This is economically inefficient, not because Chip has Susan's $100, but because Chip could have spent his time doing something productive, such as painting a house, mowing a lawn, or even watching television. Also, Susan's belief that someone may steal from her may have led her to spend money on extra locks or a security system that she could have spent on something she would enjoy, such as a new car. For these reasons, theft is economically inefficient. The economic inefficiency increases when theft involves an item with sentimental value to its owner. If Chip were to steal from Susan a necklace that belonged to her grandmother, Susan's loss would far exceed Chip's gain.

Now suppose that a poor woman steals $100 from a rich man. Some people may argue that the gain to the poor woman is larger than the loss to the rich man, so the theft may be economically efficient. Economics alone cannot answer questions that require comparing one person's happiness with another's. Economics has no method for interpersonal comparisons of utility or happiness. Some people might believe that the poor woman gains more happiness from the $100 than the rich man loses, but other people may disagree. Even if the poor woman's gain were to exceed the rich man's loss, the social policy of permitting such thefts may be economically inefficient because it would create incentives for rich people to spend time and money to protect their property and for poor people to steal rather than produce.

Theft is economically efficient in certain situations with high transactions costs. Other crimes, such as speeding, can also be economically efficient in certain cases. Suppose, for example, that a person who is lost in the woods and starving finds a cabin. No one is home, but the owner has left food inside. The lost person breaks in and eats the food. Most people would say that the thief, who would have died without the food, placed a higher value on it than the victim, who was not home and not starving.

This example illustrates three points. First, the starving person may have been willing to pay for the food, but the transactions costs were too high: the cabin's owner was not present to accept payment for the food, nor was anyone else present to sell food. Transactions costs were too high for a voluntary trade to occur, but a court would have good reason to think that a trade would have occurred if the owner of the cabin had been home. In that sense, this theft would almost certainly be economically efficient. The second point is that when transactions costs are high, as in this example, it is economically efficient to make the thief pay the cabin owner later for the food and for any damage to the cabin caused by the break-in. Otherwise, the law would encourage people to steal goods instead of buying them. The law, in this case, tries to recreate the contract that the lost person and the cabin owner would have made if the cabin owner had been home. Finally, courts may find it hard to determine whether a person who steals something would actually have been willing to pay for it. When transactions costs are low, the law requires that people demonstrate their willingness to pay for a good by actually paying for it rather than stealing it.

OTHER APPLICATIONS

It is economically efficient to have rules, such as speed limits, for driving on roads because the rules reduce accidents. However, even if the rules were set to maximize economic efficiency—and they may not be—it would not be economically efficient to enforce them perfectly, even if it were possible.[9] In some cases, such as medical emergencies, speeding is economically efficient. The transactions costs of making deals with other drivers to compensate them for the increased risk of accidents are too high to make such deals. To keep people from exceeding speed limits for minor reasons, it is economically efficient to make speeders pay fines. This raises the expected marginal cost of speeding and reduces the incentive to speed, except in extreme emergencies.

The fact that crimes, such as theft and speeding, are sometimes economically efficient has an important implication: a very high punishment for these crimes would be economically inefficient. Life imprisonment for speeding would surely reduce the number of speeders, but it would be economically inefficient because it would prevent people from speeding in emergencies. This raises the issue of economically efficient punishments for crimes.

ECONOMICS OF CRIMINAL LAW

In the large body of literature on criminal behavior, many criminologists and decision theorists agree that incentives affect all behavior, including crime. The economic analysis of criminal law starts from this sometimes controversial idea. Raising the benefits of crime increases the crime rate, and raising the cost of crime reduces it.

ECONOMICALLY EFFICIENT AMOUNT OF CRIME

It would not be economically efficient for society to eliminate crime completely. The economically efficient amount of crime is the amount at which the marginal benefit of reducing crime equals the marginal cost.

EXPLANATION Crime could be reduced by deploying larger numbers of well-paid, highly trained police, increasing lighting at night, improving social and economic conditions, expanding education and job opportunities, increasing drug treatments, offering more mental-health care, installing more high-tech security systems or better locks, and so on. These measures are expensive. Your bicycle might be stolen when you leave it outside the library, so you may buy a bicycle lock to reduce the chance of theft. Professional thieves can cut through most locks, though. You could reduce the chance of a theft further by buying a larger, heavier lock, by installing an alarm on your bicycle, by paying someone to watch it, or by never letting it out of your sight. For most people, these precautions would not be worth the cost.

ECONOMICALLY EFFICIENT METHODS OF REDUCING CRIME

The previous paragraph listed many ways to reduce crime. The government could also reduce crime by raising the expected cost of crime to criminals. It could increase the chance of being caught and punished or raise the severity of punishment for criminals who are caught.

The expected cost of crime to the criminal equals the chance of being caught multiplied by the punishment if caught. For example, suppose that the chance of catching a criminal is 10 percent and the punishment is a $1,000 fine. The expected punishment, which is the expected cost of crime to the criminal, is

---

[9]Examples of inefficiently set rules might be speed limits that are either too high or too low.

Victims of violent crimes increasingly sue for damages—and many win big awards

Not only are the perpetrators of violent crimes being hit for damages. Increasingly, the owners and managers of properties where the crimes occur are also targets of civil actions for restitution.

This increased emphasis on victims' rights, many law-enforcement officials and criminal-justice experts agree, is likely to prompt far-reaching changes in how courts operate and how they punish criminals.

Third-Party Targets

Civil suits are frequently aimed at third parties because the average criminal doesn't have the resources to pay damages; courts have been known to make multimillion-dollar awards.

Some lawmakers and critics denounce the practice of victims suing third parties with deep pockets.

Would it be economically efficient to replace criminal law with tort law?

Source: "Victims of Violent Crimes Increasingly Sue for Damages—and Many Win Big Awards," *The Wall Street Journal,* December 5, 1986, p. 33.

$100. The expected punishment rises to $500 if the chance of being caught rises to 50 percent or the fine increases to $5,000.

Either method of raising the expected cost of crime to criminals—raising the chance of being caught and convicted or punishments for convicted criminals—has a cost. The economically efficient chance of catching criminals is the chance at which the marginal benefit of raising the chance equals the marginal cost. Similarly, the economically efficient punishment for a convicted criminal is the punishment at which the marginal benefit of raising the punishment equals the marginal cost.

It would be economically inefficient to set the same expected punishment for every crime because criminals would have no incentive not to commit more severe crimes (to steal more money, for example). If the expected penalties for armed and unarmed robberies were the same, more thieves would commit armed robberies rather than unarmed robberies. The marginal expected punishment—the extra expected punishment for a more severe crime—must be high enough to deter criminals from committing more severe crimes.

The economically efficient method of punishment is often a fine rather than a prison sentence, and the economically efficient way to reduce crime might be to accept low chances of catching and convicting criminals, but to impose high punishments for convicted criminals. Some people argue that criminals should pay fines to victims, as compensation, rather than to the government. At the extreme, criminal law could be replaced entirely by tort law; the victim of a crime or the victim's family would sue the criminal in court, and the court would decide on the appropriate level of compensation. In most cases, the economically efficient level of expected punishment for a prisoner would exceed the economically efficient level of victim compensation. (Too much victim compensation would prevent potential victims of crimes from taking enough precautions against crime, such as locking doors or protecting valuables.) If so, the criminal could pay the economically efficient fine, the victim could collect the efficient level of compensation, and the government could collect the difference.

EXPLANATION   Society can increase the chance of catching a criminal by spending more resources to improve the police and court systems. Society can increase punishments by raising fines, extending prison sentences, and increasing the severity of other punishments. The marginal benefit of either action is less crime.

The marginal cost of a higher chance of conviction is the added spending on police and courts along with the loss to society from the risk of falsely convicting and punishing innocent people. The marginal cost of a higher punishment depends on the type of punishment; the law can increase a fine at a very small cost, but the cost of increasing the length of a prison sentence may be large because the government must pay for the prison building, guards, and so on. In contrast, fines generate revenue for the government.

A sufficiently high fine is likely to have the same deterrent effect as a prison sentence. Prison sentences have two advantages over fines, however. First, besides acting as a deterrent, prison sentences directly prevent repeat offenses while the criminal is in prison.[10] This implies that to reduce crime by the same amount, a fine would have to be high enough to have a larger deterrent effect than

---

[10]By 1988 federal government estimates, it costs an average of $25,000 per year to maintain a prisoner including costs of building prisons, but the new crimes committed by released prisoners cost society an average of $430,000 per year for *each* released prisoner. This Justice Department estimate includes victim losses from those crimes, police and court work, and private security expenses.

a prison sentence. Second, some criminals lack the resources to pay large fines; then deterrence requires other punishments, such as prison.[11] When fines are possible, however, the economically efficient way to reduce crime may involve a high fine and a low chance of being caught because this would keep the costs of law enforcement low.[12]

―――――――――――― **FOR REVIEW** ――――――――――――

22.9 Explain why a strict liability rule may not be economically efficient.

22.10 What makes a product-liability case different than an automobile accident case? Why do some people suggest that contract law should apply to product-liability cases?

22.11 Explain why theft is usually economically inefficient, but can sometimes be economically efficient.

―――――――――――― **QUESTIONS** ――――――――――――

22.12 Would it be economically efficient to impose a severe punishment (the death penalty, life imprisonment, or a giant fine) for every crime? How would this affect crime?

22.13 When a court finds someone liable for an injury, the court may require payment of punitive damages as extra punishment in addition to compensation for the person who was injured. Is this economically efficient? Explain.

CONCLUSIONS

PUBLIC CHOICE

Governments are not single decision makers; they consist of many people with various interests that sometimes conflict and who often lack important information for the formulation of policies. The public-choice method of evaluating government policies takes into account the incentives and constraints that create a political equilibrium.

The median-voter theorem states that, under certain conditions, the equilibrium government policy chosen in political markets is the policy favored by the median voter. Although the median-voter model explains the tendency of politicians to establish positions in the political center, the model has several limitations. For example, it does not apply to certain situations in which voters' choices are limited by previously established voting agendas.

―――――――――――

[11]Suppose that the punishment for a crime is a fine, but people who cannot afford to pay the fine go to jail instead. This raises the notion, distasteful to many people, that rich people would pay fines while poor people would go to jail. Earlier comments apply here; values other than economic efficiency may have important influences on the law. Nevertheless, when fines are possible, they are cheaper for the government than prison sentences.

[12]Note a caveat to this conclusion. Even the best criminal justice system will falsely convict some people of crimes they did not commit. A severe punishment, even with a low chance of conviction, means that when this occurs, innocent people suffer a loss. Of course, a lower overall chance of conviction may also lower the chance of falsely convicting an innocent person. Alternatively, if capricious justice often convicts innocent people of crimes, the deterrent effects of the criminal justice system decline and the amount of crime rises.

The Arrow impossibility theorem shows that, under very general conditions, the results of voting can be inconsistent. When voters choose among three alternatives, they may vote for Policy A over Policy B and Policy B over Policy C, but not for Policy A over Policy C, even if each voter has consistent first, second, and third choices. This result shows a fundamental problem in defining an unambiguous public interest, and it shows the importance of setting agendas prior to voting because the order of voting can determine the outcome of the vote.

Logrolling allows voters with very strong preferences on one issue to obtain support on that issue by trading their support on other issues. Logrolling can increase the economic efficiency of the political equilibrium.

Groups of people with concentrated interests may have more political power than groups with more diffuse interests. Information costs reduce the incentives of people in groups with diffuse interests to learn about government policies that hurt them. Organization costs may prevent them from eliminating such government policies, even if they learn about them.

The likelihood that any one person's vote will directly affect the outcome of an election is very small; the observation that people vote suggests that they see other benefits of voting, such as fulfilling civic responsibilities or pure pleasure of voting for or against certain people or issues.

ECONOMIC ANALYSIS OF LAW

Laws can promote or hinder economic efficiency because they affect incentives and behavior. Economic efficiency is one important criterion (in addition to justice or fairness) for choosing laws.

Contract law deals with agreements between people and consequences of breaking contracts. Courts can create incentives for economically efficient choices by imposing damages for breach of contract that give people and firms incentives to honor contracts when it is economically efficient to do so, and incentives to break contracts when that is economically efficient.

Tort law deals with accidents. Liability rules state who is responsible under what conditions for injuries or other harms. An economically efficient liability rule would give everyone the incentive to exercise the economically efficient degree of care so that the marginal cost of care equals its marginal benefit. Some economists believe that the government and courts should choose and interpret laws to maximize economic efficiency. Other people criticize the idea that liability rules should maximize economic efficiency on the grounds that this would ignore fairness or justice. If people involved in an accident could have gathered before the accident, they could have chosen the precautions that each would take, the penalties for failing to take those precautions, and who must pay how much money to whom if an accident were to occur anyway. Although people usually cannot sign contracts to resolve these issues before an accident occurs, economically efficient tort law can try to duplicate the contracts that people would have chosen if they had been able to meet in advance. Some analysts believe that contracts should replace tort law in cases where it is easy and inexpensive for people to negotiate contracts, such as product-liability cases.

The economically efficient enforcement of property rights occurs when the marginal cost of enforcing rights equals the marginal benefit. Theft (a violation of property rights) is usually, but not always, economically inefficient.

The economically efficient level of crime is the level at which the marginal benefit of reducing crime equals the marginal cost. The cost of crime to a criminal, the expected punishment, can be increased by raising either the chance of being caught and convicted or the level of punishment for a convicted criminal. Each method has costs, though fines are a less costly method of punishment (for the government) than prison sentences. Under some conditions, the economically efficient method of punishment is to levy a high fine and accept a low chance of catching and convicting criminals. Economically efficient punishments differ across crimes; the marginal expected punishment for a more severe crime must be large enough to achieve the economically efficient amount of crime at each level of severity.

KEY TERMS

political equilibrium

median voter

median-voter theorem

Arrow impossibility theorem

tort

liability rule

QUESTIONS AND PROBLEMS

22.14 Suppose that Anna, Bob, and Clara would vote on complete versus partial national health insurance (NHI) as in the following table:

Person	First Choice	Second Choice	Last Choice
Anna	Complete NHI	Partial NHI	No NHI at all
Bob	Partial NHI	No NHI at all	Complete NHI
Clara	No NHI at all	Complete NHI	Partial NHI

a. Suppose that people must first vote on the type of national health insurance to consider—complete coverage versus partial coverage. People would then vote on whether to adopt national health insurance at all. Which policy would win?

b. Suppose that people must first vote for or against national health insurance with partial coverage. If they chose to have some national health insurance, they then vote on expanding the program. Which policy would win?

22.15 Consider the example in Table 22.1, but suppose that the three people decide to vote on the order of voting. Can they decide? Suppose that they vote on a way to decide how to decide the order of voting. Can they decide that? Explain.

22.16 In what ways does a political equilibrium differ from an equilibrium in the market for pizzas, houses, or auto repair?

22.17 Aaron wants to raise taxes by $100 billion to eliminate the government budget deficit. Butch wants to raise taxes by $60 billion. Cory wants to raise taxes by $20 billion. Danny wants to cut taxes by $40 billion. Emmy wants to cut taxes by $60 billion. Assume that two candidates are running for office, the size of taxes is the only issue, and the candidates care only about winning the election. Use the logic of the median-voter theorem to explain what positions the candidates will support.

22.18 Suppose that candidates for public office care about supporting the policies that seem best to them. How would this affect the median-voter theorem?

22.19 Suppose that everyone could legally buy and sell their votes. What would determine the equilibrium prices of votes? Discuss the likely effects.

22.20 Make up a court case in which you think justice and economic efficiency conflict. Explain why they conflict and how courts should balance these two goals.

22.21 What is the economically efficient way to assign property rights when someone finds lost treasure? Should finders get property rights to what they take from a shipwreck? Should they be able to exclude other people from visiting the shipwreck before they have time to remove all of the valuable items? (These issues have arisen in several court cases in the last decade.)

22.22 What levels of punishments would be economically efficient for various types of crimes? What information would you need to determine the answers?

22.23 An intrauterine birth control device made in the 1970s, the Dalkon Shield, severely damaged the reproductive systems of many women, causing pain and infections and leaving them unable to have children. It also apparently caused several deaths. About 200,000 women later filed suits against the manufacturer with claims totaling $4 billion. In August 1985, the manufacturer filed for bankruptcy with the intent of preventing any new lawsuits by other women; the court handling the bankruptcy ordered the firm to set up a trust fund of $2.4 billion to pay compensation. Most of the money for this trust comes from the company that bought the manufacturer when it went bankrupt.

a. What is the best procedure for determining the sizes of damages, obtaining payments for the women who were injured, and setting incentives to reduce the chance of a similar disaster in the future?

b. Suppose that a corporation loses a product-liability suit and goes bankrupt so that it cannot pay all legitimate claims. What should the law do about these situations? What incentives for firms are created by the ability to avoid payments by declaring bankruptcy?

22.24 Suppose that an accident occurs at a nuclear power facility, causing injuries such as higher risks of cancer or other diseases to people working in the plant and people living nearby. How would you decide (a) who should pay the costs of this accident, and (b) how much they should pay?

22.25 Is it economically efficient or inefficient to allow criminals to profit from books, magazine articles, and television interviews related to the crimes they commit? Discuss this again from the standpoint of your ideas of justice or fairness; do the answers differ?

INQUIRIES FOR FURTHER THOUGHT

22.26 What is the economically efficient punishment for a college student who cheats on an exam or plagiarizes a paper? What is the correct marginal punishment for more severe cheating or plagiarism?

22.27 Marriage is a contract; divorce means breaking the contract.

    a. What would be the economically efficient legal rules in a divorce? Discuss economically efficient compensation of a spouse, division of property, and responsibilities for children.

    b. Courts have enforced so-called *palimony* suits in recent years, ruling that implicit promises or promises explicitly made in private are like marriage contracts and palimony takes the place of alimony when the couple separates. Is it economically efficient to enforce these contracts? How might a court decide if a contract existed?

22.28 Under what conditions, if any, should courts decline to enforce private, voluntary contracts?

22.29 What are the effects of laws making bars legally responsible, to some degree, for accidents committed by drunk drivers who leave those bars? Under what conditions, if any, should a smoker (or a family after a smoker's death) be able to sue a cigarette manufacturer and collect damages for health problems?

22.30 Do you think that people respond to incentives in their decisions to commit crimes?

    a. Are incentives more important for some kinds of crimes than other kinds?

    b. Would you be more likely to commit a crime—say, shoplifting, driving faster than the speed limit on a road, drinking alcohol while underage, or cheating on an exam—if the chance of being caught were lower? Would you be less likely to do this if the chance of being caught were higher? Would you be more likely to commit this crime if the punishment (if you were caught) were lower, and less likely to commit the crime if the punishment were more severe?

22.31 A convicted criminal might pay damages, as in tort law, to victims or their families.

    a. Would it be economically efficient to require victim compensation in criminal cases?

    b. How would the requirement of victim compensation affect the economically efficient level of other punishments such as fines or prison terms?

    c. How should the sizes of victim compensation be determined for various crimes? Should they depend on criminals' ability to pay?

    d. What if a criminal cannot afford to pay victim compensation?

22.32 Should the government set liability limits in lawsuits related to medical malpractice, accidents, or product-liability cases?

    a. How should courts decide the maximum liability levels in these cases?

    b. The deep-pocket theory says that when courts make bad decisions in liability cases, after accidents, people tend to sue anyone who has a deep pocket (anyone who is rich enough). Discuss this statement: "The deep-pocket lawsuits would be eliminated by maximum legal limits on liability."

22.33 How should a court determine the dollar amount that an airline must pay in damages to families of people killed or injured in an airline crash?

    a. Should the dollar amount of damages be related to the age of the person killed (an 80-year-old retiree versus a 20-year-old college student)?

b. Should it be related to the discounted present value of the lost future earnings of the person killed?

c. Should the amount of damages be the same for everyone?

d. Should it take into account pain and suffering?

e. Should it take into account inability or reduced ability to enjoy life? If so, how can one translate these losses into dollar terms? Does this require the ability to make interpersonal comparisons of utility?

22.34 Would it be economically efficient for courts to consider the *fear* of damages, even if the fear is scientifically unfounded, when deciding liability or the size of damages? What would be the effects?

a. Suppose that a person fears contracting AIDS from casual contact with another person. Does the first person have grounds for a lawsuit?

b. Suppose that someone fears getting cancer after using some product, that this fear is completely unjustified scientifically, but that the fear causes the person enough anxiety to bring on high blood pressure and a heart attack. Should the fearful person be able to sue the company for damages?

c. Suppose that someone has a good scientific basis for fear of cancer caused by a product because everyone agrees that 10 percent of all people who have used a product will get cancer. Should *everyone* who used the product be allowed to collect damages, or only those people who actually develop cancer?

22.35 The U.S. Supreme Court ruled in a 1992 case, *Lucas* v. *South Carolina Coast Commission,* that the government must compensate people who effectively lose the entire value of private property due to a government regulation. The ruling was based on the eminent domain clause in the fifth amendment to the U.S. Constitution, which says "Nor shall private property be taken for public use without just compensation." In the *Lucas* case, David Lucas bought two beach-front lots, on which he planned to build two houses. Two years later, before construction began, the state government instituted an environmental regulation that banned construction on the lots, severely reducing the value of the property. The Supreme Court said that the U.S. Constitution requires the state government to compensate Lucas for the loss of "all economically viable use" of his land.

Should the government compensate people for all losses in property values due to any changes in regulations, or only large losses, or only in certain cases? Why? What about losses due to changes in taxes?

22.36 The first amendment to the U.S. Constitution protects freedom of speech. Would it be economically efficient or inefficient for a court to rule that this applies to advertising? To libel or defamation of character? To pretrial publicity in criminal court cases? To threats?

22.37 Should losers in lawsuits have to compensate winners for their legal costs (lawyer fees, time spent on the case, and other expenses) as is required in many countries outside North America? Should losers also pay court costs (the judge's salary and so on)?

22.38 Lawyers sometimes take tort cases on contingency fees, which means that they collect some fraction of court-ordered awards if they win and nothing if they lose. Proponents of contingency fees argue that this helps many people who cannot afford lawyer fees to assert their rights in court. Opponents of contingency fees argue that they give incentives for lawyers to overuse the courts by bringing lawsuits without much merit in hopes of winning. What would be the effects of prohibiting such contingency fees?

TAG SOFTWARE APPLICATIONS

TUTORIAL EXERCISES

▶ The module contains a review of the key terms from Chapter 22.

MACROECONOMIC EQUILIBRIUM

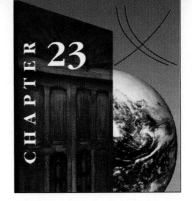

CHAPTER 23

MACROECONOMIC PUZZLES AND CHALLENGES: MEASUREMENT AND THEORY

WHAT THIS CHAPTER IS ABOUT

▶ Total output of all goods in the economy

▶ The average level of prices in the economy

▶ Main issues of macroeconomics: growth, inflation, and business cycles

Many of the momentous events of the 20th century have been connected with economics, and macroeconomic issues have often dominated the headlines. Macroeconomics is the study of the economy as a whole, including aggregate (total) production of goods and services, aggregate employment and unemployment, the economy's growth rate, the average level of prices and the rate of inflation, interest rates, foreign exchange rates, stock market performance, and similar issues. Macroeconomics is concerned with the overall effects of changes in government spending, taxes, budget deficits, and monetary policies. It is also concerned with the overall effects of consumers' decisions to spend or save, firms' decisions to hire workers and invest in new equipment, banks' decisions to lend money, and the effects of technical change on the economy.

Macroeconomic issues appear in the news every day. They often dominate political campaigns and determine the courses of people's lives. Massive hyperinflation in Germany helped Adolf Hitler's rise to power. The Great Depression brought the end of Herbert Hoover's presidency and the onset of Roosevelt's New Deal, which changed the scope of government in the United States. Macroeconomic events have delayed attempts by European countries to create a single United States of Europe. Economic catastrophes in the former Soviet Union and eastern Europe helped to bring down communism, to end the cold war, and to spread freedom and democracy in some formerly communist countries;

economic issues affected the direction and pace of all this change. Elections around the world turn on economic issues such as unemployment, inflation, and taxes. No one is isolated from these events. Macroeconomic issues such as economic growth, business cycles, and international trade will affect the kind of job you get, your salary and job stability, and the challenges and opportunities that will shape your life.

SOME MACROECONOMIC QUESTIONS

A nation's income is the total income of all people living in that country. Unless a country is fortunate enough to receive income from foreign countries (or it must pay money to other countries), its income equals its production of goods and services. As a result, the most central issue of macroeconomics is an economy's total production of goods and services.

The dollar value of total output of goods and services, called *nominal GDP,* approaches $7 trillion per year in the United States, or nearly $27,000 per person. **Figure 23.1** shows nominal GDP for the United States in recent decades. From 1960 to 1995, U.S. nominal GDP increased by 8.0 percent per year, on average. Over the same period, Japanese nominal GDP increased by 6.3 percent per year, on average, and German nominal GDP increased by 3.2 percent per year, on average. World nominal GDP is now about $30 trillion ($30,000,000,000,000). With about 5.8 billion people in the world, average world nominal GDP per person is about $5,200, about one-fourth of the U.S. level.

Part of the increase in nominal GDP over time reflects inflation, the rise in the average level of nominal (money) prices of goods and services. **Figure 23.2a** shows that prices in the United States now average about twice as high as prices in

FIGURE 23.1

NOMINAL GDP IN THE UNITED STATES, 1950–1995

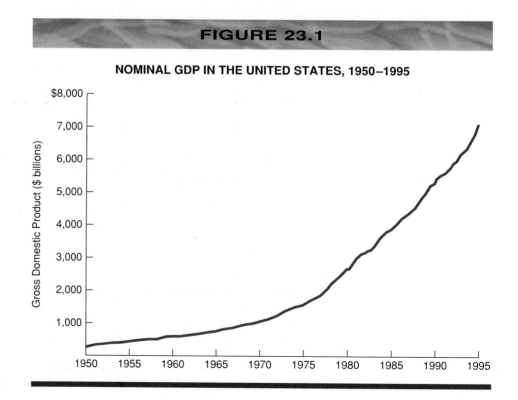

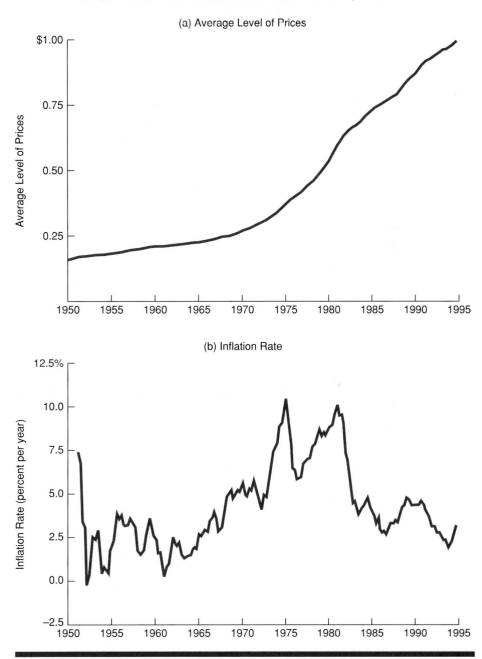

FIGURE 23.2

PRICES AND INFLATION IN THE UNITED STATES, 1950–1995

(a) Average Level of Prices

(b) Inflation Rate

1980, four times as high as prices in 1970, and six times as high as prices in 1950; a typical good that now costs $1.00 cost only about $0.25 in 1970. Figure 23.2b shows the rate of inflation in the United States. The chapter will discuss this subject later.

Most other countries have also experienced inflation. Prices in Germany now average about $2\frac{1}{2}$ times their 1970 levels and prices in Japan now average about 3 times their 1970 levels. Prices in Italy and Great Britain have increased faster than those in the United States, and inflation in Argentina, Bolivia, Brazil, Nicaragua, and Peru has temporarily reached several thousand percent per year, with prices rising significantly every day.

> Why have prices increased? Why do prices increase faster in some years than in others? Why do prices increase faster in some countries than in others? How fast will prices rise in the future? What government policies can help stop or prevent inflation?

Adjusting increases in nominal GDP for inflation reveals the true increase in a country's total output of goods and services, called *real GDP.* **Figure 23.3** shows trends in real GDP in the United States, Germany, and Japan. **Figure 23.4a** demonstrates that real GDP *per person* in the United States has roughly doubled since the mid-1950s; the U.S. economy produces about twice as many goods and services per person as it did 40 years ago. Real GDP per person grew even more rapidly over that time in some countries, such as Hong Kong and Singapore, while it changed little over that period in many sub-Saharan African countries.

> Why do some countries produce more output per person than others? Why does output per person rise over time in most countries but fall in others? Why does it rise faster in some countries than others or in some years than others? What government policies can help increase total output and the rate at which it grows?

Figure 23.5 shows changes in population, total employment, and unemployment in the United States in recent decades. The unemployment rate rose in certain years such as 1970, 1975, 1980, 1982, and 1990 to 1991. Figure 23.4 shows

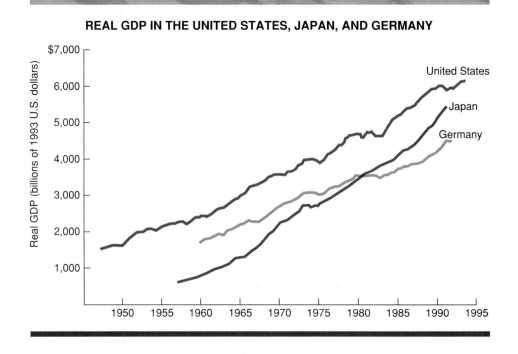

FIGURE 23.3

REAL GDP IN THE UNITED STATES, JAPAN, AND GERMANY

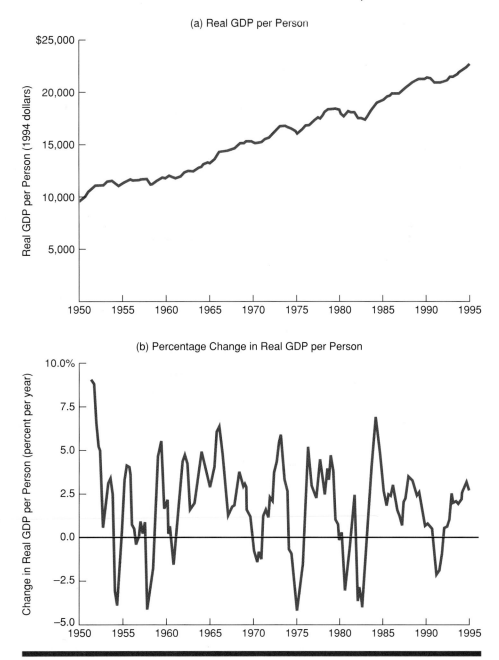

FIGURE 23.4

REAL GDP PER PERSON IN THE UNITED STATES, 1950–1995

(a) Real GDP per Person

(b) Percentage Change in Real GDP per Person

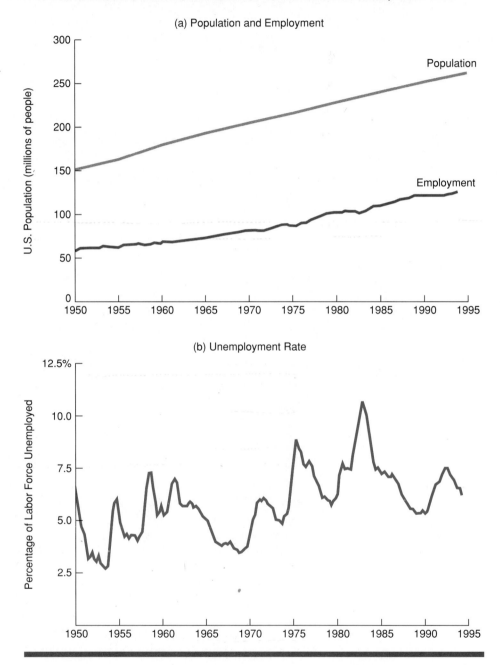

FIGURE 23.5

POPULATION AND EMPLOYMENT IN THE UNITED STATES, 1950–1995

(a) Population and Employment

(b) Unemployment Rate

decreases in real GDP per person in those same years. These are years in which the United States experienced recessions, or large decreases in the growth of real GDP accompanied by increases in unemployment. When real GDP per person falls, its percentage change is negative, as in Figure 23.4b.

> Why do economies experience recessions? What happens during recessions? What government policies might help to reduce the severity of recessions?

Definitions and Measurement of Macroeconomic Variables

real gross domestic product (GDP) — a measure of a country's total output of final market goods and services during some year

nominal gross domestic product (GDP) — the dollar value of a country's output of final market goods and services during some year

Real GDP is (roughly) a country's total output of goods and services. More precisely,

> **Real gross domestic product** is a measure of a country's total output of final market goods and services ~~during some year~~. in base year.

Nominal GDP is (roughly) the dollar value of a country's total output of goods and services. More precisely,

> **Nominal gross domestic product** is the dollar value of a country's output of final market goods and services ~~during some year.~~ in current year.

Notice the phrase "final market goods and services." Final goods are products or services intended for sale to consumers, such as automobiles and taxi rides; this excludes goods that become inputs into the production of other goods. In other words, GDP measures the economy's output of cars; it does not measure the output of steering wheels or engines separately from the cars themselves. That way each steering wheel or engine is counted only once, as part of the car. Market goods are goods or services that producers sell for pay. GDP does not measure services that people perform without explicit pay (such as housework and child care by parents). The word *goods* will frequently refer to both goods and services.

Example

Suppose that the National Sugar Company produces sugar and sells it to Nabisco for $1,000 while Hershey sells chocolate to Nabisco for $500. Nabisco uses sugar and chocolate to make 100,000 Oreo cookies, which are final goods. If people pay $0.03 per cookie, they spend $3,000 to buy 100,000 cookies. If this is the only final market good in the economy, nominal GDP is $3,000 and real GDP is 100,000 cookies. Nominal GDP equals the price of cookies times the number of cookies that people buy.

It would not be correct to include the $1,000 that Nabisco spent on sugar and the $500 that it spent on chocolate in GDP because the sugar and chocolate are inputs into the production of a final good; their value is already included in GDP as part of the cookies. The sugar and chocolate that people buy to use at home, however, are final goods and are included in GDP.

Price Levels

price level — an average of the prices of an economy's goods and services

GDP price deflator — one measure of the price level, equal to nominal GDP divided by real GDP

> The economy's **price level** refers to an average of the prices of its goods and services.

One measure of the economy's price level is the GDP deflator.

> The **GDP price deflator** equals nominal GDP divided by real GDP.

$$\text{GDP price deflator} = \frac{\text{Nominal GDP}}{\text{Real GDP}} \qquad \textbf{(23.1)}$$

It can be a useful simplification to imagine that the economy produces only one type of good, such as cookies, that real GDP is the economy's total output of that good, such as 10 million cookies per year, and that the GDP price deflator is the good's price, such as $0.03 per cookie.[1]

Rearranging Equation 23.1 shows that nominal GDP equals real GDP multiplied by the GDP price deflator:

$$\text{Nominal GDP} = \text{Real GDP} \times \text{GDP price deflator} \qquad \textbf{(23.2)}$$

Nominal GDP equals the total dollar value of the economy's output. Think of nominal GDP as the economy's dollar income, the GDP price deflator as the price of a particular good, and real GDP as the total quantity of the good that people can then afford to buy. For example, if real GDP is 100 goods per year, and the price deflator is $2, then nominal GDP is $200 per year. The combined income of everyone in the economy totals $200 per year and goods cost $2 each, and people can afford to buy 100 goods per year.

The GDP price deflator is not the only measure of the price level. Two other commonly reported measures are the consumer price index (CPI) and the producer price index (PPI). The next section discusses differences in these measures of the price level.

GROWTH RATES

Growth rates are important in macroeconomics. They will appear in almost every remaining chapter of this book.

> The **annual growth rate,** or **rate of growth,** of any economic variable is its percentage change from one year to the next.

annual growth rate (rate of growth) — the percentage change in a variable from one year to the next

Chapter 5 defined the percentage change in a variable as 100 times its change divided by the average of its original level and new level:

$$\text{Percentage change in a number} =$$

$$100 \times \frac{\text{Change in the number}}{\text{Average of (or midpoint between) the original number and the new number}}$$

This book will represent the percentage change per year in any variable X (its growth rate) as:

$$\%\Delta X$$

For example, the growth rate of GDP from 1995 to 1996 is:

$$\%\Delta\text{GDP} = 100 \times \frac{\text{GDP in 1996} - \text{GDP in 1995}}{\text{Average of GDP in 1995 and 1996}}$$

The average growth rate of GDP over a longer period of time is its percentage change over the longer period divided by the number of years. For example, the average growth rate of GDP from 1980 to 1996 is:

$$\%\Delta\text{GDP} = 100 \times \frac{\text{GDP}_{1996} - \text{GDP}_{1980}}{16 \times (\text{Average of GDP}_{1980} \text{ and GDP}_{1996})}$$

---

[1] A later section, "Measuring GDP and the Price Level," will show how to measure GDP and the price level in real-life economies, which produce many different kinds of goods.

Rule of 72

The rule of 72 is useful to estimate growth rates.

rule of 72 — the rule that if the growth rate of a variable is X percent per year, then the variable doubles after about $72/X$ years

> The **rule of 72** says that if the growth rate of a variable is X percent per year, then the variable doubles after about $72/X$ years.

For example, if GDP grows at 2 percent per year, it doubles after about 36 years. If the price level rises at 4 percent per year, it doubles in about 18 years.

Similarly, if a variable doubles in X years, then its average growth rate is about $72/X$ percent per year. For example, the price level in the United States roughly quadrupled from 1970 to 1994. Because it doubled about twice in that 24-year period, on average it doubled every 12 years. This means that the price level grew at a rate of about $72/12$, or 6 percent per year over that period.

Applications: Inflation and Economic Growth

Inflation is the growth rate of the price level.

inflation — the growth rate of the economy's price level

> **Inflation** is the growth rate of the economy's price level.

One measure of inflation is the growth rate in the GDP price deflator. For example, if the GDP price deflator in 1996 is 4 percent higher than that in 1995, then inflation from 1995 to 1996 is 4 percent per year. Figure 23.2b shows the annual growth rate of the U.S. GDP deflator.

Will the average person in your generation have a higher or lower standard of living than the average person in your parents' generation? How much higher or lower? The answers depend largely on the future rate of economic growth.

rate of economic growth — the annual growth rate of GDP per person

> A country's **rate of economic growth** is the annual growth rate of its GDP per person.

Figure 23.4b shows the annual growth rate of GDP per person in the United States. Economic growth has been positive in the past in most countries, and the United States now produces about twice as many goods and services per person as it did 40 years ago. Later chapters will discuss important questions regarding factors that affect the rate of economic growth and whether growth will continue or stop in the future. For now, note that real U.S. GDP per person has grown at an average rate of 1.8 percent per year since 1900. The rule of 72 says that at this rate, real GDP per person doubles every $72/1.8$ years, or every 40 years. Based on the U.S. experience in the 20th century, real GDP per person doubles in about 40 years or quadruples in about 80 years.

If this trend continues, real U.S. GDP per person will reach almost $42,000 (in today's dollars) by 2020. Of course, the growth rate might rise or fall. Some people fear that it will even stop or become negative, so that future generations will have lower standards of living than their parents.[2]

Most other countries have experienced growth in real GDP per person similar to that in the United States. World real GDP per person has grown at a rate of about 1.7 percent per year since 1900; most of this growth has occurred in the second half of the century.

─────────────── **For Review** ───────────────

23.1 What is the difference between real GDP and nominal GDP?

---

[2]Later chapters will discuss these issues.

23.2 Roughly how large is the U.S. GDP? Roughly how large is world GDP? How big is GDP per person in the United States? GDP per person in the world?

QUESTIONS

23.3 Use the rule of 72 to calculate how long it would take real GDP per person to double if the rate of economic growth were 2 percent per year. What if the rate of economic growth were 3 percent per year?

23.4 Use the rule of 72 to find the average rate of inflation if the price level doubles in 12 years.

MEASURING GDP AND THE PRICE LEVEL

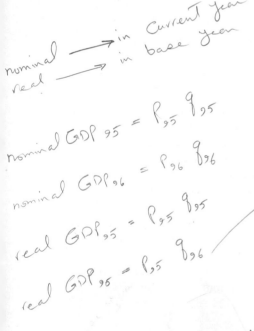

Nominal GDP is relatively easy to measure. It is the total amount of money that buyers spend on all goods that the economy produces in a year. Real GDP would also be easy to measure in an economy that produced only one type of good. The real GDP of an economy that produced only cookies would be the number of cookies it produced in a year.

Measurement of real GDP in real-life economies is complicated, however, by the fact that people produce a variety of goods, such as cookies, milk, and cartoons. It would not make sense to add the number of cookies, quarts of milk, and cartoons that the economy produces to calculate real GDP. Instead, economists measure real GDP as a money amount in base-year dollars (or pesos or yen). First, they choose some past year (such as 1992) and call it the *base year.* They then use the prices from that base year instead of current prices to calculate the value of the economy's current output. The answer measures the economy's real GDP in the dollars of the base year (such as real GDP in 1992 dollars). Real GDP in dollars of the base year shows what the money value of the economy's current output would be if prices had not changed since that base year.

Economists compare real GDPs in different years by using the same base-year prices to measure real GDP in each year. For example, U.S. real GDP in 1994 was $5.4 trillion measured in 1987 dollars. This was about 10 percent higher than U.S. real GDP in 1990, which was $4.9 trillion measured in 1987 dollars, indicating that total output of goods and services in the United States increased by about 10 percent over those four years.

EXAMPLE

Suppose that the economy produces six videos and eight pillows in 2002, as **Table 23.1** shows, and that videos cost $20 each and pillows cost $10 each in that year.

Nominal GDP in 2002 = (Output of videos in 2002)(Price of videos in 2002)

+ (Output of pillows in 2002)(Price of pillows in 2002)

= (6 videos)($20 per video) + (8 pillows)($10 per pillow)

= $120 + $80 = $200

TABLE 23.1

MEASURING GDP IN AN ECONOMY WITH VIDEOS AND PILLOWS

	Videos	Price of Videos	Pillows	Price of Pillows	Nominal GDP	Real GDP in 1990 Dollars
1990	4	$10	4	$ 5	$ 60	$ 60
1998	6	18	8	8	172	100
2002	6	20	8	10	200	100
2005	9	21	12	10	309	150
2010	9	21	16	10	349	170

Now choose a base year, such as 1990, and calculate real GDP.

Real GDP in 2002 measured in 1990 dollars

= (Output of videos in 2002) (Price of videos in 1990)

+ (Output of pillows in 2002)(Price of pillows in 1990)

Suppose that, as Table 23.1 shows, videos cost only $10 each in 1990 and pillows cost only $5 each. Then real GDP in 2002 measured in 1990 dollars equals:

(6 videos in 2002)($10 per video in 1990)

+ (8 pillows in 2002)($5 per pillow in 1990)

= $60 + $40 in 1990 dollars

= $100 in 1990 dollars

Real GDP in 2002 is $100 measured in 1990 dollars. Table 23.1 shows similar calculations for other years.

This measurement of real GDP allows sensible comparisons of the economy's output of goods and services in different years. To see why, suppose that the economy produces the same number of videos and pillows in 2002 as it did in 1998, but prices are higher in 2002 than in 1998. Nominal GDP rises between 2002 and 1998, though real GDP remains the same from 2002 to 1998; real GDP is $100, measured in 1990 dollars, in both years. This is a sensible answer. If production of goods does not change, real GDP does not change. If the economy produces 9 videos and 12 pillows in 2005, 40 percent more of each good than in 2002, then:

Real GDP in 2005 measured in 1990 dollars

= (9 videos in 2005)($10 per video in 1990)

+ (12 pillows in 2005)($5 per pillow in 1990)

= $90 + $60 in 1990 dollars

= $150 in 1990 dollars

Real GDP in 2005 is $150 measured in 1990 dollars. Real GDP rises by 40 percent from 2002 to 2005 because production of each good rises by 40 percent.

Finally, suppose that the economy produces 9 videos and 16 pillows in 2010. Real GDP in 2010 rises to $170 in 1990 dollars. The change in real GDP between any two years is an average of the changes in output of the goods that the economy produces, weighted by their base-year prices.

The price deflator in 2002 is:

$$\text{GDP price deflator in 2002 (base year 1990)}$$

$$= \frac{\text{Nominal GDP in 2002}}{\text{Real GDP in 2002 in 1990 dollars}}$$

$$= \frac{\$200}{\$100 \text{ in 1990 dollars}} = 2 \text{ (relative to base year 1990)}$$

This shows that prices double between 1990 and 2002. Notice that Equations 23.1 and 23.2 apply to this example. Nominal GDP in 2002 is $200, the price deflator is 2, and real income in 1990 dollars is $100.

OTHER MEASURES OF THE PRICE LEVEL

The GDP price deflator is not the only measure of the price level. Two other measures are the *consumer price index* (*CPI*) and the *producer price index* (*PPI*). The consumer price index measures the average nominal prices of goods and services that a typical family living in an urban area buys. The CPI is a weighted average; goods such as salt and shoelaces (on which people spend small fractions of their incomes) receive less weight in the average than goods like beef and housing, on which people spend more money. The PPI is a weighted average of the prices of inputs that producers buy to make final goods.

The CPI and PPI are constructed from government surveys. Every several years, the U.S. Census Bureau conducts a Consumer Expenditure Survey to see what goods the typical family buys. The survey compiles a list of about 400 goods and services. Each month the Bureau of Labor Statistics (BLS), part of the Department of Labor, visits about 50 stores to find out the prices of these 400 goods and services. The BLS then computes the total cost of buying the quantities of those 400 goods that the typical family buys. The BLS also makes this calculation for a base year. It then calculates the consumer price index from the formula:

$$CPI = \frac{\text{Total cost of the goods now}}{\text{Total cost of the goods in the base year}} \times 100$$

EXAMPLE

Suppose that the typical family buys ten pizzas, eight half-gallons of ice cream, and two bottles of antacid tablets every month, and that pizzas cost $10, ice cream costs $4 per half-gallon, and antacids cost $3 per bottle (see **Table 23.2.**). This gives total spending of:

$$(10)(\$10) + (8)(\$4) + (2)(\$3) = \$138$$

TABLE 23.2

MEASURING THE CPI IN AN ECONOMY WITH PIZZAS, ICE CREAM, AND ANTACIDS

Good	Price in 1985	Current Price	Quantity Purchased
Pizza	$ 7	$10	10
Ice cream	3	4	8
Antacids	2	3	2
Total cost of goods	98	138	

Suppose that in 1985 pizzas cost $7, ice cream cost $3, and antacids cost $2. At these prices, ten pizzas, eight half-gallons of ice cream, and two bottles of antacids would have cost:

$$(10)(\$7) + (8)(\$3) + (2)(\$2) = \$98$$

The CPI, measured in 1985 dollars, is then:

$$CPI = \frac{\$138}{\$98} \times 100 = about\ 141$$

This means that a family must spend about $141 to buy the same goods that it could have bought for only $100 in 1985, or that prices have increased by about 33 percent, on average, since 1985.

LIMITATIONS OF PRICE INDEXES

Figure 23.6 shows inflation in the United States as measured by the growth rates of the CPI and the PPI. The CPI and PPI differ from the GDP deflator because the GDP deflator includes all final goods produced in the economy, while the CPI includes only the goods that an average household buys and the PPI includes only the goods that an average producer buys. As the figure shows, the PPI usually fluctuates more than the CPI.

The GDP deflator, the CPI, and the PPI all measure average prices only imperfectly, and each has some limitations. It is difficult to compare prices in different years because changes in quality, such as safer cars and faster computers, alter results, as does the creation of new goods that did not even exist in an earlier year, such as CD players, portable phones, personal satellite dishes, virtual reality machines, and in-line skates. Another problem is that people buy different goods

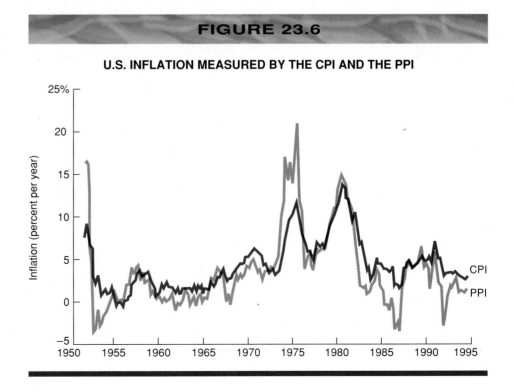

FIGURE 23.6

U.S. INFLATION MEASURED BY THE CPI AND THE PPI

and firms produce different goods as time passes. The typical family buys different products now than it did several years ago when the last consumer expenditure survey was taken; this introduces errors into the CPI.

When the relative price of a good rises, people tend to substitute other goods in its place, which creates a related problem for comparing the average levels of prices in different years. For example, suppose that people buy mostly orange juice and very little apple juice when orange juice costs $2.00 and apple juice costs $1.00. Now suppose that the price of orange juice doubles, while the price of apple juice rises 20 percent, leading people to buy mostly apple juice and very little orange juice. Does this suggest that the price level nearly doubled, or that it increased only about 20 percent, or something in between? There is no correct answer to this question, yet questions like it arise routinely when economists calculate price indexes. For these reasons, all price indexes are imperfect. Nevertheless, they can provide useful information about the economy.

FOR REVIEW

23.5 What does it mean to say that in 1994, U.S. real GDP was $5.4 trillion in 1987 dollars?

23.6 How is the consumer price index calculated?

QUESTION

23.7 Use Table 23.1 to calculate:
   a. Real GDP in 2010 measured in 2002 dollars
   b. The GDP deflator in 2010 measured in 2002 base-year dollars

---

CIRCULAR FLOW AND AGGREGATE DEMAND

CIRCULAR FLOW

The circular flow of economic activity in **Figure 23.7** gives a useful picture that can help organize thoughts about macroeconomics. This figure simplifies the circular flow in several important ways. Most importantly, the figure shows an economy that does not trade with other countries. Adding realistic complications does not affect the main points of the following discussion, however.[3]

The outside circle shows the flow of money in the economy. People pay money to firms in exchange for goods and services. Firms pay people to work for them, and they pay profits to their owners. Money travels clockwise around the circle.

The flow of money from firms to people is the economy's *aggregate* (or total) *nominal income*. The word *nominal* indicates a measurement of income in terms of money. The flow of money from people to firms is called *aggregate nominal spending*. Aggregate nominal income and aggregate nominal spending are equal; each measures the flow of money around the circle. They are equal for a simple reason: someone can earn $1 of income only when someone else spends that dollar.

The inside circle in Figure 23.7 shows flows of goods and services. The arrow from people to firms represents the flow of inputs, such as labor and capital ser-

Total expenditure = Total income

---

[3]See the last footnote in the appendix to this chapter.

FIGURE 23.7

CIRCULAR FLOW OF ECONOMIC ACTIVITY

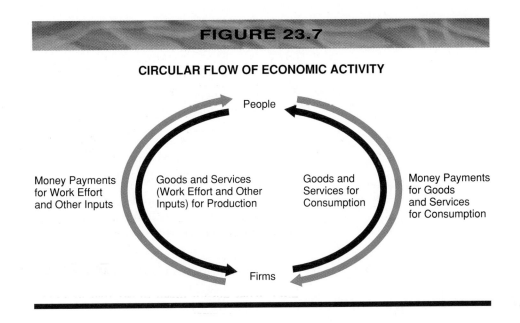

vices, from people to firms.[4] The arrow from firms to people represents the final goods that people buy from firms. While the outside circle shows aggregate nominal income and spending, measured in money terms, the inside circle shows *aggregate real income and spending,* measured in terms of actual goods and services. The word *real* indicates a measurement of an actual amount of goods and services, not the money value of these goods and services.[5]

USING THE CIRCULAR FLOW: THE EQUATION OF EXCHANGE

Suppose that the circular flow in Figure 23.7 occurs once per year. The money in the economy flows once each year from people to firms and back to people. Each dollar in the economy is used once each year by people to buy goods and once each year by firms to pay people. In this case, the flows in Figure 23.7 show the economy's GDP for one year.

Now suppose, instead, that the circular flows in the figure occur twice each year. The money in the economy flows from people to firms and back to people twice each year, so the production of final goods and services that people buy each year is twice the amount shown by the arrow in Figure 23.7. This means that GDP each year is *twice* the amount shown by the arrows in the figure.

Consider a simple economy without credit cards or checks. People exchange only dollar bills (paper money) printed by the government. The nominal money supply in this economy is the amount of money in the economy at any time. Perhaps the government has printed $1,000 in money for people to use. We can extend this idea to our more complex, real-life economy, though it is useful to keep the simplified economy in the back of your mind.

---

[4]For example, a person who starts a pizza shop supplies equipment to that shop. More generally, the owners of any firm (such as a corporation's stockholders) own the firm's buildings, land, and equipment, and they supply these inputs to the firm. (They let the firm use them.)

[5]Aggregate real income and aggregate real output are the same because every final good that the economy produces is income to someone—someone owns it or sells it.

nominal money supply — the total amount of money in the economy, measured in monetary units such as dollars or yen

The **nominal money supply** is the total amount of money in the economy, measured in monetary units such as dollars or yen.

The nominal money supply flows from people to firms and then back to people, each time the circular flow occurs. If the circular flow occurs *once* each year, then each dollar is spent once per year, so nominal GDP equals the nominal money supply, and both equal the flow of money shown by the outer arrows in Figure 23.7. If the circular flow occurs *twice* each year, then each dollar is spent twice per year on goods, so the economy's total output of goods is twice the money supply, that is, nominal GDP equals twice the nominal money supply. Because the money is spent twice each year in this case, economists say that the velocity of money is 2 per year.

velocity of money — the average number of times per year that money is spent in the circular flow

The **velocity of money** is the average number of times per year that money is spent in the circular flow; velocity equals nominal GDP divided by the nominal money supply.

If the circular flow occurs three times per year, then the velocity of money is 3 per year. In that case, nominal GDP equals three times the circular flow in Figure 23.7 because the entire money supply is spent on goods each time the circular flow occurs. More generally:

Nominal GDP equals the nominal money supply multiplied by the velocity of money.

Representing the nominal money supply by M and velocity by V, this sentence can be written as the equation:

$$\text{Nominal GDP} = MV \tag{23.3}$$

Recall that nominal GDP equals real GDP multiplied by the GDP price deflator. Representing the GDP price deflator by P and real GDP by y gives:

$$MV = Py \tag{23.4}$$

Equation 23.4 is called the *equation of exchange.*
The **equation of exchange** says that $MV = Py$.

equation of exchange — the equation that shows the nominal money supply multiplied by its velocity equal to the GDP price deflator multiplied by real GDP

In words, the equation of exchange says that the nominal money supply multiplied by the velocity of money equals the GDP price deflator multiplied by real GDP.

Figure 23.8 shows the nominal money supply and its velocity in the United States. To represent the money supply, it plots a measure of money called M1, which includes money in checking accounts as well as cash. (A later chapter will discuss various measures of the nominal money supply.) As the figure shows, the nominal money supply in the United States has grown rapidly over time while velocity has changed more slowly to its current level of about 6 or 7 times per year.

GROWTH RATES OF MONEY AND PRICES

A mathematical rule allows economists to rewrite the equation of exchange in terms of growth rates of the money supply, velocity, the price level, and real GDP:

$$\%\Delta M + \%\Delta V = \%\Delta P + \%\Delta y \tag{23.5}$$

Equation 23.5 says that the growth rate of the nominal money supply plus the growth rate of velocity equals the growth rate of the price level (the rate of inflation) plus the growth rate of real GDP. For example, the nominal money supply may grow at 5 percent per year while velocity remains constant (with a growth

FIGURE 23.8

U.S. NOMINAL MONEY SUPPLY (M1) AND ITS GROWTH RATE

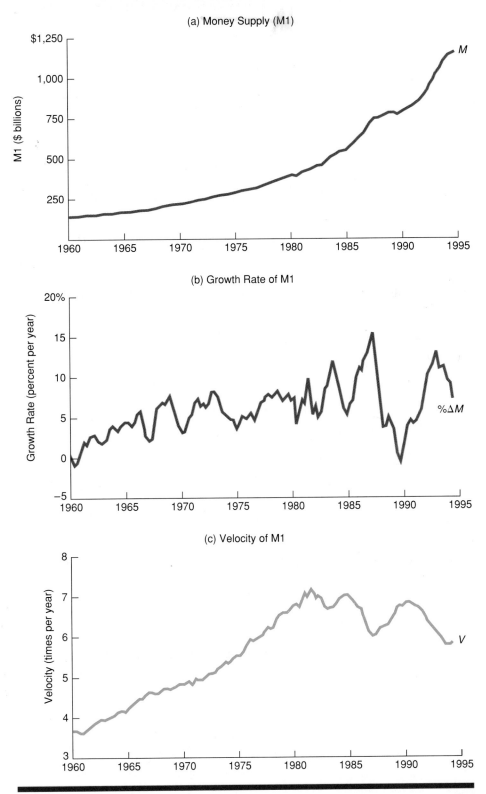

(a) Money Supply (M1)

(b) Growth Rate of M1

(c) Velocity of M1

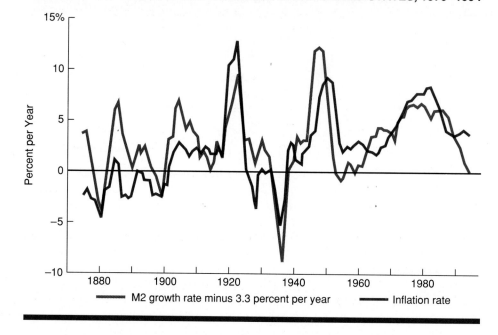

FIGURE 23.9

MONEY SUPPLY GROWTH AND INFLATION IN THE UNITED STATES, 1870–1994

M2 growth rate minus 3.3 percent per year   Inflation rate

rate of zero); the rate of inflation may then be 3 percent per year, and real GDP may grow at 2 percent per year.

In most countries, the growth rates of their nominal money supplies and price levels change more than the growth rates of their velocities or real GDPs. As a result, the growth rate of the nominal money supply and inflation tend to move together, as in **Figure 23.9,** which shows inflation and the growth rate of the money supply in the United States since 1870.[6]

AGGREGATE DEMAND

A graph of the equation of exchange, as in **Figure 23.10,** shows the economy's aggregate demand curve.[7]

> A country's **aggregate demand** refers to total demand for the goods and services produced in that country in a year. Its **aggregate demand curve** shows the total quantity demanded for its goods and services at various price levels.

The term *real aggregate demand* refers to the total quantity of goods and services purchased (such as 1,000 cookies), while *nominal aggregate demand* refers to the dollar value of those goods and services (such as $200). The aggregate demand curve shows the quantity of goods and services that people, business

aggregate demand — the total demand for the goods and services currently produced in a country

aggregate demand curve — a graph showing the total quantity demanded for an economy's goods and services at various price levels

---

[6]The money supply in the figure is another measure called M2, which will be discussed in a later chapter.

[7]The aggregate demand curve in Figure 23.10 holds both *M* and *V* fixed. Economists often draw the aggregate demand curve allowing *V* to change along the curve rather than holding it fixed. Later chapters will explain why *V* changes when *P* and *y* change.

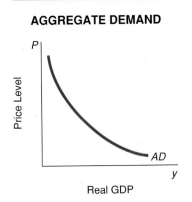

FIGURE 23.10

AGGREGATE DEMAND

The aggregate demand curve graphs the equation of exchange, *MV = Py*. Holding *M* and *V* constant, an increase in real GDP is associated with a fall in the price level.

firms, the government, and foreign countries would buy at various price levels. The vertical axis of Figure 23.10 shows the economy's price level while the horizontal axis shows real aggregate demand.

Recall that the nominal money supply, *M,* measures the total amount of money in the economy, and velocity, *V,* measures how many times per year people spend that money. Therefore, *MV* measures total dollar spending each year:

$$\text{Nominal aggregate demand} = MV$$

Total dollar spending on all goods in the economy equals the money supply multiplied by the velocity of money. Because *MV* shows total dollar spending, *MV/P* shows the quantity of goods that people buy when they spend those *MV* dollars, that is, it shows real aggregate demand:

$$\text{Real aggregate demand} = MV/P$$

The equation of exchange implies that:

$$y = \frac{MV}{P} \tag{23.6}$$

This says that for given levels of *M* and *V,* increases in *P* reduce *y.* In other words, a higher price level reduces the amount of goods and services that people can afford to buy, given their total dollar spending, *MV.* For example, suppose that the money supply is $100 and velocity is 2 per year. Then *MV* is $200 per year, so *Py* must be $200 per year. If the price level is $10 per good, then *y* is 20 goods per year. If the price level is $20 per good, then *y* is 10 goods per year, so the aggregate demand curve slopes downward, as in Figure 23.10. Later, we will combine this aggregate demand curve with an aggregate supply curve to obtain a graph that summarizes the economy's equilibrium.

TYPES OF SPENDING

The circular flow shows total spending, and the equation of exchange describes aggregate demand by relating the money supply, velocity, the price level, and real GDP. Economists describe aggregate demand in another way by adding different types of spending together. This is useful partly because different economic forces affect different types of spending.[8] Economists usually decompose spending into four parts: consumer spending, investment, government purchases of goods and services, and net exports.

Consumption refers to purchases of goods and services by people for current enjoyment or use in households. Consumption does not include goods that become inputs in production of other goods. People consume goods when they use them—when they eat, wear, or drive them.

consumption (consumer spending) — spending by people on final goods and services for current use

> **Consumption,** or **consumer spending,** is spending by people on final goods and services for current use.

People often buy goods, such as cars and houses, partly for future use. Spending by consumers on such durable goods is not included in this definition of consumption; economists consider spending by consumers on goods for future use as investment. **Figure 23.11a** shows consumption spending in the United States.

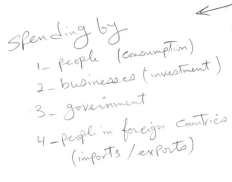

---

[8]The next chapter will discuss these forces and their effects.

FIGURE 23.11

CATEGORIES OF U.S. SPENDING, 1950–1995

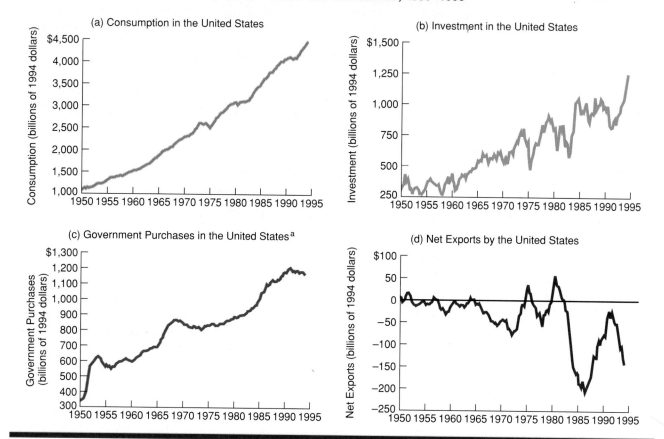

(a) Consumption in the United States

(b) Investment in the United States

(c) Government Purchases in the United States[a]

(d) Net Exports by the United States

[a] Includes federal, state, and local governments.

Investment refers to spending on new capital, such as machines, equipment, inventories of goods for future use, human skills, and knowledge.

investment — spending to create new capital goods, such as machines, equipment, inventories, human skills, and knowledge

Investment refers to spending to create new capital goods, such as machines, equipment, inventories, human skills, and knowledge.

Firms invest when they buy new capital, perhaps constructing new factories or offices, purchasing new equipment, training employees, or upgrading laboratories for research and development. People invest when they go to school or buy computers or cars. The government invests when it spends money on roads, buildings, and other capital goods. However, economists include all such government spending in a separate category, government purchases of goods and services, to be discussed next. Think of the term *investment* as shorthand for *private investment* (investment spending by everyone except the government). Figure 23.11b shows investment spending in the United States.

Government purchases refer to all spending by the government to buy goods and services or to produce them. Total government spending includes government purchases (such as police or court services, national defense, and roads) plus transfer payments (sometimes called *entitlements*), in which the government provides money to people but does not actually buy any goods or services. The Social Security program is the largest transfer payment program in the United States. Figure 23.11c shows U.S. government purchases of goods and services in 1994 dollars. Total government spending includes both government purchases and transfer payments.

government purchases — all spending by the government except transfer payments (direct payments of money to people)

> **Government purchases** refers to all spending by the government except transfer payments (direct payments of money to people).

Government purchases include investment spending by the government, such as its spending on roads, planes, and schools. Economists separate government purchases from spending by people and private firms because the factors that affect government spending differ from the factors that affect spending by people and private firms.

A fourth category of spending is spending by people in foreign countries on products and services produced in the home country, called *exports*.

exports — sales of goods and services to people and firms in other countries

imports — purchases of goods and services from people and firms in other countries

net exports (balance of international trade) — exports minus imports

> **Exports** are sales of goods and services to people and firms in other countries.

> **Imports** are purchases of goods and services from people and firms in other countries.

> **Net exports,** or the **balance of international trade,** equals exports minus imports.

When a country's net exports are positive (its exports exceed its imports), the country has an international trade surplus; when its net exports are negative (its exports fall short of imports), the country has an international trade deficit. Figure 23.11d shows net exports by the United States.

Every good produced in the economy is either consumed, invested, purchased by the government, or exported.[9] If a firm produces a good and no one buys it, economists count the good as an investment in the firm's inventory of goods not yet sold.

Consumption, investment, and government purchases include spending on goods imported from other countries. Therefore, total spending on goods produced in this country equals consumption plus investment plus government purchases plus exports minus imports. An equation can summarize this:

$$GDP = C + I + G + NEX \tag{23.7}$$

C is consumption, I is investment, G is government purchases, and NEX is net exports (exports minus imports). Gross domestic product is the sum of consumption, investment, government purchases, and net exports, as **Figure 23.12** shows. Consumption is almost two-thirds of GDP in the United States, investment varies between about 12 percent and 16 percent of GDP, government purchases amount to about 20 percent of GDP, and net exports are negative, but small.[10]

---

[9]If you buy an ice cream cone and it melts before you eat it, you might not want to say that you consumed it. Still, this counts as consumption in economic data.

[10]While exports and imports each exceed 10 percent of GDP, their difference, net exports, has varied only between 1 percent to −3 percent of GDP over the last half-century.

FIGURE 23.12

REAL GDP AND FOUR TYPES OF SPENDING IN THE UNITED STATES, 1950–1995

GDP is the sum of consumption, investment, government purchases, and net exports.

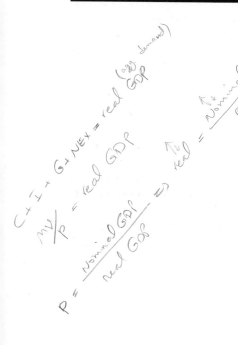

RETURN TO AGGREGATE DEMAND

Figure 23.10 graphed the equation of exchange to show the economy's aggregate demand curve. We now have a second way to describe aggregate demand, as the sum of consumption, investment, government purchases, and net exports:

$$\text{Aggregate demand} = C + I + G + NEX \qquad (23.8)$$

Equation 23.8 shows aggregate demand as the sum of four different types of spending. Part of aggregate demand is consumption, *C,* by people who live in the home country; part is investment, *I;* part is government purchases, *G;* the rest is net exports to foreigners, *NEX.* When you visit a store, your total demand for products at that store might consist of demand for shirts plus demand for pants plus demand for socks. Similarly, aggregate demand sums all of the types of spending in the economy: consumption, investment, government purchases, and net exports.

Recall that *MV* shows total nominal spending each year, and *MV/P* shows total real spending. *MV/P* and *C + I + G + NEX* both equal aggregate demand. They are two different ways to describe the same thing. Consequently, they always change together; any change in one must accompany a change in the other.

For example, suppose that the nominal money supply is $1 billion and velocity is 6 per year. This gives *MV* of $6 billion per year. If the price level is $10 per good, then aggregate demand is 600 million goods per year. Perhaps people buy 400 million goods for consumption, 100 million goods for investment, the government purchases 100 million goods, and net exports are zero. If *MV/P* rises to

700 million goods per year, then either consumption, investment, government purchases, or net exports must also rise so that they sum to 700 million goods. Additional information would be required to determine how the increase in aggregate demand is divided among changes in *C, I, G,* and *NEX.* The point is simply that if people spend more money each year, they must spend it on *something;* Equation 23.8 simply shows how they spend it.

Similarly, if an increase in investment or government purchases raises $C + I + G + NEX$, then MV/P rises by the same amount. Later chapters will explain how this happens.[11]

WORD OF CAUTION

The aggregate demand curve differs from the demand curves for individual products introduced in Chapter 4. Those demand curves relate the quantity of a good demanded to its relative price. The aggregate demand curve, in contrast, represents the equation of exchange and relates total demand to the economy's price level.

MACROECONOMIC MODELS

Macroeconomic models, like any economic models, describe logical thought about the economy. Macroeconomic models usually involve the economy as a whole, so they must take into account interactions and feedbacks between different parts of the economy. Like other economic models, they explain how certain variables would change if underlying conditions were to change. The variables that the models try to explain are called *endogenous variables,* while the term *exogenous variables* describes underlying economic conditions that the models do not try to explain, but use to help explain the endogenous variables. For example, in the basic model of supply and demand for a product, if demand for the product increases, then its price rises and the quantity traded rises; demand is an exogenous variable and the product's price and quantity traded are endogenous variables.

Variables that are exogenous in one model can be endogenous in other models. For example, one ecological model of the growth of a rain forest may treat the weather as an exogenous variable and use it to help explain the growth of plant and animal life in the forest. Other models might treat the weather as an endogenous variable, explaining changes in weather due to human activities, volcanoes, and other variables that the first model treats as exogenous. Still other models might treat volcanic activity as endogenous.

Similarly, while one economic model might treat demand for gasoline as exogenous, another model might treat that demand as endogenous, explaining changes in the demand for gasoline by changes in consumers' incomes, government fuel-efficiency regulations, development of mass transit systems, and prices of alternative transportation methods.

Economists refer to models that deal with only part of the economy as *partial-equilibrium models.* They describe models that deal with the whole economy as *general-equilibrium models.* The exogenous variables in a general-equilibrium

---

[11]Chapter 25 will show that changes in aggregate demand affect equilibrium interest rates. Later chapters will explain why these changes in interest rates affect the velocity of money and the nominal money supply, so they affect *MV/P.*

model might include technology, peoples' tastes, the weather, government economic policies, economic conditions in other countries, and so on. Endogenous variables may include real GDP, unemployment, inflation, interest rates, and the country's balance of international trade. Most macroeconomic models are based on microeconomics; the model's logic deals with the behavior of individual people and firms and how they all interact with each other. When feedbacks between various parts of the economy are not important, economists use partial-equilibrium models; when feedbacks between parts of the economy play important roles, economists use general-equilibrium models.

AGGREGATE SUPPLY AND AGGREGATE DEMAND

Many macroeconomists summarize the economy's equilibrium with a graph of aggregate demand and aggregate supply like **Figure 23.13**.

aggregate supply — the total supply of all goods and services currently produced in an economy

aggregate supply curve — a graph showing the total quantity supplied of an economy's goods and services at various price levels

A country's **aggregate supply** is the total supply of all of the goods and services produced in that country in a year. Its **aggregate supply curve** shows the total quantity supplied at various price levels.

Figure 23.13a shows the long-run equilibrium of the economy. Long-run aggregate supply is a vertical line because, in the long run, a country's aggregate supply of goods and services is unaffected by its price level. Instead, its aggregate supply depends on its available technology and inputs such as capital and labor, and on the laws, property rights, regulations, and taxes that affect peoples' incentives to use technology and inputs efficiently.

The long-run aggregate supply curve shifts rightward over time as technology improves and the economy adds more capital equipment and other inputs to pro-

FIGURE 23.13

AGGREGATE DEMAND AND AGGREGATE SUPPLY MODELS

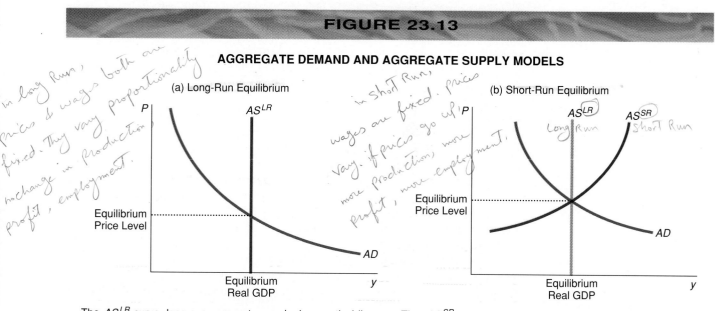

(a) Long-Run Equilibrium

(b) Short-Run Equilibrium

The AS^{LR} curve, long-run aggregate supply, is a vertical line. Equilibrium real GDP is determined by the economy's technology and available resources in long-run equilibrium.

The AS^{SR} curve, short-run aggregate supply, may slope upward for reasons to be discussed in later chapters.

duce goods. This is the process of long-run economic growth, which a later chapter will discuss.

Economists distinguish long-run aggregate supply from short-run aggregate supply. Long-run aggregate supply refers to the total supply of goods and services after the economy has had time to adjust fully to a change in conditions. Short-run aggregate supply refers to the total supply during a time before the economy has fully adjusted to the change.

Most economists believe that the short-run aggregate supply curve slopes upward, as in Figure 23.13b. Later chapters will discuss possible reasons for the upward slope. Some economists disagree about the shape of the short-run aggregate supply curve, and later chapters will also discuss their views. Economists do not yet have sufficient evidence about the economy to resolve the disagreements.

BUSINESS CYCLES

Economists generally agree that the long-run aggregate supply curve is vertical. The aggregate supply curve shifts rightward over time with advances in technology, increases in the availability of inputs, and changes in laws, property rights, regulations, and taxes that increase incentives for efficient use of technology and inputs. This process of economic growth creates an upward trend in real GDP.

Economic growth does not always occur at a steady pace, though. Fluctuations in real GDP around its trend rate of growth, accompanied by related fluctuations in investment, unemployment, and other variables, are called *business cycles.*

business cycles — 2-year to 5-year fluctuations around trends in real GDP and other, related variables

Business cycles are 2-year to 5-year fluctuations around trends in real GDP and other, related variables.

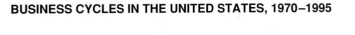

FIGURE 23.14

BUSINESS CYCLES IN THE UNITED STATES, 1970–1995

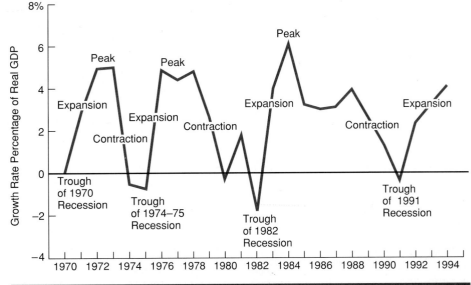

Figure 23.14 shows evidence of business cycles in the United States. Real GDP in the United States rose rapidly in the 1960s. This growth slowed in 1967 and stopped in 1970. Real GDP then increased rapidly for a few years before falling in 1974 to 1975. It began increasing again in the late 1970s before falling in 1980, rising in 1981, and falling 2.5 percent in 1982 in the deepest U.S. recession since the Great Depression of the 1930s. Real GDP then increased throughout the remainder of the 1980s until 1990 to 1991, and it began rising again in 1992. Fluctuations in unemployment, investment, and other endogenous variables accompanied these fluctuations in real GDP.

A fall in real GDP relative to its trend is called a *recession* when the drop becomes sufficiently large.

recession — a large fall in the growth of real GDP and related variables

A **recession** is a large fall in the growth of real GDP and related variables.

A depression, such as the Great Depression in the 1930s, is an especially large recession.

Some endogenous variables, such as investment and employment, move procyclically; they increase when real GDP increases and fall when real GDP falls relative to trend. Other endogenous variables, such as unemployment, move countercyclically; they fall when real GDP increases and rise when real GDP falls relative to trend. The National Bureau of Economic Research, a private, nonprofit organization, is the generally recognized authority on when recessions in the United States begin and end.

CONTROVERSIES ABOUT THE SHORT RUN

Some economists believe that business cycles result mainly from shifts in the long-run aggregate supply curve. Most economists, however, believe that short-run fluctuations are more complicated. Most assert that the short-run aggregate supply curve slopes upward, as in Figure 23.13b and that business cycles result mainly from shifts in aggregate demand, as in **Figure 23.15.**

Similarly, economists have not yet gathered enough evidence about the economy to resolve disagreements about the short-run effects of the government's monetary policy, which refers to changes in the nominal money supply, or its fiscal policy, which refers to changes in government spending, taxes, or the budget deficit (the difference between government spending and tax revenue).

Because a complete explanation of business cycles raises many controversies and entails added complications, it is useful to study equilibrium macroeconomics and long-run issues before studying business cycles. Accordingly, the next chapter discusses decisions that underlie aggregate demand, such as decisions that affect the economy's total savings and investment, that have importance in both the short run and the long run. Chapter 25 discusses the equilibrium effects of changes in underlying economic conditions such as technology, consumer preferences for spending or saving, and government fiscal policies. Chapter 26 discusses perhaps the most important issue in macroeconomics—long-run economic growth. Later chapters discuss inflation and the monetary system before returning to business cycles and completing a more systematic discussion of government policies. These later chapters will build on the less controversial economic theory that appears in the next several chapters.

FIGURE 23.15

ONE VIEW OF BUSINESS CYCLES

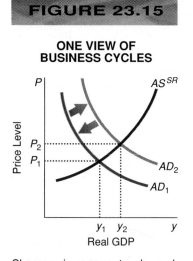

Changes in aggregate demand, which appear as shifts in the aggregate demand curve between AD_1 and AD_2, may cause increases and decreases in real GDP and the price level in the short run.

─────────────── **FOR REVIEW** ───────────────

23.8 Explain the equation of exchange and how it relates to the circular flow of economic activity.

Economists disagree about short-run macroeconomic issues. Later chapters will discuss alternative views about the short run.

Source: The Wall Street Journal, May 16, 1989.

23.9 What does the aggregate demand curve show? How is aggregate demand related to the equation of exchange and to the types of spending in the economy?

23.10 What does the aggregate supply curve show? Why is it vertical in the long run?

——————————————— QUESTIONS ———————————————

23.11 Suppose that advances in technology cause real GDP to double while the nominal money supply and the velocity of money remain unchanged.
   a. What happens to the economy's price level?
   b. Illustrate this change using the graph of aggregate supply and aggregate demand.

23.12 Suppose that real GDP grows at a rate of 3 percent per year, the rate of inflation is 2 percent per year, and velocity grows at a rate of 1 percent per year. What is the rate of growth of the nominal money supply?

CONCLUSIONS

SOME MACROECONOMIC QUESTIONS

Macroeconomics is the study of the economy as a whole, including the level and growth rate of its GDP and its price level, total employment and unemployment, interest rates, foreign exchange rates, and participation in international trade. Macroeconomics is concerned with the overall effects of changes in government spending, taxes, budget deficits, and monetary policies, as well as the effects of consumers' decisions to spend or save, firms' decisions to hire workers and invest, banks' decisions to lend, and technical progress.

DEFINITIONS AND MEASUREMENT OF MACROECONOMIC VARIABLES

Real GDP, or gross domestic product, measures a country's total output of final market goods and services. Nominal GDP is the dollar value of that output. The total income of people in an economy equals the economy's GDP plus income received from foreigners (or minus payments to foreigners).

The economy's price level is an average of the prices of its many goods and services. One measure of the price level, the GDP deflator, equals the economy's nominal GDP divided by its real GDP.

The growth rate of any economic variable is its annual percentage change. The rule of 72 says that if a variable grows at X percent per year, then it doubles after about $72/X$ years. Inflation is the growth rate of the economy's price level. A country's rate of economic growth is the growth rate of its GDP per person.

MEASURING GDP AND THE PRICE LEVEL

Economists measure real GDP in base-year dollars, which show what the value of the economy's current output would be if prices had not changed since some base year. This allows economists to compare real GDPs for different years.

The consumer price index, or CPI, and the producer price index, or PPI, are two other measures of the economy's price level. The CPI measures the average price of goods that a typical consumer buys, while the PPI measures the average price of goods that a typical producer buys. No price indexes are perfect; all have limitations.

CIRCULAR FLOW AND AGGREGATE DEMAND

The circular flow of economic activity is a simplified picture that shows the overall flows of money and goods in the economy. The nominal money supply is the total amount of money in the economy, measured in monetary units such as dollars or yen. The velocity of money is the number of times per year (on average) that money is spent in the circular flow. Therefore, nominal GDP equals the nominal money supply multiplied by the velocity of money. Since nominal GDP is real GDP multiplied by the GDP deflator, the money supply times its velocity equals real GDP times the GDP deflator. This is the equation of exchange.

A graph of the equation of exchange gives the economy's aggregate demand curve. A country's aggregate demand is the total demand for its goods and services; its aggregate demand curve shows the total quantities demanded at various price levels. Nominal aggregate demand equals the money supply times its velocity, MV, while real aggregate demand equals the money supply times velocity divided by the price level, MV/P.

Aggregate demand also equals consumption plus investment plus government purchases plus net exports. Consumption, or consumer spending, measures spending by people on goods and services for current use; investment measures spending for creation of new capital goods, such as machines, equipment, inventories, human skills, and knowledge; government purchases measures all spending by the government except transfer payments (direct payments of money to people); net exports equal the difference between sales of goods and services to other countries and purchases from those countries.

MACROECONOMIC MODELS

Macroeconomic models try to explain endogenous economic variables on the basis of exogenous variables that describe underlying economic conditions. General-equilibrium models deal with the economy as a whole. Many macroeconomists summarize the economy's equilibrium with a graph that combines aggregate demand with aggregate supply, which shows the total supply of all goods and services currently produced in the economy.

Economic growth shifts the aggregate supply curve rightward over time. Economic growth does not occur at a steady pace, though; the economy experiences fluctuations around trends in real GDP and other, related variables. These fluctuations, or business cycles, usually last about 2 to 5 years. A recession is a large fall in the growth of real GDP accompanied by changes in related variables. Economists currently lack sufficient evidence to resolve disagreements about the causes of business cycles.

LOOKING AHEAD

The next chapter discusses key factors underlying aggregate demand—interest rates, factors that affect consumption, and factors that affect investment. The material in that chapter will prove important for understanding both long-run and short-run macroeconomic issues. The subsequent chapter builds on that material to discuss the effects of changes in government policies and other underlying economic conditions. Later chapters deal with long-run economic growth and discuss inflation and the monetary system. This will lead to exploration of controversial issues involving the short-run behavior of the economy and business cycles. Discussions of government fiscal and monetary policies follow, along with consideration of the financial system, international trade, and the role of the government in the economy.

KEY TERMS

real gross domestic product (GDP)

nominal gross domestic product (GDP)

price level

GDP price deflator

annual growth rate (rate of growth)

rule of 72

inflation

rate of economic growth

nominal money supply

velocity of money

equation of exchange

aggregate demand

aggregate demand curve

consumption (consumer spending)

investment

government purchases

exports

imports

net exports (balance of international trade)

aggregate supply

aggregate supply curve

business cycles

recession

QUESTIONS AND PROBLEMS

23.13 About what fractions of U.S. GDP are spent on consumption, investment, and government purchases of goods and services?

23.14 Suppose that the nominal money supply rises by 10 percent, velocity does not change, and real GDP does not change. How much does the price level change? Suppose that the nominal money supply rises by 6 percent in some year, while velocity falls by 1 percent and real GDP rises by 3 percent. What would inflation be in that year?

23.15 Between 1870 and 1897 the GDP deflator in the United States fell in half. Use the rule of 72 to estimate the average rate of inflation during that period.

23.16 The United States imports crude oil. Suppose that an increase in the price of crude oil leads the United States to spend 1 percent more of its GDP to buy the same quantity of crude oil as before the increase. In what sense does this make the typical U.S. citizen roughly 1 percent poorer?

INQUIRIES FOR FURTHER THOUGHT

23.17 Figure 23.4 shows that in a typical recession, average real GDP per person falls by only about 2 to 5 percent, back to its level of just a few years earlier. If that level of GDP per person was satisfactory a few years earlier, why do people consider recessions to be so bad?

23.18 What factors are likely to affect consumption? Investment? Government purchases? Net exports?

23.19 What factors are likely to affect the velocity of money?

TAG SOFTWARE APPLICATIONS

TUTORIAL EXERCISES
▶ The module contains a review of the key terms from Chapter 23.

CHAPTER 23 APPENDIX — MEASURING PRODUCTION AND INCOME: NATIONAL INCOME ACCOUNTING

Table 23A.1 shows an accounting table that reports GDP for the United States in 1994. This table is in the form reported by the government and uses the government's terminology. The left side of the table shows GDP as total spending, $C + I + G + EX - IM$. This corresponds to the arrows on the right side of the circular flow in Figure 23.7. Personal consumption spending, C, was about $4.6 trillion in 1994. GDP was $6.7 trillion, so consumption was about two-thirds of GDP. Purchases of goods and services by all levels of government totaled about $1.2 trillion, or approximately 18 percent of GDP. Investment was $1 trillion, or 15 percent of GDP. Exports and imports were each about one-ninth of GDP, and net exports were only about −1.5 percent of GDP.[1]

---

[1]Exports and imports include labor and capital factor services, so $C + I + G + EX - IM$ equals gross *national* product. Subtracting the net exports of these factor services gives gross *domestic* product.

TABLE 23.A1

U.S. NATIONAL INCOME AND PRODUCT, 1994 ($ BILLIONS)

Personal consumption expenditure (C)	$4,627	Compensation of Employees	$4,005
Durables	591	Wages and salaries	3,279
Nondurables	1,394	Supplements	726
Services	2,642	Proprietors' Income	473
Gross private domestic investment (I)	1,037	Farm	39
Business fixed investment	698	Nonfarm	434
Residential investment	282	Rental income of persons	28
Inventory change	57	Corporate profits	536
Net exports (exports minus imports)	−102	After-tax profits	325
Exports (EX)	716	Profits-tax liability	206
Imports (IM)	818	Adjustments	5
Government purchases (G)	1,175	Net interest	400
Federal	437	Indirect business taxes[a]	554
State and local	738	Other items, net	25
Gross national product (GNP)	$6,737	Sum of above = net national product = $6,021	
Minus net exports of labor and		Capital consumption (depreciation)	716
capital factor services from		Gross national product (GNP)	$6,737
foreign countries (included		Income from foreign countries	
in net exports above)	0	(included in wages and net interest above)	0
Gross domestic product (GDP)	$6,737	Gross domestic product (GDP)	$6,737

[a]Includes federal, state, and local sales taxes, such as the sales tax you paid when you bought this book at the bookstore, and property taxes.

Notes: The national income and product accounts of the United States are prepared by the Bureau of Economic Analysis, which is a division of the U.S. Department of Commerce. It uses data from tax returns of people and firms and censuses (surveys) of people and firms. For further information, see Roy Webb, "The National Income and Product Accounts," *Macroeconomic Data: A User's Guide,* Federal Reserve Bank of Richmond, 1990, available free of charge by writing to the Public Service Department, Federal Reserve Bank of Richmond, P.O. Box 27622, Richmond, VA 23261. Other Federal Reserve Banks also offer similar publications on macroeconomic data. You can call or write to any of them and ask for pamphlets and publications on macroeconomic data. Also see "An Introduction to National Income Accounting," *Survey of Current Business* (published by the U.S. Department of Commerce), March 1985; and "National Income and Product Accounts: When They Are Released, Where They Are Available, and How They Are Presented," *Survey of Current Business,* July 1988. The Bureau of Economic Analysis of the Department of Commerce also calculates gross state products—GDPs for individual states. California has the highest gross state product of any U.S. state, followed by New York and Texas.

The right side of Table 23A.1 shows GDP as total income. This corresponds to the arrows on the left side of the circular flow in Figure 23.7. Firms pay people to work, and "compensation of employees" means wages and salaries plus payments that firms make for employee fringe benefits, pensions, Social Security contributions, and so on; this was just under 60 percent of GDP in 1994. "Proprietors income" is the income people earn from their own businesses. "Rental income of persons" is income from renting apartments and land, plus the money that government accountants calculate that people would pay if they rented the houses they own, plus royalties from recordings, movies, books, and so on. "Corporate profits" means total accounting profits of corporations. (Firms pay some of this to stockholders as dividends and keep the rest in the form of business savings to help pay for their investments.) After-tax corporate profits were about 4 percent of GDP. "Net interest" is the interest payments that people receive from all loans and investments except those the government provides, minus the interest payments they make to other people or businesses; net interest income was 9 percent of

GDP. "Indirect business taxes" represent income to the government, mainly sales taxes and property taxes; corporate profits taxes and indirect business taxes added to about 11 percent of GDP.

Adding these sources of income results in the "net national product." The table adds depreciation of capital because some of the investment spending on the left side goes to replace worn-out machinery and equipment. Depreciation is about 10 percent of GDP; this means that about one-tenth of total output of final goods in the economy replaces worn-out capital equipment. Adding depreciation to net national product and subtracting income from foreign countries gives gross domestic product, GDP.

The money figures in the left-hand side of Table 23A.1 represent the money flows from firms to people in Figure 23.7. The money figures on the right side represent the money flows from people to firms in Figure 23.7. These money flows both equal nominal GDP. The money flows on both sides of the circular flow are equal for the same reason that the totals on both sides of Table 23A.1 are equal: one person's spending is another person's income.

One way to measure nominal GDP is to add consumption, investment, government spending, and net exports. Table 23A.1 also shows a second way: add all types of income together. The table shows that payments for labor services account for about two-thirds to three-quarters of total GDP, while the other one-fourth to one-third represents payments for the services of capital.

PROBLEMS WITH MEASURING GDP

Measurements of most economic data are not ideal. Gross domestic product, for example, leaves out certain kinds of production such as housework, meals cooked at home, and child care provided by parents because these services are not sold for pay. When you clean your own apartment, the cleaning services do not appear in GDP. If two people clean each others' apartments, however, and pay each other $25, this adds $50 to GDP. Similarly, GDP excludes at-home child care provided by parents, but it includes child care that people pay for.

The output of the underground economy (or black market) does not appear in GDP. This includes both production of illegal goods and services and legal production that producers keep secret to avoid income taxes. Many estimates suggest that the underground economy in the United States is between 5 and 10 percent of GDP; this figure is even larger in many other countries. The underground economy in Peru a few years ago was roughly as large as its official GDP.[2]

Some goods, such as owner-occupied housing and environmental cleanups, present special problems for measurement of GDP. GDP includes payments that people make to rent houses or apartments; this is a payment for housing services. To treat the services of owner-occupied housing in a similar way, GDP includes the government's estimate of the amount of rent that the owners would pay themselves if they rented the houses to themselves. GDP also includes the costs of environmental cleanups. Ideally, GDP would include the value of these services—the amount of money that people would be willing to pay for the cleaner environ-

---

[2]See Hernando de Soto, *The Other Path* (New York: Harper & Row, 1989). Some estimates put the underground economy at more than 10 percent of GDP in Belgium, Canada, Germany, Italy, Spain, and Sweden. It appears to be smaller in Japan and Switzerland. The underground economy was very large in the socialist economies of eastern Europe and the Soviet Union, though it has declined in those countries somewhat as free markets have developed.

ment. Because this is difficult to measure, GDP includes the costs of the environmental cleanups, which may be smaller or larger than the values of the benefits.

It is important to emphasize that GDP is intended to measure production, not human happiness. GDP can rise because people work harder; it does not measure leisure time, pollution, crime, health, the quality of goods, or the quality of life. It is merely a convenient, if incomplete, summary measure of the total production of final goods sold on markets.

GDP AND GNP

While gross domestic product, GDP, measures a country's total output of final market goods and services, gross *national* product, or GNP, measures a country's total income. GNP differs from GDP when people receive income from working in foreign countries or investments in foreign countries. This income is part of GNP, but not part of GDP; GNP equals GDP plus net income received from foreign countries.

> GNP (gross national product) is the value of a country's total income in some year.

Nominal GNP is measured in dollars (or another country's money), while real GNP is measured in base-year dollars. The word *real* (as in *real* GDP or *real* GNP) refers to measurements of purchasing power, adjusted for inflation as in the earlier example of an economy that produces videos and pillows. Figure 23.7 shows the basic circular flow for an economy with zero net income from foreign countries, so GDP and GNP are equal in the figure.[3]

---

[3]The circular flow changes only slightly if an economy has positive net income from foreign countries. In that case, you need to draw another circle connecting people to foreign countries where they work or invest. The flow of money to people from foreign countries represents the income they receive from work or investments in those countries. For example, people in the United States may earn 1 million pesos from investments in Mexico. The flow of money from people to foreign countries represents their purchases of goods or assets from those countries. For example, people may spend the 1 million pesos on products from Mexico, or they may reinvest those pesos in Mexico. (When economists say *foreign countries,* they mean people or firms located in those countries, or the governments of those countries.)

INTEREST RATES, SAVINGS, AND INVESTMENT

WHAT THIS CHAPTER IS ABOUT

▶ Forces that determine interest rates and make them change

▶ Relationship between interest rates and inflation

▶ Forces that determine consumer spending, savings for the future, and investment

Your future standard of living, your wage or salary and the products that the economy makes available for you to buy, will depend partly on how the economy provides for its future. Just as people provide for their own futures by saving money, they provide for the economy's future by investing—by producing machines, equipment, buildings, tools, inventories of goods, human skills, and knowledge that the economy can use in the future and by conserving natural resources for the future.

What decisions affect the economy's future and what, in turn, affects these decisions? Which choices help an economy to grow and provide better opportunities for future generations? Which affect current opportunities?

Two key decisions that affect long-run economic opportunities involve savings and investment. These decisions are closely related to interest rates, which affect people's decisions to spend or save, and firms' decisions about how much to invest. Rising interest rates make it more attractive to save money and less attractive to borrow. Interest rates affect your opportunities to borrow to pay for an education, or for a car or a house; they also affect the returns that savers earn on their savings. Your current and future job opportunities depend partly on people's decisions to spend or save and firms' decisions to invest.

Interest rates play an important role in aggregate demand because they affect consumer spending and investment. Savings and investment also affect future aggregate supply and long-run economic growth. The incomes of future generations will depend on the resources that current generations leave for them. Your future wage or salary will depend on your future productivity, which depends partly on the investments that the economy makes today. This chapter examines these key decisions.

INTEREST RATES AND DISCOUNTED PRESENT VALUES

An interest rate is the price of a loan.

An interest rate is the price of a loan, expressed as a percentage of the amount loaned per year.

$100
1 yr.

1/12 interest year
1 yr.

EXAMPLES

If you borrow $100 for one year at an interest rate of 12 percent per year, you owe the lender $112 at the end of the year. The interest on the loan is the extra $12 you must pay; the interest rate expresses this amount as a percentage of the $100 loan; paying $12 on a loan of $100 gives an interest rate of 12 percent per year. If you borrow $200 for one year at an interest rate of 12 percent, you owe the bank $224 at the end of the year. You pay $24 in interest, which is 12 percent of the $200 loan.

not 120

If you borrow $100 for two years at an interest rate of 10 percent per year, you will owe $121 at the end of two years. The interest rate is 10 percent per year, *each year*. Your debt is $110 after one year ($100 plus $10 interest), so the interest on the second year of the loan is $11 (10 percent of $110), and you owe $121 at the end of two years. The $21 interest that you pay reflects an interest rate of 10 percent per year for two years.

INTEREST RATE FORMULA

If you borrow X dollars for one year, you must pay back:

future

$$X(1 + i)$$

$100(1.1) = 110 \quad 1\ yr.$
$110(1.1) = 121 \quad 2\ yr.$

dollars the next year, where i is the interest rate on the loan, measured as a decimal, so that an 8 percent interest rate means i is 0.08, and a 10 percent interest rate means i is 0.10.

DISCOUNTED PRESENT VALUE

One of the most useful formulas in economics is the formula for a discounted present value. The discounted present value of some amount of money in the future is its value today.

> The discounted present value of an amount of money in the future is the amount of money you would need to save now to end up with that specific amount of future money. It is the value today (at the present time) of that money.

> The main idea is simple: it is better to receive money today than in the future, because if you receive it today you can save it and earn interest. (You might put it in a bank account, for example.) If you have $100 today and a bank offers an interest rate of 5 percent per year, you can turn your money into $105 next year. This makes a dollar today more valuable than a dollar in the future.[1]

EXAMPLES

Suppose that you have $100 now and the interest rate is 6 percent per year. If you invest your money for one year, you will have $106 next year, so the discounted present value of $106 next year is $100 now. In effect, $106 next year has the same value as $100 today when the interest rate is 6 percent per year; you can trade one amount for the other. If you have $100 now, you can trade it for $106 next year by lending your money or putting it in a bank account. If someone is going to pay you $106 next year, you can trade that money for $100 now

---

[1]This statement assumes that the interest rate is higher than the inflation rate, so that the real interest rate, discussed later, is positive.

by borrowing $100 and using the $106 you receive next year to repay the loan with interest.

If the interest rate is 10 percent per year, the discounted present value of $121 paid after two years is $100. As before, $121 in two years and $100 now have the same value when the interest rate is 10 percent per year. People can trade one for the other by borrowing or lending $100 for two years. The statement that you would owe $121 if you were to borrow $100 for two years at 10 percent per year interest is the same as the statement that the discounted present value of $121 in two years at an interest rate of 10 percent per year is $100.

GENERAL FORMULA

The general formula for a discounted present value is:

$$X \text{ dollars payable 1 year from now is worth } \frac{X}{1 + i} \text{ dollars now}$$

where i is the interest rate, measured as a decimal (12 percent is the number 0.12). You are likely to use this formula many times in your future personal and business decisions. You should remember both the formula and the main idea: a dollar today is worth more than a dollar in the future, because if you have the dollar today you can save it and earn interest.

EXPLANATION If you have $X/(1 + i)$ dollars now, you can save it (put it in the bank or make another investment) and earn interest. Next year you will have:

$$\frac{X}{1 + i} (1 + i) = X \text{ dollars}$$

The value *now*, the *present value*, of the X dollars next year is $X/(1 + i)$ dollars. You can turn $X/(1 + i)$ dollars now into X dollars next year, and you can turn X dollars next year into $X/(1 + i)$ dollars now.[2] X dollars next year and $X/(1 + i)$ dollars now have the same value.[3]

USING THE FORMULA: EXAMPLES

To find the discounted present value of $20,000 next year, replace X in the formula with $20,000. If the interest rate is 8 percent, then 1 plus the decimal form of the interest rate is 1.08. Divide $20,000 by 1.08 and get $18,518.52. This is the discounted present value of $20,000 next year when the interest rate is 8 percent. If you put $18,518 in the bank this year and earn 8 percent interest, you will have $20,000 next year.

If the interest rate is 10 percent per year, the discounted present value of $100 next year is $100/(1.10), which is about $91.91. If you save $91.91 and earn 10 percent interest for a year, you will have $100 next year.

MORE COMPLICATED APPLICATIONS

1. Apply the general formula twice to find the discounted present value of $1,000 paid in two years. Suppose that in 1996 the interest rate is 10 percent per year. Someone will pay you $1,000 in 1998, and you want to find

---

[2] You can do this by borrowing X dollars now and repaying $X/(1 + i)$ dollars next year.

[3] Notice that the term *discounted present value* refers to the fact that X dollars in the future has the same economic value as $X/(1 + i)$ dollars at the present time.

the discounted present value, in 1996, of that money. First, apply the formula to find out how much $1,000 payable in 1998 is worth in 1997; the formula shows that it is worth $1,000/(1.10), or $909.09 in 1997. Then apply the formula again to find out how much $909.09 in 1997 is worth in 1996. (This time, substitute $909.09 for X in the formula.) The formula shows that it is worth $909.09/(1.10), or $826.45. The discounted present value of $1,000 paid two years from now is $826.45 if the interest rate is 10 percent per year.

2. Apply the general formula N times to find the discounted present value of $1,000 in N years from now. The formula for the discounted present value of X dollars paid N years from now is:

next N year

$$X \text{ dollars payable } N \text{ years from now is worth } \frac{X}{(1 + i)^N} \text{ dollars now}$$

where i is the interest rate per year.

3. Suppose that someone will pay you $1,000 one year from now and another $1,000 two years from now. What is the discounted present value of these payments? The discounted present value of $1,000 paid one year from now is $1,000/(1 + i). The discounted present value of $1,000 paid two years from now is $1,000/(1 + i)^2$. So the discounted present value of both payments is:

$$\frac{\$1,000}{1 + i} + \frac{\$1,000}{(1 + i)^2}$$

If the interest rate is 10 percent per year, this is $909.09 plus $826.45, or $1,735.54.

4. The discounted present value of $1,000 per year paid *every year, forever* turns out to be:

$$\frac{\$1,000}{i}$$

If the interest rate is 10 percent per year, this equals $10,000. This is also a rough approximation to the discounted present value of $1,000 paid every year for more than about 30 years.[4]

─────────────── **FOR REVIEW** ───────────────

24.1 What is an interest rate?

24.2 What is a discounted present value? Explain it in words.

─────────────── **QUESTIONS** ───────────────

24.3 If the interest rate is 10 percent per year, what is the discounted present value of $200 paid one year from now? What if the interest is 5 percent?

24.4 If the interest rate is 10 percent per year, what is the discounted present value of $20,000 two years from now?

──────────────────────

[4]The discounted present value of $1,000 paid every year for 30 years is $9,370 if the interest rate is 10 percent per year.

REAL AND NOMINAL INTEREST RATES

In 1990, interest rates reached more than 1,000 percent per year in Argentina and Brazil, but they were only about 35 percent per year in Mexico and 8 percent per year in the United States and Japan. Why do interest rates differ so much between countries? Are they connected with inflation, which was above 1,000 percent per year in Argentina and Brazil, much lower in Mexico, and even lower in the United States and Japan?

The interest rates that people usually talk about or read about are nominal interest rates. *is the actual rate of interest. The extra money borrowers have to pay back to lending, in excess of the loan amount expressed as % per year of the loan.*

nominal interest rate — the annual dollar interest payment on a loan expressed as a percentage of the dollar amount of the loan

The **nominal interest** rate on a loan is the annual dollar interest payment expressed as a percentage of the dollar amount of the loan.

The formula for the discounted present value of a certain amount of money to be delivered in the future uses the nominal interest rate. The nominal interest rate is actually a relative price.

> 1 plus the nominal interest rate is the relative price of $1 this year in terms of dollars next year.

In other words, people can buy $500 this year at a price of $500(1 + i) next year; people do this when they borrow $500. (If the nominal interest rate is 6 percent per year, then 1 plus the nominal interest rate is 1.06, so the relative price of $500 this year is 1.06 times $500, or $530 next year. This is the amount that a borrower must repay on the loan.)

real interest rate — inflation-adjusted interest rate; equals the relative price of goods this year in terms of the same goods next year, minus 1

The real interest rate corrects the nominal interest rate for inflation; the real interest rate is sometimes called the *inflation-adjusted interest rate*. Economists define the real interest rate as the relative price of a single good at two points in time.

> 1 plus the **real interest rate** is the relative price of goods this year in terms of the same goods next year. (*Percentage increase in purchasing power*)
>
> $r = i - \pi$

To see how real interest rates correct nominal interest rates for inflation, suppose that you lend someone $100 for one year at 10 percent interest; you get back $110 at the end of the year, which is 10 percent more money than you originally loaned to the borrower. If inflation has occurred, however, the borrower repays you in dollars that have lower purchasing power. Each dollar buys less at the end of the year than it bought at the beginning of the year. The nominal interest rate shows how much you gain in dollar terms from the loan; the real interest rate adjusts for inflation to measure your gain in purchasing power.

FISHER EQUATION

Real and nominal interest rates are connected by a formula called the *Fisher equation,* named after the famous American economist, Irving Fisher. The Fisher equation says:[5]

$$i = r + \pi$$

nominal interest rate ← i · *real* r · π → *rate of inflation*

where i is the nominal interest rate, r is the real interest rate, and π is the rate of inflation.

---

[5]This version of the Fisher equation is an approximation for interest that is not continuously compounded; the actual equation in that case is $(1 + r)\, e^{\pi} - 1$ where e is the natural exponent. The formula in the text is exact for continuously compounded interest.

The Fisher equation shows why countries with high rates of inflation have high nominal interest rates. Whatever the level of the real interest rate, a high rate of inflation, π, causes a high nominal interest rate, i. **Figure 24.1** shows the nominal interest rate, inflation rate, and real interest rate in the United States since 1955.[6] Notice that the big increases in the nominal interest rate in the 1970s accompanied increases in the rate of inflation, while the real interest rate fell. Rearranging the Fisher equation gives the real interest rate in terms of the nominal interest rate and inflation:

$$r = i - \pi$$

EXAMPLES

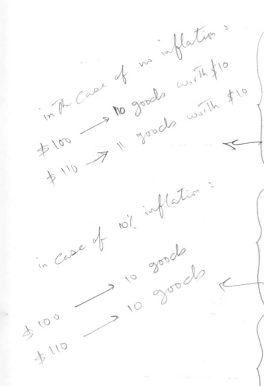

Suppose that the nominal interest rate is 10 percent per year. If you lend someone $100, that borrower pays you $110 next year. If there is no inflation, then π equals 0 and the Fisher equation gives a real interest rate of 10 percent ($r = 0.10 - 0 = 0.10$). You have 10 percent more dollars and 10 percent more purchasing power. (You can buy 10 percent more goods next year with $110 than you could buy this year with $100.) Your 10 percent gain in purchasing power means that you can buy 11 goods worth $10 each next year instead of 10 goods this year, so the relative price of each good this year is 1.10 goods next year. In other words, 1 plus the real interest rate is 1.10, so the real interest rate is 0.10, or 10 percent per year.

Now suppose that inflation is 10 percent per year while the nominal interest rate remains at 10 percent per year. In this case, the Fisher equation gives a real interest rate of zero (because $r = 0.10 - 0.10 = 0$). Prices next year will be 10 percent higher than prices this year, so you will need $110 next year just to buy the *same* amount of goods you could have bought for $100 this year. Lending money gives you a 10 percent gain in dollars, but no increase in your purchasing power. (This is the meaning of a zero real interest rate.) The relative price of goods now in terms of goods in the future is 1.

Finally, suppose that the nominal interest rate is 10 percent per year and inflation is 4 percent per year. In this case, the Fisher equation gives a real interest rate of 6 percent per year, because 0.10 minus 0.04 equals 0.06. If you lend $100 for one year at 10 percent interest, you collect $110 at the end of the year. The $110 gives you 6 percent more purchasing power next year than you would have had with $100 this year. In other words, the relative price of goods this year in terms of goods next year is 1.06. Since this relative price is 1 plus the real interest rate, the real interest rate is 6 percent per year.

These three examples illustrate an important point: the real interest rate states the interest rate in terms of the purchasing power that a borrower pays and a lender receives on a loan.

RELATIVE PRICES OVER TIME

Higher real interest rates mean that goods now (this year) are relatively more expensive in terms of future goods in the sense that people sacrifice more future goods for each good they buy now. This occurs because higher real interest rates give people higher returns, measured in purchasing power, on their savings.

---

[6]For the nominal interest rate, the figure shows the 3-month Treasury bill rate, which is the interest rate that the federal government pays to borrow money for three months.

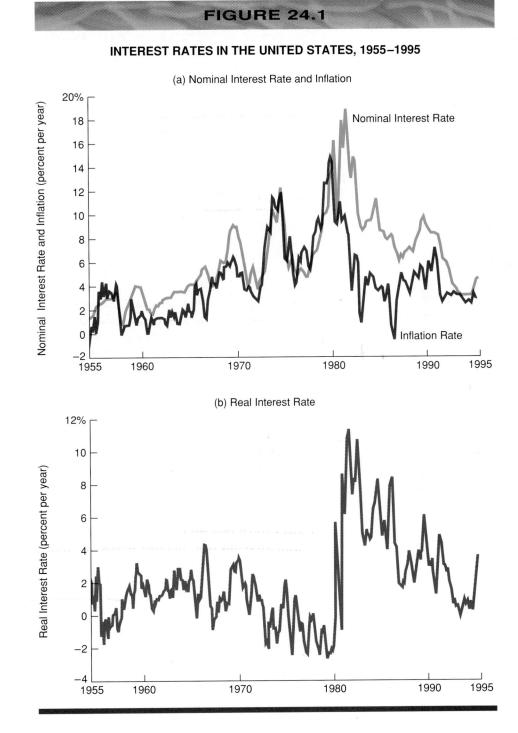

FIGURE 24.1

INTEREST RATES IN THE UNITED STATES, 1955–1995

(a) Nominal Interest Rate and Inflation

(b) Real Interest Rate

Lower real interest rates make goods now relatively cheaper in terms of future goods; people sacrifice fewer future goods for each good they buy now. This is the same as saying that future goods are relatively more expensive measured in terms of current goods.

EXAMPLE

Suppose that soda pop costs $0.50 per can this year and is expected to cost $0.55 per can next year (a 10 percent increase). Bob loans Tom $10.00 for one year at a 15 percent nominal interest rate; Tom will repay $11.50 to Bob next year. If Bob had used his $10.00 to buy soda pop this year, he could have bought 20 cans, so Bob's opportunity cost of loaning Tom $10.00 is 20 cans of soda pop this year. What does Bob get from the loan? With the $11.50 he collects from Tom next year, if soda pop really does cost $0.55, he will be able to buy (almost) 21 cans of soda pop next year.[7] This is a 5 percent increase in soda compared to the 20 cans he would be able to buy this year. This implies that the real rate of interest on the loan, measured in soda pop, is 5 percent per year; the relative price of soda pop this year in terms of soda pop next year is 1.05.

If the nominal interest rate is 20 percent per year instead of 15 percent per year, then Tom repays Bob $12.00 next year. In this case, Tom would have enough money to buy (almost) 22 cans of soda pop next year; the relative price of soda pop this year in terms of soda pop next year would be 1.10. The higher nominal interest rate, combined with the same rate of inflation of soda-pop prices, means that the real interest rate is higher; the higher real interest rate means that the relative price of soda pop this year is higher in terms of soda pop next year.

UNCERTAINTY AND EXPECTED INFLATION

In real life, inflation is uncertain. No one knows what the rate of inflation will be over the next year. The Fisher equation still applies, though. The term π actually represents the *expected* rate of inflation, the rate of inflation that people, on average, believe will occur.

Uncertainty about inflation also creates uncertainty about the real interest rate on a loan. For example, if the nominal interest rate is 10 percent and people do not know whether inflation will be 3 percent, 4 percent, or 5 percent over the next year, then they do not know whether the real interest rate will turn out to be 7 percent, 6 percent, or 5 percent. If people expect inflation of 4 percent, then the expected real interest rate is 6 percent. Economists distinguish the expected (or ex-ante) real interest rate from the actual (or ex-post) real interest rate, which may range from 7 percent to 5 percent in this example, depending on what inflation turns out to be.1

expected real interest rate — the nominal interest rate minus the expected rate of inflation

actual real interest rate — the nominal interest rate minus the actual rate of inflation during the period of the loan

The **expected real interest rate** equals the nominal interest rate minus the expected rate of inflation. The **actual real interest rate** equals the nominal interest rate minus the actual rate of inflation during the period of the loan; no one knows what the actual real interest rate will be until the time for repayment of the loan arrives.

When this chapter refers to the real interest rate, it means the expected real interest rate.

---

[7]He is $0.05 short of the price of 21 cans. This reflects the fact that the Fisher equation is an approximation when interest is not continuously compounded. See footnote 5.

─────────────────────── **FOR REVIEW** ───────────────────────

24.5 What is the real interest rate? Explain in words. What relative price equals 1 plus the real interest rate?

24.6 What is the relationship between the real interest rate, the nominal interest rate, and the expected rate of inflation?

24.7 What is the difference between the expected real interest rate and the actual real interest rate?

─────────────────────── **QUESTIONS** ───────────────────────

24.8 When the real interest rate rises, do current goods become cheaper or more expensive compared to goods in the future? Explain.

24.9 Concert tickets cost $20 now, but the price will rise to $24 next year. The nominal interest rate is 10 percent per year. What is the relative price of concert tickets this year in terms of concert tickets next year?

SAVINGS AND THE SUPPLY OF LOANS

The real interest rate affects all decisions that involve time, including savings decisions and investment decisions. An increase in the real interest rate raises total savings, reduces total consumption spending, and reduces investment. In this way, the real interest rate plays an important role in aggregate demand.

SAVINGS AND CONSUMPTION

Consumption measures consumer purchases of goods and services for current use; savings includes income preserved for future use (all income not currently spent or paid in taxes).

disposable income — after-tax income

savings — disposable income minus consumption

> **Disposable income** is after-tax income. **Savings** equals disposable income minus consumption.[8]

An equation can state savings as:

$$S = Y - T - C$$

where S is savings, Y is income before taxes, T is taxes (so $Y - T$ is disposable income), and C is consumption.

People save so they can consume more in the future. Each person's decision to spend now or save is really a choice of when to spend—now or in the future. This decision depends on wealth, disposable income, the real interest rate, and tastes or preferences for spending now versus waiting (a person's degree of patience or willingness to plan for the future).

AVAILABLE OPPORTUNITIES

A person's consumption/savings decision depends on individual tastes and available opportunities (feasible choices). This discussion begins with those opportunities.

─────────────────

[8]The word *savings* here means private savings, which includes savings by households and business firms, but not government savings.

[handwritten: The net value of all the assets a person owns]

wealth — the total value of savings accumulated in the past plus the discounted present value of expected future labor income after taxes (or human capital)

Wealth is the total value of savings accumulated in the past plus the discounted present value of expected future labor income after taxes (or human capital).[9]

Increases in wealth raise consumption and decreases in wealth reduce it.

Think about a simple case with an interest rate of 5 percent per year. A person has no savings, earns $30,000 this year, and will earn $30,000 next year. (To keep the discussion from getting too complicated, think about only two years.) This person's wealth is:

$$\$30,000 + \frac{\$30,000}{1.05} = \$58,571$$

[handwritten left margin: 30,000 − 58,571 = 28,571   discounted present value]

because the discounted present value of $30,000 paid one year from now is $28,571 at an interest rate of 5 percent per year.

What are this person's opportunities for total consumption spending? If she saves all of this year's income (spending nothing on consumption this year) she will earn 5 percent interest on $30,000 savings ($1,500 interest) and she will have $61,500 to spend on consumption next year. **Table 24.1** shows that she could also spend $20,000 on consumption this year, save $10,000 and earn $500 interest, providing $40,500 to spend on consumption next year. Or she could spend her $30,000 income on consumption this year, save nothing, and spend next year's $30,000 income on consumption next year. Finally, she could borrow and spend more than $30,000 on consumption this year. If she borrows $5,000 and spends $35,000 on consumption this year, she must repay $5,250 next year, leaving $24,750 to spend on consumption next year. If she borrowed $28,571, she would need all of next year's income to repay the loan, leaving no money to spend on consumption next year.

Figure 24.2 graphs these consumption opportunities as a budget line for consumption this year and consumption next year. This budget line shows the various combinations of consumption that this person can afford.

budget line — a graph of a person's consumption opportunities

A **budget line** between consumption this year and consumption next year shows a person's opportunities for consumption each year.

A budget line shows the various combinations of goods that a person can afford to buy with a limited budget. Each point in the graph represents a possible choice of consumption this year and next year. The person can afford any point on the budget line, such as Points A, B, or C, but not points above the budget line. The chosen point depends on individual tastes. For example, someone might choose Point A with consumption this year of $20,000 and savings of $10,000. Evidence suggests that most people, most of the time, prefer to smooth their consumption over time. They would rather spend roughly the same amount each year than spend a lot in one year and carry over little to spend the next year (or vice versa—

---

[9]For example, a person who has $10,000 invested in bank accounts and the stock market and personal goods (a car, a stereo, and so on) worth $12,000 has $22,000 in accumulated savings. Suppose that this person expects to earn $30,000 per year after taxes for the next 40 years and the interest rate is 10 percent per year. That person's human capital is the discounted present value of $30,000 per year every year for the next 40 years, which is:

$$\frac{\$30,000}{1.05} + \frac{\$30,000}{1.05^2} + \frac{\$30,000}{1.05^3} + \cdots + \frac{\$30,000}{1.05^{39}} + \frac{\$30,000}{1.05^{40}} = \$514,773$$

[handwritten: ? ? why not 1.10]

(This assumes that the person collects the first $30,000 payment 1 year from now.) The person's wealth sums to $536,773.

TABLE 24.1

CURRENT AND FUTURE CONSUMPTION OPPORTUNITIES WITH AN INTEREST RATE OF 5 PERCENT PER YEAR

Consumption Spending This Year	Saving or Borrowing	Consumption Spending Next Year
$ 0	Save $30,000	$61,500
20,000	Save $10,000	40,500
30,000	Save $0	30,000
35,000	Borrow −$5,000	24,750
58,571	Borrow −$28,571	0

This table shows opportunities for a person who earns $30,000 in each of two years when the interest rate is 5 percent per year. For simplicity, this table considers only two years.

FIGURE 24.2

BUDGET LINE FOR CONSUMPTION THIS YEAR AND NEXT YEAR

If income is $30,000 this year and $30,000 next year, and if the interest rate is 5 percent per year, points on this budget line, such as Points A, B, or C, represent feasible consumption choices.

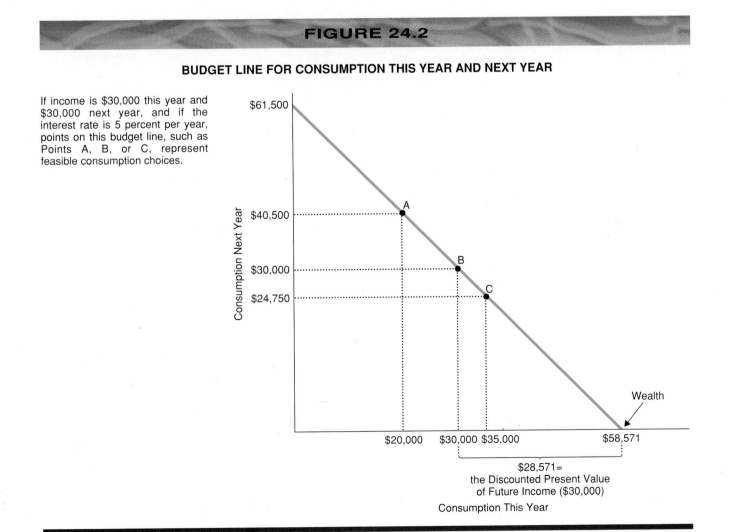

spending very little one year and a large amount the next year). People who prefer to save more for the future and consume less now are said to be more *patient;* aggregate consumption and savings depend partly on the average degree of patience of people in the economy.

EFFECTS OF CHANGES IN OPPORTUNITIES

Changes in income and interest rates affect consumption and savings decisions by changing people's opportunities. First, think about a permanent increase in income in the earlier example (an increase in both years) from $30,000 to $40,000. This expands consumption opportunities and shifts the budget line, as in **Figure 24.3,** from BL$_1$ to BL$_2$. The new budget line shows that the person has become richer and can afford more consumption both this year and next year. The consumption point that a person actually chooses depends on individual tastes. Evidence indicates that people usually respond to permanent increases in income by raising consumption spending in both years (along with income), and that permanent increases in income have little effect on savings; a typical person's consumption may move from Point B to Point B′ in Figure 24.3.

FIGURE 24.3

PERMANENT INCREASE IN INCOME

A permanent increase in income from $30,000 to $40,000 shifts the budget line outward without changing its slope. Wealth rises from $58,571 to $78,095.

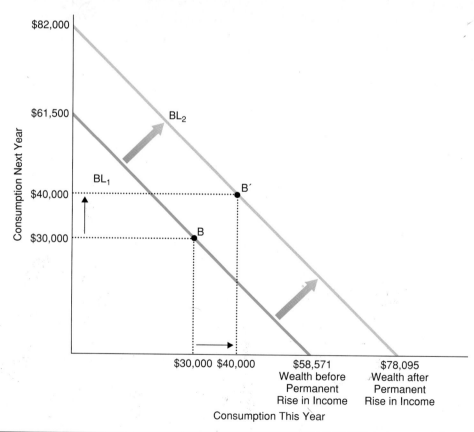

Suppose instead that the increase in income to $40,000 is only temporary, and next year's income remains at $30,000. This does not raise consumption opportunities as much as a permanent increase in income would, perhaps shifting the budget line from BL_1 to BL_3, as in **Figure 24.4.** A temporary increase in income makes people richer, but not as rich as they would have become if the income increase were permanent. Evidence indicates that people tend to spend part of the temporary increase in income and save the other part, so they can spend more on consumption in each year. (They smooth their consumption over time.) For example, a person's consumption might move from Point B to Point B′ in Figure 24.4. Temporary increases in future income raise both consumption and savings.

Now think about an increase in (expected) *future* income. Income this year remains at $30,000, but income next year rises to $40,000. This raises consumption opportunities as in **Figure 24.5,** and the budget line shifts from BL_1 to BL_4. Evidence indicates that people tend to save less or borrow more when they expect higher incomes in the future. (Again, they smooth their consumption over time.) For example, a person's consumption might move from Point B to Point B′ in Figure 24.5. Increases in expected future income raise consumption and reduce savings.

FIGURE 24.4

TEMPORARY INCREASE IN INCOME

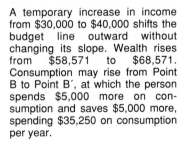

A temporary increase in income from $30,000 to $40,000 shifts the budget line outward without changing its slope. Wealth rises from $58,571 to $68,571. Consumption may rise from Point B to Point B′, at which the person spends $5,000 more on consumption and saves $5,000 more, spending $35,250 on consumption per year.

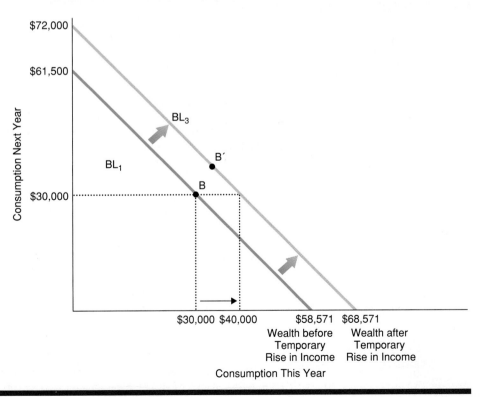

FIGURE 24.5

INCREASE IN FUTURE (EXPECTED) INCOME

An increase in expected future income from $30,000 to $40,000 shifts the budget line outward without changing its slope. Wealth rises from $58,571 to $68,095. Consumption may rise from Point B to Point B′, at which the person spends $5,000 more on consumption by borrowing $5,000 and spending $34,750 on consumption next year (which equals $40,000 minus the loan repayment of $5,250).

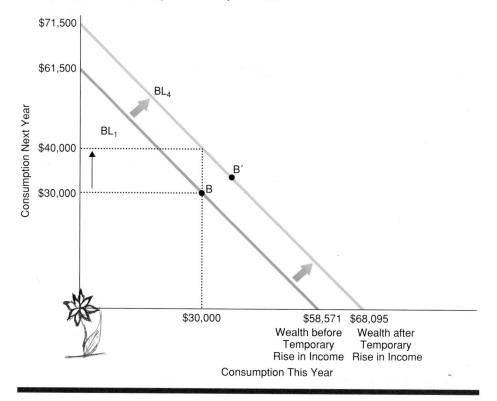

Finally, think about an increase in the real interest rate. This raises the relative price of goods this year in terms of goods next year, so it makes the budget line steeper, as in **Figure 24.6.** An increase in the real interest rate has two effects: an income effect and a substitution effect. (See Chapter 4.) The income effect is easy to understand. Savers gain from higher interest rates because they earn more interest on their savings, so they may move from Point A to Point A′. Borrowers lose from higher interest rates because they must pay more interest on their loans, so they may move from Point C to Point C′. A person who spends all available income each year and does not save or borrow (Point B) could go on doing the same thing despite the change in the real interest rate; a change in the real interest rate would have no income effect for this person.

The substitution effect of an increase in the real interest rate is more subtle. It results from the fact that the rise in the real interest rate creates new opportunities that make savings more advantageous. If the real interest rate is 5 percent, a person can buy 105 goods next year for every 100 fewer goods bought this year; if the real interest rate rises to 10 percent, that person can buy 110 more goods next year by buying 100 fewer goods this year. An increase in the real interest rate makes savings more attractive and tends to raise savings.

Overall, an increase in the real interest rate tends to raise savings and reduce consumption because the income effect of a change in the interest rate tends to

FIGURE 24.6

INCREASE IN THE REAL INTEREST RATE

An increase in the real interest rate from 5 percent per year to 10 percent per year rotates the budget line and makes it steeper. A saver who originally consumes at Point A now consumes at Point A′. A borrower who originally consumes at Point C now consumes at Point C′. A person who neither borrows or lends originally consumes at Point B, and switches to Point B′ because of the increased benefit of saving money (the substitution effect of the change in the real interest rate).

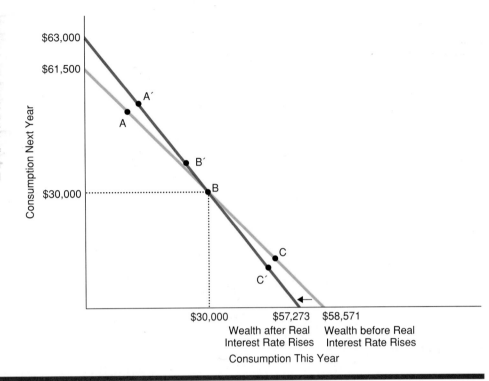

FIGURE 24.7

SAVINGS AND THE REAL INTEREST RATE

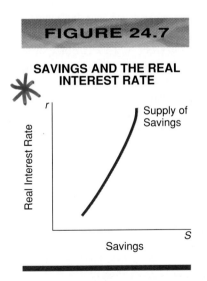

marginal propensity to consume — the increase in consumption when disposable income rises by $1

cancel out across borrowers and lenders in the economy. Because there is a borrower for every lender, the *average* person in the economy tends to be neither a borrower or a lender; the average person consumes near Point B in Figure 24.6. This leaves the substitution effect as the main effect of a change in the real interest rate on aggregate consumption, so an increase in the real interest rate tends to reduce consumption and increase savings, as in **Figure 24.7.**

The decrease in consumption spending this year and the increase in savings and future consumption spending that result from an increase in the real interest rate provide an example of intertemporal substitution in consumption, or substitution between different times.

CONSUMPTION AND INCOME   This discussion suggests that the effect of a change in income on consumption and savings depends on whether the change is temporary or permanent. In fact, most changes in aggregate (total) income are close to permanent, so aggregate consumption spending in the economy tends to move fairly closely with income, as **Figure 24.8** shows. The increase in consumption that accompanies a $1 rise in income is sometimes called the *marginal propensity to consume.*

The **marginal propensity to consume** is the increase in consumption when disposable income rises by $1.

MPC

FIGURE 24.8

U.S. CONSUMPTION AND INCOME, 1947–1994

A $1,000 increase in income has been associated, on average, with a $900 increase in consumption, so the marginal propensity to consume has averaged about 0.9.

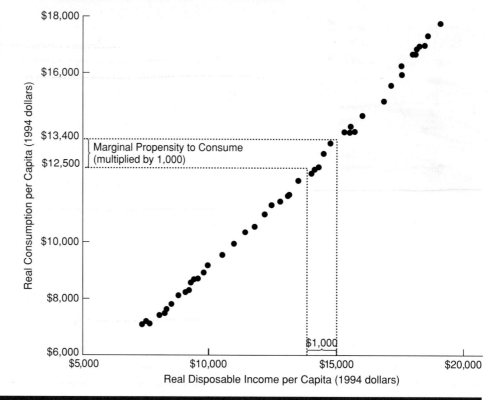

The marginal propensity to consume usually ranges between 0 and 1. For example, if an increase in disposable income of $1,000 raises consumption by $900 and savings by $100, the marginal propensity to consume would be 0.9. (This is about the average in aggregate U.S. data.) The earlier discussion implies that a permanent increase in income creates a larger marginal propensity to consume than a temporary increase in income.

SUPPLY OF LOANS

Savers lend money to borrowers, so the savings supply curve in Figure 24.7 also shows the supply of loans. When a saver puts money in a bank account or a money-market account, or buys Treasury bills, corporate bonds, or other financial assets (discussed in a later chapter), the saver becomes a lender. Banks and other financial firms that lend money often serve as intermediaries in this process. They bring borrowers and lenders together by finding people to borrow savers' money. Savers are lenders, and the supply of savings is a supply of loans, as in **Figure 24.9**.[10]

---

[10]If a person saves to start a business, then we can think of that person as lending money to her own business.

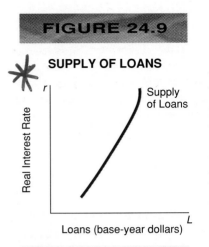

FIGURE 24.9

SUPPLY OF LOANS

Real Interest Rate (vertical axis, *r*)

Supply of Loans

Loans (base-year dollars) (horizontal axis, *L*)

supply of loans — the amounts of money that people would want to save and lend at various possible real interest rates

The **supply of loans** shows the amounts of money that people would want to save and lend at various possible real interest rates.

Economists can measure the quantity of loans supplied in either nominal terms (dollars) or real terms (base-year dollars). The supply curve for loans slopes upward, as in Figure 24.9, because an increase in the real interest rate tends to raise total savings. Chapter 24 Appendix discusses another source of the supply of loans: loans from foreigners that reflect a country's trade deficit.

Total savings by people and businesses in the United States equal about $1 trillion per year. About three-fourths of this money reflects loans to businesses to pay for investments;[11] the other one-fourth reflects loans to the federal government, which borrows money to pay for spending in excess of its tax receipts, and a small fraction reflects loans to households to buy cars and houses, to take vacations, and for other purposes.

─────────────── **FOR REVIEW** ───────────────

24.10 How does a temporary increase in income affect consumption and savings? How does a permanent increase in income affect consumption and savings?

24.11 How does an increase in the real interest rate affect the amount that people save and the amount that they spend on consumption? Explain why.

─────────────── **QUESTIONS** ───────────────

24.12 How would an increase in expected future income affect the supply of loans?

24.13 How would a temporary increase in income affect the supply of loans?

INVESTMENT AND THE DEMAND FOR LOANS

investment — an increase in the economy's capital stock, which includes its machinery, equipment, buildings, tools, inventories of goods for future use, human skills, and knowledge

demand for investment — the demand for new capital goods; the amount of money that firms would want to invest at various possible interest rates

While the supply of loans represents savings, the demand for loans mainly represents investment. Firms borrow money to pay for new investments in equipment, machinery, buildings, research, and other capital goods. The demand for investment creates a demand for loans. Combining the demand for loans with the supply determines the equilibrium real interest rate, which helps to determine consumption, savings, investment, and real GDP in macroeconomic equilibrium.

Investment is an increase in the economy's capital stock, which includes its machinery, equipment, buildings, tools, inventories of goods for future use, human skills, and knowledge.

Higher investment this year increases the economy's capital stock, K in the future.

The **demand for investment** refers to the demand for new capital goods; it shows the amount of money that firms would want to invest at various possible interest rates.

───────────────

[11]This includes money that firms borrow from themselves, that is, investments funded by their own profits.

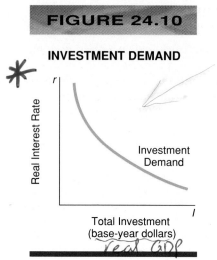

FIGURE 24.10

INVESTMENT DEMAND

Real Interest Rate (vertical axis, *r*)

Investment Demand

Total Investment (base-year dollars)
real GDP

The demand for investment, like the demand for consumption goods, is part of aggregate demand.

An increase in the real interest rate reduces the quantity of investment demanded. This makes the investment demand curve slope downward, as in **Figure 24.10.** It slopes downward because the real interest rate is an opportunity cost of investment. The investor must pay the interest rate to borrow money for the investment, so fewer investments are profitable when the real interest rate is higher.

DOWNWARD SLOPE OF THE INVESTMENT DEMAND CURVE

It is easy to become confused about the effect of the real interest rate on investment. You might think, it is more profitable to invest my money if I can earn a high interest rate on my investment, so I would be willing to invest more at a higher interest rate. This statement confuses *investment* with *savings;* a higher interest rate means that you receive greater future benefits from your savings, but *investment* refers to the creation of new capital goods, such as machines or factories. At a higher real interest rate, a firm must pay more interest if it borrows money to pay for the new machine. (If it uses its own money to pay for the machine, it sacrifices more by spending the money on the machine rather than lending the money.)

If a business firm borrows money to pay for its new capital goods, it must pay interest on the loan. A higher real interest rate raises the cost of the investment. If a firm has enough of its own money to pay for its new capital goods, it need not borrow. In this case, the interest rate is an opportunity cost of investment; if the firm did not use the money to invest, it could lend the money to someone else and earn interest on the loan, or put the money in a bank account and collect interest. A higher real interest rate raises the opportunity cost of the investment, so the interest rate is a cost of investment, whether a firm has its own money to finance the investment or it must borrow the money. A rise in the real interest rate lowers investment because it allows fewer investment projects to remain profitable.

EXAMPLE

Bo's Sports Store must evaluate an idea for an investment project. The firm can spend $20,000 to buy a new machine to produce 6,000 baseball caps that the store can sell for $1.00 per cap at the end of each of the next four years. If Bo's spends $20,000 now, the store gets $6,000 at the end of one year, another $6,000 at the end of the second year, another $6,000 at the end of the third year, and $6,000 more at the end of the fourth year. After the fourth year, the machine becomes worthless. The discounted present value of the extra revenues the store will earn from cap sales is:

$$\frac{\$6{,}000}{1+i} + \frac{\$6{,}000}{(1+i)^2} + \frac{\$6{,}000}{(1+i)^3} + \frac{\$6{,}000}{(1+i)^4}$$

Should Bo's invest in the machine? This discounted present value exceeds the $20,000 cost, making the investment profitable, if the interest rate is less than 7.71 percent per year. (You can verify this with a calculator.) At a higher interest rate, however, the discounted present value of the revenues would be less than the $20,000 cost and the investment would be unprofitable. Because the economy includes many firms and many different investment projects, any increase in interest rates causes some investment projects to become unprofitable, and this creates a downward-sloping investment demand curve.

WHY THE *REAL* INTEREST RATE MATTERS

It is important to understand why the real interest rate, not the nominal interest rate, affects investment. If the nominal interest rate and expected inflation rise equally, the Fisher equation, $i = r + \pi$, indicates that the real interest rate does not change. This change in the nominal interest rate does not affect investment because the increase in expected inflation raises the firm's expected income in the future from its investment. This increase in future dollars earned offsets the increase in the nominal interest rate in the discounted present value formula, so only changes in the real interest rate affect investment, not changes in the nominal interest rate due to changes in expected inflation.

EXAMPLE

Suppose that expected inflation in the last example is zero and the real interest rate is 5 percent per year. The Fisher equation gives a nominal interest rate of 5 percent per year. In this case, the discounted present value of the store's extra revenues from its investment is $21,276, so it earns a $1,276 profit on the investment.

Now suppose that expected inflation is 10 percent per year and the real interest rate remains at 5 percent per year. The Fisher equation gives a nominal interest rate of about 15 percent per year. In fact, as footnote 5 explained, when interest is not continuously compounded, the Fisher equation has another term, so the nominal interest rate is actually 16.04 percent per year. Because expected inflation is 10 percent per year, the price of baseball caps is expected to rise at 10 percent per year from its current level of $1.00 to $1.105 next year, $1.2214 two years from now (another 10 percent increase), $1.3499 three years from now, and $1.4918 four years from now. The discounted present value of the store's extra revenue from buying the machine is:

$$\frac{(6,000)(\$1.105)}{1.1604} + \frac{(6,000)(\$1.2214)}{1.1604^2} + \frac{(6,000)(\$1.3499)}{1.1604^3} + \frac{(6,000)(\$1.4918)}{1.1604^4}$$

$$= \$21,276$$

So the store earns the same $1,276 profit as it earns with zero expected inflation. This example shows that if the real interest rate remains unchanged, changes in the nominal interest rate associated with changes in expected inflation have no effect on the profitability of an investment.

DEMAND FOR LOANS

demand for loans — the amounts of money that people, firms, and the government would want to borrow at various possible real interest rates

The **demand for loans** shows the amount of money that people, firms, and the government would want to borrow at various possible real interest rates.

The demand for loans has two main parts: loan demand by firms to pay for investments and loan demand by the government to finance its budget deficit.[12] Firms often borrow money to pay for investments, so investment demand creates a demand for loans. If firms pay for investment projects with money they already have, economists count this as borrowing the money from themselves. Because

---

[12]For simplicity, this section discusses only investments by firms, but this category also includes consumer borrowing for investments in houses, cars, and other durable goods.

investors are borrowers, investment demand is one source of the demand for loans, as illustrated in **Figure 24.11.**

The government budget deficit is the second major source of the demand for loans.

$$GBD = G - T$$

government budget deficit —
government spending in excess of tax receipts

The **government budget deficit** in some year equals government spending in excess of tax receipts, $G - T$, during that year.

When the government must finance a budget deficit, it borrows money. The government spends G dollars, receives T dollars in taxes, and borrows the other $G - T$ dollars. For example, the U.S. government had a budget deficit of $140 billion per year in 1994, meaning that the federal government borrowed $140 billion that year. The combined budget deficit of federal, state, and local governments in the United States was $112 billion that year, meaning that units of government in the United States borrowed $112 billion. **Figure 24.12** shows the connection between investment demand, the government budget deficit, and the demand for loans.

The total demand for loans equals investment demand plus the government budget deficit.

$$D_L = I_D + GBD$$

LOAN MARKET EQUILIBRIUM

Figure 24.13 shows equilibrium in the loans market at the point where the quantity of loans demanded equals the quantity supplied. The equilibrium real interest rate is r_1 and the equilibrium quantity of loans—equilibrium savings—is S_1. To find the equilibrium nominal interest rate, use the Fisher equation and add the expected rate of inflation to the equilibrium real interest rate.

Equilibrium investment in Figure 24.13 (the quantity of investment demanded at the equilibrium interest rate) is S_1 minus the government budget deficit, or I_1. For example, if the equilibrium quantity of loans is $950 billion and the government budget deficit is $150 billion, then equilibrium investment is $800 billion.

Equilibrium in the loans market is closely connected with equilibrium in aggregate demand and aggregate supply discussed in the previous chapter. As Chapter 24 Appendix shows, when the quantity of loans supplied equals the quan-

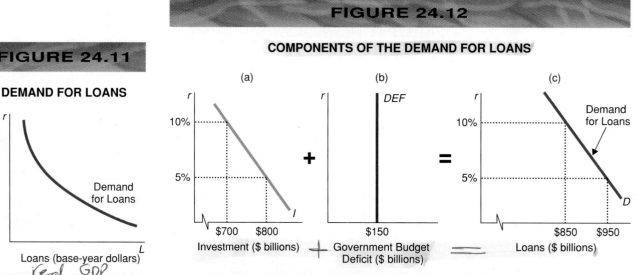

FIGURE 24.12

COMPONENTS OF THE DEMAND FOR LOANS

FIGURE 24.11

DEMAND FOR LOANS

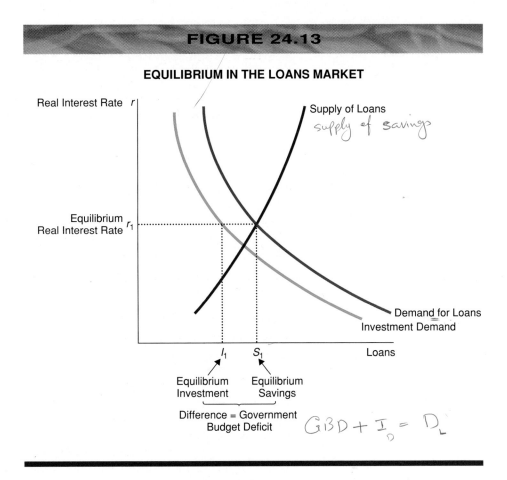

FIGURE 24.13

EQUILIBRIUM IN THE LOANS MARKET

Real Interest Rate r

Supply of Loans

supply of savings

Equilibrium
Real Interest Rate r_1

Demand for Loans
Investment Demand

I_1 S_1 Loans

Equilibrium   Equilibrium
Investment   Savings

Difference = Government
Budget Deficit $GBD + I_D = D_L$

---

tity demanded, the aggregate quantity of goods and services demanded also equals the aggregate quantity supplied, that is:

$$GDP = C + I + G + NEX$$

Figure 24.13 summarizes general equilibrium in the economy. The next chapter will discuss equilibrium real GDP and use a graph like Figure 24.13 to illustrate the effects of changes in exogenous variables on the economy, including changes in technology, changes in the willingness of consumers to spend, and changes in government spending, taxes, and budget deficits.

FOR REVIEW

24.14 Discuss this statement: "An increase in the interest rate raises the incentive to invest."

24.15 Explain why the investment demand curve slopes downward.

QUESTIONS

24.16 Explain how an increase in the government budget deficit affects the demand for loans.

24.17 How are savings, investment, and the government budget deficit related in equilibrium?

CONCLUSIONS

INTEREST RATES AND DISCOUNTED PRESENT VALUES

An interest rate is the price of a loan, expressed as an annual percentage of the amount of the loan. The discounted present value of some amount of money in the future is its value today; it is the amount of money you would need to save now to end up with that amount of future money. (It is the value today of that money.) The discounted present value of X dollars next year is $X/(1 + i)$ dollars now, where i represents the interest rate (measured as a decimal so that an 8 percent per year interest rate means i equals 0.08).

REAL AND NOMINAL INTEREST RATES

The nominal interest rate on a loan is the dollar interest payment expressed as a percentage of the dollar amount of the loan. The nominal interest rate enters into the calculation of the discounted present value of a certain amount of money in the future. Adding 1 to the nominal interest rate gives the relative price of $1 this year in terms of dollars next year.

The real interest rate corrects the nominal interest rate for inflation. The real interest rate measures the interest rate in terms of purchasing power. Adding 1 to the real interest rate gives the relative price of goods this year in terms of the same goods next year. Higher real interest rates mean that goods this year are relatively more expensive in terms of future goods; lower real interest rates mean the opposite.

The Fisher equation shows the connection between real and nominal interest rates: the nominal interest rate is the real interest rate plus the expected rate of inflation. Because future inflation is uncertain in real life, economists distinguish between the expected and actual real interest rates. The expected real interest rate is the nominal interest rate minus the expected rate of inflation; the actual real interest rate is the nominal interest rate minus the actual rate of inflation during the period of the loan.

SAVINGS AND THE SUPPLY OF LOANS

Decisions about spending or saving amount to decisions about when to spend (now or in the future). These decisions depend on opportunities and tastes, such as a person's degree of patience. A person's budget line between consumption this year and consumption next year shows his available opportunities, that is, the various combinations of goods that the person can afford to buy.

A permanent increase in income expands consumption opportunities. It raises consumption spending each year with little effect on savings. A temporary increase in income also raises consumption opportunities; it raises both consumption and savings. (People save so they will have more to spend in the future.) Because most changes in the economy's total income are roughly permanent, total consumption spending and total income move fairly closely together.

An increase in expected future income raises consumption and reduces saving. An increase in the real interest rate has two effects. First, savers gain from higher interest rates (they earn more interest on their savings) and borrowers lose (they must pay more interest on loans). Second, a rise in the real interest rate creates new opportunities that make saving more attractive and tends to raise savings. On net, an increase in the real interest rate tends to raise savings and reduce consumption.

The supply of savings creates a supply of loans, which shows the amount of money that people would want to save and lend at various possible real interest rates.

INVESTMENT AND THE DEMAND FOR LOANS

Investment is an increase in the economy's capital stock. Higher investment this year raises the economy's future capital stock. The demand for investment comes from the demand for new capital goods. It shows the amount of money that firms would want to invest at various real interest rates. An increase in the real interest rate reduces the quantity of investment demanded because the real interest rate is an opportunity cost of investment.

The real interest rate, not the nominal interest rate, has important effects on savings and investment decisions. Consumption, savings, and investment do not change substantially when the nominal interest rate and expected inflation rise equally, leaving the real interest rate unchanged.

The demand for loans shows the amount of money that people, firms, and the government would want to borrow at various possible real interest rates. This demand has two main parts: loan demand by firms to pay for investments and loan demand by the government to finance its budget deficit (government spending in excess of tax receipts). When the government has a budget deficit, it borrows money; this raises the demand for loans. The total demand for loans equals investment demand plus the government budget deficit.

EQUILIBRIUM

The equilibrium real interest rate adjusts so that the quantity of loans supplied equals the quantity demanded. This implies that the quantity of savings supplied equals the quantity of goods demanded for investment plus the quantity of goods demanded by the government minus tax revenues. Equilibrium in the loan market implies that the total quantity of goods demanded by people for consumption, by people and firms for investment, and by the government must equal the total quantity supplied (real GDP). This means that the total quantity of goods demanded in the economy equals the total quantity supplied.

LOOKING AHEAD

Chapter 25 discusses equilibrium real GDP and shows how equilibrium consumption, savings, and investment are affected by changes in technology, tastes, taxes, and government spending. It also discusses equilibrium employment and unemployment. Chapter 26 applies a similar analysis to long-run economic growth and development. It discusses why economies grow or stagnate, and why some countries are much richer than others.

KEY TERMS

nominal interest rate	budget line
real interest rate	marginal propensity to consume *mpc*
expected real interest rate	supply of loans
actual real interest rate	investment
disposable income	demand for investment
savings	demand for loans
wealth	government budget deficit

QUESTIONS AND PROBLEMS

24.18 Find the discounted present value of $540 to be paid one year from now if the nominal interest rate is 8 percent per year.

24.19 Your employer promises to pay you a $1,000 bonus 10 years from now. If the nominal interest rate is 10 percent per year, approximately what is the discounted present value of your bonus? (You may want to use a calculator.)

24.20 A state lottery promises to pay the winner $1 million, in the form of a $50,000 payment each year for 20 years. Use a calculator or computer to find the discounted present value of the prize if the nominal interest rate is 8 percent per year.

24.21 A perpetuity is a financial asset that pays interest every year, forever. If the nominal interest rate is 10 percent per year, what is the discounted present value of a perpetuity that pays $1,000 every year?

24.22 If the nominal interest rate is 8 percent per year and the expected rate of inflation is 5 percent per year, what is the real interest rate? If the real interest rate is 2 percent per year and expected inflation is 4 percent per year, what is the nominal interest rate?

24.23 Draw your budget line for consumption this year and next year and show how it changes if:
  a. The real interest rate falls
  b. Your income rises temporarily
  c. Your income rises permanently

24.24 Suppose that the nominal interest rate rises by 3 percent per year because the expected rate of inflation rises by 3 percent per year. Explain why this change does not affect investment.

24.25 Discuss this statement: "The interest rate plays no role in the investment decisions of firms that use their own profits to pay for investments in new equipment."

24.26 Explain the flaw in the following argument: "A fall in the real interest rate reduces savings. Because savings equals investment plus the government budget deficit in equilibrium, a fall in the real interest rate must also reduce equilibrium investment." (*Hint:* Recall the difference between changes in demand and changes in the quantity demanded.)

24.27 (*This problem requires knowledge of microeconomics*) Show in a diagram how a tax on interest income affects the economy's savings and investment.

INQUIRIES FOR FURTHER THOUGHT

24.28 Some economists believe that people in the United States do not save enough for the future.
  a. What affects the amount of money that people choose to save? How much should people save? Who should decide?
  b. Do people voluntarily save the amount that they should save, or should government policies provide incentives for people to save more? What government policies might lead people to save more? Do any current government policies encourage or discourage saving?

24.29 Suppose that lenders are not willing to lend money to a person at any legal interest rate, perhaps because they worry that the borrower will go bankrupt and not repay the loan.

a. Draw the budget line between consumption this year and next year for a person who cannot borrow more than a few hundred dollars.

b. How do you think this person's consumption and savings change due to a temporary fall in income? What if the person's income rises temporarily?

24.30 The Social Security system taxes workers' incomes and gives money to retired people.

a. How do you think the Social Security system affects the amount of money that people choose to save? Why?

b. How do you think the Social Security system affects equilibrium investment? Explain.

TAG SOFTWARE APPLICATIONS

TUTORIAL **E**XERCISES
▶ The module contains a review of the key terms from Chapter 24.

GRAPHING **E**XERCISES
▶ The graphing segment contains questions on the supply of and demand for loans and the determination of the interest rate

CHAPTER 24 APPENDIX — INTERNATIONAL TRADE AND THE SUPPLY OF LOANS

Recall that the demand for loans equals the demand for investment plus the government budget deficit. Chapter 24 explained that if net exports are zero, the supply of loans equals the supply of savings. More generally, an economy's net exports add to its supply of loans.

A country with positive net exports (a trade surplus) lends to people in other countries. For example, if Japan sells goods worth ¥20 trillion to other countries and imports goods worth only ¥18 trillion, then Japan lends ¥2 trillion to other countries. People in those countries receive only ¥18 trillion from buyers in Japan, but spend ¥20 trillion. They spend more yen than they receive by borrowing the remaining ¥2 trillion. Similarly, a country with negative net exports (a trade deficit) borrows from people in other countries. The United States has borrowed from other countries in recent years; in 1994, for example, it borrowed $138 billion from other countries.

In loan market equilibrium, the quantity of loans supplied must equal the quantity of loans demanded. The quantity of loans supplied equals savings plus loans from other countries, that is, savings minus net exports. The quantity of loans demanded equals investment plus the government budget deficit. Therefore, loan market equilibrium requires that savings minus the economy's net exports must equal investment plus the government budget deficit:

$$S - NEX = I + (G - T) \qquad (24\text{A}.1)$$

where S is savings, NEX is net exports, I is investment, and $(G - T)$ is the government budget deficit.

Recall that savings, S, equals disposable income minus consumption, $y - T - C$, so Equation 24A.1 becomes:

$$y - T - C - NEX = I + G - T$$

Rearranging this equation gives:

$$y = C + I + G + NEX \qquad (24\text{A}.2)$$

This restates the condition that aggregate supply (real GDP) equals the sum of consumption, investment, government purchases, and net exports. This shows why equilibrium in the loan market is closely related to equilibrium between aggregate demand and aggregate supply. When the quantity of loans supplied equals the quantity demanded, the aggregate quantity of goods and services supplied equals the aggregate quantity demanded.

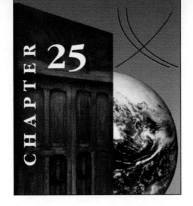

EQUILIBRIUM MACROECONOMICS

WHAT THIS CHAPTER IS ABOUT

▶ Factors that determine the economy's total output of goods and services, or real GDP

▶ How consumer spending affects the economy

▶ How technology and business investment affect the economy

▶ How government spending, taxes, and government budget deficits affect the economy

▶ Unemployment and how the economy creates new jobs

Stranded on his island, Robinson Crusoe had his own small economy. He could consume fish and berries. He could save, but only by investing, that is, by planting more food, constructing new equipment for fishing, or expanding his hut. When pirates stole his food, he consumed less and invested less; he spent less time building a boat and more time finding berries to eat. He also worked harder. Crusoe was never unemployed, except by choice. He created his own jobs.

Our modern economy is more complicated than Crusoe's. We can save by lending money to others, firms borrow money and invest in new equipment, we seldom encounter pirates, few people create their own jobs, and (of course) we consume many more goods and services than Crusoe did. Nevertheless, our economy resembles Crusoe's in many ways. While each person can save by lending to others, the *economy as a whole* saves for the future only by investing in new capital. While pirates seldom steal food, people must pay taxes. Like Crusoe, we produce goods with labor effort and capital equipment, subject to our limited technical knowledge. While Crusoe worked for himself, people in a modern economy work for each other and create jobs when they trade with each other.

How does our economy fit together? What happens if consumers decide to spend more and save less? What if businesses decide to invest more because technical progress makes investment more profitable? How do changes in government spending, taxes, and budget deficits affect the economy? How does the economy generate jobs? What causes unemployment? Why haven't large increases in population caused equally large increases in unemployment? Why has the number of jobs available increased with population? These are the subjects of this chapter.

EQUILIBRIUM

general (macroeconomic) equilibrium — a situation in which prices have adjusted to equate demands and supplies in all markets

Macroeconomics—the study of the economy as a whole—is concerned with equilibrium in *every* market in the economy.

General (macroeconomic) equilibrium is a situation in which prices have adjusted to equate demands and supplies in all markets:

1. Demand for every product equals its supply.

2. Demands for labor and other inputs equal their supplies.

3. Demands for all financial assets, including stocks, bonds, and money, equal their supplies.

The first condition requires equilibrium in the markets for all goods and services. Rather than analyzing these markets simultaneously, macroeconomists usually analyze factors that affect total gross domestic product (GDP). (Microeconomics studies the division of total GDP into production of various goods, such as food, housing, health care, and entertainment.) The second condition specifies *full employment* of labor; a later section of this chapter ("Equilibrium Employment and Unemployment") discusses this condition.[1]

REAL GDP IN GENERAL EQUILIBRIUM

Equilibrium real GDP is determined by technology, available inputs of labor and people's choices of how much and how hard to work, available inputs of capital and natural resources (and people's decisions about how much to use them), and other factors such as taxes, government regulations, enforcement of property rights, entrepreneurship, and the amount of competition in the economy.

TECHNOLOGY

The economy's available technology encompasses the state of scientific and engineering knowledge in the economy. This includes knowledge written in books and technical reports and knowledge in the minds of people that can help them to produce goods and services by combining inputs of labor and capital. Economists describe this technical knowledge with a production function.

production function — a mathematical description of technology showing the quantity of output (real GDP) the economy can get from its inputs of capital and labor

A **production function** describes the economy's technology in a mathematical equation, showing the amount of output (real GDP) the economy can get from its inputs of capital and labor.

The economy's production function shows how much output it could produce with various amounts of labor and capital. The economy's actual output in long-run equilibrium depends on the amounts of labor and capital that are actually available.

INPUTS OF LABOR AND CAPITAL

Supply and demand conditions for labor determine the economy's equilibrium input of labor. Labor supply depends on people's decisions about whether and how much to work.[2] The demand for labor depends on forces, such as technology, that determine labor's productivity. The equilibrium of the supply and

---

[1]Further discussions of unemployment appear in Chapters 29 to 31.

[2]The alternatives include going to school, retiring, relying on another person for income, working part-time rather than full-time, working overtime, working at more than one job, and so on.

demand for labor determines the economy's equilibrium input of labor. For now, suppose that people decide to work a total of $\overline{L}$ labor-hours per month, and that this equilibrium labor input is a fixed number. (Chapter 25 Appendix B discusses changes in the equilibrium labor input.)

The economy's equilibrium input of capital depends on the amount of capital, such as machinery, equipment, and natural resources, that is available and decisions about the use of this capital (for example, the number of hours per week a firm chooses to operate a machine). For now, suppose that the economy's capital input is fixed at $\overline{K}$ machine-hours per month. (Chapter 25 Appendix B discusses the forces that determine this choice, as well.)

In macroeconomic equilibrium, the quantity of labor demanded equals the quantity supplied, $\overline{L}$, and the quantity of capital demanded equals the quantity supplied, $\overline{K}$. In other words, labor and capital are fully employed; the economy uses all $\overline{L}$ person-hours and $\overline{K}$ machine-hours to produce goods and services. A later section of this chapter discusses unemployment.

The economy's production function shows that it can produce a certain quantity of goods and services with these inputs of labor and capital.[3] That quantity is its aggregate supply, which can be graphed, as in **Figure 25.1.** This aggregate supply curve is a vertical line that shows the economy's equilibrium real GDP. As Chapter 23 indicated, the long-run aggregate supply curve is a vertical line because, in the long run, a country's aggregate supply of goods and services does not depend on its price level. Long-run aggregate supply depends instead on available technology and inputs such as capital and labor, and on the laws, property rights, regulations, and taxes that affect people's incentives to use technology and inputs efficiently. Chapter 23 also explained that most economists believe that the short-run aggregate supply curve slopes upward, though others believe that it is roughly vertical even in the short run. Later chapters will discuss an upward-sloping short-run aggregate supply curve and the associated complications it brings to the discussion; the remainder of this chapter deals with the vertical aggregate supply curve like that in Figure 25.1.

OTHER ISSUES

The production function and available inputs determine the total output of goods and services that the economy could produce with efficient operations. Equilibrium real GDP also depends on factors that affect the economy's use of its resources. Those factors range from taxes and government regulations to enforcement of property rights, entrepreneurship, and the level of competition in the economy.[4] Taxes, regulations, poor enforcement of property rights, and insufficient competition can cause the economy to operate inefficiently and produce

---

[3]Economists write a production function mathematically, as $y = F(K,L)$. This indicates that if the economy uses K units of capital (machines) and L person-hours of labor (adjusted for skill level), it will produce y units of output. That output, y, is its real GDP. The production function $y = AK^{\frac{1}{3}}L^{\frac{2}{3}}$ is a good approximation of the real-life production functions in many countries, including the United States. A stands for a number that represents the level of technology; that number rises over time with technical progress. Economists have shown mathematically that this production implies that total wages equal two-thirds of GDP and that the other one-third of GDP is paid to owners of capital. This is also a good approximation to real life in many countries, though the numbers are closer to three-quarters and one-quarter in some countries.

[4]*Entrepreneurship* refers to people's anticipation of new economic opportunities and initiative to take advantage of those new opportunities through actions (such as starting new business firms or launching new products). Entrepreneurship, like labor and capital, is an input to production.

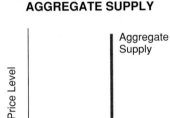

FIGURE 25.1

AGGREGATE SUPPLY

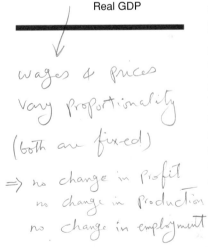

Aggregate Supply

Price Level

Real GDP

[handwritten notes:] wages & prices vary proportionality (both are fixed) ⟹ no change in profit no change in Production no change in employment

FIGURE 25.2

EQUILIBRIUM OF AGGREGATE SUPPLY AND AGGREGATE DEMAND

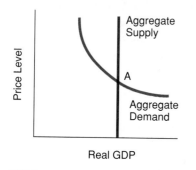

less output than the production function would indicate. The discussion in this chapter assumes that the economy operates reasonably efficiently; the main results, however, also apply to economies that operate inefficiently, though such an economy would produce a lower real GDP than its production function would indicate.

To focus on key issues without unnecessary complications, this chapter discusses an economy that cannot borrow from foreign countries or lend to them. This implies net exports of zero; exports equal imports. Chapter 25 Appendix A discusses international borrowing and lending and the associated deficits or surpluses in the balance of international trade.

MACROECONOMIC EQUILIBRIUM

Macroeconomic equilibrium requires that the aggregate quantity demanded must equal the aggregate quantity supplied, as at Point A in **Figure 25.2.** At Point A, the total number of goods that people, firms, and government want to buy this year must equal the total quantity of goods that the economy produces this year.

The previous chapter indicated that the economy is at Point A in a graph like Figure 25.2 when the quantity of loans supplied equals the quantity demanded, so we can graph the equilibrium as in **Figure 25.3.**[5] The equilibrium real interest rate is r_1, and equilibrium savings is S_1. Equilibrium investment, I_1, equals S_1 minus the government budget deficit. Because net exports are zero, equilibrium consumption equals GDP minus investment and minus government purchases:[6]

$$C = \text{GDP} - I_1 - G$$

Figure 25.3 shows the equilibrium real interest rate. The Fisher equation, discussed in Chapter 23, implies that the equilibrium nominal interest rate equals the equilibrium real interest rate plus the expected rate of inflation.

CHANGES IN ECONOMIC CONDITIONS

We now have a simple macroeconomic model that can show how changes in underlying economic conditions—exogenous variables such as the economy's technology and government policies—affect endogenous variables such as the economy's aggregate consumption, savings, investment, and the real interest rate. The next several sections discuss these changes for fixed equilibrium inputs of labor and capital services, L and K. (Chaper 25 Appendix B discusses changes in the equilibrium quantities of these inputs and the resulting effects on the economy's real GDP.)

This discussion will conclude with the following results:

▶ An increase in consumer patience, that is, an increase in people's desire to save for the future, reduces the equilibrium real interest rate, raises equilibrium savings and investment, and reduces current consumption, though it increases future consumption.

▶ Technical progress that permanently raises productivity (the output that the economy can produce with any amounts of labor and capital inputs)

---

[5]See Chapter 24 Appendix for further discussion.

[6]Another way to express equilibrium consumption, which always gives the same answer, is GDP minus taxes and minus savings, or $\text{GDP} - T - S_1$.

FIGURE 25.3

EQUILIBRIUM IN THE MARKET FOR LOANS

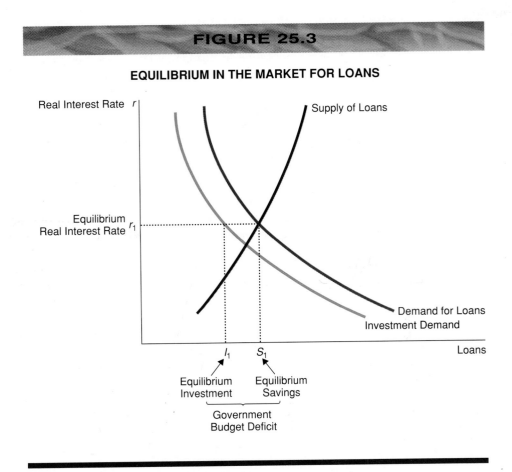

raises real GDP, the real interest rate, consumption, savings, and investment. The rise in investment increases the economy's future capital stock, so real GDP and consumption rise more in the long run than in the short run.

▶ A permanent increase in government spending financed by higher taxes reduces consumption and may leave real GDP, savings, investment, and the real interest rate unchanged. However, increases in certain types of government spending may raise investment, the real interest rate, and savings, and reduce consumption further. In addition, equilibrium savings and investment may fall if the higher tax reduces incentives to save and invest.

▶ A temporary increase in government spending financed by higher income taxes raises the real interest rate and reduces consumption, savings, and investment. Equilibrium savings and investment also depend partly on the type of government spending and the type of tax, as they do when government spending rises permanently.

▶ Controversy surrounds the effects of a tax cut that raises the government budget deficit. Based on available evidence, most economists believe that such a tax cut raises the real interest rate and consumption and reduces investment. Some economists, however, see little effect on the real interest rate, consumption, and investment in available research evidence.

The next sections follow the economist's usual procedure, discussing the effects of just one change at a time. For example, the discussion of the effects of a change in consumer tastes assumes that technology, taxes, and government spending all remain stable. In real life, of course, many changes occur at the same time, but economists study the effects of changes in one exogenous variable at a time for two reasons. First, it helps them to develop an understanding of the economic forces at work. Second, combining the answers can help them to determine the effects of simultaneous changes in several exogenous variables.

INCREASE IN CONSUMER PATIENCE

Suppose that people become more concerned about the future and decide to spend less money on current consumption and save more for the future. This kind of change is sometimes called an *increase in consumer patience* or a *fall in consumer confidence.* This raises the supply of loans, as in **Figure 25.4,** lowering the real interest rate and raising the equilibrium quantity of loans. It increases equilibrium savings from S_1 to S_2, along with the equilibrium quantity of loans. Equilibrium investment rises from I_1 to I_2, the same amount as savings increases, because savings equals investment plus the government budget deficit and savings rises while the deficit stays constant. Firms invest more because the fall in the real interest rate makes more investment projects profitable, raising the quantity of investment demanded. Equilibrium consumption falls because consumption equals GDP minus investment minus government purchases, and investment rises while GDP and government purchases remain the same. Equilibrium consumption falls by the same amount as the rise in equilibrium investment.

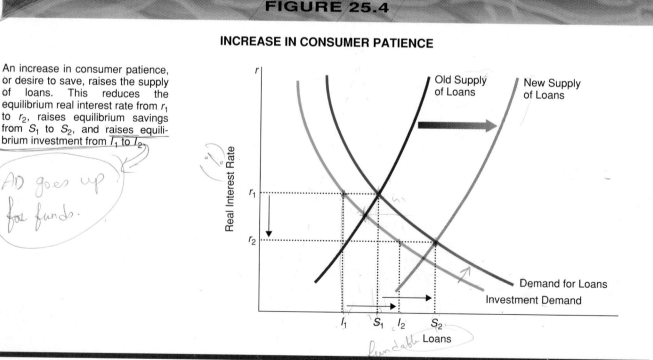

FIGURE 25.4

INCREASE IN CONSUMER PATIENCE

An increase in consumer patience, or desire to save, raises the supply of loans. This reduces the equilibrium real interest rate from r_1 to r_2, raises equilibrium savings from S_1 to S_2, and raises equilibrium investment from I_1 to I_2.

The increase in investment eventually raises the economy's capital stock, so it eventually raises the economy's real GDP. Real GDP rises even if the economy's labor input remains constant because each worker works with more capital (such as machinery or equipment), and this raises each worker's productivity. This increase in future real GDP makes more goods available for future consumption. In this way, the economy responds to the desires of consumers; if people want to reduce current consumption and raise future consumption, the economy makes fewer goods available for current consumption and more goods available for future consumption. The next chapter discusses long-run issues in greater detail.

TECHNICAL PROGRESS

Suppose now that technical progress permanently increases productivity. This raises the quantity of output that the economy can produce with each level of labor and capital inputs. This increase in productivity has two main effects. First, it raises current production of goods and services, or real GDP. Second, it raises the benefits from new investments by making new capital goods more productive. For example, technical progress might make it possible to produce a new generation of computers that are faster than older computers, or new farm equipment that allows farmers to produce more output per acre.

First, think about the effects of a permanent increase in the economy's production of goods and services. This permanently raises the economy's income. The previous chapter explained that a permanent increase in income shifts budget lines (as in Figure 24.3) and that people generally respond to a permanent increase in income with permanently higher consumption demand and stable supplies of savings. Because permanent technical progress raises the economy's income permanently, it raises consumption demand, but has little effect on the supply of savings. As a result, permanent technical progress has little effect on the supply of loans.

Now think about the effect of technical progress on investment demand. Because technical progress raises the productivity of new investment, it raises investment demand as firms buy new machinery and equipment to take advantage of the productivity increase. This increase in investment demand raises the demand for loans, as in **Figure 25.5.**

Figure 25.5 shows the short-run results of permanent technical progress. The increase in the demand for loans raises the equilibrium real interest rate, equilibrium savings, and equilibrium investment. Although consumption may increase, it increases less than the rise in real GDP. For example, real GDP may rise by $10 billion per year in 1996 dollars, with consumption rising by $3 billion and investment rising by $7 billion. Savings would also rise by $7 billion because real GDP, the economy's total income, would rise by $10 billion while consumption would rise by only $3 billion.

The increase in investment due to technical progress raises the economy's future capital stock. This provides the economy with a larger available input of capital, raising future real GDP even higher. For example, the increase in capital might eventually raise real GDP by $20 billion per year, with consumption eventually rising by $18 billion per year and investment rising by $2 billion per year. Chapter 26 discusses the long-run effects of technical progress in more detail.

The economy's precise response to technical progress depends on the desires of consumers. Notice that the economy faces a tradeoff. It could use a permanent $10 billion annual increase in real GDP due to technical progress to raise

FIGURE 25.5

EFFECTS OF TECHNICAL PROGRESS

Technical progress that permanently raises productivity has little effect on the supply of loans, but raises the demand for investment and the demand for loans. The equilibrium real interest rate rises to r_2, equilibrium savings rises to S_2, and equilibrium investment rises from I_1 to I_2.

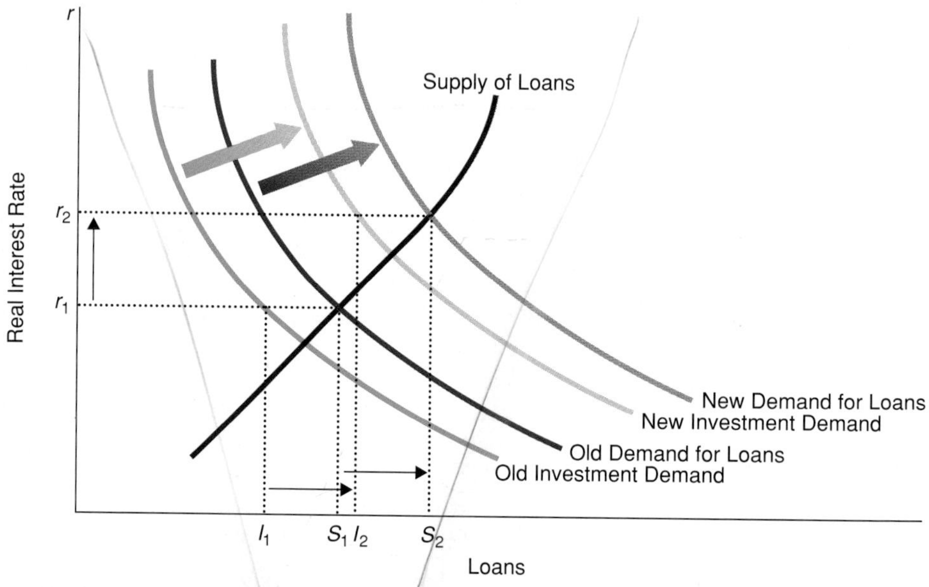

consumption by $10 billion per year, or it could raise investment by $10 billion, leaving current consumption unchanged but raising the future capital input, future real GDP, and future consumption. For example, consumption might rise permanently by $12 billion per year starting next year if investment were to rise by $10 billion this year. As a third alternative, the economy might raise both current consumption and current investment by $5 billion this year, with the increased investment raising consumption permanently by $11 billion per year starting next year.

How the economy resolves this tradeoff depends on its available opportunities for investment and the preferences of consumers. These forces operate through the supply and demand for loans. Would people rather consume $10 billion more each year starting this year or $5 billion more this year and $11 billion more each year starting next year? Would they prefer to consume $12 billion more each year starting next year but less this year? The economy's investment opportunities determine the precise combinations of current and future consumption from which consumers can choose. Consumers then decide which particular combination of current and future consumption they most prefer.

If consumers prefer to have $10 billion per year more consumption starting this year, they will spend the entire $10 billion increase in real GDP on consumption; in this case, the supply of loans would remain stable, as would the equilibrium quantities of savings and investment. This would allow consumers to raise their consumption permanently by $10 billion per year, starting immediately.

Suppose, instead, that consumers would rather use the technical progress to raise this year's consumption by only $5 billion while raising consumption by $11 billion per year permanently starting next year. In that case, people would save $5 billion of the $10 billion increase in current real GDP, raising the economy's investment by $5 billion and raising its GDP permanently by $11 billion per year starting next year. In this way, the economy responds to technical progress in the way that consumers most desire.

─────────────── **FOR REVIEW** ───────────────

25.1 What is a production function and how is it related to equilibrium real GDP?

25.2 Explain the effects of an increase in consumer patience (or decrease in consumer confidence) on consumption, savings, investment, and the real interest rate.

25.3 Explain the effects on consumption, savings, investment, and the real interest rate of technical progress that permanently raises productivity. In what way does the economy's response to technical progress depend on the desires of consumers?

─────────────── **QUESTIONS** ───────────────

25.4 Use a graph to help explain the effects of a fall in consumer patience (or a rise in consumer confidence) on consumption, savings, investment, and the real interest rate.

25.5 Use a graph to help explain the effects of a *temporary* increase in productivity on consumption, savings, investment, and the real interest rate.

PERMANENT INCREASE IN GOVERNMENT SPENDING AND TAXES

Now suppose that the government permanently raises its purchases of goods and services, and it raises taxes enough to pay for this spending increase. (The government budget deficit does not change.) Because people must pay higher taxes, they have less after-tax income, so they must either spend less or save less. You might expect people to do some of both, but Chapter 24 showed that a permanent change in income alters consumption, but not savings, because it permanently shifts the budget line as in Figure 24.3. A permanent increase in government spending and taxes permanently reduces after-tax income, so consumption demand falls and the supply of savings does not change. As a result, a permanent increase in government spending and taxes does not affect the supply of loans.

A permanent increase in government spending and taxes may also leave the *demand* for loans unchanged. Recall that the demand for loans is the sum of two parts: investment demand and the government budget deficit. The government budget deficit does not change, so the demand for loans changes only if the increase in government spending and taxes affects investment demand.

If government spending does not affect investment demand, then the demand for loans remains unchanged. In this case, no curve in Figure 25.3 shifts, so the real interest rate, savings, and investment remain unchanged. Equilibrium consumption falls by the amount of the increase in government spending and

---

[7]This result makes sense. If people were to save less, they would have even less money to spend in the future because they would have higher taxes to pay *and* less accumulated savings.

taxes.[8] In this case, the main effect of the increase in government spending is to leave fewer goods available for everyone else—the government gets more and consumers get less. This does not necessarily imply that the increase in government spending harms consumers. After all, consumers may benefit from the change in government spending. Regardless of whether people like or dislike the increase in government spending, however, it must reduce either private spending on consumption or investment. If the increase in government spending and taxes does not affect investment demand, then it must reduce private consumption spending by an equal amount.

Whether an increase in government spending affects investment demand depends partly on *what* the government buys. Government spending to build roads or repair bridges (so-called *infrastructure* spending) may raise the benefits from certain kinds of investment, such as investment in new trucks, raising investment demand. Similarly, if the government spends its money to create or enhance an electronic data superhighway, the benefits of investments in computers may rise. In these ways, certain types of government spending may raise investment demand and the demand for loans.

Now think about a permanent increase in government spending that raises investment demand, and continue to suppose that the government raises taxes to pay for its spending. The increase in investment demand raises the demand for loans, so it raises the equilibrium real interest rate, equilibrium savings, and equilibrium investment. In this case, consumption falls by more than the increase in taxes and government spending. For example, government spending may rise by $10 billion and investment may rise by $2 billion, while consumption falls by $12 billion.

A final complication arises from the effect on people's incentives of the tax increase to pay for the rise in government spending. An increase in the tax on any good or service typically reduces the equilibrium quantity of that good or service. A higher tax on gasoline, for example, typically reduces the equilibrium quantity of gasoline bought and sold.[9] Similarly, an increase in taxes on income from savings and investment tends to reduce equilibrium savings and investment. If the government pays for an increase in spending with a tax on investment income, equilibrium investment may fall rather than increase. A fall in investment demand decreases the demand for loans, reducing the equilibrium real interest rate and preventing consumption from falling by as much as the rise in government spending.

If a permanent increase in taxes and government spending raises investment, then it eventually raises the economy's capital stock and real GDP. If it reduces investment, then it eventually lowers the capital stock and real GDP. In either case, the change in future real GDP affects future consumption. The economy's precise response to the increase in taxes and government spending, like its response to technical progress, depends on its investment opportunities and on the desires of consumers, as well as the effects of the higher taxes on incentives.

TEMPORARY INCREASE IN GOVERNMENT SPENDING AND TAXES

Suppose that government raises its spending only *temporarily,* and it raises taxes by an equal amount. Because people pay higher taxes, they must either consume

---

[8]Recall that real GDP equals consumption plus investment plus government purchases (plus net exports, which are zero in this case). With real GDP and investment unchanged, every $100 increase in government purchases must reduce consumption by that same $100.

[9]The last section of Chapter 3 discussed the effects of taxes on incentives.

FIGURE 25.6

TEMPORARY INCREASE IN GOVERNMENT SPENDING AND TAXES

A temporary increase in government spending and taxes reduces the supply of loans. This raises the equilibrium real interest rate from r_1 to r_2, reduces equilibrium savings from S_1 to S_2, and reduces equilibrium investment from I_1 to I_2.

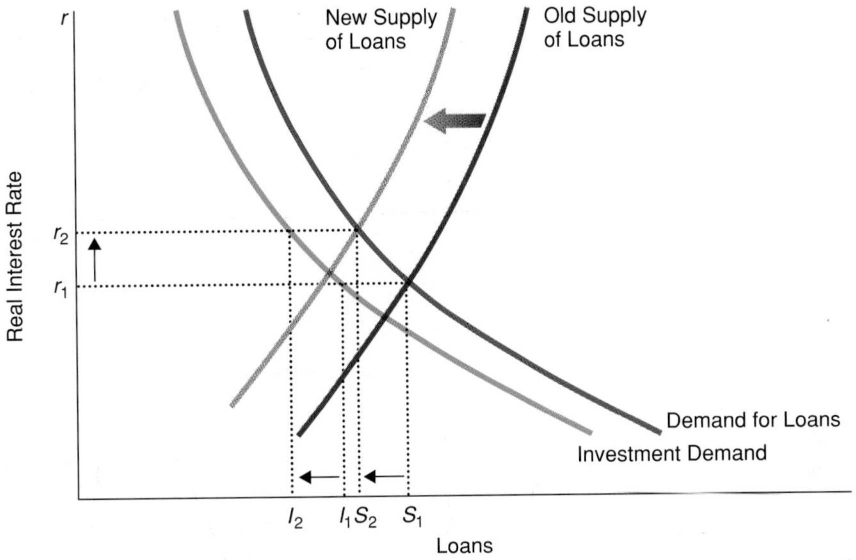

less or save less. The tax increase temporarily reduces disposable income, which reduces both consumption demand and the supply of savings.[10] This fall in the supply of savings decreases the supply of loans.

If higher government spending does not change investment demand, then it does not change the demand for loans. In this case, the decrease in the supply of loans raises the equilibrium real interest rate and reduces equilibrium savings and investment, as in **Figure 25.6**.[11]

GOVERNMENT BUDGET DEFICIT CAUSED BY A TAX CUT

Suppose that the government reduces taxes, but not its spending. This raises the government budget deficit, and the government must borrow more to finance the larger deficit.[12] Economists disagree about the effects of a tax cut that causes a larger deficit. As in all controversies in macroeconomics (later chapters will explore others), evidence from real-life economies is not yet strong enough for

---

[10]Chapter 24 showed that a temporary change in income changes both consumption demand and the supply of savings; see the discussion of Figure 24.4.

[11]If the government raises taxes on income from investment, then investment may fall further, reducing equilibrium savings and investment by even more, as described in the earlier discussion of the effects of a permanent increase in government spending. Similarly, if the increase in government spending raises private investment demand, then the demand for loans increases and reinforces the rise in the real interest rate, helping to offset the fall in equilibrium savings and investment.

[12]Financing a deficit does not mean eliminating it. The government borrows money to pay for spending that it cannot afford with its tax receipts; this borrowing is called *financing the deficit*. The government eliminates the deficit only if it reduces spending or raises taxes so that it collects enough tax revenue to pay for its spending. The government can also finance its deficit by printing money, as Chapter 27 will explain. For now, assume that the government borrows money to finance its deficit.

economists on either side of the controversy to convince those on the other side.[13] This section first discusses the view held by the majority of economists, and then it considers a minority view of deficits.

Both views agree that an increase in the government budget deficit raises the demand for loans, as in **Figure 25.7a.** The demand for loans shifts horizontally to the right by the amount of the tax cut ($50 billion in the figure) because that represents the increase in government borrowing. To keep matters simple, assume that the tax cut does not affect the demand for investment.[14] While the two views agree about the shift in the demand for loans, they disagree about what happens to the supply.

MAJORITY VIEW

According to the majority view, people save some of the money from the tax cut and spend the rest. If people save only a small amount of the tax cut, then the supply of loans increases by a small amount, as in Figure 25.7b. In that figure, the government budget deficit begins at zero, so the demand for loans initially equals the demand for investment, the initial equilibrium interest rate is r_1, and the initial equilibrium levels of savings and investment, S_1 and I_1, are equal. When the government cuts taxes by $50 billion, the demand for loans shifts to the right by $50 billion, and the supply of loans shifts to the right but not as far, perhaps by $10 billion. This creates a $40 billion shortage of loans at the initial equilibrium interest rate, so the equilibrium moves from Point A to Point B. The equilibrium interest rate rises to r_2, equilibrium savings rises to S_2, and equilibrium investment falls to I_2.[15]

A fall in investment caused by an increase in government borrowing is called *crowding out* investment. Government borrowing crowds out borrowing for private investment by business firms. Although the tax cut raises savings, savers lend more to the government to finance the budget deficit and less to business firms to finance private investments.

Crowding out of private investment occurs when government borrowing raises the real interest rate, which reduces the equilibrium amount of investment.

The increase in government borrowing in Figure 25.7b is the distance from Point C to Point B, that is, the amount by which the demand curve shifts to the right. This amount exceeds the amount of the increase in the equilibrium quantity of loans, which rises from S_1 to S_2, so part of the increase in government borrowing comes from an increase in savings, and part comes from a decrease in investment. For example, if government borrowing rises by $50 billion but savings rises by only $30 billion, then the government borrows $20 billion from money that firms would otherwise have borrowed to finance investment. In this way, government borrowing crowds out $20 billion in investment.

crowding out — a reduction in private investment when government borrowing raises the real interest rate and reduces the equilibrium amount of investment

---

[13]That evidence consists mainly of statistical studies of real-life economic changes following tax cuts and tax increases.

[14]If the tax cut were to raise the demand for investment, then the demand for loans would increase by more than the $50 billion in this example. The demand curve for loans would shift further to the right.

[15]Investment falls because the rise in the real interest rate leads firms to invest less. See the discussion of investment in the previous chapter.

FIGURE 25.7

TAX CUT THAT RAISES THE GOVERNMENT BUDGET DEFICIT

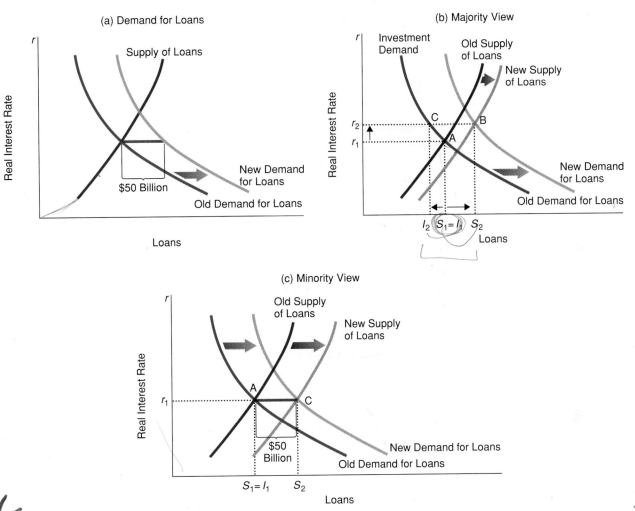

(a) Demand for Loans

(b) Majority View

(c) Minority View

(a) A $50 billion increase in the government budget deficit increases the demand for loans by $50 billion; the demand curve shifts to the right by $50 billion. (b) Most economists believe that a $50 billion tax cut that raises the government budget deficit by $50 billion also raises the demand for loans by $50 billion, but people spend part of the money from the tax cut, so the supply of savings, and the supply of loans, rises by less than $50 billion. As a result, the equilibrium real interest rate rises from r_1 to r_2, equilibrium savings rises from S_1 to S_2, and equilibrium investment falls from I_1 to I_2. In equilibrium, government borrowing rises by $50 billion; part of the increase in loans to the government comes from the increase in savings, and the rest comes from the fall in investment. The increase in government borrowing crowds out some private investment. (c) The Minority view assumes that people save all of the money from the tax cut, so the supply of loans increases by the same amount as the demand for loans. The tax cut leaves the real interest rate and investment unchanged, and it raises equilibrium savings by the same amount as the tax cut. A $50 billion tax cut raises savings by $50 billion from S_1 to S_2, but leaves investment at I_1 and the real interest rate at r_1.

IN THE NEWS

Retailers see public using fall tax cut mostly for Christmas buying, not saving

What's in store?

Administration officials who expect much of the tax reduction to be saved point to the aftermath of the Kennedy-era tax cut. In 1964, 1965, and 1966, personal savings rose by an amount equaling about

75 percent of the tax cut, and in 1967 the rise in savings equaled 121 percent of the tax cut. This time around, the Treasury Department estimates that at least 50 percent and perhaps 60 percent of the tax cut will be saved. Stephen Entin, a deputy assistant

Treasury secretary, describes this projection as "deliberately conservative."

JCPenney Co. believes it isn't nearly conservative enough. Penney expects taxpayers to save only one-third of the initial tax cut.

If people spend part of the money from a tax cut, then the majority view applies.

Source: "Retailers See Public Using Fall Tax Cut Mostly for Christmas Buying, Not Saving," *The Wall Street Journal*, July 29, 1981, p. 46.

MINORITY VIEW

According to the minority view, people save *all* the money that they get from a tax cut, so the supply of loans increases by the same amount as the increase in demand. As a result, the equilibrium real interest rate does not change. The equilibrium moves from Point A to Point C as in Figure 25.7c,

This view denies that government borrowing crowds out private investment. The real interest rate does not rise, so investment does not fall. Instead, equilibrium savings rises by the same amount as the rise in government borrowing, from S_1 to S_2, while consumption and investment remain constant.

Advocates of the minority view point out that when the government cuts taxes without cutting spending, it collects the same amount of money from taxpayers as before. It simply calls some of this money loans rather than taxes. People pay the government less money in the form of taxes, but more money in the form of loans. Either way, the government collects the money required to finance its spending. The difference between paying taxes and lending money to the government, of course, is that the government promises to repay loans. However, if the government will get the money to repay these loans by raising taxes in the future, then people will not benefit from the loan repayments. You do not gain if the government repays you $100 by raising your taxes by $100. According to the minority view, it does not matter whether one calls the money that the government takes a *tax* or a *loan*. If the government raises future taxes to repay its loans, then taxes and government borrowing are roughly equivalent. As a result, a tax cut with an increase in government borrowing has little or no effect on the economy.[16]

WHY PEOPLE MIGHT SAVE AN ENTIRE TAX CUT Why would people save an entire tax cut, as the minority view assumes? If the government borrows money this year, it will owe more in the future. Therefore, the government must either raise

IN THE NEWS

"**I** am not worried about losing my job or anything, but I feel more like saving," says a shopper at Bloomingdale's in Manhattan. "The budget deficit is in the paper every day, and every day the dollar is dropping against everybody. I feel like something has to happen."

If increased budget deficits make people save more, then the supply of loans increases along with the demand.

Source: The Wall Street Journal, November 28, 1988, p. B1.

---

[16]The main effect of a tax cut, in this view, is to postpone economic distortions due to taxes (the effects of incentives) to a future date.

future taxes or reduce its future spending to pay higher interest on its debt. The minority view assumes that the government will raise taxes in the future rather than reduce its spending. If so, the discounted present value of those higher future taxes equals the current tax cut. If people save all of the money they get from a tax cut, their extra savings (including interest) will just pay their higher future taxes. If, however, people do not save all of the money from a tax cut, they will have to spend less on future consumption in order to pay the higher future taxes. By saving all of the money from a tax cut, people prevent the change in taxes from upsetting their prior decisions about how much money to spend on current consumption and how much to save for future consumption.

EXAMPLE 1 An example shows why people may have an incentive to save all of the money they obtain from a tax cut. Suppose that the government cuts taxes by $100 per person and the interest rate is 10 percent per year. The government owes $110 more next year and raises taxes next year by $110 to pay its debt. If people save all the money from the tax cut and earn 10 percent interest on their savings, they will have $110 next year; that is exactly the amount that they need to pay the higher taxes next year.

EXAMPLE 2 Again, suppose that the government cuts taxes by $100 per person and the interest rate is 10 percent per year, but now suppose that the government never repays its debt; instead, it pays $10 per year interest on that debt every year, forever.[17] The government raises taxes by $10 per year, permanently, to make interest payments.

If people save all of the money from the tax cut and put it in a bank account earning 10 percent interest, they earn enough interest each year to pay the higher taxes forever. After 1 year, people have $110 in the bank account; they can withdraw $10 to pay the higher taxes and leave the $100 in the account. Next year they will have $110 again, and they can again withdraw $10 to pay the higher taxes and leave $100 in the account. They can repeat this every year for as long as the government pays interest on this debt. By saving all of the money from the tax cut, people can afford to pay the higher future taxes without reducing their future consumption spending.

FOR REVIEW

25.6 Use a graph to help explain the effects of a permanent increase in government spending, financed by a permanent increase in taxes, on consumption, savings, investment, and the real interest rate.

25.7 Explain the majority and minority views of the effects of a tax cut that causes a budget deficit.

QUESTIONS

25.8 Use a graph to help explain the effects on consumption, savings, investment, and the real interest rate of a permanent reduction in government spending accompanied by a permanent decrease in taxes.

25.9 Use a graph to help explain the effects on consumption, savings, investment, and the real interest rate of an increase in government spending without any increase in current taxes.

---

[17]The government may borrow another $100 each year to repay the principal on the previous loan.

EQUILIBRIUM EMPLOYMENT AND UNEMPLOYMENT

Although the macroeconomic model in this chapter is very simple, many of its conclusions carry over to more complicated models that add extra features and that economists often solve using computers. (Chapter 25 Appendix A and Appendix B discuss two of these extra features: international trade and choices of labor and capital inputs.) This chapter's analysis so far has relied on the limiting assumption that the economy fully employs labor and capital. However, the reasoning in this chapter continues to apply in situations of unemployment. We begin with a discussion of causes of unemployment.

Some unemployment results from continuing economic changes. Changes in demand and supply cause some industries to expand and others to contract; this raises the demand for labor in some industries and regions and reduces it in others. For example, steel manufacturers lay off workers when the demand for steel falls; computer firms hire workers when the demand for computers rises. Some people suffer unemployment because it takes time to find suitable jobs. Although someone who is willing to take a low-paying job can usually find one quickly, it takes longer to find a good job that suits a person's interests and skills. Unemployment occurs partly because continuing changes always force some people to look for new jobs.

Some jobs go unfilled while people are unemployed and looking for work. This occurs because it takes time for firms to find suitable employees who match their needs for skills, experience, and other characteristics. If all firms were to offer the same jobs at the same pay while all workers had the same skills, experience, and desired work environments, then workers would not care which jobs they took and firms would not care which workers they hired. Jobs and workers differ, however, so it takes time to match workers and firms to satisfy each. This matching process takes time, so continuing changes—in technology, consumer tastes, population, weather, government policies, international competition, and other factors—cause unemployment.[18] These continuing changes create unemployment, even in macroeconomic equilibrium.

equilibrium unemployment — unemployment that results from continuing changes in supplies and demands and the costs of searching for and matching jobs in labor markets

Equilibrium unemployment refers to unemployment that results from continuing changes in supplies and demands and the costs of searching for and matching jobs in labor markets.

When economists refer to *full employment,* they do not mean zero unemployment; they mean unemployment equal to its equilibrium rate.

Full employment means equilibrium unemployment.

The labor input described earlier in this chapter, $\bar{L}$, amounts to total employment when unemployment is at its equilibrium level. At this level, unemployment does not affect any of the results discussed in the chapter.

---

[18]Unemployment also results from temporary layoffs as some firms reduce production and lay off workers in response to temporary decreases in demand. (For example, construction firms often employ fewer workers in the winter.) Workers who are temporarily unemployed while waiting to be recalled to their jobs may not search for new jobs.

DETERMINANTS OF EQUILIBRIUM UNEMPLOYMENT

Equilibrium unemployment occurs when the rate of job creation equals the rate of job destruction.[19]

rate of job creation — the number of new workers hired each month

rate of job destruction — the number of people who quit or lose their jobs each month

> The **rate of job creation** is the number of new workers hired each month.

> The **rate of job destruction** is the number of people who quit or lose their jobs each month.

The rate of job destruction depends on the size and speed of changes in technology, government policies, and other factors that reduce the demand for labor in certain industries. The rate of job creation depends partly on the speed with which workers can learn about job opportunities and the speed with which firms can learn about possible employees. The rate of job creation also depends on the number of people unemployed; when more people look for jobs and more firms look for workers, more new job matches occur each month. For example, if 20 percent of unemployed workers find jobs each month, then the rate of job creation is 1 million jobs per month if 5 million people are unemployed and 2 million jobs per month if 10 million people are unemployed.

Equilibrium unemployment occurs when job destruction equals job creation, that is, when the number of people who lose their jobs each month equals the number of unemployed people who find jobs, leaving total unemployment unchanged. If unemployment exceeds its equilibrium level, then the rate of job creation exceeds the rate of job destruction and unemployment falls. If unemployment falls below its equilibrium level, then the rate of job creation falls below the rate of job destruction and unemployment rises. In this way, the rate of unemployment tends to move toward its equilibrium level.

EXAMPLE

Suppose that continuing changes in demand and supply cause 1 million job losses each month, and each month one-third of all unemployed people find jobs. In this case, equilibrium unemployment is 3 million people. Each month one-third of these 3 million people find jobs, so the rate of job creation is 1 million jobs per month. Because 1 million jobs are destroyed each month, unemployment stays at 3 million people, composed of 2 million people who were already unemployed and did not find jobs plus 1 million newly unemployed people.

To see why unemployment tends toward its equilibrium level, suppose that 6 million people are unemployed at the beginning of January. Because one-third of them find jobs in January, only 4 million remain unemployed by February. Because 1 million other people lose their jobs, however, total unemployment in February falls to 5 million, 1 million less than in January. One-third of these 5 million people (about 1,667,000 people) find jobs in February, and 1 million new people lose their jobs, so unemployment falls by 667,000 people, to 4.333 million, by March.

---

[19] When the labor force—the number of people who have or want jobs—grows over time, perhaps due to population growth, equilibrium unemployment occurs when the rate of job creation equals the rate of job destruction plus the increase in the labor force. Employment then rises along with the size of the labor force and unemployment is constant.

Each month, unemployment falls toward its equilibrium level of 3 million people, though the process takes time.

WHAT IF THERE ARE NOT ENOUGH JOBS?

What if the economy does not create enough jobs? What if the number of workers looking for jobs exceeds the number of firms looking for workers? The answer is that people and firms then create new jobs. Jobs are not products like houses and food. The number of jobs available in the economy is not limited by available resources. Jobs are *trades*—voluntary agreements in which people exchange labor services and money. The only limit to the number of jobs the economy can create comes from the number of voluntary trades that people are willing to make. As long as a worker can produce something that other people find valuable, those people are willing to hire that worker at some price (wage). So, the economy can always create enough jobs for everyone who can produce something valuable and who is willing to accept a wage equal to or below the value of the goods that he produces.

> Jobs are trades; the number of jobs the economy can create is limited only by the number of trades that people are willing to make.

While the economy can create jobs almost without limit, it takes time for people to find good jobs that suit their interests and skills. The problem of unemployment results not from a problem of creating enough jobs, but from problems matching people with firms. The jobs that people can find quickly are often not the kinds of jobs they want; some people choose unemployment while they search for better job opportunities.

Sometimes firms choose not to hire workers who would seem to add to their profits. Consider a person without much work experience or specialized skills who drops out of college after one year to look for a job. Why would this worker have trouble finding a job? Why doesn't almost *every* firm offer him a job at a wage slightly below the value of what he would produce for them? Some firms may not make the offer because they believe that the worker will soon quit to go back to school; the firms do not want to spend money to hire and train a worker whom they will soon lose. Other firms might gain extra output worth $3.00 per hour from this worker's effort. These firms would not offer a job because minimum-wage laws prevent them from hiring people at such low wages. The worker's effort might add extra output worth $6.00 per hour at another firm, but that firm may not offer him a job because it pays $8.00 per hour to other workers doing similar tasks and it believes that worker morale, and therefore productivity, would suffer if it were to employ similar workers at very different rates of pay. Factors like these increase the time it takes to find a suitable job. These factors reduce the rate of job creation and raise equilibrium unemployment.

Why don't unemployed people create jobs by becoming self-employed? They might offer services as barbers, carpenters, caterers, designers, painters, plumbers, maintenance workers, baby-sitters, consultants, or taxi drivers. They might sell handicrafts or provide lawn and landscape care, music lessons, tutoring services, laundry services, or start restaurants or video-rental stores. Centuries ago, when most people were self-employed, unemployment was virtually unknown, and it was certainly not the major public issue it is today. Although self-employment eliminates the need to search for a suitable employer, it requires a search for customers. In addition, some people would not earn much in business for themselves. A self-employed person may need a business location (for a barber shop or restaurant), tools (to work as a carpenter), money for advertising, and so on. The person may also require organizational skills, marketing skills, lawyer services, and other inputs that an employer would have provided. It can be difficult and costly to buy all these inputs, so many people prefer to remain unemployed while they search for suitable jobs working for established firms.

AUTOMATION

People have worried throughout history about automation causing unemployment as new machines replace workers at lower cost. How does the economy create new jobs to replace those that automation destroys? The answer is not that some-one must produce the new machines, creating some jobs, because one worker may produce a machine that replaces ten workers. Instead, the answer is that the economy creates new jobs through new trades; firms are willing to hire the people who lose their jobs to automation because those people offer valuable labor services. Because it takes time to create suitable matches between firms and these workers, automation drives unemployment above its equilibrium level temporarily, but in time it falls back toward its equilibrium level. People who lose their jobs may suffer greatly from unemployment, and the new jobs they find might not be as good as the jobs they lost, but the new machines raise the economy's aggregate GDP. The economy produces more goods and services for people. Although automation creates losses for *some* people (particularly those who lose their jobs), the *average* person gains from automation and other technical progress.[20]

─────────────────────── **FOR REVIEW** ───────────────────────

25.10 List some reasons for unemployment.

25.11 Explain why the rate of unemployment tends to move toward its equilibrium level.

─────────────────────── **QUESTION** ───────────────────────

25.12 Discuss this statement: "Advances in technology that replace workers with machines are likely to raise the rate of unemployment over the next several decades by reducing the number of jobs available in the economy."

CONCLUSIONS

EQUILIBRIUM

In general (macroeconomic) equilibrium, prices have adjusted to equate demands and supplies in all markets. Economists usually study macroeconomics by studying factors that affect total gross domestic product (GDP) and its composition.

An economy's equilibrium real GDP depends on its technology, available inputs of labor and people's choices of how much and how hard to work,

---

[20]Enormous advances in technology over the past two centuries and the invention of a vast array of machinery and equipment have destroyed jobs by replacing workers at lower cost. Despite these changes, and despite huge increases in population, the number of jobs in the economy has expanded about as fast as the population. On average, automation over the past two centuries has created tremendous increases in wages and material standards of living.

available inputs of capital and people's decisions about how much to use them, and other factors such as taxes, government regulations, enforcement of property rights, entrepreneurship, and the amount of competition in the economy. Economists summarize technology with a production function that shows the amount of real GDP the economy can produce with its available inputs of capital and labor. The equilibrium inputs of labor and capital are determined by the equilibrium between the supply and demand for each; this chapter assumed that the equilibrium labor and capital inputs are fixed numbers. In macroeconomic equilibrium, the economy fully employs labor and capital in the sense that it keeps unemployment at the equilibrium level. The economy's production function, with these equilibrium quantities of inputs, determines equilibrium real GDP.

Equilibrium in an economy without international trade requires equality between the total number of goods that people, firms, and the government want to buy each year and the total quantity of goods that the economy produces. This is the same as saying that the quantity of loans demanded equals the quantity supplied, so a graph of the supply and demand for loans can help economists to analyze equilibrium savings, investment, consumption, and the real interest rate.

CHANGES IN ECONOMIC CONDITIONS

This chapter's simple macroeconomic model showed how endogenous variables (the real interest rate, consumption, savings, and investment) respond to changes in exogenous variables.

An increase in consumer patience (that is, in people's desire to save for the future) reduces the equilibrium real interest rate, raises equilibrium savings and investment, and reduces current consumption, though it increases future consumption.

Technical progress that permanently raises productivity (the output that the economy can produce with any amounts of labor and capital inputs) raises real GDP, the real interest rate, consumption, savings, and investment. The rise in investment increases the economy's future capital stock, so real GDP and consumption rise more in the long run than in the short run.

A permanent increase in government spending financed by higher taxes reduces consumption and may leave real GDP, savings, investment, and the real interest rate unchanged. However, increases in certain types of government spending may raise investment, the real interest rate, and savings, and reduce consumption further. In addition, if the tax increase falls on income from investments, then it may reduce equilibrium savings and investment.

A temporary increase in government spending financed by higher income taxes raises the real interest rate and reduces consumption, savings, and investment. As in the case of a permanent increase, equilibrium savings and investment also depend partly on the type of government spending and the types of taxes.

The effects of a tax cut that raises the government budget deficit are controversial. Most economists believe that evidence supports the view that it raises the real interest rate and consumption and reduces investment. Some economists, however, believe the evidence indicates that it has little effect on the real interest rate, consumption, and investment.

EQUILIBRIUM EMPLOYMENT AND UNEMPLOYMENT

Continuing changes in technology, consumer tastes, population, weather, government policies, international competition, and other economic factors cause unemployment. Some industries contract while others expand. It takes time for unemployed people to find jobs that suit their interests and skills. It also takes time for firms to find workers who match their needs. Unemployment occurs partly because workers differ and jobs differ, so this matching process takes time.

The term *full employment* means the equilibrium level of unemployment—unemployment that results from continuing changes in supplies and demands and the costs of searching for and matching jobs in labor markets. Unemployment is at its equilibrium level when the rate of job creation equals the rate of job destruction. At this level, the number of people who lose their jobs each month equals the number of unemployed people who find jobs, so total unemployment does not change. If unemployment exceeds its equilibrium level, then the rate of job creation exceeds the rate of job destruction and unemployment falls. If unemployment falls below its equilibrium level, then the rate of job creation falls below the rate of job destruction and unemployment rises. This activity moves the rate of unemployment toward its equilibrium level.

Jobs are trades, not products with limited supplies. The only limit to the number of jobs the economy can create is the number of profitable, voluntary trades that people can create. Anyone who can produce something of value to other people can obtain a job at some wage. Unemployment occurs, not because the economy offers too few jobs, but because searching and matching take time; some people choose unemployment while they search for better opportunities.

LOOKING AHEAD

The next chapter will use the results of this chapter to discuss economic growth, the process by which real GDP per person rises over time. Later chapters then discuss inflation, money, the financial system, then issues related to unemployment and the disequilibrium forces that cause the economy to move away from its equilibrium in the short run.

KEY TERMS

general (macroeconomic) equilibrium	equilibrium unemployment
production function	rate of job creation
crowding out	rate of job destruction

QUESTIONS AND PROBLEMS

25.13 Explain why government borrowing may crowd out investment.

25.14 Suppose that the government has a budget deficit and raises taxes to eliminate the deficit. What are the effects (a) according to the majority view? (b) According to the minority view?

25.15 Why might it be rational for people to save all the money that they receive from a tax cut? Why might it not be rational?

25.16 Comment on this statement: "A tax increase to reduce a government budget deficit is more likely to reduce the real interest rate if people pay the higher taxes by saving less instead of spending less."

25.17 A fall in business confidence means that firms invest less in new equipment because of increased uncertainty about future demand for their products. Discuss the effects of a fall in business confidence on the real interest rate, savings, investment, and consumption.

25.18 Explain why the effects of an increase in government spending depend partly on whether the new spending affects investment demand. Why might it affect investment demand?

25.19 The baby-boom generation (people born in the 1950s) will retire after two or three more decades. Most retired people spend more than their incomes. The U.S. population now has about five workers for each retired person; by 2030, it will probably have only about <u>three</u> workers for each retired person.

   a. Explain how this change will affect total savings in the United States.

   b. Explain how this change will affect the real interest rate, savings, consumption, and investment.

25.20 How large is equilibrium unemployment if the rate of job destruction is 300,000 workers per month, and one-tenth of unemployed workers find jobs each month? Suppose that 10 million people are currently unemployed and explain why unemployment falls over time toward its equilibrium level.

INQUIRIES FOR FURTHER THOUGHT

25.21 **a.** How much should people save? How much should the economy save?

   b. Discuss this statement: "Free market economies do not provide enough savings, investment, and other resources for future generations. The government should adopt policies to raise savings and investment for future generations."

25.22 Why are people unemployed? Why don't unemployed people create their own jobs by going into business for themselves? What could governments do to reduce unemployment? What government policies add to unemployment?

25.23 Why don't people buy unemployment insurance like they buy fire insurance or automobile insurance?

TAG SOFTWARE APPLICATIONS

TUTORIAL EXERCISES
▶ The module contains a review of the key terms from Chapter 25.

GRAPHING EXERCISES
▶ The graphing segment contains questions on equilibrium in the loans market, the factors that lead to a change in the real interest rate, and factors that change the supply of and demand for labor.

CHAPTER 25 APPENDIX A — INTERNATIONAL TRADE

International trade adds a new issue to the discussion in the chapter: international borrowing and lending. Chapter 23 explained that real GDP equals consumption plus investment plus government purchases plus net exports, *NEX,* or exports to other countries minus imports from them. In equation form, this is:

$$GDP = C + I + G + NEX \qquad \text{(25A.1)}$$

where C is consumption, I is investment, and G is government purchases. Recall that another name for *net exports* is the *balance of international trade.* A country has an international trade surplus if its exports exceed its imports and an international trade deficit if its imports exceed its exports.

Chapter 24 Appendix showed that a country with a trade surplus lends to people in other countries, while a country with a trade deficit borrows from other countries.[1] For example, if Japan sells goods worth ¥20 trillion to other countries and imports goods worth only ¥18 trillion, then Japan lends ¥2 trillion to other countries. People in other countries receive only ¥18 trillion from buyers in Japan, but spend ¥20 trillion; they spend more yen than they receive by borrowing the remaining ¥2 trillion. The United States has borrowed hundreds of billions of dollars from other countries in recent years.

The appendix to Chapter 24 also showed that when a country can borrow from or lend to other countries, equilibrium in its loan market requires that its savings minus its net exports equal investment plus the government budget deficit:

$$S - NEX = I + (G - T) \qquad \text{(25A.2)}$$

where S is savings, NEX is net exports, I is investment, and $(G - T)$ is the government budget deficit. Because a country's trade deficit is the *negative* of its net exports, Equation 25A.2 says that savings plus the trade deficit equals investment plus the government budget deficit.

THE SUPPLY OF LOANS INCLUDES THE CURRENT ACCOUNT DEFICIT

International borrowing and lending imply that loans can come from two sources: savings by people within the country or loans from people in other countries (the trade deficit). The left-hand side of Equation 25A.2 shows the supply of loans and the right-hand side shows the demand for loans. The supply of loans equals savings plus loans from other countries. Because foreign lenders find lending more profitable when the interest rate is high, the supply of loans slopes upward, as usual.

TWIN DEFICITS

The United States has experienced large international trade deficits for over a decade. They increased substantially soon after the government budget deficit increased in the early 1980s. Many economists, seeing a relationship between these two deficits, dubbed them *twin deficits.* **Figure 25A.1** shows a loose

---

[1]This section ignores the subtle distinction between the balance of trade and another concept called the *current account balance.*

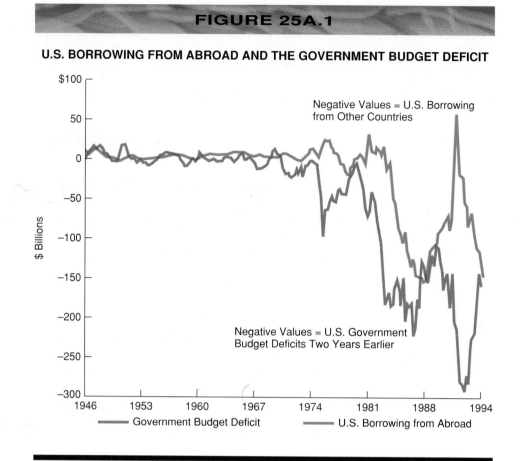

FIGURE 25A.1

U.S. BORROWING FROM ABROAD AND THE GOVERNMENT BUDGET DEFICIT

connection between the trade deficit in the United States and the federal government budget deficit two years earlier.

Many economists have interpreted these combined deficits as results of U.S. tax cuts in the 1980s. Chapter 25 discussed the majority view of a tax cut that raises the government budget deficit; this view also predicts that tax cuts cause international trade deficits. **Figure 25A.2** shows why. Initially, the equilibrium real interest rate is 2 percent per year and the United States invests $800 billion, $780 billion from U.S. savings and $20 billion from loans by people or firms in other countries. A tax cut causes a $100 billion budget deficit, increasing the demand for loans by $100 billion and increasing the supply of loans by a small amount as people save a small amount of the money that they get from the tax cut and spend the rest. The equilibrium real interest rate rises to 3 percent per year and the equilibrium quantity of loans rises from $800 billion to $860 billion. The increase in the real interest rate percent raises the quantity of loans supplied by foreign lenders by $40 billion, from $20 billion to $60 billion. Total savings in the U.S. economy rises by $20 billion from $780 billion to $800 billion, so total lending in the United States reaches $860 billion. The government borrows $100 billion, so equilibrium investment falls from $800 billion to $760 billion. Foreign countries obtain the additional $40 billion to lend to the United States by spending $40 billion less on exports from the United States or by earning $40 billion more from increased U.S. imports. The

FIGURE 25A.2

EFFECTS OF A TAX CUT ON BORROWING FROM FOREIGN COUNTRIES

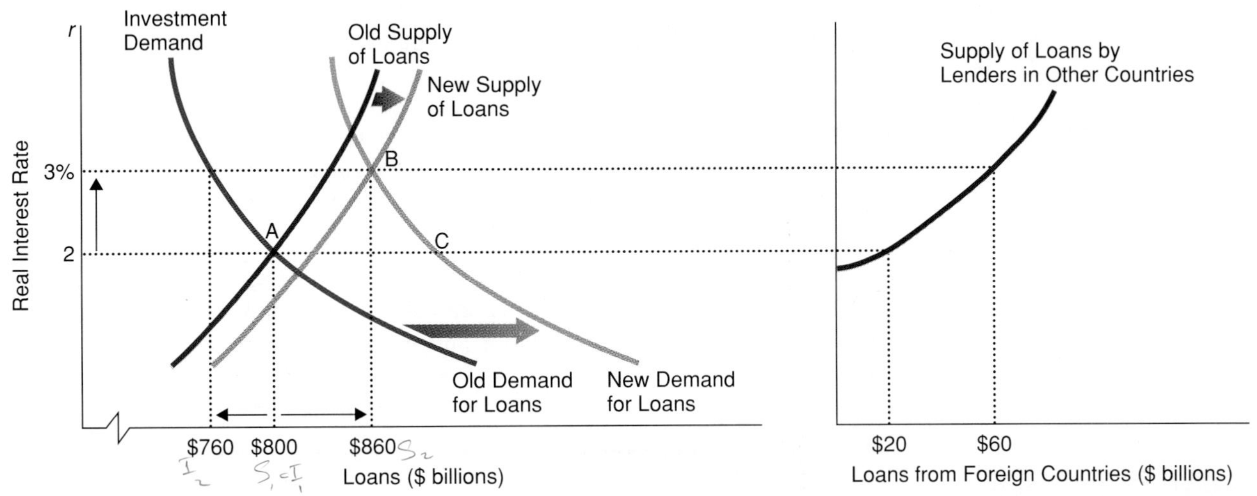

A $100 billion tax cut raises the budget deficit and the demand for loans by $100 billion. According to the majority view, the supply of loans rises by less because people save only part of the money they get from the tax cut. The equilibrium moves from Point A to Point B; the equilibrium real interest rate rises from 2 percent to 3 percent per year, and the equilibrium quantity of loans rises from $800 billion to $860 billion. The government borrows $100 billion, so equilibrium investment falls from $800 billion to $760 billion. The rise in the real interest rate causes the quantity of loans supplied from foreign countries to increase by $40 billion, from $20 billion to $60 billion. Because total loans rise by $60 billion, equilibrium savings in the United States must rise by $20 billion, from $780 billion to $800 billion.

$40 billion increase in foreign lending to the United States is the same as a $40 billion increase in the U.S. international trade deficit.

The increase in foreign lending to the United States helps to keep the real interest rate from increasing as much as it would otherwise increase. It also helps to reduce the amount by which the budget deficit *crowds out* private investment in the United States; because foreign lenders provide $40 billion in additional loans, the $100 billion budget deficit absorbs only $60 billion of loans from lenders in the United States. In Figure 25A.2, the $100 billion tax cut raises the international trade deficit by $40 billion, raises U.S. savings by $20 billion, and reduces U.S. investment by $40 billion.

QUESTIONS AND PROBLEMS

25A.1 How would a fall in the supply of loans from lenders in foreign countries affect the real interest rate, savings, investment, and consumption in the United States?

25A.2 Problem 25.19 noted that the baby-boom generation will retire and begin dissaving after another 2 or 3 decades, and that the current ratio of about five workers for each retired person in the United States seems likely to fall to only three workers for each retired person by 2030. If this were to happen only in the United States, how would it affect net U.S. exports?

CHAPTER 25 APPENDIX B — CHANGES IN LABOR AND CAPITAL INPUTS AND EQUILIBRIUM REAL GDP

utilization rate of capital — the number of hours per week firms use capital equipment

Chapter 25 assumed that inputs of labor and capital remain fixed in the short run. In real life, people choose the quantities of these inputs, and their decisions depend on economic conditions such as wage rates, wealth, and the real interest rate. This appendix discusses factors that affect the equilibrium inputs of labor and capital and equilibrium real GDP, and it explains how changes in consumer patience, technology, and government policies affect real GDP.

FACTORS THAT AFFECT EQUILIBRIUM INPUTS

FIGURE 25B.1

INCREASE IN WEALTH CAUSES A FALL IN LABOR SUPPLY

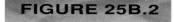

FIGURE 25B.2

INCREASE IN PRODUCTIVITY CAUSES A RISE IN LABOR DEMAND

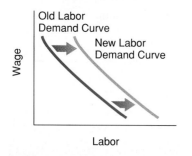

INCREASE IN WEALTH AND A REDUCTION IN LABOR SUPPLY

An increase in wealth reduces labor supply, as in **Figure 25B.1.** When people become richer, they want to buy more leisure time. An increase in wealth raises the demand for leisure time, so people buy leisure time by working less. The decrease in labor supply reduces the equilibrium quantity of labor, which tends to reduce real GDP.

INCREASE IN LABOR PRODUCTIVITY AND A RISE IN LABOR DEMAND

An increase in labor productivity raises the demand for labor, as **Figure 25B.2** illustrates. Firms are willing to pay higher wages because workers are more productive. This increase in labor demand raises the equilibrium quantity of labor, which tends to raise real GDP.

INCREASE IN THE REAL INTEREST RATE AND A TEMPORARY RISE IN THE SUPPLIES OF LABOR AND CAPITAL

An increase in the real interest rate raises the supplies of labor and capital temporarily through a process called *intertemporal substitution.* First, consider labor supply. An increase in the real interest rate makes working this year more profitable relative to working next year. A person may choose to work more now and less next year, perhaps by postponing a vacation or working more overtime hours this year. This person can take advantage of the higher interest rate that savings can earn. Intertemporal substitution of labor supply occurs when an increase in the real interest rate (or a temporary increase in the wage rate) leads people to work more now and postpone some leisure time until a future date.[1]

An increase in the real interest rate also raises the supply of capital temporarily by making it profitable to increase the utilization rate of capital.

The **utilization rate of capital** refers to the fraction of hours per week that firms use capital equipment rather than letting it sit idle.

Firms increase the utilization rate of capital by working machinery more hours per day or more days per week. An increase in the utilization rate of capital tends to

---

[1]You can think of this as intertemporal substitution in consumption of leisure; people buy less leisure (they work more) when leisure is more expensive, and they buy more leisure (they work less) when leisure costs less. An increase in the real interest rate or a temporary increase in wages raises the cost of leisure.

make machines wear out faster and break down more often, raising the cost of repairs. An increase in the real interest rate gives firms an incentive to raise the utilization rate of capital because it raises the benefit of producing goods this year rather than next year. (It raises the relative price of goods this year in terms of goods next year.) Put another way, letting a machine sit idle—not using it—amounts to an investment. The firm sacrifices output this year and gains a less worn-out machine next year. An increase in the real interest rate reduces investment and, by the same reasoning, reduces the number of hours that firms leave machines idle. In this way, an increase in the real interest rate raises the utilization rate of capital and the supply of capital.

EFFECTS OF CHANGES IN EXOGENOUS VARIABLES

Because an increase in the real interest rate temporarily increases the supplies of labor and capital, it temporarily raises their equilibrium quantities, $\bar{L}$ and $\bar{K}$, and real GDP. This section discusses the effects on equilibrium inputs and real GDP of changes in consumers' desires to save for the future, advances in technology, and changes in government spending. This extends the discussion in the chapter.

SAVING MORE FOR THE FUTURE

An increase in consumers' desires to save for the future raises labor and capital inputs and real GDP. People can save more by spending less, as discussed in the chapter, or by working more and earning higher incomes. When people decide to save more for the future, they tend to do both, so labor supply rises, as in **Figure 25B.3**. This raises the equilibrium quantity of labor from $\bar{L}_1$ to $\bar{L}_2$ and it reduces the wage rate. The increase in the equilibrium quantity of labor raises real GDP. People save more partly

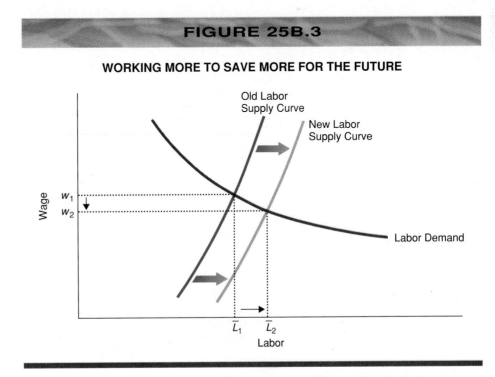

FIGURE 25B.3

WORKING MORE TO SAVE MORE FOR THE FUTURE

FIGURE 25B.4

PERMANENT INCREASE IN PRODUCTIVITY

A permanent increase in productivity raises labor demand and reduces labor supply. Evidence suggests that the long-run equilibrium quantity of labor remains about the same, while the wage rate rises.

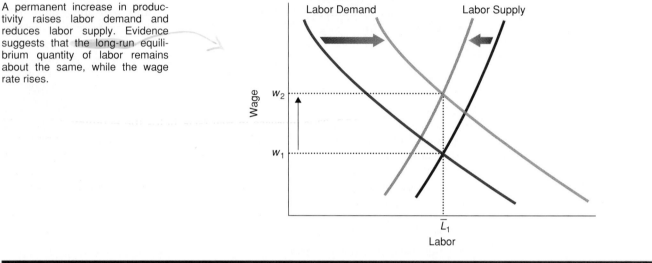

by consuming less and partly by earning higher incomes (producing more). For example, if real GDP rises by $10 billion, savings and investment can rise by $30 billion while consumption falls by only $20 billion.[2]

PERMANENT INCREASE IN PRODUCTIVITY

A permanent increase in productivity raises the demand for labor, as Figure 25B.2 showed. In addition, it raises wealth (that is, it increases the discounted present value of future income), which decreases labor supply, as in Figure 25B.1. Most evidence suggests that the long-run effects of these changes on the equilibrium quantity of labor tend to cancel, as in **Figure 25B.4.** The long-run equilibrium quantity of labor remains at about $\overline{L}_1$ in Figure 25B.4, while the wage rate rises.

Huge increases in productivity during the last century have reduced the amount of time that people spend working by a much smaller percentage. You might think that people would work much less and take much more leisure time than people did a century ago because today's workers are much wealthier than those of a century ago. The increases in productivity have also raised wages, however, so they have raised the opportunity cost of leisure time. On net, people tend to work only somewhat less in the long run (after a permanent increase in productivity than they worked before that increase).

In the short run, however, a permanent increase in productivity raises the equilibrium labor input, which reinforces the rise in real GDP. As the chapter explained, an increase in productivity raises investment demand, which raises the

[2]In addition, the increase in savings raises the supply of loans, so it raises equilibrium savings and investment and reduces the equilibrium real interest rate, as the discussion in the chapter explained. This fall in the equilibrium real interest rate limits the increase in labor supply and may temporarily reduce the supply of capital; this limits the short-run rise in real GDP.

real interest rate. This temporarily increases the supplies of labor and capital through intertemporal substitution, which reinforces the increase in real GDP in the short run. The increase in real GDP helps the economy to raise investment; if real GDP rises by $90 billion, the economy can raise investment by $100 billion while reducing consumption by only $10 billion.

PERMANENT INCREASE IN GOVERNMENT SPENDING AND TAXES

The chapter discussed the effects of a permanent increase in government spending and taxes when short-run inputs of labor and capital remain fixed. The fact that quantities of inputs may change adds one new element to that discussion because the tax increase makes people poorer. This tends to raise the supply of labor as in Figure 25B.3, which raises the equilibrium quantity of labor from $\bar{L}_1$ to $\bar{L}_2$ and raises real GDP. This increase in real GDP helps the economy to provide the extra goods that the government buys without large cuts in consumption. For example, a permanent $50 billion increase in government spending would reduce private consumption by about $50 billion if real GDP remained constant (and if savings and investment also remain constant). If, however, real GDP rises by $20 billion due to an increase in labor supply, consumption falls by only $30 billion.

TEMPORARY INCREASE IN GOVERNMENT SPENDING AND TAXES

Chapter 25 also discussed the effects of a temporary increase in government spending and taxes, holding fixed inputs of labor and capital in the short run. Changes in the quantities of inputs add two new elements to that discussion. First, a tax increase makes people poorer, which raises labor supply. A tax increase that people expect to be temporary, however, does not reduce wealth as much as one that they expect to be permanent. For this reason, a temporary tax increase does not raise labor supply by as much as a permanent tax increase would. Instead, people tend to pay some of the temporarily higher taxes by saving less for the future or borrowing more.

The temporary tax increase adds a second new element to the discussion because the fall in savings reduces the supply of loans, raising the real interest rate. This increase in the real interest rate raises labor supply temporarily through intertemporal substitution as people postpone leisure time. These two factors both tend to raise the supply of labor in the short run, temporarily raising real GDP and helping the economy to provide the extra goods that the government buys.

QUESTIONS AND PROBLEMS

25B.1 Explain why a change in the real interest rate affects labor supply.

25B.2 What is the utilization rate of capital? Explain why a change in the real interest rate affects the supply of capital.

25B.3 Explain the effect on real GDP of:
   a. An increase in the supply of labor
   b. A permanent increase in productivity
   c. A permanent increase in government spending and taxes
   d. A temporary increase in government spending and taxes

25B.4 Discuss this statement: "High real interest rates are bad for the economy."

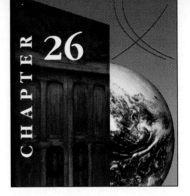

ECONOMIC GROWTH

WHAT THIS CHAPTER IS ABOUT

read pp. 757 — 763

▶ What makes the economy grow

▶ Why some countries grow faster than others

▶ Effects of government policies on economic growth

▶ Whether economic growth will slow down or stop in the future

Long-run economic growth—a continuing rise in per-capita real GDP over a long period of time—is one of the most important topics in economics. For most of history, most people have lived in conditions of extreme poverty without even the basic goods that we now regard as necessities. Life was brutal, filled with hard work and little food or health care. Lifetimes were short and infant mortality rates were high. Economic growth has lifted billions of people out of these conditions, though many people continue to live in poverty.[1] World per-capita real GDP is about $5,200 today, roughly 12 times higher than the level in 1800, and 5 times higher than the level in 1900. Per-capita real GDP in the United States is about $27,000 today, about 20 times higher than the level during the American Revolution, 10 times higher than the level during the Civil War, 5 times higher than the level in 1900, and more than twice as high as the level at the end of World War II. The economies of some countries, such as Hong Kong, Japan, Singapore, South Korea, and Taiwan, have grown much faster than that of the United States in recent years, while others have grown much more slowly. Not only has the *level* of per-capita real GDP risen over time, but the *rate of economic growth* has also increased over most of the last 200 years. Economic growth has been much higher in the last 200 years than over all of the rest of history.

Will the economy continue to grow rapidly in your lifetime and raise your material standard of living, or will economic growth slow down or stop? These issues have profound effects on people's lives. As one economist puts it:

> The consequences for human welfare involved in questions [of economic growth] like these are simply staggering: Once one starts to think about them, it is hard to think about anything else.[2]

---

[1] Life expectancy in developed countries (those that are members of the Organization for Economic Cooperation and Development) rose from 49 years at birth in 1900 to 76 in the 1980s; life expectancy in the developing countries rose from 35 to 63 years over the same time.

[2] Robert E. Lucas, "On the Mechanism of Economic Development," *Journal of Monetary Economics,* vol. 22, no. 1, July 1988, pp. 3-42.

Losing faith: Many Americans fear U.S. living standards have stopped rising

They believe their children face a tougher future; but 'Boomers' have hope

By Alan Murray
Staff Reporter of The
Wall Street Journal

For nearly three decades after World War II, the rise in American living standards was as reliable as a Maytag washer.

The march of material prosperity created the easy assurance that each generation would live better than the last. Today, that has changed.

The economic confidence of the postwar years has faded. In a painful awareness striking at the heart of American life, many no longer assume that their children will be better off than they are.

Expectations about the future may vary—but what is that future really likely to hold? Has the American dream of ever-rising living standards vanished, dwindled to a faint hope or merely gone into hibernation?

Source: Alan Murray, "Losing Faith: Many Americans Fear U.S. Living Standards Have Stopped Rising," *The Wall Street Journal,* May 1, 1989, p. A1.

BASICS OF GROWTH

Chapter 25 explained that the economy's real GDP in long-run equilibrium depends on its technology; its available inputs of capital and labor; its laws, regulations, and taxes; and other factors that affect people's incentives to use technology and inputs efficiently. A country's real GDP per capita equals its real GDP divided by its population. *Economic growth* refers to an increase in real GDP per capita, which occurs when real GDP rises at a faster rate than population increases.

economic growth — a rise in real GDP per capita

Economic growth is a rise in real GDP per capita.

Economists distinguish between short-run or temporary increases in real GDP per capita and long-run economic growth, which is a continuing increase in real GDP per capita over a long period of time. This chapter concerns long-run economic growth.

Real GDP can rise due to technical progress, increases in inputs of capital or labor, or increases in the efficiency with which the economy uses its resources.

technical progress — an increase in the quantity of output that the economy can produce with efficient use of the same quantities of capital, labor, and other inputs

Technical progress occurs when efficient use of the same quantities of capital, labor, and other inputs can produce more output.

Technical progress results from applications of new inventions and discoveries to production of goods and services. Technical progress may occur *exogenously,* as when an accidental discovery increases productivity, or because people spend time and other resources on research and development, as when firms conduct scientific and engineering research. Economists measure technical progress by the growth of total factor productivity.[3]

---

[3]As footnote 3 in Chapter 25 explained, the production function $y = AK^{\frac{1}{3}}L^{\frac{2}{3}}$ is a good approximation of the real-life production function in the United States and many other countries. The number A represents total factor productivity or the level of technology, and increases in A represent technical progress. Real GDP rises when A, K, or L rises.

total factor productivity growth — a measure of technical progress that represents increases in production with given amounts of inputs

Total factor productivity growth refers to increases in the amount of goods and services that the economy can produce with given amounts of inputs.

Most economic growth occurs because of technical progress, investment in physical capital, and investment in human capital.

physical capital — machinery, equipment, tools, and buildings

human capital — people's knowledge, education, and skills

Physical capital refers to machinery, equipment, tools, and buildings.

Human capital refers to people's knowledge, education, and skills.

Investments in physical capital increase the quantities of machinery, equipment, and tools that people can use to produce goods. Investments in human capital increase the education levels and skills of workers, making them more productive. Increases in human capital function like increases in the economy's input of labor. They raise the economy's effective amount of labor because a more skilled worker effectively provides more labor services than a less skilled worker provides.

RATE OF ECONOMIC GROWTH

The growth rate of a variable is its annual percentage increase. Economists have found that the growth rate of total real GDP equals approximately:

$$\text{Growth rate of real GDP} = (\tfrac{1}{3})(\text{Growth rate of capital})$$
$$+ (\tfrac{2}{3})(\text{Growth rate of labor})$$
$$+ \text{Growth rate of total factor productivity} \quad \textbf{(26.1)}$$

Economic growth is an increase in GDP per person.

rate of economic growth — the average annual percentage increase in per-capita real GDP

The **rate of economic growth** is the average annual percentage increase in per-capita real GDP.

The rate of economic growth equals the rate of growth of real GDP minus the rate of population growth:

$$\text{Rate of economic growth} = (\tfrac{1}{3})(\text{Growth rate of capital})$$
$$+ (\tfrac{2}{3})(\text{Growth rate of labor})$$
$$+ \text{Growth rate of total factor productivity}$$
$$- \text{Growth rate of population.} \quad \textbf{(26.2)}$$

A classic study of American economic growth found that from 1929 until recently:[4]

▶ Aggregate real GDP in the United States grew at a rate of 2.8 percent per year.

▶ About half of this growth in real GDP (1.5 percent) resulted from increases in the amounts of capital (0.6 percent) and labor (0.9 percent).

▶ The other half of the growth in real GDP in the United States resulted from increases in technology, knowledge, and education (1.2 percent) and from increases in economic efficiency, meaning that the economy made better use of its resources.

---

[4]Edward Denison, *Trends in American Economic Growth, 1929-82* (Washington, D.C.: Brookings Institution, 1985).

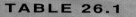

TABLE 26.1

RISING ECONOMIC GROWTH IN THE UNITED STATES

Time Period	Growth Rate of Per-Capita Real GDP in the United States (percent per year)
1800–1855	1.1%
1855–1900	1.6
1900–1950	1.7
1950–1995	1.9

Because the U.S. population grew at about 1 percent per year over this period, the rate of economic growth in the United States was 2.8 percent minus 1 percent, or 1.8 percent per year. Roughly two-thirds of growth in U.S. per-capita real GDP resulted from increases in technology, knowledge, and education, and about one-third resulted from increases in the economy's capital inputs. These facts represent part of a broader picture of world-wide economic growth and its causes.

MAIN FACTS ABOUT ECONOMIC GROWTH

WORLD ECONOMIC GROWTH

World per-capita real GDP is about $5,200 today. In 1900, it was only $1,200 to $1,300, and in 1800, it was only about $500 (all in today's dollars). Rates of economic growth have increased over time in most countries, except very recently. This means that the average person has recently been getting richer at a faster rate than in the past. World real GDP per capita grew at about 1 percent per year in the 19th century and 1.7 percent per year in the 20th century. World economic growth averaged 1.1 percent per year from 1900 to 1950, and it has averaged 2.1 percent per year since 1950. Per-capita world real GDP is now more than 4 times as high as in 1900.

One important exception qualifies this experience. World economic growth has slowed since 1973; it averaged less than 1.3 percent per year from 1973 to 1995. Still, the rate of economic growth was much lower in earlier centuries and throughout most of history.[5]

ECONOMIC GROWTH IN THE UNITED STATES AND THE UNITED KINGDOM

Table 26.1 shows economic growth in the United States for the last two centuries. The rate of U.S. economic growth has generally increased over time, though it has fallen to an average of 1.4 percent per year for the period from 1973 to 1995.

---

[5]Although economists can refer to few statistics on economic growth in earlier centuries, they know that the rate of economic growth was much lower in those centuries. Recall that in 1800, per-capita world real GDP was about $500 (in today's dollars). If economic growth had averaged 1 percent per year in earlier centuries (its rate in the 19th century), then world real GDP per person would have been only $25 in the year 1500, and about $0.16 in 1000 (measured in today's dollars). This is impossible: people need more food than this to survive. Moreover, historical records prove that incomes were much higher than this at those times. Therefore, the rate of world economic growth must have been much lower before the 19th century.

TABLE 26.2

PER-CAPITA REAL GDP IN 1994 DOLLARS

Year	United States	United Kingdom
1776	$ 1,300	$ 1,230
1860	2,300	2,700
1900	4,950	4,800
1950	11,380	7,400
1994	25,850	17,500

Gross domestic product per capita in the United States is about $27,000 today. At the time of the American Revolution in 1776, per-capita real GDP was about $1,300 (in 1994 dollars). Output per person was just slightly higher in the United States than in England and France. By 1860, on the eve of the Civil War, per-capita real GDP was $2,300 (in 1994 dollars). **Table 26.2** shows levels of real GDP per person in selected years in the United States and the United Kingdom. U.S. output of goods and services per person is now about 20 times its level at the time of the American Revolution, and about 10 times its level at the time of the Civil War. It has more than doubled since the end of World War II.

You can use the rule of 72 (see Chapter 23) to estimate the annual growth rate of per-capita real GDP in the United States since 1776. Real GDP per capita was more than 18 times higher in 1994 than its level in 1776, so it doubled more than 4 times over that 218-year period.[6] Multiplying 72 by 4 gives 288, so you can estimate the average growth rate of the U.S. economy since 1776 to be 288/218, or 1.33 percent per year.[7] At this rate, output per person has doubled every 54 years.

ECONOMIC GROWTH IN JAPAN

In 1860, at the time of the U.S. Civil War, per-capita real GDP in Japan was about $750, or about one-third that of the United States. The Japanese economy then grew at about the same rate as the U.S. economy, so Japanese real GDP per capita stayed at about one-third the U.S. level, until World War II. That war cut Japanese per-capita real GDP in half; when the war ended, it was about one-sixth of U.S. per-capita real GDP. After the war, Japan began to grow rapidly. By 1960, Japanese real GDP per capita was again one-third of the U.S. level. This rapid growth continued, and by 1994, per-capita real GDPs in Japan and the United States were about equal, depending on the method of comparison.[8]

ECONOMIC GROWTH IN OTHER COUNTRIES

Economic growth rates differ substantially across countries. Japan's economy has grown much faster than that of the United States in recent years. **Table 26.3** shows the rate of economic growth in several countries. (For comparison, recall that U.S. economic growth in the 20th century has averaged 1.8 percent per year.)

---

[6]It doubled once to $2,600, doubled a second time to $5,200, doubled a third time to $10,400, doubled a fourth time to $20,800, and then increased further after that.

[7]Since real GDP actually increased more than this (it continued increasing after doubling four times), the actual growth rate over this period is 1.36 percent per year.

[8]One way to compare amounts in Japanese yen with those in U.S. dollars is to use the foreign exchange rate between yen and dollars. Another way adjusts for differences in the prices of goods in Japan and the United States.

TABLE 26.3

ANNUAL RATES OF ECONOMIC GROWTH IN VARIOUS COUNTRIES

Country	Growth Rate, 1900–1994	Country	Growth Rate, 1950–1994
Japan	3.2%	Taiwan	6.1%
Finland, Norway	2.6	Japan	6.0
Canada	2.3	South Korea	5.7
Switzerland	2.0	Germany	3.6
Belgium, Mexico	1.6	Thailand	3.7
Australia	1.5	Mexico	2.3
United Kingdom	1.4	India	1.7
Argentina	1.1	Chile	1.0
Bangladesh	0.1	Bangladesh	0.3

Source: Maddison, "The World Economy in the 20th Century," (Paris: OECD, 1989). Figures updated by author.

Per-capita real GDP has grown despite the fact that people work less! The number of worker-hours per person in developed countries has fallen by about one-fourth since the mid-19th century.[9] Despite the decrease in work per person, real GDP per person is much higher.

Economic growth is not inevitable. Chapter 23 noted that India, China, Bangladesh, Indonesia, and Pakistan experienced negative economic growth from 1900 to 1950; their per-capita GDPs fell. Similarly, Afghanistan, Angola, Chad, Madagascar, Mozambique, and Zambia have experienced negative economic growth since 1960. Many other countries have experienced negative economic growth over 5-year or 10-year periods.

Other countries, such as the so-called *four tigers* of Asia (Hong Kong, Singapore, South Korea, and Taiwan) have posted rapid economic growth. Between 1965 and 1994, annual economic growth averaged 7.8 percent in Hong Kong, 7.5 percent in Singapore, and 9.5 percent in South Korea; growth averaged about 6.6 percent in Taiwan from 1951 to 1973.

Low-income countries are sometimes called *third-world countries* or *LDCs* (for *less developed countries*).

LDC (less developed country) — a country with a relatively low real GDP per capita

An **LDC,** or **less developed country,** is a country with a relatively low real GDP per capita.

Most high-income countries are members of the OECD, or Organization for Economic Cooperation and Development.

OECD (Organization for Economic Cooperation and Development) — an organization of countries with relatively high per-capita real GDPs

The **OECD,** or **Organization for Economic Cooperation and Development,** is an organization of countries with relatively high per-capita real GDPs.

---

[9]An average worker in the United States, England, France, Germany, and Japan worked about 2,600 hours per year in 1913, but only 1,700 hours by the 1980s. A higher fraction of the population worked, however, so the average number of hours worked per person (not per worker) stayed about the same from 1913 to 1950, rose from 1950 to 1973, and has fallen since 1973, except in the United States and Japan.

TABLE 26.4

OECD COUNTRIES

Australia	Greece	Norway
Austria	Iceland	Portugal
Belgium	Ireland	Spain
Canada	Italy	Sweden
Denmark	Japan	Switzerland
Finland	Luxembourg	Turkey
France	Netherlands	United Kingdom
Germany	New Zealand	United States

Table 26.4 lists the OECD countries. The richest of these nations account for 20 percent of world population and about 60 percent of world GDP. The second-richest 20 percent of the world population gets about 20 percent of world GDP. LDCs account for 60 percent of world population and only 20 percent of world GDP. An average person in the OECD countries has an income about nine times higher than an average person in an LDC. The low-income countries had faster economic growth (about 3.1 percent per year) from 1965 to 1994 than the OECD countries, which grew at about 2.4 percent per year in that period.

FOR REVIEW

26.1 List three ways in which economic growth can occur.

26.2 What is technical progress and what creates it?

26.3 Roughly what fraction of growth in U.S. per-capita real GDP has resulted from technical progress? What explains the rest?

26.4 At what rates did the U.S. and world economies grow in the 20th century? How much larger are U.S. and world real GDP per capita now than they were in 1900? Than in 1800?

QUESTION

26.5 What are some important goods and services that many people have now, but did *not* have 100 years ago? 300 years ago? Why are these products available now when they were not available in the past?

LOGIC OF ECONOMIC GROWTH: A BASIC MODEL

Discussions of international differences in growth rates raise the question of *models* of economic growth—logical thinking about the process of growth. Why do some countries grow faster than others? This section begins with a simple model of growth. It then discusses the problems with it and adds some more realistic features. Economist Robert E. Lucas explains why economists need models of economic growth:

At the close of World War II, South Korea was less than twice as well off as India. . . . By 1980 Korea's income was four times higher than India's. If present trends continue, by the year 2000 Korea's per-capita income will be over 10 times India's . . . comparable to those in the U.S. and Western Europe today.

With such a range of experience, why do we need theoretical models? Why not simply use success stories—like Korea—as models? Why can't India send a fact-finding delegation to Korea, find out how they do it, and then go home and get Indians to do the same?

This sounds easy enough, but it is not really operational. . . . An economy is just too complex an entity—there are just too many things going on at once—for getting all the facts to be either possible or useful.

Faced with so much data, an observer who is unequipped with a theory sees what he wants to see, or what his hosts want to show him. One needs some principles for deciding which facts are central and which are peripheral. This is exactly the purpose of an economic theory: to isolate some very limited aspects of a situation and focus on them to the exclusion of all others. . . . We need to make some hard choices about what to emphasize and what to leave out before we can think in an organized way at all.[10]

This chapter's discussion of models will reach the following conclusions:

1. An economy can grow for a while by saving and investing to raise its capital stock. However, growth would slow down and eventually stop without continual technical progress or increases in human capital.

2. Continuing technical progress can create continuing growth.

3. The economy can grow faster than technical progress by increasing its inputs of both physical and human capital. Increases in human capital raise the economy's effective labor input along with the increase in physical capital.

4. Fixed quantities of certain natural resources such as land and fossil fuels may cause growth to slow down and eventually stop. However, growth may continue indefinitely without slowing down if technical progress can create new ways for the economy to use fewer resources or to substitute replenishable resources (such as trees and sunlight) for fixed or exhaustible resources.

5. The economy may be able to increase technical progress and long-run growth through investments in education, research, and development.

BASIC MODEL OF GROWTH

The basic model of economic growth, which is intended to develop logical thinking about the key issues, has several implications.

1. The economy grows as it invests and adds to its capital stock. However, when the amount of capital per worker reaches a certain level, the economy reaches a long-run equilibrium and economic growth stops.

2. The equilibrium quantity of savings and investment determines how fast the economy adds to its capital, so it determines the equilibrium rate of economic growth. A higher equilibrium quantity of investment supports a higher rate of growth.

3. The rate of growth slows down as the economy gets close to its long-run equilibrium because of diminishing returns to capital.

---

[10]Robert E. Lucas, 1991 Fisher-Schultz lecture, European meetings of the Econometrics Society, September 1991.

The **steady state** is the economy's long-run equilibrium in which the quantity of capital per worker does not change.

The **steady state capital stock** is the long-run equilibrium quantity of capital per worker.

Diminishing returns to capital means that the benefit of additional investment falls over time as the capital-labor ratio rises; with more capital equipment per worker, the economy gets a smaller benefit of investing in even more capital.[11]

The basic model of growth says that an economy invests and grows when its capital per worker is below its steady state capital stock. When its quantity of capital reaches the steady state capital stock, the economy stops growing and remains at its steady state.

EXPLANATION

The economy grows because people save and lend money and firms borrow and invest; investment raises the capital stock, K. If capital rises faster than the population, each person works with more machines and tools, so output per person (per-capita real GDP) rises.[12] The rate of growth depends on the amount of investment; more investment means faster growth in capital per worker and output per worker.

As the economy grows and capital per worker rises, the benefit of additional investment falls. **Table 26.5** shows an example for an economy with 5 workers. If the economy has 4 machines, it has four-fifths of a machine per worker and total output is 35 goods per year. If, instead, the economy has 5 machines, it has 1 machine per worker and total output is 41 goods per year. More machines mean more output. (The economy produces 6 more goods per year with 5 machines than with 4.) The extra output the economy gets from adding additional units of capital falls, though. With 6 machines, the economy produces 46 goods per year; the sixth machine raises output by only 5 goods per year (from 41 to 46 goods per year). A seventh machine raises output by only 4 goods per year. These diminishing returns to capital reflect the fact that doubling the amount of equipment without doubling other inputs produces a less-than-double rise in output. For examples, tools, tractors, and other pieces of equipment help farmers to produce food, but once farmers accumulate a certain amount of equipment, further increases in equipment add little value. This lesson holds generally: the benefit of additional investment falls as capital per worker rises.

Because an increase in capital per worker reduces the benefit of additional investment, it reduces investment demand, as in **Figure 26.1.** As the economy grows, the demand for loans falls from D_1 to D_2 to D_3 to D_{SS}, reducing equilibrium investment from I_1 to I_2 to I_3 to I_{SS} and the real interest rate from r_1 to r_2 to r_3 to r_{SS}. Because equilibrium investment falls over time, economic growth slows down as the economy approaches its steady state.[13]

---

[11]The law of diminishing returns states that if you increase the amount of one input while keeping the amounts of other inputs fixed, you eventually reduce the productivity of the input that you are adding.

[12]Capital per person rises when the growth rate of the capital stock exceeds the growth rate of the population. The percentage change in capital per worker, K/L, equals the percentage change in K minus the percentage change in L.

[13]Capital per worker rises faster—so the rate of growth is higher—when investment is I_1 than when it is I_2 or I_3.

TABLE 26.5

DIMINISHING RETURNS TO CAPITAL (WITH 5 WORKERS)

Total Quantity of Capital	Capital per Worker	Total Output (goods per year)	Extra Output from Adding the Last Unit of Capital
0	0	2.00	
1	$\frac{1}{5}$	12.00	10.00
2	$\frac{2}{5}$	20.00	8.00
3	$\frac{3}{5}$	28.00	8.00
4	$\frac{4}{5}$	35.00	7.00
5	1	41.00	6.00
6	$\frac{6}{5}$	46.00	5.00
7	$\frac{7}{5}$	50.00	4.00
8	$\frac{8}{5}$	53.00	3.00
9	$\frac{9}{5}$	55.00	2.00
10	2	56.00	1.00
11	$\frac{11}{5}$	56.10	0.10
12	$\frac{12}{5}$	56.11	0.01

FIGURE 26.1

ECONOMIC GROWTH TOWARD A STEADY STATE

When the economy has low capital per worker, investment demand is D_1, so equilibrium investment is I_1 and the equilibrium real interest rate is r_1. Investment adds to the economy's capital stock, but, because there are diminishing returns to capital, investment demand falls as the economy's capital stock rises. As the economy grows and adds to its capital per worker, equilibrium investment and the real interest rate fall. Eventually, the economy reaches a steady state. Steady state investment, I_{SS}, is just enough to replace capital that wears out so the economy's capital stock stops rising. The steady state real interest rate is r_{SS}. (Note: This figure assumes that all loans fund investments, so the demand for loans is investment demand.)

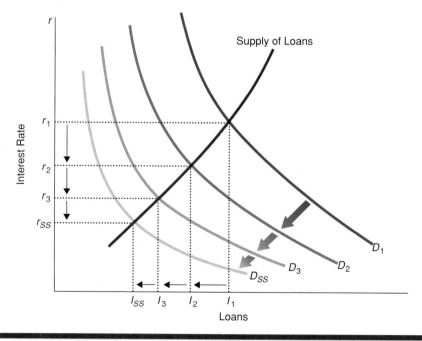

When capital per worker is sufficiently high and equilibrium investment is sufficiently low, the economy produces just enough new machines to replace those that wear out and to keep up with population growth.[14] At that point, capital per worker stops rising and the economy reaches its steady state. In Figure 26.1, the economy reaches its steady state (economic growth stops) when investment demand falls to D_4; steady state investment is I_{SS} and the steady state real interest rate is r_{SS}. According to this basic model, economic growth is temporary; the economy grows only until it reaches steady state.

EFFECT OF HIGHER SAVINGS

A temporary increase in the supply of savings raises the supply of loans, which raises equilibrium investment and the speed at which the economy grows toward its steady state. A permanent increase in savings also has a second effect: it raises the steady state capital stock. For this reason, a permanent increase in savings raises both the temporary rate of economic growth and the economy's steady state output.[15]

EXPLANATION

An increase in savings raises the supply of loans, which raises equilibrium investment and reduces the equilibrium real interest rate. The increase in investment raises the rate of growth of the capital stock and output. If the increase in savings is permanent, it also raises the steady state capital stock because it raises equilibrium investment permanently. The economy reaches its steady state when its investment exactly replaces the capital that wears out each year without increasing the quantity of capital. A higher supply of savings raises the equilibrium level of investment and the amount of capital that the economy can afford to replace each year. To see why a permanent increase in savings also raises the steady state capital stock, suppose that an economy saves and invests $50 billion a year and 10 percent of its capital equipment wears out each year. This economy's steady state capital stock is $500 billion, and capital equipment worth $50 billion wears out each year to be replaced by the economy's equilibrium savings and investment. If, instead, the economy saves $70 billion each year, then its steady state capital stock is $700 billion, and capital equipment worth $70 billion wears out each year to be replaced by the economy's equilibrium investment.

EXAMPLES

The basic growth model explains many real-life situations. World War II destroyed much capital in Germany and Japan (buildings, machinery, and so on). After the war, investment levels in Germany and Japan far exceeded those in countries such as the United States, where little capital had been destroyed. Germany and Japan had high rates of economic growth as they caught up by rebuilding their capital stocks. The same increase in investment and rapid growth typically occurs after cities are struck by natural disasters such as earthquakes.

TWO PROBLEMS WITH THE BASIC MODEL

While the basic model explains many real examples of growth, it has two main problems. It implies that economic growth slows down and eventually stops and

---

[14]This keeps capital per worker constant.

[15]Notice that an increase in savings does not permanently raise the rate of economic growth, according to the basic model, because the economy eventually reaches a steady state.

that the real interest rate falls over time as the economy approaches its steady state, as Figure 26.1 illustrated. These implications conflict with the evidence. First, there is little evidence that long-term economic growth has slowed down. Second, real interest rates have not fallen over time; they are not much higher or lower than they were a century ago. An economist might defend the basic model by suggesting that it takes a long time for an economy to approach its steady state—so long that a century or two of data do not reveal the slow down in growth and the fall in real interest rates. However, studies do not support this position. When economists study the basic model in detail on a computer, they get predictions that an economy would approach its steady state after only a few decades, rather than centuries. This result is consistent with growth in Germany and Japan, which grew fast after World War II and caught up with their long-term trends within a few decades. The basic model is missing certain important features of economic growth, such as technical progress, as the next section discusses.

FOR REVIEW

26.6 Explain the diminishing return to capital.

26.7 What is the steady state capital stock?

26.8 Explain the basic model of economic growth (without considering technical change) and list two problems with it.

QUESTIONS

26.9 Why can't a country with slow economic growth send a fact-finding delegation to a country with a faster-growing economy to find out what makes that economy grow so fast, and then raise its own economic growth by simply copying the faster-growing country?

26.10 How would a fall in the willingness of people to save for the future affect the rate of economic growth in the basic model?

LOGIC OF ECONOMIC GROWTH: ADDITIONAL ISSUES

FIRST COMPLICATIONS: TECHNICAL CHANGE AND HUMAN CAPITAL INVESTMENT

Technical change raises output per worker without any increase in capital per worker. An economy grows indefinitely if technical change continues indefinitely. Technical change results from progress in science and engineering and application of scientific knowledge to create better capital equipment and production methods. Some technical change occurs by accident and some may always result from the human quest for knowledge, but much technical change results from intentional investments in research and development and in human capital.[16] In this sense, technology amounts to a kind of capital in the form of scientific articles, books, human knowledge, and machinery and equipment that make use of that knowledge. An economy adds to its technology through savings and investment in research and education just as it adds to its physical capital through savings and investment in new machinery.

---

[16]Productivity also increases with practice and experience; economists call this *learning by doing*.

Can technical change continue indefinitely without slowing? No one knows the answer, but the rate of future technical change certainly depends to some extent on investments in research. In the basic model discussed earlier, a permanent increase in savings raises economic growth only temporarily. (It helps the economy to reach its steady state more quickly.) Remember, however, that the basic model ignored technical change. If a permanent increase in the supply of savings permanently raises investment in research and development, it may permanently raise technical progress and the rate of economic growth. On the other hand, technology is a form of capital and physical capital suffers diminishing returns. Does technical change also suffer from diminishing returns? Do the benefits of additional knowledge fall as the economy adds to its stock of knowledge? If so, the logic from the last section would apply: equilibrium investment in scientific research would fall over time and technical change would slow down. The economy would approach a steady state, and growth would eventually stop. If knowledge does not have diminishing returns, then continuing technical change may cause economic growth to continue indefinitely; growth need not even slow down.

INVESTMENT IN HUMAN CAPITAL

Future economic growth might not slow down, even if technical change were to slow. Economic growth could continue indefinitely if the economy could add continually to its *effective* labor input through education and training (investments in human capital). To see why, suppose that technical change stops; the number A in the production function (Equation 25.3) stops growing. Economic growth can then continue only if inputs of capital (K) and labor (L) continue to grow. *Both* inputs must grow; if the economy adds to its capital input without adding to its labor input, diminishing returns to capital make economic growth slow down and eventually stop. The economy can add to its capital stock by producing more machinery and equipment (investing in physical capital), but how can it add to its labor input? People could work harder or more hours per year, but there are clear limits to effort and hours per person. Improvements in skills and knowledge can make people more effective workers, however. If investments in human capital (education and training) can raise the amount of effective labor, L, per person, then the economy can raise both its capital *and* its effective labor input per person, which raises output per person.

effective labor input — labor input adjusted for knowledge and skills

> An economy's **effective labor input** is its labor input adjusted for knowledge and skills.

Because one skilled, educated person may do the work of two less knowledgeable people, increases in human capital resemble increases in the quantity of labor. They add to the economy's effective labor input. If investments in human capital can continue indefinitely, along with investments in physical capital that raise K, then economic growth can also continue indefinitely, even without technical change. Because the economy's effective labor input rises, investment demand does *not* fall, as Figure 26.1 predicted.[17] Equilibrium investment and the equilibrium real interest rate remain constant as capital, effective labor, and output rise indefinitely. In this case, economic growth may continue indefinitely without slowing down or stopping. The strong world-wide economic growth of the last two centuries, which shows no clear tendency to slow down or to reduce the real

---

[17]Investment demand remains the same because capital per effective worker stays constant as the economy adds capital.

interest rate, is consistent with the idea that economies can grow by adding to their effective labor inputs as well as their inputs of physical capital.

SECOND COMPLICATION: FIXED AND EXHAUSTIBLE NATURAL RESOURCES

Economic growth may eventually slow down and perhaps stop because we have fixed physical quantities of natural resources. We can distinguish three types of natural resources:

renewable resource — a natural resource that can be replenished, such as trees

fixed resource — a natural resource that cannot be replenished, but is not depleted in production, such as land

exhaustible resource — a resource that cannot be physically replenished and that is depleted in production, such as coal

Renewable resources are natural resources that can be replenished, such as trees.

Fixed resources are natural resources that cannot be replenished, but are not depleted in production, such as land.[18]

Exhaustible resources are resources that cannot be physically replenished and that are depleted in production, such as coal.[19]

Renewable resources play the same role that capital played in the earlier discussions. They create no complications for economic growth. In contrast, fixed resources may prevent economic growth from continuing indefinitely without slowing. By the law of diminishing returns, as the economy adds more capital and labor to a fixed quantity of land and other fixed resources, the benefits of further increases in capital and labor fall. At some point, the economy reaches a steady state at which economic growth stops. In this way, fixed resources could limit per-capita real GDP. Exhaustible resources may create even more severe problems. The remaining quantities of oil, other fossil fuels, and metals fall over time. Once these resources are gone, they cannot be used again.

MALTHUS ON POPULATION

The idea that fixed resources restrain economic growth goes back to Thomas Malthus and his famous "Essay on the Principle of Population," published in 1798. Malthus argued that as the population rises and more people work with a fixed amount of land, diminishing returns to land would reduce output of food per person. As a result, Malthus predicted that wages would fall over time as the population rose. When the wage fell far enough, he theorized, malnourishment and death would stop the population increase, and the population would stabilize at a subsistence wage just large enough for people to live and reproduce with zero population growth. This Malthusian view of growth became very popular and led people to call economics "the dismal science."

Was Malthus right? The world population numbered about 275 million people in the year 1000. It reached 750 million by 1750, 3.0 billion by 1960, and 5.7 billion by 1995. Obviously, the growth rate of the world population has increased rapidly. From 1000 to 1750, the human population grew at about 0.13 percent per year; from 1750 to 1960 it grew at about 0.66 percent per year, and from 1960 to 1995 it grew at more than 1.9 percent per year.[20] (If this 1.9 percent annual rate of increase were to continue, world population would double every 37 years.)

World population pace quickens

The world's population, about 5.4 billion, could soar to about 10.2 billion by 2050—about 25 years sooner than previously projected, the United Nations said.

The rapid growth could increase pressures on natural resources needed for global survival, said the U.N. Population Fund's annual report, issued in London, and after 2050, "significant growth will continue for another 100 years."

Source: "World Population Pace Quickens," *The Wall Street Journal,* May 14, 1991, p. A18.

---

[18]Of course, *fertile* land can be depleted as well as replenished.

[19]People deplete a resource if they transform it into a less valuable resource.

[20]Simon Kuznets, *Modern Economic Growth* (New Haven, Conn.: Yale University Press, 1966).

Malthus assumed that the population would rise as long as people had incomes high enough to survive. Modern studies of fertility and population growth show clearly that people choose family sizes in relation to their incomes, the usefulness of children (to help raise food or support parents in old age), and other factors. People do not choose to have enough children to drive their wages down to the subsistence level.[21] Instead, wages have increased over time as the world population has grown; these wage increases have resulted from technical advances and increases in physical and human capital that have raised the demand for labor faster than population growth has raised the supply. A century after Malthus published his book in Britain, that country's population had quadrupled and people's incomes were much higher.[22]

SCARCITY OF NATURAL RESOURCES

Economists cannot dismiss Malthus's argument about diminishing returns to a fixed quantity of land as easily as his predictions on population. Even with less population growth than Malthus assumed, his argument implies that economic growth will slow down and eventually stop. Many modern commentators make similar arguments, contending that diminishing returns to fixed resources imply that population growth reduces economic growth. According to this argument, population growth may even create *negative* economic growth in which real GDP per person falls. Negative economic growth may also result from falling quantities of exhaustible resources. Population increases with fixed quantities of land may also reduce the quality of life through crowding, pollution, and other factors that GDP calculations ignore.

The counter argument states that when a resource becomes scarce, people respond with innovations. People often replace scarce resources with more plentiful resources. History is filled with examples as the nearby Social and Economics Issues box illustrates. The evidence suggests that, at least in the past, scarcity of natural resources has not limited economic growth. When people deplete the remaining quantity of an exhaustible resource, its supply falls and its price rises. If economic growth were limited due to depletion of exhaustible resources, the prices of those natural resources would rise. However, the evidence suggests the opposite; historically, the relative prices of most exhaustible resources have remained about constant or fallen over time.

For example, **Figure 26.2** illustrates changes in the price of copper, adjusted for inflation. While it rises and falls over short periods, the figure shows a long-term fall; the same is true for most other raw materials.

Prices of exhaustible resources have fallen for two reasons. First, technical progress has increased their supply (for example, by locating new mines, reducing the cost of mining, and decreasing waste). Second, technical progress has reduced the demand for these resources by creating substitutes. (For example, satellite links and fiber-optic lines have replaced copper wires for telephone calls.)[23] If technical

---

[21]Throughout history, people have practiced various methods of birth control.

[22]Even in the years from 1500 to 1700, when technical progress was slow, the situation differed from Malthus's scenario. The population grew at a rate well below the biological maximum. Europeans lived in conjugal rather than extended families, and married in their mid-20s rather than at puberty to keep fertility low; priests enforced prohibitions on premarital sex with reasonable success. Average living standards remained well above the subsistence level.

[23]Though the quantity of land is physically finite, it has not inhibited economic growth in the past. The development of better techniques for land use (for irrigation, fertilization, cropping, and breeding) have reduced the importance of land for agriculture. Similarly, the developments of elevators and high-rise buildings have helped to reduce the importance of land in cities.

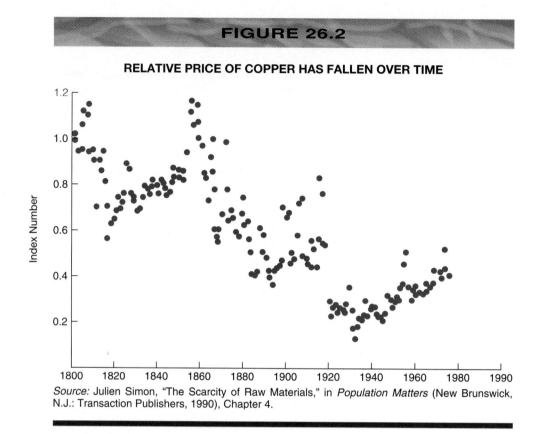

FIGURE 26.2

RELATIVE PRICE OF COPPER HAS FALLEN OVER TIME

Source: Julien Simon, "The Scarcity of Raw Materials," in *Population Matters* (New Brunswick, N.J.: Transaction Publishers, 1990), Chapter 4.

change provides methods to produce more output with fewer fixed and exhaustible resources, then economic growth may continue indefinitely without slowing down, stopping, or becoming negative.

This debate on the future of economic growth continues today, as the Social and Economic Issues box demonstrates. One side says that economic growth will slow down and eventually stop because of diminishing returns to finite resources, and perhaps because real GDP per capita will fall as the economy depletes exhaustible resources. The other side says that economic growth can continue indefinitely, driven by technical change and the accumulation of knowledge and human capital. Many past predictions that the world would soon run out of some finite resource have turned out to be wrong.[24] This does not, however, prove that similar claims will be wrong in the future.

---

[24]In his famous book *The Coal Question: An Enquiry Concerning the Progress of the Nation* (London, U.K.: Macmillan, 1865), economist Stanley Jevons warned that the world would soon run out of coal. The U.S. Federal Oil Conservation Board said in 1926 that the United States had only a 7-year supply of oil left. In *The Population Bomb* (New York: Ballantine Books, 1968), Paul Ehrlich warned that "The battle to feed humanity is over. In the 1970s the world will undergo famines—hundreds of millions of people are going to starve to death." Ehrlich warned that "nothing can prevent a substantial increase in the world death rate." He predicted that "America's vast agricultural surpluses are gone." In Ehrlich's book with Anne Ehrlich, *The End of Affluence,* the authors warned of a "nutritional disaster that seems likely to overtake humanity in the 1970s (or, at the latest, in the 1980s)," and said that "before 1985 mankind will enter a genuine age of scarcity" in which "the accessible supplies of many key minerals will be nearing depletion." So far, these predictions have been false.

◣SOCIAL AND ECONOMIC ISSUES

Will the Finite Quantity of Natural Resources Cause Economic Growth to Slow Down or Stop?

Yes

There is a finite amount of many important natural resources. Some of these, like total land area, don't change over time, but population growth reduces the amount available per person. The economy is actually using up many others, such as fossil fuels (like oil and natural gas) and metals. Future generations will have less available, even if the population stops growing.

World population growth shows no indication of slowing anytime soon. Most experts expect world population to increase massively over the next century. Population growth is already outstripping the world's supplies of fresh water, food, and minerals.

The fact that people have warned of doom in the past is irrelevant. They were, of course, wrong at the time, but *now* is different.

These finite natural resources will soon get more expensive, because they are being used up. The fact that some commodities have become cheaper in the past proves nothing, because people were not near the point of running out; we are near that point now.

No

We haven't run out yet, and for a good reason. When resources become scarce, people respond with innovations and substitutes. This has happened throughout history. The Greeks moved from the Bronze Age to the Iron Age 3,000 years ago because wars in the eastern Mediterranean disrupted trade and reduced the supply of tin for bronze production. The Greeks responded to the bronze crisis by starting to use iron instead. Timber shortages in 16th-century Britain led to the use of coal as a substitute fuel. People find alternative ways to produce the services that the scarce resources previously produced, and the alternatives usually turn out to be better. The supply of human ingenuity is unlimited, and that is the most important natural resource to produce new ideas.

As a result, neither the finite physical quantities of natural resources or population growth will limit economic growth. An increase in population growth causes short-term problems because children do not produce, but it does not create long-term problems because adults produce both goods and new ideas.

Serious people have claimed many times in the past—wrongly—that the world was about to run out of some natural resource. The current claims are wrong for the same reason that similar people were wrong in the past.

Many physically finite natural resources have become cheaper rather than more expensive over time because of new discoveries that raise their supplies or the development of substitutes that reduce their demand. We can expect similar changes in the future.

EXTERNALITIES AND GROWTH

People and firms have an incentive to invest in research and development to create technical change because the results of the research can add to their profits. These additional profits are the private benefits of investing in research and development. Other people may gain directly from these investments, as well, however, so the social benefits of investments in research may exceed the private benefits.

private benefit — the benefit to the people who produce a good or invest

social benefit — the benefit to everyone in society of private production or investment

The **private benefit** of producing a good or investing in research is the benefit to the people who produce it or invest. The **social benefit** is the benefit to everyone in the society of the production or investment.

Firms often copy technical changes that they see at other firms or in other industries. Countries copy technical changes they see in other countries.[25] New

---

[25]The extent of legal copying is limited by patent and copyright laws.

SOCIAL AND ECONOMIC ISSUES

Is Economic Growth Good or Bad?

Good

Economic growth brings people out of poverty. It raises health and expected life-span, increases literacy, and opens new opportunities for people to have fulfilling lives. It gives people both the material goods they want and more leisure time. People can use this leisure time as they choose, for recreation or to pursue other goals and promote nonmaterial values.

It provides the resources that can help the environment. A good summary measure of environmental quality as it affects people is expected life-span, which has increased with economic growth, largely due to improvements in health and medicine that accompany growth. Economic growth also provides the resources that offer people some insurance against many risks, such as famine and disease. While economic growth requires change, and any change has risks, changes can be good as well as bad.

Economic growth creates new opportunities for people to pursue fulfillment through work. Anyone who wants to be an artist or small farmer—or even self-dependent, growing one's own food, and so on—can still do so. In fact, with the increased technical knowledge made possible by economic growth, a self-dependent person can have a higher standard of living now than people could in the past. The romantic image of life and jobs before economic growth is completely different than the reality that life and work are, for most people, better after economic growth, not worse. Future economic growth can continue to improve the quality of life.

Economic growth allows some people to become rich. Although it may initially raise income inequality, it eventually reduces inequality. (For example, compare the amount of income inequality in developed countries and LDCs.) Any government policies to reduce economic growth would not reduce inequalities, they would entrench existing ones and reduce opportunities for people to advance themselves through innovation, hard work, or luck.

Bad

Economic growth reduces the quality of life by leading people to focus on material goods that do not provide real satisfaction and to ignore the nonmaterial values that are important to a satisfying life.

It ruins the beauty of nature, harms the environment, and threatens a fragile ecosystem. It threatens the welfare of future generations of people as well as nonhuman life. The ecosystem is complex, and scientists have an imperfect understanding of it. A change in any one part of it could have major effects on the whole system.

It alienates people from the most important values in life. It moves people from basic, fulfilling work such as farming, craft work, and building to unfulfilling jobs in factories and offices. With economic growth, people do not understand their work or have feelings of creating something or helping other people. Some jobs, like investment banking, encourage gross materialism and discourage important values like honesty and charity. The increased specialization that goes with economic growth alienates people from each other; it reduces shared experiences, makes it harder for people to understand each other, and breaks down the social bonds that support a civilized community.

Economic growth reduces important opportunities. Big corporate farms make it impossible for small farmers to maintain their previous lifestyles. Automation eliminates jobs that provide people with fulfillment. A craftsman in a small town may not be able to compete with machine-produced items coming from big cities. A small farmer loses income when big corporate farms can produce food at a lower cost. (Of course, anyone can still have a small farm, but only by accepting a lower standard of living than before; so economic growth really does eliminate opportunities.)

Economic growth increases income inequality and allows some people to get rich.

IN THE NEWS

The pump on the well

Unforeseen consequences of technology

Tom Wicker

WEST BERLIN — When a solar-powered water pump was provided for a well in India, the village headman took it over and sold the water, until stopped. The new liquid abundance attracted hordes of unwanted nomads. Village boys who had drawn water in buckets had nothing to do, and some became criminals. The gap between rich and poor widened, since the poor had no land to benefit from irrigation. Finally, village women broke the pump, so they could gather again around the well that had been the center of their social lives.

Moral: technological advances have social, cultural, and economic consequences, often unanticipated.

Source: Tom Wicker, "The Pump on the Well," *New York Times*, September 24, 1987, p. A27.

ideas often lead to even more ideas. Technical knowledge and ideas tend to spread throughout the economy, whether written in books and technical reports or embodied in products that can be studied by reverse engineering (in which people take apart products to see how they work). You may know of many examples such as clones of brand-name computers, designer clothes, or other consumer products. Knowledge can be so valuable that some firms undertake industrial espionage (spying) to learn about technical developments at other firms.

positive externality — when the social benefit of an action (such as producing a good or investing in research) exceeds the private benefit

A **positive externality** occurs when the social benefit of producing a good or investing in research exceeds the private benefit.

Some economists believe that positive externalities play important roles in economic growth. Countries that invest more than other countries may grow faster partly because the new ideas generated by these investments create positive externalities that spread throughout the investors' economies.

If investments in knowledge or human capital have positive externalities, then the economically efficient quantity of these investments exceeds the equilibrium quantity. This fact has led some economists to suggest that government policies should encourage savings and investment, perhaps through subsidies or lower taxes.

If investments in knowledge or human capital have positive externalities, then doubling the amounts of physical and human capital may more than double real GDP. While doubling inputs of physical and human capital at any one firm may double that firm's output, the increase may also have positive externalities that raise output at other firms. Some economists cite this as one reason for the increase in the rate of economic growth over time. Of course, no one knows whether the rate of growth will continue to increase in the future, but the suggestion that growth results partly from positive externalities suggests that this is a possibility.

FOR REVIEW

26.11 How is investment in human capital connected with the economy's effective labor input and with economic growth?

26.12 Explain why some people believe that fixed and exhaustible natural resources will cause the rate of economic growth to fall in the future. Why do some remain confident that economic growth may not fall in the future, despite the finite physical quantities of fixed and exhaustible natural resources?

26.13 What is a positive externality and how are externalities related to growth?

— QUESTION —

26.14 Why would economic growth eventually slow down and stop if investments in knowledge and technical change had diminishing returns?

ECONOMIC DEVELOPMENT: GROWTH IN LESS DEVELOPED COUNTRIES

The term *economic development* refers to growth of per-capita real GDP in countries with low incomes. Economic development is generally accompanied by increases in life expectancy, health, and literacy, and by decreases in infant mortality. In 1900, the average life expectancy at birth was 49 years in the OECD countries and 35 years in the LDCs (less developed countries). With economic growth in the 20th century, life expectancy had risen by 1990 to 76 years in OECD countries and 63 years in the LDCs. More developed countries also tend to have more political freedom, more stable governments, fewer coups and revolutions, and fewer government restrictions on their economies. Overall, incomes are more equal in developed countries, though development often tends to increase inequality in the short run.

Why do some countries have lower levels of real GDP per person than others? Why can't (or why don't) poorer countries just copy the actions of rich countries to raise their incomes? Why have some poorer countries grown very fast while others have grown much more slowly? Are poorer countries catching up with richer countries? What can a poor country do to stimulate growth?

DIFFERENCES BETWEEN COUNTRIES

Countries' real GDPs per capita have become more unequal in the last several decades. Two centuries ago, no country was as rich as developed countries are today, but no one was much poorer than the poorest country today; this suggests that the difference between the richest and poorest countries has grown wider. The ratio of real GDP per person in the richest country to that in the poorest country was about 8 to 1 in 1900.[26] It had risen to 60 to 1 by 1995.[27] In contrast, incomes in OECD countries have become more equal in the 20th century, especially since 1950.[28]

In 1900, average per-capita GDP in the OECD countries was 5 times that of Asian countries and 3 times that of Latin American countries. These ratios have increased over time, so per-capita GDP in the OECD countries is now 8 times

---

[26]This was the ratio between income per person in Australia or the United States to per-capita income in Bangladesh or India.

[27]This is the ratio between income per person in Switzerland to income per person in Ethiopia.

[28]Asia is an exception; incomes in Asian countries have become less equal over this period.

IN THE NEWS

The development gap

Most developing countries will gain little from new technologies

Developing countries face a series of obstacles in their efforts to participate in the Third Industrial Revolution. First, a pool of highly trained scientific and technical personnel is essential for the successful diffusion of the new technologies. But only 13 percent of the world's scientists and engineers are in the third world, and they are concentrated in only a few countries in East Asia and in Brazil, India, and Mexico.

Second, new technologies require large amounts of capital. But many developing countries lack access to capital markets and already are heavily burdened by debt.

Third, shifts in world consumption and technical innovation have cut demand for traditional raw materials—bad news for the nearly 40 developing countries that depend on raw materials for at least 15 percent of their total export earnings.

Source: John W. Sewell, "The Development Gap," *New York Times*, May 22, 1988, p. F3.

Asian per-capita real GDP and 3.6 times Latin American real per-capita GDP. Evidence suggests that a country tends to grow faster if it starts out poor, it has an educated or skilled population, its government places few restrictions on international trade, and it generates high levels of investment. Countries in Africa and Latin America have grown more slowly than similar countries elsewhere, perhaps because they tended to suffer more political instability and less certainty about property rights with resulting uncertainty about benefits of investment and production.

The fact that a poor country tends to grow faster than a rich one does not necessarily mean that poorer countries are catching up with richer countries. Although a country tends to grow faster if it starts out poor, it tends to grow more slowly if its population is not educated, and education levels are lower in poor countries. Furthermore, governments of poor countries tend to restrict international trade more than governments of richer countries, which slows their growth even more. Poorer countries also tend to have less stable political systems and less predictable property rights, and this uncertainty reduces investment. Whether a poor country is likely to catch up with richer countries depends on the net result of all these factors.

INVESTMENT AND GOVERNMENT POLICIES

Very poor countries tend to save smaller fractions of their incomes than richer countries. These poor countries would have very low levels of investment in equilibrium unless they borrowed from richer countries. Foreign investment in poor countries can increase their income, partly by bringing equipment to make their workers more productive and partly by bringing technical knowledge, organizational skills, and information about how to export their products. Foreigners have an incentive to invest in a poor country if it offers sufficiently low wages compared to worker productivity. In long-run equilibrium, wages would be the same for workers in different countries with the same level of skills.

In practice, poor countries attract little foreign investment and wages remain much lower in poor countries than in richer countries. This may reflect low skill levels of workers in poor countries, which offsets the benefits of their lower wages, or risks of investing in those countries because of uncertainty about property rights. Potential investors evaluate the risk that the government of a less developed country may confiscate their property in the future, impose new taxes or regulations that reduce the returns on their investments, or limit their ability to take their profits out of the country.

Other factors further limit foreign investment in LDCs. Many LDCs have poor infrastructures with unreliable or nonexistent transportation and communication systems (roads, telephone systems, and so on). Governments of LDCs often limit foreign investment to avoid the perception that foreigners are taking over their countries or in response to political pressures from people who would lose from foreign investments. Government bureaucrats, for example, often benefit from the status quo.

Many governments of LDCs adopt economically inefficient policies such as limiting international trade and controlling domestic trade. Economists may see these inefficient policies as mistakes, but the policies may also benefit powerful special-interest groups within these countries, at the expense of reduced economic growth.[29] Government policies also affect the amounts of resources that

---

[29]A fascinating description of some of these problems and their effects on the economy in Peru appears in Hernando de Soto, *The Other Path* (New York: Harper & Row, 1989).

people use to produce goods and promote economic growth and the amounts of resources that they devote to obtaining political influence through lobbying, bribes, legal battles, and other activities to acquire larger shares of the country's existing output. Countries that spend more resources fighting over the distribution of current output have lower levels of real GDP and lower rates of economic growth.

SUCCESS STORIES

Among the most famous economic development successes are the so-called "four tigers" of Asia mentioned earlier: Hong Kong, Singapore, South Korea, and Taiwan. These countries have averaged more than 6 percent annual growth of per-capita real GDP—more than four times the world average—since 1965. (The rule of 72 estimates that 6 percent annual growth would double these countries' incomes every 12 years, or quadruple them every 24 years.)

Why did these countries succeed so well at development? Economists do not yet have a complete answer, but the reason seems partly related to free markets and international trade. Evidence shows that economic growth is connected with increased international trade, particularly for small countries. All four Asian tigers imposed less government regulation and control than most LDCs, and all experienced large increases in international trade along with their rapid growth. Their governments left more economic decisions to free markets than those in low-growth countries; this promoted economic efficiency and probably raised economic growth. International trade promotes efficiency by allowing countries to specialize in the products at which they have comparative advantages (see Chapter 3), which raises their income. In addition, increased specialization can raise the rate of economic growth under certain conditions.[30] Increased international trade also raises competitive pressures on firms, which may reduce inefficiencies and raise output. Finally, increased international trade can help pressure governments to follow more economically efficient policies.

Some economists look at the evidence on development and conclude that countries can develop and grow most rapidly if their governments eliminate restrictions on international trade, promote private property rights and free markets, reduce regulations and controls on the economy, and encourage foreign investment. Others believe that economic development can speed up if the government actively promotes international trade by subsidizing exports. While most agree that governments of less developed countries follow many policies that cause inefficient uses of resources, some question the extent to which changes in government policies alone can raise economic growth rates.

───────────────────────── **FOR REVIEW** ─────────────────────────

26.15 List some factors that make countries grow faster.

26.16 How can foreign investment raise the rate of growth in a less developed country?

───

[30]If production in an industry located in one country generates positive externalities or if people learn from experience so that increased specialization raises productivity, then increased specialization can raise the rate of growth.

CONCLUSIONS

BASICS OF GROWTH

Economic growth is a rise in real GDP per capita. The rate of economic growth is the average per-year percentage increase in per-capita real GDP. Economic growth occurs because an economy experiences technical progress, investments in physical capital, and investments in human capital. Technical progress results when the economy produces more usable output with the same quantities of capital and labor. A classic study of the American economy found that roughly two-thirds of economic growth was associated with increases in technology, knowledge, and education, while increases in capital accounted for about one-third.

MAIN FACTS ABOUT ECONOMIC GROWTH

World real GDP per capita grew at about 1.0 percent per year in the 19th century and 1.7 percent per year in the 20th century (1.1 percent per year from 1900 to 1950 and 2.1 percent per year since 1950). This growth rate is much higher than rates in earlier centuries and throughout most of history. The rate of economic growth in the United States has increased over the last two centuries from 1.1 percent per year in the first half of the 19th century to 1.9 percent per year in the last half-century. Output per person doubles every 40 to 50 years. Some countries, such as Japan, have grown much faster than the United States since World War II, with the Japanese GDP per person rising from one-third of the U.S. level to about the U.S. level today. Other countries, such as Bangladesh, have experienced almost no economic growth in the last century.

LOGIC OF ECONOMIC GROWTH

An economy can grow temporarily by saving and investing, but continuing growth requires technical progress or continued investment in human capital; otherwise, growth would slow down and eventually stop as the economy reaches a steady state. Fixed and exhaustible natural resources create diminishing returns for investments in physical and human capital, so they may lead growth to slow down and eventually stop. However, growth may continue indefinitely without slowing down if technical progress allows the economy to use fewer fixed and exhaustible resources or to substitute replenishable resources such as trees and sunlight for those resources. Some technical change may occur by accident, but the economy may be able to increase technical progress and long-run growth by increasing investments in education, research, and development.

ECONOMIC DEVELOPMENT: GROWTH IN LESS DEVELOPED COUNTRIES

Countries tend to grow faster if they are poor, have educated or skilled populations, feature few government restrictions on international trade, and stimulate high levels of investment. In addition, countries in Africa and Latin America have grown more slowly than similar countries elsewhere, perhaps because they have tended to suffer more political instability and less certain property rights. The fact that poor countries tend to grow faster does not mean that poor countries are catching up with rich countries. Many countries remain poor because of frequent wars and inefficient government policies.

LOOKING AHEAD

The next two chapters turn attention away from real economic magnitudes, such as real GDP, to *nominal* magnitudes, such as the level of prices and the rate of inflation. The next chapter discusses inflation, and later chapters discuss money and the financial system, possible connections between nominal economic variables and real GDP, and the short-run economic problems associated with unemployment, recessions, and the effects of government policies.

KEY TERMS

economic growth

technical progress

total factor productivity growth

physical capital

human capital

rate of economic growth

LDC (less developed country)

OECD (Organization for Economic) Cooperation and Development

steady state

steady state capital stock

diminishing returns to capital

effective labor input

renewable resource

fixed resource

exhaustible resource

private benefit

social benefit

positive externality

QUESTIONS AND PROBLEMS

26.17 Explain why a country cannot keep growing at the same rate indefinitely simply by adding indefinitely to its physical capital.

26.18 Use a graph of the supply and demand for loans to help explain why an increase in savings raises the speed at which the economy grows toward its steady state.

26.19 How might increases in savings and investment raise the rate of economic growth as well as the level of per-capita real GDP?

26.20 Why is it reasonable to expect the relative price of an exhaustible resource to rise over time?

26.21 Explain Malthus's belief about population growth, then criticize it.

26.22 Discuss this statement: "Poor countries are likely to catch up, eventually, with rich countries."

26.23 Why do some countries grow faster than others?

26.24 Suppose that people in France begin saving more and people in England begin saving less. Is this likely to raise the rate of economic growth in France and reduce the growth rate in England? (*Hint:* What happens to international borrowing and lending and to the world equilibrium real interest rate?)

INQUIRIES FOR FURTHER THOUGHT

26.25 Are we at a turning point in history beyond which economic growth is likely to decline?

26.26 Does economic growth create winners and losers? Who are they?

26.27 **a.** Would further economic growth in the United States be good or bad? Why? If you are opposed to more economic growth, would you have opposed more growth in 1800? In 1900? In 1950?

b. How fast *should* countries' economies grow? What general principles should guide the answer to this kind of question?

26.28 What government policies would you recommend for an LDC that wants fast economic growth?

26.29 Discuss this statement: "To feed starving populations is desirable, but if new crops help add a billion new people to a crowded globe, is that necessarily good?"[31]

26.30 Discuss these statements.

    a. "Population growth may raise economic growth, because it adds more brains as well as more mouths and hands."

    b. "Population growth that increases the volume of trash may increase our problems in the short run, but it bestows benefits on future generations. The pressure of new problems leads to the search for new solutions. The solutions constitute the knowledge that fuels the progress of civilization, and leaves us better off than if the original problem had never arisen. That is the history of the human race."[32]

26.31 Suppose that a higher population would reduce per-capita real GDP, but raise aggregate real GDP. Would this increase in population be good or bad?

26.32 Discuss this statement: "Allowing foreigners to immigrate to our country can raise our rate of economic growth, particularly if the immigrants are well educated."

TAG SOFTWARE APPLICATIONS

TUTORIAL EXERCISES

▶ The module contains a review of the key terms from Chapter 26.

---

[31]Daniel Koshland, quoted in *The Wall Street Journal,* July 28, 1987, p. A32.

[32]Julian Simon, *Population Matters* (New Brunswick, N.J.: Transaction Publisher, 1990), Chapter 51, "Dump on Us, Baby, We Need It," p. 459.

MONEY AND INFLATION

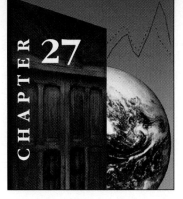

CHAPTER 27

INFLATION

WHAT THIS CHAPTER IS ABOUT

▶ Level of money prices and inflation

▶ Causes of inflation

▶ Who loses and who gains from inflation

▶ Biggest episodes of inflation in history

example

The 1908 Sears, Roebuck catalog listed regulation basketballs for $1.45 and $2.70. A recent Sears catalog listed a price of $28.44 for a Michael Jordan basketball, or $24.61 for a Rawlings MVP ball. On average, prices in the United States in 1994 were more than 18 times higher than prices in 1900 and twice as high as those in 1979.

inflation — the growth rate of the price level (the percentage increase in the average nominal price of goods and services)

> **Inflation** is the growth rate of the price level (the percentage increase in the average nominal price of goods and services).

Economists measure inflation by the growth rate of a price index such as the GDP deflator, consumer price index (CPI), or producer price index (PPI), as an earlier chapter explained. Inflation reduces the purchasing power of money, that is, the amount of goods and services that a unit of money (a dollar or a peso) will buy.

Inflation in the United States, measured by the GDP deflator, averaged 4.3 percent per year from 1980 to 1994, slightly above its 4.0 average from 1947 to 1994. Inflation was negative (the price level fell) in 1949 and 1953, but it exceeded 9.0 percent in 1974 and 1980. Since 1984, inflation has averaged 3.6 percent per year.[1] The purchasing power of money in the United States has fallen with inflation so that, by 1995, a dollar was worth only 16 percent of its 1950 value; $1.00 in 1995 was the same as $0.16 in 1950.

Inflation has not always been this high. The price level in 1940, at the beginning of World War II, was only about one-third higher than its level when George Washington took the oath of office as the nation's first president. The continuing inflation that people in the United States take for granted today is a relatively recent phenomenon.

Some periods of inflation have been much higher. In Germany from August 1922 to November 1923, inflation averaged 322 percent per *month*. Prices at the

---

[1]Measured by the consumer price index, inflation was slightly higher.

A weary Buenos Aires family wonders how to keep afloat

By James Brooke
Special to The
New York Times

BUENOS AIRES, June 15—With his 2-year-old son squirming on his lap, Guillermo Dietrich pondered how to keep his family afloat in Argentina's rising sea of inflation.

"My wife, my mother and my aunt are the antibodies of hyperinflation," the drawn father of two said, cracking a rare smile. "Every morning, they pool price information and try to save before prices are marked up again."

Last month, food prices jumped 78 percent, a record here. Argentina's working class neighborhoods erupted in the worst riots in a decade.

'We Live Day to Day'
This month, prices are expected to jump 100 percent.

With businessmen projecting this year's inflation to be 12,000 percent, Argentina's middle class feel pushed to the edge.

"We live day to day," Mr. Dietrich said. "We only pay bills when the money comes in."

The descendants of immigrants from Europe, the Dietrichs grew up to think of themselves as middle class. Guillermo was a construction foreman. Elida, his wife, is a lawyer.

"We grew up with inflation of 7 to 15 percent a month," Mr. Dietrich, 31 years old, said of the annual inflation rate common to Argentina in the 1970s and 1980s. "But now, prices don't mean anything any more."

"I bought this last week at 37 australes," he said, toying with a half-smoked pack of L&M Light cigarettes. "Now it is selling for 55 australes. Next week, it will be 78 australes. What is the price?"

Elida Dietrich juggled her 4-year-old daughter, Valeria, and said: "It makes you feel very insecure."

"This morning, I went into one store, looking for detergent," she continued. "In one place, it was 140. The next place, 100. Finally, I bought it at a third store at 80. But tomorrow all the prices will change."

In late May, sudden rises of food prices triggered the sacking of hundreds of food shops across Argentina. In a shock to the nation, 15 people were killed, dozens were injured, and hundreds were arrested.

Living with inflation.

Source: James Brooke, "A Weary Buenos Aires Family Wonders How to Keep Afloat," *New York Times,* June 18, 1989, p. A16.

end of that German hyperinflation (a term for particularly high inflation) were 10 billion times the original level.[2] More recently, inflation has reached nearly 5,000 percent per year in Argentina, 2,000 percent per year in Brazil, over 1,000 percent per year in Peru, and several hundred percent in Israel. Bolivia's inflation rate reached 1,282 percent in 1984 and accelerated to a rate of 60,000 percent per year in the summer of 1985, before falling again in August.

Who gains from inflation? Who loses? Why do some countries have higher rates of inflation than others? What causes inflation and what can stop it? How can it be prevented? These are the subjects of this chapter.

---

[2]Someone who lived through hyperinflation once offered the following definition: hyperinflation is when it's cheaper to pay for your lunch before you start eating it than after you finish.

Hunger spreading in Peru inflation

Food is plentiful in markets but soaring prices put it out of reach for many

*By Alan Riding
Special to The
New York Times*

LIMA, Peru—Wandering around a street market near her home with the equivalent of just 60 cents in her pocket,

Sara Chaverry seemed almost in a daze as she tried to imagine how she would provide the next three meals for the 10 members of her household.

"There's plenty of food in the stalls," the 28-year-old mother said, waving at unsold chickens and cuts of meat, "but things I could afford a couple of months ago are now out of reach. Sometimes I just buy the tail,

skin, and head of a fish and boil it up with rice."

Since this country's deepening economic crisis brought a surge of inflation of 114 percent in September alone, food—or the lack of it—has become the central concern of millions of Peruvians who were already living below the poverty line.

Inflation creates winners and losers.
Source: Alan Riding, "Hunger Spreading in Peru Inflation," *New York Times,* October 30, 1988, p. A3.

EQUATION OF EXCHANGE

nominal variable — a variable measured in terms of money, such as U.S. dollars, Mexican pesos, or Japanese yen

real variable — a variable that refers to a quantity of goods and services, often measured in base-year dollars

nominal price — a money price

relative price — the opportunity cost of one good in terms of other goods (equal to one nominal price divided by another or divided by a price index)

To understand inflation, it is essential to understand the distinction between nominal and real variables.

Nominal variables are measured in terms of money, such as U.S. dollars, Mexican pesos, or Japanese yen.

Real variables refer to quantities of goods and services; economists often measure real variables (such as real GDP) in base-year dollars.

The dollar value of automobile sales is a nominal variable; the number of automobiles sold is a real variable. Other examples include nominal GDP (measured in dollars) and real GDP (measured in base-year dollars).

A related distinction concerns nominal and relative prices.

Nominal prices are money prices of goods and services.

Relative prices show the opportunity costs of goods in terms of other goods.

If P_1 and P_2 are the nominal prices of Goods 1 and 2, the relative price of Good 1 in terms of Good 2 is P_1/P_2.

The term *price level* refers to the average level of nominal prices of goods and services. Since inflation represents increases in the price level, economists analyze inflation by first examining the forces that affect the price level. Changes in the price level can occur without any changes in relative prices. If, for example, all nominal prices double, then the price level doubles but all relative prices remain unchanged.

Figure 27.1 shows the basic version of the circular flow of economic activity that an earlier chapter introduced to discuss the price level. The outer circle

FIGURE 27.1

CIRCULAR FLOW

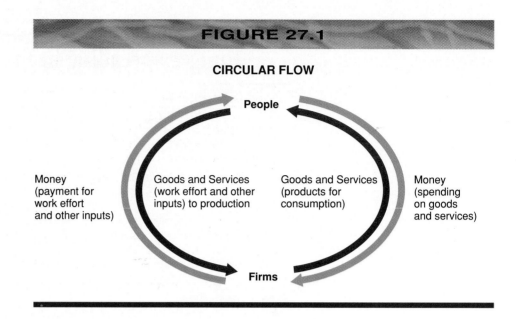

People

Money
(payment for
work effort
and other inputs)

Goods and Services
(work effort and other
inputs) to production

Goods and Services
(products for
consumption)

Money
(spending
on goods
and services)

Firms

shows money flowing from people to firms as people buy goods and services (aggregate nominal spending), and money flowing back to people as firms pay wages and distribute profits (aggregate nominal income). The inner circle shows the flow of final goods from firms to people (real GDP) and the flow of work effort and other inputs from people to firms (another way to measure real GDP).

A previous chapter defined the *nominal money supply* as the total quantity of money in the economy, measured in monetary units such as dollars or yen. For now, think of the nominal money supply as the total amount of dollar bills that the government has printed, minus those lost or destroyed. (The next chapter will discuss several alternative definitions that economists frequently use to analyze the economy.)

nominal money supply — the total dollar value of all paper money and coins in the economy

The **nominal money supply,** M, is the total dollar value of all paper money and coins in the economy.[3]

The velocity of money, V, equals the number of times someone spends each dollar (or yen) each year, on average. The price level, P, is the average nominal price of goods and services in the economy, measured by a price index such as the GDP deflator or the consumer price index.

The equation of exchange says that the nominal quantity of money multiplied by the velocity of money equals nominal GDP, or the price level multiplied by real GDP:

$$MV = Py \qquad (27.1)$$

This implies that the price level equals the nominal money supply times velocity, divided by real GDP:

$$P = MV/y \qquad (27.2)$$

---

[3]This is the currency definition of money, to be discussed in the next chapter.

Equation 27.2 shows that the price level depends on the nominal money supply, *M,* real GDP, *y,* and the velocity of money, *V.* Increases in the nominal money supply or velocity raise the price level, while increases in real GDP reduce the price level.

EXAMPLES

Think about an economy that produces 10 final goods each month, for a real GDP of 120 goods per year. Suppose also that its nominal money supply is $60. Each time through the circular flow, people spend $60 on goods. If people spend the money once per month, that is, if velocity equals 1 per month (or 12 per year), then they buy 10 goods per month with $60, implying that each good costs $6. In this case, the equation of exchange becomes:

$$(\$60)(1 \text{ per month}) = (\$6 \text{ per good})(10 \text{ goods per month})$$

On an annual basis:

$$(\$60)(12 \text{ per year}) = (\$6 \text{ per good})(120 \text{ goods per year})$$

These equations can be rewritten to show the price level is $6 per good:

$$\$6 \text{ per good} = \frac{(\$60)(1 \text{ per month})}{10 \text{ goods per month}} = \frac{(\$60)(12 \text{ per year})}{120 \text{ goods per year}}$$

If, instead, people spend the nominal money supply *once per year,* so annual velocity equals 1, then they spend $60 each year to buy 120 goods, so each good must cost $0.50. In this case, the equation of exchange becomes:

$$(\$60)(1 \text{ per year}) = (\$0.50 \text{ per good})(120 \text{ goods per year})$$

SUPPLY AND DEMAND FOR MONEY

While the equation of exchange shows the relationship of the price level to the nominal money supply, real GDP, and velocity, it does not indicate the forces that affect those variables. Who controls the economy's nominal money supply? What determines the velocity of money and what factors affect it? These questions lead to a discussion of the supply and demand for money.

MONEY SUPPLY

The government controls the economy's nominal supply of money, as defined earlier.[4] Only the government has the legal right to print paper money and mint coins. The nominal money supply in the United States, by this definition, was about $350 billion in 1995. This figure is about 7 times higher than the 1970 figure ($48 billion), 14 times higher than the figure at the end of World War II, and 350 times higher than the figure in 1900. Governments of other countries have also increased their nominal money supplies. For example, the nominal money supply in Japan, by the same definition, is now about ¥30 trillion, 6 times its 1970 level.

The real money supply measures the purchasing power value of the nominal money supply.

---

[4]The next chapter discusses other measures of the money supply and shows that the government does not have complete control over them. This does not affect the conclusions in the current chapter.

real money supply — the purchasing power of the nominal money supply, or the amount of goods that the nominal money supply could buy at current prices

The **real money supply** is the purchasing power of the nominal money supply, that is, the amount of goods and services that the nominal money supply could buy at current prices.

If the letter *M* represents the nominal money supply and *P* represents the price level, then the real money supply is *M/P*. For example, if the nominal money supply is $100 and goods cost $5 each, then the real money supply is 20 goods. Although the government directly controls the nominal money supply, it does not directly control the real money supply because it does not directly control the price level. When economists use the term *money supply* without specifying the nominal or real money supply, they nearly always mean the nominal money supply.

MONEY DEMAND

Most people own some money; perhaps they carry some in their wallets. What affects the amount of money that people choose to own? What guarantees that the amount that people choose matches the amount that is actually available? What if too little or too much money is available? Examining the demand for money provides answers to these questions.

Money is just one of many assets that people own. It is a particularly important asset because people use money to buy goods and services that they want. Assets are valuable, durable goods that people can use to store their wealth. Assets other than money include stocks, bonds, bank accounts, land, gold, fine art, automobiles, jewelry, and so on. Everyone who has saved money in the past must decide which assets to own. The expected benefits and costs of owning each asset affect people's decisions. If the expected benefit of holding an asset increases, people want to hold more of it. An increase in the expected cost, perhaps due to taxes, storage costs, or riskiness, leads people to hold less of it.[5]

COSTS AND BENEFITS OF HOLDING MONEY

Stocks, bonds, and bank accounts pay interest or dividends, but *paper money and coins pay nothing*. In fact, money *loses value* in times of inflation because after prices increase, each dollar can buy fewer goods and services. The real interest rate that people earn by holding money equals the negative of the rate of inflation. A higher rate of inflation erodes the purchasing power of a dollar faster.

The opportunity cost of holding money is the nominal interest rate that a person could earn by holding another asset, such as a government bond or a savings account. The nominal interest rate is a benefit of holding that other asset, and an opportunity cost of holding money. At a higher nominal interest rate, the opportunity cost of holding money is higher and people choose to hold less money. The Fisher equation showed that (holding fixed the real interest rate) increases in inflation raise the nominal interest rate. The nominal interest rate incorporates the loss that people suffer when their money loses value due to inflation.

Of course, holding money has benefits as well as costs. You cannot exchange a stock certificate, corporate bond, or piece of land for food at the grocery store. The special benefit of money is that you can spend it to buy goods and services.[6] The size of this benefit of holding money (the opportunity to spend it) depends

---

[5]A subsequent chapter discusses risk.

[6]This fact ought to strike you as rather peculiar—why should other people give you goods and services you want in exchange for certain pieces of paper? Why will they accept some kinds of paper and not others?

on many factors, such as the extent to which stores accept credit cards or checks, the time involved in writing checks and providing identification to store personnel, and so on.

QUANTITY OF MONEY DEMANDED

Recall that a person's quantity demanded of any good at some price is the amount that the person would choose to buy at that price, given current conditions such as the person's income, wealth, and tastes; the usefulness of the good; and the prices of other goods. Similarly, a person's *quantity of money demanded* at some price level is the amount of money that the person would choose to own, given current conditions such as the person's income, wealth, and tastes; the usefulness of money; and the costs and benefits of other assets (such as the nominal interest rate that the person could earn on a bond or a bank account).

quantity of money demanded — the amount of money that a person would choose to own, given current conditions such as the person's income and wealth, the price level, the usefulness of money, and the costs and benefits of owning other assets

> A person's **quantity of money demanded** at some price level is the amount of money that the person would choose to own, given current conditions such as the person's income and wealth, the usefulness of money, and the costs and benefits of owning other assets.

Nominal money demand measures the quantity of money demanded in monetary units such as dollars, pesos, or yen. Real money demand measures the quantity of money demanded in purchasing power units, often base-year dollars. Studies of money demand have established several relationships:

1. **The nominal quantity of money demanded is proportional to the price level.** When the price level doubles, given a stable real GDP and nominal interest rate, the nominal quantity of money demanded doubles and the real quantity of money demanded remains unchanged. It is easy to understand why—when nominal prices double, people need twice as much money to buy the same goods and services as before. If the economy's real GDP remains unchanged, then people do buy the same amount of goods and services as before. (On average, their money incomes have doubled along with prices, allowing them to afford the same goods and services at the higher prices.) With nominal prices twice as high as before, people carry twice as much money in their wallets.

2. **The quantity of money demanded rises as real GDP rises.** On average, over long periods of time, and across many countries, each 1 percent increase in real GDP raises the quantity of money demanded by about 1 percent. It is easy to understand why—people who have higher incomes buy more goods and services, so they carry more money in their wallets.

3. **The quantity of money demanded falls when the nominal interest rate rises.** Because the nominal interest rate is an opportunity cost of holding money, a higher nominal interest rate leads people to hold less money. An increase in the nominal interest rate from 5 percent per year to 6 percent per year (an 18 percent rise in the interest rate) typically reduces the quantity of money demanded by between 2 percent and 10 percent.

4. **The demand for money has changed in recent decades in the United States and many other countries.**

Economists summarize the demand for money with a formula stating that the quantity of money demanded is proportional to GDP,

$$M^d = kPy \tag{27.3}$$

where M^d is the quantity of money demanded, P is the price level, y is real GDP, and k is a factor of proportionality, such as 1/10. The number k measures the fraction of GDP that people choose to hold in the form of money rather than other assets. This number is not a constant; instead, it rises when the nominal interest rate falls and falls when the nominal interest rate rises. This reflects the fact that the nominal interest rate is an opportunity cost of holding money.

EQUILIBRIUM PRICE LEVEL

The supply of money and demand for money help economists to analyze the equilibrium price level.

equilibrium price level — the price level that equates the quantity of money demanded with the quantity supplied

> The **equilibrium price level** is the price level that equates the quantity of money demanded with the quantity supplied.

In equilibrium, the quantity of money demanded must equal the quantity supplied by the same reasoning as for any other product. The quantity of money demanded is the amount of money that people choose to hold; the quantity supplied is the amount available for them to hold (in the earlier definition, the amount the government has printed). Earlier we asked, "What guarantees that the amount of money that people choose to hold is the amount that is actually available? What if too little or too much money is available?" This section answers these questions.

In equilibrium, the quantity of money supplied equals the quantity demanded. Expressed mathematically:

$$M = kPy \qquad \text{(27.4)}$$

where M is the nominal quantity of money supplied and kPy is the nominal quantity of money demanded. The number k—the fraction of GDP that people choose to hold in the form of money—equals the inverse of the velocity of money:

$$V = 1/k \qquad \text{or} \qquad k = 1/V \qquad \text{(27.5)}$$

Because k falls when the nominal interest rate rises, velocity rises when the nominal interest rate rises. At a higher nominal interest rate, people spend money faster. Think about a country with a very high rate of inflation where people spend money as soon as they can after they receive it, before the money loses much of its value due to inflation; velocity would be very high.

Because velocity is the inverse of k, Equation 27.4 is the same as the equation of exchange, $MV = PY$. Therefore, the equilibrium price level, the price level at which the quantity of money demanded equals the quantity supplied, is:

$$P = \frac{MV}{y} \qquad \text{(27.6)}$$

This is Equation 27.2 from the section on the circular flow. This equation shows how the equilibrium price level depends on the nominal money supply, real GDP, and the nominal interest rate, which affects k. It shows that the equilibrium price level rises when

▶ Nominal money supply, M, rises

▶ Nominal interest rate rises, raising V

▶ Real GDP, y, falls

What happens if the economy is not in equilibrium, that is, if the supply of money does not equal demand? Suppose, for example, that the quantity of money supplied exceeds the quantity demanded. This means that people have more money than they want to hold, given current conditions. Do not get confused by the apparent paradox in supposing that people have more money than they want. Of course, people always like to have more money. They may have more money than they want, however, if, *given their wealth,* they would like to hold less money and instead hold more of other assets such as savings accounts, stocks, bonds, land and houses, gold, art, cars, audio equipment, old comic books, jewelry, and so on. If the quantity of money supplied exceeds the quantity demanded, then people have more money than they want to hold, and they tend to spend it to buy these other assets with their excess money. This raises the demands for these assets, raising their prices.

Any one person can get rid of excess money by spending it, but what is true for an individual is not true for society as a whole.[7] Society as a whole is stuck with the additional money that the government has printed. As each person spends money, someone else receives it. As people spend the money, nominal prices rise. The increase in the price level, P, raises the nominal quantity of money demanded, kPy. The price level keeps rising until the nominal quantity of money demanded equals the nominal quantity of money supplied. At that point, the economy reaches its equilibrium.

Similarly, if the quantity of money supplied is less than the quantity demanded, the price level tends to fall, reducing the quantity of money demanded, kPy. The price level falls until the quantity of money demanded has fallen enough to equal the quantity supplied, bringing the economy to its equilibrium.

EXPLANATION

The government has created a certain amount of money, which is the economy's nominal money supply. In equilibrium, people must choose to hold this quantity of money. The amount of money that people choose to hold depends on their incomes, the usefulness of money, interest rates, and other conditions. One important condition is the price level.

At a higher price level, it takes more money to buy goods and services. Given a stable real GDP, a higher price level means that people pay more to buy goods, and sellers receive more when they sell goods. Because it takes more money to buy goods, people hold more money in their wallets to pay for their purchases. Because people receive more money when they sell goods, on average, people have higher money incomes and they can afford to hold this additional money. In this way, an increase in the price level raises the quantity of money demanded.

If the quantity of money supplied exceeds the quantity demanded, people spend the excess money on goods and assets. This increases demand for these goods and assets, raising their prices and the overall price level. This increase in the price level raises the quantity of money demanded, bringing the quantity demanded into equality with the quantity supplied. The price level rises until people want to hold exactly the amount of money that the government has printed. That is the equilibrium price level.

If the government has printed less nominal money than people want to hold, the price level falls. As prices fall, it takes less nominal money to buy the goods and services that the economy produces, so people choose to hold less money. Therefore, the nominal quantity of money demanded falls. The price level falls

---

[7]This is an example of the *fallacy of composition,* discussed in Chapter 2.

until the nominal quantity of money demanded equals the nominal supply. That is the equilibrium price level.

The equilibrium price level equals MV/y as well as M/ky because V and $1/k$ are the same number. The number k is the fraction of a year's GDP that people hold in the form of money rather than other assets. A lower k indicates that people choose to hold a smaller fraction of a year's GDP in the form of money and that velocity is higher (people spend each dollar bill faster, on average). A higher k indicates that people choose to hold a larger fraction of GDP as money and that velocity is lower (people spend each dollar bill more slowly, on average).[8]

INCREASE IN THE MONEY SUPPLY

Changes in the nominal money supply, the nominal interest rate, or real GDP cause changes in the price level. Equation 27.6 shows that the price level rises if the nominal money supply rises, if the nominal interest rate rises, or if real GDP falls. It also shows that a rise in velocity for some other reason, such as an increase in the availability of credit cards, raises the price level.

Suppose that the government prints additional money and uses it to finance a tax cut. The government does not change the amount of money it spends, but it reduces taxes and prints the additional money it needs to keep its spending constant. This raises the quantity of money supplied, above the quantity demanded. As explained earlier, the price level tends to rise when the quantity of money supplied exceeds the quantity demanded. People spend their excess money on goods and other assets that they want to hold, raising demands for these goods and assets and raising their prices. As the price level rises, the nominal quantity of money demanded (kPy) rises, until the quantity demanded equals the new quantity supplied. Equation 27.6 implies that a change in the nominal supply of money, with no change in the nominal interest rate or real GDP, raises the price level by the same percentage. The new equilibrium has three characteristics:

▶ All real variables, such as real GDP and the real interest rate, remain unchanged.

▶ All relative prices of goods and services remain unchanged.

▶ All nominal prices and nominal variables such as nominal GDP (except the nominal interest rate) are higher.

---

[8]To see why, suppose velocity is 2, that is, people spend each dollar *2 times per year*. The circular flow occurs twice per year, so people spend the nominal money supply twice per year on the economy's real GDP. Each time they spend it, they buy half of the economy's real GDP that year. The equation of exchange with $V = 2$ becomes:

$$2M = Py$$

so the real quantity of money demanded equals one-half of real GDP, or:

$$M/P = y/2$$

This shows that when velocity equals 2, k equals $\frac{1}{2}$.

Now suppose that velocity is *10 times per year*. The circular flow occurs 10 times per year, so each time people spend the nominal money supply on the economy's real GDP, they buy one-tenth of the economy's real GDP. Because $V = 10$, the equation of exchange implies that:

$$10M = Py$$

so the real quantity of money demanded equals one-tenth of real GDP:

$$M/P = y/10$$

This shows that when velocity equals 10, k equals $\frac{1}{10}$.

Similarly, a decrease in the nominal money supply, as occurred in the United States in 1921, reduces the price level by the same proportion.

The economy may take time to reach its new equilibrium level. In the long run, a change in the money supply changes the price level by the same proportion without affecting real variables such as real GDP or relative prices. Still, the short-run effects may be more complex, and they spark controversies among economists. Later chapters will explore the possible short-run effects of changes in the money supply.

───────────── **FOR REVIEW** ─────────────

27.1 State and explain the equation of exchange.

27.2 Explain why an increase in the nominal interest rate reduces the quantity of money demanded. *nominal i rate measures the opportunity cost of holding money. So, at a higher i rate, q. of money demanded is reduced.*

27.3 Explain why an increase in the price level raises the quantity of money demanded. *They are proportional. ??? $m^d = kPy$*

27.4 Explain the relationship between the velocity of money and the quantity of money demanded. How is velocity affected by the nominal interest rate?

27.5 What happens if the price level is below its equilibrium? Explain why. *?? It tends to rise until reaches the ...*

───────────── **QUESTIONS** ─────────────

27.6 Discuss this claim: "The quantity of money demanded is infinite because people always want more money."

27.7 How would the equilibrium price level react to an increase in the money supply? An increase in the nominal interest rate? An increase in real GDP?

CURRENCY REFORMS

currency reform — replacement of an old form of money with a new form of money, with automatic adjustment of all nominal values in existing contracts such as nominal wages and nominal debts to keep real values the same

A currency reform presents an interesting example of a change in the nominal money supply.

A **currency reform** occurs when the government of a country (a) replaces one kind of money with another, new kind of money, and (b) automatically adjusts all nominal values in existing contracts (such as nominal wages in employment contracts and nominal debts in loan contracts) for the change in money to keep *real* values the same.

The new money often has a different name. Usually each unit of the new money is worth many units of the old money. For example, each unit of the new money may be worth 1,000 units of the old, and Part b of the definition means that nominal values specified in existing contracts automatically fall to 1/1,000 of their previously stated levels. For example, if a firm owes a bank $2 million in old dollars, and each new dollar is worth $1,000 in old dollars, then the firm owes $2,000 in new dollars after the reform.

A currency reform does not affect the amount of goods and services a country produces, consumes, or invests; it leaves real variables unchanged. Also, it does not affect relative prices, but it does affect nominal values, because the nominal values are measured in a new, different money. When the new money is worth

IN THE NEWS

Argentina slims peso by stripping off 0,000

By a Wall Street Journal Staff Reporter

With the Argentine peso wracked by a 210 percent inflation rate last year, the military government has decided to lop four zeros off each peso note.

When the measure takes effect in about a month's time, a current 10,000-peso note will be called 1 peso. By the end of the year, the government hopes to phase out all the old notes and replace them with new units.

In 1967, the authorities resorted to a similar measure during a bout of inflation by converting 100 pesos into 1 peso. The new Argentine peso will be the equivalent of 1 million pesos of 1966.

A currency reform that reduced money and prices to 1/10,000 of their previous levels.

Source: "Argentina Slims Peso by Stripping Off 0,000," *The Wall Street Journal,* January 6, 1983.

1,000 units of the old money, all nominal prices measured in the new money equal 1/1,000 of the prices measured in the old money; nominal GDP and other nominal variables fall to 1/1,000 of their values before the currency reform. (There is one exception: the nominal interest rate does *not* change in this way.)

EXPLANATION AND EXAMPLE

The following fictional news report gives an example of exactly what happens every several years in some country, somewhere in the world: "President Announces New Money: One 'New Dollar' Worth Ten Old Dollars; Crossing off Zeros; Prices Fall"—*America Today,* February 1, 1999.

> The president announced today that the United States would immediately issue "New Dollars" in place of old ones. Effective immediately, every $10 bill is now called one "New Dollar," every old $1 bill is now called one "New Dime." Every old $5 bill is now called 50 "New Cents," and so on. People must cross a zero off each $10 and $20 bill they own (making the bills $1 and $2 bills). The same applies to larger bills (a $100 becomes a $10 bill, for example). Also, people must relabel $1 bills as 10 cents, and so on. Pennies become 0.1 cent coins, and nickels become 0.5 cent coins. The government has announced that it will soon issue "New Dollars," which will look different than the familiar green paper money.
>
> As part of the change, all wages, salaries, debts, and payments stated in all contracts will automatically fall to one-tenth of their previous levels. For example, anyone who has earned $10 per hour will now earn One New Dollar per hour. Anyone who owed a debt of $2,000 in old dollars automatically owes 200 New Dollars.
>
> In a related development, major retailers announced reductions in prices to one-tenth of their previous levels. For example, a television that previously sold for $300 will now sell for 30 New Dollars. The president described the measure as a "victory for consumers." He called the policy a "currency reform" and said similar policies have been very successful in other countries.
>
> The speaker of the House, a long-time political foe of the president, opposed the measure. "This is just a political ploy by the president," he said. "Sure, a bag of groceries that used to cost $40 will now cost $4, but so what? It still takes the same four $10 bills as before to pay for those groceries—all we've done is to cross a zero off of each bill and rename it. Now we'll call each of those $10 bills 'one dollar' and say that we pay only $4 for those groceries. Any fool can see this does not change anything except the name of the dollar bills. It doesn't change anything of real importance to American consumers."

If the United States were really to do this, the move would have almost no effect on real GDP, real consumption and savings, real investment, employment, and so on.[9] Everything real in the economy would continue as before, except the names of the pieces of paper money that people exchange to buy and sell. Where once people paid $10 they would pay one (new) dollar; where they once paid $4.50 they would pay 45 (new) cents.[10] The currency reform would affect only nominal values. Each person would have one-tenth as many dollars and collect one-tenth of her previous nominal wage, and all nominal prices would fall to one-tenth of their previous levels. This is what has happened in real-life currency reforms throughout the world.[11]

---

[9] The word *almost* appears in this sentence because a currency reform could make the economy somewhat more efficient by reducing the time it takes to count money and make change when people buy and sell goods. It takes less time to count the zeros on paper money after the currency reform.

[10] Where people once paid 25 cents for something, they would pay 2.5 new cents. If the government had issued no half-cent coin, then payments involving half cents would have to be rounded up or down to the nearest whole cent. The effect of this rounding on real GNP (and so on) would be very small.

[11] Economists' use of the term *nominal* reflects the fact that only the name of the money changes in a currency reform.

IN THE NEWS

Brazil creates new currency to replace the cruzeiro

By Ian Simpson
Reuters

BRASILIA, Brazil—Brazilian President Itamar Franco ordered a new currency Wednesday to replace the inflation-weakened cruzeiro, a presidential spokesman said.

The currency, to be called the cruzeiro real, will be Brazil's fifth since 1980. Brazil, the world's ninth biggest economy, is suffering from a deep recession and inflation now hitting 30 percent a month.

Brazil will cut three zeroes from the cruzeiro to create the new currency, Franco spokesman Glaucio Veloso said.

A recent currency reform in Brazil.

Source: Ian Simpson, "Brazil Creates New Currency to Replace the Cruzeiro," *Journal of Commerce*, June 30, 1993, p. 2A.

REAL-LIFE CURRENCY REFORMS

History reports many cases of currency reforms. In every case, nominal prices changed by the same percentage as the nominal money supply, and the change had no perceptible effect on real variables such as real GDP or on relative prices. For example, in 1989, Brazil introduced a new money, the cruzado novo, to replace its old money, the cruzado. The cruzado novo was worth 1,000 old cruzados, so the nominal money supply (the number of cruzados) fell to 1/1,000 of the previous level, and nominal prices (in cruzados per good) fell to 1/1,000 of their previous levels. This was a typical currency reform.[12]

Since 1989, Brazil has replaced the cruzado with another new money, the cruzeiro. In 1994, it replaced the cruzeiro with yet another new money, the real, through a slightly more complicated currency reform.

On January 1, 1960, France introduced the new franc, worth 100 old francs. On January 1, 1963, Bolivia created the Bolivian peso to replace the boliviano; one peso was worth 1,000 bolivianos. On January 1, 1987, after a period of hyperinflation described later in this chapter, Bolivia replaced the peso with a new boliviano, worth 1,000,000 pesos. (The new boliviano was worth 1,000,000,000 of the pre-1963 bolivianos.)

Argentina has gone through a series of inflationary periods and currency reforms. On January 1, 1970, Argentina replaced its old peso with a new peso worth 100 old pesos. On June 1, 1983, 13 years later, a period of severe inflation brought an even newer peso worth 10,000 old pesos (or 1,000,000 of the pre-1970 pesos). Still, inflation continued, and on June 14, 1985, Argentina replaced its most recent peso with the austral, worth 1,000 pesos (or 1,000,000,000 of the pre-1970 pesos). Inflation raged on, reaching nearly 5,000 percent per year by 1989, before falling in the next 2 years. In 1992, Argentina replaced the austral with a new peso worth 10,000 australs.

Israel replaced the Israeli pound with the sheckel on February 22, 1980; 1 sheckel was worth 10 pounds. On September 4, 1985, Israel replaced the old sheckel with a new sheckel worth 1,000 old sheckels.

CURRENCY REFORM IN REVERSE

Inflation resembles a currency reform in reverse. A currency reform usually replaces an old money with a new money worth more than the old (1 unit might be worth 1,000 units of the old currency). This causes a fall in nominal prices. Think about a currency reform that does the reverse, introducing a new money worth less than the old money it replaces. For example, suppose that the government tells people to *add* a zero to every piece of money, so that $1 becomes $10, $5 becomes $50, and so on. The nominal money supply would be 10 times higher, and all nominal prices would rise to 10 times their previous levels. Real variables and relative prices would not change, though. Inflation works like a reverse currency reform. The main difference is that a currency reform does not redistribute income, so it does not create major winners and losers. In real-life episodes of inflation, however, some people may gain and others may lose as inflation redistributes income. A later section, Effects of Inflation, discusses these redistributions.

---

[12]Some countries impose government controls on nominal prices that prevent prices from changing in proportion to the money supply. Uncontrolled prices and black-market prices, however, change in rough proportion to the money supply.

And in Bolivia: Weary from inflation that has hiked the price of a hamburger to 3 million pesos ($1.56), Bolivia will create a new currency by lopping six zeros from the peso's value and renaming it boliviano. One U.S. dollar now buys 1.9 million pesos; after Jan. 1, it will be worth 1.9 bolivianos. Argentina, Brazil, and Israel have taken similar steps.

A currency reform in Bolivia.
Source: USA Today, December 31, 1986.

Argentina returns to peso, saving numerous zeroes

By Nathaniel C. Nash
Special to The
New York Times

BUENOS AIRES, Feb. 8—For the fifth time in 21 years, Argentina has switched currencies. The country has officially stopped using the austral and returned to the peso, the name of the currency in many Spanish-speaking countries.

In leaving the austral behind last month, the administration of Carlos Saúl Menem is hoping to send a signal that stable times are here.

Introduced in June 1985, the austral, whose name refers to the southernmost extremes of Argentina, was at first worth $1.40. Then hyperinflation took over. By the end of last year, the austral was worth one-hundredth of 1 cent. That implies that the dollar's appreciation against the austral was 1.39 million percent.

When the switch was made on Jan. 1, $1 was equal to almost 10,000 australs. With 10,000 australs converted to one peso, the dollar and the peso are equal in value.

"When we came to the point of considering the need to print a bill of a million australs, that touched off an alarm that said we had to change," said Alvaro Otero, a spokesman for the country's central bank. "The calculator and computers we import do not have the capacity to do such large sums."

But lopping off zeros—this time four—is not new for Argentina. In the last 21 years, the national currency has lost 13 zeros. If no such changes had occurred, the price tag for a $1,400 stereo system in an electronic shop on Avenida Florida in downtown Buenos Aires would have to read 14,000,000,000,000,000.

A currency reform in Argentina.
Source: Nathaniel C. Nash, "Argentina Returns to Peso, Saving Numerous Zeros," *New York Times,* February 10, 1992, p. D5.

EQUILIBRIUM INFLATION

equilibrium rate of inflation — the growth rate of the equilibrium price level

The rate of inflation is the growth rate of the price level.

The **equilibrium rate of inflation** is the growth rate of the equilibrium price level.

Economists take growth rates of the variables in Equation 27.6 to solve for the equilibrium rate of inflation:

$$\%\Delta P = \%\Delta M + \%\Delta V - \%\Delta y \qquad (27.7)$$

As in earlier discussions, $\%\Delta$ indicates the percentage change in the variable, which is its growth rate.

Equation 27.7 says that the rate of inflation equals the growth rate of the nominal money supply plus the growth rate of velocity minus the growth rate of real GDP. For example, if the growth rate of the money supply is 8 percent per year, the growth rate of V is zero (which means that velocity remains constant over time), and the growth rate of real GDP is 3 percent per year, then inflation is 5 percent per year.[13] Nothing affects the equilibrium rate of inflation unless it affects either growth rate of the money supply, the growth rate of velocity, or the growth rate of real GDP.

---

[13]If something remains constant, its growth rate is zero.

FIGURE 27.2

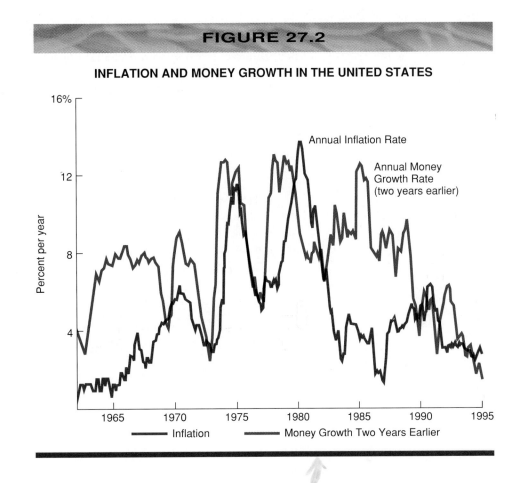

INFLATION AND MONEY GROWTH IN THE UNITED STATES

Equation 27.7 shows the sense in which inflation is caused by "too much money chasing too few goods," as a famous quote explains. If velocity is constant so that its growth rate is zero, then inflation occurs if the growth rate of the nominal money supply exceeds the growth rate of real GDP. An increase in the growth rate of real GDP reduces the rate of inflation.

SHORT-RUN AND LONG-RUN INFLATION AND MONEY SUPPLY GROWTH

A figure in an earlier chapter showed changes in inflation and the money supply in the United States since 1870. On average, the inflation rate is higher when the growth rate of the nominal money supply is higher, and lower when money growth is lower. The growth rate of the money supply and inflation differ due to changes in velocity and real GDP.

Over short periods of time, however, the growth rate of the money supply can increase without raising inflation, and it can decrease without reducing inflation. **Figure 27.2** shows the annual inflation rate and growth rate of money in recent years in the United States.[14] As the figure indicates, money growth and

---

[14]The next chapter will discuss the definition of the nominal money supply in Figures 27.2 and 27.3, called *M2*.

inflation are <u>not closely</u> related in the short run. Although a large increase in the money growth rate preceded large increases in inflation in 1973 through 1975 and 1978 through 1980, short-run changes in inflation and money growth have not usually been closely connected.

Over longer periods of time, however, money growth and inflation move more closely together. **Figure 27.3** shows the relationship between the average inflation rate and the average growth rate of the nominal money supply in the United States in various decades from 1870 to 1990. With only three exceptions (the decades of the 1880s, the 1930s, and the 1950s) the rate of inflation and the rate of money growth lie closely along a line. This figure shows that nominal money growth and inflation are closely connected in the long run.

Similarly, differences in average inflation rates between countries over periods of several years or more are also related to differences in money growth rates. Countries whose nominal money supplies show high growth rates have high rates of inflation, and countries with low rates of nominal money growth have low rates of inflation.

FIGURE 27.3

U.S. INFLATION AND MONEY GROWTH RATE BY DECADES, 1870–1990

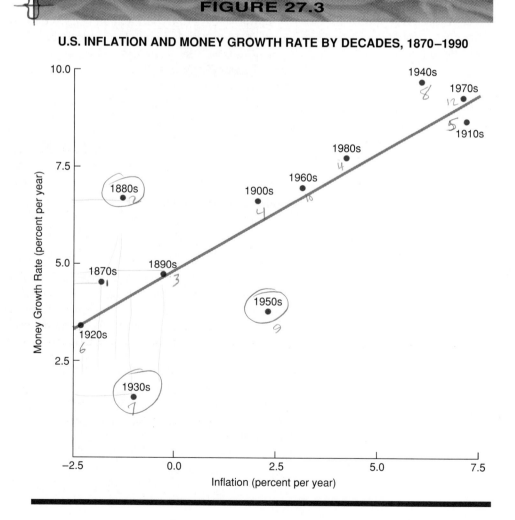

FAMOUS EPISODES OF INFLATION

Many examples demonstrate how governments have increased rates of money supply growth (often to pay for wars), causing inflation. This section reviews some of the most famous examples.

During the American Revolution, the colonies printed Continental Currency to pay for the war. This increased the money supply and caused inflation of 8.5 percent per month. Similarly, an increase in the growth rate of the money supply during the French Revolution caused inflation to average 10 percent per month.

During the Civil War, the money supply doubled in the North as the government printed paper money called *greenbacks* to pay for the war; the inflation rate was high enough that the wholesale price level doubled between 1861 and 1864.

The Confederacy (the South) also printed money to pay its cost of the U.S. Civil War. Inflation averaged 10 percent per month from October 1861 to March 1864. In May 1864, the Confederacy stopped increasing the money supply and actually reduced it with dramatic results. As one study put it, "Dramatically, the general price index dropped . . . in spite of invading Union armies, the impending military defeat, the reduction in foreign trade, the disorganized government, and the low morale of the Confederate army. Reducing the stock of money had a more significant effect on prices than these powerful forces."[15]

A famous case of hyperinflation occurred in Germany after World War I. The Treaty of Versailles that ended the war forced Germany to make large reparation payments to the Allied countries. The German government printed money rapidly to meet this obligation, and between August 1922 and November 1923, its money supply grew at an average rate of 314 percent per month. Inflation averaged 322 percent per month. The money supply and price level both increased by a factor of 10 million. In October 1923 alone, prices increased by 32,000 percent.

In this case, as in many other times of hyperinflation, money lost value so fast that people could not wait to spend it. People would go to work, get paid (daily), and quickly spend the money before it lost value. Later in the episode, people were often paid two or three times a day; they would go to work in the morning, get paid, go out and spend the money before it lost value, then go back to work in the afternoon, get paid again, and then quickly spend that money before it lost value. People took wheelbarrows of money to stores to buy goods. Often the money weighed more than the groceries people could buy with it. Money became so worthless that people gave it to children as toys. It was cheaper to tie bundles of money together to make blocks than to buy blocks for children.

Other hyperinflations followed World War I. In Austria's hyperinflation from October 1921 to August 1922, the government increased the money supply at a rate of 31 percent per month, and inflation averaged 47 percent per month. Hungary had hyperinflation from March 1923 to February 1924 when the money supply grew at 33 percent per month and inflation averaged 46 percent per month. Poland had hyperinflation from January 1923 to January 1924; the money supply grew at 81 percent per month and inflation averaged 72 percent per month. Russia had hyperinflation from December 1921 to January 1924; the money supply grew at 57 percent per month and inflation averaged 49 percent per month.

---

[15]Eugene Lerner, "Inflation in the Confederacy," in *Studies in the Quantity Theory of Money,* ed. by Milton Friedman (Chicago: University of Chicago Press, 1956).

When inflation rate is 116,000%, prices change by the hour

In Bolivia, the pesos paid out can outweigh purchases; No. 3 import: More pesos

By Sonia L. Nazario
Staff Reporter of The
Wall Street Journal

LA PAZ, Bolivia—A courier stumbles into Banco Boliviano Americano, struggling under the weight of a huge bag of money he is carrying on his back. He announces that the sack contains 32 million pesos, and a teller slaps on a notation to that effect. The courier pitches the bag into a corner.

"We don't bother counting the money anymore," explains Max Loew Stahl, a loan officer standing nearby. "We take the client's word for what's in the bag." Pointing to the courier's load, he says, "That's a small deposit."

At that moment the 32 million pesos—enough bills to stuff a mail sack—were worth only $500. Today, less than two weeks later, they are worth at least $180 less. Life's like that with quadruple-digit inflation.

A 116,000% Rate?
Bolivia's inflation rate is the highest in the world. In 1984, prices zoomed 2,700 percent, compared with a mere 329 percent the year before. Experts are predicting the inflation rate could soar as high as 40,000 percent this year. Even those estimates could prove conservative. The central bank last week announced January inflation of 80 percent; if that pace continued all year, it would mean an annual rate of 116,000 percent.

Prices go up by the day, the hour, or the customer. Julia Blanco Sirba, a vendor on this capital city's main street, sells a bar of chocolate for 35,000 pesos. Five minutes later, the next bar goes for 50,000 pesos. The two-inch stack of money needed to buy it far outweighs the chocolate.

Changes in the dollar exchange rate—and thus in vendors' own prices—pass by word of mouth. One egg costs 10,000 pesos this week, up from 3,000 pesos last week.

Bolivians aren't yet lugging their money

about in wheelbarrows, as the Germans did during the legendary hyperinflation of the Weimar Republic in the 1920s, when prices increased 10 billionfold. But Bolivia seems headed in that direction.

Tons of paper money are printed to keep the country of 5.9 million inhabitants going. Planeloads of money arrive twice a week from printers in West Germany and Britain. Purchases of money cost Bolivia more than $20 million last year, making it the third-largest import, after wheat and mining equipment.

Weighing In
The 1,000-peso bill, the most commonly used, costs more to print than it purchases. It buys one bag of tea. To purchase an average-size television set with 1,000-peso bills, customers have to haul money weighing more than 68 pounds into the showroom. (The inflation makes use of credit cards impossible here, and merchants generally don't take checks, either.) To ease the strain, the government in November came out with a new 100,000-peso note, worth $1. But there aren't enough in circulation to satisfy demand.

"This isn't even good as toilet paper," says pharmacist Ruth Aranda, holding up a 100-peso bill. Indeed, she points out, admission to a public toilet costs 300 pesos.

Three years ago, she says, she bought a new luxury Toyota auto for what she now sells three boxes of aspirin for.

"We're headed for the garbage can," says Jorge von Bergen, an executive of La Papelera S.A., a large paper-products company, who lugs his pocket-money around in a small suitcase. "When it comes to inflation, we're the international champs."

Mr. von Bergen says his wife has to take the maid along to the market to help carry the bales of cash needed for her shopping. But all that money buys so little that Mrs. von Bergen easily carries her purchases back home on her own.

Food shortages abound, and fights break out as people try to squeeze into line to buy sugar at several times the official price. Some companies have resorted to barter.

The situation has upset all phases of life in Bolivia. Private banks were closed a few days ago because of worries about executive safety. Strikes frequently close the factories. Many shops have closed. Because pesos are practically worthless, dollars now are being demanded for big-ticket purchases. People get their dollars from the 800 or so street-side money vendors who line Avenida Camacho, long La Paz's Wall Street. Banking, in effect, has moved outside.

The current crisis dates to the late 1970s, when large oil reserves the country thought it had didn't materialize and when large international loans began to come due. Meanwhile, the price of tin, the second-largest legal export, collapsed, and the market for the largest legal export, natural gas, turned sour because of the problems of its main customer, Argentina. (Bolivia's largest export is coca base, used in making cocaine; but it's illegal and doesn't help the government's payments crunch.)

President Siles Zuazo was elected in 1980, but the military, which historically has played a dominant role here, wouldn't let him take office for nearly three more years. By the time he got in, the government was spending more than it was taking in. It began to print more and more money.

"Look at what democracy has brought us," says Severino Quispe Pari, who lives with his wife and two barefoot children in an adobe and mud hut in the small rural town of Yaurichambi. Mr. Pari says he used to trade the potatoes and yellow corn he grows on his half-acre plot for sugar, coffee, meat, and fish. Now he has been reduced to eating only yellow corn.

In the neighboring town of Batallas, some people think this is the apocalypse. Petronila Loguidis stands on a street corner with her six children clinging to her colorful Indian skirts. "They don't understand why there is no longer any bread," she says, pointing to the children. "The Bible says things would get very costly. You could no longer buy bread. There would be earthquakes and wars. I think this is coming."

Living with hyperinflation.

Source: Sonia L. Nazario, "When Inflation Rate Is 116,000%, Prices Change by the Hour," *The Wall Street Journal,* February 7, 1985.

Fed chief warns of higher rates caused by fears

Greenspan sees no reason for concern but frets over financial markets

By Rose Gutfeld
Staff Reporter of The Wall Street Journal

WASHINGTON—Federal Reserve Board Chairman Alan Greenspan warned of "dangerously high interest rates" if financial markets' fears of accelerating inflation start "to mushroom."

Rising expectations of inflation cause nominal interest rates to rise.

Source: Rose Gutfeld, "Fed Chief Warns of Higher Rates Caused by Fears," *The Wall Street Journal,* October 5, 1987, p. 2.

During World War II, Greece had hyperinflation in which the money supply grew at 365 percent per month from November 1943 to November 1944, and inflation averaged 220 percent per month.

The largest hyperinflation in recorded history occurred in Hungary after World War II. From August 1945 to July 1946, the money supply grew at 12,200 percent per month, and inflation averaged 19,800 percent per month. This is 19.3 percent per day, or 0.74 percent per hour. Prices rose by less than 1 percent per hour, but this turned into almost 20,000 percent in a month. In a year—the length of this period of hyperinflation—Hungary experienced an inflation rate of $3,810,000,000,000,000,000,000,000,000 = 3.81 \times 10^{27}$ percent. (Note that inflation compounds; a 10 percent per month inflation rate amounts to 214 percent per year, not 120 percent per year.)

INFLATION AND THE NOMINAL INTEREST RATE

Inflation causes high nominal interest rates. The Fisher equation says that the nominal interest rate, i, equals the real interest rate, r, plus the expected rate of inflation, π^e:

$$i = r + \pi^e \qquad (27.8)$$

Suppose that the real interest rate does not change when expected inflation changes. In this case, Equation 27.8 shows that each 1 percentage point increase in expected inflation raises the nominal interest rate by 1 percentage point. Studies show that the real interest rate does not change, at least not very much, when inflation changes. Some studies show that the real interest rate falls slightly with higher inflation, but that the fall in r is smaller than the rise in π^e, so an

Daily inflation struggle obsesses Brazil

Nation looks to president-elect for relief from price shock

By Thomas Kamm
Staff Reporter of The Wall Street Journal

RIO DE JANEIRO—It was a balmy evening in Rio, the sort of weather that invites one to relax at an outdoor cafe in Copacabana or Ipanema and take in the beachfront action.

But on this particular recent evening the hottest spot in town wasn't one of the cafes, bars, or restaurants that line the city's coast. The place to be was the gas station.

"The price of gas is going up 60% at midnight, so I want to fill up my tank before that happens," explained a taxi driver as he pulled into the line at the Petrobras gas station on Copacabana's Avenida Atlantica. It was close to 11:30 p.m. and there were a good 30 cars ahead of him. "I hope I reach the pump before midnight," he said. "Otherwise, my money will buy only 20 liters instead of 34."

In the 12 months ended in February, consumer prices here increased 2,751 percent. Restaurant patrons complain that the cost of their meals goes up as they eat. Shoppers complain that prices are marked up while they wait in checkout lines.

High inflation diverts people's time and resources from producing goods or enjoying life.

Sources: Thomas Kamm, "Daily Inflation Struggle Obsesses Brazil," *New York Times,* January 29, 1990, p. A10; and "A New Assault on Brazil's Woes," *The Wall Street Journal,* March 15, 1990, p. D1.

increase in expected inflation raises the nominal interest rate. **Figure 27.4** shows the nominal interest rate and actual inflation in the United States from 1962 to 1995. When inflation rises, the nominal interest rate tends to rise also because *expected* inflation also tends to rise. So, countries with high inflation also experience high nominal interest rates.

───────────────────── **FOR REVIEW** ─────────────────────

27.8   Describe how a currency reform works. Explain why it changes nominal prices, but not relative prices, and does not affect real variables.

27.9   Cite examples of (a) currency reforms and (b) periods of high inflation or hyperinflation. What caused such high inflation?

27.10   Why would a reverse currency reform resemble inflation?

───────────────────── **QUESTION** ─────────────────────

27.11   If the growth rate of the money supply is 1 percent per year, the growth rate of velocity is 2 percent per year, and the growth rate of real GDP is 3 percent per year, what is the equilibrium rate of inflation?

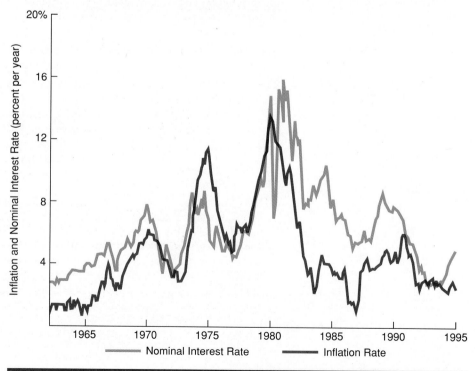

FIGURE 27.4

INFLATION AND THE NOMINAL INTEREST RATE IN THE UNITED STATES, 1962–1995

WHAT AFFECTS— AND DOESN'T AFFECT— INFLATION?

Equation 27.7 is the key equation for inflation. Anything that raises inflation must either raise the growth rate of the money supply, raise the growth rate of velocity, or reduce the growth rate of real GDP. This section discusses commonly cited forces that do—and do not—cause inflation.

News reporters and commentators often blame inflation on some special forces that may affect relative prices, but do not affect the overall price level, which is an average of the nominal prices of the economy's goods and services. While relative prices depend on the supplies and demands for particular goods and services, the economy's price level is determined by the supply and demand for money.

A second common fallacy appears in many claims of news reporters and other commentators who confuse a high price level and a rising price level. Some factor, such as a low level of real GDP, may cause the price level to be high without causing it to continue to rise. The words *high* and *rising* do not mean the same thing! Equation 27.6, $P = MV/y$, implies that the price level is high when y, real GDP, is low. It also implies that the price level rises when real GDP falls. It does not say, however, that a low level of real GDP causes the price level to rise, so it does not say that a low level of real GDP causes inflation.[16]

Any change in conditions can raise inflation if the change causes the government to raise the growth rate of the money supply. Similarly, any change in conditions can raise the price level, raising inflation temporarily, if it causes people to reduce the quantity of money they demand, raising velocity. Except as indicated, the following paragraphs assume that the government does not change the money supply.

SUGGESTED CAUSES OF INFLATION

1. GREED

Business firms want high profits, but greed for high profits does not cause inflation. Two fallacies mar the reasoning that greed causes inflation. First, sellers almost always want more profits. If sellers could increase their profits by raising their prices, they would already have done so![17] While greed might make prices high, it does not cause prices to *increase* over time. (This is an example of the fallacy of equating high prices with rising prices.) The episodes of high inflation discussed earlier in this chapter did not occur because sellers suddenly became greedy—they were always greedy. Nor did hyperinflation end because sellers became less greedy. Inflation did not increase in the United States in the 1970s because sellers became more greedy or fall in the 1980s because sellers became less greedy. Greed has nothing to do with inflation.

The second fallacy in the claim that greed causes inflation results from ignoring equilibrium between the quantity of money demanded and quantity supplied.

---

[16]An analogy may help to explain the distinction. If your effort level in a class is high, the grades you receive on exams in the class are likely to be high. A high level of effort does not imply that your exam grades will increase as the class continues, though. Improving grades would require increases in effort as the class continues. High levels of effort and increasing levels of effort are not the same thing.

[17]Why doesn't a seller increase its profit by raising its prices? Because the seller would lose enough sales to competitors, including sellers of other, substitute products, that raising prices would not increase its profits. That is, sellers charge the prices that give them the highest profits they can get, so any further price increases would reduce profits by changing prices from their profit-maximizing levels.

If the nominal money supply, velocity, and real GDP do not change, then the equilibrium price level does not change.

Suppose that sellers were to increase prices without any changes in the nominal supply of money, velocity, or real GDP. The increase in the price level would raise the quantity of money demanded, kPy, making the quantity demanded larger than the quantity of money supplied. People would hold less money than they wanted, so they would add to their holdings of money by spending less. The fall in spending would reduce prices. The price level would fall, reducing the nominal quantity of money demanded, until the nominal quantity of money demanded came to equal the nominal quantity supplied. In conclusion, if sellers were to try to raise prices while the nominal money supply, velocity, and real GDP remained unchanged, they would create a situation in which nominal prices would tend to fall and bring the price level back to its equilibrium level.

2.   MONOPOLY SELLERS

Monopoly sellers charge higher prices than sellers that face more competition, but monopolies do not cause inflation. The idea that they do suffers from the same two fallacies as the idea that greed causes inflation. First, it confuses high levels of prices with increasing prices, as discussed above. A monopoly does not continually raise prices; it charges the price that gives it the highest profit and keeps its price at that level. Second, the idea that monopolies cause inflation ignores equilibrium between the demand and supply of money, confusing relative prices with the price level. A monopoly charges a high relative price, but the equilibrium price level, which averages nominal prices of goods and services, reflects equilibrium between the quantities of money demanded and supplied, as in Equation 27.6.

3.   LOW PRODUCTIVITY

Low productivity means that real GDP is lower than it would be if productivity were higher. Low productivity, therefore, means that the price level is higher than it would otherwise be, but not that the price level is increasing. Low productivity does not cause inflation.

A low *growth rate* of productivity, however, may cause a low growth rate of real GDP and therefore a higher rate of inflation.[18] Equation 27.7 shows that inflation is high when the growth rate of real GDP is low. The effect on inflation of low productivity growth, however, is small. A 1 percentage point fall in the growth rate of real GDP from 3 percent per year to 2 percent per year (which represents a substantial fall in the growth rate of real GDP) raises inflation by only 1 percentage point, such as from 3 percent per year to 4 percent per year. Changes in the growth rate of real GDP explain only a small fraction of changes in real-life inflation. Similarly, differences among countries' growth rates of real GDP explain only small fractions of cross-country differences in inflation rates.

4.   GOVERNMENT REGULATIONS

Government regulations, like low productivity, may cause real GDP to be low and the price level to be high. Regulations cause inflation, however, only if they reduce the growth rate (not just the level) of real GDP. As in the case of low productivity growth, the effect of regulations on inflation is very small.

---

[18]This is an example of a change in aggregate supply, as discussed in later chapters.

5. INCREASE IN THE PRICE OF AN IMPORTANT GOOD

News reporters and commentators *[handwritten: one who discusses news]* often say that inflation results from an increase in the price of some particular good or set of goods. This is usually a mistake. An increase in the price of any particular good or service can cause inflation only if it raises the growth rate of money or the growth rate of velocity or if it reduces the growth rate of real GDP.

It is easy to see why someone might make this mistake. Whenever inflation occurs, most prices rise, so someone might easily think, incorrectly, that the price increases cause inflation when, in fact, the price increases *are* inflation. Saying that a price increase causes inflation is like saying that falling raindrops cause rain.[19]

Think about a change in demand. If people decide to eat more vegetables and less meat, then the demand for vegetables rises and the demand for meat falls. This raises the relative price of vegetables and reduces the relative price of meat, but it does not change the overall price level because the money supply, velocity, and real GDP do not change. Because the price level does not change, the nominal price of vegetables rises to create a rise in the relative price of vegetables. Similarly, the nominal price of meat falls to create a fall in the relative price of meat. The change in demand causes a change in both *relative* prices, but it does not affect the price level.

Now think about a change in supply. The price level may change if the price of vegetables rises due to a fall in the supply. The result depends on why the supply falls. If farmers grow fewer vegetables and raise more chickens instead, then the supply of vegetables falls but the supply of chickens rises. This raises the price of vegetables but reduces the price of chicken, and it is unlikely to affect the overall price level. Suppose, however, that the supply of vegetables falls because of a bad harvest, perhaps due to bad weather. This may reduce the economy's real GDP and raise the price level. The effect is likely to be small—if vegetables constitute 1 percent of GDP, GDP will fall by only 0.5 percent even if the quantity of vegetables sold falls by half, so the price level rises by 0.5 percent. The price of vegetables might triple, but the size of the change in the price of vegetables is affected by the supply and demand for vegetables, while the change in the overall price level is affected by the supply and demand for money.

In conclusion, a fall in the supply of some good—without any increases in supplies of other goods—can raise the price level. Inflation occurs as the price level rises, but only temporarily. A permanent fall in real GDP causes a permanent rise in the price level, but only temporary inflation. Once the price level reaches its higher level, it stops rising.[20] The point is simple: you are permanently taller than you were as a child, even though you grew only temporarily.

6. *[handwritten: Not]* HIGH WAGES *[handwritten: but increase in wages]*

High wages, perhaps due to strong unions, do not cause inflation. The idea that they do confuses levels with changes, as discussed earlier. High wages might cause high prices, or vice versa, but high wages do not cause *rising* prices.

Increases in wages can raise the price of a good by reducing its supply. If unions were to become more powerful and raise wages throughout the economy,

---

[19]A similar fallacy states that unemployment is caused by people losing their jobs, a famous observation of President Calvin Coolidge.

[20]If the fall in supply is only temporary (if good weather and a good harvest return the following year), then the price level falls back to its original level.

IN THE NEWS

Auto insurance, clothing push consumer prices up

Inflation advances

Sharp increases in the cost of clothing and auto insurance helped send inflation back into the 5 percent annual range last month.

Food price rises push up inflation

By Emma Tucker
Economics Staff

Sharper price increases for food were the main influence behind the rise in inflation last month, official figures showed yesterday.

Fallacies about inflation in the news media.

Sources: "Auto Insurance, Clothing Push Consumer Prices Up," *Washington Post,* November 23, 1988; and "Food Price Rises Push Up Inflation," *Financial Times,* April 17/18, 1993, p. 5.

[handwritten margin notes: P = MV/y ; %DP = %∆M+%∆V−%∆y]

FIGURE 27.5

DEMAND FOR LABOR

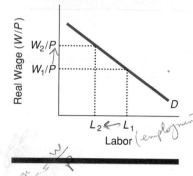

employment would be likely to fall. **Figure 27.5** shows the demand for labor by firms. The demand for labor depends on the *real wage* (the purchasing power of the nominal wage). Figure 27.5 represents the real wage by the nominal (money) wage, W, divided by the price level, P. This indicates that if the money wage, W, and the price level, P, rise by the same percentage (for example, if they both double), then the purchasing power of the wage remains unchanged.

If unions raise the nominal wage from W_1 to W_2 when the price level does not change, the real wage rises from W_1/P to W_2/P and the quantity of labor demanded falls from L_1 to L_2. This reduces employment from L_1 to L_2, and increases unemployment. This fall in employment reduces the economy's total output of goods and services, real GDP, which raises the equilibrium price level. This creates temporary *cost-push inflation* (inflation due to an increase in wages or other costs of production) as the price level rises to reach its new, higher equilibrium level. This effect is small in real life, however. Even a permanent 2 percent fall in real GDP, which would be fairly large compared to most real-life changes in real GDP, would raise the price level permanently by only 2 percent, temporarily adding 2 percentage points to inflation. This increase in inflation is small compared to most real-life inflation experiences.

Cost-push inflation may occur for a second reason. The increase in unemployment resulting from an increase in wages above the equilibrium level might lead the government to increase the money supply.[21] Such an increase in the money supply, sometimes said to "validate the wage increase," would raise the price level. The rise in the price level in turn reduces the real wage (the increase in P reduces W/P), raising the quantity of labor demanded, and employment, back to L_1, and reducing unemployment. Although firms pay higher nominal wages than before, they can charge higher prices for their products, making it profitable to hire L_1 workers.

If unions and the government act this way, a wage-price spiral can result. Unions see that the increase in the price level reduces the real wage, so they raise nominal wages again. Similarly, the government may again increase the money supply, raising the price level even higher. Inflation continues, and the rate may even increase, until either the unions or the government change their behavior. While the wage-price spiral may be important in some episodes of inflation, especially in countries with strong unions that operate in many industries, it is not the main explanation for most episodes of inflation. Evidence shows that there is no strong connection between a country's rate of inflation and the strength of its unions.[22]

7.   RISE IN IMPORT PRICES

A rise in import prices can cause inflation, but only temporarily, by reducing real GDP. A country that must pay more for its imports becomes poorer as a result. Its real GDP may fall because costs of imported inputs increase. The fall in real GDP raises the price level, creating temporary inflation as the price level rises to its new, higher equilibrium level. The size of this effect, however, is usually small. For example, think about the effect on inflation of an increase in the price of imported oil. If a country spends 3 percent of its GDP on oil imports and the price of oil doubles, the country must spend 6 percent of its GDP to buy the same amount of

---

[21]Later chapters will discuss possible reasons for this reaction.

[22]Of course, wages do usually rise with prices during inflation, but this is part of the process of inflation (as raindrops are part of the process of rain), not a cause of inflation.

A rise in nominal interest rate raises the velocity.

IN THE NEWS

Higher pay may be pushing up prices

By Mark Memmott
USA TODAY

Our wages and benefits are rising at a faster pace and may soon land in shopping bags as slightly higher prices.

The Labor Department says private industry labor costs in the 12 months that ended in March rose 3.9 percent, a sharper increase than the 3.1 percent rise in the previous 12-month period.

Robert Dederick, chief economist at Northern Trust Co. in Chicago, says you can bet businesses "will certainly make every effort to pass those costs on to consumers."

Another fallacy about inflation in the news media—the article never mentions the fact that the price level will increase only if the government raises the money supply.

Source: Mark Memmott, "Higher Pay May Be Pushing Up Prices," *USA Today*, April 27, 1988, p. A1.

---

oil. It would probably not buy as much oil as before, but even if it did, the country would become only 3 percent poorer. The doubling of oil prices would work like a 3 percent fall in real GDP, raising the price level by 3 percent, so even a major increase in the price of imported oil would create relatively moderate inflation. The same reasoning applies to increases in the prices of other imports.

8. RISING INTEREST RATES

Sometimes people claim that inflation results from rising interest rates. They see interest rates as a cost of doing business, so rising interest rates seem to them to raise business costs and create higher prices. This argument confuses relative prices with the nominal price level by forgetting that the equilibrium nominal price level is determined by Equation 27.6, which equates the supply and demand for money. A rise in the nominal interest rate is more likely to *result* from an increase in inflation (as discussed earlier) than to cause an increase.

A rise in the nominal interest rate can add to inflation in another way, however. When the nominal interest rate rises, the velocity of money increases. The growth rate of velocity becomes positive temporarily as velocity rises to its new, higher equilibrium level. This temporary increase in the growth rate of velocity causes temporary inflation. In other words, temporary inflation takes the price level upward to its new, higher equilibrium level.

The changes in velocity that result from changes in nominal interest rates can complicate the responses of the price level to changes in the money supply. For example, an increase in the growth rate of money raises inflation more in the short run than in the long run. This results from the effect of the nominal interest rate on the velocity of money. An increase in the growth rate of the money supply affects inflation in two ways. The first effect is obvious from Equation 27.7—the increase in the growth rate of money directly raises inflation by the same amount. The second effect, however, is more subtle. The increase in inflation raises the nominal interest rate, which raises velocity. This increase in velocity temporarily raises inflation even higher as velocity rises to its new, higher equilibrium level. In

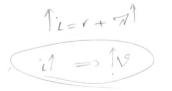

$\uparrow_{i = r + \uparrow\pi}$

$i\uparrow \Rightarrow \uparrow v$

$\uparrow\%\Delta P = \%\Delta M + (\%\Delta V - \%\Delta y)$

this way, an increase in the growth rate of the money supply rate can raise inflation more in the short run than in the long run.

9.   GOVERNMENT BUDGET DEFICITS

Government budget deficits can cause inflation in two ways. When the government spends more than it collects in taxes, it must choose from two options:

1. Print money to spend in excess of its tax revenue

2. Borrow money to spend in excess of its tax revenue

If the government prints money, the money supply and the price level increase. In this way, a deficit causes temporary inflation, and deficits that continue year after year can create continuing inflation if the government finances them by printing money.

If the government borrows money to finance its deficit, the increased demand for loans can raise the interest rate, which, in turn, raises the velocity of money and the price level. An earlier chapter described the majority view of the effects of a government budget deficit, which says that the deficit raises the real interest rate. (According to the minority view, a deficit does not increase the real interest rate, so it would not raise the nominal interest rate and velocity.)

Government budget deficits and inflation show no close relationship in the United States, however. For example, inflation in the United States decreased during the 1980s as government budget deficits rose. In some countries, though, particularly less developed countries, governments often finance budget deficits by printing money, and deficits and inflation tend to occur together.

10.   EXPECTED INFLATION

Suppose that people begin to believe that inflation will increase soon. (The reason for this belief is not important; it may result from political changes, for example.) This change in beliefs can actually cause inflation, even if the money supply does not change. An increase in expected inflation raises the nominal interest rate, which raises velocity. The increase in velocity raises the equilibrium price level, so inflation occurs, temporarily, as the price level rises to its new equilibrium level.[23]

--- FOR REVIEW ---

27.12 Explain the effects on inflation of:
   a. Greed
   b. Low productivity
   c. An increase in food prices
   d. High wages
   e. An increase in the nominal interest rate
   f. A government budget deficit

---

[23]Suppose that a small increase in the nominal interest rate causes a large rise in velocity, causing a large rise in the price level and a high rate of inflation. When people see this high rate of inflation, they may expect inflation to rise even more, raising the nominal interest rate and velocity even further, and creating even higher inflation. In this case, inflation would continue to accelerate into hyperinflation. This is an example of self-fulfilling expectations. While economists have documented no confirmed cases of this happening, some evidence indicates that this occurred at the end of the German hyperinflation.

------- QUESTIONS -------

27.13 Would an increase in the availability of credit cards cause inflation? How would the increase affect the price level? (*Hint:* How would it affect the quantity of money demanded?)

27.14 Explain why an increase in the growth rate of money can change velocity and, therefore, raise inflation more in the short run than in the long run.

EFFECTS OF INFLATION

inflation tax — the loss that people suffer when inflation reduces the purchasing power of their assets

WINNERS AND LOSERS

Some people lose from inflation, but others gain. Everyone who holds money loses because the real value of the money (its purchasing power) falls.

The loss that people suffer when inflation reduces the purchasing power of their assets is called the **inflation tax.**

Inflation acts like a tax on holding money. Your money loses 10 percent of its value if prices rise 10 percent. You suffer the same loss as if there were no inflation, but you were required to give 10 percent of your money to the government as a tax payment.

The government gains when it prints money because it can spend the money. (Saying that "the government gains" really means that certain people gain—those people who benefit from whatever the government buys with the money.) Suppose that the government raises the money supply by 10 percent, raising prices 10 percent. The government's gain from printing money equals 10 percent of the money supply. Because prices rise 10 percent, the money that people already have in their wallets loses 10 percent of its value. The people who hold money pay an inflation tax equal to 10 percent of the money supply. In this case, the government gains what holders of money lose from the inflation tax.

The government also gains in another way. Tax laws in most countries, including the United States, guarantee that inflation automatically raises certain taxes. For example, people pay taxes on nominal capital gains, that is, increases in the nominal values of assets such as stocks, bonds, or houses. Suppose that you bought a share of stock last year for $100, before 10 percent annual inflation. Suppose also that the stock price exactly kept up with inflation, so its price is $110 this year. If you sell it for $110, you earn a $10 nominal capital gain, but a zero real capital gain—a zero increase in purchasing power. Nevertheless, you must pay taxes on your nominal capital gain. A higher rate of inflation produces a higher nominal capital gain and raises the tax. In this way, inflation reduces the real after-tax return on the asset.

The U.S. personal income tax increased automatically with inflation until 1985, when the government indexed income tax rates for inflation. The United States, like most other countries, has graduated income tax rates; people with higher incomes pay higher percentages of income in taxes. Think about a single person with taxable income of $15,000 in 1980, before the U.S. government indexed income tax rates. This person paid $2,605 in federal income taxes, leaving her with $12,395. Inflation from 1980 to 1981 was 10 percent, as measured by the consumer price index. Suppose that this person's pretax income rose by 10 percent to keep up with inflation, so it reached $16,500 in 1981. The taxpayer's after-tax income would have had to rise 10 percent, from $12,395 to $13,634, to keep up with inflation. Together, however, inflation and the graduated income tax raised the *percentage* of her income that she owed in taxes, so she paid $3,055 in federal income taxes in 1981. This left her with $13,445 after taxes in 1981, $189 short of the $13,634 needed to keep up with inflation. Until 1985, when the United States began indexing tax rates to inflation, inflation automatically raised income tax rates in the United States.

indexing — automatically adjusting a nominal value for changes in the price level

> **Indexing** the tax rate to inflation means adjusting tax rates so that the real tax payment does not depend on inflation.

Indexing eliminates one of the effects of inflation on people by eliminating the automatic tax increases that inflation would otherwise create. Canada has indexed income tax rates since 1973.

UNEXPECTED INFLATION

If inflation is unexpected—if inflation is higher than people thought it would be—then:

▶ Debtors (people who have borrowed money) gain.

▶ Creditors (people who have loaned money) lose.

Debtors gain because they repay loans in dollars with lower purchasing power. They pay the same number of dollars, but each dollar buys fewer goods, so the purchasing power of the debt repayment is smaller. Unexpected inflation reduces the opportunity cost of paying off the loan. Creditors lose what debtors gain because they collect dollars with lower purchasing power.

Similarly, if inflation is lower than people had expected, debtors lose and creditors gain. The nominal interest rate reflects the inflation rate that people had expected, so unexpectedly low inflation means that the nominal interest rate overcompensates lenders for debt repayments in dollars with lower purchasing power.[24]

EXPECTED INFLATION

When inflation is fully expected—when people correctly anticipate the actual rate of inflation—the nominal interest rate exceeds the real interest rate by the rate of inflation. In this way, the interest rate on the loan becomes high enough to offset the lower purchasing power of the dollars with which the borrower repays the loan. Even though each dollar that a borrower repays to a lender buys fewer goods due to inflation, the higher nominal interest rate causes borrowers to pay enough to counteract the lower purchasing power of each dollar. Neither debtors or creditors gain or lose from fully expected inflation.

INDEXING CONTRACTS

Unexpected increases in inflation help debtors at the expense of creditors only if loans are not indexed to inflation, as most loans are not. Similarly, labor contracts often specify nominal wages (such as $10 per hour) that firms must pay to work-

---

[24]Some people don't like the idea of reducing the rate of inflation rapidly because creditors (who may be wealthier than debtors) would gain and debtors would lose.

IN THE NEWS

Inflation: Some like it

Just when you thought inflation was history, here it comes again. But while most of us nervously await its arrival, some are secretly rolling out the red carpet.

They're the USA's closet inflation-lovers, the ones for whom the gains of rising prices outweigh the losses.

To the rest of us, though, inflation is still a bogeyman. "Inflation is bad and has a very insidious effect in that it erodes value while people aren't looking," says Wayne Gantt, an economist at SunTrust Banks Inc. in Atlanta. "For every winner in inflation, there's a loser."

Some people gain from inflation.

Source: "Inflation: Some Like It," *USA Today,* May 20, 1988, pp. 1B–2B.

ers. In these cases, an unexpected increase in inflation reduces the real wage (the purchasing power of the wage), so firms gain and workers lose. Firms are like debtors because they promise to pay some money in the future, namely certain nominal wages. The workers are like creditors, collecting these future wage payments. Just as unexpected inflation benefits debtors at the expense of creditors, it can benefit firms at the expense of workers when labor contracts specify nominal wages in advance. Similarly, people who live on fixed nominal incomes, such as retired persons whose pensions pay fixed amounts of dollars each month, resemble creditors; they lose from unexpected inflation that erodes the purchasing power of their fixed incomes.

The gains to firms and losses to workers from unexpected inflation do not occur when inflation has been fully expected. In that case, workers and firms know that future wage payments will be made in dollars with reduced purchasing power, and they can choose a nominal wage that compensates for this reduced purchasing power. Even unexpected inflation may not redistribute income from workers to firms if wage contracts are indexed to inflation. Labor contracts often have cost-of-living adjustments, or COLA clauses, that raise nominal wages automatically with the price level. If an increase in the price level raises the nominal wage by the same proportion, and if the wage increase does not occur after a long delay, then cost-of-living adjustment clauses eliminate the effects of unexpected inflation on real wages.[25]

IS INFLATION BAD?

If inflation worked exactly like a reverse currency reform, no one would care much about it. After all, nominal prices are not very important. In a currency reform, all nominal prices change, but nothing real changes: relative prices, real GDP, and people's real incomes remain unaffected.

Most people think that inflation is bad because higher prices reduce the amount of goods that people can afford. This is true for an individual with a fixed income, but it is false for society as a whole. As a whole, inflation does not necessarily make people poorer. A country's real income is its real GDP, which is determined primarily by technology, available inputs, and other factors that do not respond to changes in nominal prices. The government cannot have any long-run effect on real GDP simply by printing pieces of paper called *money.*

Some economists, in fact, believe that inflation is not very important as long as it remains steady so that everyone can learn to expect it and adjust to it. In that case, inflation does not redistribute income from creditors to debtors. Although people lose from inflation as the purchasing power of their money falls (the inflation tax), the government gains by printing the extra money that causes prices to rise. In this case, the inflation tax is like any other tax, and the government must collect *some* taxes, after all, to finance its spending. According to this view, steady inflation has little or no effect on the economy's real income, so steady inflation is not a serious problem as long as it does not become too high. (A reasonable limit might fall around 5 percent per year.)

---

[25]Several years ago, Vietnam had a high rate of inflation, and some salaries were indexed to the cost of rice. According to the *New York Times* (April 25, 1989, p. A4), professors of computer science were paid each month whatever amount of money it took that month to buy 33 pounds of rice. Whenever the price of rice increased, nominal salaries automatically increased by the same proportion, keeping their real wages, measured in rice, unchanged.

IN THE NEWS

Argentina in chaos as prices rise hourly

By James Brooke
Special to The
New York Times

BUENOS AIRES, June 1—
"Weimar Germany never had an I.B.M. computer," Adrián Rodríguez Boero said today, explaining with a wry smile how he manages to keep his supermarket ahead of Argentina's annual inflation rate of 12,000 percent.

"Every four hours, these prices lose 1 percent of their value," he said, surveying the well-stocked aisles of the Disco supermarket. With all produce tagged with bar codes, the prices are adjusted daily on a central computer.

The rub for Argentines is that their salaries do not increase by 1 percent every four hours.

In the last week, food prices jumped 27 percent. With food climbing out of reach, poor people responded by sacking hundreds of food stores across the nation.

The riots have left 15 people dead and about 80 wounded. In addition, about 1,700 people have been arrested around the country.

Here, at the Disco in downtown Buenos Aires, shoppers pushed loaded carts through the aisles in panic shopping.

"People want their money in something solid," Mr. Rodríguez Boero said, grasping a box of oatmeal for emphasis.

Redistributions of income caused by inflation create social problems.

Source: James Brooke, "Argentina in Chaos as Prices Rise Hourly," *New York Times,* June 2, 1989, p. A2.

Other economists believe that inflation is a serious problem that creates economic inefficiencies and harms people. Inflation differs from a reverse currency reform because it redistributes income and continually changes the basic unit of measurement for prices, the dollar (or yen, franc, or peso). A currency reform changes the amount of money that everyone has by the same proportion, but inflation redistributes income. When the government prints more money, most people don't get any! Furthermore, critics of inflation point out, low and predictable inflation might not be a serious problem; however, few if any real-life episodes of inflation have stayed low and predictable over any sustained period of time. While a relatively harmless low and predictable inflation is a theoretical possibility, it appears unlikely in real life.

We can summarize the main points on both sides. Inflation may be *bad* for several reasons:

▶ It takes time and resources for people to adjust to rising prices, so inflation wastes valuable time and resources. For example, inflation raises the nominal interest rate and reduces the quantity of money demanded, raising velocity and reducing the benefits to people of money as a convenient method of payment. During hyperinflations, people try to spend the money they receive very quickly before it loses value. Sometimes they resort to barter and other inefficient methods of trade. Inefficient use of time and resources can waste tremendous wealth in a hyperinflation.

▶ Inflation wastes resources in financial markets by creating new but costly methods for people to avoid personal losses due to inflation.

▶ Inflation is like changing the length of an inch every year or continually changing the definition of a pound or a quart. Inflation distorts nominal prices and makes it harder for people to compare prices of different goods at different

IN THE NEWS

When inflation runs out of control, when no one really knows if next month's inflation will be 50 or 500 percent, only the most rudimentary transactions can take place in the currency.

Turning to Dollars

Generally, of course, wages go up almost as fast as prices or people wouldn't be able to survive. But the uncertainty wreaks havoc on the daily lives of ordinary people.

That explains why Latin American economies in the midst of hyperinflation typically end up using United States dollars as the medium of exchange, whether or not government authorities make such transactions legal. It also explains why the remedy for hyperinflation usually combines a change in the name and look of the local currency with more tangible measures to rebuild confidence in the economy.

Inflation creates uncertainty and erodes confidence.

Source: New York Times, July 6, 1989, p. A1.

IN THE NEWS

Inflation has spawned an inflation of work, ideas, and even jobs designed to deal with inflation. Isak Marcel Aizim Diamante, the 29-year-old general manager of a Sao Paulo company that makes blinds, says he spends about 2 hours a day reading business newspapers to decide what to do with his money.

Some don't have the time to do this themselves, so they leave it to their secretaries.

Running to the Bank

"That's all I do in the morning," says 25-year-old Maria Claudia Gebaili, a secretary at a Sao Paulo newspaper. "When I come in, the first thing I do is call the bank. Usually it's busy because everybody else is trying to do the same thing. So I have to go over to the bank and wait on line to talk to the manager and ask him to take money out of my boss's short-term funds and put some in the checking account to cover the checks he wrote overnight. On Fridays, I always have to make sure that my boss's checking account is emptied because the money left there would get devalued over the weekend. But on Monday morning, some of the checks he wrote over the weekend have already appeared at the bank. So I have to race over to make sure he doesn't get an overdraft. It wears you down."

Inflation leads people to waste time and resources.

Source: "Daily Inflation Struggle Obsesses Brazil," *The Wall Street Journal,* January 29, 1990, p. A10.

times. This leads people and business firms to make mistakes in their economic decisions, creating economic inefficiencies.

▶ Inflation creates uncertainty that causes economic inefficiency. For reasons that economists do not yet fully understand, high rates of inflation seem to be more variable and unpredictable. People generally dislike the increased uncertainty associated with inflation.

▶ Inflation raises certain taxes in a subtle way without an open and honest government policy of raising taxes.

▶ Unexpected inflation harms many people by redistributing income. Unexpected inflation penalizes people who work and save because savers usually become creditors who lose from unexpected inflation. In this way, even a risk of inflation may discourage savings and investment. Similarly, the redistributions caused by inflation are bad because they take from some people and give to others with no regard either for people's property rights or any notions of fairness.

On the other hand, inflation may have *good* effects:

▶ People may feel happier, perhaps irrationally, when their nominal wages rise (for which they take credit), even if their real wages remain the same because their nominal wages rise only enough to keep up with price-level increases.

▶ Inflation may have other good effects, at least in the short run, as later chapters will discuss.

SUPPRESSED INFLATION

Many governments have imposed price controls and wage controls to try to reduce inflation, often while they were printing money at a rapid rate.

suppressed inflation — inflation that would occur without government controls on wages and prices, but that does not fully occur due to those controls

Suppressed inflation refers to inflation that would occur without government controls on wages and prices, but that does not fully occur due to those controls.

Government efforts to suppress inflation have a long history. The money supply in the Roman Empire rose rapidly starting in 296 A.D. under the Emperor Diocletian. This caused inflation, and Diocletian tried to stop it by imposing wage and price controls in 301 A.D. His famous Edict on Maximum Prices set maximum legal prices on 900 goods, maximum legal wages for 130 types of work, and imposed the death penalty for violation for both the buyer and seller. Numerous people were executed and Diocletian abdicated the throne in 305. President Nixon imposed price controls in the United States in 1971 in response to inflation of 4.5 percent per year. Many people considered that rate of inflation outrageously high and thought that controls would help. Between the Roman and U.S. episodes, many other tries at price controls (often during wartime bouts of inflation) nearly always created shortages and economic inefficiencies, led to black markets (illegal transactions to avoid the controls), and ultimately failed to stop inflation.[26]

─────────────────────── **FOR REVIEW** ───────────────────────

27.15 Who gains from inflation? Who loses? Does it matter whether inflation is expected or unexpected? Why?

27.16 Is inflation bad? Defend both *yes* and *no* answers to this question.

─────────────────────── **QUESTIONS** ───────────────────────

27.17 How does inflation impose a tax? What does it tax? Who collects the tax revenue?

27.18 Explain why fully expected inflation does not redistribute income from creditors to debtors.

CONCLUSIONS

EQUATION OF EXCHANGE
The circular flow of economic activity illustrates the equation of exchange, $MV = Py$, where M is the nominal money supply, V is velocity, P is the price level, and y is real GDP. The equation of exchange implies that the price level can be expressed as $P = MV/y$.

SUPPLY AND DEMAND FOR MONEY
The government controls the nominal money supply, defined as the total dollar value of all paper money and coins in the economy. The quantity of money

───────────────

[26]Some people argue for wage and price controls in periods of high inflation on the grounds that such controls allow a government to show people that it is serious about reducing inflation. This could help reduce expected inflation, reducing the nominal interest rate and the velocity of money and helping to hold down price increases until the government can attack inflation in other ways. However, wage and price controls can create serious distortions in the economy and cannot ultimately reduce inflation unless the government also reduces the rate of growth of the money supply. Moreover, if people view wage and price controls as a desperate measure by a government, or an indication that the government lacks the political will to fight inflation by reducing the rate of money growth, then wage and price controls may raise inflationary expectations and make it more difficult to stop inflation.

A fascinating history of wage and price controls appears in Robert Schuettinger and Eamonn Butler, *Forty Centuries of Wage and Price Controls: How Not to Fight Inflation* (Thornwood, N.Y.: Caroline House Publishers, 1979).

demanded at some price level is the amount of money that people would choose to own, given current conditions such as real GDP, the usefulness of money, and the costs and benefits of owning other assets. The nominal interest rate is an important benefit of holding other assets such as bank accounts or bonds. The nominal interest rate measures the opportunity cost of holding money. Evidence shows that the nominal quantity of money demanded is proportional to the price level, rises as real GDP rises, and falls as the nominal interest rate rises.

Economists summarize the demand for money with a formula that defines the quantity of money demanded as proportional to GDP, $M^d = kPy$, where k is a factor of proportionality that decreases when the interest rate rises. This factor of proportionality k equals the inverse of the velocity of money. The equilibrium price level, the price level for which the quantity of money demanded equals the quantity supplied, can be expressed as $P = MV/y$. Whenever the quantity of money supplied exceeds the quantity demanded, the price level tends to rise toward its equilibrium level as people spend their excess money; whenever the quantity of money demanded exceeds the quantity supplied, the price level tends to fall toward its equilibrium level. An increase in the nominal money supply raises the long-run equilibrium price level by the same percentage without affecting real variables such as equilibrium real GDP and relative prices. The short-run effects of a change in the money supply may be more complex, as later chapters explain.

CURRENCY REFORMS

A currency reform occurs when the government of a country replaces an old unit of money with a new unit of money and automatically adjusts all nominal values in existing contracts (such as nominal wages and debts) for the change in money to keep real values the same. Each unit of new money is usually worth more than a unit of old money. (The new money often crosses off several zeros from the old money.) A reverse currency reform would add zeros to money, effectively raising the nominal money supply and nominal prices. Inflation resembles a reverse currency reform, except that inflation may create winners and losers by redistributing income in ways that a currency reform does not.

EQUILIBRIUM INFLATION

The equilibrium rate of inflation is the growth rate of the equilibrium price level. The equilibrium rate of inflation equals the growth rate of the nominal money supply plus the growth rate of velocity minus the growth rate of real GDP. Over long periods of time, inflation and the growth rate of the money supply are closely related. Over short periods of time, however, they are not closely related. High rates of inflation raise the nominal interest rate.

WHAT AFFECTS—AND DOESN'T AFFECT—INFLATION?

Anything that raises inflation must either raise the growth rate of the money supply, raise the growth rate of velocity, or reduce the growth rate of real GDP. News commentators commonly blame inflation on special forces that do not affect those variables; this involves a fallacy of confusing changes in relative prices with changes in the price level, which is an average of nominal prices. In another common source of error, people often confuse a high price level with a rising price level, although the words *high* and *rising* have different meanings.

These fallacies explain why the greed of business firms, the actions of monopoly sellers, low levels of productivity, or high levels of government regulation do not cause inflation. Similarly, they explain why an increase in the price of a particular good, however important that good, need not cause inflation unless it

$$P = \frac{MV}{y}$$

$$/_\Delta P = /_\Delta M + /_\Delta V - /_\Delta y$$

IN THE NEWS

Keener competition among producers keeps price increases, inflation at bay

By Erle Norton and David Wessel Staff Reporters of The Wall Street Journal

In most recoveries, companies use increased demand as an excuse to raise prices—and with them, the inflation rate. But not this time.

The difference is intense competition. In this recovery, producers have been plagued by a fear that cutthroat rivals will rob them of market share if they raise prices. That market-share mentality, particularly in industries without dominant producers, has fostered intense competition that outweighs the normal tendency toward higher prices and profit margins.

Producers in many industries—diaper makers, tire manufacturers, food companies, clothing peddlers, and electronics concerns, among others—are complaining that competition has kept price increases off the books. That keeps inflation at bay.

Find the economic errors in this news article.

Source: Erle Norton and David Wessel, "Keener Competition among Producers Keeps Price Increases, Inflation at Bay," *The Wall Street Journal*, August 2, 1993, p. A2.

accompanies a fall in the economy's overall real GDP. For the same reasons, high wages do not cause inflation. *Increases* in wages, however, may lead the government to raise the nominal money supply, and in this way create inflation.

An increase in import prices can raise the price level, creating temporary inflation as the price level reaches its new, higher equilibrium level. Similarly, an increase in the nominal interest rate can raise inflation temporarily by raising the velocity of money, which raises the equilibrium price level.

A government budget deficit causes inflation if the government prints money to finance the deficit. If, instead, the government borrows money to finance the deficit, the increased demand for loans may raise the real and nominal interest rates, raising velocity and temporarily adding to inflation as the equilibrium price level rises. The deficit has a large effect on inflation in real life only when the government prints money to finance the deficit. Temporary inflation can also result from an increase in expected inflation, regardless of the source of the change in belief. A rise in expected inflation raises the nominal interest rate, which raises velocity, causing temporary inflation as the price level rises to its new, higher equilibrium level.

EFFECTS OF INFLATION

Some people lose and others gain from inflation. Everyone who holds money loses because inflation reduces the purchasing power of the money. This loss is the inflation tax. The government collects revenue from the inflation tax because it prints and spends the money that causes the inflation. The government also gains from inflation because some taxes (those not indexed to the price level) automatically rise with inflation.

Unexpected inflation redistributes income from creditors to debtors. Debtors gain from unexpectedly high inflation because they repay loans in dollars with lower purchasing power; creditors lose for the same reason. When people fully expect inflation, in contrast, the nominal interest rate exceeds the real interest rate by the rate of inflation, and this higher nominal interest rate offsets the reduction in purchasing power. Although each dollar that a borrower repays buys fewer goods because of inflation, borrowers pay sufficiently more dollars that they do not gain and creditors do not lose from fully expected inflation.

Unexpected inflation can also redistribute income from workers to firms if wages previously set in nominal terms do not automatically rise with inflation. Similarly, unexpected inflation can redistribute income away from other people such as retired persons who live on pensions that are fixed in nominal terms.

If inflation worked exactly like a reverse currency reform, no one would care much about it. High, unexpected inflation can disrupt the economy by creating massive redistributions of income. Suppressed inflation can create serious economic inefficiencies. Economists disagree, however, over the question of whether low, steady inflation poses a serious problem.

LOOKING AHEAD

The next chapter discusses alternative measures of the nominal money supply and the roles of banks and other financial intermediaries in the monetary system. It also begins the discussion of the short-run effects of changes in the money supply that will carry into subsequent chapters and into a discussion of business cycles and recessions.

KEY TERMS

inflation	quantity of money demanded
nominal variable	equilibrium price level
real variable	currency reform
nominal price	equilibrium rate of inflation
relative price	inflation tax
nominal money supply	indexing
real money supply	suppressed inflation

QUESTIONS AND PROBLEMS

27.19 How is an increase in the growth rate of the nominal money supply likely to affect the nominal interest rate?

27.20 Comment on this statement: "If the demand for money rises over time, then eventually the government will be forced to increase the supply."

27.21 Suppose that velocity rises at 1 percent per year and real GDP grows at a rate of 2 percent per year. If the money supply rises at 6 percent per year, what is the equilibrium rate of inflation?

27.22 Suppose that velocity is constant and real GDP grows at a rate of 2 percent per year.
   a. Explain why the government can increase the money supply at a rate of 2 percent per year without causing inflation.
   b. Note that the government can spend the new money it prints. Who loses the purchasing power that the government gets from printing money? What would happen—and who would gain—if the government did not raise the money supply at a rate of 2 percent per year?

27.23 What would happen if unions were to raise wages, sellers were to raise nominal prices to "pass along the higher wage costs to consumers," and the money supply were to remain unchanged?

27.24 A counterfeiter prints money and spends it. Does this hurt anyone? Explain.

27.25 Comment on this situation: In an old movie, Doris Day plays a teenager whose father is a banker. Her boyfriend, trying to impress her father, asks him for a $10 bill and then tears it up, saying, "See? Money is really worthless! Even though I have destroyed this money, there is no less food, clothing, cars, houses, or love in the world than there was before!" Doris's father is not impressed. Is the boyfriend correct? Who (if anyone) gained or lost when he tore up the money?

27.26 Discuss the following quotation from Milton Friedman:

> Money is a veil. The "real" forces that determine the wealth of a nation are the capacities of its citizens, their industry and ingenuity, the resources at their command, their mode of economic and political organization, and the like.[27]

---

[27]Milton Friedman and Rose Friedman, *Free to Choose* (New York: Harcourt Brace, 1979), p. 238.

27.27 Discuss the likely effects of suppressed inflation.

27.28 Disinflation means a fall in the (positive) rate of inflation. Who gains and who loses from disinflation? Deflation refers to negative inflation (a falling price level). What could cause deflation? Who would win and who would lose from deflation?

27.29 Identify at least one error in economics in the news article two pages back, "Keener Competition among Producers Keeps Price Increases, Inflation at Bay," and explain why it is an error.

INQUIRIES FOR FURTHER THOUGHT

27.30 Is inflation good or bad? Is deflation good or bad? If both are bad, why are both increases *and* decreases in the price level bad? What is so good about the current price level that makes you want to keep it?

27.31 Why isn't every nominal wage indexed for inflation? Why don't people have cost-of-living adjustments for everything?

27.32 Discuss this statement:

Inflation is a disease, a dangerous and sometimes fatal disease, a disease that if not checked in time can destroy a society. Examples abound. Hyperinflations in Russia and Germany after World War I . . . prepared the ground for communism in one country and nazism in the other. The hyperinflation in China after World War II eased Chairman Mao's defeat of Chiang Kai-shek.[28]

27.33 Why do people in the United States exchange dollars and not Swiss francs? Why don't Canadians and Mexicans trade U.S. dollars? Why do you spend dollars and not Swiss francs?

TAG SOFTWARE APPLICATIONS

TUTORIAL EXERCISES

▶ The module contains a review of the key terms from Chapter 27.

---

[28]Milton Friedman and Rose Friedman, *Free to Choose* p. 242.

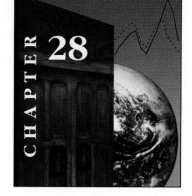

CHAPTER 28

MONEY SUPPLY AND FINANCIAL INTERMEDIARIES

WHAT THIS CHAPTER IS ABOUT

▶ Money—definitions and measurement, why people use it, and how it changes

▶ Federal Reserve and its policies

▶ How banks help to create money

▶ History of money and the gold standard

▶ Bank runs and deposit insurance

▶ Short-run effects of changes in the money supply

Horse would you like to grow your own money? In some southern colonies before the American Revolution, people did. Tobacco was money, and people could literally grow their own money and use it to buy other goods.

Today, people think of money mainly as paper printed by the government. Throughout much of the 19th century in the United States, however, people used paper money that regular private banks created. Each bank's money was a little different. (Imagine owning your own bank, printing your own money with your picture on it, and watching people spend your money to buy groceries!) Today, people use paper money issued by the government, but banks still affect the money supply in ways that this chapter will explain.

Although the government's monetary policies may profoundly affect your life, few people know much about the Federal Reserve System, the independent government agency that controls the country's monetary policy. This chapter will introduce you to the Federal Reserve, its operations, and its monetary policy tools.

FINANCIAL INTERMEDIARIES AND THE MONEY SUPPLY

Earlier chapters discussed the supply and demand for loans and used these concepts as tools of thought to examine the effects of changes in consumer spending, government budget deficits, and other macroeconomic issues. The supply of loans mainly reflects lending by people who save, while the demand for loans mainly reflects borrowing by firms for investments and by governments to finance budget

821

deficits. In modern economies, a large fraction of borrowing and lending transactions occur through firms called *financial intermediaries.*

A **financial intermediary** bridges the gap between borrowers and lenders.

Financial intermediaries serve several important functions in the economy. They help borrowers and lenders to find each other, they combine small savings by many people into large sums of money to lend, they help savers to reduce risk by diversifying their investments, and they help lenders to determine which borrowers are likely to repay their loans on time. Financial intermediaries also play an important role in the money supply process: they actually help to "create" money. The best-known financial intermediaries are *banks.*[1]

MONEY IN THE BANK

The last chapter defined the *nominal money supply* as the total nominal value of all paper money and coins in the economy. This chapter will discuss other, broader definitions of *money.* These broader definitions reflect the facts that you can pay for some goods by writing checks and that money in the bank is *almost* like money in your wallet.

Money as defined in the previous chapter is actually called *currency held by the nonbank public.*

Currency held by the nonbank public includes all paper money and coins owned by people and business firms, not including banks or the government.

Economists work with several broader definitions of money. One such alternative is M1.

M1 is a measure of the money supply that includes currency held by the nonbank public, traveler's checks, and balances in accounts at banks and other financial intermediaries against which people or firms can write checks.

M1 measures money based on the idea that money in the bank *is* money, just like cash in a wallet, if people can spend that money by writing checks. A $50 checking account balance is similar to $50 cash in your wallet, after all. Paying with a check works like paying with cash, though one method may be more convenient than the other.[2] M1 includes all checking account balances owned by people and business firms (except balances owned by banks and the government), plus balances in other kinds of accounts that allow people to write checks.[3]

---

[1]Other financial intermediaries include savings and loan associations, credit unions, investment banks, and mutual funds. Different types of financial intermediaries operate under different laws and regulations.

[2]Not all sellers accept checks, especially checks from out-of-town banks. Writing a check may also take more time than using cash because a seller may require the buyer to show identification. On the other hand, checks may be safer to carry since thieves steal checkbooks less often than cash.

[3]The technical term for a regular checking account is a *demand deposit,* which means a bank deposit that you can withdraw on demand by writing a check without notifying the bank in advance that you plan to withdraw. M1 includes the balances of other checkable accounts: NOW (negotiated order of withdrawal) accounts, super-NOW accounts, and ATS (automatic transfer from savings) accounts.

---

financial intermediary — an organization that bridges the gap between lenders (savers) and borrowers (spenders)

currency held by the nonbank public — all paper money and coins owned by people and business firms, not including banks or the government

M1 — a measure of the money supply that includes currency held by the nonbank public, traveler's checks, and balances in accounts at banks and other financial intermediaries against which people or firms can write checks

BASICS OF CHECKING ACCOUNTS

Suppose that you have money in a checking account at a bank. When you pay for food at a grocery store by writing a check for $20, the store takes the check to its bank. That bank gets $20 from your bank, and adds it to the balance in the store's bank account. In that way, the store gets your $20.[4]

When you deposit $100 in paper money in a bank account, the bank does not keep all of this $100 in its vault. Instead, it lends most of that money to someone who wants to borrow. The money that the bank keeps (the part of the $100 that it does not lend) adds to the bank's reserves.

bank reserves — the money that banks hold to back up their deposits

Bank reserves are the money that banks hold to back up their deposits.

In the United States, the legal definition of bank reserves includes the paper money and coins that banks keep in their offices and vaults, plus the balances in banks' own accounts at the Federal Reserve (an independent agency of the federal government).

Banks hold reserves for two reasons. First, they need money to give to people who make withdrawals from their accounts. The practice of keeping only a fraction of deposits as reserves and lending the rest is called *fractional reserve banking*. Fractional reserve banking provides banks with funds to lend, turning them into intermediaries between borrowers and lenders rather than simply safe places to store money or bookkeeping firms that record who owes how much to whom. However, fractional reserve banking also creates the possibility that people may try to withdraw more money on a certain day than the bank has available. Because only a small fraction of depositors typically withdraw money each day, banks generally have enough reserves to satisfy those depositors.

Banks also hold reserves because the government *requires* them to hold a certain fraction of deposits as reserves. In recent years, banks have been required to hold reserves equal to 3 percent of their total checking-account deposits up to about $50 million, and 10 percent of remaining deposits. Every day, some banks find that they have more reserves than they want while other banks have less, so some banks borrow reserves from other banks.[5]

Banks earn profits by lending the money that people deposit and charging higher interest rates to borrowers than the interest rates that they pay to depositors. For example, you may earn 4 percent interest on the money in your bank account, but the bank lends most of the money you deposited, perhaps charging 12 percent interest. The difference covers the bank's costs and provides a profit for the bank's owners. Reserves have an opportunity cost for banks because they could lend the money that they hold as reserves and earn interest on those loans. Banks balance the costs and benefits of reserves when they choose the amount of reserves to hold.

---

[4] Banks send money to each other through clearinghouses. The Federal Reserve, which a later section of this chapter discusses, is one clearinghouse for U.S. banks. Each bank has its own account at the Federal Reserve. When your bank owes $20 to a store's bank, the Federal Reserve takes money from your bank's account and adds it to the account of the store's bank. The store's bank can withdraw the money from its account at the Federal Reserve whenever it wants. The Federal Reserve is not the only bank clearinghouse in the United States; several private clearinghouses also operate in competition with the Federal Reserve.

[5] The banks actually borrow and lend their deposits at the Federal Reserve. When Bank A lends $1 million to Bank B, the Federal Reserve subtracts $1 million from the balance in Bank A's Federal Reserve account and adds it to the balance in Bank B's account.

ALTERNATIVE DEFINITIONS OF THE MONEY SUPPLY

Currency held by the nonbank public and M1 are not the only important concepts of money supply. Economists measure the money supply by the following main operational definitions:

> The **monetary base** is a measure of the money supply that includes currency held by the nonbank public and bank reserves.

> **M2** is a measure of the money supply that combines M1 with balances in most savings accounts and similar accounts.[6]

> **M3** is a measure of the money supply that combines M2 with balances in most other accounts at financial intermediaries.[7]

> **L** (for *liquidity*) is a measure of the money supply that combines M3 with certain short-term financial assets (loans).[8]

These alternative operational definitions of money are called *monetary aggregates*. **Figure 28.1** plots these monetary aggregates and their growth rates for the United States since 1960.

Table 28.1 shows how the financial pages of *The Wall Street Journal* report data on monetary aggregates. Look first at the top of the table called *Monetary Aggregates.* It shows the daily average of the money supply during the latest week and the previous week. The first two lines show M1 in billions of dollars. The first line, "Money Supply (M1) sa," shows the seasonally adjusted money supply; the second line, labeled *nsa* shows the nonseasonally adjusted money supply. The nonseasonally adjusted data are the actual money supply data. The seasonally adjusted money supply data reflect a technical adjustment to the numbers that makes them more useful for economic analysis.[9]

The next lines in Table 28.1 show M2 and M3. You can see that M2 is about three times as large as M1. The bottom of the table shows total bank reserves (in millions of dollars), required reserves, and excess reserves, which are the reserves that banks have in excess of what the Fed requires them to hold. The last line in the table shows the seasonally adjusted monetary base.

CHOOSING AMONG MEASURES OF MONEY

Which definition best describes the money supply? The answer depends on what *best* means. For some purposes, economists might want the definition that best

---

monetary base — a measure of the money supply that includes currency held by the nonbank public and bank reserves

M2 — a measure of the money supply that combines M1 with balances in most savings accounts and similar accounts

M3 — a measure of the money supply that combines M2 with balances in most other accounts at financial intermediaries

L (liquidity) — a measure of the money supply that combines M3 with certain short-term financial assets (loans)

[handwritten margin note: — The easier it can be converted to cash, the more liquid it is. — money is the most liquid acid.]

---

[6]Specifically, M2 includes M1 plus balances in savings accounts except special accounts called *time deposits* over $100,000, plus balances in money market deposit accounts, money market mutual funds (except balances owned by certain types of institutions), and certain other balances such as overnight repurchase agreements and overnight Eurodollars. The chapter on financial markets discusses these and other types of assets in more detail.

[7]Specifically, M3 includes M2 plus balances in time deposits over $100,000, plus balances in money market deposit accounts owned by firms, plus certain other balances such as term repurchase agreements and term Eurodollars.

[8]Specifically, L includes M3 plus short-term loans made to the federal government (short-term Treasury securities) and to businesses (commercial paper), plus savings bonds, plus certain other balances such as bankers' acceptances.

[9]The main idea of seasonal adjustment is that in a typical year, monetary aggregates such as M1 and M2 rise in December and fall in January, reflecting holiday shopping rather than the country's monetary policies. (A later section will explain how this occurs.) Seasonal adjustment takes these and other changes that occur regularly each year out of the data. Seasonal adjustment makes it easier for economists to compare money supply data in different months and provides a better measure of a country's monetary conditions.

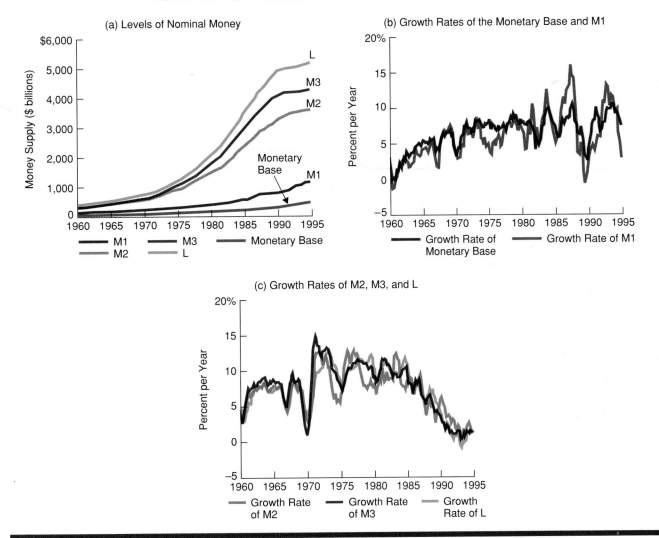

FIGURE 28.1

MONETARY AGGREGATES IN THE UNITED STATES, 1960–1995

(a) Levels of Nominal Money

(b) Growth Rates of the Monetary Base and M1

(c) Growth Rates of M2, M3, and L

matches their idea of what money really is, the pieces of paper, coins, or other things such as stones or tobacco that people exchange to buy and sell goods and services. Economists call such things _generally accepted media of exchange._ For other purposes, economists might want to use the definition of money that the government (the Federal Reserve in the United States) can most easily control. For still other purposes, economists might want the definition that best suits the need to predict future economic conditions.

Defining or measuring money, therefore, is somewhat like defining or measuring intelligence. Scientists could measure a person's ability to learn mathematics, memorize poetry, recognize and deal with complex issues in human relationships, succeed in creating a happy life, and so on, but the many different ways to

TABLE 28.1

FEDERAL RESERVE DATA

Monetary Aggregates (daily average in billions)

	One Week Ended	
	January 9	January 2
Money supply (M1) sa	$1,145.7	$1,141.8
Money supply (M1) nsa	1,191.9	1,182.4
Money supply (M2) sa	3,606.8	3,605.9
Money supply (M2) nsa	3,655.3	3,635.5
Money supply (M3) sa	4,289.9	4,291.5
Money supply (M3) nsa	4,326.7	4,304.0

Reserve Aggregates (daily average in millions)

	Two Weeks Ended	
	January 18	January 4
Total reserves (sa)	$ 59,018	$ 58,705
Nonborrowed reserves (sa)	58,951	58,459
Required reserves (sa)	57,533	57,586
Excess reserves (nsa)	1,485	1,119
Borrowings from Fed (nsa)-a	67	246
Free reserves (nsa)	1,418	873
Monetary base (sa)	419,015	417,061

a—Excluding extended credit. nsa—Not seasonally adjusted. sa—Seasonally adjusted.
Source: The Wall Street Journal, January 20, 1995, p. C20.

measure intelligence have different purposes, and not all people are intelligent in the same ways. To predict how well a person will succeed in an engineering course, one would choose some definition or measurement of intelligence that could predict that kind of success. Similarly, to predict inflation, economists want to use a measure of the money supply suited to that purpose. No one can supply a unique answer to the question of which is the best definition of money.

The government has more control over some measures of money supply than others. The government—in the United States, the Federal Reserve—has nearly complete control over the monetary base. The monetary base changes only when the government changes it or when money disappears, for example, in a shipwreck.

The government has less than complete control over broader measures of the money supply, such as M1 and M2. While government actions can change the broader measures of money, these measures also react to actions of people and financial intermediaries. To see why, the next section explains how banks create money.

HOW FINANCIAL INTERMEDIARIES HELP CREATE MONEY

Suppose that you take $100 from your wallet and deposit it in your bank account. The bank might keep $12 of this money as reserves and lend the other $88 to your economics professor. Your professor then has $88 in cash and you have $100 in your bank account. Even though your professor has $88 of the paper money you deposited, you still feel as if you have the entire $100. In a sense, you do; you have a $100 balance in your bank account. Your actions, along with those of your bank and your professor, have increased the M1 measure of the money supply by $88. (The even broader measures, M2 through L, also increase by $88.)

Mystery of the Missing Money

Who has all of the paper money? By 1995, the total amount of U.S. currency (paper money and coins) in circulation totaled over $400 billion. That amounts to an average of about $1,500 per person for everyone (including children) in the United States. You probably don't have that much cash. (I don't.) Where is the missing money?

Some of it is held by people in other countries. People in less developed countries, particularly countries with high inflation rates, often hold U.S. dollars. People also use dollars to buy goods on black markets in many countries. Currency is also used for illegal transactions such as those in the drug trade. Some of it, obviously, has been lost at the bottoms of lakes and burned in fires. So far, however, economists lack convincing data to explain just where all of the currency is.

The story does not end there. M1 and the broader measures of money will rise by more than $88 when your professor does something with the borrowed money. When your professor puts the $88 into a bank account, that bank lends most of the money to someone else. This process continues through many rounds, and eventually the M1 measure of the money supply rises by a larger amount that depends on how much reserves banks hold and how people choose to divide their money between cash in their wallets and money in the bank.

EXAMPLE

Suppose that banks always hold reserves equal to 10 percent of the balances in checking accounts. **Table 28.2** shows the results. Initially, you take $100 in cash from your wallet and deposit it in your checking account. The monetary base does

IN THE NEWS

Overseas travels by U.S. dollar follow in tracks of world economy

By B. J. Phillips
Knight-Ridder
Newspapers

In the ad, a little boy in Arab dress leads a confused American couple down side streets and through a crowded market, finally depositing them triumphantly in front of an automated teller machine.

The Americans, who'd just gotten cleaned out buying a driverless camel, gasp with amazement to discover that, no matter where they go, there's easy access to American money.

Obviously it was their first trip abroad or they wouldn't be the least bit surprised to find greenbacks in even the remotest corners of the world. In fact, to currency experts, the definition of *overseas* is that vast place where most American money is kept.

According to the Federal Reserve, 60 percent of all American currency in circulation—$365 billion at last count—is held somewhere outside the United States. Other experts think the number could be as high as 80 percent. What's more, the dollar outflow may be matched by a similar movement of other hard currencies.

Some of the money is in drugs and the underground economy, but most is used as legal tender.

Source: B. J. Phillips, "Overseas Travels by U.S. Dollar Follow in Tracks of World Economy," *Journal of Commerce*, March 9, 1994.

R = required reserve %. = deposits/reserves

1/R = money multiplier

initial deposit × 1/R

max Total deposit = money supply

= $1000 (money supply)

100 × 1/.1 10%

90 × 1/.1

= $1000 (Total money supply)

= $900 (Total M.)

TABLE 28.2

HOW THE BANKING SYSTEM CREATES MONEY: AN EXAMPLE

Actions	Effects on Money Supply
You take $100 cash from your wallet and put it in your checking account.	No change in monetary base or M1.
The bank keeps $10 (10 percent of your $100 deposit) as reserves and lends $90 to Andrea.	No change in monetary base; M1 rises by $90.
Andrea spends the $90 to buy something from Bob, who deposits the $90 in his checking account. Bob's bank keeps $9 (10 percent of $90) as reserves, and lends the other $81 to Celine.	No change in monetary base; M1 rises another $81, bringing its total increase to $171
Celine spends the $81 to buy something from Dave, who deposits the $81 in his checking account. Dave's bank keeps $8.10 (10 percent of $81) and lends the other $72.90 to Elaine.	No change in monetary base; M1 rises another $72.90, bringing its total increase to $243.90
Elaine uses the money to buy something from Fran, who deposits the money in her checking account, and the process continues. . . .	Eventually, M1 rises by $900[a].

[a]The $900 figure comes from adding

$$\$90 + (.9)(\$90) + (.9)^2(\$90) + (.9)^3(\$90) + (.9)^4(\$90) + \ldots$$
$$\qquad \$81 \qquad \$72.90 \qquad \$65.61 \qquad \$59.05$$

which equals

$$\$90(1 + .9 + .9^2 + .9^3 + .9^4 + .9^5 + \ldots)$$
$$= \$90/(1 - .9)$$
$$= \$90/.1$$
$$= \$900$$

not change because, although currency in the hands of the nonbank public (that is, you) falls by $100, bank reserves rise by $100 because the bank has your money. Broader measures of the money supply also remain unchanged, because although currency in the hands of the nonbank public falls by $100, the balance in your checking account rises by that amount.

The bank, however, keeps only $10 of the money you deposited and lends the other $90 to Andrea. At this point, M1 rises by $90 because you still have $100 in your bank account, but Andrea has $90 that she did not have before. Andrea spends the $90 to buy boots from Bob, who deposits it in his bank account. His bank keeps $9 (10 percent of the $90) as reserves and lends the other $81 to Celine. At this point, M1 rises by another $81, for a total increase of $171, because Celine now has $81 that she did not have before, while you still have your $100 in the bank and Bob still has his $90 in the bank. Celine spends the $81 to buy daggers from Dave, who deposits it in his bank account. His bank keeps $8.10 (10 percent of the $81.00 deposit) and lends the other $72.90 to Elaine, raising M1 by another $72.90. By this time, M1 has increased by $243.90. Next, Elaine spends the money to buy flowers from Fran, and this process continues. After three more rounds, M1 rises by a total of $421.70; eventually, M1 rises by a total of $900 as a result of your initial $100 deposit.

MONEY MULTIPLIER

The last example showed how M1 eventually rises by $900 when a person deposits $100 in the bank and banks hold reserves equal to 10 percent of their deposits. Because a $100 rise in deposits raises M1 by $900, economists say that the money multiplier is 9 in this case.

money multiplier — the ratio of a broad measure of the money supply, such as M1, M2, M3, or L to the monetary base

A **money multiplier** is the ratio of a broad measure of the money supply, such as M1, M2, M3, or L, to the monetary base.

For example, the money multiplier for M1 is defined as:

$$\text{M1 money multiplier} = \frac{\text{M1}}{\text{Monetary Base}}$$

Economists calculate similar money multipliers for M2 and other measures of money.

In the last example, the M1 money multiplier was 9 because the ratio of bank deposits to reserves equaled 9, that is, banks lent $9 for every $1 they held in reserves. For each dollar of deposits, banks lent $0.90 and kept $0.10 as reserves. In that example, the M1 money multiplier equaled:

$$\text{M1 money multiplier} = \frac{\text{Deposits}}{\text{Reserves}}$$

In that example, however, each seller deposited *all* newly received money into a bank account. More generally, a seller may keep some of that money as cash in a wallet. A more general formula for the M1 money multiplier takes this into account:

$$\text{M1 money multiplier} = \frac{1 + \text{Currency-Deposit Ratio}}{\text{Reserve-Deposit Ratio} + \text{Currency-Deposit Ratio}}$$

The currency-deposit ratio shows how much currency (paper money and coins) people hold as a fraction of their total checking-account balances; the reserve-deposit ratio shows how much reserves banks hold as a fraction of total checking-account balances.[10]

---

[10]One can derive the M1 money multiplier from the definitions of M1 and the monetary base. If C stands for currency (cash), D stands for deposits, and R stands for bank reserves, then M1 equals:

$$\text{M1} = D + C$$

and the monetary base, B, equals

$$B = R + C$$

The M1 money multiplier equals the ratio of M1 to B:

$$\text{M1 Money Multiplier} = \frac{\text{M1}}{B}$$

Substituting definitions for M1 and B:

$$= \frac{D + C}{R + C}$$

Dividing numerator and denominator by D:

$$= \frac{\left(1 + \dfrac{C}{D}\right)}{\left(\dfrac{R}{D} + \dfrac{C}{D}\right)}$$

This is the expression in the text. Money multipliers for broader measures of money can be derived in a similar way, with more complicated results.

MONEY MULTIPLIERS IN THE UNITED STATES

The M1 money multiplier in the United States currently hovers about 2.60. The currency-deposit ratio has averaged about 0.40 in the last decade, and the reserve-deposit ratio has averaged about 0.13 (13 percent), implying a multiplier of 2.64. **Figure 28.2** shows the changes in the U.S. M1 money multiplier over the last 30 years. The U.S. M2 money multiplier is about 11, the M3 money multiplier is about 14, and the L money multiplier is about 17.

USING THE MONEY MULTIPLIER

The money multiplier can illustrate how a change in the monetary base affects M1. Suppose that the government raises the monetary base by printing $1,000 in new money and spending it to buy something. The seller now has the $1,000, so the monetary base has risen by $1,000. The M1 money multiplier of 2.64 suggests that M1 will eventually rise by $2,640 (2.64 times $1,000). The general rule is:

Change in M1 = M1 money multiplier × Change in monetary base

EXPLANATION AND EXAMPLE   Suppose that the government prints $1,000 in new currency and buys something from Megan, a typical person whose currency-deposit ratio of 0.4 indicates that she holds $0.40 in currency for each $1.00 in her bank account. Therefore, as a typical person, Megan puts $714 of her newly earned $1,000 into her checking account and keeps $286 as currency ($286 is 40

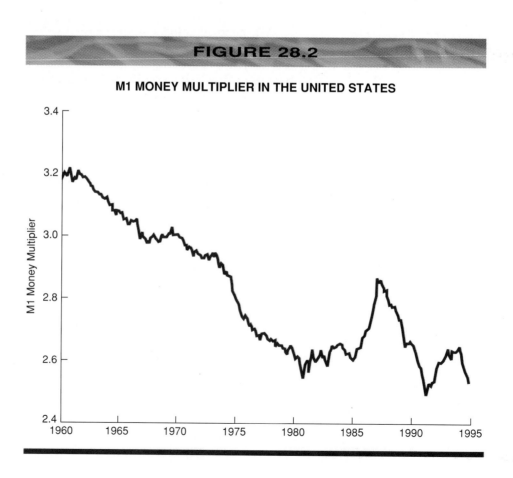

FIGURE 28.2

M1 MONEY MULTIPLIER IN THE UNITED STATES

ALTERNATIVE DEFINITIONS OF THE MONEY SUPPLY

Concept of Money	Includes	Affected by Actions of
Currency held by the nonbank public	All paper money and coins owned by the nonbank public (people and business firms, not including banks and the government)	Government, people, and banks
Monetary base	Currency held by the nonbank public plus bank reserves	Only the government
M1	Currency held by the nonbank public plus traveler's checks, balances in accounts at banks or at other financial intermediaries against which people or firms can write checks	Government, people, and banks
M2	M1 plus balances in most savings accounts and similar accounts	Government, people, and banks
M3	M2 plus balances in most other accounts at financial intermediaries	Government, people, and banks
L	M3 plus certain short-term financial assets (loans)	Government, people, and banks

percent of $714). These actions appear in the first row of **Table 28.3**. Megan's bank has a reserve-deposit ratio of 13 percent, so it keeps $92.82 of Megan's deposit as reserves and lends the other $621.18 to Ned.

Ned, another typical person with a currency-deposit ratio of 0.4, keeps $177.66 in cash and deposits $443.52 into his checking account. His bank keeps $57.66 as reserves on this deposit, and lends the other $385.86 to Oprah, another typical person. The money supply grows as the process continues down the rows of Table 28.3. Eventually, by the eighth round of this process (when Tom's bank has loaned $22.17 to someone), M1 has increased by $2,603.42, as shown in the last row of Table 28.3. If the table were to continue even farther, it would show that M1 eventually rises by $2,640. The money multiplier simply gives a quick way to calculate the final change in M1.

─────────────── FOR REVIEW ───────────────

28.1 If you pay for a new shirt with a check, how does the store get your money?

28.2 How can you (with the help of a bank) increase the money supply? Explain.

28.3 Define and explain who controls (a) the monetary base, (b) M1, and (c) M2.

28.4 Explain how the banking system creates money.

TABLE 28.3

HOW A CHANGE IN THE MONETARY BASE RAISES M1

	Starting Amount	Kept as Currency	Deposit in Bank	Bank Reserves	Bank Loans	Cumulative M1 Increase
Megan	$1,000.00	$286.00	$714.00	$92.82	$621.18	$1,621.18
Ned	621.18	177.66	443.52	57.66	385.86	2,007.04
Oprah	385.86	110.36	275.51	35.82	239.69	2,246.74
Pete	239.69	68.55	171.14	22.25	148.89	2,395.63
Quentin	148.89	42.58	106.31	13.82	92.49	2,488.12
Robert	92.49	26.45	66.04	8.58	57.45	2,545.57
Sandra	57.45	16.43	41.02	5.33	35.69	2,581.26
Tom	35.69	10.21	25.48	3.31	22.17	2,603.42

─────────────────── **QUESTIONS** ───────────────────

28.5 Suppose that banks hold $0.10 of reserves out of every $1.00 of deposits and that the currency-deposit ratio is 0.5. How large is the M1 money multiplier?

28.6 Suppose that people choose to increase the fraction of their money that they hold in the form of currency and reduce the fraction that they hold in the form of bank deposits. How would this affect M1 and M2?

FEDERAL RESERVE SYSTEM

central bank — a bank for banks

Federal Reserve System — a semi-independent agency of the U.S. government that serves as the central bank in the United States

Many countries, including the United States, operate central banks that serve as banks for banks. The U.S. central bank is the Federal Reserve System, often simply called the *Fed.*

> A **central bank** is a bank for banks. The **Federal Reserve System,** a semi-independent agency of the U.S. government, is the central bank in the United States.

The Fed conducts monetary policy (controlling the money supply) and handles most bank regulation in the United States. Similar agencies in other countries include the Bank of Canada, Bank of England, Bank of Japan, Bank of Mexico, and the German Central Bank (Bundesbank). These central banks conduct monetary policies and regulate banks in their countries. Most central banks are government agencies, though not all; the Bank of England began as a private bank.

The Fed was created by the Federal Reserve Act in 1913. Before that time, the United States had no central bank. Although the Fed affects the lives of every citizen through its policies, most people know little about how it operates. The Federal Reserve System consists of three main parts:

1. The Board of Governors, a seven-member panel in Washington, D.C., employs a large supporting staff of statisticians and researchers. Members of the board are appointed by the president and confirmed by Congress to serve 14-year terms. The long terms are intended to help shield board members from political pressure, much as judges' life terms shield them. The terms are staggered so that one becomes vacant every 2 years. The president appoints one governor as chairman for a 4-year term. The chairman, currently Alan Greenspan, has more influence and power, partly through control of the agendas at meetings, than the other governors.

2. Regional Federal Reserve Banks are centered in 12 cities around the country.[11] Each Federal Reserve Bank has nine directors, three appointed by the Board of Governors and six elected by private banks in the Federal Reserve Bank's district. These nine directors choose the president of the Federal Reserve Bank. The New York Federal Reserve Bank carries out most of the Fed's policy actions.

3. The Federal Reserve Open Market Committee, or FOMC, is a committee that meets about every six weeks in Washington to discuss the economy, set the nation's monetary policy, and choose Fed policy actions. The FOMC's 12 mem-

───────────

[11]Federal Reserve Banks are located in New York, Boston, Philadelphia, Cleveland, Richmond, Atlanta, Chicago, St. Louis, Minneapolis, Kansas City, Dallas, and San Francisco.

bers include the 7 Fed governors in Washington D.C., the president of the Federal Reserve Bank of New York, the presidents of 4 of the 11 other Federal Reserve Banks, who take turns serving on the committee. The bank presidents who do not serve on the FOMC can participate in its meetings, but cannot vote on policy. The Federal Reserve Bank of New York is responsible for carrying out the policies chosen by the FOMC.

The Fed, unlike most government agencies, operates somewhat independently of the rest of the government. This independence is intended to isolate the Fed from political forces that might compromise its choice of the best policies for the economy.[12] The Fed does not receive money directly from Congress. Instead, the Fed pays its expenses (staff salaries and so on) out of the interest that it earns on its financial assets, mostly U.S. Treasury bills and government bonds.[13] After paying its expenses, it returns any leftover money to Congress. In addition, the Fed does not undergo audits by the General Accounting Office, a federal government accounting agency that audits the books of most other government agencies. This also helps to reduce political pressures on the Fed.

FEDERAL RESERVE POLICY TOOLS: HOW THE MONEY SUPPLY CHANGES

The Fed has three main tools of monetary policy:

Open market operations

Discount window lending

Reserve requirements and other bank regulations

OPEN MARKET OPERATIONS

The Fed's primary policy tool is the open market operation.

open market operation — Federal Reserve purchase or sale of financial assets

In an **open market operation,** the Fed buys or sells financial assets, usually U.S. government Treasury bills and Treasury bonds.

In an open market purchase, the Fed buys financial assets; in an open market sale, the Fed sells financial assets.

An open market purchase increases the monetary base because the Fed spends newly created money to buy financial assets. This increase in the monetary base sets into motion the money-multiplier process described earlier, raising broader measures of money such as M1 and M2. When the Fed buys financial assets from a bank in an open market purchase, rather than actually paying the bank with newly printed paper money, the Fed deposits its payment into the bank's account at the Fed. This raises the bank's reserves, increasing the monetary base. The actual supply of paper money may rise when those banks lend some of their newly acquired reserves in the money-multiplier process described earlier. Because open market purchases raise bank reserves, economists and news analysts often describe such purchases by saying that the Fed *injects reserves* into the banking system.

An open market sale shrinks the monetary base because the Fed collects payment for the assets it sells by taking reserves out of the accounts of the banks that

---

[12]A later chapter returns to issues of Fed independence.

[13]Financial assets are covered in a later chapter.

buy those assets. (Think of the Fed as destroying the money that it receives for selling the assets.) Because open market sales reduce bank reserves, economists and news analysts often describe such sales by saying that the Fed *withdraws reserves* from the banking system. This fall in reserves sets into motion the money-multiplier process described earlier, so the open market sale reduces broad measures of the money supply such as M1 and M2. The FOMC makes decisions about open market operations, and the Federal Reserve Bank of New York does the actual buying and selling.

DISCOUNT WINDOW LENDING

The Fed sometimes lends reserves to banks. The bank is said to borrow at the Fed's *discount window,* and the interest rate the bank pays is called the *discount rate.*[14]

Federal Reserve discount rate — the interest rate that the Fed charges banks for short-term loans

> The **Federal Reserve discount rate** is the interest rate that the Fed charges banks for short-term loans.

When the Fed lends reserves to a bank, the monetary base rises. Broader measures of the money supply then increase through the money-multiplier process. By raising and lowering the discount rate, the Fed can affect the amount of bank borrowing at the discount window.

As noted earlier, banks borrow and lend reserves among themselves every day. Banks with more reserves than they want lend to other banks with fewer reserves than they want. The interest rate that banks charge each other for short-term loans of reserves is called the *federal funds rate.*

federal funds rate — the interest rate that banks charge each other for short-term loans of reserves

> The **federal funds rate** is the interest rate that banks charge each other when they borrow and lend reserves for short periods.

The federal funds rate has nothing to do with the federal government, although, as a later chapter will explain, it is often a target of Federal Reserve monetary policy.

Figure 28.3 shows changes in the Federal Reserve discount rate and the federal funds rate since 1960. When the federal funds rate is less than the Federal Reserve discount rate, banks find it cheaper to borrow from other banks than from the Fed. When the discount rate is less than the federal funds rate, banks would prefer to borrow from the Fed than from other banks. The Fed discourages banks from borrowing too much or too often at the discount window, however, and it does not always lend to banks that want to borrow.[15]

The Fed lends reserves to banks at the discount window for two purposes: acting as a lender of last resort in an emergency situation and conducting monetary policy. The original reason for the discount window was to make the Fed a lender of last resort, a source of loans to banks that cannot easily borrow funds elsewhere and that need reserves so depositors can withdraw their money (or for other purposes such as meeting legal reserve requirements).[16] If only one bank

---

[14]Each Federal Reserve Bank has the power to choose its own discount-window policy, but in practice their policies differ little across Federal Reserve Banks. The discount rate applies to very short-term loans. Federal Reserve Banks often charge banks interest rates higher than the discount rate for longer-term loans.

[15]Banks that try to borrow from the Fed too often or too much would attract increased scrutiny by Federal Reserve bank regulators, creating inconvenience and costs for those banks.

[16]Banks that borrow at the discount window frequently could borrow in the federal funds market, but only at a higher interest rate.

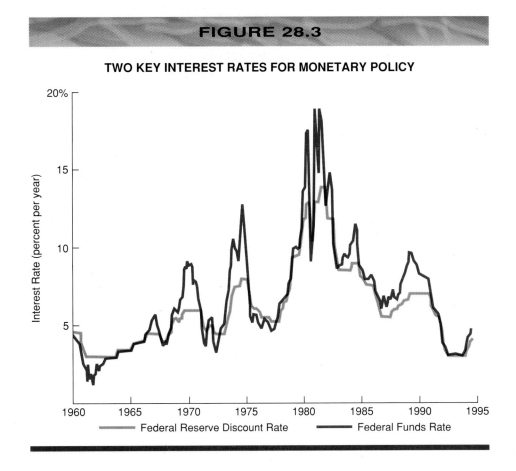

FIGURE 28.3

TWO KEY INTEREST RATES FOR MONETARY POLICY

Federal Reserve Discount Rate — *Federal Funds Rate*

needs to borrow reserves for depositors to withdraw, it can borrow from other banks, but if *all* (or many) banks simultaneously experience large withdrawals, they may be unable to borrow enough because the entire economy may not contain enough currency to allow all depositors to withdraw at once.[17] A lender of last resort provides additional currency in such a situation; by assuring people that they can always withdraw their money whenever they want, it can help to prevent such a situation from developing out of panic. This was originally intended as the main role of the Federal Reserve, and discount window lending was the main tool of Fed policy in its early years.

The second purpose of discount window lending is to help conduct monetary policy, that is, to control the money supply. By lending reserves to banks, the Fed can raise the monetary base and broader measures of the money supply.

REQUIRED RESERVES AND OTHER BANK REGULATIONS

As an earlier section noted, the Fed requires banks to hold minimum levels of reserves per dollar of deposits, currently 3 percent to 10 percent of checking-account balances.

---

[17]As an option, banks might give people only, say, $0.90 for each $1.00 in their accounts. This is what actually happened in many banking panics, as a later section discusses.

required reserves — the reserves that the Fed requires banks to hold, based on their total deposits

Required reserves are the reserves that the Fed requires banks to hold, based on their total deposits.

The Fed can increase the M1 money multiplier by reducing the required reserves on checkable deposits. A bank lends a larger fraction of each deposited dollar if it holds a smaller fraction as reserves. This result appears in the formula for the M1 money multiplier: a fall in the ratio of reserves to deposits (or an increase in the ratio of deposits to reserves) raises the multiplier. Similarly, the Fed can reduce the M1 money multiplier by raising required reserves, which reduces the amount of bank lending per dollar of deposits. Although reserve requirements can affect money multipliers and change M1 and M2, the Fed seldom changes reserve requirements much.

The Fed also supervises and regulates banks. The Fed makes sure that banks actually hold the reserves that they are required to hold. It monitors their investments to make sure that they meet certain legal requirements, such as those intended to prevent banks from choosing particularly risky investments. The Fed also enforces a variety of other bank regulations. Other functions of the Federal Reserve include acting as a clearinghouse to clear checks and distributing new currency.

FOR REVIEW

28.7 Describe the Federal Reserve System and its three main policy tools.

28.8 Explain open market operations and how they affect the money supply.

28.9 What is the Federal Reserve discount rate? The federal funds rate?

QUESTION

28.10 Why might the Federal Reserve be more effective than a private bank as a lender of last resort?

HISTORY AND ROLES OF MONEY

It is important to view the Federal Reserve and the current U.S. monetary system in perspective. The current system is only one of many possible systems. It differs from previous monetary systems and likely will change in the future.

MONEY AND BARTER

Not all civilizations have used money. Certainly not all used money as people know it today. Some primitive societies relied mainly on barter.[18] Barter was common during the Middle Ages (roughly the 5th through 15th centuries), except for international trade. Barter was also common in America in the early 16th century, though money transactions became common later in the 16th century.

ADVANTAGES OF MONEY OVER BARTER

People use money because it is more convenient than barter. It avoids the problem of creating a double coincidence of wants in which someone both has goods

---

[18]When the government of ancient Egypt collected taxes (which were high), people paid by giving goods, not money, to the government. The same was true in medieval Europe under the feudal system; serfs paid goods rather than money to lords.

that you want and wants goods that you have. A double coincidence of wants makes barter easy, but real life is not usually as simple as this. Can you imagine professors trying to barter lectures on chemistry or economics for food and rent? Money makes it easier to trade. People can sell goods for money and then spend that money to buy the goods they want from other sellers. A monetary transaction requires no double coincidence of wants. This is the main role of money: as a medium of exchange.

medium of exchange — an asset that sellers generally accept as payment for goods, services, and other assets

A **medium of exchange** is an asset that sellers generally accept as payment for goods, services, and other assets.

Money also acts as a store of value and a unit of account.

store of value — any good or asset that people can store while it maintains some or all of its value

A **store of value** is any good or asset that people can store while it maintains some or all of its value.

Many goods can serve as stores of value, but most services cannot. Although inflation reduces the value of money, very few goods or assets maintain all of their value as time passes. Some goods function better than others as stores of value because they maintain their values better over time. No good that loses its value quickly would be a very useful medium of exchange because people must accept it in payment before they spend it.

unit of account — a measure for stating prices

A **unit of account** is a measure for stating prices.

The usual unit of account in the United States is the dollar. People quote prices in dollars and write totals on price tags in dollars. When buyers and sellers negotiate a price, they discuss dollar amounts.

TYPES OF MONEY

Although people exchange paper money and coins today, cigarettes served as money in World War II prisoner-of-war camps and in Germany immediately after the war ended.[19] People have traded shells, salt, silk, cattle, furs, dried fish, beads, and even stones as money in various societies. Gold, silver, copper, tin, iron, and other metals have been used as money. Some Native Americans used seashells (called *wampum*) as money. Tobacco served as money in the colonies of Virginia, Maryland, and North Carolina in the 1600s and 1700s. Of course, since farmers could grow tobacco, they could literally grow money, and they did, boosting the supply of money 40-fold over half a century, which caused a giant surge of inflation.

GOLD AND SILVER COINS

Coins first circulated in China in 1091 B.C. and in Greece in about 750 B.C.[20] Nearly 2,000 years later the Chinese first invented and traded paper money around 900 A.D.

In economies that designated gold or silver coins as money, the money supply could increase in three ways. First, governments could debase coins by making more of them from the same amount of gold or silver, either by making each coin slightly smaller (shaving the edges and using the shavings to make more coins) or by mixing other, cheaper, metals with the gold or silver. Debasement

IN THE NEWS

Soviet barter: The haves and have-nots

*By Felicity Barringer
Special to The
New York Times*

SVERDLOVSK, U.S.S.R.—
Goods Are the Currencies
Mr. Nazarenko is a middleman in the middle of an economic maelstrom. His suppliers are in flight from the currency now derisively called "wooden rubles." For him and tens of thousands of other businessmen in the Soviet Union, metal, meat, and wheat are the currencies of choice.

Barter became common in the final years of the Soviet Union.

Source: Felicity Barringer, "Soviet Barter: The Haves and Have-Nots," *New York Times,* September 19, 1991, p. 1.

---

[19]Cigarettes also substituted for official forms of money to some extent in the Soviet Union and eastern European countries as they began turning away from socialism in the later 1980s and early 1990s.

[20]Cheng, the second King of Chou, circulated the first coins in China.

IN THE NEWS

Panama's once-sophisticated economy, squeezed by U.S., slips to barter system

By Jose de Cordoba
Staff Reporter of The
Wall Street Journal

PANAMA CITY, Panama—Six months after the U.S. put the squeeze on Panama, one of Latin America's most sophisticated economies has deteriorated into a cash-poor, makeshift barter system.

Most Panamanians are making do. Take Adolfo Berrios, the president of an electrical contracting company. Since the crisis began, Mr. Berrios has been paid—and has canceled debts—with products ranging from chickens and eggs to bicycles. He

says 80 percent of his business is based on barter deals and jokes that instead of a central bank, Panama should open a central barter office.

As payment on one contract, Mr. Berrios received $4,000 worth of live chickens, some of which he exchanged for certificates redeemable for groceries at a supermarket. Mr. Berrios, who has laid off 35 of his 47 workers, pays one-quarter of their salary with these grocery bonds.

Ready to Emigrate
When a cement producer gave him about 500 bicycles

valued at about $80,000 to cancel a debt, Mr. Berrios became a bicycle salesman. He dedicates one day a week to exchanging bicycles, chickens, eggs, and anything else he has received as payment for cash, debts, or the materials he needs to work with. "Bicycles are easy," he says. "It's the eggs and chickens that are difficult." Mr. Berrios thinks he can keep going this way for six or seven months, but if things don't improve he will move his family to Costa Rica, where he has already set up a company.

Barter often becomes common in poorly functioning economies.

Source: Jose de Cordoba, "Panama's Once-Sophisticated Economy, Squeezed by U.S., Slips to Barter System," *The Wall Street Journal*, September 7, 1988, p. 22.

gave governments more coins to spend and imposed an inflation tax on people, as described in the previous chapter. Inflation occurred in ancient Rome because the government debased its money frequently. Rome first used copper coins, then switched to silver coins, and then switched again to gold coins. The government debased them all. The money supply in the Roman empire rose rapidly starting in 296 A.D. under Emperor Diocletian who, as the previous chapter mentioned, tried and failed to stop inflation with wage and price controls. In contrast, coins suffered no debasement in ancient Athens and other Greek city states, even in times of war. As a result, ancient Greece did not experience inflation. Greece was an exception, however. Debasement of coins has been a common practice throughout history.

New discoveries of gold or silver provide a second way for the money supply to increase in an economy that uses gold or silver coins as money. Such discoveries raise the supply of gold or silver to make coins. For example, gold discoveries in the United States and Australia in 1848 to 1851 increased world gold output by 8 percent per year for 15 years, leading to higher prices.

Finally, the money supply increases if such a country imports gold or silver from other countries to make more coins. Suppose that an increase in the supply of gold money in Spain raised the Spanish price level. Goods and services would cost more gold coins than before. People in Spain would have an incentive to buy goods in other countries where prices had not changed, such as England, and bring those goods to Spain. To buy English goods, they would pay gold coins to English sellers, raising the supply of gold in England. As England exported goods and imported gold, the gold imports would raise the English money supply and price level. Meanwhile, the Spanish money supply would fall as Spaniards spent their gold coins in England. The fall in the Spanish money supply would reduce the Spanish price level. At the same time, the price level in England would rise until prices were again equal in the two countries. At that point, Spanish people would stop exporting gold to England.

During the Middle Ages, when barter was common, people often exchanged gold coins in international trade—coins minted by the Byzantine Empire before the 8th century and Moslem Arabic coins after that. Later, in medieval Europe, various feudal lords, kings, and ecclesiastics minted, and frequently debased, silver coins for local use. International trade expanded in the 13th century, and gold coins issued in Florence became the medium of exchange for international trade. By the 14th century, England, France, Germany, and other European countries had issued gold coins.

Europe experienced a long period of inflation in the 16th and early 17th centuries. Commonly known as the *Price Revolution,* this was the longest period of inflation in history up to that time. At this time Spanish pesos were popularly called *pieces of eight,* as viewers of pirate movies know well. The high inflation rates of this period may appear low by today's standards. In the 16th century, inflation averaged 2.1 percent per year in France, 1.7 percent per year in England, and probably more than 2.0 percent per year in Spain, high rates by historical standards. The Price Revolution resulted mainly from gold and silver discoveries in the New World. By 1660, these discoveries had nearly doubled the European gold stock and more than tripled the silver stock.

In the 18th century, the Bank of England began issuing paper money, which began to replace silver and gold coins. The Bank of Amsterdam did the same in Holland, and paper money began to replace coins in Spain, as well.

GOLD STANDARD

Of the many types of commodities that have served as money throughout history, gold is the most historically important, and the gold standard is the most historically important commodity standard. Two main kinds of gold standards define currency values.

> In a **pure gold standard,** people trade gold coins as money, and there is no paper money.

> In a **gold exchange standard,** people trade paper money that is backed by gold stored in a warehouse.

pure gold standard — a system in which people trade gold coins as money, and there is no paper money

gold exchange standard — a system in which people trade paper money that is backed by gold stored in a warehouse

A silver standard resembles a gold standard, based on silver instead of gold. Both are special cases of commodity standards.

A pure gold standard functioned for many centuries, eventually to be replaced by a gold exchange standard. Paper money initially served as a sort of warehouse certificate for gold, and people found the certificates more convenient to trade than gold coins. Although anyone could theoretically exchange paper money for the gold that backed it in a gold exchange standard, few people did.

Imagine that the U.S. government were to adopt a gold exchange standard at a $400-per-ounce gold price by allowing anyone to bring $400 to a government office to buy an ounce of gold, or to sell 1 ounce of gold to the government office for $400. The government would be a *residual buyer or seller* of gold at $400— it would sell as much gold as anyone would want to buy for $400 an ounce and buy as much as anyone would want to sell for that price. This would fix the price of gold at $400.[21] No one would ever pay more than $400 per ounce to buy gold when the government would sell it for $400 per ounce, and no seller would ever sell it for less when the government would buy it for $400 per ounce. Gold would back the paper money in the sense that anyone could trade either for the other at the $400 price.

Under any commodity standard, paper money works like a warehouse certificate to the commodity. However, if people are willing to hold and accept paper money without exchanging it for the gold or other commodity in the warehouse, then the commodity in the warehouse may seem to lose its importance. Why store the commodity in the warehouse rather than using it for some other purpose? Why not simply rely on the paper money and eliminate the possibility of exchanging it for the commodity? When the government does not back its paper money with any commodity (like gold or silver)—when people cannot trade the paper money for a commodity at a fixed price—it distributes fiat money.

fiat money — paper money that is not backed by a commodity in the sense that people cannot trade it for a particular commodity at a fixed nominal price

> **Fiat money** is paper money that is not backed by a commodity in the sense that people cannot trade it for a particular commodity at a fixed nominal price.

MONEY IN AMERICAN HISTORY

Before the American Revolution, the 13 American colonies relied on paper money called *bills of credit* denominated in British pounds. (Paper money in the United States today consists of Federal Reserve Notes denominated in dollars.)[22]

During the American Revolution, the colonies printed paper money known as *continental currency* to pay for the war; inflation averaged 8.5 percent per month during that time. The continental money consisted of *dollars,* which was a word for the Spanish pesos (pieces of eight). From 1775 to 1779, the colonial money supply rose to ten times its previous level and caused massive inflation, driving prices to as much as 100 times their previous levels. In a famous phrase, something utterly worthless was said to be "not worth a continental."

Then the Continental Congress stopped printing money. It asked the states to allow people to pay taxes with the continental money and to count 40 paper dollars as equal to one silver dollar until 1783. After 1783, the continental currency became worthless.

The Constitution gave Congress the sole right to "coin Money and regulate the Value thereof" and made it illegal for the states to "coin Money; emit Bills of Credit; (or) make anything but gold and silver coin a Tender in Payment of Debts." In 1794, the federal government opened its first mint in Philadelphia. Inflation

---

[21]The government must hold enough gold to sell to people who want to buy it for $400 an ounce. If the government does not have enough gold, it cannot fix the price at $400.

[22]The colonies experienced several episodes of large increases in the money supply and inflation. Between 1715 and 1741, the money supply in New England (Massachusetts, New Hampshire, Connecticut, and Rhode Island) rose by a factor of 3.9, and prices rose by a factor of about 3.4. Then the money supply quadrupled by 1749 and prices roughly doubled. Massachusetts decided in 1750 to eliminate paper money and to return to silver coins. Increases in the money supply and inflation also occurred in North and South Carolina in the 1700s.

remained virtually zero for the first 70 years after U.S. independence. From the time that George Washington became the first president in 1789 until the Civil War, the U.S. price level stayed about the same.

The U.S. monetary system is complicated because the Coinage Act, passed in 1792, established a practice called *bimetallism.* This system defined the dollar in two different ways: (1) as a certain amount of gold and (2) as a certain amount of silver. In practice, this meant that the United States was on a silver standard until 1834 and a gold standard after that.[23]

States could not print or mint money, but they could let privately owned banks do so. Private banks, under license from state governments, issued banknotes, pieces of paper like dollar bills today, that people exchanged as paper money. The banknotes of each bank looked different, and people tended to use banknotes issued by banks in their own cities or nearby cities. Banknotes were supposed to be backed by stores of silver (before 1834) or gold (after 1834). Banks found, however, that they could increase their profits by printing more paper dollars than they could exchange for silver or gold, and they did.[24] Some of the time, from 1791 to 1811 and from 1816 to 1836, a government-owned Bank of the United States also issued paper money. Even then, private banks rather than the government issued most of the paper money in circulation.

In 1862, the federal government printed paper money, fiat money that people could not exchange for gold, to help pay for the Civil War. These so-called *greenbacks* were measured in dollars. The government made them *legal tender,* meaning that sellers were legally required to accept greenbacks in payment for goods and services; sellers could not legally require buyers to pay with gold or any other kind of money. The federal government roughly doubled the U.S. money supply

---

[23]Under the silver standard of the 1792 law, the U.S. dollar was worth 371.25 grains of silver (about $\frac{3}{4}$ of an ounce). Anyone with this much silver could take it to a U.S. government mint, and the mint would exchange it for a $1 silver coin. Anyone with a $1 silver coin could melt it and get 371.25 grains of silver to use for jewelry or some other purpose.

The 1792 Coinage Act also defined a dollar as 24.75 grains of gold. Anyone with this much gold could take it to a U.S. government mint and exchange it for a $1 gold coin. Anyone with a $1 gold coin could melt it and get 24.75 grains of gold.

The law intended to encourage use of both gold and silver coins as money, but it created a problem: 24.75 grains of gold was worth more to people than 371.25 grains of silver. Anyone with a $1 gold coin could trade it to someone for more than 371.25 grains of silver. That person could then get a $1 silver coin and still have some silver left! (That person could also get more than $1 worth of silver coins.) Also, the owner of the gold coin might melt it and use the gold in some way other than as money. For this reason, only silver served as money, and virtually no one used gold as money.

This is an example of Gresham's Law, which says that when a money is defined as two different things (such as a certain amount of gold and a certain amount of silver), the bad money drives out the good money, meaning that people stop using the more valuable thing (the good money) as money, and spend only the less valuable, bad money. Gresham's Law also applied when tobacco served as money in southern American colonies; people would spend the lowest-quality tobacco as money, and smoke the best-quality tobacco. For this reason, only the lowest-quality tobacco served as money.

Later, in 1834, Congress passed a new Coinage Act that defined a dollar as 23.20 grains of gold or 371.35 grains of silver. Because 23.20 grains of gold was worth less to people than 371.25 grains of silver, people started using only *gold* as money and keeping the silver for other purposes. As a result, after 1834, the United States was on a gold standard, and it remained on a gold standard for most of the next 150 years, until 1971.

[24]In some states, *anyone* could open a bank and print paper money, even without a license. To start a bank, a person would need only to abide by certain regulations on reserve requirements and making banknotes redeemable in gold.

between 1859 and 1862, causing inflation. The U.S. wholesale price index doubled in 3 years between 1861 and 1864.

Before 1863, only states licensed banks. In 1863, the federal government began licensing banks to print money, creating so-called *national banks.* This was the start of the national banking system that the United States still has today (and why many banks have names like the "First National Bank of Mudville"). All of the paper money issued by the national banks looked basically the same.

In 1865, the federal government ended the state-licensed banking system by placing a 10 percent tax on banknotes issued by state-licensed banks. This tax was high enough to prevent state-licensed banks from competing with nationally licensed banks, that did not have to pay the tax, and state-licensed banks went out of business. This had two effects. First, it made all paper money the same for the first time in U.S. history. Second, it helped the federal government. Every national bank that issued paper money was required to buy (and keep) some U.S. government bonds. This requirement raised the demand for government bonds, raising the price of the bonds and effectively allowing the government to borrow money at a lower interest rate.

After the Civil War, the government began reducing the supply of greenbacks, creating deflation (negative inflation). By 1879, the wholesale price level had fallen all the way back to its pre–Civil War level. People could exchange banknotes for gold again, as they had done under the previous gold standard. Deflation continued in most years until 1896, as inflation averaged −5 percent per year from 1864 to 1879, and −1.6 percent per year from 1879 to 1896.[25] Because this deflation was unexpected, it helped creditors and hurt debtors.[26] In 1875, debtors formed a new political party, the Greenback Party, to fight against deflation and to favor faster money growth and inflation. Important political debates of the period centered around gold and silver standards, inflation versus deflation, and their effects on the distribution of income.

The United States remained on the gold exchange standard from 1879 until 1914, when World War I began. Countries had often suspended the gold standard temporarily during wars, and World War I was no exception. Germany returned to the gold standard in 1924, after its hyperinflation discussed in the last chapter. Britain and France returned to the gold standard in 1925 and 1928, respectively. The Federal Reserve System began operation as the United States returned to the gold standard after World War I.

--- **FOR REVIEW** ---

28.11 Why is trade based on money often more efficient than barter?

28.12 Name some commodities that have served as money.

28.13 What are three important properties of money?

--- **QUESTION** ---

28.14 What is a gold standard? Use a supply-demand diagram to explain how it worked.

---

[25]Meanwhile, the growth rate of aggregate real GNP averaged 4 percent per year from 1870 to 1896.

[26]The previous chapter explained how unexpected inflation helps debtors and hurts creditors; this is the opposite case.

During the bank run, $250 million an hour left First Republic

By Michael J. Lyon

The silent run was accelerating at the First RepublicBank Corporation's offices in Texas—silent because retail customers were not lining up on the streets. This run was being fueled by large institutions, including other banks, racing to electronically withdraw uninsured deposits. Alarm bells went off around Washington, as the nation's top bank regulators met in an emergency session.

Today, bank runs can occur electronically.

Source: New York Times, January 8, 1989, p. B1.

BANK RUNS AND DEPOSIT INSURANCE

bank run — when many people try at the same time to withdraw their money from a bank that lacks sufficient reserves

banking panic — many simultaneous bank runs

BANKING PANICS

Congress created the Federal Reserve to "furnish an elastic currency" to help prevent bank runs and banking panics.

A **bank run** occurs when many people try at the same time to withdraw their money from a bank and the bank lacks enough reserves to accommodate all of them. In a **banking panic,** many banks face runs at the same time.

When a bank lacked sufficient reserves to let people withdraw money from their accounts, it often suspended convertibility, that is, it stopped letting people withdraw their money. *Convertibility* means being able to convert bank deposits into currency; in suspending convertibility, a bank refused to let people make this conversion. Banking panics over suspensions of convertibility occurred frequently in the United States prior to the beginning of the Federal Reserve System. Banking panics occurred in 1814, 1819, 1837, 1839, 1857, 1873, 1893, and 1907 to 1908.

Banks that closed during banking panics were not usually bankrupt. A bank closed when it lacked enough currency at the time to provide to depositors who wanted to withdraw funds. In most cases, though, banks could and did eventually allow depositors to withdraw all of their money once people who had borrowed from those banks repaid their loans. Some banks went out of business permanently during banking panics, usually because people who borrowed money from them failed to repay their loans. (Loans to farmers, which were common, exposed banks to great risk because bad weather could prevent farmers from repaying.) In these cases, depositors divided up whatever money the bank had, but did not get all of their money. The vast majority of banks, however, reopened after runs without any ultimate losses to depositors. Even in the worst banking panic, in 1893, 98.7 percent of banks later reopened. On average, depositors lost about $0.02 out of every dollar of their deposits in banks.[27] Of course, averages do not always accurately portray effects on people; this average loss of $0.02 per dollar reflects little or no loss for many people, but major losses of lifetime savings for a few people.

[27]The banking panic during the Great Depression of the 1930s was worse than this, however.

Banking panics were often associated with recessions—periods of low real GDP and high unemployment. Real GDP fell 8.5 percent from 1907 to 1908. To put this in perspective, note that no recession in the United States since the Great Depression of the 1930s has seen such a large decline. Although real GDP increased the following year, many people became convinced that the United States needed a central bank to prevent banking panics. The Federal Reserve System was intended to accomplish this by acting as a lender of last resort.

DEPOSIT INSURANCE

Despite the actions of the Federal Reserve System, the United States (and many other countries) experienced banking panics in the Great Depression from 1929 through much of the 1930s. In 1934, following the banking panic associated with the Great Depression, the federal government started the Federal Deposit Insurance Corporation (FDIC) to insure bank deposits. Deposit insurance was intended to protect people from losing their deposits if a bank had insufficient funds or went out of business. If a bank lacks sufficient funds for people to withdraw their deposits, the FDIC provides those funds. Banks pay the FDIC for this deposit insurance.

Without deposit insurance, a bank run may occur simply because people *believe* that it will occur. Suppose you believe that a bank run will occur at your bank tomorrow, and the bank has no deposit insurance. What would you do? Most people would quickly go to the bank and withdraw all of their money while the bank still has it—before other people withdraw all their money and the bank runs out of funds. In other words, everyone wants to be near the beginning of the line at the bank to withdraw their money, because the people at the end of the line may find the vault empty. As many people rush to the bank to withdraw simply because they expect a bank run, they cause that bank run. The bank run becomes a *self-fulfilling belief*—when the bank run occurs, people see their beliefs confirmed.

Deposit insurance can prevent bank runs. Even if people expect a bank run, deposit insurance takes away their incentive to rush to the bank to be near the front of the line, because deposit insurance guarantees that all of them can withdraw their money. Because people have no incentive to rush to the bank to withdraw, a bank run becomes less likely.[28]

PRIVATE DEPOSIT INSURANCE

Many banks in the United States arranged private deposit insurance in the 19th century. Banks often joined together and agreed that if any one of them failed, the others would pay depositors their money. In this way, the banks jointly acted as an insurance company for one another.

These insurance arrangements differed across states because of differences in state laws. Some states prohibited branch banking and required each bank to have only one office (one bank building). These laws were intended to protect small banks by preventing large banks from opening many conveniently located branch

---

[28]Some economists believe that by preventing a banking panic, deposit insurance can prevent a repeat of the Great Depression, when a large number of bank failures caused a large fall in the M1 and M2 measures of the money supply. Later chapters will discuss the connection between money-supply changes and the Great Depression.

"Yeah, but who guarantees the federal government?"

Source: *The Wall Street Journal,* August 15, 1986, p. 15.

offices that would draw customers away from small competitors. However, larger banks usually took the leadership roles in creating private deposit insurance, so states that prohibited branch banking often lacked effective deposit insurance.

Bank clearinghouses began to provide deposit insurance in the mid-19th century. A clearinghouse moves money between banks to clear checks. If you wrote a $50 check to pay for a new horse, the seller would deposit the check in a local bank. The seller's bank would then collect money from your bank. If the seller's bank already owed your bank $30, then your bank would owe a net amount of $20 to the seller's bank. The clearinghouse figures out all of this and moves the money. Privately operated clearinghouses flourished in the 19th century, as they also acted as lenders of last resort. Unfortunately, the benefits of clearinghouses, including deposit insurance and lender-of-last-resort services, were limited by state laws against branch banking. The creation of the Federal Reserve essentially put an end to private deposit insurance and many private clearinghouse activities. Today, the Federal Reserve and several private firms function as bank clearinghouses in the United States.

PROBLEMS WITH DEPOSIT INSURANCE

Until the 1980s, government-provided deposit insurance seemed safe. Then the government agency that provided deposit insurance for savings-and-loan associations went bankrupt. (Savings-and-loan associations, or S&Ls, resemble banks, but are legally distinct.) The FSLIC (Federal Savings and Loan Insurance Corporation) lacked enough money to reimburse depositors of failed savings-and-loan associations, and the country plunged into a savings-and-loan crisis.

IN THE NEWS

Bonfire of the S&Ls

It's the biggest financial mess in U.S. history, and the bills will be coming due for the next 40 years. And that isn't all: the nation's banks may be next.

Deposit insurance offered by the U.S. government affected the incentives of savings and loans and led to bankruptcies of many.

Source: "Bonfire of the S&Ls," *Newsweek,* May 21, 1990, p. 20.

Deposit insurance changes the incentives of banks or S&Ls, allowing them to make riskier investments than they would choose otherwise. With good luck, these risky investments pay off well and the bank or savings-and-loan association makes a high profit. With bad luck, it goes out of business and deposit insurance covers depositors' balances.

Suppose that a bank without deposit insurance can choose between investing depositors' money in a safe way or a risky way. If the risky investment pays off, the bank's owners make a big profit. If not, they suffer a big loss. If the bank goes out of business, the bank's owners lose, but so do the depositors, who lose part or all of the money in their accounts. This gives depositors, particularly people with large balances, an incentive to monitor the bank and prevent it from making risky investments. Any bank that began to make risky investments would lose deposits as people put their money in other banks with safer investments.

Deposit insurance takes away the incentives of depositors to monitor their banks. Knowing that they can get their money out of the bank no matter what happens, depositors do not care whether or not banks make risky investments. The insurer, such as the FDIC, has an incentive to establish rules that limit the riskiness of banks' investments and to monitor banks to make sure that they follow these rules. If a bank suffers losses from risky investments, after all, the insurance company must pay.

In the 19th century, private deposit insurers regulated and monitored bank investments. Similarly, when the government provides deposit insurance, it could either establish regulations that prevent banks from making risky investments or charge higher insurance premiums to banks with riskier investments, just as private health and life insurance companies charge higher insurance premiums to people who smoke.

SAVINGS-AND-LOAN CRISIS

However, the U.S. federal government did not adequately monitor the investments of savings-and-loan associations, and government regulations did not prevent S&Ls from making risky investments. In fact, the government increased the amount of deposit insurance it provided to S&Ls in the early 1980s at the same time that it reduced regulations on them and reduced the staffs of regulatory agencies that monitored them. Because the government charged the same deposit-insurance fees to all S&Ls (rather than charging higher fees to S&Ls with riskier investments), S&Ls began to make increasingly risky investments.[29] Good luck on some of these risky investments made huge profits for owners of some S&Ls. Bad luck on other risky investments caused many other S&Ls to suffer huge losses and many went bankrupt, creating large losses for the FSLIC, which insured their deposits. The FSLIC ran out of money in 1986—it did not have enough money to reimburse depositors in all failed S&Ls—and the federal government provided the FSLIC with more money from taxpayers.

The government eliminated the FSLIC 3 years later and formed other agencies to pay depositors and to guarantee deposits at the remaining S&Ls, which the government allowed to remain in operation. People were even willing to leave their

---

[29]For various reasons, many S&Ls also lost money when inflation fell between 1979 and 1982, reducing nominal interest rates.

IN THE NEWS

Perils of insuring bank deposits

By Lindley H. Clark Jr.

Any insurance plan has to deal with a basic problem: something insurance men call "moral hazard." The idea is simple. If you have no fire insurance on your home, you are extra careful. If, on the other hand, you are insured, you relax. You may not let the kids play with matches, but you don't stay awake nights trying to smell smoke.

Similarly, when a bank deposit is insured, the depositor doesn't worry about the safety of his funds. He has little incentive to check up on the bank to try to learn if its operations are safe and sound. The bank, for its part, pays a fixed rate for deposit insurance regardless of the riskiness of its assets. If the bank's loans go bad, it knows the government will be standing by to pick up the pieces. There's a substantial incentive to make riskier loans to improve bank profits.

Deposit insurance, like all insurance, creates a problem of moral hazard.

Source: Lindley H. Clark, Jr., "Perils of Insuring Bank Deposits," *The Wall Street Journal,* May 8, 1989, p. A1.

deposits at bankrupt S&Ls because the government provided deposit insurance. Because deposit insurance kept these S&Ls in business, their owners continued to make risky investments. As before, the owners could collect big profits if they were lucky and these risky investments paid off well, while the owners had virtually nothing to lose (because the S&L was already bankrupt) if they were unlucky and their risky investments failed! This was truly a situation of "Heads I win, tails you lose." In the end, the government eventually reimbursed depositors from tax revenues and took over the assets of bankrupt savings and loans.

The cost of this savings-and-loan crisis to taxpayers averaged several hundred dollars per person for everyone in the United States, making it the most costly financial scandal in history. Even today, no one knows the exact cost because when S&Ls went bankrupt, the government took over many of their assets, such as real estate, that it still owns and for which it cannot determine precise values.

FOR REVIEW

28.15 What is a bank run and why might one occur?

28.16 How is deposit insurance intended to prevent bank runs?

28.17 What problem does deposit insurance create? How was this problem connected with the U.S. savings-and-loan crisis?

QUESTION

28.18 Suppose that a banking panic occurs and banks close, reducing the amount of bank deposits enough to raise the currency-deposit ratio from 1 to 2. If the reserve-deposit ratio is 10 percent, how does the money multiplier change? How would M1 change if the monetary base were to remain constant?

FIGURE 28.4

EFFECTS OF AN OPEN MARKET PURCHASE

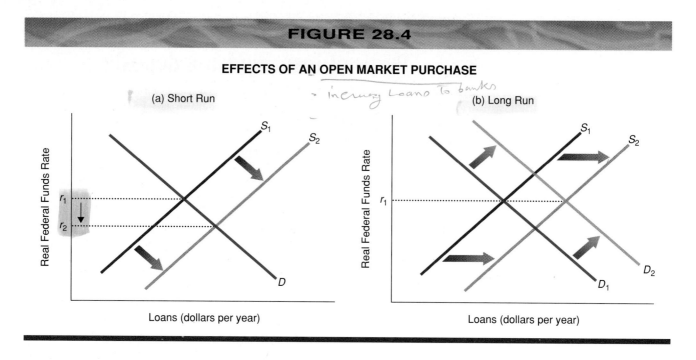

(a) Short Run

→ increay Loans To banks

(b) Long Run

SHORT-RUN EFFECTS OF FEDERAL RESERVE POLICIES

The Federal Reserve can raise the money supply through an open market purchase, an increase in its loans to banks, or a reduction in its reserve requirements for banks. In the long run, an increase in the money supply raises all nominal prices in the same proportion. For example, a 10 percent rise in the money supply eventually raises all nominal prices by 10 percent, so that relative prices do not change. Like a currency reform in reverse, an increase in the money supply has no long-run effects on real GDP, employment, or other real economic conditions.[30] Similarly, in the long run, a fall in the money supply reduces all nominal prices by the same proportion, without altering relative prices or real economic conditions.

In the short run, however, an increase in the money supply engineered by a Federal Reserve open market purchase may affect real economic conditions. These effects have inspired much economic research and controversy, as the next two chapters explain. Most economists agree, however, that real interest rates fall in the short run when the Fed raises the money supply.

Think about the supply and demand for short-term loans among banks. The equilibrium interest rate on these loans is the equilibrium federal funds rate. When the Fed adds reserves to the banking system through an open market purchase, the supply of loans increases, as in **Figure 28.4a,** reducing the equilibrium federal

---

[30]Unlike a currency reform in reverse, however, the change in the money supply may redistribute income, creating winners and losers. In a reverse currency reform, everyone would share the increase in the money supply (essentially by adding zeros to their money). However, not everyone receives additional money when the money supply rises through an open market purchase, so the open market operation can redistribute wealth from some people to others.

IN THE NEWS

Fed cuts discount rate to 6.5%; move signals concern on economy

Lower funds rate is also seen backed at earlier meeting

By David Wessel
Staff Reporter of The
Wall Street Journal

WASHINGTON—The Federal Reserve Board, signaling its concern about the weakening U.S. economy, cut the highly visible discount rate one-half percentage point to 6.5 percent.

The unanimous decision by the six Fed governors came hours after a meeting of the Fed's larger policy-making committee. The committee is believed to have authorized an immediate reduction of one-quarter percentage point in the key federal funds rate, which banks charge on loans to one another.

Market reaction to the cut in the discount rate—which the Fed charges on loans to banks—was swift and enthusiastic. Stock and bond prices rose, driving interest rates down.

The discount-rate move, and the expected reduction in the federal funds rate to 7 percent as early as today, are likely to force banks to finally cut their lending rates.

Just two weeks ago, the Fed cut the federal funds rate one-quarter percentage point and made the unusual move of reducing the fraction of deposits that banks must hold as reserves—two moves aimed at stimulating the economy.

Symbolic Move

Moves in the discount rate have little direct effect on the economy, but are used by the Fed to send loud and clear signals. "Symbolism is important," said Mr. Moran. "This will be on the front pages rather than the credit market columns. It will be on the evening news. It will be seen by individuals and small-business people who might not otherwise know [what the Fed is doing]. It will be a boost to confidence."

The Fed governors directly set the discount rate in response to requests from district Fed banks. But the Fed's Open Market Committee—for which the voting members consist of the six current governors plus five of the 12 district bank presidents—controls the federal funds rate by buying and selling Treasury securities. The fed funds rate is more significant in determining the level of interest rates in the economy.

Federal Reserve policy actions affect interest rates.

Source: David Wessel, "Fed Cuts Discount Rate to 6.5%; Move Signals Concern on Economy," *The Wall Street Journal,* December 19, 1990, p. A2.

---

funds rate. Similarly, the supply of loans decreases when the Fed withdraws reserves from the banking system through an open market sale.

If the demand for loans were to increase by the same amount as the supply increase, then the equilibrium real federal funds rate would not change. Because an increase in the money supply raises all nominal prices proportionally in the long run, the nominal quantity of loans demanded also rises proportionally in the long run, and the equilibrium real federal funds rate does not react to the open market operation in the long run. Figure 28.4b shows the long-run effect of the open market purchase on the federal funds market. An open market operation has no long-run effects on the real federal funds interest rate.

In the short run, however, an open market purchase tends to reduce the real federal funds rate. Economists differ on the precise explanation for the difference between the short-run and long-run responses, though most economists believe

looser monetary policy — an increase in the growth rate of the monetary base and the broader measures of the money supply or a decrease in the federal funds rate

tighter monetary policy — a reduction in the growth rate of the monetary base and the broader measures of the money supply or an increase in the federal funds rate

IN THE NEWS

Fed votes against cutting short-term rates for now

Open Market panel opposes immediate move, signals inaction in weeks ahead

By David Wessel
Staff Reporter of The
Wall Street Journal

WASHINGTON—Federal Reserve policy makers decided this week against any immediate cut in short-term interest rates, people familiar with the Fed's deliberations said.

The Fed influences the federal funds rate, which banks charge each other for overnight loans, by buying and selling government securities.

Source: David Wessel, "Fed Votes against Cutting Short-Term Rates for Now," *The Wall Street Journal,* May 21, 1992, p. A2.

IN THE NEWS

Federal Reserve's chief suggests a new rate rise may be needed

By Keith Bradsher
Special to The
New York Times

WASHINGTON, July 20—The chairman of the Federal Reserve said today that the four increases in interest rates this year might not have been enough to keep inflation under control.

Marc W. Wanshel, an economist at J. P. Morgan in New York, said that the comment made likely an additional tightening of monetary policy and higher interest rates.

The Fed tightens monetary policy to fight inflation.

Source: Keith Bradsher, "Federal Reserve's Chief Suggests a New Rate Rise May Be Needed," *New York Times,* July 21, 1994, p. A1.

that it is related to the time that nominal prices need to adjust to a change in the money supply. Whatever the precise mechanism, the fall in the real federal funds rate also tends to reduce the nominal federal funds rate, though the nominal federal funds rate may rise if the money-supply increase causes a sufficiently large rise in expected inflation. The nominal federal funds rate might rise or fall depending on the size of any change in expected inflation. (Recall the Fisher equation discussed in previous chapters. A fall in the real interest rate tends to reduce the nominal interest rate, while an increase in expected inflation tends to raise it.)

Most economists agree that the change in the federal funds rate alters other interest rates, as well. A fall in the federal funds rate reduces the cost to banks of borrowing reserves, and competition then leads banks to reduce the interest rates that they charge to borrowers. Similarly, a rise in the federal funds rate raises the cost to banks of borrowing reserves, leading banks to raise the interest rates that they charge. An open market operation has no long-run effects on real interest rates. After changing in the short run, real interest rates return to their original levels.

Because open market purchases temporarily lower the real federal funds rate and open market sales temporarily raise it, commentators often describe Federal Reserve policies in terms of their effects on interest rates. The Fed itself often describes its policies in this way—as raising or lowering interest rates.

A **looser monetary policy** increases the growth rate of the monetary base and the broader measures of the money supply or decreases the federal funds rate.

The Fed loosens monetary policy by conducting more open market purchases or lending more reserves to banks at the discount window.

A **tighter monetary policy** reduces the growth rate of the monetary base and the broader measures of the money supply or increases the federal funds rate.

The Fed tightens monetary policy by conducting fewer open market purchases (or more open market sales) or lending less to banks at the discount window.

The next two chapters explore the short-run effects of monetary policy, and a later chapter discusses alternative views of the role of monetary policy.

--- FOR REVIEW ---

28.19 How does a Federal Reserve open market purchase affect the federal funds rate? Why? How do the short-run effects differ from the long-run effects?

28.20 What does it mean to loosen or tighten monetary policy?

--- QUESTION ---

28.21 If an open market sale raises the real interest rate by 1 percentage point and reduces expected inflation by 2 percentage points, how does it affect the nominal interest rate?

CONCLUSIONS

FINANCIAL INTERMEDIARIES AND THE MONEY SUPPLY

Financial intermediaries, such as banks and similar kinds of firms, play an important role in the money-supply process. Banks hold only a fraction of their deposits as reserves and lend the rest of the money that people deposit. Bank reserves represent money that banks hold to back up their deposits. The monetary base is a measure of the money supply that includes currency held by the nonbank public plus bank reserves. Currency held by the nonbank public includes all paper money and coins owned by people and business firms other than banks or the government.

Financial intermediaries help to create money. An increase in bank reserves leads to an increase in bank lending, which raises broad measures of the money supply. Definitions of the money supply broader than the monetary base include M1, which includes currency held by the nonbank public, plus traveler's checks, plus balances in accounts at banks or other financial intermediaries against which people or firms can write checks; M2, which combines M1 with balances in most savings accounts and similar accounts; M3, which combines M2 with balances in most other accounts at financial intermediaries; and L, which combines M3 with certain short-term financial assets (loans). A money multiplier is the ratio of a broad measure of the money supply, such as M1 (or M2, M3, or L) to the monetary base.

FEDERAL RESERVE SYSTEM

A central bank is a bank for banks. The Federal Reserve, a partially independent agency of the U.S. government, is the central bank of the United States. The Federal Reserve consists of the Board of Governors, 12 regional Federal Reserve Banks, and the Federal Open Market Committee (FOMC).

FEDERAL RESERVE POLICY TOOLS: HOW THE MONEY SUPPLY CHANGES

The Fed's three main tools of monetary policy are open market operations, discount window lending, and changes in reserve requirements and other bank regulations. The primary tool of monetary policy is the open market operation in which the Fed buys or sells financial assets, usually U.S. government Treasury bills and Treasury bonds. In an open market purchase, the Fed buys financial assets; in an open market sale, the Fed sells financial assets.

HISTORY AND ROLES OF MONEY

Many commodities have served as money, and some civilizations have not used money at all. Money has advantages, however, because it avoids the problem with barter of creating a double coincidence of wants. In its main role as a medium of exchange, money acts as an asset that sellers generally accept as payment for goods, services, and other assets. Money also serves as a store of value and a unit of account.

The most common form of commodity standard for money has been a gold standard. In a pure gold standard, people use gold coins as money, and there is no paper money. In a gold exchange standard, people trade paper money that is backed by gold stored in a warehouse. A silver standard resembles a gold standard, but silver instead of gold backs paper money. Fiat money is paper money that is not backed by a commodity in the sense that people cannot trade it for a particular commodity at a fixed nominal price.

BANK RUNS AND DEPOSIT INSURANCE

When the Federal Reserve System was created, one of its main purposes was to help prevent bank runs and banking panics. A bank run occurs when many people try at the same time to withdraw their money from a bank and the bank lacks enough reserves. A banking panic refers to a situation in which many bank runs occur at the same time.

Deposit insurance can help to prevent bank runs, but it changes the incentives of financial intermediaries (like banks), making them more willing to choose risky investments and reducing the incentive of depositors to monitor banks' investments and choose less risky banks in which to hold deposits. The U.S. savings-and-loan crisis was partly a result of these incentives, coupled with a failure of the insurer (the government, in that case) to prevent these risky investments or raise insurance premiums to riskier institutions.

SHORT-RUN EFFECTS OF FEDERAL RESERVE POLICIES

In the long run, an increase in the money supply raises all nominal prices proportionally and does not affect relative prices or the real interest rate. In the short run, however, most economists agree that an open market purchase may reduce the real interest rate on federal funds (loans of reserves from one bank to another), leading to reductions in other real interest rates. Nominal interest rates may also fall, or they may rise if the increase in the money supply raises expected inflation sufficiently.

People commonly describe Fed policies in terms of raising or lowering interest rates. A looser monetary policy increases the growth rate of the money supply or decreases the federal funds rate, usually by increasing open market purchases. A tighter monetary policy reduces the growth rate of the money supply or increases the federal funds rate, usually by reducing open market purchases or increasing open market sales.

LOOKING AHEAD

The following three chapters discuss short-run macroeconomic issues, particularly issues associated with business cycles—recessions and recoveries—and the short-run effects of policies of the Federal Reserve and other government agencies. These chapters prepare the way for a more thorough discussion of government macroeconomic policies (monetary and fiscal policies) in later chapters.

KEY TERMS

financial intermediary	federal funds rate
currency held by the nonbank public	required reserves
M1	medium of exchange
bank reserves	store of value
monetary base	unit of account
M2	pure gold standard
M3	gold exchange standard
L (liquidity)	fiat money
money multiplier	bank run
central bank	banking panic
Federal Reserve System	looser monetary policy
open market operation	tighter monetary policy
Federal Reserve discount rate	

QUESTIONS AND PROBLEMS

28.22 What is a double coincidence of wants?

28.23 When and why was the Fed created?

28.24 Why do banks hold reserves?

28.25 Suppose that banks hold reserves equal to 20 percent of deposits in checking accounts and that people always keep equal amounts of currency and checking-account balances (making the currency-deposit ratio equal to 1). If the Fed raises the monetary base by $1 million with an open market purchase, how much will M1 increase? Explain why.

28.26 What does it mean to say that a government *debases coins*?

28.27 Suppose that the United States and Russia were on a gold standard and that large quantities of gold were discovered in Russia. Explain the process by which this discovery would affect prices in the United States.

28.28 Suppose that it takes 6 months for prices to increase after the Fed increases the money supply. Suppose that the Fed raises the money supply by 10 percent through open market purchases.
a. Explain why this could reduce the real interest rate for 6 months.
b. Explain why this would not reduce the long-run real interest rate (after nominal prices have increased by 10 percent).

INQUIRIES FOR FURTHER THOUGHT

28.29 a. Why are sellers willing to trade goods for the pieces of paper that people call *dollar bills*? What makes those pieces of paper different from other pieces of paper that sellers would refuse to accept as payment?
b. Why do sellers in the United States usually insist on payment in U.S. dollars rather than Canadian dollars while Canadian sellers display the opposite preference? (Notice that if a Canadian dollar were worth only $0.75 in U.S. money, a seller could require payment of $2.00 Canadian

for a product that costs $1.50 in U.S. money. Nevertheless, sellers are seldom willing to do this. Why?)

    c. Why do people use the money issued by their own governments? Why not other moneys? What advantages and disadvantages might accompany attempts by people in another country to use U.S. dollars rather than their own country's money?

28.30 What would happen if banks were allowed to issue their own money, as they were in 19th-century America?

28.31 What would happen if the government were to stop providing deposit insurance to banks? What would happen if the government were to privatize deposit insurance?

28.32 Do you think that people will use money 50 years from now? Some people have predicted that cash will disappear as computers keep track of who owes what to whom. How might that work? Could inflation exist with that system?

28.33 Some people have proposed that the United States eliminate pennies. (The federal government mints about 12 billion pennies each year, about 50 for every person in the country. Sales clerks at stores take a few extra seconds to deal with pennies, and this time adds up to a large expense, in the millions of dollars, for these stores. Banning the penny would eliminate these expenses.) If the penny were abolished and all prices were rounded to the nearest $0.05, would stores always round the price upward, or would they maintain the psychological advantages of a $12.98 price by rounding down to $12.95? What would happen? Who would gain and who would lose from eliminating the penny? Would it be a good or bad idea?

TAG SOFTWARE APPLICATIONS

TUTORIAL EXERCISES
▶ The module contains a review of the key terms from Chapter 28.

ANALYTICAL EXERCISES
▶ The analytical section includes questions on the money-multiplier process and how to calculate the money multiplier.

BUSINESS CYCLES

CHAPTER 29

STICKY PRICES AND SHORT-RUN DISEQUILIBRIUM

read
p. 857 – 873

WHAT THIS CHAPTER IS ABOUT

▶ Why slow changes in prices affect the economy

▶ Why the economy may experience business cycles, with recessions and expansions

▶ Why changes in underlying conditions have different short-run and long-run effects

▶ Short-run effects of changes in investment or consumer spending

▶ Short-run effects of government monetary and fiscal policies

From 1929 to 1933, real GDP in the United States fell by 30 percent. The price level fell by more than 20 percent, and nominal GDP fell by half. The unemployment rate in the United States rose to almost 25 percent, idling roughly one out of every four workers. This period is appropriately called the *Great Depression.*

Most economists believe that the Great Depression and other business cycles defy explanation by the tools of equilibrium macroeconomics presented in previous chapters. They believe that economists can explain business cycles only by adding some new features to the model. This chapter discusses such features.

Real-life economic relationships appear to suggest complex connections between changes in the *nominal* money supply, nominal prices, and real GDP and unemployment. These connections between nominal and real variables are controversial and economists do not fully understand them. For example, during the Great Depression, the M2 measure of the money supply fell by almost one-third.[1] Many economists believe that if the Federal Reserve had prevented the fall in the money supply, it would have averted the Great Depression or made it much less severe.

Half a century later, in 1982, the United States experienced its largest recession since the Great Depression as inflation fell rapidly. In 1979, the Federal

---

[1]The government did not purposely reduce the money supply. The Federal Reserve kept the monetary base roughly constant, but the money multiplier (discussed in the last chapter) fell as banks failed and the currency-deposit ratio increased.

Reserve had decided to change monetary policy to reduce the rate of inflation. Inflation fell from 13.3 percent in 1979 to 3.8 percent in 1982, but the unemployment rate rose from 5.8 percent in 1979 to more than 10.0 percent in the last half of 1982 and early 1983. Also, real GDP fell 1.6 percent from fall 1979 to fall 1982.[2] More recently, the United States experienced a recession in 1990 to 1991 as the Federal Reserve followed tight monetary policies to fight inflation. The Great Depression, the 1982 recession, and other, similar episodes suggest connections between nominal variables (such as the money supply and inflation) and real variables (such as real GDP and unemployment).

Most economists believe that short-run *disequilibrium* forces explain the connections between real and nominal variables, and play major roles in business cycles. Earlier chapters discussed the main forces that affect the equilibrium levels of GDP, interest rates, consumption, savings, investment, and employment. This chapter discusses the forces that can cause short-run disequilibrium in the economy.[3]

PRICE STICKINESS AND DISEQUILIBRIUM

sticky nominal price — a nominal price that takes time to adjust to its new equilibrium level following a change in supply or demand.

Almost any change in supply or demand causes a change in some equilibrium price. If prices adjust very quickly following an increase in the nominal money supply or another change in underlying economic conditions, the economy moves quickly from one equilibrium to another.[4] Most economists believe, however, that nominal prices are sticky in the short run.

Sticky nominal prices take time to adjust to their new equilibrium levels following a change in supply or demand.

Some prices adjust very quickly to changes in demand or supply; they are not sticky. Prices of metals such as gold, silver, and tin or commodities such as wheat or soybeans can change every few seconds on an organized market such as the Chicago Mercantile Exchange. Other prices adjust more slowly, such as the prices of magazines at newsstands and the prices of steel, cement, chemicals, and glass bought by manufacturing firms. Prices in some industries remain unchanged for periods of several years.[5]

Sticky prices can create short-run disequilibrium in the economy.

disequilibrium — a situation in which the quantity supplied of some good does not equal the quantity demanded

In **disequilibrium,** the quantity supplied of some good does not equal the quantity demanded.

Many economists believe that disequilibrium due to sticky prices plays an important role in business cycles. The equilibrium economic forces discussed in earlier

---

[2]Real GDP fell more than 3.0 percent from fall 1981 to fall 1982.

[3]This is the main focus of this chapter and the next. The chapter after that discusses a different view held by a minority of economists.

[4]Still, the economy might take a long time to reach a new long-run equilibrium. For example, Chapter 5 discussed the effects of a decrease in the supply of gasoline. The price of gasoline rises. In the short run, most people continue to drive the same cars as before, possibly enduring poor gasoline mileage. As time passes, people replace their old cars with new ones that get more miles per gallon. They also learn to conserve gasoline in other ways, by driving less, car-pooling, and so on. After the decrease in supply, the economy moves immediately to a new short-run equilibrium (see Chapter 5), and then it moves slowly to its new long-run equilibrium.

[5]The next chapter discusses some reasons for sticky prices.

chapters describe the economy's long-run behavior, but its short-run reactions to changes in government policies or other changes in conditions differ from its long-run reactions.

EFFECTS OF SHORT-RUN PRICE STICKINESS

A 10 percent fall in the nominal money supply reduces all nominal prices by 10 percent in the long run. This includes nominal wages and salaries (the prices of labor); they also fall by 10 percent in the long run so that real wages and salaries—the purchasing power of nominal wages and salaries—remain unchanged. A change in the money supply does not affect long-run levels of real economic variables such as production, employment or unemployment, the real interest rate, savings, consumption, investment, and economic growth. In the short run, however, a change in the money supply can affect real economic variables because prices are sticky.

To see why, consider the equation of exchange:

$$MV = Py \tag{29.1}$$

The long-run effect of a 10 percent fall in the nominal money supply (M) is to lower the price level (P) by 10 percent, leaving velocity (V) and real GDP (y) unchanged. Sticky prices, however, prevent P from falling in the short run. The 10 percent fall in M then makes the left-hand side of the equation, MV, smaller than the right-hand side. To balance the equation, either V must rise or y must fall. Typically, V rises *and* y falls, as a later section will soon explain.

KEY EXAMPLE

Now consider a simple example called the *key example* to help explain the effects of price stickiness. Suppose:

1. *V* cannot change. Velocity is 1 per year; people always spend all of the money in the economy exactly 1 time every year, not more or less.

2. *P* is completely sticky for a year or more; it cannot change at all during this time.

While these conditions are not realistic, they will help you to understand the real-life case in which *V* can change and prices are not completely sticky.

Figure 29.1 shows the circular flow diagram from an earlier chapter. At first, the money supply is $1,000, velocity is 1 per year, and real GDP is 100 goods per year, so the equilibrium price level (P) is $10 per good. The money supply then falls to $900. With P fixed at $10 per good and velocity equal to 1 per year, people spend $900 each year to buy goods that cost $10 each. *These people can afford to buy only 90 goods each year.* They cannot afford to buy all 100 goods that the economy can produce each year. Because firms cannot sell all 100 goods that they could produce each year—they can sell only 90—they reduce production by laying off workers, and unemployment rises. Because of sticky prices, a fall in the money supply causes a fall in real GDP and a rise in unemployment in the short run. This is an example of a recession.

WHEN THE SHORT RUN BECOMES THE LONG RUN

Prices are not permanently sticky. They eventually rise or fall to their long-run equilibrium levels. In the key example, the price level falls from $10 to $9 in the long run, allowing people to buy 100 goods with the $900 they have to spend each year. Real GDP then rises back to its original level of 100 goods per year, the

FIGURE 29.1

KEY EXAMPLE

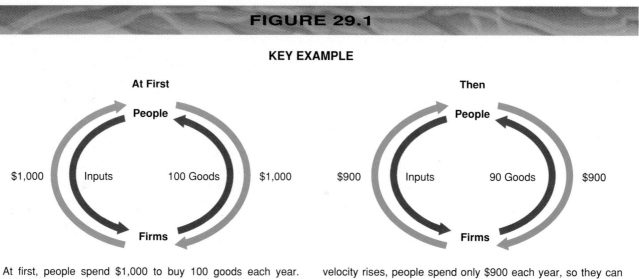

At first, people spend $1,000 to buy 100 goods each year. Velocity is 1 per year, and the price is $10 per good. The money supply then falls from $1,000 to $900. The completely sticky price level keeps the cost of goods at $10 each. Unless

velocity rises, people spend only $900 each year, so they can afford to buy only 90 goods each year. Firms reduce output from 100 goods per person to 90 goods per person, and a recession occurs.

amount that the economy can produce with its available labor, capital, and technology, and the recession ends. The fall in the money supply reduces real GDP in the short run, but not in the long run.

How Short Is the Short Run?

The answer depends on how fast prices can change toward the equilibrium level. Most economists believe that prices take several years to adjust completely to new equilibriums following a major change in the money supply. They claim that this explains why recessions typically last 1 or 2 years.

Aggregate Demand

A country's aggregate demand, as an earlier chapter explained, refers to the total demand for the goods and services produced in that country in a given year. An aggregate demand curve graphs the total quantity demanded at various price levels, as in **Figure 29.2**. The vertical axis shows the price level and the horizontal axis shows real aggregate demand. The aggregate demand curve in Figure 29.2 holds fixed the money supply and velocity.[6]

As an earlier chapter explained, economists can describe aggregate demand in two ways. First, they can state nominal aggregate demand as the product of the nominal money supply, *M,* and the velocity of money, *V:*

$$\text{Nominal aggregate demand} = MV \qquad\qquad (29.2)$$

[6]More advanced formulations of the aggregate demand curve hold fixed the money supply and all factors that affect velocity except the nominal interest rate. (Recall from an earlier chapter that an increase in the nominal interest rate raises the velocity of money.) To avoid unnecessary complications, this book uses the simpler formulation of aggregate demand that holds velocity fixed.

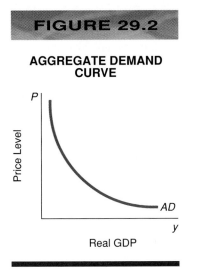

FIGURE 29.2

AGGREGATE DEMAND CURVE

Real aggregate demand then equals nominal aggregate demand divided by the price level, P:

$$y = MV/P$$

$$\text{Real aggregate demand} = MV/P \qquad (29.3)$$

(This measures real aggregate demand in the same way as real GDP, in terms of base-year dollars, as discussed in an earlier chapter.) The first way to describe aggregate demand reflects the equation of exchange.

The second way to describe aggregate demand adds different types of spending together. This states aggregate demand as the sum of consumption, investment, government purchases, and net exports:

$$(y) \quad \text{Real aggregate demand} = C + I + G + NEX \qquad (29.4)$$

Equation 29.4 shows that aggregate demand equals consumption by people living in the home country (C), plus investment (I), plus government purchases (G), plus net exports to foreigners (NEX). Nominal aggregate demand is $P \times (C + I + G + NEX)$.

$$(y)$$

EXPLANATION

The two descriptions of aggregate demand amount to two ways to describe a person's total purchases at a store. As one way to describe total purchases, one could look at the total amount of money that the person spends at the store; as another way, one could add the person's spending on each type of good (spending on marshmellows, plus spending on graham crackers, plus spending on chocolate). In the same way, economists can describe aggregate demand either by the total amount of money that people spend each year—the money supply times the velocity of money (the average number of times people spend each dollar during the year); they can also describe aggregate demand by total consumption spending plus investment spending plus government purchases plus net exports. MV/P and $C + I + G + NEX$ both equal aggregate demand; they are two different ways to describe it.

EXAMPLE

Suppose that people spend $4 billion on consumption and $1 billion on investment. Also suppose that the government spends $1 billion, and exports equal imports, so net exports equal zero. Total spending on goods produced in the country, aggregate demand, then equals:

$$P \times (C + I + G + NEX) = \$6 \text{ billion}$$

$$(\$4 + \$1 + \$1 + \$0 = \$6)$$

If the money supply is $1 billion, then people must spend each dollar 6 times per year, on average, so the velocity of money is 6 times per year:

$$MV = \$6 \text{ billion per year}$$

$$V = \$6 \text{ billion per year}/M$$

$$= \$6 \text{ billion per year}/\$1 \text{ billion}$$

$$= 6 \text{ times per year}$$

DIFFERENT ANSWERS TO EQUATIONS 29.3 AND 29.4?

You may wonder how economists can have two equations for aggregate demand. How can they guarantee that both give the same answer? What if the

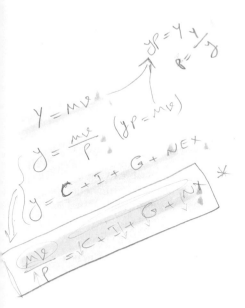

answers differ? The equations *always* give the same answer. To see why, suppose that you have $60 in your wallet when you walk into a store. After you buy some things, you leave the store with $20. Two equations can describe your total spending at the store. One equation says that you spent $60 − $20, or $40. (Your spending equals the $60 you had to start minus the $20 you had left.) The second equation adds up your spending on the different things you bought; it says that you spent $20 on a shirt, $10 on magazines, and $10 on snack food, which add up to $40. Both equations for your total spending must give the same answer.

Because both equations for aggregate demand always give the same answer, any change in one equation must also change the other equation. For example, if consumption rises while *I, G,* and *NEX* stay the same, then Equation 29.4 says that real aggregate demand rises, so something must also change in Equation 29.3; either *M* rises or *V* rises or *P* falls. (If the government keeps the money supply *M* fixed and *P* is sticky, then it turns out that the interest rate rises and this raises *V;* a later section of the chapter, *Changes in Aggregate Demand,* discusses this.) Both equations *always* give the same answer for aggregate demand.

CHANGES IN AGGREGATE DEMAND

Many factors affect aggregate demand, and the aggregate demand curve holds constant all factors except the price. Changes in these various factors, such as the money supply, the velocity of money, people's tastes for savings versus spending, the investment opportunities available to business firms, taxes, and government spending, shift the aggregate demand curve.

Any change in underlying economic conditions that affects aggregate demand affects both *MV/P* and *C + I + G + NEX*. The two quantities always change together because both describe the same thing (aggregate demand). Any change in one must be accompanied by a change in the other. For example, a technical change that increases investment spending, *I*, raises *C + I + G + NEX* directly. It also raises the interest rate, raising velocity and, therefore, *MV/P*. In this way, both descriptions of aggregate demand rise when investment rises due to a technical change.

EXAMPLE

Suppose that the money supply is $1 billion, and velocity falls from 6 per year to 5 per year. (People begin spending money more slowly, so each dollar bill changes hands an average of 5 times per year instead of 6 times per year.) Total spending each year, *MV,* then falls from $6 billion to $5 billion per year. If *P* equals $1 per good, then Equation 29.3 says that real aggregate demand must also fall by 1 billion goods per year.

What about Equation 29.4? *C + I + G + NEX* must also fall by 1 billion goods per year. No one can say how this increase breaks down among changes in *C, I,* and so on, without additional information; perhaps consumption spending falls by 800 million goods per year and investment spending falls by 200 million, so real aggregate demand falls by 1 billion goods per year. The point is that if people spend less each year, they must spend less on something; Equation 29.4 simply shows how they reduce spending.

SLOPE OF THE *AD* CURVE

The aggregate demand curve slopes downward. To see why, recall that the aggregate demand curve holds constant the money supply and velocity, so it holds con-

FIGURE 29.3

EXAMPLE OF AN AGGREGATE DEMAND CURVE

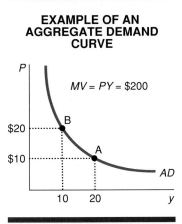

stant the product MV.[7] MV equals Py, however, so the aggregate demand curve must hold constant Py. This means that when P is higher, y must be lower, and vice versa. Therefore, the aggregate demand curve slopes downward.

For example, suppose that the money supply is $100 and velocity is 2 per year. Then MV is $200 per year, so Py must be $200 per year. At a price of $10 per good, y equals 20 goods per year (Point A in **Figure 29.3**). At a price of $20 per good, however, y equals only 10 goods per year (Point B in Figure 29.3). This shows, again, that the aggregate demand curve slopes downward.

The second equation for aggregate demand can also show that the aggregate demand curve slopes downward. An increase in the price level reduces aggregate demand in Equation 29.4 in two ways: it reduces consumption (C) and reduces investment (I).

An increase in the price level reduces consumption because it reduces the amount of products people can afford to buy with the money they have available. (Remember that the aggregate demand curve holds constant the money supply, M, and velocity, V.) For this reason, an increase in the price level reduces consumption, which reduces aggregate demand.[8]

An increase in the price level reduces investment because it raises the real interest rate. When the price level rises in the short run (without a rise in M), people try to borrow more money to buy goods. (They also save less.) This raises the demand for loans and decreases the supply of loans, which raises the real interest rate as an earlier chapter explained. This increase in the real interest rate reduces investment, I, so an increase in the price level reduces investment, which reduces aggregate demand.[9]

A higher price level reduces consumption, C, and investment, I, and it reduces aggregate demand, $C + I + G + NEX$. Similarly, a fall in the price level raises C and I (by raising the amount of goods that people can afford to consume and by reducing the real interest rate), so it raises aggregate demand. For this reason, the aggregate demand curve slopes downward as Figure 29.2 shows.

REMINDER

The aggregate demand curve differs from the demand curves for individual products introduced in Chapter 4. Those demand curves involve *relative prices* of goods, not the *nominal price level*. The aggregate demand curve, in contrast, involves the nominal price level. This is important because the long-run equilibrium levels of real GDP, the real interest rate, and other real variables do not depend on the nominal price level. The nominal price level matters only when prices are sticky in the short run.

─────────── **FOR REVIEW** ───────────

29.1 What does it mean to say that prices are sticky in the short run?

---

[7]More advanced formulations of the aggregate demand curve do not hold constant velocity, but instead hold constant various factors that affect velocity.

[8]Why don't people just spend the money faster so velocity rises and people can buy the same amount of goods? Because a person who spends money faster after receiving it has less money available on a typical day. (Imagine a person who spends money minutes after receiving it. Payday comes once a week and the person immediately spends the money. As a result, *most of the time,* the person would have no money. An earlier chapter discussed the *demand for money;* people usually want to have some of their wealth in the form of money. This limits the speed at which people spend money—it limits the velocity of money.

[9]The higher interest rate also raises V, which partly offsets the fall in aggregate demand.

29.2 Draw a circular flow diagram and explain why a decrease in the money supply leads to a fall in real GDP if prices are completely sticky and velocity remains constant.

QUESTIONS

29.3 Write down two equations for aggregate demand. Explain each in words. Why do both equations give the same answer for aggregate demand?

29.4 Why does the aggregate demand curve slope downward?

SHORT-RUN EFFECT OF CHANGES IN AGGREGATE DEMAND

The aggregate demand curve holds constant a variety of factors such as the money supply, the velocity of money, consumer tastes for consumption spending versus saving, technology, and the willingness of firms to invest in new capital, government purchases of goods and services, and net exports. Exogenous changes in these underlying factors—changes not precipitated by changes in prices, interest rates, or income—cause changes in aggregate demand, shifting the aggregate demand curve, as in **Figures 29.4** and **29.5.** This section considers the short-run effects of exogenous changes in these factors.

AGGREGATE DEMAND INCREASES

MONEY SUPPLY RISES

[handwritten: i is the cause of saving not the effect. So, if people save more, it won't effect i.]

When the money supply rises, someone in the economy gets the new money and decides how to use it. If people spend the new money on consumption goods, then consumption rises. If they save the new money, the supply of loans increases, reducing the real interest rate and raising equilibrium investment, as an earlier chapter showed. In one of these ways, aggregate demand rises whether people spend or save the new money.

VELOCITY RISES EXOGENOUSLY

An increase in velocity means that people spend each dollar in the economy more times per year, raising total spending and aggregate demand. Whether this increase in spending boosts consumption or investment goods, $C + I + G + NEX$ rises by the same amount as the rise in MV/P.

CONSUMPTION SPENDING RISES EXOGENOUSLY

Consumption is part of aggregate demand ($C + I + G + NEX$), so an exogenous increase in consumption raises aggregate demand. Because people spend more on consumption, they save less, reducing the supply of loans and raising real and nominal interest rates. The rise in the nominal interest rate increases velocity, as explained in a previous chapter, raising MV/P by the same amount as $C + I + G + NEX$.

INVESTMENT SPENDING INCREASES EXOGENOUSLY

Investment is part of aggregate demand ($C + I + G + NEX$), so an exogenous increase in investment raises aggregate demand. The increase in investment demand raises the demand for loans as firms borrow more to finance the addi-

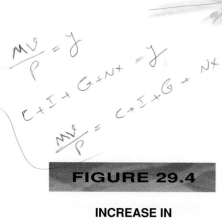

[handwritten equations:
$$\frac{MV}{P} = y$$
$$C + I + G + NX = y$$
$$\frac{MV}{P} = C + I + G + NX$$
]

FIGURE 29.4

INCREASE IN AGGREGATE DEMAND

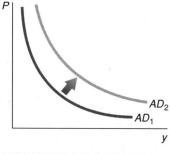

[graph axes labeled P and y, with curves AD_2 and AD_1]

tional investment, raising real and nominal interest rates. The rise in the nominal interest rate increases velocity, as explained in a previous chapter, raising MV/P by the same amount as $C + I + G + NEX$.

GOVERNMENT PURCHASES OF GOODS AND SERVICES INCREASE EXOGENOUSLY

Government purchases, like consumption and investment, are part of aggregate demand, so an exogenous increase in G raises $C + I + G + NEX$. MV/P again rises by the same amount as $C + I + G + EX - IM$, because V rises.

To see why velocity rises in this case, think about how the government pays for the spending increase. If it raises taxes, people will have less after-tax income and they will likely save less, decreasing the supply of loans and raising the real and nominal interest rates. (This reasoning assumes that the increase in government spending is temporary; a permanent change in government spending introduces additional complications.) If taxes do not increase, the government budget deficit rises and the increase in government borrowing raises the demand for loans, raising the real and nominal interest rates. In either case, the increase in the nominal interest rate raises velocity.

FOREIGN DEMAND FOR DOMESTIC GOODS INCREASES EXOGENOUSLY

Aggregate demand includes demand for domestic products by people, businesses, and governments in foreign countries, so an exogenous increase in foreign demand for U.S. goods raises U.S. aggregate demand directly. MV/P rises by the same amount as $C + I + G + NEX$ because V rises. When net exports increase as foreigners buy more U.S. goods without selling more of their own goods in the United States, foreign buyers pay for the U.S. goods by borrowing from the United States, raising the U.S. demand for loans, real and nominal interest rates, and the velocity of money.

DOMESTIC DEMAND FOR IMPORTS OF FOREIGN GOODS DECREASES EXOGENOUSLY

An exogenous fall in imports directly raises aggregate demand by raising net exports. MV/P rises by the same amount as $C + I + G + EX - IM$ because V rises. Velocity rises because the fall in imports gives foreigners less income from selling products in the domestic market, so foreign residents borrow more from the domestic country to pay for their imports (domestic exports). This increases the demand for loans and raises interest rates and velocity.

RELATIVE PRICES OF FOREIGN GOODS

Net exports are related to the relative prices of foreign goods in terms of domestic goods, that is, the amount of domestic goods that a person sacrifices to buy one foreign good. These relative prices are, in turn, related to the foreign exchange rate.

The **foreign exchange rate** is the price of one unit of foreign money.

foreign exchange rate — the price of one unit of foreign money

For a person in the United States, the foreign exchange rate between the U.S. dollar and the Japanese yen is the number of dollars it costs to buy ¥1. (The same relationship holds for other foreign moneys such as the Mexican peso or German mark.) For example, the foreign exchange rate between dollars and British pounds might be $1.70 per pound. This means that each unit of British money (the pound sterling) costs $1.70. Sometimes foreign exchange rates are stated the other way

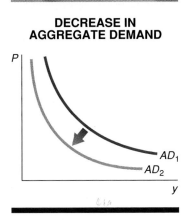

FIGURE 29.5

DECREASE IN AGGREGATE DEMAND

around; if you read that the exchange rate between the U.S. dollar and the Japanese yen is ¥100 (where ¥ is the symbol for yen), this means you can buy ¥100 for $1, so the price of ¥1 is $1/100, or $0.01.

The relative price of foreign goods in terms of domestic goods also depends on the price levels in the two countries. The term *foreign price level* refers to the amount of foreign money it takes to buy foreign goods; the *domestic price level* refers to the price level in the home country. The relative price of foreign goods in terms of domestic goods rises when:

1. The foreign exchange rate (the price of foreign money) rises, holding constant the foreign and domestic price levels. If it takes more dollars to buy the same amount of foreign money (at a constant foreign price level), then it takes more dollars to buy foreign goods. For example, suppose it takes $0.075 (three-fourths of 1¢) to buy a Japanese yen, and a Japanese VCR costs ¥40,000, then it takes $300 to buy the VCR ($300 buys ¥40,000, which buys the VCR). If the price of yen rises to $0.01 per yen, then it takes $400 to buy the VCR (since it takes $400 to buy the ¥40,000). Suppose that the price of an American VCR is $350; then the relative price of the Japanese VCR in terms of the American VCR has increased (from 300/350 to 400/350).

2. The foreign price level rises, holding constant the exchange rate and the domestic price level. This raises the number of dollars it takes to buy foreign goods. For example, suppose that it takes $0.075 (three-fourths of 1¢) to buy a Japanese yen, and a Japanese VCR costs ¥40,000. Then it takes $300 to buy the VCR ($300 buys ¥40,000, which buys the VCR). Suppose that the foreign price level rises to ¥60,000 for a VCR. Then it takes $450 to buy that VCR (since it costs $450 to buy ¥60,000). This raises the relative price of the Japanese VCR in terms of American goods.

3. The domestic price level falls, holding fixed the exchange rate and the foreign price level. The dollar price of a Japanese VCR does not change, so a fall in the dollar price of the American VCR raises the relative price of the Japanese VCR.

An increase in the relative price of foreign goods raises aggregate demand, as in Figure 29.4. As a country trades more with other countries, a change in its foreign exchange rate has a larger effect on its aggregate demand.

TIMING AND SIZES OF CHANGES IN AGGREGATE DEMAND

The aggregate demand curve does not usually shift instantly in response to an exogenous change in the money supply or spending. Instead, the shift in the *AD* curve often begins after a lag, and its motion takes time. For example, when the money supply rises, it may take time for people to begin spending the extra money. When the relative price of foreign goods changes, it often takes time for people to begin switching between foreign and domestic goods. (People may learn about the price change with a lag, and they may adjust their spending over a longer time.) The exact timing of a shift in aggregate demand is not completely predictable. This complicates the formation of economic policy, as later chapters will explain.

MULTIPLIER

A $100 exogenous increase in spending can raise aggregate demand by either more than $100 or less than $100. The size of the change in aggregate demand depends on the multiplier.

aggregate demand multiplier —
a measure of the ultimate increase in aggregate demand that results from an exogenous $1 rise in spending

The **aggregate demand multiplier** shows the ultimate increase in aggregate demand that results from an exogenous $1 rise in spending.

For example, if spending rises exogenously by $100 and the multiplier is 2, then aggregate demand rises by $200. If the multiplier is 1, aggregate demand rises by $100. If the multiplier is $\frac{1}{2}$, aggregate demand rises by $50; see **Figure 29.6.**

The main idea behind the multiplier is simple: when someone's spending rises, someone else's income rises. The person who earns a higher income also spends more, and someone else earns more income and spends more, and so on. When one person spends more, it leads other people to spend more, too, so total spending can rise by more than the original increase in spending.

Unfortunately, higher spending has indirect effects as well as direct effects. Someone who spends more saves less (unless her income has risen). The fall in savings decreases the supply of loans, so it decreases the amount of money that other people can borrow. The people who borrow less also spend less, which reduces the incomes of other people, leading them to spend less, too.

Taking into account all the direct and indirect effects, a change in spending changes aggregate demand:

▶ An exogenous increase in spending raises aggregate demand.

▶ The multiplier can be larger or smaller than 1, depending on how people behave.

EXPLANATION AND EXAMPLE

Suppose that spending rises exogenously because Al decides to save $100 less and spend $100 more to buy bread from Bill the baker. This raises Bill's income by $100. Bill decides to save $50 of this extra income and spend the other $50 to buy candy from Cindy, so Cindy's income rises by $50. She decides to save $25 of this

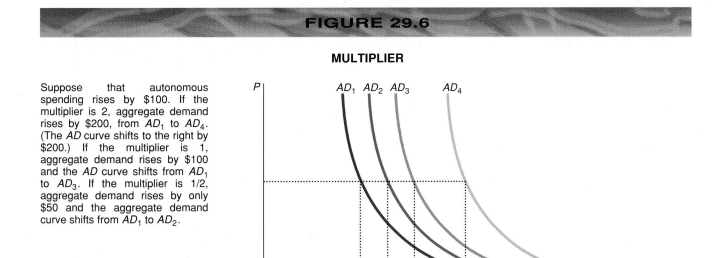

FIGURE 29.6

MULTIPLIER

Suppose that autonomous spending rises by $100. If the multiplier is 2, aggregate demand rises by $200, from AD_1 to AD_4. (The AD curve shifts to the right by $200.) If the multiplier is 1, aggregate demand rises by $100 and the AD curve shifts from AD_1 to AD_3. If the multiplier is 1/2, aggregate demand rises by only $50 and the aggregate demand curve shifts from AD_1 to AD_2.

FIGURE 29.7

WHY THE MULTIPLIER EXCEEDS ZERO

An increase in consumption spending reduces saving, which reduces the supply of loans from S_1 to S_2. This raises the real interest rate from r_1 to r_2, which raises the nominal interest rate and velocity. Therefore, aggregate demand (MV) rises.

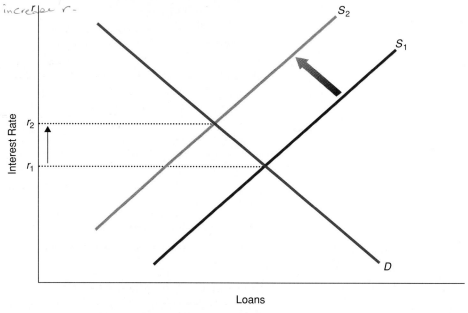

(handwritten: ⇒ increase r-)

Consumption, the engine of the economy

A decline in consumer confidence often points toward recession because lower confidence is generally translated into lower sales of such things as cars and refrigerators. The effect of canceled or postponed purchases ripples through the economy as, say, the automobile salesman decides he'll wait another year to add a patio to his house and the mason's helper begins to worry about being laid off.

———

A change in spending has indirect effects that ripple through the economy.

Source: New York Times, November 29, 1987, p. E5.

extra income and spend the other $25 to buy dishes from Dave. Dave earns $25 more income, and so on. If each person spends half of any increase in income and saves the other half, total spending eventually rises by $200. If nothing else were to happen, the multiplier would equal 2.[10]

Now think about indirect effects. Because Al raises his spending by $100, he reduces his saving by $100. He puts $100 less in his bank account for the bank to lend, so someone else—say, Marcia—borrows $100 less. Marcia has $100 less to spend on nachos from Ned. Because Marcia spends $100 less, Ned's income falls by $100, so Ned spends $50 less on oranges from Ollie. Ollie's income then falls, and so on. Because Marcia spends $100 less, she can no longer borrow Al's savings from the bank. The decrease in Marcia's spending exactly cancels the increase in Al's spending. Also, the decrease in Ned's spending cancels the increase in Bill's spending, the decrease in Ollie's spending cancels the increases by Cindy, and so on. In such a case, the initial increase in spending would not raise aggregate demand.[11] The multiplier would be 0.

In fact, the indirect effects are *smaller* than the direct effects, so real-life aggregate demand rises and the multiplier is positive, but smaller than 2. To see why, look at the supply and demand for loans in **Figure 29.7.** When Al spends

———

[10]More generally, if people spend a fraction *MPC* (for *marginal propensity to consume*) of their extra income and save the rest, then when Al decides to spend $100 more and save $100 less, total spending rises by $100/(1 − *MPC*). The multiplier is $1/(1 - MPC)$. In the example, $MPC = \frac{1}{2}$, so the multiplier is 2 and total spending rises by $200.

[11]Al spends $100 more but Marcia spends $100 less, Bill spends $50 more but Ned spends $50 less, Cindy spends $25 more but Ollie spends $25 less, and so on. This example ignores bank reserves (discussed in the previous chapter) for simplicity.

$100 more and saves $100 less, the supply of loans falls. This raises the equilibrium real interest rate from r_1 to r_2. *This increase in the interest rate raises velocity.*[12] The increase in velocity, in turn, raises nominal aggregate demand, *MV.* In other words, total spending rises because the higher interest rate leads people to spend money faster than before. (It reduces real money demand.) So Al's decision to spend more and save less really does raise aggregate demand.

The size of the increase in aggregate demand depends on how much people raise the velocity of money when the interest rate rises, and how changes in income and the interest rate affect consumption and investment spending. Aggregate demand might rise by either more or less than the original increase in Al's spending, so the multiplier is positive, but less than 2 (and possibly less than 1).

This same reasoning applies to any exogenous change in spending. An increase in investment, government spending, or net exports also raises aggregate demand. Due to the positive multiplier, the ultimate increase in aggregate demand can be larger or smaller than the original increase in spending.

--- **FOR REVIEW** ---

29.5. List five changes in economic conditions that shift the aggregate demand curve and explain why.

29.6. What is the connection between the relative price of foreign goods and the foreign exchange rate?

29.7. Explain the direct effects and indirect effects of an exogenous increase in spending, and how they affect the multiplier.

--- **QUESTIONS** ---

29.8. If spending rises exogenously by $1 million, by how much does nominal aggregate demand ultimately rise? Explain.

29.9. How would aggregate demand react to global warming that reduced the amount of money that people spend on heating bills, winter coats, skiing and skating equipment, and vacations in warm climates?

AGGREGATE SUPPLY

As an earlier chapter explained, a country's aggregate supply is the total supply of all goods and services produced in that country in a given year. Its aggregate supply curve graphs the total quantities supplied at various price levels.

LONG-RUN AGGREGATE SUPPLY

Economists distinguish long-run aggregate supply from short-run aggregate supply. Long-run aggregate supply measures the total supply of goods and services after the economy has had time to adjust to a change in conditions (in particular, after prices have adjusted). Short-run aggregate supply refers to the total supply of goods and services before prices have adjusted fully to a change in conditions.

---

[12]The increase in the real interest rate raises the nominal interest rate, which raises velocity.

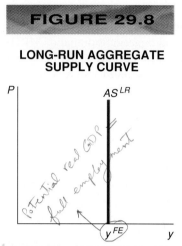

FIGURE 29.8

LONG-RUN AGGREGATE SUPPLY CURVE

The long-run aggregate supply curve is a vertical line at the full-employment level of output, y^{FE}.

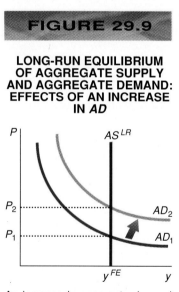

FIGURE 29.9

LONG-RUN EQUILIBRIUM OF AGGREGATE SUPPLY AND AGGREGATE DEMAND: EFFECTS OF AN INCREASE IN *AD*

An increase in aggregate demand raises the price level in the long run and leaves real GDP unchanged at the full-employment level of output, y^{FE}.

short-run aggregate supply curve — curve showing the total supply of all goods and services produced in the economy in the short run with sticky prices

The long-run aggregate supply curve is a vertical line, as in **Figure 29.8,** because in the long run, a country's output of goods and services does not relate to its price level and depends solely on available technology and inputs such as capital and labor, and on the laws, property rights, regulations, and taxes that affect people's incentives to use technology and inputs efficiently. It does not depend on the nominal price level because changes in the nominal price level do not have any long-run effects on the economy's technology or available inputs of capital and labor.

> The long-run aggregate supply curve, AS^{LR}, is a vertical line. The long-run level of aggregate supply is the full-employment level of output, y^{FE}, which is the equilibrium level of output discussed in an earlier chapter.

The full-employment level of output rises over time with long-run economic growth, so growth shifts the long-run aggregate supply curve to the right. The curve shifts right whenever technology improves or when the available inputs of labor or capital increase.

LONG-RUN EQUILIBRIUM OF AGGREGATE SUPPLY AND DEMAND

The intersection of the long-run aggregate supply and aggregate demand curves, as in **Figure 29.9,** shows real GDP and the price level in long-run equilibrium.

Suppose that aggregate demand increases, for one of the reasons discussed earlier, from AD_1 to AD_2. Figure 29.9 shows the long-run effects of this change: it raises the price level from P_1 to P_2 and leaves real GDP unchanged at y^{FE}, the full-employment rate of output.

EXAMPLE

Suppose that aggregate demand rises because the government raises the money supply by 10 percent. The price level rises by 10 percent in the long run, and real GDP does not change. You may wonder how one can know that the price level will rise by 10 percent rather than 5 percent or 15 percent. To get this answer, use the equation of exchange, $MV = Py$. An increase in the money supply does not change real GDP or velocity in the long run, so y and V do not change. The increase in M raises the left-hand side of the equation $MV = Py$, however, so P must rise to balance the equation by raising the right-hand side by the same amount as the left-hand side. When M rises by 10 percent, the equation is balanced by a 10 percent rise in P. That determines exactly how far the AD curve shifts in Figure 29.9.

SHORT-RUN AGGREGATE SUPPLY

> The **short-run aggregate supply curve,** AS^{SR}, shows the total supply of all goods and services produced in the economy in the short run with sticky prices.

Economists disagree about the shape of the short-run aggregate supply curve. Some believe that it runs roughly horizontally, at least some of the time, as in **Figure 29.10a,** where it is labeled AS^{SR}. Others believe it slopes upward most of the time, as in Figure 29.10b. Others believe it usually runs close to vertically like the long-run aggregate supply curve. Economists do not yet have enough evidence to resolve this disagreement.

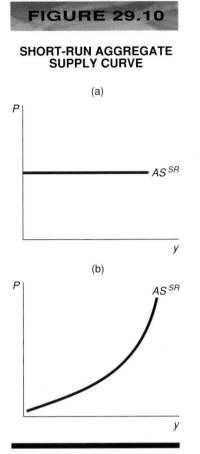

FIGURE 29.10

**SHORT-RUN AGGREGATE
SUPPLY CURVE**

For now, think about the extreme Keynesian case of a horizontal short-run aggregate supply, as in Figure 29.10a. *Keynesian* is pronounced *Kān' zē en,* after early followers of British economist and statesman John Maynard Keynes, the most famous economist of the 20th century. His 1936 book, *The General Theory of Employment, Interest, and Money,* revolutionized economics. The Keynesian revolution in economics led to economic models like the ones in this chapter and the next.[13]

It is useful to think about this extreme case because it is the easiest to understand. It will also set the stage for more realistic cases in the next chapter.

HORIZONTAL SHORT-RUN AGGREGATE SUPPLY CURVE

The short-run aggregate supply curve runs horizontally under two conditions:

1. All nominal prices are *completely sticky*—that is, *fixed*—in the short run.

2. Unemployment occurs because firms cannot find enough buyers to buy the extra output that they could produce with full employment. (If firms were to produce more, no one would buy the extra output.) This happens if the price level is fixed above its equilibrium level.

The short-run aggregate supply curve may become vertical at some point. (See Figure 29.12 later in the chapter.)

EXPLANATION AND EXAMPLE **Figure 29.11a** shows an example of the supply and demand for furnaces. Suppose that the price of furnaces is fixed at P_2, which lies above the equilibrium price, P_1. The quantity supplied is Q^S, but the quantity demanded is only Q^D. Each year there is a surplus of furnaces equal to $Q^S - Q^D$. In this situation, furnace manufacturers would reduce output to Q^D, because they could not sell more than that amount without reducing the price, which cannot happen with completely sticky prices.[14] Employment and use of capital equipment in the furnace industry fall.

Now suppose that the demand for furnaces increases. Figure 29.11b shows that the price stays the same (remember, this case assumes that it cannot change), and the output of furnaces rises from Q_1^D to Q_2^D. In this case, an increase in demand raises output.[15]

The furnace example could extend to all goods in the economy. If the nominal price level exceeds the equilibrium nominal price level, the economy can produce a surplus of all (or almost all) goods. Firms reduce production to the amounts that they can sell, as in the key example earlier in this chapter. (See Figure 29.1.)

---

[13]Keynes was also an important statesman and social critic. He represented Great Britain at the Versailles peace conference at the end of World War I, where he tried unsuccessfully to convince other countries not to punish Germany as much for that war. His 1919 book, *Economic Consequences of the Peace* (New York: Harcourt, Brace & Howe, 1920), criticized the Treaty of Versailles. Keynes argued that the treaty would create instability in Germany and Europe and threaten another war. The treaty was, of course, followed by the German hyperinflation and the rise of Hitler.

[14]The price of furnaces might be sticky because the furnace manufacturers have distributed catalogs with prices printed in them, and the costs of quickly printing and distributing new catalogs or price-change announcements is prohibitively high.

[15]This occurs whenever the quantity demanded is less than Q^S. If demand were to increase enough to intersect the supply curve above Q^S, then the equilibrium price would be higher than P_2. In this case, the price P_2 would no longer be above the equilibrium; further increases in demand would not raise output.

FIGURE 29.11

SUPPLY AND DEMAND FOR FURNACES

(a) Supply and Demand with the Price above Equilibrium

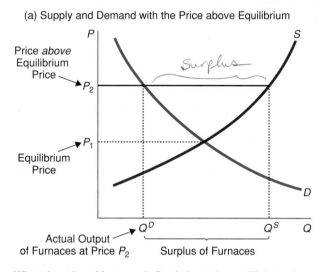

(b) Increase in Demand

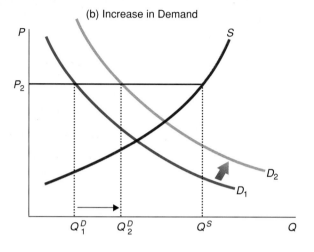

When the price of furnaces is fixed above the equilibrium price, an increase in the demand for furnaces raises output of furnaces without changing the price.

In the key example, the equilibrium nominal price level began at $10, then the money supply fell from $1,000 to $900, so the equilibrium price level fell to $9. *P* remained fixed at $10 in the short run, though, so the nominal price level was too high; it exceeded the equilibrium level. As a result, people bought only 90 goods each year. Although firms could have produced 100 goods, they chose to produce only 90 goods because they could sell no more.

Suppose that the money supply rises in the key example from $900 to $950. People can then afford 95 goods rather than 90. The price level stays fixed at $10, but output rises from 90 goods per year to 95 goods per year. In this case, as in the furnace example, an increase in demand raises output (real GDP) without changing the price. When changes in aggregate demand cause changes in real GDP without changing the price level, the economy has a perfectly elastic (horizontal) aggregate supply curve, as in Figure 29.10.

Now suppose that the money supply rises to $1,100, while the price level remains fixed in the short run at $10. People would like to buy 110 goods per year, but the economy can produce only 100 goods per year in the long run with its current technology and its inputs of labor and capital. If the economy can produce no more, even in the short run, the short-run aggregate supply curve becomes vertical at 100 goods per year, as in **Figure 29.12a.** When the money supply rises to $1,100, the economy does not produce enough goods to allow people to spend all of the money that they have. (People spend only $1,000 to buy 100 goods for $10 each. They can find no goods on which to spend the extra

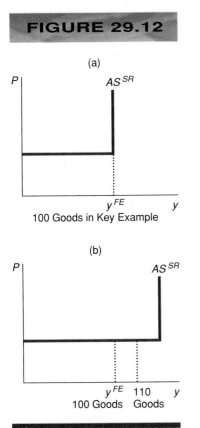

FIGURE 29.12

(a)

100 Goods in Key Example

(b)

100 Goods   Goods

money.) In this case, velocity falls in the short run from 1 per year to less than 1 per year. Because the equilibrium price level is $11 and the actual $10 price level is below this equilibrium level, prices rise to $11 in the long run.

The economy may be able to produce more than 100 goods in the short run, however. Firms might operate machinery more hours per day in the short run, but not in the long run (perhaps because the machinery would break down too often if it had to run so many hours per day on a continuing basis). In that case, the short-run aggregate supply curve could look like Figure 29.12b. If the money supply were to increase to $1,100 with prices fixed at $10 in the key example, output could increase to 110 goods per year in the short run. In the long run, output would fall back to its full-employment level of 100 goods per year as the price level rose to $11.

CONCLUSION ON THE SHAPE OF THE SHORT-RUN AGGREGATE SUPPLY CURVE

In this extreme Keynesian case, the short-run aggregate supply curve runs horizontally for levels of output lower than the full-employment level of output (that is, to the left of the long-run aggregate supply curve). It may become vertical at the full-employment level of output, as in Figure 29.12a, or it may remain horizontal for higher levels of output and become vertical at some higher level of output, as in Figure 29.12b. This depends on whether the economy can produce more than the full-employment level of output for a short time and whether firms are willing to produce this extra output in the short run while their prices remain fixed. The remainder of this chapter applies to the second case in which the short-run aggregate supply curve looks like Figure 29.12b.

COMBINING SHORT-RUN AGGREGATE SUPPLY AND DEMAND

Economists combine the short-run aggregate supply and aggregate demand curves on a single graph, as in **Figure 29.13.** The intersection shows real GDP and the price level in the short run. The price level, P_1, is completely sticky (fixed) in the short run.[16] Output, y_1, changes whenever aggregate demand changes.

Figure 29.13 also shows the effects of an increase in aggregate demand, perhaps because the government raises the money supply or because spending rises exogenously. The increase in aggregate demand raises real GDP in the short run and leaves the price level unchanged. Similarly, a decrease in aggregate demand reduces GDP.

FROM THE SHORT RUN TO THE LONG RUN

The price level does not remain sticky in the long run. As prices finally adjust to a change in economic conditions (any change that affects the equilibrium price level), the short-run aggregate supply curve rotates toward the long-run aggregate supply curve, as in **Figure 29.14.**

Figure 29.15 shows the effects of a decrease in aggregate demand. In the short run, real GDP falls from y^{FE} (Point A) to y_2 (Point B) and the price level remains unchanged. As the price level eventually begins falling, real GDP rises

---

[16]The price level, P_1, is higher than the equilibrium price level; see the earlier section, *Horizontal Short-Run Aggregate Supply Curve.*

FIGURE 29.13

SHORT-RUN EFFECTS OF AN INCREASE IN AGGREGATE DEMAND

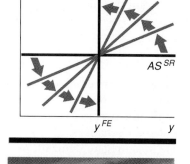

FIGURE 29.14

AGGREGATE SUPPLY FROM THE SHORT RUN TO THE LONG RUN

FIGURE 29.15

SHORT-RUN AND LONG-RUN EFFECTS OF A DECREASE IN AGGREGATE DEMAND

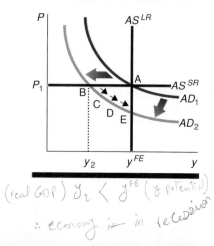

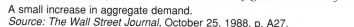

"Whether the marriage lasts or not, we've certainly given the economy a boost."
A small increase in aggregate demand.
Source: The Wall Street Journal, October 25, 1988, p. A27.

toward its full-employment level, y^{FE} (from Point B through Points C and D toward Point E).[17] In the long run, when prices have adjusted to their equilibrium levels, real GDP equals y^{FE} (Point E).

Figure 29.16 shows the effects of an increase in aggregate demand, starting from a long-run equilibrium. In the short run, real GDP rises from y^{FE} (Point A) to y_2 (Point B) while the price level holds steady. As the price level begins rising, real GDP falls toward its full-employment level, y^{FE} (from Point B through Points C and D toward Point E). In the long run, when prices have adjusted to their equilibrium levels, real GDP equals y^{FE} (Point E).[18]

Figure 29.17 shows the effects of a small increase in aggregate demand when the economy starts with unemployment. In the short run, real GDP rises from y_1 to y_2 (Point A to Point B) and the price level remains stable. Since the price level lies above its long-run equilibrium (the cause of the unemployment), it eventually falls. Real GDP then rises toward its full-employment level (from Point B toward Point C). In the long run, the price level reaches its equilibrium level and real GDP equals y^{FE} (Point C).

---

[17]The movement through Points C and D occurs as the aggregate supply curve rotates in Figure 29.14.

[18]Suppose that after the economy reaches Point E, aggregate demand rises again. The same thing happens again, but the process starts at Point E instead of Point A, and it ends up at a point higher than Point E.

(real GDP) $y_2 < y^{FE}$ (y potential)
∴ economy is in recession

Colombians fear for the economy

Sudden halt to drug trade could bring recession, economists declare

By Joseph B. Treaster
Special to The
New York Times

BOGOTA, Colombia, Sept. 10—As Colombia's stepped-up campaign against drug trafficking goes into its fourth week, many Colombians are divided over the wisdom of trying to abruptly shut down the country's most lucrative industry.

Both government and independent economists say that a sudden halt to the drug trade, which last year yielded $4 billion, would throw the country into a deep recession that might run four or five years.

"It should be reduced gradually over five or six years," said a leading economist, who requested anonymity.

A fall in aggregate demand reduces real GDP.

Source: Joseph B. Treaster, "Colombians Fear for the Economy," *New York Times,* September 11, 1989, p. A5.

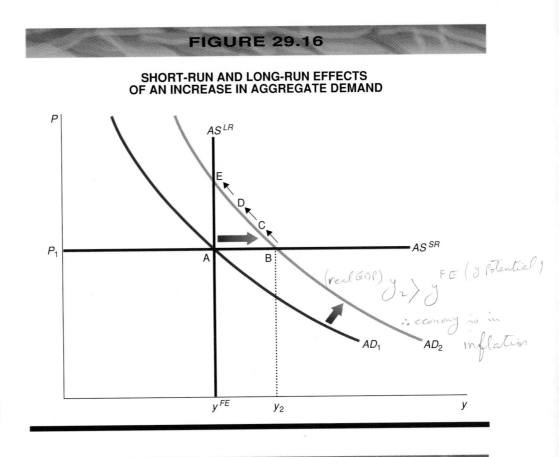

FIGURE 29.16

SHORT-RUN AND LONG-RUN EFFECTS OF AN INCREASE IN AGGREGATE DEMAND

(Handwritten annotations on figure: (real GDP) $y_2 > y$ FE (y Potential) ∴ economy is in inflation)

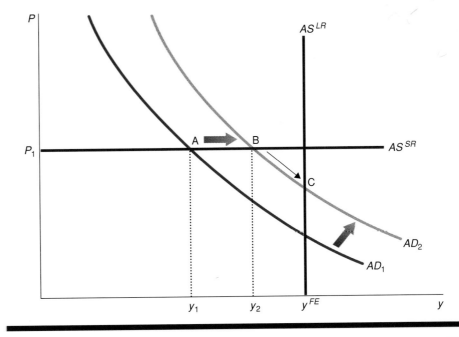

FIGURE 29.17

SHORT-RUN AND LONG-RUN EFFECTS OF AN INCREASE IN AGGREGATE DEMAND STARTING BELOW FULL EMPLOYMENT

IN THE NEWS

Defense cuts to cost nearly 2 million jobs

By Laurence Jolidon
USA TODAY

Nearly 2 million jobs will be extinct by 1998 as a result of defense cutbacks, the Defense Base Closure and Realignment Commission was told Monday.

Ronald Kutscher of the Bureau of Labor Statistics told the commission that 900,000 jobs have been lost since 1987 and another 1.8 million will be eliminated before 1998.

"We're dealing with a very poignant economic and human issue," said commissioner Harry McPherson Jr.

The commission is conducting hearings on whether to recommend the closing of more than 30 military bases.

Its final report is due July 1.

Kutscher's estimate of job losses includes:

► 594,000 in manufacturing.
► 286,000 in services.

► 139,000 in trade.
► 62,000 in transportation.

But the bottom line "need not necessarily translate into unemployment for the workers involved," Kutscher said.

Paul Dempsey of the Pentagon's Office of Economic Adjustment said most communities where bases have been closed were able to replace lost jobs within a few years.

A fall in government spending on the military reduces aggregate demand, causing a fall in real GDP and employment in the short run. In the long run, the economy returns to full employment.

Source: Laurence Jolidon, "Defense Cuts to Cost Nearly 2 Million Jobs," *USA Today,* April 13, 1993, p. A1.

MONEY AND INTEREST RATES IN THE SHORT RUN

If a rise in the money supply were to lead to an immediate rise in prices of the same percentage (say, 10 percent), then the economy would move to the new long-run equilibrium immediately. Real GDP, unemployment, and the real interest rate would not change. With sticky prices in the short run, however, a rise in the money supply can raise real GDP and reduce unemployment and the real interest rate.

Price stickiness can explain how a Federal Reserve open market purchase (which raises the money supply) can reduce the real interest rate in the short run. The open market operation raises the supply of loans, but, because prices do not rise along with the money supply in the short run, the demand for loans remains unchanged and the real interest rate falls.

The real interest rate also falls when the government spends newly printed money. Suppose, for example, that the government of a country prints money to buy military equipment. The increase in spending does not directly affect the supply and demand for loans, but it raises the incomes of people who own or work in the military-equipment firms. These people then save some of their extra income, raising the supply of loans and reducing the real interest rate. In this way, an increase in the money supply reduces the real interest rate in the short run regardless of whether the government initially spends the money or loans it, as the Fed does when it buys financial assets in an open market purchase. The fall in the real interest rate due to an increase in the money supply is often called the *liquidity effect* of a money-supply change.

liquidity effect — a short-run inverse change in interest rates associated with a change in the money supply

The **liquidity effect** of a change in the money supply refers to a short-run fall in interest rates associated with a rise in the money supply and a rise in interest rates associated with a fall in the money supply.

IN THE NEWS

Experts say a lack of hiring stems from weak spending

By Louis Uchitelle

Americans are being bombarded with explanations of why the nation cannot generate enough jobs: a shortage of skilled workers, they are told, holds down hiring, along with higher taxes, global competition, expensive government regulations, technology that automates work, and cutbacks in military spending.

All of these play a role, many experts say, but the biggest problem is simply a lack of robust economic growth—the most basic source of job creation. Until the national economy kicks into higher gear, they say, faster job growth will be hard to come by.

They say that American consumers—and for that matter European consumers who buy American goods—have simply not purchased with their usual gusto. As a result, fewer workers are needed to make goods or provide services to the nation. The problem, in short, is weak demand, not a new world that has found a way to prosper without workers.

Low aggregate demand can cause low real GDP in the short run.

Source: Louis Uchitelle, "Experts Say a Lack of Hiring Stems from Weak Spending," *New York Times,* July 17, 1993, p. 1.

The liquidity effect is important because a change in the real interest rate can affect investment spending. By reducing the real interest rate in the short run, an increase in the money supply can raise investment spending. By raising the real interest rate in the short run, a fall in the money supply can reduce investment spending. A fall in the interest rate also raises consumption spending due to intertemporal substitution; people find it less worthwhile to save when the interest rate is lower, so they save less and spend more instead. Many economists see the liquidity effect as an important channel through which changes in the money supply affect aggregate demand and real GDP in the short run.

In the long run, when prices adjust to their equilibrium levels, the liquidity effect disappears. When all nominal prices have eventually increased in the same proportion as the money supply, the nominal quantity of loans demanded rises in that same proportion. Although lenders may have 10 percent more dollars to offer, borrowers want to borrow 10 percent more dollars. Therefore, in the long run, the demand for dollar loans increases—the demand curve shifts to the right—by the same amount as the supply of loans, and the real interest rate returns to its original level. An increase in the money supply can reduce the real interest rate in the short run, but not in the long run. Similarly, a fall in the money supply can raise the real interest rate in the short run, but not in the long run.

FOR REVIEW

29.10 Draw a graph to show the long-run effect of a fall in aggregate demand on real GDP and the price level.

29.11 State the two conditions under which the short-run aggregate supply curve is horizontal.

QUESTION

29.12 What is the liquidity effect? Why does it occur and why does it vanish in the long run?

CONNECTIONS BETWEEN REAL AND NOMINAL VARIABLES

This chapter opened with remarks about the Great Depression and the 1982 recession. Recall the suggestion that evidence from these and other episodes leads most economists to believe that short-run disequilibrium forces like those discussed in this chapter create important connections between nominal variables (like the money supply) and real variables (like real GDP).

The equilibrium model of earlier chapters implies that an increase in the nominal money supply has no effect on real GDP (or its components: real consumption, real investment, government spending, and the current account), unemployment, or the real interest rate. It implies that an increase in the nominal money supply affects *only* nominal prices. Economists summarize this relationship by saying that in the equilibrium model, money is neutral; it has no effects on real economic variables such as real GDP, though it does affect nominal variables.

neutrality of money — position that a change in the money supply affects only nominal prices and not real variables

> **Neutrality of money** means that a change in the money supply does not affect real GDP or other real variables.

Some evidence suggests, however, that money is not neutral. Changes in the money supply do appear to affect real GDP, real investment, real consumption, unemployment, and the real interest rate in the short run. The evidence is controversial, but the majority of economists accept its major components; a later chapter will discuss a minority view. Evidence suggests that *in the short run* an increase in nominal money supply or its rate of growth:

1. Reduces the real interest rate
2. Raises real investment spending
3. Raises real consumption spending by less than investment spending
4. Raises real GDP
5. Raises employment and lowers the unemployment rate

In the long run, the unemployment rate and the real interest rate rise back to their original levels while real GDP, employment, consumption, and investment return to their original levels adjusted for long-run economic growth.[19]

The short-run connection between the nominal money supply and the real interest rate is strong enough that the Federal Reserve usually describes its policies in terms of changing interest rates rather than changing the money supply. To reduce the nominal interest rate in the short run, the Fed raises the growth rate of the nominal money supply by conducting open market purchases or lending more at the discount window, as discussed in the previous chapter. The increase in the

---

[19]That is, if the long-run rate of growth of real GDP grows 2 percent per year in the long run, then after, say, 3 years real GDP returns to its original level *plus* 6 percent, reflecting 3 years of growth at 2 percent per year.

growth rate of the money supply leads to higher inflation in the long run, but it has little effect on inflation in the short run.

The real interest rate falls with a rise in the money supply for two reasons. First, the nominal interest rate falls. Second, expected (future) inflation rises. In the long run, the real interest rate returns to its original level. If the growth rate of the money supply remains higher in the long run, it creates higher long-run inflation, so the nominal interest rate rises in the long run. If the rate of money growth returns to its original level, the inflation rate and the nominal interest rate also return to their original levels in the long run, though the price level remains higher.[20]

Similarly, the Fed raises the nominal and real interest rates in the short run by reducing the rate of money growth. This reduces aggregate demand and, in the short run, real GDP. If the lower rate of money growth continues, then in the long run inflation falls, the nominal interest rate falls, and real GDP and the real interest rate return to their original levels, adjusted for long-run growth in real GDP.

The *disequilibrium* model discussed in this chapter—the model of aggregate demand and aggregate supply with completely sticky (fixed) prices in the short run—is consistent with this evidence. The disequilibrium model does not treat money as neutral in the short run; changes in money affect real variables. The evidence that money is not neutral helps to support the disequilibrium model, which the next chapter will develop further.

The disequilibrium model also explains involuntary unemployment.

Involuntary unemployment means it is impossible to find a suitable job, even by offering to work for a lower wage.

involuntary unemployment — unemployment resulting from inability to find a suitable job, even at a lower wage

A legal minimum wage above the equilibrium wage creates involuntary unemployment, for example. If the legal minimum wage, W_{min}, exceeds the equilibrium wage, as in **Figure 29.18,** L_S people want jobs, but only L_D people can find jobs. $L_S - L_D$ people are involuntarily unemployed. Voluntary unemployment, in contrast, occurs when people could take jobs but choose to remain unemployed instead, perhaps because available jobs pay too little, require work that is too unpleasant, or do not match the person's training or desires. To say that unemployment is voluntary does not imply that it is fun. Even voluntary unemployment may be extremely unpleasant, psychologically damaging, harmful to self-esteem, and a source of many other problems. A voluntarily unemployed person may be very unhappy; the choice not to work indicates that they see their opportunities as even worse.

The model in this chapter can explain involuntary unemployment. Suppose, for example, that aggregate demand decreases, as in Figure 29.15. In the short run, the economy moves from Point A to Point B. Real GDP falls from its full-employment level to y_2. At Point B, aggregate demand limits real GDP; firms could produce more than y_2, but they would be unable to sell it, so they don't produce more. They have no incentive to hire more workers, even if they could pay the extra workers lower wages, because the goods produced by these extra workers would go unsold.

Typically, a slowdown in money-supply growth leads to slower overall economic growth. And indeed, Japan's economy already is slowing somewhat, owing to the tight monetary policy the central bank has pursued since May 1989, when it began a series of interest-rate increases.

A slower growth rate of the money supply in Japan raises real interest rates there and reduces real GDP in the short run.

Source: The Asian Wall Street Journal, April 22, 1991, p. 6.

---

[20]For example, suppose (in the equation $MV = Py$) that $M = 100$, $V = 1$, $P = 100$, and $y = 1$. Also, suppose that nothing is changing so inflation is zero. Now suppose that M begins rising at 10 percent per year. After 1 year, $M = 110$. If V and y do not change, P rises to 110 after 1 year. If the money supply stops increasing (leaving it at 110, permanently higher than before), the price level stays at 110. In this case, the price level is higher, but inflation returns to its original level (zero).

FIGURE 29.18

INVOLUNTARY UNEMPLOYMENT DUE TO A MINIMUM LEGAL WAGE

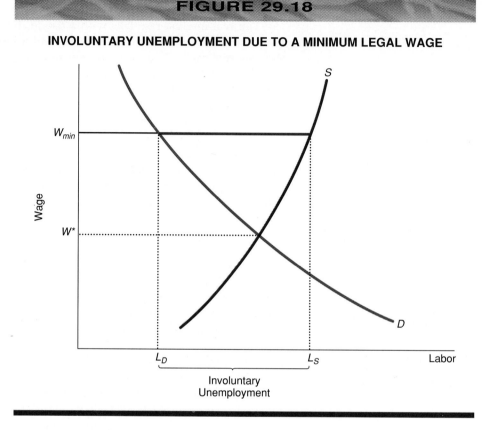

The earlier equilibrium model, in contrast, cannot explain involuntary unemployment. That model implies that people can always find jobs by offering to work at lower wages. Firms will hire them because those firms can always sell their extra output at lower prices. Firms are willing to hire more workers as long as they can pay sufficiently low wages, so they make a profit by hiring the workers and selling the extra output. If the equilibrium model were correct, all unemployment would be voluntary.

Is most unemployment voluntary or involuntary? This question is not easy to answer because hard evidence of involuntary unemployment is elusive. Nevertheless, many people believe that much unemployment during recessions is involuntary. If so, this supports the disequilibrium model and not the equilibrium model.

Finally, direct evidence does suggest that some prices are sticky. This raises the questions of why prices are sticky and how markets operate in the short run with sticky prices. No one has yet developed a good explanation for sticky prices. The next chapter will return to these issues and examine aggregate supply in more detail.

--- **FOR REVIEW** ---

29.13 Draw a graph to show how an exogenous increase in spending affects real GDP and the price level in the short run and in the long run.

29.14 What does it mean to claim that money is neutral?

―――――――――――――――――――― QUESTION ――――――――――――――――――――

29.15 What is involuntary unemployment? Explain why a fall in aggregate demand can cause involuntary unemployment if prices are sticky in the short run.

―――

CONCLUSIONS

PRICE STICKINESS AND DISEQUILIBRIUM

Economists say that nominal prices are sticky if they adjust to their new equilibrium levels only after a period of time following a change in supply or demand. Price stickiness may play a role in business cycles. In the long run, a fall in the money supply reduces nominal prices and does not affect real GDP. If prices are sticky in the short run, however, a fall in the money supply reduces real GDP as in the key example.

AGGREGATE DEMAND

Aggregate demand is the total demand for goods produced in the economy in a year. Aggregate demand can be described by two equations. First, real aggregate demand equals $C + I + G + EX - IM$. This shows the division of total spending on the economy's output among consumption, investment, government spending, and net exports. Second, real aggregate demand equals MV, the nominal money supply multiplied by the velocity of money, divided by the price level. This shows total spending each year, since $MV = Py$ and Py is total nominal spending. Economists graph aggregate demand with real GDP on the horizontal axis and the nominal price level on the vertical axis; the aggregate demand curve slopes downward.

CHANGES IN AGGREGATE DEMAND

Certain factors are held constant along the aggregate demand curve; a change in any of these factors shifts the aggregate demand curve. Aggregate demand increases if the nominal money supply increases, the velocity of money increases, spending on consumption or investment increases exogenously, government spending increases, foreign demand for domestic products increases exogenously, or domestic demand for foreign products decreases exogenously.

An exogenous $1 increase in spending can raise aggregate demand by more or less than $1. The increase in aggregate demand that results from an exogenous $1 rise in spending is called the *aggregate demand multiplier.*

AGGREGATE SUPPLY

Aggregate supply is the total supply of all goods and services produced in the economy this year. The long-run aggregate supply curve is a vertical line at the full-employment level of output. The short-run aggregate supply curve shows the total supply of all goods and services produced in the economy in the short run when prices are sticky. The short-run aggregate supply curve is horizontal if prices are completely sticky (fixed) in the short run.

COMBINING SHORT-RUN AGGREGATE SUPPLY AND DEMAND

The short-run aggregate demand curve is horizontal when prices are completely sticky. As time passes and prices begin to adjust, the aggregate supply curve

SOCIAL AND ECONOMIC ISSUES

Does the United States Spend Too Much? Should the United States Save More?

Since the middle of the 20th century, Japan has saved a much larger fraction of its GDP than the United States has. As an earlier chapter indicated, the Japanese economy has also grown much faster over that period than the U.S. economy. Japan's GDP per person grew from about one-sixth of the U.S. level in 1950 to one-third of the U.S. level in 1960 (its pre–World War II ratio), to near equality with the United States today. For the past decade, Japan has saved about one-third of its GDP, more than twice as much as the United States has saved. (These data refer to gross savings, that is, savings not adjusted for replacement of worn-out capital.)

Many economists argue that the United States should save more. Because an economy needs savings to provide investment, which is necessary for long-run economic growth, they argue that the United States is sacrificing the incomes of future generations (and of current generations when they become older) by saving only a small fraction of GDP.

Some respond to the assertion that people should save more by saying that if people would benefit by saving more and spending less, they would do so. (Don't they know what is best for themselves? Do economists, or the government, really know better?) Whether people should sacrifice the benefits of current spending for higher future incomes is a question that economics alone cannot answer. Perhaps every person should make that decision personally.

Many economists believe, however, that government policies are partly to blame for low savings in the United States. Government policies reduce savings in three main ways. First, most economists believe that government budget deficits reduce savings, and that high budget deficits of the U.S. federal government have contributed to low savings in the United States. An earlier chapter explained that an increase in the budget deficit raises the demand for loans as the government borrows more to finance its spending. That chapter also presented the majority view among economists that a deficit affect the supply of loans less than the demand, so the deficit raises the real interest rate and reduces savings. In essence, a government budget deficit means that the government dissaves (saves a negative amount), reducing total U.S. savings.

Government policies also reduce saving through the Social Security system. The Social Security system reduces private savings by helping to provide income for people at older ages, thereby reducing the amount that people need to save for themselves. In essence, people consider their Social Security taxes as contributions to a retirement account operated by the government from which they will collect income when they are older. However, unlike private retirement accounts, the U.S. government does not actually *save* the money that people pay in Social Security taxes. Until recently, the government simply collected Social Security taxes from workers and immediately paid that money to Social Security recipients. Currently, the government saves the excess of Social Security tax revenue over Social Security payments, but it does not save most of the money that

rotates until, in the long run, it is vertical. In the short run, an increase in the money supply reduces interest rates, and a decrease in the money supply raises interest rates; this is called the *liquidity effect* of a change in the money supply.

CONNECTIONS BETWEEN REAL AND NOMINAL VARIABLES

The equilibrium model of earlier chapters implied that money is neutral—changes in the money supply affect nominal prices but not real variables such as real GDP or unemployment. The sticky-price model, however, implies that money is *not* neutral—changes in the money supply have short-run effects on real GDP and other real variables. This is consistent with evidence that money is not neutral.

The sticky-price model can also explain short-run involuntary unemployment when workers cannot find suitable jobs, even by offering to work for lower

people pay in Social Security taxes. As a result, the Social Security system reduces U.S. national savings.

Finally, tax policies of the government tend to reduce savings. The tax system reduces the incentive to save by taxing income when people earn it, and then taxing the interest that people earn if they save their money. Taxes on investments also reduce the benefits of saving and investing, thereby reducing the incentive to save.

Together, the government budget deficit, the Social Security system, and the incentive effects of taxes probably reduce U.S. savings below the level that people would choose without these policies. In that sense, one could say that the United States saves too little.

Suppose that the U.S. government were to adopt policies to raise savings by changing the tax system, reducing the government budget deficit, or by encouraging people in other ways to save more for the future. How would an increase in savings affect the economy? Economists generally agree that it would raise investment, which in turn would raise the economy's future productive capacity and its future real GDP. An increase in savings, therefore, would raise people's incomes in the long run.

The models of aggregate demand and supply in this chapter imply, however, that in the short run an increase in savings would reduce real GDP by reducing consumption and aggregate demand, as in Figure 29.15. (An increase in savings would raise the supply of loans, reducing real and nominal interest rates. The fall in the nominal interest rate would reduce

velocity, decreasing aggregate demand, MV/P.) The idea that increased savings can reduce real GDP and that increased consumption spending can raise real GDP has a long history. Many noneconomists wrote about this idea in the 19th century, but economists rejected their arguments as incorrect. John Maynard Keynes first made the argument intellectually respectable in his famous book, *The General Theory of Employment, Income, and Prices.* Many Keynesian economists (those who adopted Keynes's arguments) influenced governments in subsequent years.

After World War II, the United States adopted policies to provide people with incentives to spend more and save less. These policies included taxes, legal limits on interest rates available to most savers, and expansion of a Social Security program that, by helping to provide income at older ages, reduced the incentive to save.

Most modern economists are more concerned with the long-run consequences of savings decisions. Some favor changes in tax and regulatory policies to raise the incentive to save. The long-run benefits of increased savings are clear. With short-run price stickiness, however, increased savings during a recession could make the recession worse rather than better. Choosing tax policies that encourage enough savings for rapid long-run growth while avoiding the short-run problems raised in this chapter is a difficult job, and it can raise questions of tradeoffs between short-run and long-run benefits.

wages. If aggregate demand is low, real GDP is below its full-employment level. In this case, unemployed workers cannot find jobs, even at lower wages, because firms would be unable to sell the goods they would produce.

Most economists believe that a model similar to the one in this chapter explains the Great Depression and other recessions, and it also explains the short-run effects of government policies and other changes in conditions that affect the economy.

LOOKING AHEAD

The next chapter discusses alternative models of aggregate supply and contrasts the models. The chapter after that discusses other theories of business cycles and connections between nominal and real variables. Those two chapters explore the

Source: *Richmond Times-Dispatch,* December 16, 1987, p. 12.

heart of the main controversies in macroeconomics today. Two subsequent chapters discuss government macroeconomic policies.

KEY TERMS

sticky nominal price

disequilibrium

foreign exchange rate

aggregate demand multiplier

short-run aggregate supply curve

liquidity effect

neutrality of money

involuntary unemployment

QUESTIONS AND PROBLEMS

29.16 Explain why aggregate demand falls if:
  a. The money supply falls
  b. The velocity of money falls
  c. Government spending decreases

29.17 Suppose that people decide to spend more going to ball games and to save less money. Explain how this affects:
  a. The real interest rate and the nominal interest rate
  b. The velocity of money
  c. Aggregate demand
  d. Real GDP and the price level in the short run and long run
  e. The current account in the short run

  If people spend $10 million more on ball games, does real GDP change by more or less than $10 million? Explain.

29.18 Suppose that the government raises spending by $20 billion and raises taxes by $20 billion to pay for the higher spending.

    a. Explain how this affects consumption and saving, interest rates, investment, velocity, the current account, and real GDP in the short run.

    b. How would your answer change if the government did not raise taxes to pay for increased spending, but borrowed the money instead?

    c. How would your answer change if the government did not raise taxes to pay for increased spending, but printed money to pay for the higher spending?

29.19 Use the aggregate demand and aggregate supply model to explain how a tax cut could raise real GDP and reduce unemployment in an economy with low output.

29.20 How would an increase in the price of imported oil affect long-run aggregate supply? Explain.

29.21 How is aggregate demand likely to react to an increase in consumer confidence about the future of the economy?

INQUIRIES FOR FURTHER THOUGHT

29.22 Should the United States adopt policies to reduce consumption spending and increase savings? What are the benefits and costs of a policy like this? Why did earlier chapters imply that an increase in saving raises productivity and future output, while according to this chapter, an increase in saving reduces aggregate demand and real GDP?

29.23 Why are prices sticky? Does price stickiness imply that the economy operates inefficiently?

TAG SOFTWARE APPLICATIONS

TUTORIAL EXERCISES
▶ The module contains a review of the key terms from Chapter 29.

GRAPHING EXERCISES
▶ The graphing segment includes questions on aggregate demand, the factors that increase or decrease aggregate demand, aggregate supply in the long and short runs, and the determination of long-run equilibrium.

350 | 40
320 | .87   87%
3°
28

530 | 60
480 | .088
500

40 | 2
36 | × 44
40

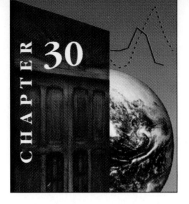

ALTERNATIVE THEORIES OF AGGREGATE SUPPLY

read
pp. 887 – 902 &
910 — 917

WHAT THIS CHAPTER IS ABOUT

▶ Relationship between inflation and unemployment

▶ Unresolved issues among economists about aggregate supply

▶ Effects of sticky prices, sticky wages, and imperfect information on aggregate supply

▶ Effects of changes in aggregate demand and supply

▶ Recessions

Government policymakers need to understand the causes of business cycles and the consequences of alternative economic policies before they can choose the best policies to adopt. Currently, however, economists lack a full understanding of business cycles and the causes of recessions. Much of this uncertainty, and resulting disagreement, concerns aggregate supply. This chapter and the next discuss alternative models of aggregate supply and their consequences for business cycles and the effects of government policies.

AGGREGATE SUPPLY AND AGGREGATE DEMAND

The last chapter examined an extreme case of a *completely* sticky price level—prices fixed at some level—in the short run. This extreme case, the simple Keynesian model, may portray some situations realistically, but most economists believe that the short-run aggregate supply curve slopes upward rather than running horizontally, as in the last chapter. **Figure 30.1** shows an upward-sloping short-run aggregate supply curve, AS^{SR}. The curve slopes upward because prices are not *completely* sticky, even in the short run.

Aggregate supply shows the total supply of all goods and services produced in the economy per month or year. Short-run aggregate supply measures the supply of goods and services before prices have fully adjusted to a change in conditions; long-run aggregate supply measures supply after prices have fully adjusted. As in the last chapter, the long-run aggregate supply curve is a vertical line at the full-employment level of output.

Each aggregate supply curve holds constant the economy's technology and factors that affect the supplies of capital, labor, and other inputs. Any change in

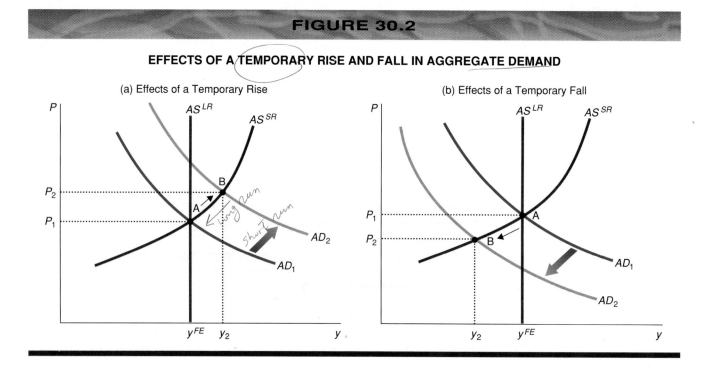

technology or these factors causes a change in aggregate supply—a shift in the aggregate supply curve. Aggregate supply increases if technology improves or if supplies of inputs increase. Aggregate supply decreases if supplies of inputs decrease (for example, if the price of imported oil rises). Changes in taxes or government regulations can shift the aggregate supply curve by changing incentives to work or to invest in new capital equipment. An increase in education and skills makes workers more productive, which raises aggregate supply.

CHANGES IN AGGREGATE DEMAND

This section uses an upward-sloping short-run aggregate supply curve to discuss the effects of changes in aggregate demand or supply. These effects depend on whether the change is temporary or permanent. Panel a of **Figure 30.2** shows the effects of a temporary increase in aggregate demand from AD_1 to AD_2. The economy starts from short-run and long-run equilibrium at Point A. In the short run, the economy moves from there to Point B as real GDP rises from y^{FE} to y_2 and the price level rises from P_1 to P_2. The increase in aggregate demand is only temporary, though. In the long run, the aggregate demand curve shifts back to AD_1 and the economy returns to its short-run and long-run equilibrium at Point A.

Panel b of Figure 30.2 shows the effect of a temporary decrease in aggregate demand from AD_1 to AD_2. In the short run, the economy moves from Point A to Point B as real GDP falls from y^{FE} to y_2 and the price level falls from P_1 to P_2. Because the change in aggregate demand is only temporary, the aggregate demand curve shifts back to AD_1 in the long run and the economy returns to its short-run and long-run equilibrium at Point A.

FIGURE 30.2

EFFECTS OF A TEMPORARY RISE AND FALL IN AGGREGATE DEMAND

FIGURE 30.3

EFFECTS OF A PERMANENT RISE AND FALL IN AGGREGATE DEMAND

(a) Effects of a Permanent Rise

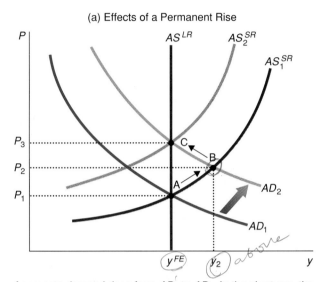

(b) Effects of a Permanent Fall

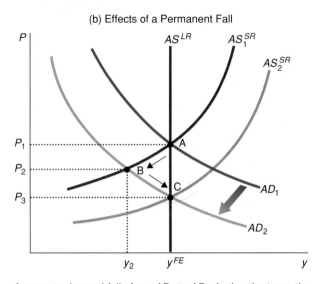

Aggregate demand rises from AD_1 to AD_2. In the short run, the economy moves from Point A to Point B as the price level rises from P_1 to P_2 and real GDP rises from y^{FE} to y_2. In the long run, the economy moves to Point C, where the new aggregate demand curve intersects the long-run aggregate supply curve. The short-run aggregate supply curve shifts from AS_1^{SR} to AS_2^{SR}, and intersects the aggregate demand curve at Point C. The price level rises all the way to P_3, and real GDP falls back to its full-employment level, y^{FE}.

Aggregate demand falls from AD_1 to AD_2. In the short run, the economy moves from Point A to Point B as the price level falls from P_1 to P_2 and real GDP falls from y^{FE} to y_2. In the long run, the economy moves to Point C, where the new aggregate demand curve intersects the long-run aggregate supply curve. The short-run aggregate supply curve shifts from AS_1^{SR} to AS_2^{SR} and intersects the aggregate demand curve at Point C. The price level falls all the way to P_3, and real GDP rises back to its full-employment level, y^{FE}.

Figure 30.3 shows the effects of permanent changes in aggregate demand. Panel a of Figure 30.3 shows a permanent increase in aggregate demand from AD_1 to AD_2. The economy starts from short-run and long-run equilibrium at Point A. In the short run, it moves from there to Point B as real GDP rises from y^{FE} to y_2 and the price level rises from P_1 to P_2. In the long run, the economy moves from Point B to Point C, where the new aggregate demand curve intersects the long-run aggregate supply curve. The price level rises to P_3 and real GDP falls back to its full-employment level, y^{FE}. Notice that in the long run, the short-run aggregate supply curve shifts from AS_1^{SR} to AS_2^{SR}, so that both the short-run and long-run aggregate supply curves intersect the new aggregate demand curve at Point C.

Panel b of Figure 30.3 shows the effects of a permanent decrease in aggregate demand from AD_1 to AD_2. In the short run, the economy moves from Point A to Point B. Real GDP falls from y^{FE} to y_2 and the price level falls from P_1 to P_2. In the long run, the economy moves from Point B to Point C as the price level falls to P_3 and real GDP rises back to its full-employment level, y^{FE}. The short-run aggregate supply curve shifts in the long run from AS_1^{SR} to AS_2^{SR}, so that both the short-run and long-run aggregate supply curves intersect the new aggregate demand curve at Point C.

FIGURE 30.4

EFFECTS OF A PERMANENT RISE AND FALL IN AGGREGATE SUPPLY

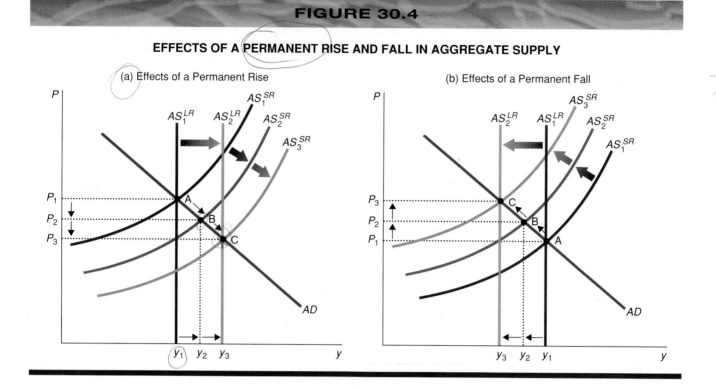

(a) Effects of a Permanent Rise

(b) Effects of a Permanent Fall

CHANGES IN AGGREGATE SUPPLY

Figure 30.4 shows the effects of permanent changes in aggregate supply. The economy begins in long-run and short-run equilibrium at Point A. In Panel a of Figure 30.4, an improvement in technology permanently raises aggregate supply, so the short-run and long-run aggregate supply curves shift to AS_2^{SR} and AS_2^{LR}. The economy moves to a new *short-run* equilibrium at Point B as real GDP rises to y_2 and the price level falls to P_2. Eventually, the economy moves to a new short-run and long-run equilibrium at Point C as real GDP rises to y_3 and prices fall to P_3. When the economy moves to its long-run equilibrium, the short-run aggregate supply curve shifts from AS_2^{SR} to AS_3^{SR} so that the new short-run and long-run aggregate supply curves intersect the aggregate demand curve at Point C.

Panel b of Figure 30.4 shows a permanent decrease in aggregate supply. A permanent rise in the price of an imported input (such as crude oil) shifts the short-run and long-run aggregate supply curves to AS_2^{SR} and AS_2^{LR}. The economy moves to a new short-run equilibrium at Point B as real GDP falls to y_2 and the price level rises to P_2. Eventually, the economy moves to a new short-run and long-run equilibrium at Point C as real GDP falls to y_3 and the price rises to P_3. As the economy moves to its new long-run equilibrium, the short-run aggregate supply curve shifts from AS_2^{SR} to AS_3^{SR}. In the long run, the new short-run and long-run aggregate supply curves intersect the aggregate demand curve at Point C.

AGGREGATE SUPPLY: THE STICKY-PRICE THEORY

The short-run aggregate supply curve sparks controversy among economists. This chapter discusses three alternative models of the short-run aggregate supply curve. The first model, the sticky-price theory of aggregate supply, is often called a *New Keynesian theory*. Like the simple Keynesian model discussed in the last chapter, it postulates that prices are sticky in the short run, but it assumes that prices are not *completely* sticky. The price level can change in the short run, but not far enough or quickly enough to reach the new equilibrium level. In the short run, prices remain stuck near their past levels. The sticky-price theory implies that the short-run aggregate supply curve slopes upward, as in Figure 30.1

In the long run, prices are no longer stuck near their past levels; prices become free to move to their new long-run equilibrium levels. When this happens, the short-run aggregate supply curve shifts. For example, consider a permanent increase in aggregate demand like that in Figure 30.3a. The economy moves from Point A to Point B in the short run because prices are sticky and do not rise all the way to P_3 (the new long-run equilibrium level). In the long run, prices escape their limits from the past, so the short-run aggregate supply curve shifts from AS_1^{SR} to AS_2^{SR} and the economy moves to Point C.

Similarly, consider a permanent fall in aggregate supply like that in Figure 30.4b. The economy begins in long-run and short-run equilibrium at Point A. A permanent rise in the price of imported oil shifts the long-run aggregate supply curve to AS_2^{LR} and the short-run aggregate supply curve to AS_2^{SR}. The economy moves to Point B in the short run because prices are sticky. Eventually, prices adjust to their new, long-run equilibrium levels. When that happens, the short-run supply curve shifts from AS_2^{SR} to AS_3^{SR} and the economy moves to Point C.

REASONS FOR PRICE STICKINESS

Some prices adjust quickly to changes in demand or supply. Others adjust slowly.[1] Although many prices appear to be sticky, economists do not yet know precisely why. They have proposed several explanations.

MENU COSTS

Some prices are sticky because they are hard or costly to change. For example, it is costly to print new catalogs or menus with new prices. These costs are called menu costs.

menu cost — a cost of changing prices

Menu costs are the costs of changing prices.

Menu costs can become large in some cases, for example, when stores must put new price tags on many separate items. Menu costs are small in other cases, for example, when a seller can simply post a new sign to announce the new price. The menu-cost idea remains controversial, and economists are currently looking for more evidence on menu costs and sticky prices.

LARGE AND SMALL PRICE CHANGES   If menu costs were the main reason for sticky prices, then sellers would not change prices very often; price changes would be large and infrequent. A seller would not issue a new catalog every time a price needed changing, but when the price moved far enough away from equilibrium,

---

[1]When the price of a product adjusts slowly, other features of the product often change instead. For example, it takes buyers longer to get the product delivered after they order it.

IN THE NEWS

Electronic price labels tested in supermarkets

By Richard Gibson
Staff Reporter of
The Wall Street Journal

Prices of more than 500 items will change today at Bauersfeld's supermarket in Topeka, Kan., but the clerks won't have to peel outdated labels off the shelves.

Instead, they will change the prices electronically, plugging a hand held computer into programmable labels clipped to the store's shelves. The computer sends a signal to a microchip in the molded plastic label, which then displays the new price in half-inch-high liquid crystal numerals.

Such devices are part of the grocery industry's continuing effort to reduce overhead with technology. Already more than half of the nation's supermarkets have electronic scanners at checkouts to ring up prices of bar-coded packages. Programmable shelf labeling promises to trim labor costs further and allow quicker price changes than are now possible.

Technology's Cost

"It's something everybody would like to do," says H. D. (Skip) Smith, vice president of information services at Super Valu Stores Inc., the

nation's largest food wholesaler. "It all depends on the cost."

The new labeling technology isn't cheap; retrofitting a typical supermarket could cost well over $100,000. But many people in the industry see advantages for customer and merchant alike. For the grocer, programmed labeling could cut labor costs. "Usually it takes one guy close to nine hours to change 600 labels," says a Bauersfeld's supervisor. Changing labels electronically should cut the repricing time significantly, he says.

Technical change can reduce menu costs.

Source: Richard Gibson, "Electronic Price Labels Tested in Supermarkets," *The Wall Street Journal*, March 31, 1988, p. 25.

the seller would issue a new catalog with a large price change. The evidence, however, shows more small price changes than economists would expect if menu costs were the main cause of sticky prices. Some economists believe that this implies that menu costs do not cause sticky prices.

STAGGERED PRICE SETTING Despite menu costs, firms may make small changes in prices if different firms change prices at different times. The amount by which each seller changes a price depends on how much that seller expects competitors to change their prices. A seller may fear losing too many customers from one sudden, large price increase, so the seller may make small price changes and wait for other sellers to follow. Prices would then adjust slowly to the equilibrium level as sellers would take turns making small price changes.

Consider, for example, a town with two grocery stores. Suppose that an increase in the demand for groceries raises the equilibrium price by 10 percent, and that Acme Foods raises its prices first. Acme will not want to raise its prices too much, because it may lose customers to the other grocery store, Big Bear, so Acme raises its prices a small amount, say, 2 percent. Big Bear also raises its prices eventually because its prices are below the new equilibrium price. When Big Bear decides to raise prices, it faces the same problem that Acme did; if it raises prices too much, it will lose many customers to the other store. Big Bear raises its prices only a little—say, 2 percent—above Acme's prices. This leaves prices at both stores below the equilibrium price, so the same thing happens again; Acme raises prices again to slightly above Big Bear's prices. Big Bear then raises prices again, above Acme's prices, by a small amount. This process continues until prices at both stores reach the new equilibrium level.

This explanation does not work as well, however, for price decreases as it does for price increases. When the equilibrium price falls, sellers have an incentive to cut prices quickly, all the way to the equilibrium level. By cutting prices a large amount, each seller gets a chance to gain customers from other stores.

STICKY INPUT PRICES

Another explanation asserts that prices of final goods and services may be sticky because the prices of certain inputs (such as labor) are sticky. Sticky input prices create stickiness in marginal costs. Of course, this raises the question of why input prices are sticky. One answer is that workers often sign contracts with their employers that set nominal wages for a year or longer, until the parties negotiate new contracts. A later section discusses nominal wage contracts.

PREFERENCES FOR STABLE PRICES

Some economists believe that prices are sticky because buyers and sellers like prices to stay constant rather than change. A stable price may be convenient when buyers and sellers deal repeatedly with each other. Buyers may reason that sometimes they pay more than the equilibrium price, and other times they pay less, so that it all evens out in the end. Sellers may reason the same way. The trouble with this explanation comes from the difficulty of explaining why people like constant nominal prices. People may benefit from stable *relative* prices, but the benefits of stable nominal prices are harder to understand.

DISCUSSION

Some evidence indicates that many prices are sticky in the short run; they remain constant or change very little despite changes in demand or supply. Evidence also shows that the price level responds slowly to changes in the nominal money supply. An increase in the money supply raises the price level by the same amount (in percentage terms) in the *long run,* but by very little in the short run. It may take several years for the price level to rise to its new, long-run equilibrium. Economists are currently debating and seeking new evidence on the issues associated with price stickiness.[2] Meanwhile, many economists believe that the model of short-run aggregate supply based on sticky prices can be a useful tool.

─────────────── **FOR REVIEW** ───────────────

30.1 Why might prices be sticky?

30.2 According to the sticky-price theory, what makes the short-run aggregate supply curve rotate to the long-run aggregate supply curve?

─────────────────────

[2]Even the results of price stickiness remain uncertain; see the next chapter.

--- QUESTIONS ---

30.3 Use the sticky-price theory to explain what happens, in the short run and the long run, when aggregate demand falls.

30.4 According to the sticky-price theory, why does the short-run aggregate supply curve not become vertical when it reaches the full-employment level of output?

AGGREGATE SUPPLY: THE STICKY-WAGE THEORY

A second model of aggregate supply, the sticky-wage theory of aggregate supply, asserts that the aggregate supply curve slopes upward, as in Figure 30.1, not because product prices are sticky, but because nominal wages are sticky in the short run.

> According to the sticky-wage theory, the nominal wage is sticky in the short run, but the prices of final products are not.[3]

Although the sticky-wage theory does not assume a sticky price level, later discussions will reveal that the theory predicts a slow movement in the price level to its new, long-run equilibrium level after a change in aggregate demand or supply. So the theory is consistent with evidence of sticky product prices.

REASONS FOR STICKY NOMINAL WAGES

Evidence shows that many workers' nominal wages remain constant for periods of months or years. Many economists view this as evidence of sticky wages. They believe that long-run equilibrium wages change more than the wages actually receive, that is, that actual wages are sticky.

Why don't wages change more often? It is tempting to suggest that workers *like* constant wages because the stability reduces uncertainty. If wages changed every week, it would be hard for workers to plan their household budgets. Perhaps sticky wages can provide workers with predictable sources of income. Unfortunately, this tempting argument overlooks two facts: more stable wages often mean less stable employment, and workers care about their real wages, not their nominal wages.

Employment becomes less stable when wages are sticky. When the demand for a product falls, its producer would lay off fewer workers if it could reduce wages instead. The workers who would lose their jobs from a fall in demand would probably prefer lower wages to unemployment![4] Although stable wages reduce one kind of risk that workers face (the risk of a fall in wages), they increase the risk of unemployment.

Nominal wages are not important to workers; real wages are.

real wage — the purchasing power of a wage

> The **real wage** is the purchasing power of a wage; the real wage is measured in base-year dollars.

---

[3]Some versions of this theory hold that product prices are *also* sticky. This section will discuss the simpler case in which product prices are not sticky.

[4]Some economists have proposed to reduce unemployment by automatically reducing wages when profits are low (which happens when product demand falls) and raising them when profits are high.

The real wage equals the nominal wage divided by the price level. For example, if you earn a nominal wage of $100 per day and goods cost $5 each, you can buy 20 goods with one day's wages. Your *real wage* is 20 goods per day. Writing this as an equation:

$$w = W/P \qquad\qquad (30.1)$$

where w is the real wage, W is the nominal wage, and P is the nominal price level.

A nominal wage shows only how much money a worker earns; a real wage shows how much the worker can *buy* with that money. Changes in nominal wages and real wages differ because of inflation. To reduce uncertainty, workers would want sticky real wages rather than sticky nominal wages.

The evidence, however, indicates that most nominal wages do not rise quickly in response to surprise (unexpected) inflation, so unexpected inflation reduces real wages in the short run. Some nominal wages are indexed to inflation so that surprise inflation does not change the real wages.

indexed wage —a nominal wage that changes automatically when the price level changes

An **indexed wage** is a wage that changes automatically when the price level changes.

Workers who receive automatic cost-of-living wage increases have indexed wages.[5] A wage is completely indexed to inflation if the nominal wage changes by the same percentage as the price level, so that the real wage does not change at all. For example, suppose that inflation is 10 percent per year. If a worker's nominal wage also rises by 10 percent, then the real wage has not changed. If the wage changes automatically to keep up with inflation, then it is completely indexed.[6] A nominal wage is incompletely indexed if it changes automatically, but by a smaller percentage than the price level. For example, suppose that 10 percent inflation automatically raises a worker's wage by 6 percent; then the wage is incompletely indexed to inflation.

In fact, most nominal wages are *not* indexed to inflation, or not completely indexed. This provides evidence of nominal-wage stickiness. Although unexpected inflation reduces real wages, nominal wages generally change with *expected* inflation so that fully expected inflation does not affect real wages.

The important question of wage stickiness hinges on whether the wages workers actually receive vary as much as equilibrium wages. Economists have little direct evidence on this question because it is difficult to estimate the equilibrium wage. They must always contend with uncertainty about the exact positions of supply and demand curves. Current evidence supports some reasonable conclusions:

Many nominal wages remain constant for months or years.

Nominal wages respond fairly quickly to changes in expected inflation.

Nominal wages do not respond quickly or fully to unexpected inflation, so unexpected inflation changes real wages.

Economists do not yet completely understand why wages are not completely indexed to inflation, nor do they yet have a good explanation for sticky nominal wages. Many economists believe that, while an explanation for sticky wages

---

[5]Cost-of-living adjustments in wages are sometimes called *COLAs*.

[6]The worker would get a 5 percent cost-of-living wage increase if inflation were 5 percent, a 15 percent increase if inflation were 15 percent, and a 3 percent cut in wages if inflation were −3 percent.

FIGURE 30.5

LABOR MARKET EQUILIBRIUM

W is the nominal wage and *P* is the price level, so *W/P* is the real wage.

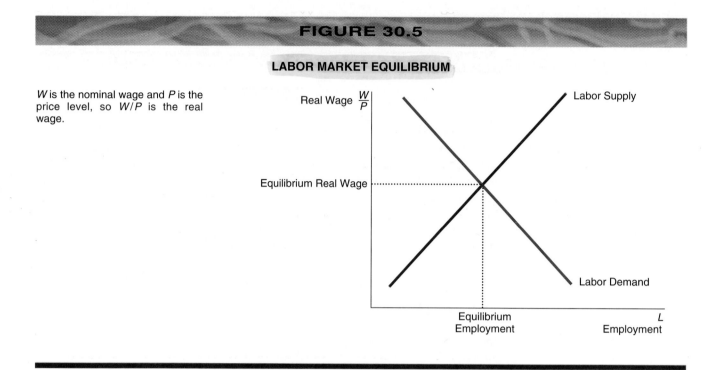

would be nice, it is not necessary for understanding the short-run behavior of the economy. They argue that wages clearly are sticky and that they need to study only the results of that stickiness. Other economists believe that the reasons for wage or price stickiness may affect the results.[7] Economists continue to debate and discuss the issues associated with wage stickiness.

AGGREGATE SUPPLY WITH STICKY NOMINAL WAGES

The sticky-wage model implies that the short-run aggregate supply curve slopes upward, as in Figure 30.1. While the curve looks the same as that in the sticky-price model, its interpretation differs slightly.

Figure 30.5 shows the demand for labor and supply of labor. The demand and supply both depend on the real wage. The intersection gives the equilibrium real wage.

EFFECTS OF A STICKY NOMINAL WAGE

If the nominal wage were not sticky, it would change whenever the price level changed so that the real wage would remain at its equilibrium level. (If *W* and *P* rise in the same proportion, then *W/P* stays constant.) The nominal wage would also change whenever the equilibrium real wage changed, due to changes in supply or demand, to move the real wage to its new equilibrium level.

With a *sticky* nominal wage, however, a change in the price level causes a change in the real wage. A fall in the price level raises the real wage (the fall in *P*

---

[7]See the next chapter.

FIGURE 30.6

EFFECTS OF A FALL AND RISE IN THE PRICE LEVEL WITH STICKY NOMINAL WAGES

(a) Effects of a Fall in the Price Level

(b) Effects of a Rise in the Price Level

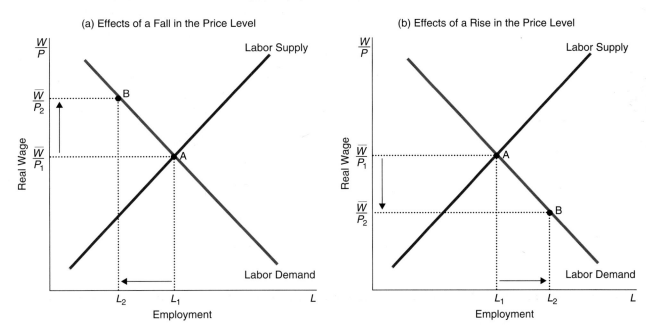

The nominal wage is fixed at $\overline{W}$. The price level falls from P_1 to P_2, so the real wage rises from $\overline{W}/P_1$ to $\overline{W}/P_2$. This reduces the quantity of labor demanded, and employment, from L_1 to L_2.

The nominal wage is fixed at $\overline{W}$. The price level rises from P_1 to P_2, so the real wage falls from $\overline{W}/P_1$ to $\overline{W}/P_2$. This raises the quantity of labor demanded, and employment, from L_1 to L_2.

raises W/P). This reduces the quantity of labor demanded, which reduces employment, as in Panel a of **Figure 30.6,** and the fall in employment reduces real GDP. Similarly, a rise in the price level reduces the real wage (the rise in P reduces W/P) and raises the quantity of labor demanded, which raises employment and real GDP, as in Panel b of Figure 30.6.

As in the sticky-price model, aggregate supply curves in the sticky-wage model hold constant the economy's technology and factors that affect input supplies. Changes in these factors shift aggregate supply. One difference separates the models:

In the sticky-*price* model, the short-run aggregate supply curve shifts when the nominal price level eventually adjusts to its long-run equilibrium.

In the sticky-*wage* model, the short-run aggregate supply curve shifts when the nominal wages eventually adjust to their long-run equilibrium.

EXPLANATION   With a sticky nominal wage, a fall in the price level raises the real wage. Suppose that workers and firms sign a 2-year labor contract in 1996 that obligates firms to pay wages of $8 per hour in 1996 and 1997. After the contract is signed, suppose that the government permanently reduces the nominal money supply, M. The fall in the money supply reduces the price level from P_1 to P_2, as in Figure 30.6a.[8] (Remember that the price level is *not* sticky in the sticky-wage model; only the nominal wage is sticky. People have less money to spend, so the price level falls.) The fall in P reduces the real wage from $w_1 = \$8/P_1$ to $w_2 = \$8/P_2$. At this higher real wage, the quantity of labor demanded (the number of workers that firms are willing to employ) falls from L_1 to L_2, so employment falls from L_1 to L_2 (Point A to Point B) in Figure 30.6a. This fall in employment reduces real GDP.

The movement from Point A to Point B in Figure 30.6a is the same as the movement from Point A to Point B in Figure 30.3b, where the fall in the money supply reduces aggregate demand from AD_1 to AD_2. The fall in employment from L_1 to L_2 in Figure 30.6a corresponds to the fall in real GDP from y^{FE} to y_2 in Figure 30.3b.

Employment and output stay at these lower levels until firms and workers sign new labor contracts in 1998 to reduce the nominal wage. This fall in the nominal wage reduces the real wage, and raises employment back to its long-run equilibrium level; the economy moves from Point B in Figure 30.6a back to Point A.[9] When firms and workers renegotiate contracts and the nominal wage falls, the short-run aggregate supply curve in Figure 30.3b shifts from AS_1^{SR} to AS_2^{SR}. The price level then falls to P_3 and output rises back to y^{FE}, moving the economy to a new short-run and long-run equilibrium at Point C. Notice that the price level falls less in the short run than in the long run even though the price level is *not* sticky.[10] (Only the nominal wage is sticky.)

Figure 30.6b shows the effects of a permanent rise in the money supply after a labor contract has been signed. The increase in the money supply raises aggregate demand from AD_1 to AD_2 in Figure 30.3a, which raises the price level from P_1 to P_2. This reduces the real wage from $w_1 = \$8/P_1$ to $w_2 = \$8/P_2$ and raises the quantity of labor demanded from L_1 to L_2 in Figure 30.6b. If labor contracts allow firms to choose employment, then employment rises from L_1 to L_2 and the economy moves from Point A to Point B in Figure 30.6b.[11] This corresponds to moving from Point A to Point B in Figure 30.3a, which takes real GDP from y^{FE} to y_2.

Eventually, in the long run, labor contracts are renegotiated and the nominal wage rises; this increases the real wage and reduces employment back to L_1 in Figure 30.6b (from Point B back to Point A). This wage increase shifts the short-run aggregate supply curve in Figure 30.3a from AS_1^{SR} to AS_2^{SR}, and output falls back to y^{FE}.

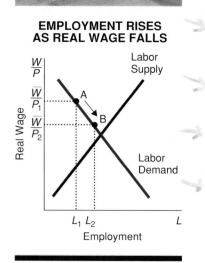

FIGURE 30.7

**EMPLOYMENT RISES
AS REAL WAGE FALLS**

---

[8]The fall in the money supply reduces the left-hand side of the equation $MV = Py$. To balance the equation, the right-hand side must fall (assuming that V does not change). In the short run, both P and y fall to reduce the right-hand side. (V is also likely to fall somewhat.) In the long run, the fall in the right-hand side occurs completely through a fall in P.

[9]Total employment and real GDP may take longer to return to their original levels because contracts are staggered. Some firms had signed contracts in 1996 just before the money supply fell, and those contracts will not come up for renewal until 1998; some firms and workers may have longer contracts that will not be renegotiated until 1999.

[10]The fall in the money supply reduces the left-hand side of the equation $MV = Py$. In the long run, the price level P will fall to reduce the right-hand side of the equation. In the short run, the fall in real GDP (y) helps to reduce the right-hand side of the equation, so P does not need to fall as much in the short run as in the long run.

[11]You might wonder why employment equals the quantity demanded at the lower real wage $w_2 = \$8/P_2$ rather than the quantity supplied. There are two answers. First, many labor contracts allow firms to choose levels of employment. Second, labor contracts might set nominal wages so that real wages start out higher than the intersection of supply and demand, as at Point A in **Figure 30.7**. This may occur for several reasons connected with the operations of labor markets, union wage-setting, or firms' attempts to raise productivity by paying above-equilibrium wages. Starting at Point A in Figure 30.7, a rise in the price level moves the economy to Point B; the real wage falls and employment rises from L_1 to L_2.

EXPECTED AND UNEXPECTED INFLATION

The sticky-wage model predicts that inflation affects employment and real GDP only if it was unexpected when the nominal wage was set. Workers and firms would have agreed on a higher real wage to adjust for any expected inflation. For example, suppose that workers and firms know that all nominal prices will rise 10 percent in the second year of the labor contract discussed in the last section. They could keep the real wage at its equilibrium level by writing a contract that would set the nominal wage at $8.00 per hour in 1996 and $8.84 per hour (10 percent higher) in 1997. The prediction that only unexpected changes in the price level affect employment and real GDP receives support from evidence that surprise (unexpected) changes in the money supply have larger effects on real output than predictable changes. This relationship remains controversial because some evidence suggests that even predictable changes in the money supply or inflation have temporary effects on real GDP. Still surprise changes in the money supply and inflation seem to have larger effects on real GDP. Surprise changes in the money supply can create surprise inflation, while predictable changes in the money supply create predictable inflation. This evidence supports the sticky-wage model.

CYCLICAL BEHAVIOR OF REAL WAGES

The sticky-wage model implies that a fall in aggregate demand raises the real wage and reduces output and that a rise in aggregate demand lowers the real wage and increases output. In other words, the model implies that shifts in aggregate demand make real wages move countercyclically, rising when real GDP falls in the short run (during recessions), and falling when output rises (during recoveries). The evidence suggests, however, that real wages in the United States move mildly procyclically; they fall when real GDP falls (during recessions), and rise when real GDP rises (during recoveries). This evidence leads some economists to question the value of the sticky-wage model to explain short-run aggregate supply.[12]

──────────────── **FOR REVIEW** ────────────────

30.5 Why might nominal wages be sticky? What evidence suggests that they are, or are not, sticky?

30.6 What is the connection between the nominal wage and the real wage?

30.7 Discuss the evidence on the cyclical behavior of real wages and the predictions of the sticky-wage model.

──────────────── **QUESTIONS** ────────────────

30.8 Suppose that aggregate demand falls.
   a. Draw a diagram of the demand and supply for labor to explain how this change affects employment and the real wage in the short run and long run.
   b. Draw a graph of aggregate demand and supply to show what happens to output and the price level in the short run and the long run.

30.9 According to the sticky-wage model, what makes the short-run aggregate supply curve rotate to the long-run aggregate supply curve?

───────────────────────────────────────

[12]The evidence is not strong enough, however, to fully refute the sticky-wage model.

AGGREGATE SUPPLY: THE IMPERFECT-INFORMATION THEORY

This section will discuss a third model of aggregate supply, the *imperfect-information theory of aggregate supply,* also called the *misperceptions theory.* This theory is usually considered a New Classical theory rather than a New Keynesian theory because it tries to explain business cycles without appealing to sticky prices or wages. (The next chapter will discuss another kind of New Classical theory.) The imperfect-information theory does not say that prices and wages are sticky. Instead, it says that the short-run aggregate supply curve slopes upward (as in Figure 30.1) because sellers sometimes make mistakes. They sometimes confuse *nominal* price changes with *relative* price changes.

Suppose that a surprise increase in the price level produces higher inflation than people expect. When a seller sees an unexpected increase in the nominal price of the good he sells, he may mistakenly believe that it represents an increase in the relative price of that good. Because the seller incorrectly believes that the relative price is higher, he raises output. As other sellers make similar mistakes, unexpected increases in the price level (unexpected inflation) raise real GDP.

Similarly, the theory says that when inflation is unexpectedly low, output falls. When a seller sees an unexpectedly small rise (or an unexpected fall) in the nominal price of the good that she sells, she may mistakenly believe that its relative price has fallen, so she reduces output. As other sellers make similar mistakes, unexpected small increases (or unexpected decreases) in the price level reduce real GDP.

The incomplete-information model implies that the short-run aggregate supply curve slopes upward, as in Figure 30.1. The curve looks the same as in the sticky-price and sticky-wage models, but it has a different interpretation.

EXPLANATION

Suppose that the economy confronts an unexpected 10 percent increase in the money supply. We will first discuss what happens if everyone knows about the money-supply increase. Then we will discuss what happens if most sellers don't know about the money-supply increase.

WHEN SELLERS KNOW *about the money supply increase :*
If the money supply rises by 10 percent and everyone knows about it, prices will quickly rise by 10 percent and real GDP will not change. Without sticky prices or imperfect information, money remains neutral—a change in the money supply does not affect real GDP or other real variables. A 10 percent increase in the money supply would raise all nominal prices and wages by 10 percent, so relative prices would remain unchanged. The short-run aggregate supply curve would be the same as the long-run aggregate supply curve, and the economy would move immediately from its old long-run equilibrium at Point A in Figure 30.3a to its new long-run equilibrium at Point C. To see why, recall the discussion on currency reforms from an earlier chapter. An increase in the money supply and all nominal prices and wages is similar to a currency reform in reverse, so if the money supply changes and people know about it, nominal prices change but relative prices and real GDP stay the same. Notice that this happens regardless of whether people expect the change in the money supply or not. What matters is that people know about it when it happens.[13]

---

[13]This discussion abstracts from the real effects of inflation on the distribution of income and incentives that the earlier chapter on inflation discussed.

FIGURE 30.8

WHAT SELLERS MAY BELIEVE WHEN THE PRICE LEVEL RISES

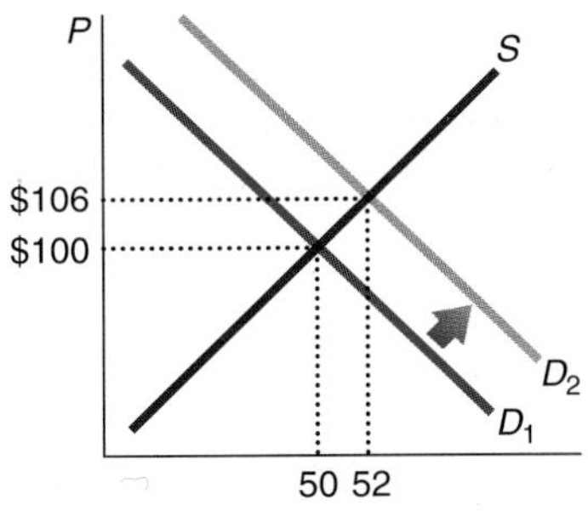

WHEN SELLERS DON'T KNOW *about the money supply increase:*

Now suppose that most sellers don't know about the money-supply increase. The 10 percent increase in the money supply then raises both the price level and real GDP in the short run. To see why, suppose that you make and sell bicycles. When people start spending the newly printed money, more people come to your store with more money to buy bicycles. You don't know about the money-supply increase, though; you think that the demand for bicycles has increased, as in **Figure 30.8,** so you raise your price from $100 to $106 and raise your output from 50 to 52 bikes per week. You produce more bicycles because you believe, incorrectly, that the relative price of bicycles has increased by 6 percent. Although you don't know it, the same thing happens throughout the economy as other sellers see people spending more money in their stores and raise their prices and outputs. No one knows that nominal prices of other products are also rising by 6 percent. For this reason, you believe (incorrectly) that the *relative price* of your bicycles is 6 percent higher, and you produce more bicycles.

The same reasoning applies throughout the economy. Most sellers, in most industries, raise output along with their nominal prices. Each seller incorrectly thinks that the increase in the nominal price of its own good is an increase in its relative price. Real GDP rises from y^{FE} to y_2 in Figure 30.3a; employment rises and unemployment falls. The economy moves from Point A to Point B.

Although prices are not sticky, the model predicts that the price level rises by less than 10 percent in the short run, because output rises. Recall that:

$$\%\Delta M + \%\Delta V = \%\Delta P + \%\Delta y$$

The money supply, *M,* rises by 10 percent. Velocity, *V,* does not change. (Its percentage change is zero.) Because the left-hand side of the equation rises by 10 percent, the right-hand side must also rise by 10 percent. In this example, prices rise by 6 percent in the short run and real GDP rises by 4 percent.[14]

Eventually, sellers learn that they have made mistakes. Each seller finds out that the price level increased and realizes that the *relative* price of its own good did *not* rise, so output falls back to its original level. Employment and unemployment return to their original levels. Real GDP falls back to its full-employment level, y^{FE} in Figure 30.3a, and the price level rises from P_2 to P_3. The short-run aggregate supply curve *shifts* from AS_1^{SR} to AS_2^{SR}, and the economy moves from Point B to Point C.

Similarly, suppose that aggregate demand falls permanently and sellers don't know about it, or aggregate demand rises more slowly than sellers believe. Each seller then mistakes a fall (or an unusually small rise) in the nominal price of its own good for a fall in its relative price. Sellers reduce output; employment falls and unemployment rises. This moves the economy from Point A to Point B in Figure 30.3b. Eventually, sellers learn that they have made mistakes. They find out that the price level rose less than they thought, so the relative prices of the goods they sell did not fall. They raise output back to its full-employment level. Real GDP and employment rise; unemployment falls. The price level falls further, and the economy moves from Point B to Point C in Figure 30.3b.

---

[14]The exact numbers depend on the shapes (the elasticities) of supply curves. Prices may rise 8 percent and real GDP may rise only 2 percent, or prices may rise only 3 percent and real GDP may rise 7 percent. The sum of the percentage changes must equal 10 percent, though.

CRITICISM OF THE INCOMPLETE-INFORMATION MODEL

The incomplete-information model explains why the short-run aggregate supply curve slopes upward if sellers don't know about the change in the price level. However, many economists have criticized this assumption. They say that sellers could learn about price-level changes either by reading news reports about the money supply and the price level (the government regularly publishes information about the consumer price index and GDP deflator), or by going shopping and looking at prices in other stores. Most economists believe that while the incomplete-information model may explain part of the relationship between the nominal money supply and real GDP, it is not the main explanation for major recessions.

FOR REVIEW

30.10 Explain why an increase in the money supply could lead a firm to believe that the relative price of its product had risen. Also explain why this would lead a seller to increase output.

30.11 According to the imperfect-information model, why does the short-run aggregate supply curve eventually rotate into the long-run aggregate supply curve?

QUESTIONS

30.12 What could sellers do to stop making the mistakes that the incomplete-information model says that they make?

30.13 Use the incomplete-information theory to explain what happens, in the short run and the long run, when aggregate demand falls.

UNEMPLOYMENT IN THE THREE MODELS

The three models of aggregate supply discussed so far differ in their interpretations of unemployment. The sticky-price model implies that unemployed people cannot find jobs *even by offering to work for a lower wage.* In that model, a fall in aggregate demand means that firms cannot sell all of the output they produce, so they reduce production and employment. An unemployed person cannot get a job, even at a lower wage, because firms cannot sell the output that the person would produce. (The firms could sell more if they could reduce their prices, but they cannot because prices are sticky in the short run.) Unemployment will fall in the long run when prices can fall, but the only way to reduce unemployment in the short run is to raise aggregate demand.

The sticky-wage theory says that unemployment occurs when the real wage exceeds its equilibrium level. Unemployed people could find jobs if firms could pay lower wages, but the sticky-wage model assumes that labor contracts or other forces prevent any reductions in nominal wages in the short run. In that model, the only way to reduce the real wage to its equilibrium level in the short run is to raise prices. In the long run, unemployment will fall because the nominal wage can fall to its equilibrium level, but in the short run, this model allows a reduction in unemployment only by raising aggregate demand. Because the sticky-price and sticky-wage models suggest that increases in aggregate demand can reduce unem-

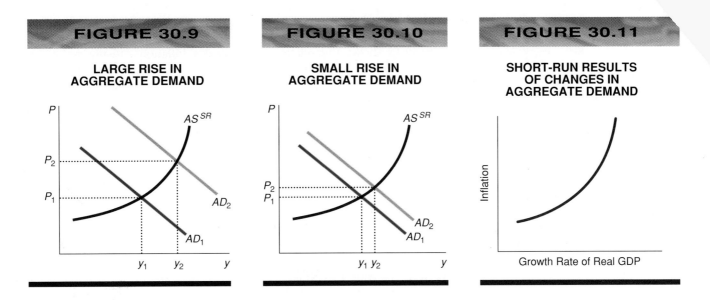

FIGURE 30.9

LARGE RISE IN AGGREGATE DEMAND

FIGURE 30.10

SMALL RISE IN AGGREGATE DEMAND

FIGURE 30.11

SHORT-RUN RESULTS OF CHANGES IN AGGREGATE DEMAND

ployment in the short run, many economists have proposed government policies to raise aggregate demand in response to high unemployment. Later chapters discuss these government-policy proposals.

The incomplete-information model sees unemployment as voluntary in the sense that any unemployed worker can find a job by offering to work at a sufficiently low wage. Wages and prices are *not* sticky in that model, so firms can pay lower wages and sell the additional output that workers produce. This model says that people are unemployed when they prefer unemployment to their current job opportunities, which may pay low wages. As the last chapter noted, it is difficult to obtain evidence on whether most unemployment is voluntary or involuntary.

PHILLIPS CURVES

Temporary changes in aggregate demand create a direct relationship between changes in output and changes in the price level. When aggregate demand rises temporarily, output and the price level both increase; when aggregate demand falls again, output and the price level both decrease. A large increase in aggregate demand creates a high growth rate of real GDP and high inflation, as in **Figure 30.9;** a smaller increase in aggregate demand creates a smaller growth rate of real GDP and lower inflation, as in **Figure 30.10.** Temporary changes in aggregate demand cause inflation and the growth rate of real GDP to move together, as in **Figure 30.11.** Permanent changes in aggregate demand also cause inflation and the growth of real GDP to move together *in the short run* (that is, until the short-run aggregate supply curve shifts from AS_1^{SR} to AS_2^{SR} in Figure 30.3).

A statistical generalization called Okun's Law indicates that each 1.0 percentage point increase in the growth rate of real GDP in the United States typically accompanies a 0.5 percentage point fall in the unemployment rate.[15] Because

---

[15]For example, a rise in the growth rate of real GDP from 3 percent to 4 percent per year typically occurs with a fall in the unemployment rate from 6 percent to 5.5 percent.

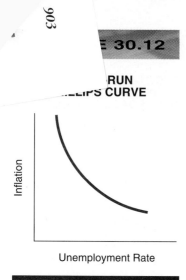

E 30.12

RUN
..IPS CURVE

(y-axis) Inflation

Unemployment Rate

short-run Phillips Curve — a
statistical relationship showing that
unemployment falls temporarily
when inflation rises, and unemployment rises temporarily when inflation falls

natural rate of unemployment
— the unemployment rate that
occurs when the economy produces the full-employment level of
output

higher growth in real GDP accompanies lower unemployment, Figure 30.11 can become **Figure 30.12.**

Figure 30.12 shows the relationship between inflation and unemployment predicted by the model with an upward-sloping short-run aggregate supply curve and temporary changes in aggregate demand, or the short-run effects of permanent changes in aggregate demand. In the short run, high inflation goes with low unemployment, and low inflation goes with high unemployment.

Evidence supports the short-run relationship in Figure 30.12. The short-run Phillips Curve represents a statistical relationship between inflation and unemployment:

> The **short-run Phillips Curve** is a statistical relationship between infla-
> tion and unemployment: in the short run, unemployment is low when
> inflation is high, and unemployment is high when inflation is low.

Figure 30.13 shows unemployment rates and inflation rates for the United States since 1986; the points show a downward-sloping relationship similar to the curve in Figure 30.12—a short-run Phillips Curve.

In the long run, the economy tends to return to the full-employment level of output, y^{FE}, and an associated level of unemployment called the *natural rate of unemployment.*

> The **natural rate of unemployment** is the unemployment rate that
> occurs when the economy produces the full-employment level of output.

The natural rate of unemployment corresponds to equilibrium unemployment discussed in an earlier chapter. Unemployment results from inevitable changes in real economies, including changes in the population, technology, consumer pref-

FIGURE 30.13

PHILLIPS CURVE FOR THE UNITED STATES, 1986–1994

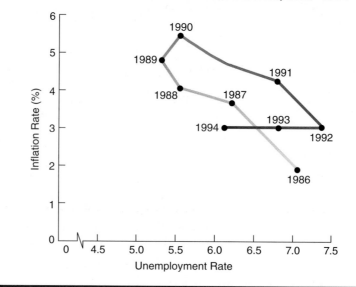

IN THE NEWS

Brazil's harsh attack on inflation is risking deep economic slump

Tight squeeze

Shrinkage of its money supply hobbles many companies, forces people to cut back

A housemaid loses her job

By Thomas Kamm
Staff Reporter of The
Wall Street Journal

SAO PAULO, Brazil—When Fernando Collor de Mello took office in March, he said he had "only one shot" to halt Brazil's hyperinflation. But instead of firing a bullet, the new president dropped a bomb.

"The monetary contraction we imposed on society is fantastic," acknowledges Ibrahim Eris, one of the architects of the harsh anti-inflation plan and now the president of the central bank. "It's probably the first time in the world that a country in time

of peace has practically destroyed its monetary standard and replaced it."

But in stopping inflation, the government has also stopped the economy. "To kill the cockroach, they set the apartment on fire," complains former Economic Planning Minister Antonio Delfim Netto.

Deprived of cash, consumers stopped buying, companies stopped producing, and exporters stopped exporting.

In any country, policies to reduce inflation may also cause a recession.

Source: Thomas Kamm, "Brazil's Harsh Attack on Inflation Is Risking Deep Economic Slump," *The Wall Street Journal,* May 10, 1990, p. A1.

FIGURE 30.14

PHILLIPS CURVES

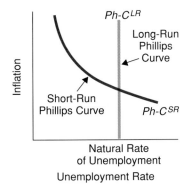

long-run Phillips Curve — a vertical line at the natural rate of unemployment

erences, government policies, and world economic conditions. The natural rate of unemployment is not a constant; it changes over time. Its size depends on the frequency and sizes of these changes in supply and demand, which determine how many people lose jobs and look for new jobs each year. The natural rate of unemployment also depends on how fast people find new jobs, which reflects how much information they have about job opportunities and how mobile they are. It depends on their incomes while they remain unemployed, which depends on incomes earned by other family members or from unemployment compensation. Finally, the natural rate of unemployment depends on the effect on job opportunities of union policies, minimum wages, government regulations, and taxes.

No one knows exactly the size of the natural rate of unemployment; economists estimate that it is currently about $5\frac{1}{2}$ to 6 percent in the United States. Economic models predict a *long-run Phillips Curve* that is a vertical line at the natural rate of unemployment, as in **Figure 30.14.** The evidence supports this long-run relationship: in the long run, unemployment equals its natural rate, UN^{nat}, regardless of the inflation rate.

The **long-run Phillips Curve** is a vertical line at the natural rate of unemployment.

Figure 30.15 shows the unemployment and inflation rates in the United States over several recent periods. Some periods show stronger evidence than others of a stable short-run Phillips Curve. Plotting data for all years, as in Panel f, does not

FIGURE 30.15

INFLATION AND UNEMPLOYMENT IN THE UNITED STATES

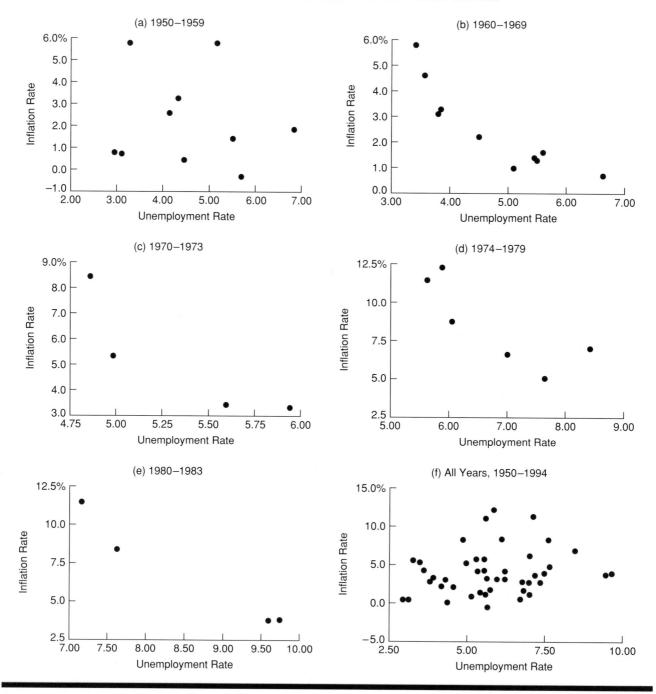

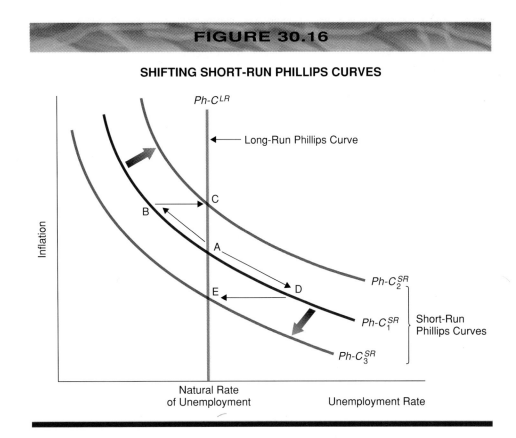

FIGURE 30.16

SHIFTING SHORT-RUN PHILLIPS CURVES

show a short-run Phillips Curve. Apparently the short-run Phillips Curve shifts over time.[16]

SHIFTS IN THE SHORT-RUN PHILLIPS CURVE

Most economists interpret the evidence as confirmation that the short-run Phillips Curve holds constant expected inflation and shifts when expected inflation changes, as in **Figure 30.16.** An increase in expected inflation shifts the short-run Phillips Curve upward and to the right; a fall in expected inflation shifts it downward and to the left. The long-run Phillips Curve, in contrast, does *not* hold constant expected inflation, so changes in expected inflation do not shift the long-run Phillips Curve.

Suppose that the economy begins at a long-run equilibrium at Point A in Figure 30.16. In a surprise policy change, the Federal Reserve then raises the growth rate of the money supply. Inflation rises above what people expected, unemployment falls, and the economy moves to Point B in the figure. After a while, people learn to expect this higher rate of inflation. The rise in expected inflation shifts the short-run Phillips Curve upward and to the right from $Ph\text{-}C_1^{SR}$

---

[16]A small number of economists believe that the evidence for a short-run Phillips Curve is a statistical illusion; they doubt the existence of a short-run Phillips Curve. See the next chapter.

IN THE NEWS

Jobs data show healthy growth in the economy

Inflation concern may rise as April unemployment dropped to 14-year low

By Rose Gutfeld
Staff Reporter of The Wall Street Journal

WASHINGTON—The April employment report, showing a drop in the jobless rate to a 14-year low and a modest rise in jobs, suggests healthy growth but is likely to add to fears of an overheating economy.

Rapid increases in real GDP may lead the Federal Reserve to believe that the economy is moving upward along a short-run Phillips Curve, making higher inflation more likely. The Fed may then choose to fight increases in inflation by tightening monetary policy.

Source: Rose Gutfeld, "Jobs Data Show Healthy Growth in the Economy," *The Wall Street Journal,* May 9, 1988, p. 3.

stagflation — a combination of inflation and a fall in real GDP

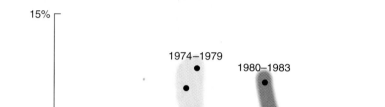

FIGURE 30.17

SHIFTING SHORT-RUN PHILLIPS CURVES FOR THE UNITED STATES, 1960–1994

to $Ph\text{-}C_2^{SR}$ until the economy reaches Point C in the long run. In the long run, inflation is higher and unemployment is back to the natural rate. A permanent increase in the growth rate of the money supply permanently raises inflation, but it reduces unemployment only temporarily.

Figure 30.16 also shows the effects of a decrease in the growth rate of the money supply. Starting from Point A, inflation falls and unemployment rises in the short run as the economy moves from Point A to Point D. As people learn to expect the lower rate of inflation, the short-run Phillips Curve shifts from $Ph\text{-}C_1^{SR}$ to $Ph\text{-}C_3^{SR}$ and unemployment falls back to its natural rate. In the long run, the economy reaches Point E. A permanent fall in the growth rate of the money supply permanently lowers inflation, but temporarily raises unemployment.[17] **Figure 30.17** shows shifting short-run Phillips Curves for the United States since 1960.

Figure 30.4b showed that a fall in aggregate supply can create inflation while real GDP falls. A fall in aggregate supply creates stagflation.

Stagflation is a combination of inflation and a fall in real GDP.

---

[17]The same results occur if inflation falls due to a fall in the growth rate of the velocity of money. See the discussion of the 1982 recession in a later section.

The United States experienced stagflation after the oil price shock of 1973 to 1974, when the price of imported oil rose four-fold. The oil shock preceded a fall in industrial production and a rise in inflation at the end of 1973 and later in 1974.

Changes in aggregate supply shift the short-run Phillips Curve. (They can also change the natural rate of unemployment and shift the long-run Phillips Curve.) Some recent changes in U.S. aggregate supply have come from changes in the price of imported crude oil. **Figure 30.18** shows the relative price of oil since 1960. Oil prices rose dramatically in 1973 to 1974 and again in 1980 to 1981; they then fell rapidly at the beginning of 1986. These changes in the price of imported oil caused shifts in both the U.S. aggregate supply curve and the short-run Phillips Curve. Notice that the price of oil remained stable in the 1960s, and nothing else caused any big changes in aggregate supply, so the graph of inflation and unemployment in the 1960s in the second panel of Figure 30.15 shows a stable short-run Phillips Curve.

───────────────────────── FOR REVIEW ─────────────────────────

30.14 Why does unemployment develop, according to the sticky-price model? Why does it develop, according to the sticky-wage model and the incomplete information model?

FIGURE 30.18

RELATIVE PRICE OF OIL SINCE 1960

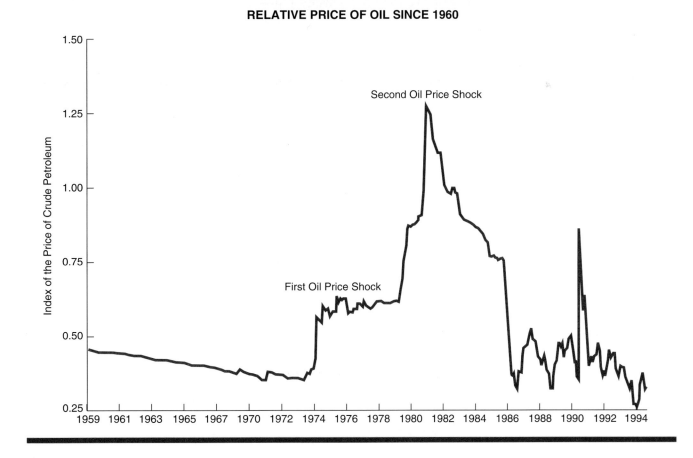

30.15 What causes short-run Phillips Curves to shift?

——————————————— **Question** ———————————————

30.16 Use the sticky-price model to explain why a graph of the U.S. inflation–unemployment data for the 1970s as a whole does not look like a short-run Phillips Curve.

Four Case Studies

Great Depression

The Great Depression, from 1929 through most of the 1930s, was the biggest recession in U.S. history. Real GDP per capita fell 30 percent from 1929 until 1933 and then rose slowly, reaching its 1929 level again only in 1940. The rise from 1933 to 1940 was interrupted by another recession in 1937 to 1938. It is customary to date the beginning of the Great Depression at the stock-market crash of October 1929, particularly October 24 (Black Thursday) and October 29 (Black Tuesday). Many people lost fortunes in the crash; some even committed suicide. As much as some people suffered from the stock-market crash, the coming depression would be far worse and affect more people.[18]

From 1929 to 1933, real GDP in the United States fell 30 percent. Deflation (negative inflation) dropped the price level fell by more than 20 percent.[19] By 1933, nominal GDP was only 56 percent of its 1929 level.

The unemployment rate in the United States rose to almost 25 percent in 1933 and 1934; roughly one out of every four workers was unemployed. In September 1932, *Fortune* magazine estimated that 34 million people (28 percent of the U.S. population) had no incomes at all.[20]

A multiplier effect magnified the decline, as discussed in the last chapter. People without jobs or other incomes could not pay taxes or rents, landlords who could not collect rents could not pay taxes, cities that could not collect taxes could not pay for social programs or schools. People without incomes could not buy much and many businesses closed.[21]

It is important not to let statistics hide the impact of the depression on people's lives—the depression caused considerable misery. That is why the models in these chapters are important. These models represent economists' attempts to understand logically what happened during the depression and during other recessions so people can try to avoid repeating them. The issues in these chapters have great, direct effects on people's lives.

---

[18]Most economists do not believe that the stock-market crash caused the depression. Recessions have occurred without stock-market crashes, and stock-market crashes have occurred (as on October 19, 1987) without recessions immediately followings.

[19]It fell 3.0 percent in 1930 and 8.7 percent in 1931 as the depression deepened, and it continued to fall until 1934.

[20]Cited in Paul Johnson, *Modern Times* (New York: Harper & Row, 1983), p. 247.

[21]Big retail stores did not suffer as badly as industry. James Thurber noted that they reduced prices and that anyone who could earn money could get bargains at these stores.

IN THE NEWS

Busy factories revive fears of inflation

So the Fed, which has been trying since March to hold off inflation by raising interest rates, will likely push rates higher. The goal: dampen demand for loans, which would discourage spending. Then businesses would have to hold off on some price increases.

▲

Job growth revives fears of inflation

By Mark Memmott
USA TODAY

If anyone out there knows when U.S. businesses will stop creating more than 10,000 jobs a day, please call Alan Greenspan.

The Federal Reserve chairman has been pushing up interest rates for a year, to slow the economy and head off what he fears is an onrushing wave of inflation.

Sources: "Busy Factories Revive Fears of Inflation," *USA Today,* December 15, 1988; and Mark Memmott, "Job Growth Revives Fears of Inflation," *USA Today,* March 13, 1989, p. B1.

WHAT CAUSED THE GREAT DEPRESSION?

In 1933, the U.S. economy produced only about two-thirds as many goods as it produced in 1929, even though it had available about the same people, equipment, and technology for production. Why did output fall so much? Economists generally agree that the Great Depression cannot be explained with the kind of equilibrium model from earlier chapters. Most economists believe that the sticky-price or sticky-wage models discussed in this chapter play a major role in the explanation.[22]

Economists generally interpret the Great Depression as the result of a huge fall in aggregate demand, but they disagree about the reasons for that fall. One prominent view, promoted by Milton Friedman and Anna J. Schwartz in a famous study, holds that the main cause of the depression was a fall in the money supply. The Federal Reserve increased the monetary base slightly from 1930 to 1933 as the economy slid into the Great Depression, but more than 9,000 banks stopped operating. People lost over $1 billion in deposits in those banks, and this made them poorer, though the loss was small compared to the $85 billion people lost in the stock market over the same period. Bank failures increased the currency-deposit ratio, which reduced the money multiplier (discussed in an earlier chapter) and caused the M2 measure of the money supply to fall by almost one-third from 1929 to 1933.[23] According to this view, the fall in the money supply reduced aggregate demand.

Another prominent view holds that an exogenous fall in spending on consumption and investment reduced aggregate demand, causing the depression. Consumption spending may have fallen because people lost money in the stock market or because consumer confidence declined and people decided to save more and spend less. Some economists see a major factor in unexpected deflation that redistributed wealth from borrowers to lenders. If lenders tend to save more and spend less than borrowers, this could reduce aggregate demand.[24] Finally, investment spending may have fallen because bank failures made it harder for firms to borrow money from people who saved it. The unexpected deflation bankrupted many firms that had borrowed money and pushed other firms to the brink of bankruptcy. It became risky for people to lend money to firms because the threat of bankruptcy increased, worrying lenders that they would not be repaid in full. With lenders more cautious about lending money, firms had more trouble obtaining funds to finance their operations and investments, which may have reduced aggregate demand and contributed to the depression.

Whatever the reason for the fall in aggregate demand, the result was a huge fall in real GDP and the price level from 1929 to 1933. This fall was followed by a long movement back toward the full-employment level of output.

Many, though not all, economists believe that if the Federal Reserve had prevented the fall in the M2 measure of the money supply, it would have avoided the

---

[22]Some economists believe that other kinds of market failures contributed; see the discussion of coordination failures in the next chapter.

[23]It is interesting that *no* bank failures or even bank runs occurred in Canada during this period. Canada's money supply fell anyway, because Canada was on the gold standard and world deflation reduced prices in all gold-standard countries. Canada endured the depression along with the United States and other countries. Canada's having experienced the depression without bank failures casts doubt on the view that bank failures alone caused the depression.

[24]Evidence supports the claim that deflation from 1929 to 1933 was mainly unexpected. See James Hamilton, "Monetary Factors in the Great Depression," *Journal of Monetary Economics* 19 (1987), pp. 145–169.

Great Depression or made it much less severe. Milton Friedman and Anna J. Schwartz took this position in their important book, *A Monetary History of the United States*.[25] They argued that every major change in the money supply in U.S. history has led to changes in real GDP in the short run and inflation in the long run, regardless of why the money supply changed. As a result, a fall in M2 by one-third, the largest fall in U.S. history, should be expected to bring about the biggest depression in U.S. history. Friedman and Schwartz argued that if the Federal Reserve had increased the monetary base to keep M2 from falling, the Great Depression would have been, at most, a mild recession. Even if aggregate demand had fallen for some reason unrelated to the fall in M2, a stable money supply would have prevented aggregate demand from falling enough to cause a depression.[26]

INTERNATIONAL COMPARISONS

The Great Depression was a world-wide event. As the price level fell in the United States, international trade transmitted deflation to other countries on the gold standard. The depression became deeper in the United States, Canada, and Germany than in most other countries.

One way for economists to learn about the effects of different policies on the economy is to compare results in countries with different policies. From 1929 to 1933, countries with the biggest deflations also had the biggest recessions. Researchers have identified three groups of countries to compare. First, many countries, such as the United States and Germany, were on the gold standard. These countries had deflations and major recessions from 1929 to 1933. Second, some countries, such as China and Spain, had no deflations because they were *not* on the gold standard. These countries had no major recessions.

Third, some countries *stopped* their deflations by abandoning the gold standard in 1931.[27] These countries put early ends to their recessions. For example, Great Britain went off the gold standard in September 1931, and its real GDP stopped falling. **Figure 30.19** shows the results. From 1929 to 1933, aggregate demand fell in the United States; Panel a shows falling prices and falling real GDP over this period. In Great Britain, aggregate demand fell between 1929 and 1931, then stayed about constant from 1931 to 1933, so the price level and real GDP fell from 1929 to 1931 in Great Britain (from Point A to Point B in Panel b of the figure). As the British economy adjusted toward the long-run equilibrium, prices fell further and real GDP increased (from Point B to Point C).

Sweden also abandoned the gold standard in 1931, and stopped its deflation immediately. Prices and the money supply remained about constant for a year, then rose slowly for the next few years. Real GDP in Sweden fell 9.1 percent in 1931, almost as much as the 11.5 percent fall in U.S. real GDP. In 1932, however, after Sweden stopped its deflation, Swedish real GDP fell only 3.2 percent while

---

[25]Milton Friedman and Anna J. Schwartz, *A Monetary History of the United States* (Princeton, N.J.: Princeton University Press, 1963).

[26]Some economists claim that an increase in the money supply would not have helped in this situation. They say that in certain situations with low nominal interest rates, as in the Great Depression, people would be unwilling to spend increases in the money supply, so those increases would not raise aggregate demand. Instead, they argue, an increase in *M* would simply reduce velocity, *V,* so that aggregate demand, *MV,* would not increase.

[27]The gold standard required countries to choose certain money-supply growth rates. In the early 1930s, these growth rates were low enough to cause deflation. Abandoning the gold standard gave governments the ability to choose any money-supply growth rate, so the country could choose to have stable prices or inflation.

FIGURE 30.19

AN INTERNATIONAL COMPARISON OF THE GREAT DEPRESSION

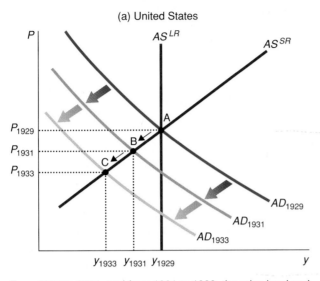

(a) United States

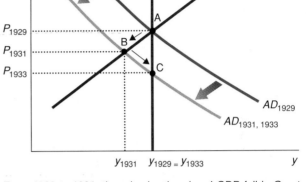

(b) Great Britain

From 1929 to 1931, and from 1931 to 1933, the price level and real GDP fell in the United States.

From 1929 to 1931, the price level and real GDP fell in Great Britain. Great Britain then abandoned the gold standard, and real GDP increased as the price level fell.

U.S. real GDP fell another 18.7 percent.[28] By 1934, Swedish real GDP was back to its 1929 level, while U.S. real GDP was only 73 percent of its 1929 level.

These episodes suggest that the United States might have been able to end the Great Depression earlier if it had raised the monetary base to keep M1 and M2 from falling and to stop the deflation.

Some people have suggested that the Hawley-Smoot Act of 1930, which raised tariffs significantly, made the depression much worse than it otherwise would have been. Economists generally agree that tariffs reduce economic efficiency, but most doubt that the Hawley-Smoot Act played a major role in the Great Depression. Its main role may have been to help spread the depression to European countries, many of which also increased their tariffs.

In the United States, the Great Depression helped Franklin Roosevelt win election over President Herbert Hoover in 1932, leading to the New Deal, Roosevelt's policies to fight the depression.[29] Real GDP started rising slowly in 1934.

The famous book by John Maynard Keynes, *The General Theory of Employment, Interest, and Money,* was published in 1936, when real GDP in the

---

[28]Why did Swedish real GDP not rise? Perhaps because depressions in other countries reduced the demand for Sweden's exports. This would have caused aggregate demand in Sweden to continue to fall, but by *less* than if Sweden had stayed on the gold standard and continued to endure deflation as the United States, Germany, and other countries did.

[29]President Hoover, who had come into office in early 1929, actually followed some policies to raise aggregate demand (such as cutting taxes and raising government spending, mainly for transfer payments), leading to a government budget deficit of almost 3 percent of GDP in 1931.

United States was still below its 1929 level. It received immediate attention as a theory of why recessions occur, and how to cure and prevent episodes like the Great Depression. Keynes's *General Theory* became the dominant influence on the development of macroeconomics over the next 40 years.

CREDIT CONTROLS IN 1980[30]

On March 14, 1980, President Carter imposed credit controls on the U.S. economy to try to reduce inflation, which had reached 12.4 percent in 1979. These credit controls subjected lenders to special regulations that effectively worked like a tax on loans.[31] They were intended to lower inflation by reducing the amount of money that consumers and businesses borrowed and spent on consumption and investment. That is, they were intended to reduce aggregate demand, and they succeeded.

The controls led some banks to stop accepting new credit-card applications and others to tighten the requirements to get credit cards, raise annual fees for credit cards, raise interest rates on the cards, and raise minimum required monthly payments. Though other controls on consumer borrowing were mainly symbolic, the publicity and confusion generated by the credit controls caused a large fall in consumer spending. Total bank loans fell 5 percent in 1 month (April 1980), and retail sales fell at the fastest rate in 29 years. **Figure 30.20** shows growth rates of consumption, investment, real GDP, and the unemployment rate and inflation rate. The shaded area indicates the period of credit controls.

The credit controls led to steep falls in consumption and investment spending, reducing aggregate demand, real GDP, and the rate of inflation and raising the unemployment rate. Although the growth rate of the monetary base did not change much, the growth rates of M1 and M2 fell because the money multiplier fell as banks reduced lending. In this way, the credit policy caused reductions in M1 and M2 as well as a fall in aggregate demand. This shows why economists must look cautiously at data. It would be easy to look at the graph and conclude, falsely, that the fall in the money-growth rate *caused* the fall in consumption and investment that led to the fall in real GDP. In fact, the fall in the money-growth rate resulted from the decrease in borrowing due to the credit controls.

RECESSION OF 1982

In October 1979, the new chairman of the Federal Reserve Board, Paul Volcker, announced that the Federal Reserve would change its operating procedures to focus more attention on the money supply and would try to reduce inflation. The Federal Reserve did just that, with some help from a change in velocity. The growth rate of the monetary base quickly fell from almost 8.0 percent per year in 1980 to about 4.5 percent per year in 1981, then it gradually rose in 1982. The growth rate of M1, however, changed little.[32] The velocity of M1 had been grow-

---

[30]This discussion is based on Stacey L. Schreft, "Credit Controls, 1980," *Economic Review* 76, no. 6 (November/December 1990), published by the Federal Reserve Bank of Richmond. Figure 30.20 comes from this paper.

[31]These controls included, for example, a special deposit requirement on lenders for certain types of unsecured consumer credit that required lenders to hold noninterest-bearing deposits at the Fed equal to 15 percent of their loans.

[32]The growth rate of M2 did not fall, but its velocity fell.

FIGURE 30.20

EFFECTS OF CREDIT CONTROLS IN 1980

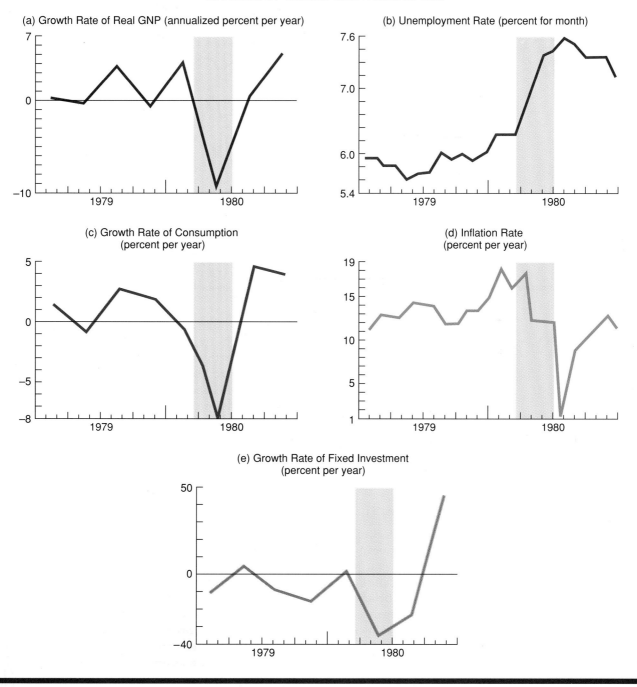

(a) Growth Rate of Real GNP (annualized percent per year)

(b) Unemployment Rate (percent for month)

(c) Growth Rate of Consumption
(percent per year)

(d) Inflation Rate
(percent per year)

(e) Growth Rate of Fixed Investment
(percent per year)

FIGURE 30.21

MONEY, OUTPUT, AND PRICES IN THE 1982 RECESSION

Output in this graph is measured by industrial production; the money supply is measured by the monetary base. Broader measures of the money supply such as M1 also fell in 1981 prior to the 1982 recession.

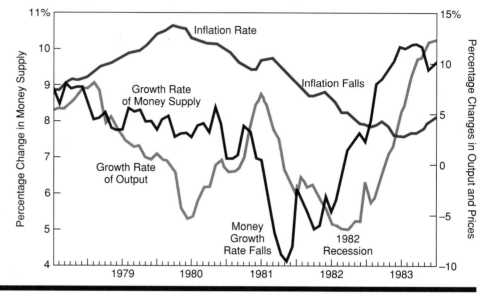

ing steadily since 1960, and it suddenly started falling in 1982 for reasons that economists do not yet understand well.[33]

The combination of a fall in the growth rate of the money supply and lower velocity reduced aggregate demand. **Figure 30.21** shows the results. Inflation was 12.4 percent in 1979, 11.6 percent in 1980, and 8.5 percent in 1981.[34] It suddenly fell to 3.8 percent in 1982, as the recession occurred, and 3.7 percent in 1983. Real GDP fell more than 3.0 percent from fall 1981 to fall 1982, down to 1.6 percent below its fall 1979 level. The unemployment rate rose from 5.8 percent in 1979 to more than 10.0 percent in the last half of 1982 and the first half of 1983. The 1982 recession was the largest in the United States since the Great Depression. (A panel in Figure 30.15 shows the Phillips Curve for this period.)

RECESSION OF 1990–1991

The 1990–1991 recession may have been partly related to monetary policy, which tightened prior to the recession. **Figure 30.22** shows the growth rate of output in the United States (measured by industrial production, which changes more than GDP during business cycles) and the growth rate of M1 $1\frac{1}{2}$ years earlier. Many economists believe that the recession had other causes, as well, including less willingness of financial intermediaries to lend that may have resulted partly from the savings-and-loan crisis. Additional research may shed new light on the causes of the 1990–1991 recession, but the data graphed in Figure 30.22 show that the recession may have been connected with money-growth rates.

---

[33]Nominal interest rates fell, which helped to reduce velocity, but velocity fell by more than economists expected based on the fall in nominal interest rates.

[34]The 1979 figure is the December-to-December inflation rate.

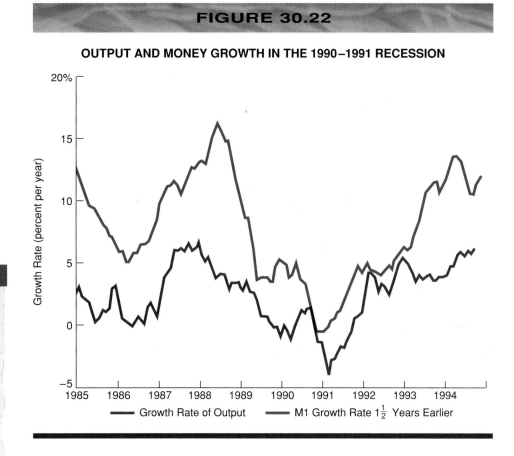

FIGURE 30.22

OUTPUT AND MONEY GROWTH IN THE 1990–1991 RECESSION

— Growth Rate of Output   — M1 Growth Rate $1\frac{1}{2}$ Years Earlier

RECESSIONS AND EXPECTED INFLATION

Some economists believe that the short-run Phillips Curve does *not* shift rapidly even when expectations change, or that people adjust their expectations slowly. These economists cite the 1982 recession as evidence that *any* attempt to reduce the rate of inflation requires a recession in the short run. The 1982 recession occurred after the Federal Reserve announced publicly that it would try to reduce inflation. This, they argue, means that people expected the fall in inflation in 1982, but that a recession occurred anyway. If the short-run Phillips Curve were to shift whenever expectations changed—if only *unexpected* inflation could affect real GDP—then, these economists say, the 1982 recession would not have happened.

Other economists argue that people did not expect inflation to fall, that people really did not believe the Federal Reserve's public announcement in October 1979 that it would fight inflation. These economists argue that politicians and government bureaucrats (including Federal Reserve officials) make many announcements and that people cannot believe all of them. After all, this was not the first time the government announced that it would fight inflation. Whether a fully expected fall in inflation causes a recession remains a topic of controversy among economists.

CONCLUSIONS

AGGREGATE SUPPLY AND AGGREGATE DEMAND

Most economists believe that the short-run aggregate supply curve slopes upward. The aggregate supply curve holds constant technology and factors that affect supplies of inputs. Changes in technology or changes in forces that determine input supplies cause changes in aggregate supply.

A temporary increase in aggregate demand raises real GDP and the price level temporarily. A permanent increase in aggregate demand raises real GDP temporarily and the price level permanently. A permanent increase in aggregate supply raises real GDP and reduces the price level permanently.

AGGREGATE SUPPLY: THE STICKY-PRICE THEORY

The New Keynesian theory asserts that the aggregate supply curve slopes upward because prices of goods and services are sticky in the short run, though not completely sticky. Prices may be sticky due to menu costs, consumer preferences for stable prices, or other reasons. Prices may adjust slowly after a change in economic conditions because sellers take turns making small price changes.

AGGREGATE SUPPLY: THE STICKY-WAGE THEORY

Another theory asserts that the aggregate supply curve slopes upward because nominal wages are sticky in the short run. If nominal wages are sticky, a fall in the money supply reduces the price level, raising the real wage. This increase in the real wage reduces the quantity of labor demanded by business firms, so employment falls, raising unemployment and reducing output. While the sticky-price model implies that the short-run aggregate supply curve shifts when the nominal price level eventually changes, the sticky-wage model implies that the short-run aggregate supply curve shifts when nominal wages eventually change.

AGGREGATE SUPPLY: THE IMPERFECT-INFORMATION THEORY

Another theory asserts that the aggregate supply curve slopes upward, not because prices or wages are sticky, but because in the short run sellers mistake nominal price changes for relative price changes. When the nominal price of a product rises, its sellers falsely believe that its relative price has increased, so they produce more. When the nominal price of a product falls, its sellers falsely believe that its relative price has decreased, so they produce less. When sellers eventually realize that they have made a mistake, the short-run aggregate supply curve shifts.

UNEMPLOYMENT IN THE THREE MODELS

All three models of short-run aggregate supply imply that the long-run aggregate supply curve is vertical at the full-employment level of output. The three models differ, however, in their interpretations of the causes of short-run unemployment. The sticky-price model implies that unemployed people cannot find jobs, even by offering to work for lower wages, because firms cannot sell the additional products that those workers would produce. The sticky-wage theory implies that unemployment occurs because the real wage exceeds its equilibrium level, and unemployed people could find jobs if they could offer to work for lower wages. The incomplete-information model implies that unemployed workers could find jobs by offering to work at lower wages.

PHILLIPS CURVES

The short-run Phillips Curve describes a statistical relationship between inflation and unemployment. Unemployment falls temporarily when inflation rises, and it rises temporarily when inflation falls. Eventually, the economy returns to the natural rate of unemployment and produces the full-employment level of output, so the long-run Phillips Curve is a vertical line at the natural rate of unemployment. Evidence indicates that the short-run Phillips Curve shifts over time, perhaps in response to changes in people's expectations of inflation.

FOUR CASE STUDIES

The Great Depression from 1929 through most of the 1930s may have resulted from a very large fall in the money supply from 1929 to 1933 that reduced aggregate demand. It may also have resulted from an exogenous fall in spending on consumption and investment that reduced aggregate demand. Redistributions of income from an unexpected fall in the price level may have contributed to the fall in aggregate demand by causing some business firms to go bankrupt and making it harder for others to borrow money to finance operations and new investments.

Many countries around the world suffered from the Great Depression, though the depression ended earlier in countries that left the gold standard and adopted monetary policies to prevent deflation. For this and other reasons, many economists believe that the depression resulted, at least in part, from monetary causes.

Credit controls imposed by the U.S. government in 1980 reduced consumption spending, causing a fall in aggregate demand and reducing real GDP. Most economists blame the 1982 recession in the United States mainly on tighter monetary policies by the Federal Reserve. The Fed intended these policies to reduce inflation from a rate exceeding 10 percent per year. Monetary policy may also have played a role in the U.S. recession in 1990 and 1991.

LOOKING AHEAD

The models of aggregate supply in this chapter suggest that recessions occur when markets do not work well. They might not work well because prices are sticky, because wages are sticky, or because people lack enough information to infer the important relative prices from the nominal prices that they observe in markets. The next chapter turns to theories of so-called *real business cycles* in which nominal variables like the money supply do not necessarily play important roles. That chapter first discusses real business cycle models in which markets work well. It then considers models in which markets sometimes work poorly, not because prices or wages are sticky, but because of so-called *coordination failures*. The chapters after that discuss government monetary and fiscal policies, and other government policies, in the context of the various macroeconomic models of this and the next chapter.

KEY TERMS

menu cost

real wage

indexed wage

short-run Phillips Curve

natural rate of unemployment

long-run Phillips Curve

stagflation

QUESTIONS AND PROBLEMS

30.17 List seven changes in conditions that can change aggregate supply and explain how each works.

30.18 Use the sticky-price model to explain stagflation.

30.19 Why might price changes by a firm affect its competitors when firms face menu costs?

30.20 Why can staggered price setting with menu costs lead to a series of small price increases?

30.21 Summarize the evidence on price stickiness.

30.22 Discuss the following claim: "Sticky nominal wages help to reduce uncertainty for workers."

30.23 What happened in the Great Depression? What may have caused it?

30.24 How did credit controls in 1980 affect aggregate demand? What happened to the U.S. economy?

30.25 What happened in the 1982 recession? What may have caused it?

30.26 Suppose that aggregate demand rises. Explain what happens in the short run and the long run (and why) according to the:
   a. Sticky-price model
   b. Sticky-wage model
   c. Incomplete-information model

30.27 In Figure 30.3b, suppose that the economy has already gone from Point A to Point B to Point C. Now suppose that another decrease in aggregate demand moves the *AD* curve downward below AD_2 in the figure. Show what happens in the short run and the long run, then repeat this problem using Figure 30.3a and assuming another increase in aggregate demand.

30.28 In Figure 30.4b, suppose that the economy has already gone from Point A to Point B to Point C. Now suppose that another decrease in aggregate supply occurs. Show what happens in the short run and the long run.

30.29 Why does unemployment return to its natural rate in long-run equilibrium?

30.30 The GDP deflator in the United States fell 18 percent from 1920 to 1921 and another 8 percent from 1921 to 1922.[35] Meanwhile, per-capita real GDP fell 11 percent from 1920 to 1921 and then rose 13 percent from 1921 to 1922. Explain, using aggregate supply and demand curves, what happened.

30.31 Great Britain had high inflation during and after World War I. The price level doubled from 1914 to 1918 and then rose 40 percent from 1918 to 1920. Then the British government decided to reduce the price level back to about its prewar level.[36] From 1920 to 1921, the GDP deflator fell 11 percent, while real GDP fell 6 percent. The next year, the price level fell another 17 percent and real GDP increased. Use the aggregate demand/aggregate supply framework to explain what happened.

---

[35]The U.S. wholesale price index fell 46 percent from 1920 to 1921!

[36]The government wanted to set the price of gold at its prewar level. This requires the price level to go back to about that level.

30.32 Use the framework in this chapter to explain why a city's real GDP may rise and its unemployment may fall if it hosts the Olympics or some other major event.

30.33 Use aggregate supply and aggregate demand curves to discuss the short-run and long-run effects of:
   a. Exogenous increase in consumer savings
   b. Earthquake
   c. Increase in government spending for defense, paid for by a tax increase
   d. Increase in the government budget deficit caused by a tax cut without any cut in government spending

INQUIRIES FOR FURTHER THOUGHT

30.34 Which model in this chapter do you think better describes the real-life economy? (If none seems close, explain what model might be better.)

30.35 If you could guide U.S. economic policies, what would you do to try to avoid recessions?

30.36 Is it worth raising inflation permanently to reduce unemployment temporarily? Is it worth reducing inflation permanently if it raises unemployment temporarily?

30.37 Suppose that you run the government's economic policies and you want to reduce inflation without causing a recession. Can you do this? How might you try?

TAG SOFTWARE APPLICATIONS

TUTORIAL EXERCISES
▶ The module contains a review of the key terms from Chapter 30.

GRAPHING EXERCISES
▶ The graphing segment examines the impact of changes in aggregate demand and aggregate supply on equilibrium GDP, and short- and long-run Phillips Curves.

REAL BUSINESS CYCLES AND COORDINATION FAILURES

WHAT THIS CHAPTER IS ABOUT

▶ Business cycles caused by changes in the rate of technical progress

▶ Rational expectations

▶ Multiple equilibria, coordination failures, and sunspots

Some economists doubt that the theories discussed in the previous chapter describe the real-life economy. This chapter discusses two important alternative theories of business cycles. Both claim that business cycles happen in equilibrium, not (or not only) from disequilibrium forces like those described in the last two chapters. One theory says that business cycles represent economically efficient equilibrium responses of the economy to changes in conditions. The other theory sees business cycles as economically inefficient situations in which the economy sometimes gets stuck in a bad equilibrium. Both theories are controversial and have stimulated current economic research. The implications for government policy of these theories differ substantially from those suggested by the theories in the previous chapter.

REAL BUSINESS CYCLE THEORIES

real business cycle theories — theories that explain business cycles mainly as results of changes in technology or other real variables, while claiming that nominal variables are unimportant

Real business cycle theories claim that business cycles result mainly from changes in technology or other real variables, and that nominal variables are unimportant.

In other words, real business cycle theories say that changes in real GDP and employment have little to do with sticky nominal prices or wages, or with changes in the nominal money supply. These theories attribute changes in real GDP only (or mainly) to real variables such as changes in the economy's technology, investment opportunities, or consumer tastes (for spending versus saving or work versus leisure time), changes in taxes, regulations, or government spending. This emphasis justifies the name *real* business cycle theories.[1] Relative prices (but not

---

[1]The name does not refer to the realism of the theories.

nominal prices) and real wages (but not nominal wages) still play roles in these theories.

There are two main types of real business cycle theories. Most imply that markets work well, that is, they see voluntary trades among people leading to an economically efficient equilibrium.[2] These types of theories imply that business cycles are normal features of well-functioning economies, that a nation's economy always remains close to its equilibrium and that the disequilibrium factors discussed in the last two chapters play little or no role. The term *real business cycle theory* usually refers to this kind of a model.

The second main type of real business cycle theory says that markets don't work well, that business cycles result from market failures in which voluntary trades can lead to an equilibrium that is not economically efficient. The models in the last two chapters explained market failures caused by sticky nominal prices, sticky nominal wages, or a certain type of incomplete information that led sellers to confuse nominal and relative prices. Those market failures all involved nominal prices or wages. The second type of theories in this chapter, called *coordination-failure theories,* refer to more subtle types of market failures that do not necessarily involve nominal variables.[3]

REAL BUSINESS CYCLE MODELS WITH EFFICIENT MARKETS

Economies usually grow over time, and it would be surprising if the rate of economic growth were the same every year. Economists expect any economy, even one that is always in equilibrium (without the disequilibrium forces of the last two chapters), to grow a lot in some years and less in others. After all, the rate of economic growth depends on the development and implementation of new technologies, accumulation of human capital, and many other factors discussed in earlier chapters. These factors change from year to year.

Real business cycle theory says *recessions* are simply times when equilibrium economic growth is slower than usual, or negative. Real business cycle theory says that the economy is always in equilibrium—that prices and wages are not sticky—so actual economic growth is the same as equilibrium growth.

Real business cycle theory explains most of what happens during business cycles as the economy's equilibrium reacts to continual changes in technology. More specifically:

▶ It claims that changes in technology, typically called *technology shocks,* cause most changes in real GDP, in both the short run and the long run. Advances in

---

[2]Recall that a situation is economically efficient if no change can make anyone better off, except by making someone else worse off by a larger amount. In such a situation, the economy is performing well; it is not wasting resources. If a situation is not economically efficient—if it is economically *inef-*ficient—then it is not performing well. In that case, some change in the economy could help some people without hurting anyone else, or without hurting them as much as it would help the others. The situation is economically inefficient without that change.

The sticky-price and sticky-wage theories in the last chapter imply that the economy does not function well. It operates inefficiently when real GDP differs from its full-employment level. For example, a fall in the nominal money supply in the sticky-wage model reduces the price level and raises the real wage, reducing employment because firms are not willing to employ as many people at the higher wage. (Their quantity of labor demanded falls.) Because people still want jobs, the fall in the money supply creates an excess supply of labor, which is economically inefficient.

[3]Some coordination-failure theories do involve nominal variables.

technology raise real GDP. The growth rate of real GDP rises when technology advances quickly and falls when it advances slowly.[4]

▶ Employment and the real wage change *procyclically* and unemployment changes *countercyclically*.[5] Advances in technology raise labor productivity, which increases the demand for labor. This raises equilibrium employment and the real wage. (The number of employees and the number of hours worked per employee both rise.) Therefore, employment and the real wage grow faster when technical progress is faster and more slowly when it slows; they move procyclically. When employment rises, unemployment falls, so unemployment moves countercyclically.

▶ Investment moves procyclically because technical advances raise the profitability of new investments and raise investment demand. This raises the demand for loans, which raises the real interest rate and equilibrium investment.

▶ Consumption moves mildly procyclically. An increase in the rate of technical change makes people richer, so they spend more on consumption. Also, people raise their consumption spending when they work more.[6]

▶ Average labor productivity, real GDP per worker-hour, moves procyclically. People work more during nonrecession periods because more rapid technical advances raise the demand for labor; these advances also make workers more productive.

Most economists believe that evidence supports the claim that changes in the money supply have major short-run effects on real GDP, unemployment, and real interest rates. Proponents of real business cycle theories, however, argue that this evidence is suspect in some cases and incorrectly interpreted in other cases. According to real business cycle models, changes in the money supply have no major effects on real GDP, unemployment, and real interest rates, even in the short run.

EXPLANATION

The economy's production function describes its technology; it shows the amount of output (real GDP) that the economy can produce with its inputs of capital and labor. Economists write a production function mathematically in the form:

$$y = F(K, L)$$

to show that if the economy uses K units of capital (machines) and L labor-hours of labor (adjusted for skill level), it will produce y units of output. That output, y, is its real GDP. A footnote in an earlier chapter noted that the production function,

$$y = AK^{\frac{1}{3}}L^{\frac{2}{3}} \tag{31.1}$$

is a good approximation for the economies of many countries, including the United States. The number A measures a variable called *total factor productivity*.

---

[4]Technical advance refers to implementation of new techniques, not basic scientific discoveries that firms have not yet implemented in equipment or used to help produce products. Technical change can also refer more broadly to changes in regulations, laws, and the enforcement of property rights that affect the amount of output people produce with given inputs.

[5]Procyclical variables rise and fall with real GDP relative to trends in business cycles. Countercyclical variables rise when real GDP falls (relative to trend), and they fall when real GDP rises (relative to trend). Acyclical variables do not change much over business cycles, or do not change in the same way every time.

[6]They may eat out at restaurants more often, for example.

total factor productivity — a number in the economy's production function that measures its level of technology; the value rises with technical progress

Total factor productivity refers to the number A in the economy's production function; it measures the level of the economy's technology, and it rises over time with technical progress.

An increase in total factor productivity means that the economy produces more output with the same amount of inputs.

The production function in Equation 31.1 implies that total wages equal two-thirds of GDP and that owners of capital receive the other one-third of GDP, which closely approximates real life.[7] Real business cycle models often use this production function to measure changes in total factor productivity. First, they rewrite it as:

$$A = \frac{y}{K^{\frac{1}{3}}L^{\frac{2}{3}}}$$

(31.2)

They then use data for y, K, and L (on the right-hand side of the equation) to calculate total factor productivity (on the left side) and its changes over time.

Economists can use these changes in total factor productivity to measure technology shocks.

technology shock — an unexpected change in technology

Technology shocks are unexpected changes in technology.

Evidence suggests that total factor productivity jumps around from year to year as it rises over time and that technology shocks are *persistent* (*not* temporary). When total factor productivity rises, it is likely to remain high for several years. Panel a of **Figure 31.1** shows total factor productivity. Panel b, in contrast, shows an example of a variable (the *growth rate* of total factor productivity) whose changes are temporary.

Real business cycle theory then uses a model based on the analysis in Chapter 25 and its Appendix B (Changes in Labor and Capital Inputs and Equilibrium Real GDP). That appendix explained why an increase in labor productivity increases the demand for labor and an increase in the real interest rate temporarily raises the supplies of labor and capital.

An increase in the real interest rate raises the supply of labor through intertemporal substitution; it raises the incentive to work more this year and less in the future. An increase in the real interest rate also raises the supply of capital services by making it profitable for firms to increase the utilization rate of capital (the number of hours per week that the firm uses its capital equipment).

Because an increase in the real interest rate temporarily raises the supplies of labor and capital, economists can graph short-run equilibrium output as in **Figure 31.2.**

short-run equilibrium output curve — a graph of the short-run level of output as changes in the real interest rate cause changes in the supplies of labor and capital inputs

The **short-run equilibrium output curve** (Figure 31.2) graphs the level of output from the economy's production function (in the short run) as changes in the real interest rate cause changes in the supplies of labor and capital inputs.

Because an increase in the real interest rate temporarily raises K and L, it temporarily raises equilibrium real GDP, which Equation 31.1 gave as:

$$y = AK^{\frac{1}{3}}L^{\frac{2}{3}}$$

---

[7]In some countries, the numbers are closer to three-quarters and one-quarter rather than two-thirds and one-third.

FIGURE 31.1

TOTAL FACTOR PRODUCTIVITY

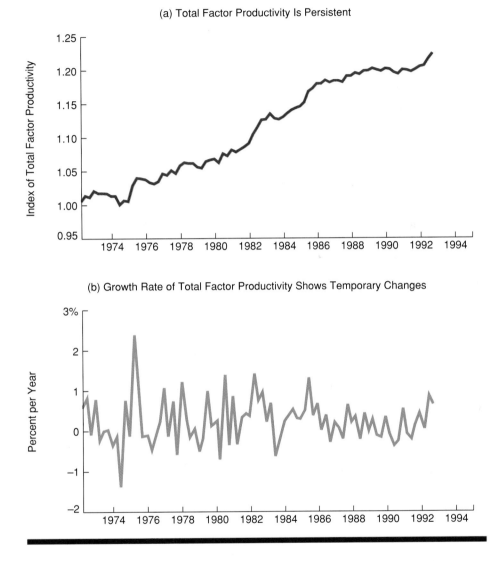

(a) Total Factor Productivity Is Persistent

(b) Growth Rate of Total Factor Productivity Shows Temporary Changes

In Figure 31.2, an increase in the real interest rate from r_1 to r_2 raises the supplies of labor and capital from L_1 and K_1 to L_2 and K_2, which corresponds to a move along the short-run equilibrium output curve from Point A to Point B. Real GDP rises from y_1 to y_2. The short-run equilibrium output curve shifts when technology changes, or when the supplies of labor and capital change for reasons other than a change in the real interest rate. An increase in total factor productivity or an increase in the supplies of labor or capital (holding fixed the real interest rate) shifts the short-run equilibrium output curve rightward.

Figure 31.3 shows two graphs. Panel a shows the supply and demand for loans; this determines the equilibrium real interest rate, as earlier chapters have

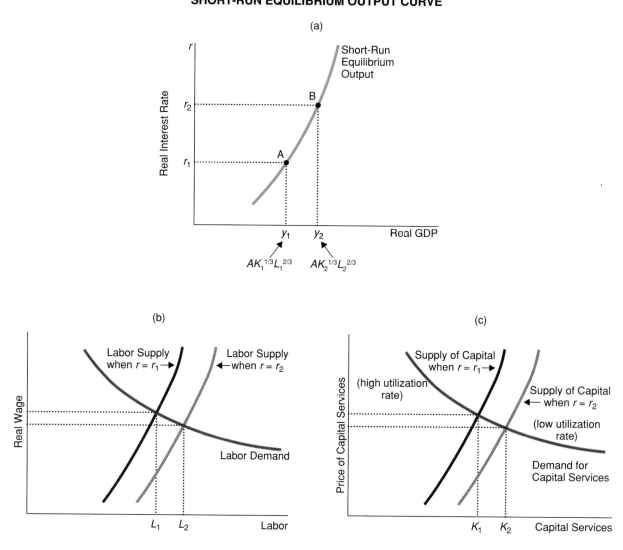

FIGURE 31.2

SHORT-RUN EQUILIBRIUM OUTPUT CURVE

explained. The graph on the right shows how short-run equilibrium output depends on real GDP. Finding equilibrium real GDP requires two steps. First, use the supply and demand for loans to find the equilibrium real interest rate, then use the short-run equilibrium output curve to find equilibrium real GDP. In Figure 31.3, the equilibrium real interest rate is r_0, so equilibrium real GDP is y_0.

After finding the equilibrium real interest rate and equilibrium real GDP, one can find equilibrium investment from the investment demand curve from earlier chapters. Equilibrium investment equals the equilibrium quantity of loans minus the government budget deficit. One can also find equilibrium savings by subtracting loans from foreigners from the total equilibrium quantity of loans. One can

FIGURE 31.3

HOW TO DERIVE EQUILIBRIUM REAL GDP

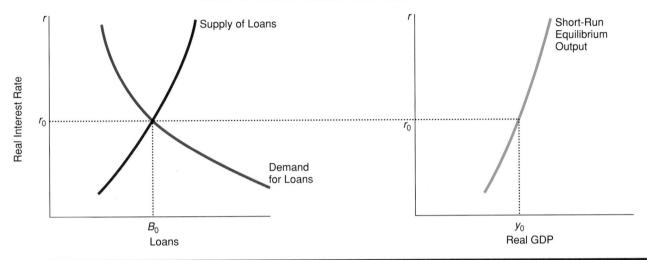

find equilibrium consumption in one of two ways, either by subtracting equilibrium savings and total taxes from equilibrium real GDP or subtracting government spending, investment, and the current account surplus from real GDP. Equilibrium employment comes from the supply and demand for labor (as in Figure 31.2) and equilibrium labor productivity (output per labor-hour) equals equilibrium real GDP divided by total labor-hours.

EXPECTATIONS

An important complication arises when economists estimate the curves in Figure 31.3 from data: the positions of the curves depend on people's expectations about the future. For example, the demand for loans depends on the expected profitability of investment. Estimating it involves the difficult work of estimating people's beliefs about the future.

Real business cycle models postulate that people behave, and form their expectations, rationally.

> People have **rational expectations** if their beliefs about the future accurately reflect the probabilities of various future events, based on all the information they currently have available.[8]

rational expectations — beliefs about the future that accurately reflect the probabilities of various future events, based on all currently available information

---

[8]If people can obtain more information at some cost, they form rational expectations if they obtain all of the information that they think is worth the cost, and then use this information to form their expectations. A more precise, but controversial, definition emerges from the following process. Various events might occur in the future; make a list of all possibilities. Based on all available information, there are certain probabilities that each of these events might occur. A person's expectations about future events are rational if the *chances* that the person attaches *psychologically* to these events equals the actual probabilities that they will occur.

For example, suppose that you want to predict the score of a basketball game. Of many *possible* scores, some are more likely than others. Based on information about the teams, you could try to estimate the probability of each possible score. You would have rational expectations if your own personal estimates of these chances matched the probabilities based on statistical analysis. Note that *one can never actually know the probabilities;* one can never be *sure* if someone's expectations are rational or not.

For example, suppose that you want to predict the number of points a team will score in the last 20 seconds of a basketball game. You may estimate a one-third chance that the team will score 0 points, a one-third chance it will score 2 points, and a one-third chance it will score 4 points. Your expectations are rational if, based on all available information, the team actually has a one-third chance of each of these outcomes.

People often state their expectations in terms of a single number rather than a list of chances that various events will occur. For example, you might say you expect the team to score 2 points. This is the *expected value,* or *mean,* of the score; it averages the numbers in all possible situations, weighted by the chances that they will happen.

To calculate an expected value:

1. Think of the number (e.g., the score) in each possible situation.

2. Multiply the number by the chance of that situation occurring.

3. Add up the answers from Step 2.

In the basketball example with a one-third chance of 0 points, plus a one-third chance of 2 points, plus a one-third chance of 4 points, the expected value of the score is:

$$(\tfrac{1}{3})(0) + (\tfrac{1}{3})(2) + (\tfrac{1}{3})(4) = 2 \text{ points}$$

A person with rational expectations may expect the team to score 2 points. That is the expected value of the score. Two-thirds of the time, however, this person will be wrong. One-third of the time the team will not score, and one-third of the time it will score 4 points. This illustrates an important point:

> People can make mistakes, even when they have formed rational expectations; they may even guess wrong most of the time. But they are not wrong in predictable ways if their expectations are rational because if people can predict their errors ahead of time, then they can correct them.

──────────────── **FOR REVIEW** ────────────────

31.1 According to real business cycle theories, why do business cycles (recessions and recoveries) happen?

31.2 What is total factor productivity? What does it mean to say it is *persistent*?

31.3 What is intertemporal substitution and how is it connected to the shapes of the loan supply curve and the aggregate supply curve?

31.4 What are rational expectations?

EFFECTS OF INCREASES IN THE RATE OF TECHNICAL PROGRESS

A technological improvement that raises total factor productivity has several effects on the economy. This section will go through the logic in several steps, but it is important to remember that all of these steps actually happen at the same time. This discussion separates them into steps only to simplify explanation.

The first effect of a rise in total factor productivity raises the amount of output that the economy can produce with the same inputs. It shifts the short-run

FIGURE 31.4

EFFECTS OF A TECHNOLOGY SHOCK—PART 1

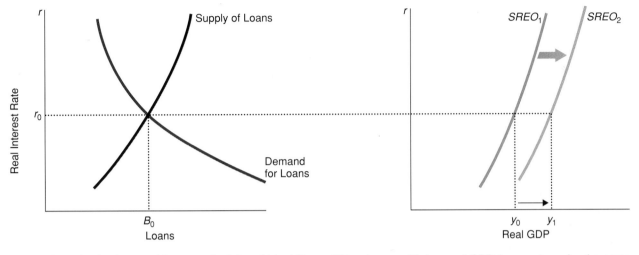

A technology shock raises total factor productivity, which shifts the short-run equilibrium output curve from $SREO_1$ to $SREO_2$.

This raises equilibrium real GDP from y_0 to y_1 by the same percentage as the increase in total factor productivity.

equilibrium output curve, as in **Figure 31.4.** This raises real GDP from y_0 to y_1 holding fixed the real interest rate and the inputs of labor and capital. Real GDP rises by the same percentage as the rise in total factor productivity.

The second effect of a rise in total factor productivity raises the demand for labor by raising the productivity of workers. This raises total employment from L_1 to L_2 and the equilibrium real wage, as in Panel b of **Figure 31.5** This increase in employment raises real GDP; it shifts the short-run equilibrium output curve from $SREO_2$ to $SREO_3$ in Panel a of Figure 31.5. Holding fixed the real interest rate, real GDP rises to y_2. (The rise in output from y_0 to y_2 occurs all at once—output does not rise first to y_1 and then to y_2 later.) The percentage increase in real GDP exceeds the percentage increase in total factor productivity.

The third effect of a productivity increase occurs because technology shocks are persistent, not purely temporary. Therefore, people expect a rise in total factor productivity to last for several years. This raises the expected future benefit from current investment, which raises investment demand and the demand for loans, as in Panel a of **Figure 31.6.** This raises the equilibrium real interest rate from r_0 to r_3 and the equilibrium quantity of loans from B_0 to B_3.[9] This increase in the real interest rate moves the economy along the short-run equilibrium output curve from Point A to Point B in Figure 31.6. Output increases because the rise in the real inter-

---

[9]The rise in the equilibrium quantity of loans includes a rise in savings *and* a rise in the amount borrowed from foreign countries. To keep this analysis from getting even more complicated, it ignores the government budget deficit for now; this does not change the reasoning in any important way. In general, one subtracts the government budget deficit from the equilibrium quantity of loans to calculate equilibrium investment.

FIGURE 31.5

EFFECTS OF A TECHNOLOGY SHOCK—PART 2

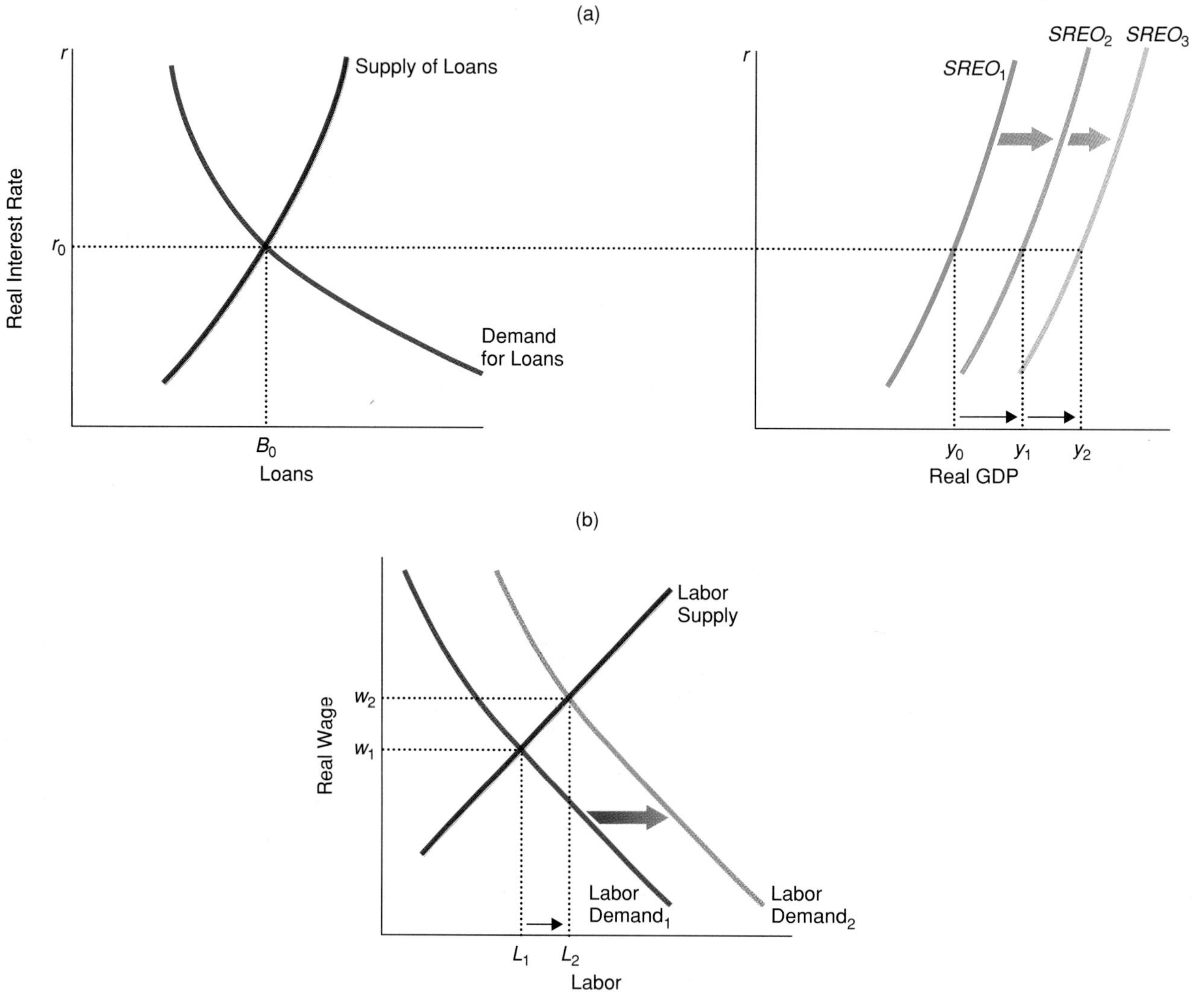

(a)

(b)

An increase in the demand for labor raises equilibrium employment from L_1 to L_2, which shifts the short-run equilibrium output curve and raises real GDP to $y_2 = AK_1^{1/3} L_2^{2/3}$. Equilibrium real GDP rises by a larger percentage than total factor productivity.

est rate raises the supply of labor through intemporal substitution. It also raises the supply of capital by raising its utilization rate. These increases in labor and capital raise real GDP from y_2 to y_3.

The fourth effect of a rise in total factor productivity is to raise people's incomes by increasing real GDP. People spend some of the higher income and save the rest. (They choose to spend more after a more persistent technology shock because this means that they can expect higher future incomes as well as higher current incomes. A more persistent technology shock causes greater increases

FIGURE 31.6

EFFECTS OF A TECHNOLOGY SHOCK—PART 3

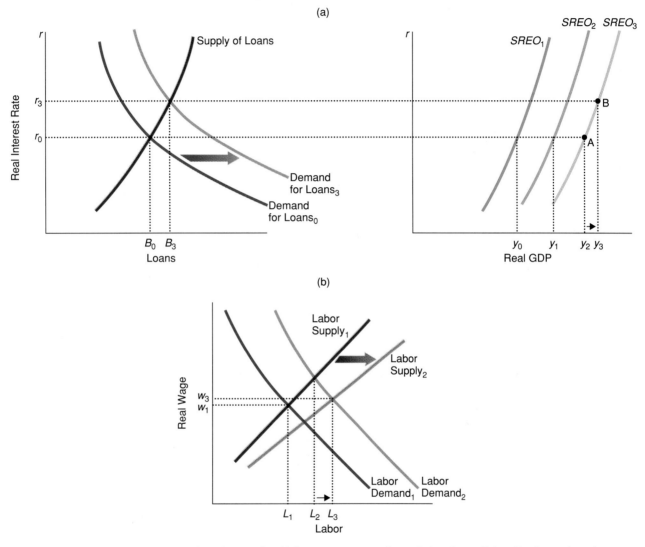

(a)

(b)

An increase in the real interest rate raises the supply of labor and increases equilibrium employment to L_3. This moves the economy from Point A to Point B along the short-run equilibrium output curve and raises real GDP to y_3.

in wealth and consumption demand.) To the extent that people raise the supply of savings, the supply of loans increases, as in **Figure 31.7.** This dampens the rise in the equilibrium real interest rate so that it rises only to r_4, not all the way to r_3, and it dampens the increase in real GDP, which rises only to y_4, not all the way to y_3.

COMBINING THE RESULTS

Overall, an increase in total factor productivity raises real GDP from y_0 to y_4. This gain comes from three sources:

FIGURE 31.7

EFFECTS OF A TECHNOLOGY SHOCK—PART 4

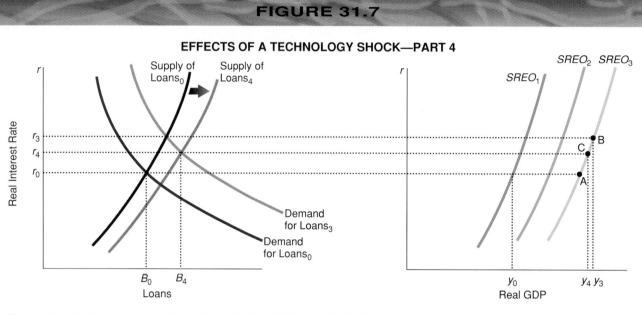

The supply of savings increases because people have higher incomes. This raises the supply of loans, which dampens the rise in the real interest rate. In equilibrium, the real interest rate rises only to r_4, and real GDP rises only to y_4.

1. The rise in productivity allows firms to produce more output with the same inputs.

2. Employment increases because the demand for labor rises, and the real wage rises.

3. Employment and the utilization rate of capital increase because of the rise in the real interest rate.

The percentage increase in real GDP is about twice as large as the increase in total factor productivity.[10] The percentage increase in investment, from B_0 to B_4, is 2 to 3 times larger than the percentage change in real GDP. (Because investment represents only about one-fifth of GDP, the actual increase in investment is smaller than the increase in GDP, even though the percentage change is larger.) Consumption rises, but by a smaller percentage than the rise in GDP. Employment rises; the percentage increase in total hours worked just about matches the percentage increase in real GDP.

The real interest rate rises from r_0 to r_4.[11] The real wage also rises as in Panel b of Figure 31.6 so, the real wage moves procyclically, as evidence confirms.[12]

---

[10]Economists use the *standard deviation,* a common measure in statistics, as one measure of variability. The standard deviation of a change in real GDP is about twice the standard deviation of a change in total factor productivity.

[11]This reduces net exports, causing an international trade deficit, because the higher interest rate raises the quantity of loans supplied by foreigners. Domestic residents borrow more from foreigners, which drives the trade deficit upward.

[12]This real business cycle model actually predicts that the real wage moves *more* procyclically than the evidence suggests.

According to the real business cycle model, business cycles result inevitably from increases and decreases in the rate of technical progress. If total factor productivity measures technology shocks effectively, then a model like this one can explain most of what happens during business cycles.

──────────────── **FOR REVIEW** ────────────────

31.5 List and explain three reasons why persistent technical progress raises real GDP.

31.6 Why does a persistent technology shock raise the real wage, the real interest rate, and equilibrium investment?

COMMENTS ON REAL BUSINESS CYCLE THEORIES

SEASONAL CYCLES

According to real business cycle theory, business cycles resemble the seasonal cycles that the economy experiences each year. In the first quarter of a typical year (January through March), real GDP is almost 4 percent below its average for that year. In the second and third quarters, real GDP about matches the year's average. In the fourth quarter, GDP is more than 4 percent above the year's average, after which it falls by almost 8 percent in the first quarter of the next year, and the seasonal cycle begins again. Seasonal cycles resemble business cycles in many ways; for example, investment varies more than output (in percentage terms) and consumption varies less. However, seasonal cycles are larger than most business cycles, and they are very predictable.

No economist attributes seasonal cycles to changes in the money supply because of sticky nominal prices or wages or confusions of nominal and relative prices. Seasonal cycles occur for other reasons (increased demand for goods before Christmas, less outdoor construction in cold winter months, and so on). Cold winter weather works like a slowdown in technical progress when it decreases output in the first quarter of each year. According to real business cycle theories, it is not surprising that seasonal cycles resemble business cycles because their causes are similar. The main difference is that seasonal cycles are shorter, larger, and more predictable than business cycles.

PERSISTENCE

If the theories of the previous chapter were right, changes in the money supply would have temporary effects on real GDP. (The temporary effects may last several years, but eventually the economy would return to its equilibrium level of output.) On the other hand, if the economy reacts mainly to permanent changes in total factor productivity, and if these changes cause business cycles, then changes in real GDP would be permanent.[13] In real life, changes in real GDP appear to combine the two.

─────────────────

[13]Temporary changes in total factor productivity could cause temporary changes in output.

A typical estimate summarizes the behavior of U.S. real GDP:

▶ If the economy is not in a recession, real GDP is likely to grow at 1.2 percent per quarter. Also, there is a 90 percent chance that it will not be in a recession in the next quarter and a 10 percent chance that it will be in a recession. (A quarter is 3 months.)

▶ If the economy is in a recession, real GDP is likely to fall at 0.4 percent per quarter. Also, it has a 75 percent chance of remaining in the recession in the next quarter, and a 25 percent chance of recovering from the recession by the next quarter.

SECTORAL SHIFTS

Some real business cycle models suggest that unemployment rises due to sectoral shifts.

> **Sectoral shifts** refer to output increases in some sectors of the economy along with output decreases in other sectors.

sectoral shift — output increase in one sector of the economy along with output decreases in one or more other sectors

For example, when compact disks replaced vinyl phonograph records, companies reduced their output of the vinyl records. People lost jobs in that industry, while the compact disk industry created jobs. Technology and consumer tastes always change, shifting supply and demand curves in various industries and leading to increases in output in some industries and decreases in others. People lose jobs in some industries and find jobs in others.

This process takes time, though. Unemployment may rise with larger sectoral shifts because more jobs are lost in some industries and created in others, and people remain unemployed for a time as they switch jobs. Economists continue to debate the importance of sectoral shifts as an explanation for changes in unemployment during business cycles.

It is interesting that every U.S. recession since World War II (with one exception in 1961) followed an increase in the price of imported crude oil.[14] One hypothesis holds that these price increases contributed to the recessions by causing sectoral shifts from industries that used oil heavily to other industries. Another hypothesis holds that the higher import prices reduced aggregate demand.

One can try to judge which hypothesis is right by watching what happens when oil prices fall. According to the sectoral shift hypothesis, this should cause sectoral shifts in the opposite direction from the shifts caused by oil price increases, which should reduce output growth and raise unemployment in the short run. According to the other hypothesis, a fall in oil prices should raise aggregate demand, raising the growth rate of real GDP and reducing unemployment. Oil prices fell dramatically in 1986. If a rise in oil prices affects the economy mainly by reducing aggregate demand, this fall in oil prices should have raised aggregate demand, raised real GDP, and reduced unemployment. This did not happen, at least not right away, as **Figure 31.8** shows. Initially, the growth rate of real GDP fell and unemployment increased slightly. This is some evidence against the view that oil prices affect the economy mainly by changing aggregate demand, and in favor of the sectoral shifts hypothesis. Over the next 3 years, though, the unemployment rate fell as the aggregate demand hypothesis says it should. As a result, this evidence does not clearly refute one hypothesis in favor of the other.

The Sun Belt gains manufacturing jobs as nation loses them

Work shift

Source: "The Sun Belt Gains Manufacturing Jobs as Nation Loses Them," *The Wall Street Journal,* April 1, 1988, p. 1.

---

[14]The 1990 recession followed only a brief increase in the price of oil at the time of Iraq's invasion of Kuwait.

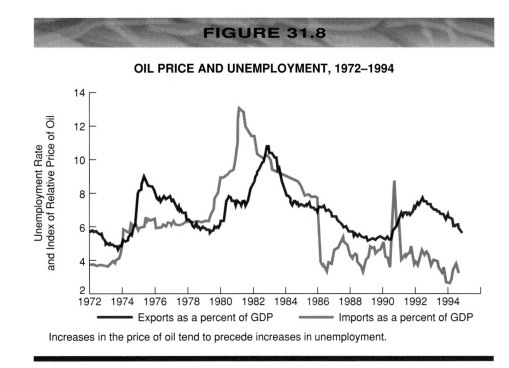

FIGURE 31.8

OIL PRICE AND UNEMPLOYMENT, 1972–1994

Exports as a percent of GDP   Imports as a percent of GDP

Increases in the price of oil tend to precede increases in unemployment.

MONEY AND REVERSE CAUSATION

Chapter 2 discussed the post-hoc fallacy of claiming that one event causes another because it precedes the other. It may always get dark soon after the street lights begin to shine, but that doesn't mean that turning on the street lights causes it to get dark. One cannot infer that one event causes another when two events occur together because one may reflect expectations of the other, or both may be results of some third event.

Many proponents of real business cycle models see the same fallacy in claims that money-supply changes cause business cycles. Money-supply changes often immediately precede changes in real GDP during business cycles, but that does not mean that they *cause* those changes in real GDP. Economists have identified two other possibilities.

First, the Federal Reserve may follow policies that lead it to raise the money supply just prior to increases in real GDP and to reduce the money supply before real GDP declines. Suppose that real and nominal interest rates rise just before real GDP rises because firms borrow more for new investments. Also, suppose that the Federal Reserve follows a policy of trying to keep the nominal interest rate roughly constant. The Fed sees the nominal interest rate rise, so it wants to reduce it. To reduce the nominal interest rate in the short run, the Federal Reserve conducts open market purchases which raise the money supply. The increase in the money supply may occur before the increase in real GDP, but it does not cause that increase.

An earlier chapter explained that the real demand for money rises when real GDP rises. A rise in the rate of technical progress—a technology shock—raises both real GDP and the real demand for money, M/P. If the Federal Reserve does not change the nominal money supply, then the price level falls to make M/P rise. The Federal Reserve may not want the price level to fall, however, so it may raise the nominal money supply to keep the price level from falling. In that case, the real demand for money, *M/P,* still rises, but through an increase in *M* rather than a fall in *P.* When this happens, economists say that the Federal Reserve *accommodates* the increase in the demand for money by changing the nominal supply. If a technology shock raises real GDP and the Federal Reserve accommodates the increase in money demand, then the money supply rises along with real GDP. Again, however, the money-supply increase does not cause the increase in real GDP.

A second series of events could explain a rise in the money supply and a subsequent rise in real GDP without one causing the other. Even if the Federal Reserve does not change the money supply, the money supply may rise just before an increase in real GDP because of an increase in the money multiplier. For example, businesses may increase their borrowing from banks before they increase investments and output. The increase in borrowing lowers both the reserve-deposit ratio and the currency-deposit ratio. This raises the money multiplier and increases the M1 and M2 measures of the nominal money supply, though not the monetary base. Because this happens *before* the increase in investment and output, changes in M1 and M2 precede changes in real GDP. Still, the money-supply change does not cause the change in real GDP.

Recall that during the 1980 credit-control episode discussed in the last chapter, decreases in bank lending reduced the money multiplier and reduced M1 and M2. According to real business cycle theories, the credit controls acted like a fall in productivity by interfering with people's productive activities, and caused a fall in real GDP. The money supply fall was a *result,* not a cause, of the recession.

Some other evidence supports this view. Changes in real GDP are much more closely related to changes in M1 and M2 than to changes in the monetary base. If business cycles resulted from money-supply changes, caused in turn by the Federal Reserve, then one might expect a stronger relationship between changes in real GDP and changes in the monetary base. Instead, money-supply changes during business cycles appear mainly as changes in M1 and M2. These changes in M1 and M2 could be results of changes in borrowing during business cycles, rather than causes of business cycles.

These arguments suggest *reverse causation* between money and real GDP. According to proponents of real business cycle theory, changes in the money supply do not cause changes in real GDP. Instead, changes in the money supply result from the same forces (such as technology shocks) that raise real GDP.

NOTE ON REAL BUSINESS CYCLE THEORIES

Real business cycle theories stir controversy. Most economists doubt that the theories are correct; they do not believe that business cycles are caused mainly by changes in the rate of technical progress or that changes in the money supply have no major short-run effects on real GDP, unemployment, and real interest rates. They also remain skeptical of the reverse-causation argument. Most economists believe that something like the sticky-price or sticky-wage model from the previous chapter explains business cycles best, perhaps combined with a coordination-failure model like the ones discussed later in this chapter.

Most economists could be wrong in this judgement, though. Science is not a popularity contest. Even if real business cycle models turn out to be flawed, however, they will have made important contributions that will form part of the models that macroeconomists will use in the future. The next section reviews criticisms of the theory and the responses of proponents of real business cycle models to these criticisms.

FOR REVIEW

31.7 What are sectoral shifts? How do they affect unemployment and real GDP?

31.8 a. What is reverse causation between money and real GDP?
How is it connected to the post-hoc fallacy?
b. What evidence supports the reverse-causation view?

CRITICISMS OF REAL BUSINESS CYCLE THEORIES

Economists have criticized real business cycle theories on five main grounds:

▶ They cannot explain decreases in real GDP during recessions.

▶ They cannot explain evidence linking money, inflation, and real GDP (such as the evidence for the short-run Phillips Curve).

▶ They cannot explain evidence that prices are sticky.

▶ They cannot explain involuntary unemployment.

▶ They do not explain business cycles as successfully as they seem to because their measure of technology shocks makes the theories look better than they are.

DECREASES IN REAL GDP

Critics of real business cycle theory say it cannot explain why real GDP actually falls during some recessions. Technical advances, the critics say, are permanent; people do not forget new technology, and equipment does not retrogress. Therefore, a slowdown in the rate of technical progress reduces the growth rate of real GDP, but it could not make the level of GDP fall, that is, the growth rate could not become negative. Yet real GDP has often fallen (its growth rate has become negative), as **Figure 31.9** clearly shows.

In response, proponents of real business cycles say three things:

▶ Real GDP does not properly measure output, since it excludes leisure, many investments in human capital, production in the home, and other activities. If real GDP included these categories to properly measure total output, it might not fall in recessions.

▶ Total factor productivity measures technical change in a broad sense. Total factor productivity changes in response to changes in regulations, laws, and the security and enforcement of property rights. This broader view of technical change does accommodate negative technical change. For example, the government may increase regulations on business to protect the environment. These regulations may lead firms to hire more people (such as environmental experts and lawyers) and to produce less output with more inputs (more labor). This would appear as a fall in total factor productivity. If the regulations produced a small benefit to the environment, they could cause negative technical change. If they produced a large benefit to the environment, they could cause positive technical change that would raise *true* output despite the fall in *measured* output, because measured real GDP does not include benefits to the environment.

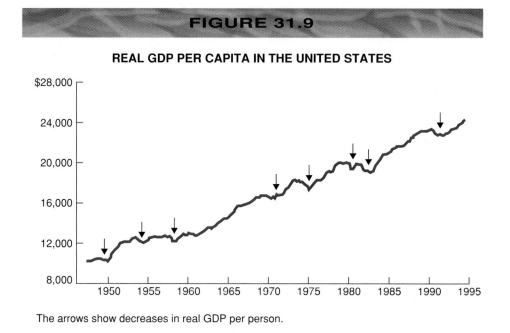

FIGURE 31.9

REAL GDP PER CAPITA IN THE UNITED STATES

The arrows show decreases in real GDP per person.

▶ Real GDP can fall, and unemployment can rise, due to sectoral shifts that occur during business cycles.

PHILLIPS CURVES

The second criticism of real business cycle models claims that they cannot explain evidence that supports a short-run Phillips Curve, as discussed in the last chapter. Critics doubt the reverse-causality argument (that changes in the money supply are results rather than causes of business cycles). They say that some changes in the money supply are results of business cycles, but the Federal Reserve creates other changes on purpose, and those money-supply changes cause short-run changes in real GDP, unemployment, and real interest rates. Some money-supply changes occur because the Federal Reserve wants to change inflation. Three examples illustrate this point:

▶ In 1974 to 1975, minutes of Federal Reserve meetings show an intention to follow policies that reduce inflation. The Fed then reduced the rate of growth of the M1 in 1974 to 1975, and the economy fell into a recession.

▶ In 1979 to 1982, the Federal Reserve announced that it would reduce inflation; inflation fell and so did real GDP in the 1982 recession.

▶ In 1936, the Federal Reserve raised reserve requirements for various reasons, reducing the growth rates of M1 and M2. An intentional reduction in the rate of growth of the monetary base followed, and the economy fell into a recession in 1937.

A long list of similar episodes suggests that the connection between changes in the money supply and real output does not rest solely on reverse causation.

Proponents of real business cycle theory present several arguments in response. First, they see only weak evidence for a short-run Phillips Curve. A graph in the last chapter showed no clear relationship between unemployment and inflation in U.S. data when all years are included in the analysis. To isolate certain sets of years, as in other panels of that figure, and argue that the Phillips Curve shifts over time amounts to adjusting evidence to fit a theory, rather than judging whether evidence is consistent or inconsistent with the theory. (Whenever data do not fit the theory, one could simply say that the Phillips Curve shifted.)

Furthermore, say proponents of real business cycle theory, critics mislead people when they concentrate attention on occasions when tighter monetary policies have preceded recessions while ignoring times when recessions have not followed tighter monetary policies. Concentrating attention on particular episodes, they argue, can distort the true picture.

STICKY PRICES AND WAGES

The third criticism of real business cycle analysis claims that it cannot explain the observation and evidence that many nominal prices and wages appear to be sticky. The last chapter noted that evidence supports the idea that prices are sticky and do not change as often as equilibrium theories imply they should. Evidence also suggests that nominal wages are sticky in the sense that they do not respond quickly or completely to unexpected inflation.

Real business cycle proponents respond with three arguments. First, they doubt the evidence that prices and wages are sticky. Economists cannot measure the equilibrium price or wage, so they can never know whether those values are their equilibrium levels. The fact that some prices do not change much may not indicate that they are sticky, because the equilibrium price may not change much, either.

The second response of real business cycle proponents notes that sticky prices may not matter. When buyers and sellers (or workers and firms) have long-term relationships, they might keep the price (or wage) constant, knowing that the buyer sometimes underpays and sometimes overpays, and the costs and benefits cancel out over time. Prices may look sticky, but it may not matter. A worker with a fixed nominal wage loses in the short run when unexpected inflation reduces the real wage, but an implicit contract (a general, unwritten agreement) with the employer may assure the worker that whenever this happens, the firm will pay an extra amount later to make up for the loss. (Similarly, the implicit contract may provide that when the worker gains from unexpectedly low inflation, a lower wage later on will make up for the short-run gain at the employee's expense.) Economists call this *ex-post settling-up*—when surprise changes in inflation cause one side to gain or lose, the implicit contract between people tells them to correct for these gains and losses at a later time.

Finally, real business cycle theorists argue that, even if prices and wages are sticky, the stickiness may not affect real GDP and employment. To see why, think about the sticky-wage model discussed in the last chapter. Suppose that the nominal wage, W, is sticky in the short run. A decrease in the money supply lowers the price level, P, which raises the real wage, W/P. If the price level falls from P_1 to P_2, the real wage rises from $w_1 = \overline{W/P_1}$ to $w_2 = \overline{W/P_2}$ in **Figure 31.10.**

According to the sticky-wage theory in the last chapter, employment falls from L_1 to L_2 (Point A to Point B), because the quantity of labor demanded is lower

FIGURE 31.10

WAGE STICKINESS MAY NOT AFFECT EMPLOYMENT

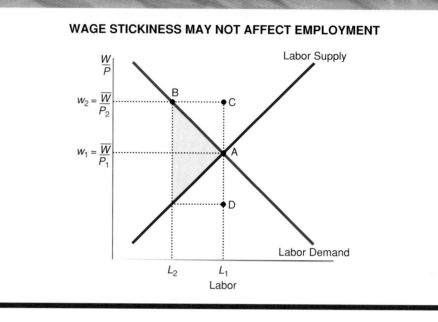

at a higher real wage; firms want fewer workers if the real wage is high. Both firms and workers could gain, however, by agreeing in advance (in a formal labor contract or in an implicit contract) to keep employment at L_1.

If employment falls to L_2, the economy suffers a *loss in economic efficiency* equal to the shaded area in the figure. This loss in economic efficiency measures lost gains from trade (see Chapter 3). The economically efficient level of employment is L_1 (where the supply and demand for labor are equal), at any price level. Firms and workers both gain by agreeing to keep employment at L_1, no matter what happens to the price level:

▶ If the price level falls, the firm loses profits and workers gain a higher real wage. The workers' gains equal the firm's losses, and the labor market is at Point C in the figure.

▶ If the price level rises, the firm gains profits and workers receive a lower real wage. The workers' losses equal the firm's gains, and the labor market is at Point D in the figure.

Fixing the nominal wage in a contract amounts to betting on the price level. The key point is that this bet should not affect employment, since the economically efficient amount of employment is L_1. Keeping employment at the efficient level creates the biggest pie for everyone to share. If employment moves from L_1, everyone loses from the losses in economic efficiency.

For this reason, rational workers and firms would agree to keep employment at the economically efficient level (L_1) even if they choose to bet on the price level by fixing the nominal wage. The changes in the money supply would not affect employment or real GDP even though wages are sticky.

Critics of real business cycle theory respond that this might happen in a theoretical rational world, but not in real life. They say that changes in real wages caused by unexpected inflation cause changes in employment (that the economy appears to move to a point like B), and that employment moves back to L_1 only when new labor contracts take effect, as the sticky-wage theory predicts.

INVOLUNTARY UNEMPLOYMENT

The fourth criticism of real business cycle theory focuses on its claim that all unemployment is voluntary. To many critics of real business cycle theory, it seems obvious that much unemployment during recessions is involuntary.

Proponents of real business cycle theory respond either that it seems obvious that the unemployment is voluntary, even though it is painful to the unemployed people, or that real business cycles are consistent with a certain kind of involuntary unemployment. To see why, suppose that you manage a firm. You have a job available for one person (technically, only one person can do it). Suppose, however, that two people who are completely alike in training, experience, and ability both want the job. You might choose one of them randomly since they are equally well qualified, leaving one person employed and the other unemployed. The unemployed person could take some other type of job somewhere, but the other job might not be as good or pay as well, so the unemployed person may choose not to take another job. That person is voluntarily unemployed in the sense that a job of some kind is available at a lower wage, but involuntarily unemployed in the sense that, despite being like the person who got the job, the jobless person cannot find any similar job at the same wage.

MEASURING TECHNICAL CHANGE

The fifth criticism of real business cycle analysis denies that it explains the economy as well as it claims to explain it. Critics say that total factor productivity does not effectively measure technology shocks, and that it makes the theory look better than it really is. Recall how economists measure total factor productivity—they look at data for y, K, and L on the right-hand side of Equation 31.2, and use the equation to calculate A, total factor productivity. Critics of real business cycle theory claim that economists' data do not accurately measure the amounts of labor and capital actually used in production. When real GDP (y) rises, Equation 31.2 says that total factor productivity (A) rises. Real business cycle theory then claims to explain the increase in real GDP by the increase in total factor productivity, but the increase in real GDP might really have resulted from increases in the amounts of labor and capital inputs, perhaps because of an increase in aggregate demand in a model like those in the last chapter. The economist might not recognize these changes because bad data on L and K would hide them. In addition, critics say, actual technical change in real life is too slow and gradual—too persistent—to cause business cycles. These issues currently spark vigorous controversy.

_____ **FOR REVIEW** _____

31.9 List and explain five criticisms of real business cycle theory. How do proponents of real business cycle theory respond?

31.10 Discuss some evidence against the reverse-causality view of money and real GDP.

COORDINATION FAILURES

coordination failure — situation that could result in any one of several equilibria, and in which the best equilibrium does not occur because people cannot jointly choose their actions

Some economists believe that business cycles are related to coordination failures in the economy.

> A **coordination failure** occurs when people fail to reach an equilibrium that would benefit everyone because they lack some way to coordinate, or jointly choose, their actions.

A coordination failure can occur when an economy allows multiple equilibria—more than one possible equilibrium. Sometimes one equilibrium is better than the others. The economy may become stuck in an economically inefficient equilibrium that voluntary trades cannot prevent without additional coordination of people's activities.

According to this view, recessions may occur when the economy enters a bad equilibrium with inefficiency, low output, and unemployment. The models in the last two chapters postulated economic inefficiencies due to sticky nominal prices, sticky nominal wages, or lack of certain information. While those models involved nominal prices or wages, coordination failures can also occur in real business cycle models.

THREE EXAMPLES

Suppose that a group of people decide to play a basketball game if enough people show up at the court this afternoon. If enough people expect other people to show up, they will go to the court ready to play. If most people do not expect other people to show up, they will not expect a game and they will not go to the court. This situation allows two equilibria, one in which people expect a game to occur, so they go and play a game, and another in which people don't expect a game to occur, so they don't go and no game occurs. Everyone might be better off playing a game, but if no one expects other people to show up, no one plays. This is the bad equilibrium.

In this coordination failure, everyone could gain if they could jointly decide to show up at the court. People solve most coordination failures in obvious ways: the people might talk to each other and jointly decide to have the game. Sometimes it is much more difficult than this to coordinate people's activities, though.

Notice that in the basketball example and the examples below, expectations may be *rational*. If people expect the good equilibrium, then it occurs. If they expect the bad equilibrium, then *it* occurs. In these examples, people's expectations are *self-fulfilling*. What people expect affects their actions, which creates the results that they expected.

A second example of coordination failures comes from countries like the old Soviet Union where people often had to wait in very long lines at government-owned stores to buy goods because the government kept prices below the equilibrium prices, which created shortages. When people spend a lot of time waiting in lines, they don't have much time left to work, so they don't produce many goods. With lower output of goods, the shortage becomes worse and lines become longer. An economy can be stuck in a bad equilibrium. If people could spend less time waiting in lines, they could spend more time working, so they could produce more goods. The shortages would then be less severe and the lines would be shorter.

trading externality — a situation
in which the costs of dealing with
other people would fall if more
people would participate in trading

Trading externalities can create a third type of a coordination failure.

> **Trading externalities** occur if the costs of dealing with other people would fall if more people would participate in trading.

Think about a country like the Soviet Union at the time socialism collapses. Normal, government-owned-and-operated stores have no food. People have two choices:

1. Grow food in their own gardens and eat it themselves (and not buy or sell any food)

2. Specialize by producing one kind of food (or another good) and trading some of it for the food or goods that other people produce

If people grow food for themselves, they must grow several kinds of foods to get important nutrients. If they specialize in one kind of food (or some other good), they can produce more through gains from specialization like those discussed in Chapter 3. If people specialize and trade, everyone can end up with more food (and perhaps more of some other goods) than if they all grow their own food in their own gardens.

Trading externalities arise because people who want to specialize and trade must find others with whom to trade. If it takes a long time to find trading partners (time that could be spent producing goods), then people are better off not trading and just growing food for their own use.

If many people decide to specialize and trade with other people, then they can easily find trading partners. If few people decide to specialize and trade, then someone who specializes must work hard to find trading partners. This creates two equilibria:

1. A bad equilibrium in which people grow their own food because no one expects many other people to try to trade

2. A good equilibrium in which all people (or many people) specialize and trade things, and everyone ends up with more food

The good equilibrium happens if everyone expects it to happen because then people find it worthwhile to specialize and trade. The bad equilibrium happens if everyone expects it because then people doubt that they can find trading partners, so they grow their own food instead of specializing and trading. The economy can get stuck in the bad equilibrium because people have no easy way to coordinate their actions so that they all participate in trading.[15]

CONNECTION WITH BUSINESS CYCLES

Some economists believe that coordination failures are related to business cycles. John Maynard Keynes wrote of the influence on investment decisions of "animal spirits"—his term for the psychology of the market. Sometimes most firms are optimistic about the future of the economy; they expect high rates of return on investments. Other times they are pessimistic about the future; they expect low rates of return on investments. Investments may depend on trading externalities.

---

[15]Another example involves well-attended and poorly attended parties. Everyone likes well-attended parties, but a party can be poorly attended simply because no one expects many other people to come, so they don't come either.

In the last example, people may need to invest to specialize and trade. If people expect a good equilibrium with much investment activity, they invest and produce a high level of output. Employment is high, consumption is high, and people gain from specializing—the good equilibrium happens. If they expect the bad equilibrium, they do not invest as much, and they produce less output. The bad equilibrium, a recession, occurs.

GOVERNMENT POLICIES

These examples all have multiple equilibria. Several things could happen, some of them perhaps better than others. The economy could get stuck in a bad equilibrium. Certain government policies might help the economy to reach a better equilibrium, though. The appropriate government policy would depend on exactly what kind of coordination failure occurs. People would benefit if someone could help to coordinate their actions. This someone could be the government, although this suggestion raises the question of what the government can do to coordinate people's actions that those people cannot do themselves, without the government.

One rationale for government action to help coordinate people's actions emerges when people face fixed costs of coordinating their actions. (The fixed costs could come from time spent organizing people, for example.) No one individual may be willing to pay the fixed costs for coordination. Perhaps each of 100 people would gain $1,000 from coordination, but the fixed costs of coordination are $20,000. The government could coordinate people because it could tax each person $200 to get the $20,000 to spend for coordination. Since each person then gains $1,000 from the coordination, each person is $800 better off than if the government had not taxed them and coordinated their actions. (In practice, people would want to take into account the government's incentives and knowledge. Does the government have enough information to coordinate people effectively? Does it have an incentive to coordinate them effectively or do political pressures create different incentives?

SUNSPOTS

Some economists believe that business cycles occur because of coordination failures that create multiple equilibria. These economists believe that recessions occur when the economy gets into a bad equilibrium, and the economy bounces around from one equilibrium to another. Sometimes it is in a good equilibrium (at the full-employment level of output) and sometimes in a recession. This bouncing around between equilibria is itself an equilibrium, called a *sunspot equilibrium.*

Suppose that, as in a real business cycle model, the nominal money supply would ordinarily not affect real GDP. Suppose, however, that people believe it affects real GDP. Suppose they believe that the economy will be in the bad equilibrium if the nominal money supply is low, and the good equilibrium if it is high. When the government chooses the nominal money supply each year and announces its level, the economy can bounce around between high and low levels of output. People have rational expectations because their expectations are self-fulfilling.

In this case, the nominal money supply creates economic sunspots. When an economy has multiple equilibria, anything can create economic sunspots if two conditions hold:

1. People believe that it affects the economy and, as a result of their actions, it has the effect that people believed it would have

2. It would not affect the economy at all, except for the fact that people believe that it does

Sunspot equilibria can occur even if everyone is rational. It is rational to believe in the economic sunspots because other people do, so the sunspots really do affect the economy. If no one else believed that the sunspots mattered, they would not affect the economy and rational people would not pay attention to them.

Logic allows many interesting types of coordination failures and sunspot equilibria. Whether sunspots are an important part of real-life business cycles is, like the real business cycle theories discussed earlier, a subject of current research and controversy.

—————————————————— FOR REVIEW ——————————————————

31.11 What is a coordination failure? What are multiple equilibria?

31.12 What are self-fulfilling expectations?

31.13 Explain trading externalities and give an example.

31.14 What is a sunspot equilibrium?

CONCLUSIONS

REAL BUSINESS CYCLE THEORIES

Real business cycle theories try to explain business cycles without referring to nominal variables like the nominal price level. They claim that business cycles are economically efficient, equilibrium responses of the economy to technology shocks. These theories take a broad view of technology shocks, including changes in regulations, laws, and enforcement of property rights as well as implementation of scientific knowledge into productive capital equipment or human capital. The theories measure technology shocks by changes in total factor productivity through a model like the one in an earlier chapter. The theories assume that people have rational expectations. The models explain how these persistent technology shocks raise or lower real GDP along with employment, productivity, consumption, investment, real wages, the real interest rate, and the current account deficit.[16]

EFFECTS OF INCREASES IN THE RATE OF TECHNICAL PROGRESS

Technical progress raises GDP in three ways: (1) it directly raises the amount of output produced with the same inputs, (2) it raises employment because real wages rise as the technology shock raises worker productivity and the demand for labor, and (3) it raises employment through rises in the real interest rate and intertemporal substitution in labor supply. The real interest rate rises because the technology shock raises the expected rate of return on investment, which raises the demand for loans.

COMMENTS ON REAL BUSINESS CYCLE THEORIES

Real business cycle theories compare business cycles to seasonal cycles in many ways. They deny that business cycles result from changes in the money supply.

———————————————

[16]This means an increase in real GDP that is faster than its trend rate of growth, or a decrease in its growth rate below its trend rate of growth (in recessions).

The theories attribute changes in the money supply during business cycles to reverse causation. The money supply changes because a productivity shock changes investment, the real interest rate, and real GDP; the money-supply change does not cause these other changes.

CRITICISMS OF REAL BUSINESS CYCLE THEORIES

Critics deny that real business cycle theories can explain decreases in the level of real GDP during recessions. They also say that the theories cannot explain evidence linking money, inflation, and real GDP (such as the evidence for the short-run Phillips Curve) or evidence that prices are sticky. They also say that most unemployment during business cycles is involuntary and that real business cycle theories cannot explain this. Critics say that the theories look more successful than they are because they rely on a bad measure of technology shocks.

COORDINATION FAILURES

Another type of model tries to explain business cycles through coordination failures, again without referring to nominal variables. Coordination-failure models allow multiple equilibria, and they claim that the economy sometimes gets stuck in a bad equilibrium. That is a recession. The theory of sunspots tries to explain why the economy sometimes has recessions by saying that changes in a sunspot variable change people's expectations. This leads people to change their behavior, and the change in behavior creates exactly the situation that people expected; expectations are self-fulfilling.

Both real business cycle theories and coordination-failure theory with sunspots are controversial. Economists do not yet agree on any theory of business cycles. Most economists place more faith in the sticky-price or sticky-wage models of the last chapter than in other theories, but truth is not a popularity contest, so economists continue to look for evidence about all these theories. They also continue to develop the theories logically, hoping to identify new predictions of the theories that they can compare to real-life economic data.

LOOKING AHEAD

Now that you have collected a nearly complete set of macroeconomic trading cards, it is time to use them to think about government economic policies. The next two chapters discuss monetary and fiscal policies.

KEY TERMS

real business cycle theories	rational expectations
total factor productivity	sectoral shift
technology shock	trading externality
short-run equilibrium output curve	coordination failure

QUESTIONS AND PROBLEMS

31.15 According to real business cycle theory, why does productivity, measured as real GDP per labor-hour, change procyclically?

31.16 What would happen to investment and the real interest rate if a technology shock were *not* persistent, but *temporary* instead? (*Hint:* Work through graphs like those in Figures 31.3 through 31.7.)

31.17 a. Explain how and why a persistent increase in the rate of technical progress affects the current account.

b. What would happen to the balance of international trade (net exports) if this increase in the rate of technical progress were to occur in all countries at the same time?

31.18 Suppose that economists find a country where *all* changes in real GDP are completely permanent. Explain how that would help economists to decide between real business cycle theories and the theories of the last chapter.

31.19 Explain why firms and workers would like to sign contracts that keep employment at the economically efficient level, even if the nominal wage is fixed in the short run so that unexpected inflation changes the real wage. If contracts do this, and if nominal wages are sticky in the short run, how would a fall in the money supply affect real wages, employment, and real GDP?

INQUIRIES FOR FURTHER THOUGHT

31.20 What happens during seasonal cycles? Why do you think the economy has these seasonal cycles? In what ways do you think they are the same as business cycles? In what ways do they differ?

31.21 Suppose that recessions occur because of coordination failures. What policies, if any, should the government follow to avoid recessions? Why might the government be able to do things to prevent a recession that people or firms outside the government could not do?

TAG SOFTWARE APPLICATIONS

TUTORIAL EXERCISES

▶ The module contains a review of the key terms from Chapter 31.

GRAPHING EXERCISES

▶ The graphing segment examines how changes in the real interest rate affect input markets, and it examines the effects of a technology shock.

MACROECONOMIC POLICIES

MONETARY POLICY

WHAT THIS CHAPTER IS ABOUT

▶ Activist and laissez-faire views of government policy

▶ Rules versus discretion in government policy

▶ Lucas critique

▶ Goals for monetary policy

▶ Alternative institutions for monetary policy

Not many people discuss monetary policy around the dinner table. Even news reports spend much less time reporting on monetary policy than on the latest political scandals or daily fluctuations in the stock market. Yet monetary policy has a more dramatic impact on your life than most of the issues discussed more frequently in the news. It determines whether you live in a country with stable prices or suffer through hyperinflation. It affects interest rates and redistributes income and wealth. In the short run, most economists believe, monetary policy affects the economy's output of goods and services, job opportunities for millions of workers, and unemployment. The Federal Reserve is one of the most powerful agencies in the world, perhaps with more impact on your life than the Supreme Court, but how much do you know of its policies and how many of its members can you name?

If you were in charge of the Federal Reserve or the central bank of another country, how would you make decisions?[1] How would you decide what the Fed should do today or next week? How would you decide whether to raise the money supply through open market purchases or by how much to raise it? How would you decide whether to raise the discount rate and by how much? How would you choose longer-term goals for your policies and what would those goals be? To keep inflation at a certain level? To avoid recessions? Would you base your decisions on some underlying principle or rule or just try to do what seems best on a day-to-day basis?

If you were a member of Congress in charge of rethinking monetary policy and perhaps redesigning the way government works, would you want Congress or the Constitution to require the Fed to follow some particular principles or rules in its monetary policies? Would you want to keep the Federal Reserve System at all or replace it with something else?

---

[1]An earlier chapter described the Federal Reserve System and its main tools of monetary policy: open market operations, discount-window lending, and reserve requirements and other bank regulations.

TYPES OF MACROECONOMIC POLICIES

monetary policy — changes in the nominal money supply through open market operations, changes in the discount rate or discount-window lending policy, or reserve requirement changes

fiscal policy — government actions that affect total government spending, tax rates or tax revenues, or the government budget deficit

The two main types of government macroeconomic policy are monetary and fiscal policy:

> **Monetary policy** refers to changes in the nominal money supply through open market operations, changes in the discount rate or discount-window lending policy, or reserve requirement changes.

The Federal Reserve conducts monetary policy in the United States. Other countries have their own central banks, such as the Bank of Japan, the Bank of England, and the Bank of Mexico, which conduct those nations' monetary policies.

> **Fiscal policy** refers to government actions that affect total government spending, tax rates or tax revenues, or the government budget deficit.

The next chapter will discuss fiscal policy.

TWO GENERAL VIEWS OF GOVERNMENT POLICIES

Two general views characterize the debate about the proper role of government economic policy.

ACTIVIST VIEW

Some economists take an activist view of policy.

activist view of policy — the view that the economy often operates inefficiently on its own and that government macroeconomic policies can make the economy more efficient

> An **activist view of policy** maintains that the economy often operates inefficiently on its own and government macroeconomic policies can make the economy more efficient.

According to this view, changes in aggregate demand and supply sometimes reduce output below its full-employment level and raise unemployment above its natural rate. Government macroeconomic policies can stabilize the economy— prevent or reduce the sizes of business cycles—by preventing or offsetting these changes in aggregate demand and supply. For example, when aggregate demand decreases, the government could increase the money supply or government spending to raise aggregate demand and real GDP, as in **Figure 32.1.**

LAISSEZ-FAIRE VIEW

Other economists take a laissez-faire (hands off) view of policy.

laissez-faire view of policy — the view that the economy usually operates efficiently on its own and that even when it does not, active government policies are more likely to aggravate inefficiencies and create new inefficiencies than to alleviate problems

> A **laissez-faire view of policy** maintains that the economy usually operates efficiently on its own and that even when it does not, active government policies are more likely to aggravate inefficiencies and create new inefficiencies than to alleviate problems.

Proponents of the laissez-faire view usually advocate a small role for government in the economy along with little government interference with individual freedom to make voluntary trades. Whenever possible, government policies should conform to a set of rules announced in advance rather than basing decisions on the discretion of government officials. For example, a rule might require the Federal Reserve to keep the growth rate of M1 between 2 percent and 4 percent per year; another rule might require the government to balance its budget each year.

Why do supporters of the laissez-faire view oppose activist policies? Don't they care about the fall in real GDP shown in Figure 32.1 without a government policy to raise aggregate demand? They do care, but they believe that activist poli-

FIGURE 32.1

AN ACTIVIST VIEW OF GOVERNMENT POLICY

If aggregate demand were to fall from AD_1 to AD_2, an activist government policy might raise the money supply or government spending to try to raise aggregrate demand back to AD_1.

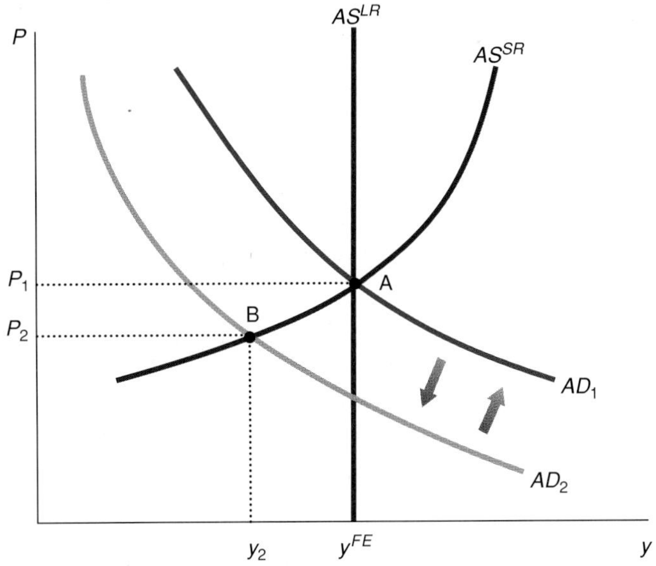

cies usually do more harm than good. They argue that rules produce better results than the discretionary policies of politicians, even well-meaning politicians. Activist government policies—policies not governed by rules—make things worse for three reasons, according to this view:

1. Economists don't know enough about the operation of the economy, particularly about lags between policy changes and changes in the economy, to know how to improve its efficiency.[2]

2. Rules for government policies make it easier for people to plan because they know what to expect. This allows people to make better decisions.

3. Rules that are announced in advance and that are credible (that is, rules that people believe the government will follow) can produce better results than policies not based on rules because credible rules change people's incentives.

The following sections will explain these arguments.

---

[2]To see why lags matter, think about turning on the water to take a shower. You turn on the hot water along with the cold water, but it takes time for the hot water to get hot; a lag separates the time you turn on the faucet and the time hot water arrives. After a minute, if the water feels too cold, you may turn on more hot water, but you may not have waited long enough for the hot water to arrive at the shower; by turning up the hot water, you will have made the shower too hot after a few minutes. The lag—the length of time hot water takes to arrive at the shower—may change from day to day depending on the outside temperature, how many other people in the building are using hot water, and so on. This may make it difficult to get the water temperature just right. You may be better off with a simple rule such as "turn up the hot and cold water each halfway regardless of the water temperature for the first several minutes."

ISSUES OF MONETARY POLICY

Monetary policy affects inflation. In the short run, it may also affect real GDP and unemployment as in the *AS/AD* (aggregate supply/aggregate demand) model of earlier chapters. Monetary policy also affects interest rates, so participants in financial markets pay close attention to Federal Reserve actions and statements by Fed officials that might foreshadow future policy changes. Some firms rely on professional Fed-watchers for up-to-date reports on Federal Reserve actions and predictions about future actions.

Three types of issues arise in debates over monetary policy:

1. What should the Federal Reserve do today?
2. What longer-term policy should the Fed follow? Should rules or discretion govern monetary policy? What kinds of rules, or principles for discretion, should guide monetary policy?
3. What institutions should carry out monetary policy?

TODAY'S ACTIONS

What should the Fed do right now? Should it conduct open market purchases to raise the monetary base by $3.2 million, $5.8 million, or some other number? Should it raise the discount rate and, if so, by how much? The question about today's Fed actions breaks down into three questions. First, what goals should the Fed pursue? Should it work to reduce inflation or to keep inflation at its current level, or to do everything possible to prevent a recession regardless of inflation? Should it do something else?

Second, what kinds of actions would best achieve the Fed's goals? Should the Fed try to control the growth rate of the M1 or M2 measures of the money supply? Should it try to control nominal interest rates, as it has often tried to do? Would some other current actions better achieve its goals?

Third, what specific actions should the Fed take today? For example, suppose that the Fed wants M1 to grow at 5 percent per year. Should it conduct $1 million or $2 million in open market purchases to accomplish this?

RULES OR DISCRETION?

Should the Federal Reserve act at its own discretion, that is, base daily actions on its judgement of the economic situation, or should it follow a policy rule?

policy rule — a statement of what policy an agency will follow

A **policy rule** is a statement of what policy an agency will follow.

For example, a policy rule might say that each month, the Fed will conduct open market operations to raise M1 at a constant rate of 5 percent per year. This is an example of a simple policy rule.

simple policy rule — a rule that requires a particular policy regardless of economic circumstances

A **simple policy rule** requires a particular policy regardless of economic circumstances.

contingent policy rule — a rule that states specifically how policies will depend on economic circumstances

A **contingent policy rule** states specifically how policies will depend on particular economic circumstances.

A contingent policy rule takes the form "if *x*, then policy will be *y*." For example, a contingent policy rule might state something like:

Each month, the Fed will look at the most recent unemployment rate. If the unemployment rate is below 7 percent, the Fed will conduct open market operations to raise M1 at a constant rate of 5 percent per year. If the unemployment rate is 7 percent or higher, the Fed will conduct open market operations to raise M1 at a constant rate of 10 percent per year.

Contingent policy rules can specify any number of conditions and involve any level of complication. A later section will discuss the benefits of rules and those of discretion.

The choice of a policy rule raises the same issues detailed above. What goals should monetary policy pursue? What kinds of actions would best achieve those goals? What kind of policy rule would best promote those actions? The Fed might impose a monetary policy rule on itself, though nothing would then prevent it from violating or changing its rule. Alternatively, Congress might pass a law requiring the Fed to follow a certain rule. This would increase the likelihood that the Fed would follow the rule.

credible policy rule — a rule that people believe policy makers will follow, perhaps because they have an incentive to follow it

A **credible policy rule** is a rule that people believe, perhaps because the policy maker has an incentive to follow the rule.

Some policy rules are more credible than others. Usually, stronger incentives for a policy maker to follow a rule make the rule more credible.

commitment to a policy rule — an action by a policy maker to guarantee implementation of the rule

A policy maker makes a **commitment to a policy rule** by doing something to guarantee implementation of the rule.

People sometimes say that a person "burns bridges behind him" when he does something that makes it hard to reverse some action. This phrase has its origins in war, when a general in an invading army might burn the bridges behind the army (after crossing them) to prevent soldiers from retreating during a battle; burning bridges commits the army to either fight or surrender. The idea of burning bridges is to increase the incentive to fight hard; it is a method of promoting commitment. Economic policy makers usually find it much harder than soldiers to commit.

discretionary policy — a policy that chooses moves day-to-day without a specific rule

Discretionary policy does not require the policy maker to follow a specific policy rule.

Most economic policy making is discretionary. The Federal Reserve, for example, continually evaluates economic conditions and acts as it considers appropriate.

MONETARY INSTITUTIONS

The third issue that arises in the debate about monetary policy concerns policy institutions. Should the Federal Reserve act as an independent agency of the government, as it does now, or should Congress or the president control the Fed more directly? What powers should the Fed have? Should the Federal Reserve exist at all? Similar questions arise in other countries. Should all the countries of Europe use the same money and have one European central bank rather than different monies and different central banks? If so, how should that central bank be organized and who should control it?

Should the law allow private firms such as banks to print their own money as they did during part of the 19th century? Should people be free to use whichever money they want as long as someone else is willing to accept it voluntarily? Should the government involve itself in the money business at all, or should it leave this activity to private producers in free markets like most other businesses?

DISCRETIONARY MONETARY POLICY

Most discussions of monetary policy focus on the first question listed earlier: What should the Fed do now? What is the best discretionary monetary policy? The answer involves choosing goals, then choosing actions to achieve them. Many economists, with the *AS/AD* model of earlier chapters in mind, believe that the Fed should try to keep real GDP near its full-employment level by taking monetary policy actions to stabilize aggregate demand. (An effort to stabilize aggregate demand uses policy actions to offset other changes.) Generally, such economists take an activist view of policy and favor discretionary policies. Other economists believe that the Fed should try to keep inflation steady and low. Most economists in this group tend to take a laissez-faire view of policy and tend to favor policy rules.[3] Some economists advocate goals that compromise between pursuit of steady, low inflation and stable real GDP. A compromise rule might try to keep the growth rate of nominal GDP constant. Another kind of compromise might place limits on discretionary policies. The Federal Reserve itself usually states its goals only vaguely, and most Fed-watchers believe that it usually compromises between these goals as it formulates its discretionary policies.

The Fed usually describes its monetary policies in terms of effects on interest rates. Recall from an earlier chapter that the federal funds rate is the interest rate on short-term loans between banks.

looser monetary policy — a policy that increases the growth rates of the monetary base and broader measures of the money supply or decreases the federal funds rate

> A **looser monetary policy** acts to increase the growth rates of the monetary base and broader measures of the money supply or to decrease the federal funds rate.

The Fed loosens monetary policy by conducting more open market purchases or lending more reserves to banks at the discount window.

tighter monetary policy — a policy that reduces the growth rates of the monetary base and broader measures of the money supply or increases the federal funds rate

> A **tighter monetary policy** acts to reduce the growth rates of the monetary base and broader measures of the money supply or to increase the federal funds rate.

The Fed tightens monetary policy by conducting fewer open market purchases (or more open market sales) or lending less to banks at the discount window.

A looser policy is also called a more *expansionary* policy; a tighter policy is said to be more *contractionary*. The Fed, and people who report on Federal Reserve actions, often describe a looser policy as *reducing interest rates* and a tighter policy as *raising interest rates*. The Fed usually tightens monetary policy when it sees inflation as the most serious problem facing the economy. It may tighten only a small amount to try to avoid causing a large fall in aggregate demand and a recession. The Fed usually loosens monetary policy when it believes that inflation is under control and it sees the threat of a recession as the most serious problem facing the economy.

Some economists argue that it is misleading to describe monetary policy in terms of its effects on interest rates. Suppose that the Fed loosens monetary policy by increasing the growth rate of the money supply from 4 percent per year to 6 percent per year. In the short run, this may reduce the federal funds rate and other short-term interest rates, but in the long run it causes higher nominal inter-

---

[3]Some of these economists advocate the real business cycle models discussed in the last chapter. They believe that monetary policy has at most a small effect on real GDP.

Most short-term interest rates rise amid talk Fed might be tightening its policy somewhat

Credit markets

By Tom Herman and Laurence Bauman Staff Reporters of The Wall Street Journal

NEW YORK—Most short-term interest rates rose amid speculation that the Federal Reserve may be tightening credit slightly in an effort to combat inflation.

While the evidence is unclear, some bond traders say the Fed appears to be reacting to signs of stronger economic growth recently. Many expect further interest rate increases in the next few weeks.

Changes in monetary policy have almost instant effects on financial markets.

Source: Tom Herman and Laurence Bauman, "Most Short-Term Interest Rates Rise Amid Talk Fed Might Be Tightening Its Policy Somewhat," *The Wall Street Journal,* November 9, 1988, p. C23.

est rates. The increase in the growth rate of the money supply raises inflation in the long run, and, because it has no long-run effect on the real interest rate, it raises the nominal interest rate. This complicates the connection between monetary policy and interest rates; policies that may reduce interest rates in the short run can raise them in the long run, and vice versa.

DISCRETIONARY MONETARY POLICY IN THE *AS/AD* MODEL

The sticky-price *AS/AD* model of earlier chapters provides a tool to examine the effects of Fed policies. Suppose that aggregate demand falls from AD_1 to AD_2, as in Figure 32.1. This temporarily reduces real GDP from y^{FE} to y_2 and raises unemployment. It also reduces the price level from p_1 to p_2 in the short run, and still further in the long run. The Fed might try to offset this temporary fall in real GDP by raising the money supply enough to prevent a fall in aggregate demand. Similarly, the Fed could tighten monetary policy to prevent an increase in aggregate demand.

Now suppose that aggregate supply falls, possibly because of a rise in the price of imported oil, from AS_1 to AS_2 in **Figure 32.2.** If the Fed keeps the nominal money supply constant, as in Panel a, the economy moves from Point A to Point B in the short run; the price level rises from p_1 to p_2 and real GDP falls from y_1 to y_2. In the long run, real GDP falls from y_1 to y_3 and the price level rises to p_3 (Point C). The Fed cannot prevent the long-run fall in real output from y_1 to y_3, but it can affect the economy in the short run. If the Fed raises the money supply enough to raise aggregate demand from AD_1 to AD_2, as in Panel b, then the economy moves from Point A to Point D in the short run; the price level rises to p_4 in the short run, but real GDP does not fall. In the long run, the economy moves to Point E; real GDP falls to y_3 and the price level rises to p_5. The Fed faced this problem when the price of imported oil quadrupled in 1973, reducing aggregate supply as in Figure 32.2. The Fed responded by keeping the growth rates of the monetary base and M1 about the same and allowing the growth rate of M2 to fall.

Many, though not all, economists view the short-run Phillips Curve of an earlier chapter as an illustration of a short-run tradeoff between inflation and

The Federal Reserve, the nation's central bank, Friday took steps to lower interest rates in an attempt to prevent even a mild recession.

The Fed loosens monetary policy or raises interest rates.

Source: Washington Post, July 16, 1990, p. A5.

FIGURE 32.2

EFFECTS OF A FALL IN AGGREGATE SUPPLY

(a) Effects with Constant Money Supply

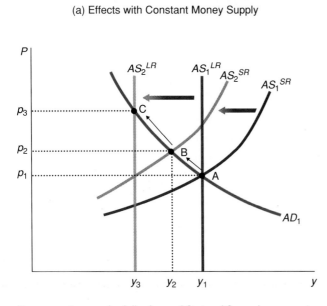

(b) Effects with Rising Money Supply

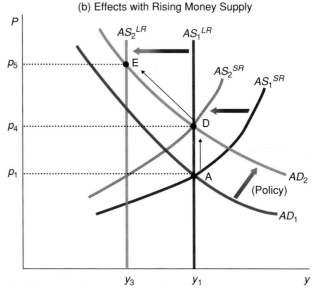

If aggregate supply falls from AS_1 to AS_2 and aggregate demand remains constant, output falls to y_2 in the short run and to y_3 in the long run. The price level rises to p_2 in the short run and to p_3 in the long run.

If aggregate supply falls from AS_1 to AS_2, an activist monetary policy might raise the money supply to try to raise aggregate demand back to AD_2. Then real GDP stays at y_1 in the short run, and the price level rises to p_4. In the long run, the economy moves to Point E, real GDP falls to y_3, and the price level rises to p_5.

unemployment. These economists believe that policy makers can temporarily choose any combination of inflation and unemployment on the short-run Phillips Curve, such as Point A in **Figure 32.3** with high inflation and low unemployment, Point B with moderate inflation and unemployment, or Point C with low inflation and high unemployment. The choice has only temporary effects because the short-run Phillips Curve shifts in the long run, as in Figure 32.3b. Whatever inflation rate policy makers choose, unemployment then returns to its natural rate.

Most proponents of discretionary monetary policy argue that the Federal Reserve should focus on both inflation and real GDP or unemployment. They believe that the Fed should follow a countercyclical monetary policy.

countercyclical monetary policy — moves to loosen monetary policy when unemployment is high and inflation is low and to tighten monetary policy when unemployment is low and inflation is high

A **countercyclical monetary policy** loosens monetary policy when unemployment is high and inflation is low and tightens monetary policy when unemployment is low and inflation is high.

The argument for this position is simple. Suppose that a fall in consumer spending or business investment spending causes a fall in aggregate demand. Real GDP falls and unemployment rises as the economy moves from Point B to Point C in Figure 32.3a. If the Fed follows a countercyclical monetary policy, it loosens mon-

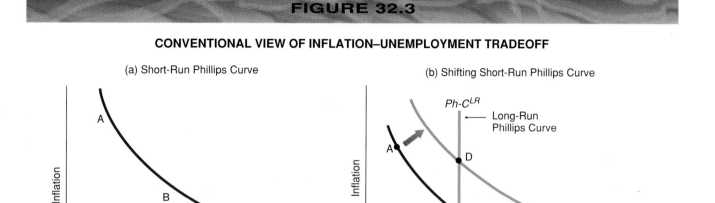

FIGURE 32.3

CONVENTIONAL VIEW OF INFLATION–UNEMPLOYMENT TRADEOFF

etary policy to bring the economy back to Point B in the figure. Unemployment falls and inflation rises as the economy moves from Point C to Point B, so the countercyclical monetary policy reduces unemployment at the cost of higher inflation. The trick is to loosen monetary policy just enough to bring the economy to Point B; further loosening might take the economy to Point A, with lower unemployment (temporarily) but higher inflation.

Similarly, if aggregate demand increases and takes the economy from Point B to Point A (with lower unemployment but higher inflation), a tighter monetary policy could bring the economy back to Point B. Again, the trick is to do enough but not too much. If monetary policy becomes too tight, it causes a recession as the economy moves to Point C. The Fed faced this problem in 1989 and in 1994 to 1995. In 1989, the Fed believed that U.S. aggregate demand was rising rapidly, so it tightened monetary policy to help prevent inflation from rising. The tighter monetary policy, however, may have contributed to the 1990 to 1991 recession. Similarly, the Fed tightened monetary policy in 1994 and early 1995 because it interpreted rapid growth of real GDP as an increase in aggregate demand and the Fed wanted to prevent inflation from rising.

All countercyclical policies involve choices of how to divide attention between inflation and real GDP or unemployment. Opinions differ about how much and for how long monetary policy can affect real GDP.[4] Opinions also differ about how bad inflation is compared to a rise in unemployment. These differences amount to disagreements over the best countercyclical monetary policy, that is,

[4]That is, opinions differ about the precise shape of the short-run Phillips Curve and the length of time before it shifts.

how loose or how tight the Fed should set policy in any given situation, and when it should change its policy.

———————————————————— **FOR REVIEW** ————————————————————

32.1 Explain and contrast the activist and laissez-faire views of the role of government policy.

32.2 Explain and contrast simple and contingent policy rules.

32.3 What does it mean to say that a policy rule is *credible*?

32.4 Use a graph to help explain the argument for countercyclical monetary policy.

———————————————————— **QUESTION** ————————————————————

32.5 Suppose that the Fed raises the growth rate of the money supply from 3 percent per year to 6 percent per year and that people expect this policy to last for at least several years. Use the model of aggregate demand and aggregate supply from earlier chapters to explain the likely short-run and long-run effects of this policy change on real GDP, unemployment, the price level, the rate of inflation, the real interest rate, and the nominal interest rate.

THREE PROBLEMS WITH DISCRETIONARY POLICY

Advocates of policy rules cite three main arguments to favor their position over discretionary policies. They claim that discretionary policy can make economic conditions worse rather than better. They see discretionary policy as inferior to rules because:

1. Two kinds of lags complicate the effects of policies.

2. The Fed lacks enough information about changes in the economy.

3. Commitment to a rule can improve economic performance by changing people's incentives.

This section discusses each issue in turn.

FIRST PROBLEM: LAGS

The first problem with discretionary policy comes from lags in the implementation and effects of discretionary policies. It takes time for any government agency, including the Fed, to react to economic changes. Furthermore, the Fed gathers the economic data that tracks the economy with a lag, so, try as it may, the Fed's information is never as fully up to date as it would like. These two factors create a lag in the implementation of policy.

Also, the effects of Fed policies occur with a lag. Changes in the money supply take time to affect aggregate demand, real GDP, and prices. Evidence suggests that the lags are not only long, but variable and unpredictable. This makes it hard for the Fed to know when and how much to change its policy. For example, the Fed may want to loosen monetary policy to help the economy out of a recession, but a policy action now might have effects only later, when the recession is over and the looser monetary policy only adds to subsequent inflation.

Why the Fed's efforts to forestall inflation have thus far failed

Delayed reaction

It pushed up interest rates, but maybe not enough; Risk of recession grows

Why has the Fed's anti-inflation campaign failed?

In part, the answer lies in the long and unpredictable lags that always separate Fed actions from desired results.

Unpredictable lags make monetary policy difficult.

Source: Why the Fed's Efforts to Forestall Inflation Have Thus Far Failed," *The Wall Street Journal,* March 20, 1989, p. 1.

EXAMPLES

The Fed is aware of the policy problems created by lags, and it tries to minimize those problems. For example, in 1994 the Fed saw signs that inflation would soon rise. Even though inflation was not yet increasing, the Fed began tightening monetary policy so that, after a lag, the tighter monetary policy would prevent inflation from rising in the future. This policy sparked controversy. Critics argued that the Fed should not tighten monetary policy because inflation was not rising and, in their view, was not likely to rise. The Fed defended its policy on the grounds that real GDP was rising very rapidly and that, based on historical experiences, higher inflation would soon follow. Because monetary policy affects the economy with a lag, argued the Fed, it could not wait for inflation to rise before tightening monetary policy. The lag in the effect of monetary policy is also evident in Figure 30.26 in Chapter 30, which shows the growth rate of output in the United States and the growth rate of M1 $1\frac{1}{2}$ years earlier.

SECOND PROBLEM: LACK OF INFORMATION

The second problem with discretionary policy comes from policy makers' lack of enough information about the economy. Policy makers need two types of important information that they do not have. First, they don't have enough information about current changes in the economy. Second, they don't have enough information about how their policy actions will affect the economy.

INFORMATION ABOUT THE ECONOMY

Neither policy makers or economists usually know whether a current change in GDP occurs because of a change in aggregate demand or a change in aggregate supply, nor do they know if a change will be temporary or permanent. Economists even disagree about the causes of many past changes in the economy, including the Great Depression. Without good knowledge of current changes in the economy, the Fed lacks sufficient information to conduct good discretionary monetary policy.[5]

Economist Milton Friedman has argued that the problems of lags and insufficient information have led the Fed's discretionary policies to magnify fluctuations in real GDP and inflation. When a fall in aggregate demand or supply raises unemployment, the Fed usually loosens monetary policy to help reduce unemployment and raise real GDP. The Fed often responds too vigorously, however, partly because it lacks sufficient information about the economy and partly because its policies affect the economy only after a lag. After the lag, when the effects of Fed policy appear, unemployment falls below its natural rate and inflation rises. However, unemployment does not remain permanently below its natural rate; it eventually begins to rise back toward its natural rate. This rise in unemployment creates political pressures for the Fed to loosen monetary policy even more to reduce unemployment. Again, unemployment falls in the short run, but only at the cost of even higher inflation. As people begin to adjust to ever-higher rates of inflation, the Fed can keep unemployment below its natural rate only by continually accelerating money growth. Eventually, inflation rises enough that people become more concerned with it than with unemployment. At that point, political pressure leads the Fed to

---

[5]This would pose a problem even without lags in the implementation and effects of policy.

IN THE NEWS

Economists see jobless decline without inflation

A key question: How low can the unemployment rate safely go?

No one, including the Fed, has enough knowledge of the economy to answer questions like this. As a result, monetary policy sometimes underreacts and sometimes overreacts.

Source: "Economists See Jobless Decline without Inflation," *New York Times,* September 20, 1987, p. 32.

Lucas critique — the proposition that people do not always respond the same way to changes in economic conditions or government policies because their responses depend partly on their expectations about the future, and those expectations can change

tighten monetary policy, raising unemployment above its natural rate and causing a recession. As inflation rises higher, the recession becomes deeper when inflation is finally reduced.

Figure 32.4 shows Friedman's argument in terms of short-run Phillips Curves. When a fall in aggregate demand moves the economy from Point A to Point B, with higher unemployment, The Fed overreacts (partly because of lags and information problems) and moves the economy to Point C, with lower unemployment and higher inflation. When the short-run Phillips Curve shifts from $Ph\text{-}C_1$ to $Ph\text{-}C_2$ and unemployment begins to rise again toward Point D, however, the Fed reacts by again raising the growth rate of the money supply and the economy moves to Point E. This may happen again, as the economy moves toward Point F but looser Fed policy takes it to Point G. Eventually, people become concerned about inflation. As the short-run Phillips Curve shifts again and the economy heads toward Point H, the Fed tightens policy and takes the economy to Point I with lower inflation, but at the cost of a big recession.[6]

INFORMATION ABOUT THE EFFECTS OF POLICIES

Policy makers lack a second type of information concerning the effects of their policies. Economists have constructed intricate mathematical models of the economy on computers to try to determine the effects of changes in policies. The computer models use data from the past to try to predict how current policy changes will affect the economy. These efforts face an important problem, though: the effects of current policy changes may differ from the effects of past policy changes if people's expectations differ from those in the past. This leads to the Lucas critique of econometric policy evaluation.

> The **Lucas critique** says that people do not always respond the same way to a change in economic conditions or government policies because their responses depend partly on their expectations about the future, and those expectations can change.

People's expectations about the future depend partly on their past experiences. The past responses of government policy to changes in underlying conditions affect how people expect the government to respond in the future and, therefore, affect the results of those policies. For example, if the Fed has usually tightened monetary policy in the past when inflation rose by more than 2 percentage points over a 6-month period, then people may expect the Fed to do so again in the future. The effects of tighter Fed policy under these conditions, when that policy is expected, may differ considerably from the effects of tighter Fed policy under other conditions, when people did not expect tighter policy.

The Lucas critique makes it difficult to specify the effects of a particular policy because the effects may depend on the situation, that is, on people's expectations. It is hard to find evidence on the effects of policies because past experience is not necessarily a reliable guide if expectations have changed. This makes it hard for computer models of the economy to predict the effects of government policies in a reliable way. Obviously, this makes discretionary policy making more difficult.

---

[6]Friedman, a winner of the Nobel Memorial Prize in Economic Science, is considered a *monetarist* due to his view that changes in the money supply are the most important cause of business cycles and due to his view that the Fed should follow a rule of keeping the growth rate of M1 or M2 at a constant rate of about 3 percent per year.

FIGURE 32.4

WHEN MONETARY POLICY OVERREACTS

A fall in aggregate demand takes the economy from Point A to Point B. The Fed loosens monetary policy, but because of lags and information problems, it takes the economy to Point C in the short run. In the long run, the economy moves toward Point D as the short-run Phillips Curve shifts. The Fed reacts to the rise in unemployment by loosening policy again, which takes the economy to Point E. This repeats, and the economy moves to Point F and then Point G. Finally, as the economy moves toward Point H in the long run, pressures to reduce inflation lead the Fed to tighten policy and reduce inflation at the expense of a recession (Point I).

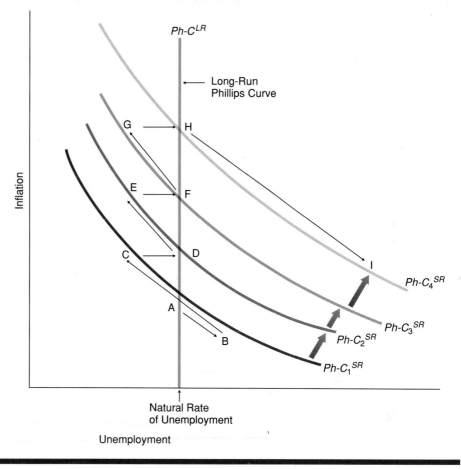

PUBLIC INFORMATION ABOUT POLICY

Discretionary policy can add uncertainty to the economy. Without a credible policy rule, it is often hard to predict what Fed officials or other policy makers will do in various situations. This makes it harder for people to form expectations about policy. In a letter to the editor of *The Wall Street Journal*, Milton Friedman wrote:

> I know, or can find out, what monetary *actions* have been: open market purchases and sales and discount rates at Federal Reserve Banks. I know also the federal funds rate and rates of growth of various monetary aggregates. What I do not know is the *policy* that produced those actions.
>
> The closest I can come to an official specification of current monetary policy is that it is to take those actions that the monetary authorities, in light of all evidence available, judge will best promote price stability and full employment—i.e., to do the right thing at the right time. But that surely is not a "policy." It is simply an expression of good intentions and an injunction to "trust us."

> I hasten to add that the present situation is not unique. On the contrary, it has persisted for nearly the entire . . . life of the Federal Reserve System. The only exception was from the outbreak of World War II to 1951, when the Fed followed an announced policy of pegging interest rates on federal government securities. For the rest, the Fed has consistently resorted to statements of good intentions . . . It has claimed credit for good results and blamed forces beyond its control—generally fiscal policy—for any bad outcomes.[7]

This third problem of information arises because discretionary policy creates uncertainty when the public lacks enough information about the Fed's policy to predict its future actions accurately. This problem highlights an important benefit of rules over discretion.

THIRD PROBLEM: THE BENEFIT OF POLICY RULES

The third problem with discretionary policy is that it gives up the benefit of commitment to a rule. A credible rule, one that people believe will be followed, affects people's expectations, incentives, and behavior. This leads to an important result:

> A credible rule for actions can lead to better results than even the best case-by-case (discretionary) actions.

A well-known example of this phenomenon concerns rules for dealing with terrorists.

EXAMPLE: DEALING WITH TERRORISTS

Suppose that you are a government official in charge of dealing with terrorist threats. Terrorists may take hostages to trade for things they want (cash, arms, freeing prisoners). A credible policy rule never to deal with terrorists leaves them little incentive to take hostages. Without a credible policy rule not to deal with terrorists, that is, with a policy toward terrorists leaves them decided by discretion (doing whatever seems best in a particular case), terrorists may expect hostages to be good bargaining chips. They may see at least, a chance of gains by taking hostages. Terrorists are more likely to take hostages if you rely on discretionary policy than if you set a credible rule not to deal with them.

TIME CONSISTENCY

The best case-by-case (discretionary) decisions are not always the same as the best rules. To see why, consider the terrorist example. Suppose that you are a discretionary policy maker (you do not have a credible rule), and terrorists take some hostages. You must decide whether to deal with the terrorists to try to save the hostages or not deal with them to take a hard-line on terrorism and try to discourage hostage-taking in the future. With discretionary policy, it might be better in some cases, to deal with the terrorists because the benefit of saving the hostages may exceed the expected future costs from giving in to the terrorists. This would be true, for example, if a hard-line stance *this time* would not affect terrorists' expectations of your future behavior. Then you could gain nothing from a hard-line reaction, while you would benefit from saving the hostages.

If you could choose a credible rule, however, the best rule would *not* allow you to deal with terrorists, even if the beat case-by-case decision would be to deal

---

[7]"The Fed Has No Clothes," *The Wall Street Journal,* April 15, 1988, p. 28.

with them. The best rule is never to deal with terrorists because that removes their incentive to take hostages to begin with.[8]

time consistent policy — when the best case-by-case decisions are the same as the decisions suggested by the best policy rule

time inconsistent policy — when the best case-by-case decisions differ from the decisions suggested by the best policy rule

In a **time consistent policy,** the best case-by-case decisions are the same as the decisions suggested by the best policy rule.

In a **time inconsistent policy,** the best case-by-case decisions differ from the decisions that the best policy rule would suggest.

Time inconsistency occurs when what *currently* seems best for today and tomorrow *no longer seems best when tomorrow comes,* even though no new information emerges. It is a little like giving in to temptation at the last minute in a rational way. In this situation, people can make themselves better off by committing to a rule that prevents them from giving in to temptation at the last minute, even though they may want to give in when the time comes.

To make a rule more credible, it helps to have some way to commit to it. A stronger commitment to the rule makes it more credible. To see why, think about the problems of getting terrorists to *believe* that you will stick to a rule never to deal with them. A policy maker who *announces* a rule may face an incentive to change the decision at the last minute, as when saving some particular hostages may seem very important. A rule becomes more credible (people believe it more strongly) if the policy maker will suffer some penalty for breaking the rule. Perhaps a law sets the policy rule and a punishment for violating it, or perhaps social or political pressures penalize policy makers for violations.[9]

OTHER EXAMPLES

Consider some other examples of situations in which a credible commitment to a policy rule makes for a better policy than discretionary policy making.

NUCLEAR DETERRENCE During the Cold War, the United States and the Soviet Union adopted policies called *Mutually Assured Destruction* to prevent a nuclear war. Each country stated a rule to respond to an attack by completely destroying the other country. Each country tried to commit to this rule as a way to prevent attack by the other. Discretionary policy would not be reliable here because if an attack were to occur, the attacked country would not have much incentive, besides revenge, to destroy the attacker.[10] (Why kill millions of people when your country is already destroyed?) The best discretionary policy in this case might be *not* to retaliate. But it would be better to deter attacks to begin with through a credible policy rule (like Mutually Assured Destruction) that would mandate retaliation *even when it would bring no benefit.*

TAXES ON CAPITAL High taxes on income from capital would discourage investment, but after someone had already invested in new capital equipment, the government could place a very high tax on the income from that capital equipment

---

[8]This assumes that terrorists' behavior responds to incentives. Evidence and general agreement among experts suggest that it does.

[9]This is why almost all policy makers stress the importance of a policy rule *never* to deal with terrorists, and to treat it as a very serious mistake if a policy maker does so, as in the Iran-Contra scandal under President Reagan. When this attitude is common, it helps to make the rule not to deal with terrorists more credible than it would otherwise be (which, unfortunately, may not be very credible). Another way to make a rule credible is to choose, as the policy maker, a hard-liner who would never deal with terrorists, even if it seemed best in a particular case.

[10]The desire for revenge may serve a useful purpose by helping people to commit to rules.

to generate revenue. Investors know that the government could do this, and their knowledge reduces the incentive to invest. Less investment gives the government less capital to tax, so even the government loses if people expect it to place high taxes on capital. Policy makers can do better if they can convince investors that they will not place high taxes on capital in the future. A more credible commitment to a policy rule of low taxes on capital encourages more investment.

APPLICATION TO INFLATION AND THE PHILLIPS CURVE

INFLATIONARY BIAS OF DISCRETIONARY POLICY   Now apply these ideas to monetary policy. In the long run, unemployment equals its natural rate and the Fed cannot affect it. The Fed can affect the long-run inflation rate, however, because it can control the money growth rate, and the Fed would choose low inflation if it could commit to a rule. Because the Fed cannot commit to a rule, however, it ends up creating inflation. This gives discretionary monetary policy an *inflationary bias.*

To see why, follow these steps:

1. If people expect low inflation, then the Fed could have an incentive to raise inflation to reduce unemployment temporarily, because the benefits of the reduced unemployment might exceed the costs of higher inflation.

2. Because enough people understand the Fed's incentive to raise inflation, however, expected inflation rises.

3. If the Fed were to create less inflation than people expect, then unemployment would rise above its natural rate temporarily. (The economy would move downward along a short-run Phillips Curve to a point with lower inflation and higher unemployment, such as from Point A to Point B in Figure 32.4.) In fact, the Fed must create the inflation that people expect just to prevent unemployment from rising above its natural rate.

This results in unemployment equal to its natural rate accompanied by high inflation.

If the Fed could follow a credible rule, it could choose a rule that would create low inflation. A credible rule would lead people to *expect* low inflation. With low actual and expected inflation, unemployment would still equal its natural rate, so the credible rule would produce better economic results than discretionary policy.

EXPLANATION   Think about an analogy. One element of excitement in a sporting event such as the Olympics comes from the chance that participants will perform exceptionally well, outperforming the expectations of spectators and judges. In an event like that, spectators know that participants have an incentive to try exceptionally hard. This raises their expectations, making it even more difficult for participants to exceed those expectations. Participants must practice more and perform even better than usual simply to create the normal level of excitement that results when their performance meets people's expectations.

Now restate the last paragraph using slightly different language. Spectators or judges are disappointed when a performance falls short of their expectations. To avoid creating disappointment, participants have an incentive to try exceptionally hard. Aware of this incentive, spectators and judges have high expectations for performers. These high expectations make it even more difficult for performers to avoid creating disappointment. They must perform particularly well simply to match expectations and avoid creating disappointment.

Now think about Fed policy. People know that low expected inflation may give the Fed an incentive to reduce unemployment by creating inflation. Aware of this incentive, people expect higher inflation. High expected inflation makes it more difficult for the Fed to reduce unemployment. (The Fed can reduce unemployment below the natural rate only by raising inflation above the expected level.) Indeed, the Fed must create some amount of inflation simply to match expectations and avoid creating unemployment in excess of the natural rate.

POLITICAL BUSINESS CYCLES

The inability of the government to commit to economic policies shows up in the political business cycle.

> The **political business cycle** refers to the apparent tendency for recessions to occur in the middle of presidents' 4-year terms, while the economy tends to improve before presidential elections

political business cycle — the apparent tendency for recessions to occur in the middle of presidents' 4-year terms, while the economy tends to improve before presidential elections

Figure 32.5 shows the unemployment rate in the United States since 1947, with vertical lines just before each presidential election. Of the nine times when unemployment rose sharply (in 1949 to 1950, 1954, 1958, 1960, 1970, 1974 to 1975, 1980, 1982, and 1990 to 1992), three were presidential election years (1960, 1980, and 1992) and in each case the incumbent party lost the presidency. The incumbent party won the six presidential elections that did not coincide with surges in unemployment. The other six sharp increases in unemployment occurred in years between presidential elections.

If voter support for political parties depends mainly on economic conditions just before elections—and not as much on conditions in previous years—

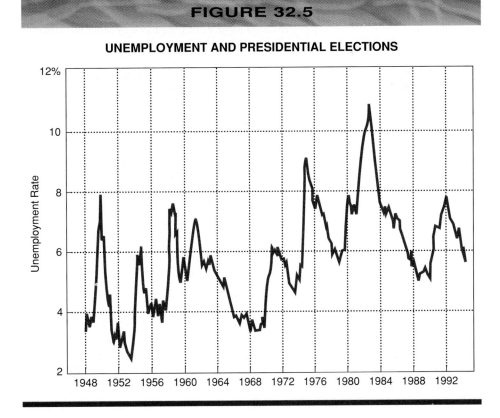

FIGURE 32.5

UNEMPLOYMENT AND PRESIDENTIAL ELECTIONS

IN THE NEWS

Recession and re-election don't mix

Scholars who have studied the effects of the economy on presidential elections have found that incumbents have serious trouble weathering election-year recessions but that voters are forgiving of recessions that occurred earlier in a president's term.

Do political pressures have short memories?

Source: "Recession and Re-election Don't Mix," *New York Times*, October 9, 1991, pp. D1 and D5.

then policy makers who want to reduce inflation would have an incentive to do so early in a presidential term, so that any recession would end well before the next election. Policy makers may also have an incentive to take actions that reduce unemployment prior to elections, even if inflation will rise later. One study found that the incumbent political party loses about 1 percentage point of votes in the election for each 1 percent fall in the growth rate of real GDP, and another 1 percentage point of votes for each 3 percentage point increase in inflation. If policy makers can raise the growth rate of real GDP by 1 percentage point while increasing inflation by less than 3 percentage points, or if they can delay the inflationary effects of a policy until after an election, then they can raise the number of votes they are likely to receive in the election.[11]

HOW TO TAME A WILD PHILLIPS CURVE

Can the Fed reduce inflation without causing a recession? Can it end a recession quickly without raising inflation? Can monetary policy somehow tame or avoid the short-run Phillips Curve?

Some economists argue that a credible change in monetary policy can reduce inflation without affecting unemployment or real GDP. The idea is that a credible change in policy leads people to change their expectations of inflation. The change in expectations shifts the short-run Phillips Curve (as described in Chapter 30 and illustrated in Figure 30.16). This allows inflation to fall without any rise in unemployment. These economists argue that the government could make its policy credible by committing to a policy rule or by taking unusual and dramatic actions that would indicate a major change in policy, showing people that policy makers were not following "business as usual."

A credible policy rule could take the form of a law or a constitutional amendment stating a required policy, though even these measures leave the possibility of loopholes or simple disobedience. Unusual and dramatic actions might include major changes in fiscal policy, such as balancing a government budget that previously had run big deficits, making big changes in taxes or government regulations, and so on. History offers only a few good examples of major policy changes of the kind that may affect expectations. For example, at the end of the German hyperinflation in 1923, the central bank was separated from the government so the government could not force it to print money to finance budget deficits, as it had during the period of hyperinflation.

Can credible changes in policy really tame the Phillips Curve? When Margaret Thatcher became prime minister of Great Britain in 1979, she promised to reduce inflation. Inflation fell, but Britain had a major recession. Some economists argue that Thatcher's promise was credible, and that this shows that policy makers cannot avoid the short-run Phillips Curve simply by adopting credible policies. They argue that even with a credible policy, a fall in inflation must be accompanied by a temporary increase in unemployment and fall in real GDP growth. Other economists argue that Thatcher's policies were *not* credible, and that is why Britain had a recession.[12]

[11]Suppose that the incumbent political party follows new policies that both raise the growth rate of real GDP by 1 percent and raise inflation. The higher growth rate of real GDP raises voter support 1 percent. If the policies raise inflation by exactly 3 percentage points, this reduces voter support back to its original level. But if inflation rises by less than 3 percentage points, voter support stays above the original level (the level of support before the new policies).

[12]See also the discussion of expected and unexpected inflation at the end of Chapter 30. Proponents of real business cycles, of course, argue that the recession is unrelated to the fall in inflation.

32.6 Why do lags create difficulties for discretionary monetary policy?

32.7 Why do information problems create difficulties for discretionary monetary policy?

32.8 Explain the Lucas critique.

32.9 Why can rules produce better results than case-by-case, discretionary policy making?

32.10 Explain why discretionary monetary policy has an inflationary bias.

ALTERNATIVE RULES FOR MONETARY POLICY

Economists have proposed several alternative rules to guide monetary policy. This section discusses some of the most prominent proposals and the main pro and con arguments. In addition to the specific arguments against individual policy rules, one important argument claims that any monetary-policy rule is too inflexible. The main argument for discretionary policy states that new situations might arise that call for new policies. Rules would prevent the flexibility to adopt the best policies in those new situations.

Advocates of policy rules respond that contingent rules have flexibility. Advocates of discretion counter that no one can think of all the situations that might arise in the future, so it is impossible to make a sufficiently flexible rule. In addition, they argue, contingent policy rules would be very complicated because they would have to consider so many possible future circumstances. A complicated rule does not help people to form expectations about policies, eliminating one of the alleged benefits of rules—that it helps people to form expectations. With these arguments in mind, consider some proposals for policy rules.

KEEP THE MONEY SUPPLY GROWTH RATE CONSTANT

One policy rule proposal urges the Fed to make the nominal money supply (measured as either M1 or M2) grow at a constant rate, such as 3 percent per year.

▶ PRO

This policy would result in a predictable, steady rate of inflation that people could learn to handle. If the Fed sets the money growth rate to equal the long-run growth rate of real GDP, inflation will average out to zero over the long run.

A requirement for constant money growth would create smaller business cycles. History shows that when the Fed tries to use monetary policy to stabilize real GDP, it usually creates even larger business cycles. When inflation rises, the Fed reduces the money supply too sharply, creating a recession. The Fed then tries to get out of the recession by raising the money supply too sharply and making inflation even worse. Because of lags and information problems, discretionary policies make business cycles worse.

If the Fed were to follow this policy, inflation would remain both low and more stable, so nominal interest rates would also be lower and more stable. This would help stabilize the velocity of money, which would help to stabilize aggregate demand.

▶ CON

This policy would not stabilize the rate of inflation because the demand for money often changes in unpredictable ways. In other words, the velocity of money changes unpredictably. The Fed could control inflation better by changing the money supply to *offset* these changes in money demand (changes in velocity).

This policy rule would create large fluctuations in interest rates, as such a policy did from 1979 to 1982. These fluctuations in interest rates would cause fluctuations in the velocity of money, leading to larger fluctuations in aggregate demand. This would create larger business cycles.

This policy does nothing to help reduce the size of business cycles. Discretionary policy makers have made mistakes in the past, but that is no reason to give up trying. Policy makers can learn from past mistakes and do better in the future than this policy rule would do.

TARGETING AN INFLATION RATE

Another proposal suggests that the Fed should change the growth rate of the money supply to keep the inflation rate at some particular level such as 3 percent per year (or zero).

▶ PRO

This policy is better than making the money supply grow at some constant rate because it takes account of changes in velocity. If velocity rises, this policy causes the money supply to grow more slowly to keep inflation from rising.

This policy shares other benefits of a requirement for constant money growth. It would prevent the Fed from making business cycles even worse by overreacting or reacting too late to changes in the economy.

▶ CON

This policy, like a requirement for a constant money growth rate, does nothing to help reduce the size of business cycles. Policy makers can do better by conducting a countercyclical monetary policy, as shown in Figure 32.1 and described later.

This policy would be very difficult to follow. The Fed's actions (such as open market operations) affect the price level only after a long and variable lag that may last several years. This would prevent the Fed from keeping the rate of inflation very close to any target level.

SET A NOMINAL GDP TARGET

A third proposal recommends that the Fed adopt a nominal GDP target and try to keep the growth rate of nominal GDP constant.

▶ PRO

This countercyclical rule shares the benefits of countercyclical policies, taking both inflation and real GDP into account. It also shares a benefit of rules if policy makers are committed to the policy.

This policy stabilizes both real GDP and the price level when aggregate demand changes. To see why, notice that a fall in aggregate demand reduces both prices and real GDP, so it reduces nominal GDP. This rule requires the Fed to loosen monetary policy enough to raise aggregate demand back to its original level (as in Figure 32.1) to stabilize nominal GDP.

▶ CON

This policy suffers from the same problems as any countercyclical policy. It is likely to make business cycles larger because of the lags and information problems discussed earlier. In addition, this policy requires inflation to rise when the growth rate of real GDP falls, and inflation to fall when the growth rate of real GDP rises. It might be better to follow a policy that would keep the rate of inflation stable.

The nominal GDP target is arbitrary. Policy makers should not take the same actions when inflation is zero and real GDP growth is 6 percent (which is a very good situation) as when real GDP growth is zero and inflation is 6 percent (which is a bad situation), even though nominal GDP growth is the same in both cases.

TARGET A FEDERAL FUNDS RATE

A fourth argument recommends that the Fed try to keep the nominal federal funds rate stable or keep it at some low level. This policy generally refers to the nominal federal funds rate because the Fed cannot affect the real interest rate in the long run.

Recall that the federal funds rate is the interest rate that banks charge each other for short-term loans of reserves. The Fed can control the federal funds rate by raising the supply of bank reserves when demand for them rises and reducing the supply when demand falls. An increase in the demand for bank reserves would ordinarily raise the equilibrium federal funds rate, but the Fed can prevent a rise by increasing the supply of reserves through open market purchases (i.e., looser monetary policy), as in **Figure 32.6.** The Fed can stabilize the federal funds interest rate by changing the supply of bank reserves to offset changes in the demand.

FIGURE 32.6

STABILIZING THE FEDERAL FUNDS RATE

An increase in the demand for reserves by banks would raise the federal funds rate from i_1 to i_2, but the Fed can keep the federal funds rate at i_1 by increasing the supply of reserves appropriately.

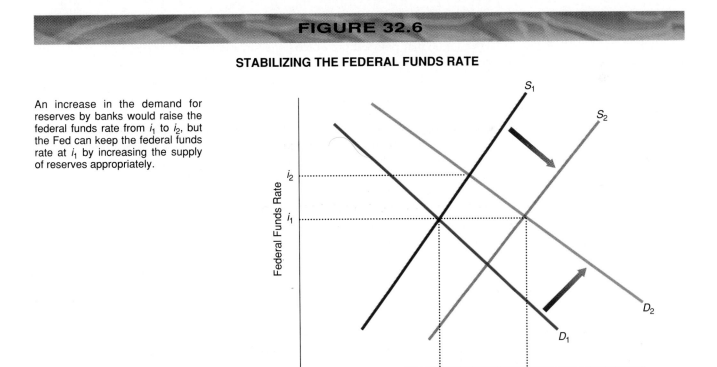

▶ PRO

This policy, which is similar to policies that the Fed has frequently followed, keeps interest rates more stable than policy rules like a requirement for a constant money growth rate. From 1979 to 1982, for example, the Fed paid more attention to the money supply and less attention to keeping the federal funds rate constant. This resulted in large fluctuations in the federal funds rate and other interest rates during those years. The Fed can avoid these big swings in interest rates by focusing its policy rules on keeping the federal funds rate stable.

▶ CON

In the long run, Federal Reserve actions can affect only nominal interest rates, not real interest rates. The Fed can stabilize nominal interest rates by stabilizing the rate of inflation. That can be done better with a rule for constant money growth or with a rule to target the rate of inflation. It is difficult to focus policy directly on interest rates because, as noted earlier, policies that reduce the nominal interest rate in the short run are likely to raise it in the long run, and vice versa.

ALTERNATIVE MONETARY INSTITUTIONS

An early section of this chapter identified the third focus of debate over monetary policy as a question of the best set of institutions for a monetary system. Institutions could be designed to help implement policy rules, to help policy makers exercise discretion with minimal political interference, or to strengthen political control over monetary policy. Some economists argue that a monetary policy rule should be written into law, perhaps even as a constitutional amendment. This would help to make the rule credible and to guarantee adherence to it. Others argue for maximum independence of the Fed from political pressures or control. They argue that political pressures generally focus on short-run goals, while monetary policy must take long-run goals into account. Independence, according to this argument, allows the Fed to pursue the best discretionary policies.

FEDERAL RESERVE INDEPENDENCE

The Federal Reserve is an *independent agency* of the federal government, as an earlier chapter explained. This is supposed to free it from political influence so it can follow the best policies without political pressures. The Fed has faced many challenges to its independence such as proposals in Congress to require the Fed to report to Congress or the executive branch of the federal government, or to place the Fed under the supervision of the General Accounting Office. (It currently escapes such control.) As an earlier chapter explained, the president of the United States appoints 7 of the 12 Federal Reserve governors, while the others are Federal Reserve Bank presidents who are appointed by the members of the boards of directors of those banks. The Board of Governors of the Fed appoints three of the nine members of those boards of directors, but the majority, six members, are elected by private banks in the Federal Reserve Bank's district.

Some critics have argued that this procedure is undemocratic and gives too much power to private banks. For example:

> The Federal Reserve Board is indefensible in theory and indispensable in practice. Twelve unelected people have their collective finger on the second most important button in America: the one that controls the money supply, the biggest con-

trollable factor in the equation of our economy. . . . Their decisions are made in secret and kept secret for 6 weeks. Their budget is also secret. They probably affect your life more than the Supreme Court. How many of them can you even name?[13]

Some people have proposed changes in the Fed's status such as submission to more control by the president or Congress; regular audits of Fed operations by the General Accounting Office; a legal requirement that the Fed announce its policy decisions right away rather than 6 weeks after making them; a requirement to announce its plans annually for the coming year; or a requirement to follow some specific, and perhaps very detailed, policies set by the president, Congress, or both.

William Greider, an editor of *Rolling Stone* magazine, wrote a book about the Fed in 1987.[14] Greider attacked the Fed as a secretive, undemocratic government organization with a probanking, anti-inflation bias that favors rich people over poor people. He argued that, while educated people often discussed money and monetary policies in the 19th century, the creation of the Fed took monetary issues out of the political arena and placed them in the hands of a bureaucracy run by supposed experts and dominated by banks. The Fed became a secretive organization whose policies, in Greider's view, often helped banks and Wall Street at the expense of ordinary people. He summarized the arguments of opponents of Fed independence as follows:

▶ The president, Congress, and the Fed fight for control over the economy.

▶ The Fed often sacrifices output and employment to bring down and control inflation.

▶ The government works like a "car with two drivers." When things go wrong, Congress and the administration blame the Fed, and the Fed blames Congress and the administration. As a result, no one accepts accountability for anything, because everyone always has someone else to blame. This makes bad policy decisions inevitable.

▶ Economic policy would improve if Congress were to control the Fed, or at least coordinate its policies with those of Congress and the president.

Despite such arguments, evidence indicates that countries with more independent central banks tend to have lower rates of inflation than countries whose central banks operate with less independence from governments.

Not everyone believes the Fed needs to be restructured. In 1990, for example, Mobil Corporation ran the following advertisement headlined "No Need to Fix the Fed":

> Our concern is that giving elected officials additional power over the Fed could politicize the process of setting interest rates and determining the money supply. And make no mistake. These are not arcane functions, of interest only to economists and bankers. They affect every American.
>
> Want to buy a house or sell one? Interest rates often determine whether or not you can. Need to borrow the money to start a business or expand one? If so, you're certainly interested in interest rates. Can your company afford to modernize the plant where you work? Once again, interest rates could hold the key, this

[13]Michael Kinsley, "TRB from Washington," *New Republic,* October 30, 1989, p. 4.
[14]William Greider, *Secrets of the Temple* (New York: Simon and Schuster, 1987).

time to your very job. What the Fed does, in short, impacts directly on the very quality of our lives.

Walking the tightrope between inflation and growth is difficult enough in a nonpolitical climate. Politicizing the Fed makes absolutely no sense at all—and would fly in the face of one of life's most sensible dictums. The Fed isn't broken. Let's not fix it.

MORE RADICAL CHANGES

Some economists favor more radical changes in monetary institutions. For example, some favor establishing a gold standard under which the Fed's main task would be to buy and sell gold to keep its nominal price fixed, as described in an earlier chapter.[15] Another radical proposal would privatize the money business; the government would stop supplying money and let private firms (banks or anyone else) print pieces of paper that people could exchange as money. Each issuing firm would put its own name on its money so people could distinguish it from other issuers' money. This idea, usually called *free banking,* would to make people free to choose whatever money they want to use, so that competition among suppliers of money could produce a money with good properties, such as a low rate of inflation. Some proposals would let anyone issue money, providing that they back it 100 percent with gold. Another reform, commonly suggested for countries that want to reduce inflation from high levels and keep it low, is to establish a currency board.

GOLD STANDARD

A gold standard is a special case of a commodity standard; the other historically important type of commodity standard is the silver standard. An earlier chapter explained the two main kinds of gold standards. In a pure gold standard, people trade gold coins as money. In a gold exchange standard, people trade paper money that is backed by gold.

The key feature of a gold exchange standard is the government's choice of a nominal money supply to keep the nominal price of gold at some fixed level, such as $350 per ounce. If something in the economy changes to reduce the price of gold below $350 per ounce, then the government increases the money supply, raising nominal prices until gold sells for $350 again. If something changes to raise the price of gold above $350 per ounce, then the government decreases the money supply, reducing nominal prices until gold sells for $350 again. The government can keep the price of gold at $350 per ounce at all times by announcing that it will act as a residual buyer and seller of gold. Precisely, it guarantees to:

1. Buy as much gold as anyone wants to sell, and at the price of $350 per ounce.

2. Sell as much gold as anyone wants to buy.

The government buys gold by printing as much new money it needs, and it sells gold out of its storage facilities, destroying the money that it receives in pay-

---

[15]In 1989, a Federal Reserve governor and several other people recommended to the former Soviet Union that it adopt a gold standard as part of its economic reforms. It did not follow this advice.

IN THE NEWS

Battle with White House never ends

The Federal Reserve Board's sweeping power over the economy—and the board's independence—has inevitably produced conflict with the White House.

That's true because, while a president can influence the economy by pushing through Congress measures like tax cuts or spending programs, what ultimately happens to

the economy depends to an enormous extent on what the Federal Reserve does with its day-to-day control over the nation's money supply.

Congress, hoping to influence future policy, pushes measures to curb Fed's independence

Fed cuts lending rates amid political pressure

Political pressures on the Fed.

Sources: "Battle with White House Never Ends," *Rochester Democrat and Chronicle,* July 26, 1981, p. 3A; "Congress, Hoping to Influence Future Policy, Pushes Measures to Curb Fed's Independence," *The Wall Street Journal,* October 21, 1989; *New York Times,* November 11, 1990; and "Fed Cuts Lending Rates Amid Political Pressure," *New York Times,* November 7, 1991, p. D8.

ment. In this way, the money supply rises automatically whenever the government buys gold and falls whenever the government sells gold.[16]

Because people can always buy gold from the government for $350 per ounce, they will never pay more to another seller. Because people can always sell gold to the government for $350 per ounce, they will never accept less from another buyer. In this way, the government can fix the nominal price of gold at $350.

While the government fixes the *nominal* price of gold, conditions of supply and demand determine its *relative* price. For example, the relative price of gold in terms of televisions might be 1.0 televisions per ounce of gold. With a nominal price of gold at $350 per ounce, the nominal price of a television is $350 per set. If the relative price of televisions in terms of gold falls (perhaps due to an increase in the supply of televisions) from 1 ounce of gold per television to $\frac{9}{10}$ of an ounce of gold per television, then the nominal price of televisions falls from $350 to $315 per set, while the nominal price of gold remains at $350 per ounce. If the relative price of gold in terms of other goods and services does not change much over time, then the price level does not change much over time. Indeed, inflation averaged about zero under the gold standard of the 19th century, with

---

[16]Notice that the government must maintain a sufficiently large quantity of gold in storage to make this work, otherwise it could run out of gold and lose the ability to keep the price of gold from rising above $350 per ounce.

varying episodes of positive and negative inflation roughly averaging out over the century.

The government has little or no discretion in monetary policy under a gold standard. It must keep the money supply at the level that guarantees the fixed nominal price of gold. If the government, or a central bank such as the Federal Reserve, were to try to raise the money supply through open market purchases, the increase in the money supply would raise the price level, which would raise the nominal price of gold above $350 per ounce. To maintain the fixed price, the government would have to reduce the money supply again. (This happens automatically if the government destroys the money that it collects in payment for gold sales.) Similarly, if the government were to try to lower the money supply through open market sales, the price level would fall, reducing the nominal price of gold below $350 per ounce. To maintain the fixed price, the government would have to raise the money supply again, which happens automatically if the government prints new money whenever it buys gold at $350 per ounce.

SUMMARY OF THE DEBATE ON THE GOLD STANDARD

▶ **PRO**   The gold standard would end political control of the money supply. This would have several beneficial effects:

1. Reduction in the long-run rate of inflation, as in the 19th century
2. Reduction in the severity of business cycles by preventing Fed actions that destabilize the economy
3. Increase in economic growth by providing a sound money that people can count on for long-term planning

▶ **CON**   Despite the low long-run rate of inflation, the economy would suffer many short-term swings in the price level, as occurred in the 19th century. While these changes were small compared to those in the 20th century, other policy rules can do a better job than the gold standard of keeping inflation low and steady.

Similarly, while the gold standard would have prevented many Fed actions that made business cycles worse, the gold standard would also prevent desirable actions. For example, the gold standard did not prevent the giant fall in the money supply from 1929 to 1933. If the Fed had prevented this fall, the Great Depression may have been only a minor recession.

A sound money that facilitates long-run planning is good, but this can be achieved better with other policy rules to keep inflation low and steady.

DEBATE ON FREE BANKING

Free banking removes the government's role in the money industry. History offers only a few cases in which governments have allowed free banking. Scotland had a form of free banking from 1716 to 1845, as did the United States in the first half of the 19th century, as an earlier chapter explained.[17]

---

[17]A few other isolated cases have been reported. In Rochester, New York, on the morning of March 6, 1933 (during the Great Depression), the presidents of several banks met and decided to issue scrip—pieces of paper like coupons with $1, $5, or $10 printed on them—a sort of private money—to meet the city's payroll. They printed $2 million in scrip and paid city workers with the scrip instead of government money. Retail stores agreed to accept the scrip as money, though no law required them to do so. (Wages were paid in cash in those days and people held virtually no credit cards.) Companies such as Kodak and General Motors also paid their workers with this scrip. While local stores accepted the scrip as money, they could spend it only in Rochester; stores elsewhere did not accept it.

This is an example of privately issued money. It circulated as money—people were willing to accept it as payment for wages or sales of goods—simply because they expected other people to accept it later.

▶ **PRO**   Free banking removes the government almost entirely from the money business and ends political control of the money supply. It allows competition in which issuers of money can experiment with different types of products and consumers (users of money) can choose what they like best. Competition would encourage a high-quality money with stable and predictable purchasing power along with innovation in the monetary and financial payments system.

▶ **CON**   Competition among private issuers' moneys would not work very well for two reasons. First, it is much cheaper, and much more convenient, for people to use only one money instead of many different kinds. Use of many kinds of moneys at once would be confusing, would cause space problems in cash registers, and would cost people time and resources to find out the values of the different issuers' moneys, exchange them, and conduct other transactions. These problems of using many forms of money have motivated European countries to try to adopt *one* money for all of Europe to replace the many current national forms of money.

Second, after a bank has printed some money and some people have decided to use it, the bank then has an incentive to print a lot of money and cause inflation. In this way, the bank could collect an inflation tax. Banks could not commit not to do this. Advocates of free banking respond that an offending bank's reputation would suffer, eliminating its incentive to do this because a loss in reputation would hurt the bank's future profits. However, this incentive may not be strong enough to prevent some banks that face dim future profit pictures anyway from inflating their currencies.

INCENTIVES OF CENTRAL BANKS

While economists disagree about the best monetary policy, they generally agree that central banks, like all government institutions, respond to incentives. The individuals at the Fed may have the best intentions, but they always operate under strong political pressures, despite the Fed's official independence. Changes in the Fed's organization, or the potential loss of its independence, would affect its incentives. Even *proposals* to take away the Fed's independence affect its incentives.

Some economists have suggested reducing the Fed's incentive to inflate by forcing it to hold assets that lose value when inflation rises and gain value when inflation falls. For example, the law could require the Fed to borrow money and index the loan to inflation (that is, sell bonds that are indexed to inflation) and lend money (buy bonds) without indexing to inflation. To see why this would work, note that a loan is indexed to inflation if the amount of money the borrower must repay the lender changes automatically to keep up with inflation. For example, if the Fed were to borrow $1,000 for 1 year at a 10 percent interest rate, it would ordinarily owe $1,100 at the end of the year. If the loan were indexed to inflation, which averaged 5 percent during the year of the loan, that $1,100 payment would automatically rise by 5 percent from $1,100 to $1,155. Higher inflation would raise the amount of money the Fed would owe on this loan. Indexing would make the real value of the loan repayment (its purchasing power) independent of the inflation rate, so it would prevent the Fed from benefiting from inflation. Similarly, as an earlier chapter explained, unexpected inflation helps borrowers and hurts lenders when loans are not indexed to inflation. (Borrowers repay the loans in deflated dollars.) If the Fed buys unindexed bonds, it loses when inflation rises.

These two requirements would prevent the Fed from gaining from inflation and would make the Fed lose from higher inflation. Although the Fed gives its profit back to the Treasury Department each year, higher revenues allow it to raise its spending on things that benefit its employees. So, the Fed, like any other government agency, generally likes higher revenues. This proposal would give the Fed an incentive to reduce inflation. A related proposal would force the government to replace its current, unindexed debt with indexed debt, so the federal government would not gain from inflation. Still another proposal would tie the salaries of Fed officials to inflation so that an increase in inflation automatically reduces their salaries.

The value of these ideas depends on whether the Fed (or the rest of the federal government) currently has an incentive to produce too much inflation. Some economists believe it does, as the argument about the inflationary bias of discretionary policy demonstrated, but other economists believe that the Fed should emphasize inflation less and focus more on short-run changes in real GDP and unemployment.

CURRENCY BOARDS

Some countries have added credibility to their monetary policies by replacing their central banks with currency boards. To establish a currency board, a government must choose a particular value of a foreign exchange rate—usually with the country's main trading partner—fix the value of that exchange rate by law, and provide the currency board with political independence and a sufficient level of assets (reserves) to keep the exchange rate fixed.

> **currency board** — an institution whose sole purpose is to keep a foreign exchange rate fixed by acting as a residual buyer or seller of the country's money at that price

A **currency board** is an institution whose sole purpose is to keep a foreign exchange rate fixed by acting as a residual buyer or seller of the country's money at that price.

The reserves of the currency board must be large enough to fund any conceivable purchase of domestic money to keep the exchange rate fixed.

Hong Kong created a currency board in 1984. More recently, Argentina, Estonia, and Lithuania have created currency boards. Currency boards essentially replace central banks as the country identifies fixing the exchange rate as its only monetary policy. As a result, a currency board disciplines monetary policy, adding credibility at the cost of flexibility to pursue other goals. Many economists believe that currency boards represent an attractive alternative for countries that suffer from high inflation or low credibility in their monetary policies.

───────────────── **FOR REVIEW** ─────────────────

32.11 Discuss the pro and con arguments of the following proposals:
  a. Monetary policy rule requiring the money supply to grow at a fixed rate
  b. Nominal GDP target for monetary policy
  c. Choosing monetary policy to keep inflation constant
  d. Choosing monetary policy to keep the federal funds rate constant

32.12 Summarize the arguments for and against the gold standard.

32.13 What is free banking? Summarize arguments for and against it.

CONCLUSIONS

TYPES OF MACROECONOMIC POLICIES

Monetary and fiscal policies are the two main types of government macroeconomic policies. Monetary policy refers to changes in the nominal money supply through open market operations, changes in the discount rate or discount-window lending policy, or reserve requirement changes. The Federal Reserve conducts monetary policy in the United States. Fiscal policy refers to changes in government spending or taxes.

Some economists hold an activist view about the proper role of government economic policy, believing that government policy actions can help to reduce inefficiencies in the economy. According to this view, the government should use monetary and fiscal policies to help stabilize real GDP, reducing economically inefficient fluctuations that move unemployment from its natural rate. Other economists hold a laissez-faire view of policy, believing that the economy usually operates efficiently on its own and that, even when it does not, active government policies usually aggravate inefficiencies and create new inefficiencies. According to this view, the economy operates better when the government plays a small role restricted to enforcing property rights and following a general set of rules for its monetary and fiscal actions. Proponents of this view argue for policy rules on the grounds that economists don't know enough about the economy's operation to improve its performance with activist policies, that policy rules make it easier for people to plan, and that credible rules can change incentives in ways that enhance economic efficiency.

ISSUES OF MONETARY POLICY

The main issues in monetary policy concern what the Fed should do on a particular day, what longer-term goals it should pursue, whether rules or discretion should guide policy, and what kinds of monetary institutions a country should have.

A policy rule, a public statement of policy makers' future actions, can be simple (noncontingent) or contingent, stating how policies will depend on circumstances. A credible policy rule is believable, perhaps because policy makers have an incentive to follow the rule. Sometimes policy makers can commit to certain rules. Most policy, however, is discretionary, with no rules to bind policy makers' actions.

DISCRETIONARY MONETARY POLICY

Discussions of discretionary monetary policy tend to focus on the issue of what the policy maker should do today. Many economists believe that the Fed should try to stabilize real GDP around its full-employment level by monetary policy actions designed to offset other changes in aggregate demand. Following such a countercyclical monetary policy, the Fed might loosen monetary policy through additional open market purchases when aggregate demand falls, raising the growth rate of the money supply or reducing the federal funds rate, it might tighten monetary policy when aggregate demand rises. While many economists, and the Fed itself, describe monetary policy in terms of its effects on interest rates such as the federal funds rate, some economists believe that this is misleading because policies that reduce nominal interest rates in the short run may raise them in the longer run.

THREE PROBLEMS WITH DISCRETIONARY POLICY

Advocates of policy rules attack discretionary policy on three main grounds. First, they note that variable lags in the implementation and effects of policies make it difficult to set effective countercyclical policies so attempts may create economic inefficiencies. Second, critics charge that discretionary policy may create rather than alleviate economic problems because policy makers lack sufficient information about both current economic conditions and the likely effects of their policies. The Lucas critique says that people do not always respond in the same way to a change in government policies because changes in those policies can change their expectations, and this makes it difficult to predict the effects of changes in policies. These information problems create difficulties for discretionary policy making.

Finally, critics of discretionary policy claim that it sacrifices the beneficial effects of credible commitment to a rule on people's expectations, incentives, and behavior, which may lead to better economic results than even the best discretionary policy could achieve. Policy is said to be *time inconsistent* if the best case-by-case (discretionary) decisions differ from decisions under the best policy rule. Time inconsistency may give an inflationary bias to discretionary monetary policy, create political business cycles under discretionary policy, and raise the cost of reducing inflation.

ALTERNATIVE RULES FOR MONETARY POLICY

Economists have proposed several alternative rules to guide monetary policy, such as making the nominal money supply grow at a constant rate, keeping inflation at a certain level, keeping the growth rate of nominal GDP at a certain level, or trying to stabilize a nominal interest rate. Each proposed rule has pros and cons.

ALTERNATIVE MONETARY INSTITUTIONS

The third source of debate about monetary policy concerns the institutions through which a society carries out its policies. How do alternative arrangements for a central bank affect incentives and monetary policy choices? Should central banks be partially independent of political processes and what are the results of that independence? What would be the effects of more radical changes such as the adoption of a gold standard, a free banking system, changes in central bank incentives, or a currency board? What is the proper role of government in the monetary system?

LOOKING AHEAD

Government spending, taxes, and budget deficits are the main subjects of the next chapter. The chapter after that discusses financial markets, and the last two chapters discuss policy issues associated with international economic events.

KEY TERMS

monetary policy	discretionary policy
fiscal policy	looser monetary policy
activist view of policy	tighter monetary policy
laissez-faire view of policy	countercyclical monetary policy
policy rule	Lucas critique
simple policy rule	time consistent policy
contingent policy rule	time inconsistent policy
credible policy rule	political business cycle
commitment to a policy rule	currency board

QUESTIONS AND PROBLEMS

32.14 What factors influence the incentives of a central bank in its choice of monetary policy?

32.15 Argue the case for policy rules rather than discretion; argue the case for discretionary policy rather than rules.

32.16 Discuss this statement from a study by the Congressional Budget Office: "Inflation could be reduced relatively painlessly by lowering inflationary expectations."

32.17 Discuss this statement: "The development of better computer models of the economy will increase the ability of policy makers to conduct effective discretionary monetary policy, but it will not improve the performance of policy rules."

32.18 How is monetary policy likely to differ between a country with a central bank that is partly independent of politics (as in the United States) and a country whose central bank is subject to more government control?

32.19 What would happen if the United States were to abolish the Federal Reserve System and replace it with some form of free banking and privately issued money? What incentives would banks face in choosing their own monetary policies?

32.20 Suppose that the United States adopts a gold standard and sets the nominal price of gold at $350 per ounce. Discuss the effects of these changes:
  a. Large gold discoveries in Russia that tend to reduce the world price of gold
  b. Increase in the rate of technical progress and economic growth

Inquiries for Further Thought

32.21 Do you agree more with the activist view of policy or the laissez-faire view? Why?

32.22 Which guides monetary policy better: rules or discretion?
  a. If you think that rules are better, which rule is best? Should the rule be part of a Constitutional amendment?
  b. If you think that discretionary policy is better than rules, who should get the discretion? How should they exercise that discretion?

32.23 What incentives guide the Fed's actions? How could they be changed? How should they be changed? Should the Fed be independent? If not, what changes should be made? Should the Federal Reserve keep its operations and the minutes of its meetings secret? Is the Federal Reserve System undemocratic? Does the Fed respond to political pressures? How?

32.24 Should the United States adopt one of the more radical changes in monetary institutions discussed in this chapter? Why or why not?

Tag Software Applications

Tutorial Exercises
▶ The module contains a review of the key terms from Chapter 32.

Graphing Exercises
▶ The graphing segment includes questions on the impact of monetary policies on aggregate demand and equilibrium GDP and the effects of monetary policies on the Phillips Curve.

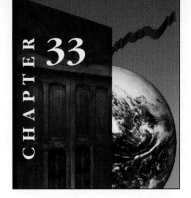

CHAPTER 33

FISCAL POLICY

WHAT THIS CHAPTER IS ABOUT

▶ Government spending and taxes
▶ Government budget deficits

Government budget deficits, taxes, and the size of government spending have generated much of the debate over public issues in the United States. Candidates in virtually every electoral campaign debate proposals to raise or reduce taxes, to reduce the budget deficit, to increase or cut government spending and the role of government in people's lives. These are the issues of fiscal policy.

The magnitudes of money involved stagger the imagination. The U.S. federal government has incurred a debt of several *trillion* dollars. Despite the importance of these issues for people's lives and the living standards of future generations, many people have little conception about the size of government spending or taxes. Many also confuse the government's debt with its deficit. Even today, with prominent reports on these issues in daily news reports and public discussions, few people realize the full extent to which government spending, taxes, and debt will affect their lives in the coming decades.

MAIN ISSUES OF FISCAL POLICY

fiscal policy — actions that change government spending, taxes, or both

Fiscal policy refers to government actions that affect total government spending, tax rates or tax revenues, or the government budget deficit.

Three general sets of issues inspire the main controversies and debates about fiscal policy. First, what are the proper roles of government spending and taxes in the economy? What is the best size for government? What are the appropriate levels of government spending, tax revenues, and budget surpluses or deficits? Second, how should government spending, tax rates, tax revenues, and the budget deficit respond to changes in economic conditions such as real GDP and unemployment? For example, should the government raise spending and reduce tax rates in the face of a recession and reduce spending and raise tax rates at other times? Finally, should formal rules or the discretion of politicians and government officials guide any such changes? What kinds of fiscal policy rules, if any, are appropriate? For example, should a rule, perhaps encoded in a Constitutional amendment, require the government to balance its budget each year or to limit its spending?

The last chapter discussed the activist and laissez-faire views of government monetary policy. This division also applies to fiscal policy. Economists who hold a laissez-faire view of fiscal policy tend to favor a smaller role for government spending and taxes than people who hold an activist view. Proponents of a laissez-faire view generally favor low levels of government spending and low tax rates, and they usually believe that the government should base spending and tax rates only on the merits of the programs involved and not on efforts to stabilize real GDP. (Most proponents of the laissez-faire view oppose fiscal policy actions designed to affect the price level or inflation, believing that rules for monetary policy should keep the price level stable and inflation low.) Some proponents of the laissez-faire view, but not all, favor formal rules for fiscal policy, such as a balanced-budget amendment or a limit on government spending as a fraction of GDP.

Proponents of an activist view of fiscal policy generally favor higher levels of government spending and higher tax rates, particularly on people with relatively high incomes. They also tend to believe that the government should vary its total spending and tax rates to try to stabilize real GDP and unemployment by offsetting, at least somewhat, other changes in aggregate demand. Most such proponents favor discretionary fiscal policies, though some favor certain kinds of fiscal policy rules such as institutions that automatically raise government spending or reduce taxes in a recession.[1]

The effects of many government regulatory policies resemble those of fiscal policies. For example, a government regulation that requires firms to buy pollution-abatement equipment may have effects similar to those of a tax on firms to fund government spending on pollution abatement. Regulations that require firms to provide workers' compensation benefits (which pay workers who suffer job-related injuries) resemble taxes on firms to fund government payments to injured workers.

RULES VERSUS DISCRETION IN FISCAL POLICY

The three main arguments for fiscal policy rules echo the arguments for monetary policy rules:

1. Two kinds of lags complicate fiscal policies—lags in *implementing* policies (actual changes in tax rates or government spending) and lags in the *effects* of fiscal policies on the economy.[2] These lags make it difficult to improve economic performance with discretionary fiscal policy.

2. Economists and the government lack sufficient information about the economy to conduct good discretionary fiscal policy. They lack relevant information about both underlying economic conditions (including current and near future conditions) and the likely effects of fiscal policies.

3. Credible rules for fiscal policy can improve economic performance by changing people's incentives.[3] Credible policy rules affect incentives and behavior in ways that discretionary policy cannot; rules can improve economic performance as compared to even the best discretionary policies.

---

[1]See the discussion of automatic stabilizers later in this chapter.

[2]In fact, implementing a change in fiscal policy usually takes longer than implementing a change in monetary policy.

[3]See the example of high taxes on capital in the previous chapter.

The main argument for discretionary fiscal policy views rules as too inflexible. New situations might arise that call for new policies, and policy rules would prevent actions required to adopt the best policies in those new situations. For example, the sticky-price model of aggregate supply and aggregate demand from earlier chapters implies that the government can help to fight a recession by raising spending and reducing taxes to increase private consumption and investment spending. A policy rule that requires the government to balance its budget might prevent it from taking these actions. Because no policy rule can take into account all situations that might arise in the future, any policy rule might limit the ability of policy makers to choose the best policy actions in the future.

TAXES, GOVERNMENT SPENDING, AND BUDGET DEFICITS IN THE UNITED STATES

In 1994, federal, state, and local governments in the United States collected $2.3 trillion ($2,300 billion) in tax revenues; they spent about $2.5 trillion. The combined government budget deficit amounted to $160 billion (according to the usual measure of the deficit, which a later section of this chapter criticizes). Nominal GDP was about $6.7 trillion, so government spending took almost 37 percent of GDP and people paid 34 percent of GDP in taxes. People paid $1.38 trillion in taxes to the federal government, which spent $1.54 trillion, for a federal budget deficit of $160 billion. Federal taxes took 20.3 percent of GDP and federal spending took 22.9 percent of GDP.

FIGURE 33.1

FEDERAL GOVERNMENT REVENUES AND EXPENDITURES, 1994

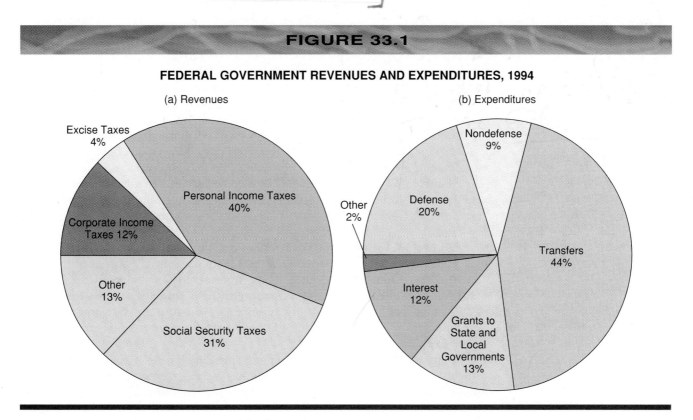

(a) Revenues

(b) Expenditures

FIGURE 33.2

TOTAL GOVERNMENT REVENUES AND EXPENDITURES (FEDERAL, STATE, AND LOCAL)

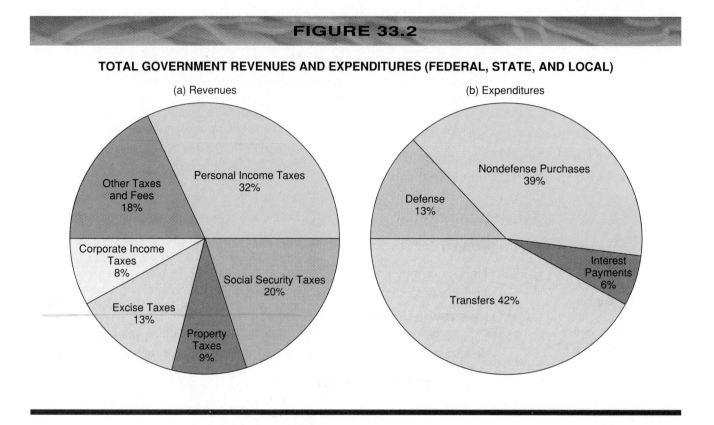

(a) Revenues

(b) Expenditures

Figure 33.1 shows where the federal government gets its money and how it spends money. About 40 percent of its revenues come from personal income taxes; another 31 percent come from Social Security taxes. Almost half of the federal government's spending covers transfer payments, one-fifth goes for defense, and one-eighth pays for aid to state and local governments. The federal government spends 12 percent of its total outlays to pay interest on its debt, and less than 10 percent pays for nondefense purchases of goods and services.

Figure 33.2 shows the sources of income for units of government at all levels, state and local as well as federal. Income taxes account for one-third of total government revenue; Social Security taxes are about one-fifth of total government revenue.

Figure 33.3 shows how government revenue has risen as a fraction of GDP since the end of World War II. Most of the increase has occurred at the state-and-local government level, though the figure shows a slight upward trend in federal government revenue as a fraction of GDP. The federal government now takes about one-fifth of GDP in tax revenue; in addition, state and local governments take about 11 percent, plus another 3 percent in grants from the federal government.

Figure 33.4 shows how government spending has risen as a fraction of GDP since the end of World War II. Spending has increased across all levels of government. Federal spending currently takes between one-fifth and one-fourth of GDP; total government spending takes between 35 percent and 40 percent of GDP. **Figure 33.5** shows that the government budget deficit has risen over the last half-

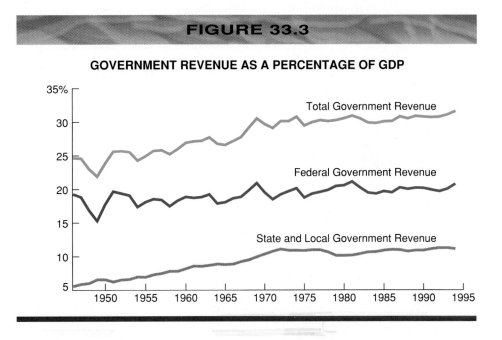

FIGURE 33.3

GOVERNMENT REVENUE AS A PERCENTAGE OF GDP

century despite increases in taxes, as government spending has increased more rapidly.

Figure 33.6 shows why federal spending has consumed a larger fraction of GDP. Though the government spends a smaller fraction of GDP on defense, spending on transfer payments has grown rapidly.

Figure 33.7 shows why total government spending has increased, whether measured in real (inflation-adjusted) terms, or as a fraction of GDP. The two main

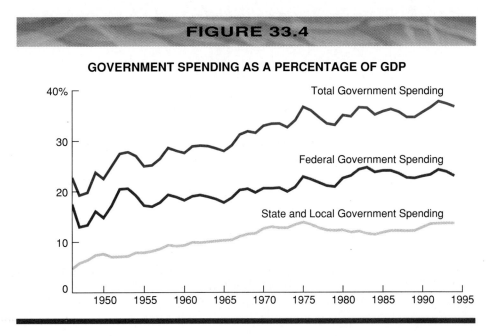

FIGURE 33.4

GOVERNMENT SPENDING AS A PERCENTAGE OF GDP

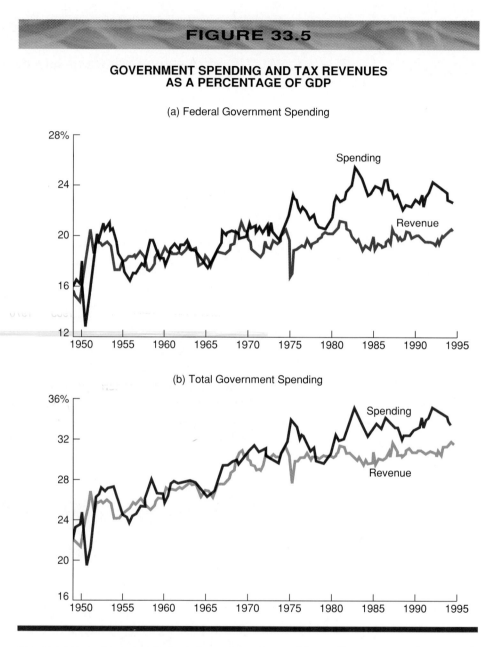

FIGURE 33.5

**GOVERNMENT SPENDING AND TAX REVENUES
AS A PERCENTAGE OF GDP**

(a) Federal Government Spending

(b) Total Government Spending

reasons are an increase in transfer payments, and in earlier years, an increase in nondefense purchases by state and local governments.

FOR REVIEW

33.1 Roughly how large is total government spending in the United States? How large a share of GDP does it take? How much of total government spending represents federal government spending? Look up the population of the United States, if you do not know it, and calculate total government spending per person.

33.2 Roughly how large is total government tax revenue in the United States? What fraction of GDP do people pay in taxes? How much of total tax pay-

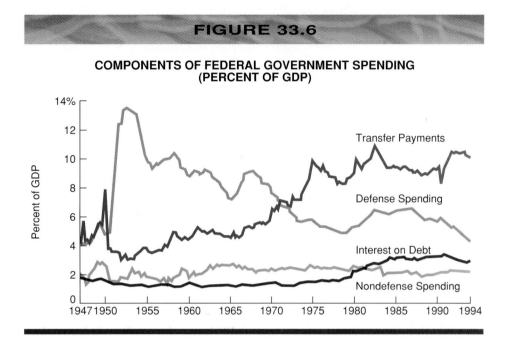

FIGURE 33.6

**COMPONENTS OF FEDERAL GOVERNMENT SPENDING
(PERCENT OF GDP)**

ments go to the federal government rather than state and local governments? Calculate average tax payments per person.

33.3 What are the main categories of government spending in the United States? How much do governments spend on these main categories?

33.4 What are the main sources of tax revenue in the United States?

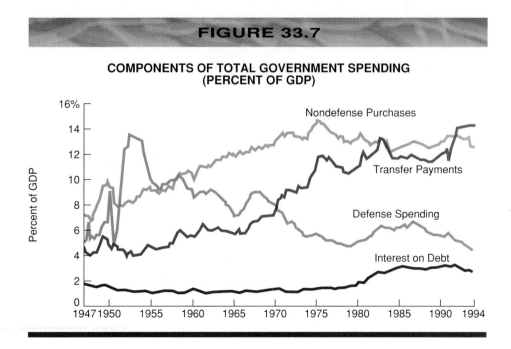

FIGURE 33.7

**COMPONENTS OF TOTAL GOVERNMENT SPENDING
(PERCENT OF GDP)**

QUESTION

33.5 In what ways do the following regulatory policies resemble fiscal policies?
   a. Minimum-wage laws
   b. Government regulations requiring new buildings to provide wheelchair access
   c. Government regulations that prohibit people from building on land deemed environmentally sensitive
   d. Regulations that establish procedures that pharmaceutical companies must follow to obtain government approval to sell a new drug

---

GOVERNMENT DEBT AND BUDGET DEFICITS

government debt — the amount of money the government owes people because it has borrowed money in the past

government budget deficit — the increase in the government's debt during 1 year

balanced budget — when tax receipts equal spending, so the deficit is zero and the government's debt does not change

budget surplus — the opposite of a deficit

Economic analysis of fiscal policy begins with a distinction between the government's debt and its deficit:

> **Government debt** (also sometimes called the *national debt*) is the amount of money the government owes people because it has borrowed money in the past.

> The **government budget deficit** is the increase in the government's debt during 1 year.

The budget deficit equals the government's spending minus its tax revenue. When the government has a budget deficit, it must either borrow money or print money to spend.[4]

> In a **balanced budget,** tax receipts equal spending, so the deficit is zero and government debt does not change.

> A **budget surplus** is a negative deficit (a decrease in government debt).

TIME PATH OF TAXES

Budget deficits and surpluses allow the government to change the time path of tax revenues. In other words, the government can collect less tax revenue now and more in the future, or vice versa. However, the discounted present value of the government's tax revenues must be as large as the discounted present value of its spending plus the initial value of its debt.

EXAMPLE

Suppose that the government will spend $100 this year and $100 next year, and the nominal interest rate is 10 percent per year. The discounted present value of government spending is:

$$\$100 + \frac{\$100}{1.10} = \$191$$

where $1 + i = 1.10$.

---

[4]In a common mistake, some people think that borrowing money or printing money eliminates the deficit—that is not true. The government still *has* a budget deficit when it borrows or prints money to spend in excess of its income. Borrowing or printing money for this purpose is called *financing the deficit.*

Consider three possible times paths of taxes:

1. The government could balance its budget each year by collecting $100 in taxes both this year and next year. This would give it tax receipts with a discounted present value of $191, the same as the discounted present value of spending.

2. The government could collect *no taxes this year* and $210 in taxes next year.[5] The government would have a $100 deficit this year, which it would finance by borrowing $100. Next year the government collects $210 in taxes to give it a $100 budget surplus. It would use $110 to pay for next year's spending ($100 for normal spending plus $10 for interest on its debt) and the other $100 to repay its loan.

3. The government could collect $191 in taxes this year and *no taxes next year*. It would then have a $91 surplus this year and a $100 deficit next year. The government would use $100 for current spending and save $91, earning 10 percent interest. This would give the government $100 for next year's spending.

The government could set up many other time paths for taxes. For example, it could collect $80 in taxes this year, running a $20 budget deficit, then collect $122 in taxes next year to pay for its $100 in normal spending and to repay its $20 debt with 10 percent interest.

CHOOSING THE TIME PATH OF TAXES

The time path of taxes affects the economy in two ways. First, the time path of taxes affects the size of the economic inefficiency caused by taxes.

EXPLANATION

Taxes create economic inefficiencies because they affect incentives. **Figure 33.8** shows how taxes drive a wedge between the price including tax that buyers pay, P_B, and the after-tax price that sellers receive, P_S. The difference, P_B minus P_S, is the per-unit tax. For example, with a 5 percent sales tax, buyers pay $10.50 for a good, sellers receive $10.00 after taxes, and the government get $0.50 in taxes; P_B is $10.50, P_S is $10.00, and the per-unit tax is $0.50. Because buyers pay a higher price (including tax) than sellers keep (after taxes), the equilibrium quantity is Q_1 (instead of Q_0, the equilibrium quantity without any tax). Since buyers must pay P_B, they want to buy only Q_1 instead of Q_0, and since sellers keep only P_S for each good they sell, they want to sell Q_1 instead of Q_0. The tax reduces the equilibrium quantity bought and sold. This causes economic inefficiency because it leads some people to forgo mutually advantageous trades (purchases and sales) because by not trading they can avoid the tax.

Each time the tax rate doubles, the amount of economic inefficiency more than doubles—it roughly quadruples. In fact, the economic inefficiency from a tax is roughly proportional to the tax rate squared. Raising a tax from $0.05 per unit to $0.10 per unit doubles the tax rate, but it raises the economic inefficiency about four times ($0.10 squared is 100, while $0.05 squared is 25; 100 is four times 25). This implies a benefit—less inefficiency—from a 5-cent tax for 2 years than a 10-cent tax for 1 year.[6] A 5-cent tax for 2 years also causes less economic

econ inefficiency =
(tax rate)²

---

[5]The discounted present value of this tax revenue is $210/1.1, or $191.

[6]Imposing a 5-cent tax for 2 years causes an efficiency loss proportional to $0.25 for 2 years, so the total loss is proportional to $0.50. Imposing a 10-cent tax for 1 year causes an efficiency loss proportional to $1.00.

FIGURE 33.8

TAXES CAUSE ECONOMIC INEFFICIENCY

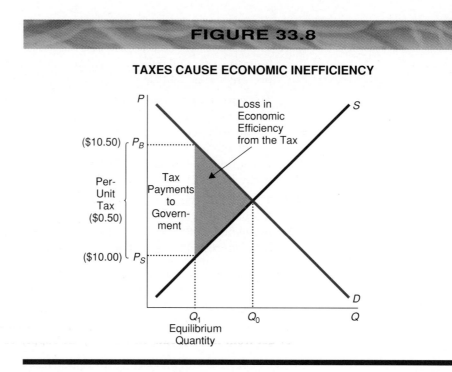

inefficiency than an 8-cent tax for 1 year and a 2-cent tax for the other year.[7] In other words, the time path of taxes affects economic efficiency.

ANALOGY

Think about an analogy. Imagine that you want to drive a car 100 miles in 2 hours. You could drive 50 miles per hour for 2 hours, or you could drive 20 miles per hour for 1 hour and 80 miles per hour for another hour. It is safer to drive 50 miles per hour for the whole trip. Raising your speed from 50 to 80 for 1 hour and lowering it from 50 to 20 for the other hour raises your risk of an accident. Similarly, raising a tax from $0.50 to $0.80 for 1 year and lowering it from $0.50 to $0.20 for the other year raises the economic inefficiency caused by the tax.

EFFECTS ON AGGREGATE DEMAND AND SUPPLY

A second effect on the economy operates through aggregate demand and supply. Changes in the time path of taxes can affect real GDP and inflation by changing aggregate demand and aggregate supply.

EXPLANATION

An earlier chapter discussed the controversy over the effects of a government budget deficit caused by a decrease in tax revenue. Most economists believe that a change in the time path of taxes affects aggregate demand. A tax cut raises con-

---

[7]A 5-cent tax causes inefficiency proportional to 25 each year for 2 years, so the inefficiency is proportional to (25)(2) = 50. An 8-cent tax causes inefficiency proportional to 64, and a 2-cent tax causes inefficiency proportional to 4, so an 8-cent tax for 1 year and a 2-cent tax for the other year cause an inefficiency proportional to 64 + 4 = 68, which is larger than the inefficiency from a 5-cent tax for 2 years.

sumption spending because people do not save all the money they get from the tax cut. In this way, the tax cut raises aggregate demand and a tax increase reduces aggregate demand. If the sticky-price model or sticky-wage model from an earlier chapter is correct, the government may be able to help stabilize aggregate demand—and thereby stabilize real GDP—by cutting or raising taxes. Changes in taxes also affect aggregate supply by changing the equilibrium inputs of labor and capital, because a tax increase may reduce the incentive to work. This implies that the government can use fiscal policy to change aggregate supply as well as aggregate demand.

TIMING OF TAXES AND AGGREGATE DEMAND

The government's budget deficit rises if it cuts taxes (revenue) without changing its spending. Because the government borrows more money, the demand for loans increases, as in Figure 33.9. Taxes fall, so people have more after-tax income. If they save some of this extra after-tax income, the supply of loans also increases.

Economists disagree about the results. According to the majority view, people spend some of the extra after-tax income. Because they do not save all of it, the supply of loans increases by less than the increase in demand so the real interest rate rises as in **Figure 33.9a**. The increase in consumption raises aggregate demand ($C + I + G + NEX$).[8]

According to the minority view, people save all of the extra after-tax income they get from the tax cut.[9] As a result, the supply of loans increases by the same amount as the increase in the demand for loans, and the real interest rate remains constant, as in Figure 33.9b. Because people do not increase consumption spending, aggregate demand remains constant.

If the majority view of tax cuts is correct, then a tax cut raises aggregate demand. Now think about the sticky-price model from earlier chapters and suppose that the economy is in a recession. The economy begins in a short-run equilibrium (not a long-run equilibrium) at Point A in **Figure 33.10.** As time passes and prices or wages adjust freely, the economy moves from Point A to its long-run equilibrium at Point B. However, this adjustment may take time and the government may want to speed up the process; to do so, it may reduce taxes.

If the government cuts taxes (but not its spending), aggregate demand increases from AD_1 to AD_2, as in Figure 33.10. The economy moves from Point A to Point B, so the tax cut raises real GDP and the price level. The tax cut also raises the government's debt, so it will owe more in the future. In the future, the

The debate: Our heavy debt

Deficits do matter; We must cut them

▲

Deficits don't matter; We must cut spending

*Arthur Laffer,
An opposing view*

The effects of deficits and government spending spark controversies among economists.
Source: USA Today, June 23, 1987, p. 10A.

---

[8]In this case, government spending, G, does not change because the government cuts taxes but not spending. You may wonder how one can be sure that aggregate demand rises—after all, the real interest rate rises and this reduces investment, I. If C is rising and I is falling, how does one know that $C + I + G + NEX$ rises? If I falls enough, might aggregate demand fall? In fact, aggregate demand rises. To see why, recall that real aggregate demand *also* equals MV/P. The money supply does not change, but the increase in the interest rate raises velocity, so MV rises, and, at any given price level, P, MV/P rises.

[9]According to this view, people have an incentive to save all the money from the tax cut because the budget deficit raises the government's debt. Unless the government cuts future spending, it will have to raise *future* taxes to pay interest on the debt, even if it never pays off the debt. The discounted present value of those higher future taxes is the same as the tax cut this year, so people will save the entire tax cut because they will need this increased savings (with interest) to pay higher taxes in the future. The minority view says that a change in taxes does not affect aggregate demand. If the government cuts taxes this year and raises taxes in the future, aggregate demand does not change because the discounted present value of taxes does not change. People don't care whether the government taxes them now or in the future; they care about the total amount (the discounted present value of the amount) that the government takes from them in taxes.

FIGURE 33.9

TWO VIEWS OF A TAX CUT

(a) Majority View

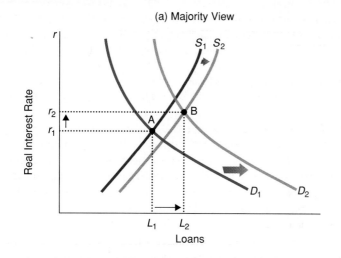

(b) Minority View

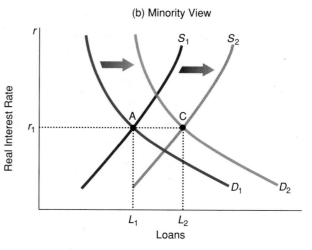

According to the majority view, a tax cut raises the demand for loans by more than the supply, so it raises the equilibrium real interest rate.

According to the minority view, a tax cut raises the demand and supply of loans equally, so the equilibrium real interest rate does not change.

FIGURE 33.10

TAXES AND AGGREGATE DEMAND

A tax cut raises aggregate demand and moves the economy from Point A to Point B.

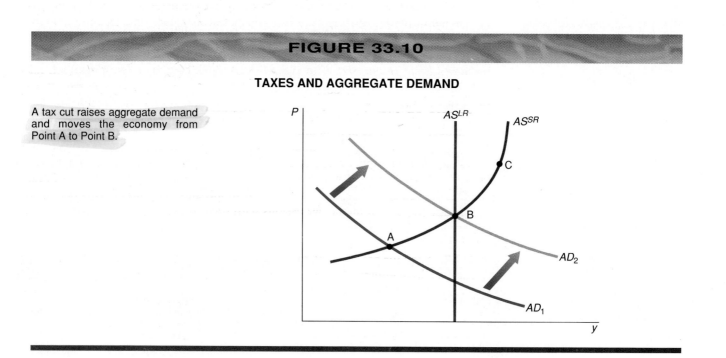

IN THE NEWS

Let's borrow more money

That's the way to end this recession.

By John Kenneth Galbraith

Some economists advocate tax cuts during recessions to raise aggregate demand (even though tax cuts would raise the budget deficit).

Source: John Kenneth Galbraith, "Let's Borrow More Money," *New York Times,* May 16, 1991, p. A23.

government will have to raise taxes to pay interest on its debt or reduce other government spending to free up money to pay interest on the debt. Whichever choice the government makes, aggregate demand will decrease in the future as the government pays higher interest on the debt, which will tend to reduce real GDP temporarily at that time.

If the government can time its policies particularly well, it can raise future taxes at a time of high aggregate demand and real GDP, that is, when the economy is at a point like Point C in Figure 33.10. This may keep the fall in future aggregate demand from reducing future real GDP by more than a small amount. For example, it may move the economy from Point C to Point B in the future. If the government can do this, it can use changes in the time path of taxes to stabilize real GDP near its full-employment level.

Tax changes can affect aggregate demand in another way by changing people's incentives to spend or save. For example, suppose that the government cuts taxes on the income that people earn from their savings. This gives people an incentive to save more for the future and reduce current consumption spending. To see how this affects aggregate demand, recall that nominal aggregate demand equals *MV*, the money supply times the velocity of money. Velocity increases when the nominal interest rate rises, as an earlier chapter explained.[10] Holding fixed the money supply, aggregate demand increases when velocity increases, and it decreases when velocity decreases. As a result, an increase in the nominal interest rate raises velocity and thereby raises aggregate demand. Similarly, a decrease in the nominal interest rate reduces velocity and thereby reduces aggregate demand. To see how the tax cut affects aggregate demand, one must find out if it raises or lowers the interest rate.

Because a tax cut raises government borrowing, it raises the demand for loans. However, the tax cut also raises the supply of loans because it raises the incentive to save. If the tax cut raises the incentive to save enough to raise the supply of loans by more than the demand, then it reduces the equilibrium real interest rate. The fall in the real interest rate reduces the nominal interest rate, which reduces velocity and decreases aggregate demand. On the other hand, if the tax cut has only a small effect on the incentive to save, so that the supply of loans rises by less than the rise in demand, then it raises the equilibrium interest rate, which raises velocity and increases aggregate demand.

TIMING OF TAXES AND AGGREGATE SUPPLY

Changes in the time path of taxes also affect aggregate supply. A cut in the income tax rate raises the after-tax wage and increases the incentive to work. This raises the equilibrium input of labor, raising total employment, hours worked per person, and real GDP. Emphasis on the incentive effects of taxes and government regulations on aggregate supply is often called *supply-side economics.* This perspective became popular in public discussions with the election of Ronald Reagan in 1980. Although some supply-side arguments have been quite controversial, other features of supply-side economics receive wide agreement among economists, and their implications for government policy amount largely to placing greater emphasis on the incentive effects of taxes and regulations when thinking about policies.

---

[10]An increase in the nominal interest rate raises the opportunity cost of holding money (instead of an asset that pays interest), raising the velocity of money.

Because a tax cut can increase both aggregate demand and aggregate supply, it can potentially raise real GDP with little effect on the price level, as **Figure 33.11** shows. Whether the price level rises or falls depends on whether aggregate supply increases more or less than aggregate demand.

CASE STUDIES: THE KENNEDY AND REAGAN TAX CUTS

The tax cuts proposed by President John Kennedy were enacted in 1964 and 1965, after Kennedy's assassination. Tax cuts proposed by President Ronald Reagan in 1980 took effect over the years from 1982 to 1984. Both the Kennedy and Reagan tax cuts were followed by longer-than-usual periods before recessions, which occurred in 1970 and 1990, respectively. Economists advising the government in the 1960s argued that the tax cuts helped the economy to grow during that decade by raising aggregate demand. Those advisors generally considered themselves as Keynesian economists, and they regarded the sticky-price or sticky-wage model as the best model of the economy. Economists advising the government in the 1980s, in contrast, argued that the tax cuts of that decade helped the economy to grow by raising aggregate supply. Those advisors generally regarded themselves as supply-side economists, and they promoted diverse views that included the imperfect-information model and real business cycle model as well as the sticky-price and sticky-wage models.

Before the Kennedy tax cuts, the top marginal federal income tax rate stood at 91 percent, although this tax rate applied only to incomes over $1 million per year in today's dollars. **Figure 33.12** shows marginal tax rates in 1963 before the Kennedy tax cut, in 1965 after the tax cut, in 1981 before the Reagan tax cut, in 1984 after the Reagan tax cut, and in 1995.

average tax rate — the fraction of income that a person must pay in taxes

The **average tax rate** is the fraction of income that a person must pay in taxes.

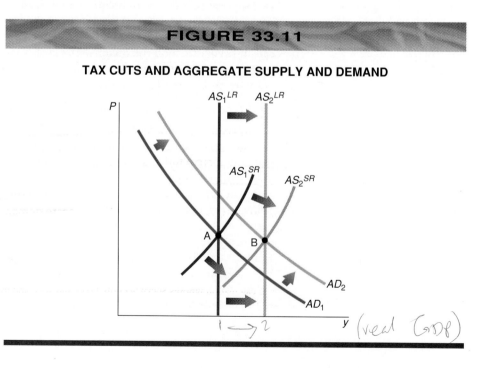

FIGURE 33.11

TAX CUTS AND AGGREGATE SUPPLY AND DEMAND

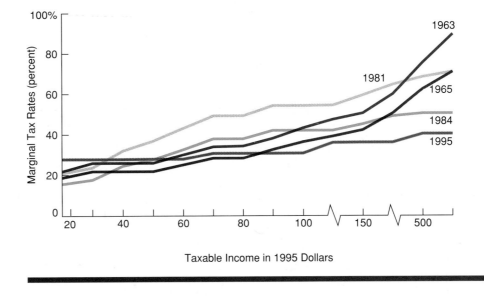

FIGURE 33.12

MARGINAL FEDERAL INCOME TAX RATES IN THE UNITED STATES

Taxable Income in 1995 Dollars

---

marginal tax rate — the fraction of each additional dollar earned that a person must pay in taxes

The **marginal tax rate** is the fraction of each additional dollar earned that a person must pay in taxes.

The marginal tax rate and the average tax rate differ because of deductions (representing income on which no tax is due) and because most people pay a lower tax rate on the first dollar they earn than on the last dollar. For example, in 1995 a single person earning $40,000 paid 15 percent of the first $28,969 of income as federal income taxes and 28 percent of the rest of that income, giving an average income tax rate of 16.25 percent and a marginal income tax rate of 28 percent.[11] The marginal tax rate affects a person's incentive to work more hours.

The Kennedy tax cuts reduced taxes by about $11.5 billion in 1965. Economists at the time estimated the aggregate demand multiplier (discussed in an earlier chapter) at between 1.3 and 2.0, so they expected the tax cut to increase real GDP by about $15 billion to $23 billion through an increase in aggregate demand. GDP actually grew by about $28 billion, above its trend rate of growth.[12] This suggests that even if one-half to three-fourths of that increase in real GDP resulted from an increase in aggregate demand due to the tax cut, the remaining one-fourth to one-half may have resulted from an increase in aggregate supply caused by the tax cut.[13]

---

[11]This calculation ignores Social Security taxes and state and local income taxes.

[12]See Lawrence Lindsey, *The Growth Experiment* (New York: Basic Books, 1990). Lindsey is now a governor of the Federal Reserve System.

[13]Lawrence Lindsey argues that the supply-side effects were larger than this; many other economists think they were smaller.

By 1981, federal income tax rates were higher again, mainly because of bracket creep, which occurs when inflation automatically raises taxes.[14] The Reagan tax cut reduced federal income taxes again, as shown in Figure 13.12. One study estimated that the increase in aggregate demand from the Reagan tax cut raised GDP by 3.2 percent in 1983 to 1984 and by 2.7 percent in 1985, while the increase in aggregate supply from the tax cut raised GDP by about half of this amount.[15]

LAFFER CURVE

Higher tax rates usually mean larger tax payments and more tax revenue for the government, but not always.

Laffer Curve — a graph showing the relationship between the marginal tax rate and the government's tax revenue

The **Laffer Curve** shows the relationship between the marginal tax rate and the government's tax revenue.

The Laffer Curve in **Figure 33.13** shows that the government does not get any tax revenue is the tax rate if either zero or very high. If the income tax rate were 100 percent, for example, people would probably stop working for pay; without any income to tax, the government would not collect any tax revenue. If the tax rate were high enough (say, at Point B in the figure), the government would get little tax revenue. In that case, the economy is said to be on the *wrong side of the Laffer Curve* and the government could increase its tax revenue by reducing the tax rate.

Some economists claimed that the U.S. economy was on the wrong side of the Laffer Curve in the early 1980s and that the Reagan tax cuts would raise the government's tax revenue. Most economists believed, however, that the economy was on the rising (left) portion of the Laffer Curve, so that a cut in tax rates would reduce tax revenue. On balance, the majority turned out to be right. If the tax cut had *not* raised real GDP, evidence suggests that the federal government would have lost about $115 billion in tax revenue each year.[16]

An increase in GDP raises the *tax base,* however, which helps to mitigate the fall in tax revenue. Evidence suggests that the increase in aggregate demand due to the Reagan tax cuts added about $40 billion to federal tax revenues in 1985, while the increase in aggregate supply from the tax cuts added about $20 billion. In addition, the decrease in tax rates raised government tax revenue by about $20 billion per year by reducing people's use of legal methods of tax

---

[14]To see how inflation pushed people into higher tax brackets, suppose that you are single and you earn $20,000 per year. Inflation doubles all prices and your pretax salary also doubles to $40,000. Before taxes, you have kept up with inflation. Everything costs twice as much as before, but you now earn twice as much. After taxes, however, you may have fallen behind. Suppose that you must pay a 15 percent tax on all income under $20,000 and a 28 percent tax on all income above $20,000. Before inflation your taxes were $3,000 (15 percent of $20,000) leaving after-tax income of $17,000. After inflation, your taxes are $8,600 ($3,000 on your first $20,000 of income and $5,600 on the rest) leaving after-tax income of $31,400. Your after-tax income did not double; it did not rise from $17,000 to $34,000. Instead, your taxes more than doubled, from $3,000 to $8,600, and your after-tax income rose from $17,000 to $31,400. The purchasing power of your after-tax income fell. This bracket creep results from inflation with unindexed taxes. Starting in 1984, federal income taxes in the United States became indexed to inflation to prevent bracket creep; the tax tables now change automatically so that, if your salary keeps up with inflation before taxes, it also keeps up with inflation after federal income taxes.

[15]Lindsey, *Growth Experiment.*

[16]This is the estimate for 1985 from Lindsey, *Growth Experiment.*

FIGURE 33.13

THE LAFFER CURVE

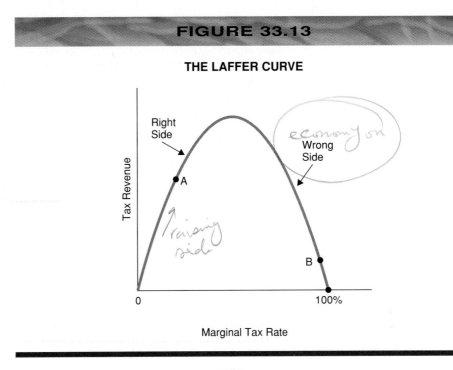

avoidance.[17] While the direct effect of the tax cut may have reduced tax revenue by $115 billion per year, these three factors indirectly raised tax revenue by about $80 billion per year, so that the government had a net loss of about $35 billion in revenue in 1985 from the tax cuts.[18]

AUTOMATIC CHANGES IN GOVERNMENT BUDGET DEFICITS WITH GDP

Business cycles affect the government budget deficit. The government's tax revenue falls automatically in recessions, raising the budget deficit, because people have less income to tax. Also, the government's tax revenue automatically rises when real GDP rises, reducing the budget deficit, because people pay taxes on a higher level of income.

A 1 percent fall in real GDP raises the federal government budget deficit by about $30 billion. To see why, recall that GDP is close to $7 trillion, so a 1 percent

---

[17]People use legal methods of tax avoidance when they choose investments that lower their taxes, even if those investments pay lower returns. For example, one investment of $1,000 might return $100 of taxable income at the end of the year. If the marginal tax rate is 40 percent, people pay $40 in taxes and keep $60 for themselves. Another investment of $1,000 might pay back only $70, but in nontaxable income. If the tax rate is 40 percent, people choose the second investment and the government gets zero tax revenue from this investment. If the government cuts the tax rate to 25 percent, however, people choose the first investment, and they pay $25 in taxes and keep $75 for themselves. The lower tax rate leads people to change their behavior in ways that raise the government's tax revenue. (Notice that the government's revenue from a tax on investment can rise from a cut in the tax rate even though the total amount of investment does not change. This occurs because the *type* of investment changes.)

[18]Some evidence supports the claim that the tax cuts in the highest tax brackets actually raised tax revenue, so the economy was on the wrong side of the Laffer Curve for *some* taxes, though not for most.

rise in GDP increases it by about $70 billion. On average, the marginal tax rate in the United States lies between one-third and one-half, so a $70 billion rise in GDP raises government tax revenue by between one-third and one-half of this amount, or about $30 billion.

Because increases in the government budget deficit during a recession (and decreases when real GDP is high) could stabilize real GDP as discussed earlier, these automatic changes in the government deficit automatically stabilize real GDP. They are examples of automatic stabilizers.

> An **automatic stabilizer** is a feature of government policy that reduces fluctuations in real GDP automatically, without any explicit actions of the government.

automatic stabilizer — a feature of government policy that reduces fluctuations in real GDP automatically, without any explicit actions of the government

In the 1995 congressional debate on a balanced-budget amendment to the U.S. Constitution, opponents focused on concern that the proposed amendment would eliminate automatic stabilizers.

FOR REVIEW

33.6 What is the government debt? What is the budget deficit? Roughly how large are they?

33.7 Explain how the government can change the time path of taxes without changing its spending?

33.8 How does a change in the time path of taxes affect aggregate demand? How does it affect aggregate supply?

33.9 Define and give an example of an average tax rate and a marginal tax rate.

QUESTION

33.10 What is the Laffer Curve? What does it mean to be on the wrong side of the Laffer Curve?

MEASURING THE BUDGET DEFICIT

Figure 33.14 shows the usual measure of the federal government's budget deficit in nominal terms. To avoid misleading comparisons between figures in different years without adjusting for inflation, **Figure 33.15a** shows the inflation-adjusted budget deficit and budget deficit or surplus of state and local governments. Notice that the federal budget deficit rose in the 1980s and 1990s above levels of earlier years, but that state and local governments had *budget surpluses* in those years.

Another way to look at the size of the government's budget deficit is to compare it to the economy's total income, GDP. Figure 33.15b shows the federal, state-and-local, and total government budget deficits or surpluses as shares of GDP. Since 1985, the federal government's budget deficit has averaged about 3.5 percent of GDP, while state–and–local budget surpluses reduced the total government budget deficit to 2.7 percent of GDP.

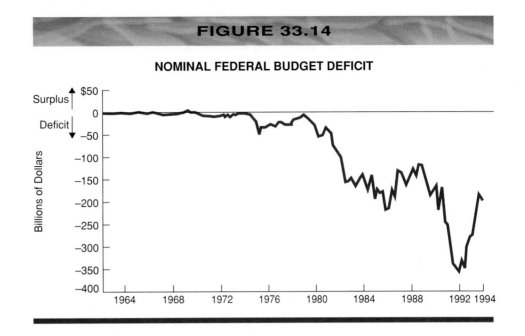

FIGURE 33.14

NOMINAL FEDERAL BUDGET DEFICIT

ACCURATE MEASUREMENT OF THE GOVERNMENT'S DEBT AND BUDGET DEFICIT

The measures of the government budget deficit in Figures 33.14 to 33.16 can be misleading, even after adjustment for inflation or conversion to shares of GDP. To measure the government's budget deficit (the change in the government's debt) properly, these figures need several adjustments.

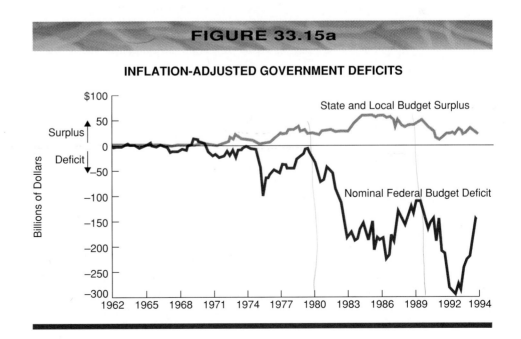

FIGURE 33.15a

INFLATION-ADJUSTED GOVERNMENT DEFICITS

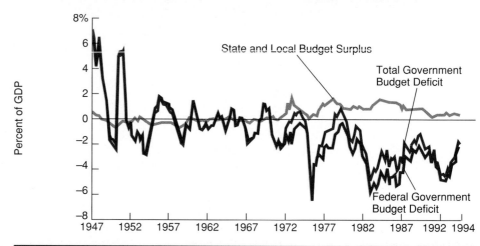

FIGURE 33.15b

GOVERNMENT BUDGET DEFICITS AS A PERCENTAGE OF GDP

State and Local Budget Surplus

Total Government Budget Deficit

Federal Government Budget Deficit

First, the government's debt should include the money the government owes to other people, but not the money that one part of the government owes to another part. News commentators usually forget to make this adjustment. For example, commentators reported the government's debt at $4.8 trillion in January 1995. But some of this total is money that the government owes to itself![19] (For example, the Treasury Department owes money to the Federal Reserve.) The government's debt to other people was about $3.6 trillion ($3,600 billion) at the beginning of 1995. This is called the *privately held government debt*.

privately held government debt — the amount of government debt owned by people and business firms outside the government

> **Privately held government debt** is the amount of government debt owned by people and business firms outside the government.

In 1995, the privately held government debt amounted to nearly $14,000 for every person in the country, including children. **Figure 33.16** shows the nominal federal government debt and the privately held debt.

A second important change to measures of the government debt and budget deficit would adjust the figures for inflation in any comparison between different years.

real government debt — the government's debt in constant (base-year) dollars, that is, adjusted for inflation

real government budget deficit—the increase in the government's real debt

> The **real government debt** is the government's debt stated in constant (base-year) dollars, that is, adjusted for inflation.

> The **real government budget deficit** is the increase in the government's real debt.

The real budget deficit differs from the deficit as usually measured because inflation lowers the real value of the government's debt—the government repays its

---

[19]It should be obvious why we don't want to count this as part of the government's debt. You could make your own debt seem very large by announcing that you owe yourself $1 million!

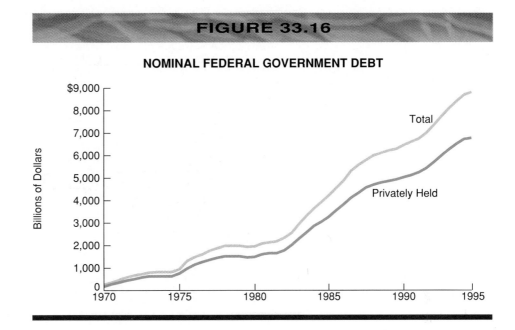

FIGURE 33.16

NOMINAL FEDERAL GOVERNMENT DEBT

debt in deflated dollars. **Figure 33.17** shows the real, privately held federal government debt in billions of 1994 dollars. The real, privately held government debt has grown rapidly in recent years. By 1995, it was about three times higher than in 1980.

Figure 33.18 shows the real federal government deficit (the change in the real debt) in recent years. Notice that the federal government had real budget surpluses several times in the 1970s. **Figure 33.19** shows the real federal government deficit as a percentage of GDP.

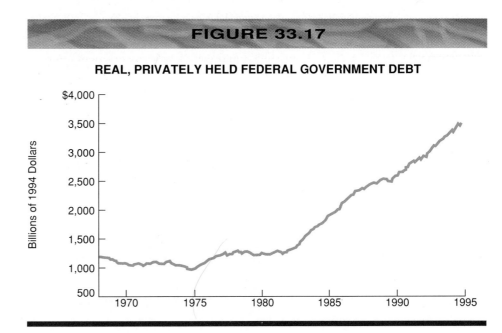

FIGURE 33.17

REAL, PRIVATELY HELD FEDERAL GOVERNMENT DEBT

An International Comparison of Government Debts and Deficits

The governments of many countries around the world have run up budget deficits and incurred large debts. Japan's central government, for example, ran deficits exceeding 4 percent of Japan's GDP in 1993, 1994, and 1995 (although, as in the United States, local government budget surpluses in the previous six years. Governments of other countries have run even larger deficits. The governments of Greece, Italy, and Sweden have recently had budget deficits larger than 10 percent of their GDPs.

The following table shows real privately-held government debt as a percent of GDP for a few developed countries. The governments of Belgium and Italy have debts higher than their countries' annual GDPs. Japan's government debt is among the smallest in the world, at about 10 percent of GDP.

ESTIMATED PRIVATELY-HELD GOVERNMENT DEBT AS A PERCENT OF GDP, 1995

Belgium	128%	Germany	47%
Italy	124	United States	40
Canada	66	Sweden	40
Netherlands	60	France	35
Spain	50	Australia	25
United Kingdom	48	Japan	10

Source: OECD Economic Outlook December 1994, Annex Table 34.

A third adjustment to measures of the government debt and budget deficit must account for money that the government owes but that the *official* statement of the government debt omits. The official measure of the government debt does not include all the government's liabilities—the money it owes people. The two biggest missing items are:

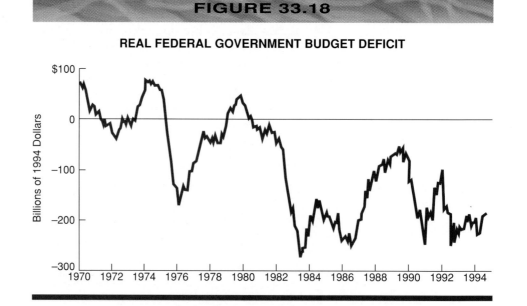

FIGURE 33.18

REAL FEDERAL GOVERNMENT BUDGET DEFICIT

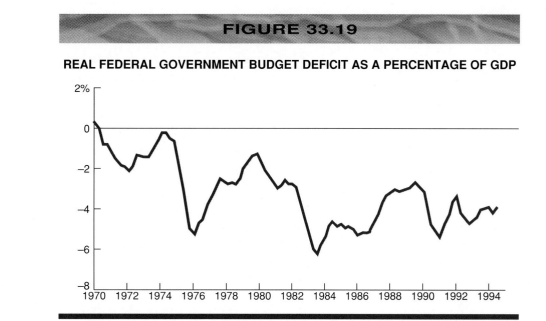

FIGURE 33.19

REAL FEDERAL GOVERNMENT BUDGET DEFICIT AS A PERCENTAGE OF GDP

1. Pensions for government employees that the government will owe in the future

2. Social Security benefits that the government has promised to pay in the future

Pensions: About $1 Trillion

The official statement of the privately held federal government debt at the beginning of 1995 was about $3.6 trillion, but this figure does not include pensions that the government owes to its employees. Some of the money the government has promised to pay as pensions is funded: money has been put aside and invested to help pay the pensions in the future. About $1,000 billion of the government's pension liabilities are unfunded, however; the government has no money saved or invested to cover these payments.[20]

This $1 trillion unfunded pension debt raised the federal government's debt to other people in 1995 to about $4.6 trillion rather than $3.6 trillion. This is roughly $18,000 for each person in the country. The government did not have many unfunded pension liabilities 40 years ago. This part of the government's debt has grown since then, so the true government deficits over that period have been bigger than the numbers in the earlier figures.

Social Security: About $4 Trillion

The official government debt numbers also omit money that the government has promised to pay for Social Security benefits in the future. Rough estimates place the discounted present value of these payments between $3 trillion and $5 trillion.

---

[20]See Henning Bohm, "Budget Deficits and Government Accounting," *Carnegie-Rochester Conference Series on Public Policy,* 1992.

Some economists argue for including this obligation in the government's debt. They see little difference between:

1. A government promise to repay a loan in the future
2. A government promise to make Social Security payments in the future

Other economists argue against including promised Social Security payments as part of the government's debt since Congress can always change Social Security laws so that the government will not owe this much money. (Some argue that this is likely to happen.) The economists who want to include Social Security respond that the government can break *any* of its promises—it can fail to repay its formal loans, for example—so the possibility that the government *might not* actually make the Social Security payments promised in current law should not prevent us from counting those payments as money the government owes. This issue remains controversial. Including the discounted present value of Social Security payments in the government's debt raises it from $4.6 trillion to somewhere around $8 trillion, around $30,000 for every person in the country.

DOES THE DEFICIT HAVE *ANY* MEANING?

The last section calculated how much the government owes other people. The government also owns assets, however, such as land, mineral rights, capital equipment, military hardware, and so on. The government collects income from some of these assets, such as lease payments on land. Perhaps the most important asset the government owns is its ability to collect taxes.

Economist Laurence J. Kotlikoff has argued that the usual measurement of the deficit, even with the corrections discussed so far, is arbitrary and misleading as a guide to fiscal policy.[21] He argues that when the government takes money from people, it arbitrarily calls some of it *taxes* and the rest *borrowing*. When it pays money to people, it arbitrarily calls some of it *spending* and some of it *principal plus interest on the debt.* Since the spending and taxes labels are both arbitrary, their difference, the deficit, is also arbitrary. The pattern of taxes and government spending has important effects, however, and can affect different people (and different generations) differently.

EXAMPLE

Consider Social Security. When the government collects money from people for Social Security, it calls this a *Social Security tax.* When it makes Social Security payments to people, it calls this *spending* on transfer payments. The government could just as well call such a payment a *loan,* though. The government could say that it borrows money for Social Security from people, and it pays back the loan when it pays Social Security benefits. This language is arbitrary, but it changes the measured deficit, so the deficit is really meaningless. It depends on the arbitrary language that describes these things. (The effects of the Social Security program, however, are real.)

If Kotlikoff's suggestion seems strange, consider what the government of France once did. The French government once imposed a forced loan on the

---

[21]He suggests an entirely new way to measure fiscal policy based on its effects on people born in different years. See Laurence J. Kotlikoff, *Generational Accounting* (New York: Free Press, 1992).

French people; it required people to lend money to the government. Is this a tax or a loan? If one considers it a loan, then the French government's debt increased; it had a deficit. When the government repays the loan, it is really a loan repayment, or should one call it a *transfer payment* to the people who earlier paid taxes? Kotlikoff argues that such a question of language has no right answer, and since it affects the measurement of the deficit, the deficit is meaningless. These issues are very controversial.

Notice that Kotlikoff's argument is related to the controversy about the effects of government budget deficits caused by tax cuts. The majority view sees taxes and loans as different. If the government lowers taxes and borrows money from people instead, they feel richer. When they give the government money and call it *lending* rather than *tax payments,* people spend more money. In contrast, the minority view says that people don't care what the payment is called; they spend the same amount in either case. In the minority view, only the total discounted present value of money that the government takes affects people's spending.

SOCIAL SECURITY SURPLUS

More babies than usual were born in the years between the end of World War II and 1960. This baby-boom generation will retire around the years 2020 to 2030, perhaps causing problems for the Social Security system. The U.S. population now includes about one retired person for every five people of working age (20 to 65 years old). The Social Security benefit payments that retired people collect come from the Social Security taxes that these workers currently pay. In other words, Social Security is (and has been, since it started) mainly a pay-as-you-go system.[22] By 2020 to 2030, the population will include only about 3.0 to 3.5 workers per retired person. This leaves three possibilities:

1. Social Security taxes will be twice as high.
2. Social Security payments will be cut in half.
3. The Social Security system will start saving more money now to accumulate a trust fund big enough to continue the same level of payments without higher taxes.

The current Social Security law is intended to produce the third solution. The Social Security system now runs a surplus, collecting tax revenue that exceeds its total payments. If the government were to save this surplus, it could accumulate a trust fund to help reduce the size of future increases in taxes or cuts in payments (depending on future economic and demographic developments).

The Social Security surplus, which now exceeds $100 billion per year and is rising over time, appears as part of the overall government budget figures. This increasing surplus will automatically reduce the overall government budget deficit in the years ahead, and it may eventually turn that deficit into a budget surplus. Some economists see a danger in this trend, because the falling government deficit numbers could reduce the government's willingness to reduce the deficit exclusive of Social Security by raising other taxes or reducing other spending. Because the government currently uses the Social Security surplus to pay for other pro-

---

[22]When people paid Social Security taxes, the government did not save and invest their money for them so that it could pay them Social Security benefits when they retired. Instead, the government distributed their money as Social Security payments to people who were already retired.

grams, it will not build up a large enough trust fund by 2020 to 2030. That would make the third solution listed earlier impossible, forcing a choice between the other two solutions—big increases in Social Security taxes or big cuts in Social Security payments.[23]

FOR REVIEW

33.11 Roughly how large is the U.S. government budget deficit? How large a share of GDP does it represent?

33.12 What do economists mean by the term *real government budget deficit*? Discuss three important adjustments to the usual measure of government deficits.

33.13 Why does the U.S. Social Security system run a surplus? What happens to that surplus?

CHANGES IN GOVERNMENT SPENDING

In 1994, 42 percent of total government spending in the United States covered transfer payments (6.0 percent covered interest on debt) and 52 percent covered purchases of goods and services (13 percent for defense and 39 percent for non-defense purchases). Transfer payments and government purchases of goods and services have different effects on the economy, and the effects of government purchases depend on what the government buys.

EFFECTS OF TRANSFER PAYMENTS

Transfer payments are simply payments of money to people. Social Security is the largest transfer payment program. Unemployment compensation payments are also transfer payments. When the government taxes one person to provide transfer payments to someone else, it redistributes income. This does not necessarily affect aggregate demand at all. It can raise aggregate demand if it redistributes income from people with low marginal propensities to spend (people whose spending does not change much when their income changes) to people with large marginal propensities to spend. It can reduce aggregate demand if it redistributes income in the opposite direction.

Transfer payments can affect aggregate supply by changing the incentives to work. For example, the Social Security program encourages people to retire earlier and not to take part-time jobs that would end their eligibility for Social Security payments. The taxes to pay for transfer payments can also affect aggregate supply.

EFFECTS OF GOVERNMENT PURCHASES

Government purchases of goods and services affect aggregate demand directly; aggregate demand equals $C + I + G + NEX$, where G represents government purchases of goods and services, *but does not include transfer payments*. The effects

---

[23]Under current law, Social Security taxes will probably exceed Social Security payments until about 2025. If the government uses the Social Security surplus for current spending, it will have to raise taxes to very high levels in the future for about 20 years or so (until the baby boomers die).

of increases in government spending on the economy depend on several conditions:

1. What the government buys, including:
   a. How well government spending substitutes for private spending
   b. How productive the government spending is
2. How the government pays for its spending

GOVERNMENT SPENDING THAT SUBSTITUTES FOR PRIVATE SPENDING

Government spending can substitute for (or replace) private spending. Suppose that the government raises taxes when it raises spending, so the budget deficit does not increase. (The next section will discuss other cases.) Assume that the government buys more of something that substitutes very well for spending that people already do on their own. Such an increase in government spending does not add to aggregate demand because a fall in consumption (*C*) or investment (*I*) offsets the rise in *G*. On the other hand, if the government raises spending on something that substitutes poorly for spending that people already do on their own, then aggregate demand rises.

EXAMPLE: LUNCH PROGRAM   Suppose that the government starts a free lunch program in which it buys your lunch for you. To keep the example simple, suppose that it buys exactly the same food that you would have bought for yourself, and it raises your taxes to pay for this program. (Ignore the salaries of government bureaucrats who run the program.)

This program has no effect on aggregate demand. You go through the cafeteria line and get your food, but you don't have to pay the cashier. Instead, you have to pay the tax collector, and the tax collector pays the cashier. This government program has no effect on anything.[24] It only introduces an intermediary—the tax collector—between you and the cashier. Government spending (*G*) rises, but private consumption spending (*C*) falls, so *C* + *I* + *G* + *NEX* does not change. The important feature of this example is the assumption that government spending substitutes very well (perfectly, in fact) for private spending because the government buys exactly the same food that you would have bought for yourself.[25] The next example will consider government spending that substitutes poorly for private spending.

EXAMPLE: GOVERNMENT SPENDING ON DEFENSE   Suppose that the government raises spending on national defense, and it raises taxes to pay for the spending increase. Government spending on national defense is not a good substitute for private spending, so aggregate demand rises. (The demand for private consumption and investment does not fall by as much as the rise in government spending.)

REAL-LIFE GOVERNMENT SPENDING

Most government purchases of goods and services fall somewhere between these two extremes; they do not substitute perfectly for private spending, as in the

---

[24]This ignores the fact that the increase in your taxes may change your incentives to work, consume, save, or invest, depending on what tax the government raises.

[25]If the government were to buy different food than you would have bought for yourself, the government spending might not substitute very well for your own private spending. You might continue to buy some food for yourself. In that case, private spending on consumption (*C*) would not fall by as much as the rise in government spending (*G*), and aggregate demand would rise.

lunch example, but they substitute better than the spending in the national-defense example. Public schools, for example, substitute partially for spending on private schooling. (Government spending on schools exceeds $200 billion.) Government spending for police services (about $30 billion) substitutes partially for private spending to fight crime (better locks and security systems on houses and businesses, private police or security guards, and so on). Government spending on natural resources, national parks, and recreation (over $100 billion) substitutes partially for private spending. Even government spending for courts and highways substitutes partially for private spending on private courts and arbitration services, more frequent replacement of cars, and construction of private roads or alternative transportation methods such as airlines and trains.

PRODUCTIVITY OF GOVERNMENT SPENDING

Some government spending helps private firms to produce goods. Government spending on infrastructure (transportation and communication systems, including roads, bridges, airports, mass transit, waterways, and so on) lowers firms' costs of producing, distributing, and selling goods and services. Government spending on police and fire services, courts, hospitals, and education can also enhance productivity and reduce firms' costs of production.[26]

An increase in government spending on productive goods or services can raise aggregate supply as well as aggregate demand. If the government spending substitutes very well for private spending (for example, if an increase in public police protection leads firms to reduce spending on their own security guards), then the increase in government spending does not have a big effect on either aggregate demand or aggregate supply.[27] If the government spending on productive goods and services does not substitute well for private spending, then it can affect both aggregate demand and aggregate supply, raising the productivity of labor and privately owned capital.

EXAMPLE   Suppose that the government raises spending to repair bridges and roads. This adds to aggregate demand; *G* rises while *C* and *I* do not fall because this spending does not substitute well for private spending. This government spending also adds to aggregate supply as better roads and bridges allow firms to obtain inputs for production and distribute output to consumers faster and at lower cost.

PAYING FOR GOVERNMENT SPENDING

Suppose now that the government raises spending without raising taxes. This has the same effects on the economy as two policies combined:

1. Raising spending and raising taxes
2. Cutting taxes back to the original level to raise the budget deficit

Earlier discussions have addressed each of these policies separately. The first policy (raising both spending and taxes) raises aggregate demand if government spending does not substitute well for private spending. The effects of the second

---

[26]This does not imply that the government *should* pay for or produce these goods and services. It only states that such government spending reduces firms' costs, just as any government subsidy would.

[27]In the extreme case, in which a $1,000 increase in government spending for police leads to a $1,000 fall in private spending on security guards, the change has no effect on aggregate demand or supply.

policy depend on whether people save or spend the tax cut. If the majority view is right, the second policy raises aggregate demand because people spend part of the money they save in taxes. If the minority view is right, the second policy has no effect on aggregate demand, but the first still raises aggregate demand.

SUMMARY OF THE EFFECTS OF CHANGES IN GOVERNMENT SPENDING

An increase in government spending paid for by higher taxes has several effects:

▶ It raises aggregate demand if the government spending does not substitute well for private spending. (It has little effect on aggregate demand if they substitute well.)

▶ It lowers aggregate supply to the extent that higher taxes reduce the incentive to work.

▶ It raises aggregate supply to the extent that the government spending enhances productivity.

▶ It lowers future aggregate supply to the extent that higher taxes reduce savings and investment.

An increase in government spending without any increase in taxes has several effects:

▶ It raises aggregate demand if the government spending does not substitute well for private spending.

▶ It raises aggregate demand even further than if taxes had increased (according to the majority view, but not to according to the minority view) because there is no tax increase to reduce C and I while G is rising.

▶ It raises aggregate supply to the extent that higher expected future taxes raise the incentive to work more this year (and less in the future).

▶ It raises aggregate supply to the extent that the government spending enhances productivity.

▶ It lowers future aggregate supply to the extent that higher taxes reduce savings and investment.

CONNECTIONS BETWEEN FISCAL AND MONETARY POLICY

Some countries' governments require their central banks to print whatever money their governments need to finance budget deficits. This is not the case in the United States, where the Federal Reserve chooses monetary policy (subject to political pressures). In the United States, the government must borrow money (sell bonds) to finance its budget deficit. It cannot directly force the Fed to print more money.

Fiscal policy can still affect monetary policy in several ways, though. For example, a government budget deficit may raise expectations of future inflation. This raises the current nominal interest rate and velocity of money, which raises the equilibrium price level (creates temporary inflation) and may change the incentives of the Federal Reserve. High levels of government debt may raise the incentive to create inflation to reduce the real value of its debt. High levels of debt and high budget deficits may raise political pressures on the Fed to increase the growth rate of the money supply.

SOCIAL AND ECONOMIC ISSUES

Arguments For and Against a Balanced-Budget Amendment

Pro

1. The government has shown it cannot balance its budget without a Constitutional amendment. Continued budget deficits raise real interest rates, reduce national saving and economic growth, and threaten the economic well-being of future generations.

2. A balanced-budget amendment would help to reduce the total level of government spending as one way to balance the budget. Lower government spending would be more economically efficient and would promote greater freedom.

3. A balanced-budget amendment would reduce the power of special-interest group lobbyists by making it more difficult for Congress to fund the programs that they desire.

4. The benefits of allowing deficit spending in certain situations (to stabilize the economy) are very small compared to the harms done by deficit spending.

5. If Congress wants to continue the *automatic stabilizer* of larger deficits during recessions, it can do so by creating a budget surplus in normal times so that the surplus falls automatically during recessions. In this way, the automatic stabilizer can function without a budget deficit.

6. While the government may find some ways around a balanced-budget amendment, it will make deficit spending more difficult for the government. The fact that no balanced-budget amendment can be perfect is not an argument against having one; it is an argument for trying to prevent loopholes such as off-budget spending.

Con

1. A balanced annual budget is a bad idea. The economy benefits from the deficit's role as an automatic stabilizer, with higher budget deficits during recessions and lower deficits or surpluses at other times. It benefits even more from the discretion to increase or reduce deficits if the automatic stabilizer does not do enough to stabilize real GDP.

2. Budget deficits are not necessarily bad. According to the minority view, they do not raise real interest rates. Even if that view were wrong, budget deficits would raise real interest rates less now than they did in the past because real interest rates are now determined on world markets for loans. Changes in government borrowing in any one country do not have big effects on the world equilibrium real interest rate.

3. Budget deficits can have good effects. Continued economic growth will make future generations better off than current generations, so budget deficits that help the current generation at the expense of future generations are good; future generations can afford it.

4. Even if a balanced budget were a good idea, the government will always be able to find loopholes in a law or Constitutional amendment. For example, the government can expand *off-budget* programs, or it can increase regulations and *mandated benefits* (regulations that force business firms to spend money in certain ways). These have almost the same economic effects as raising government spending and taxing those firms, but they do not show up in official tax revenue or government spending. Further, it would be particularly dangerous to modify the Constitution to require something that the government would avoid by finding loopholes.

COMMITMENT AND POLICY RULE CREDIBILITY

Fiscal policy, like monetary policy, can be discretionary or subject to rules. The government finds it difficult to commit to policy rules, however. For example, Congress passed the Gramm-Rudman-Hollings Act in an effort to reduce the budget deficit in the late 1980s and early 1990s. When the time came for lower deficits, however, the government exploited loopholes that allowed the deficits to continue. Finally, it changed the law.[28] Some people favor a Constitutional amendment to require a balanced government budget. When Congress voted down such an amendment in 1995, some opponents argued that it would remove the flexibility of discretionary fiscal policy. Others argued that enforcement of such a rule would ultimately prove impossible.

Some analysts have argued that budget deficits affect future government spending because higher budget deficits create political pressures to reduce the growth in government spending. As the budget deficit raises the government debt, interest payments on the debt rise, leaving less tax revenue for other spending programs, unless the government raises taxes. In such a scenario, people who favor less government spending might support tax cuts to create budget deficits, knowing that those deficits would tend to reduce future increases in government spending. This is one reason why some political conservatives support tax cuts even in the face of budget deficits.

─────────────────────── **FOR REVIEW** ───────────────────────

33.14 Discuss this statement: "An increase in government spending on transfer payments raises aggregate demand."

33.15 Why do the effects of government spending depend on what the government buys? Explain specifically and give at least two examples.

33.16 Explain how a change in government spending can affect aggregate supply.

33.17 Discuss the arguments for and against a Constitutional amendment to balance the government's budget.

─────────────────────── **QUESTION** ───────────────────────

33.18 Which raises aggregate demand by a larger amount, an increase in government spending financed by higher taxes or an increase in government spending without a tax increase that raises the budget deficit and is financed by increased government borrowing? Explain.

───

FISCAL POLICIES AND ECONOMIC GROWTH

national savings — private savings plus government savings

Fiscal policies can affect long-run economic growth by changing national savings.

National savings equals private savings plus government savings.

The government saves when it has a budget surplus; a budget deficit amounts to negative savings. Private savings equals disposable income (income after taxes) minus consumption spending. For the country as a whole, income is GDP, so disposable income is GDP minus taxes. This gives private savings as:

$$\text{Private savings} = y - T - C$$

Government savings equals $T - G$. Adding these together gives national savings:

$$\text{National savings} = (y - T - C) + (T - G)$$

$$= y - G - C$$

───────────────────────

[28]The original law was supposed to bring the deficit to zero by 1991.

An earlier chapter showed that:

$$y = C + I + G + NEX$$

where *NEX* is the current account, which indicates domestic lending to people in foreign countries. This equation says that real GDP equals aggregate demand. Subtracting *G* and *C* from both sides gives an equation for national savings:

$$\text{National savings} = I + NEX$$

This equation shows two uses for higher national savings:

1. Investment in the nation's economy (*I*)
2. Lending (investing) in foreign countries *NEX*.

Investment in the nation's economy adds to its future capital stock and production, so it adds to economic growth. Investment in foreign economies (*NEX*) adds to the nation's future income as foreigners pay interest or dividends on the investments. (It also adds to the foreign capital stock and promotes world economic growth.)

DEFICITS AND NATIONAL SAVINGS

Most economists blame government budget deficits in part for low rates of saving in the United States. To see why, recall the controversy about the effects of government budget deficits caused by tax cuts. Suppose that the government cuts taxes by $100 per person without changing its spending. According to the minority view of deficits (Figure 33.9b), people save the extra $100 in after-tax income and lend it to the government; private savings rise by $100 while government savings fall by $100, leaving national savings unchanged. According to the majority view (Figure 33.9a), however, people spend part of the $100 they save on taxes, so private savings rise by less than $100 while government savings fall by $100, reducing national savings. In this way, a tax cut can reduce national savings and long-run economic growth.

The Social Security program also reduces national savings, according to the majority view. People expect to receive Social Security payments when they retire, so they save less than they would without the Social Security system. Therefore, the Social Security system reduces private savings. If the government were to save all of the money that people pay in Social Security taxes, then this higher government savings would offset lower private savings and the Social Security system would not affect national savings. (People would save less, but the government would save more.) Of course, the government has not saved all of the money that people have paid in Social Security taxes. Instead, Social Security has operated as a pay-as-you-go system, so it has, according to the majority view, reduced economic growth.

Some economists favor replacing the current income tax with a consumption tax. This would free people from paying income tax on money they save, taxing only money they spend. Many economists believe that a consumption tax would be more economically efficient than an income tax because a consumption tax would not distort people's incentives to save, as an income tax does. By encouraging savings, replacement of the income tax with a consumption tax would also raise long-run economic growth.

TAXES AND AGGREGATE SUPPLY

Some economists argue that taxes have their most important effects on aggregate supply rather than aggregate demand. They argue that high taxes reduce savings, investment, and long-run economic growth. According to this view, a tax cut raises economic growth even if the government does not reduce spending, that is, even if the tax cut raises the budget deficit. A reduction in marginal tax rates can raise aggregate supply by raising the incentive to work. It can also raise future aggregate supply by raising the incentives to save and invest because it raises the expected after-tax returns from investments.

If the government cuts taxes, but does not reduce spending, it must raise taxes or reduce spending in the future to repay its higher debt. Will the benefits of lower taxes this year be offset by lower national saving and economic growth due to higher future taxes? They may not. If tax cuts raise economic growth today, they raise the future tax base—the amount of income on which people pay taxes. This raises the tax revenue generated by higher future tax rates, so future increases in tax rates can be smaller than the current decreases in tax rates.

INCENTIVES AND RENT SEEKING

Some economists, including most proponents of real business cycle theory, argue that discretionary fiscal policies reduce long-run economic growth. Discretionary changes in taxes create uncertainty, which reduces investment in physical and human capital and slows technical progress by reducing investment in research and development. They also argue that discretionary changes in government spending can create economic inefficiency. This can occur if the level of government spending on a program (national defense, roads, and so on) is not justified by the costs and benefits of that program.

Discretionary government policies also reduce economic efficiency by encouraging rent seeking.

> **Rent seeking** is the use of time, money, and other resources to try to get government benefits (government spending, tax changes, or regulations targeted to some special-interest group).

rent seeking — the use of time, money, and other resources in pursuit of government benefits (government spending, tax changes, or regulations targeted to some special-interest group)

The very possibility that the government will take discretionary policy actions that benefit or harm various special groups creates rent seeking. Rent seeking is economically inefficient because the resources devoted to rent seeking have an opportunity cost; they could be used to produce goods and services. Investing those resources in physical capital, human capital, or research and development would raise real GDP; it would increase the size of the economic pie rather than funding the fight about how to divide the pie. The government might reduce rent seeking if it could credibly commit to fiscal policy rules.

——————————————— **FOR REVIEW** ———————————————

33.19 Explain why government budget deficits may reduce national savings.

33.20 Explain why the Social Security system may reduce national savings.

CONCLUSIONS

RULES VERSUS DISCRETION IN FISCAL POLICY
The main arguments for fiscal policy rules (as for monetary policy rules) are based on lags in the implementation and effects of policies, lack of sufficient information about the economy and the effects of policies, and the benefits of credible rules on incentives.

Taxes, Government Spending, Debt, and Budget Deficits in the United States

Total government spending and tax payments in the United States are slightly above one-third of GDP. The government debt reflects the amount of money the government owes from past borrowing. The government budget deficit measures the increase in the government debt during any year. Budget deficits and surpluses allow the government to change the time path of taxes. The time path of taxes affects the size of the economic inefficiency caused by taxes. It also affects aggregate demand and aggregate supply. The effects of taxes on aggregate supply work mainly through the marginal tax rate, which is the fraction of each additional dollar earned that a person must pay in taxes. In contrast, the average tax rate is the fraction of income a person must pay in taxes. The Laffer Curve graphs the relationship between the marginal tax rate and the government's tax revenue; higher tax rates do not always lead to higher tax revenue. Tax laws can automatically raise or lower taxes when GDP rises or falls, and these tax changes may affect aggregate demand as an automatic stabilizer.

Measuring the Budget Deficit

The usual measures of government debt and the budget deficit are misleading, partly because the government owes some of its debt to itself. The privately held government debt is the amount of money the government owes to people and business firms outside the government. In 1995, the privately held government debt was nearly $14,000 for every person in the country. Any comparison of debt or deficit figures for different years should adjust for the effects of inflation. The real government debt is the government's debt in constant (base-year) dollars, that is, adjusted for inflation. Similarly, the real government budget deficit is the increase in the government's real debt. Finally, the government owes large amounts of money that the official government statement of its debt omits. The two biggest missing items are pensions for government employees that the government will owe in the future, which total about $1 trillion (in discounted present value), and Social Security payments that the government has promised to pay in the future, which total about $4 trillion (also in discounted present value).

Changes in Government Spending

The effects of government spending depend on what the government buys. Over 40 percent of total government spending in the United States covers transfer payments. Transfer payments redistribute money from some people to other people and do not necessarily affect aggregate demand at all. About half of government spending goes to purchase goods and services (13 percent for defense and 39 percent for nondefense purchases). If government spending substitutes well for private spending, then changes in government spending have little effect on aggregate demand, as in the lunch-program example. If, however, government spending substitutes poorly for private spending, then increases in government spending raise aggregate demand, as in the defense spending example. Some government spending enhances productivity and raises aggregate supply (when it does not substitute closely for similar, private spending).

Fiscal Policies and Economic Growth

National savings equals private savings plus government savings, that is, private savings minus the government budget deficit. Most economists blame government budget deficits in part for low rates of saving in the United States. A similar argument shows that the Social Security system reduces national savings. Through the connection between national savings and investment, budget deficits may reduce economic growth.

LOOKING AHEAD

The next chapter discusses the economics of financial markets: interest rates, stocks, bonds, and corporate finance. The two chapters after that deal with international economic policy issues.

KEY TERMS

fiscal policy	Laffer Curve
government debt	automatic stabilizer
government budget deficit	privately held government debt
balanced budget	real government debt
budget surplus	real government budget deficit
average tax rate	national savings
marginal tax rate	rent seeking

QUESTIONS AND PROBLEMS

33.21 Suppose that the government decides to build a giant pyramid in Washington, D.C., as a way to provide jobs for construction workers and stimulate the economy. Assume also that the government raises personal income taxes to pay for the additional spending. How is this likely to affect total employment? How will it affect employment in different industries, real GDP, and the price level?

33.22 Summarize the effects on aggregate demand and supply of:
   a. An increase in government spending financed by higher taxes
   b. An increase in government spending without any increase in taxes

33.23 Suppose that the government's debt on January 1 is $2,000, and the real interest rate is 2 percent per year.
   a. If the government's nominal deficit is $100 this year, the nominal interest rate is 2 percent per year, and the inflation rate is zero, calculate its nominal debt at the end of the year and its real budget deficit.
   b. If the government's nominal deficit is $300 this year, the nominal interest rate is 12 percent per year, and the inflation rate is 10 percent per year, calculate its nominal debt at the end of the year and its real budget deficit.

33.24 Explain the argument that the government's budget deficit is poorly measured or even a meaningless concept.

33.25 Discuss this statement: "Large government budget deficits raise interest rates. To keep interest rates at a reasonable level (to keep them from rising too much), the Fed must pursue a policy of loose money." (*Hint:* Distinguish between real and nominal interest rates and between the short run and the long run.)

33.26 Discuss this statement: "The government could reduce unemployment to almost zero by guaranteeing a government job to anyone who is unemployed. The people could work to clean up city streets and national parks and do other useful tasks, and everyone would benefit."

33.27 Suppose that the government kept its total real (inflation-adjusted) spending at the current level, and kept tax revenue as a percentage of GDP at its current level. If economic growth continues at its historical rate (discussed in a previous chapter), how many years would it take before the government budget were balanced?

INQUIRIES FOR FURTHER THOUGHT

33.28 Many people blame the high budget deficits of the 1980s and 1990s on the Reagan tax cuts in the early 1980s. Look carefully at the graphs in this chapter and argue (a) that the tax cuts caused the high deficits and then (b) that they did not.

33.29 Should the government exercise discretionary fiscal policy? What should guide the government's fiscal policy? Why?

33.30 Do you think that government budget deficits help to reduce the growth in government spending?

33.31 Should the United States add a balanced-budget amendment to the U.S. Constitution?

33.32 Should the government repay the national debt? What effects would this move have?

33.33 What will eventually happen if the government budget deficit keeps rising every year?

TAG SOFTWARE APPLICATIONS

TUTORIAL EXERCISES
▶ The module contains a review of the key terms from Chapter 33.

GRAPHING EXERCISES
▶ The graphing segment includes questions on the efficiency loss from taxation, different views of tax cuts, and the effects of tax cuts in the long run.

PART

12

TOPICS IN MACROECONOMICS

CHAPTER 34

FINANCIAL MARKETS

WHAT THIS CHAPTER IS ABOUT

▶ Stocks, bonds, and other financial assets

▶ How to read the financial pages of a newspaper

▶ Risk and diversification

▶ Ownership and control of firms, hostile takeovers, and leveraged buyouts

Every day, television news reports, newspapers, and business magazines are filled with news about stock markets and other financial markets. Despite all this information, financial markets mystify most people. This chapter provides the basic knowledge necessary to understand these news reports and to construct informed opinions about financial matters. You can refer back to this chapter for the background you will need for your personal and business decisions in the future.

FINANCIAL ASSETS AND MARKETS

financial asset — a right to collect some payment or series of payments in the future

rate of return — income the owner receives from an asset over some period of time plus the increase in its value during that period, all as a percentage of the original value of the asset

A **financial asset** is a right to collect some series of payments in the future.

A financial market is a set of formal or informal trading arrangements for financial assets. The *rate of return* on a financial asset is the income the owner receives from the asset over some period of time plus the increase in its value during that period, all as a percentage of the original value of the asset:

$$\text{Rate of return} = \frac{\text{Interest (or other) payments} + \text{Increase in asset price}}{\text{Beginning-of-period asset price}}$$

For example, suppose that General Television stock sells for $50 in February 1996 and for $52 after 1 year. Also, each share of stock pays its owner $1 in dividends during that year. The rate of return on this stock is:

$$\text{Rate of return} = \frac{\$1 + (\$52 - \$50)}{\$50} = \frac{\$3}{\$50} = \frac{\$6}{\$100} = 6 \text{ percent per year}$$

Financial markets trade many types of financial assets.

Debt is a borrower's promise to pay.

A person, business firm, or government that borrows money incurs a debt. The debt is the borrower's promise to repay the loan; it is the IOU. People can buy and sell that IOU, and when they do, they buy and sell the right to collect the money that the borrower will repay. Debt securities include government bonds, corporate bonds, and Treasury bills.

Equities (shares of stock) represent legal rights of ownership to part of a firm.

The stockholders of a firm own that firm. They own its assets and liabilities, including its equipment and buildings, legal rights to its brand names, and its debts and other legal obligations. Stockholders in a corporation have limited liability for debts, however, meaning that they cannot lose more than the value of their stock.

Futures contracts are agreements to buy or sell goods at some future date at a price set today.

You might buy 5,000 bushels of corn or 5,000 shares of General Motors stock to be delivered and paid for next July, at a price set today.

Options are legal rights, but not obligations, to buy or to sell a certain amount of goods or assets in the future at a price set today.

The term *option* refers to the choice that such a contract gives to its owner. Suppose that you own an option to buy 100 shares of American Express stock at a price of $25 per share sometime within the next 4 months. You can choose whether to buy that stock at the pre-set price of $25. Similarly, if you own an option to sell 500 shares of Xerox stock at a price of $50 per share sometime within the next 2 months, you can choose whether or not to sell at that price. When people buy and sell options, they trade these rights to buy or sell at pre-set prices.

These assets change hands in two kinds of markets. *Primary markets* handle transactions where issuers sell financial assets for the first time, as when a firm issues new stock or new bonds to borrow money. In *secondary markets*, investors (people or firms) buy and resell previously issued assets. Most financial-market trades occur on secondary markets such as the New York Stock Exchange.

FUNCTIONS OF FINANCIAL MARKETS

Financial markets provide opportunities and promote economic efficiency. Financial markets allow people to save for the future by lending to other people. (Without financial markets, people could save only by stockpiling food and other storable goods.) Financial markets allow thousands of people to pool small amounts of savings into one large sum of money to lend, giving them the highest possible return on their savings. Financial markets allow people to borrow money to buy houses or cars, to modernize factories, to start new businesses, and to finance development of new products. They allow borrowers to obtain loans at the lowest possible cost. They help to channel the economy's resources into their most valuable uses. Financial markets allow people to reduce risks through insurance and diversification of investments. Financial markets are essential for any modern economy, and for the economic development of poor countries and formerly socialist countries such as Russia.

RISK AND INSURANCE

The future is uncertain, so everyone faces risks. People can base their plans for the future only on their expectations.

EXPECTATIONS

An expectation is a guess about the future. A rational guess (or rational expectation) about some future variable, such as the score of a future ball game or a future price, is its expected value.

expected value — an average of every possible value that a variable can take, weighted by the chance of that value occurring

> The **expected value** of a variable is an average of every possible value for that variable, weighted by the chance of that value occurring.

The expected value is also called the *mean.* You can calculate an expected value in three steps:

1. Write down each *possible* value of the variable.
2. Multiply each value by its chance of occurring.
3. Add the answers from Step 2.

EXAMPLES

EXAMPLE 1   Suppose that you estimate a one-half chance that the rate of return on an investment will be 5 percent and a one-half chance that it will be 15 percent. The expected value of the rate of return (or the *expected return,* for short) is:

$$(1/2)(5\%) + (1/2)(15\%) = 10 \text{ percent}$$

EXAMPLE 2   Suppose that you lend someone $100. You estimate a 95 percent chance that the borrower will repay the loan and a 5 percent chance of default. Your expected payback is:

$$(95/100)(\$100) + (5/100)(\$0) = \$95$$

EXAMPLE 3   Suppose that you lend someone $100 for 1 year and charge 10 percent interest. The borrower owes you $110 at the end of the year. If you estimate a 95 percent chance of repayment and a 5 percent chance of default, your expected payback is:

$$(95/100)(\$110) + (5/100)(\$0) = \$104.50$$

Notice that this gives you the same expected payback as a loan charging $4\frac{1}{2}$ percent interest with certain repayment.

RISK

A situation is *risky* for you when several things could happen, and some are better (for you) than others. The amount of risk you face depends on how much better or worse some of your possible situations are. Scholars have developed a complicated mathematical theory of risk, but the basic ideas can be understood with examples. These examples introduce important ideas, and later discussions will refer back to them.

EXAMPLES (CONTINUED)

EXAMPLE 4   If you know for sure that your income next year will be $20,000, then your income is not risky. If, however, you face a one-half chance that you will earn $30,000 and a one-half chance that you will earn $10,000, your income is risky. If you face a one-half chance of earning $40,000 and a one-half chance of earning zero, your income is even riskier. Notice that your expected income is the same in all three cases.

EXAMPLE 5 (*PORTFOLIO RISK 1*)   Suppose that you bet $10 that Team A will win a football game. If Team A wins, you win $10; if Team B wins, you lose $10. (If they tie, the bet is canceled.) Your income from the bet is risky. If you *also* bet $10 on Team B to win, then you can be sure of winning one bet and losing the other. Your betting income is no longer risky; you have hedged your bets. Although no sports fan would place opposing bets like this, the example shows how combining two risky investments (or bets) can reduce overall risk (to zero, in this case).

EXAMPLE 6 (*PORTFOLIO RISK 2*)   Larry lends someone $100 for 1 year and charges 10 percent interest. The loan brings a 95 percent chance that the borrower will pay Larry back and a 5 percent chance of default, so Larry's expected payback is $104.50 (as in Example 3).

Barb also has $100 to lend, but she lends $1 to each of 100 different people at 10 percent interest. Each loan presents a 5 percent chance of default, and the chance that any one borrower will repay the loan is completely unrelated to whether any other borrowers repay. It is *very* unlikely, then, that all or even most of the borrowers will fail to repay. In this case, it turns out to be quite likely that about 95 of the borrowers will repay their loans (each paying Barb $1.10) and about 5 of them will not repay, so it becomes very likely that Barb will collect about $104.50.[1] Her expected payoff is the same as Larry's, but her risk is lower. This shows how diversification, lending to many people rather than to one ("putting all your eggs in one basket") as Larry did, can reduce risk.

EXAMPLE 7 (*PORTFOLIO RISK 3*)   You have $100 to lend for 1 year at 10 percent interest. You could lend it all to David, who will repay the loan next year unless he loses his job making Silly Putty. David faces a 5 percent chance that he will lose his job because a new firm, Crazy Putty, may cut into Silly Putty's sales, so you would face a 5 percent chance that David would not repay the loan. This leaves a 95 percent chance that you would collect $110 next year and a 5 percent chance that you would collect nothing. Alternatively, you could lend $50 to David and $50 to Jay, who works for Crazy Putty. This exposes you to a 5 percent chance that Crazy Putty will not sell at all, and Jay will lose his job and not repay the loan.

This presents three possible outcomes:

1. A 5 percent chance exists that Crazy Putty will put Silly Putty out of business, so David will not repay the loan, but you will collect $55 from Jay.

2. A 5 percent chance exists that Crazy Putty will not sell at all, so Jay will not repay the loan, but you will collect $55 from David.

3. This leaves a 90 percent chance that David and Jay will *both* repay their loans, as Crazy Putty will succeed but Silly Putty will stay in business, too. You collect $110 in this case.[2]

Your risk is lower if you lend to David and Jay rather than lending only to David. If you lend only to David, you face a 95 percent chance that you will collect $110 and a 5 percent chance that you will collect *nothing*. If you lend to both, however, you face a 90 percent chance of collecting $110 and a 10 percent

---

[1]This is a situation in which the decisions to repay or not are *statistically independent* of each other.
[2]The example assumes that there is no chance that both fail to repay the loan.

chance of collecting $55. You have the same expected payback of $104.50 in either case, but two borrowers reduce the risk of this payback. Like the football-bet example, this example shows how you can reduce risk by choosing investments (bets or loans) that move out of step with each other. Risk diminishes for combinations of investments in which *some* pay off well in situations when others pay off poorly.

DIVERSIFICATION

The previous examples show how people can reduce the risks of their investments by diversifying.

diversification — spreading risks by choosing many unrelated investments or investments whose payoffs are out of step

> **Diversification** refers to spreading risks by choosing many unrelated investments or investments whose payoffs are out of step.[3]

Diversification restates the old adage not to "put all your eggs in one basket." This is good advice for reducing investment risk.

INSURANCE

Insurance is an investment specifically designed to move *out of step* with other investments. If you buy insurance against theft, the insurance company pays you only if you are robbed. Robbery gives you a *negative* payoff on your investment in the stolen property. Because you collect insurance payments in this case, your payoffs from investments in the property and in insurance move out of step. In the same way, you can insure against losing a bet on a football game by making another bet on the opposing team, as in the example above. (Obviously, this is one type of insurance that many people don't want.[4]) In Example 7, by lending money to Jay, you can partially insure against the chance that David will default.

RISK AVERSION

People tend to be risk averse in most real-life situations.

risk averse — a characteristic of a person who prefers less risk to more risk

risk neutral — a characteristic of a person who does not care about risk, only about the expected return on an investment

> A **risk averse** person prefers less risk to more risk.

> A **risk neutral** person does not care about risk, only about the expected return on an investment.[5]

People are usually willing to pay to reduce risk; they accept *lower* expected returns on investments with correspondingly lower risk. People buy insurance and diversify their investments because they are risk averse. Later sections will show that riskier financial assets have higher expected returns than less risky assets; the riskier assets must pay higher expected returns to get anyone to invest.

─────────── **FOR REVIEW** ───────────

34.1 What is a financial asset? What is its rate of return?

34.2 What are debts, equities, and options?

─────────────────

[3]In technical terms, the payoffs are negatively correlated.

[4]Most people do want this insurance, so they choose not to bet on the game.

[5]A person who likes risk is said to be a *risk preferrer.*

QUESTIONS

34.3 If a stock price has a 4/10 chance of being at $5 next year, a 1/2 chance of being at $10, and a 1/10 chance of being $80, what is the expected value of the stock price?

34.4 What is diversification? Explain how combining two risky investments can reduce overall risk.

DEBT INVESTMENTS: BOND MARKETS AND MONEY MARKETS

bond — an IOU for a long-term debt, typically on a loan lasting 10 years or more

Debt is a borrower's promise to repay a loan. Suppose that IBM borrows money from you for 20 years. It gives you a written promise (an IOU) to repay the loan after 20 years, that is, the debt matures after 20 years. Before then, you can sell it to another buyer on secondary markets. Buying and selling a debt means buying and selling the right to collect repayment on the loan.

BOND MARKETS

A **bond** is long-term debt, typically a loan lasting 10 years or more.

Corporate bonds are issued by corporations, government bonds by the federal government, and municipal bonds by state and local governments.[6] Most bonds pledge to make interest payments each year called *coupon payments*.

coupon payment — an interest payment that a borrower makes to bondholders

Coupon payments are payments of interest that borrowers make to bondholders.

For example, suppose that Walt Disney Corporation borrows money for 10 years by issuing a $10,000 bond. Disney borrows money by selling this bond. An investor might be willing to pay $8,000 for the bond; this means that the investor lends $8,000 to Disney for 10 years and earns $2,000 in interest when Disney repays the loan. The bond's *face value*—the money that Disney will repay in 10 years—is $10,000. The bond may also have *5 percent coupons,* which means that Disney pays $500 *every year* (5 percent of $10,000) to the bondholder. Disney makes these coupon payments in addition to the $10,000 repayment of the debt when the bond matures after 10 years. Some bonds, called *zero-coupon bonds,* have no coupons; they pay bondholders only at maturity.

MARKETS FOR SHORTER-TERM LOANS

Many kinds of short-term financial assets are available to investors. The government borrows money for several months by selling IOUs called *Treasury bills,* and for longer periods by selling Treasury notes.

Treasury bill (T-bill) — a short-term debt security issued by the U.S. government, typically for a 3-month to 6-month loan

Treasury note — debt security issued by the U.S. government, typically for a loan of 1 to 10 years

Treasury bills (or **T-bills**) are short-term debts issued by the government, mostly for 3-month and 6-month loans. **Treasury notes** are similar IOUs for loans of 1 year to 10 years.

---

[6]You may be familiar with bond issues for public schools. A vote of the community is usually required to allow a school system to borrow money by issuing bonds.

A business firm can borrow money for a short period by issuing commercial paper.

commercial paper — short-term debt (usually with a 30-day maturity) issued by a private firm

> **Commercial paper** is short-term debt (usually with a 30-day maturity) issued by a private firm.

Markets for loans of 1 year or less are sometimes called *money markets*. To simplify the discussion, the term *bond* will include these short-term assets as well as long-term assets for the remainder of this chapter.

DEFAULT RISK

The examples detailed earlier illustrated the risk of default on a loan.

default — failure to repay a loan in full

> A borrower who fails to repay a loan in full **defaults.**

Note that a borrower can default by repaying some but not all of the loan.

The risk of default, affects interest rates. A higher chance that a borrower will default leads lenders to demand a higher interest rate to compensate for that risk.

risk-free interest rate — the interest rate on a loan with no chance of default

> The **risk-free interest rate** is the interest rate on a loan with no chance of default.

The interest rate on a *risky* loan includes a risk premium.

risk premium — an extra payment that compensates investors for risk

> A **risk premium** is an extra payment that compensates investors for risk.

The interest rate on a risky loan is the sum of the risk-free rate and a risk premium:

$$\text{Interest rate on a risky loan} = \text{Risk-free interest rate} + \text{Risk premium}$$

Higher risk raises the risk premium. The size of the risk premium depends on economic forces. People trade risks in financial markets, and the equilibrium of supply and demand in the market for risk determines the equilibrium risk premium.

EXAMPLE

Earlier, Example 3 considered a $100 loan at 10 percent interest to someone with a 5 percent chance of defaulting. It showed an expected payback on the loan of $104.50 instead of $110.00, the payback with no risk of default. This gave an expected rate of return on the loan of $4\frac{1}{2}$ percent per year.

Suppose that a safe borrower (one who will not default) is willing to pay you $4\frac{1}{2}$ percent interest for a 1-year, $100 loan. Another person, who has a 5 percent chance of defaulting on a loan, also wants to borrow $100 from you for 1 year. If you were risk neutral (caring only about the expected return on your investment), you would be indifferent between lending to the safe borrower at $4\frac{1}{2}$ percent interest and lending to the risky borrower at a 10 percent interest rate. If the equilibrium interest rate on safe loans is $4\frac{1}{2}$ percent per year, then the equilibrium interest rate on loans with a 5 percent chance of default is 10 percent per year.[7] This example shows that even a risk neutral lender charges a higher interest rate to riskier borrowers. Because most lenders are risk averse, risky bonds pay even higher interest rate differentials than this example indicates.

---

[7]If the interest rate on these risky loans were lower than 10 percent, no one would lend to the risky borrowers. If the interest rate on these risky loans were higher than 10 percent, all lenders would try to lend to the risky borrowers instead of the safe borrowers, and this would drive the interest rate down to 10 percent.

Bond Prices and Yields to

The price of a bond is the discounted present value (*DPV*) of its expected payments. A higher interest rate reduces the DPV of a set of expected payments, so the price of the bond falls.[8] To calculate a DPV requires an interest rate. For a bond with no chance of default, investors use the risk-free interest rate. For a bond with a chance of default, investors use a higher interest rate to compensate for the chance of default in the calculation of the DPV of the bond's expected future payments. One important measure of the rate of return on a bond is its yield to maturity.

> The **yield to maturity** on a bond is (roughly) the average annual interest rate you would get if you were to hold the bond until its maturity rather than selling it sooner.[9]

yield to maturity — roughly, the average annual interest rate the owner would get from holding a bond until its maturity rather than selling it sooner

Examples[10]

Example 1   A typical Treasury bill pays $10,000 after 3 months. (It makes no coupon payments.) If you pay $9,750 for this T-bill, you loan the government $9,750. When the T-bill matures in 3 months, it pays $10,000, so you get (roughly) a $2\frac{1}{2}$ percent interest rate on the loan. This is roughly a 10 percent annualized (per year) return on your investment because you could reinvest your money in this way four times during 1 year, earning $2\frac{1}{2}$ percent each time, for a total return of about 10 percent.[11] The equilibrium price of the T-bill is $9,750 if (and only if) the equilibrium nominal annual interest rate on T-bills is about 10 percent.

Example 2   Suppose that the nominal interest rate is 8 percent per year and people expect it to remain constant. The price of a 20-year, $1,000 zero-coupon bond is $215 because the discounted present value of $1,000 to be paid 20 years in the future is:

$$\$1,000/(1 + i)^{20}$$

This is (about) $215 if $i = 0.08$ (8 percent) per year.

Example 3   The price of a 20-year, $1,000 bond with 5 percent (or $50) annual interest (coupon) payments is:

$$\frac{\$50}{1 + i} + \frac{\$50}{(1 + i)^2} + \frac{\$50}{(1 + i)^3} + \ldots + \frac{\$50}{(1 + i)^{20}} + \frac{\$1,000}{(1 + i)^{20}}$$

This is about $705 if the nominal interest rate is 8 percent per year.

Holding Period Yields and Capital Gains

Another important measure of the rate of return on a bond is its holding period yield.

---

[8]For example, if the interest rate is 5 percent per year, the DPV of $100 to be paid 1 year from now is $100/1.05, or $95.24. If the interest rate is 10 percent per year, however, the *DPV* is $100/1.10, or $90.91.

[9]More precisely, it is the constant interest rate at which the discounted present value of all of the bond's future payments would equal its current price.

[10]Many assets have features that complicate these calculations. For example, corporate bonds typically pay interest twice per year rather than once.

[11]This is not exact because it ignores *compound interest,* or interest earned on earlier interest income.

holding period yield — the rate of return the owner would get on a bond over some specified period of time that might be less than the time until the bond matures

The **holding period yield** on a bond is the rate of return you would get on the bond over some specified period of time that might be less than the time until the bond matures.

EXAMPLE

Suppose that an asset sells for $100 in June 1997. It pays $10.00 in interest in June 1998 and $110.00 when it matures in June 1999. Suppose also that it carries no risk of default, and the interest rate in June 1997 is 10 percent per year. The discounted present value of the asset's payments comes to:

$$\$10.00/1.10 + \$110.00/1.10^2 = \$100.00$$

so the price of the asset is $100.00.

Now suppose that the market interest rate unexpectedly falls in June 1998 to 5 percent per year. If you own the asset, you own the right to a $110 payment 1 year later in June 1999. The discounted present value in 1998 of that payment is:

$$\$110.00/1.05 = \$104.76$$

so the price of the asset in June 1998 is $104.76. (Investors are willing to pay $104.76 for the asset because that is the present value of its future payment.) If you sell this asset for $104.76 in June 1998, just after you collect the $10.00 interest payment, then you get a $4.76 capital gain on your investment.

capital gain (or capital loss) — an increase (or decrease) in the value of an asset

A **capital gain** (or **capital loss**) is an increase (or decrease) in the value of an asset that you own.

The capital gain brings your total return on the asset from June 1997 to June 1998 to $14.76, $10.00 in interest and $4.76 in capital gains. Therefore, your holding period return from 1997 to 1998 on this asset is:

$$\frac{\$14.76}{\$100.00} = 0.1476 = 14.76 \text{ percent per year}$$

The person who buys the asset from you may hold it until it matures in June 1999 to earn a 5 percent holding period return.

Bonds can produce capital gains in two ways. First, the price of a bond changes over time even if the interest rate does not change. For example, at an interest rate of 8 percent per year, the price of the zero-coupon bond in the earlier example was about $215 at a time 20 years before the bond's maturity. After 15 years, however, 5 years before the bond's maturity, the price would be:

$$\$1,000/(1 + i)^5$$

This is (about) $681 if the interest rate remains at 8 percent per year. Over the first 15 years, then, the bond generates a capital gain of $466 ($681 minus $215).

Second, the price of a bond rises—the bondholder gets a capital gain—if the nominal interest rate falls. If the nominal interest rate had fallen to 6 percent per year (0.06) from 8 percent per year, the price of the 20-year, zero-coupon bond in the example would have risen to $312. Someone who bought the bond when the interest rate was 8 percent per year and saw the interest rate fall to 6 percent per year would have earned an immediate capital gain of $97 ($312 minus $215).

DEFAULT RISK AND YIELDS

Debt securities issued by the U.S. federal government are almost completely safe from default.[12] In contrast, all private firms have some chance of going bankrupt and defaulting on their debt. Two private firms, Standard & Poor's Corporation and Moody's Investors Services, Inc., rate bonds based on their chances of default. The best bonds, rated AAA or Aaa, have the lowest chances of default, followed by bonds rated AA or Aa, A, BBB or Baa, and so on, down to C (the riskiest bonds). Because of these risk differences, yields to maturity on Baa bonds exceed yields on Aaa bonds, which exceed yields on government bonds. The differences reflect increasing risks of default.

Bonds rated below Baa often carry the pejorative label *junk bonds.* Before the 1980s, it was hard for firms to sell bonds rated below Baa.[13] In 1977, Michael Milken of the firm Drexel Burnham Lambert (later sentenced to prison for violating certain federal laws on financial markets) started helping firms to sell junk bonds by helping them to find buyers, that is, lenders willing to accept high chances of default for sufficiently high interest rates. Junk bonds made it easier for firms with high default risk to borrow. They also became very controversial because of their use in takeovers, as discussed later. Nevertheless, they remain an important source of finance for many small, startup firms. The long-distance telephone company, MCI, for example, was financed with junk bonds.

TERM STRUCTURE OF INTEREST RATES

The term structure of interest rates is the relationship between interest rates on short-term loans and those on longer-term loans. Long-term interest rates are averages of the many short-term interest rates that people expect during the period of the long-term loan.

EXAMPLE

Suppose that you want to borrow $100.00 for 2 years. You could borrow $100.00 for 1 year, and then take out another 1-year loan next year to pay off the first loan. Suppose you can borrow $100.00 now for 1 year at an interest rate of 5 percent per year, so you will owe $105.00 at the end of the year. Suppose also that you believe you can borrow $105.00 next year for 1 year at an interest rate of 15 percent. You can use this $105.00 to pay off the first loan, then after 2 years you will owe $120.75 (= $105.00 plus 15 percent interest on $105.00, which is $15.75).

As an alternative, you can take out a 2-year loan now. If the interest rate on a 2-year loan is 9.886 percent per year, then at the end of 2 years you will owe:

$$(\$100.00)(1 + 0.09886)^2 = \$120.75$$

At this interest rate, you would owe the same amount at the end of 2 years whether you (a) take out a 1-year loan now, then take out another 1-year loan a year from now, or (b) take out a 2-year loan now. If the interest rate on 2-year loans were lower than 9.886 percent per year, people would try to make a profit by borrowing for 2 years and lending the money for 1 year now, then lending the

---

[12]Although they do not default in nominal terms, inflation reduces their real returns. In that sense, unexpectedly high inflation caused by the government is like a partial default on U.S. government debt in real terms.

[13]In language to be discussed later in this chapter, *investment banks* would not *underwrite* bonds rated below Baa.

proceeds again next year for 1 year. This would raise the demand for 2-year loans and the interest rate on these loans would also rise. If the interest rate on 2-year loans were higher than 9.886 percent per year, people would try to make a profit by borrowing now for 1 year and lending the money for 2 years, borrowing again next year to repay the first loan. This would raise the supply of 2-year loans and lower their interest rate. In equilibrium, the interest rate on 2-year loans would be 9.886 percent per year. This is a weighted average of the two interest rates on 1-year loans: 5 percent and 15 percent.

This example shows that if people expect short-term interest rates to rise in the future, the long-term interest rate is higher than the short-term interest rate. In the example, the short-term rate is the rate on 1-year loans and the long-term rate is the rate on 2-year loans. People expect the short-term interest rate to rise from 5 percent now to 15 percent in the future, so the long-term interest rate of 9.886 percent per year exceeds the current short-term rate.

Figure 34.1 graphs the term structure of interest rates. When long-term interest rates are above short-term interest rates, the term structure is rising. When long-term rates are below short-term rates, the term structure is falling. When they are equal, the term structure is flat.

READING BOND QUOTES IN THE FINANCIAL PAGES

Most bonds are traded over the counter (by telephone or computer links) among bond dealers. **Figure 34.2** shows how to read bond tables from the financial pages of a newspaper like *The Wall Street Journal.*

Figure 34.3 shows quotes for various short-term interest rates, including:

▶ *Treasury bill rate.* The interest rate on Treasury bills

▶ *Commercial paper rate.* The interest rate that firms pay for short-term loans in the form of commercial paper

▶ *Federal funds rate.* The interest rate that banks charge other banks for overnight loans

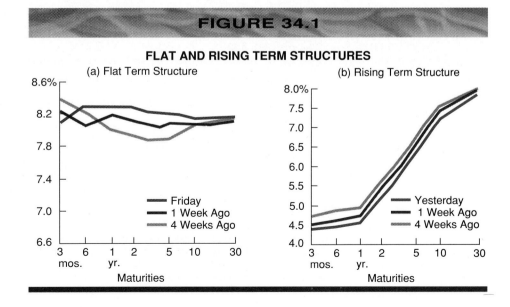

FIGURE 34.1

FLAT AND RISING TERM STRUCTURES

(a) Flat Term Structure — Friday, 1 Week Ago, 4 Weeks Ago; Maturities: 3 mos., 6, 1 yr., 2, 5, 10, 30

(b) Rising Term Structure — Yesterday, 1 Week Ago, 4 Weeks Ago; Maturities: 3 mos., 6, 1 yr., 2, 5, 10, 30

FIGURE 34.2

FINANCIAL-PAGE QUOTES FOR BONDS AND T-BILLS

(a)

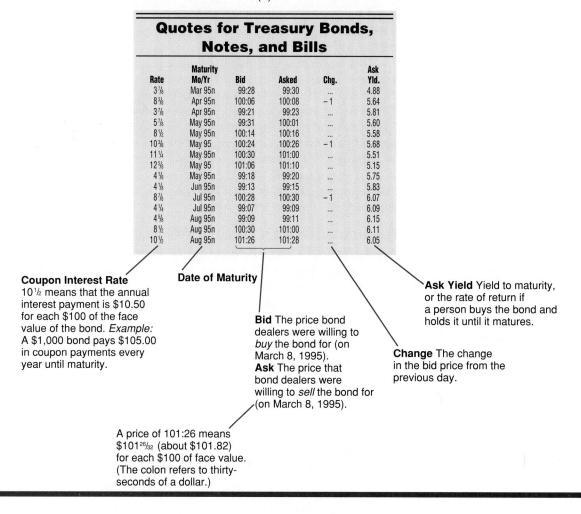

Quotes for Treasury Bonds, Notes, and Bills

Rate	Maturity Mo/Yr	Bid	Asked	Chg.	Ask Yld.
3⅞	Mar 95n	99:28	99:30	...	4.88
8⅜	Apr 95n	100:06	100:08	−1	5.64
3⅞	Apr 95n	99:21	99:23	...	5.81
5⅞	May 95n	99:31	100:01	...	5.60
8½	May 95n	100:14	100:16	...	5.58
10⅜	May 95	100:24	100:26	−1	5.68
11¼	May 95n	100:30	101:00	...	5.51
12⅝	May 95	101:06	101:10	...	5.15
4⅛	May 95n	99:18	99:20	...	5.75
4⅛	Jun 95n	99:13	99:15	...	5.83
8⅞	Jul 95n	100:28	100:30	−1	6.07
4¼	Jul 95n	99:07	99:09	...	6.09
4⅝	Aug 95n	99:09	99:11	...	6.15
8½	Aug 95n	100:30	101:00	...	6.11
10½	Aug 95n	101:26	101:28	...	6.05

Coupon Interest Rate
10½ means that the annual interest payment is $10.50 for each $100 of the face value of the bond. *Example:* A $1,000 bond pays $105.00 in coupon payments every year until maturity.

Date of Maturity

Bid The price bond dealers were willing to *buy* the bond for (on March 8, 1995).
Ask The price that bond dealers were willing to *sell* the bond for (on March 8, 1995).

Ask Yield Yield to maturity, or the rate of return if a person buys the bond and holds it until it matures.

Change The change in the bid price from the previous day.

A price of 101:26 means $101 26/32 (about $101.82) for each $100 of face value. (The colon refers to thirty-seconds of a dollar.)

▶ *Prime rate.* The interest rate banks charge their best customers for loans[14]

▶ *Federal Reserve discount rate.* The interest rate that Federal Reserve Banks charge commercial banks for loans

FOR REVIEW

34.5 Name some types of debt.

34.6 Explain why default risk affects the interest rate on a loan.

34.7 What is a capital gain? Why do bondholders receive capital gains if interest rates fall?

---

[14]Sometimes, though, banks lend to very good customers at interest rates below their prime rates.

FIGURE 34.2 (CONT.)

(b)

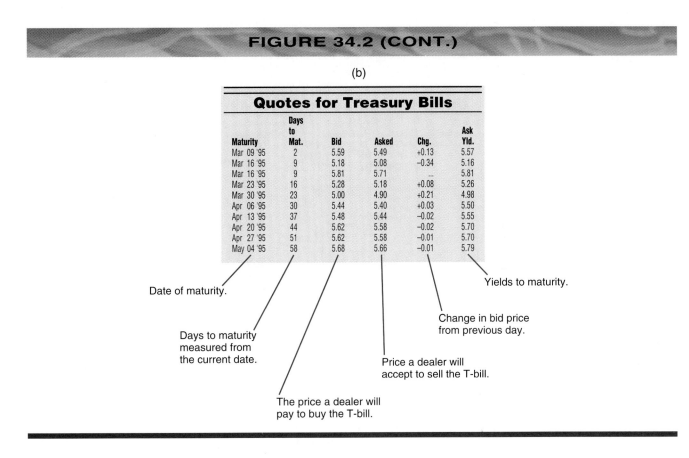

Quotes for Treasury Bills

Maturity	Days to Mat.	Bid	Asked	Chg.	Ask Yld.
Mar 09 '95	2	5.59	5.49	+0.13	5.57
Mar 16 '95	9	5.18	5.08	−0.34	5.16
Mar 16 '95	9	5.81	5.71	...	5.81
Mar 23 '95	16	5.28	5.18	+0.08	5.26
Mar 30 '95	23	5.00	4.90	+0.21	4.98
Apr 06 '95	30	5.44	5.40	+0.03	5.50
Apr 13 '95	37	5.48	5.44	−0.02	5.55
Apr 20 '95	44	5.62	5.58	−0.02	5.70
Apr 27 '95	51	5.62	5.58	−0.01	5.70
May 04 '95	58	5.68	5.66	−0.01	5.79

Date of maturity.

Yields to maturity.

Days to maturity measured from the current date.

Change in bid price from previous day.

Price a dealer will accept to sell the T-bill.

The price a dealer will pay to buy the T-bill.

QUESTIONS

34.8 Governments of many developing countries have borrowed money by issuing bonds. In some cases, recessions or other economic problems in countries with large debt burdens have drastically reduced the prices of their bonds. Why would such problems cause bond prices to fall?

34.9 Suppose that looser monetary policy leads people to expect inflation to increase over the next several years. Would this be more likely to cause a rising or falling term structure of interest rates?

STOCKS AND STOCK MARKETS

A share of stock (also called an *equity*) represents a legal right of ownership in part of a company. A firm's stockholders own that firm. A stockholder who owns most of the stock in a firm has a controlling interest in the firm; that stockholder can choose the managers, from the CEO or chief executive officer on down, and make other decisions for the firm. If no one owns enough stock to have a controlling interest in a firm, groups of stockholders control it. Stockholders choose the firm's board of directors by voting, and they also vote on some issues that

FIGURE 34.2 (CONT.)

(c)

Quotes for Corporation Bonds

Bonds	Cur Yld	Vol	Close	Net Chg.		Bonds	Cur Yld	Vol	Close	Net Chg.	
CORPORATION BONDS Volume, $31,698,000						ClevEl 8⅜12	9.7	415	86	...	
						Coastl 10¼04	9.2	10	111½	+	⅞
						Coeur 7s02	cv	65	106	+	1
AMR 9s16	9.0	159	100	+	⅜	Coeur 6⅜04	...	49	79	...	
AMR 8.10s98	8.1	16	99⅞	–	⅞	ColeWld zr13	...	60	28⅜	+	⅜
AMR 6½24	cv	3	90¾	–	¾	ViColuG 8¾s95f	...	22	125⅝	...	
ATT 7½06	7.6	230	98⅛	–	½	viColuG 9⅛s95f	...	15	124¾	...	
ATT 4¾98	5.1	15	93⅜	+	¼	viColuG 7½97M f	...	10	116⅜	–	⅞
ATT 4⅜96	4.6	7	96¼	–	¾	viColuG 9s93f	...	20	128	...	
ATT 4⅜99	4.9	6	88⅞	–	½	viColuG 10½12f	...	30	133½	...	
ATT 6s00	6.4	61	93⅞	–	¼	CmwE 8⅜07D	8.4	4	96¾	+	½
ATT 5⅛01	5.8	20	88⅜	–	1⅛	CmwE 8¼07	8.5	26	97¼	+	¼
ATT 8⅝31	8.5	63	101⅝	–	⅜	CompUSA 9¼00	10.4	191	91½	+	⅛
ATT 7⅛02	7.3	190	97⅛	–	⅛	ConrPer 6¾01	cv	37	74¾	+	¾
ATT 8⅛22	8.2	152	98½	–	½	ConrPer 6½02	cv	98	75¼	+	¾
ATT 8⅛24	8.2	23	98½	–	½	Consec 8⅛03	9.2	365	88½	+	1⅞
ATT 6¾04	7.2	125	93⅝	+	⅛	ConNG 7¼15	cv	25	99½		

Bonds issued by AT&T with 6¾ percent coupon payments to mature in 2004.

Net Change
Change in closing price from the previous day.

Current Yield
An approximation to the yield to maturity on the bond—7.2 percent for this AT&T bond. *Note:* "cv" means that a bond is convertible into stock, which complicates the meaning of the yield.

Volume
Previous day's volume of buying and selling of this bond, in thousands of dollars.

Close
Closing price in dollars per $100 of the face value. AT&T bonds sold for $93.625 per $100 of the face value. So, a $1,000 bond sold for $936.25

Sources: The Wall Street Journal, March 9, 1995, p. C17; and March 6, 1995, p. C22.

affect its operations. The board of directors chooses the firm's managers. Each share of stock usually gives the stockholder one vote.[15]

Stockholders earn income from their shares through dividends and capital gains.

dividend — a regular cash payment from a firm to stockholders

Dividends are cash payments that firms make to stockholders, usually quarterly (four times per year).

The rate of return, or holding period yield, on a stock is:

$$\text{Rate of return} = \frac{\text{Dividend} + \text{Increase in stock price}}{\text{Beginning-of-period stock price}}$$

where the increase in the stock price is the capital gain.

---

[15]Common stock is ordinary stock. Preferred stock is slightly different; it resembles bonds more than common stocks in some ways.

FIGURE 34.3

QUOTES FOR CURRENT INTEREST RATES

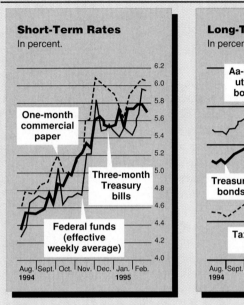

The New York Times

Short-Term Rates

	Last Week (In Percent)		Last Week (In Percent)
Prime Rate	**9.00**	**Certificates of Deposit**	**5.95**
The rate posted by large banks as a base rate for loans to consumers and smaller businesses.		Offering yield on the secondary market for one-month certificates of large banks in blocks of $1 million or more.	
Discount Rate	**5.25**	**Eurodollar Time Deposits**	**6.06**
The interest rate charged by Federal Reserve banks on loans to depository institutions.		Rates paid on one-month dollar deposits outside the United States.	
Federal Funds*	**5.93**	**London Interbank Offered Rate**	**6.25**
The rate for overnight loans among financial institutions.		The rate paid in London on three-month dollar deposits from other banks, used as a base rate in internatinal lending.	
Treasury Bills*	**5.68**		
Discount rates for three-month Treasury bills traded in the secondary market.			
Commercial Paper*	**6.05**	**Long-Term Rates**	
Discount rate for unsecured 30-day notes of high quality corporate borrowers.		**Tax-Exempt Bonds***	**6.18**
		An index of yields for long-term A-rated general obligation bonds compiled weekly by The Bond Buyer.	
Broker Call Loans	**7.75**		
The rate charged on bank loans to securities dealers with stocks as collateral.		**Aa Utility Bonds***	**8.33**
		Salomon Brothers estimate for new long-term issues.	
Bankers Acceptances	**5.91**	**Treasury Bonds***	**7.70**
Discount rate in the secondary market for bank credits created to finance trade.		Weekly average yield of Treasury issues, with maturities of 10 years or more.	
*Rate depicted in chart.			

Source: New York Times, February 20, 1995, p. D4.

When a firm earns profits, it pays part to stockholders as dividends, and it keeps part as *retained earnings*. Firms use retained earnings to pay for investments in equipment, research, and expansion. Retained earnings increase the price of stock and generate capital gains for reasons discussed in a later section.

How Firms Issue Stock

A firm can raise money to finance new investments by borrowing from a bank, issuing bonds or commercial paper, or issuing new equity (shares of stock). More than half of all money firms raise from external sources (as opposed to retained earnings) comes from bank loans; about one-third comes from issuing bonds and commercial paper, and only about 2 percent comes from issuing new stock. Firms often sell newly issued stock to an investment banker who finds buyers for the stock. Sometimes investment bankers underwrite the stock—they buy it themselves and then resell it. This helps the firm that issues the stock by eliminating the risk that buyers will not be willing to pay much for the stock. Investment bankers, of course, charge fees for their services.

Firms that have never issued stock are called *privately held firms,* while firms that have stock traded among the public are called *publicly held firms.* (This should *not* be confused with firms owned by the government!) When a privately held firm issues stock, it *goes public,* it becomes a publicly held firm. Its first sale of stock is called an *initial public offering (IPO).* After the IPO, owners of the stock can trade it on a stock exchange. On average, IPOs appear to be *underpriced* in the sense that their prices on the primary market (when people buy shares from underwriters) average about 10 or 15 percent below their eventual selling prices in the first trades on the stock exchange. Attempts to explain why have generated some controversy among financial economists, who ask why more people don't try to profit by buying IPOs if they are predictably underpriced.

Reading Stock Tables

The New York Stock Exchange (NYSE) is a firm that operates the world's largest equities market. The American Stock Exchange (AMEX) operates another large U.S. stock market, and smaller, regional exchanges also trade stock in the United States, such as the Pacific Exchange, the Philadelphia Exchange, the Boston Exchange, and the Midwest Exchange. Important foreign stock exchanges are in Tokyo, London, Toronto, Montreal, Brussels, Hong Kong, Mexico, Paris, Amsterdam, Milan, Stockholm, Sydney, and Switzerland.

Figures 34.4 and **34.5** show how to read stock market quotations in the newspaper. Look first at the table for the New York Stock Exchange. It lists company names, for example, CampblSoup for the Campbell Soup Company. To the right of the name is the company's abbreviated trading symbol, CPB. These abbreviations show up in many summaries of stock prices, such as those on the Financial News Network on television. To the left of the company's name, the quote lists the highest price (Hi) and lowest price (Lo) for one share of the company's stock during the previous year (52 weeks).[16] The price of one share of

---

[16]The letters or symbols to the left of these 52-week highs and lows are footnotes. The newspaper explains their meanings.

FIGURE 34.4

SAMPLE STOCK MARKET QUOTATIONS, NEW YORK STOCK EXCHANGE

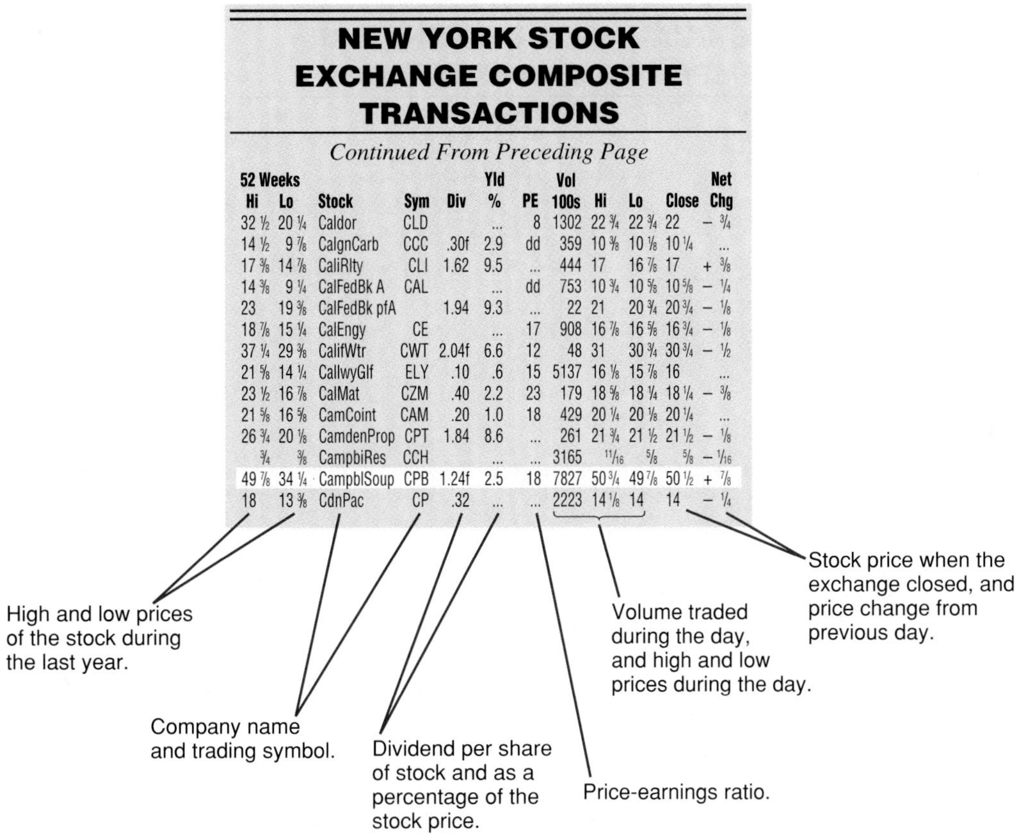

NEW YORK STOCK EXCHANGE COMPOSITE TRANSACTIONS

Continued From Preceding Page

52 Weeks Hi	Lo	Stock	Sym	Div	Yld %	PE	Vol 100s	Hi	Lo	Close	Net Chg
32 1/2	20 1/4	Caldor	CLD		...	8	1302	22 3/4	22 3/4	22	− 3/4
14 1/2	9 7/8	CalgnCarb	CCC	.30f	2.9	dd	359	10 3/8	10 1/8	10 1/4	...
17 3/8	14 7/8	CaliRlty	CLI	1.62	9.5	...	444	17	16 7/8	17	+ 3/8
14 3/8	9 1/4	CalFedBk A	CAL		...	dd	753	10 3/4	10 5/8	10 5/8	− 1/4
23	19 3/8	CalFedBk pfA		1.94	9.3	...	22	21	20 3/4	20 3/4	− 1/8
18 7/8	15 1/4	CalEngy	CE		...	17	908	16 7/8	16 5/8	16 3/4	− 1/8
37 1/4	29 3/8	CalifWtr	CWT	2.04f	6.6	12	48	31	30 3/4	30 3/4	− 1/2
21 5/8	14 1/4	CallwyGlf	ELY	.10	.6	15	5137	16 1/8	15 7/8	16	...
23 1/2	16 7/8	CalMat	CZM	.40	2.2	23	179	18 5/8	18 1/4	18 1/4	− 3/8
21 5/8	16 5/8	CamCoint	CAM	.20	1.0	18	429	20 1/4	20 1/8	20 1/4	...
26 3/4	20 1/8	CamdenProp	CPT	1.84	8.6	...	261	21 3/4	21 1/2	21 1/2	− 1/8
3/4	3/8	CampbiRes	CCH		...	...	3165	11/16	5/8	5/8	− 1/16
49 7/8	34 1/4	CampblSoup	CPB	1.24f	2.5	18	7827	50 3/4	49 7/8	50 1/2	+ 7/8
18	13 3/8	CdnPac	CP	.32	...	...	2223	14 1/8	14	14	− 1/4

High and low prices of the stock during the last year.
Company name and trading symbol.
Dividend per share of stock and as a percentage of the stock price.
Price-earnings ratio.
Volume traded during the day, and high and low prices during the day.
Stock price when the exchange closed, and price change from previous day.

Source: The Wall Street Journal, March 20, 1995, p. C4.

Campbell Soup stock varied between $34\frac{1}{4}$ ($34.25 per share) and $49\frac{7}{8}$ ($49.875) in the year before this quote appeared.

The second column from the right, labeled *Close,* shows the price of the stock when the market closed at 5 P.M. eastern standard time the day before the quote appeared. Campbell Soup closed at $50.50 per share of stock. The arrow pointing upward at the far left indicates that this is the highest closing price within the last year. The last column, labeled *Net Chg,* shows the change in the stock's closing price from the previous day; the price of Campbell Soup stock rose $0.875 from the previous day. (It had closed at $49.625 the previous day.)

Just to the left of the closing price the quote lists the high (Hi) and low (Lo) prices for the previous day's trading during that day, the price of Campbell's stock varied from $49.875 to $50.50 per share. Moving further to the left, the column labeled *Vol 100s* shows the volume of trading in the stock in hundreds of shares; traders exchanged 782,700 shares of Campbell Soup stock.

FIGURE 34.5

SAMPLE STOCK MARKET QUOTATIONS, AMERICAN STOCK EXCHANGE

AMERICAN STOCK EXCHANGE
COMPOSITE TRANSACTIONS

52 Weeks Hi	Lo	Stock	Sym	Div	Yld %	PE	Vol 100s	Hi	Lo	Close	Net Chg		52 Weeks Hi	Lo	Stock	Sym	Div	Yld %	PE	Vol 100s	Hi	Lo	Close	Net Chg
6	4 3/8	CertlFdCda g	CEF	01	...	...	1222	5	4 7/8	4 15/16	+ 1/8		13 5/8	9	Heico	HEI	.15	1.2	15	22	12 3/8	12 3/8	12 3/8	...
18	14 5/8	CentlSec	CET	1.61e	9.4	...	37	17 1/8	17	17 1/8	+ 3/8		11 1/2	5 5/8	HeistCH	HST	...	...	81	10	8 7/8	8 7/8	8 7/8	...
8 3/4	5 3/4	ChadThraput	CTU	stk	...	23	15	8 5/8	8 1/2	8 5/8	...		11 3/4	8 1/4	HemloGold g	HEM	.20a	...	...	1613	9 1/4	9	9	− 1/4
4 1/4	1 13/16	ChambrDev A	COVA	...	dd	4	663	4 1/8	4	4	− 1/10		27 5/8	15 3/4	HeritgMedia	HTG	...	...	cc	373	24 7/8	24 3/8	24 3/8	− 1/8
4 1/4	2	ChambrDev B	COVB	...	dd	4	10	4	4	4	+ 1/16		n14 3/4	3 3/8	HiShear Tch	HSR	...	...	dd	91	10 7/8	10 5/8	10 7/8	+ 1/4
40 5/8	22 3/4	ChampEnt	CHB	...	...	10	350	34 1/2	34 1/4	34 1/4	+ 1/8		n15 1/4	11	Highlandrinco	HLA	1.25	10.6	...	24	11 7/8	11 3/4	11 3/4	− 1/8
n 10	7	ChampnHlthcr	CHC	...	...	...	20	8 3/4	8 5/8	8 1/8	...		3 7/16	1 3/8	HolcoMtg	HOLA	.83e	39.1	7	1	2 1/8	2 1/8	2 1/8	− 1/16
28 1/2	13 7/8	CharterMed	CMD	...	dd	4	1479	17 3/4	17 3/8	17 1/2	− 1/4		33 3/4	23	HollyCp	HOC	.40	1.7	10	20	24 1/4	24 1/4	24 1/8	+ 1/8
22	9 3/4	ChartPwr	CHP	.11	.6	14	110	19 1/2	19 3/8	19 1/2	− 1/4		15 1/2	9 3/8	HomeOil	HO	...	...	66	9 7/8	9 5/8	9 7/8	+ 1/4
s 30 1/4	6	CheynSftwr	CYE	...	...	17	4228	17 3/4	16 1/4	16 3/4	− 5/8		22	5 3/4	HondoO&G	HOG	...	...	dd	189	12 1/4	10 7/8	11 3/4	+ 1/2
34 3/8	25 3/4	ChiRivet	CVR	1.20a	4.3	9	6	28	27 7/8	28	+ 3/8		14 3/4	5 3/4	HooprHolm	HH	.12m	1.5	19	14	7 7/8	7 5/8	7 3/4	...

52 Weeks Hi	Lo	Stock	Sym	Div	Yld %	PE	Vol 100s	Hi	Lo	Close	Net Chg		52 Weeks Hi	Lo	Stock	Sym	Div	Yld %	PE	Vol 100s	Hi	Lo	Close	Net Chg
28	23 1/8	PacGE pfP		2.05	8.2	...	14	25 1/4	24 7/8	25 1/8	...		39 1/2	28 3/4	SalomonORCL	OLK	2.30	5.9	...	14	39	38 5/8	39 7/8	− 1/8
25 1/2	20 1/8	PacGE pfQ		1.86	7.9	...	1	23 1/2	23 1/2	23 1/2	− 1/8		97	80 1/4	SalomonMSFT	MEK	3.99	4.1	...	9	97 1/2	97 1/4	97 1/4	+ 1/4
24 1/2	18 3/8	PacGE pfX		1.72	8.0	...	15	21 3/8	21 3/8	21 3/8	+ 1/4		59	41	SalomonAMGN	AEK	3.19	5.7	...	22	56 1/2	56 3/8	56 3/8	+ 3/8
18 3/8	13 1/8	PacGE pfD		1.25	7.9	...	5	15 3/4	15 1/2	15 3/4	+ 1/8		28	15 1/8	SalomonSNPL	SEK	2.12	13.8	...	432	15 1/2	15 3/8	15 3/8	...
25 1/4	19 3/4	PacGE pfU		1.76	8.1	...	29	21 5/8	21 3/8	21 5/8	+ 1/8		49 1/4	29 7/8	SalomonPRI	PLK	3.02	8.1	...	20	37 1/2	37 3/8	37 3/8	− 1/4
4 5/8	2 7/8	PacGateway	PGP	...	dd	20	3 3/8	3 3/8	3 3/8	− 1/8		37 1/2	23 7/8	SalomonDEC	DLK	2.53	7.6	...	17	33 3/8	33	33 3/8	+ 1/2
18 1/2	12 3/4	PacGulfProp	PAG	1.56	9.9	...	58	15 3/4	15 5/8	15 3/4	...		4 3/8	3 5/8	SalomnPhbOil	SPO	...	...	...	364	4 1/8	4 1/8	4 1/8	...
70	55 1/2	PacifiCp pf		5.00	7.8	...	z275	64	64	64	+ 2		14 1/8	11	SanDgoGE pfA		1.00	8.2	...	3	12 3/8	12 1/4	12 1/8	...
5 3/4	2 1/2	PageAmGp	PGG	...	dd	164	2 7/8	2 3/4	2 3/4	− 1/4		12 1/2	9 1/2	SanDgoGE pfC		.88	8.2	...	1	10 3/4	10 3/4	10 3/4	− 1/4
n 6 7/8	1 5/8	PnWbrUSD Jpn	wt	...	...	277	2 1/2	1 3/4	2 1/2	+ 7/8		98	81 5/8	SanDgoGE pfG		7.20	8.6	...	1	84 1/8	82	84 1/8	+ 1/8
n 3 3/4	3/8	PnWbrUSJ Yen	wt	...	...	260	7/16	7/16	7/16	...		25 3/4	20	SandgoGE prH		1.82	7.9	...	1	23 7/8	23 1/8	23 1/8	− 1/4

Source: The Wall Street Journal, March 6, 1995, p. C11.

Further to the left appear three columns labeled *Div, Yld %,* and *PE. Div* shows the annual dividend per share, $1.24 for Campbell Soup. Dividing this dividend by the stock price ($50.50) gives 0.025, or 2.5 percent per year. This shows the rate of return on the stock from dividends only, ignoring capital gains or losses. The column labeled *PE* shows price-earnings ratios, the stock price divided by the firm's earnings per share. To calculate the price-earnings ratio, divide the company's accounting profit by the total number of shares of stock in the company. The result shows earnings (or profits) per share of stock. Divide the stock price by earnings per share to get the price-earnings (PE) ratio. Campbell Soup, had a PE ratio of 18, so the price of one share of stock was 18 times the amount of earnings (profit) per share of stock. In other words, the Campbell Soup Company earned profits of $1 for each $18 of its stock. The American Stock Exchange table and the NASDAQ National Market Issues table (for so-called *over-the-counter stocks*) are the same as that for the New York Stock Exchange, as **Figure 34.6** illustrates.[17]

---

[17]More details on foreign stocks are available in foreign newspapers or in publications such as the *Financial Times* of London, which is also available in the United States.

FIGURE 34.6

NASDAQ NATIONAL MARKET ISSUES

Quotations as of 4 p.m. Eastern Time
Wednesday, March 8, 1995

52 Weeks Hi	Lo	Stock	Sym	Div	Yld %	PE	Vol 100s	Hi	Lo	Close	Net Chg
		-A-A-A-									
n 16³⁷/₆₄	9⁴⁹/₆₄	AAON Inc	AAON	p	..	13	96	11 ½	11 ⅛	11 ½	+ ⅜
14	12	ABC Bcp	ABCB	.29e	2.3	...	40	12 ⅞	12 ½	12 ⅞	+ ⅜
23 ⅜	15 ¾	ABC RailPdt	ABCR		...	22	22	23	23	23 ⅜	...
s 23 ¾	10 ¼	ABR InfoSvc	ABRX		...	...	536	24 ¾	22 ¾	24 ¼	+ ⅞
16 ¾	11 ½	**ABS Ind**	ABSI	.20	1.6	13	19	12 ½	11 ¾	12 ½	+ ¾
29 ½	11 ⅞	BldgPdt	ABTC		...	9	293	15 ⅛	14 ¾	15	+ ¼
26 ¼	12 ¾	ACC	ACCC	.12	.6	dd	2981	19 ¼	17 ¾	18 ¾	+ ⅞
21 ¼	5 ½	ACS Ent	ACSE		...	dd	472	13 ¼	12 ½	13 ¼	+ ½
40 ¾	31 ¼	ACX Tch	ACXT		...	26	139	40	39 ¼	40	+ ½

52 Weeks Hi	Lo	Stock	Sym	Div	Yld %	PE	Vol 100s	Hi	Lo	Close	Net Chg
3 ⅛	1 ⅝	Amistar	AMTA		...	12	89	2 ¹/₁₆	1¹⁵/₁₆	2 ¹/₁₆	+ ⅛
n 7 ⅞	7	AmpaceCp	PACE		...	...	163	7 ⅜	7 ⅛	7 ⅛	− ¼
9 ¼	5 ¼	AMRESCO	AMMB	.20	3.0	4	756	7 ⅛	6 ⁹/₁₆	6 ¾	− ¼
15	5 ¾	Amrion	AMRI		...	17	230	7	6 ¾	7	...
2 ¾	⅜	AmserHltcher	AMSR		...	dd	10	2 ¼	2 ¼	2 ¼	+ ⅜
33 ¼	7 ¼	**AmtechCp**	AMTC	.08	1.0	15	1392	7 ⅝	7 ¼	7 ⅝	+ ⅜
10 ¾	6	Amtran	AMTR		...	33	95	10	9 ¼	9 ½	− ⁵/₁₆
22 ½	13 ½	AMTROL	AMTL	.20	1/3	,,,	45	16 ½	15 ¾	15 ¾	− ½
14 ½	4 ¾	AmylinPharm	AMLN		...	,,,	361	6	5 ½	5 ¾	...
21	14 ⅝	Analogic	ALOG		...	16	37	19	18 ¼	18 ¼	− ½
21 ¾	14 ½	AnlyInt	ANLY	.52	2.6	16	1325	21 ¼	20 ¼	20 ¼	...
s16	13 ¼	Anangel	ASIPY	1.00e	6.9	19	254	14 ⅝	14 ¼	14 ½	+ ⅜
38 ¾	22	AnchrBcpWis	ABCW	.30	.8	11	15	35 ⅞	35 ¾	35 ⅞	− ⅜

CANADIAN MARKETS

Quotations as of 4 p.m. Eastern Time
Wednesday, March 8, 1995

TORONTO

Sales	Stock	High	Low	Close	Chg.
26400	Cineplex	340	325	325	− 10
11600	Co Steel	$26	26	26 ½	+ ⅞
6500	CoCaCBev	$ 5 ¼	5 ⅛	5 ⅛	− ⅛
2001	Conwest	$21 ¾	21 ⅜	21 ⅜	... ...
3000	DY 4 syst	$11 ¼	11 ¼	11 ¼	... ...
19180	Delrina C o	$20 ¼	19 ⅜	19 ¾	− ⅜

Sales	Stock	High	Low	Close	Chg.
30200	Loblaw Co	$25 ⅛	25	25 ⅛	... ...
309479	M. L. Foods	$14 ⅜	14 ¼	14 ⅜	+ ⅛
500	MDS H A	$14 ⅛	14 ⅛	14 ⅛	+ ⅛
72700	Mackenzie	$ 8 ⅛	7 ⅞	8	... ...
193778	Magna A f	$50 ⅝	50	50 ⅝	+ ⅝
15176	Maritime f	$21 ⅛	20 ¾	21	+ ¼
29500	Sherritt w	345	335	345	... ...
17670	Southam	$12 ⅞	12 ⅝	12 ¾	... ...
99032	Spar Aero	$13 ½	13 ⅛	13 ⅛	− ⅛
491500	Stelco A	$ 6 ⅞	6 ½	6 ¾	... ...
145529	TIPS	2230	2215	2225	+ 5
362094	Talisman	$24 ⅜	24	24 ¼	+ ¼

FOREIGN MARKETS

LONDON (in pence)			AMSTERDAM (in guilders)			FRANKFURT (in Marks)			TOKYO (in yen)	Close	Prev. Close
Abbey National	440	441	ABN Amro	58	58.40	AEG	133.50	137.80			
Allied-Domecq	502	500.5	Aegon	108.6	109	Allianz	2443	2501	ANA	972	976
Argyll Group	280	276	Ahold	51.30	51.40	Asko	605	610.50	Aiwa	2110	2150
Ario Wiggins	245.5	248	Akzo Nobel	183.2	185.9	BASF	297.50	304.50	Ajinomoto	1040	1060
Assoc Brit Fds	583	580.5	AMEV	74	73.10	Bayer	341.50	346	Alps Elec	1040	1070
BAA PLC	424	417	Bols Wessanen	27.60	27.70	Byr Vereinsbk	434.50	438	Amada Co	968	970
Barclays	588.5	582.5	DSM	127.2	129.1	BMW	723	735	Ando Elec	1150	1160
Bass	490	497	Elsevier	15.50	15.40	Commerzbank	333.50	337.50	Anritsu'	1070	1060
BAT Indus	420.5	413	Fokker	10.80	10.90	Continental	210	214.50	Asahi Chem	608	635
Blue Circle	267	267				Daimler Benz	651.20	659	Asahi Glass	1060	1070

Source: The Wall Street Journal, March 9, 1995, pp. C7 and C13.

The Dow Jones Industrial Average (DJIA) is an average of the prices of 30 industrial stocks. The Standard & Poor's 500 (S&P 500) index is an average of the prices of 500 stocks.[18] **Figure 34.7** shows stock market indexes for major foreign exchanges. The Nikkei Average, an average of 225 stock prices on the Tokyo

---

[18]The Wilshire 5,000 is an even broader average of the prices of 5,000 stock issues.

FIGURE 34.7

FOREIGN EXCHANGE STOCK MARKET INDEXES

Stock Market Indexes

EXCHANGE	3/3/95 CLOSE		NET CHG		PCT CHG
Tokyo Nikkel 225 Average	17039.62	+	76.44	+	0.45
Tokyo Nikkel 300 Index	251.09	+	1.86	+	0.75
Tokyo Topix Index	1362.34	+	8.16	+	0.60
London FT 30-share	2301.6	–	9.7	–	0.42
London 100-share	3025.1	–	13.1	–	0.43
London Gold Mines	na				
Frankfurt DAX	2109.49	–	9.17	–	0.43
Zurich Swiss Market	2586.5	–	30.7	–	1.17
Paris CAC 40	1795.24	–	12.11	–	0.67
Milan MIBtel Index	10010	–	142	–	1.40
Amsterdam ANP-CBS General	272.7	–	2	–	0.73
Stockholm Affarsvarlden	1489.5	–	14.8	–	0.98
Brussels Bel-20 Index	1332.57	+	1.39	+	0.11
Australia All Ordinaries	1902.4	–	13.3	–	0.69
Hong Kong Hang Seng	8185.15	–	68.18	–	0.83
Singapore Straits Times	closed				
Taiwan DJ Equity Mkt	159.78	+	1.37	+	0.86
Saturday Market	159.85	+	0.07	+	0.04
Johannesburg J'burg Gold	1479	–	17	–	1.14
Madrid General Index	281.22	–	2.71	–	0.95
Mexico I.P.C.	1519.52	+	2.44	+	0.16
Toronto 300 Composite	4097.04	+	15.83	+	0.39
Euro, Aust., Far East MSCI-p	1011.1	+	13.8	+	1.38

p-Preliminary
na-Not available

Source: The Wall Street Journal, March 16, 1995, p. C17.

Stock Exchange, resembles the Dow Jones Industrial Average or the S&P 500 in the United States. Other important stock indexes include the TSE 300 Index for the Toronto exchange and the *Financial Times* 30-share and 100-share indexes for the London exchange. Some newspapers, such as the *Financial Times* of London, report stock market indexes for stock exchanges around the world and for the world market as a whole. Some also report stock-price indexes measured in alternative currencies. For example, one can compute a stock-price index for Japanese stocks measured in either Japanese yen or U.S. dollars by converting yen prices to dollars using *foreign exchange rates,* as described in a later chapter. Most investors in the United States are mainly interested in the dollar values of their stocks, while most investors in Japan are mainly interested in the yen values of their stocks. People who do business in other countries may be interested in both.

MECHANICS OF STOCK MARKET TRADES

People buy stocks through stockbrokers, who place orders to buy or to sell stocks either through their firms' New York offices or other stock exchange members. Members of the New York Stock Exchange own seats on the NYSE; these seats can be bought and sold, and they have sold for over $1 million each. Specialists at the New York Stock Exchange assume responsibility for trading in each stock; they match orders to buy that stock with orders to sell it at the same price. Besides over 400 specialists, about 200 floor traders buy and sell stocks on the NYSE for their own profit. Floor traders are not allowed to trade stocks for other people.

A buyer pays a slightly higher price for a stock than the seller receives. The difference is the bid-ask spread. Buyers pay the (higher) bid price and sellers receive the (lower) ask price. The difference covers the broker's cost of buying or selling the stock. Stockbrokers also charge commissions to place orders; some stockbrokers also charge for investment advice.

EQUILIBRIUM STOCK PRICES AND RETURNS

A variable follows a random walk if its changes are unpredictable. It came as a surprise to many investors a few decades ago when a thorough examination of the evidence showed that stock prices are close to random walks.

> Stock prices are (close to) random walks.

Stock prices are (almost) equally likely to rise or fall at any given time. On average, they rise slowly over time.

This is sometimes called the *efficient markets theory.*

efficient markets theory — theory that stock prices are (almost) random walks

> The **efficient markets theory** states that stock prices follow (almost) random walks.

With a few well-known exceptions, research evidence strongly supports the efficient markets theory.

EXPLANATION

If you could accurately predict changes in stock prices, you could become a millionaire. You could achieve the age-old investment goal: buy low and sell high. You could buy each stock before its price rises and sell each stock before its price falls. Of course, many people would like to be millionaires, so many people study stock prices and try to predict whether they will rise or fall. If many investors could gather information that would help predict stock prices, they would also try to buy a stock before its price rises and sell before its price falls. When many people try to buy a stock before its price rises, however, the increased demand drives up its current price until investors think it will not rise any further; also, when many people try to sell a stock because they think its price will fall, the increased supply reduces its current price until the price is no longer expected to fall. As a result, in equilibrium, stock prices follow random walks.

Suppose, for example, that investors expect the price of XYZ stock to rise to $15 from its current level of $10 over the next month. They will try to profit by buying XYZ stock *now, before the price rises.* This raises current demand for XYZ stock, which *immediately* raises its price to $15. Anyone who tries to buy the stock must then pay $15. The people who gain from this price increase are those who already owned the stock *before* investors started predicting the price increase and drove the price upward.

Why must the stock price immediately rise to $15? To see why, suppose (falsely) that it rises to only $12. Investors who expect the price to rise to $15 would expect to earn another $3 profit over the next month if they buy the stock. If many investors expect this, they will try to buy the stock today for $12. The increased demand will continue to raise the current price to $15. At any price below the expected future price, investors would see potential profits; their attempts to obtain these profits would increase the stock price until it came to equal the expected future price. Their efforts will raise the stock price to $15 *today.*

> A stock's price always rises or falls enough each day that most investors do *not* expect large rises or falls in the future.

In this sense, an asset's price fully reflects all publicly available information. Any public information—information available to most investors—that affects people's beliefs about a future stock price causes a change in that price as soon as the information becomes available. This makes it impossible to predict stock prices with publicly available information. If this were not true, many investors could easily become millionaires, and people who work as investment advisors wouldn't be working at all—they would be vacationing on their yachts.

IMPLICATIONS

The fact that stock prices follow random walks has several implications. First, technical analysis (attempts to predict a future stock price by studying its past trends) is nearly useless. The history of a stock's price is public information, so it is already reflected in the current price. Considerable evidence confirms that technical analysts do not do any better playing the stock market than anyone else, though they do make money by selling their analyses to other people![19]

Second, fundamental analysis of a stock (efforts to predict a future stock price by examining public data such as that in an annual report about a firm's profits, sales, and so on) is unlikely to help most investors. This information is publicly available, so it is already reflected in current stock prices. The main exception applies to a person with special knowledge that is not available to everyone and who, as a result of this special knowledge, can interpret public information better than almost everyone else.

Third, people can make a big profit in the stock market only with either luck or inside information (information about a firm's prospects available to very few other people). Inside information allows people to buy or sell stocks *before* the information becomes public—before other investors raise or lower demand for the stock, causing its price to rise or fall. Evidence clearly indicates that people with inside information can profit from its use (though such trading is illegal in many cases).

Luck plays a bigger role in investment success than many people may think. If a million people invest in the stock market, it is very likely that a few hundred of them will get rich just by chance. In fact, it would be very surprising if some of them *didn't.* Perhaps *most* of the million investors began trading with a great deal of confidence in their ability to choose good investments. The few hundred people who get rich will believe (incorrectly) that their success confirms their initial confidence; they will be even more certain than before that they know how to

---

[19]Be careful to avoid common mistakes in thinking about this issue. Technical analysts who do better than average by chance are able to attract customers and stay in business longer than those who do worse by chance, illustrating sample selection bias (see Chapter 2); the technical analysts who stay in business longer are the ones who happened to be lucky in the past. This means that the past performance of technical analysts who remain in business is better than average and better than the performance that would be expected by pure chance. That is consistent with the idea that their performance is the result of pure chance, because the evaluation counts only the technical analysts who were lucky enough to remain in business!

The concept is embedded in the ancient joke: "But where are the *customers'* yachts?"

The editors of this magazine have never found the random walk theory persuasive. We know lots of investors who own yachts.

Not everyone believes the efficient markets theory.

Source: Forbes, June 26, 1989, p. 178.

earn money in the stock market. Other people are likely to believe them, since the few hundred people who *lost* a lot of money in the stock market won't go around talking about it. (If they did, people might view them as rather stupid.)

If you flip a coin, the chance that you will flip 10 heads in a row is almost 1 out of 1,000. Because stock prices are close to random walks (with equal chances of rising or falling), think of stock prices as rising if you flip heads and falling if you flip tails. If 1 million people flip coins, about 1,000 of them will flip 10 heads in a row. (About 122 of them will flip heads 13 times in a row!) Picking 10 winning stocks in 10 tries looks pretty impressive, but 1,000 out of every 1 million investors will do it by chance. Picking 13 winning stocks in 13 tries looks even more impressive, but 122 out of every 1 million investors will do it by chance.

People sometimes ridicule the efficient markets theory by telling the fable of an efficient markets believer who wouldn't pick up a $20 bill lying on the sidewalk because he was convinced that it couldn't really be there. Considerable evidence indicates that the efficient markets theory closely approximates reality.[20] On the other hand, no one believes that it describes reality *exactly.* After all, if stock prices always reflected all publicly available information, people might stop collecting information. The search for profits leads people to seek information about values of financial assets (like stocks). The efficient market theory amounts to a generalization that it is extremely difficult to find these profit opportunities, and impossible to find them consistently.

EX-DIVIDEND STOCK PRICES

Stock prices do change predictably immediately after stocks pay dividends. To see why, suppose that a firm will pay a $5 dividend to the owner of a share of its stock as of 3 P.M. eastern time on March 1. Is the stock as valuable at 4 P.M. as it was at 2 P.M. It isn't; if you buy the stock at 2 P.M. you will get it in time to collect the dividend, but if you buy it at 4 P.M., you are too late—the previous owner gets the dividend. This makes the stock worth about $5 less at 4 P.M. than it was at 2 P.M. All investors know this, so they all expect the stock price to fall $5 just after 3 P.M., when the dividend is paid.

LEVEL OF STOCK PRICES

Ultimately, stocks are valuable because they pay dividends (or they will at some time in the future).

fundamental price — the discounted present value of a stock's expected future dividends

The **fundamental price** of a stock is the discounted present value of its expected future dividends.

The present value of expected future dividends is:[21]

DPV of expected future dividends

$$= \frac{d_1}{1 + i} + \frac{d_2}{(1 + i)^2} + \frac{d_3}{(1 + i)^3} + \ldots \text{forever}$$

[20]The efficient markets theory says that most people cannot "beat the market" except by luck, but it doesn't deny that people sometimes get lucky. Someone who sees a $20 bill should not stubbornly refuse to realize that gains are possible simply by luck!

[21]This simplified formula assumes that firms pay dividends once every year at the end of the year, rather than quarterly.

where d_1, d_2, and so on, are the expected dividends after 1 year, 2 years, and so on, and i is the interest rate.

This equation gives the stock's fundamental price. It turns out that the fundamental price also equals:[22]

Fundamental stock price at beginning of 1997

$$= \frac{d_{1997}}{1 + i} + \frac{\text{Fundamental stock price at beginning of 1998}}{1 + i}$$

The fundamental price of the stock rises currently whenever expected future dividends rise. For example, if investors believe that the firm will pay more dividends 5 years from now, d_5 rises. This increases the current fundamental price of the stock. For example, stock prices of firms selling condoms in the United States and Japan immediately rose about 5 percent when basketball star Magic Johnson reported in 1991 that he had contracted the human immunodeficiency virus, which causes AIDS. Investors presumably expected this to raise the future profits and dividends of condom makers. The fundamental price falls if the interest rate rises.

DRIFT IN STOCK PRICES

Stock prices are almost random walks, but not *exactly*. The current equilibrium price of a stock does not exactly equal its expected future price because owning stocks has an opportunity cost. For every dollar you invest in stocks, you sacrifice the interest you could have earned on other investments (T-bills, for example). People invest in stocks because they expect rates of return from stocks high enough to compensate for this opportunity cost.

For example, suppose that the interest rate is 6 percent per year. If investors expect a stock price to be $106 next year, then they might be willing to pay only $100 for the stock this year. Their expected capital gain on the stock is about 6 percent per year, so equilibrium stock prices rise predictably. They have risen, on average, about 6 percent per year since the end of World War II. This leads a rational investor to expect a stock selling for $10.00 today to sell for about $10.01 after 1 week, giving a $0.01 capital gain during the week.

For this reason, today's stock price does not exactly equal the expected stock price next week or next year, but it is close. A stock price follows a random walk with a drift. The drift is the slow, average upward movement of stock prices.

STOCKS ARE RISKY

Stocks are risky investments. The expected rate of return on stocks equals the risk-free rate of return plus a substantial risk premium:

Expected rate of return on stocks = Risk-free interest rate + Risk premium

Figure 34.8 shows the extreme volatility of stock prices. It tracks the Dow Jones Industrial Average and the annual return on the S&P 500 after the end of World War II in nominal terms and after adjustment for inflation. Stock prices vary a lot, even daily; changes of more than 1 percent *per day* are fairly common. (If

---

[22]If you are mathematically inclined, you might be able to prove that these two equations for the stock's fundamental value are equivalent. (*Hint:* Use the first equation to write the fundamental value in both 1997 and 1998, then substitute both into the second equation and try to prove that the second equation is true.)

FIGURE 34.8

STOCK PRICES AND RATES OF RETURN

(a) Nominal Stock Price Indexes

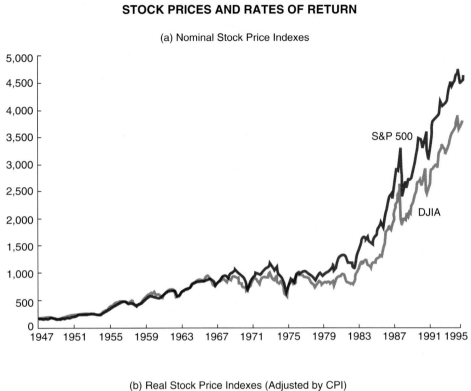

(b) Real Stock Price Indexes (Adjusted by CPI)

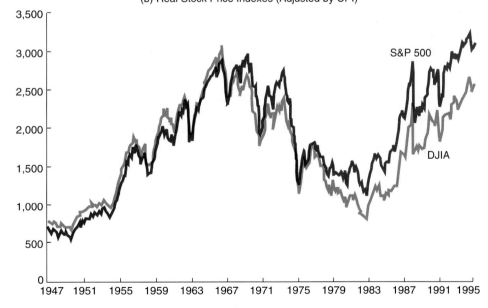

FIGURE 34.8 (CONT.)

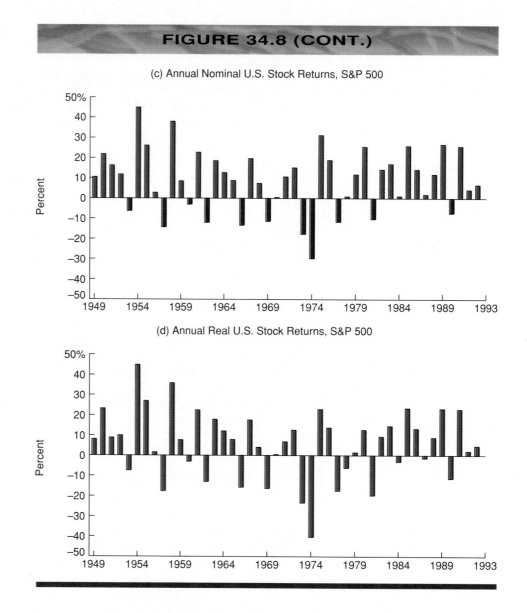

(c) Annual Nominal U.S. Stock Returns, S&P 500

(d) Annual Real U.S. Stock Returns, S&P 500

the DJIA is 4,000, a 1 percent change is a change of 40 points.)[23] The biggest daily change in recent U.S. history was the stock market crash on Black Monday, October 19, 1987, when the DJIA fell 22 percent.[24]

It may seem surprising, but price volatility alone does not make stocks risky. Instead, the risk of any stock is measured by how much uncertainty it adds to the overall wealth of a typical investor.

---

[23]An increase of 1 percent per day is very large. If it were to continue for a full year, a stock selling for $1 at the beginning of the year would sell for over $37 at the end of the year, a 3,600 percent annual increase in price!

[24]It had also fallen 17 percent in the 6 weeks before the crash, so stock prices fell almost 40 percent in 6 weeks.

A stock is risky if owning it adds uncertainty to an average investor's wealth.

Stocks that move in step with other stocks expose an investor to more risk than stocks that move out of step with other stocks.[25] Stocks that move out of step make it easier for investors to diversify their investments. Riskier stocks pay higher risk premiums than less risky stocks; they pay higher expected rates of return to induce investors to own them.

EXAMPLE

If it rains a lot this summer, Umbrellas Unlimited will earn a $1 million profit and its stock price will rise, while Picnic Supplies Incorporated will suffer a $1 million loss and its stock price will fall. If the weather is good, the opposite will occur. Forecasters project a one-half chance of good weather and a one-half chance of a lot of rain.

If you own stock only in Umbrellas Unlimited, your wealth depends on the uncertain weather. The same is true if you own stock only in Picnic Supplies Unlimited. If you invest in both stocks, however, you reduce your risk. In fact, if you invest equally in the two stocks, you may have no risk; one of your stocks will rise in value, and the other will fall, whatever the weather. (The upward drift in stock prices still earns you money because the drift implies that the rise in one stock price will be bigger than the fall in the other.) When you already own stock in either company, investing in the *other* stock reduces uncertainty in your wealth because the two stocks move out of step.

A stock's risk to an average investor depends on whether that stock moves in step or out of step with all of that investor's other investments. Riskier stocks— those that move in step with other investments—have higher rates of return on average than less risky stocks, which move out of step with other investments.

TRADEOFFS BETWEEN RISK AND EXPECTED RETURN

From 1926 to 1993, the average nominal rate of return on the stock market (represented by Standard & Poor's 500) was 11.4 percent per year. Since inflation averaged 3.1 percent per year over this period, the average real rate of return on the stock market was 8.7 percent per year. Over this same period, the average real return on long-term government bonds was only 1.7 percent per year, and the average real return on Treasury bills was only 0.4 percent per year. See **Table 34.1.**

U.S. Treasury bills have almost *zero* risk of default, so people think of 3.5 percent per year as the average *risk-free nominal interest rate* over this period. This means that the risk premium on common stock averaged 7.9 percent per year (11.4 minus 3.5) over this period. In other words, an investor who accepted the extra risk involved in owning stocks instead of T-bills earned, on average, 7.9 percent per year more than an investor who preferred the safety of T-bills.[26]

DO STOCK PRICES EQUAL THEIR FUNDAMENTAL PRICES?

Many economists believe that stock prices do not always equal their fundamental prices. They believe that stock prices sometimes change even when fundamental

---

[25]That is, stocks that are positively correlated with other stocks are riskier than stocks that are uncorrelated or *negatively* correlated with other stocks.

[26]This is the return on the CRISP value-weighted portfolio of U.S. stocks.

TABLE 34.1

ANNUAL RATES OF RETURN, 1926–1993

Asset	Nominal Rate of Return	Real Rate of Return
Common stock	11.4%	8.3%
Corporate bonds	5.2	2.1
Government bonds	4.8	1.7
1-month Treasury bills	3.5	0.4

Source: Center for Research in Securities Prices, University of Chicago, and author's calculations.

---

prices do not. For example, most economists doubt that fundamental stock prices fell 22 percent in one day on Monday, October 19, 1987. What could happen on that day (or over the weekend just before it) to cause such a big change in fundamental stock prices (the discounted present value of expected future dividends)? No one knows. Most economists believe that stock prices are more volatile than their fundamental prices for two reasons:

Speculation crumbles in face of reality

Bubbles can burst.

Source: "Speculation Crumbles in Face of Reality," *USA Today,* November 19, 1991, p. C4.

▶ Bubbles may affect stock prices. A bubble occurs when people are willing to pay more for an asset (like a stock) simply because they believe that other people will be willing to pay even more later! In theory, bubbles can occur even when all investors act rationally. Bubbles can also burst, sending prices into sudden falls. Many economists believe that episodes like the 1987 stock market crash reflect bursting bubbles. Others disagree, claiming that fundamental stock prices can change quickly and that economists should not conclude that big stock price changes are *bubbles* simply because they have not discovered the specific events that caused the changes. It is hard to tell who is right because economists lack a good measure of fundamental stock prices.

▶ Some investors may be irrational or poorly informed about investments. If these investors believe that Digmore Mining Company stock is a good deal, they may buy it and drive up its price above its fundamental value. These movements can become fads if enough irrational or uninformed investors participate. Some economists believe that fads help to make stock prices volatile. Others disagree, saying that rational investors sell the stocks that rise above their fundamental values and buy stocks that fall below their fundamental values. Enough rational investors can keep stock prices from moving far from their fundamental values. Again, it is hard to know which side is right because economists lack a good measure of fundamental stock prices.

MUTUAL FUNDS

A mutual fund is a firm that pools money from many small investors, buys and manages a portfolio of financial assets, and pays the earnings back to the investors. Because a mutual fund buys many assets at once, it incurs lower transactions costs than individual investors through volume discounts on commissions. A mutual fund can also diversify its investments, so an individual investor can achieve automatic diversification just by owning shares in the mutual fund.

IN THE NEWS

Unlike October dives, this stock market fall is due to fundamentals

Basic correction

As profits fall and rates rise, many buyers stand aside and look for the bottom

A 250-point drop in 3 weeks

By Douglas R. Sease And Craig Torres Staff Reporters of The Wall Street Journal

Reality is suddenly battering Wall Street.

Now, the raw essentials— earnings and interest rates— are driving the market. And as earnings fall and interest rates rise, the fundamentals are driving the market steadily lower.

Yields on long-term Treasury bonds have risen steeply.

Meantime, economic data continues to paint a gloomy picture of what lies ahead.

Recession or not, a slower economy means lower corporate earnings. And although investors were prepared for some deterioration in fourth-quarter profits, they didn't anticipate the flood of disappointing earnings announcements they have been seeing in recent weeks.

Changes in fundamentals affect stock prices.

Source: "Unlike October Dives, This Stock Market Fall Is Due to Fundamentals," *The Wall Street Journal,* January 26, 1990, p. A8.

In an *open-end fund,* people can buy or sell shares whenever they want at a price near the value of the mutual fund's assets.[27] Most open-end mutual funds are no-load funds, funds that charge no commissions for buying and selling shares. Shareholders do pay fees to cover the wages and other costs of the funds' managers.[28]

Some mutual funds own stocks, some own bonds, some own both, and some money-market mutual funds own only short-term debt securities. Prices of closed-end mutual funds are reported in financial pages of newspapers, and many financial magazines also rate the performance of various closed-end and open-end mutual funds.

FUTURES MARKETS

futures market — a market for contracts that provide for future delivery of goods or assets

A **futures market** is a market for contracts that provide for future delivery of a good or asset.

---

[27]If you want to invest more in the mutual fund, you send your money and the mutual fund buys more assets. If you want to withdraw money, you redeem shares; the mutual fund sells some of its assets and sends you the money.

[28]Closed-end funds are less common. Such a fund issues a fixed number of shares when it begins operations. People can then buy and sell shares, but the share price is not necessarily equal to the value of the financial assets the mutual fund owns. In fact, closed-end mutual funds sell, on average, for less than the values of their assets. (The value of all the parts of the fund—the assets the mutual fund owns—are worth more than the mutual fund itself!) This apparently means that investors in such closed-end mutual funds would gain if the funds were converted to open-end funds. The fact that this does not happen is an example of a situation in which a firm's managers fail to act in the interest of the firm's owners. A later section will discuss this in more detail.

In a futures market, you may agree *today* to buy or sell a certain amount of a good or asset in the future at a price set today.[29] You may buy wheat futures, contracting for 5,000 bushels of wheat to be delivered next March 1 at a price of $3.50 per bushel. Like most other people who buy these futures, you do not want 5,000 bushels of wheat, but you believe that the price of wheat will rise, giving you a chance to profit. To do this, you lock in the $3.50 price today. If you are right and the price rises by March 1, you buy the wheat for $3.50 per bushel and simultaneously sell it at the higher future price without ever actually seeing any wheat. Futures markets allow people to place bets on whether a price will rise or fall. For example, if wheat sells for $4.00 per bushel on March 1, then you earn a profit of $0.50 per bushel. On the other hand, if the price of wheat falls to $3.00 per bushel by March 1, you are stuck paying $3.50 for wheat that you can sell for only $3.00, so you lose $0.50 per bushel. When you buy futures, you are betting that the price of the good will rise, and you are said to *go long* in the good.

If you think that the price of a good will fall, you can sell futures. You might sell silver futures if you think that the price of silver will fall; you might agree to deliver 5,000 troy ounces of silver next December 1 to someone who has agreed to pay you $4.00 per ounce. If the price of silver falls to $3.00 per ounce by December 1, you can buy the silver you have agreed to deliver for $3.00 per ounce and sell it for $4.00 per ounce, earning a profit of $1.00 per ounce. On the other hand, if the price of silver rises to $5.00 per ounce, you lose money; you must pay $5.00 per ounce for something that you have already agreed to sell for only $4.00 per ounce. When you sell futures in a good, you are said to *go short* in it.

TRADING FUTURES

Traders buy and sell futures in commodities like soybeans, barley, pork bellies, cocoa, orange juice, and heating oil in organized futures markets like the Chicago Mercantile Exchange (CME); the Chicago Board of Trade (CBT); the Commodity Exchange (COMEX) in New York; the Coffee, Sugar, and Cocoa Exchange (NYC-SCE), and many other exchanges. You can also buy and sell futures in financial assets like Treasury bills, government bonds, and many foreign currencies (like the Japanese yen). Some of these futures trade on other exchanges, like the Financial Instrument Exchange (FINEX), a division of the New York Cotton Exchange, and the International Monetary Market (IMM), a division of the CME in Chicago.

You can even buy or sell futures in stock indexes. For example, you can buy futures on the S&P 500 if you expect the index to rise, or you can sell futures on the S&P 500 if you expect it to fall. Futures exchanges also offer contracts on the Nikkei Index of Japanese stock prices. **Figure 34.9** shows how to read a futures table in a newspaper.

OPTIONS

Traders buy and sell two kinds of options contracts: call options (rights to buy) and put options (rights to sell).

A **call option** is a legal right to buy some underlying asset during some specified period of time at some preset strike price. If you own a call option, you have the choice (or option) of deciding whether to exercise

call option — a right to buy some underlying asset during some specified period of time at some preset strike price

---

[29]This discussion ignores slight differences between *futures markets* and *forward markets*.

FIGURE 34.9

SAMPLE FUTURES QUOTATIONS

FUTURES
THURSDAY, MARCH 16, 1995

FINANCIAL

Lifetime High	Low	Date	Open	High	Low	Settle	Chg	Open Int

3-MO. T-BILLS (CME)
$1 million; pts of 100%

94.24	92.55	Jun. 95	94.02	94.08	94.01	94.05	+ .02	18,629
93.92	92.25	Sep. 95	93.79	93.88	93.79	93.86	+ .03	9,757
93.78	92.14	Dec. 95	93.69	93.75	93.65	93.71	+ .03	6,516

Est vol 4,073; prev vol 3,395; open int 34,938; −573

JAPANESE YEN (CME)
12.5 million yen; cents per yen

| 1.1325 | .9776 | Jun. 95 | 1.1298 | 1.1340 | 1.1183 | 1.1192 | −.0080 | 57,760 |
| 1.1441 | 1.0175 | Sep. 95 | 1.1430 | 1.1470 | 1.1310 | 1.1318 | −.0081 | 2,533 |

Est vol 26,301; prev vol 66,875; open int 60,989; −36,066

S&P 500 (CME)
$500 X index

494.30	441.45	Mar. 95	491.80	496.00	491.60	495.85	+3.85	65,227
498.45	451.00	Jun. 95	496.00	500.10	495.65	499.55	+3.45	168,360
502.50	456.55	Sep. 95	500.40	504.40	500.40	503.95	+3.30	5,431
507.20	475.60	Dec. 95	506.10	509.00	506.10	508.60	+3.35	2,908

Est vol 127,660; prev vol 97,915; open int 241,930; −6,610

NIKKEI 225 (CME)
$5 X index

| 21195. | 16245. | Jun. 95 | 16480. | 16675. | 16460. | 16635. | −110. | 26.094 |

Est vol 1,370; prev vol 1,821; open int 26,110; +334

AGRICULTURAL

Lifetime High	Low	Date	Open	High	Low	Settle	Chg	Open Int

CORN (CBT)
5,000 bu.; $ per bu.

2.82½	2.20½	Mar. 95	2.41½	2.42¾	2.40½	2.41	−.01¼	4,177
2.85	2.28	May 95	2.47¾	2.48¾	2.46½	2.47	−.01½	114,777
2.85½	2.32½	Jul. 95	2.54¼	2.55¼	2.53	2.53½	−.01¼	104,015
2.70½	2.38	Sep. 95	2.58¾	2.59¼	2.57½	2.58¼	−.01	19,867
2.62½	2.47¾	Dec. 95	2.62	2.62½	2.60¾	2.62	−.00¼	86,109
2.68¾	2.66	Mar. 96	2.68	2.68½	2.67	2.68	−.00½	8,302
2.74¾	2.55½	Jul. 96	2.74	2.74½	2.73	2.74¼	−.00½	4,114
2.63	2.35½	Dec. 96	2.58	2.58	2.57	2.57½	−.00¾	2,238

Est vol 45,000; prev vol 48,524; open int 344,000; + 5,300

OATS (CBT)
5,000 bu.; per bu.

1.52¾	1.16½	May 95	1.25½	1.25½	1.24¾	1.24¾	−.00¾	71
1.51	1.22¼	May 95	1.29¾	1.29¾	1.28¾	1.29¼	−.00½	6,884
1.42½	1.27½	Jul. 95	1.34¾	1.34¾	1.34	1.34¼	−.00½	4,358

COFFEE (CSCE)
37,500 lb.; per lb.

244.00	78.90	Mar. 95	178.00	178.00	171.75	172.00	−6.75	191
244.40	82.50	May 95	180.80	182.40	170.55	171.20	−7.60	17,920
245.10	85.00	Jul. 95	181.95	183.50	172.00	172.50	−7.50	9,345
238.00	151.80	Sep. 95	183.50	184.75	175.30	175.30	−6.00	4,997
242.00	81.80	Dec. 95	179.50	179.50	174.90	174.90	−6.00	4,650

Est vol 13,658; prev vol 8,425; open int 37,804; + 74

METALS AND ENERGY

Lifetime High	Low	Date	Open	High	Low	Settle	Chg	Open Int

GASOLINE, unleaded (NYM)
42,000 gal.; per gal.

60.30	52.10	Apr. 95	52.90	55.70	53.95	54.93	+ .89	23,104
59.00	52.30	May 95	53.50	55.40	54.18	54.85	+ .61	21,863
58.20	52.40	Jun. 95	53.80	55.25	54.45	54.77	+ .38	9,322
57.94	51.60	Jul. 95	54.25	55.20	54.35	54.67	+ .18	6,707
57.35	53.40	Aug. 95	54.10	54.60	54.17	54.17	+ .07	2,612
56.35	52.20	Sep. 95	53.25	53.85	53.32	53.32	+ .07	2,182
54.75	50.30	Dec. 95	51.20	51.30	51.07	51.07	+ .07	1,007

Est vol 38,206; prev vol 30,068; open int 68,768; + 851

HEATING OIL (NYM)
42,000 gal.; per gal.

55.15	43.05	Apr. 95	44.35	45.90	45.05	45.37	+ .23	31,744
54.30	44.60	May 95	45.05	46.25	45.45	45.79	+ .17	29,525
53.50	45.50	Jun. 95	45.75	46.70	46.20	46.34	+ .12	14,977
54.30	46.50	Jul. 95	46.50	47.30	46.90	46.94	+ .07	12,687
55.60	42.70	Aug. 95	47.35	48.05	47.69	47.69	+ .02	6,545
53.10	48.15	Sep. 95	48.15	48.90	48.59	48.59	+ .02	4,123
53.95	49.08	Oct. 95	50.00	50.00	49.49	49.49	+ .02	3,533
54.40	49.98	Nov. 95	50.00	50.70	50.39	50.39	+ .02	2,726
57.60	50.85	Dec. 95	51.00	51.65	51.29	51.29	+ .02	9,448
53.30	51.43	Feb. 96	51.60	51.90	51.60	51.89	+ .02	2,355

Est vol 33,009; prev vol 28,394; open int 126,280; −220

SILVER (CMX)
5,000 troy oz.; per oz.

604.00	416.50	Mar. 95	467.00	472.50	466.50	466.50	+.10	94
606.50	418.00	May 95	471.00	477.00	467.50	467.50	−.20	65,123
610.00	420.00	Jul. 95	476.50	482.00	473.00	473.00	−.20	14,985
603.50	446.00	Sep. 95	481.50	486.40	477.00	477.00	−.30	11,238
628.00	454.00	Dec. 95	489.50	494.20	486.00	486.00	−.40	16,183
622.00	466.50	Mar. 96	497.50	502.30	497.50	497.50	−.50	9,786

Est vol 14,000; prev vol 17,153; open int 131,030; −70

Lifetime High, Low Recent high and low futures prices.

Date of delivery specified in the futures contract.

High and Low High and low prices during previous day's trading.

Settle Previous day's closing price.

Change Change in closing price from the previous day's close.

Open Interest Number of futures contracts open (someone has sold and someone else has bought each contract).

Source: New York Times, March 17, 1995, p. D13.

put option — a right to sell some underlying asset during some specified period of time at some preset strike price

it, that is, to buy the underlying asset. If you do not choose to exercise your right to buy, you let the option expire.

A **put option** is a legal right to sell some underlying asset during some specified period of time at some preset strike price. If you own a put option, you can decide whether to exercise it by selling the underlying asset or let it expire.

You can buy (go long) or sell (go short) in either kind of option. You need not own an option to sell one; you can simply have a broker issue the option contract and sell it for you. If you buy an option, you have the right to decide whether to exercise it. If you sell an option, the person who buys it from you has the right to decide whether to exercise it.

If you buy a call option, you are betting that the price of the underlying asset will rise. If you buy a put option, you are betting that it will fall. When you buy an option, your potential profits are unlimited, while your potential loss is limited to the price of the option contract.

If you sell a call option, you are betting that the price of the underlying asset will fall. If you sell a call option, you are betting that it will rise. When you sell an option, your potential profits are limited, but your potential loss may be unlimited. For example, if you sell a call option, nothing limits how high the price of the underlying asset may rise, so your possible loss has no limit.[30]

Because options are rights to trade other assets, they are examples of *derivative securities*—assets whose values derive from prices of other assets. Futures markets in assets are also derivative securities. Derivatives became controversial when Orange County, California, went bankrupt in 1994, partly due to losses on risky derivative securities, and due to Nick Leeson, a 28-year-old trader working for a 200-year-old British firm, who bankrupted the firm when he lost $1.3 billion in the futures markets in 1995.

EXPLANATION AND EXAMPLES

Suppose that you buy a call option on stock in Levi Strauss & Company. The call option costs you $300, and it gives you the right to buy up to 100 shares of Levi stock before next March at $110 per share. Suppose that the price of Levi stock is currently $104 per share. If the stock price stays below $110 until March, you simply let the option expire; you don't buy Levi stock for $110, and you lose the $300 you paid for the call option. You cannot lose more than the money you paid for the option. If the price of Levi stock rises to $115 by March, you *exercise* the option; you buy Levi stock for $110 per share, and you can sell it for $115 per share, so you gain $5 per share on 100 shares, a profit of $500. Since you paid $300 for the option, your net profit is $200. Your potential profit is *unlimited* because the potential price of Levi stock is unlimited; for every $1 increase in the price of Levi stock above $110, your profit rises by $100.

Suppose that you buy a put option on stock in the Boeing Corporation. The put option costs you $200 and gives you the right to sell 100 shares of Boeing stock before next February at a price of $45 per share. If the price of Boeing stock at the end of January exceeds $45 per share, you let the put option expire and you lose the $200 you paid for the option. If the stock price is below $45 per share, you exercise the put option. You profit from the option if the stock price falls

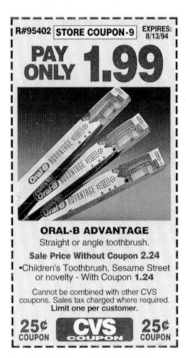

A simple call option with strike price $1.99.

---

[30]However, you can limit your potential loss by combining two options.

below $43. For example, if the stock price falls to $40 per share, you buy 100 shares of Boeing stock for $40 per share and exercise your option to sell it for $45 per share. You collect $500, a $300 profit (since you paid $200 to buy the option). As the stock price falls lower, your profit rises.

TRADING OPTIONS

People can buy and sell options on stocks, bonds, and Treasury bills, foreign currencies, commodities like cattle and sugar, stock-price indexes like the S&P 500, and even options on futures contracts. Option contracts trade on the Chicago Board Options Exchange (CBOE) and other organized markets. **Figure 34.10** shows how to read options tables in the financial pages.

Options are like bets; the seller of the option bets one way and the buyer bets the other way. The price of an option depends on what people believe might happen to the price of the underlying asset in the future. Unlike other

FIGURE 34.10

SAMPLE OPTIONS QUOTATIONS

LISTED OPTIONS QUOTATIONS

Option/	Strike	Exp.	-Call- Vol.	-Call- Last	-Put- Vol.	-Put- Last
15 7/8	15	May	10	1 11/16	50	11/16
15 7/8	22 1/2	Aug	225	3/8	...	...
Exxon	65	Mar	373	1/4	...	...
65 1/4	65	Apr	39	1 1/8	105	5/8
65 1/4	65	Oct	17	2 3/4	102	2 1/4
65 1/4	70	Oct	76	3/4	...	...
FHP s	30	Mar	...	...	80	1 1/8
FTP Sf	25	Mar	155	4 7/8	...	...
29 11/16	30	Apr	...	...	50	2 3/8
FedExp	60	Mar	65	5 1/2	...	...
65 3/4	65	Mar	183	1/2	40	1/16
65 3/4	65	Apr	105	2 1/4	10	1 1/2

Option/	Strike	Exp.	-Call- Vol.	-Call- Last	-Put- Vol.	-Put- Last
36 7/8	40	May	216	1 1/8	...	...
Humana	20	Mar	50	4 5/8	...	...
24 3/8	22 1/2	Mar	55	1 3/4	...	...
24 3/8	25	Apr	20	7/8	300	1 1/8
24 3/8	25	May	...	...	292	1 5/8
24 3/8	25	Aug	45	2 1/8	...	...
I-STAT	25	Apr	...	...	148	2
ICN Ph	15	Mar	47	1/16	446	1/8
14 7/8	15	Apr	92	1	108	1 1/8
14 7/8	15	Jun	85	1 1/16	20	2
IMC Gl	40	Mar	200	10 1/2	...	...
50 1/2	50	Mar	463	1/2	50	1/16

Option/	Strike	Exp.	-Call- Vol.	-Call- Last	-Put- Vol.	-Put- Last
43 7/8	45	Jul	1394	1 9/16	59	2
43 7/8	45	Oct	365	2 1/4	30	2 3/8
Merril	30	Mar	1603	13 3/4	...	...
44	35	Mar	186	9	...	...
44	35	Apr	1521	8 3/4	1524	1/16
44	35	Jul	10	10 1/2	60	3/8
44	40	Mar	655	4 1/8	...	...
44	40	Apr	199	4 3/8	30	7/8
44	40	Jul	17	6 1/8	240	1 1/4
44	45	Mar	144	1/16	87	3/8
44	45	Apr	146	1 1/8	278	1 7/8
44	45	Jul	92	2 1/2	...	...

Company name and current stock price.

Strike price and expiration date for option on shares of stock.

Price of calls.

Price of puts.

OPTIONS

PHILADELPHIA EXCHANGE

		Calls Vol.	Calls Last	Puts Vol.	Puts Last
Japanese Yen					**112.00**
6,250,000 Japanese Yen -100ths of a cent					
107	Jun	...	...	190	1.00
108	Apr	...	...	2	0.50
108	Jun	...	...	5	1.11
109	Apr	1	3.88	10	0.83

		Calls Vol.	Calls Last	Puts Vol.	Puts Last
109	May	...	...	1	1.12
109	Jun	5	5.45	5	1.50
110	Apr	...	...	6	1.02
110	Jun	...	...	193	1.88
111	Jun	7	4.26	7	2.20
112	Jun	50	3.50	203	2.60
113	Jun	2	3.15	1	3.18
117	Jun	20	1.68	...	...

It costs $388 per million yen to buy a call option on yen with a strike price of 109 yen per dollar and an expiration date of April.

Source: The Wall Street Journal, March 20, 1995, pp. C12 and C15.

◣ **PERSONAL DECISION MAKING**

Investments

The best investment advice is fairly simple.

Rule 1: Diversify your investments. You can do this on your own; choosing five or ten stocks at random usually provides a fairly high degree of diversification. (*The Wall Street Journal* reports occasionally on the performance of professional investment advisors compared to the performance of a set of stocks chosen by throwing a dart at a dart board; the professionals usually don't do much better than the dartboard stocks!) As an alternative, you can invest in a mutual fund that diversifies for you. Many no-load mutual funds charge low fees and do a very good job of diversifying—probably better than you can do on your own, and with lower transactions costs.

Rule 2: Buy and hold. Don't keep changing your investments. You probably won't do much better, and you might do worse. Also, every time you buy and sell assets, you pay commissions and other transactions costs. You can also use your time in much more valuable ways than continually following your investments. Unless you have some inside information about a firm, you are unlikely to beat the market, anyway. Take transactions costs (fees, commissions, bid-ask spreads, and the value of your time) into account.

Rule 3: Consider stocks, despite the risk. For long-term investments, remember that the average rate of return on a diversified portfolio of stocks has been much higher in the past than the average rates of return on bonds or Treasury bills. Stocks are riskier, but they may be worth the risk, especially if you plan to hold them for a long time.

Rule 4: Plan around taxes. Some investments, such as individual retirement accounts, pay tax-deferred returns; you don't have to pay taxes on them until you take income from them in the future, for example, when you retire. Unless you think that taxes are going to be much higher then, this can help you; the discounted present value of your taxes is lower if you pay them in the future than if you pay them now. (In other words, you gain the annual interest on the money you will owe in taxes.) Also, remember to focus on the after-tax, real return on your investments. Taxes and transactions costs can have big effects on the rate of return you get.

Rule 5: Remember a penny saved is no longer a penny earned. It was close in Ben Franklin's day, but today taxes are higher, so *$1.00 saved is about $1.50 earned.* (It is exactly that much, if you are in the $33\frac{1}{3}$ percent marginal tax bracket, including federal and state income taxes and Social Security tax). If you buy a VCR for $300, it takes about $450 in before-tax income to pay for it. Every $67 you save is like earning $100 more.

Rule 6: Don't waste your money. Besides minimizing transactions costs, don't bother with so-called *technical analysis* of stocks. Instead of spending your

financial assets, more uncertainty actually makes options more valuable. To see why, consider a call option on stock in The Limited. Greater uncertainty about the future price of this stock—higher likelihood that it will either rise or fall by a lot—means that an investor stands to gain more from buying the option. If the stock price rises a lot, the option owner profits. Greater uncertainty has little effect on the investor's potential loss, however, which is limited to the cost of the option.

—————————— **FOR REVIEW** ——————————

34.10 Discuss the claim that stock prices follow a random walk; discuss some of the implications of random-walk stock prices.

time with technical or fundamental analysis of stocks, you are probably better off spending more time working toward a promotion, figuring out how to start your own business, writing the Great American Novel, producing a hot music video, or enjoying yourself.

Rule 7: Budget your time. Most people gain less from an hour spent following their investments closely than from an hour spent clipping coupons for the grocery store or driving to a more distant store with lower prices.

Rule 8: Diversify your investments internationally. Stocks in different countries do *not* move completely in step, so they can reduce your risk at a lower cost in expected return than if you invest only in U.S. stocks.

Rule 9: Don't pay a lot of money for investment advice. Don't put much extra faith in people with financial planning degrees or certifications. Most people who call themselves financial planners have little training, and most will recommend that you buy things on which they earn commissions. No law prohibits conflicts of interest in this business! If you can, find a financial advisor who (a) will give you a list of customers who have stayed with that person for several years, (b) gets good recommendations from those customers, and (c) charges a flat fee or hourly rate instead of getting commissions from selling recommended assets.

Ask the financial planner what percentage of his or her revenues come from commissions (ask even "fee-only" advisors) and whether the advisor accepts any kind of payment (including free trips and gifts) from people selling specific financial assets. You can also ask outright: "How might your interests in this matter differ from mine?"

You can get a form called the *ADV form* from the Securities and Exchange Commission (SEC) that lists the education and past jobs of financial planners. (See the *Economics Yellow Pages* for the address and phone number of the SEC.) You can also check on a financial planner with your state government (ask especially for information on complaints or lawsuits) and with the National Association of Securities Dealers in Rockville, Maryland. The National Association of Personal Financial Advisors can provide information on financial planners who don't get commissions.

Finally, remember that the investment advice of financial advisors will not help you to beat the market. Roughly two-thirds of advisors' recommendations end up doing worse than the S&P 500. When an advisor generates an expected return higher than that of the S&P 500, it is usually at the cost of higher risk, with higher returns in some years and lower returns in other years.

34.11 How large (roughly) are the average rates of return on stocks, bonds, and Treasury bills?

34.12 What are mutual funds? What are Treasury bill futures?

34.13 Suppose that you buy a call option on General Cinema stock. Under what conditions do you earn a profit? Under what conditions do you suffer a loss?

QUESTIONS

34.14 The price of DullCo stock never changes by more than a few percent per year. The price of WildCorp stock is highly variable. Is WildCorp stock riskier than DullCo stock? Explain.

34.15 What affects the fundamental price of a stock? Why might stock prices deviate from their fundamental prices? Do economists have any way to tell if and when this happens? How?

OWNERSHIP AND CONTROL OF FIRMS

Stockholders in a firm own that firm. They collect its profits, that is, any revenue that remains after workers, suppliers of material inputs, bondholders, and so on, have been paid. Stockholders are *residual income recipients*—they get what is left (if something is left). Stockholders also have the right to make the firm's decisions and to hire and fire its managers.

Although stockholders have the *right* to control the firm's decisions, actual control is difficult in a big firm. One person or a few people may own and manage a small firm as at many small retail stores and restaurants. The same people own and control these privately held firms. However, publicly held corporations, which have issued stock, often have many stockholders.[31] The stockholders do not control the firm directly. Instead, they choose managers to run it for them. Stockholders vote—each share of stock usually gives its owner one vote—to choose the firm's board of directors, which then chooses managers who make the firm's operating decisions.

This may create a *separation of ownership and control* so that the owners do not fully control the firm's decisions. The managers may make different decisions than the stockholders would have made, decisions that do not always serve the stockholders' best interests. Separation of ownership and control can allow the managers to make decisions that are best for *themselves,* even if the owners (the stockholders) lose. The managers might concentrate more on the firm's short-run profits and less on its long-run profits than owners would like, particularly if the managers do not expect to remain in their jobs for a long time, or they simply might work less hard than if they owned the firm.

The owners try to maintain control of the corporation in two ways. First, they monitor the managers—they watch what the managers do. Monitoring efforts confront two main problems. Managers usually have more information about details of the firm's operations and investment opportunities than owners have, which makes it hard for owners to know if managers are making the choices that benefit the owners most. Also, monitoring takes time and resources, so each of many stockholders may prefer to wait for some *other* stockholders to monitor the managers rather than spending their own time and resources.

Owners also try to keep control of the firm by giving managers incentives to make the decisions that are best for the owners. They have devised many ways to do this, though none works perfectly. Rather than paying managers flat salaries,

---

[31]Privately held firms can also be incorporated. This limits the liability of the owners. In a sole proprietorship or a partnership, the owners (usually) have *unlimited liability;* if the firm borrows money and goes bankrupt, the *owners* must repay the loans, or if someone sues the firm in court, the owners are legally responsible for paying any judgement. A *corporation,* however, becomes (legally) like a person; if the corporation borrows money, only the corporation is responsible for repaying the loan. If the corporation goes bankrupt, the owners do *not* have to use their own money to repay the loans. Similarly, the owners are not responsible for paying lawsuits against the firm. The only money the owners of a corporation can lose is the money they have already invested in the firm.

owners often pay managers more when the firm earns higher profits. Owners might require managers to own shares of stock in the firm to make the managers part-owners and give them some of the same incentives as other owners. This does not solve the problem completely, however. To see why, suppose that a manager must decide whether to spend $1 million of the firm's money on a new office building. Suppose that the new building would add $600,000 to the discounted present value of the firm's profits—$400,000 less than it costs. Stockholders would choose *not* to spend the money because the total value of the firm's stock—the *value of the firm*—would fall by $400,000. If the manager owns 0.1 percent of the firm's stock, this amounts to a personal loss of only $400. The manager may want a new office, however, and may be willing to pay more than $400 to get it. Consequently, the manager may spend the $1 million even though the owners would have chosen not to do so.

Another problem arises in plans to pay managers more when the firm earns higher profits, perhaps by requiring them to own stock: managers do not like risk. As the manager's ownership of stock in the firm rises, the manager's wealth becomes less diversified. This reduces the manager's incentive to choose risky investments for the firm—even risky investments that other owners with *diversified* investments would want the firm to choose. As a result, profit-based compensation is not a perfect solution to the problems caused by separation of ownership and control; in fact, no perfect solution is possible.

TAKEOVERS

If a firm has bad managers whose decisions fail to maximize the value of the firm's stock, the stockholders have an incentive to replace them. If they don't replace the managers, someone who notices this situation may buy enough stock in the firm to take control of it and then try to profit by replacing the managers or by taking other actions to change their incentives and improve the firm's performance.

> A **takeover** occurs when one person, a group of people, or another company buys enough stock in a firm to guarantee a majority vote at stockholder meetings.
>
> A **leveraged buyout (LBO)** is a form of takeover financed by extensive borrowing, often pledging the assets of the takeover target as collateral for the loans.
>
> A **merger** occurs when two firms join together voluntarily.

In a hostile takeover, the top managers of the target firm oppose the takeover, usually for fear that they will lose their jobs, which often happens. They may try to convince stockholders *not* to sell their stock to the would-be acquirers. They may try to use legal tricks to prevent a takeover by delaying it and making it expensive for the potential acquirers. In some U.S. states, managers are partly protected from takeovers by antitakeover laws that make it more costly to take over a firm. If these laws work, they protect entrenched managers at the expense of stockholders.

Managers may also try other tricks to make a takeover so expensive that no one will try. They may institute poison pills, which raise the cost of a takeover by allowing old stockholders to buy new shares of stock at extra-low prices if someone begins a hostile takeover. They may pay greenmail, a bribe paid to the acquirers to get them to abandon the takeover. Managers might establish golden parachutes to pay themselves (very well, usually) if they lose their jobs in a takeover!

takeover — when one person, a group of people, or another company buys enough stock in a firm to guarantee a majority vote at stockholder meetings

leveraged buyout (LBO) — a form of takeover financed by extensive borrowing, often pledging the assets of the takeover target as collateral for the loans

merger — when two firms join together voluntarily

(It sounds unfair, but golden parachutes can make top managers more willing to accept a takeover that would benefit stockholders rather than fight it.)

Fear of a takeover (as well as fear of being fired and replaced by the current owners) helps to give managers some incentive to act in the interests of the stockholders. Friendly takeovers occur when current managers of a firm want the takeover. (In such a case, obviously, the top managers do not expect to be replaced.) A friendly takeover can raise a firm's stock value by improving the efficiency of its operations. They can also help managers to fend off *other* takeovers that are not so friendly (and in which the managers might be replaced). Sometimes managers look for a white knight—someone friendly to the current managers who is willing to take over the firm before a more hostile takeover can occur.

ARE MERGERS AND TAKEOVERS SOCIALLY WASTEFUL?

Takeovers raise economic efficiency. Measures of productivity show that takeover targets usually have low productivity levels that improve after the takeovers. The number of managers and the firm's overhead spending usually fall after a takeover, though employment, wages, and production do not. Stock prices of takeover targets usually rise and stay higher long after the takeovers. Also, the stock prices of the acquiring firms do not fall, so total stock market values—the discounted present values of expected future dividends—rise because of takeovers. Investors clearly expect firms to become more profitable after being taken over (and, usually, having the old managers replaced).[32]

People sometimes complain that mergers, takeovers, and leveraged buyouts harm the economy by wasting large amounts of money. People who say this incorrectly believe that the money a company spends to take over another company is money that could have paid for something else, such as health care for the poor. This view is misleading. Suppose that Company A buys Company B for $100 million, that is, it buys most of the stock in Company B from that firm's previous stockholders. Company A then has less money to spend, but the previous stockholders of Company B have the money. The money does not just disappear! (The same is true if you buy stock on the New York Stock Exchange—you have less money, but the person who sold you the stock has more.) Spending money for a takeover does not reduce the amount of other goods that society can afford; it does not reduce the amount of goods that society can produce.

Note one qualification to this result, though. The takeover may consume valuable resources such as lawyers' time. This prevents use of those resources in some other way. That time is the true social cost of takeovers. Still, remember that takeovers raise the total value of stock in the firms involved by raising economic efficiency, so takeovers add to the economy's wealth.

Sometimes people say that the individuals involved in finance, takeovers, mergers, and similar activities don't really produce anything (like cars or food), and that this causes a problem for the economy. This argument ignores the value of services. Accountants and people in the insurance industry don't make tangible goods, either, but they provide valuable services. Without their work, production of tangible goods would be lower rather than higher. Similarly, people

---

[32]Evidence also suggests that the increase in profitability does not result from an increase in monopoly power. However, some of the gains in stock market value may occur because of reductions in wages paid to workers rather than because of increases in productivity.

involved in takeovers and mergers produce a more efficient economy through their actions. The increase in total stock market value from takeovers is a rough measure of the value of their production. (Their actions are really more valuable than this, because the mere threat of takeovers also creates better incentives for managers.)

STOCKHOLDERS VERSUS BONDHOLDERS

Stockholders and bondholders in the same firm often have different incentives and want the firm to make different decisions. One important area of disagreement concerns the riskiness of the firm's investments. Stockholders prefer riskier investments than bondholders for a simple reason: if a firm makes a risky investment, it might win big or lose big. If it wins big, the stockholders get the benefits (higher profits), while the bondholders get only their usual interest payments. Bondholders usually do not gain if the risky investment turns out well. On the other hand, if the investment is a big loser, the firm may go bankrupt and bondholders may lose the chance for repayment in full! Bondholders view stockholders as saying "Heads, I win; tails, you lose" when they choose risky investments for a firm. For this reason, bondholders dislike risky investments and stockholders like them.[33] To help protect their interests, bondholders often insist on *bond covenants,* special conditions in the terms of debt contracts that limit the risks the firm can take. Bond covenants help to protect bondholders from increases in risk. Conflict arises between bondholders and stockholders in many other areas, and many of the features of debt contracts and corporate law exist to try to help resolve those conflicts and to provide incentives for economically efficient decisions.

FOR REVIEW

34.16 Explain separation of ownership and control.

34.17 What is a takeover? How and why does a takeover typically affect the stock price of the takeover target?

QUESTIONS

34.18 Greedyblood Corporation spends $1 billion on a hostile takeover of the Goodfrus Corporation. Is this likely to be money that society could have put to a more useful purpose? Explain.

34.19 What creates a conflict of interests between stockholders and bondholders?

CONCLUSIONS

The financial industry is world-wide and very competitive. Financial markets are always innovating by creating new securities, sometimes very complicated ones, that help investors and add to the efficiency of the economy.

---

[33]Stockholders like risky investments as long as they generate expected rates of return high enough to justify the risk.

FINANCIAL ASSETS AND MARKETS

A financial asset is a right to collect some payment or series of payments in the future. Its rate of return is the income the asset pays, plus the increase in its price, all as a percentage of the original asset price. Financial markets increase opportunities for people and make the economy more efficient by helping people to borrow and lend, to diversify risk, and to direct resources toward their most economically efficient uses.

RISK AND INSURANCE

Most people are risk averse; they dislike risk enough that they are willing to take lower expected rates of return in order to reduce risk. This means that risky assets must pay higher expected rates of return than safer assets in equilibrium. People try to reduce their risks by diversifying their investments. They can reduce risk by choosing investments whose returns move out of step with each other.

DEBT INVESTMENTS: BOND MARKETS AND MONEY MARKETS

Debt is a borrower's promise to repay a loan. Bonds, Treasury bills, and commercial paper are examples of debt securities. The price of a bond is the discounted present value of its expected future payments. The discounted present value calculation uses a higher interest rate for a bond with a bigger risk of default.

STOCKS AND STOCK MARKETS

Shares of stock are certificates that represent part-ownership in a corporation. The return on stock consists of dividends and capital gains. The fundamental price of a stock is the discounted present value of its expected future dividends. The discounted present value calculation uses a higher interest rate for a riskier stock. The risk of a stock depends on how much uncertainty it adds to the overall wealth of investors, which depends on whether its rate of return moves in step or out of step with other investments. Stock prices are approximately random walks; they rise slowly over time, but big changes in stock prices are not predictable with publicly available information. Stocks are riskier than bonds, but they pay much higher expected rates of return.

OTHER ASSETS

A mutual fund pools investors' money to buy a diversified set of financial assets. They provide an easy and cheap way for individual investors to diversify. A futures market is a market for future delivery of a good or an asset. A call option is a legal right to buy an asset during some specified period of time at a preset price. A put option is a similar right to sell. Options allow investors to bet on a wide variety of financial events and to hedge a wide variety of risks.

OWNERSHIP AND CONTROL OF FIRMS

Stockholders own a corporation, but they do not completely control it; they hire managers to make decisions for them, creating a separation of ownership and control. Managers' interests are not the same as stockholders' interests, so stockholders use a variety of methods to alter managers' incentives to make decisions that benefit the owners. If a firm has bad managers whose decisions differ substantially from the decisions that the owners would make, then the firm may be subject to a takeover. A takeover raises the efficiency of the acquired firm and raises its stock market value. Managers usually oppose hostile takeovers because they are likely to lose their jobs. They have developed many ways to try to fight hostile takeovers.

Bondholders and stockholders also have conflicting interests. Bondholders want the firm to make decisions that reduce its chance of bankruptcy and default, which raises the value of its bonds. Bondholders want the firm to choose less risky investments than stockholders want, even though the less risky investments pay lower expected rates of return.

KEY TERMS

financial asset	risk premium
rate of return	yield to maturity
expected value	holding period yield
diversification	capital gain (or capital loss)
risk averse	dividend
risk neutral	efficient markets theory
bond	fundamental price
coupon payment	futures market
Treasury bill (T-bill)	call option
Treasury note	put option
commercial paper	takeover
default	leveraged buyout (LBO)
risk-free interest rate	merger

QUESTIONS AND PROBLEMS

34.20 Why do stock prices follow almost random walks? Why *almost*?

34.21 Suppose that a company discovers a new product that is likely to double its profits next year. What would happen to its stock price? How can the stock price follow a random walk?

34.22 How would you expect reductions in government defense spending to affect the prices of stock in firms that make military equipment? What if the cuts in defense spending were already expected by investors?

34.23 Explain why diversifying your investments reduces your risk. Does diversification always reduce your expected profit?

INQUIRIES FOR FURTHER THOUGHT

34.24 If investment advisors are so smart, why aren't they rich? Why are they giving other people advice or writing about investing instead of making money and retiring, or making money to give to needy people, medical research, or other worthy causes?

34.25 Why do financial markets offer so many different kinds of assets? What functions (if any) do they perform? What good (if any) do they do?

34.26 What are the incentives of a stockbroker? Why not compensate a broker by paying a fraction of your winnings if you win, and ask the broker to pay part of your losses if you lose? Why not pay doctors in a similar way?

34.27 Do you think that bubbles or fads move stock prices? Do stock prices usually equal their fundamental values?

34.28 Why do people work for firms? Why doesn't everyone work for himself or herself as a separate, private contractor or consultant, perhaps doing the same work?

34.29 Why can't you buy insurance against low grades in college?

TAG SOFTWARE APPLICATIONS

TUTORIAL EXERCISES

▶ The module contains a review of the key terms from Chapter 34.

CHAPTER 35

INTERNATIONAL TRADE

WHAT THIS CHAPTER IS ABOUT

▶ Gains from international trade

▶ Trade deficits and surpluses

▶ Restrictions on international trade

International trade conjures up images of romance and danger in foreign lands, of spices from China, tea from India, oranges from Morocco, fashions from France and Italy, and the latest consumer electronics from Japan, of established business opportunities in the European Union or entrepreneurial opportunities in newly developing economies. It also invokes fears of competition from foreign sellers and worries over future prospects for local jobs and family economic security.

Most of the 5.8 billion people in the world earn wages far below those of a typical American worker. As advances in technology, transportation, and communication create a more integrated world economy, American firms and workers will face increased competition from firms and workers in other countries. How will this competition affect the American economy and your future standard of living? Can American workers expect to earn the high incomes to which they have become accustomed when workers in other countries are willing to work for lower wages? Will American wages fall to world levels as international trade expands? What would be the consequences of shutting off the nation from the rest of the world economy? Why does the United States have a trade deficit? Is this a sign that America cannot compete in the world marketplace? This chapter addresses the reasons for international trade and its economic consequences.

SCOPE OF INTERNATIONAL TRADE

export — a sale of goods or services to people in another country

import — a purchase of goods or services from people in another country

International trade promotes economic efficiency; the ability to buy from foreign sellers helps consumers, and the ability to sell to foreign buyers helps producers. International trade adds to the competition facing domestic producers; it allows countries to specialize in producing the goods and services that they can produce at lowest cost, and it helps to spread modern technology around the world, raising world output and economic growth.

Trade has two components: exports and imports.

Exports are sales of goods and services to people in other countries.

Imports are purchases of goods and services from people in other countries.

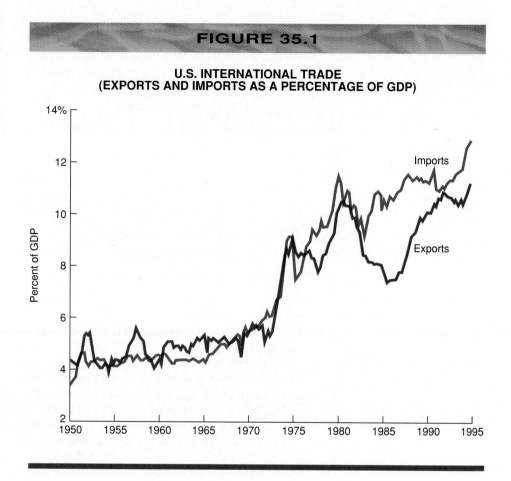

FIGURE 35.1

**U.S. INTERNATIONAL TRADE
(EXPORTS AND IMPORTS AS A PERCENTAGE OF GDP)**

The United States exports about one-tenth of all goods and services that it produces, that is, U.S. exports are about 10 percent of GDP. People in the United States also import about one-tenth of everything they buy.[1] **Figure 35.1** shows that the U.S. currently imports and exports a higher fraction of its GDP than it did in the past. **Figure 35.2** shows that international trade is even more important for smaller countries such as Italy and Canada than for large countries such as the United States and Japan.[2]

A country that exports more than it imports has a trade surplus; a country that imports more than it exports has a trade deficit.

balance of international trade — the value of a country's exports minus that of its imports

trade surplus — exports in excess of imports

trade deficit — imports in excess of exports

A country's **balance of international trade** equals its exports minus its imports. When the balance is positive (exports exceed imports), the country has a **trade surplus;** when the balance is negative (imports exceed exports), it has a **trade deficit.**

The United States had a trade surplus in most years from 1947 to 1976, but it has had a trade deficit since then. See **Figure 35.3.**

---

[1]The phrase "a country trades" means that people, business firms, or the government in that country trade. Many imports are inputs in the production of other products rather than final products themselves.

[2]*Smaller* and *larger* refer to the relative sizes of economies (measured by total GDP), not to land areas.

FIGURE 35.2

INTERNATIONAL TRADE AS A PERCENTAGE OF GDP

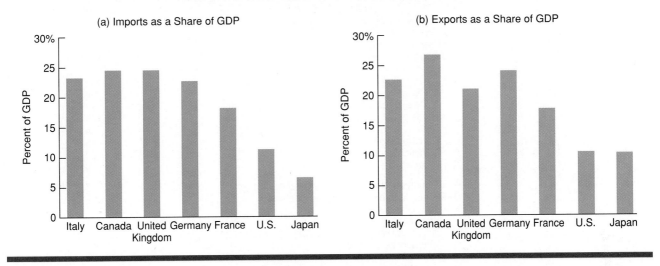

(a) Imports as a Share of GDP

(b) Exports as a Share of GDP

FIGURE 35.3

U.S. BALANCE OF TRADE ON GOODS AND SERVICES

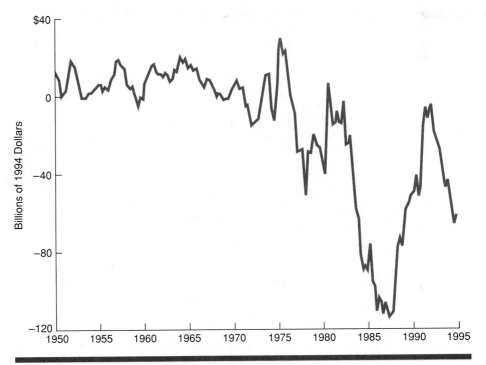

FIGURE 35.4

CATEGORIES OF U.S. IMPORTS AND EXPORTS IN 1993 ($ BILLIONS)

Total exports of merchandise and services	$642
Merchandise (excluding military goods)	458
Foods, beverages, feeds	40
Industrial supplies and materials	111
Capital goods (excluding autos)	182
Automobiles and parts	52
Nonfood consumer goods	54
Other exports	15
Services	184
Travel	58
Transportation	40
Royalties and license fees	20
Other private services	66
Total imports of merchandise and services	$717
Merchandise (excluding military goods)	589
Foods, beverages, feeds	27
Industrial supplies and materials	152
Capital goods (excluding autos)	152
Automobiles and parts	102
Nonfood consumer goods	134
Other imports	22
Services	128
Travel	40
Transportation	35
Royalties and license fees	5
Other private services	48

Source: Survey of Current Business.

FIGURE 35.5

U.S. TRADING PARTNERS

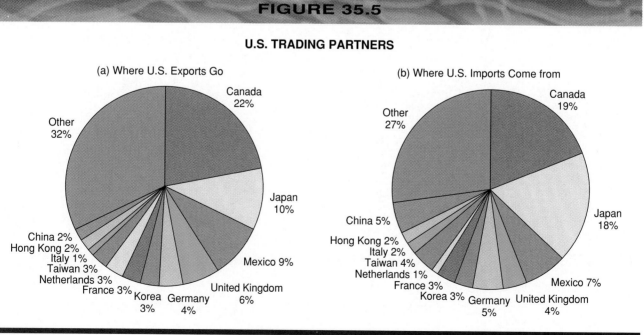

(a) Where U.S. Exports Go

Canada 22%
Japan 10%
Mexico 9%
United Kingdom 6%
Germany 4%
Korea 3%
France 3%
Netherlands 3%
Taiwan 3%
Italy 1%
Hong Kong 2%
China 2%
Other 32%

(b) Where U.S. Imports Come from

Canada 19%
Japan 18%
Mexico 7%
United Kingdom 4%
Germany 5%
Korea 3%
France 3%
Netherlands 1%
Taiwan 4%
Italy 2%
Hong Kong 2%
China 5%
Other 27%

News reports about trade deficits can be confusing because they report two different measures of the balance of trade:

merchandise trade balance — the difference between exports of goods (but not services) and imports of goods (but not services)

balance of trade on goods and services — the difference between exports of goods and services and imports of goods and services

The **merchandise trade balance** refers to trade in goods only (not services). The **balance of trade on goods and services** covers *both*.

The merchandise trade balance includes international trade in food, industrial supplies, machinery and equipment, automobiles, and other consumer goods. The balance of trade on goods and services also includes international trade in services such as travel and transportation services. **Figure 35.4** breaks down the main categories of U.S. exports and imports.

Figure 35.5 shows that Canada and Japan are the two biggest trading partners of the United States; about one-third of all U.S. international trade involves exchanges with Canada and Japan. Mexico, the United Kingdom, Germany, South Korea, and Taiwan are also major U.S. trading partners. As **Figure 35.6** shows, the United States is Japan's biggest trading partner.

COMPARATIVE ADVANTAGE AND THE GAINS FROM TRADE

International trade is like a good technology. When one country loads wheat on a boat and ships it to another country, and boats come back filled with television sets, international trade works like a technology that turns wheat into television sets.

People gain from international trade for the same reason that they gain from an improvement in technology. Of course, some people also lose from an improvement in technology (producers of horse-drawn carriages lost business when changes in technology led to mass production of cars). The gains to the winners (buyers who

FIGURE 35.6

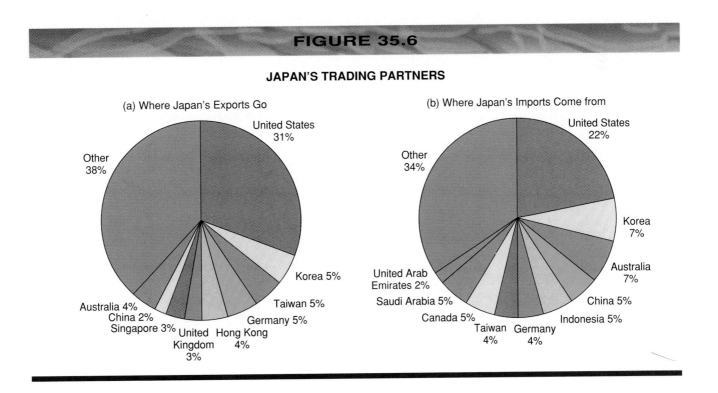

JAPAN'S TRADING PARTNERS

(a) Where Japan's Exports Go

- United States 31%
- Other 38%
- Korea 5%
- Taiwan 5%
- Germany 5%
- Hong Kong 4%
- United Kingdom 3%
- Singapore 3%
- China 2%
- Australia 4%

(b) Where Japan's Imports Come from

- United States 22%
- Other 34%
- Korea 7%
- Australia 7%
- China 5%
- Indonesia 5%
- Germany 4%
- Taiwan 4%
- Canada 5%
- Saudi Arabia 5%
- United Arab Emirates 2%

chose cars over carriages and the car producers) exceed the losses to the losers, however. Similarly, domestic car manufacturers lose when people buy foreign cars instead of domestic cars. However, while some people lose from international trade, the gains to the winners are larger than the losses to the losers, just as they are when technology improves. That is why international trade is economically efficient.

PRINCIPLE OF COMPARATIVE ADVANTAGE

Costs of production differ across countries. A country gains from trade when it exports goods in which it has a comparative advantage.

comparative advantage — the ability to produce a product at a lower opportunity cost than other countries

> A country has a **comparative advantage** in a product when it can produce that product at a lower opportunity cost than other countries.

Countries gain from international trade by doing more of what they do best. Each country produces more of the products in which it has a comparative advantage, and each produces less of other products. This raises world output and allows people to consume more of *every product,* a result sometimes called the *law of comparative advantage.*

EXAMPLE

Table 35.1 shows the hypothetical costs of producing one music video or one computer program in the United States and in Japan. The costs are measured in the number of person-days each country takes to produce one unit of each good. It takes 1 person-day of work in the United States to produce a music video; it takes 4 person-days in Japan. On the other hand, it takes 3 person-days in the United States to write a computer program; it takes only 2 person-days in Japan. Notice that in the United States, the cost of writing a computer program is three times the cost of producing a music video; in Japan, it is one-half of the cost of a music video. The United States has a comparative advantage in music videos because it can produce them at a lower opportunity cost than Japan can, and Japan has a comparative advantage in computer programming because the opportunity cost of computer programming is lower there than in the United States.

Table 35.2 shows productivity levels in each country in this example, that is, the quantity of each product that one person can produce in 1 day. Tables 35.1 and 35.2 present the same information in two different ways. The numbers in Table 35.2 are the *inverses* of the numbers in Table 35.1

Table 35.3 shows the opportunity cost of producing each good in each country. The opportunity cost of producing a computer program in the United States

TABLE 35.1

COSTS OF PRODUCTION: AMOUNT OF LABOR TIME NEEDED TO PRODUCE 1 UNIT OF A PRODUCT

	United States	Japan
One music video	1 person-day	4 person-days
One computer program	3 person-days	2 person-days

TABLE 35.2

PRODUCTIVITY: HOW MUCH ONE PERSON CAN PRODUCE IN 1 DAY

	United States	Japan
Music videos	1 video	$\frac{1}{4}$ video
Computer programs	$\frac{1}{3}$ program	$\frac{1}{2}$ program

TABLE 35.3

OPPORTUNITY COST OF PRODUCING ONE UNIT OF A PRODUCT

	United States	Japan
Opportunity cost of one music video	$\frac{1}{3}$ computer program	2 computer programs
Opportunity cost of one computer program	3 music videos	$\frac{1}{2}$ music video

is three music videos. (The reason should be obvious; the United States could produce three music videos in the time it takes to produce one computer program). Similarly, the opportunity cost of a music video is one-third of a computer program. In Japan, the cost of a computer program is one-half of the cost of producing a music video, so the opportunity cost of producing a computer program is one-half of one music video and the opportunity cost of producing a music video is two computer programs. The United States has a comparative advantage in music videos and Japan has a comparative advantage in computer programs.

GAINS FROM TRADE IN THE EXAMPLE

This example offers chances for gains from trade. Suppose that each country has 60 million person-days available for work (writing computer programs or producing music videos), and that people in each country want twice as many music videos as computer programs.[3] **Table 35.4** summarizes the results. Without international trade, Japan would spend 48 million person-days to produce 12 million music videos. Japan would spend its other 12 million person-days writing 6 million computer programs. (This would give Japan twice as many music videos as computer programs, which is what people want to buy.) The United States would spend 24 million person-days to produce 24 million music videos. The United States would spend its other 36 million person-days writing 12 million computer programs. World output (in the United States and Japan together) would total 36 million music videos and 18 million computer programs.

With international trade, the United States would spend all 60 million person-days producing music videos and Japan would spend all 60 million person-days working on computer programs. Total world output would rise to 60 million music videos (all produced in the United States) and 30 million computer programs (all produced in Japan). International trade would raise world output of

---

[3]This means that music videos and computer programs are (perfect) complements.

TABLE 35.4

(a) Total World Output without International Trade

	United States	Japan	World
Music videos	24	12	36
Computer programs	12	6	18

(b) Total Output with International Trade

Music videos	60	0	60
Computer programs	0	30	30

Note: People in each country work 60 million person-days, and buyers in each country want exactly twice as many music videos as computer programs.

both products. That is why international trade resembles an improvement in technology. Although no one works harder, the world produces more output. World output rises because international trade raises economic efficiency.

In real life, the United States appears to have a comparative advantage in farm products and high-tech products. Specific products include aircraft, computers, medicines, organic chemicals, and wheat. The United States appears to have a comparative *dis*advantage in goods such as auto parts, electronic parts, inorganic chemicals, semiconductors, and televisions. Evidence suggests that the United States has a comparative advantage in products that use relatively large quantities of land or skilled labor as inputs. It has a comparative disadvantage in products that use relatively large amounts of unskilled labor or capital equipment.

FOR REVIEW

35.1 What is the balance of international trade?

35.2 Which countries are the biggest trading partners of the United States?

35.3 What is comparative advantage? What is the law of comparative advantage?

35.4 Explain why international trade resembles a good technology.

QUESTION

35.5 Suppose that the numbers in Table 35.1 change to:

COSTS OF PRODUCTION: AMOUNT OF LABOR TIME NEEDED TO PRODUCE ONE UNIT OF A PRODUCT

	United States	Japan
One music video	1 person-day	3 person-days
One computer program	2 person-days	4 person-days

Which country has a comparative advantage in which product?

GAINS FROM INTERNATIONAL TRADE: GRAPHICAL ANALYSIS

production possibilities frontier (PPF) — a graph showing the combinations of products that an economy can produce with its available resources and technology

PRODUCTION POSSIBILITIES

Without international trade, each country is limited to consuming the goods that it can produce. International trade allows each country to consume more of every good. How much more? The answer depends on world equilibrium prices and the country's production possibilities frontier.[4]

> A country's **production possibilities frontier (PPF)** shows the combinations of products that it can produce with its available resources and technology.

Figure 35.7 shows a country's PPF. The PPF answers the question, "How much of Product Y (such as fabric) can the economy produce if it produces a given amount of Product X (such as cars)?" Each point on the PPF shows one combination of products that the economy can produce. It can produce any one of many combinations:

▶ 750 million yards of fabric and 10 million cars

▶ 700 million yards of fabric and 20 million cars

▶ 600 million yards of fabric and 30 million cars

▶ 400 million yards of fabric and 40 million cars

▶ 100 million yards of fabric and 50 million cars

With its currently available resources and technology, the economy cannot produce at a point above the PPF, such as Point E in Figure 35.7.

The negative slope of a PPF shows the tradeoff between producing the two products. If the economy produces more fabric, it has fewer resources left to produce cars. The absolute value of the slope of the PPF shows the opportunity cost in terms of fabric of producing cars.

CONSUMPTION POSSIBILITIES

Without international trade, a country's PPF also shows its consumption possibilities. People can buy any combination of goods that the economy can produce, such as Points A, B, or C, but they cannot consume at points above the PPF, such as Points D or E.

International trade, however, allows people to buy more than the country can produce! To see why, look at the world price line in **Figure 35.8.** The world price line shows opportunities for trading with other countries. Its slope (in absolute value) shows the world relative price of cars in terms of fabric. People can consume at any point on the world price line, such as Points B, D, or E. To consume at Point D the country produces at Point B (30 million cars and 600 million yards of fabric), and then it trades along the world price line to Point D by exporting cars and importing fabric. The slope of the world price line (in absolute value) shows the amount of fabric the country can import for each car it exports. Similarly, if people in the country want to consume at Point E, they can produce at Point B, then export fabric and import cars.

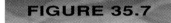

FIGURE 35.7

PRODUCTION POSSIBILITIES FRONTIER

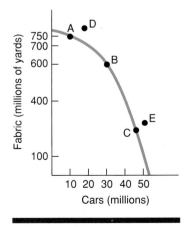

---

[4]See the appendix to Chapter 3 for further discussion.

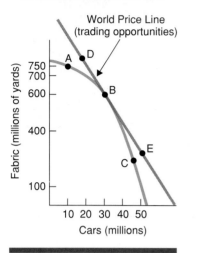

FIGURE 35.8

CONSUMPTION POSSIBILITIES WITH INTERNATIONAL TRADE

Supply and Demand on World Markets

The absolute value of the slope of the world price line—the equilibrium relative price of the two goods—depends on world supply and demand. **Figure 35.9** shows how to find the world supply and world demand for any good in international trade, its world equilibrium price, and the equilibrium exports and imports of each country. Figure 35.9a shows the supply and demand for fabric in the United States. If the United States does not trade with other countries, the equilibrium U.S. price is $12 and the equilibrium U.S. quantity is 20 units of fabric. Figure 35.9b shows the supply and demand for fabric in Mexico. If Mexico does not trade with other countries, its equilibrium price of fabric is $7 and its equilibrium quantity is 15 units. Without international trade, the price differs across countries. This difference gives people an incentive to trade; people want to buy the good in the country where its price is low, and firms want to sell in the country where its price is high.[5]

With international trade, the world demand and supply in Figure 35.9 give a world equilibrium price of $10 and a world equilibrium quantity of 40. To obtain the world supply and demand curves, add the supply curves and demand curves from all countries that engage in international trade horizontally.[6] In equilibrium, people in the United States buy 28 units of fabric.[7] U.S. firms produce and sell only 14 units of fabric, so the United States imports the other 14 units of fabric. Firms in Mexico produce and sell 26 units of fabric, while people in Mexico buy only 12, so Mexico exports 14 units of fabric; U.S. imports equal Mexican exports.

Winners and Losers: The Size of the Gain from Trade

Some people gain from international trade, and others lose:

1. *Consumers in the importing country gain.* International trade allows them to buy the good at a lower price.

2. *Producers in the importing country lose.* They sell the good at a lower price, and they sell less. The losers include the owners (stockholders) of firms that face additional foreign competition and workers at those firms.

3. *Producers in the exporting country gain.* International trade allows them to charge a higher price and sell more.

4. *Consumers in the exporting country lose.* They pay a higher price for the good.

Figure 35.10 shows the sizes of these gains and losses from international trade.[8]

---

[5]Supplies and demands for most goods differ across countries, so equilibrium prices without international trade also differ across countries. International trade makes relative prices (nearly) equal in all countries. The reason for the qualifying *nearly* is that transportation costs and transactions costs can keep prices higher in some countries than in others. A Big Mac, for example, does not sell for the same price in all countries, or even in all cities within a country. Figure 35.9 ignores transportation costs and transactions costs.

[6]This example assumes that only the United States and Mexico buy and sell fabric.

[7]The quantity demanded in the United States at the world equilibrium price is 28 units.

[8]The sizes of these gains and losses are a topic in microeconomics. They reflect the fact that when a person buys a good, the value that the buyer places on that good typically exceeds its price. (Otherwise, the buyer would probably not buy the good!) For example, if you value a concert ticket at $40 in the sense that the highest price you would be willing to pay to see the concert is $40, and if the concert ticket actually costs $25, then your gain from buying the ticket equals $15. Similarly, when a seller sells a good, the value that the seller places on the good is usually less than its price. (Otherwise, the seller would probably not sell it.) These observations make it possible to measure the gains from trade to buyers and sellers and to compare the sizes of the gains (as in the various trades between the two students discussed in Chapter 3).

FIGURE 35.9

EQUILIBRIUM IN WORLD MARKETS

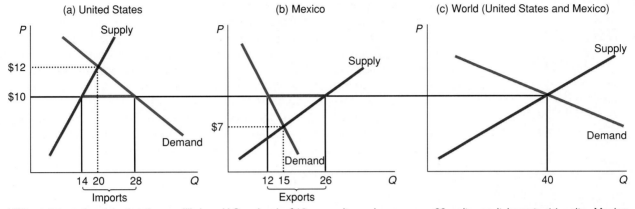

(a) United States   (b) Mexico   (c) World (United States and Mexico)

Without international trade, the equilibrium U.S. price is $12 and the United States produces and consumes 20 units of fabric. The equilibrium price is $7 in Mexico, and Mexico produces and consumes 15 units of fabric. With international trade, the world equilibrium price is $10 (that is, a unit of fabric sells for $10 in each country). The United States produces 14 units and consumes 28 units, so it imports 14 units. Mexico produces 26 units and consumes 12 units, so it exports 14 units. In equilibrium, Mexican exports of fabric equal U.S. imports of fabric. In Panel c, world equilibrium occurs when the world quantity supplied equals the world quantity demanded.

FIGURE 35.10

MEASURING GAINS FROM TRADE

Without international trade, the equilibrium price is $12 in one country and $7 in the other. With international trade, the world equilibrium price is $10. (a) Consumers in the importing country gain Areas A + B from international trade, while producers in the importing country lose Area A; on net, the importing country gains Area B from international trade. (b) Consumers in the exporting country lose Area C from international trade, but producers in the exporting country gain Areas C + D; on net, the exporting country gains Area D from international trade.

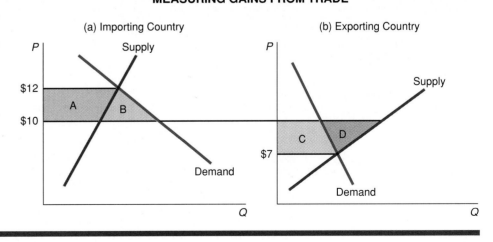

(a) Importing Country   (b) Exporting Country

1. *Consumers in the importing country gain Areas A + B.*
2. *Producers in the importing country lose Area A.*

Trade accord would create winners and losers

Tariff reduction can be harmful to some American industries.

"There will be winners and losers," says Frank Vibert, deputy director of the Institute of Economic Affairs in London. "But the momentum [toward economic integration] is unstoppable."

Indeed, the pact will force some countries and businesses to make difficult transitions. Workers in Sweden, Norway, and Finland might, under stiffer competition from cheap southern labor, have to forsake parts of their extensive social security systems. EFTA farmers will face competition from lower-cost producers in the EU.

Some people gain and others lose from international trade, though the gains to winners exceed the losses to losers.

Sources: "Trade Accord Would Create Winners and Losers," *New York Times*, November 29, 1990, p. D1.

gains from trade — the net benefits to people (as consumers and producers) from trading

On net, the importing country gains Area B.

3. *Producers in the exporting country gain Areas C + D.*

4. *Consumers in the exporting country lose Area C.*

On net, the exporting country gains Area D.

The importing country gains on net because its consumers gain more than its producers lose. The exporting country gains on net because its producers gain more than its consumers lose. The winners in each country gain enough that they could compensate the losers for their losses and still gain from international trade. In this sense, the world as a whole gains from international trade; the net world gain is Areas B + D in Figure 35.10.

This result on the gains from international trade is one of the most famous results in economics. The result implies that (on net) countries lose when they restrict international trade.

The **gains from trade** are the net benefits to people (as consumers and producers) from trading.

The total of Areas B and D in Figure 35.10 measure each country's gains from international trade in this product. The total gains from international trade sum these gains across all traded products.

Countries earn *larger* gains from trade when their equilibrium prices without international trade *differ more* from each other. In this sense, people benefit from diversity. **Figure 35.11** shows international trade between two countries that do not differ from each other very much; the gains from trade in this case are much smaller than those in Figure 35.10. People gain more in Figure 35.10 than in Figure 35.11 because international trade changes relative prices more.

RETURN TO PRODUCTION AND CONSUMPTION POSSIBILITIES

International trade allows people in each country to consume more of every product. Figure 35.8 showed that people can consume at any point on the world price line. The absolute value of the slope of that world price line gives the equilibrium price from supply and demand on world markets, as in Figure 35.9.[9]

EXAMPLE

Figure 35.12 shows the PPFs for the United States and Japan for the example from Tables 35.1 to 35.3. These PPFs are straight lines. Each country has 60 million person-days available for work, so the United States can produce 60 million music videos and zero computer programs, or zero music videos and 20 million computer programs, or some combination along the PPF in Figure 35.12a. Japan can produce 15 million music videos and zero computer programs, or zero music videos and 30 million computer programs, or some combination along its PPF in Figure 35.12b.

Without international trade, people in the United States may consume 24 million music videos and 12 million computer programs, and people in Japan may

---

[9]Recall that the price in a supply/demand graph is always the relative price of the good. (See Chapter 4.) The $10 equilibrium price in Figure 35.10 takes as given the average level of other nominal prices. The equilibrium price would be $20 if other nominal prices were twice as high.

FIGURE 35.11

GAINS FROM TRADE BETWEEN SIMILAR COUNTRIES

Because the countries' equilibrium prices without trade differ less in this figure than in Figure 35.10, their gains from international trade (Areas B and D) are smaller than in Figure 35.10.

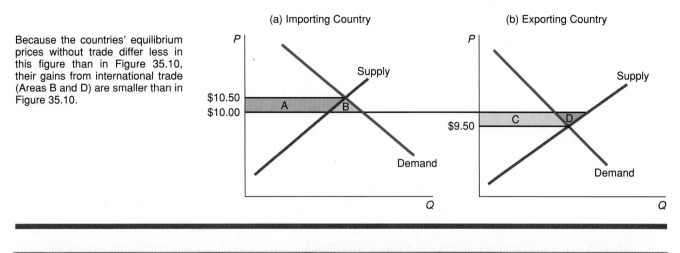

FIGURE 35.12

PRODUCTION POSSIBILITY FRONTIERS FROM TABLES 23.1 TO 23.3

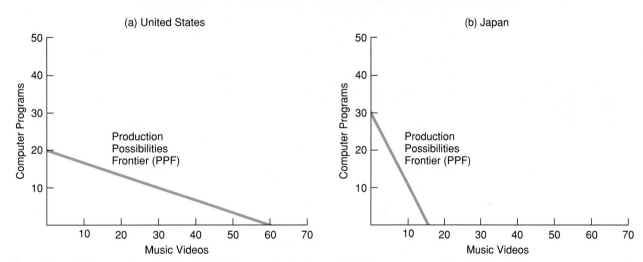

consume 12 million music videos and 6 million computer programs.[10] With international trade, their opportunities depend on prices. Suppose that the world

[10]The slopes of the PPFs show the relative prices of music videos and computer programs in the two countries without international trade. The relative price of computer programs in terms of music videos is 3 in the United States (equal to the opportunity cost listed in Table 35.3); one computer program costs the same as three music videos. The relative price of computer programs in terms of music videos is $\frac{1}{2}$ in Japan; one computer program costs half as much as one music video. Because music videos are relatively cheaper in the United States and computer programs are relatively cheaper in Japan, people in the United States may consume relatively more music videos and people in Japan may consume relatively more computer programs.

FIGURE 35.13

WORLD EQUILIBRIUM RELATIVE PRICE

The world equilibrium relative price is one-half of a music video per computer program.

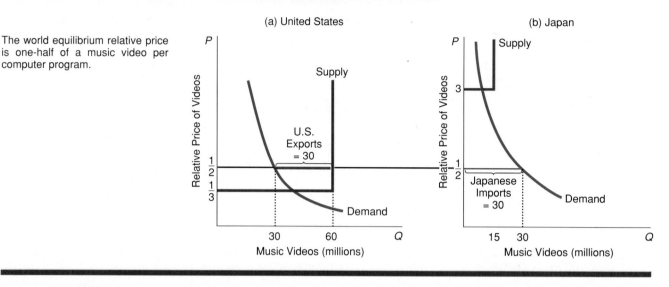

(a) United States   (b) Japan

equilibrium relative price is *one-half of a computer program per music video,* that is, a computer program costs twice as much as a music video, as in **Figure 35.13.** This defines a slope for the world price line (in absolute value) of one-half, as in **Figure 35.14,** which shows consumption opportunities in each country. The United States produces at Point A with 60 million music videos and no computer programs. It exports 30 million videos and imports 15 million computer programs, so people in the United States consume 30 million music videos and 15 million computer programs. Japan produces at Point B with 30 million computer programs and no music videos. It exports 15 million computer programs and imports 30 million music videos, so people in Japan consume 30 million music videos and 15 million computer programs. International trade, like an improvement in technology, allows everyone to consume more of every product.[11]

FOR REVIEW

35.6 What is a production possibilities frontier (PPF)?

35.7 Why does international trade increase a country's consumption possibilities?

QUESTION

35.8 How does international trade between two countries affect consumers and producers in each country? Draw a graph to show the sizes of the gains and losses from international trade to consumers and producers in each country.

---

[11]In this example, Japan gains more from international trade than does the United States. The division of the gains from international trade between the two countries depends on the world equilibrium relative price.

FIGURE 35.14

TRADE EXPANDS CONSUMPTION OPPORTUNITIES

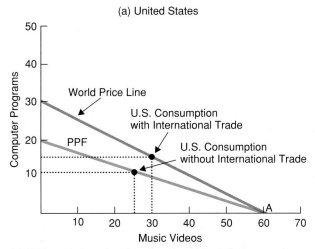

(a) United States

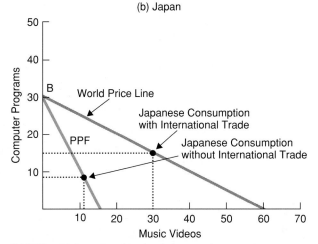

(b) Japan

(a) Without international trade, the United States produces and consumes 24 million music videos and 12 million computer programs. With international trade, it produces 60 million music videos, exports 30 million, and imports 15 million computer programs, so the United States consumes 30 million music videos and 15 million computer programs.

(b) Without international trade, Japan produces and consumes 12 million computer programs and 6 million music videos. With international trade, it produces 30 million computer programs, exports 15 million, and imports 30 million music videos, so Japan consumes 30 million music videos and 15 million computer programs.

REASONS FOR COMPARATIVE ADVANTAGE

Countries gain from trade because they differ in some way—they differ in either their PPFs or their consumer tastes. Production possibility frontiers differ across countries with different technologies or different supplies of inputs.

Technologies differ across countries partly because some countries have more advanced technical knowledge than others. They also differ because some countries work with newer, more advanced machinery and equipment that incorporates more recent technology while other countries work with older, less advanced machinery and equipment. Input supplies differ across countries partly because some countries have more abundant natural resources like oil resources, minerals, and farmland than others. Some countries have more capital (machinery and equipment) than others because they have invested more in the past. Some countries have more people—more potential workers—than others, and workers are more educated and more skilled in some countries than in others. Countries with small amounts of capital per worker tend to produce and export more labor-intensive products, which require relatively little capital per worker to produce, while countries with larger amounts of capital per worker tend to produce and export more capital-intensive products, which need more capital per worker. Countries with more *human capital* (skills, education, and knowledge) tend to produce and export goods that make use of their skills.[12] As noted earlier, the

---

[12]While differences in input supplies affect the pattern of international trade, international trade also affects input supplies. People who live in a country that exports goods whose production requires highly skilled labor have a greater incentive to acquire those skills.

TABLE 35.5

PRODUCTIVITY OF ONE PERSON

	Country A	Country B
Food	6 bushels	3 bushels
Sneakers	9 pairs	6 pairs

United States has relatively large relative quantities of land and skilled labor, and smaller relative quantities of capital and unskilled labor than other countries.

EVERY COUNTRY'S COMPARATIVE ADVANTAGE

Every country has a comparative advantage in something.[13] Even if a country has lower productivity than others in every industry, it still has a comparative advantage. **Table 35.5** shows lower productivity for Country B as compared to Country A in both the food industry and the sneakers industry. A worker in Country A can produce either 6 bushels of food or 9 pairs of sneakers in 1 day; a worker in Country B can produce only 3 bushels of food or 6 pairs of sneakers in a day.

Although workers in Country A are more productive in every industry, Country B has a comparative advantage in producing sneakers and Country A has a comparative advantage in producing food. The opportunity cost of one pair of sneakers produced in Country B is 1/2 (or 3/6) of a bushel of food. This is lower than the opportunity cost of one pair of sneakers produced in Country A, 2/3 (or 6/9) of a bushel of food. Even though Country B has lower productivity in every industry, it has a comparative advantage in producing sneakers and can gain from international trade by exporting sneakers and importing food.

HOW BIG ARE THE GAINS FROM INTERNATIONAL TRADE?

It is difficult to estimate precisely the total gains from international trade in real life, but evidence suggests that the gains are big. To see why, think about the gains from intercity trade, trade between cities in the same country. How much would your standard of living decline if you could not buy any products produced outside the city where you live? Most people would live much less well; each city would have to produce all of the food its people would eat, all of the materials for its housing, all of its consumer products, and so on. Most cities have few natural resources to become inputs into production of these goods. Most cities also lack sources of energy such as oil or natural gas. Trade between cities and between states clearly brings huge gains.[14]

The gains from international trade may be larger than Figure 35.10 suggests for three reasons. The economy benefits from dynamic gains from trade, extra gains from trade in industries with economies of scale, and political gains from trade.

---

[13]If two countries have exactly the same opportunity costs, the choice of which country has a comparative advantage in which good is arbitrary.

[14]The gains from international trade in small countries, such as Hong Kong or Luxembourg, resemble the gains from intercity trade in larger countries. People in larger countries reap somewhat smaller gains from international trade because they can trade with many other people within their own countries.

The gains from trade shown in Figure 35.10 are often called the *static gains from international trade.* The gains become larger if international trade helps countries to raise their productivity. This can occur if increased specialization increases the speed at which workers and firms learn from experience. In this way, international trade may accelerate increases in productivity and economic growth.

dynamic gains from trade — the benefits of increased economic growth and development due to international trade

Dynamic gains from trade refer to the benefits of increased economic growth and development due to international trade.

International trade can also contribute to economic efficiency and the incentive to innovate by providing firms with increased competition from foreign sellers. Some estimates suggest that the dynamic gains from trade exceed the static gains.

In some industries, *economies of scale* reduce the average cost of producing a product in larger quantities. (Per-unit costs fall with larger-scale operations.) International trade allows countries to specialize more, so it can reduce the costs of production in these industries. This adds to the gains from international trade.

Increased specialization also reduces the cost of producing a larger variety of sizes, colors, styles, and models of a product. People gain from an increase in variety because they can choose which style to buy. This also adds to the gains from international trade.

The political gains from trade refer to benefits of increased international dependencies, increased trust, better communication and understanding, increasingly frequent cultural exchanges, and reductions in chances of war due to international trade. People are less willing to shoot other people when those other people are their customers. By encouraging economic interactions and interdependencies, increased international trade may have many political and social benefits.

BALANCE OF TRADE AND THE CURRENT ACCOUNT

current account — the amount that a country lends to or borrows from other countries

current account surplus — net lending to other countries

current account deficit — net borrowing from other countries

People gain from international trade in *financial assets* as well as trade in goods and services. Trade in financial assets allows countries to borrow and lend and to diversify investments to reduce risk. When a country lends money to other countries or invests in those countries, it has a current account surplus.

The **current account** measures the amount that a country lends to or borrows from other countries. A country has a **current account surplus** when it lends and it has a **current account deficit** when it borrows.

The phrase "a country borrows" means that people, business firms, and units of government in one country borrow from people, business firms, and units of government in other countries.

A country that owes money on net to other countries because it has borrowed money in the past is a net debtor. A country to which other countries owe money is a net creditor. Net debtor countries pay interest and make loan repayments to other countries. Net creditor countries earn income by collecting interest and repayments of past loans.

The balance of trade and current account are closely related. A country's current account surplus equals its trade balance surplus plus its net income from investments in other countries:

Current account surplus = Trade balance surplus

+ Net income from foreign investments and transfer payments   **(35.1)**

In 1994, the United States exported goods and services worth $718 billion, and it imported goods and services worth $818 billion. U.S. GDP was $6.7 trillion, so the United States exported about 11 percent (or about one-ninth) of the goods and services it produced. Because imports exceeded exports by $100 billion, the United States had a $100 billion trade deficit.[15] Other countries shipped more goods and services to the United States than it shipped to them. Other countries were willing to make those shipments because the United States gave them financial assets (stocks, bonds, money, and other assets). In other words, the United States borrowed the money to pay for the excess of imports over exports; it borrowed the money to pay for its trade deficit.

The United States also borrowed from other countries to make transfer payments, mainly foreign aid and gifts, to other countries. The United States gave $36 billion more to other countries as gifts and foreign aid—transfer payments to foreigners—than it received. At the same time, foreigners earned slightly more on their U.S. investments ($162 billion) than the United States earned on its investments in other countries ($156 billion), leaving net income from foreign investments of −$6 billion. On transfer payments and income on foreign investments combined, the United States paid other countries $42 billion more than it collected from them in 1993. This means that the United States now owes these countries $42 billion more than before. These countries hold U.S. financial assets that resemble IOUs from the United States. The United States owes goods and services to these countries in the future. They get these goods and services by spending the interest payments on the financial assets or selling the financial assets to buy goods from the United States.

U.S. borrowing from other countries exceeded the trade balance deficit by $42 billion:

1994 U.S. current account surplus	=	1994 U.S. trade balance surplus	+	1994 U.S. net income from foreign investments and transfer payments
−$142 billion	=	−$100 billion	+	−$42 billion

Note that a *negative* surplus represents a *deficit;* the United States had a $100 billion trade deficit and a $142 billion current account deficit. This means that the United States borrowed $142 billion from other countries.

Similarly, a country with a trade surplus lends to people in other countries. If Germany sells goods worth 20 billion marks to other countries and imports goods worth only 16 billion marks, then Germany lends 4 billion marks to other countries. People in those countries receive only 16 billion marks from German buyers, but spend 20 billion marks, so they borrow the other 4 billion marks to spend on German goods.

Causes of Current Account Deficits

A country has a current account deficit when it saves less than it invests. A country can save less than it invests only by borrowing the extra money for investment from other countries. A country has a current account surplus when it saves more than it invests. A country can save more than it invests only by lending the extra savings to people in other countries.

---

[15]In Equation 35.1, this shows up as a negative number for the trade balance surplus.

Figure 35.15 shows three supply and demand diagrams. Panel a shows the supply of loans and the demand for loans in the United States. Panel b shows the supply and demand for loans in other countries. Panel c shows the world supply and demand for loans. This graph resembles Figure 35.9, which showed exports and imports of goods in international trade. Figure 35.15, in contrast, shows exports and imports of loans. If the United States could not borrow from other countries in this example, the U.S. interest rate would be 10 percent per year and the foreign interest rate would be 5 percent per year. International borrowing and lending, however, gives a world real interest rate of 7 percent per year. The United States borrows $142 billion from foreign countries, so the U.S. current account deficit is $142 billion. Other countries lend $142 billion to the United States, so the rest of the world has a current account surplus of $142 billion.

The current account changes when the demand or supply of loans changes in any country. Most economists believe that U.S. government budget deficits are a main cause of U.S. current account deficits. According to the majority view, a tax cut that causes a government budget deficit raises the U.S. demand for loans more than the supply. Without international borrowing and lending, the deficit would raise the real interest rate in the United States. By borrowing and lending on international markets, however, the United States can meet part of its increased demand for loans. Borrowing from other countries raises the U.S. current account deficit.

The evidence on government budget deficits and current account deficits issue is mixed. U.S. current account deficits increased substantially in the mid-1980s soon after government budget deficits increased, but the two deficits are not tightly linked in other periods. **Figure 35.16** shows that the current account deficit appears to follow the budget deficit after a lag of 1 or 2 years.

FIGURE 35.15

WORLD LOAN MARKET EQUILIBRIUM

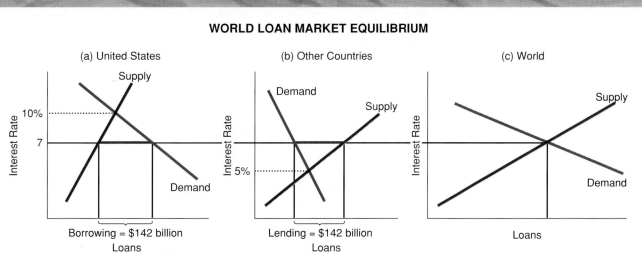

Without international borrowing and lending, the equilibrium interest rate in the United States is 10 percent per year. With international borrowing and lending, the world equilibrium interest rate is 7 percent per year and the United States borrows $142 billion from other countries. (It has a $142 billion current account deficit.)

FIGURE 35.16

TWIN U.S. DEFICITS: GOVERNMENT BUDGET DEFICIT AND CURRENT ACCOUNT DEFICITS

Real government budget deficit measured by increases in the real value of the federal government debt held by the public.

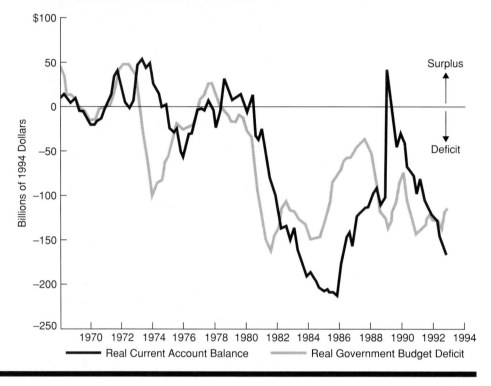

Several other factors also affect the current account deficit. Tax policies affect both the supply of loans and the demand for loans by affecting investment demand. Changes in technology raise the demand for loans by increasing the demand for investment. Changes in people's tastes for spending or saving money, or changes in expected future incomes, affect savings and the supply of loans. These and other factors affect the current account by affecting the supply or demand for loans.

EFFECTS OF CURRENT ACCOUNT DEFICITS

Are trade deficits good or bad? The term *deficit* sounds bad, and people often express concern about trade deficits. Some people appear to believe that exports create jobs (so exports are good) and imports destroy jobs (so imports are bad); they conclude that trade deficits reduce domestic employment.[16] Against this view, one might argue for the benefits of imports; they give a country products to consume without producing them, while exports require people to work to produce goods for other countries to enjoy.

Both arguments are misleading. Current account deficits and surpluses occur because people borrow from and lend to people in other countries. These loans

---

[16]This is the argument behind buy-American campaigns.

are voluntary trades, and people expect to benefit from them. A country has a current account deficit when it trades away future products to get more current products. Similarly, a current account surplus occurs when a country trades current products to get more future products.

Trade deficits may *appear* to reduce the total number of jobs available because jobs supported by exports are easier to identify than jobs supported (indirectly) by imports. U.S. imports, for example, create American jobs indirectly by providing foreigners with dollars to spend on American products. (When the foreign sellers do not spend those dollars, they lend the money to borrowers who *do* spend it.) Both imports and exports create local jobs. For the same reason, buying strictly American goods does not create more American jobs. It simply changes the composition of those jobs by creating more jobs in import-competing industries and fewer jobs in export industries and other industries.

Some people mistakenly believe that trade deficits reduce total spending on domestic goods, that is, aggregate demand. With sticky nominal prices in the short run, a fall in aggregate demand (total spending on domestic products) can reduce real GDP and employment in the short run. When a country such as the United States has a trade deficit, foreigners earn more dollars selling imports to America than they spend on American products. Foreigners do not simply keep those dollars, though.[17] They either lend the dollars or invest them in American assets such as real estate or stocks. When they lend the dollars, the borrowers spend them on American products; when foreigners buy real estate, stocks, or other assets, the people who sold those assets have more dollars to spend. So trade deficits do not necessarily reduce aggregate demand.

In fact, trade deficits usually accompany high aggregate demand. To see why, recall that an increase in the demand for loans in the United States can cause a U.S. trade deficit (and a current account deficit). That increase in the demand for loans also raises the equilibrium world interest rate. The higher interest rate raises the velocity of money, which raises aggregate demand.[18] The demand for loans may rise due to an increase in the government budget deficit or due to an exogenous increase in consumption or investment spending. In either case, the trade deficit rises along with the increase in aggregate demand. Similarly, a fall in the demand for loans may result from either an exogenous fall in consumption or investment spending or a fall in government borrowing. In either case, it reduces the interest rate, velocity, and aggregate demand while it reduces the trade deficit. That is why the trade deficit tends to be smaller in recessions.

When a recession begins, people may blame the trade deficit for the economy's rising unemployment and suggest trade restrictions to reduce the deficit. Trade restrictions are unlikely to raise aggregate demand, however, so they are unlikely to reduce unemployment. After all, the trade deficit does not cause unemployment to rise; both result from a fall in aggregate demand. Trade

---

[17]If they did, the United States would enjoy immense gains because it could trade away paper money (which is cheap to produce) for useful goods and services produced in other countries.

[18]Recall that nominal aggregate demand equals *MV,* the money supply times the velocity of money. With a constant money supply, an increase in velocity raises aggregate demand. As an earlier chapter explained, velocity rises when the nominal interest rate rises. An increase in the demand for loans raises the real interest rate. This raises the nominal interest rate (unless expected inflation falls at the same time), which raises both velocity and aggregate demand.

restrictions would raise jobs in import-competing industries by destroying jobs in other industries, but no evidence suggests that trade deficits reduce the total number of available jobs.

In summary, trade deficits *per se* are neither good or bad. They may reflect good or bad underlying economic conditions, but trade deficits are at least as likely to reflect high aggregate demand and low unemployment as the opposite. People have no more reason to be concerned about current account deficits—borrowing from people in foreign countries—than they have to worry about borrowing from a local bank to buy a car or take a vacation. A country with a current account deficit would have a higher real interest rate if it could not borrow from other countries. Borrowing always means trading future goods to obtain more current goods. A borrowing country incurs a debt, which it must repay (or pay interest on indefinitely).[19] When a country repays its loans or makes interest payments on them, it exports more than it imports. In other words, current account deficits do not last forever.

FOR REVIEW

35.9 What are the dynamic gains from trade? What are the political gains from trade?

35.10 What is the current account? How is it related to the balance of trade?

35.11 What can cause a current account deficit?

QUESTIONS

35.12 Are current account deficits necessarily bad for the economy?

35.13 Suppose that an increase in consumer confidence in the United States leads people to spend more on entertainment and save less. Draw a graph of the supply and demand for loans similar to Figure 35.14 to show how this affects the current account.

PROTECTIONISM

protectionism — government policies that restrict imports

Governments often act to restrict international trade. Because restrictions on imports protect domestic firms from foreign competition, government restrictions on imports are often referred to as *protectionism.*

Protectionism refers to government policies that restrict imports.

Allowing free international trade usually enhances economic efficiency for the reasons discussed earlier in this chapter; protectionist policies almost always cause economic inefficiency. Some people gain and some people lose from restricting imports, but the losses to the losers (such as consumers) exceed the gains to the winners (mainly domestic firms protected from foreign competition). Trade restrictions help domestic firms to keep their prices high by reducing competition. The restrictions prevent consumers from buying products from foreign com-

---

[19]A country can repay its loans by borrowing again; by rolling over loans in this way, the country ends up paying interest on them forever.

petitors or impose special taxes on purchases from those foreign competitors. Trade restrictions tend to occur when the groups that stand to benefit have greater political influence than the groups that stand to lose.

TYPES OF TRADE RESTRICTIONS

The two most prominent forms of restrictions on international trade are tariffs and import quotas.

tariff — a tax on imports

> A **tariff** is a tax on imports.

import quota — a restriction on the number of imported goods of a certain type

> An **import quota** is a direct limit on the number of imported goods of a certain type.

The U.S. government has imposed tariffs in recent years on computers, ball bearings, and many other goods. It has imposed import quotas on steel, sugar, textiles, ice cream, and many other products. Japan has set quotas for imports of beef, oranges, and rice.

Other forms of trade restrictions include voluntary export restraints (VERs), which work like unofficial quotas in which the government of a country agrees "voluntarily" to limit its exports to another country. A country may agree to limit its exports to avert a threat of another country placing tariffs or quotas on its exports if it does not voluntarily restrict them.[20] The United States induced Japan to begin voluntary export restraints on its cars starting in 1981. According to one estimate, this raised the U.S. prices of Japanese cars by about $2,500 each and raised the prices of American cars by about $1,000 each. U.S. pressure led Japan to reduce its automobile exports further (to 1.65 million cars per year) in 1992. Under similar pressure, other countries have put VERs on a variety of other goods.

Another form of trade restriction, *a local content requirement*, creates a legal minimum fraction (perhaps one-half) of the value of the parts of a good (such as a car) that must come from producers in the domestic country rather than from imports. Another form of protectionism, *bureaucratic (red tape) protectionism*, prevents sellers from a foreign country from legally selling their goods until they complete a set of bureaucratic procedures. Those bureaucratic procedures are designed to raise costs to foreign producers. Government regulations, sometimes disguised as health and safety regulations, also serve as trade restrictions. Suppose, for example, that foreign firms and domestic firms use different types of inputs in their products. The inputs may be identical in every important respect, but a government may ban the input used by foreign firms and try to justify the move on health or safety grounds. The effect is still to restrict imports from the foreign firms, though.

EFFECTS OF TARIFFS

Figure 35.17 shows the effects of a tariff. This figure applies to tariffs that do not affect the world price of the good. For example, the United States buys only a small fraction of the world's tea, so a fall in purchases of tea by people in the United States reduces the world demand for tea—and the world price—by such a small amount that economists can ignore it in practice.

---

[20]The restriction is often voluntary in the same sense that a crime victim voluntarily gives up a wallet to a mugger.

Some U.S. Trade Restrictions

Quotas restrict imports of foreign ice cream to about 1 teaspoonful per American per year, imports of foreign peanuts to about 2 per person per year, and cheese to about 1 pound per person per year.

Tariffs on imports of low-priced watch parts have recently reached 151 percent; tariffs on some shoe imports have been 67 percent. The tariff on orange juice has been 40 percent; the tariff on mushrooms has been 25 percent. Tariffs have reached 41 percent on grapefruit juice, 20 percent on watermelon, 35 percent on dates, and 20 percent on yogurt. The tariff on imports of brooms is 42 percent, and 25 percent on imported flashlights. The U.S. imposed a 100 percent tariff on Japanese computers in 1987.

Source: James Bovard, *The Fair Trade Fraud* (New York: St. Martin's Press, 1991).

Suppose that the U.S. government puts a tariff on imports of tea. P^{US} is the price including tax (that is, including the tariff) that buyers pay for imported tea. Foreign sellers receive the after-tax world price P^W. The difference, $P^{US} - P^W$, is the per-unit tariff that the government collects.

As the tariff raises the U.S. price of tea above the world price, tea producers in the United States also raise their prices to P^{US}, so they benefit from the tariff, raising their production and sales from 10 to 15 units. Area A shows the gain to U.S. producers (the increase in their profits) from the tariff. The tariff

FIGURE 35.17

EFFECTS OF A TARIFF

Without a tariff, the United States produces 10 goods, imports 24, and consumes 34. With a tariff, the U.S. price rises from P^W to P^{US}, U.S. production rises to 15 goods, U.S. imports fall to 9, and U.S. consumption falls to 24. U.S. consumers lose Areas A + B + C + D from the tariff. U.S. producers gain Area A, and the U.S. government gains Area C in tariff (tax) revenue. The difference, Area B + D, is a deadweight social loss from the tariff.

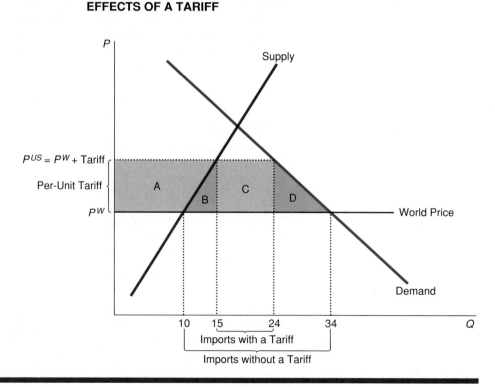

IN THE NEWS

Hong Kong agrees to limit exports of textiles to U.S.

*By Eduardo Lachica
Staff Reporter of The
Wall Street Journal*

WASHINGTON—Hong Kong agreed to sharply curb the growth of its textile and apparel exports to the U.S. through 1991.

"Obviously, we aren't happy about it, but like it or not there is a lot of protectionist pressure (in the U.S.) that forced us to make a realistic assessment of what we could get," said Hamish MacLeod, chief textile negotiator for Hong Kong.

▲

Japanese quota extension pleases Detroit

But car-export limit is likely to hurt U.S. consumers

*By Joseph B. White
Staff Reporter of The
Wall Street Journal*

The Japanese government's decision to keep a cap on car exports to the U.S. pleased Detroit's auto makers, who will keep the benefit of trade restraint even though they may report record profits for 1988.

Detroit's gain, however, is likely to come at the expense of U.S. consumers. For them, Japan's decision announced yesterday to maintain a 2.3 million-car limit on annual exports to the U.S. means the most popular Japanese cars probably will remain expensive and in short supply.

"The impact of the quotas is quite heavy on the consumer," said a spokesman for Toyota Motor Corp.'s U.S. sales arm. "You're just making people pay more for products, and the extra money is going into Detroit's pocket, and ours."

Begun in 1981

The quotas were first established in 1981 as a device to give U.S. auto makers time to recover from the nation's deep recession. Detroit's Big Three, however, have earned near-record profits in the past 2 years, so the auto makers are using different arguments to press for continued quotas. Chief among them: the overall U.S. trade deficit is so bad that almost any measure is justified to reduce it.

Trade restrictions imposed by the United States.

Sources: Eduardo Lachica, "Hong Kong Agrees to Limit Exports of Textiles to U.S." *The Wall Street Journal,* June 1, 1986, p. 30; and Joseph B. White, "Japanese Quota Extension Pleases Detroit," *The Wall Street Journal,* January 11, 1989, p. A9.

hurts American consumers because it raises the U.S. price of tea.[21] Total sales of tea in the United States fall from 34 (10 from U.S. firms and 24 imported from foreign firms) to 24. Imports fall from 24 to 9. American consumers lose Areas A, B, C, and D from the tariff. The U.S. government gains Area C because people pay the government ($P^{US} - P^{W}$) for each of the 14 units they continue to import.

The total benefit to the government and to U.S. producers—Areas A + C — is smaller than the loss to U.S. consumers—Areas A + B + C + D. The tariff creates

---

[21]Even though the tariff applies only to imports, the higher price of imported goods reduces the foreign competition facing U.S. producers, so U.S. producers also raise their price. The price increase applies to tea produced anywhere, not just imported tea.

Big tariff put on sweetener

BRUSSELS, Nov. 29 (Reuters) — The European Commission today imposed large duties on cut-price imports of the low-calorie sweetener aspartame from the United States and Japan to protect the only European producer of the product.

The duties, which will add 70 percent to the imported prices almost overnight, came just days before the final phase of talks on liberalizing trade were scheduled to begin here.

Another trade restriction.

Source: "Big Tariff Put on Sweetener," *New York Times,* November 30, 1990, p. D6.

winners and losers, but the losers lose more than the winners win. The difference is a deadweight social loss, or loss to society as a whole, because the tariff causes economic inefficiency. The deadweight social loss equals Areas B + D in Figure 35.17.

This deadweight social loss is similar to the loss in the two-student example of Chapter 3 if the students clean and paint their own apartments rather than trading. In that example, each student gains leisure time by trading. Tariffs reduce international trade, so people get fewer gains from trade than they would get without tariffs.

TARIFFS AND WORLD PRICES

When a country buys a large enough fraction of total world sales of a good, a tariff can actually reduce the world price of that good. This benefits the country that imposes the tariff by reducing the price it pays for imports. If this benefit is large enough (larger than the deadweight social loss from the tariff), then a country can gain by imposing a tariff. The country's gain, though, comes at the expense of even bigger losses in foreign countries, that is, greater world economic inefficiency.

Although a country can sometimes gain at the expense of other countries from a tariff, evidence indicates that countries usually lose on net from the tariffs they impose. In most real-life situations, governments impose tariffs not because their countries stand to gain overall from the tariffs, but because the winners (firms that want to reduce foreign competition) have more political influence than the losers (such as consumers).

Tariffs can provoke foreign retaliation. If the United States imposes tariffs on imports of a product from the European Union (EU), the EU may in turn impose tariffs on its imports of American products. In the end, all countries are likely to lose. Even if a country could gain from some tariff considered in isolation, it may lose after evaluating all the effects of the tariff, including the political forces that create retaliation.

EFFECTS OF NONTARIFF TRADE RESTRICTIONS

Import quotas have effects similar to those of tariffs, but with one main difference: the government collects no tax revenue from a quota. A quota limits the *quantity* of imports. Figure 35.17 shows the effects of a tariff, and it also shows the effects of a quota that limits U.S. imports to 14 units. The interpretation of the figure changes only slightly. Area C represents a profit to the people who are legally allowed to import the 14 units of foreign goods, instead of a gain to the government. They profit because they can buy those imported goods at the low world price, P^W, and resell them at the higher U.S. price, $P^{US};$ Area C shows the profits from these resales. Otherwise, a quota has the same effect as a tariff; the U.S. loses Area B + D from the import quota.

A voluntary export restraint (VER) has almost the same effect as a quota, with one difference: the people who gain the Area C in Figure 35.17 are the *foreign producers* whom the foreign government allows to export the 14 units of the product. The effects of bureaucratic restrictions are also similar to the effects of a tariff, since paying employees to handle the red tape is like paying a tax. The main difference is that the government does not collect the tariff revenue. Instead, Area C in Figure 35.17 represents spending by foreign firms to comply with the government's bureaucratic procedures.[22]

---

[22]Trade with some countries requires paying bribes to appropriate officials; the effects of these bribes resemble the effects of tariffs.

TABLE 35.6

LOSSES AND GAINS DUE TO PROTECTIONISM (1990 $ MILLIONS)

Protected Industry	Loss to American Consumers	Gain to American Producers	Gain to U.S. Government	Net Loss to U.S. Economy
Ceramics and tiles	$ 241	$ 63	$ 173	$ 5
Costume jewelry	103	46	51	5
Frozen concentrated orange juice	281	101	145	35
Glassware	266	162	95	9
Luggage	211	16	169	26
Rubber footwear	208	55	141	12
Women's footwear (excluding athletic shoes)	376	70	295	11
Apparel	21,158	9,901	3,545	7,712 (2,301)[a]
Textiles	3,274	1,749	632	894 (181)[a]
Canned tuna	73	31	31	10 (4)[a]
Machine tools	542	157	0	385 (35)[a]

[a]The first figure shows the net loss to the U.S. economy; the second figure (in parentheses) shows that loss after including the gains to foreign firms from U.S. protectionism.

Source: Gary Clyde Hufbauer and Kimberly Ann Elliott, *Measuring the Costs of Protection in the United States* (Washington, D.C.: Institute for International Economics, 1994).

SCOPE OF PROTECTIONISM

How much does protectionism cost? A recent study estimates that in 1990, protectionism cost U.S. consumers about $70 billion per year (about $270 per person each year).[23] Domestic producers gained about $35 billion from these restrictions, and they brought the government about $13 billion in revenue, so the net loss to the U.S. economy from protectionism was about $22 billion per year (about $85 per person each year). **Table 35.6** summarizes the losses to consumers and gains to producers in certain industries.

Governments engage in less protectionism now than they did in the past. The average U.S. tariff rate in 1920 was 16 percent. It increased to 38 percent in 1922 partly because the government raised tariffs and partly because tariff rates rose automatically due to falling prices.[24] The Smoot-Hawley Act of 1930 and more increases in tariff rates due to falling prices raised the average U.S. tariff rate to 53 percent, though tariffs applied to only about one-third of U.S. imports.

In 1947, many countries signed the General Agreement on Tariffs and Trade (GATT) to reduce trade restrictions. The GATT also established an international organization in Geneva, Switzerland, to assist trade negotiations and work to

---

[23]See Gary Clyde Hufbauer and Kimberly Ann Elliott, *Measuring the Costs of Protection in the United States* (Washington, D.C.: Institute for International Economics, 1994).

[24]If a good costs $10 and the tariff is $2, then the tariff rate is 20 percent. If the price of the good falls to $5 and the tariff stays at $2, the tariff rate rises to 40 percent. Prices fell from 1920 to 1922, which raised tariff rates automatically.

reduce restrictions on trade. The most recent round of international trade talks has renamed the GATT as the World Trade Organization (WTO).

World Trade Organization (WTO) — formerly the General Agreement on Tariffs and Trade (GATT), a 117-country organization and a series of related treaties that reduce trade restrictions

The **World Trade Organization (WTO),** formerly the General Agreement on Tariffs and Trade (GATT), is a 117-country organization and a series of related treaties that reduce trade restrictions.

The GATT has helped to reduce world protectionism in the last half of the 20th century. The United States reduced its tariffs to an average of about 25 percent, covering only about one-tenth of its imports, by 1960. Other countries also reduced trade restrictions. The Kennedy Round of GATT talks in 1967 reduced tariffs further; U.S. tariffs fell to an average of about 12 percent, covering only 7 percent of imports. The Tokyo Round in 1979 reduced U.S. tariff rates to 6 percent, covering only 4 percent of imports, with similar reductions in other countries.

The WTO now includes 117 countries. The latest agreement, the Uruguay Round, concluded in 1993 after 8 years of negotiations. In that agreement, the United States and the European Union agreed to cut tariffs on each others' goods in half (on average) and to cut tariffs on goods from other countries by a smaller amount. On average, the Uruguay Round reduced world tariffs by about one-third, and it requires countries to replace import quotas on many products with more visible tariffs. It also includes pioneering agreements on certain products, such as farm products and intellectual property (protection of patents, copyrights, and trademarks).[25] The agreement also gave the WTO new powers to resolve trade disputes more quickly and at lower cost than previous arrangements. Estimates suggest that the agreement will eventually raise U.S. real GDP by about $100 billion per year and world real GDP by about $300 billion.

The North American Free Trade Agreement (NAFTA) began with a 1989 agreement between Canada and the United States to reduce and eliminate many trade restrictions between the two countries. Restrictions will be eliminated gradually through January 1, 1999, at which point Canada and the United States are supposed to have completely free international trade with each other. The NAFTA was extended in 1993 to include Mexico and is likely soon to include Chile. It may eventually include other countries in the American continents.

European countries are not left out of the trend toward freer international trade. Recently, countries in the European Union have established free trade with each other. EU member countries jointly set trade restrictions with non-EU countries. The EU was created in 1957 by France, Germany, Italy, Belgium, the Netherlands, and Luxembourg, though free trade within the EU is more recent. **Table 35.7** lists the 12 current member countries of the EU and members of the European Free Trade Association (EFTA), which includes European countries that are not members of the EU, but want to participate in free trade with EU countries. The EU plans further steps toward European economic integration, perhaps including creation of a single money to be used in all or most EU countries.

The increasing economic integration of Europe has important consequences for the United States and other countries. About 400 million people live in EU and EFTA countries, roughly as many as in the United States and Japan combined.[26] Free trade within Europe will help to raise European standards of living in the

---

[25]It failed to resolve trade disputes, however, on certain products such as movies, television shows, music, and shipping and financial services.

[26]Of these, only 40 million live in the EFTA countries: those countries have relatively small populations.

U.S. and Europe clear the way for a world accord on trade, setting aside major disputes

Big cut in tariffs

Movies, TV, and financial services are some of the areas left out

By Keith Bradsher
Special to The
New York Times

GENEVA, Dec. 14—The United States and Europe agreed to put aside major trade disputes today, clearing the way for a world trade accord covering more indus-

tries in more countries than any other trade agreement in history.

"The stakes are immense," the President said. "This would be the single largest trade agreement ever. It writes new rules of the road for world trade well into the next century."

▲

Japan ends ban on rice imports

Coalition government acts at brink of deadline for trade talks

By T. R. Reid
Washington Post
Foreign Service

TOKYO, Dec. 14 (Tuesday)— Prime Minister Morihiro Hosokawa reversed three decades of agriculture policy with a predawn announce-

ment today that Japan will end its ban on rice imports to fulfill its obligations under the General Agreement on Tariffs and Trade.

The policy shift has provoked weeks of fury from farmers and their political allies.

But Hosokawa, arguably Japan's most skillful political analyst, seems once again to have gauged the popular will better than his fellow politi-

cians. Every national poll for the past few months has shown that most people agree the time has come to import rice.

Still, rice import liberalization in Japan is a political issue similar to gun control in the U.S. Even with majority support in the polls, the step is tough for politicians, because opponents tend to be intensely motivated, single-issue voters.

▲

GATT, at last

The new trade agreement might best be understood by looking at one U.S. company, Caterpillar Inc. The big construction equipment maker sells worldwide, so eliminating tariffs on its goods will save its foreign customers $100 million a year. That makes the company's machines more affordable. And because many foreign tariffs are higher than those in this country, Cat's products are also more competitive.

But the GATT deal goes well beyond tariff cuts, and Caterpillar and others stand to benefit in these areas as well. For example, the new trade deal phases out laws that require manufacturers to buy some of their components in the countries where they do business—so-called local content rules. Caterpillar, like many U.S. companies, has been forced to buy parts and supplies where it didn't

make economic sense so it could keep selling in some key markets. That will end.

Likewise, Caterpillar— and all companies—will benefit from new global protections on trademarks and patents. Since most countries have agreed to beef up safeguards in these areas, the $455 million Caterpillar invested in new processes and products last year is better protected.

The U.S. government has signed two important free trade accords in recent years: the NAFTA and the GATT.

Sources: Keith Bradsher, "U.S. and Europe Clear the Way for a World Accord on Trade, Setting Aside Major Disputes," *New York Times,* December 15, 1993, p. 1; T. R. Reid, "Japan Ends Ban on Rice Imports," *Washington Post,* December 14, 1993, p. A19; *Journal of Commerce,* April 15, 1994, p. 6A.

TABLE 35.7

EUROPEAN TRADING ORGANIZATIONS AND COUNTRIES

European Union (EU) Members[a]		European Free Trade Association (EFTA) Members[a]	
Belgium	Ireland	Austria	Norway
Britain	Italy	Finland	Sweden
Denmark	Luxembourg	Iceland	Switzerland
France	Netherlands	Liechtenstein	
Germany	Portugal		
Greece	Spain		

[a]As of 1991.

future. If trade restrictions between Europe and other countries remain low, the gains will be even larger, and most of the world will share those gains. If the European countries impose bigger trade barriers with countries outside the continent, however, this could hurt the United States, Japan, and other countries. Some analysts are concerned that regional free trade agreements in Europe and North America reduce the incentives for world free trade; other analysts see these agreements as steps toward that goal.

FOR REVIEW

35.15 What is protectionism?

35.16 What are tariffs, import quotas, and voluntary export restraints?

35.17 What is the WTO? What is the NAFTA? What is the EU?

QUESTION

35.18 Draw a graph to illustrate the effects of a tariff. Who gains and who loses from the tariff? Show the sizes of the gains and losses on your graph.

COMMON ARGUMENTS FOR PROTECTIONISM

Groups that favor trade restrictions (usually to benefit themselves) have advanced many arguments to justify their positions. Economists generally agree that these arguments are usually incorrect, and that legitimate arguments do not apply to most real-life cases of trade restrictions. This section considers some of the most common arguments for protectionism.

ARGUMENT 1.   DOMESTIC FIRMS NEED TRADE RESTRICTIONS TO COMPETE IN WORLD MARKETS

This argument is fallacious. Every country has a comparative advantage in certain products. Domestic firms can profitably sell those products in world markets if they produce them. Firms that produce other products, those in which the country has no comparative advantage, fail to compete on world markets because their costs are higher than the costs of foreign firms. Losses at those firms, along with profits at firms producing the products at which the country has a comparative advantage, provide incentives to direct the nation's resources to their most economically efficient uses.

One form of the argument for protection to bolster domestic competitiveness states that domestic producers cannot compete on world markets because foreign countries pay lower wages in every industry. This means, the argument goes, that no domestic producers in any industry can compete in world markets. Imagine what would happen if this were true, if every domestic firm faced competition from foreign sellers who could charge lower prices based on lower costs. All domestic firms would lose most of their customers to foreign competitors. Domestic firms would lay off workers, and the demand for labor would fall. This fall in the demand for labor would reduce its price (the wage rate), so wages would fall. This fall in wages would continue until some domestic firms' costs would fall to or below the levels of foreign competitors. These firms would produce the products in which the country would have a comparative advantage. In summary, the level of wages adjusts so that (in equilibrium) firms in every country can compete in world markets.[27]

ARGUMENT 2.   TRADE RESTRICTIONS PROTECT JOBS

Trade restrictions save jobs in some industries, but they eliminate jobs in other industries. Suppose that the United States imposes a tariff on imports of foreign cars. This raises the price of cars in the United States and raises sales of American-made cars. The tariff creates jobs in the protected American car industry, but it destroys jobs in other industries for two reasons. First, American consumers spend more on cars, leaving them less income to spend on other products (movies, clothes, food, and so on). Sales of these other products fall, destroying jobs in those industries. Second, foreigners earn fewer dollars because they sell fewer cars to U.S. buyers; this reduces their spending on American products and destroys jobs in various American industries. While trade restrictions create jobs in protected industries, they destroy jobs in other industries. On net, trade restrictions have little effect on total employment.[28]

NOTE ON TRADE DEFICITS

What happens if foreigners do not spend the dollars they earn to buy American products? This creates a trade deficit for the United States. For example, in 1994 the United States imported $818 billion in goods and services from other countries, and exported only $718 billion. On net, foreigners earned $100 billion by selling products in the United States. (They also obtained $42 billion from the United States in gifts, foreign aid, and net income on U.S. investments.) They did not spend all $142 billion on American products. Instead, they loaned some of those dollars back to people in the United States and invested the rest in assets such as American real estate and stocks. Notice that the Americans who borrowed the money or sold the assets had the dollars available to spend. As a result, a trade

---

[27]Wages in the United States are higher than wages in most other countries of the world, but American firms are nevertheless able to compete in world markets because productivity at American firms is substantially higher than the levels in most other countries.

[28]Much international trade occurs in intermediate products, those that become inputs into the production of other, final products. Restricting imports of intermediate products raises costs at domestic firms producing final products. The higher costs reduce those firms' supplies of final products, reduce their equilibrium sales, and reduce employment at those firms.

deficit does not necessarily affect total spending on American-made products. Foreigners spent $142 billion less on American products than Americans spent on foreign products and gave as gifts, but foreigners lent $142 billion back to Americans to spend.

However, a trade deficit can *result* from a change in total spending (aggregate demand). A country's trade deficit can rise for one of two reasons: either loan demand in that country rises (people want to borrow more), or loan supply in other countries rises (foreigners want to lend more). In the first case, the equilibrium interest rate rises; in the second case, it falls. In the first case, the velocity of money rises, while in the second case, it falls. Overall, rising domestic loan demand raises aggregate demand, while rising foreign loan supply reduces aggregate demand.[29] As earlier chapters explained, changes in aggregate demand can change real GDP in the short run if nominal prices or wages are sticky, so a trade deficit may occur along with an increase in aggregate demand and a rise in total employment. (This happens over the course of a business cycle; trade deficits tend to rise when real GDP rises, and they tend to fall in recessions.) A trade deficit may also occur along with a fall in aggregate demand and a fall in total employment. When this happens, people may blame the trade deficit for the economy's rising unemployment, though the trade deficit does not really cause the rise in unemployment. Instead, both result from the fall in aggregate demand. Trade restrictions are unlikely to raise aggregate demand, so they are unlikely to reduce unemployment. In summary, trade restrictions save jobs in some industries by destroying jobs in other industries. No evidence supports the claim that trade restrictions protect the total number of available jobs.

ARGUMENT 3. TRADE RESTRICTIONS RAISE WAGES

Trade restrictions do not necessarily raise domestic wages. If a country has a comparative advantage in producing a product that requires a relatively large input of labor, then international trade is likely to raise wages and trade restrictions will likely reduce wages. In other circumstances, however, international trade may reduce wages, so restricting international trade can raise wages. Even in these circumstances, however, international trade reduces the economy's total income.

While expanding international trade has been good for the United States as a whole, it has created winners and losers. Some evidence indicates that the expansion of international trade has contributed to the fall in wages of low-skilled U.S. workers that has occurred since the early 1970s. Trade restrictions would redistribute income, raising wages in certain industries at the expense of people who do not work in those industries and causing a net loss in income to the economy. If the government wants to redistribute income, it is likely to do so more efficiently by redistributing income directly, taxing some people and transferring the money to other people, rather than redistributing indirectly through trade restrictions.

ARGUMENT 4. TRADE RESTRICTIONS LEVEL THE PLAYING FIELD

Some people argue for trade restrictions to keep a so-called "level playing field" in international trade. ("Other countries have them, so we should, too.")

---

[29]Recall that nominal aggregate demand equals *MV*, the money supply times the velocity of money. In this case, the money supply does not change, but changes in velocity resulting from changes in the interest rate cause changes in aggregate demand.

International trade is not like a football game or a war, though. International trade, like all voluntary trade, occurs because both sides expect to gain, and both sides usually do. Trade restrictions reduce economic efficiency and redistribute income from domestic consumers to protected domestic producers, whether or not other countries impose their own trade restrictions.

Suppose that subsidies by the Korean government lead Korean firms to reduce the prices of goods they sell in the United States. Should the United States respond with trade restrictions to protect American firms that compete with those Korean firms? Notice that the Korean government subsidies help American consumers because they can buy the Korean products at lower prices. The subsidies hurt American producers who compete with the Korean firms. Korean taxpayers lose because they pay for the subsidies, while Korean firms benefit from the subsidies.

How large are these gains and losses? It is easy to show that American consumers gain more than American firms lose. To see why, notice that American firms lose because they must reduce prices to compete, but every dollar they lose from reduced prices is a gain to American buyers who pay those lower prices! In fact, American consumers gain even more because they buy some Korean products at prices subsidized by Korean taxpayers. Therefore, the United States *gains* on net when a foreign government subsidizes its nation's producers. Trade restrictions would prevent the domestic country from getting those gains.[30]

Another version of the level playing field argument for trade restrictions claims that foreign firms sometimes charge lower prices on exports than they charge for sales in their own countries. This is popularly called *dumping*. Dumping is illegal, and most countries restrict imports of goods from foreign firms that they find guilty of dumping. For example, in 1985, the United States required Japanese semiconductor producers to raise the prices they charged to American buyers. Who gains and who loses from dumping? The answer resembles the case of foreign subsidies. Consumers benefit from low prices if a foreign firm dumps. Firms that compete with the foreign firm lose because they must charge lower prices. Gains to domestic buyers match all the losses to domestic firms from charging lower prices, however. Buyers also gain when they buy foreign products at the lower price, so dumping benefits domestic consumers more than it hurts domestic producers.[31] One study estimated that U.S. trade restrictions imposed in retaliation for dumping cost American consumers $2.6 billion per year and create a net annual loss to the U.S. economy of roughly $1 billion.

ARGUMENT 5.   TEMPORARY TRADE RESTRICTIONS HELP INDUSTRIES GET STARTED

Some people argue that infant industries—new industries that are not yet well-established—need protection from foreign competition if they have high start-up costs. Without trade restrictions, the argument claims, these firms would not be

---

[30]Sometimes people argue that a foreign government may subsidize its producers only long enough to drive domestic firms out of business, then eliminate the subsidies. No evidence suggests that this happens in real life. If domestic firms expect a foreign government to discontinue its subsidy in the future, they will reduce production only temporarily and resume production when the subsidies stop. So this argument provides little justification for trade restrictions.

[31]Dumping is illegal in most countries, presumably, because domestic firms (that are harmed by dumping) have stronger political influence on this issue than domestic consumers.

IN THE NEWS

Imported sweaters face duty

U.S. finds dumping by Far East makers

*By Clyde H. Farnsworth
Special to The
New York Times*

WASHINGTON, April 23—In an action that could lead to higher prices for sweaters in the United States and increase trade tensions with nations in the Far East, the Commerce Department ruled today that Hong Kong, South Korea, and Taiwan were dumping sweaters on the American market and that importers should pay penalty duties.

Dumping can provide governments with an excuse for trade restrictions.

Source: Clyde H. Farnsworth, "Imported Sweaters Face Duty," *New York Times*, April 24, 1990, p. D1.

able to compete with foreign firms for the first few years, even though they would be able to compete in the future. This argument suggests a need for temporary trade restrictions to give the new firms a chance to develop.

The main problem with this argument comes from the capital market. If expected future profits are high enough to justify the infant firms' losses for the first few years, then investors would be willing to accept short-term losses in return for the prospects of future profits. If expected future profits are not high enough to compensate investors for losses in the first few years, then the infant industry is economically inefficient—the economy's resources could be used better in other industries. Because trade restrictions would allow infant firms to raise domestic prices high enough to profit in the short run, they essentially force buyers to subsidize infant industries by paying the higher prices.

ARGUMENT 6. TRADE RESTRICTIONS HELP NATIONAL DEFENSE

Some people argue that free trade is politically dangerous because it creates too much specialization. Suppose that a country has no comparative advantage in producing military equipment or some other product important for national defense. With free trade, the country may import these products rather than produce them. The national-defense argument sees danger in this arrangement because a country cannot rely on imports in wartime. (It might even fight the country from which it imports war material.) This national-defense argument suggests that a country may benefit militarily (at the cost of some economic inefficiency) from trade restrictions in certain industries with critical importance to national defense.

ARGUMENT 7. STRATEGIC TRADE POLICY

A strategic trade policy is a national policy to encourage other governments to reduce their trade restrictions. Strategic trade policies often involve threats to impose more trade restrictions unless other nations reduce their own restrictions. Some people believe that strategic trade policy can help to reduce world-wide trade restrictions. Others emphasize the potential danger that strategic trade policy may cause trade wars in which both countries raise trade restrictions with each other and every country loses.

CAUSES OF PROTECTIONISM

Most restrictions on international trade result from political action by the interest groups who benefit from those restrictions. Trade restrictions, like many other government policies, create winners and losers. The winners, often relatively small numbers of people or firms, have strong incentives to lobby the government for the policies that help them and to provide campaign contributions for cooperative politicians. Industry associations can make it easy for some groups to organize for effective political persuasion. Losers from trade restrictions are often large numbers of people whose per-person losses are relatively small, so each individual has less incentive to spend the time and money to organize effective opposition to the trade restrictions. The losers may even be unaware of the trade restrictions that raise the prices they pay. For these reasons, the groups that lose from trade restrictions often wield less political power than the groups that gain. Restrictions on imports of children's pajamas may raise the price by $0.50 per pair, hardly noticeable to any one consumer. A firm selling 1 million pairs of pajamas, however, may earn an extra $500,000 from the import restrictions. The

IN THE NEWS

U.S. tariff appears to backfire

Japan is retaliating for 63% charge on computer screens

By David E. Sanger
Special to The
New York Times

TOKYO, Sept. 25—A month and a half after the United States imposed a 63 percent tariff on the most advanced screens for laptop and notebook computers, the Japanese have begun to retaliate.

Some companies have said they will stop sending the screens to the United States, and the Toshiba Corporation, one of the largest Japanese companies to make computers in the United States, has said it is moving its operations abroad to obtain the screens without paying the tariffs.

Thus, the retaliation will hurt the many American computer makers that rely on the Japanese screens and could lead to a loss of American jobs. The tariff was intended to protect a nascent sector of the American computer industry.

▲

Canada puts levies on steel sheets of U.S., 5 nations

By John Urquhart
Staff Reporter of The
Wall Street Journal

OTTAWA—Canada, in a retaliatory move, placed stiff antidumping levies on steel sheet imports from the U.S. and five other countries.

The case is one of three antidumping actions that were initiated by Canadian steel producers last year after the U.S. steel industry filed unfair trade complaints against steelmakers in Canada and 18 other countries.

Strategic trade policy may reduce foreign trade restrictions, but at the risk of causing a trade war.

Sources: David E. Sanger, "U.S. Tariff Appears to Backfire," *New York Times,* September 26, 1991, p. D1; and John Urquhart, "Canada Puts Levies on Steel Sheets of U.S., 5 Nations," *The Wall Street Journal,* February 1, 1993, p. A6.

incentives for producers to lobby for restrictions is much stronger than the incentives for individual consumers to give the matter a second thought, let alone take the time to obtain more information, organize with other consumers, and lobby to eliminate the restrictions.

TRANSITION TO FREE TRADE

Eliminating trade restrictions creates losers as well as winners. Some firms lose sales as buyers choose to import foreign products; other firms gain sales as foreigners spend the dollars they earn from their exports. Because it takes time for workers who lose their jobs to find new ones, the removal of trade barriers can cause short-term unemployment. Some people argue that the government should help workers who lose from the removal of trade restrictions, perhaps by providing increased unemployment compensation or job training. Some people argue that this adjustment assistance is not only fair, but that it also encourages free trade by making it easier politically to remove trade restrictions. Other people

IN THE NEWS

As U.S. urges free markets, its trade barriers are many

By Keith Bradsher
Special to The
New York Times

In comparison with Japan and America's other major trading partners, the United States is less protectionist— but many barriers to imports remain.

Quotas double the price of sugar in morning coffee and limit imports per American to no more than seven peanuts, a pound of dairy cheese, and a lick of ice cream each year. Fresh cream and milk are banned; frozen cream may be purchased only from New Zealand. And the Customs

Service recently turned back a shipment of buttered croissants from France because it violated a quota on French butter shipments.

Imports of men's heavy and worsted wool suits are capped at 1.2 million, the equivalent of one for each male manager and professional every dozen years. The Commerce Department has imposed punitive duties on martial arts uniforms from Taiwan, awning window cranks from El Salvador, and the tiny pads for woodwind instrument keys from Italy after determining that they were being sold, or

"dumped," at unfairly low prices.

Sprawling and Inconsistent

This sprawling and inconsistent collection of quotas, tariffs, and other barriers reflects lobbying by many industries, as well as the occasional national-security concern. The result has been higher prices for American consumers and fewer opportunities for millions of people in developing countries to escape poverty by growing crops or stitching clothes for people in wealthy countries.

Political forces, such as the relative political power of various groups, affect a country's trade policies.

Source: Keith Bradsher, "As U.S. Urges Free Markets, Its Trade Barriers Are Many," *New York Times,* February 7, 1992, p. A1.

argue against adjustment assistance, partly on the grounds that *most* changes in government policy help some people and hurt others, so they see nothing special about removing trade restrictions; these critics claim that the government could not possibly help everyone who is hurt by any change in government policies.

FOR REVIEW

35.19 Do some countries need trade restrictions so they can compete in world markets? Explain.

35.20 Do trade restrictions protect jobs? Explain.

35.21 Who loses and who gains if a foreign government subsidizes the exports of its country's producers?

35.22 What is a strategic trade policy? Cite one argument for and one argument against a strategic trade policy.

CONCLUSIONS

SCOPE OF INTERNATIONAL TRADE

International trade is an important and growing part of the world economy. Imports and exports each consist of about one-tenth of U.S. GDP. Some countries have trade deficits, importing more than they export, while others have trade surpluses, exporting more than they import.

COMPARATIVE ADVANTAGE AND THE GAINS FROM TRADE

International trade, like a good technology, expands opportunities. International trade raises economic efficiency. Because all countries can share the gains from trade, international trade allows every country to consume more products than it can produce.

A country gains from trade by producing more products in which it has a comparative advantage—a lower opportunity cost—and fewer products in which it has a comparative disadvantage. It then exports the former products and imports the latter. This raises world output and consumption in every country.

GAINS FROM INTERNATIONAL TRADE: GRAPHICAL ANALYSIS

Without international trade, each country's consumption is limited to what it can produce. Its production possibilities frontier (PPF) shows the combinations of products it can produce with its available resources and technology. International trade allows each country to consume more of every good by trading along a world price line, exporting some products and importing others. The absolute value of the slope of the world price line is the world relative price of the product on the horizontal axis of the graph. The relative price is determined by the equilibrium of world supply and demand.

Some people gain from international trade, and others lose. When a country imports a good, its consumers gain because international trade reduces the good's price, and firms whose products compete with the imported good lose. Consumers gain more than producers lose, however, in the sense that they could compensate the losers and still gain from international trade. Foreign exporters gain increases in sales, and foreign consumers lose because they pay a higher price for the good. Producers gain more than consumers lose, so, on net, both the importing country and the exporting country gain from trade.

REASONS FOR COMPARATIVE ADVANTAGE

Countries gain from trade because they differ in their opportunity costs of production or in their consumer tastes. Costs may differ across countries because they have different technologies or different supplies of inputs.

BALANCE OF TRADE AND THE CURRENT ACCOUNT

A country that lends money to other countries has a current account surplus; a country that borrows has a current account deficit. A country's current account surplus equals its trade balance surplus plus its net income from past investments in other countries. A country has a current account deficit when it saves less than it invests and borrows to finance the extra investment. It has a current account surplus when it saves more than it invests and lends the difference to people in other countries. Trade deficits are neither good or bad per se. They reflect underlying economic conditions, and they are at least as likely to accompany high aggregate demand and low unemployment as the opposite.

PROTECTIONISM

Protectionism advocates government policies to restrict imports to protect domestic producers from foreign competitors. Trade restrictions almost always hurt the country as a whole (ignoring the distribution of income), but they also create winners and losers. The two most prominent forms of restrictions on international trade are tariffs (taxes on imports) and import quotas (restrictions on the number of imports of a particular product). Other trade restrictions include voluntary export restraints, local content requirements, and bureaucratic (red tape) protectionism. Tariffs raise the domestic price of a product by taxing imported goods. Domestic producers benefit, but domestic consumers lose more than the producers gain. The effects of other trade restrictions are similar. Trade restrictions may also provoke foreign retaliation in the form of higher foreign tariffs on domestic exports.

The costs of protectionism are difficult to estimate. U.S. protectionism alone probably costs consumers about $70 billion per year (about $270 per person each year), while providing about a $35 billion gain to domestic producers and a $13 billion gain to the government. This leaves a net loss to the U.S. economy from U.S. protectionism of about $22 billion per year (about $85 per person each year). Many countries have signed treaties with other countries to remove trade restrictions. The World Trade Organization (WTO) involves 117 countries. Other important agreements include the North American Free Trade Agreement (NAFTA), the European Union (EU), and the European Free Trade Association (EFTA).

COMMON ARGUMENTS FOR PROTECTIONISM

Some people claim that domestic producers need trade restrictions to compete in world markets, but the argument for this claim is fallacious. The level of wages adjusts so that, in equilibrium, firms in every country can compete in world markets. Some people also claim that trade restrictions save jobs. While trade restrictions protect jobs in some industries, they eliminate jobs in other industries. Trade restrictions have little effect on overall employment.

Some people argue for trade restrictions to keep wages high, because low foreign wages give cost advantages to foreign producers. In some circumstances, restrictions on international trade can keep wages higher than they would be with free trade, but even in these circumstances, restricting international trade reduces the economy's total income.

Trade restrictions are not necessary to level the playing field in international trade. International trade differs from a sporting contest or a war because both sides win when they trade. (Everyone can gain from a voluntary trade.) Trade restrictions reduce economic efficiency and redistribute income from domestic consumers to protected domestic producers, whether or not other countries impose trade restrictions.

Another argument for trade restrictions urges temporary protection for infant industries with high start-up costs until they become well-established. If expected future industry profits were high enough to justify the losses for a few years, however, then investors would be willing to accept short-term losses in return for future profits; the industry would not need temporary protection from foreign competition. Trade restrictions essentially force buyers to subsidize economically inefficient industries.

Some people argue that trade restrictions are necessary to protect national defense. This argument may be important for a limited number of industries, but probably has little bearing on most real-life trade restrictions. Finally, some people argue that trade restrictions can help to provide leverage in bargaining with other countries to reduce their own restrictions. Such a strategic trade policy may invite further foreign retaliation and start a trade war, however, in which trade restrictions increase and every country loses.

Most real-life restrictions on international trade result from political action by the interest groups who benefit from those restrictions. The benefits of trade restrictions are usually concentrated in a small group of winners, who have an incentive to lobby for those restrictions, while the (larger) costs are spread out among many people, each of whom has little individual incentive to actively oppose the restrictions.

KEY TERMS

export	gains from trade
import	dynamic gains from trade
balance of international trade	current account
trade surplus	current account surplus
trade deficit	current account deficit
merchandise trade balance	protectionism
balance of trade on goods and services	tariff
comparative advantage	import quota
production possibilities frontier (PPF)	World Trade Organization (WTO)

QUESTIONS AND PROBLEMS

35.23 Make up a simple numerical example to show the gains from international trade.

35.24 Draw a graph to illustrate the effects of an import quota. Who gains and who loses from the quota? Show the sizes of the gains and losses on your graph. How large are the gains and losses to each country and to the world as a whole?

35.25 Consider the example from Figures 35.13 and 35.14, but suppose that the world equilibrium relative price of videos is one computer program per music video (that is, they have the same price).
  a. Draw graphs like those in Figure 35.14 to show consumption opportunities in the United States and Japan if they trade.
  b. Does the United States gain more from international trade if the relative price of music videos is one-half or one computer program? Explain why.

35.26 Suppose that the United States and Japan can produce either CD players or wheat. Each country has 60 person-days available for work. The table below shows the labor required to produce each product.

COSTS OF PRODUCTION: LABOR TIME TO PRODUCE 1 UNIT OF A PRODUCT

	United States	Japan
CD player (1 unit)	10 person-days	12 person-days
Wheat (1 ton)	1 person-day	2 person-days

a. Draw (to scale) each country's production possibilities frontier (PPF).

b. Which country has a comparative advantage in which product?

c. Suppose that the world equilibrium price of a CD player is $80 and the world price of wheat is $10 per ton. What is the relative price of CD players in terms of wheat? Which country would produce which product at these prices?

d. Add world price lines to your PPF graphs and use those graphs to show why international trade allows each country to consume more than it could without international trade.

INQUIRIES FOR FURTHER THOUGHT

35.27 What imported goods do you consume? What goods that you use have some imported parts (perhaps inside)?

35.28 Suppose that states in the United States could not trade with each other. What goods or services would you not be able to buy?

a. How much would your standard of living fall? (Be sure to think about inputs into production of goods that you buy.)

b. How much would your standard of living fall if governments were to prohibit international trade? How much would it rise if governments were to eliminate all restrictions and taxes on international trade?

35.29 What jobs in the United States depend on international trade?

35.30 When the U.S. government chooses its trade policies, should it take into account *only* the effects on people in the United States, or should it also consider the effects on people in other countries? For example, suppose that a policy would help the United States by $5 million and hurt people in other countries by $6 million. Should the government adopt that policy? What if it would hurt people in other countries by $60 million? What if the policy would hurt people in the United States by $5 million, but help people in other countries by $6 million or by $60 million?

35.31 Why would the government impose import quotas rather than levying tariffs? (It could collect revenue from tariffs, but the gains from quotas go to foreign sellers.)

35.32 The government of Italy subsidizes its steel industry. Italy also exports steel to the United States. How does Italy's subsidy affect U.S. consumers and U.S. steel producers? Some people say that the United States should impose an import quota or tariff in a case like this. (The U.S. government does set quotas in the form of voluntary export restraints.) Do you agree that Italian steel imports should face trade restrictions? If so, how big should they be, and who would gain and lose from the quota or tariff?

Tag Software Applications

Tutorial Exercises
▶ The module contains a review of the key terms from Chapter 35.

Analytical Exercises
▶ The analytical segment contains questions on the calculation of opportunity costs.

Graphing Exercises
▶ The graphing segment includes questions on production possiblitites frontiers, imports and exports, consumption possibitities with international trade, and the effects of a tariff.

CHAPTER 36

INTERNATIONAL MONEY AND FINANCE

WHAT THIS CHAPTER IS ABOUT

▶ Foreign exchange rates

▶ Connections between prices in different countries

▶ Exchange rate systems

Foreign exchange, someone said, is as romantic as young love and every bit as difficult to understand. While this claim certainly exaggerates the interest that international monetary issues generate in normal humans, it also exaggerates their complexities. Different countries use different moneys, and some are more valuable than others. The issues of international monetary economics lie in the connections between these different moneys, and the factors that affect their values. Why does it cost only about $0.01 to buy a Japanese yen, but about $1.50 for a British pound? Why does a U.S. dollar buy about 1,600 Italian lira but only about $1\frac{1}{2}$ German marks? What happens when a country devalues its money? Young love it isn't, but no one can doubt the significant consequences of international monetary issues for people's material standards of living.

FOREIGN EXCHANGE MARKET

foreign exchange (FX) market — a market for purchases and sales of the moneys of various countries

exchange rate — a price of one money in terms of another

Most countries have their own forms of money. People buy and sell moneys on the foreign exchange (FX) market.

> The **foreign exchange (FX) market** refers to purchases and sales of the moneys of various countries.

> An **exchange rate** is a price of one money in terms of another.

Table 36.1 from *The Wall Street Journal* shows foreign exchange rates between the U.S. dollar and the moneys of some other countries. The first column shows the country and the name of its money. (For example, Argentina uses pesos.) The next two columns show the price of the foreign money in terms of U.S. dollars (on the most recent trading day and the day before that). The last two columns show two days' prices of the U.S. dollar in terms of the foreign money. For example, the table shows that one Japanese yen cost $0.01122, or just above 1¢. It also shows

TABLE 36.1

CURRENCY TRADING

EXCHANGE RATES

Friday, March 17, 1995

The New York foreign exchange selling rates below apply to trading among banks in amounts of $1 million and more, as quoted at 3 p.m. Eastern time by Bankers Trust Co., Dow Jones Telerate Inc. and other sources. Retail transactions provide fewer units of foreign currency per dollar.

Country	U.S. $ equiv. Fri.	U.S. $ equiv. Thur.	Currency per U.S. $ Fri.	Currency per U.S. $ Thur.
Argentina (Peso)	1.00	1.00	1.00	1.00
Australia (Dollar)	.7341	.7461	1.3623	1.3404
Austria (Schilling)	.10222	.10259	9.78	9.75
Bahrain (Dinar)	2.6529	2.6529	.3769	.3769
Belgium(Franc)	.03489	.03468	28.66	28.83
Brazil(Real)	1.1148272	1.1210762	.90	.89
Britain (Pound)	1.5840	1.5880	.6313	.6297
30-Day Forward	1.5838	1.5878	.6314	.6298
90-Day Forward	1.5825	1.5866	.6319	.6303
180-Day Forward	1.5789	1.5834	.6334	.6316
Canada (Dollar)	.7083	.7072	1.4118	1.4140
30-Day Forward	.7068	.7059	1.4149	1.4166
90-Day Forward	.7045	.7037	1.4195	1.4211
180-Day Forward	.7020	.7012	1.4245	1.4260
Czech. Rep. (Koruna)				
Commercial rate	3.085223	.0384187	25.9590	26.0290
Chile (Peso)	.002441	.002437	409.65	410.35
China (Renminbi)	.118662	.118652	8.4273	8.4280
Colombia (Peso)	.001157	.001157	864.25	864.50
Denmark (Krone)	.1789	.1780	5.5912	5.6171
Ecuador (Sucre)				
Floating rate	.000417	.000417	2400.50	2398.50
Finland (Markka)	.23030	.22955	4.3422	4.3564
France (Franc)	.20186	.20105	4.9540	4.9740
30-Day Forward	.20148	.20065	4.9632	4.9838
90-Day Forward	.20064	.19997	4.9840	5.0008
180-Day Forward	.19980	.19926	5.0050	5.0185
Germany (Mark)	.7215	.7161	1.3860	1.3965
30-Day Forward	.7226	.7168	1.3839	1.3951
90-Day Forward	.7242	.7183	1.3808	1.3923
180-Day Forward	.7265	.7205	1.3765	1.3880
Greece (Drachma)	.004404	.004373	227.05	228.65
Hong Kong (Dollar)	.12936	.12934	7.7305	7.7315
Hungary (Forint)	.0083843	.0083836	119..2700	119.2801
India (Rupee)	.03179	.03175	31.45	31.50
Indonesia (Rupiah)	.0004491	.0004493	2226.75	2225.50
Ireland (Punt)	1.5830	1.5870	.6317	.6301
Israel (Shekel)	.3369	.3369	2.9684	2.9686
Italy (Lira)	.0005731	.0005884	1745.00	1699.50
Japan (Yen)	.011220	.011085	89.13	90.22
30-Day Forward	.011263	.011121	88.78	89.92
90-Day Forward	.011341	.011199	88.18	89.30
180-Day Forward	.011471	.011326	87.17	88.29
Jordan (Dinar)	1.4556	1.4556	.6870	.6870
Kuwait (Dinar)	3.3870	3.3870	.2953	.2953
Lebanon (Pound)	.000611	.000611	1636.50	1636.50
Malaysia (Ringgit)	.3920	.3921	2.5510	2.5505
Malta (Lira)	2.8729	2.8729	.3481	.3481
Mexico (Peso)				
Floating rate	.1434720	.1398601	6.9700	7.1500
Netherland (Guilder)	.6433	.6380	1.5545	1.5675
New Zealand (Dollar)	.6473	.6507	1.5450	1.5369
Norway (Krone)	.1609	.1600	6.2166	6.2514
Pakistan (Rupee)	.0324	.0324	30.85	30.85
Peru (New Sol)	.4442	.4449	2.25	2.25
Philippines (Peso)	.03890	.03864	25.71	25.88
Poland (Zloty)	.42553191	.42372881	2.35	2.36
Portugal (Escudo)	.006807	.006768	146.90	147.75
Saudi Arabia (Riyal)	.26664	.26664	3.7504	3.7504
Singapore (Dollar)	.7082	.7077	1.4120	1.4130
Slovak Rep. (Koruna)	.0342583	.0342583	29.1900	29.1900
South Africa (Rand)	.2779	.2801	3.5980	3.5700
South Korea (Won)	.0012891	.0012866	775.75	777.25
Spain (Peseta)	.007768	.007797	128.72	128.25
Sweden (Krona)	.1384	.1388	7.2278	7.2024
Switzerland (Franc)	.8689	.8587	1.1509	1.1645
30-Day Forward	.8707	.8606	1.1485	1.1619
90-Day Forward	.8744	.8643	1.1436	1.1570
180-Day Forward	.8801	.8697	1.1362	1.1498
Taiwan (Dollar)	.038436	.038404	26.02	26.04
Thailand (Baht)	.04045	.04044	24.72	24.73
Turkey (Lira)	.0000239	.0000240	41768.51	41731.52
United Arab (Dirham)	.2723	.2723	3.6727	3.6727
Uruguay (New Peso)				
Financial	.167645	.167926	5.97	5.95
Venezuela (Bolivar)	.00589	.00589	169.78	169.78
SDR	1.54169	1.54172	.64864	.64863
ECU	1.30325	1.30680	....	....

Special Drawing Rights (SDR) are based on exchange rates for the U.S., German, British, French and Japanese currencies. Source: International Monetary Fund.

European Currency Unit (ECU) is based on a basket of community currencies.

The Wall Street Journal. Monday, March 20, 1965. C15

that $1 cost ¥89.13. Similarly, one French franc costs about 20.186¢ and $1 cost 4.954 French francs.

To keep the discussion clear, this chapter will define the exchange rate as the price of foreign money—the amount of domestic money it takes to buy one unit of foreign money. This corresponds to the first two columns of numbers in Table 36.1. (Sometimes people quote exchange rates the other way around, as the amount of foreign money it takes to buy one unit of domestic money, as in the last two columns of the table.) The letter *e* will represent an exchange rate.

The exchange rate *e* between a domestic and a foreign currency is the price of foreign money—the amount of home money required to buy one unit of foreign money.

When the exchange rate changes, the money that becomes more valuable (in terms of the other money) appreciates and the money that becomes less valuable (in terms of the other) depreciates.

appreciation of a currency — a rise in the value of a money on the foreign exchange market so that one unit buys more foreign money

depreciation of a currency — a fall in the value of a money on the foreign exchange market so that one unit buys less foreign money

Appreciation of a currency refers to a rise in its value on the foreign exchange market so that one unit buys more foreign money.

Depreciation of a currency refers to a fall in its value on the foreign exchange market so that one unit buys less foreign money.

Because the exchange rate is the price of foreign money, a domestic currency appreciates when the exchange rate falls. (The domestic money becomes more valuable, so you need less of it to buy one unit of foreign money.) The domestic currency depreciates when the exchange rate rises. (The domestic money becomes less valuable, so you need more of it to buys one unit of foreign money.)

Table 36.1 shows that the Japanese yen appreciated against the dollar (and the dollar depreciated against the yen) from Thursday to Friday; on Thursday ¥1 was worth 1.1085¢, while on Friday its value had increased to 1.1220¢.[1] It took more cents to buy ¥1 on Friday than it did on Thursday; equivalently, it took fewer yen to buy \$1.

Figure 36.1 shows how five U.S. dollar exchange rates have changed since 1960. Each graph shows the U.S. dollar price of a foreign money. Notice that a falling curve indicates appreciation of the dollar (because the dollar can buy more foreign money when the price of foreign money falls). A rising curve indicates depreciation of the dollar (because the dollar cannot buy as much foreign money).

MECHANICS OF THE FOREIGN EXCHANGE MARKET

People buy foreign money to pay for imports of foreign goods or foreign assets. If you run a music store that sells imported compact disks, you buy them from a U.S. distributor who imports them from other countries. You pay U.S. dollars to the distributor for the CDs, but the distributor pays British pounds to manufacturers in England or Spanish pesetas to those in Spain. The distributor buys these pounds and pesetas on the foreign exchange market through a bank, which actually carries out the transaction. Table 36.1 showed a price of about \$1.58 for each British pound and 3/4¢ for each Spanish peseta. The distributor *sells U.S. dollars* and *buys pounds* or *pesetas* on the foreign exchange market. People also buy foreign currencies to pay for investments in foreign countries.

The foreign exchange market operates mostly through banks.[2] People and business firms trade bank deposits denominated in one currency for deposits denominated in another. Most trades take place over the telephone. Currency traders often talk on several phones at once as they watch computer screens that display the latest information.

---

[1]Notice that the exchange rate changed by more than 0.67 percent in just 1 day. (If it changed this much every day for one month, the exchange rate would change by 20 percent!) These large daily changes in exchange rates are common; exchange rates are highly variable.

[2]Some firms, such as corporations involved in international trade and brokerage firms, sometimes trade in the FX market directly without going through banks.

FIGURE 36.1

U.S. DOLLAR FOREIGN EXCHANGE RATES

(a) Japanese Yen, German Mark, and French Franc Exchange Rates

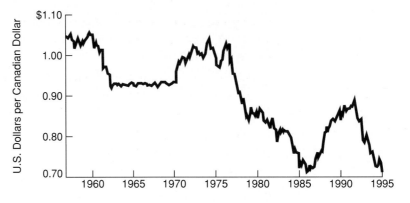

(b) Canadian Dollar Exchange Rates

(c) British Pound Exchange Rates

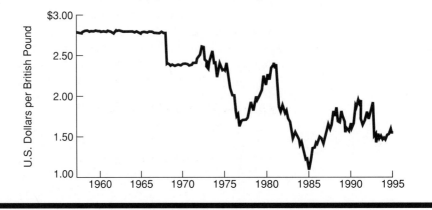

The foreign exchange market is by far the biggest financial market in the world. Trades take place 24 hours per day around the world, and the total value of trade on world FX markets exceeds $1 trillion worth of various currencies per day. Most FX trades are not connected with purchases of foreign goods and services; most FX trades occur so that people can buy foreign financial assets, speculate, or hedge risks.

USING THE EXCHANGE RATE TO CONVERT PRICES

The exchange rate allows people to compare prices in different countries. Suppose that a compact disk costs 30 DM (30 German marks) in Germany. If the exchange rate between the mark and the dollar is $0.70 per mark, then a CD in Germany costs $21.00. To restate a foreign-money price in domestic money, multiply the foreign price by the exchange rate, where the exchange rate is defined as the price of foreign money.

> If P^f is an amount of foreign money and e is the exchange rate (the price of one unit of foreign money), then the equivalent amount of domestic money is eP^f.

If the foreign price P^f is 30 DM and the exchange rate e is $0.70 per German mark, then the equivalent dollar price is:

$$(\$0.70/\text{DM}) \ (30 \text{ DM}) = \$21$$

If it costs e dollars to buy a unit of foreign money, it costs $1/e$ units of foreign money to buy $1. To convert domestic money into foreign money, then, divide by the exchange rate:

> If P is an amount of domestic money and e is the exchange rate (the price of one unit of foreign money), then the equivalent amount of foreign money is P/e.

If the dollar price P is $15 and the exchange rate e is $1.50 per British pound (£), then the equivalent pound price is:

$$(\$15)/(\$1.50/\text{pound}) = £10$$

The price of a good is the same in two countries if:

$$P = eP^f$$

where P is the domestic-money price, e is the exchange rate, and P^f is the foreign-money price of the good. If $P \ (>) \ eP^f$ then the good is cheaper in the foreign country. If $P \ (<) \ eP^f$ then the good is cheaper in the home country. To see why, notice that if you buy a good in the United States, you pay P dollars. If you buy the same good in Canada, you must spend P^f Canadian dollars. Each Canadian dollar costs e U.S. dollars, so it costs eP^f to buy the good in Canada.

FORWARD EXCHANGE RATES

When an American firm sells products in Germany, it receives German marks from buyers. The American firm wants U.S. dollars to pay wages and other costs of production, so it sells the German marks for dollars on the foreign exchange market.

Suppose that a firm expects to receive a certain amount of foreign money at some future date. For example, if a U.S. firm sells machinery to a German firm, the German firm might pay the U.S. firm 1 million German marks after 90 days. If

---

IN THE NEWS

Exchange rate deters Canadians from entering the U.S. to shop

All's quiet along the world's longest undefended border.

Too quiet for John Warriner, manager of the Record Town outlet in the sleek St. Lawrence Centre shopping mall in Massena, N.Y., across the river from Cornwall, Ontario.

"The days of people loading their families in the car to come to the mall" from Canada are gone, laments Mr. Warriner. Canadians used to account for 25 percent of his store's sales, but the proportion has plunged lately. Despite a Canadian holiday last Friday, for example, "we just didn't take in any Canadian money at all," he says.

From northern New England to Washington state, retailers tell much the same story. Canadian consumers, who jammed the parking lots and shopping aisles of U.S. malls a couple of years ago, are increasingly staying home.

The main reason is "the darn exchange rate," says Mark Erickson, marketing director at Columbia Mall in Grand Forks.

People use exchange rates to convert prices of goods in other countries into units of their own country's money.

Source: Christopher J. Chipello, "Mighty Barrier Stops Canadians at U.S. Border: Exchange Rate," *The Wall Street Journal*, July 7, 1994, p. B1.

---

the firm waits until it receives the marks in 90 days to sell them for dollars, then its profit will depend on whether the foreign exchange rate rises or falls within the next 90 days. If the German mark appreciates relative to the dollar, then the U.S. firm can buy more dollars with its 1 million German marks, raising its dollar profit. If, however, the German mark depreciates relative to the dollar within 90 days, the U.S. firm receives fewer dollars in exchange for its German marks, lowering its dollar profit.

Uncertainty about the future exchange rate makes the firm's dollar profit risky. The firm can hedge this risk in the forward foreign exchange market.

forward foreign exchange market — a market in which people agree now to buy and sell currencies in the future at prices set today

The **forward foreign exchange market** is a market in which people agree now to buy and sell currencies in the future at prices set today.

The forward foreign exchange market allows traders to lock in an exchange rate for a future transaction. If the American firm can sell 1 million German marks on the 90-day forward market at a price of $0.7242 per mark, then it can lock in a price of $724,200 for the 1 million German marks that it will sell in 90 days. By trading on the forward market, the American firm converts its German mark receipts into U.S. dollar receipts, eliminating its risk from a change in the exchange rate.

FOR REVIEW

36.1 What does it mean to say that a currency *depreciates* on foreign exchange markets?

36.2 What is the forward exchange rate? How can an exporter use the forward market to reduce risk?

--- QUESTIONS ---

36.3 In Table 36.1, find out how many French francs you can buy with $1; find out how many dollars it would take to buy one Indian rupee.

36.4 You want to buy a T-shirt in Mexico that costs 50 pesos. If the exchange rate is $0.15 per peso, how many dollars does the T-shirt cost? A hotel in Italy charges 68,000 lira for a room for the night. If the exchange rate is 1,700 lira per dollar, what is the price of the room in dollars?

EQUILIBRIUM EXCHANGE RATES

The equilibrium exchange rate is determined by supply and demand on foreign exchange markets. A person who buys Japanese yen with U.S. dollars, demands yen and supplies dollars on the foreign exchange market. A person who buys U.S. dollars with Japanese yen supplies yen and demands dollars. The exchange rate between the U.S. dollar and Japanese yen depends on supply and demand on the market for trading yen and dollars. **Figure 36.2** shows the supply and demand for yen on the FX market. Notice that the supply of yen is the same as the demand for dollars, and the demand for yen is the same as the supply of dollars. The equilibrium exchange rate in the figure is 1¢ per yen.

FIGURE 36.2

SUPPLY AND DEMAND ON THE FOREIGN EXCHANGE MARKET

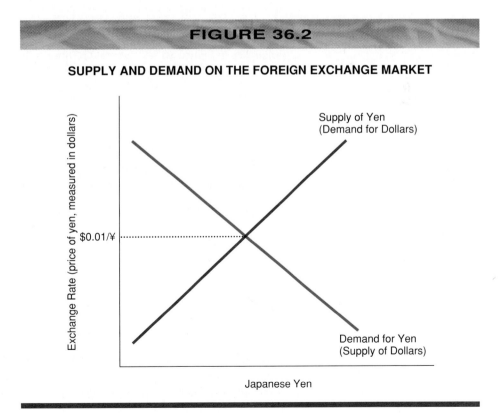

FIGURE 36.3

CHANGES IN SUPPLY OR DEMAND ON THE FOREIGN EXCHANGE MARKET

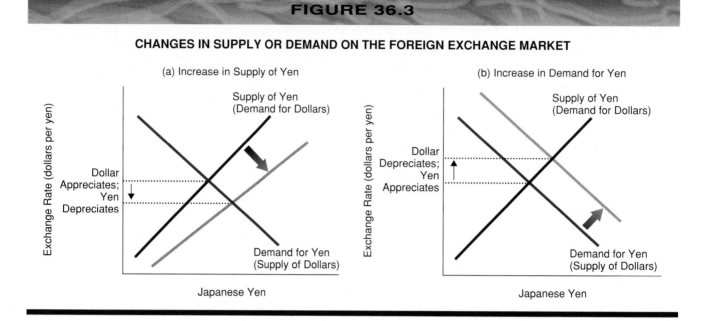

Changes in supply or demand on the foreign exchange market cause changes in the equilibrium exchange rate. An increase in the supply of Japanese yen causes depreciation of the yen (appreciation of the dollar), as in **Figure 36.3a.** An increase in the demand for yen causes appreciation of the yen (depreciation of the dollar), as in Figure 36.3b. Several factors can lead to changes in supply or demand on foreign exchange markets, including arbitrage, changes in supplies or demands for internationally traded goods, and changes in supplies or demands for internationally traded assets.

ARBITRAGE AND THE FX MARKET

Arbitrage refers to a process of buying something in a low-price location and reselling it in a high-price location. Because arbitrage raises demand in the low-price location, it raises the price there. Because it raises supply in the high-price location, it reduces the price there. In this way, arbitrage reduces price differences across locations.

If prices are higher in Japan than in the United States, people may arbitrage by buying products in the United States and reselling them in Japan. The arbitragers need U.S. dollars to buy products in the United States, and they receive yen from buyers when they resell the products in Japan. Suppose that the arbitragers are Japanese. As they sell yen to buy dollars on the foreign exchange market (to pay for U.S. purchases), their arbitrage raises the supply of yen on the foreign exchange market, as in Figure 36.3a. The same thing happens if the arbitragers are Americans. They receive yen when they resell the products in Japan, and as they use these yen to buy dollars, they supply yen on the foreign exchange market. Arbitrage by either group raises the supply of yen on the foreign exchange market, as in Figure 36.3a.

The higher prices in Japan may also cause some buyers to switch their purchases from Japan to the United States. This raises the demand for U.S. dollars to buy the U.S. products. Because these buyers sell yen to buy dollars, this raises the supply of yen on the foreign exchange market, as in Figure 36.3a. In addition, some firms may decide to sell their products in Japan, where prices are high, rather than in the United States. If an American firm sells its products in Japan, people pay yen for those products. The American firm sells the yen for dollars to pay its wages and other dollar costs. This raises the supply of yen on the foreign exchange market, as in Figure 36.3a.

For all these reasons, the exchange rate between two countries' currencies tends to change if prices are higher in one country than in the other. (We use the exchange rate to convert prices into common units, as previously explained, before comparing prices.) The money of the high-price country tends to depreciate and the money of the low-price country tends to appreciate.

> If prices are higher in one country than in another, then the money of the high-price country tends to depreciate and the money of the low-price country tends to appreciate.

If prices are higher in Japan than in the United States, for example, the dollar tends to appreciate and the yen tends to depreciate, as in Figure 36.3a. Evidence shows that this does not happen quickly, though; these changes in exchange rates can take years to occur. A later section returns to this issue.

PURCHASING POWER PARITY (PPP)

Suppose that goods produced in two countries are perfect substitutes (people view them as identical) and arbitrage costs are negligable (buying in one location to resell in another location takes virtually no time or resources). Then the equilibrium price is the same in both locations. This result is sometimes called the *law of one price*.

law of one price — proposition that if arbitrage is costless, then the equilibrium price of a product is the same in any location

> The **law of one price** says that if arbitrage is costless, then the equilibrium price of a product is the same in any location.

The costs of arbitrage for some products, such as crude oil, wheat, rice, cotton, gold, and silver, are very low.[3] Furthermore, these products are virtually identical regardless of their countries of production. Consequently, the law of one price applies to these products: they sell for roughly the same price everywhere.

The theory of purchasing power parity (or PPP) applies the law of one price to the entire bundle of goods that a country produces or consumes.

purchasing power parity (PPP) theory — the theory that the exchange rate adjusts to make the prices of goods and services, expressed in a single currency, equal in all countries

> The **purchasing power parity (PPP) theory** says that exchange rates adjust to equalize the prices of goods and services, expressed in a single currency, in all countries, at least in the long run.

The PPP theory says that if the U.S. price level is P and the Canadian price level is P^f, then the long-run equilibrium exchange rate between the Canadian and U.S. currencies is:

$$e = P/P^f$$

---

[3]These goods allow low-cost arbitrage at the wholesale level, but not necessarily at the retail level, so the law of one price applies to them closely at the wholesale level, but not necessarily at the retail level.

The ratio P/P^f is called the *PPP exchange rate.* The PPP theory says that the market exchange rate adjusts, at least in the long run, to equal the PPP exchange rate.

Recall that products are more expensive in the domestic country than in the foreign country if $P > eP^f$, and products are more expensive in the foreign country than in the domestic country if $P < eP^f$. With costless arbitrage, prices must be the same in both countries, so $P = eP^f$.

EXPLANATION

Suppose that prices are lower in the United States than in England, meaning that $P^{USA} < eP^{England}$. People will try to buy products in the United States rather than in England, where prices are higher. English buyers need dollars to buy products in the United States, so they trade pounds for dollars. This raises the supply of pounds and demand for dollars on the foreign exchange market, which creates dollar appreciation, reducing e. This continues until e falls enough that $P^{USA} = eP^{England}$. At this point, the market reaches equilibrium with purchasing power parity.

USING PPP THEORY

Earlier chapters discussed the equation of exchange:

$$MV = Py$$

where M is the nominal money supply, V is the velocity of money, P is the price level, and y is real GDP. Those chapters showed that the equilibrium price level is:

$$P = MV/y$$

Similarly, the equilibrium price level in the foreign country is:

$$P^f = M^f V^f / y^f$$

where P^f is the foreign price level, M^f is the foreign nominal money supply, V^f is foreign velocity, and y^f is foreign real GDP.

Substituting these results into the purchasing power parity equation gives the equilibrium exchange rate as:

$$e = \frac{MVy^f}{M^f V^f y}$$

This equation has several implications for the exchange rate between the two countries:

Causes of Depreciation (Rise in *e*)	Causes of Appreciation (Fall in *e*)
1. Rise in the domestic money supply, *M*	1. Rise in the foreign country's money supply, *M*^f
2. Rise in the domestic velocity of money, *V*	2. Rise in the foreign country's velocity of money, *V*^f
3. Rise in the foreign country's real GDP, *y*^f	3. Rise in domestic real GDP, *y*

Changes in expectations about the future can affect the exchange rate. For example, an increase in expected inflation in some country can raise its nominal interest rate. This raises its velocity, which raises its exchange rate, that is, its money depreciates.[4]

---

[4]Recall from an earlier chapter that velocity rises when the nominal interest rate rises (and it falls when the nominal interest rate falls). Also recall that the nominal interest rate equals the real interest rate plus the expected rate of inflation.

FIGURE 30.4

PURCHASING POWER PARITY: BRAZILIAN–U.S. RELATIONSHIP

EVIDENCE ON PPP

The PPP theory fits real-life data well when inflation rates of two countries differ a lot. **Figure 36.4** shows the exchange rate between the Brazilian cruzeiro and the U.S. dollar and the PPP exchange rate during a period of extremely rapid inflation in Brazil.[5] Notice that the exchange rate and the price level change together, as the PPP theory implies.

Figure 36.5 shows the U.S. dollar's exchange rates with the Canadian, Japanese, German, and British currencies since 1965 along with the PPP exchange rates, calculated as ratios of consumer price indexes.[6] The PPP theory works poorly in the short run, though it fits long-run data somewhat better. Statistical evidence shows that an exchange rate above its PPP level usually tends to move toward that level in the long run. Although the PPP theory works better in the long run than the short run, the relationship is not exact, even in the long run.

The law of one price fails in the short run for many goods. While the law of one price applies closely to the wholesale prices of *some* commodities, prices of most goods differ across countries. Price differences may occur when arbitrage is costly because of large time costs or resource costs of buying in one country and selling in another. Arbitraging most goods becomes profitable only if the price difference exceeds the per-unit cost of arbitrage.

---

[5]The figure expresses the exchange rate as the cruzeiro price of dollars and the PPP exchange rate as the Brazilian price level divided by the U.S. price level.

[6]Because price indexes measure base-year prices, the *level* of P/P^f is arbitrary. The PPP theory applied to these indexes says that e and P/P^f change proportionately, not that they are equal.

FIGURE 36.5

EXCHANGE AND PPP RATES OF THE U.S. DOLLAR

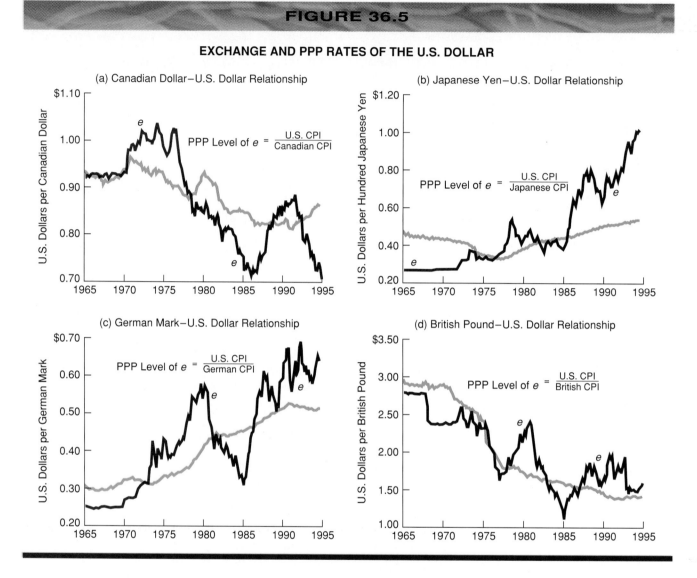

(a) Canadian Dollar–U.S. Dollar Relationship

PPP Level of $e = \dfrac{\text{U.S. CPI}}{\text{Canadian CPI}}$

(b) Japanese Yen–U.S. Dollar Relationship

PPP Level of $e = \dfrac{\text{U.S. CPI}}{\text{Japanese CPI}}$

(c) German Mark–U.S. Dollar Relationship

PPP Level of $e = \dfrac{\text{U.S. CPI}}{\text{German CPI}}$

(d) British Pound–U.S. Dollar Relationship

PPP Level of $e = \dfrac{\text{U.S. CPI}}{\text{British CPI}}$

Each year, for example, *The Economist* magazine publishes a comparison of Big Mac prices at McDonald's restaurants around the world. **Table 36.2** shows that a Big Mac sold in the United States for an average price of $2.32, while in Japan, a Big Mac cost ¥391 on average.[7] The second column of the table shows the exchange rate that the *law of one price* would imply, based on Big Mac prices. In other words, if the exchange rate were $0.006 per yen (or ¥169 per dollar), then the price of a Big Mac would be the same in Japan as in the United States, and $P = eP^f$ would apply to Big Macs. In fact, the exchange rate was 100 percent higher than this level, at $0.012 per yen (or ¥84.2 per dollar), so Big Macs were twice as expensive in Japan as in the United States. In that sense, the dollar was undervalued by 100 percent, compared to its purchasing power parity value

---

[7]The price differs between cities within each country.

TABLE 36.2

THE HAMBURGER STANDARD

United States[b]	Big Mac Prices		Implied PPP[a] of the Dollar	Actual Dollar Exchange Rate 7/4/95	Local Currency Under(-)/over(+) Valuation[c], %
	In Local Currency $2.32	In Dollars $2.32	—	—	—
Argentina	Peso3.00	3.00	1.29	1.00	+29
Australia	A$2.45	1.82	1.06	1.35	-22
Austria	Sch39.0	4.01	16.8	9.72	+73
Belgium	BFr109	3.84	47.0	28.4	+66
Brazil	Real 2.42	2.69	104[d]	0.90	+16
Britain	£1.74	2.80	1.33[d]	1.61[d]	+21
Canada	C$2.77	1.99	1.19	1.39	-14
Chile	Peso950	2.40	409	395	+4
China	Yuan9.00	1.05	3.88	8.54	-55
Czech Republic	CKr50.0	1.91	21.6	26.2	-18
Denmark	DKr26.75	4.92	11.5	5.43	+112
France	FFr18.5	3.85	7.97	4.80	+66
Germany	DM4.80	3.48	2.07	1.38	+50
Holland	F15.45	3.53	2.35	1.55	+52
Hong Kong	HK$9.50	1.23	4.09	7.73	-47
Hungary	Forint191	1.58	82.3	121	-32
Indonesia	Rupiah3,900	1.75	1,681	2,231	-25
Israel	Shekel18.90	3.01	3.84	2.95	+30
Italy	Lire4,500	2.64	1,940	1,702	+14
Japan	¥391	4.65	169	84.2	+100
Malaysia	M$3.76	1.51	1.62	2.49	-35
Mexico	Peso10.9	1.71	4.70	6.37	-26
New Zealand	NZ$2.95	1.96	1.27	1.51	-16
Poland	Zloty3.40	1.45	1.47	2.34	-37
Russia	Rouble8,100	1.62	3,491	4,985	-30
Singapore	S$2.95	2.10	1.27	1.40	-9
South Korea	Won2,300	2.99	991	769	+29
Spain	Ptas355	2.86	153	124	+23
Sweden	Skr26.0	3.54	11.2	7.34	+53
Switzerland	SFr5.90	5.20	2.54	1.13	+124
Taiwan	NT$65.0	2.53	28.0	25.7	+9
Thailand	Baht48.0	1.95	20.7	24.6	-16

[a]Purchasing-power parity: local price divided by price in United States.
[b]Average of New York, Chicago, San Francisco, and Atlanta.
[c]Against dollar.
[d]Dollars per pound.

Source: McDonald's.

measured in Big Macs. An appreciation of the dollar that doubled its value would have equalized the prices of Big Macs in both countries.

The table makes similar comparisons for other countries.[8] Although Big Macs are virtually identical in different places (though they may be consumed in different climates, surroundings, and so on), the law of one price does not hold closely for Big Macs, even across cities within the United States. No one travels from one city to another—or one country to another—simply to pay less for a Big Mac.

---

[8]A 1993 study of numerous other products found large price differences between countries. For example, Kelloggs' cornflakes and Palmolive hand-wash liquid were $2\frac{1}{2}$ times as expensive in Italy as in England; Coca Cola was twice as expensive in Ireland as in France; Nescafé was twice as expensive in Germany as in Ireland. *Source: Financial Times,* January 4, 1993, p. 7.

IN THE NEWS

Big MacCurrencies

Our Big Mac index confirms that the dollar is undervalued against other main currencies

The Big Mac index was devised in 1986 as a light-hearted guide to whether currencies are a "correct" level. It is not a precise predictor of currencies, simply a tool to make exchange-rate theory a bit more digestible. Burgernomics is based upon one of the oldest concepts in international economics; the theory of purchasing-power parity (PPP). This holds that, in the long run, the exchange rate of two currencies should move towards the rate that would equalize the prices of an indentical basket of goods

and services in each country.

Our 'basket" is a McDonald's Big Mac: made to more or less the same recipe in 79 countries. The Big Mac PPP is the exchange rate that would leave hamburgers costing the same in America as abroad. Comparing actual exchange rates with PPP is one indication of whether a currency is under or overvalued.

The first column of [Table 36.2 on the next page] shows the local-currency price of a Big Mac; the second shows the dollar one. The cheapest Big Mac is in China: it costs $1.05, compared with an average price in four American cities of $2.32 (all prices include sales tax). At the other extreme, Big Mac munchers in Switzerland pay a beefy $5.20. This is another

way of saying that the yuan is the most undervalued currency, the Swiss franc the most overvalued.

The third column calculates Big Mac PPP. For example, dividing the Japanese price by the American one gives a dollar PPP of ¥169. On April 7, the rate was ¥84, implying that the yen is 100 percent overvalued against the dollar—or looking at it from the other point of view, that the dollar is 50 percent undervalued. On the same basis, the D-mark is 50 percent overvalued against its PPP of DM2.07; sterling is 21 percent overvalued.

Studies have found that although PPP does hold in the very long run, currencies can indeed deviate from their equilibrium for lengthy periods.

Source: "Big MacCurrencies," *Economist,* April 15, 1995, p. 88.p 75.

Arbitrage of this good is costly, so changes in the demand or supply of Big Macs in Japan can affect the Japanese price of Big Macs without changing prices in Italy or the United States.[9] Similarly, changes in the demand and supply for Japanese products in general can affect the relative prices of Japanese and American products in general, causing the exchange rate to differ from its PPP value.

PRODUCT MARKETS AND THE FX MARKET

Supplies and demands of currencies on the foreign exchange market also react to other factors, such as changes in the demands or supplies of domestic and foreign products. Because two goods of the same type produced in different countries may differ somewhat, they may sell for different prices.[10]

---

[9]Some products, such as haircuts, have such high costs of arbitrage that they are not traded internationally.

[10]If consumers do not consider Korean-produced VCRs and Japanese-produced VCRs to be perfect substitutes, then they would not sell for the same price, even if arbitrage were free.

Strong dollar aids travelers to Europe

By Cathy Lynn Grossman
USA TODAY

Europe is looking a bit greener for U.S. vacationers now that the dollar has rebounded to last summer's level in buying power.

Prices differ between countries, often reflecting changes in exchange rates.

Source: Cathy Lynn Grossman, "Strong Dollar Aids Travelers to Europe," *USA Today,* April 22, 1991, p. C3.

TABLE 36.3

RELATIVE PRICES AND EXCHANGE RATES

Cause	Effect on Relative Price	Likely Effect on Exchange Rate
Increase in demand for foreign goods	Increase in relative price of foreign goods (eP^f/P rises)	e rises
Increase in demand for domestic goods	Decrease in relative price of foreign goods (eP^f/P falls)	e falls
Increase in supply of foreign goods	Decrease in relative price of foreign goods (eP^f/P falls)	e falls
Increase in supply of domestic goods	Increase in relative price of foreign goods (eP^f/P rises)	e rises

One can represent the relative price of Japanese goods in terms of American goods as eP^J/P^{US} where P^J is the price of Japanese goods, P^{US} is the price of American goods, and e is the exchange rate, measured in dollars per yen. This relative price shows the opportunity cost of Japanese goods, that is, the number of American goods a buyer sacrifices to buy a Japanese good. Similarly, P^{US}/eP^J is the relative price of American products in terms of Japanese products. For example, suppose that an American car sells for \$15,000 and a similar Japanese car sells for ¥1.8 million. If the exchange rate is \$0.01 per yen per dollar, the Japanese car costs \$18,000. The relative price of the Japanese car in terms of the American car is:

$$\text{Relative price} = \frac{(\text{¥}1,800,000 \text{ per Japanese car}) (\$0.01 \text{ per yen})}{\$15,000 \text{ per American car}}$$

$$= \frac{\$18,000 \text{ per Japanese car}}{\$15,000 \text{ per American car}}$$

$$= \frac{6}{5} \text{ American cars per Japanese car}$$

Similarly, the relative price of the American car in terms of the Japanese car is $\frac{5}{6}$.

The equilibrium relative price of Japanese goods in terms of American goods, eP^J/P^{US}, depends on the supplies and demands for the goods produced in each country. The relative price of Japanese goods rises if the demand for those goods increases, and it falls if the demand for American products increases. An increase in the supply of Japanese goods lowers their relative price in terms of American goods, while an increase in the supply of American goods raises the relative price of Japanese goods.[11] **Table 36.3** summarizes the effects of changes in the demands or supplies of a country's goods.

An increase in the relative price of foreign goods in terms of domestic goods, eP^f/P, can occur either through an increase in the exchange rate, e, through a rise

---

[11]An increase in the supply of American products reduces their relative price, P/eP^f, so it raises the relative price of Japanese products, eP^f/P.

in foreign prices, P^f, or through a fall in domestic prices, P. If domestic and foreign monetary policies prevent the change in supply or demand from affecting prices P^f and P, then an increase in eP^f/P causes a rise in e, the exchange rate. As a result, an increase in eP^f/P implies an increase in e—a depreciation of the domestic money and an appreciation of foreign money, as the third column of Table 36.3 indicates. Similarly, a decrease in eP^f/P implies a decrease in e—an appreciation of domestic money and a depreciation of foreign money.

SPECULATION, ASSET MARKETS, AND THE FX MARKET

A third set of effects on the foreign exchange market comes from the supplies and demands for financial assets such as stocks, bonds, and real estate in various countries. Just as an increase in the demand for American goods can cause a dollar appreciation, an increase in the demand for American assets can cause a dollar appreciation by raising the demand for dollars to purchase those assets. Similarly, an increase in the demand for German assets causes depreciation of the dollar and appreciation of the German mark as people sell dollars and buy marks to purchase those assets.

Because people invest in the assets that they expect earn the most profits, asset demands depend on expectations about the future. Investors speculate in the FX market by buying currencies that they believe will appreciate (in anticipation of selling them later at higher prices), and selling currencies that they expect to depreciate. As a result, expectations for the future also affect demands and supplies on the foreign exchange market. An increase in expected future appreciation of a currency increases the demand for that currency on foreign exchange markets, causing immediate appreciation. Similarly, an increase in expected future depreciation of a currency decreases the demand for that currency on FX markets, causing it to depreciate immediately.

For example, suppose that changing expectations about the future lead investors to expect dollar depreciation against the British pound (that is, they expect the pound to appreciate against the dollar). Investors would try to sell assets denominated in dollars, such as U.S. government bonds, and buy assets denominated in pounds, such as British government bonds. To do this, investors would sell dollars and buy pounds on the foreign exchange market. The rise in demand for pounds and fall in demand for dollars cause the pound to appreciate and the dollar to depreciate. In this way, changes in expectations about the future affect current exchange rates.

Investors may also trade currencies when interest rates change. An increase in interest rates in Japan may lead investors to sell U.S. assets and to buy Japanese assets (that pay higher interest rates). Investors then sell U.S. dollars and buy Japanese yen, causing dollar depreciation and yen appreciation.

Figure 36.5 showed that exchange rates often change by much more than their PPP levels change, particularly in the short run. Many economists believe that speculation in FX markets has been responsible for these large, short-run fluctuations in exchange rates. Some economists believe that speculative bubbles, like those discussed in an earlier chapter on financial markets, may also play a role in exchange rate fluctuations.

--- **FOR REVIEW** ---

36.5 Suppose that prices are higher in Switzerland than in Spain. Is arbitrage likely to make the Swiss franc appreciate or depreciate against the Spanish peseta? Why?

36.6 What is purchasing power parity?

36.7 If eP^f/P is the relative price of a Japanese product in terms of an American product, what is the relative price of an American product in terms of a Japanese product?

--------------------------------- QUESTIONS ---------------------------------

36.8 Suppose that the exchange rate between the U.S. dollar and the Russian ruble is 3,000 rubles per dollar and Russian inflation is 100 percent per year, while U.S. inflation is close to zero. What is the exchange rate likely to be after 1 year?

36.9 How would a large increase in the demand by Americans for vacations on the Greek islands affect the exchange rate between the U.S. dollar and Greek drachma?

EXCHANGE RATES AND RELATIVE PRICES

Back in 1970, it cost about $2.40 to buy 1 British pound; by 1995, a pound cost only about $1.60. Did that make it cheaper for an American to visit Great Britain in 1995 than in 1970? Not necessarily. Between 1970 and 1995 inflation was higher in Great Britain than in the United States. On average, British products that cost £1 ($2.40) in 1970 cost almost £8 by 1995, or almost (8)($1.60), or $12.80. Prices in the United States increased by less over that period; on average, products that cost $2.40 in the United States in 1970 cost $9.40 by 1995. Although British pounds were cheaper in terms of U.S. dollars in 1990s than in 1970, products that had cost the same in the two countries in 1970 cost about $\frac{1}{3}$ more in Great Britain than the United States by 1995. The change in the pound-dollar exchange rate did not reflect the change in the relative price of goods in the two countries.[12] **Figure 36.6** shows the exchange rate between the dollar and the pound and an index of the relative price of British goods in terms of American goods, measured by the exchange rate (dollars per pound) times the British consumer price index divided by the U.S. consumer price index.

Although changes in exchange rates do not always reflect changes in relative prices of goods between countries in the long run, they often move together in the short run.[13] Figure 36.6 shows that the relative price of British goods and the exchange rate usually move up together and down together in the short run. The same is true for exchange rates and relative prices with other countries, as **Figure 36.7** shows. When a country's money appreciates, the goods and services it produces become more expensive compared to similar goods and services in other countries. When a country's money depreciates, its goods and services become less expensive compared to similar goods and services in other countries.

Why does the relative price of foreign goods move so closely with the exchange rate in the short run? One answer suggests that the exchange rate

---

[12]The relative price of goods between countries is sometimes called the *real exchange rate*.

[13]This statement applies only to countries whose inflation rates are similar. It does not apply, for example, to the changes in the exchange rate between Brazil and the United States graphed in Figure 36.4.

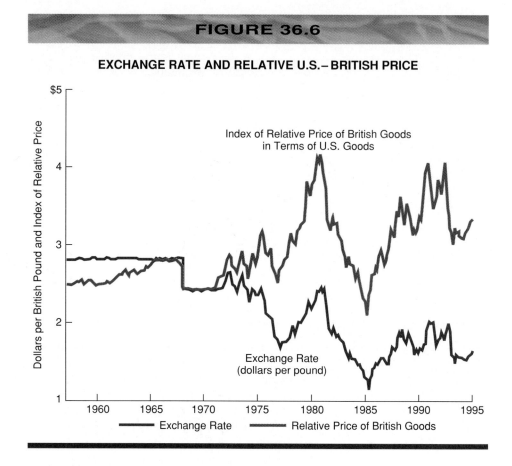

FIGURE 36.6

EXCHANGE RATE AND RELATIVE U.S.– BRITISH PRICE

(Chart: Dollars per British Pound and Index of Relative Price, vertical axis $1 to $5; horizontal axis years 1960 to 1995. Lines labeled "Index of Relative Price of British Goods in Terms of U.S. Goods" and "Exchange Rate (dollars per pound)". Legend: — Exchange Rate, — Relative Price of British Goods)

responds to changes in supplies and demands for goods. These changes affect the equilibrium relative price of foreign goods in terms of domestic goods, which affects the exchange rate. For example, an increase in the supply of French products reduces their relative price, reducing the demand for French francs to purchase French products and causing the franc to depreciate.

Most economists believe, however, that the causal relationship works the other way around, that depreciation of a country's currency causes a fall in the relative price of its goods. Most economists interpret the evidence to indicate that changes in monetary policies and speculators' expectations about the future cause changes in the exchange rate, as discussed earlier. Because price levels in each country, P and P^f, are sticky in the short run according to this view (as discussed in earlier chapters), changes in the exchange rate cause changes in the relative price of foreign goods in terms of domestic goods, eP^f/P. Because P and P^f do not change in the short run, changes in e cause changes in eP^f/P.

Suppose that a change in investors' expectations about the future causes depreciation of a foreign currency (appreciation of the domestic currency). This reduces the relative price of foreign goods in terms of domestic goods, eP^f/P.[14] In

---

[14]Of course, this means that the change raises the relative price of domestic goods in terms of foreign goods.

FIGURE 36.7

EXCHANGE RATES AND RELATIVE PRICES

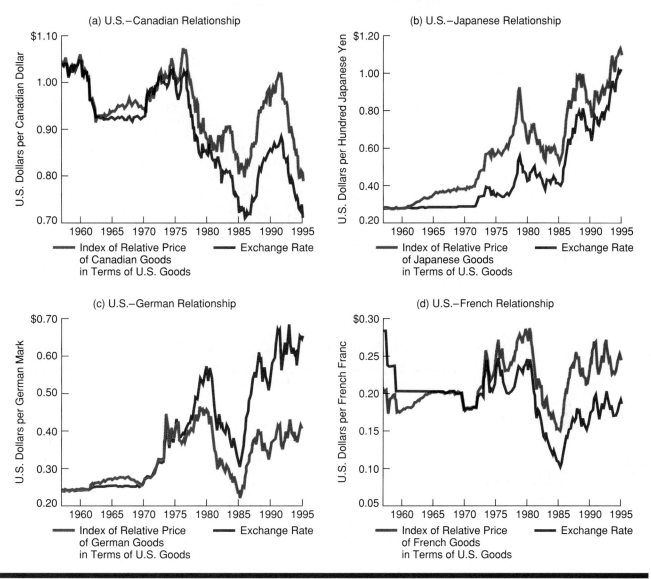

(a) U.S.–Canadian Relationship

Index of Relative Price of Canadian Goods in Terms of U.S. Goods — Exchange Rate

(b) U.S.–Japanese Relationship

Index of Relative Price of Japanese Goods in Terms of U.S. Goods — Exchange Rate

(c) U.S.–German Relationship

Index of Relative Price of German Goods in Terms of U.S. Goods — Exchange Rate

(d) U.S.–French Relationship

Index of Relative Price of French Goods in Terms of U.S. Goods — Exchange Rate

the long run, people would buy fewer domestic goods and more foreign goods instead because they are cheaper, and this would increase the demand for foreign money on the FX market, raising the exchange rate. This increase in the exchange rate would tend to raise eP^f/P back toward its original level. However, arbitrage can be costly in the short run, so the relative price of foreign goods in terms of domestic goods may remain low for some time.

In the short run, while the exchange rate remains low and the relative price of foreign goods in terms of domestic goods remains below its long-run value, the

IN THE NEWS

Weak dollar makes U.S. world's bargain bazaar

By Sylvia Nasar

The weak dollar has turned the world's wealthiest economy into the Filene's basement among industrial countries. Despite its rebound during the European currency crisis, the dollar, which fell to record lows this summer, remains extraordinarily weak by historical standards.

To the Swiss businessman just off the Concorde, the $120 tab for a room at the Plaza looks like the lunch check back home. To the teenager from Paris, the $9 sticker on the tape at Tower Records or the $30 tag on a pair of Levi 501's read like big signs that say buy one, get one free.

For foreigners in strong-currency countries, coming here is almost cheaper than staying at home. The weekend rate at the Hyatt Regency Chicago, for example, is $89 for a double per night. Comparable hotels in Munich, London, or Rome charge two to three times that. A Big Mac is one-third to one-half cheaper here. A movie ticket is one-fifth to one-half as much.

Or take that classic, a trip to Disney World. For a Frankfurt family, a week at Walt Disney World in Orlando could easily cost less than a visit to Euro Disney. As it turns out, one-third more foreign tourists than last year have been arriving at Orlando International Airport. "The devalued dollar has played a strong role in making Disney World a great bargain," said John Dreyer, manager of Walt Disney World publicity.

Changes in exchange rates and relative prices often occur together, making goods cheaper in countries whose currencies have depreciated.

Source: Sylvia Nasar, "Weak Dollar Makes U.S. World's Bargain Bazaar," *New York Times,* September 28, 1992, p. A1.

FIGURE 36.8

EFFECTS OF AN OVERVALUED CURRENCY

An overvalued domestic currency means that the exchange rate is below its equilibrium level (perhaps its purchasing power parity level), so the relative price of domestic goods in terms of foreign goods is above its equilibrium level. This reduces the quantity demanded of domestic goods by foreign buyers, so it reduces exports from Q_1 to Q_2.

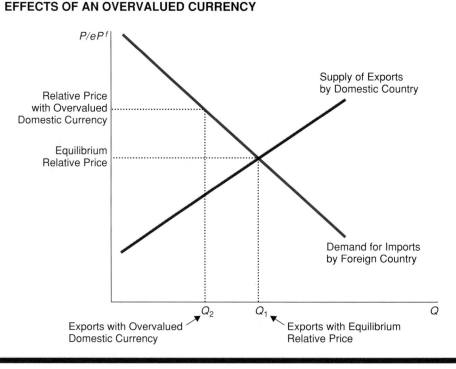

domestic money is said to be *overvalued* and the foreign money is described as *undervalued.* Many economists believe that evidence indicates that an overvalued currency reduces a country's exports by making them less competitive in world markets. For example, suppose that the U.S. dollar appreciates (the exchange rate, e, falls) while U.S. and foreign price levels, P^{US} and P^f, remain sticky in the short run. The fall in e raises the relative price of American goods in terms of foreign goods, P^{US}/eP^f, making American goods less competitive (more expensive) on world markets. As a result, foreigners may buy fewer American goods, and Americans may buy more of the less expensive imported goods. American firms would sell fewer products, so they would reduce output and employment. **Figure 36.8** shows how an overvalued domestic currency raises the relative price of domestic goods above its equilibrium and reduces a country's sales of goods to other countries from Q_1 to Q_2.[15]

ALTERNATIVE EXCHANGE RATE SYSTEMS

floating (or flexible) exchange rate system — a system in which the government does not actively trade in foreign exchange markets to try to influence exchange rates

fixed (or pegged) exchange rate system — a system in which the government buys or sells its currency in foreign exchange markets in whatever amounts are necessary to keep its exchange rate fixed (pegged) to some foreign currency

managed-float exchange rate system — a system in which the exchange rate floats, but the government sometimes trades in foreign exchange markets to try to influence it

While supply and demand on the foreign exchange market determine the exchange rate, governments often adopt policies to change the exchange rate or prevent it from changing. They follow two main kinds of exchange rate systems:

> In a **floating (or flexible) exchange rate system,** the government does not actively trade in foreign exchange markets to try to influence exchange rates.

> In a **fixed (or pegged) exchange rate system,** the government buys or sells its currency in foreign exchange markets in whatever amounts are necessary to keep its exchange rate fixed (pegged) to some foreign currency.

A third system combines these two:

> A **managed-float exchange rate system** refers to a combination system in which the government sometimes trades in foreign exchange markets to try to influence the exchange rate, but does not keep it fixed.

SYSTEMS OF FIXED EXCHANGE RATES

The gold standard of the 19th century was one type of fixed exchange rate system. Each country on the gold standard fixed the nominal price of gold in its currency by acting as a residual buyer or seller of gold. Because the law of one price applies to gold, this fixed the country's exchange rate. For example, suppose that the United States fixes the dollar price of gold at $35 per ounce while the British government fixes the pound price of gold at £7 per ounce. Arbitrage (the law of one price) implies that the price of gold must be the same in both countries, so £7 must equal $35, implying that £1 is worth $5. The gold standard

---

[15]By a similar argument, a country's currency may become undervalued on FX markets in the short run if domestic and foreign price levels are sticky and a change in expectations about the future causes the country's currency to depreciate.

IN THE NEWS

How dollar's plunge aids some companies, does little for others

Few quick bucks

It spurs exports and improves profits sent back home, but also can raise costs

A Wall Street Journal News Roundup

The dollar's plunge against other major currencies is helping U.S. companies enormously, right?

Well, yes, no, and maybe. [T] he weak dollar clearly is helping many U.S. companies.

"As the dollar goes down," says James Blair, general counsel of Tyson Foods Inc., a giant poultry processor

and major exporter, "it makes our products more competitive" abroad. Overseas sales of the Springdale, Ark., concern have been brisk recently. In the second week of October, Tyson exported more than 6 million pounds of poultry, up 14 percent from the year-earlier period. "A year ago, the dollar was a lot stronger," Mr. Blair notes.

Many American companies see the dollar's decline mainly in terms of the improvement in their currency translations: The foreign currencies that they earn can be converted into more dollars when profits are brought back to the U.S. Gian Camuzzi, assistant treasurer of Gillette Co., calls the dollar's decline

"very beneficial" because about 60 percent of its earnings come from outside the U.S., and its products are sold in European currencies.

However, the dollar is causing the Irvine, Calif., company problems, too. Western Digital makes disk drives in Singapore and circuit-board parts in Ireland. In both countries, some of the company's expenses must be paid in local currency, which now costs more in dollars. To protect itself against future swings in exchange rates, Mr. Markovich says Western Digital uses forward contracts and other currency-hedging techniques.

Changes in exchange rates may affect international trade and create winners and losers.

Source: "How Dollar's Plunge Aids Some Companies, Does Little for Others," *The Wall Street Journal,* October 22, 1990, p. A1.

keeps the exchange rate between two countries fixed as long as each country keeps the price of gold fixed.

The gold standard evolved, and in 1944 it led to the Bretton Woods System of fixed exchange rates, which lasted until 1971. The Bretton Woods agreement set the U.S. dollar price of gold at $35 per ounce and required other countries to keep their own exchange rates fixed against the dollar.[16] For example, the British pound exchange rate was fixed at $4.80 per pound, and the Japanese yen exchange rate was fixed at 0.278¢ per yen (or ¥360 per dollar). To keep its exchange rate fixed,

---

[16]The Bretton Woods agreement also set up two major international organizations. It created the International Monetary Fund (IMF) to monitor exchange rate and balance of payments policies and to encourage governments to allow people to exchange currencies of different countries, which makes international trade easier. The IMF lends money to governments of countries with large debts to other countries to help them pay interest and principal on their loans. It tries to promote economic policies that it believes will help long-run economic growth of its borrowers, and it often requires that countries adopt some of these policies as preconditions for loans. The Bretton Woods agreement also created the World Bank to help rebuild the countries that were destroyed in World War II and to help the economic development of poor countries around the world.

each country's government would sell as much of its own currency as people wanted to buy at the fixed exchange rate, and buy as much as people wanted to sell.[17] When a country sold its own money and bought U.S. dollars on the foreign exchange market, it was said to have a *balance of payments surplus.* When it bought its own money by selling U.S. dollars on the foreign exchange market, it was said to have a *balance of payments deficit.*

Under the Bretton Woods system of fixed exchange rates, governments bought and sold their own money for U.S. dollars rather than buying and selling gold, as they would under a gold standard. Whenever a government bought its own currency (with dollars) on the foreign exchange market, its money supply fell. Whenever it sold its own currency (for dollars), its money supply increased. In this way, the requirement that a government fix its exchange rate dictated the extent to which the government changed the money supply, just as a requirement that you drive at 30 miles per hour would dictate the extent to which you must press the accelerator pedal in a car. While a country fixed its exchange rate to the U.S. dollar, it could not use monetary policy to pursue other goals.

DEVALUATIONS

For many reasons, governments did not like the constraint that the fixed exchange rate system placed on their monetary policies. They frequently wanted to increase their money supplies more rapidly (or sometimes more slowly) than fixed exchange rates would allow. Countries that tried to increase their money supplies more rapidly experienced balance of payments deficits. A country with a large balance of payments deficit risked exhausting its supply of U.S. dollars to sell, which would make it unable to continue to fix its exchange rate. This prospect often led to devaluations.

> A **devaluation** of a currency occurs when a country that fixes its exchange rate at a certain level changes that level so that its money loses value in terms of foreign money. (The exchange rate, *e*, rises.)

devaluation — when a country changes the level at which it fixes its exchange rate so that its currency loses value in terms of foreign currencies

In the long run, a devaluation raises nominal prices of all goods and services along with the nominal money supply without affecting relative prices, real GDP, or employment. A devaluation works like a currency reform in reverse. To see why, imagine that a country decides to add a zero to every unit of its money. A 1-peso bill becomes a 10-peso bill, a 10-peso bill becomes a 100-peso bill, and so on. The foreign exchange rate must also change. If 1 peso was originally worth $1.00, the devaluation reduces its value to only $0.10 (so that 10 pesos are worth $1). This currency reform in reverse, which would amount to a huge inflation that would raise prices by a factor of 10, is the same as a devaluation.

SHORT-RUN EFFECTS OF DEVALUATION

In the short run, however, a devaluation can have real effects if nominal prices or nominal wages are sticky. With sticky prices in the short run, a devaluation lowers the foreign-currency prices of domestically produced products and raises the domestic-currency prices of foreign products. For example, suppose that a country devalues its money from 10 francs per dollar to 12 francs per dollar. A product that sells for 100 francs cost foreigners $10.00 before the devaluation but costs

---

[17]This worked somewhat like the gold-exchange standard or the currency boards discussed in earlier chapters.

IN THE NEWS

Turmoil erupts in aftermath of African franc's fall

By Michelle Faul
Associated Press

ABIDJAN, Cote d'Ivoire—People fought in supermarkets and scrambled to fill shopping carts while clerks raced to double prices, the day after the African franc lost half its value.

The devaluation of the French-backed currency caused turmoil across the 14 former French colonies as prices abruptly shot up. Labor leaders warned that strikes and food riots could break out.

"It will cause economic and social catastrophe," said Mathias Ndzon, director general of Banque Internationale du Congo.

Under pressure from world financial institutions which said the currency was overvalued, 14 nations grudgingly agreed last Tuesday to slash the value from 50-1 to the French franc to 100-1—the first change since it was established in 1948.

Shoppers throughout the west and central African nations cleared off shelves before prices could be changed.

The International Monetary Fund, World Bank, and French government had pressured the countries to devalue their currency because it had overvalued prices for the African nations' main exports, such as cocoa and coffee.

But many Africans feared the increased competitiveness of their exports would be wiped out by the sudden rise in the prices of essential imports, such as food and fuel.

At Froid Industriel supermarket in Cote d'Ivoire, a bag of rice zoomed from 1,700 CFAs—about $5.80 at the old rate—to 3,100, or $5.34 at the new rate.

Though the price was actually cheaper by foreign exchange standards, it still represented a shocking climb for impoverished Africans whose wages remained unchanged.

Devaluations can affect people's lives.

Source: Michelle Faul, "Turmoil Erupts in Aftermath of African Franc's Fall," *Journal of Commerce,* January 18, 1994, p. 4A.

only $8.33 after the devaluation; a foreign product that sells for $100 cost 1,000 francs before the devaluation, but costs 1,200 francs after the devaluation. These price changes may lead people to buy more domestically produced goods and fewer foreign goods, reducing imports, raising exports, and possibly affecting the country's employment and real GDP.

Just as unexpected inflation can redistribute income, creating winners and losers, devaluations usually redistribute income. Losers include workers whose nominal wages are fixed in the short run. By raising prices of imported products, a devaluation reduces their real wages. People whose savings or pensions are fixed in nominal units of the domestic currency also lose real income from the devaluation. Winners include owners of some firms that export more products as a result of the devaluation, while paying the same nominal wages and lower real wages. Indeed, countries with fixed exchange rates sometimes devalue their currencies specifically to try to make their goods more competitive in world markets, creating these winners and losers.

As a whole, however, a devaluation makes a country poorer because it makes foreign goods and services more expensive. In the short run, a country cannot trade its products for as many foreign products after a devaluation as before. In the long run (after prices and wages fully adjust), the devaluation does not affect relative prices or make a country more competitive, though the effects of the redistribution of income may linger.

When speculators believe that a country might devalue its money, they try to avoid losses or make profits by selling that currency and buying others instead. This can create a balance of payments crisis in which people rapidly sell a country's money, forcing the country's government to spend a large amount of resources to continue to fix the exchange rate. Balance of payments crises usually result in devaluations because governments are unwilling to spend so many resources to continue to fix their exchange rates. For example, in late 1994, speculators began to expect that the government of Mexico would devalue the Mexican peso. As a result, speculators tried to sell pesos and buy other currencies, such as U.S. dollars. This raised the amount of pesos that Mexico's central bank had to buy (with U.S. dollars) to keep the exchange rate fixed. Mexico spent billions of dollars to try to keep the exchange rate fixed. Finally, rather than lose more dollars, Mexico devalued the peso in December 1994.[18]

A government may try to continue fixing the exchange rate by increasing regulations and controls that make it more difficult for people to sell the country's money. Although these regulations and controls reduce the losses that the government incurs to keep the exchange rate fixed, they can also cause large economic inefficiencies. Also, they seldom prevent devaluation in the long run.

WHICH EXCHANGE RATE SYSTEM IS BEST?

Many countries abandoned the system of fixed exchange rates in 1973 because of continuing balance of payments crises and devaluations. Japan and most European countries adopted floating exchange rates, as Canada had done in 1970. Since that time, European countries have alternated between floating exchange rate systems and managed-float systems. The European Monetary System (or EMS) and its associated Exchange Rate Mechanism (ERM) operates much like a pegged exchange rate system in which several European countries peg their currencies loosely to the German mark. Major European countries formed the EMS and ERM to limit the sizes of exchange rate changes. Rather than completely fix exchange rates, the ERM allows them to move between certain official upper and lower limits—2.25 percent above or below a central parity, or target exchange rate, for most countries, and up to 6.00 percent above or below the central parity for others.

Economists disagree about the relative merits of fixed exchange rates and flexible exchange rates. Part of the disagreement results from the absence of sufficient evidence on the economic effects of these alternative systems.

Some economists argue for a floating exchange rate system because it allows a government to choose its monetary policy without the restriction of keeping its exchange rate fixed. This frees a country to use monetary policy to pursue low inflation or other goals. With a fixed exchange rate, in contrast, a country cannot use monetary policy for these goals. While the purchasing power parity theory implies that a country with a fixed exchange rate has the same long-run inflation rate as the rest of the world, a floating exchange rate system allows the country to choose its own inflation rate and monetary policies.

---

[18]At that time, Mexico switched from a fixed exchange rate system to a floating exchange rate system.

Governments do not need to spend resources to keep their exchange rates fixed under a floating-rate system, so this system frees resources for other uses. In addition, balance of payments crises under fixed exchange rate systems often lead governments to restrict international trade in goods and financial assets to help keep their exchange rates fixed.[19] These restrictions reduce economic efficiency and may affect a country's exports, imports, real GDP, and employment. These economically inefficient restrictions become unnecessary under a system of floating exchange rates because the government allows supply and demand in foreign exchange markets to determine the equilibrium exchange rate without its interference. A floating exchange rate system also prevents governments from using devaluations, along with regulations on international trade in goods and financial assets, to keep exchange rates at levels that are not consistent with equilibrium in foreign exchange markets.

Other economists argue for a fixed exchange rate system as much more convenient than a floating-rate system. Because the exchange rate does not change every day, even every minute, it reduces information costs. People can plan more easily because they know what the exchange rate will be. This helps to promote international trade. In contrast, the constant change in a floating exchange rate system creates uncertainty that hinders international trade. A fixed-rate system also imposes discipline on governments by preventing them from raising their money supplies rapidly and creating high inflation. This fosters international cooperation in setting policies.

Exchange rates change too often and by too much under a floating exchange rate system, argue advocates of fixed exchange rates. Speculation causes large, unpredictable changes in exchange rates. Because prices are sticky in the short run, these changes affect relative prices between domestic and foreign goods. The resulting overvaluations or undervaluations cause economic inefficiencies and may affect a country's exports, imports, real GDP, and employment. Evidence shows that the relative prices of foreign goods in terms of domestic goods change much less under a fixed exchange rate system than under a floating exchange rate system. Figures 36.6 and 36.7, for example, show smaller changes in relative prices with fixed exchange rates in the 1960s than with floating exchange rates since the early 1970s. A fixed exchange rate system can avoid the problems of overvaluation and undervaluation of currencies if countries follow appropriate monetary and fiscal policies to avoid balance of payments crises. Proponents of floating exchange rates respond that countries with fixed exchange rates have seldom followed the necessary policies to prevent balance of payments crises.

Perhaps economists will begin to agree on this issue at some point in the future, when more evidence becomes available about the effects of each type of exchange rate system. Even with more evidence, however, disagreements may continue if they reflect differences in value judgements about the effects of each system.

FOR REVIEW

36.10 What is an overvalued money? How might overvaluation affect a country's exports?

---

[19]Restrictions on international trade in financial assets help to keep the exchange rate fixed by making it more difficult for people to sell the domestic currency and buy foreign currencies.

36.11 What is a floating exchange rate system? What is a fixed exchange rate system?

36.12 What is a balance of payments deficit? What is a devaluation?

―――――――――――――――――― **QUESTION** ――――――――――――――――――

36.13 How does a fixed exchange rate system prevent a country from changing its monetary policy whenever it wants?

CONCLUSIONS

FOREIGN EXCHANGE MARKETS

A foreign exchange rate is the price of one money in terms of another, often expressed as the amount of domestic currency required to buy one unit of foreign currency. A currency appreciates when its value rises (requiring less domestic money to buy one unit of foreign money), and it depreciates when its value falls (requiring more domestic money to buy one unit of foreign money).

People use exchange rates to convert prices from one currency into units of another. To convert the price of a product measured in foreign currency per good, P^f, to domestic units, multiply by the exchange rate, e, measured as the domestic price of one unit of foreign currency. The result, eP^f, is the price measured in domestic currency. A forward foreign exchange rate is the price of foreign money to be delivered at a future date.

EQUILIBRIUM EXCHANGE RATES

Supply and demand on foreign exchange markets determine equilibrium exchange rates. A person who buys Japanese yen with U.S. dollars demands yen and supplies dollars; a person who does the opposite supplies yen and demands dollars. Changes in supply and demand cause changes in equilibrium exchange rates.

Arbitrage (buying in a low-price country and reselling in a high-price country) affects supplies and demands on foreign exchange markets. If prices are higher in one country than another, then the currency of the high-price country tends to depreciate and the currency of the low-price country tends to appreciate; this works to equalize prices in different countries, measured in the same monetary units. The law of one price says that if arbitrage were costless, then the equilibrium price of a product would be the same in every country. The purchasing power parity theory says that the exchange rate adjusts in the long run to equalize prices of goods and services in all countries, expressed in the same monetary units. Changes in supplies or demands of goods or financial assets can affect the exchange rate by changing the supplies and demands for currencies on foreign exchange markets. When people expect a currency to depreciate in the future, they tend to sell it to avoid losses in value due to the depreciation; their attempts to sell the currency can cause it to depreciate immediately.

EXCHANGE RATES AND RELATIVE PRICES

In the short run, the relative price of a country's goods and services usually falls when its currency depreciates and rises when its currency appreciates. In the short run, changes in the exchange rate and changes in the relative price between countries usually occur together. In the long run, in contrast, changes in the exchange rate are not closely connected with changes in the relative price of one country's goods in terms of another country's goods. Most economists believe that the short-run connections between relative prices and exchange rates result from sticky nominal prices of goods and services, expressed in the currencies of the countries in which they are produced, and that exchange rate changes that cause a country's money to be temporarily overvalued or undervalued cause relative price changes, perhaps with effects on international trade, output, and employment in each country.

ALTERNATIVE EXCHANGE RATE SYSTEMS

In a floating (or flexible) exchange rate system, the government does not actively trade in foreign exchange markets to try to influence its currency's exchange rate. In a fixed (or pegged) exchange rate system, the government buys or sells its currency in foreign exchange markets in whatever amounts are necessary to keep the exchange rate fixed (pegged). A managed-float system combines fixed and floating exchange rate systems.

A country devalues its money when it changes the exchange rate under a fixed exchange rate system so that its currency loses value in terms of foreign currency (that is, the price of foreign money rises). In the long run, devaluations cause inflation without affecting real variables. (They resemble currency reforms in reverse.) In the short run, however, devaluations redistribute income, just as unexpected inflation does. With sticky nominal prices or wages, devaluations may also affect international trade, employment, and real GDP.

Economists disagree about how a country's exchange rate system affects international trade, real GDP, employment, inflation, and other economic variables. As a consequence, they disagree about which exchange rate system is better.

KEY TERMS

foreign exchange (FX) market

exchange rate

appreciation of a currency

depreciation of a currency

forward foreign exchange market

law of one price

purchasing power parity (PPP) theory

floating (or flexible) exchange rate system

fixed (or pegged) exchange rate system

managed-float exchange rate system

devaluation

QUESTIONS AND PROBLEMS

36.14 A souvenir in India costs 900 rupees. Use Table 36.1 to calculate approximately how much it costs in dollars. A meal in Paris costs 100 francs; use Table 36.1 to calculate approximately how much it costs in dollars.

36.15 An airline ticket from London to New York costs $300 in the United States or £220 in England. Where is it cheaper to buy the ticket? (Use Table 36.1.)

36.16 What is the law of one price? Why does it not always apply?

36.17 Use Figure 36.6 to determine in which years a vacation in Great Britain would have been particularly expensive or particularly cheap, measured in

U.S. dollars. Use Figure 36.7 to determine in which years a vacation in Canada, France, Germany, or Japan would have been particularly expensive or particularly cheap, measured in U.S. dollars.

36.18 Suppose that people decide to start buying more U.S. goods and fewer Japanese goods. How would that affect the exchange rate between dollars and yen? Explain why.

36.19 Use Table 36.1 to calculate the exchange rate between French francs and German marks. (The answer is not in the table; you must calculate it from information in the table.)

36.20 You work for an international business firm that expects to receive 1 million French francs 30 days from now and 2 million German marks 90 days from now. Your boss in New York is worried that exchange rates might change within the next month or two and reduce your firm's dollar profit.
   a. Would an appreciation or depreciation of the dollar reduce your firm's dollar profit?
   b. What action would you suggest to your boss to avoid this risk? (Be specific.)

INQUIRIES FOR FURTHER THOUGHT

36.21 Summarize the case for (a) a floating exchange rate system and (b) a fixed exchange rate system. If you were an economic advisor to the government of some country, which system would you recommend? Why?

36.22 Why do people in different countries use different currencies? Why don't they all use the same one?

TAG SOFTWARE APPLICATIONS

TUTORIAL EXERCISES
▶ The module contains a review of the key terms from Chapter 36.

GRAPHING EXERCISES
▶ The graphing segment includes questions on supply and demand in the foreign exchange market and the appreciation and depreciation of a currency.

ECONOMICS YELLOW PAGES

These Economics Yellow Pages list some of the main sources of economic information and data, and where you can obtain it. Information Source Numbers refer to publications *listed inside the back cover of this book.*

Index to Economic Information by Chapter and Topic

Internet Sources

See *Resources for Economists on the Internet*, by Bill Goffe, available by anonymous FTP from many sites, such as rtfm.mit.edu, in the /pub/usenet/sci.econ.research directory, where the file is called econ-resources-faq. On the World Wide Web, look for this document through a menu service (such as Yahoo) under Economic Resources, or use a search service and search for it by name or by the author's name. Or try

http://econwpa.wustl.edu/EconFAQ/EconFAQ.html
or http://alfred.econ.lsa.umich.edu/EconFAQ/EconFAQ.html
or http://sosig.esrc.bris.ac.uk/Goffe/EconFAQ/EconFAQ.html

Web Resources for Economists, another useful site to begin searching for economic information, can be found at http://minerva.cis.yale.edu/~amiyake/econ.html.

Discussion of economic issues occurs in two Usenet news groups. An unmoderated newsgroup, sci.econ contains some economics-related discussion, but mostly of poor quality (though it is a good place to test your ability to find fallacies in arguments). A better discussion occurs in the moderated news group, sci.econ.research.

Research Institutes and Media

Many research institutes publish discussions of economic policy issues. For example, the CATO Institute (1000 Massachusetts Avenue N.W., Washington DC 20001) publishes analyses of current policy issues in *Policy Analysis*, discussions of government regulations in the magazine, *Regulation*, and other publications. The Brookings Institution (1775 Massachusetts Avenue N.W., Washington DC 20036) publishes analyses of economic issues in *Brookings Papers on Economic Activity* and other publications.

Many magazines and newspapers report economic stories and economic data. Some of the major U.S. periodicals with economic information include *Business Week*, *The Economist* (weekly news magazine), *Financial Times* (London), *Forbes*, *Fortune*, *Investors Business Daily*, and *The Wall Street Journal*. Many other periodicals discuss economic issues. Among the best publications with nontechnical articles on current economic research are the *NBER Digest* and *NBER Reporter*, published by the National Bureau of Economic Research, a private economic research institute, and *Economic Perspectives*, published by the American Economic Association.

(continued on inside back cover)

GLOSSARY

accounting profit — total revenue minus total cost as measured on accounting statements (p. 335)

activist view of policy — the view that the economy often operates inefficiently on its own and that government macroeconomic policies can make the economy more efficient (p. 954)

actual real interest rate — the nominal interest rate minus the actual rate of inflation during the period of the loan (p. 708)

adverse selection — a situation in which two people might trade with each other and one person has relevant information about some aspect of the product's quality that the other person lacks (p. 551)

agent — the person hired by a principal to do something (p. 544)

aggregate demand — the total demand for the goods and services currently produced in a country (p. 684)

aggregate demand curve — a graph showing the total quantity demanded for an economy's goods and services at various price levels (p. 684)

aggregate demand multiplier — a measure of the ultimate increase in aggregate demand that results from an exogenous $1 rise in spending (p. 867)

aggregate supply — the total supply of all goods and services currently produced in an economy (p. 690)

aggregate supply curve — a graph showing the total quantity supplied of an economy's goods and services at various price levels (p. 690)

annual growth rate (rate of growth) — the percentage change in a variable from one year to the next (p. 674)

antitrust law — a law that prohibits monopolies and cartels or monopoly-like behaviors (p. 372)

appreciation of a currency — a rise in the value of a money on the foreign exchange market so that one unit buys more foreign money (p. 1109)

arbitrage — buying a good at a place where its price is low and selling it where its price is higher (p. 170)

arbitrage opportunity — a recognized price differential that exceeds the costs of arbitrage (p. 170)

area — a number that measures the size of some specific region in a graph (p. 40)

Arrow impossibility theorem — under very general conditions, the results of voting can inconsistent (in the sense that A can beat B in an election while B beats C, but A does not beat C) even if all voters make consistent choices (p. 639)

automatic stabilizer — a feature of government policy that reduces fluctua-tions in real GDP automatically, without any explicit actions of the government (p. 1002)

average cost — total cost divided by the quantity produced (p. 281)

average product — a firm's total output divided by the quantity of an input (p. 441)

average revenue — total revenue divided by the quantity produced (p. 281)

average tax rate — a person's tax payment as a fraction of income (p. 627, 998)

average variable cost — total variable cost divided by the quantity produced (p. 281)

backward-bending labor supply curve — a labor supply curve with a negatively sloped portion (p. 467)

balance of international trade — the value of a country's exports minus that of its imports (p. 1066)

balance of trade on goods and services — the difference between exports of goods and services and imports of goods and services (p. 1069)

balanced budget — when tax receipts equal spending, so the deficit is zero and the government's debt does not change (p. 992)

bank reserves — the money that banks hold to back up their deposits (p. 823)

bank run — when many people try at the same time to withdraw their money from a bank that lacks sufficient reserves (p. 843)

banking panic — many simultaneous bank runs (p. 843)

barrier to entry — a cost high enough to prevent potential competitors from entering an industry (p. 363)

Bertrand model — a model of oligopoly in which each firm believes that other firms will react to its decisions by changing the quantities they sell to keep their prices fixed (p. 404)

best response — the action that maximizes a firm's profit, given the actions of rivals (p. 404)

best responses (or best strategy) — the strategy that maximizes a player's payoff given the strategies or other players (p. 419)

black market — an illegal market (p. 200)

bond — an IOU for a long-term debt, typically on a loan lasting 10 years or more (p. 1028)

budget line — a graph of a budget set (p. 235); a graph of a person's consumption opportunities (p. 710)

budget set — a person's opportunities or feasible choices (p. 235)

budget surplus — the opposite of a deficit (p. 992)

business cycles — 2-year to 5-year fluctua-tions around trends in real GDP and other, related variables (p. 691)

call option — a right to buy some underlying asset during some specified period of time at some preset strike price (p. 1052)

capacity output — the level of output that minimizes average cost (p. 283)

capital gain (or capital loss) — an increase (or decrease) in the value of an asset (p. 1031)

capital good — an input that a firm can use repeatedly to produce other goods (p. 334)

capital stock — the quantity of durable inputs (p. 450)

capture view of regulation — the view that regulatory agencies originally established to serve the general public interest end up serving the special interests of the industries they were intended to regulate (p. 612)

cartel — a group of firms that try to collude to act as a monopoly (p. 368)

central bank — a bank for banks (p. 832)

change in demand — a change in the numbers in the demand schedule and a shift in the demand curve. An increase in demand shifts the demand curve to the right; a decrease shifts it to the left. (p. 78)

change in supply — a change in the numbers in the supply schedule and a shift in the supply curve. An increase in supply shifts the supply curve to the right; a decrease shifts it to the left. (p. 87)

commercial paper — short-term debt (usually with a 30-day maturity) issued by a private firm (p. 1029)

commitment to a future action — doing something now to limit future options or to change future incentives to take that action (p. 430)

commitment to a policy rule — an action by a policy maker to guarantee implementation of the rule (p. 957)

common resource — a resource that belongs to no one or to society as a whole (p. 578)

comparative advantage — the ability to produce a product at a lower opportunity cost than other people or countries (p. 48, 1070)

compensating differential — a difference in wages that offsets differences in nonpay features of a job (p. 473)

competition — the process by which people attempt to acquire scarce goods for themselves (p. 11)

complement — two goods are complements if an increase in the price of one reduces demand for the other (p. 82)

complement inputs — two inputs for which an increase in the price of one raises demand for the other (p. 448)

concentrated interest — a benefit to a small group of people or firms (p. 612)

constant cost — long-run marginal cost and long-run average cost that do not change with the level of output (p. 284)

constant-cost industry — an industry with a perfectly elastic long-run supply curve (p. 342)

consumer surplus— the benefit to a consumer of the chance to buy a good at the equilibrium price, rather than being unable to buy the good at all (p. 232)

consumption (consumer spending) — spending by people on final goods and services for current use (p. 685)

consumption of a good — the amount of a good people use for their current benefit (wearing, eating, driving, or watching the good, for example) (p. 164)

contingent policy rule — a rule that states specifically how policies will depend on economic circumstances (p. 956)

coordination failure — situation that could result in any one of several equilibria, and in which the best equilibrium does not occur because people cannot jointly choose their actions (p. 944)

correlation — a measure of how closely two variables are related (p. 28)

cost-benefit analysis — the process of finding and comparing the costs and benefits of a regulation, tax, or other policy (p. 604)

countercyclical monetary policy — moves to loosen monetary policy when unemployment is high and inflation is low and to tighten monetary policy when unemployment is low and inflation is high (p. 960)

coupon payment — an interest payment that a borrower makes to bondholders (p. 1028)

Cournot model — a model of oligopoly in which each firm believes that other firms will react to its decisions by changing their prices to keep their levels of output and sales fixed (p. 405)

credible policy rule — a rule that people believe policy makers will follow, perhaps because they have an incentive to follow it (p. 957)

cross-price elasticity of demand (or supply) — the percentage change in the quantity demanded (or supplied) of one good when the price of another good rises by 1 percent (p. 121)

crowding out — a reduction in private investment when government borrowing raises the real interest rate and reduces the equilibrium amount of investment (p. 738)

currency board — an institution whose sole purpose is to keep a foreign exchange rate fixed by acting as a residual buyer or seller of the country's money at that price (p. 980)

currency held by the nonbank public — all paper money and coins owned by people and business firms, not including banks or the government (p. 822)

currency reform — replacement of an old form of money with a new form of money, with automatic adjustment of all nominal values in existing contracts such as nominal wages and nominal debts to keep real values the same (p. 795)

current account — the amount that a country lends to or borrows from other countries (p. 1081)

current account deficit — net borrowing from other countries (p. 1081)

current account surplus — net lending to other countries (p. 1081)

deadweight social loss — the amount that people would be willing to pay to eliminate an inefficiency (p. 311)

decreasing cost — long-run marginal cost and long-run average cost that fall with an increase in output (p. 284)

default — failure to repay a loan in full (p. 1029)

demand curve — a graph of a demand schedule (p. 75)

demand for investment — the demand for new capital goods; the amount of money that firms would want to invest at various possible interest rates (p. 717)

demand for loans — the amounts of money that people, firms, and the government would want to borrow at various possible real interest rates (p. 719)

demand schedule — a table that shows various possible prices and a person's quantity demanded at each price (p. 75)

depreciation — the fall in the value of a good over time (p. 334)

depreciation of a currency — a fall in the value of a money on the foreign exchange market so that one unit buys less foreign money (p. 1109)

deregulation — a decrease in government regulations (p. 601)

devaluation — when a country changes the level at which it fixes its exchange rate so that its currency loses value in terms of foreign currencies (p. 1129)

differentiated product — a product that buyers consider to be a good, but not perfect, substitute for another (p. 389)

diffuse interest — a benefit that is spread across many people (p. 612)

diminishing returns to capital — the

decline in the benefit of additional investment over time as the capital-labor ratio rises; with more capital equipment per worker, the benefit of investing in even more capital declines (p. 765)

discounted present value (of a future amount of money) — the money you would need to save and invest now to end up with that specific amount of money in the future (p. 288)

discretionary policy — a policy that chooses moves day-to-day without a specific rule (p. 957)

disequilibrium — a situation in which the quantity demanded and the quantity supplied are not equal at the current price (pp. 94, 858)

disposable income — after-tax income (p. 709)

distribution of prices — a situation in which some sellers charge higher prices than others (p. 537)

diversification — spreading risks across many different, unrelated investments (p. 541)

diversification — spreading risks by choosing many unrelated investments or investments whose payoffs are out of step (p. 1027)

dividend — a regular cash payment from a firm to stockholders (p. 1036)

dominant strategy — a strategy that is best regardless of what other players do (p. 419)

durable input — an input that a firm buys for future use or one that the firm can use repeatedly (p. 449)

dynamic gains from trade — the benefits of increased economic growth and development due to international trade (p. 1081)

economic costs — all of a firm's costs, explicit and implicit (p. 335)

economic growth — a rise in real GDP per capita (p. 758)

economic model — a description of logical thinking about an economic issue stated in words, graphs, or mathematics (p. 18)

economic profit — total revenue minus total economic cost (p. 335)

economic rent — the price of an input minus the economy's opportunity cost of using that input (p. 452)

economically efficient — a situation that cannot be changed so that someone gains unless someone else loses (p. 50)

economically efficient method of production — the technically efficient method with the lowest cost (p. 270)

economically efficient (or Pareto efficient) situation — a situation that allows no potentially Pareto-improving change (p. 307)

economically inefficient — a situation that can be changed so that at least one person gains while no one else loses (p. 50)

economically inefficient (or Pareto inefficient) situation — a situation that is not economically efficient, so a potentially Pareto-improving change *could* be made (p. 307)

economics — the study of how a society uses its limited resources to produce, trade, and consume goods and services; also the study of people's incentives and choices and what happens to coordinate their decisions and activities (p. 7)

effective labor input — labor input adjusted for knowledge and skills (p. 769)

efficiency wage — a wage above equilibrium intended to raise worker productivity (p. 490)

efficient markets theory — the argument that stock prices are random walks (p. 1043)

egalitarianism — the view that fairness requires equal results (p. 513)

elastic demand (or supply) — elasticity with an absolute value greater than 1 (p. 112)

elasticity of demand (or supply) — the percentage change in the quantity demanded (or supplied) divided by the percentage change in price (p. 111)

entrepreneur — a person who conceives and acts on a new business idea and takes the risk of its success or failure (p. 332)

entry — when a firm begins producing and selling a product (p. 336)

equation of exchange — the equation that shows the nominal money supply multiplied by its velocity equal to the GDP price deflator multiplied by real GDP (p. 682)

equilibrium — a situation that has no tendency to change unless some underlying condition changes (p. 93)

equilibrium price — the price at which quantity supplied equals quantity demanded (p. 93)

equilibrium price level — the price level that equates the quantity of money demanded with the quantity supplied (p. 792)

equilibrium quantity — the quantity at which quantity supplied equals quantity demanded (p. 93)

equilibrium rate of inflation — the growth rate of the equilibrium price level (p. 798)

equilibrium unemployment — unemployment that results from continuing changes in supplies and demands and the costs of searching for and matching jobs in labor markets (p. 742)

evidence — any set of facts that helps to convince people that a positive statement is true or false (p. 18)

excess capacity — the opportunity for a firm to reduce its average cost by raising its output (p. 395)

excess demand (shortage) — a situation in which the quantity demanded exceeds the quantity supplied (p. 95)

excess supply (surplus) — a situation in which the quantity supplied exceeds the quantity demanded (p. 96)

exchange rate — a price of one money in terms of another (p. 1107)

exhaustible resource — a resource that cannot be physically replenished and that is depleted in production, such as coal (p. 770)

exit — when a firm stops selling a product (p. 336)

expected real interest rate — the nominal interest rate minus the expected rate of inflation (p. 708)

expected value — an average of every possible value that a variable can take, weighted by the chance of that value occurring (pp. 535, 1025)

explicit cost — a cost that requires some direct payment (p. 335)

exports — sales of goods and services to people and firms in other countries (pp. 164, 687, 1065)

externality — a difference between the private and social costs or benefits (p. 562)

fallacy of composition — false reasoning that what is true for one person must be true for the economy as a whole (p. 24)

family — people living with others to whom they are related by nature or marriage (p. 496)

federal funds rate — the interest rate that banks charge each other for short-term loans of reserves (p. 834)

Federal Reserve discount rate — the interest rate that the Fed charges banks for short-term loans (p. 834)

Federal Reserve System — a semi-independent agency of the U.S. government that serves as the central bank in the United States (p. 832)

fiat money — paper money that is not backed by a commodity in the sense that people cannot trade it for a particular commodity at a fixed nominal price (p. 840)

financial asset — a right to collect some payment or series of payments in the future (p. 1023)

financial intermediary — an organization that bridges the gap between lenders (savers) and borrowers (spenders) (p. 822)

firm — an organization that coordinates the activities of workers, managers, owners, lenders, and other participants to produce and sell a good or service (p. 267)

n-firm concentration ratio — the total sales of the largest *n* firms in an industry as a percentage of total industry sales (p. 401)

fiscal policy — actions that change government spending, taxes, or both (pp. 954, 985)

fixed (or pegged) exchange rate system — a system in which the government buys or sells it currency in foreign exchange markets in whatever amounts are necessary to keep its exchange rate fixed (pegged) to some foreign currency (p. 1127)

fixed cost — an unavoidable cost of a fixed input (p. 276)

fixed input — an input whose quantity a firm cannot change in the short run (p. 276)

fixed resource — a natural resource that cannot be replenished, but is not depleted in production, such as land (p. 770)

floating (or flexible) exchange rate system — a system in which the government does not actively trade in foreign exchange markets to try to influence exchange rates (p. 1127)

foreign exchange (FX) market — a market for purchases and sales of the moneys of various countries (p. 1107)

foreign exchange rate — the price of one unit of foreign money (p. 865)

forward foreign exchange market — a market in which people agree now to buy and sell currencies in the future at prices set today (p. 1112)

free entry or exit — entry or exit opportunities with no legal barriers (p. 336)

fundamental price — the discounted present value of a stock's expected future dividends (p. 1045)

futures market — a market in which people buy and sell goods for future delivery (pp. 185, 1051)

futures price — the price of a good for delivery at a future date (p. 185)

gains from trade — the net benefits to people (as consumers and producers) from trading (p. 1076)

game theory — the general theory of strategic behavior (p. 417)

GDP price deflator — one measure of the price level, equal to nominal GDP divided by real GDP (p. 673)

general (macroeconomic) equilibrium — a situation in which prices have adjusted to equate demands and supplies in all markets (p. 728)

Gini coefficient — a summary of income inequality equal to twice the area enclosed in a Lorenz curve graph (p. 504)

gold exchange standard — a system in which people trade paper money that is backed by gold stored in a warehouse (p. 839)

goods — (also *goods and services*) things that people want (p. 8)

government budget deficit — government spending in excess of tax receipts (p. 720)

government budget deficit — the amount of money that the government borrows each year when it spends more than it collects in taxes (p. 184)

government budget deficit — the increase in the government's debt during 1 year. (p. 992)

government budget deficit — the money that the government must borrow when it spends more money than it collects in taxes (p. 136)

government debt — the amount of money the government owes people because it has borrowed money in the past (p. 992)

government purchases — all spending by the government except transfer payments (direct payments of money to people) (p. 687)

government regulation — a limit or restriction on the actions of people or firms, or a required action (p. 600)

historical cost — a price paid for something in the past (p. 333)

holding period yield — the rate of return the owner would get on a bond over some specified period of time that might be less than the time until the bond matures (p. 1031)

household — a family or an individual living alone (p. 496)

human capital — people's knowledge, education, and skills (pp. 474, 759)

implicit cost — a cost that does not require any direct payment; solely an opportunity cost (p. 335)

implicit labor contract — an informal agreement or understanding about the terms of employment (p. 489)

implicit rental price — the cost of owning and using a capital good over some period of time (p. 334)

import quota — a restriction on the number of imported goods of a certain type (pp. 219, 1087)

imports — purchases of goods and services from people and firms in other countries (pp. 164, 687, 1065)

incentive — the expected benefit of a decision minus its opportunity cost (p. 10)

income — the value of money and goods that a person receives over some time period (pp. 81, 495)

income effect of a price change — the change in quantity demanded that results from a change in the amount of goods that buyers can afford (p. 84)

income elasticity of demand — the percentage increase in the quantity demanded of a good divided by the percentage change in buyers' incomes (p. 121)

increase in economic efficiency — a change that is a potential Pareto improvement (p. 307)

increasing cost — long-run marginal cost and long-run average cost that rise with increase in output (p. 284)

increasing returns to scale — a situation in which average cost of production decreases with higher output (p. 365)

increasing-cost industry — an industry with an upward-sloping long-run supply curve (p. 343)

indexed wage — a nominal wage that changes automatically when the price level changes (p. 895)

indexing — automatically adjusting a nominal value for changes in the price level (p. 812)

indifference curve — a graph of combinations of goods between which a person is indifferent (p. 254)

inelastic demand (or supply) — elasticity with an absolute value less than 1 (p. 112)

inferior good — a good whose demand decreases if income rises (p. 81)

inflation — the growth rate of the price level (the percentage increase in the average nominal price of goods and services) (pp. 675, 785)

inflation tax — the loss that people suffer when inflation reduces the purchasing power of their assets (p. 811)

interest rate — the price of a loan, expressed as a percentage of the loaned amount per year (p. 287)

internalizing an externality — changing the private costs or benefits so that they equal social costs or benefits; making people responsible for all the costs to other people of their own actions (p. 568)

intertemporal substitution (substitution over time) — a change in the current demand or supply of a good caused by a change in its expected future price (p. 82)

inventories — goods that a firm owns, including raw materials or other inputs, partially finished goods (goods in process), or finished goods that the firm has not yet sold (p. 333)

investment — an increase in the economy's capital stock, which includes its machinery, equipment, buildings, tools, inventories of goods for future use, human skills, and knowledge (pp. 450, 717); spending to create new capital goods (p. 686)

involuntary unemployment — unemployment resulting from inability to find a suitable job, even at a lower wage (p. 879)

L (liquidity) — a measure of the money supply that combines M3 with certain short-term financial assets (loans) (p. 824)

labor force — all the people who work in the market or who are looking for a job in the market (p. 466)

labor turnover — the continuing flows of people into and out of the labor force, employment and unemployment, and various jobs (p. 480)

labor union — an organization of workers intended to improve the working conditions and pay of its members (p. 486)

Laffer Curve — a graph showing the relationship between the marginal tax rate and the government's tax revenue (p. 1000)

laissez-faire view of policy — the view that the economy usually operates efficiently on its own and, even when it does not, active government policies are more likely to aggravate inefficiencies and create new inefficiencies than to alleviate problems (p. 954)

law of diminishing returns — the generalization that raising the quantity of an input eventually reduces its marginal product, if the quantity of another input remains fixed (p. 442)

law of one price — proposition that if arbitrage is costless, then the equilibrium price of a product is the same in any location (p. 1115)

LDC (less developed country) — a country with a relatively low real GDP per capita (p. 762)

leveraged buyout (LBO) — a form of takeover financed by extensive borrowing, often pledging the assets of the takeover target as collateral for the loans (p. 1059)

liability rule — a legal statement of who is responsible under what conditions for injuries or other harms in a tort (p. 647)

liquidity effect — a short-run inverse change in interest rates associated with a change in the money supply (p. 876)

long run — a period of time over which people fully adjust their behavior to a change in conditions; a period of time over which a firm can change the quantities of all its inputs (p. 272)

long run — the time people need to fully adjust to a change (p. 122)

long-run demand (or supply) curve — a curve that shows prices and quantities demanded (or supplied) at each price after buyers (or sellers) have adjusted completely to a price change (p. 122)

long-run equilibrium — an equilibrium over a time long enough to allow firms to enter or exit the industry (p. 331); a situation in which entry or exit has adjusted the market until each firm earns zero economic profit (p. 338)

long-run Phillips Curve — a vertical line at the natural rate of unemployment (p. 905)

looser monetary policy — a policy that increases the growth rates of the monetary base and broader measures of the money supply or decreases the federal funds rate (pp. 850, 958)

Lorenz curve — a graph that shows percentages of the population on the horizontal axis and percentages of income that they receive on the vertical axis (p. 503)

Lucas critique — the proposition that people do not always respond the same way to changes in economic conditions or government policies because their responses depend partly on their expectations about the future, and those expectations can change (p. 964)

M1 — a measure of the money supply that includes currency held by the nonbank public, traveler's checks, and balances in accounts at banks and other financial intermediaries against which people or firms can write checks (p. 822)

M2 — a measure of the money supply that combines M1 with balances in most savings accounts and similar accounts (p. 824)

M3 — a measure of the money supply that combines M2 with balances in most other accounts at financial intermediaries (p. 824)

managed-float exchange rate system — a system in which the exchange rate floats, but the government sometimes trades in foreign exchange markets to try to influence it (p. 1127)

marginal benefit — the increase in total benefit from doing something once more (p. 241)

marginal cost — the increase in total cost from doing something once more (p. 243)

marginal product — the increase in a firm's total output when it adds one more unit of an input while keeping the quantities of other inputs fixed (p. 441)

marginal propensity to consume — the increase in consumption when disposable income rises by $1 (p. 715)

marginal rate of substitution — the largest amount of one good that you would be willing to trade away for one unit of another (p. 256)

marginal revenue — the increase in total revenue as the quantity produced rises by 1 unit (p. 271)

marginal tax rate — the fraction of each additional dollar earned that a person must pay in taxes (pp. 627, 999)

marginal utility — the increase in total utility that you gain from an additional unit of a good (p. 260)

market — the activity of people buying and selling goods (p. 12)

market demand — demand for a good by all buyers, including the private sector and the government (p. 133)

market demand curve — a graph of the market demand schedule (p. 77)

market demand schedule — a table of many hypothetical prices of a good and the quantity demanded by *all buyers* in the economy at each price (p. 77)

market equilibrium — a situation, described by a combination of price and quantity traded, in which the quantity supplied equals the quantity demanded (p. 93)

market process — the coordination of people's economic activities through voluntary trades (p. 12)

market quantity demanded — the total amount of a good that *all buyers* in the economy would buy during a time period if they could buy as much as they wanted at a given price (p. 77)

market quantity supplied — at a given price, the total amount of a good that all sellers in the economy would sell during a time period if they could sell as much of the good as they wanted (p. 87)

market supply curve — a curve graphing the market supply schedule (p. 87)

market supply schedule — a table showing many hypothetical prices of a good and the quantity supplied at each price (p. 87)

markup (or profit margin) — price minus average cost (p. 331)

maximum legal price (or price ceiling) — the highest price at which the government allows people to buy or sell a good (p. 193)

mean income — total income divided by the number of people (p. 496)

median income — the income level at which half of the people have more income and half have less (p. 496)

median voter — the voter whose views on a policy issue are in the middle of the spectrum, with half of the other voters on one side and half on the other side (p. 637)

median-voter theorem — the proposition that, under certain conditions, the equilibrium government policy chosen in political markets is the policy favored by the median voter (p. 637)

medium of exchange — an asset that sellers generally accept as payment for goods, services, and other assets (p. 837)

menu cost — a cost of changing prices (p. 891)

merchandise trade balance — the difference between exports of goods (but not services) and imports of goods (but not services) (p. 1069)

merger — when two firms join together voluntarily (p. 1059)

minimum legal price (or price floor) — the lowest price at which the government allows people to buy or sell a good (p. 201)

misleading comparison — a comparison of two or more things that does not reflect their true differences (p. 26)

monetary base — a measure of the money supply that includes currency held by the nonbank public and bank reserves (p. 824)

monetary policy — changes in the nominal money supply through open market operations, changes in the discount rate or discount window lending policy, or reserve requirement changes (p. 954)

money income — before-tax income including transfer payments, excluding noncash transfers and noncash benefits paid by employers (p. 496)

money multiplier — the ratio of a broad measure of the money supply, such as M1, M2, M3, or L to the monetary base (p. 829)

monitoring — obtaining information about an agent's actions (perhaps by watching) (p. 546)

monopolistic competition — an industry in which (1) each firm sells a differentiated product, (2) the industry has enough firms that when one cuts its price, every other firm loses only a small quantity of its sales, and (3) the industry has free entry (p. 390)

monopoly — a firm that faces a downward-sloping demand curve for its product and makes decisions without considering the reactions of other firms (p. 355)

monopsony — a buyer that faces an upward-sloping supply curve and makes decisions without considering the reactions of other buyers (p. 381)

moral hazard — a situation in which a principal cannot observe the actions of an agent who lacks an incentive to act in the best interests of the principal (p. 544)

multipart price — a price with several components (p. 367)

Nash equilibrium — a situation in which each firm makes its best response, that is, maximizes its profit, given the actions of rival firms (p. 404); a situation in which each player makes her best response (p. 419)

national savings — private savings plus government savings (p. 1015)

nationalized firm — a firm that the government owns (p. 620)

natural monopoly — an industry with increasing returns to scale over sufficiently large quantities (p. 366)

natural rate of unemployment — the unemployment rate that occurs when the economy produces the full-employment level of output (p. 904)

negative correlation — a relationship between variables that tend to move in opposite directions (inversely) (p. 28)

negative externality — the result of a social cost of a good in excess of its private cost (p. 562)

negative slope — the shape of a curve that runs downward and to the right (p. 39)

net benefit (or profit) — total benefit minus total cost (p. 244)

net exports (balance of international trade) — exports minus imports (p. 687)

net present value of a durable input — the discounted present value of the future value of the input's marginal product minus the discounted present value of its cost (p. 449)

neutrality of money — position that a change in the money supply affects only nominal prices and not real variables (p. 878)

nominal gross domestic product (GDP) — the dollar value of a country's output of final market goods and services during some year (p. 673)

nominal interest rate — the annual dollar interest payment on a loan expressed as a percentage of the dollar amount of the loan (p. 705)

nominal money supply — the total amount of money in the economy, measured in monetary units such as dollars or yen (pp. 681, 682, 788)

nominal (money) wage — the wage rate measured in money (such as dollars, yen, or pesos) (p. 469)

nominal price — a money price (pp. 101, 787)

nominal variable — a variable measured in terms of money, such as U.S. dollars, Mexican pesos, or Japanese yen (p. 787)

nondurable input — an input that a firm uses soon after acquiring it and can use only once to produce a product (p. 446)

nonexcludable good — a good that is prohibitively costly to provide only to people who pay for it while excluding other people from obtaining it (p. 588)

nonprice competition — competitive rivalry based on better-quality products or product characteristics designed to match the preferences of specific groups of consumers (p. 397)

nonprice rationing — a system for choosing who gets how many goods in a shortage (p. 397)

nonrival good — a good for which the quantity available to other people does not fall when someone consumes it (p. 588)

normal (accounting) profit — the level of accounting profit required for a zero economic profit (p. 339)

normal good — a good whose demand increases if income rises (p. 81)

normative statement — a statement that expresses a value judgment or says what *should be;* such a statement cannot be true or false (p. 18)

OECD (Organization for Economic Cooperation and Development) — an organization of countries with relatively high per-capita real GDPs (p. 762)

oligopoly — an industry in which (1) firms are not price takers (each faces a downward-sloping demand curve), and (2) each firm acts strategically, taking into account its competitors' likely reactions to its decisions and how it will be affected by their reactions (p. 399)

open market operation — Federal Reserve purchase or sale of financial assets (p. 833)

opportunity cost — the value of what someone must sacrifice or give up to get something (p. 9)

optimal contract — an agreement that maximizes the principal's profit while providing an incentive for the agent to participate in the agreement (p. 544)

optimal taxation — a system of tax rates that minimizes the total deadweight social loss from taxes while raising a certain amount of revenue for the government (p. 625)

other-conditions fallacy — false reasoning that two events will always occur together in the future because they occurred together in the past (p. 25)

ownership — the right to make decisions about a good (p. 13)

Pareto improvement — a change that helps at least one person without hurting anyone (p. 305)

payoff — the amount that a player wins or loses in a particular situation in a game (p. 418)

percentage change — 100 times the

change in a number divided by the average (or midpoint) of the original number and the new number (p. 110)

perfect competition — competition among price-taking sellers (p. 331)

perfect price discrimination — charging each customer the highest price that that customer is willing to pay (p. 376)

perfectly elastic demand (or supply) — infinite elasticity illustrated by a demand (or supply) curve that is a horizontal line (p. 114)

perfectly inelastic demand (or supply) — elasticity equal to zero, illustrated by a demand (or supply) curve that is a vertical line (p. 114)

physical capital — machinery, equipment, tools, and buildings (p. 759)

policy rule — a statement of what policy an agency will follow (p. 956)

political business cycle — the apparent tendency for recessions to occur in the middle of presidents' 4-year terms, while the economy tends to improve before presidential elections (p. 969)

political equilibrium — a situation, characterized by peoples' votes and campaign contributions, the positions and strategies of candidates for office, and the decisions and actions of government officials, that shows no tendency for a change unless some underlying condition changes (p. 636)

positive correlation — a relationship between variables that tend to rise or fall together (p. 28)

positive externality — the result of a social benefit of a good in excess of its private benefit (p. 562)

positive externality — when the social benefit of an action (such as producing a good or investing in research) exceeds the private benefit (p. 775)

positive slope — the shape of a curve that runs upward and to the right (p. 38)

positive statements — a statement of fact, of what *is* or what *would be* if something else were to happen; such a statement is either true or false (p. 18)

positive-sum game — environment in which everyone can gain at the same time (p. 50)

post-hoc fallacy — false reasoning that because one event happened before another, the first event must have caused the second event (p. 25)

potential Pareto improvement — a change that could allow the winners to compensate the losers to make the change a Pareto improvement (p. 305)

predatory pricing — selling goods at prices below their average costs to try to drive a competitor out of business (p. 372)

price — the amount of something that a

buyer trades away (pays) per unit of the good he receives (p. 56)

price differential — a difference between the prices of identical goods in two different locations (p. 170)

price discrimination — charging different prices to different buyers for the same good (p. 374)

price level — an average of the prices of an economy's goods and services (p. 673)

price rigidity — slow adjustments of prices to changes in costs or demand (p. 403)

price taker — a firm that faces a perfectly elastic demand for its product (p. 292)

price taker in an input market — a firm that faces a perfectly elastic supply of an input (p. 446)

principal — a person who hires someone else to do something (p. 544)

private benefit — the benefit to people who buy and consume a good (p. 562); the benefit to the people who produce a good or invest (p. 773)

private cost — the cost paid by a firm to produce and sell a good (p. 561)

private demand — demand for a good by people and nongovernment businesses (p. 133)

private ownership — a property right held by one person or a small group of people (p. 577)

private property — something that a person owns (p. 13)

privately held government debt — the amount of government debt owned by people and business firms outside the government (p. 1004)

privatization — creation of private property rights in a nationalized firm so that it becomes privately owned (p. 620)

producer surplus — the benefit to a producer from being able to sell goods at the equilibrium price, rather than being unable to sell them at all (p. 294)

production function — a mathematical description of technology showing the quantity of output (real GDP) the economy can get from its inputs of capital and labor (p. 728)

production possibilities frontier (PPF) — a graph showing the combinations of products that an economy can produce with its available resources and technology (pp. 61, 1073)

profit — total revenue minus total cost (p. 271)

property rights — people's legal rights to decide whether and how to use scarce resources or to sell them to others (pp. 13, 577)

protectionism — government policies that restrict imports (p. 1086)

public good — a nonrival and nonexcludable good (p. 589)

public-interest view of regulation — the view that government regulations serve the public interest (p. 612)

purchasing power parity method — a method of comparing incomes in different areas by adjusting for price differences between those areas (p. 507)

purchasing power parity (PPP) theory — the theory that the exchange rate adjusts to make the prices of goods and services, expressed in a single currency, equal in all countries (p. 1115)

pure gold standard — a system in which people trade gold coins as money, and there is no paper money (p. 839)

put option — a right to sell some underlying asset during some specified period of time at some preset strike price (p. 1054)

quantity demanded (at a given price) — the amount of a good that a person would buy during a time period if she could buy as much as she wanted at that price (p. 74)

quantity of money demanded — the amount of money that a person would choose to own, given current conditions such as the person's income and wealth, the price level, the usefulness of money, and the costs and benefits of owning other assets (p. 791)

quantity supplied (at some price) — the amount that a seller would offer to sell during some time period if she could sell as much as she wanted at that price (p. 86)

random walk — a price pattern that is equally likely to rise or fall by the same amount, so, on average, people do not expect it to change (p. 186)

rate of economic growth — the annual growth rate of GDP per person (pp. 675, 759)

rate of job creation — the number of new workers hired each month (p. 743)

rate of job destruction — the number of people who quit or lose their jobs each month (p. 743)

rate of return — income the owner receives from an asset over some period of time plus the increase in its value during that period, all as a percentage of the original value of the asset (p. 1023)

rate of return on investment — a firm's accounting profit per dollar of its previous investments, expressed as a percentage per year (p. 403)

rational behavior — the actions of people when they do the best they can, based on their own values and information, under the circumstances they face (p. 23)

rational choice — the choice in your budget set that you most prefer (p. 240)

rational expectations — beliefs about the future that accurately reflect the probabilities of various future events, based on all currently available information (p. 929)

real business cycle theories — theories that explain business cycles mainly as results of changes in technology or other real variables, while claiming that nominal variables are unimportant (p. 923)

real government budget deficit — the increase in the government's real debt (p. 1004)

real government debt — the government's debt in constant (base-year) dollars, i.e., adjusted for inflation (p. 1004)

real gross domestic product (GDP) — a measure of a country's total output of final market goods and services during some year (p. 673)

real interest rate — inflation-adjusted interest rate; equals 1 plus the relative price of goods this year in terms of the same goods next year (p. 705)

real money supply — the purchasing power of the nominal money supply, or the amount of goods that the nominal money supply could buy at current prices (p. 790)

real variable — a variable that refers to a quantity of goods and services, often measured in base-year dollars (p. 787)

real wage — the wage rate adjusted for inflation, that is, measured in purchasing power units (pp. 471, 894)

recession — a large fall in the growth of real GDP and related variables (p. 692)

relative price — the opportunity cost of one good in terms of other goods (equal to one nominal price divided by another or divided by a price index) (p. 787)

relative price of one good in terms of another — the opportunity cost of the first good measured in units of the second good (p. 101)

renewable resource — a natural resource that can be replenished, such as trees (p. 770)

rent seeking — competition for favors from the government (p. 380)

rent seeking — the use of time, money, and other resources in pursuit of government benefits (government spending, tax changes, or regulations targeted to some special interest group) (p. 1017)

repeated game — a game that the same players play more than once (p. 432)

required reserves — the reserves that the Fed requires banks to hold, based on their total deposits (p. 836)

risk averse — a characteristic of a person who prefers a less risky income, holding fixed the expected value of the income (pp. 542, 1027)

risk neutral — a characteristic of a person who does not care about risk, only about the expected return on an investment (pp. 543, 1027)

risk premium — an extra payment that compensates investors for risk (p. 1029)

risk-free interest rate — the interest rate on a loan with no chance of default (p. 1029)

rule of 72 — the rule that if the growth rate of a variable is X percent per year, then the variable doubles after about $72/X$ years (p. 675)

rules of a game — statements of who can do what, and when (p. 418)

savings — disposable income minus consumption (p. 709)

search cost — the time and money cost of obtaining information about a price or a product (p. 536)

sectoral shift — output increase in one sector of the economy along with output decreases in one or more other sectors (p. 936)

selection bias — use of data that are typical, but are selected in a way that biases results (p. 26)

sequential game — a game in which players make decisions at different times (p. 427)

share of stock — legal right of ownership in a business firm, traded on a stock market (p. 186)

shift — a change in the position of a curve on a graph (p. 36)

short run — a period of time over which people cannot fully adjust their behavior to a change in conditions; a period of time over which a firm cannot vary the quantities of all its inputs (p. 275)

short-run aggregate supply curve — curve showing the total supply of all goods and services produced in the economy in the short run with sticky prices (p. 870)

short-run equilibrium output curve — a graph of the short-run level of output as changes in the real interest rate cause changes in the supplies of labor and capital inputs (p. 926)

short-run equilibrium — an equilibrium with a fixed number of firms (p. 331)

short-run Phillips Curve — a statistical relationship showing that unemployment falls temporarily when inflation rises, and unemployment rises temporarily when inflation falls (p. 904)

shortage — a situation in which the quantity demanded exceeds the quantity supplied at the current price (p. 194)

simple policy rule — a rule that requires a particular policy regardless of economic circumstances (p. 956)

slope — a number that shows the distance by which a curve goes up or down as it moves one unit to the right (p. 39)

social benefit — the benefit to everyone in society of private production or investment (pp. 562, 773)

social cost — the total cost of a good to everyone in society (p. 562)

special-interest view of regulation — the view that government regulations serve special-interest groups (p. 612)

speculation — buying a good when its price is low and storing it to sell in the future when its price might be higher (p. 175)

spot price — the prices of a good for current delivery (p. 185)

stagflation — a combination of inflation and a fall in read GDP (p. 908)

statistical analysis — the use of mathematical probability theory to draw inferences in situations of uncertainty (p. 18)

statistical discrimination — using the fact that a person is a member of a certain group to make predictions about that person (p. 520)

steady state — the economy's long-run equilibrium in which the quantity of capital per worker does not change (p. 765)

steady state capital stock — the long-run equilibrium quantity of capital per worker (p. 765)

sticky nominal price — a nominal price that takes time to adjust to its new equilibrium level following a change in supply or demand (p. 858)

stock price — price of a share of stock (p. 186)

store of value — any good or asset that people can store while it maintains some or all of its value (p. 837)

strategy — a plan for actions in each possible situation in a game (p. 418)

subgame perfect Nash equilibrium — a Nash equilibrium in which every player's strategy is credible (p. 429)

substitute — two goods are substitutes if an increase in the price of one raises demand for the other (p. 81)

substitute inputs — two inputs for which an increase in the price of one reduces demand for the other (p. 448)

substitution effect of a price change — the change in quantity demanded that results from a change in the opportunity cost of the good (p. 84)

sunk cost — a cost that you have already paid and cannot recover (p. 249)

supply curve — a graph of a supply schedule (p. 86)

supply of loans — the amounts of money

that people would want to save and lend at various possible real interest rates (p. 717)

supply schedule — a table that shows various possible prices and the quantity supplied at each price; the *market* supply schedule includes *all* sellers (p. 86)

suppressed inflation — inflation that would occur without government controls on wages and prices, but that does not fully occur due to those controls (p. 815)

surplus — a situation in which the quantity demanded is less than the quantity supplied at the current price (p. 201)

takeover — when one person, a group of people, or another company buys enough stock in a firm to guarantee a majority vote at stockholder meetings (p. 1059)

tariff — a tax on an import (pp. 217, 1087)

tax rate — the per-unit tax on a good, expressed as a percentage of its price (p. 205)

technical efficiency — a situation in which an economy cannot produce more of one good without producing less of something else (p. 62)

technical inefficiency — a situation in which an economy could alter its use of resources so that it produces more output of some good without producing less of anything else. (p. 62)

technical progress — an increase in the quantity of output that the economy can produce with efficient use of the same quantities of capital, labor, and other inputs (p. 758)

technically efficient method of production — a method that does not waste any inputs, so the firm cannot produce the same amount of output using less of any input without using more of other inputs (p. 269)

technology shock — an unexpected change in technology (p. 926)

tie-in sale — a sale in which a seller sells only to buyers who also agree to buy some other product (p. 198)

tighter monetary policy — a policy that reduces the growth rates of the monetary base and broader measures of the money supply or increases the federal funds rate (pp. 850, 958)

time consistent policy — when the best case-by-case decisions are the same as the decisions suggested by the best policy rule (p. 967)

time inconsistent policy — when the best case-by-case decisions differ from the decisions suggested by the best policy rule (p. 967)

time price — the time necessary to buy, prepare, and use a good (p. 142)

tit-for-tat — a strategy in which players

cooperate unless one of them fails to cooperate in some round of the game, in which case others do in the next round what the uncooperative player did in the current round (p. 433)

tort — an act that injures other people, either intentionally or by accident (p. 647)

total factor productivity — a number in the economy's production function that measures its level of technology; the value rises with technical progress (p. 926)

total factor productivity growth — a measure of technical progress that represents increases in production with given amounts of inputs (p. 759)

total gain from trade — the sum of consumer and producer surplus (p. 304)

total revenue — total receipts from selling a good (p. 271)

trade deficit — imports in excess of exports (p. 1066)

trade surplus — exports in excess of imports (p. 1066)

trading — buying and selling (p. 12)

trading externality — a situation in which the costs of dealing with other people would fall if more people would participate in trading (p. 945)

tragedy of the commons — the overuse of a common resource relative to its economically efficient use (p. 578)

transactions costs — the costs of finding people with whom to trade, and the costs of buying, selling, or negotiating agreements, paying for products or services, and enforcing contracts (pp. 456, 571)

Treasury bill (T-bill) — a short-term debt security issued by the U.S. government, typically for a 3-month to 6-month loan (p. 1028)

Treasury note — debt security issued by the U.S. government, typically for a loan of 1 to 10 years (p. 1028)

underemployed person — someone who does not have a job that makes full use of his or her training and skills, but wants one (p. 481)

unemployed person — someone who wants a job, but does not have one (p. 481)

unit of account — a measure for stating prices (p. 837)

unit-elastic demand (or supply) — elasticity with an absolute value equal to 1 (p. 112)

util — a unit of utility (p. 260)

utilitarianism — the view that justice consists of maximizing the total amount of human happiness (p. 514)

utility — the benefit people get from the goods that they buy (p. 260)

utilization rate of capital — the number of hours per week firms use capital equipment (p. 752)

value of a firm — the discounted present value of the firm's expected future profits (p. 287)

value of the marginal product — the increase in the money value of a firm's output when it adds one more unit of an input, keeping the quantities of other inputs fixed (p. 445)

variable cost — an avoidable cost of a variable input (p. 276)

variable input — an input whose quantity a firm can change in the short run (p. 276)

variables — names of a set of numbers analyzed with a graph (ranged along the horizontal and vertical axes) or with mathematical methods (p. 33)

velocity of money — the average number of times per year that money is spent in the circular flow (p. 682)

wealth — the total value of savings accumulated in the past plus the discounted present value of expected future labor income after taxes (or human capital) (pp. 81, 495, 710)

World Trade Organization (WTO) — formerly the General Agreement on Tariffs and Trade (GATT), a 117-country organization and a series of related treaties that reduce trade restrictions (p. 1092)

yield to maturity — roughly, the average annual interest rate the owner would get from holding a bond until its maturity rather than selling it sooner (p. 1030)

zero-sum game — environment in which one person's gain is another person's loss (p. 50)

CREDITS

INDEX

equation for, 703
examples of, 702-703
formula for, 288-290
Discretionary [monetary] policy, 957
in AS/AD model, 959-962
benefit of policy rules as problem with, 966-970
inflationary bias of, 968-969
information about effects of, 964
lack of information as problem with, 963-966
lags and, 962-963
looser monetary policy, **958**
Phillips Curve and, 970
problems with, 962-970
public information about, 965-966
tighter monetary policy, **958**
Discrimination
equilibrium with, 522-523
in insurance rates for men and women, 530
in labor markets, 518-522
laws requiring, 523, 523n.
pro-Christian bias, 530
remedies for, in United States, 524
reverse discrimination, 524
sex bias in schools and child-rearing practices, 520
statistical discrimination, **520**-521
typical study of, 522
wage discrimination against, women, 518-521, 521n.
wage discrimination against blacks, 518-519, 521-522
Disequilibrium. *See also* Equilibrium
definition of, 94, **858**
interest rates and, 879
involuntary unemployment and, 879
price stickiness and, 858-860
Disk jockeys, bribery of, 147-148, 149
Disney Corporation, 109, 116, 398
Disney World, 1126
Disposable income, 709
Distribution of prices, 537
Diversification, 1027
definition of, **541**
risk and, 541-542, 543
Dividends, 1036-1037
DJIA. *See* Dow Jones Industrial Average (DJIA)
Dodd, Bill, 191
Dolan, Brian, 1134
Dominant strategy, of a game, **419**
Donagan, Alan, 515n.
Donahue, John D., 622
Donnelly, Barbara, 543
Dow Jones Industrial Average (DJIA), 1041-1042
Dowries, 154-155, 156, 158
Drexel Burnham Lambert, 480
Dreyer, John, 1126
Drug regulations, 619-620
Drug trade, 875
Duncan Hines, 391
Durable inputs, 449-450
Dworkin, Ronald M., 643n.
Dynamic gains from trade, 1081

Earnings. *See* Income; Wages
Eastern Europe, 667, 698n., 837n.
EC. *See* European Community (EC)

Economic Consequences of the Peace (Keynes), 871n.
Economic costs, 335
Economic development, in LDCs, 776-778
Economic efficiency
and barter and money trades, 51-52
comparative advantage and, 51
competitive equilibrium as, 309-310
crime reduction and, 655-657
definition of, **50, 307**
in environmental economics, 563-567, 567n.
and equilibrium with positive externalities, 586-588
examples of, 50-51
goodness of, 56-58, 308-309
increase in, 307
Pareto improvement and, 305-310
of perfect competition, 348-349
property rights law and, 652, 654-655
real business cycles and, 924-930
of rules, 655
side payments and, 570
torts and, 648-650
tradeoff between equity and, 57, 309, 626
Economic growth
advantages and disadvantages of, 774
basic model of, 763-768
basics of, 758-760
definition of, 69, **758**
effect of higher savings on, 767, 767n.
externalities and, 773, 775
and fixed and exhaustible natural resources, 770-773
historical trends in, 757, 760, 760n.
in Japan, 761
logic of, 763-775
production possibilities frontier (PPF) of, 69-71
rate of, 675, 759-760
statistics on, 3-4
and technical change and human capital investment, 768-770
in United Kingdom, 760-761
in United States, 757, 760-761
world economic growth, 760-763
Economic inefficiency, 50-51, 57, **307,** 993-994, 994n.
Economic models
as artificial economies, 23
assumptions underlying, 19
conclusions drawn from, 19
definition of, **18**
good and bad models, 19-20
and interpretation of data as evidence, 21-23
prediction and, 21
purposes of, 20-23
rational behavior and, 23-24
as simplified versions of reality, 20-21
Economic profits, 335-336
Economic rent, 340-341, 451-453, **452**
Economically efficient method of production, 270
Economically efficient (or Pareto efficient) situation, 307
Economically inefficient (or Pareto inefficient) situation, 307
Economics
definitions of, **7**-8
disagreements within field, 29
of everyday life, 154-157

Economist, The, 1118, 1120
EEOC. *See* Equal Employment Opportunity Commission (EEOC)
Effective labor input, 769-770
Efficiency. *See* Economic efficiency; Technical efficiency
Efficiency wages, 489-**490**, 489n.
Efficient markets theory, 1043-1045, 1045n.
EFTA, 1091, 1091n.
Egalitarianism, 513-514
Ehrlich, Anne, 772n.
Ehrlich, Paul, 772n.
Elastic demand (or supply), 112, 113, 116
Elasticities. *See also* Elasticity of demand; Elasticity of supply
and changes in equilibrium, 119-120
cross-price elasticity of demand (or supply), **121**
definition of, 110, 116
formulas for, 124-126
income elasticity of demand, **121**
of labor demand, 469
slopes and, 130
taxes and, 211-214
Elasticity of demand
and availability of substitutes, 120
and change in demand, 118-119
and changes in equilibrium, 119-120
definition of, 110, **111**
elastic demand, **112, 113**
for firm's output, 330
formula for, 111, 124
and fraction of income spent on the good, 120-121
graphs of, 109-110, 112, 113, 115
income elasticity of demand, **121**
inelastic demand, **112,** 113
long-run, 122-123, 124
percentage changes and, **110**-111
perfectly elastic demand, **114**
perfectly inelastic demand, **114**
and shape of demand curve, 111-114
short-run, 122-123, 124
slope and, 111
spending and, 114-116
unit-elastic demand, **112,** 113
Elasticity of supply
and availability of substitutes, 120
and change in supply, 119
definition of, **111,** 116
elastic supply, **112,** 113, 116
formula for, 116
graphs of, 117
inelastic supply, **112,** 113, 116
perfectly elastic supply, **114,** 116
perfectly inelastic supply, **114,** 116
unit-elastic supply, **112,** 113, 116
Electronic superhighway, 579
Elliott, Kimberly Ann, 1089n., 1090
Emergencies, gain from, 153
Employment. *See* headings beginning with Labor
EMS. *See* European Monetary System (EMS)
End of Affluence, The (Ehrlich and Ehrlich), 772n.
Endogenous variables, 689-690
England, 839. *See also* United Kingdom
Entin, Stephen, 740
Entitlements, 687

Printed Sources of Economic Data and Information

For an index to the sources listed here and a discussion of Internet resources, see the **Economics Yellow Pages Index** preceding the book's glossary on G-1. Printed sources listed below are available at major libraries. U.S. government publications are also available from the Superintendent of Documents, U.S. Government Printing Office. Letters in brackets below refer to addresses in the address section. For example, the U.S. Government Printing Office is **[A]**.

General Sources of Economic Information

Sources (1) and (2) are the first two places to look (in printed format) for almost any economic data.

(1) The *Statistical Abstract of the United States*, annual, Bureau of the Census, U.S. Department of Commerce, the single best general source of economic and social data for the United States **[A]**. It is available in many bookstores under the title, *The American Almanac*, published by the Reference Press (800-486-8666).

(2) The *Economic Report of the President*, an annual summary of the U.S. economy and many tables of U.S. economic statistics. **[A]**.

(3) *User's Guide to BEA Information* — summary of additional economic data available from the Bureau of Economic Analysis at the U.S. Department of Commerce **[B]** or electronically on the Internet.

(4) The *Survey of Current Business*, monthly, U.S. Department of Commerce **[B]**.

(5) *Historical Statistics of the United States: Colonial Times to 1970* (two volumes) **[B]**.

(6) *Business Statistics*, annual, U.S. Department of Commerce **[A]**.

(7) The Congressional Budget Office (CBO) **[C]** publishes many detailed studies of current economic issues and proposed government policies (with titles such as *Reducing the Deficit: Spending and Revenue Options*, or *The Tax Treatment of Health Insurance*).

Other Sources of Microeconomic Data

(8) *Handbook of Labor Statistics*, annual, Bureau of Labor Statistics at the U.S. Department of Labor **[D]**.

(9) *Monthly Labor Review*, U.S. Department of Labor **[D]**.

(10) *Employment and Earnings* (monthly), U.S. Department of Labor **[D]**.

(11) *Employment and Wages* (annual), U.S. Department of Labor **[D]**.

(12) *Real Earnings* (monthly), U.S. Department of Labor **[D]**.

(13) *Statistics of Income Bulletin*, quarterly, U.S. Internal Revenue Service **[F]**.

(14) *Vital Statistics of the United States*, annual, National Center for Health Statistics **[E]**.

(15) *Current Population Reports* and the *Census of Population*, Bureau of the Census **[G]**.

(16) Information about business firms from the Bureau of the Census **[G]** appears in the *Census of Retail Trade*, the *Census of Wholesale Trade*, the *Census of Service Industries*, the *Census of Manufacturers*, and the *Annual Survey of Manufacturers*.

(17) Dun and Bradstreet Corporation publishes several reports on business firms, including: *Monthly Business Starts Report*, *Monthly Business Failure Report*, *Monthly New Business Incorporations Report*, and *Business Failure Record* (annual), available in most libraries.

Other Sources of Macroeconomic Data

(18) *National Income and Products Accounts of the United States*, published by the U.S. Department of Commerce **[B]** provides detailed information on Gross Domestic Product and its components.

(19) *Producer Price Indices* (monthly) and *CPI Detailed Report*, (monthly), U.S. Department of Labor **[G]**.

(20) *The Budget of the United States Government*, annual, Office of Management and Budget (OMB) **[I]**.

(21) *Treasury Bulletin*, quarterly, U.S. Department of the Treasury **[H]**, contains data on government finances.

(22) *Federal Reserve Bulletin* and *Annual Statistical Digest*, Board of Governors of the Federal Reserve System **[J]**.

(23) Federal Reserve Bank publications with data include *Annual U.S. Economic Data*, *National Economic Trends*, *Monetary Trends*, and *International Economic Conditions*, Federal Reserve Bank of St. Louis (PO Box 442, St. Louis, MO 63166) and *Economic Trends*, Federal Reserve Bank of Cleveland (PO Box 6387, Cleveland, OH 44101).

Publications with articles about economic issues include:

Economic Review, Federal Reserve Bank of Atlanta, 104 Marietta St. NW, Atlanta, GA 30303.

New England Economic Review, Federal Reserve Bank of Boston, 600 Atlantic Avenue, Boston, MA 02106.

Economic Perspectives, Federal Reserve Bank of Chicago, PO Box 834, Chicago, IL 60690.

Economic Review and *Economic Commentary*, Federal Reserve Bank of Cleveland, PO Box 6387, Cleveland, OH 44101.

Economic Review, Federal Reserve Bank of Dallas, Station K, Dallas, Texas 75222.

Economic Review, Federal Reserve Bank of Kansas City, Kansas City, MO 64198.

Quarterly Review, Federal Reserve Bank of Minneapolis, 250 Marquette Avenue, Minneapolis, MN 55480.

Quarterly Review, Federal Reserve Bank of New York, 33 Liberty Street, New York, NY 10045.

Business Review, Federal Reserve Bank of Philadelphia 19106, Ten Independence Mall, Philadelphia, PA 19106.

Economic Quarterly and *Cross Sections*, Federal Reserve Bank of Richmond, PO Box 27622, Richmond, VA 23261.

Review, Federal Reserve Bank of St. Louis, PO Box 442, St. Louis, MO 63166.

Economic Review, Federal Reserve Bank of San Francisco, PO Box 7702, San Francisco, CA 94120.